W9-AGE-389

# Criminal Investigation

# Criminal Investigation

EIGHTH EDITION

Charles R. Swanson UNIVERSITY OF GEORGIA

Neil C. Chamelin ASSISTANT STATE ATTORNEY, LEON COUNTY, FLORIDA

Leonard Territo UNIVERSITY OF SOUTH FLORIDA

Boston Burr Ridge, IL Dubuque, IA Madison, WI New York San Francisco St. Louis
Bangkok Bogotá Caracas Kuala Lumpur Lisbon London Madrid Mexico City
Milan Montreal New Delhi Santiago Seoul Singapore Sydney Taipei Toronto

**McGraw-Hill Higher Education** 

*A Division of The* ***McGraw-Hill*** *Companies*

**Criminal Investigation**

Published by McGraw-Hill, a business unit of The McGraw-Hill Companies, Inc., 1221 Avenue of the Americas, New York, NY, 10020.


This book is printed on acid-free paper.

4 5 6 7 8 9 0 DOW/DOW 0 9 8 7 6 5 4

ISBN 0-07-248592-2

Editorial director: *Phillip A. Butcher*
Senior sponsoring editor: *Carolyn Henderson Meier*
Senior marketing manager: *Daniel M. Loch*
Project manager: *Christina Thornton-Villagomez*
Production supervisor: *Susanne Riedell*
Lead designer—cover/interior: *Matthew Baldwin*
Media producer: *Shannon Rider*
Senior supplement producer: *Marc Mattson*
Manager, photo research: *Brian Pecko*
Cover image: Roberto Borea © Wide World Photos/AP Photos
Typeface: *10.5/12 New Caledonia*
Compositor: *GAC Indianapolis*
Printer: *R. R. Donnelley & Sons Company*

**Library of Congress Cataloging-in-Publication Data**

Swanson, Charles R., 1942–
Criminal investigation / Charles R. Swanson, Neil C. Chamelin, Leonard Territo.—8th ed.
p. cm.
Includes bibliographical references and index.
ISBN 0-07-248592-2 (alk. paper)
1. Criminal investigation. 2. Criminal investigation—United States. I. Chamelin, Neil C., 1942– II. Territo, Leonard. III. Title.
HV8073 .S84 2003
363.25—dc21

2002067873

www.mhhe.com

# DEDICATION

*From Charles R. Swanson:* For my wife, Paige,
for her endless cheer and support; the kids—Ben, Cole, Colin, Kellie, Maggie, and Traci; my good friends and critics Russ Abernathy, Bob Miller, Mark Foster, and Joe Markham; and the men and women out there, 24-7-365.

*From Neil C. Chamelin:* For my wife, Vicki,
and our children, Chris and Todd.

*From Leonard Territo:* For my wife, Jurema,
and our children, Lorraine, Daniel, Mauricio, and Michelle, and our grandchildren, Matthew, Branden, João Vitor, and Leonardo.

# ABOUT THE AUTHORS

**Charles R. "Mike" Swanson** enlisted in the Marine Corps when he was 17 years old. He then joined the Tampa Police Department, working as a uniformed officer in the highest-crime areas of the city before being promoted to detective. Subsequently, he worked as the senior police planner, and later as the acting deputy director, of the Council on Law Enforcement in the Office of the Florida Governor. While working in Florida, Mike earned his bachelor's and master's degrees in criminology from Florida State University. Then, after a teaching stint at East Carolina University, Mike accepted a faculty position in the University of Georgia's Institute of Government, where he received a Doctor of Public Administration degree and rose through the administrative ranks, retiring as the interim director in late 2001.

In addition to cowriting this book, Mike has coauthored four other books, including *Police Administration: Structures, Processes, and Behavior,* and has authored or coauthored a number of monographs, articles, and conference papers pertaining to policing.

Mike has extensive experience in designing promotional systems for state, county, and municipal public safety agencies, including the Georgia State Patrol. He has conducted over 60 job analysis studies and written more than 125 promotional tests. He has designed and implemented at least 75 assessment centers, as well as written the exercises. Mike has trained assessors from 13 different states. He has testified in federal court as an expert witness on promotional matters. In retirement, he is very active consulting with police agencies on custom-designed promotional systems, written tests, and assessment centers.

**Neil C. Chamelin** is an assistant state attorney in Leon County, Florida. He previously served as a hearing officer in the Florida Division of Motor Vehicles; director of Criminal Justice Programs for Troy State University—European Region; director of the Florida Police Standards and Training Commission; division director, Standards and Training Division, Florida Department of Law Enforcement; administrator of the Police Science Division, Institute of Government, at the University of Georgia; and director of the Florida Institute for Law Enforcement. He has also served as a police officer in Sarasota, Florida. Chamelin is coauthor of *Criminal Law for Police Officers, Introduction to Criminal Justice,* and *Police Personnel Selection Process.*

**Leonard Territo** is a professor of criminology at the University of South Florida, Tampa. Previously he was chief deputy (undersheriff) of the Leon County, Florida, Sheriff's Office, and served for nine years in the patrol, traffic, detective, and personnel and training divisions of the Tampa Police Department. He is a former chairperson of the Department of Police Administration at St. Petersburg Junior College, where he directed specialized continuing education programs for police officers through the Florida Institute for Law Enforcement. In addition to writing numerous articles, book chapters, and technical reports, he has authored or coauthored nine books, the most recent of which are *Stress Management in Law Enforcement; Police Administration: Structures, Processes and Behavior;* and *Crime and Justice in America.* His books have been used in over 1,000 colleges and universities in all 50 states.

# BRIEF CONTENTS

# CONTENTS

## Chapter 4 Interviewing and Interrogation



## Chapter 5 Field Notes and Investigative Reporting

## Chapter 6 The Follow-Up Investigation



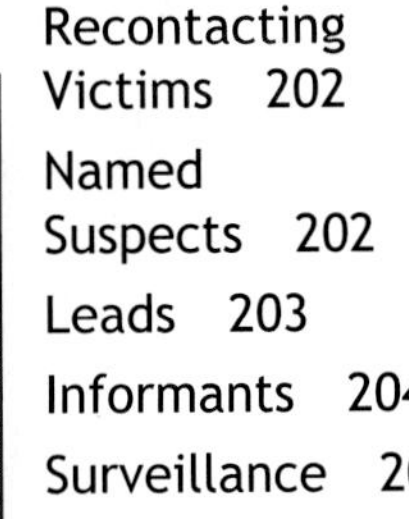

## Chapter 7 The Crime Laboratory

## Chapter 8 Investigative Resources



## Chapter 9 Injury and Death Investigations

## Chapter 10 Sex-Related Offenses

## Chapter 11 Crimes against Children

## Chapter 15 Vehicle Thefts and Related Offenses



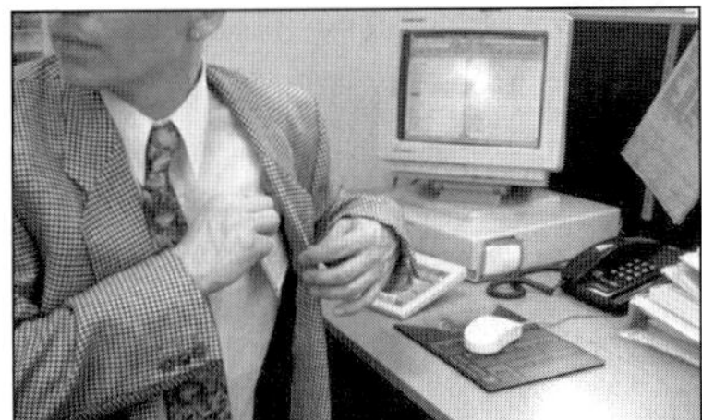

## Chapter 16 Computer Crime

POLICE

## Chapter 21 The Investigator and the Legal System

# PREFACE

For reasons that we can all articulate, crime is a terrible burden on society. The men and women who will, or presently do, investigate crime play a crucial role in combating it. More than anything, this book is intended as a tool for those trying to make life safer for all of us.

*Criminal Investigation* continues to differ from other texts for this course, and it is important to understand the differences, as they are again reflected throughout this edition.

First, investigation generally has been conceived of, and touted as, an art. This approach depreciates the precision required to conduct inquiries; it denies the existence of, and adherence to, rigorous methods; and it associates investigation with unneeded mysticism. Investigation is in large part a science. The fact that criminals are not always apprehended does not make it less so. The rational scientific method will, of necessity, be supplemented by initiative and occasional fortuitous circumstances, but it is the application of the method rather than shrewd hunches that most frequently produces results. The most successful investigators are those who know how to apply the rational scientific method; therefore, it is this method that we consistently use in *Criminal Investigation.*

A second major difference between this text and others arises from our belief that writing about techniques takes on more substance if one understands something of the nature of the event being investigated. Thus, we have discussed typologies—including offenses, offenders, and victims—in depth, so that our readers not only take away a more comprehensive understanding of criminal investigation than they would from another textbook but also have substantial information to refer back to later, when they are using the text as a reference.

Third, because crime prevention technology has been a significant milestone for both the police and the public, we have inserted short sections on prevention in chapters where appropriate. The complexity of crime prevention dictates that it is a specialization within police departments. Yet at the scene of a crime, the investigator may be in a unique position to make a few helpful, if rudimentary, suggestions to a victim on how to avoid further loss. *Criminal Investigation's* crime prevention sections give investigators the tools to accomplish this task.

Finally, most investigative books tend to blur the distinction between the roles of uniformed officers and detectives; we draw this line distinctly. While everyone may not agree with our dichotomizing, it is essential that the uniformed officer's role be recognized for the contribution it makes to the ultimate success of an investigation.

## THE EIGHTH EDITION

Criminal investigation is always evolving due to scientific, legal, and social developments, as well as changes in the behavior of criminals. While many investigative techniques are fundamental and remain basically the same over time, there are also significant changes that occur on a continuing basis. In addition to having updated photographs, tables, figures, and citations, this edition reflects both the ongoing and the changing dimensions of criminal investigation by including the following text updates and revisions:

- Chapter 1, "The Evolution of Criminal Investigation and Criminalistics," a historically oriented chapter, has undergone more modest revision than other chapters. However, a new chapter-ending section on institutional initiatives in investigation and criminalistics through 2001 ensures that the chapter remains relevant for today's readers.
- Chapter 2, "Investigators, the Investigative Process, and the Crime Scene," is a major

rewrite, a dynamic new chapter on the cutting edge of practice. The section on preliminary investigation has been greatly expanded and now covers in depth the protocols for releasing the scene to follow-up investigators. Also included is a new discussion of primary and secondary crime scenes, as well as macroscopic and microscopic scenes.

- Chapter 3, "Physical Evidence," has been carefully updated to reflect changes in protocols for locating, collecting, marking, and preserving physical evidence.
- Chapter 4, "Interviewing and Interrogation," combines these two critical and interrelated investigative techniques, describing in detail their commonalities and their differences—something reviewers have asked us to do.
- Chapter 5, "Field Notes and Investigative Reporting," includes several new sections—among them, sections on the National Incident Based Reporting System (NIBRS) and the use of mobile data terminals—as well as a number of new model reporting forms from various police agencies.
- Chapter 6, "The Follow-Up Investigation," is a substantially rewritten chapter. While the title is not new, the coverage is. The chapter now includes new model forms on the building/neighborhood canvass, the vehicle canvass, and lead assignments, as well as an expanded section on sources of information internal to police departments (e.g., intelligence files, impounded-vehicle reports, and field interview or information cards). The polygraph and psychological stress evaluator section is entirely new, as are the guidelines for conducting photo, automated photo, and live lineups and show-ups.
- Chapter 7, "The Crime Laboratory," now includes coverage of the role of the National Institute of Justice in promoting new forensic science research technologies as well as material on the identification and collection of DNA evidence, new developments in DNA-testing technologies, and postconviction DNA testing. The chapter also features updated coverage of the Integrated Automated Fingerprint Identification System and the new National Integrated Ballistic Information Network Program.
- Chapter 8, "Investigative Resources," is a brand-new chapter offering a fast-paced look at intelligence units, the intelligence cycle, methods of crime analysis, and ways in which intelligence is disseminated, as well as methods of criminal and geographic profiling and tools such as time-event charting and telephone record analysis. An array of federal investigative resources is covered, including the Combined DNA Index System (CODIS), the Child Abduction and Serial Murder Investigative Resources Center (CASMIRC), Law Enforcement On-Line (LEO), and more.
- Chapter 9, "Injury and Death Investigations," features revised coverage of stalking, including cyberstalking and a significantly expanded section on serial murder.
- Chapter 10, "Sex-Related Offenses," contains a new section on the different categories of sexual murders and another on drug-facilitated sexual assault (by means of Rohypnol and GHB, for instance).
- Chapter 11, "Crimes against Children," now includes sections on runaways and abduction, sex-offender registration, and the investigation of crime in schools.
- Chapter 12, "Robbery," has been updated in regard to statistics and references and includes new case studies, new figures, and new sections on carjackings, ATM robberies, truck hijackings, and taxi-driver and convenience-store robberies.
- Chapter 13, "Burglary," now includes an important new section on criminal fences and their operations as well as investigative techniques for detecting them, including stings.
- Chapter 14, "Larceny and Fraud," now features coverage of mail fraud, the use of the Internet to launder money, and identity theft.
- Chapter 15, "Vehicle Thefts and Related Offenses," contains new material on cargo theft, the NCIC 2000, and the National Equipment Register.
- Chapter 16, "Computer Crime," is another significantly revised chapter. It now features an easy-to-understand "typology of computer crime" that focuses on the computer as the target of a criminal act, the computer as the instrumentality of a crime, the computer as

incidental to a crime, and crimes often associated with computer use. New, in-depth discussions of computer-based money laundering, child pornography and pedophilia, and intellectual-property violation highlight this presentation. There is also an extensive discussion of malicious attack codes sent through new Trojan horse, virus, and worm programs aimed at the destruction of Internet sites. Finally, the chapter highlights new investigative techniques involved in the detection, prevention, and prosecution of computer crimes, with a special discussion on crime scene techniques and digital forensic analysis.

- Chapter 17, "Agricultural, Wildlife, and Environmental Crimes," features a revised section on environmental crime and continues to emphasize the connection between rural crime and the urban setting, including the sale of rustled horses for slaughter, the theft of dinosaur fossils from public land, seasonal theft of Christmas-type trees along expressways and parkways, and specialized investigative resources such as the EPA's National Enforcement Investigation Center (NEIC) and the U.S. Fish and Wildlife National Forensics Laboratory.
- Chapter 18, "Arson and Explosives Investigations," now includes new material on burn indicators, as well as a detailed guide for explosion and bomb scene investigations.
- Chapter 19, "Recognition, Control, and Investigation of Drug Abuse," has been updated and now includes discussion of OxyContin, ecstasy, and other "new" drugs.
- Chapter 20, "Terrorism," is new to the book and examines what terrorism is, which domestic and international terrorist groups are presently on the U.S. radar scope, the aims and methods of these groups, and the role of state and local officers in investigating and preventing terrorism.
- Chapter 21, "The Investigator and the Legal System," describes pretrial and trial procedures and offers a detailed discussion on the law enforcement investigator's role in court.

## ORGANIZATION

As with previous editions, we have attempted to craft in this revision a book that unfolds along the same logical continuum as an investigation. We start with the basics—fundamentals and history—in Chapter 1, "The Evolution of Criminal Investigation and Criminalistics," and move on to actual crime scenes and an overview of investigatory procedures in Chapter 2, "Investigators, the Investigative Process, and the Crime Scene." From the crime scene, we go to physical evidence in Chapter 3, interviewing and interrogation in Chapter 4, and field notes and reporting in Chapter 5. Thus, by the close of Chapter 5—just over a hundred pages into the text—readers have mastered all the basics of criminal investigation.

The next three chapters are pivotal, elevating the reader's view from the crime scene to a wider perspective of investigation, including a more detailed understanding of the follow-up investigation, the role of the crime laboratory, and the myriad of federal and state resources that can be brought to bear on an investigation. Then, Chapters 9 through 20 explore crime-specific offenses in depth, presenting practical information about offenders, offenses, and offense investigations of everything from injury and death to fraud, computer and environmental crimes, and terrorism. The closing chapter, "The Investigator and the Legal System," addresses the legal system as the investigator interacts with it, describing pretrial and trial procedures in detail.

## LEARNING AIDS

Working together, the authors and editor have developed a format for the text that supports the goal of a readable, practical, user-friendly book. In addition to all the changes already mentioned, we have added a host of new photographs, figures, and tables to this edition to amplify the text coverage. A more visual presentation of the book's many lists—which are so critical in a text that teaches professionals or future professionals "how to" investigate crime—makes this material easier than ever to digest. The learning aids in the eighth edition go beyond these visual elements, however:

- **New, chapter-opening photographs, detailed outlines, and learning objectives** draw readers in and serve as a road map to the chapter.

- **New, expanded chapter-opening overviews** provide readers with a snapshot of the entire chapter and will prove to be excellent review tools when readers are preparing for exams.
- **New, detailed captions accompany photographs,** clarifying precisely what readers should be looking for and learning from when examining each piece of art.
- **New end-of-chapter review sections featuring key-term lists, review questions, and Internet activities** make preparing for exams easier than ever.
- **A new end-of-book glossary** includes definitions for all the text's key terms—a valuable review tool now and a superb reference resource later.

We have, of course, retained our plentiful, widely acclaimed "cases" within the body of every chapter, ensuring that the eighth edition is not only the most current, definitive text on criminal investigation but also the most practical and relevant. And with the enhancements we have made to the learning aids, *Criminal Investigation* is, simply put, the most mastery-oriented text available for the course.

## SUPPLEMENTS

As a full-service publisher of quality educational products, McGraw-Hill does much more than just sell textbooks. The company creates and publishes an extensive array of print, video, and digital supplements for students and instructors. This edition of *Criminal Investigation* is accompanied by an extensive supplements package.

### FOR THE STUDENT

- *Making the Grade CD-ROM (by Chris Perillo, Atlantic County Community College):* This free electronic study guide, packaged with every text, includes chapter quizzes with feedback indicating why each answer is right or wrong, an Internet guide, a study skills primer, and much more.
- *Online Learning Center Website (by Chris Perillo and Maryann Carol, Atlantic County Community College):* This unique, book-specific website features interactive cases that are not only fun to explore but terrific learning tools; the website also includes flashcards that can be used to master vocabulary and a wealth of other chapter review tools.

### FOR THE INSTRUCTOR

- *Instructor's Manual and Testbank (by Max Bromley, University of South Florida):* Rewritten from scratch, this instructor supplement now includes detailed chapter outlines, key terms, overviews, lecture notes, transparency masters, and a complete testbank.
- *Computerized Testbank:* This easy-to-use computerized testing program is for both Windows and Macintosh computers.
- *PowerPoint Slides:* Complete chapter-by-chapter slide shows feature text, art, and tables.
- *Online Learning Center Website:* Password-protected access is provided for important instructor support materials and additional resources.
- *PageOut:* This easy-to-use tool allows the instructor to create his or her own course web page and access all material at the *Criminal Investigation* Online Learning Center.
- *Videotapes:* A wide variety of videotapes from the *Films for the Humanities and Social Sciences* series is available to adopters of the text.

All the above supplements are provided *free of charge* to students and instructors. Orders of new (versus used) textbooks help us defray the cost of developing such supplements, which is substantial. Please contact your local McGraw-Hill representative for more information on any of the above supplements.

## ACKNOWLEDGMENTS

Without the kindness of many people throughout the country—literally from Alaska to Maine—this book could not have been written. We are grateful for the support of our colleagues around the country who have contributed case histories, reviewed portions of the manuscript within their areas of expertise, written sections for inclusion in the book, contributed photographs, forms, and other illustrations, or otherwise gone out of their way to be helpful. Our continuing concern in writing these acknowledgments is that, inadvertently, we may have omitted someone. If this is so, let us know so that we may correct this oversight and also please accept our apologies. Our acknowledgments include persons who have contributed to this edition and those who helped with earlier editions. Some of the people identified have retired or taken on new responsibilities since assisting us, but unless otherwise requested, we include their organizational affiliation and status at the time of the original contribution, since we feel that the agencies then employing them are also deserving of continued recognition.

Colleagues who have contributed photographs, forms, and other illustrations are identified on page xxviii; thank you one and all. We would also like to thank another group of individuals who helped out in a variety of ways. Bob Hopkins, Hillsborough County, Florida, Sheriff's Office, gave us information to strengthen the section on follow-up investigations; Commander Michael Frazier, Phoenix, Arizona, Police Department, was helpful with information on arson and explosives, as were Chief Richard Pennington and Officer R. Bonelli from the New Orleans Police Department; Chief Lee Donahue and Major William Gulledge, Honolulu, Hawaii, Police Department; Kenneth V. Lanning, Supervising Special Agent of the Federal Bureau of Investigation and the National Center for Missing and Exploited Children, allowed us to reprint in Chapter 11—"Crimes against Children"—from his previously published material on the topics of child molestation and child pornography. Major Andy Garrison and Frank Broadrick, Northeast Georgia Police Academy, reviewed the chapter on report writing and made good suggestions for its revision. Steven Gottlieb, executive director of the Alpha Group Center for Crime and Intelligence Analyst Training, allowed us to adopt portions of his textbook to explain the critical role of crime analysis in law enforcement investigations. Ron French, Ecorse, Michigan, Fire Department, provided updated commentary on where and how fires start, as well as on fire setting and related mechanisms. Leigh Herbst from the University of Nebraska helped with the new chapter-opening and -closing material.

Gene Lazarus, Florida State Fire College, Ocala, and Steve Mraz, formerly with the Pinellas County, Florida, Fire Academy, reviewed and contributed to the arson chapter. Bob Quinn, Tom Costigan, Mike Rendina, Jim Wilder, and Richard Frank, presently or formerly with the Drug Enforcement Administration; Tom Matthews, Temple Terrace, Florida, Police Department; and Mike Sciales, formerly with the Hillsborough County, Florida, Sheriff's Office, reviewed and contributed to the chapter on drug abuse. Richard Souviron, Chief Forensic Odontologist, Dade County Florida, Medical Examiners Office, was the principal author of the material dealing with bite marks and dental evidence. Dr. Wally Graves, Medical Examiner for Lee, Henry, and Glades Counties, Florida, provided information on dental evidence. John Valor, forensic artist and photographer, provided illustrations for the dental section. Dick Williams, FBI Crime Laboratory, read the questioned-documents section and made a number of suggestions to clarify and strengthen it. Don Hampton, Springfield, Missouri, Police Department, did the same for parts of the crime scene chapter. Bob Taylor, University of North Texas, who has yet to master the nuances of steelhead fishing, coauthored the chapter on computer crime. We benefited also from the reviews and research materials provided by Jim Halligan, formerly with the Florida Department of Law Enforcement and then a professor at Florida State University's School of Criminology. He was a superb teacher and a real friend.

This eighth edition of the book benefited from the counsel of reviewers: Thanks to James M. Adcock, University of New Haven; William J. Vizzard, California State University, Sacramento; Anthony C. Trevelino, Camden County College; Norman J. Raasch, Lakeland Community College; Dennis M. Payne, Michigan State University; Richard H. DeLung, Wayland Baptist University; C. Wayne Johnston, Arkansas State University; Michael J. McCrystle, California State University, Sacramento; Daniel K. Maxwell, University of New Haven; Steven Brandl, University of Wisconsin, Milwaukee; Joseph Morris, Northwestern State University; Tere Chipman, Fayetteville Technical College; Stephan D. Kaftan, Hawkeye Community College; Alexandro del Carmen, University of Texas, Arlington; and Michael Grimes, Miami Dade Community College.

Maryellin Territo devoted long hours to researching sources for the most current information relating to all facets of criminal investigation.

Manuscript typing and revisions were handled by Marianne Bell and Carole Rennick, who worked hard and were patient with our changes and deadlines. Thanks to all of you.

Finally, a few words about the hard-working people at McGraw-Hill who helped make this a better book: We would like to thank Senior Editor Carolyn Henderson Meier; Project Manager Christina Thornton-Villagomez; Senior Designer Matt Baldwin; Photo Research Manager Brian Pecko; Senior Marketing Manager Dan Loch; Media Producer Shannon Rider; Copy Editor Susan Gottfried; and everyone else from the McGraw-Hill production staff in Burr Ridge who worked on this edition of the text.

Charles R. "Mike" Swanson
Neil C. Chamelin
Leonard Territo

# IN APPRECIATION

We are grateful to our colleagues from around the country who have been kind enough to contribute photographs, forms, or other figures to the text. The inclusion of such material helps ensure the relevancy and usefulness of the text for all readers in all states. For this, we are indebted to the following individuals, departments, and agencies:

**Alaska**

State of Alaska Scientific Crime Detection Laboratory

**Arizona**

Phoenix, Arizona, Police Department

**California**

California Bureau of Livestock Identification
Kern County, California, Sheriff's Department
Los Angeles County Sheriff's Department
Riverside County, California, Sheriff's Department
San Bernardino County, California, Sheriff's Department
San Diego County Sheriff's Department
Santa Ana, California, Police Department
Santa Barbara County, California, Sheriff's Department

**Colorado**

Westminster, Colorado, Police Department

**Delaware**

Delaware State Police

**Florida**

Big Bend Bomb Disposal Team, Tallahassee, Florida
Dade County Medical Examiner Department, Miami, Florida
Leon County Sheriff's Department, Tallahassee, Florida
Miami-Dade Police Department
Pinellas County, Florida, Public Health Unit, Sexual Assault Victim Examination Program
Pinellas County, Florida, Sheriff's Office
Port Orange, Florida, Police Department
St. Petersburg, Florida, Police Department
Tallahassee Regional Crime Laboratory, Florida Department of Law Enforcement
Tampa, Florida Fire Department,
Tampa, Florida Police Department

**Georgia**

Athens-Clarke County, Georgia, Police Department
Atlanta Police Department

**Idaho**

Idaho Bureau of Investigation

**Illinois**

Chicago Crime Laboratory
Chicago Police Department
Cook County, Illinois, Sheriff's Department
Illinois State Police

**Indiana**

Indiana State Police

**Iowa**

Iowa Criminalistic Laboratory, Department of Public Safety
State Historical Society of Iowa

**Kansas**

Wichita, Kansas, Police Department

**Kentucky**

Kentucky State Police

**Maine**

Lewiston, Maine, Police Department

**Massachusetts**

Massachusetts Environmental Police

**Michigan**
Ecorse, Michigan, Fire Department
Sterling Heights, Michigan, Police Department

**Mississippi**
Yoknapatawpha County, Mississippi, Sheriff's Department

**Missouri**
Regional Criminalistics Laboratory, Metropolitan Kansas City, Missouri
Springfield, Missouri, Police Department
St. Louis County, Missouri, Police Department
St. Louis Police Department

**New Jersey**
New Jersey State Police

**New York**
Nassau County, New York, Police Department
New York City Police Department

**Ohio**
Geauga County, Ohio, Sheriff's Department

**Pennsylvania**
Pennsylvania State Police
Philadelphia Police Department

**South Carolina**
Georgetown, South Carolina, Police Department

**Tennessee**
Nashville Police Department
Tennessee Bureau of Investigation

**Texas**
Austin, Texas, Police Department
Dallas Police Department
Texas Department of Public Safety
Texas Parks & Wildlife

**Virginia**
Alexandra, Virginia, Police Department
Fairfax County, Virginia, Police Department

**Washington**
Clark County Sheriff's Office, Vancouver, Washington

**Wisconsin**
Madison Police Department
Milwaukee County Department of Social Service

**Wyoming**
Lincoln County, Wyoming, Sheriff's Office
Wyoming Game and Fish Department
Wyoming State Archives and Historical Department

**National & Federal Agencies**
Bureau of Justice Statistics, U.S. Department of Justice
Centers for Disease Control
Chester A. Higgins, Jr., and the U.S. Department of Justice, Office of Justice Programs, Drug Enforcement Administration
Environmental Protection Agency
Federal Bureau of Investigation
Federal Emergency Management Agency
Immigration and Naturalization Service, Forensic Document Laboratory
National Automobile Theft Bureau
National Center for Missing and Exploited Children
National Institute of Justice
National Insurance Crime Bureau
National Park Service
Office of Justice Programs, National Institute of Justice
Pinkerton's Archives
U.S. Customs Service
U.S. Department of the Treasury Bureau of Alcohol, Tobacco and Firearms
U.S. Forest Service
U.S. Public Health Service

**International Agencies**
London Metropolitan Police
Royal Canadian Mounted Police

# VISUAL WALK-THROUGH

Criminal investigation is always evolving due to scientific, legal, and social developments, as well as changes in the behavior of criminals. While many investigative techniques are fundamental and remain basically the same over time, there are also significant changes that occur on a continuing basis. This edition of *Criminal Investigation* features the most up-to-date coverage of the important changes in the field.

## New Chapters

Two completely new chapters focus on recent developments: one on terrorism, which is particularly relevant in the aftermath of 9/11, and another on cutting-edge investigative resources, tools, and techniques.

EIGHT

Investigative Resources

*Today, law enforcement agencies make use of state-of-the-art technology to assist in criminal investigations. For example, software is now available to use eyewitness description information to produce reasonable likenesses of potential suspects, like this one, made with EFIT. (Courtesy of Royal Canadian Mounted Police (RCMP))*

TWENTY

Terrorism

*Ground Zero, where the Twin Towers stood prior to the murderous Al-Qaeda attacks on September 11, 2001. This tragic act of terrorism brought about significant changes in the frequency and types of information shared between federal and local law enforcement regarding suspected terrorists and their organizations. (© AFP/Corbis)*

## Dramatic Updating

Dramatic updating of the computer crime chapter keeps the text current and accurate in this ever-changing arena.

SIXTEEN

Computer Crime

Robert W. Taylor and D. Kall Loper

*University of North Texas*

*Given the major advances in computer technology, it is not surprising that there are so many different types of computer crimes today. These range from network intrusion and data altering to the use of computers as facilitators for committing crimes. (© Hannah Gal/Corbis)*

## Extensive Chapter Revisions

Extensive revision of these chapters ensures that the text's presentation of tools and techniques remains unmatched in its currency, comprehensiveness, and accuracy.

S E V E N

### The Crime Laboratory

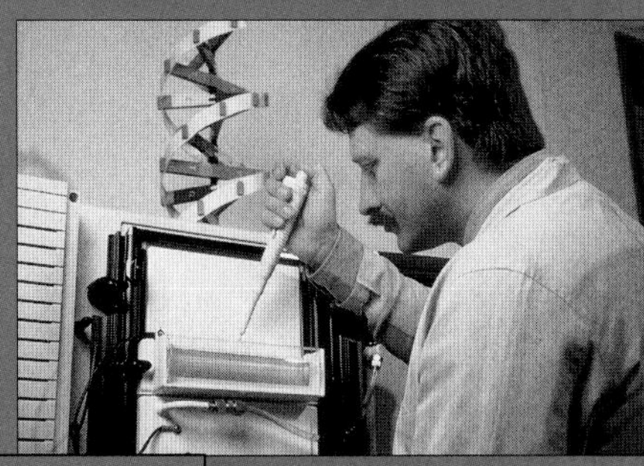

cognized as one of the most comprehensive and prestigious crime labs inception in 1932, the FBI crime lab has provided valuable services for ment agencies at the state, county and municipal level free of charge. (© R. Crandall (The Image Works))

T W O

### Investigators, the Investigative Process, and the Crime Scene

nt, such as a barricaded criminal or a hostage situation, an incident scene to take control of the situation. In fast-moving situations, the to operate out of his/her assigned vehicle until a mobile command , the police will use an existing building, with the permission of the o operate. Following the attack of September 11, 2001, members of epartment established a temporary headquarters near ground zero. (Courtesy Andrea Booher, Federal Emergency Management Agency)

S I X

### The Follow-Up Investigation

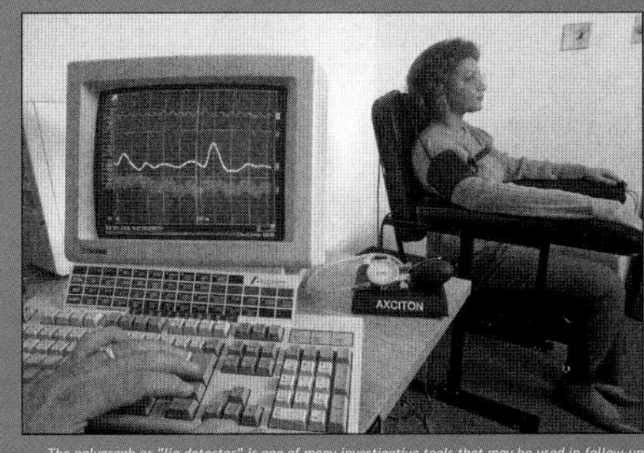


The polygraph or "lie detector" is one of many investigative tools that may be used in follow-up investigations. Today's polygraphs are often computerized, like this one from the Montgomery County Police Department. (© Richard T. Nowtiz/Corbis)

## Chapter-Opening Photographs

Chapter-opening photographs draw the reader in.

## Expanded Chapter Introductions

Expanded chapter introductions provide a snapshot of the entire chapter and will prove invaluable when the reader is studying for exams.

NINE

Injury and Death Investigations

*The investigation of deaths, whether by accidental or felonious cause, can often be aided by modern technology. For example, the underwater search for missing bodies can be facilitated by sonar tracking devices such as the one shown in the photo from Hennepin County, Minnesota, where deputies are using a side scan sonar unit to attempt to locate a body. (© AP/Wide World Photos)*

CHAPTER OUTLINE



CHAPTER OBJECTIVES

1. Describe the four motivational models for classification of homicide.
2. Identify the investigator's responsibilities when responding to the scene of a suspected homicide or assault.
3. Comprehend the importance of personal identification of a victim in a homicide investigation.
4. Outline the major elements in a search for buried bodies.
5. Understand the individual observations used collectively to determine the time of death.
6. Discuss the five most common types of wounds encountered in injury and death investigations.
7. Assess information used by investigators to distinguish between a homicide and a suicide.
8. Outline facts that need to be determined in the investigation of fire deaths.
9. Define stalking, and identify common categories of stalking.
10. Describe what items are needed for a psychological profile.

INTRODUCTION

The investigation of felonious injuries and criminal homicides can be the most important, yet difficult, responsibility assigned to a police investigator. First, these crimes are viewed as being among the most serious offenses committed in our society. The seriousness is reflected in all state statutes, which impose severe penalties for acts resulting in the grave bodily injury or death of a human being. Second, in the beginning stages of some homicide investigations, the inability to identify the decedent greatly complicates the investigative process and prevents it from moving forward. In all homicides, questions such as "Who were the victim's enemies?" and "Who would benefit most from the victim's death?" must be answered before any significant progress can be made in the investigation. Estimating the time of death also needs to be done early in the investigation.

Third, the interview and interrogation process for the investigator in both felony assaults and homicides can be very difficult. For felony

273

## Outlines and Learning Objectives

Chapter-opening outlines and learning objectives serve as the reader's road map to the chapter.

CHAPTER OUTLINE



CHAPTER OBJECTIVES

1. Understand the role of the investigator and the skills and qualities he or she must possess.
2. Discuss the major events in the investigation of a crime.
3. Explain the seven major steps in a preliminary investigation.
4. Describe the activities conducted in a follow-up investigation.
5. Define a crime scene.
5. Outline the purposes and functions of a crime scene investigation.
6. Explain the "rules" for the crime scene investigator.
7. Identify potential threats to investigators' health and safety.
8. Be familiar with the five major considerations that dominate the crime scene search.

INTRODUCTION

Although crime is a national problem, its control is primarily the responsibility of local government. When officials fail to prevent or cannot deal effectively with crime, there are negative consequences. First, if individuals commit crime and escape prosecution, future illegal acts are encouraged. Second, an escalating crime rate requires that resources, which could be devoted to other social problems, be diverted to crime control, resulting in further entrenchment of such ills as poverty, substandard housing, and inadequate medical care. Third, as crime increases, our system of government faces the real possibility of a crisis of confidence in its ability to maintain public welfare. Finally, crime tears the fabric of social relations and living patterns. People become fearful of strangers and of being on the streets after dark, homes become fortresses, and families move to new locations in search of a secure life. A terrible reality is that until significant inroads are made in controlling crime, the overall quality of life is lower than it could be.

While good investigative work will not significantly reduce crime by itself, the investigation of any crime places important responsibilities on the investigator. First, successful investigators must possess essential qualities such as good communication skills, strong ethics, initiative, resourcefulness, and compassion. Second, investigators must ensure that crimes are investigated effectively and thoroughly. This responsibility includes not only complete

## Easy-to-Read Lists

A more visual presentation of the book's many lists makes the material easier than ever to digest.



D.C., area who may have entered more than 100 homes that were being offered for sale, stealing furs, tape recorders, silverware, and other valuables worth between $200,000 and $300,000.[15]

### MAINTAIN DOCUMENTATION

Documentation of the crime scene is a constant activity, starting with the rough, shorthand record created by field notes. Other types of documentation that need to be maintained include:

1. The **crime scene entry log sheet,** which was shown in Figure 2–2.
2. The **administrative log,** which is the responsibility of the crime scene coordinator and details such things as who is assigned to what function at the crime scene and the sequence of events at the scene, including its release.
3. **Assignment sheets,** which are completed by each individual who is given specific work to do and which document the results—both positive and negative.
4. The incidence/offense report, which is the responsibility of the first officer on the scene.
5. **Photographic logs,** detailing who took which shots, from where, when, and under what circumstances (e.g., type of lighting). Typical photo logs are video, digital, conventional 35 millimeter, Polaroid, and aerial (see Figure 2–4).
6. The rough sketch of the crime scene, the data from which are used to prepare the finished or final diagram, which may be drawn by hand or by computer.
7. The **evidence recovery log,** which lists each item of evidence; the names of the collector and witness; the location, date, and time of the collection, and documentation such as photos or diagrams. (See Figure 2–5.)
8. Emergency medical personnel documents.
9. The **lifted-prints log,** which contains the same type of basic information as does the evidence recovery log.
10. If applicable, consent search form or search warrant.

In lesser offenses, a single officer may be the only representative of the police department at the scene. Thus, everything that is learned will be a result of his or her investigation. In such cases the only documentation that may exist is the officer's field notes and the incident/offense report.

### CRIME SCENE SAFETY ISSUES

There are numerous threats to investigators' health and safety. For example, at outdoor scenes people

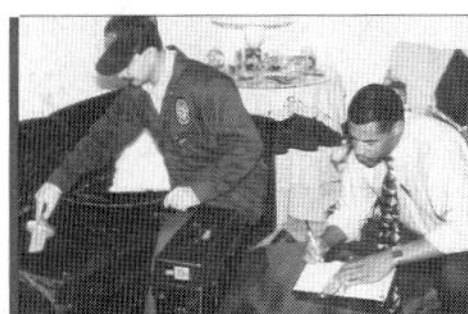

Trace Evidence Vacuum
A crime scene technician uses a trace evidence vacuum on a sofa where a sexual assault took place, while the detective working with him makes notes. Processing the sofa in this manner allows for recovery of hairs, fibers, and even certain types of drugs.
(Courtesy Westminster, Colorado, Police Department)



Figure 2-4a Photo Log Sheet
(Courtesy Imprimus Forensic Services, © 2000, by permission)

PHOTO LOG SHEET
Supplement to Evidence Report

Basic case and photograph information

Individual photos are listed here in numerical sequence and accompanied by notes

may be stung by insects (which could produce anaphylactic shock, a life-threatening allergic reaction), get lyme disease from ticks, be bitten by animals, or get a severe skin reaction from poison ivy, oak, or sumac.[16] More often, however, investigators are at risk of contracting infectious pathogens (disease-causing agents), such as HIV, hepatitis B, hepatitis C, and tuberculosis. After the September 11, 2001, attacks on the Twin Towers in New York City biological terrorism came to the fore in the form of anthrax sent through the mail. Beyond biological warfare are chemical, radiological, and nuclear threats. This section discusses the self-protection measures officers at crime scenes should take with respect to the more usual infectious diseases; the following section covers precautions regarding potential or actual terrorist events.

### INFECTIOUS DISEASES

#### HIV/AIDS

The **human immunodeficiency virus (HIV)** is a blood-borne pathogen that is also present in other body fluids. There is some question as to whether all body fluids can transmit HIV, since evidence indicates that naturally occurring proteins in tears and saliva inhibit HIV. However, investigators must always take all appropriate precautions to protect themselves. If HIV progresses into acquired immunodeficiency syndrome (AIDS), the body's natural defenses against many types of diseases are substantially reduced, leaving victims vulnerable to "opportunistic infections," such as pneumonia, from which they ultimately die. There is no HIV/AIDS vaccine.

## Newly Designed Tables and Figures

Redesigned tables and figures highlight material and make key points more understandable.



feeble-minded or insane, and (5) if the person is a child who is under the age of consent as fixed by statute. Rape is generally considered a woman-centered issue, but growing awareness has led to a rise in reports of male rape. Keep in mind that society places greater stigma on male rape victimization. Fear, shame and this stigmatization still prevent a large number of male victims from reporting their experience. Whether the victims are male or female, the offenders are overwhelmingly male but it is certainly possible for a female to perpetrate rape.[2]

When police and medical examiners are confronted with a dead body, they are obviously not able to interview the deceased victim to obtain an explanation for what has occurred. Investigators must rely on their initial impression of the scene, such as the state of the victim's clothing, positioning of the body, items found, and the presence or absence of injuries related to sexual activity (e.g., bite marks, hickeys, direct genital or oral injury), in deciding whether sexual activity or attempted sexual activity was related to the cause of death. The investigator must be mindful, however, in weighing the significance of the presence of sexual evidence. Although the victim may have engaged in sexual activity with another person before death, the intercourse might not be related to the cause of death.

In the case of a homicide involving a female victim, it is a frequent and ordinary occurrence for investigators to question whether a rape has taken place. However, it is imperative that the question of rape also arise when the victim of a homicide is male. This is especially true when a male child is involved. Currently, the U.S. Department of Justice estimates that about 1 out of every 10 rape victims over the age of 12 is male and that fully half of all underage sexual-abuse victims are male.[3] Sex is a major motivator and modifier of human behavior. Therefore, a determination of sexual activity may be of great value not only in a rape-murder case but also in natural, suicidal, or accidental deaths. Careful observation of the scene and the body may indicate a need for a rape investigation. Even if sexual intercourse does not seem to have any direct bearing on the cause of death, it may explain motives or timing of death or simply provide a check on the veracity of a suspect or witness. The following cases illustrate these points:

A 53-year-old businessman was found dead in a motel room. There was no evidence of foul play. The bed was in slight disarray, with one of the pillows on the floor. The bed covers were bunched in an unusual position. The body on the floor was dressed in a shirt, loosened tie, trousers, underclothes, and socks. Shoes were neatly laid out next to a chair, and a jacket was on the back of a chair. Examination of the contents of the deceased's trouser pockets revealed the usual items, except for a pair of female panties. Autopsy revealed a massive heart attack and no vaginal cells on the penis. A logical reconstruction of the events preceding death suggested sexual foreplay with a female, in the course of which a wrestling match ensued during which the man took the woman's panties and then suffered a heart attack.

Although establishing the absence of sexual intercourse in this case did not significantly add to the medical solution of the problem, it did explain why the victim was found at a motel when he was supposedly having lunch.

A furnace repairman was found dead, slumped over the front seat of his van. There was no evidence of foul play, and the medical examiner was not called to the scene. Observation at the morgue revealed that there were peculiar parallel linear abrasions over the victim's knees, tearing of the overalls at the same region, and his underwear. His boots were reversed and loosely laced. Penile washings were positive for vaginal cells. Further investigation disclosed that he had visited a woman at 7 in the morning under the pretext of cleaning her furnace and had been stricken by a heart attack during intercourse. The woman hastily dressed him and dragged him across the back alley to his truck, not realizing that his underwear was neatly tucked under her bed.

A 15-year-old girl's body was found in a vacant lot. The absence of clothing on the lower body suggested sexual intercourse immediately before the time of death. Faint abrasions were present on the back of the neck, and marked hemorrhages were present in the eye. The medical examiner believed that this was a case of rape-

## Chapter Cases

Plentiful, widely acclaimed "cases" within the body of each chapter ensure the text's real-world applicability.

## Expanded Figure and Photo Captions

Detailed captions now accompany photographs and figures to clarify precisely what the reader should be looking for and learning from when examining each piece of art.



Footwear Impression Photography
Here a crime scene technician is recording the location of a shoe impression in dirt. The shoe print runs left to right, roughly between the two front legs of the tripod. The small slip of white paper is just "north" of the impression and has the necessary case identification information on it. The most important of a series of photographs will be shot from directly above the impression using a tripod and will include a ruler alongside the impression.
(Courtesy Nassau County, New York, Police Department)

#### Preserving Shoe Impressions in Snow

Dental stone is also the preferred material for casting impressions in snow, replacing the more difficult and time-consuming process of using sulfur, which has to be heated. Impressions in snow should first be photographed in the manner previously described. A red-colored product called **Snow Print Wax** is sprayed on the impression at a 30- to 45-degree angle until the highlights are lightly tinted. A dark-colored spray paint will also serve the same purpose. In either case, the spray can must be held 30 to 40 inches away so that the force of the aerosol does not disturb the details of the impression. The impression is then rephotographed (see photos in the right-hand column on page 76). The casting process is continued, with the impression being sprayed with enough Snow Print Wax to form a layer of wax, followed by the dental-stone casting process. Because some heat is generated when dental stone is mixed, use snow or cold water instead of water to form a consistency somewhat thinner than pancake batter. A box should be placed over the cast as it dries for at least 1 hour before it is moved.

### PAINT

During many investigations there is the possibility of encountering paint that has been transferred accidentally or deliberately, from one object to another.[23] The paint is transferred as fresh smears, dried chips, or "chalking" from old, dry paint. Cases in which such transfers occur include burglaries and hit-run-run accidents.[24] In these offenses, the paint may be found on tools in the suspect's possession or on clothing. In hit-and-run cases, the make and model of the involved vehicle might be identified by comparing paint evidence to FBI reference files on original-manufacturer finishes.

Usually, paint is class-characteristic evidence, although in some cases it reaches the level of individual evidence. If the chips are large enough, it may be possible to make a physical match between a

The Evolution of Criminal Investigation and Criminalistics . . . . 21

over the past decade there have been a number of discoveries in the area of DNA profiling, and they have led to quicker procedures with excellent reliability. While individual and team-driven scientific breakthroughs will continue to foster progress, another important factor has been initiatives at the institutional and system levels.

Characteristically, these initiatives are put forth by agencies blending old and new technologies and by agencies creating and managing new databases. The quickening pace of such initiatives can be seen in Table 1–1, on pages 19 and 20, which lists some of the major institutional and system initiatives of recent years in chronological order. As explained in the table, the Combined DNA Index System (CODIS) uses computer technology and scientific discoveries about DNA to create electronic comparisons of DNA profiles. The creation and management of a new database is typified by the Jewelry and Gem (JAG) database, which includes descriptions and images of stolen items. A number of the initiatives identified in Table 1-1 are discussed in greater detail in subsequent chapters, such as Chapter 8, "Investigative Resources."

## Key Terms

**anthropometry**
**Bertillon, Alphonse**
**bobbies**
**Bow Street Runners**
**criminalistics**
**dactylography**
**deoxyribonucleic acid (DNA)**
**Drug Enforcement Administration (DEA)**
**Enderby cases**
**Fielding, Henry**
**Fielding, John**
**Galton, Francis**
**Girard, Stephen**
**Goddard, Calvin**
**Goddard, Henry**
**Gross, Hans**
**Henry system**
**Kirk, Paul**
**Lattes, Leone**
**Locard, Edmond**
**Metropolitan Police Act (1829)**
**Mulberry Street Morning Parade**
**National Academy**
**National Crime Information Center (NCIC)**
**Osborn, Albert**
**palo verde seedpod case**
**Peel, Robert**
**Pinkerton, Allan**
**"police spies"**
**Popay, Sergeant**
**rogues' gallery**
**Scotland Yard**
**T-men**
**Vollmer, August**
**Vucetich, Juan**
**West case**

## Review Questions

1. Who were the Bow Street Runners, and of what historical importance are they?
2. Why did the British public object to the use of detectives after enactment of the Metropolitan Police Act of 1829?
3. Why did the profession of detective in this country basically evolve in the private sector?
4. What assessment can be made of the work of Pinkerton and his National Detective Agency?
5. What is a rogues' gallery?
6. What parallels can be drawn between Allan Pinkerton and J. Edgar Hoover?
7. What is anthropometry, and why was it abandoned in favor of dactylography?
8. What are the milestones in the development of dactylography?
9. Why does the Henry classification system enjoy greater use than Vucetich's system?
10. What are the different human sources of DNA material identified in this chapter?
11. Of what significance is the palo verde case?
12. What are the milestones in the development of firearms identification?

22 . . . . Chapter One

## Internet Activities

1. Research your local, county, and state police agencies. Do these agencies have a criminal investigation unit? Is there more than one unit that specializes in particular types of crimes (burglary, robbery, homicide, etc.)? How many investigators are assigned to such units? Do officers have to meet a certain criteria to be assigned to these units? Is there any history on the creation of these units?
2. Find out more about DNA forensics by logging onto the U.S. Department of Energy's Human Genome Program website at www.ornl.gov/hgmis. Under the heading "Ethical, Legal and Social Issues" click on "Forensics." Is DNA an effective identifier? What are some interesting uses of DNA forensics? What are the ethical, legal, and social issues associated with DNA data banking?

## Notes

1. Material on the evolution of criminal investigation is drawn, in part, from Thomas R. Phelps, Charles R. Swanson, Jr., and Kenneth Evans, *Introduction to Criminal Justice* (New York: Random House, 1979), pp. 42–55.
2. T. A. Critchley, *A History of Police in England and Wales*, 2nd ed. (Montclair, N.J.: Patterson Smith, 1972), p. 34.
3. Ibid.
4. A. C. Germann, Frank D. Day, and Robert J. Gallati, *Introduction to Law Enforcement and Criminal Justice* (Springfield, Ill.: Charles C. Thomas, 1970), pp. 54–55.
5. Melville Lee, *A History of Police in England* (Montclair, N.J.: Patterson Smith reprint, 1971), p. 240.
6. Thomas A. Reppetto, *The Blue Parade* (New York: Free Press, 1978), p. 26.
7. Ibid., pp. 26–28.
8. Ibid., p. 29.
9. Ibid., p. 29, states three of four; John Coatman, *Police* (New York: Oxford, 1959), pp. 98–99, notes only one such conviction. Vincent's CID was based on his study of the Paris centralized detective system.
10. Coatman, *Police*, pp. 98–99.
11. Ibid., p. 99.
12. James F. Richardson, *The New York Police* (New York: Oxford, 1970), p. 37.
13. James D. Horan, *The Pinkertons* (New York: Bonanza Books, 1967), p. 25.
14. Ibid., p. 23.
15. Ibid., p. 25.
16. Jurgen Thorwald, *The Marks of Cain* (London: Thames and Hudson, 1965), p. 129.
17. Reppetto, *The Blue Parade*, p. 258.
18. Thorwald, *The Marks of Cain*, p. 129.
19. Reppetto, *The Blue Parade*, p. 257. There seems to be some dispute over whether there was ever any real threat and, if so, whether Pinkerton or New York City Police actually discovered it.
20. Ibid., pp. 257–258.
21. Ibid., p. 258. Reppetto asserts that as a military analyst Pinkerton was a failure and that his overestimates of enemy strength made General McClellan too cautious, contributing to McClellan's dismissal as head of the Union army.
22. Ibid.
23. William J. Bopp and Donald Shultz, *Principles of American Law Enforcement and Criminal Justice* (Springfield, Ill.: Charles C. Thomas, 1972), pp. 70–71.
24. Thorwald, *The Marks of Cain*, p. 131.
25. Reppetto, *The Blue Parade*, p. 259, notes that in two separate instances a total of eight Reno gang members arrested by the Pinkertons were subsequently lynched. In the first instance, three gang members reportedly were taken from Pinkerton custody.
26. Thorwald, *The Marks of Cain*, p. 131.
27. Reppetto, *The Blue Parade*, p. 261.
28. Ibid., p. 263.
29. Clive Emsley, *Policing and Its Context 1750–1870* (New York: Schocken Books, 1983), p. 106.
30. Augustine E. Costello, *Our Police Protectors* (Montclair, N.J.: Patterson Smith, 1972 reprint of an 1885 edition), p. 402.
31. Richardson, *The New York Police*, p. 122.

# End-of-Chapter Review

Each chapter closes with a list of key terms, review questions, and Internet activities.

# End-of-Book Glossary

A new end-of-book glossary includes definitions for all the text's key terms—a valuable review tool now and a superb reference resource later.

# GLOSSARY

**AAMVANET** Maintained by the American Association of Motor Vehicle Administrators, a computerized network linking state and Canadian province agencies on driver's license and motor vehicle matters of highway usage and safety.

**accelerant** In fire starting, any flammable fluid or compound that speeds the progress of a fire. Also called *booster*.

**action stereotyping** Occurs when an officer expects an event will unfold in a particular way; it can result in the officer's failure to see the event the way it actually occurred.

**active system (theft deterrent)** A type of vehicle antitheft device which requires that the driver do something to activate and deactivate the system every time the vehicle is parked or driven.

**administrative log** A written record of the actions taken by the crime scene coordinator, including assignments and release of the scene.

**admissibility** A legal criterion used to determine whether an item of evidence can be presented in court; requires that the evidence have relevance, materiality, and competence.

**admission** A person's acknowledgment of certain facts or circumstances that tend to incriminate him or her with respect to a crime but are not complete enough to constitute a confession.

**affidavit** A sworn, written statement of the information known to an officer that serves as the basis for the issuance of an arrest warrant.

**affirmation** The process in which a witness acknowledges that he or she understands and undertakes the obligation of an oath (i.e., to tell the truth with a realization of the penalties for perjury); a means of establishing a witness's competence.

**AFIS** *see* **Automated Fingerprint Identification System.**

**agrichemical** Any of various chemical products used on farms; includes pesticides, fertilizers, and herbicides.

**agroterrorism** The use of biological agents as weapons against the agricultural and food supply industries.

**AIDS** *see* **human immunodeficiency virus**.

**algor mortis** The decrease in body temperature that occurs after death.

**alligatoring** The checking of charred wood, which gives it the appearance of alligator skin.

**ALS** *see* **alternative light systems.**

**alternative light systems (ALSs)** Portable lasers and handheld ultraviolet lighting used to locate physical evidence at the crime scene; particularly helpful in locating trace evidence.

**amateur burglars** Burglars who operate on the basis of impulse or opportunity, with no planning; often use sheer force to enter, ransack the premises for anything of value, and may become violent if detected and commit secondary crimes (e.g., murder, rape).

**ambush** A robbery that involves virtually no planning and depends on surprise and the use of force against victims; usually produces a small score.

**American Society of Crime Laboratory Directors (ASCLD)** An international society devoted to maintaining the highest standards of practice at crime laboratories; conducts an accreditation program for laboratories and education programs for lab personnel.

**amido black** A dye that is sensitive to blood and thus is used in developing fingerprints contaminated with blood.

G

Glossary . . . . G-1

**amphetamines** Stimulants that increase blood pressure and heart, respiratory, and metabolic rates; produce decreased appetite, hyperalert senses, and a general state of stress that last a prolonged period.

**anthrax** An acute infectious disease with three forms (cutaneous, intestinal, and inhalation), which differ in means of transmission, symptoms, and lethality; also, a biological agent.

**anthropometry** Developed by Alphonse Bertillon in the late 19th century, the study and comparison of body measurements as a means of criminal identification.

**archaeological looting** The illegal, unscientific removal of archaeological resources from public, tribal, or private land.

**arrest** The process of taking a person into legal custody to answer a criminal charge.

**arrest warrant** A judicial order commanding that a particular person be arrested and brought before a court to answer a criminal charge.

**assignment sheets** Written reports completed by persons assigned tasks at a crime scene that document what they have done and found.

**associative evidence** Bidirectional evidence that connects the perpetrator to the scene or victim or connects the scene or victim to the perpetrator.

**attack code** A malicious software program intended to impair or destroy the functioning of a computer or a network resource.

**autoerotic death** Death from accidental asphyxiation as a result of masochistic activities of the deceased. Also called *sexual asphyxia*.

**Automated Fingerprint Identification System (AFIS)** A computerized system, maintained by the FBI, that stores and compares millions of fingerprints and is used to find matches for identification purposes.

**autopsy** The medical examination of a body to determine the time of and cause of death; required in all cases of violent or suspicious death.

**avionics** The electronic equipment (e.g., radio, navigation) on an aircraft.

**back doors** Code breaks used in debugging a computer program that are designed to evade normal security procedures; targeted by exploit programs as a means of illegal access to files.

**barbiturates** Short-, intermediate-, and long-lasting depressants (e.g., secobarbital, amobarbital) strongly associated with the tendency for abrupt withdrawal to cause convulsions and death; nicknamed after the capsule or pill color or the manufacturer's name.

**basic yellow 40** Used after superglue fuming, a dye that causes latent prints to fluoresce under alternative lighting.

**battered-child syndrome** The clinical term for the injuries sustained by a physically abused child.

**be-on-the-lookout (BOLO)** Part of the preliminary investigation, a notification broadcast to officers that contains detailed information on suspects and their vehicles.

**behavioral evidence analysis (BEA)** A deductive and evidence-based method of criminal profiling.

**Biggers-Brathwaite Factors Test** A test that balances the reliability of eyewitness identification (as determined by five factors specified by the Supreme Court) with the corrupting effect of any suggestive procedures; enables a highly reliable identification to be used in court even if something jeopardized the fairness of the identification procedure.

**biological agents** Certain microorganisms and toxins produced by organisms (e.g., smallpox, anthrax, plague, botulism) that cause human illness or death and could be used as terrorist weapons; typically slower acting than chemical agents.

**bobbies** A colloquial term used in reference to British police constables; derived by the public from the first name of Sir Robert Peel, whose efforts led to the creation of the first metropolitan police force in London.

**body language** Gestures, demeanor, facial expressions, and other nonverbal signals that convey, usually involuntarily, a person's attitudes, impressions, truthfulness, and so on.

**BOLO** *see* **be-on-the-lookout**.

# Supplements

## Making the Grade CD-ROM

A free electronic study guide is packaged with the text to help readers improve their grades on exams.

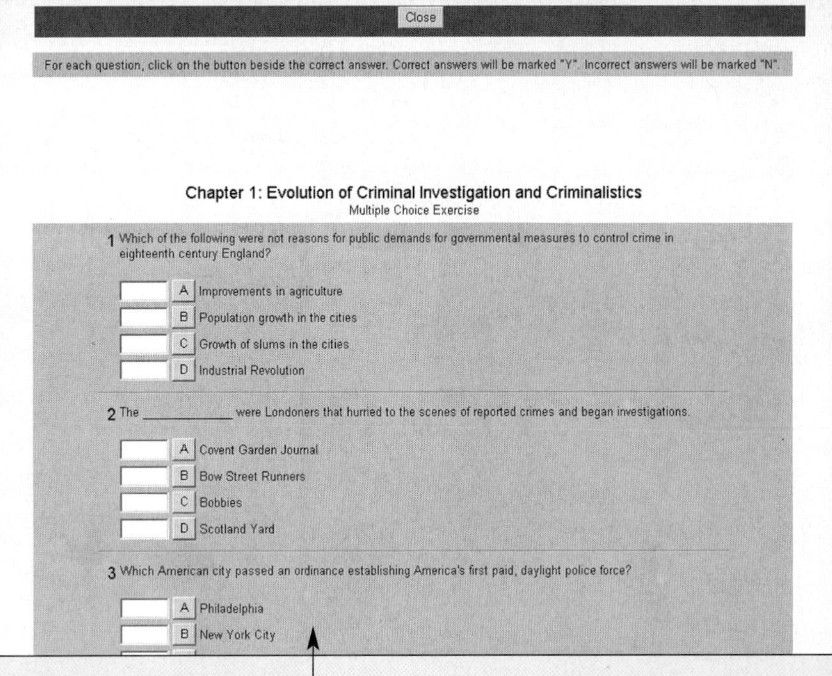


## Quizzes

Multiple-choice quizzes with feedback indicating why each answer is right or wrong enable students to master chapter material as they prepare for exams.

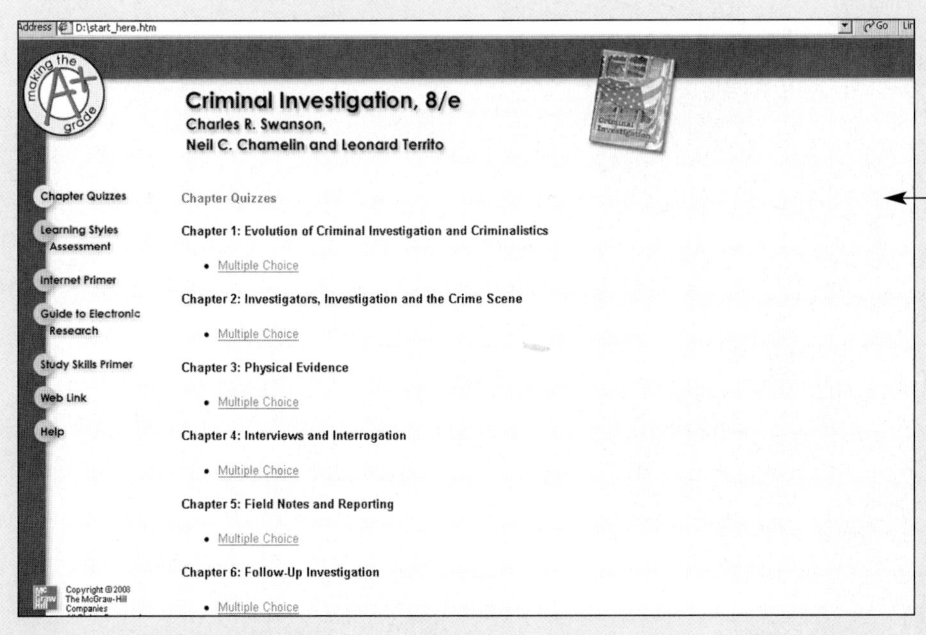


## More Resources

In addition to 21 separate quizzes, the *Making the Grade* electronic study guide includes such important resources as an Internet guide, a study skills primer, and more.

## Online Learning Center Website

The unique, book-specific website is available to students at no extra charge. The website features interactive cases that are not only fun to explore but terrific learning tools, flashcards that can be used to master vocabulary, and many other chapter review tools.

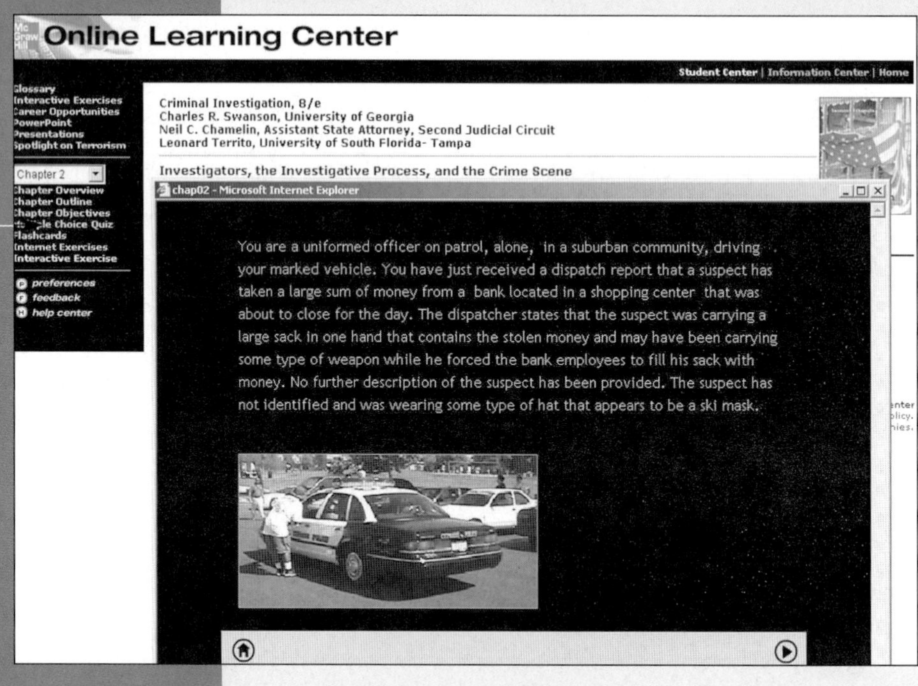


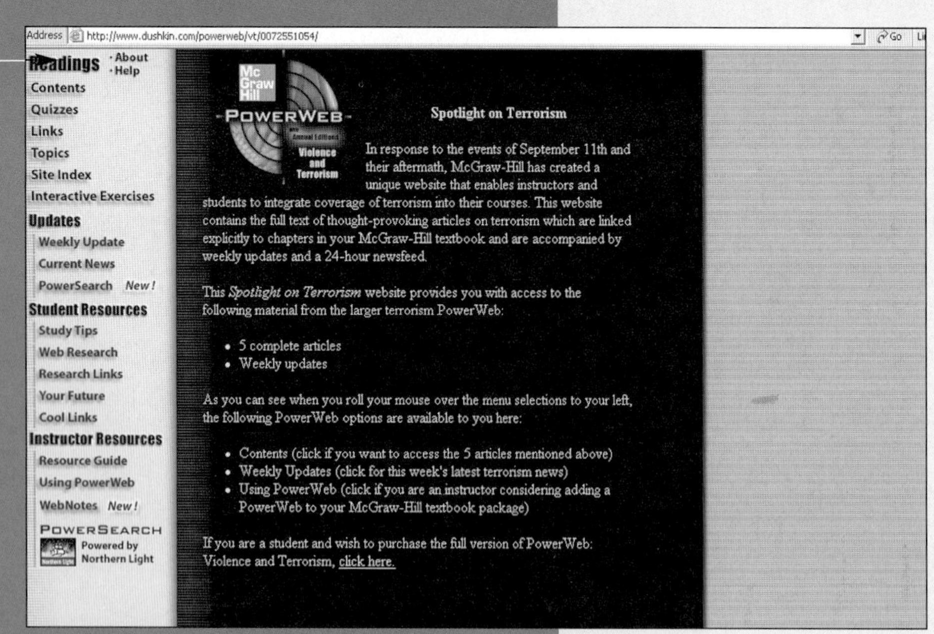

# Criminal Investigation

# ONE

# The Evolution of Criminal Investigation and Criminalistics

*A group of Texas Rangers, circa 1880. Note that the Rangers are well-armed, carrying repeating rifles, revolvers, and knives. In 1823, Stephen Austin hired 10 veterans of the frontier to serve as "rangers" in a punitive raid on hostile Indians. It was another 12 years before the Rangers were officially created by the Texas legislature. (Courtesy Texas Department of Public Safety)*

## CHAPTER OUTLINE



## CHAPTER OBJECTIVES

1. Explain the importance of the Bow Street Runners.
2. Discuss the contribution of Sir Robert Peel's reform to early policing in the United States.
3. Explain the history and function of the Pinkerton National Detective Agency.
4. Highlight the first major federal investigative agencies and their responsibilities.
5. Explain the Supreme Court's "due process revolution" and its impact on policing.
6. Discuss Bertillon's method of anthropometry.
7. Summarize the historical development of fingerprint identification.
8. Explain the concept and practice of DNA typing.
9. Outline the milestones in the development of firearms identification.

# INTRODUCTION

The roots of criminal investigation can be traced back to England in the eighteenth century, a period marked by numerous social, political, and economic changes. These changes were catalysts in the creation of the first modern detective force, the Bow Street Runners. In addition, London was the home of the first police reformer, Robert Peel. Both of these factors contributed to the subsequent development of police organizations and criminal investigation in the United States.

Within the criminal investigation process, investigators and detectives frequently use various scientific methods found in criminalistics to help identify suspects, gather evidence, and collect information—all of which is done in the effort to convict criminal offenders. Criminalistics draws from diverse disciplines, such as geology, physics, chemistry, biology, and mathematics, to study physical evidence related to crime. If it is suspected that a person has died from poisoning, for example, a toxicologist, who specializes in identifying and recognizing poisons and their physiological effects on humans and animals, can assist in the investigation. Experts in other areas, such as botany, forensic pathology, entomology and archaeology, may also provide helpful information to criminal investigators.

This chapter presents a brief history of criminalistics and criminal investigation, and it highlights major developments in the field. In addition, it discusses the creation and use of personal identification systems, such as anthropometry, fingerprint identification, and DNA typing, as well as providing an overview on the use of firearms identification in criminal investigation. Writing about these two separate but intertwined topics is a difficult task. Many volumes have been written on each, but the space that can be devoted to them here is limited. Sufficient broad perspectives and supporting details, however, are included in this chapter to enable readers intrigued by these subjects to independently pursue their interest armed with a working knowledge of the basics.

## THE EVOLUTION OF CRIMINAL INVESTIGATION

For present purposes, the evolution of criminal investigation began in eighteenth-century England, when massive changes were being unleashed. To fully appreciate the development of criminal investigation, you should first understand the social, economic, political, and legal contexts in which it evolved. Thus, this section provides this background and offers a brief history of criminal investigation from its early days in England to more recent times in the United States.

### THE IMPACT OF THE AGRICULTURAL AND INDUSTRIAL REVOLUTIONS

During the eighteenth century two events—an agricultural revolution and an industrial revolution—began a process of change that profoundly affected how police services were delivered and investigations conducted. Improved agricultural methods, such as the introduction in 1730 of Charles Townshend's crop rotation system and Jethro Tull's four-bladed plow, gave England increased agricultural productivity in the first half of the eighteenth century.[1] Improvements in agriculture were essential preconditions to the Industrial Revolution in the second half of the eighteenth century, because they freed people from farmwork for city jobs. As the population of England's cities grew, slums also grew, crime increased, and disorders became more frequent. Consequently, public demands for government to control crime grew louder.

### THE FIELDINGS: CRIME INFORMATION AND THE BOW STREET RUNNERS

In 1748, **Henry Fielding** became chief magistrate of Bow Street and set out to improve the administration of justice. In 1750, he established a small group of volunteer, nonuniformed home owners to "take thieves." Known as the **"Bow Street Runners,"** these Londoners hurried to the scenes of reported crimes and began investigations, thus becoming the first modern detective force. By 1752, Fielding began publishing *The Covent Garden Journal* as a means of circulating the descriptions of wanted persons. Upon his death in 1754, Henry Fielding was succeeded by his blind half-brother, **John Fielding,** who carried on Henry's ideas for another 25 years.[2] Under John Fielding, Bow Street became a clearinghouse for information on crime, and by 1785 at least four of the Bow Street Runners were no longer volunteers but paid government detectives.[3]

### THE METROPOLITAN POLICE ACT OF 1829

In 1816, in 1818, and again in 1822, England's Parliament rejected proposals for a centralized professional police force for London. Highly different political philosophies were at odds. One group argued that such a force was a direct threat to personal liberty. The other group—composed of reformers such as Jeremy Bentham and Patrick Colquhoun—argued that the absence, rather than the presence, of social control was the greater danger to personal liberty. Finally, in 1829, due in large measure to the efforts of **Sir Robert Peel,**

Parliament passed the **Metropolitan Police Act,** which created a metropolitan police force for London. Police headquarters became known as **"Scotland Yard,"** because the building formerly had housed Scottish royalty. Police constables were referred to as **"bobbies,"** a play on Peel's first name, Robert. Peel selected Charles Rowan and Richard Mayne as police commissioners, responsible for the development of this new force, and important new principles governing police work were stated:

1. The police must be stable, efficient, and organized along military lines.
2. The police must be under government control.
3. The absence of crime best proves the efficiency of police.
4. The distribution of crime news is essential.
5. The development of police strength both over time and by area is essential.
6. No quality is more indispensable to a police officer than a perfect command of temper; a quiet, determined manner has more effect than violent action.
7. Good appearance commands respect.
8. The securing and training of the proper people is at the root of efficiency.
9. Public security demands that every police officer be given a number.
10. Police headquarters should be centrally located and easily accessible to the people.
11. Police should be hired on a probationary basis.
12. Police records are necessary to the correct distribution of police strength.[4]

Because French citizens had experienced oppression under centralized police, the British public was suspicious of and at times even hostile to the new force. In response to the high standards set for the police force, there were 5,000 dismissals and 6,000 forced resignations from the force during the first three years of operations.[5] This record was a clear indication to the public that police administrators were requiring that officers maintain high standards of conduct. Within a few years, the London Metropolitan Police had won a reputation for fairness, and it became the international model of professional policing. Despite the growing popularity of the uniformed bobbies, however, there was fear that the use of **"police spies"**—detectives in plain clothes—would reduce civil liberties.

In the years immediately following 1829, some Metropolitan Police constables were temporarily relieved from patrolling in uniform to investigate crimes on their beats.[6] As the distinction between the use of uniformed constables to prevent crime and the use of plainclothes detectives for investigation and surveillance became clear, the public became uneasy. Illustratively, in 1833, a **Sergeant Popay** was dismissed following a parliamentary investigation which revealed that he had infiltrated a radical group, acquired a leadership position, and argued for the use of violence. Until 1842, Metropolitan Police constables assigned to investigate crimes competed with the Bow Street Runners; in that year, a regular detective branch was opened at Scotland Yard, superseding the Bow Street forces.[7] Under Commissioner Mayne, the detective force was limited to no more than 16 investigators, and its operations were restricted because of his distrust of "clandestine methods."[8]

Following a scandal in which three of four chief inspectors of detectives were convicted of taking bribes,[9] a separate, centralized Criminal Investigation Department (CID) was established in 1878 at Scotland Yard. It was headed by an attorney, Howard Vincent.[10] Uniformed constables who had shown an aptitude for investigation were recruited to become CID detectives.[11] Interestingly, at least since Vincent's time, the use of strong central control has been a recurrent theme in the reform of police organizations to correct for abuses. (See photo.)

## AMERICAN INITIATIVES

The success of Peel's reform in England did not go unnoticed in the United States. **Stephen Girard** bequeathed $33,190 to Philadelphia to develop a competent police force. In 1833, Philadelphia passed an ordinance creating America's first paid, daylight police force. Although the ordinance was repealed just three years later, the concept of a paid police force would reappear as American cities staggered under the burdens of tremendous population growth, poverty, and massive crime. In 1836,

**New Scotland Yard**
In 1890, the Metropolitan Police left their original quarters and were housed in New Scotland Yard, which is pictured here circa 1895. Subsequently, in 1967, the Metropolitan Police moved again, to their present facilities, which are also referred to as New Scotland Yard.
(Courtesy London Metropolitan Police)

New York City rejected the notion of a police force organized along the lines advocated by Peel. The committee studying the idea concluded:

> Though it might be necessary, at some future period, to adopt a system of police similar to that of London . . . the nature of our institution is such that more reliance may be placed upon the people for aid, in case of any emergency, than in despotic governments.[12]

Thus, before midcentury, few American cities had police service, and what existed was inadequate. Many cities had paid police service only at night or treated day and night police services as entirely separate organizations. Finally, in 1844, the New York state legislature created the first unified police force in the country, although New York City did not actually implement the measure until a year later. Other cities rapidly followed New York's lead: Chicago in 1851, New Orleans and Cincinnati in 1852, and Baltimore and Newark in 1857. By 1880, virtually every major American city had a police force based on England's Peelian reforms of 1829 and pioneered in this country by New York City.

If one of the problems of the London Metropolitan Police had been getting the public to accept some constables' working out of uniform as detectives, in this country the problem was getting the police to wear uniforms in the first place. American officers felt that a uniform made them easy targets for public harassment and made them look like servants. Only after the Civil War did the wearing of a uniform—invariably blue—become widely accepted by American police officers.

## Pinkerton's National Detective Agency

American cities needed reliable detectives for several reasons. First, graft and corruption were common among America's big-city police officers. Second, police jurisdiction was limited. Third, there was little communication of information among departments in different cities. Thus, offenders often fled from one jurisdiction to another with impunity.

In 1846, seeing the need for reliable investigators, two former St. Louis police officers formed the first recorded private detective agency.[13] But the major private detective agency of the nineteenth century was formed by **Allan Pinkerton** (1819–1884). In 1849, Chicago's Mayor Boone appointed Pinkerton as the city's first detective. Pinkerton enjoyed great success, but he resigned due to political interference and took a job as a special U.S. mail agent to solve a series of post office thefts and robberies in the Chicago area.[14] In 1850, after succeeding in this job, Pinkerton, by then a well-known public figure, formed a private detective agency with a Chicago attorney, Edward Rucker.[15] Pinkerton's trademark was an open eye above the slogan "We never sleep."[16] The trademark

**Pinkerton at Work**
Allan Pinkerton, President Lincoln, and General McClellan at Antietam, Maryland, about October 3, 1862. Born in Scotland, Allan Pinkerton was the son of a police sergeant. He found employment as a barrel maker and advanced to supervisor. At the same time, this red-headed, strong-willed man advocated more voice in government for ordinary people, a position which resulted in him becoming a wanted man. Narrowly avoiding arrest on his wedding day, Pinkerton and his wife fled to America, surviving a shipwreck while enroute. He started a successful barrel making company. While owner of that business, his initiative led to the arrest of counterfeiters. This gave him an appetite for police work, his father's profession, and changed his life and American policing forever.
(Courtesy Pinkerton's Archives)

gave rise to the use of the term "private eye" in reference to any private investigator.[17] The Pinkertons enjoyed such enormous success in the United States and throughout the world that some people thought "Pinkerton" was a nickname for any American government detective.[18]

The list of achievements by Pinkerton and his operatives is impressive. Pinkerton reportedly discovered and foiled an assassination attempt on President-elect Lincoln in Baltimore as Lincoln traveled to his inauguration in Washington, D.C.[19] At the outbreak of the Civil War in 1861, Pinkerton organized a Secret Service Division within the army (not to be confused with the U.S. Secret Service, which was organized after that war) and worked closely with Union General George McClellan until 1862, when McClellan was dismissed (see photo).[20] Although Pinkerton infiltrated Confederate lines in disguise on several occasions, he usually functioned as a military analyst.[21]

Following the Civil War, the Pinkertons were primarily engaged in two broad areas: (1) controlling a discontented working class, which was pushing for better wages and working conditions, and (2) pursuing bank and railroad robbers.[22] Unrestricted by jurisdictional limits, Pinkerton agents roamed far and wide pursuing lawbreakers. In a violent time, they sometimes used harsh and unwise methods. For instance, suspecting that they had found the hideout of Jesse James's gang, Pinkerton agents lobbed in a 32-pound bomb, killing a boy and injuring a woman.[23]

Pinkerton understood the importance of information, records, and publicity and made good use of all of them. For example, in 1868, Pinkerton agent Dick Winscott was assigned responsibility for smashing a group of bandits known as the Reno gang. Taking a camera with him, Winscott located Fred and John Reno and, after a drinking bout, persuaded them to let him photograph them.[24] He sent the photographs to Pinkerton files, and within a year the Reno gang was smashed.[25] Pinkerton also collected photographs of jewel thieves and other types of criminals and photographed horses to prevent illegal substitutions before races.[26] The Pinkertons also pushed Butch Cassidy (Robert Parker) and the Sun Dance Kid (Harry Longabaugh) into leaving the United States for South America, where they were reportedly killed by Bolivian soldiers at San Vincente in 1909 (see photo).

The Pinkertons investigated other major types of crimes as well. They caught two safecrackers who stole $1,250,000 from a Massachusetts bank and a state treasurer of South Dakota who had embezzled $300,000.[27] Because of their better-known

No. P.N.D.A. - 1597.
Name Geo Cassidy alias Butch Cassidy al
Alias Ingerfield. right name, Robt. Parker
Age 32 Height 5 ft 9" Weight 165
Complexion Light Hair Flaxen
Eyes Blue Beard Teeth
Nationality American
Marks and Scars 2 cut scars back hea
Small red scar under left eye.
eyes deep set. Small brown
mole calf of leg.
Arrested for Grd. Lar. Fremont Co. Wyo
Remarks July-15-94. Pardoned Jan 19
by Gov. Richards
Home is in Circle Valley, Utah
Sandy beard & Mustache if any

**Butch Cassidy's Pinkerton Record**

Note the "P.N.D.A." initials on the first line, which stand for Pinkerton National Detective Agency. Pinkerton agents were highly successful in combating the bank and train robbers of the Old West, such as the Hole in the Wall gang, so named because of the small opening through rocky walls that led to the valley in Johnson County, Wyoming, used as their hideout. As many as 40 bandits may have lived there in six cabins. Butch Cassidy and the Sun Dance Kid were both members of the Hole in the Wall gang at various times.

(Courtesy Wyoming State Archives and Historical Department)

antilabor activities, the Pinkertons' other work often is overlooked. But they were the only consistently competent detectives available in this country for over 50 years[28] and provided a good model for government detectives.

## The Emergence of Municipal Detectives

As early as 1845, New York City had 800 plainclothes officers,[29] although not until 1857 were the police authorized to designate 20 patrol officers as detectives.[30] In November 1857, the New York City Police Department set up a **rogues' gallery**—photographs of known offenders arranged by criminal specialty and height—and by June 1858, it had over 700 photographs for detectives to study so that they might recognize criminals on the street (see photo).[31] Photographs from rogues' galleries of that era reveal that some offenders grimaced, puffed their cheeks, rolled their eyes, and otherwise tried to distort their appearance to lessen the chance of later recognition.

To assist detectives, in 1884, Chicago established this country's first municipal Criminal Identification Bureau.[32] The Atlanta Police Department's Detective Bureau was organized in 1885 with a staff of one captain, one sergeant, and eight detectives.[33] In 1886, Thomas Byrnes, the dynamic chief detective of New York City, published *Professional Criminals in America,* which included pictures, descriptions, and the methods of all criminals known to him.[34] Byrnes thereby contributed to

**NYPD Rogues' Gallery**
Uniformed officers of the New York City Police Department maintaining a rogues' gallery in the detective bureau, circa 1896. Police departments have used rogues' galleries since the late 1850s.
(Courtesy Library of Congress)

information sharing among police departments. To supplement the rogues' gallery, Byrnes instituted the **Mulberry Street Morning Parade.** At 9 o'clock every morning, all criminals arrested in the past 24 hours were marched before his detectives, who were expected to make notes and to recognize the criminals later.[35] Despite such innovations, Byrnes was tragically flawed; in 1894 he was forced to leave the department when he admitted that he had grown wealthy by tolerating gambling dens and brothels. In spite of such setbacks, by the turn of the century many municipal police departments used detectives.

## State and Federal Developments

From its earliest days, the federal government employed investigators to detect revenue violations, but their responsibilities were narrow and their numbers few.[36] In 1865, Congress created the U.S. Secret Service to combat counterfeiting. In 1903—two years after President McKinley was assassinated by Leon Czolgosz in Buffalo—the previously informal arrangement of guarding the president was made a permanent Secret Service responsibility.[37]

In 1905, the California Bureau of Criminal Identification was set up to share information about criminal activity, and Pennsylvania governor Samuel Pennypacker signed legislation creating a state police force. Widely regarded then by labor as "strikebusters on management's side," the Pennsylvania State Police nevertheless was the prototype for modern state police organizations (see photo). New York and Michigan in 1917 and Delaware in 1919 adopted the state police concept. One function that state police forces since have assumed is providing local police with help in investigations.

After Prohibition was adopted nationally in 1920, the Bureau of Internal Revenue was responsible for its enforcement. Eventually the ranks of the bureau's agents swelled to a massive 4,000.[38] Because the Bureau of Internal Revenue was lodged in the Department of the Treasury, these federal agents were referred to as **T-men.**

In 1908, U.S. Attorney General Charles Bonaparte created the embryo of what was later to become the Federal Bureau of Investigation (FBI) when he ordered that investigations were to be handled by a special group. In 1924, J. Edgar Hoover (1895–1972) assumed leadership of the Bureau of Investigation; 11 years later Congress passed a measure giving the FBI its present designation. When Prohibition was repealed by the Twenty-first Amendment to the U.S. Constitution

**The Pennsylvania State Police**

Troop D, Pennsylvania State Police, Punxsutawney, Pennsylvania, 1906. Note that both plainclothes and uniformed personnel are represented.

(Courtesy Pennsylvania State Police)

in 1933, many former bootleggers and other criminals turned to bank robbery and kidnapping.[39] During the Depression, some people saw John Dillinger, "Pretty Boy" Floyd, Bonnie and Clyde, and Ma Barker and her boys as "plain folks" and did not grieve over a bank robbery or the "snatching" of a millionaire.[40] Given the restricted roles of other federal investigative agencies, it became the FBI's role to deal with these criminals.

Under Hoover, who understood the importance and uses of information, records, and publicity as well as Allan Pinkerton had, the FBI became known for investigative efficiency.

In 1932, the FBI established a crime laboratory and made its services available free to state and local police. In 1935, it started the **National Academy,** a training course for state and local police. In 1967, the **National Crime Information Center (NCIC)** was made operational by the FBI, providing data on wanted persons and property stolen from all 50 states. Altogether, these developments gave the FBI considerable influence over law enforcement throughout the country. Although some people argue that such federal influence is undesirable, others point out that Hoover and the FBI strengthened police practices in this country, from keeping crime statistics to improving investigation.

**Clyde Barrow**

Clyde Barrow (1909–1934) was captured after his escape from the Waco County Jail and served two years in prison. Upon his release, he and Bonnie began their rampage. Outside of Black Lake, Louisiana, they were killed by law enforcement officers who had persistently been pursuing them.

(Courtesy Federal Bureau of Investigation)

**Bonnie Parker**

Texas-born Bonnie Parker (1910–1934) was part of the murderous Barrow gang, which robbed and murdered its way across Oklahoma, Missouri, Texas, and New Mexico. In 1930, she smuggled a gun into the Waco (Texas) County Jail, helping Clyde Barrow and a companion to escape. From 1932 until 1934, Bonnie and Clyde left a deadly trail before they were stopped.

(Courtesy Federal Bureau of Investigation)

The Hague Conference in 1914 called for international action against illicit drugs. Subsequently, Congress passed the Harrison Act, making the distribution of nonmedical drugs a federal crime. Enforcement responsibility was initially given to the Internal Revenue Service, although by 1930 a separate Narcotics Bureau was established in the Treasury Department. In 1949, a federal commission noted that federal narcotics enforcement was fragmented among several agencies, resulting in duplication of effort and other ills. In 1968, some consolidation of effort was achieved with the creation of the Bureau of Narcotics and Dangerous Drugs in the Department of Justice, and in 1973, with the creation of its successor, the **Drug Enforcement Administration (DEA).** Today the DEA devotes many of its resources to fighting international drug traffic. Like the FBI, the DEA trains state and local police in investigative work. The training focuses on recognition of illegal drugs, control of drug purchases, surveillance methods, and handling of informants.

### The Police and the U.S. Supreme Court

As the highest court in this country, the Supreme Court is both obligated and well positioned to review cases and to make decisions that often have considerable impact. From 1961 to 1966, a period known as the "due process revolution," the Supreme Court became unusually active in hearing cases involving the rights of criminal suspects and defendants. Its decisions focused on the two vital areas of search and seizure and the right to legal representation. Among those cases was *Miranda* v. *Arizona* (1966), which established the well-known "Miranda rights"

*Miranda* and other decisions infuriated the police, who felt that the Supreme Court had "tied their hands" and "prevented them from doing their jobs." Crime was surging and politicians running for public office played to public fears by running on "law-and-order" platforms. Chief Justice Earl Warren was often blamed for the "sorry state of affairs" and soon "Impeach Warren" billboards dotted the landscape. In fact, the Supreme Court was simply doing its job, that only a few brave souls were willing to articulate then.

So what did the due process revolution and subsequent Supreme Court decisions really change? Questionable and improper police procedures and tactics were greatly reduced. In turn, this created the need to develop new procedures and tactics and to make sure that officers were well trained in their uses. There has been an ongoing cycle of decisions and adaptation to them by the police since the due process revolution. To no small extent, this cycle has hastened the continuing professionalization of the police while also asserting the principle that the action of police officers anywhere may be subject to close scrutiny by the Supreme Court.

## HISTORICAL MILESTONES OF CRIMINALISTICS

The origins of criminalistics are largely European. **Criminalistics** draws from diverse disciplines, such as geology, physics, chemistry, biology, and mathematics, to study physical evidence related to crime. The first major book describing the application of scientific disciplines to criminal investigation was written in 1893 by **Hans Gross,** a public prosecutor and later a judge from Graz, Austria.[41] Translated into English in 1906 under the title Criminal Investigation, it remains highly respected today as the seminal work in the field.

Criminalistics, like other scientific disciplines, enjoys periods of stability, but on the whole it is dynamic and in constant progress. To illustrate this principle of dynamic change, the histories of two commonly used services—personal identification and firearms identification—are traced in this section.

## PERSONAL IDENTIFICATION

There are three major scientific systems for personal identification of criminals: anthropometry, dactylography, and deoxyribonucleic acid (DNA) typing. The first was relatively short lived. The second, dactylography, or fingerprint identification, remains in use today throughout the world. The third, DNA typing, is a contemporary development.

### Anthropometry

Anthropometry was developed by **Alphonse Bertillon** (1853–1914), who is rightly regarded as the father of criminal identification (see photo). The first method of criminal identification that was thought to be reliable, **anthropometry** "was based on the fact that every human being differs from every other one in the exact measurements of their body, and that the sum of these measurements yields a characteristic formula for each individual."[42] The photo at lower right depicts a New York City police detective taking one type of measurement used in the "Bertillon system."

There was little in Alphonse Bertillon's early life to suggest that he would later make significant contributions. The grandson of a well-known naturalist and mathematician and the son of a distinguished French physician and statistician, who was also the vice president of the Anthropological Society of Paris,[43] Bertillon came from a family with a strong scientific tradition.[44] Moreover, in the late nineteenth century, there was a basic belief that all of life's problems could be solved by scientific knowledge, precise thinking, and scholarly deductions.[45] Yet Bertillon's early life reflected several failures

**Bertillon**
Alphonse Bertillon (1853–1914), the father of personal identification. In 1882, he began using his system on those incarcerated in Paris's Palais de Justice.
(Courtesy Jacques Genthial)

and suggested little ability. He was expelled from several schools for poor grades, dismissed from an apprenticeship in a bank after only a few weeks, performed poorly as a tutor in England, and while in the army had difficulty telling the difference between the bugle signals for reveille and roll call.[46] He was, therefore, able to obtain only a minor position in 1879, filing cards on criminals for the Paris police, because of his father's good connections.[47] The cards described criminals so vaguely that they might have fit almost anyone: "stature: average . . . face: ordinary."[48]

With growing resentment over the dreariness and senselessness of his work, Bertillon asked himself why so much time, money, and human energy were wasted on a useless system of identifying criminals.[49] Bertillon became a source of jokes and popular amusement as he began comparing photographs of criminals and taking measurements of those who had been arrested.[50] Bertillon concluded that if 11 physical measurements of a person were taken, the chances of finding another person with the same 11 measurements were 4,191,304 to 1.[51] His report outlining his criminal identification system was not warmly received. After reading it, the chief said:

> If I am not mistaken, you are a clerk of the twentieth grade and have been with us for only eight months, right? And already you are getting ideas? . . . Your report sounds like a joke.[52]

Yet in 1883, the "joke" received worldwide attention, because within 90 days of its implementation on an experimental basis, Bertillon correctly

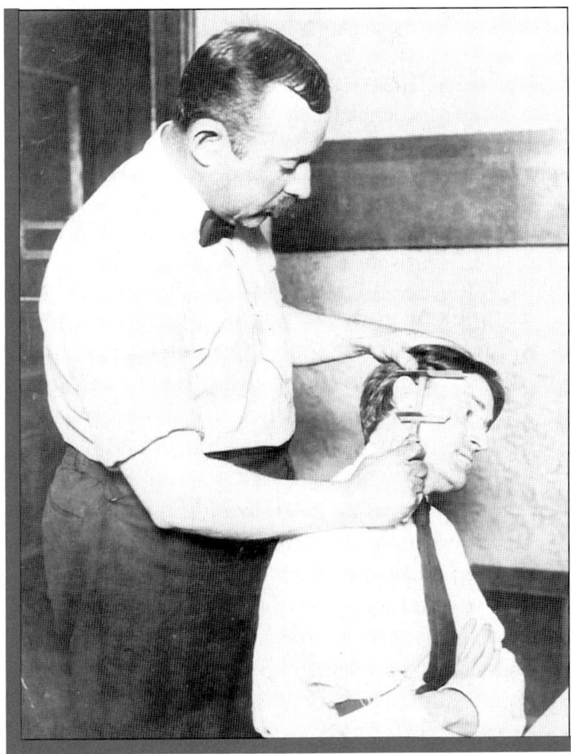

**Taking a Bertillon Measurement**
A New York City Police detective taking a Bertillon measurement of the right ear, one of the 11 measurements which made up anthropometry. This photograph was taken around 1896. Note in the two illustrations which immediately follow that the right ear is consistently part of the meaurements made.
(Courtesy Library of Congress)

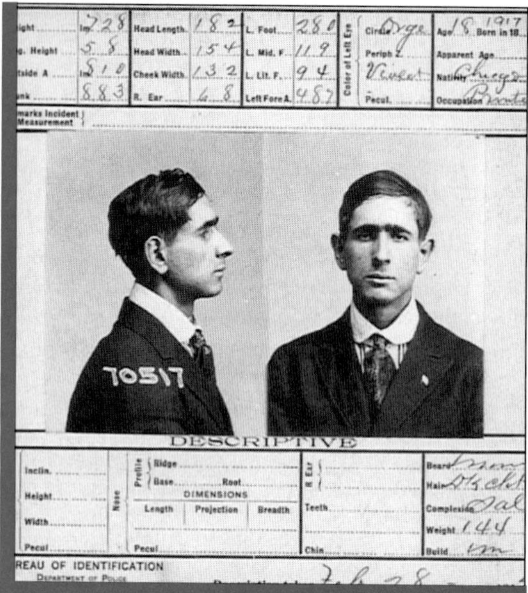


**Early Identification Card**
A Bertillon-style identification card, combining both personal measurements and photographs, prepared on February 28, 1917, by the Chicago Police Department.
(Courtesy Chicago Police Department)

made his first criminal identification. Soon almost all European countries adopted Bertillon's system of anthropometry. In 1888, Bertillon's fertile mind produced yet another innovation, the *portrait parlé* or "speaking picture," which combines full-face and profile photographs of each criminal with his or her exact body measurements and other descriptive data onto a single card (see illustration).

After the turn of the century, many countries abandoned anthropometry and adopted the simpler and more reliable system of fingerprints instead. Bertillon himself was not insensitive to the potential of fingerprints. In 1902, he solved the murder of Joseph Riebel when he discovered the prints of Henri Scheffer on the pane of a glass cupboard.[53] Yet Bertillon's rigid personality would not allow him to acknowledge the clear superiority of dactylography to anthropometry. In 1906, Bertillon testified as an expert in handwriting—although he was unqualified—and his testimony helped to convict Captain Alfred Dreyfus of spying for Germany. Although the French government later admitted that the Dreyfus conviction had been an injustice, Bertillon refused to admit his error.[54] The Dreyfus incident tarnished Bertillon's reputation on two counts: (1) acting as an expert out of one's field and (2) refusing to admit error. It also illustrates from another perspective his rigid character.

Even so, Bertillon's place in history is secure as the father of criminal identification. His portrait parlé—an ancestor of the "mug shot"—was a significant innovation, to which Bertillon reluctantly added fingerprints, at first only four from the left hand but later all ten fingerprints from both hands.[55] Bertillon was also a pioneer in police photography beyond its application in the portrait parlé; when Bertillon found the fingerprint in the 1902 Riebel murder, his primary interest was in how to best photograph it. Ironically, his success in photographing this fingerprint found at the crime scene not only underscored the practical use of photography in criminal investigation; it also illustrated the value of dactylography, which even then was quickly gaining favor over Bertillon's anthropometry. Upon Bertillon's death in 1914, France became the last major country to replace anthropometry with dactylography as its system of criminal identification.

## Dactylography

***Early Discoveries*** Although in 1900 England became the first country to use **dactylography** as a system of criminal identification, fingerprints have a long, legal and scientific history. In a legal context, in the first century, the Roman lawyer Quintilianus introduced a bloody fingerprint in a murder trial, successfully defending a child against the charge of murdering his father.[56] Fingerprints also were used on contracts during China's T'ang Dynasty in the eighth century as well as on official papers in fourteenth-century Persia and seventeenth-century England.[57]

In a scientific context, in 1684 in England, Dr. Nehemiah Grew first called attention to the system of pores and ridges in the hands and feet.[58] Just two years later, Marcello Malpighi made similar observations.[59] In 1823, John Perkinje, a professor at the University of Breslau, named nine standard types of fingerprint patterns and outlined a broad method of classification.[60] Despite these early stirrings, dactylography as a system of criminal identification took nearly another 75 years to emerge.

***The Herschel-Faulds Controversy*** Beginning in 1858, William Herschel, a British official in India, requested the palm prints and fingerprints of those with whom he did business, thinking that it might awe people into keeping agreements.[61] Over the next 20 years, Herschel noted from his records that the patterns of the lines on the fingerprints never changed for an individual; a person might grow and undergo other physical changes, yet the fingerprints remained the same. Excited by the prospects of applying this knowledge to the identification of criminals, Herschel wrote in 1877 to the inspector general of the prisons of Bengal. The reply was kindly in tone, but it was clear that the inspector general thought that Herschel's letter was the product of delirium. Herschel was so dispirited by the reply that he made no further efforts to pursue his discovery. Meanwhile, Henry Faulds, a Scottish physician teaching physiology in Tsukiji Hospital in Tokyo, had been interested in fingerprints for several years before 1880. When a thief left a sooty print on a whitewashed wall, Faulds was able to tell that the person in police custody was not the thief[62] and to match another suspect's fingerprints with those on the wall.[63] Faulds reported his findings in the journal *Nature* in 1880. Herschel read the account and published a reply, claiming credit for the discovery over 20 years before. A controversy broke out that was never resolved to anyone's satisfaction. Because there was also no official interest in using fingerprints, both Herschel and Faulds were even further frustrated.

***Galton's and Vucetich's Systems*** In 1888, Sir **Francis Galton** (1822–1911), a cousin of Charles Darwin, turned his attention to criminal identification.[64] When the thorough Galton contacted the editor of *Nature* for both Herschel's and Faulds's addresses, he was by chance sent only Herschel's. Contacted by Galton, Herschel unselfishly turned over all of his files in the hopes that this revived interest would lead to practical uses of fingerprints.[65] In 1892, Galton published the first definitive book on dactylography, *Finger Prints.* It presented statistical proof of the uniqueness of fingerprints and outlined many principles of identification by fingerprints.[66] In Argentina, in 1894, **Juan Vucetich** (1858–1925) published *Dactiloscopia Comparada,* outlining his method of fingerprint classification. In 1892, a disciple of Vucetich's, an Inspector Alvarez, obtained South America's first criminal conviction based on fingerprints by using Vucetich's system to convict a woman of beating her two children to death.[67]

***The Henry System*** The final breakthrough for the fingerprint method of personal identification was made by Edward Henry. At the age of 23 he went to India and by 1891 had become the inspector general of police of Nepal, the same province in which Herschel had worked some 15 years earlier.[68] Subject to many of the same influences as Herschel, but apparently working independently, Henry developed an interest in fingerprints[69] and instituted Bertillon's system with the addition of fingerprints to the cards. In 1893, Henry obtained a copy of Galton's book and began working on a simple, reliable method of classification. The governor general of India received a report from Henry in 1897 recommending that anthropometry be dropped in favor of Henry's fingerprint classification system. It was adopted throughout British India just six months later.[70] In 1900, **Henry's system** was adopted in England. The next year, Henry enjoyed two personal triumphs, the publication of his *Classification and Use of Finger Prints* and his appointment as assistant police commissioner of London,[71] rising to the post of commissioner two years later.

***Faurot and "James Jones"*** In 1904, New York City Detective Sergeant Joseph Faurot was sent to England to study fingerprints, becoming the first foreigner trained in the use of the Henry classification system. Upon Faurot's return, the new police commissioner told him to forget about such "scientific notions" and transferred him to walking a beat.[72] In 1906, Faurot arrested a man dressed in formal evening wear, but not wearing shoes, as the man crept out of a suite in the Waldorf-Astoria Hotel.[73] Claiming to be a respectable citizen named "James Jones," the man demanded to see the British consul and threatened Faurot with nasty consequences.[74] Faurot sent the man's fingerprints to Scotland Yard[75] and got back a reply that "James Jones" was actually Daniel Nolan, who had 12 prior convictions of hotel thefts and who was wanted for burglarizing a home in England. Confronted with this evidence, Nolan confessed to several thefts in the Waldorf-Astoria and received a sentence of seven years.[76] Newspaper stories about the case brought Faurot appropriate credit and advanced the use of fingerprints in this country.

***The West Case*** Despite the fame achieved by Faurot, the most important incident to advance the use of fingerprints in this country was the **West case.** In 1903, Will West arrived at the U.S. penitentiary at Leavenworth, Kansas. While West was being processed in through identification, a staff member said that there were already a photograph and Bertillon measurements for him on file. But a comparison of fingerprints showed that despite identical appearances and nearly identical Bertillon measurements, the identification card on file belonged to a William West, who had been in Leavenworth since 1901 (see illustration). The incident accelerated the recognition that fingerprints were superior to anthropometry as a system of identification.

***Rivalry of Vucetich's and Henry's Systems*** Vucetich's book on fingerprint classification was published in 1894, seven years before Henry's, but Henry's system has become much more widely used. To this day, however, some experts prefer Vucetich's system.[77] The rivalry between partisans of the two classification systems deserves attention.

In 1911, the provincial government of Buenos Aires passed a law requiring fingerprint registration for all adults subject to military service and eligible to vote.[78] By 1913 Vucetich had completed the task and decided to travel. In his travels, he was showered with decorations for his classification system. But when he visited Bertillon to pay his respects to the father of criminal identification,[79] Bertillon kept Vucetich waiting and finally opened the door just long enough to yell, "Sir, you have done me great harm," before slamming it shut again.[80] They were never to meet again. Upon his return to Argentina, Vucetich was to face further humiliation. When Buenos Aires planned an expansion of fingerprint registration, there were strong protests. In 1917 the Argentine government canceled registrations, seized Vucetich's records, and forbade him to continue his work.[81] In 1925, much as Bertillon had in 1914, Vucetich died a disappointed man.

### The Two Wests

William West had been in Leavenworth Prison since 1901; Will West arrived two years later. Given their similar appearances and nearly identical anthropometry measurements, it is easy to understand the confusion created upon Will West's arrival.

(Courtesy Federal Bureau of Investigation)

| | William West | Will West |
|---|---|---|
| Bertillon Measurements (in centimeters) | | |
| Height | 177.5 | 178.5 |
| Outstretched arms | 188.0 | 187.0 |
| Trunk | 91.3 | 91.2 |
| Head length | 19.8 | 19.7 |
| Head width | 15.9 | 15.8 |
| Cheek width | 14.8 | 14.8 |
| Right ear | 6.5 | 6.6 |
| Left foot | 27.5 | 28.2 |
| Left middle finger | 12.2 | 12.3 |
| Left little finger | 9.6 | 9.7 |
| Left forearm | 50.3 | 50.2 |

Although Vucetich's system is in use in South America today, Vucetich did not live long enough to see the vindication of his life's work.

In contrast, Henry became the head of what was then the world's most prestigious police organization and enjoyed the support of his government. These advantages, coupled with Vucetich's loss of support in his own country, meant that the Henry classification would become adopted virtually throughout the world.

## DNA Typing

***DNA as "Blueprint"*** Although **deoxyribonucleic acid (DNA)** was discovered in 1868, scientists were slow to understand its role in heredity.[82] During the early 1950s, James Watson and Francis Crick deduced the structure of DNA, ushering in a new era in the study of genetics.[83] Such developments were seemingly of peripheral interest to forensic scientists until 1985, when research into the structure of the human gene by Alec Jeffreys and his colleagues at Leicester University, England, led to the discovery that portions of the DNA structure of certain genes can be as unique to individuals as are fingerprints.[84] In fact, according to Jeffreys, the chance of two persons having identical DNA patterns is between 30 billion and 100 billion to 1.[85]

In all life forms—with the exception of a few viruses—the basis for variation lies in genetic material called DNA.[86] This DNA is a chemical "blueprint" that determines everything from hair color to susceptibility to diseases.[87] In every cell of the same human that contains DNA, this blueprint is identical, whether the material is blood, tissue, spermatozoa, bone marrow, tooth pulp, or a hair root cell.[88] Thus, with the exception of identical twins, every person has distinctive DNA. Initially, the process of isolating and reading this genetic material was referred to as "DNA fingerprinting," but currently the term DNA typing is used to describe this practice.

***The Enderby Cases*** The first use of DNA typing in a criminal case was in 1987 in England,[89] in regard to the **Enderby cases.** In 1983, Lynda Mann, age 15, was raped and murdered near the village of Enderby. This case was unsolved. Three years later, another 15-year-old, Dawn Ashworth, was a victim in a similar offense. Comparing the DNA "fingerprints" derived from semen recovered from both victims' bodies, investigators realized that the same man had raped and killed both women. A 17-year-old man was initially arrested and a sample of his blood was subjected to DNA typing. This man's innocence, however, was clearly established by the lack of a DNA match, and he was released. Subsequently, all males in the Enderby area between 13 and 30 years of age were asked by the police to voluntarily provide blood samples for DNA typing. Of 5,500 men living in the area, all but 2 complied with the request. A man then came forward and told the police that he had used false identification to supply a blood sample in the name of a friend. This friend, Colin Pitchfork, was subsequently arrested and convicted of Ashworth's murder, with DNA evidence playing a crucial role in the prosecution's case.

***The Orlando Cases*** During 1986, a series of rapes and assaults occurred in Orlando, Florida, which set the stage for the first use of DNA typing in the United States.[90] The crimes shared a common pattern: the attacks occurred after midnight, in the victims' homes, by a knife-wielding perpetrator. The perpetrator was quick to cover the eyes of the victims with a sheet or blanket, so none of them could give detailed descriptions of their assailant. During early 1987, investigators staking out a neighborhood in which it was believed the rapist might strike saw a blue 1979 Ford speeding out of the area. They followed the car for a short distance before it crashed into a utility pole while making a turn. The suspect, Tommie Lee Andrews, lived just 3 miles from the home of the first victim, who identified him at a photographic lineup the next morning. The prosecutor's case was certainly not ironclad. The identification rested on the victim's having seen the defendant for 6 seconds in a well-lit bathroom nearly a year before the photo lineup. Standard forensic tests comparing characteristics of the suspect's blood with characteristics derived from the semen found on the victim suggested only that Andrews could have committed the offense; but 30 percent of the male population of the United States shared these same characteristics. In short, there was enough evidence to prosecute, but a conviction was by no means a certainty. However, upon learning about the Enderby cases, the prosecutor secured DNA processing of the evidence and Andrews was convicted.

***DNA Analysis*** In 1988, the FBI became the first public-sector crime laboratory in the United States to accept cases for DNA analysis.[91] Since that time, there has been a substantial increase in the number of crime laboratories providing this type of service. Private firms also offer DNA typing, including Cellmark Diagnostics in Germantown, Maryland.

While DNA analysis of blood and other evidence from humans in criminal investigation cases is widely understood and used, there was no application of "genetic fingerprinting" to plant evidence in criminal cases until the 1992 **palo verde seedpod case** in Phoenix, Arizona.[92] Joggers found the body of a female who had been strangled. At the scene, investigators found a beeper, which led them to a suspect. The suspect admitted that (1) he had been with the victim the evening she disappeared, (2) the victim had been in his vehicle, (3) he and the victim had had sex, and (4) he and the victim had struggled. However, the suspect also maintained that the victim had run off with his beeper when he refused to help her get drugs and that he had not been anywhere near the place the body was found in 15 years. Investigators had found two seedpods from a palo verde tree in the bed of the suspect's truck. A University of Arizona plant geneticist was asked to determine if the seedpods came from a palo verde tree at the scene. The Maricopa County Sheriff's Office collected a total of 41 samples of palo verde seedpods from the crime scene and the surrounding region. The geneticist was able to exactly match the seedpods from the bed of the suspect's truck with those seized from the crime scene as part of the sample of 41 seedpods. Additionally, none of the 41 seedpods exactly matched each other. This evidence was admitted at the trial. The defense attacked the evidence, properly arguing that the findings from a study based on 41 trees had substantial limitations and did not establish conclusively that the suspect could have gotten the seedpods only at the crime scene. However, along with other evidence, the testimony given by the geneticist had sufficient weight for the jury to convict the suspect.

## FIREARMS IDENTIFICATION

Personal identification grew as several rival systems, with one of them finally predominating. In contrast, firearms identification moved forward in a series of successive steps. In this country, the frequency of shootings has made firearms identification extremely important.[93] As a specialty within criminalistics, firearms identification extends far beyond the comparison of two fired bullets. It includes identification of types of ammunition, knowledge of the design and functioning of firearms, restoration of obliterated serial numbers on weapons, and estimation of the distance between a gun's muzzle and a victim[94] when the weapon was fired.

In 1835, **Henry Goddard,** one of the last of the Bow Street Runners, made the first successful attempt to identify a murderer from a bullet recovered from the body of a victim.[95] Goddard noticed that the bullet had a distinctive blemish on it, a slight gouge. At the home of one suspect, Goddard seized a bullet mold with a defect whose location corresponded exactly to the gouge on the bullet. The owner of the mold confessed to the crime when confronted with this evidence.[96]

Professor Lacassagne removed a bullet in 1889 from a corpse in France; upon examining it closely, he found seven grooves made as the bullet passed through the barrel of a gun.[97] Shown the guns of a number of suspects, Lacassagne identified the one that could have left seven grooves. On the basis of this evidence, a man was convicted of the murder.[98] However, any number of guns manufactured at that time could have produced seven grooves. There is no way of knowing whether the right person was found guilty.[99]

In 1898, a German chemist named Paul Jeserich was given a bullet taken from the body of a man murdered near Berlin. After firing a test bullet from the defendant's revolver, Jeserich took microphotographs of the fatal and test bullets and, on the basis of the agreement between both their respective normalities and abnormalities, testified that the defendant's revolver fired the fatal bullet, contributing materially to the conviction obtained.[100] Unknowingly at the doorstep of scientific greatness, Jeserich did not pursue this discovery any further, choosing instead to return to his other interests.

Gradually, attention began to shift from just bullets to other aspects of firearms. In 1913, Professor Balthazard published perhaps the single most important article on firearms identification. In it, he noted that the firing pin, breechblock, extractor, and ejector all leave marks on cartridges and that these vary among different types of weapons. With World War I looming, Balthazard's article was not widely read for some years.

**Calvin Goddard** (1858–1946), a U.S. physician who had served in the army during World War I, is the person considered most responsible for raising firearms identification to a science and for perfecting the bullet-comparison microscope. To no small degree, Goddard's accomplishments were contributed to heavily by three other Americans—Charles Waite, John Fisher, and Phillip Gravelle—working as a team on firearms identification. In 1925, Goddard joined Waite's team and upon Waite's death a year later, Goddard became its undisputed driving force and leader.[101] Like many pioneers, Waite's contributions are often overlooked. He had been interested in firearms since 1917, and from 1920 on he visited firearms manufacturers to get data on those manufactured since 1850. Because of Waite, the first significant cataloged firearms collection in this country was assembled. Nonetheless, ultimately it was Goddard who raised firearms identification to the status of a science.

## OTHER CONTRIBUTORS

There are many other contributors to the evolution of investigation and criminalistics. For example, in 1910 **Albert Osborn** (1858–1946) wrote *Questioned Documents*, still regarded as a definitive work. From at least 1911 onward, **Edmond**

**Table 1-1** Major Institutional and System Initiatives, 1990-2001

| Year | Innovation | Description |
|---|---|---|
| 1990 | Combined DNA Index System (CODIS) | Began as an FBI pilot project to combine forensic science and computer technology into a tool for combating violent crime; includes major databases such as the Offender Index (profiles of convicted violent-crime offenders contributed by states) and the Forensic Index (DNA evidence recovered at crime scenes). CODIS consists of the National DNA Index System (NDIS), State DNA Information System (SDIS), and Local DNA Information System (LDIS). CODIS software can be used to link together crimes in the Forensic Index, revealing the existence of a predatory violent offender. When such profiles are run against the Offender Index, identification of the offender may be established. |
| 1992 | Jewelry and Gem (JAG) database | Created by the FBI to combat increasing jewelry and gem thefts by organized criminal enterprises working across jurisdictional lines; provides information about modus operandi, descriptions and images of stolen property, and case analysis and coordination for cases submitted by other agencies nationally. |
| 1992 | Exceptional Case Study Project (ECSP) | A five-year project run by the Secret Service, National Institute of Justice, and Bureau of Prisons; covered 83 subjects who in the previous 50 years had attacked or come close to attacking a U.S. government official. |
| 1995 | Justice Prisoner and Alien Transport System (JPATS) | Created by combining the air fleets of the Marshals Service and Immigration and Naturalization Service; moves criminals and aliens between judicial districts, correctional facilities, and foreign countries. |
| 1997 | National Drug Pointer Index (NDPIX) | Run by the DEA; uses the National Law Enforcement Telecommunications System (NLETS) as its communication backbone. Participating local, state, and federal agencies submit active case data and get back "pointer" information, so agencies know of common targets and can enhance safety of undercover operatives. By mid-2000, 86,000 cases were in the system. |
| 1998 | National Instant Criminal Background Check System (NICS) | Mandated by the Brady Handgun Prevention Act of 1994; requires that federal firearms licensees request background checks on individuals and refuse sales to those not eligible under the Brady Act. In 1998, the FBI, in cooperation with the ATF, implemented the permanent provisions of the Brady Act. |
| 1998 | National Infrastructure Protection Center (NIPC) | Established within the FBI, with support from other agencies and the private sector; designed for threat assessment, warning, investigation, and response to threats or attacks against energy and water systems, banking and finance, and government operation systems. |

**Table 1-1** Major Institutional and System Initiatives, 1990–2001, *continued*

| Year | Innovation | Description |
|---|---|---|
| 1998 | Child Abduction and Serial Murder Investigative Resources (CASMIRC) | Authorized by Congress; provides investigative support, training, assistance, and coordination to federal, state, and local agencies in matters involving child abductions, disappearances of children, and child violence and serial homicides. |
| 1999 | National Crime Information Center (NCIC) | The FBI's much enhanced, online information center. NCIC has been operational since 1967. |
| 1999 | Safe School Initiative (SSI) | Conducted by the Secret Service's National Threat Assessment Center, in partnership with the Department of Education; uses threat assessment to help prevent incidents of school-based violence. |
| 2000 | National Threat Assessment Center (NTAC) | Officially mandated by Congress, although already operational for more than a year. Part of the impetus for the Secret Service's creation of NTAC was the final ECSP report. |
| 2000 | Internet Fraud Complaint Center (IFCC) | A joint venture between the FBI and the National White Collar Crime Center (NW3C); addresses fraud committed over the Internet. |
| 2001 | National Integrated Ballistic Information Network (NIBIN) | A joint venture between the Bureau of Alcohol, Tobacco, and Firearms (ATF) and the FBI; NIBIN was intended to enhance the use of firearms evidence conducted in a few regions of the country in 2001. |
| 2001 | Trade Partnerships Against Terrorism (TPAT) | A U.S. Customs program developed in response to the events of September 11, 2001; designed to fight terrorism by establishing a cooperative relationship with carriers, manufacturers, exporters, importers, and others. Cooperators receive benefits, such as priority services and processing. |
| 2001 | Missing Persons Index (MPI) | Became a CODIS database; contains DNA from skeletal remains and DNA reference samples from maternal relatives of missing persons in order to match known remains with missing persons' reports. |

**Source:** Data drawn from the websites of the agencies mentioned. Readers are encouraged to visit them to obtain more details.

**Locard** (1877–1966) maintained a central interest in locating microscope evidence; all crime scenes processed today are based on the presumed validity of Locard's principle: There is something to be found. **Leone Lattes** (1887–1954) developed a procedure in 1915 that permits blood typing from a dried bloodstain, a key event in forensic serology. Although more an administrator and innovator than a criminalist, **August Vollmer** (1876–1955), through his support, helped John Larson produce the first workable polygraph in 1921, and Vollmer established America's first full forensic laboratory in Los Angeles in 1923. In 1935, Harry Soderman and John O'Connell coauthored *Modern Criminal Investigation*, the standard work for the field for decades until the publication of *Crime Investigation* by **Paul Kirk** in 1953. A biochemist, educator, and criminalist, Kirk helped develop the careers of many criminalists.

## THE RECENT PAST: INSTITUTIONAL AND SYSTEM INITIATIVES

As shown in this chapter, individuals and teams working together have historically provided the scientific breakthroughs that have fueled the development of new forensic capabilities. For example, over the past decade there have been a number of discoveries in the area of DNA profiling, and they have led to quicker procedures with excellent reliability. While individual and team-driven scientific breakthroughs will continue to foster progress, another important factor has been initiatives at the institutional and system levels.

Characteristically, these initiatives are put forth by agencies blending old and new technologies and by agencies creating and managing new databases. The quickening pace of such initiatives can be seen in Table 1–1, on pages 19 and 20, which lists some of the major institutional and system initiatives of recent years in chronological order. As explained in the table, the Combined DNA Index System (CODIS) uses computer technology and scientific discoveries about DNA to create electronic comparisons of DNA profiles. The creation and management of a new database is typified by the Jewelry and Gem (JAG) database, which includes descriptions and images of stolen items. A number of the initiatives identified in Table 1-1 are discussed in greater detail in subsequent chapters, such as Chapter 8, "Investigative Resources."

## Key Terms

**anthropometry**
**Bertillon, Alphonse**
**bobbies**
**Bow Street Runners**
**criminalistics**
**dactylography**
**deoxyribonucleic acid (DNA)**
**Drug Enforcement Administration (DEA)**
**Enderby cases**
**Fielding, Henry**
**Fielding, John**
**Galton, Francis**
**Girard, Stephen**
**Goddard, Calvin**
**Goddard, Henry**
**Gross, Hans**
**Henry system**
**Kirk, Paul**
**Lattes, Leone**
**Locard, Edmond**
**Metropolitan Police Act (1829)**
**Mulberry Street Morning Parade**
**National Academy**
**National Crime Information Center (NCIC)**
**Osborn, Albert**
**palo verde seedpod case**
**Peel, Robert**
**Pinkerton, Allan**
**"police spies"**
**Popay, Sergeant**
**rogues' gallery**
**Scotland Yard**
**T-men**
**Vollmer, August**
**Vucetich, Juan**
**West case**

## Review Questions

1. Who were the Bow Street Runners, and of what historical importance are they?
2. Why did the British public object to the use of detectives after enactment of the Metropolitan Police Act of 1829?
3. Why did the profession of detective in this country basically evolve in the private sector?
4. What assessment can be made of the work of Pinkerton and his National Detective Agency?
5. What is a rogues' gallery?
6. What parallels can be drawn between Allan Pinkerton and J. Edgar Hoover?
7. What is anthropometry, and why was it abandoned in favor of dactylography?
8. What are the milestones in the development of dactylography?
9. Why does the Henry classification system enjoy greater use than Vucetich's system?
10. What are the different human sources of DNA material identified in this chapter?
11. Of what significance is the palo verde case?
12. What are the milestones in the development of firearms identification?

## Internet Activities

1. Research your local, county, and state police agencies. Do these agencies have a criminal investigation unit? Is there more than one unit that specializes in particular types of crimes (burglary, robbery, homicide, etc.)? How many investigators are assigned to such units? Do officers have to meet a certain criteria to be assigned to these units? Is there any history on the creation of these units?
2. Find out more about DNA forensics by logging onto the U.S. Department of Energy's Human Genome Program website at www.ornl.gov/hgmis. Under the heading "Ethical, Legal and Social Issues" click on "Forensics." Is DNA an effective identifier? What are some interesting uses of DNA forensics? What are the ethical, legal, and social issues associated with DNA data banking?

## Notes

1. Material on the evolution of criminal investigation is drawn, in part, from Thomas R. Phelps, Charles R. Swanson, Jr., and Kenneth Evans, *Introduction to Criminal Justice* (New York: Random House, 1979), pp. 42–55.
2. T. A. Critchley, *A History of Police in England and Wales*, 2nd ed. (Montclair, N.J.: Patterson Smith, 1972), p. 34.
3. Ibid.
4. A. C. Germann, Frank D. Day, and Robert J. Gallati, *Introduction to Law Enforcement and Criminal Justice* (Springfield, Ill.: Charles C. Thomas, 1970), pp. 54–55.
5. Melville Lee, *A History of Police in England* (Montclair, N.J.: Patterson Smith reprint, 1971), p. 240.
6. Thomas A. Reppetto, *The Blue Parade* (New York: Free Press, 1978), p. 26.
7. Ibid., pp. 26–28.
8. Ibid., p. 29.
9. Ibid., p. 29, states three of four; John Coatman, *Police* (New York: Oxford, 1959), pp. 98–99, notes only one such conviction. Vincent's CID was based on his study of the Paris centralized detective system.
10. Coatman, *Police*, pp. 98–99.
11. Ibid., p. 99.
12. James F. Richardson, *The New York Police* (New York: Oxford, 1970), p. 37.
13. James D. Horan, *The Pinkertons* (New York: Bonanza Books, 1967), p. 25.
14. Ibid., p. 23.
15. Ibid., p. 25.
16. Jurgen Thorwald, *The Marks of Cain* (London: Thames and Hudson, 1965), p. 129.
17. Reppetto, *The Blue Parade*, p. 258.
18. Thorwald, *The Marks of Cain*, p. 129.
19. Reppetto, *The Blue Parade*, p. 257. There seems to be some dispute over whether there was ever any real threat and, if so, whether Pinkerton or New York City Police actually discovered it.
20. Ibid., pp. 257–258.
21. Ibid., p. 258. Reppetto asserts that as a military analyst Pinkerton was a failure and that his overestimates of enemy strength made General McClellan too cautious, contributing to McClellan's dismissal as head of the Union army.
22. Ibid.
23. William J. Bopp and Donald Shultz, *Principles of American Law Enforcement and Criminal Justice* (Springfield, Ill.: Charles C. Thomas, 1972), pp. 70–71.
24. Thorwald, *The Marks of Cain*, p. 131.
25. Reppetto, *The Blue Parade*, p. 259, notes that in two separate instances a total of eight Reno gang members arrested by the Pinkertons were subsequently lynched. In the first instance, three gang members reportedly were taken from Pinkerton custody.
26. Thorwald, *The Marks of Cain*, p. 131.
27. Reppetto, *The Blue Parade*, p. 261.
28. Ibid., p. 263.
29. Clive Emsley, *Policing and Its Context 1750–1870* (New York: Schocken Books, 1983), p. 106.
30. Augustine E. Costello, *Our Police Protectors* (Montclair, N.J.: Patterson Smith, 1972 reprint of an 1885 edition), p. 402.
31. Richardson, *The New York Police*, p. 122.

32. Bopp and Shultz, *Principles of American Law Enforcement and Criminal Justice,* p. 66.
33. William J. Mathias and Stuart Anderson, *Horse to Helicopter* (Atlanta: Community Life Publications, Georgia State University, 1973), p. 22.
34. Thorwald, *The Marks of Cain,* p. 136.
35. Ibid.
36. Reppetto, *The Blue Parade,* p. 263.
37. Ibid., p. 267.
38. Ibid., p. 278.
39. Ibid., p. 282.
40. Ibid., p. 283.
41. Richard Saferstein, *Criminalistics* (Englewood Cliffs, N.J.: Prentice-Hall, 1977), p. 5.
42. Jurgen Thorwald, *Crime and Science* (New York: Harcourt, Brace & World, 1967), p. 4.
43. Jurgen Thorwald, *The Century of the Detective* (New York: Harcourt, Brace & World, 1965), p. 6.
44. Thorwald, *Crime and Science,* p. 233.
45. Ibid.
46. Thorwald, *The Century of the Detective,* p. 6.
47. Ibid.
48. Ibid., p. 7.
49. Ibid., p. 9.
50. Ibid.
51. Ibid., p. 10.
52. Ibid., p. 12.
53. Ibid., pp. 83–84.
54. Ibid., p. 89.
55. Raymond D. Fosdick, *European Police Systems* (Montclair, N.J.: Patterson Smith, 1969 reprint of the 1915 original), p. 323.
56. Anthony L. Califana and Jerome S. Levkov, *Criminalistics for the Law Enforcement Officer* (New York: McGraw-Hill, 1978), p. 20.
57. Ibid.; also see Frederick R. Cherrill, *The Finger Print System at Scotland Yard* (London: Her Majesty's Stationery Office, 1954), p. 3.
58. Cherrill, *The Finger Print System at Scotland Yard,* p. 2.
59. Califana and Levkov, *Criminalistics for the Law Enforcement Officer,* p. 20.
60. Cherrill, *The Finger Print System at Scotland Yard,* p. 4.
61. Thorwald, *The Century of the Detective,* pp. 14–16.
62. Ibid., p. 18.
63. Ibid.
64. Ibid., p. 32.
65. Ibid., p. 33.
66. Saferstein, *Criminalistics,* p. 4.
67. Thorwald, *The Marks of Cain,* p. 81.
68. Thorwald, *The Century of the Detective,* p. 58.
69. Ibid.
70. Ibid., p. 60.
71. Ibid., p. 62.
72. Thorwald, *The Marks of Cain,* p. 138.
73. Ibid.
74. Ibid.
75. Ibid., p. 139.
76. Ibid.
77. Saferstein, *Criminalistics,* p. 281.
78. Thorwald, *The Century of the Detective,* p. 88.
79. Ibid.
80. Ibid., p. 87.
81. Ibid., p. 88.
82. Richard Saferstein, *Criminalistics: An Introduction to Forensic Science,* 5th ed. (Englewood Cliffs, N.J.: Prentice-Hall, 1995), p. 384.
83. Tod W. Burke and Walter F. Row, "DNA Analysis: The Challenge for Police," *The Police Chief,* October 1989, p. 92.
84. Saferstein, *Criminalistics,* 5th ed., p. 383.
85. "British Police Use Genetic Technique in Murder Arrest," *The Atlanta Constitution,* September 22, 1987, p. A3.
86. David Bigbee et al., "Implementation of DNA Analysis in American Crime Laboratories," *The Police Chief,* October 1989, p. 86.
87. Saferstein, *Criminalistics,* 5th ed., p. 384.
88. Bigbee et al., "Implementation of DNA Analysis," p. 86.
89. The account of the role of DNA in solving the Mann-Ashworth murders is drawn, in part, from Clare M. Tande, "DNA Typing: A New Investigatory Tool," *Duke Law Journal,* April 1989, p. 474.
90. This information is from Ricki Lewis, "DNA Fingerprints: Witness for the Prosecution," *Discover,* June 1988, pp. 44, 46.
91. Bigbee et al., "Implementation of DNA Analysis," p. 88.

92. This account is drawn from several sources: Jim Erickson, "Tree Genes: UA Professor's DNA Work Helps Convict Killer," *The Arizona Daily Star,* May 28, 1993, Metro/Region Section, p. 1; and Tim Henderson, "Report on Analysis of Palo Verde Samples," University of Arizona, April 14, 1993.
93. Saferstein, *Criminalistics,* 5th ed., p. 438.
94. Ibid., p. 30.
95. Thorwald, *The Marks of Cain,* p. 161.
96. Ibid.
97. Thorwald, *The Century of the Detective,* pp. 418–419.
98. Ibid., p. 419.
99. Thorwald, *The Marks of Cain,* p. 164.
100. Ibid.
101. Thorwald, *The Century of the Detective,* p. 434.

# TWO

# Investigators, the Investigative Process, and the Crime Scene

*When there is an unusual event, such as a barricaded criminal or a hostage situation, an incident commander will come to the scene to take control of the situation. In fast-moving situations, the incident commander may have to operate out of his/her assigned vehicle until a mobile command van arrives. In other situations, the police will use an existing building, with the permission of the owner, as a point from which to operate. Following the attack of September 11, 2001, members of the New York City Police Department established a temporary headquarters near ground zero. (Courtesy Andrea Booher, Federal Emergency Management Agency)*

## CHAPTER OUTLINE



## CHAPTER OBJECTIVES

1. Understand the role of the investigator and the skills and qualities he or she must possess.
2. Discuss the major events in the investigation of a crime.
3. Explain the seven major steps in a preliminary investigation.
4. Describe the activities conducted in a follow-up investigation.
5. Define a crime scene.
5. Outline the purposes and functions of a crime scene investigation.
6. Explain the "rules" for the crime scene investigator.
7. Identify potential threats to investigators' health and safety.
8. Be familiar with the five major considerations that dominate the crime scene search.

## INTRODUCTION

Although crime is a national problem, its control is primarily the responsibility of local government. When officials fail to prevent or cannot deal effectively with crime, there are negative consequences. First, if individuals commit crime and escape prosecution, future illegal acts are encouraged. Second, an escalating crime rate requires that resources, which could be devoted to other social problems, be diverted to crime control, resulting in further entrenchment of such ills as poverty, substandard housing, and inadequate medical care. Third, as crime increases, our system of government faces the real possibility of a crisis of confidence in its ability to maintain public welfare. Finally, crime tears the fabric of social relations and living patterns. People become fearful of strangers and of being on the streets after dark, homes become fortresses, and families move to new locations in search of a secure life. A terrible reality is that until significant inroads are made in controlling crime, the overall quality of life is lower than it could be.

While good investigative work will not significantly reduce crime by itself, the investigation of any crime places important responsibilities on the investigator. First, successful investigators must possess essential qualities such as good communication skills, strong ethics, initiative, resourcefulness, and compassion. Second, investigators must ensure that crimes are investigated effectively and thoroughly. This responsibility includes not only complete preliminary and follow-up investigations, but also understanding the importance of physical evidence in a criminal investigation. The contributions of physical evidence to an investigation are diminished primarily by the inability, unwillingness, or failure to locate, properly collect, mark, and preserve the evidence and by the drawing of improper conclusions from its analysis.

Investigators must also recognize that searching the crime scene for physical evidence is not limited to the location at which the offense was committed; it involves a wider area, including the perpetrator's lines of approach and flight. Thus, a crime scene search must include the specific setting of the crime and its general environs. Finally, there may be situations when even the most organized and well-planned crime scene investigation experiences obstacles. Investigators must always be cautious and aware of potential problems at a crime scene and address these issues appropriately.

## TYPES OF OFFENSES

A **crime** is the commission (doing) of any act that is prohibited or the omission (failing to do) of any act that is required by the penal code of an organized political state. There can be no crime unless there is advance notice of the conduct that is prohibited or required.

Legislatures enact criminal laws that distinguish between felonies and misdemeanors. In most states a **felony** is an act punishable by imprisonment for a term of one or more years or by death. Generally, violations of the criminal code that are not felonies are designated as **misdemeanors,** lesser offenses that may be punishable by a fine not to exceed $500 and/or imprisonment for no more than a year. Some states have a third crime category called **violation** (e.g., criminal littering), which is punishable only by a fine of no more than $250.

## THE INVESTIGATOR AND THE IMPORTANCE OF INVESTIGATION

An **investigator** is someone who gathers, documents, and evaluates evidence and information. This is accomplished through the process of *investigation.* The investigative process has the following objectives:

1. To establish that a crime was actually committed.
2. To identify and apprehend the suspect(s).
3. To recover stolen property.
4. To assist in the prosecution of the person(s) charged with the crime.

The investigator must have special knowledge and skills to achieve these objectives. The most important skill is the ability to converse equally well with a wide range of people, from corporate officers to prostitutes. This is essential because much of what we learn during an investigation comes from people. The competent investigator is aware of the difference between knowing things and doing things. Such an investigator will therefore consistently translate his or her special knowledge into actual investigative behaviors.

The investigation of any crime places significant responsibilities on the investigator. These responsibilities are particularly heavy during an arrest for a violent felony, since the investigator may have to use deadly force: investigators cannot legally use such force prematurely, but from a tactical standpoint they cannot be even a split second too late in responding to deadly force directed at them. When a person is arrested, whether for a felony or a misdemeanor, the arrest is often publicized and the person, even if not convicted, incurs economic and/or social costs. The more heinous the charge, the greater these costs will be. If a criminal charge is sustained, the person may suffer any of the penalties authorized for conviction of a felony, misdemeanor, or violation, which run from a fine to execution. This means that investigators must evaluate information accurately and use sound judgment in making investigative decisions. Other qualities are also required, as discussed below.

## ESSENTIAL QUALITIES OF THE INVESTIGATOR

Some investigators have a reputation of being lucky, and good fortune sometimes does play a role in solving a case. Most often, however, the "lucky" investigator is someone with strong professional training and solid experience who, by carefully completing every appropriate step in an investigation, leaves nothing to chance. By doing so, he or she forfeits no opportunity to develop evidence. In addition, successful investigators:

1. Invariably have a strong degree of self-discipline. (It is not the presence or absence of a supervisor that causes them to get things done.)
2. Use legally approved methods and are highly ethical.
3. Have the ability to win the confidence of people with whom they interact.
4. Do not act out of malice or bias.
5. Include in their case documentation all evidence that may point to the innocence of the suspect, no matter how unsavory his or her character.
6. Know that investigation is a systematic method of inquiry that is more science than art.
7. Realize that successful investigations are not always produced by rote application of the appropriate steps and therefore supplement the investigative procedures with their own initiative and resourcefulness.
8. Have wide-ranging contacts across many occupations.
9. Are not reluctant to contact experts from many different fields to help move the investigation forward.
10. Use both **inductive** and **deductive reasoning.** (Inductive reasoning moves from the specific details to a general view. It uses the factual situation of a case to form a unifying and logically consistent explanation of the crime. In contrast, deductive reasoning creates a hypothesis about the crime. The explanation is tested against the factual situation. If the fit is not good, the hypothesis is reformulated and tested again. The process is repeated until everything "fits together.")
11. Know that inductive and deductive reasoning can be distorted—by untenable inferences, logical fallacies, the failure to consider all alternatives, and bias—and self-monitor themselves to ensure effective use of these reasoning processes.
12. Learn something from every person with whom they come into contact, knowing that the wider their understanding of different lifestyles, occupations, vocabularies, views, and other factors, the more effective they will be.
13. Have the sensitivity and compassion to do their job without causing unnecessary anguish (e.g., when interviewing a rape suspect).
14. Avoid becoming calloused and cynical from their constant contact with criminals, keeping in mind that the criminal element does not represent everyone. (The failure to keep this distinction in mind can be the precursor of unethical behavior.)

# ORGANIZATION OF THE INVESTIGATIVE PROCESS

The major events in the investigation of crime are depicted in Figure 2–1. A discussion of these and their subelements will provide an overview of the investigative process and introduce concepts covered in greater detail in subsequent chapters.

Once a criminal offense has been committed, three immediate outcomes are possible. It may go undetected, as in the case of a carefully planned and conducted murder by organized-crime figures, in

Figure 2-1 Major Events in the Investigation of a Crime

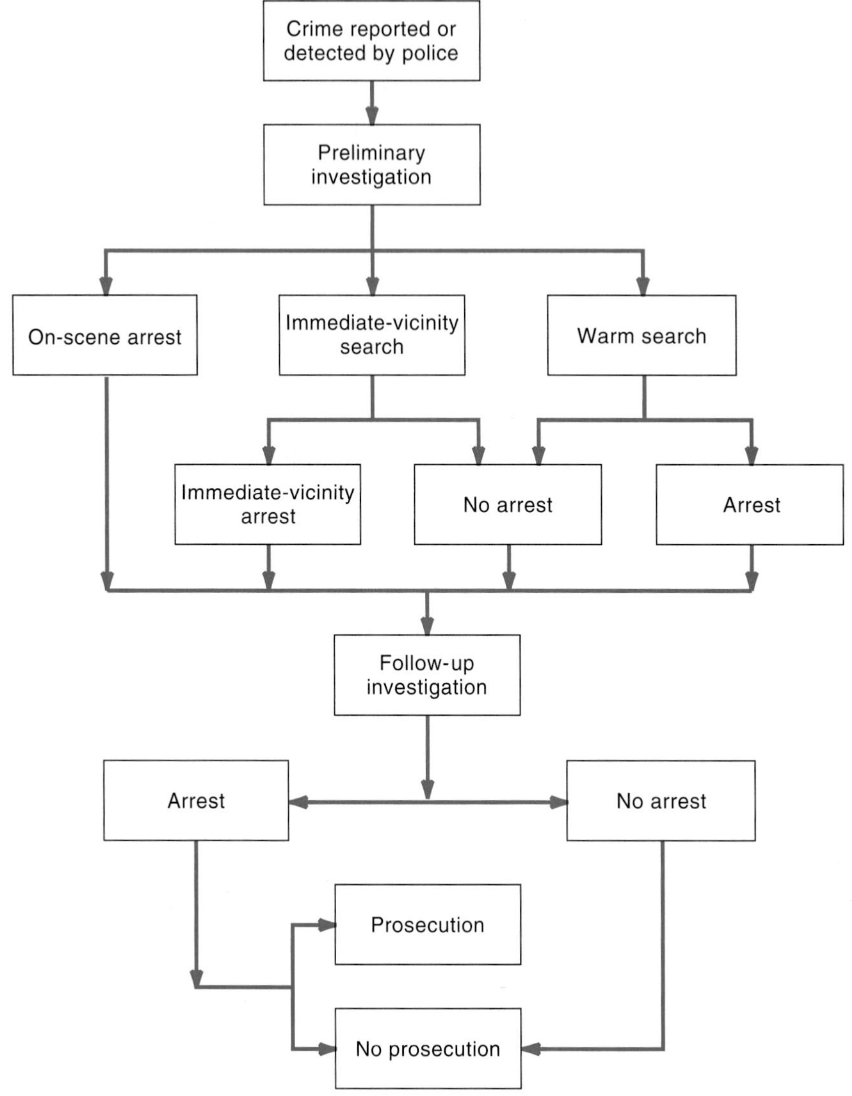


which the body is disposed of in such a way that it will remain undiscovered. If a violation is detected, it may not be reported, such as when a proprietor finds that his or her business premises have been burglarized but does not contact the police because the loss is minor or because the insurance coverage would be adversely affected. Finally, the crime may come to the attention of the police through their observation, a complaint by the victim or witnesses, or a tip.

Regardless of the outcome, a crime has occurred in each of the three preceding instances. However, only in the last case, when it is both detected and reported, is the offense of concern to the investigator, because only at that time does it become subject to formal processing.

## THE PRELIMINARY INVESTIGATION

The actions taken by the first officer to arrive at the scene of a crime after its detection and reporting are collectively termed the **preliminary investigation.** Normally the preliminary investigation is conducted by a uniformed officer from the Patrol Division and consists of the seven major steps explained below.

## 1. Receipt of Information and Initial Response

a. Note all dispatch information: time, date, type of call, location, names of parties involved, past history of incidents at the location, and, if known, whether any weapons are involved in this call.[1] Continue taking **field notes** throughout your preliminary investigation.

b. Be alert for people and cars leaving the crime scene; do not deviate from your assignment, except for the strongest reasons (e.g., discovering a violent crime in progress or being fired upon).

c. Approach the scene cautiously, scan the entire area thoroughly, assess the scene, and be aware of people and vehicles in the vicinity that may be related to the call.

d. In assessing the scene, use all of your senses: look, listen, smell. Be alert for dangers from people and from situations (e.g., natural gas or gasoline leaks; possible packages of explosives; biological, chemical, radiological, and other threats); inform other responders about dangers and request specialized help as the situation dictates.

e. Remain alert and attentive. Assume that the crime is in progress until you can safely conclude—not assume—that it is over and the suspects are no longer on the scene.

f. Treat the location as a crime scene until you conclude otherwise. Sometimes this is not an easy determination (see photo on page 32):

OVER a four-year period a woman was tormented by a person dubbed the "Poet" because he sent threatening mail in verse form to her, as well as committing other acts. Among the acts reported to the police were having her telephone line cut, chunks of concrete thrown at her home, and being abducted and stabbed. When the woman was discovered mailing a "poet" letter to herself at the Post Office, along with her normal bills, the truth came out. A psychologist speculated that the Poet incidents were motivated by the prior victimization of the woman, at that time age 16, when she was drugged, assaulted, and branded on both thighs by an assailant.[2]

## 2. Emergency Care

a. Maintain a safe distance, and put on appropriate protective gear if warranted. You can't warn or help anybody if you are incapacitated or dead.

b. Assess the need for medical personnel.

c. Point out potential evidence to medical personnel, and ask them to have no contact with it or to have minimum contact with it. Instruct emergency personnel to preserve all clothing and personal effects; do not allow them to cut clothing through or along bullet holes or knife openings. Document all movement of people and items by medical personnel.

d. If there are no satisfactory options, remember that saving a life has a higher value than preserving physical evidence.

e. Get the names of attending medical personnel, as well as their locator information, including their units and shield, telephone, and pager numbers.

f. If there is a chance that the victim may die, attempt to get a dying declaration. Document other statements, comments, and exclamations by victims, suspects, and witnesses.

## 3. Crime Scene Control

Maintaining **crime scene control** is a crucial element in the preliminary investigation. To the extent possible while meeting emergency care and other responsibilities, prevent individuals at the scene from committing any acts of theft, altering or destroying evidence, or attacking others. Identify all individuals at the scene. Secure and separate suspects, and separate witnesses, asking them not to discuss whatever they may know. If bystanders are not witnesses, they should be removed from the scene.

## 4. Issue a Be-on-the-Lookout

If the suspect is not arrested at the scene, conduct interviews and issue a **be-on-the-lookout (BOLO)** notice, which is broadcast to other officers. The

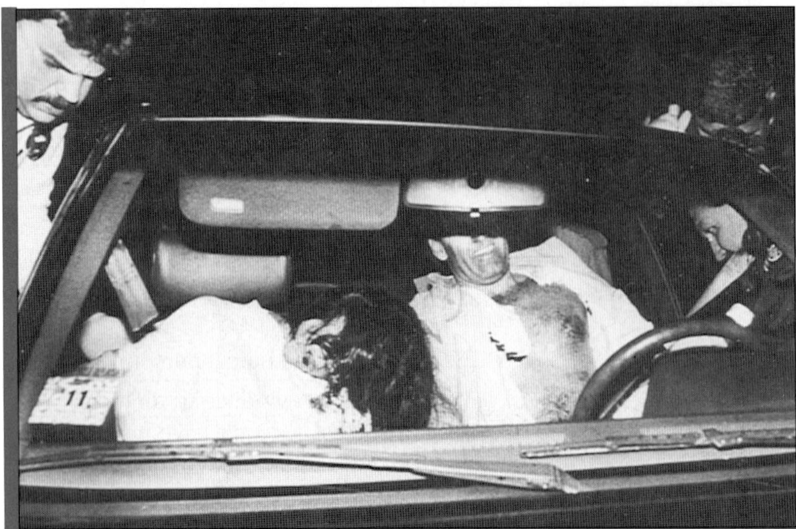

**The Scene of the False Report of a Murder/Robbery**
Mortally wounded wife and wounded husband, who used his car phone to describe the incident as a robbery, being helped by emergency personnel. Subsequent investigation revealed that the husband had shot his wife and then himself to make it appear they had both been shot by a third party.
(Photograph © 1989 by Evan Richman-The Boston Herald)

BOLO is crucially important because without its information other officers could be caught in the situation of approaching someone whom they think is a minor traffic violator when they have actually stumbled on a violent criminal fleeing the scene. Whenever possible, a BOLO should include the following points: number of suspects, age, race, sex, height, weight, build, coloration, names and/or nicknames, clothing, scars, marks, tattoos, jewelry worn, deformities (e.g., missing finger), and accent, as well as whether the suspects were unarmed or armed, numbers and descriptions of weapons, the method and direction of flight, and a full description of their vehicle, including year, make, model, color, stickers, damage, things hanging from the mirror, and loud mufflers. The importance of details in BOLO is demonstrated by the following case:

A convenience store was hit by an armed robber. The initially responding officer determined that a toy gun may have been used and that the suspect's vehicle had a white "hard hat" on the rear shelf. This information was included, along with a description of the suspect and his vehicle. Another officer found a vehicle matching the suspect's behind a tavern. A toy gun box was found on the rear floorboard and a white hard hat was on the rear shelf. The bartender said a man matching the suspect's description had entered the tavern, called a taxi, knocked down a drink, and left in the taxi when it arrived. The cab company reported that the fare was taken to the airport. There it was learned that he had boarded a flight to another city, where he was arrested when he got off the plane.

## 5. Crime Scene Determination

a. Determine the focus of the crime scene; that is, where the crime was committed.

b. Working outward from the focal point, identify the paths of entry and exit for the victim, suspect, and witnesses.

c. Set up a physical barrier. Use yellow crime scene tape, for example, or use natural barriers such as doors, walls, gated areas, additional personnel, or official vehicles.

d. Maintain a crime scene entry log of persons coming to and leaving the scene (see Figure 2–2).

## 6. Evidence

a. In smaller departments that do not have specialists, roughly those with 20 or fewer sworn personnel, the responding officer must recognize and identify physical evidence, document its location through sketching and photographs, collect it and mark it, package it, and take it to the station for storage in the evidence room, where a written receipt for it will be given to the officer. This receipt is then attached to the incident/offense report,

**Figure 2-2** Crime Scene Entry Log Sheet

**CRIME SCENE ENTRY LOG SHEET**

*ALL PERSONS ENTERING THE CRIME SCENE MUST SIGN THIS SHEET*

AGENCY:____________________ INCIDENT #: ____________________

SCENE LOCATION: ________________________________________

NOTE: Officers assigned to maintain scene security must also log in and out on this sheet and should state their reason as "Log Officers".

| | | | IN | OUT | |
|---|---|---|---|---|---|
| NAME & TITLE | INITIALS | AGENCY | DATE / TIME | DATE / TIME | REASON FOR ENTERING |
| | | | / | / | |
| | | | / | / | |
| | | | / | / | |
| | | | / | / | |
| | | | / | / | |
| | | | / | / | |
| | | | / | / | |
| | | | / | / | |
| | | | / | / | |
| | | | / | / | |
| | | | / | / | |
| | | | / | / | |
| | | | / | / | |
| | | | / | / | |
| | | | / | / | |
| | | | / | / | |

which the officer subsequently writes. When serious crimes are committed in smaller jurisdictions, assistance with the crime scene may be available through mutual aid agreements with larger agencies or from the state investigative agency.

b. At all stages of handling the evidence, the chain of custody or control of it must be established. The **chain of custody** is the witnessed, unbroken, written chronological history of who had the evidence when. It also accounts for any changes in the evidence, noting, for example, if any portion was used for laboratory analysis.

c. In larger agencies that have sworn and/or civilian crime scene technicians, these specialists will process the crime scene (see photo below). More detailed information about this subject is presented later in this chapter. When such specialists are used, one or more plainclothes investigators may also come to the scene, depending on the severity of the crime. If they do, the initially responding officer has the following crime scene turnover responsibilities: (1) briefing the personnel taking charge, (2) assisting in controlling the scene, (3) turning over responsibility for starting another crime scene entry log, and (4) remaining at the scene until relieved.

## 7. The Incident/Offense Report

The officer assigned to the call must prepare an **incident/offense report** on his or her part of the investigation. After the initiating officer's supervisor reviews and approves the report, a copy of it is sent to the unit of the police department responsible for the follow-up investigation. Additional information on this subject is presented in Chapter 5, "Field Notes and Investigative Reporting."

**Technician Collecting Blood Evidence**
The evidence/crime cone has been placed both to mark the location of the blood and to prevent its accidental loss, destruction, or alteration. Small flags, which can either be stuck in the ground or mounted on tripods, are also available for this purpose.
(Courtesy Nassau County, New York, Police Department)

## THE FOLLOW-UP INVESTIGATION

The **follow-up investigation** is the effort expended by the police in gathering information during the period between the initiation of the original report and the time the case is ready for prosecution or closed.

Upon receipt of a major-case offense report, a supervisor in the investigative unit will assign it to a particular individual who will be responsible for the latent or follow-up work. Although the follow-up investigation will vary depending on the circumstances, the investigator conducting it will usually engage in most of the following activities:

1. Read the offense report and become thoroughly conversant with it.
2. Evaluate the case in regard to potential or existing leads and next steps.
3. If there is an arrested suspect, conduct a custodial interrogation.
4. Liaison with the officer initiating the report to clarify any matters that are unclear.
5. Liaison with other units or agencies as needed.
6. Talk to informants.
7. Search special databases (e.g., the National Crime Information Center and automated mug shot "books").
8. Conduct and document a neighborhood canvas to see if area residents, businesspeople, or others saw anything that is material to the investigation. If the crime was committed near a public transit system, visit the system at the same time and perhaps on the same day of the week as the time and day of the crime.
9. Visit the scene, reinterview the victim, and reinterview witnesses on an as-needed basis.
10. Evaluate the scientific and legal significance of evidence and laboratory findings.
11. Use specialized investigative procedures if appropriate (e.g., physical, technical, and

electronic surveillance and polygraph examinations).

12. Obtain search and arrest warrants as needed.
13. Identify, locate, and apprehend the suspect.
14. Conduct lineups.
15. Recover stolen property.
16. Meet with the prosecuting attorney.

These steps may vary in terms of the sequence in which they are done, and some may be conducted simultaneously by different investigators assigned to the case. The remaining sections of this chapter address the crime scene and its handling. Bear in mind that even as the crime scene processing is going on, some elements of the follow-up investigation, such as the neighborhood canvas, will have already started. A fuller discussion of the follow-up investigation is found in Chapter 6.

A final note is required with respect to various perceptions of what constitutes a successful investigation. In the public's mind that status is attained when the perpetrator is arrested, property is recovered, and the person charged is subsequently convicted. In administrative terms success is achieved when the offense is accorded one of two classifications: it may be **"exceptionally cleared,"** in that a factor external to the investigation, such as a complainant's refusal to testify, results in no charge being filed against a suspect; or it may be **"cleared by arrest,"** which occurs when the perpetrator has been arrested and there is sufficient evidence to file a formal charge. Here it must be observed that not every arrest will result in prosecution; the police can and do make mistakes, or the evidence may be found to be legally insufficient.

An examination of the data in Table 2–1 leads to the conclusion that in many types of major-case offenses the investigator will not experience success as defined by the public or administrative classifications. What, then, should be the investigator's attitude? How can feelings of frustration be avoided? The investigator knows that many crimes are highly resistant to clearance and some crimes are simply insoluble because of insufficient evidence or legal restrictions. Therefore, success for the investigator must rest in the knowledge that the case was vigorously pursued and all avenues leading to clearance were examined.

**Table 2-1** Crimes Cleared by Arrest

| Offense | % Cleared by Arrest |
|---|---|
| Murder | 63.1% |
| Aggravated assault | 56.9 |
| Forcible rape | 46.9 |
| Robbery | 25.7 |
| Larceny-theft | 18.2 |
| Motor vehicle theft | 14.1 |
| Burglary | 13.4 |

**Source:** Federal Bureau of Investigation, *Crime in the United States–2000* (Washington, DC: Government Printing Office, Oct. 22, 2001), p. 206.

## THE CRIME SCENE

The fundamental assumption on which crime scene searches rest is Locard's principle: There is something to be found. Crime scenes vary in regard to the amount of physical evidence that is ordinarily expected to be recovered; a murder scene will yield more than a yard from which a lawn mower was stolen. At the most basic level, a **crime scene** is the location where the offense was committed. Of necessity, the search of the crime scene for physical evidence must include a wider area, such as the perpetrator's lines of approach to and flight from the scene.

The basic definition works well for many crimes such as a burglary or a robbery at a liquor store. But where is the crime scene when a victim is abducted from a mall parking lot, raped by one accomplice while the other one drives the van around, and then is taken to a secluded area, removed from the van, further abused, and executed and the body is dumped into a ravine? Clearly, we need additional ways to think about what a crime scene is:

1. Criminal incidents may have more than one crime scene. The **primary scene** is the location where the initial offense was committed; the locations of all subsequent connected events are **secondary scenes.**[3]
2. On the basis of size, there are macroscopic and microscopic scenes.[4] A **macroscopic**

Locard's Principle: "There Is something to be found"

**scene** is the "large view." It includes things such as the relevant location(s), the victim's and the suspect's bodies, cars, and buildings. The **microscopic scene** consists of the specific objects and pieces of evidence that are associated with the commission of the crime, including knives, bite marks, hairs and fibers, shoe and tire impressions, cigar butts, blood, and so on.[5]

3. Other useful ways of thinking about crime scenes are based on the type of crime (larceny versus aggravated assault), the location (indoors or outdoors), the condition of the scene (organized or disorganized), and the type of criminal action (active or passive). Some further breakdown of these types may also be useful, such as if outside, whether the body is on the surface, buried, or underwater.[6]

The usefulness of having several frames of reference for crime scenes is that they can help organize your thinking about how to approach and process a crime scene. If there are multiple crime scene locations, the primary and secondary scenes may be located in different legal jurisdictions, a situation requiring a high level of cooperation and informational exchange between agencies. In cases where a serial offender is active and working across several jurisdictions, the case may be assigned to a standing interagency investigative task force, or a special one may be created. In such situations it is important that departmental jealousies, the issue of who is going to get credit for solving the case, and other factors do not impede the success of the operation.

## ORGANIZATION OF THE CRIME SCENE INVESTIGATION

Crime scene investigation is purposeful behavior and is intended to accomplish the following objectives:

1. Reconstruct what happened.
2. Determine the sequence of events.
3. Find out what the suspect did or didn't do.
4. Establish the modus operandi, the method of operation, used by the suspect.
5. Determine what property was stolen and what articles were left by the suspect.
6. Reveal the motive. For example, if the crime appears to be a home invasion that resulted in a murder, why wasn't the victim's cash and jewelry taken? Did the perpetrator panic and flee the scene before taking them, or is something else at work, such as a love triangle?
7. Locate and interview witnesses.
8. Document and recover physical evidence.[7]

In order to achieve these objectives, the work at the crime scene is divided into three major functions: overall coordination of the scene, technical services, and investigative services.

### OVERALL COORDINATION

Ordinarily, this function is vested in the senior investigator at the scene and she or he will have the ultimate responsibility for what is done at the scene and what types of additional resources are requested. For example, in some situations, it may be necessary to get a search warrant. If there is a dead body, the medical examiner or the coroner must be called to the scene; generally this official has jurisdiction over a dead body, and it should not be searched or removed from the scene without his or her prior consent.[8] The overall coordinator will make sure that all the members of the crime scene team are briefed simultaneously by the first officer on the scene so that everyone hears and knows the same thing. This person is also responsible for ensuring that there is a continuous flow of information between members of the team when, for example, a piece of evidence is recovered. Other duties include making his or her own evaluation of potential safety issues, reviewing the actions of the person who conducted the preliminary investigation, allocating resources among the primary and any secondary scenes, establishing a secure area for the temporary storage of evidence, and establishing a command post and media function if the situation warrants them. The senior investigator will also do a walk-through of the scene with those responsible for technical services to make sure there is a common understanding of how the scene will be approached and processed.[9]

Processing the scene for evidence

### TECHNICAL SERVICES

This function is the responsibility of the ranking representative of the department's central crime

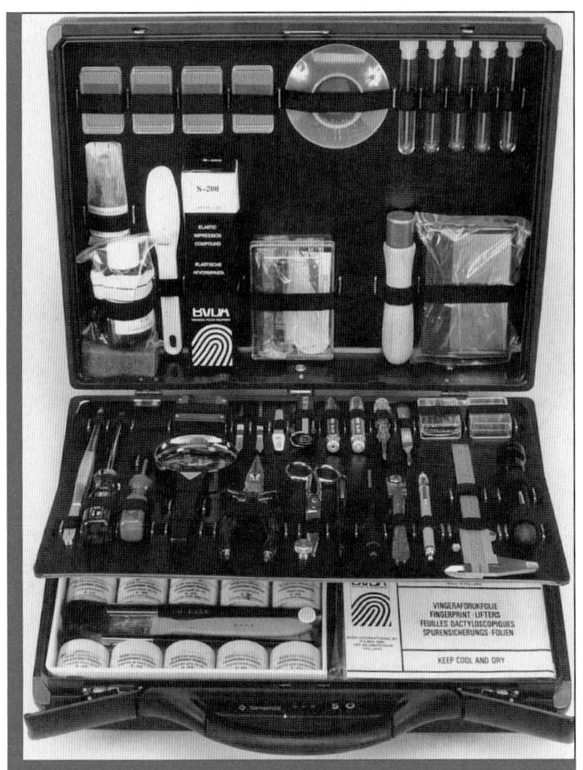


**Universal Crime Scene Kit**

A Universal Crime Scene Investigation Kit, the contents of which go well beyond those of a compact kit, adding such features as the materials for casting toolmarks.

(Courtesy ODV Incorporated, South Paris, Maine)

laboratory or its crime scene processing unit, along with any subordinate specialists who are assigned to the scene. They may arrive to process the scene carrying a universal crime scene investigation kit (see photo above) or may have all the additional resources of a crime scene van (see photo below, right) and Figure 2–3). Some jurisdictions also make use of a mobile crime laboratory in which technicians can carry out limited scientific tests. The technical services function is concerned with the actual processing of the scene for physical evidence. This includes establishing a point for trash generated by processing the scene, including biohazard bags for the collection of disposable evidence equipment and personal protection equipment, and carrying out the identification, documentation, collection, marking, packaging, and transmission of physical evidence to the evidence room or the crime laboratory. Technicians process the scene on the basis of priorities established by the situation. For example, if there are both indoor and outdoor scenes, inclement weather may require that the outdoor scene be protected by tarps or tents and processed first. The presence of crowds or a hostile environment (which can occur, e.g., when there has been a shooting by a police officer, may also affect the sequencing of processing.[10]

## INVESTIGATIVE SERVICES

Investigative services include interviewing witnesses, conducting and documenting the neighborhood canvass (discussed earlier) and a field interrogation of the suspect if he or she is in custody, and carrying out and recording the results of a vehicle information canvass. Occasionally a suspect may not have time to get to his or her car before the

**Philadelphia Police Department Mobile Crime Scene Unit**

Units of this type vary in their capabilities. Some contain the full range of materials needed to process a crime scene, while others have that capability, plus the instrumentation needed to analyze some types of evidence.

(Courtesy Philadelphia Police Department)

**Figure 2-3** Crime Scene Investigation Equipment List

## Supplies for Scene Security

- Crime scene barrier tape ("Police Line, Do Not Cross"— available in several languages)
- Crime scene flags (marked "Sheriff," "Police," or "Evidence")
- Tents, rain-repellent tarps
- Sawhorses
- Spray paints (various colors)
- Marked police vehicles
- Cord, rope
- Flares, high-intensity lighting on poles
- Preprinted signs and poles (e.g., "Command Post," "Media Relations")
- Traffic cones

## Telecommunications

- Fax machine
- Cell phones, pagers
- Portable copier/printer
- Laptop with modem
- Videoconferencing capability
- Departmental handheld radios
- Palm Pilots

## Miscellaneous

- Audio recorder
- Handheld global positioning system (GPS)
- Magnetic compass
- Portable generator
- Refrigeration/cooling capability
- Flashlights, spare batteries
- Business cards
- Chalk (various colors)
- Hard-metal scribes
- Thermometers
- Logbooks
- Metal-detection sweeper
- Telephone directories, phone numbers of special and/or important contacts
- Extension cord, adapters
- Area map
- Small mirrors for viewing hard-to-see places
- Ladders for reaching difficult-to-check places (e.g., rooftop) for evidence
- First-aid kit
- Magnifying glasses
- Binoculars

## Equipment for Crime Scene Documentation

*Photography*

- Video recorder
- Digital camera
- 35-mm camera
- Tripods
- 1:1 or close-up camera
- Tripods
- Stepladder for "shooting" the scene from different perspectives
- Scales, rulers
- Color and black-and-white film, videotapes, batteries (ample supply of each)
- Lens filters
- Remote flash units
- Auxiliary lighting
- Small tent-style plastic "signs" for showing the location of evidence (may be numbers, letters, or arrows)
- Photo evidence ruler tape, 30-foot rolls (sticks to surface and shows distances between evidence items), flexible vinyl scale and magnetized scale to place on metal objects

**Figure 2-3** Crime Scene Investigation Equipment List, *continued*

*Sketching Equipment*

- Tape measures, lengths of 6 to 50 feet (several)
- Measuring wheels with visible readers for establishing longer distances (e.g., up to 1,000 feet)
- Paper
- Sketching templates (e.g., crime scene, traffic, curves, home furnishings, architect's, human figures, office plan)
- Pencils, colored markers
- Large clipboards or lap-size drawing board
- Straight-edge ruler, clear, 12 inches
- T-square, clear plastic triangles (e.g., 30/60 and 45 degrees)
- Protractor
- Laser or sonic measuring "meter/tape"
- Laptop computer, crime scene sketching software

## Equipment and Materials for Processing Crime Scenes

*General Collection Equipment*

- Tweezers, forceps
- Common hand tools (saws, drills, screwdrivers, chisels, etc.)
- Assorted yard tools (rakes, trowels, buckets, shovels, etc.)
- Nets for flying insects
- Framed screen sifters/sieves
- Tongue depressors
- Knives
- Disposable scalpels/scrapers
- Scissors

*Special Evidence Collection Kits*

- Latent fingerprint
- Imprint and impression
- Trace evidence with evidence vacuum
- Blood
- Excavation
- Sexual assault (separate ones for victim and suspect)
- Gunshot residue
- Casting (e.g., silicon, dental stone, and Snow Impression Wax)
- Forensic lighting
- Ultraviolet light source
- Presumptive/field drug testing
- Laser trajectory
- Blood splatter

*Evidence Packaging Materials*

- Evidence tags, general identification labels
- Assorted Kraft/manila paper evidence bags and envelopes
- Special sticky labels (e.g., "Biohazard," "Latent Print Evidence")
- Evidence collection boxes (in which to mount guns, small tools, etc.)
- Clear tubes for syringes and small knives
- Evidence sealing tape, 1/2 inch to 3 inches wide (often marked "Evidence," "Security Seal, No Tampering," or similar wording)
- "Peel and seal" integrity evidence bags
- Pillboxes, jars, cans, tubes
- Sterile swabs, swab boxes
- Latent-fingerprint lifters (assorted)
- Butcher paper
- Blood tubes with and without preservatives
- Zip-Lock bags (assorted sizes)
- Evidence control/chain-of-custody labels
- Document sleeves

**Source:** Content drawn from Henry C. Lee, Timothy M. Palmbach, and Marilyn T. Miller, *Crime Scene Handbook* (San Diego: Academic Press, 2001), pp. 321-324, and Technical Working Group on Crime Scene Investigation, *Crime Scene Investigation* (Washington, DC: U.S. Department of Justice, 2000), pp. 33-36; additional content supplied by the authors.

police arrive, so the suspect simply walks away, intending to return later. Checking the registrations of the cars identified in the vehicle canvass may reveal additional witnesses and possible suspects.

## TYPES OF EVIDENCE

There are three broad categories of evidence in which investigators have a particular interest: corpus delicti, associative, and tracing. The task of developing such evidence is spread across the three main crime scene functions, but the data from the different types of evidence are combined to create a larger and more unified picture of the crime. This picture helps determine, to a large extent, how the follow-up investigation will be conducted.

### Corpus Delicti Evidence

Each criminal offense contains a distinct set of elements whose commission or omission must be demonstrated to have occurred in order to prove a case; **corpus delicti evidence** substantiates these elements. Thus, at each crime scene the investigator must keep in mind the unique requirements of proof for the case and attempt to locate related evidence.

### Associative Evidence

**Associative evidence** is bidirectional in that it connects the perpetrator to the scene or victim or connects the scene or victim to the suspect. A case history illustrates this:

A silent burglary alarm was triggered at a bar in a high-crime area. Officers responding to the scene found a point of forced entry at a rear window of the building. An individual was detected hiding in a small shed attached to the building. His statement was that when walking up the alley, he suddenly saw police cars, panicked, and hid in the shed. The search of this person following his arrest revealed the presence of valuables and materials taken from the burglarized premises, connecting the suspect with the scene.

### Tracing Evidence

The identification and location of the suspect are the goals of **tracing evidence;** corpus delicti and associative evidence may also serve these purposes:

A 20-year-old female was at a laundromat washing her clothes. A male loitered nearby, observing her. When the woman was alone, he walked rapidly to the laundromat and entered the men's room. A few minutes later, with his pants and underwear around his ankles, he approached the woman, shook his genitals at her, pulled up his clothing, and ran off. The officer who responded to the call found a man's wallet on the floor of the men's rest room. A records check on the identification contained in it revealed that the owner of the wallet had a history of sex offenses and lived in the neighborhood of the laundromat. When the victim identified the suspect from a series of photographs, a warrant for the suspect's arrest was obtained.

## TYPICAL CRIME SCENE PROBLEMS

Although the procedures to be followed at a crime scene investigation may be neatly delineated in theory, any number of conditions may render their accomplishment a good bit less orderly than the ideal. The resources of a police department are finite, and considerable demands are made upon them. Ideally, every crime scene should be fastidiously processed. In reality, the scenes of misdemeanor offenses receive at best a cursory examination, and even the thoroughness with which felony crime scenes are processed will frequently be affected by the severity of the offense. To the person victimized, the situation is of considerable importance, possibly even traumatically so, and may have brought him or her into direct contact with the police for the first time. From the police standpoint, the offense committed may be a nonpriority crime that—due to limitations of personnel and time—does not warrant employing the full range of technical and investigative services. However, even when investigating a nonpriority case, officers must display a genuine interest in their work.

At the scenes of violent crimes, especially those that are interracial, emotions may run high. Even a small crowd may add considerable confusion to the process of ascertaining what has happened and along what lines the investigation should proceed.

In such situations it is not unusual for witnesses to be lost, for their versions and perceptions of what occurred to be altered by contamination through contact with the crowd, or even for so-called witnesses to be added. In this last circumstance, an individual standing in the crowd may have been at, or very near to, the scene when the crime occurred, without actually viewing the offense. However, in the emotionally charged atmosphere, hearing the comments and descriptions of people standing nearby, the person suddenly and earnestly believes that he or she has something of value to share with the investigative team.

Limitations on the availability of equipment may force an investigator to use less-desirable procedures or to eliminate a particular step. Police officers and supervisors occasionally make investigations more difficult when they drop by to see if they "can be of help" when in reality they are simply curious. Too many people at the scene may lead to confusion of assignments or accidental alteration or destruction of evidence. Finally, at the scenes of major crimes, such as bank robberies and criminal homicides, members of the press typically arrive shortly after the investigation and immediately attempt to obtain information from any police officer or witness, creating no small amount of confusion and sometimes producing erroneous reports.

## RULES FOR THE CRIME SCENE INVESTIGATOR

Regardless of the type of crime involved, five fundamentals must be observed.

### MAINTAIN CONTROL

Without control a life might be lost, evidence destroyed, assignments overlooked, or the investigation conducted in a generally slovenly manner. At the scene of sensational crimes, particularly those involving well-known figures, the crime scene coordinator will be approached by members of the press who want to photograph or videotape the scene as well as obtain information for their newspapers or television stations. Properly responding to such individuals is an essential aspect of control. The person in charge of the crime scene should cooperate with the press, but the scope of cooperation is limited by the need to avoid interference with the investigation, to protect the legal rights of a suspect, and to avoid placing a witness in danger, as well as by other factors. Although some states have enacted "shield laws" so that news media personnel are not required to divulge their sources, as a general matter reporters have no legal rights beyond those granted each citizen. Although news officials may be permitted to enter a crime scene, they do so at their own risk; if their presence in any way jeopardizes police operations, it should not be allowed. The arrest of a news media worker at a crime scene should be made only upon the most serious provocation and with full awareness of the adverse publicity that is certain to follow for the police department.

News media personnel may photograph or report anything that they observe while legally at a crime scene or covering any other incident involving the police. If in this process they obtain information that could endanger people or adversely affect the investigative process, both they and their supervisors should be notified of the possible consequences.

When suspects have been interviewed but not arrested, their identities should not be disclosed. It is appropriate for the crime scene coordinator to generally describe to reporters the physical evidence found at the scene, proceeds of the crime, weapons, and the issuance and service of search warrants. However, detailed descriptions of evidence, proceeds, or weapons should not be disclosed, nor should information pertaining to how physical evidence, proceeds of the crime, or weapons were located.

In some investigations it is appropriate to withhold certain details about the crime scene, such as how a victim was mutilated, messages left at the scene by the perpetrator, particular types of evidence seized, or the exact words spoken to a rape victim. Such information could be vital in solving the case, evaluating informants' tips, or determining the authenticity of statements or confessions made by subsequently identified suspects. If a suspect has been identified and an identity established or a likeness generated by an artist's sketch or by facial composite software (see Chapter 12, "Robbery"), it may be advantageous to widely publicize this information if it is not likely to hinder apprehension of the suspect.

Relevant information can be supplied in **media statements** if it cannot be characterized as being prejudicial to a fair trial for the defendant. Among the actions and statements that are impermissible under the policies of many departments are the following:

1. Requiring the suspect to pose for photographers.
2. Reenacting the crime.
3. Disclosing that the suspect told where weapons, proceeds of the crime, or other materials were located.
4. Referring to the suspect as a "depraved character," "real no-good," or "sexual monster" or in similar terms.
5. Revealing that the suspect declined to take certain types of tests or that the suspect did take certain tests (e.g., a blood alcohol test to determine the degree, if any, to which the suspect was under the influence of drugs or alcohol).
6. Telling the press the results of any tests to which the suspect submitted.
7. Making statements as to the guilt or innocence of a suspect.
8. Releasing the identities of prospective witnesses or commenting on the nature of their anticipated testimony or credibility.
9. Making statements of a purely speculative nature about any aspect of the case.

If a suspect is arrested, it is permissible in most states to release the following types of information:

1. The defendant's name, age, sex, residence, employment, marital status, and similar background information, unless the defendant is a juvenile.
2. The nature of the crime for which the arrest was made and the identity of the complainant (as long as disclosing this information does not create a danger for the complainant and is not seriously embarrassing to him or her (as can be the case for victims of sexual offenses) or does not run counter to other reasons of good judgment or applicable laws.
3. The identities of any other agencies participating in the investigation and/or making the arrest, as well as those of the individual officers involved.
4. The circumstances surrounding the arrest, such as the time and place, extent of any pursuit, amount of resistance, possession and use of weapons, injuries (notification to the family should precede disclosing an individual officer's identity), and a general description of items seized at the time of arrest.

## CONCEPTUALIZE EVENTS

Inexperienced investigators sometimes jump to conclusions after taking a brief look at a crime scene. This can result in their looking for evidence that supports their "theory" or conceptualization of the crime and ignoring evidence that does not fit into their explanation—a dangerous and potentially disastrous practice. In processing the crime scene, it is necessary to keep both known facts and inferences in mind. This facilitates the reconstruction of the offense and identification of the perpetrator's method of operation, suggests the possible existence of certain types of physical evidence, and assists in establishing appropriate lines of inquiry:

MULTIPLE female murder victims were found strangled and stabbed in an apartment. The lead investigator studied the crime scene very carefully. One of the victims was lying near the doorway to one of the bedrooms with a pillow under her head. The investigator concluded that the perpetrator may have touched the very lowest portion of the door to steady himself as he stood up after killing that victim. The crime scene technician processed that portion of the door and located the only fingerprint of the suspect found at the crime scene. The suspect was identified by this print and subsequently convicted of the murders.

Without the investigator's thoughtful examination of the crime and reconstruction of how the perpetrator may have acted, that lower portion of the door would not have been dusted for fingerprints because it would have been illogical to expect to find a fingerprint there. Consequently, the most important piece of evidence would never have been located.

Assumptions that are made must be checked for accuracy as quickly as possible. The failure to do so may result in an offender's escaping prosecution and in embarrassment for the investigator and the department. It may also produce confusion in, or misdirect, the investigation. For example, a woman in a large city was murdered in her apartment. The investigators assumed that the woman's husband had thoroughly searched the apartment for their missing infant child when he first arrived and found his wife's body. Thus, they further assumed that the baby had been kidnapped. Some four days later the baby's body was found by the grandmother in the apartment under a sofa cushion.[11]

Human behavior is rich in its variety; in reconstructing the crime, investigators must be alert to the danger of imparting their own probable motives or actions to the perpetrator unless there are solid grounds for so doing. Alternatively stated, this proposition dictates that simply because, under the same or a similar set of circumstances, we would not have acted in a particular fashion does not preclude the possibility that the perpetrator may have acted in that way. Two cases illustrate the importance of this point: In Woodbridge, New Jersey, a series of burglaries was cleared when it was established that two inmates had been breaking out of a correctional facility to commit the offenses, returning nightly to the facility.[12] In Palm Beach, Florida, a guard at a bank was surprised one night by an intruder who took $50,000 in gold coins. Unable to find a point of entry, investigators were puzzled until they received an anonymous tip that the intruder had shipped himself into the bank in a crate and broken out of it after the regular employees had gone home.[13]

Large physical evidence, such as a handgun used in a criminal homicide, is often easily found at the crime scene and requires little in the way of conceptualization. However, there is the possibility that much smaller types of evidence are also present; these will be located only if the investigator is able to conceptualize events:

A university student claimed that several hours ago her date had raped her at his apartment. This had been their second date. In addition to being able to identify her assailant, the victim gave the investigator a Polaroid photograph taken of the two of them earlier in the evening. In examining the photograph, the investigator noticed that the victim was wearing a sorority pin in the photograph, but the victim's pin was now missing. Believing that the pin could have been lost at the crime scene, the investigator went to the suspect's apartment. The suspect's version of events was that he told the victim he no longer wanted to date her and she swore to get even for "being dumped." The suspect also said that the woman had never been in his apartment and consented to a search. The investigator found the missing sorority pin in the perpetrator's bedroom, and the suspect subsequently gave her a confession.

It does not take a great deal of conceptualization to recognize larger items of evidence at a crime scene. Where this ability pays substantial dividends is in locating **trace evidence,** which is present in extremely small or limited amounts. Such evidence may be, but is not exclusively, microscopic in size.

Often this trace evidence is located using **alternative light systems (ALS).** Illustrations include portable lasers, such as Sirchie's Crime Sweeper, Polilight, BlueMaxx, and Luma-Lite (see photo on page 44) and handheld ultraviolet (UV) lighting. As illumination from ALSs sweep over a crime scene, the various colored lights cause many types of evidence to fluoresce. Trace evidence that reacts to such illumination includes fingerprints, bodily fluids, hairs, fibers, drugs, glass and metal fragments, bite marks, bruises, human bone fragments, and gunshot residues. The following case illustrates the value of ALSs:

A small leaf was found on the windowsill where a burglar entered the building. He had been barefooted, and investigators located a portion of his footprint on the leaf using a Luma-Lite. This print was developed and in light of this and other evidence the suspect pled guilty.[14]

Portable **trace evidence vacuums** (see photo on page 45) are also quite useful in locating very small items of evidence. In order to prevent the accidental contamination of evidence, the nozzle and evidence filter unit (which sits on top of the vacuum's nozzle) is packaged and sealed at the factory's "clean room." At the crime scene, as each different area is vacuumed (such as the sofa in the photo), the nozzle and the filter are detached. A lid is snapped onto the filter, and then the nozzle and filter are sealed in a clear plastic envelope. After the appropriate identifying information is placed on the plastic envelope, it is sent to the crime laboratory, where the material caught in the filter is analyzed. These systems are particularly effective in gathering hairs, fibers, and certain types of drug evidence, such as cocaine. Thus, trace-evidence vacuum systems can often be effectively used in assault, rape, and some drug cases. However, if clothing is seized as evidence and fiber, hair, or other evidence from the suspect or victim may be on it, crime laboratories generally prefer that the clothing not be vacuumed but be sent to the laboratory for processing to prevent the possibility that other valuable evidence may be lost during the vacuuming.

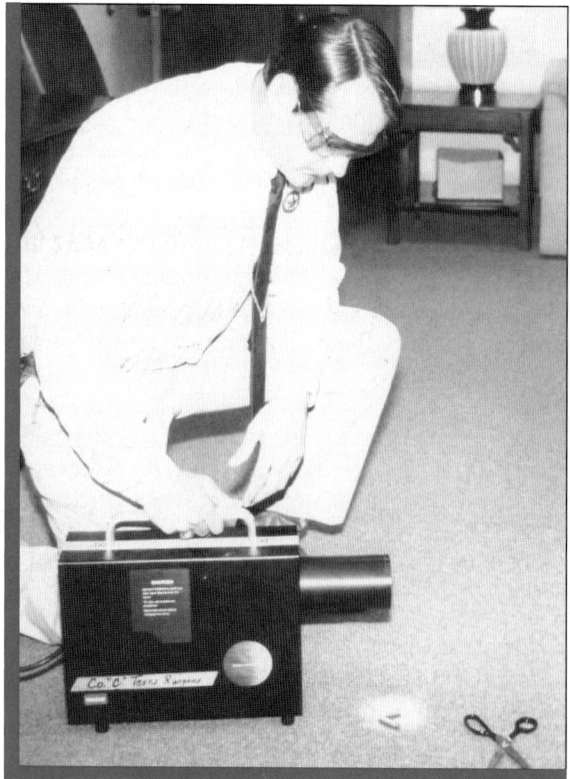

**Use of Luma-Lite**

A Texas Ranger demonstrates the use of a Luma-Lite at a simulated crime scene. The use of such an alternative light system at a crime scene results in finding evidence which otherwise would not have been detected.

(Courtesy Texas Department of Public Safety)

## PROCEED WITH CAUTION

Many crime scenes provide an immediate focus; in criminal homicide, for example, there is a tendency to move directly to the body. Such action, when the person is obviously deceased, has a number of disadvantages. In approaching the point of focus, minute but extremely important evidence may be altered or destroyed; the area to be searched may be too rapidly defined; and other areas that might be fruitfully explored are overlooked or given only a cursory examination.

## APPLY INCLUSIVENESS

The rule of inclusiveness dictates that every available piece of evidence be obtained and, where there is a question as to whether a particular item constitutes evidence, be defined as such. The rationale is that mistakes made in excluding potential evidence often cannot be rectified. One cannot always return to the crime scene and recover evidence. The rule of inclusiveness also requires that standard samples and elimination prints always be obtained when appropriate. If, for example, a burglary has been committed and a safe inside the building successfully attacked, exposing the insulation of the safe, then standard samples of the insulation should be obtained. This will ensure that if at some future time a suspect is identified, comparisons can be made between the standard sample of safe insulation and any traces of safe insulation that might be recovered from the soles of the suspect's shoes or his or her car floormat. Elimination prints are useful in determining whether a latent fingerprint found at a crime scene belongs to the suspect. In the case of a residential burglary, for example, if a latent print was developed inside the house on the window ledge where the perpetrator entered, the residents of the household should be fingerprinted and a comparison made between the latent fingerprint and those of the residents. If the latent fingerprint does not belong to any of the residents, there is a good possibility that it belongs to the perpetrator. In some instances, the fingerprint might belong to someone having authorized access to the dwelling. In cases where this is found to be true, however, the possibility cannot be overlooked that the person with authorized access may be the perpetrator. An example of this is the case of a licensed real estate dealer operating in the Washington,

D.C., area who may have entered more than 100 homes that were being offered for sale, stealing furs, tape recorders, silverware, and other valuables worth between $200,000 and $300,000.[15]

### MAINTAIN DOCUMENTATION

Documentation of the crime scene is a constant activity, starting with the rough, shorthand record created by field notes. Other types of documentation that need to be maintained include:

1. The **crime scene entry log sheet,** which was shown in Figure 2–2.
2. The **administrative log,** which is the responsibility of the crime scene coordinator and details such things as who is assigned to what function at the crime scene and the sequence of events at the scene, including its release.
3. **Assignment sheets,** which are completed by each individual who is given specific work to do and which document the results—both positive and negative.
4. The incidence/offense report, which is the responsibility of the first officer on the scene.
5. **Photographic logs,** detailing who took which shots, from where, when, and under what circumstances (e.g., type of lighting). Typical photo logs are video, digital, conventional 35 millimeter, Polaroid, and aerial (see Figure 2–4).
6. The rough sketch of the crime scene, the data from which are used to prepare the finished or final diagram, which may be drawn by hand or by computer.
7. The **evidence recovery log,** which lists each item of evidence; the names of the collector and witness; the location, date, and time of the collection; and documentation such as photos or diagrams. (See Figure 2–5.)
8. Emergency medical personnel documents.
9. The **lifted-prints log,** which contains the same type of basic information as does the evidence recovery log.
10. If applicable, consent search form or search warrant.

In lesser offenses, a single officer may be the only representative of the police department at the scene. Thus, everything that is learned will be a result of his or her investigation. In such cases the only documentation that may exist is the officer's field notes and the incident/offense report.

## CRIME SCENE SAFETY ISSUES

There are numerous threats to investigators' health and safety. For example, at outdoor scenes people

**Trace Evidence Vacuum**
A crime scene technician uses a trace evidence vacuum on a sofa where a sexual assault took place, while the detective working with him makes notes. Processing the sofa in this manner allows for recovery of hairs, fibers, and even certain types of drugs.
(Courtesy Westminster, Colorado, Police Department)

**Figure 2-4a** Photo Log Sheet

(Courtesy Imprimus Forensic Services, © 2000, by permission)

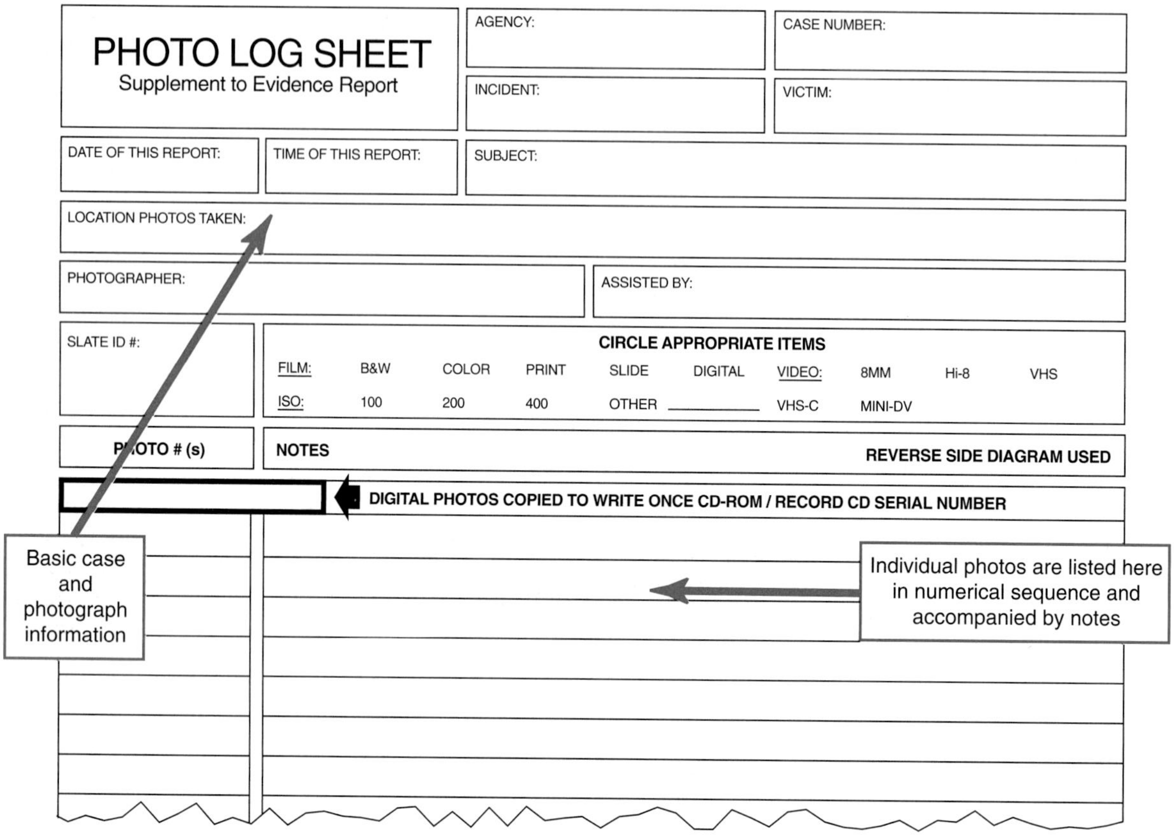

PHOTO LOG SHEET
Supplement to Evidence Report

AGENCY:

CASE NUMBER:

INCIDENT:

VICTIM:

DATE OF THIS REPORT:

TIME OF THIS REPORT:

SUBJECT:

LOCATION PHOTOS TAKEN:

PHOTOGRAPHER:

ASSISTED BY:

SLATE ID #:

CIRCLE APPROPRIATE ITEMS

FILM: B&W COLOR PRINT SLIDE DIGITAL VIDEO: 8MM Hi-8 VHS

ISO: 100 200 400 OTHER ________ VHS-C MINI-DV

PHOTO # (s)

NOTES

REVERSE SIDE DIAGRAM USED

DIGITAL PHOTOS COPIED TO WRITE ONCE CD-ROM / RECORD CD SERIAL NUMBER

Basic case and photograph information

Individual photos are listed here in numerical sequence and accompanied by notes

may be stung by insects (which could produce anaphylactic shock, a life-threatening allergic reaction), get lyme disease from ticks, be bitten by animals, or get a severe skin reaction from poison ivy, oak, or sumac.[16] More often, however, investigators are at risk of contracting infectious pathogens (disease-causing agents), such as HIV, hepatitis B, hepatitis C, and tuberculosis. After the September 11, 2001, attacks on the Twin Towers in New York City biological terrorism came to the fore in the form of anthrax sent through the mail. Beyond biological warfare are chemical, radiological, and nuclear threats. This section discusses the self-protection measures officers at crime scenes should take with respect to the more usual infectious diseases; the following section covers precautions regarding potential or actual terrorist events.

## INFECTIOUS DISEASES

### HIV/AIDS

The **human immunodeficiency virus (HIV)** is a blood-borne pathogen that is also present in other body fluids. There is some question as to whether all bodily fluids can transmit HIV, since evidence indicates that naturally occurring proteins in tears and saliva inhibit HIV. However, investigators must always take all appropriate precautions to protect themselves. If HIV progresses into acquired immunodeficiency syndrome (AIDS), the body's natural defenses against many types of diseases are substantially reduced, leaving victims vulnerable to "opportunistic infections," such as pneumonia, from which they ultimately die. There is no HIV/AIDS vaccine.

Figure 2-4b Photo Log Sheet, *continued*

(Courtesy Imprimus Forensic Services, © 2000, by permission)

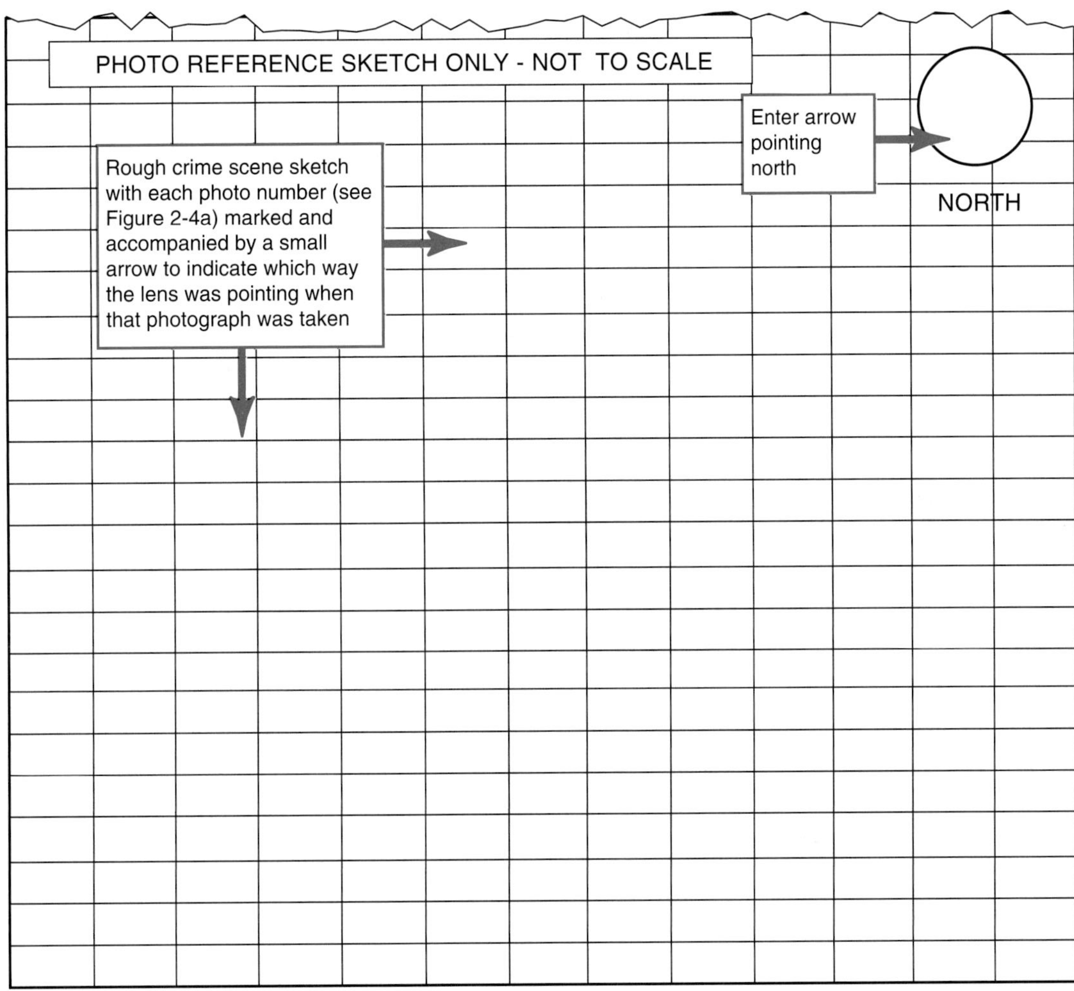


As 2001 began, 36.1 million people worldwide had AIDS.[17] In the United States, about 900,000 people have AIDS, and it is estimated that one-third of them do not know it.[18] The first report of AIDS in America was in 1981. Approximately 40,000 new HIV infections occur each year in the United States; 70 percent of those infected are men, and 30 percent are women.[19] About half of these newly infected people are under 25 years of age.[20] Typically, men become infected through homosexual intercourse (60 percent), injection drug use (25 percent), and heterosexual intercourse (15 percent).[21] Among women, the causes of infection roughly parallel those among men. The transmission of HIV cascades when infection spreads from injection drug users (IDUs) to their sexual and needle-sharing partners, then to the partners' partners, and so on, and from pregnant IDUs to their unborn children.[22] AIDS is now the fifth leading cause of death in the United States among people age 25 to 44.[23]

HIV is not spread from casual contact. You cannot get it from toilet seats, telephones, swimming pools, or air.[24] There is no present evidence that HIV is

**Figure 2-5** Evidence Recovery Log

| Incident # | Offense: | Victim: | Location: |
|---|---|---|---|

| Item No. | Description | Collector | Witness | Location | Time/Date Collected | Photos | | Diagramed | |
|---|---|---|---|---|---|---|---|---|---|
| | | | | | | Y | N | Y | N |
| 1 | | | | | | | | | |
| 2 | | | | | | | | | |
| 3 | | | | | | | | | |
| 4 | | | | | | | | | |
| 5 | | | | | | | | | |
| 6 | | | | | | | | | |
| 15 | | | | | | | | | |

| Recorded by: | Date: | Recorded by: |
|---|---|---|
| Name: ______ | ______ | Name: ______ |
| | Start Time: ______ | |
| ID No.: ______ | End Time: ______ | ID No.: ______ |
| Unit: ______ | | Unit: ______ |

Page___of___Pages

spread through sweat, tears, urine, or feces.[25] However, the presence of blood is not always obvious in such materials, nor is blood necessarily immediately apparent on clothing, guns, knives, cars, drugs, and hypodermic needles; therefore, consistent caution is always warranted. It should be noted that HIV (and hepatitis B and C) can also be spread through shared razors, toothbrushes, and other personal care items. Although saliva is generally not believed to be a means of HIV transmission, the risk of infection from "deep kissing" and the exchange of large amounts of saliva is not known.[26] Biting insects, such as mosquitoes, do not transmit HIV.[27]

## HIV/AIDS and Investigators

The approximate risk of HIV infection after an accidental needle stick is 0.3 percent.[28] Given the frequency with which investigators deal with special populations, such as IDUs, homosexuals, and prostitutes, the risk for them may be somewhat greater. The greatest danger to officers arises when they are making arrests, seizing drug-related evidence, and processing crime scenes and accidents where blood and other bodily fluids are exposed.

At crime, accident, and other scenes with a potential or known HIV risk, investigators should be knowledgeable about and employ self-protection techniques, including the following:

1. Be cautious when conducting all types of searches; never put your hands anywhere you cannot see. Instead, use a mirror, or probe with a flashlight, wooden dowel, or metal rod.
2. The most important protective barrier against HIV infection is intact skin. Even the

slightest opening in the skin can be a portal through which HIV enters the body. Protect skin wounds, abrasions, and openings with 360-degree fluid-proof bandages.

3. About 20 percent of AIDS patients develop raised, purplish-colored lesions, which may be present anywhere on the body. Some of these are "weeping lesions" that let out an HIV-carrying fluid. You should be particularly careful around such lesions.
4. If you are bitten by a suspect, seek medical assistance and have an assessment made because many types of infection are possible from such a wound.[29]
5. Bites, needle sticks, cuts, or similar incidents involving broken or punctured skin, however slight, should be washed immediately with soap in warm water for at least 30 seconds and treated medically.[30] Use soap from a dispenser, not a shared bar. (Some agencies recommend the use of germicidal wipes approved by the Environmental Protection Agency [EPA].) There is no evidence that squeezing or "milking" wounds reduces the risk of HIV.
6. If splashed in the eyes or on mucous membranes (e.g., inside the nose), flush the area for 15 minutes using water, sterile water, or a saline solution.
7. Do not attempt to recap hypodermic needles seized as evidence, and use care when seizing any other sharp items (e.g., knives, razor blades, broken glass, scissors, and metal pieces) at crime scenes. When handling sharp objects, use disposable tongs or forceps and place the objects in appropriate rigid, puncture-resistant containers.
8. There is a direct correlation between the type of gloves one wears and the tactile sensitivity they provide.[31] While "double gloving" reduces the sense of touch somewhat, it does offer additional level of protection. Remove any rings that could tear a glove. Wear latex gloves when contact with blood, body fluids, body parts, weeping lesions, body membranes, or nonintact skin of others is possible. Do not touch or handle petroleum products when wearing latex gloves; such products "eat" or degrade them. Wear vinyl gloves instead.[32] Use nitrile gloves if you are latex-sensitive.
9. The use of gloves may reduce the amount of blood transferred by an accidental needle stick by 50 percent.[33] Cut-resistant glove liners further reduce the chance of accidental needle sticks and other wounds. Because some new gloves may have leaks, supplies should be periodically evaluated and only the appropriate quality should be purchased for use.
10. Check your gloves frequently for wear and tear; replace them often. When you replace gloves, wash your hands and use a germicidal wipe on them.
11. Maintain a high sense of personal awareness at potential HIV scenes. When you are wearing gloves, do not handle personal items (such as your pen or clipboard) and do not put your hands in your pockets, touch your face, or scratch your head. If you do touch personal items or body areas, they should be disinfected (see Figure 2–6).
12. Always carry a flashlight, even during daylight hours, so that you can search dark areas more safely.
13. Do not eat, drink, smoke, handle contacts, or apply lip balm or cosmetics at HIV-risk crime scenes.
14. Wear a mask and a face shield or similar protective gear when scraping dried blood.
15. In addition to gloves, other **personal protection equipment (PPE)** may be necessary at high-risk scenes with exposed blood and splatters. Examples of such equipment are listed in Figure 2–7.
16. If you must give cardiopulmonary resuscitation (CPR), use protective eyewear and use a CPR device with a one-way valve to prevent blood or other bodily fluids from entering your mouth. A resuscitation bag is an attractive alternative because it eliminates direct contact between the person giving the CPR and the person receiving it.
17. Contaminated evidence should be collected, marked, and packaged as appropriate for the

**Figure 2-6** Common Disinfectants Used for HIV/AIDS Blood Exposure

*Equipment*

Use a 1:10 mix of EPA-registered bleach and water, which requires 9 cups, or other measurement, to each cup of water. Bleach-and-water mixes should not be used if they were mixed more than 24 hours earlier because bleach loses some of its potency. The best practice is to prepare the mix immediately before using it. If there has been significant contact with blood, contact time for the mix and equipment is 20 minutes.

*Personal*

Wipe the exposed area with an EPA-approved germicide, such as 70 percent isopropyl, and let it air dry; immediately report the exposure to your supervisor.

**Source:** Colleen Wade, ed., Handbook of Forensic Services (Washington, DC: Federal Bureau of Investigation, 1999), pp. 103-104.

particular type of evidence. If the evidence might be contaminated, mark it prominently as such or apply a "Biological Hazard" sticker.

18. All disposable worn PPE should be placed in a biohazard waste bag when you have completed your work at the crime scene. Many departments use specially colored bags, such as red or orange, for this purpose.
19. Know and follow your department's procedures for disinfecting uniforms and equipment. If you have not worn protective "booties," make sure you disinfect your shoes as you leave the crime scene; then wash your hands.
20. Report all exposures immediately to a supervisor.
21. Make sure you understand your state's confidentiality laws that pertain to disclosing information about HIV to others, including the news media.

## Hepatitus B and C

**Hepatitis B (HBV)** is the most common serious disease in the world and is the leading cause of liver cancer.[34] It also results in cirrhosis (scarring) of the liver and liver failure. In the United States, 5 percent of the population has been infected with HBV, and there are 200,000 new cases annually.[35] In about 50 percent of the cases, those infected have no symptoms; the balance have a variety of symptoms, including fever, fatigue, muscle or joint pain, loss of appetite, nausea, and vomiting.[36] Officers are likely to contract HBV in the same way that they would HIV: through exposure to blood and bodily fluids. However, HBV is much more potent than HIV, so officers are more likely to contract it in the absence of precautions. Since 1982 there has been a safe and effective HBV vaccine.

Spread by contact with the blood of an infected person, **hepatitis C (HCV)** is emerging as a major health concern. The cause of chronic liver disease, HCV may be more serious for one person than another. In the United States, 3.9 million people (nearly 2 percent of the population) have been infected by HCV, and 2.7 million of them are chroni-

**Figure 2-7** Crime Scene Personal Protection Equipment

- Gloves: cotton, latex, nitrile, vinyl, heavy rubber, neoprene
- Cut-resistant glove liners
- Protective or impermeable "booties" or shoe covers, disposable gowns, coveralls or jumpsuits, aprons, hoods, chin-length face shield, eyewear with side shields
- Masks: infiltration mask for protection from highly contagious people and situations; nuisance odor mask for reduction of unpleasant odors; and half-mask particulate respirator for protection from fumes, particulate/dust, and airborne pathogens
- Self-contained breathing apparatus (SCBA)
- EPA-registered bleach, germicidal disinfectants, and wipes
- First aid kit
- Biohazard bags
- Insect repellant

**Source:** Content drawn from Henry C. Lee, Timothy M. Palmbach, and Marilyn T. Miller, *Crime Scene Handbook* (San Diego: Academic Press, 2001), pp. 321-324, and Technical Working Group on Crime Scene Investigation, *Crime Scene Investigation* (Washington, DC: U.S. Department of Justice, 2000), pp. 33-36; additional content supplied by the authors.

cally afflicted; about 40,000 new cases are seen annually.[37] Unless effective new therapies are developed, deaths due to HCV will double or even triple over the next 15 to 20 years simply because 80 percent of those infected have no signs or symptoms and therefore may have been infected for a long time without knowing it.[38] The symptoms include jaundice, dark urine, fatigue, abdominal pain, nausea, and loss of appetite. There is no vaccine for this disease. Neither HBV nor HCV is spread by casual contact such as hugging.

### Tuberculosis

**Tuberculosis (TB)** is a chronic bacterial infection that is spread by air. Accountable for more deaths worldwide than any other infectious disease, it usually infects the lungs, although other organs may be involved.[39] One-third of the world's population is infected with TB, although most will never develop active TB; it is estimated that 10 to 15 million Americans have TB and roughly 10 percent of them will develop active cases, which can usually be cured.[40] The death rate for untreated active cases of TB is between 40 and 50 percent, while the mortality rate for treated cases is about 10 percent.[41] The relatively recent dramatic rise in drug-resistant strains of TB is of concern to public health officials.[42]

When a person with active TB coughs into the air, infectious droplets are released; repeated exposure to them can cause the disease. People who eat healthy diets and lead healthy lifestyles are less at risk that others when such exposure occurs. Conversely, IDUs, the homeless, alcoholics, drug addicts, and people in poor health are at greater risk.

A vaccine (BCG) is given to infants in some parts of the world where the disease is common; the effectiveness of BCG in adults varies widely, and in the United States its general use is not recommended.[43] Several drug therapies are available for people who have a high risk of developing active TB, that is, those who are in close contact with persons who are infected with TB or have active TB.[44]

The infectious diseases discussed in this section may also occur in combination; for example, some people have both TB and HIV, and every year 8 percent of these people develop active TB.[45] Therefore, officers working with high-risk populations should take every reasonable protection to prevent their own exposure and infection.

### THE AMERICANS WITH DISABILITIES ACT

Investigators who contract the infectious diseases discussed above may be covered by the federal **Americans with Disabilities Act (ADA).** Under this act, it is illegal to discriminate against an otherwise qualified employee in regard to employment actions—such as assignments and promotions—solely because the employee is thought to have or actually has a covered disability. Employers may be required to make "reasonable accommodations" for such employees. Reasonable accommodations include redesigning jobs, offering part-time hours, and modifying equipment and facilities. The legal provisions of ADA are broad and cover more than just infectious diseases; additional information is readily obtainable in personnel offices, from police unions, and on the Internet.

As a final note, some police agencies have taken the view that if an officer cannot fully perform all of the functions required of a certified peace officer, she or he may be separated from the service or placed on involuntary medical retirement, depending on the situation. Other police departments have chosen to inventory their positions each year in order to determine how many of them could, with reasonable accommodations, be staffed by persons covered by ADA.

## THE CRIME SCENE SEARCH

The purpose of the crime scene search is to obtain physical evidence useful in establishing the fact that an offense has been committed; identifying the method of operation employed by the perpetrator; reducing the number of suspects; and identifying the perpetrator. Five major considerations dominate the crime scene search. Each is discussed below.

### BOUNDARY DETERMINATION

In terms of the boundary of the crime scene, it is useful to think of an inner perimeter and an outer perimeter. The inner perimeter delineated the area where the specific items of evidence are known to be, along with the lines of entry into and exit from the scene. The outer perimeter is set further back than the inner perimeter and helps establish control of and entry into the scene.

The crime scene coordinator is responsible for deciding the positions of the inner and outer perimeters, which are determined by the locations of the primary and any secondary crime scenes—such as the perpetrator's lines of approach to and from the scene. Along these lines the perpetrator may have accidentally left or dropped valuable evidence, such as items taken from the scene, the perpetrator's wallet or distinctive jewelry, matches from an establishment he or she works at or frequents, a water bottle the perpetrator drank from while waiting for the victim, and the butt from a cigarette he or she smoked. Saliva traces from the bottle and the butt could yield key DNA evidence.

For an indoor crime scene, the physical limitations of the building can help determine where the inner and outer boundaries should be. More problematic is determining the boundaries for an outdoor crime scene. When a person is found shot to death in a large field, for instance, how narrow or broad should the perimeters be? As a general rule, in such situations, it is better to establish the perimeters more broadly. While doing so, may result in some "wasted" resources, items of evidence are occasionally found.

## CHOICE OF SEARCH PATTERN

There are five basic **crime scene search patterns** from which the crime scene coordinator may choose. The spiral, depicted in Figure 2–8a is usually employed in outdoor scenes and is normally executed by a single person. The searcher walks in slightly decreasing, less-than-concentric circles from the outermost boundary determination toward a central point. This pattern should not be operated in the reverse—beginning at some central point and working toward the perimeter of the crime scene in increasing, less-than-concentric circles—as there is a real danger that some evidence may be inadvertently destroyed while walking to the central point to initiate the search. Use of the strip/line search, shown in Figure 2–8b, involves the demarcation of a series of lanes down which one or more persons proceed. Upon reaching the starting point, the searchers proceed down their respective lanes, reverse their direction, and continue in this fashion until the area has been thoroughly examined. If multiple searchers are being used, then whenever physical evidence is encountered, all searchers should stop until it is properly handled and they have received information with respect to its nature. The search is then resumed in the fashion described above. The photo on page 54 shows a single searcher using a metal detector to look for a bullet casing while conducting a strip search in lanes established by landmarks. A variation of the strip search is the grid, depicted in Figure 2–8c. After completing the strip pattern, the searchers double back perpendicularly across the area being examined. While more time-consuming than the strip search, the grid offers the advantage of being more methodical and thorough; examined from two different viewpoints, an area is more likely to yield evidence that might otherwise have been overlooked.

Figure 2–8d shows the zone/quadrant search pattern, which requires that an area be divided into four large quadrants, each of which is then examined using any of the methods already described. If the area to be searched is particularly large, each of the quadrants can be subdivided into four smaller quadrants. The pie/wheel search, shown in Figure 2–8e, entails dividing the area into a number of pie-shaped sections, usually six. These are then searched, usually through a variation of the strip method.

In actual practice, both the spiral and the pie search patterns are rarely employed. When the area to be searched is not excessively large, the strip or grid pattern is normally used. When the crime scene is of significant size, the zone search pattern is normally employed.

## INSTRUCTION OF PERSONNEL

Although instruction of personnel was mentioned earlier in the chapter, its importance requires some further elaboration. Even when the same type of criminal offense has been committed, the variation among crime scenes may be enormous. These variations are due to such factors as the physical settings, the manner and means that the perpetrators

**Figure 2-8** Crime Scene Search Patterns

**(a) Spiral**

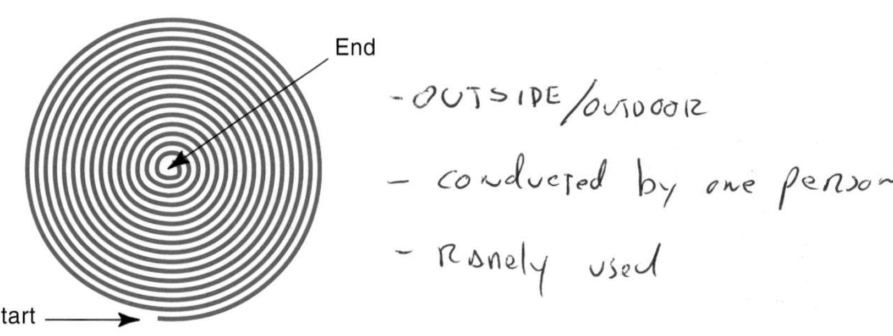


**(b) Strip/Line**

**(c) Grid**

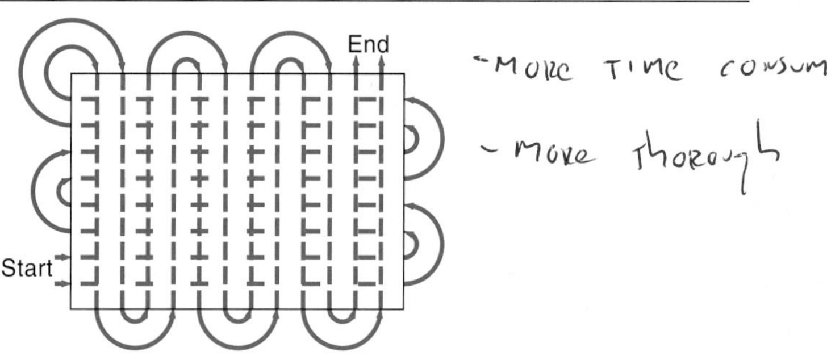


**(d) Zone/Quadrant**

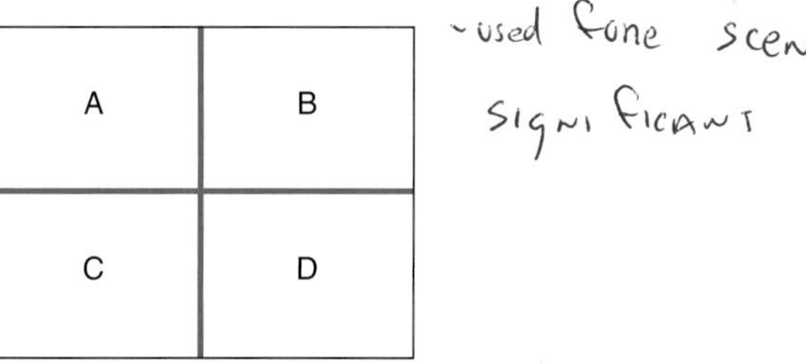


**(e) Pie/Wheel**

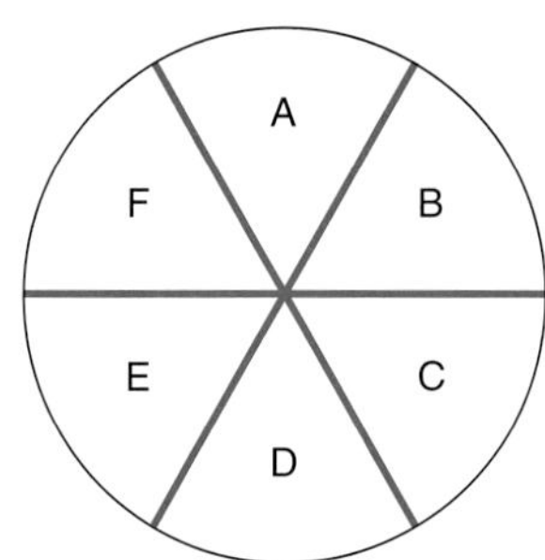

**Conducting a Strip Search**
This police officer is walking a lane using a metal detector while conducting a strip search for a bullet casing. Metal detectors vary in their capabilities and how well they work in different types of soils. The more advanced ones are computerized and can tell you how deep an object is, as well as suggest the nature of the item detected.

used to execute the offenses, and the lengths to which they may have gone to eliminate or destroy evidence. Thus, it is of paramount importance that the crime scene coordinator call together all the individuals who will be, in various capacities, processing the scene and share with them all the available information concerning the case. Doing so serves to minimize the possibility of excluding any available evidence. On receipt of this information, the members of the crime scene processing team may then begin their work.

## COORDINATION

As discussed earlier, one of the most important responsibilities of the person in charge of the crime scene is integrating the efforts of those assigned to the technical and investigative service functions, along with ensuring the timely flow of pertinent information. For example, if a suspect is in custody and the interrogation yields information concerning the weapon or tool that may have been used, or where it may be located, then the crime scene coordinator should rapidly relay this information to those involved in technical services at the scene so that they will be alert to specific possibilities for the recovery of physical evidence. Conversely, as significant physical evidence is recovered, the information should be conveyed to the crime scene coordinator, who can then transmit it to the investigators so that they can move toward apprehending a suspect or be assisted in the interrogation of a possible perpetrator already in custody.

# SUSPENDED SEARCHES, DEBRIEFING, AND RELEASE OF THE SCENE

The amount of time required to process a crime scene varies considerably, depending on such factors as the extent and nature of the area to be examined, the complexity of the case, the abundance or scarcity of physical evidence, and available personnel. Once it has been established that a crime has been committed, under no circumstances should the search be terminated until all possible fruitful avenues for developing physical evidence have been thoroughly explored. Occasionally it may be necessary to suspend an operation temporarily. In one of the most common situations, a priority crime with evidence subject to decay requires the temporary diversion of personnel from a scene where delayed processing will not result in any loss of physical evidence. If it becomes necessary to stop the examination of a scene for a time, that scene should be secured in such a fashion that there is no possibility of contamination, alteration, or accidental destruction of any evidence that may exist.

Immediately before the **crime scene release,** the coordinator calls all team members together. In addition to ensuring that assignments were properly executed, the coordinator checks to make sure that all equipment brought to the scene has been retrieved and that all trash generated in processing the scene has been removed. Because all participants share information during the debriefing, additional opportunities to develop evidence may be identified and all parties leave the scene with a common understanding of the crime and of what the next steps are going to be. When the scene is finally released, the name of the party to whom it is released and his or her locator information should be noted in the administrative log.

Generally, you get only one chance to process a crime scene; any mistakes made may not be rectifiable. Once a scene is released, the person to whom it is released will often clean it up. Additionally, if the person is living there, the countless small things he or she does each day will alter and contaminate the scene so that returning to it for further processing is not a viable option. Therefore, the decision to release a scene must be well thought out.

## COLLECTION AND CARE OF EVIDENCE

The location of physical evidence during the crime scene search merely marks the first step in its long journey toward presentation in court. To satisfy legal requirements related to its introduction in a judicial proceeding, investigators must be able to:

1. Identify each item of evidence that they collected or handled.
2. Describe the location and condition of the evidence at the time it was collected.
3. State who had contact with or handled the evidence.
4. State when or during what time periods the evidence was handled.
5. Declare under what circumstances and why the evidence was handled.
6. Explain what changes, if any, were made to the evidence.[46]

Chapter 3, "Physical Evidence," deals with various types of evidence and the specific ways to properly collect and package it. In general, investigators have many different options when it comes to packaging evidence. Among them are paper bags, paper cartons, Kraft envelopes, tamper-evident evidence sealing tape, seamless all-metal cans, cardboard tubes, pillboxes, document sleeves, clear evidence pouches (see photo on page 56) which may be heat-sealed or be closed using the pouch's double adhesive strips. Many of these items have preprinted forms incorporated into them. This eliminates having to attach forms, which can become separated and lost. The essence of packaging any evidence is to do it in a way that will make any tampering with it clearly evident. For example, if evidence is placed in a Kraft envelope, the envelope should be sealed with tamper-evident evidence tape. As a further measure, when the officer signs her or his initials or signature, the writing can start on the envelope, cross the tape, and go back onto the envelope.

Some evidence may be so large that packaging it is not reasonable; in such cases, attaching an evidence tag to the item is an approved way of identifying it. The information on an evidence tag is fundamentally the same as that required on printed forms incorporated into the packaging, and all entries should be made in permanent ink:

1. Collecting officer's full name.
2. Collecting officer's identification number (e.g., badge or serial number).
3. Street address of, or other applicable information about, the place where the evidence was seized.
4. Exact location from which the evidence was collected (e.g., from the rearview mirror).
5. Time and date that the evidence was seized.
6. Content description, including size, condition, and/or amount.
7. Other related information, including case control number, type of offense, and witnesses to the collection.
8. Collecting officer's signature.[47]

The entries made on evidence forms and tags, along with strong evidence room procedures (such as the use of bar codes to track evidence handling) help in the introduction of evidence in a courtroom.

## VISUAL DOCUMENTATION OF THE CRIME SCENE

Occasionally, the value of an otherwise excellent investigation is reduced by improper or inadequate

**Clear Plastic Evidence Envelope**
Pictured above is a heat-sealed clear plastic envelope containing four unfired bullets. Case information has been entered on the label.
(Courtesy St. Louis County, Missouri, Police Department)

visual documentation of the scene. People process information differently, so the more ways a crime scene is properly documented, the greater the likelihood that other people will accurately understand the scene and what happened there. This section examines three major methods of documenting crime scenes: videotaping, photographing, and sketching. In general, the methods should be used in the order presented here, with documentation moving from the general to the more specific.

## VIDEOTAPING

Using a video camera, or **videotaping,** to document the crime scene offers several advantages. Such cameras are relatively inexpensive, they incorporate audio, their use can be quickly learned, the motion of videotapes holds the attention of viewers, and the images collected can be played back immediately. On the downside, neither the resolutions or the color accuracy can compete with those in 35-millimeter photography, and tapes may be damaged by electromagnetic waves. Videotaped images are not an acceptable alternative to high-resolution still photographs. Listed below are guidelines for the use of crime scene videotaping:

1. Keep the camera's heads and lens clean to produce sharper images.
2. The use of appropriate lighting will speed up the focusing of the camera, thereby producing true colors and higher resolution. Battery-operated lights should be used to avoid dragging electrical cords through the scene.
3. Most crime scenes can be documented on a 30-minute tape, although longer-time tapes should be immediately available for more complicated situations.
4. Once you begin, keep the camera running; gaps in the tape may be hard to explain satisfactorily to jurors.
5. The use of a tripod with the camera will produce smoother, less jerky images.
6. Use the camera's title generator for future reference.
7. Begin with a short narrative of the situation, including the case number, the type of offense, the location, and other pertinent information. Plan your shots so that you can tell the viewer where you took them and what he or she will be seeing.
8. Department policies vary on whether there should be continuous narration as the entire scene is videotaped. On the plus side, it can provide viewers with additional understanding However, if extraneous and nonobjective comments are made, portions or all of the tape may be ruled inadmissible.
9. The most common mistake in videotaping is going too fast; the speed you think is right is probably 50 percent too quick. Take your time and use the camera's capabilities for wide-area pans, close-ups, and very tight shots of the evidence.

When the videotaping of the scene is completed, the tape is evidence and needs to be packaged and marked in the same manner as are other types of evidence. Tapes should be stored in an area free from dust and machinery that generates magnetic fields. If the tape is going to be viewed more than once or twice, a copy should be made to avoid the possibility of degrading the tape through repeated showings.

## PHOTOGRAPHING

In addition to videotaping, **photographing** is an important means of documenting major crime scenes. It offers the benefits of various types of cameras and techniques. Aerial photography is effective in showing the point of interest and its position relative to other evidence in a broad area. Infrared aerial photographs are particularly useful when the need to show contrasting terrain features exists.

Digital cameras store images in a numeric format. High-end digital cameras, which are for professional use, offer features such as interchangeable lenses that make them more expensive, but they are a better option than the low-end ones intended for the consumer market.[48] The advantages of a digital camera are that the images can be immediately viewed, can be printed on-site, and can be quickly transmitted and disseminated.[49] Among the disadvantages are that the stored images are subject to electromagnetic degrading, the storage media can be obtained only at special stores, and, because the technology continues to evolve rapidly, accessing older archived images may not be possible with newer equipment.[50]

Conventional silver-based film used in a 35-millimeter camera is still the primary means of capturing crime scene images. Such cameras offer high resolutions, the best color range, and the most durable storage medium, and they can be used with a variety of films.[51] These advantages are countered by the need for a processing and printing facility, the longer processing time required, and the inability to immediately evaluate the image.[52]

Polaroid cameras are easy to use and provide photographs very quickly. However, enlargements and duplicates of the photographs may take some time to get. Among their other uses, Polaroids can be useful in orienting the crime scene team, and pictures of suspects just arrested at the scene can be taken and used in the neighborhood canvass.

The guidelines listed below are general ones, appropriate for photographing almost any scene:

1. Keep a photo log of all shots taken.
2. Photograph the scene as soon as possible, showing the condition of the evidence before its recovery.
3. Document all stages of the investigation, including physical-evidence discoveries.
4. Establish a progression of overall, medium, and close-up views.
5. Photograph from eye level to present the normal view, unless there is a need to use a stepladder to provide a different perspective.
6. Take at least two shots of each item of evidence: the first consists of only the item of itself, and the second includes the item plus a ruler or measuring tape, as well as a card showing the photographer's initials, the

**Documenting the Crime Scene**
A pump shotgun found near a crime scene lies in the snow. Its location is being documented with a camera by the officer.
(Courtesy Lewiston, Maine, Police Department)

time, and the date. The first photograph establishes the evidence at the scene as it was actually discovered; the second one is used for administrative and investigative purposes.

7. Photograph interior and outdoor scenes overall and with overlapping shots.
8. Shoot the exterior view of a building to establish the scene's location; for outdoor scenes, try to include a landmark if there is one.
9. If the scene is a building, take pictures of all doors and exits.
10. Whether the scene is indoors or outdoors, photograph the lines of approach to and flight from the scene.
11. Consider the use of aerial photography.[53]

## SKETCHING

It is critical that measurements shown on the sketch be as accurate as possible and that they be made and recorded uniformly; if one aspect is inaccurate, such as the dimensions of a field in which a body was found, the distortion introduced renders the sketch relatively useless. The coordinate distances of an item in the sketch must be determined in the same manner; one coordinate leg should not be paced and the other measured. It is also a poor practice to pace off a distance and then show it on the sketch in feet and inches. Such an indication connotes a greater degree of accuracy than actually exists. If the point arose in court, the inconsistency would significantly detract from the value of the sketch. An erroneous measurement in a drawing, once discovered, is difficult to explain and may introduce doubt as to the competency of the entire investigation.

### Sketching Methods

Discussed below are various techniques for preparing sketches, particularly the methods that can be used to establish the location of evidence and other important items. Refer to Figure 2–3 for the equipment used in crime scene sketching.

***Baseline/Coordinate*** This technique involves measuring the distance of an object from two fixed points. One form of the coordinate uses a baseline drawn between two known points. The baseline may also be a wall or be drawn as the mathematical center of a room, the exact dimensions of which are known. The measurements of a given object are then taken from left to right along the baseline to a point at right angles to the object that is to be plotted. The object is indicated on the sketch by a number, and the object is identified by a corresponding number in the legend. Figure 2–9 illustrates this method. The simplest form of a sketch, it is the two-dimensional presentation of the scene as if viewed directly from above, using a number keyed to a description of the item located in the sketch. Figure 2–9 incorporates the full range of information essential to a proper sketch; however, this is omitted from subsequent diagrams to avoid needless repetition.

***Triangulation*** This method, illustrated in Figure 2–10, is particularly useful in an outdoor situation where there are no easily identifiable edges of fields or roads for use as baselines. Two or more widely separated reference points are located, and the item of interest is located by measuring along a straight line from each of the reference points. The reference points must be ones that are not likely to disappear. Note in Figure 2–10 that a metal light pole, the corner of a brick house, and a fire hydrant were used.

***Cross-Projection*** Depicted in Figure 2–11, the cross-projection method is useful when the items or locations of interest are on or in the walls as well as elsewhere in an enclosed space. The walls, windows, and doors in a cross-projection sketch are drawn as though the walls had been folded flat on the floor. The measurements from a given point on the floor to the wall are then indicated.

***Rough and Smooth Sketches*** A **rough sketch** is one drawn by the investigator at the scene of the crime. Changes should not be made after the investigator leaves the scene. The rough is not drawn to scale but indicates accurate distances and dimensions. To eliminate excessive detail, it may be necessary to prepare more than one sketch. For example, one sketch may be devoted to the position of the victim's body and a limited number of critical evidence items. Additional sketches might depict the location of other evidence with respect to the point of entry or other critical areas.

**Figure 2-9** Baseline/Coordinate Method of Sketching

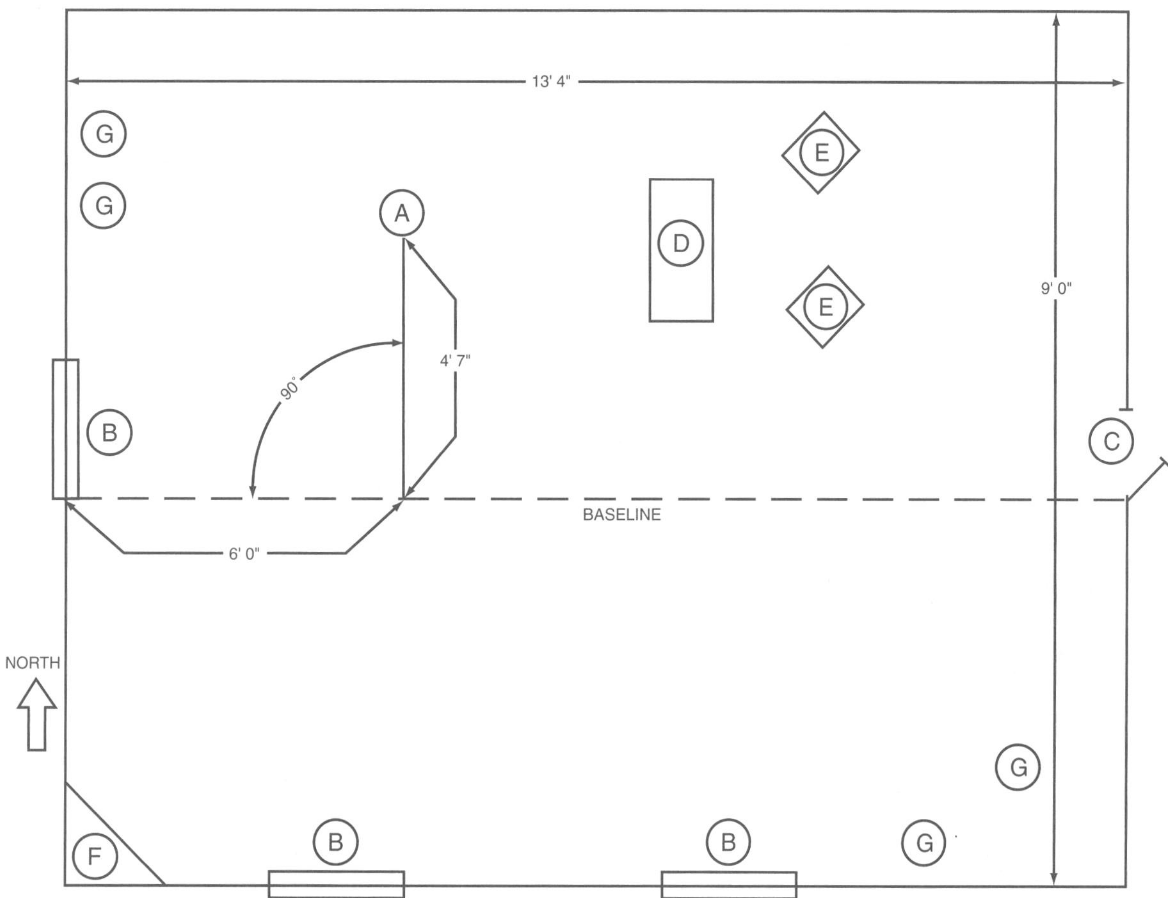


| Legend | **Offense:** Burglary **Case Number:** 062202-849 |
|---|---|
| | **Drawn By:** Officer Kellie Pless, ACCPD, #551 |
| A. Face-up, U.S. dollar bill, #B17481980P, face covered with light-colored powdery substance | **Assisted By:** Officers Colin Cummings, ACCPD, #723 and T. L. Swanson, ACCPD, #675, made the measurements |
| B. Sash windows, 36" wide and 42" tall | **Complainant:** Mrs. Juanita Alvarez 5416 Duncan Springs Road |
| C. Door enters into the kitchen | **Offense/Location/Area:** Aggravated Assault/5416 Miller Road/Den |
| D. Grey cloth, 3-seat couch, facing east | **Drawn:** 0735 hrs, June 22, 2002 |
| E. Matching black leather easy chairs | **Scale:** Tape Measured, but not drawn to scale |
| F. 7' brown wood, built-in corner cupboard | **Weather Conditions:** Steady, hard rain creating a lot of mud outside |
| G. Matching high back, blond wood chairs | **Signature:** Kellie Pless #551 |

**Figure 2-10** Triangulation Method of Sketching

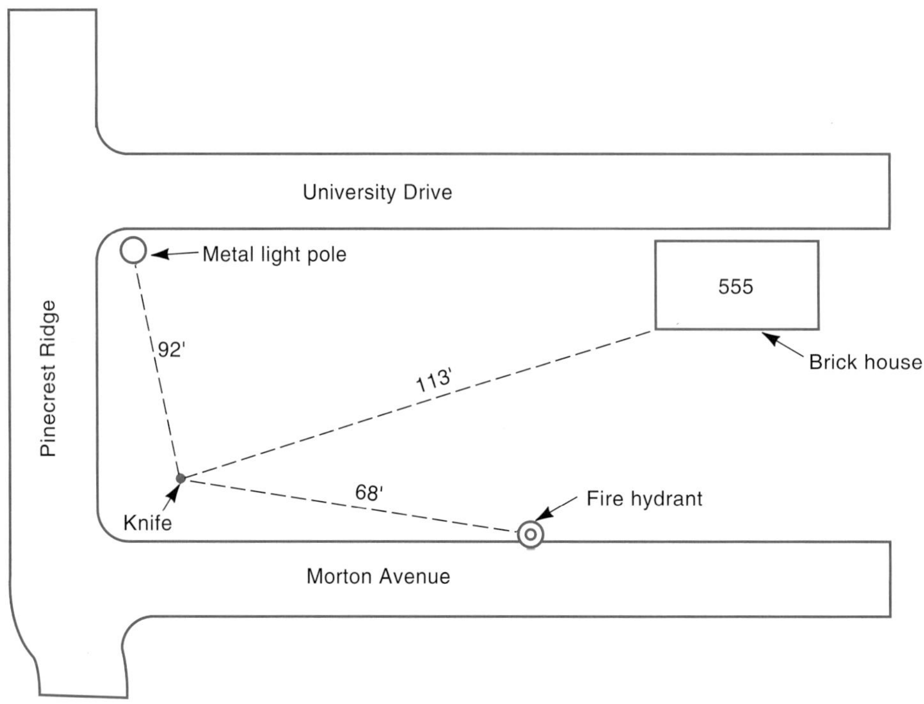


A **smooth sketch** is simply one that is finished, frequently being drawn to scale using information contained in the rough sketch. In a scaled diagram, the numbers concerning distances can be eliminated; if the smooth sketch is not drawn to scale, these distances must be shown. The person preparing the rough sketch must verify the accuracy of the final product whenever the smooth sketch is drafted by someone else.

While many law enforcement agencies continue to make crime scene sketches by hand, some use computer technology to produce them. Several software programs are used for this purpose (see Figure 2–12).

## SUBMISSION OF EVIDENCE TO THE LABORATORY

Evidence submitted to a crime laboratory is most often transmitted by courier, air express, or registered mail.[54] In the ideal situation, the investigator most knowledgeable about the case takes it to the laboratory, where he or she can discuss the case with appropriate examiners. Given the caseloads all crime laboratories have, this situation is the exception. In general, the method of transmitting evidence is determined by the nature of the evidence and the urgency of getting an analyst's conclusions. Federal and state agency rules specify how some special classes of evidence must be sent. Examples of these classes are chemicals, blasting caps, flammable materials, and biological and chemical agents. With these materials, the safest procedure is to contact the laboratory to which the evidence is being sent to give lab personnel advance notice and to get their guidance on how to properly package and send the evidence.

In submitting evidence to the FBI laboratory, certain protocols must be followed. The **letter of transmittal** should include the following information:

1. The submitting person's agency, address, and telephone number.
2. Current and any previous case identification numbers, the associated evidence

Figure 2-11 Cross-Projection Method of Sketching

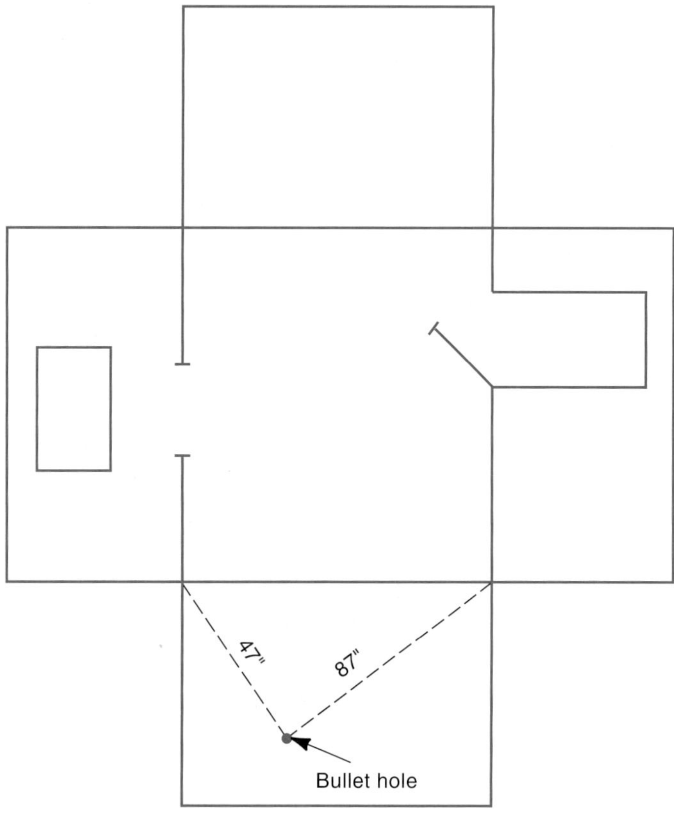


submissions, and all communications relating to them.

3. A description of the nature of the offense and the basic facts related to it.
4. Names of and descriptive data about the individuals involved (e.g., subject, suspect, or victim).
5. A list of the evidence "herewith" (enclosed) or being sent under separate cover. If the evidence is herewith, all writing or other pressure on the envelope should be completed before the letter and evidence are inserted and the envelope is sealed. When the nature of the evidence or the amount of it precludes sending it herewith, the evidence is submitted under separate cover. In this case, the method of transmittal should be specified.
6. An indication of what examinations are requested (e.g., did the gun enclosed fire the bullet recovered from the victim's head).
7. A statement as to whether the evidence was examined by another expert, whether there is local controversy, and whether other law enforcement agencies have an interest in the case.
8. The need and reason for an expeditious examination of the evidence if speed is warranted. (Do not routinely request such handling.)
9. Where and to whom the evidence is to be returned and to whom the laboratory report should be sent.

Each letter and package of evidence should deal with only one case. Evidence being sent to the FBI

Figure 2-12 Computer-Generated Sketch

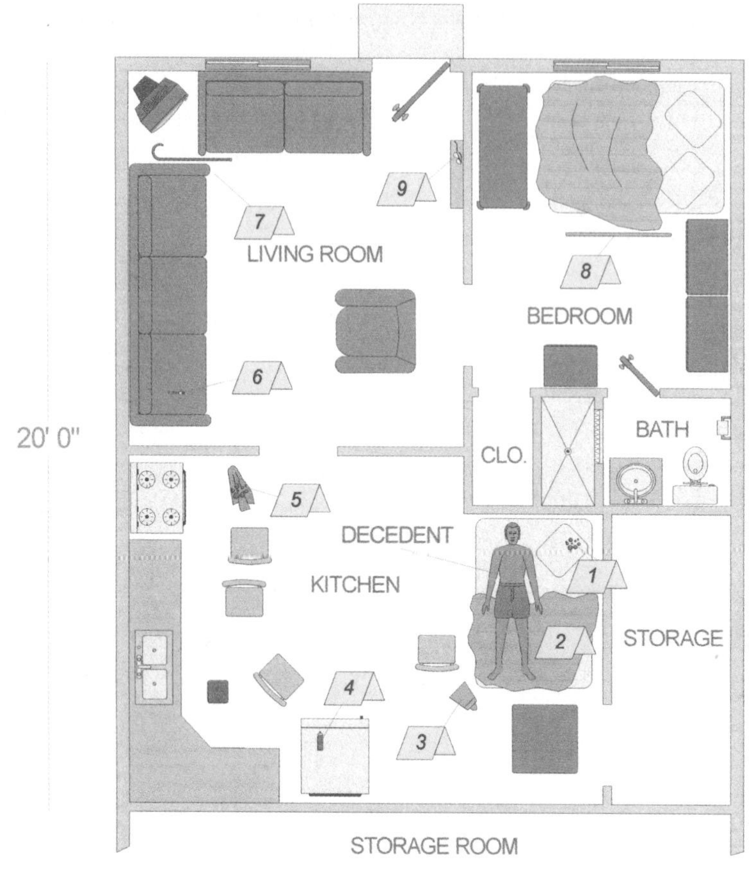


laboratory must be properly packaged and shipped. The following guidelines are applicable:

1. Before packaging the evidence, call the appropriate unit of the laboratory for specific instructions.
2. Take precautions to preserve the evidence.
3. When requesting latent-print examinations, put evidence items in individual protective coverings. For example, place a nonporous item in a thick transparent envelope or suspend it in a container so that there is minimal surface contact; place a porous item in a paper envelope. Stabilize the evidence to avoid movement or friction during shipment.
4. Wrap and seal each item of evidence separately to avoid contamination.
5. Place the evidence in a clean, dry, and previously unused inner container.
6. Seal the inner container with tamper-evident or filament tape.
7. Affix an "Evidence" label, and a "Biohazard" or "Hazardous Material" label, if appropriate, to the inner container.
8. If any of the evidence needs to be examined for latent prints, put a "Latent" label on the inner container.
9. Attach the evidence examination request and all case information to the inner container.

10. Place the sealed inner container in a clean, dry, and previously unused outer container. Protect it with clean packing materials. (Do not use loose Styrofoam.)
11. Completely seal the outer container in such a way that opening of the container would be evident.
12. Label the outer container with a "Biohazard" or "Hazardous Material" label if appropriate.
13. Address the outer container as follows: FBI Laboratory, Attention: Evidence Control Center, 935 Pennsylvania Avenue NW, Washington, DC 20535-0001.
14. Ship the evidence via U.S. Postal Service registered mail, United Parcel Service, or Federal Express. Record the method of shipment and the tracking number on the chain-of-custody form.
15. Rendered-safe explosive devices must be shipped via United Parcel Service.
16. Live ammunition must be shipped via Federal Express. U.S. Department of Transportation regulations mandate the following: Live ammunition must be packaged in a cardboard container and must be shipped separately from firearms; invoices must be labeled "Federal Express," and the shipper's certification for restricted articles must be included; the outside of the container must be labeled "ORM-D Air Cartridges Small Arms"; and the shipping papers must include the weight in grams.
17. *The Interstate Shipment of Etiologic Agents* (42 CFR Part 72) provides packaging and labeling requirements for etiologic agents (viable microorganisms or toxins that cause or may cause human disease) shipped in interstate traffic. Additional information is available at the website of the Centers for Disease Control and Prevention (www.cdc.gov/od/ohs/biosfty/shipregs.htm). Package and label etiologic agents in volumes of less than 50 milliliters in glass tubes sealed with waterproof tape. Place each tube containing a culture inside a capped container packed with absorbent materials. Package this primary container in a secondary capped container labeled with the specimen record (CDC 3.203). Surround the secondary container with dry ice and seal it in a capped shipping container marked with the destination address and the appropriate infectious-substance or etiologic-agent label.

## Key Terms

**administrative log**
**alternative light systems (ALSs)**
**Americans with Disabilities Act (ADA)**
**assignment sheets**
**associative evidence**
**be-on-the-lookout (BOLO)**
**chain of custody**
**cleared by arrest**
**corpus delicti evidence**
**crime**
**crime scene**
**crime scene control**
**crime scene entry log sheet**
**crime scene release**
**crime scene search patterns**
**deductive reasoning**
**evidence recovery log**
**exceptionally cleared**
**felony**
**field notes**
**follow-up investigation**
**hepatitis B (HBV) and hepatitis C (HCV)**
**human immunodeficiency virus (HIV)**
**incident/offense report**
**inductive reasoning**
**investigator**
**letter of transmittal**
**lifted-prints log**
**macroscopic scene**
**media statement**
**microscopic scene**
**misdemeanor**
**personal protection equipment (PPE)**
**photographic log**
**photographing**
**preliminary investigation**
**primary scene**
**rough sketch**
**secondary scenes**
**sketching**
**smooth sketch**
**trace evidence**
**trace evidence vacuum**
**tracing evidence**
**tuberculosis**
**videotaping**
**violation**

## Review Questions

1. What are the objectives of the investigative process?
2. How would you describe the "lucky" investigator?
3. Contrast inductive and deductive reasoning.
4. What are the preliminary and follow-up investigations?
5. Name the major steps in the preliminary investigation.
6. How is a crime scene entry log properly used?
7. What is scene turnover?
8. What is scene release?
9. Define primary scene and secondary scenes.
10. What are macroscopic and microscopic scenes?
11. Identify and explain the major crime scene functions.
12. State and explain three broad categories in which investigators have a particular interest.
13. What are the rules for crime scene investigators, and what do they mean?
14. State at least 12 measures police officers at crime scenes can take to protect themselves against health risks from blood-borne pathogens, such as HIV/AIDS.
15. Identify and discuss three means by which a crime scene can be visually documented.
16. Draw a rough crime scene sketch of the room in which you live, assuming that there are two shell casings on the floor, one bullet hole in the west wall, and one in the north wall.
17. What kind of information should be included in a letter of transmittal accompanying evidence being sent to the crime laboratory?

## Internet Activities

1. The Crime Scene Investigation website at www.crime-scene-investigator.net/index.html contains many helpful articles on crime scene investigation and evidence collection. Go to this website and click on "Evidence Collection." Read the article "Evidence Collection Guidelines," which discusses procedures for collecting various types of physical evidence at a crime scene.
2. Learn more about the importance of understanding a crime scene and documenting crime scene evidence by reading the article "Crime Scene Interpretation" at www.feinc.net/cs-int.htm.

## Notes

1. The information on the preliminary investigation is drawn from several sources, including Technical Working Group on Crime Scene Investigation, *Crime Scene Investigation: A Guide for Law Enforcement* (Washington, DC: U.S. Department of Justice, January 2000), pp. 11–17, and the authors' own experiences.
2. "Mysterious Poet Assailant Proves to Victim Herself," *Atlanta Journal and Constitution*, Oct. 3, 1981, p. A3.
3. Henry C. Lee, Timothy Palbach, and Marilyn T. Miller, *Crime Scene Handbook* (San Diego, CA: Academic Press, 2001), pp. 2–3.
4. Ibid., p. 4.
5. Ibid.
6. Ibid., pp. 4–5, from which the content of this point is summarized.
7. Barry A. J. Fisher, *Techniques of Crime Scene Investigation*, 6th ed. (Boca Raton, FL: CRC Press, 2000), p. 46, with some restatement.
8. Ibid., p. 32.
9. Some of the points in this paragraph are restatements from *Crime Scene Investigation*, pp. 19–23.
10. Ibid.
11. Bill Berkeley, "Wrong Assumptions Ruined Probe," *Atlanta Journal*, Feb. 17, 1982, pp. A1, A13.
12. "But Some Have Ins and Outs," *St. Petersburg* (Florida) *Times*, Feb. 24, 1979, p. A1.

13. "Man Accused of Shipping Self to Bank," *Atlanta Journal,* May 10, 1979, p. A18.
14. John Lester, "Forensic Expert Uses Tiny Clues to Solve Crimes," *Tampa Tribune,* Sept. 9, 1992, pp. 1–2.
15. "Real Estate Agent Pleads Guilty to 5 'Lock Box' Thefts," *Washington Post,* Sept. 12, 1978, p. B5.
16. Fisher, *Techniques of Crime Investigation,* pp. 67–68.
17. National Institutes of Health, "Fact Sheet: HIV/AIDS Statistics" (Washington, DC: Oct. 20, 2001), p. 1.
18. Ibid., p. 2.
19. Ibid.
20. Ibid.
21. Ibid.
22. Lawrence O. Gostin et. al., "Prevention of HIV/AIDS and Other Blood-Borne Diseases among Injection Drug Users," *Journal of the American Medical Association,* Vol. 277, Jan. 1, 1997, p. 254.
23. National Institutes of Health, "Fact Sheet," p. 2.
24. National Institutes of Allergy and Infectious Diseases, "Basic Information on HIV Infection and AIDS," www.aricone.org/imm/basic/basicinf.html, Oct. 21, 2001, p. 1.
25. Ibid.
26. National Institutes of Allergy, "Basic Information on HIV."
27. Centers for Disease Control, "HIV and Its Transmission" (Washington, DC: Oct. 21, 2001), p. 4.
28. National Conference of State Legislatures, Health Policy Tracking Service, "Occupational Exposure to HIV" (Washington, DC: Mar. 1, 2000), p. 1.
29. National Institute for Occupational Safety and Health and the Centers for Disease Control, "Guidelines for Prevention of Transmission of Human Immunodeficiency Virus and Hepatitis B Virus to Health-Care and Public Safety Workers: A Response to P.L. 100-607, The Health Omnibus Programs Extension Act of 1988" (Washington, DC: June 23, 1989). These protective guidelines remain in effect unless they have been specifically changed by subsequent announcements.
30. Ibid., p. 9.
31. Ibid.
32. Ibid., p. 13.
33. S. T. Mast, G. D. Woolwine, and J. L. Gerberding, "Efficacy of Gloves in Reducing Blood Volumes Transferred during Simulated Needle Stick," *Journal of Infectious Diseases,* 1993, Vol. 168, No. 6, pp. 1589–1592.
34. Hepatitis B Foundation, "Facts on Hepatitis B," www.hepb.org, Oct. 24, 2001, p. 1.
35. Ibid., p. 2.
36. Ibid.
37. Centers for Disease Control, "Viral Hepatitis C," www.cdc.gov/ncidod/diseases/hepatitis/c/fact.htm, Aug. 25, 2001, p. 3.
38. Centers for Disease Control, "What You Should Know about Hepatitis C," www.niaid.nih.gov/dmid/hepatitis/hepcfacts.htm, Jan. 18, 2002, p. 3, and "Viral Hepatitis C," p. 1.
39. National Institute of Allergy and Infectious Diseases, "Fact Sheet: Tuberculosis," www.hiaid.nih.gov/factsheets/tb.htm, Jan. 13, 2001, p. 1.
40. Ibid.
41. Ibid., p. 7.
42. Ibid., p. 1.
43. Ibid., p. 10.
44. Ibid., p. 7.
45. Ibid., p. 10.
46. California Commission on Peace Officer Standards and Training, "Basic Course Workbook Series: Learning Domain 30, Preliminary Investigation," Version 2 (Sacramento, CA: 2001), p. 2–14, with some additions.
47. Ibid., pp. 2–12, with minor restatement.
48. National Forensic Science and Technology Center, Scientific Working Group on Imaging Technologies, "Draft Guidelines for Field Application of Imaging Technology," Version 2.2, www.for-swg.org, June 7, 2001, p. 4.
49. Ibid.
50. Ibid.
51. Ibid., p. 2.
52. Ibid., p. 3.
53. This section is taken with minor restatement from Colleen Wade, ed., *Handbook of Forensic Services* (Washington, DC: Federal Bureau of Investigation, 1999), pp. 116–117.
54. Ibid., p. 4–10.

# THREE

# Physical Evidence

*Police Officers in Falls Church, Virginia, search the crime scene of a sniper attack in front of a Home Depot. There were a total of 13 sniper attacks in the Washington DC area. Subsequent investigations led to the arrest of two men in 2002.*

## CHAPTER OUTLINE



## CHAPTER OBJECTIVES

1. Distinguish between class and individual characteristics.
2. Outline procedures for locating and handling soil and pollen evidence.
3. Understand processes for preserving footwear and tire prints and impressions.
4. Summarize techniques for collecting glass and paint evidence.
5. Discuss methods of collecting and storing fibers, cloth fragments, and impressions.
6. Understand how to locate, identify, and use tools to obtain fingerprints.
7. Describe the importance of forensic dentistry.
8. Discuss the identification and analysis of bloodstains.
9. Identify the determinations that can be made from firearm evidence.
10. Outline techniques for identifying questioned documents.

# INTRODUCTION

A common theme in all criminal investigations, and one of the most important throughout this text, is the collection of physical evidence. While the topic of physical evidence is addressed in several chapters of this book, this chapter specifically focuses on the techniques used to identify, collect, package, and store particular types of physical evidence for subsequent examination.

Several types of physical evidence are covered in this chapter: soil and pollen, footwear and tire prints, paint, glass, fibers, hair, lip prints, and tool marks. Details on collection and packaging techniques are provided for fingerprints, dental evidence, bloodstains, firearm evidence, and questioned documents. In addition, several software programs and investigative tools for each type of evidence is discussed. The importance of consulting specialized forensic and medical experts is emphasized throughout the chapter.

Due to inattention, neglect, or simply oversight, there may be occasions when investigators fail to collect potentially important physical evidence at a crime scene. As a rule of thumb, investigators should immediately collect any and all types of physical evidence. Even if the source of crime scene samples is unknown at the time, investigators may later be able to connect the samples to a source in the same, or perhaps in another, criminal investigation. In short, once a crime scene is released, the chance of collecting any evidence that has not either been destroyed or been contaminated from a variety of factors is essentially nonexistent. Lack of evidence significantly hampers investigators' ability to produce a strong criminal case against a defendant; in addition, most investigators agree that there is nothing worse than being questioned at a trial about their lack of or careless collection of evidence.

## CLASS VERSUS INDIVIDUAL CHARACTERISTICS

To fully appreciate the potential value of physical evidence, the investigator must understand the difference between class and individual characteristics. Characteristics of physical evidence that are common to a group of objects or persons are termed **class characteristics.** Regardless of how thoroughly examined, such evidence can be placed only into a broad category; an individual identification cannot be made because there is a possibility of more than one source for the evidence.[1] Examples of this type of evidence include glass fragments too small to be matched to broken edges and tool marks or shoeprints in instances where microscopic or accidental markings are insufficient for positive individual identification. Evidence with individual characteristics can be identified, with a high degree of probability, as originating with a particular person or source.[2] The ability to establish individuality distinguishes this type of physical evidence from that possessing only class characteristics. Some examples of evidence with individual characteristics are fingerprints, palm prints, and footprints.

Conceptually, the distinction between class and individual characteristics is clear. But as a practical matter, the crime scene technician or investigator often may not be able to make this differentiation and must rely on the results yielded by crime laboratory examination. For example, a shoeprint collected at one scene may yield only class characteristics: left by a man's shoe of a particular brand from the left foot and of such newness as to yield no individual markings. However, the photos below illustrate a situation in which a heel print yielded not only class characteristics but also individual ones. Thus, while the investigator must recognize that physical evidence that allows for individualization is of more value, for no reason should he or she disdain evidence that appears to offer only class characteristics, as it may show individual characteristics through laboratory examination. Furthermore, a preponderance of class-characteristic evidence tying a suspect or tools in the suspect's possession to the scene strengthens the case for prosecution. It should also be noted that occasionally class-characteristic evidence may be of such an unusual nature that it has much greater value than that ordinarily associated with evidence of this type. In an Alaska case a suspect was apprehended in the general area where a burglary had been committed; the pry bar found in his possession contained white stucco, which was of considerable importance, as the building burglarized was the only white stucco building in that town.[3] Finally, class-characteristic evidence can be useful in excluding suspects in a crime, resulting in a more effective use of investigative effort.

## COMPARISON SAMPLES

Much of the work of forensic science involves comparing various types of samples. Special terms are used to refer to these samples, and it is important to know what they mean so that you can communicate with the laboratory and understand lab reports. At the most general level, comparison samples may be from unknown or questioned sources or from known sources; each of these two main categories has three subcategories.

## Unknown or Questioned Samples

1. *Recovered crime scene sample whose source is in question:* This evidence may have been left, for example, by either victims or suspects. (It leads to questions such as, Did the suspect leave the fingerprint recovered at the point of entry for the burglary?)
2. *Questioned evidence that may have been transferred to an offender during the commission of a crime and been taken away by him or her:* When compared with the evidence from a known source, this evidence can be used to link the suspect to a person, vehicle, tool, or weapon. (For example, do any of the hairs combed from the suspect's hair match those of the victim?)
3. *Evidence from an unknown or questioned source that can be used to link multiple offenses:* This material might link crimes that were committed by the same person, tool, or weapon. (Illustratively, were the bullets recovered from the victims' bodies in three separate murders fired by the pistol the suspect was carrying when he was arrested?[4]

## Known Samples

1. *Standard or reference sample:* This is material from a known or verifiable source. It is compared to similar material from an unknown source to determine whether an association or linkage exists between a crime scene, a victim, and the offender. (For example, a sample of blood is taken under medical conditions from the suspect so that it can be compared with blood on the victim's shirt.)
2. *Control or blank sample:* This is material from a known source that was uncontaminated by the crime (e.g., carpet fibers taken from the far corner of a room in which a body was found). It is used to make sure that the material on which evidence was deposited (e.g., carpet fibers, under the body, on which there is blood) does not interfere with laboratory testing.

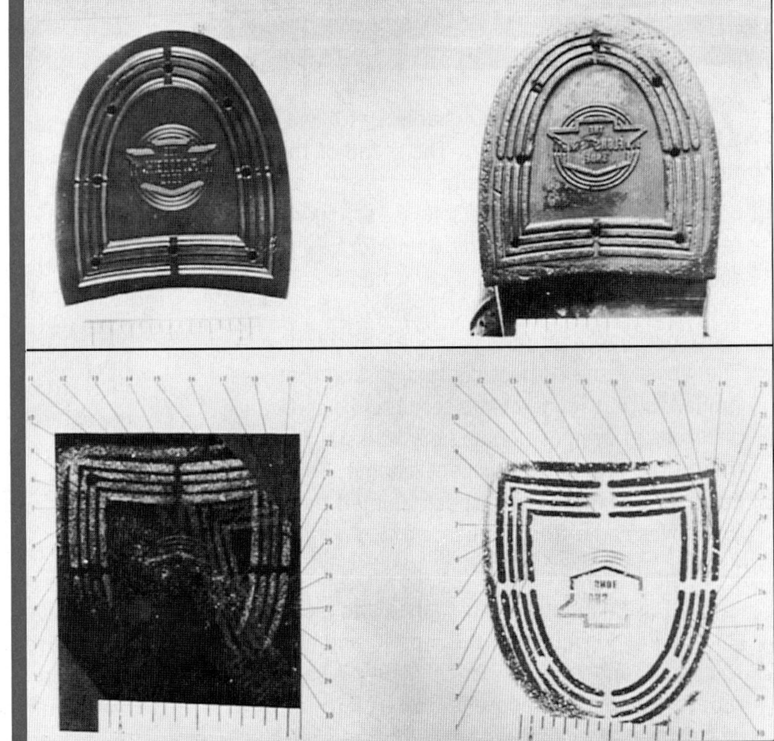

**Class versus Individual Characteristics**

*Upper left:* a new Florsheim shoe heel representing class characteristics; *upper right:* a suspect's shoe heel, incorporating both class and individual characteristics. *Lower left:* a shoe-heel print left on a piece of carbon paper at the scene of a burglary; *lower right:* an inked print of the suspect's shoe heel, indicating positive identification as the print on the carbon paper.

(Courtesy Chicago Crime Laboratory)

3. *Elimination sample:* This type of sample is taken from a source known to have had lawful access to the crime scene (such as a police officer, medical technician, or occupant). It is compared with unknown samples of the same type from the scene so that matches can be eliminated, thereby highlighting nonmatches. (An example is elimination prints. If latent fingerprints recovered at a crime scene do not match the fingerprints of those who have lawful access to the area, they immediately become of investigative interest in terms of determining whose prints they are.[5]

## SOIL AND POLLEN

Soil is the natural accumulation of earth materials, such as weathering rocks, minerals, and decomposing plants, along with pollen; soil may also contain human-made materials, including pieces of brick, concrete, glass, and paint.[6] How soil develops depends on many factors, such as the basic materials, climate, and time.[7] By comparing color, texture, and composition, soil examinations can determine whether soils share a common origin.[8] Although soil is class-characteristic evidence, its analysis can help focus investigations and discredit alibis:

A man was arrested and charged with the beating of a young girl. The scene of the crime was a construction site adjacent to a newly poured concrete wall. The soil was sand, which had been transported to the scene for construction purposes. As such, it had received additional mixing during the moving and construction process and was quite distinctive. The glove of the suspect contained sand that was similar to that found at the scene and significantly different in composition and particle size from that in the area of the suspect's home. This was important because the suspect claimed the soil on the gloves came from his garden.[9]

AN elderly woman was robbed and murdered in a Washington, D.C., park, and her body was found under a park bench. Within a short time, a suspect was apprehended as a result of a description given by a witness who had seen the person leaving the park on the night of the murder. It was obvious that the suspect had been involved in a struggle and had soil adhering to his clothing and inside his trouser cuffs. He claimed to have been in a fight in another part of the city and gave the location of the fight. Study of the soil near the park bench and of that collected from the scene of the alleged fight revealed that the soil from the suspect's clothing was similar to soil near the park bench but did not compare favorably with samples from the area of the described fight. These comparisons strongly suggested that the suspect had been in contact with the ground in that area and cast strong doubt on his statement that he had not been in the park for years. Furthermore, the lack of similarity between the clothing soil samples and those from the area in which he claimed to have been fighting questioned the validity of his alibi.[10]

The pollen in soil or on plants and grass can also be very significant in determining whether or not a suspect was at the scene:

IN a case of alleged sexual assault, the pollen content of samples from a grassy crime scene were compared to pollen recovered from the suspect's clothes and shoes. A very strong correlation with the variety of pollens present on the suspect's clothing and the sample collected at the scene very strongly supported the conclusion that the suspect was at the scene.[11]

Although soil and pollen are class-characteristic evidence, their specificity can approach the level of individual characterization:

IN a rape case, the knees of the suspect's trousers contained encrusted soil samples; the sample from the right knee was different from that collected from the left. In examining the crime scene, two impressions were found in the soil corresponding to a right and left knee; samples taken from these two impressions were different. The soil sample from the left-knee impression compared with that removed from the left trouser knee of the suspect, as did the right-knee impression and the right trouser knee soils. The significant difference in soil type between the two knee impressions and their consistency with samples obtained from the suspect's trousers strongly indicated his presence at the scene.[12]

## LOCATING AND HANDLING SOIL EVIDENCE

Soil evidence may be important when the suspect drives or walks on unpaved areas, since it is picked up by tire treads or the bottom of shoes and the cuffs of pants. It may also be recovered in a number of other places, such as on the floorboard of the subject's car or on articles in the trunk of the vehicle, including shovels and blankets. If there was a struggle with the victim, the suspect may also have soil on his or her body and clothing. If this soil is different from that in the area where the body was found, this may suggest that the victim was killed elsewhere. In hit-and-run accidents, soil samples may be encountered, for example, on the clothing of victims and on the road. In one unusual case, a solid soil sample in the rough shape of a triangle with 3-inch sides was found and later matched to a space on the underside of the suspect's vehicle.

The guidelines below should be followed in handling soil evidence:

1. Soil conditions at the scene can change, so gather the soil as quickly as sound action permits.
2. Collect soil not only from the crime scene but from the logical points of access to and escape from the scene.
3. Collect soil samples where there are noticeable changes in composition, color, and texture.
4. Collect soil samples from a depth that is consistent with the depth at which the questioned soil may have originated.
5. When possible, collect soil samples from alibis areas, such as the worksite, yard, or garden of the suspect.
6. Make a map documenting where and at what depth you collected the soil samples.
7. Do not remove soil adhering to shoes, clothing, and tools. Do not process tools for latent prints at this time. Air-dry the soiled garments and package them separately in paper bags.
8. Carefully remove soil adhering to vehicles. Air-dry the soil and also package it separately in paper bags.
9. Submit unknown or questioned soil and known samples in separate leakproof containers such as film canisters or plastic pill bottles. Avoid the use of paper envelopes or glass containers. If there are lumps in the soil, pack in a way that keeps them intact.[13]
10. In packaging soil or other types of evidence, take care to avoid **cross-contamination** of the samples.

The guidelines for collecting pollen evidence are consistent with those for soil evidence. It may be necessary to take grass or other clippings from different heights.

# FOOTWEAR, FEET, AND TIRES: PRINTS AND IMPRESSIONS

Prints from footwear (shoes, boots, etc.), feet, and tires are common types of evidence, as are foot and tire impressions. Footwear prints, footprints, and tire prints (hereafter referred to inclusively as **footwear prints**) are formed when the soles are contaminated with foreign matter such as blood or dust and leave a print on a firm base, such as a floor a chair, paper, or cloth (see the photo at the top of page 72).[14] Such prints are called residue prints. In contrast, footwear, foot, and tire impressions (hereafter, collectively, **footwear impressions**) occur when the footwear treads in some moldable material, such as earth, clay, and snow.[15]

## PRESERVING FOOTWEAR PRINTS

Footwear prints may or may not be readily visible. If they are not immediately apparent, turn off the lights and search for prints using a flashlight held close to, but obliquely from, the surface you are examining. When you find prints:

1. Take general crime scene photos showing the location of the footwear prints.

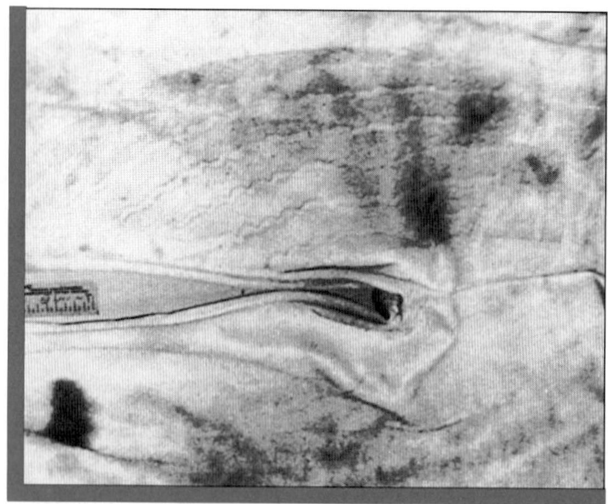

## Tire Print on Fabric

Tire prints from the striking car were found on the pants of a hit-and-run victim. Later, police located the vehicle, which they believe was involved in the hit and run. A comparison of the tire prints taken from the suspect's car with the tire marks on the victim's trousers along with other physical evidence recovered from the grille established that the vehicle was involved in the crime. However, the police still needed to put the car's owner behind the wheel at the time of the hit and run. The police confronted the suspect with the evidence, which destroyed his claim that the car was in his driveway all night. Ultimately, the man confessed.

2. Take photos from directly overhead using lighting and a tripod. Include a linear scale next to, and on the same plane as, the footwear prints. Place a label in the area being photographed to correlate photos with crime scene and photo log records.[16]

There are several methods by which footwear prints can be recovered. The best approach is to send the original evidence to the lab. It should be taped in a rigid container so that there is no opportunity for accidental erasure of the footwear print; do not wrap it in plastic, as this can cause a partial erasure of the image. Footwear prints may be collected by using a transparent adhesive lifter, which measures roughly 6 feet by 15 feet, and then mounting the lifter on an appropriately colored card. Similarly, an appropriately colored and sized rubber-gelatin lifter can be employed. Coated with a thin film of very sensitive gelatin, the lifter is carefully placed over the print and then removed (see photo below). Transparent, black, and white lifters are available. Transparent and white lifters can be used for dark prints, while a black lifter should be used for light prints.

Dust prints can also be lifted through the use of an electrostatic device. These devices use static electricity to attract the dust particles of the print onto a dark-colored lift film. The special film is taped over the dust print, an electrical probe is touched to the film to charge it with electricity, and

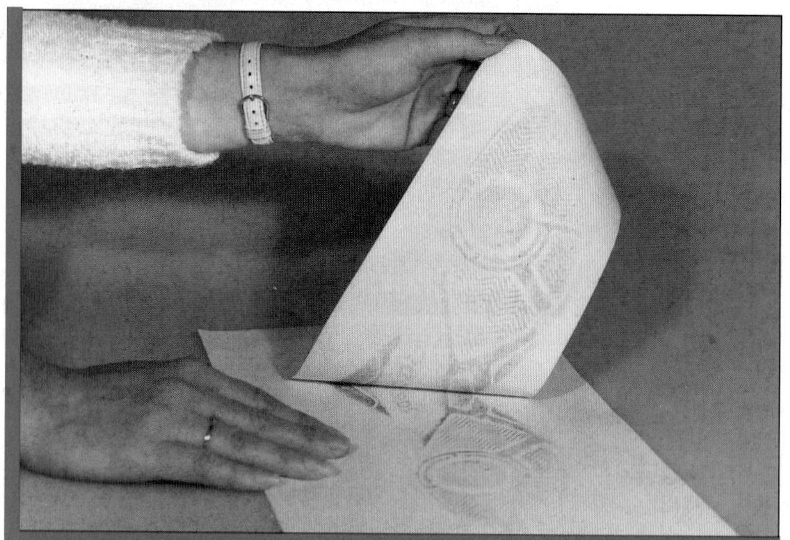

## Rubber-Gelatin Lifter

A rubber-gelatin lifter being used to lift a footwear print. Because such lifters are elastic, they are often bought in sheets and then cut into smaller sections to lift fingerprints and palm prints from rounded surfaces.

(Courtesy Lightning Powder Company, Salem, Oregon)

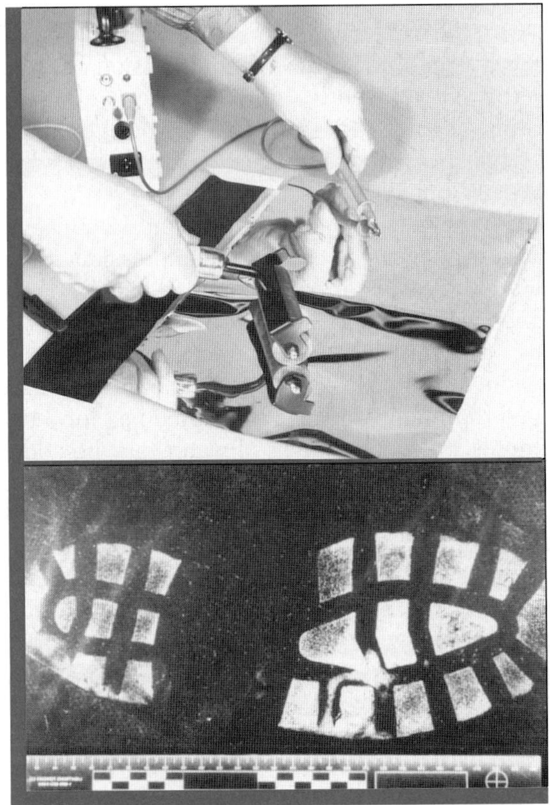

**Use of a Dust-Mark/Electrostatic Lifter**
A charged electrostatic lifter being rolled *(top)* and the image that was lifted *(bottom)*.
(Courtesy Lightning Powder Company, Salem, Oregon)

a roller is then used on the top surface of the film to ensure maximum contact between the film and the dust print (see photos above). The resulting image must be photographed as soon as possible as it is in dust and therefore not permanent.

## COMPARING SHOE-PRINT EVIDENCE

The **Shoeprint Image Capture and Retrieval System (SICAR)** is a software package that classifies, archives, and identifies shoe prints (see photos below). It allows the operator to create a coded description of a shoe print, which can then be compared against a database of known shoe prints by make and model. SICAR can also do a search against an operator-created database of suspects' shoe prints in other cases. Final identification of matches is always confirmed by an individual examiner.

## PRESERVING FOOTWEAR IMPRESSIONS

As in the case with footwear prints, the location of footwear impressions (see photo on page 74) should

**Shoe-Print Image Capture and Retrieval**
In the top photograph, the examiner has scanned an image of a shoe print recovered at the crime scene into the computer. In the bottom photograph, he is coding the scanned image so it can be compared to both known samples from manufacturers, for example, Nike, as well as other suspect shoes in the database. Examinations of this type may establish the manufacturer and model of a shoe, tie shoes seized from the suspect to shoe prints recovered at the scene, or link several cases together where the suspect is still at large.
(Courtesy Foster and Freeman)

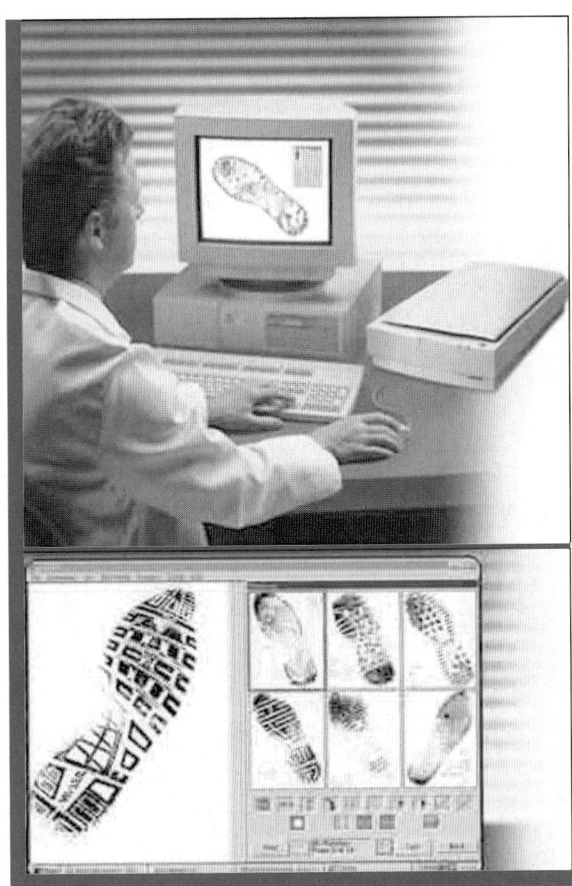

be photographed as part of the general scene and then with a scale (see photo on 75). Note that in the photograph on page 75, the camera is on a tripod directly over the impression and the flash is being held at a low oblique angle to enhance the detail in the shot and the photo scale next to the impression.

Plaster of paris is no longer recommended for use in casting impressions. **Dental stone** is the preferred medium because of its greater strength, quicker setting time, and ease of use and because it provides more detailed impressions.

The first step in casting is the preparation of the impression. The rule is that the impression itself should not be disturbed. Thus, if twigs, leaves, or other materials are stuck *in* the impression, they should remain there. Loose water lying in the impression should be allowed to remain there. Only loose material lying *on* the impression, such as leaves, should be moved. The impression does not need to be sprayed to "fix" it in place before the casting begins. There is no need to use a casting form around the impression unless it is on a hill or on uneven ground.[17]

About 2 pounds of dental stone and 12 ounces of water are needed to cast a shoe impression. To facilitate the casting process, 2-pound bags of dental stone can be premeasured into 8- by 12-inch zip-lock bags. Initially, 9 to 10 ounces of water should be added to the zip-lock bag and the mixture massaged thoroughly through the closed bag for 3 to 5 minutes.[18] Several ounces of water may be added to adjust the mixture until it has the consistency of pancake batter.[19] The dental stone is then poured alongside the impression and allowed to flow into it, or it can be gently laid onto the impression. To prevent the accidental destruction of detail, the fall of the dental stone into the impression can be broken by using a spoon or tongue depressor. The impression should be filled until the dental stone overflows from the impression.

Dental stone sets fairly rapidly. In warm weather it can be moved in 20 to 30 minutes, but a longer time should be allowed when the weather is colder. When the cast is firm, but still soft, basic identifying information should be scratched on its back. Moving the cast requires that it be packed carefully, but without the use of plastic materials. The laboratory examiner will clean the cast and examine it in the laboratory after it has dried for at least 48 hours (see top left photo on page 76).

If there is standing water in the impression, the following procedure should be used: (1) build a retaining wall around the impression so that a cast 2 inches deep can be made; (2) sift dental stone that has not been mixed with water directly into the impression to a depth of about 1 inch; (3) add enough mixed dental stone to form a second 1-inch layer; and (4) allow the cast to set in place for at least 1 hour.[20]

Soil evidence should be collected from the bottom of the impression after the cast is removed. The crime scene technician or other person casting the footwear impression should enter her or his initials, the date, and other relevant details on the bottom of the cast before it dries.[21] For submission to the laboratory, wrap the cast in clean paper, bubble wrap, or paper bags.[22]

### Footwear Impressions

Below are shoe impressions left in the insulation of a safe at the scene of a burglary. In this initial photograph, just the impressions are shown, without a ruler. Subsequent photographs from the scene would include a ruler to indicate sizes. Later still, an attempt would be made to cast the shoe impressions.

(Courtesy Tampa, Florida, Police Department)

### Footwear Impression Photography

Here a crime scene technician is recording the location of a shoe impression in dirt. The shoe print runs left to right, roughly between the two front legs of the tripod. The small slip of white paper is just "north" of the impression and has the necessary case identification information on it. The most important of a series of photographs will be shot from directly above the impression using a tripod and will include a ruler alongside the impression.

(Courtesy Nassau County, New York, Police Department)

### Preserving Shoe Impressions in Snow

Dental stone is also the preferred material for casting impressions in snow, replacing the more difficult and time-consuming process of using sulfur, which has to be heated. Impressions in snow should first be photographed in the manner previously described. A red-colored product called **Snow Print Wax** is sprayed on the impression at a 30- to 45-degree angle until the highlights are lightly tinted. A dark-colored spray paint will also serve the same purpose. In either case, the spray can must be held 30 to 40 inches away so that the force of the aerosol does not disturb the details of the impression. The impression is then rephotographed (see photos in the right-hand column on page 76). The casting process is continued, with the impression being sprayed with enough Snow Print Wax to form a layer of wax, followed by the dental-stone casting process. Because some heat is generated when dental stone is mixed, use snow or cold water instead of water to form a consistency somewhat thinner than pancake batter. A box should be placed over the cast as it dries for at least 1 hour before it is moved.

## PAINT

During many investigations there is the possibility of encountering paint that has been transferred accidentally or deliberately, from one object to another.[23] The paint is transferred as fresh smears, dried chips, or "chalking" from old, dry paint. Cases in which such transfers occur include burglaries and hit-run-run accidents.[24] In these offenses, the paint may be found on tools in the suspect's possession or on clothing. In hit-and-run cases, the make and model of the involved vehicle might be identified by comparing paint evidence to FBI reference files on original-manufacturer finishes.

Usually, paint is class-characteristic evidence, although in some cases it reaches the level of individual evidence. If the chips are large enough, it may be possible to make a physical match between a

**Forensic Comparison**
Evidence technician making a comparison between a cast made at a crime scene and the suspect's shoe.
(Courtesy Fairfax County, Virginia, Police Department)

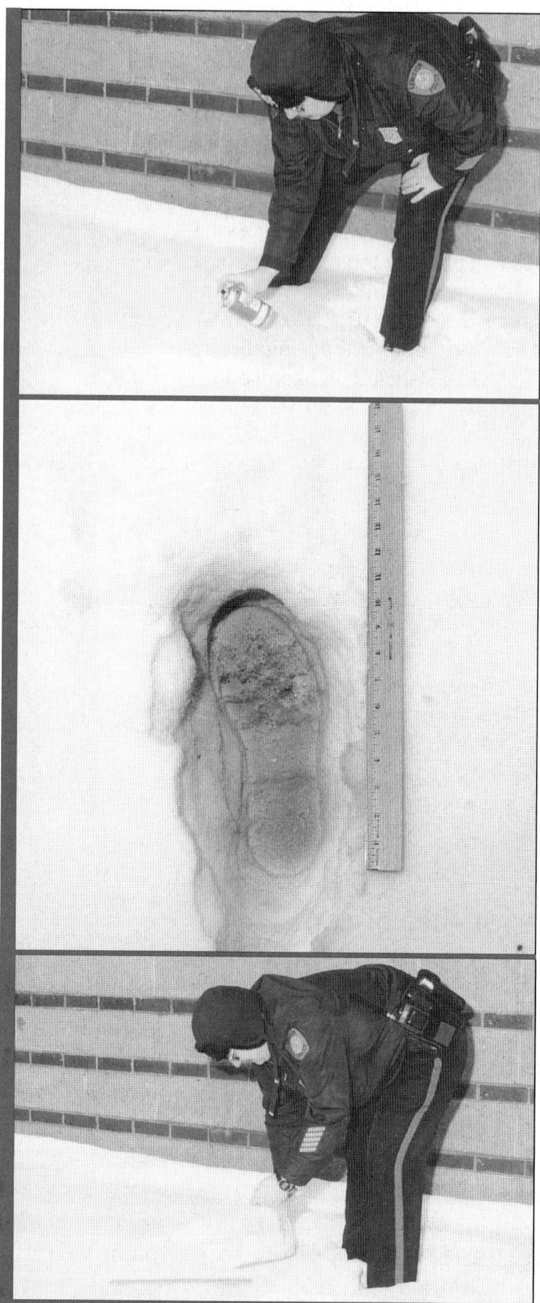

**Snow Print-Wax Use**
Having already photographed the shoe impression in the snow, the officer sprays red-colored Snow Print Wax on the impression (*top*); the impression is rephotographed (*middle*); and the dental-stone mix is poured from a plastic pouch onto the impression (*bottom*).
(Courtesy Lewiston, Maine, Police Department)

questioned and a known source. An example is matching recovered paint chips to a particular location, such as the point of entry in a burglary.

Paint is examined in several ways in the laboratory. Factors of importance in its identification are shade, composition, number of coats and their characteristics, texture, and weathering.[25]

In no case should paint chips or particles be collected with transparent tape or mounted on a card using this material, because doing so makes separation in the laboratory difficult to do without damage. Similarly, small particles should not be placed in cotton because it is difficult to separate them.[26] Paint evidence should not be placed in envelopes because the chips may slip out or be broken; small plastic bags should be avoided because they have a static electric charge that makes it extremely difficult to remove the chips in the crime laboratory.[27] Clear plastic containers are ideal because the paint evidence can be seen. Where it is particularly difficult to gather paint samples, a small portion of the surface to which the paint has adhered should be cut or chipped off.

## GLASS

Glass is important as physical evidence because of the frequency with which it is encountered. Although it is ordinarily class-characteristic evidence, glass has high evidentiary value because of its variations in density, refractive index, and light-dispersion characteristics. Additionally, if the fragments are sufficiently large to allow for a **fracture match,** glass may assume individuality. Most commonly this will occur in hit-and-run cases where a piece of the headlight lens found at the scene or embedded in the victim's body or clothing aligns with a missing portion of lens from a suspect's vehicle (see photo below). Before the accident, cleaning or other actions may have created surface striations on the headlight lens. Along with a fracture match, these further strengthen the condition of individuality.

Glass is a common form of evidence, particularly at the scenes of burglaries where a window has been the point of entry. When a suspect is apprehended soon after the commission of an offense, his or her clothing should be carefully examined for minute traces of glass evidence.[28] Although they may be so small that they permit only the conclusion that they are consistent with samples obtained at the scene, this conclusion can strengthen the case for the prosecution. At other times, the clothing of a burglary suspect may contain pieces of glass large enough to make fracture matches. A case history illustrates this possibility:

WALKING a beat in a downtown business section in the late evening hours, a uniformed officer heard an alarm go off and saw an individual round the corner and run toward him at full speed. Upon seeing the officer, the individual started to double back the other way and then stopped. As the officer approached, the man started to flee, but he stopped upon being commanded to do so. The

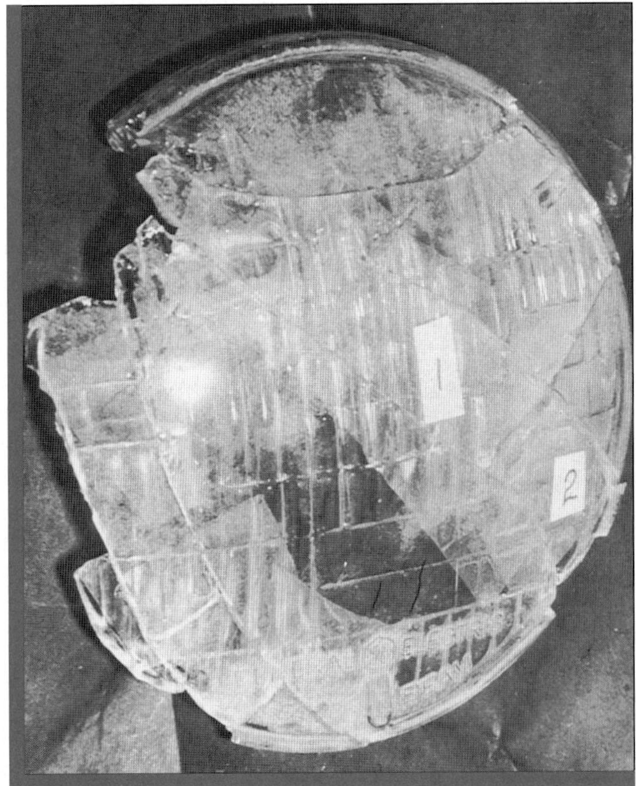


**Glass Fracture Match of Headlight Lens**
Pieces 1 and 2 were recovered at the scene of a hit-and-run automobile accident. The remaining pieces were obtained from the grille and light housing of the suspect's vehicle. Notice how perfectly the recovered pieces fit into the remaining headlight on the suspect's vehicle.
(Courtesy Regional Criminalistics Laboratory, Metropolitan Kansas City, Missouri)

man then told the officer that he had observed two people standing in front of a jewelry store window take a brick from a shopping bag and throw it through the window. The person said that, upon seeing this, he became frightened and ran. Subsequent investigation revealed that the person who had rounded the corner was in fact the perpetrator of the offense and that he had fled before obtaining any material from the display window because a lookout had seen a police car responding to a call in an adjacent block and had given warning. Processing of the perpetrator's clothing revealed pieces of glass in the cuff of his pants sufficiently large to make fracture matches with glass at the scene.

It is essential that the crime scene technician and investigator understand the ways in which glass reacts to force. Often this knowledge is critical in determining whether a crime has been committed and in establishing the credibility of statements given by parties at the scene. A case history illustrates this:

POLICE were called to a residence where the occupant alleged that while standing in his living room he was suddenly fired on by someone standing outside the window. The occupant further related that he immediately fell to the floor and crawled to a desk in which a handgun was kept and after a short period of time stood up, when second and third shots were fired from outside the building. The complainant stated he could clearly see the person and, in turn, fired one shot. The perpetrator identified by the complainant lived a short distance away and was at home when contacted by the police. The alleged suspect maintained that he was walking by the home of the complainant, with whom there had been a history of ill feelings, and was suddenly fired on three times, but he admitted firing one shot in return.

Figure 3–1 illustrates the four bullet holes found in the window by the police. When a glass window is broken by a shot, both radial and concentric fracture lines may develop. Radial fractures move away from the point of impact, while concentric fracture lines more or less circle the same point. From Figure 3–1 we know that shot B came before shot A, because the radial and concentric fracture lines of shot B stop those of shot A. From examination, we know nothing of the relationship of holes C and D. However, as suggested in Figure 3–2, it is possible to determine the direction from which a bullet penetrated glass: on the side opposite the surface of initial impact, there will be a characteristic cone-shaped area. In the case being illustrated, shots A, B, and D all contained a cone-shaped characteristic on the inside of the window, indicating that these three shots had been fired from the outside. Shot C had the cone-shaped area on the outside, revealing that it had been fired from inside the house. Thus the physical evidence substantiated the complainant's statement.

**Figure 3-1** Bullet Holes Found in Window

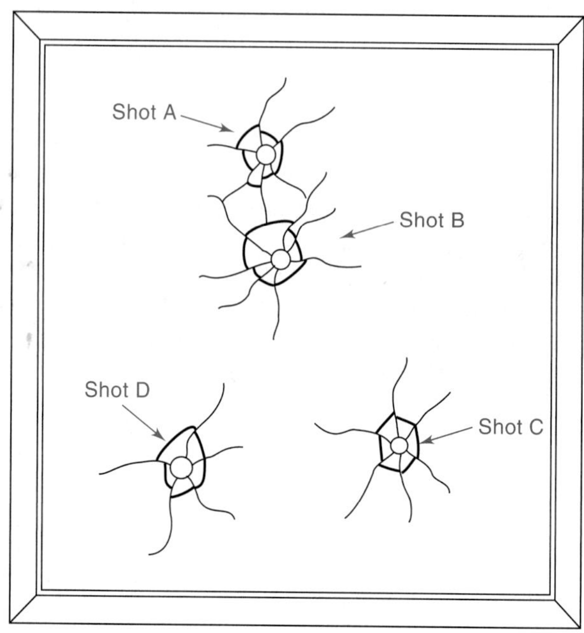


Before any glass or window pane is moved at all, it should be photographed in detail to reflect the exact nature of the existent glass fractures. Moving the evidence may cause fracture extensions that could confuse or reverse the findings of the investigator and laboratory examiner. This same principle applies to fractures of automobile glass when a vehicle is pulled to the side of the road by a wrecker operator. Such examples underscore the importance of the investigator's paying particular attention to what

**Figure 3-2** Determining the Direction of a Bullet's Penetration of Glass

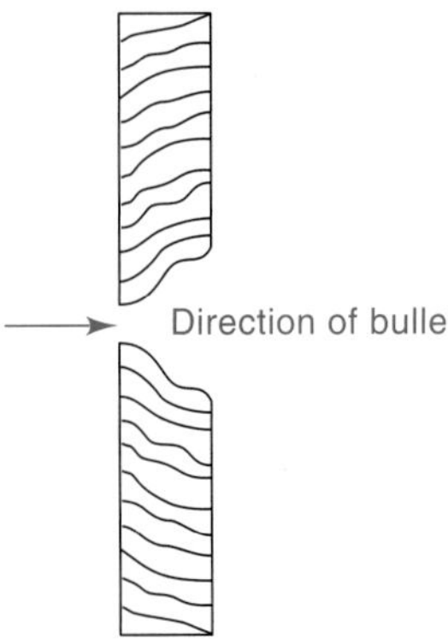


has occurred between the time of the crime and the time that he or she arrives at the scene. In this light, a key question that the investigator must attempt to answer with all types of evidence is whether the characteristics could have been caused by someone other than the suspect, such as a witness, the victim, emergency medical personnel, or another officer.[29]

### HANDLING GLASS EVIDENCE

Tape should not be used to collect glass evidence since any processing for latent prints is ordinarily done in the laboratory.[30] Glass should be packed in a rigid, leakproof container such as a film canister or a plastic pill bottle; paper and glass containers should not be used.[31] Samples gathered from different sides of a window or windshield should be marked as such and packaged separately.[32] If a vehicle is involved, use a vacuum to collect the glass from each area of the vehicle; evidence collected from different areas should be packaged separately.[33] If glass evidence is involved with suspects and/or victims, their hair, skin, and wounds must be inspected for particles; if their clothing is wet, allow it to dry and package it separately to avoid cross-contamination.[34]

If the laboratory is to make a fracture match, the glass should be marked appropriately (e.g., "top, inside, left").[35] Do not place any objects in holes in the glass; if large pieces of glass are involved, pack them securely between pieces of plywood or sturdy cardboard.[36]

## FIBERS, CLOTH FRAGMENTS, AND IMPRESSIONS

Fibers are of greater value as evidence than are rootless hairs because they incorporate such variables as material type, number of fibers per strand, number of strands, thickness of fibers and strands, amount and direction of twists, dye content, type of weave, and the possible presence of foreign matter embedded in them (see photos on pages 80 and 81). When something composed of fibers, such as clothing, comes into contact with other clothing or objects, there is the opportunity for the exchange or transfer of fibers. Fibers may also be located on the body of the victim or the suspect, serving to connect one to the other.

Cloth fragments may be found at the scene of violent crimes or along the perpetrator's point of approach to or exit from a crime scene. They may be found on such diverse points as a chain fence, the splintered edge of a wooden building, or protruding nails. In hit-and-run offenses, cloth fragments may be found in the grille or undercarriage of the striking vehicle (see top left photo on page 81). Cloth impressions are found infrequently in investigations, usually on wet paint or some surface of a vehicle involved in striking a pedestrian (see bottom right photo on page 81).

Both fibers and cloth fragments should be packaged in a pillbox or in folded paper that is taped shut. Only on rare occasions will it be possible to obtain a cast of a cloth impression. This effort, however, should invariably be preceded by the taking of several photographs; at least one of these photos should show a scale to allow for comparisons at some future date.

## STRING, CORD, AND ROPE

String, cord, and rope evidence is usually found in robbery, criminal homicide, rape, and abduction cases.[37] Less frequently it is found in accidental hangings by children and accidental sexual asphyxiations. Cord and rope have essentially the same characteristics as string, and all have some characteristics of fibers. Known samples of these types of evidence can be compared to crime scene evidence on the basis of composition, diameter, color, and

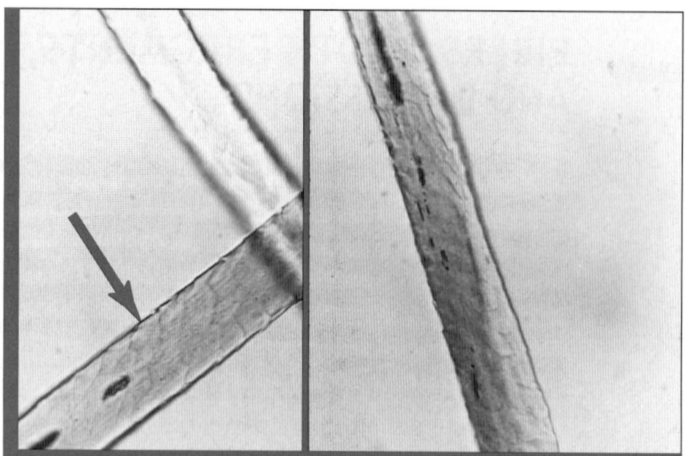

### Comparison of Wool Fibers

Photomicrographic comparison of wool fiber from the victim's sweater *(right)* versus wool fiber recovered from the trousers of the suspect who sexually assaulted her, resulting in a finding that the two fibers matched in all characteristics.

(Courtesy Royal Canadian Mounted Police)

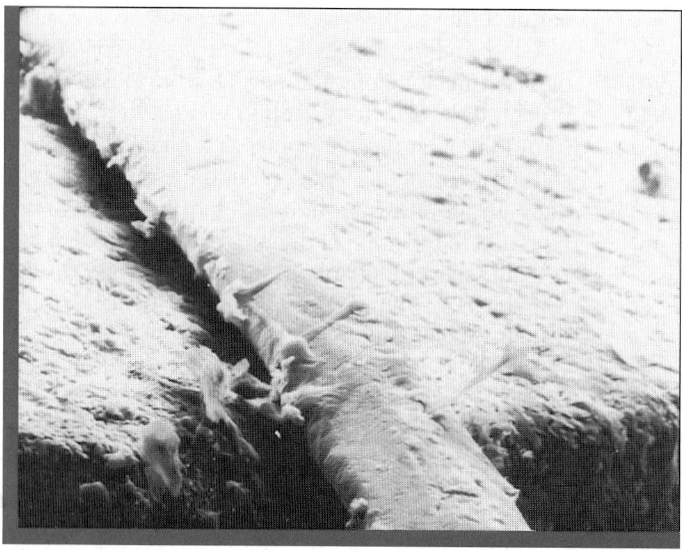

### Scanning Electron Micrograph

Scanning electron micrograph (570 ×) of a nylon fiber removed from a sheet used to transport the body of a murder victim. The fiber, associated with a carpet in the offender's residence, was manufactured only in small quantities about a decade before it was recovered as part of the investigation.

(Courtesy Federal Bureau of Investigation)

construction; if a tracer is present, it is possible to identify the manufacturer. In instances where the victim was tied, it may be possible to match the ends of rope, cord, twine, and tape with the rest of the roll in the suspect's possession (see photos on page 82). When rope evidence is removed from a victim or from anyplace, knots should never be severed. Instead, a place away from the knot should be cut and a piece of twine used to loop the two ends together. A tag should be attached to indicate that the investigator has cut the rope. Ordinarily, because of its resilient nature, the packaging of this type of evidence poses no particular problem when standard procedures are followed.

## FINGERPRINTS

Several different parts of the body—such as palms, fingers, toes, and the soles of the feet—have friction ridges that can form a "fingerprint." All such prints are collected, preserved, and identified in the same way. Moreover, it may not be immediately apparent which part of a body made the print. As used here, "fingerprint" includes all prints made by friction ridges.[38] Basically, a **fingerprint** is a replica of the friction ridges that touched the surface on which the print was found. These ridge characteristics are also called **minutiae.**

Fingerprints of offenders are found on a wide variety of surfaces and in various states. In all cases, however, the prints are fragile and susceptible to destruction by any careless act. They are also in many instances difficult to locate.

With just a few exceptions—that is, some persons who are physically impaired—everyone has fingerprints. This universal characteristic is a prime factor in establishing a standard of identification. Since a print of one finger has never been known to duplicate exactly another fingerprint—even of the same person or an identical twin[39]—it is possible to identify an individual with just one impression. The relative ease with which a set of inked fingerprints can be taken as a means of identification is a further reason for using this standard. Despite such factors as aging and environmental influences, a person's fingerprints do not change. This unaltering pattern is a permanent record of the individual throughout life.

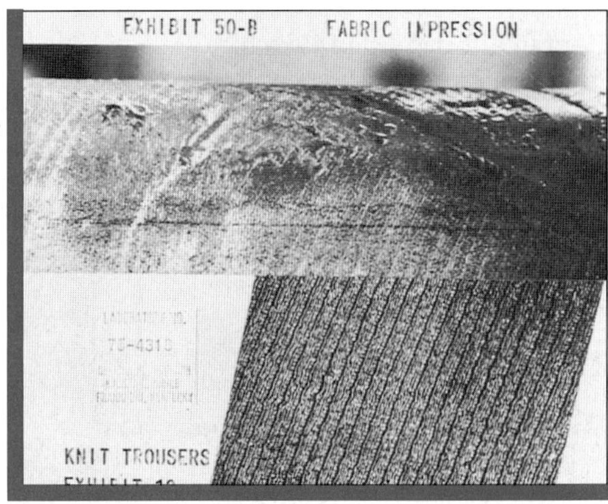


## Fabric Impression

In hit and run cases involving pedestrians, there is often a great deal of evidence, such as shards of a broken headlight embedded in the victim, blood on the grille of the vehicle, and fabric impressions. In this unusual case, the driver drove over the victim, who bounced off of the pavement and into the undercarriage of the car, leaving a fabric impression of his pants on the residue covering the tailpipe. As in the above case, the suspect's vehicle is conclusively tied to the crime scene.

(Courtesy Kentucky State Police)

## Fabric Match

The inserted fragment was found in the grille of the suspect's vehicle, which had been involved in a hit-and-run case. The fragment fitted the victim's shirt and conclusively establishes the contact between the suspect's vehicle and the victim.

(Courtesy Federal Bureau of Investigation)

Although there are several different filing systems for fingerprints, each is based on classification of common characteristics. The **fingerprint classification** system works to categorize a set of fingerprints readily as well as to provide quick access to a set of prints with a given characteristic.

There are three broad categories of latent fingerprints:

1. **Plastic prints** are created when fingers touch material such as a newly painted surface, the gum on envelopes and stamps, oil films, explosives, thick layers of dust, edible fats, putty, and adhesive tape (see top left photo on page 83).
2. **Contaminated/visible prints** result after fingers, contaminated with foreign matter such as soot, oils, face powder, ink, and some types of safe insulation, touch a clean surface. The most common type of contaminated print results when a finger is pressed into a thin layer of dust before touching a smooth

### Electrical Cord Edge Match

Photomicrograph of electrical-cord edge match. The piece on the left was seized in the suspect's custody and matched with the end on the right, which was part of the length used to tie up a homicide victim. (Courtesy Regional Criminalistics Laboratory, Metropolitan Kansas City, Missouri)

surface. Fingerprints that result from blood contamination (see bottom right photo on page 83) are sometimes less distinct than those that result from other types of contamination.

3. **Latent/invisible prints** are associated with the small amounts of body perspiration and oil that are normally found on the friction ridges. A latent fingerprint is created when the friction ridges deposit these materials on a surface. While latent prints are easily developed on smooth, nonabsorbent surfaces, under favorable conditions they may also be developed on rough surfaces, such as starched shirts. Latent fingerprints are typically invisible to the unassisted eye. "Developing" a latent fingerprint refers to the process of making it visible.[40]

Note that the term "latent prints" can be used in two different ways: (1) to refer to all three categories of prints identified above, in the sense that they have been found at the scene of the crime or on items of investigative interest, and (2) to refer specifically to latent/invisible prints. Ordinarily, the context in which the term is used helps in understanding which meaning is intended.

## BASIS OF IDENTIFICATION OF FINGERPRINTS

The ridge detail of fingerprints—including ends of ridges, their separations, and their relationship to each other—constitutes the basis for identification of fingerprints. There are as many as 150 ridge

### Tape Match

In a home-invasion robbery and attempted murder, the suspects used filament strapping tape to tie the victim up. The victim was left for dead, but she managed to crawl out of an open door and hide in nearby bushes. The suspects panicked when they noticed she was gone, and they fled the scene. The lower portion of the photograph is the filament tape recovered from the victim's arms. The top part of the photograph is the end of the filament-tape roll found in the suspects' vehicle when they were arrested. By showing that these two ends of the filament tape match, a physical match is established. (Courtesy Illinois State Police)

**Plastic Print**
A plastic print found in windowsill caulking.
(Courtesy Delaware State Police)

characteristics in an average-size fingerprint.[41] The major **fingerprint patterns** are shown in Figure 3–3. About 65 percent of the population has loops, roughly 30 percent has whorls, and the remaining 5 percent has arches.[42] Points are identical characteristics that are found in fingerprints from known and questioned sources. Positive identification cannot be made when an unexplained difference appears, regardless of the points of similarity.

There is no standard requirement of print size for positive identification. It is necessary only that the partial print be large enough to contain the necessary points of individuality. This number may be found in an area as small as the flat end of a pencil. Thus, the rule whenever an investigator develops a partial latent print that appears to have only a few ridges is that it should be submitted to the laboratory.

Some persons erroneously believe that the points used for identification of the fingerprint occur only in the pattern area of the finger. In fact, all the different types occur outside the pattern area on the finger as well as on the first and second joints of the finger and the entire palm of the hand. They are also present on the toes and the entire sole of the foot; they may be found in any area where friction ridges occur.

## CONDITIONS AFFECTING THE QUALITY OF LATENT FINGERPRINTS

The quality of latent fingerprints is affected by a number of conditions, including the following:

1. *The surface on which the print is deposited:* Plastic prints can last for years if undisturbed. Latent prints on smooth surfaces, such as

**Contaminated/Visible Print**
A blood-contaminated/visible print found on the blade of a knife.
(Courtesy Delaware State Police)

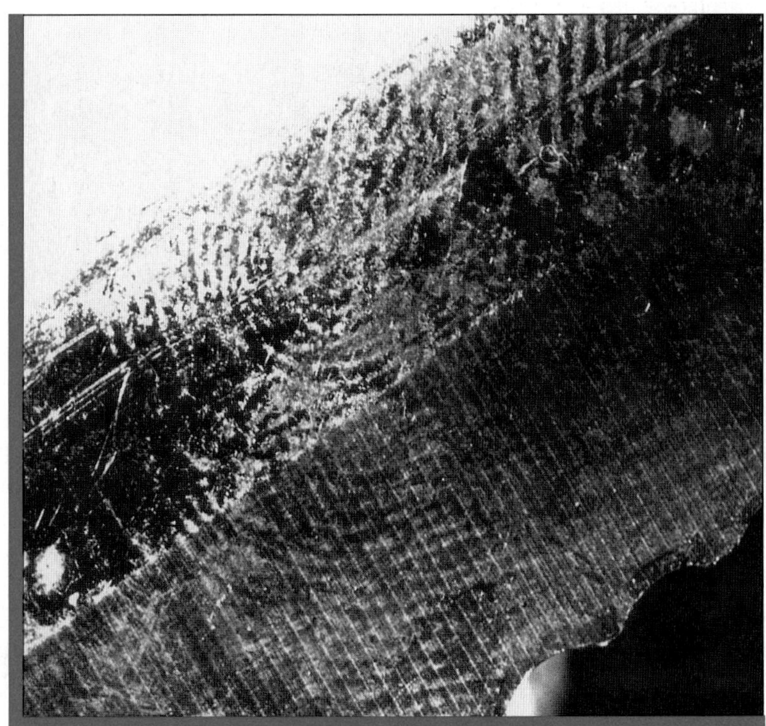

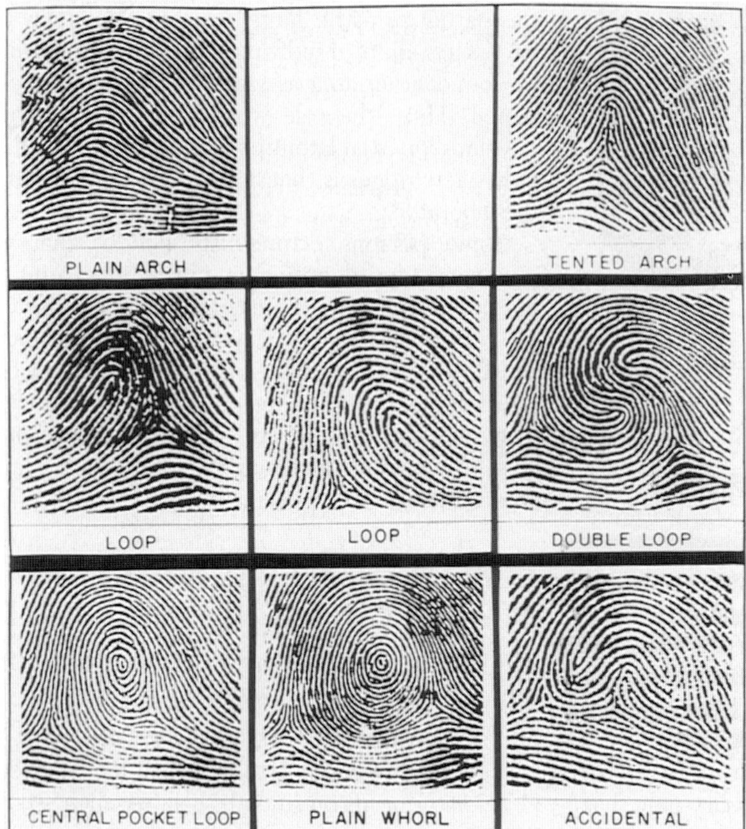


**Figure 3-3**

Major Fingerprint Patterns

(Courtesy Wichita, Kansas, Police Department)

porcelain and glass, can be developed after a similar period, while those left on porous material like paper vary more in how long they can survive. Latent prints on documents can fade or deteriorate beyond the point of being useful it they are subject to high humidity or if they become wet. Otherwise, latent prints on paper are fairly stable and can be developed even years after they were made.

2. *The nature of the material contaminating the fingerprint:* Latent fingerprints resulting from contamination by soot, safe insulation, and face powder are quickly destroyed, while those made with blood, ink, or oil can last longer periods of time under favorable conditions.[43]
3. *Any physical or occupational defects of the person making the print.*
4. *How the object on which the prints appear was handled:* The distance between friction ridges is very small, and if the finger moves even slightly, that ridge detail can be lost.
5. *The amount of the contamination:* When the finger leaving the print is very contaminated, both the ridge surfaces and their "valleys" get filled up, resulting in a smeared appearance with little value as evidence.

## LOCATING LATENT FINGERPRINTS

Latent prints are such valuable evidence that extraordinary efforts should be made to recover them. The investigator must adopt a positive attitude about this, regardless of apparent problems or past failures.

It is imperative that the investigator thoroughly search all surface areas in and around the crime scene that might retain prints. Shining a flashlight at an oblique angle to the surface being examined is often helpful in this search. The fact that an individual may have worn gloves in no way lessens the need for a complete search. On occasion, gloves themselves leave impressions as individualized as fingerprints. Moreover, although it is unusual, it may be possible to develop a latent fingerprint on the inside of a glove recovered at a crime scene.[44] Particular attention should be paid to less obvious places, such as the undersides of toilet seats, toilet handles, tabletops, and dresser drawers; the surfaces of dinner plates and filing cabinets; the backs of rearview mirrors; and the trunk lids of automobiles. Frequently handled objects, such as doorknobs and telephones, ordinarily do not yield good prints. But because they are likely to have been touched, they should always be processed.

It is never safe to assume that the offender took precautions against leaving prints or destroyed those left. The commission of a criminal offense involves stress, and the offender may have made a mistake. If gloves were worn, for example, the suspect may have removed them for some operation.

It helps to attempt to view the scene as the criminal did. Such conditions as time of day, weather, and physical layout may suggest that certain surfaces should be more closely examined. In conducting the examination for latent prints in a burglary case, for example, the search should begin at the point of entry. For other crimes, such as the issuance of worthless checks, the point of entry often takes on less importance. Ordinarily, however, whatever the crime and its attending circumstances, reconstruction by the investigator gives direction to the search.

A person who is familiar with the environment, such as the owner of the building or the occupant of an apartment, may give valuable aid in obtaining latent prints. The person should be allowed to observe the scene so that he or she can indicate any items out of place or brought to the scene by the suspect.

The development of latent fingerprints often involves the use of lasers, alternative light, ultraviolet light, powders, and chemicals that can be irritating or toxic. Therefore, appropriate safety precautions should be taken (see photo below).

## METHODS OF DEVELOPING LATENT FINGERPRINTS

Plastic and contaminated prints may require no or little development. However, there are numerous ways to develop latent prints. Five methods that investigators should be familiar with are (1) use of traditional powders, (2) use of fluorescent powders, (3) application of chemicals, (4) cyanoacrylate or superglue fuming, and (5) visualization under laser, alternative light, and ultraviolet illumination. The

**Locating Prints**

A crime scene technician using protective equipment while dusting for fingerprints. Several developed prints can be seen in the area the technician is dusting.

(Courtesy Nassau County, New York, Police Department)

most common method of developing latent/invisible prints is through the use of traditional powders.

## Traditional Powders

Commercially prepared **traditional powders** come in a number of colors, including black, white, silver, red, and gray. To provide a good contrast between the print and the background on which it has been made, darker powders are used to locate latent/invisible prints on lighter-colored surfaces and lighter ones are used on darker backgrounds. There are also dual-use powders, which will appear black when dusted on a light-colored surface and silver when applied to a dark one. The tip of the brush is gently placed into the wide-mouthed powder container and then lightly tapped to allow excess powder to drop away. Caution must be used when applying the powder to a latent print. Too much powder creates a print in which the details are difficult to identify (see photo below). This is why powder is never sprinkled directly on the surface to be dusted. The entire area to be dusted should be covered with smooth, light brush strokes until the ridge detail begins to show. Then, the brush strokes should follow the contours of the ridges until the latent/invisible print is fully visible. Even if the first attempt to develop a print is not successful, a second one may be.

The choices of brushes include squirrel hair, the Zephyr—a fiberglass brush—and feather dusters. There are also applicators that use special magnetic powders. These powders commonly come in black, gray, and white. There are also dual-use magnetic powders. When the magnetic applicator is dipped into the iron powder particles—which are covered with a color pigment—streamers of powder are created that develop a latent print when brought into contact with the surface being examined; the excess powder is then removed from the print by a magnet.[45]

## Fluorescent Powders

Low concentrations of some naturally occurring substances will cause a latent print to fluoresce, or glow, under laser, alternative light, or ultraviolet (UV) illumination. However, the intensity of the glow varies considerably, perhaps due to the accidental acquisition of fluorescent materials from the environment.[46] To compensate for the typically low level of naturally occurring fluorescence, the area to be examined can be dusted with a special **fluorescent powder**, which chemically enhances the print when viewed under laser, alternative light, or UV illumination. Fluorescent powders are also available in several colors for use with a magnetic applicator.

## Chemicals

A variety of chemicals are used to develop and enhance latent prints. These chemicals are applied by spraying or brushing the surface being examined, by fuming, or by dipping the object on which there may be prints in a solution.[47] Because chemicals may interfere with processes like blood typing, a forensic serologist should be consulted before using them.[48] Some of these chemicals will develop prints that are immediately visible, while others—such as DFO, rhodamine 6G, and basic yellow 40—fluoresce under an alternative light source. Among chemicals in use are the following:

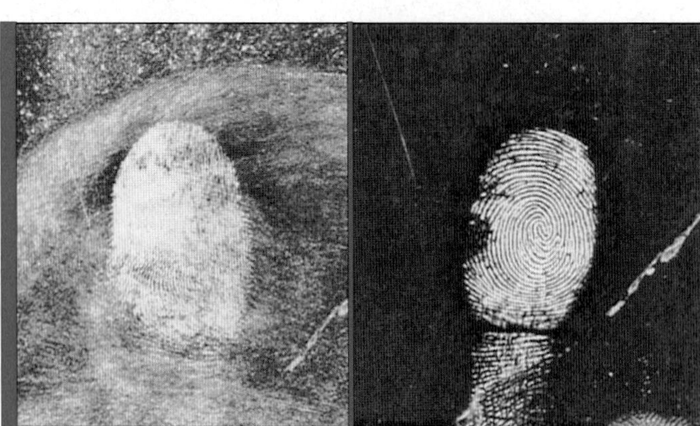

**Application of Fingerprint Powder**
The photograph on the left illustrates the use of too much fingerprint powder in developing a latent print, resulting in the needless destruction of detail. The photograph on the right shows a latent fingerprint developed by the use of the correct amount of powder.
(Courtesy Wichita, Kansas, Police Department)

- **Amido black:** Amido black is a dye sensitive to properties in blood and may be used with contaminated/visible prints involving blood. It has the capability to turn blood proteins to a blue-black color. As in the case of any procedure aimed at developing prints, a photographic record of the print should be made both before and after treatment.
- **Crystal violet:** Crystal violet is used to develop latent prints on the adhesive side of almost any kind of tape. It may also be useful on plastic surfaces. Crystal violet is mixed with water, and the tape is soaked in the solution. The tape is then rinsed with tap water; any latent print that appears is dyed a purple color. The results produced by crystal violet can be enhanced by viewing the treated area under laser illumination.
- **Iodine:** One of the oldest and most proven methods of developing latent prints on both porous—particularly paper—and nonporous surfaces is iodine fuming. If use of ninhydrin is required, the iodine fuming should be done first.
- **Ninhydrin:** This chemical is also used to develop latent prints on paper and cardboard, producing purplish prints. It should not be used with money because it turns the entire bill purple.[49] Ninhydrin may be applied by fuming, dipping, or spraying.
- **DFO (1, 8-diazafluren-9-one):** While it functions similarly to ninhydrin, DFO is about three times more effective than ninhydrin in developing latent prints on paper. These red prints may be immediately visible to the naked eye. DFO prints fluoresce under almost all laser and alternative light sources. Both DFO and ninhydrin may be used on paper, but DFO must be used first to get any fluorescence.
- **Small-particle reagent (SPR):** SPR is used for developing latent prints that have been immersed in water, as when a perpetrator has attempted to dispose of a firearm used in a crime by throwing it into a river or lake. It is also used to develop prints on dew- or rain-soaked cars; on surfaces covered with a residue, such as salt from being on or near the ocean; and on waxed materials, plastics, tile, and glass. Developed prints appear dark gray on a light surface and light gray on a dark surface. Although SPR can be sprayed on an object, immersion of the object for about 30 seconds in an SPR solution produces better results.
- **Rhodamine 6G:** This is an excellent fluorescent chemical dye to use on metal, glass, leather, plastic, wood, and many other types of nonabsorbent surfaces. Rhodamine 6G may enhance latent prints already developed and also reveal others.
- **Basic yellow 40:** After superglue fuming, basic yellow 40 can be effectively used on surfaces such as cans, leathers, and plastics. The article is soaked in the basic-yellow-40 solution for about 1 minute; it will then fluoresce well under alternative lighting.

## Cyanoacrylate or Superglue Fuming

**Superglue fuming** was developed in 1978 and its use quickly spread. The three factors associated with its rapid acceptance were ease of use, remarkable results, and low cost. The mechanics of superglue fuming are fairly straightforward. Cyanoacrylate is heated in a high-humidity chamber. As the fumes condense, they develop white-colored latent prints in 5 to 15 minutes. The developed prints may be further enhanced with powders or soaked in chemicals that fluoresce under alternative light sources.

In the "early days," 10-gallon fish tanks were used as fuming chambers and ordinary superglue was heated. While this procedure for fuming is still effective, it carries with it the risk of developing a toxic fume, hydrogen cyanide, which is caused by overheating of the cyanoacrylate or its vapors. This risk is pronounced at 200°F.

Today, there is a vast array of fuming options. Large programmable fuming chambers are available for use in the laboratory; these units, which may be 6 feet wide, 5 feet deep, and 7 feet high, can process large objects such as doors and long guns or process dozens of object simultaneously. At the other end of the spectrum, investigators may employ a handheld superglue **fuming wand** (see top left photo on page 88), which was developed through the collaboration of the Alaska State

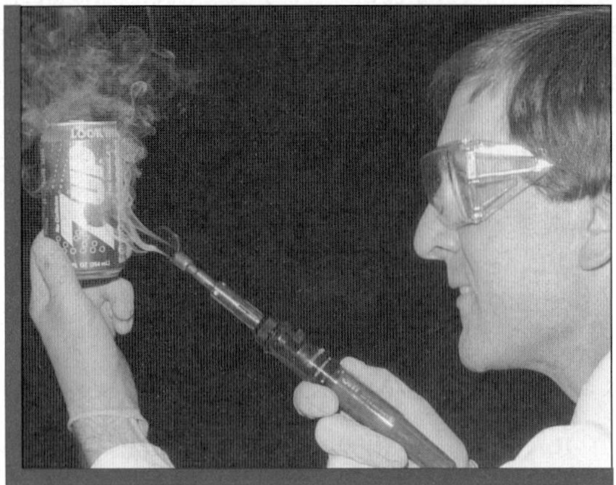

**Superglue Wand**

Use of a superglue wand, which was developed at the crime laboratory in Anchorage. This handheld device works well for fuming of smaller objects like this soda can.

(Courtesy State of Alaska Scientific Crime Detection Laboratory)

Troopers and 3M. Additional options for cyanoacrylate fuming include compact, portable systems, weighing about 30 pounds that can fume entire rooms and the interior and exterior of vehicles (see photo below).

## Visualization under Laser, Alternative Light, and Ultraviolet Illumination

The use of alternative light sources—such as the Polilight, BlueMaxx, Omnichrome, and Luma-Lite—and UV illumination was covered in Chapter 2. Therefore, the discussion here deals with using laser illumination and the reflected ultraviolet imaging system to detect latent fingerprints.

***Laser Illumination*** Early work on the forensic use of lasers dates from 1976 and is based on the efforts of the Ontario Provincial Police Department and the Xerox Research Center in Toronto.[50] When excited by **laser illumination,** latent fingerprints fluoresce or glow a vivid yellow-orange when viewed through a special lens. Without such illumination, the prints might not be found. Fingerprints detected in this manner can be photographed. After latent fingerprints are located by lasers, other means of developing them, such as conventional powders and chemicals or dyes, can be used.

Lasers can be used on porous and nonporous surfaces with great effectiveness (see photos on page 89). Among these surfaces are Styrofoam cups, cloth, and documents nearly 30 years old. However, if latent fingerprints are located on surfaces that also fluoresce when excited by the laser, the print image will not stand out sharply from the background on which it rests. This difficulty can be overcome by developing the fingerprints in a manner (e.g., with chemicals or dyes) that causes them to stand out much more distinctly from their background.

***Reflected Ultraviolet Imaging System*** The term **reflected ultraviolet imaging system (RUVIS)** is the generic name for a class of lighting and imaging systems that have been increasingly

**Portable Superglue Fuming Chamber**

This portable superglue unit is being used to process the inside and outside of a car for latent fingergprints much more efficiently than would be the case with the superglue wand shown above.

(Courtesy Sirchie)

### Laser Illumination of Prints

Following unsuccessful conventional processing of a Styrofoam cup for prints (*left*), the laser was used and produced identifiable latent prints on the cup (*right*).

(Courtesy Tallahassee Regional Crime Laboratory, Florida Department of Law Enforcement)

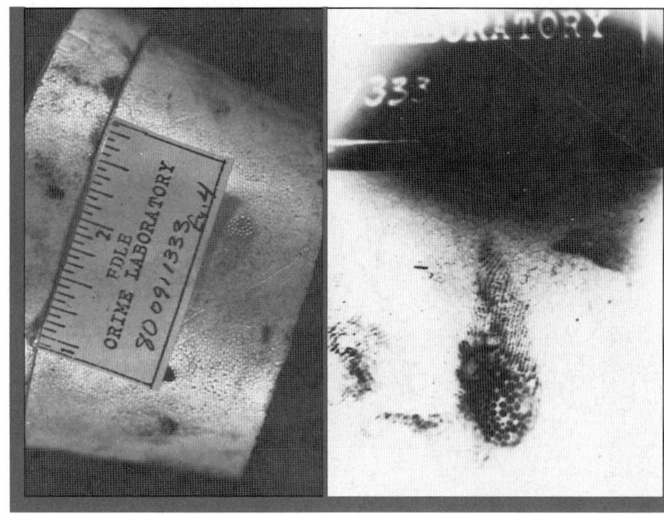


used in the past several years. An example of this type of equipment is SPEX Forensic's SceneScope. While conventional ultraviolet (UV) lighting causes many types of evidence to fluoresce, RUVIS operates on a different principle. When the UV light strikes an undetected fingerprint on most nonporous surfaces, it is "bounced" back to the RUVIS and the image is highly intensified. Prints located in this manner can then be developed and photographed. When no prints are initially found, superglue fuming can be used and the scene reexamined using RUVIS. The complete SceneScope system enables the technician to have hands-free operation, and prints can be videotaped or photographed using other capabilities of the system (see photo on page 90).

## MARKING AND IDENTIFYING PRINT LIFTS

When a latent print has been developed, lifted, and placed on a card, it is necessary that the card be properly identified. Information recorded on the card should include the date, type of case, case number, address of the crime scene, name of the officer who made the lift, exact place of the lift, and type of object from which the print was lifted. Regardless of how well the latent was developed and lifted, if the card is not properly marked with all the data required or if the fingerprint specialist is not furnished with the information required, the entire process may be wasted effort. In describing the exact place that the lift was made, it is sometimes helpful to draw a simple sketch of the object. The sketch should be made on the fingerprint card that is sent to the laboratory. The inclusion of corresponding numbers on both the lift and the sketch establishes the location of the latent print.

## DEVELOPING LATENT FINGERPRINTS ON BODIES

For the most part, the history of trying to locate and develop latent fingerprints on the bodies of deceased victims is one of failure. There have been occasional success stories but no methods that regularly produced results. Once in a while, the application of powder directly on the deceased's skin developed usable prints.

However, glue fuming of the deceased's body, followed by the application of magnetic powders, is a recommended approach to developing latent prints on the bodies of deceased victims.[51] If possible, a body at the crime scene should be processed immediately after the medical examiner has completed the initial examination and released the body. At a minimum, the body should be fumed at the scene to preserve the prints and to prevent their obliteration when the body is moved. Ideally, bodies should not be refrigerated before they are fumed. Condensation from refrigeration can wash away prints and interfere with the proper functioning of glue fuming and application of magnetic powder. Refrigerated bodies should not be processed until

**Reflected Ultraviolet Imaging System**

RUVIS is being used to locate physical evidence, such as fingerprints, at the scene.

(Courtesy SPEX Forensics)

all moisture has evaporated naturally, a matter of several minutes. A trial application should be done, on an area of the body where latent prints are least likely to be found to ensure that the moisture isn't reacting to the glue and washing possible prints away and that the powder can be used without its caking and destroying the prints. Skin that is warm or near normal body temperature should be glue-fumed for 5 to 10 seconds. Colder skin should be fumed for not more than 15 seconds.

## COLLECTING AND PRESERVING LATENT PRINTS

Occasionally items such as beer cans or glasses that have condensation on them need to be processed for prints. Heat lamps or any other source of artificial heat should not be used to dry the object quickly. Such objects should be allowed to air-dry naturally. Similarly, articles that have been frozen and need to be processed for prints must be allowed to thaw and dry naturally.

Once a print is found—regardless of whether it is plastic, contaminated/visible, or a latent that has been developed with powders—it should be photographed immediately with a rigid scale in view. The ruler allows a one-to-one, or actual-size, picture of the print to be made. This provides a permanent record of the print in the event that collecting the print, attempting to further develop and enhance it, or transporting it results in its accidental alteration or destruction. Many law enforcement agencies are using digital cameras to record important crime scene evidence such as latent fingerprints. This type of camera digitizes the image, which can then be put into a computer and enhanced through software such as **Adobe Photoshop**. In years past, every aspect of fingerprint examination was labor-intensive. However, computerized **Automated Fingerprint Identification Systems** (**AFISs;** see Chapter 7 for more information on this subject) have speeded up the process of fingerprint identification and comparison enormously. An AFIS can supply a list of potential matches for the submitted latent print(s) from the records on file. At that point, however, an experienced examiner then personally makes the comparison to see if there is indeed a match.

Whenever possible, a plastic print should be taken to the laboratory on the object on which it was found. If this is not practical, the photographic record of it may be supplemented by a cast of the print made of a material such as silicone.

Most latent prints are lifted with a clear strip of tape or clear flap lifter after they have been developed with powders (see top photo on page 91). One end of the clear tape is placed on the surface just before the latent print appears. Pressure is

### Clear Flap Lifter

Lifting a latent fingerprint using a clear flap lifter. Flap lifters are made with the lifting surface permanently attached to the backing card onto which the lifted print is laid.

(Courtesy Nassau County, New York, Police Department)

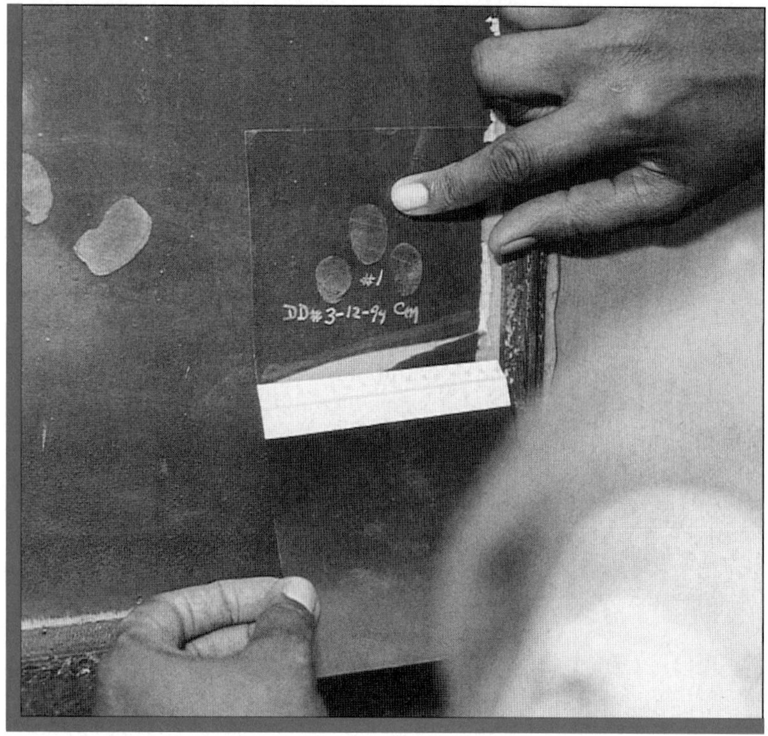


then applied to progressively lay the tape over the print, taking care not to leave air bubbles. If air bubbles are accidentally created, the tape should be carefully smoothed over to eliminate them. The tape may be left on the object if the object is to be submitted to the laboratory. Alternatively, the pattern of the print is lifted by pulling up the tape, starting at one end and moving progressively to the other end. Now the powder that shows the print pattern is stuck to the sticky side of the tape. This tape is then laid back down on an appropriately colored backing card. For example, assume that a latent print is developed with dark powder on a clear window. The clear tape used to lift it would then be placed on a white card for maximum contrast. Occasionally prints are found on uneven or curved surfaces, such as light bulbs, clothes hangers, and doorknobs. In these cases a rubber-gelatin lifter, described earlier in this chapter, can be used to lift the print. Such prints can first be photographed with a Rotorgraph, a device invented in 1992 by Turner Pippin of the State of Alaska Crime Laboratory. The Rotorgraph makes it possible to accurately take photographs of developed latent prints on rounded surfaces (see photo at right).

### Fingerprint from Rounded Surface

Fingerprint on a 9-mm cartridge photographed with the Rotorgraph invented by Turner Pippin. The Rotorgraph makes it possible to accurately take photographs of developed latent prints on rounded surfaces like this cartridge.

(Courtesy State of Alaska Scientific Crime Detection Laboratory)

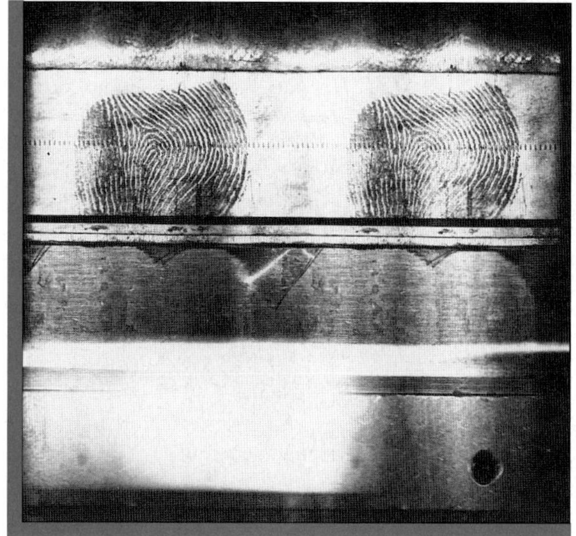

## DENTAL EVIDENCE

**Forensic dentistry** is a specialty that relates dental evidence to investigation.[52] The dental apparatus, including teeth, prosthetic appliances, and morphological (shape and form) peculiarities, is of primary importance in the identification of mutilated, decomposed, or otherwise visually unrecognizable human remains. Teeth themselves leave patterns in the skin, and analysis of bite marks has played a major role in many criminal cases. Teeth marks left in food (see photo below), pencils, Styrofoam cups, and other objects at crime scenes can be analyzed for the bite record; in addition, they can be the source of saliva samples for comparison of blood-type groups. Analysis of a bite mark in and of itself can be of great value in helping investigators eliminate suspects as well as identify a suspect.

### HISTORY

The teeth and facial bones are a major means of identifying skeletal remains and have been used by anthropologists for many years. It is interesting to speculate that the first forensic dentist in the United States may have been Paul Revere. In 1775, he constructed a silver bridge for his friend General Joseph Warren, who was later killed by the British during the Battle of Bunker Hill. Warren was buried in a mass grave, and Revere later identified his remains by the bridgework he had constructed for Warren—the earliest-known dental identification in the United States.

Nearly 100 years after Revere's identification, the body of President Lincoln's assassin, John Wilkes Booth, was identified by a gold "plug tooth" on the right side of his jaw. Probably the most publicized bite-mark case involved Ted Bundy, who allegedly committed homicides in Washington, California, Utah, Colorado, and Florida. He was arrested for murdering several women in a sorority house in 1978. At trial, the positive relationship between bite-mark evidence obtained from one of the victims and the teeth of the accused contributed to his successful prosecution.

#### Bite Mark in Food

A partially eaten "Moon Pie" bitten by one of the suspects in a double homicide. From the bite marks it can be determined that the individual making them had two nonequally protruding upper front teeth. Such information can play an important role in determining probable cause for arrest and/or search warrants.

(Courtesy Dr. Richard R. Souviron, D.D.S., ABFO, Chief Forensic Odontologist, Dade County Medical Examiner Department, Miami, Florida)

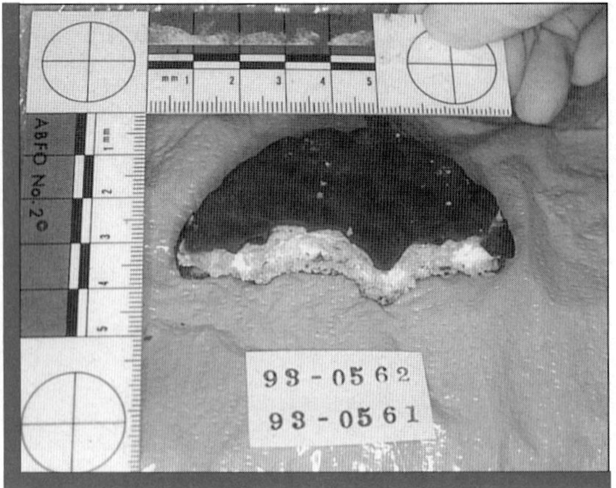


### DENTAL IDENTIFICATION

Dental records include, but are not limited to, dental X-rays, dentagrams, dental charts, prosthetic molds, and dental casts. In **dental identification**, the forensic dentist compares antemortem (before death) records with postmortem (after death) findings to determine if there is a positive match. No set number of points is required for a positive match. Sometimes one unique feature of the teeth can be enough for a positive identification. This usually includes some type of human-made anomaly, such as a root canal, a post, a crown, pins in the tooth, or a unique cavity or crown preparation form.

Like human fingerprints, human dentitions (teeth) are unique. The average adult has 32 teeth. Tooth form and arrangement, missing teeth, and mechanical alterations from dental fillings or accidents produce hundreds of thousands of possible combinations. It is important that the crime scene search not overlook dental evidence that appears to be useless. A single tooth with unusual anatomy may provide a basis for identification of the individual. On the basis of skull and jaw formations, a forensic dentist may be able to give investigators valuable opinions and information as to the victim's age, race, sex, and, possibly, unusual habits. A forensic dentist can state with reasonable certainty the approximate age within six months of an individual through age

13. From age 14 through 25, a one-year plus-or-minus estimate is possible. After age 25, sophisticated tests can be performed to approximate age.

Certain groups—Asians and Indians—have deep grooves in the inner aspect of the upper front teeth. These are referred to as shovel-shaped incisors. Functioning third molars (wisdom teeth) are common among blacks but are found in less than 20 percent of whites, who are likely to have had their wisdom teeth extracted to prevent crowding of their remaining teeth. Crowding of the teeth is common among whites but not among blacks or Native Americans. The absence of certain teeth may help identify age and race. For example, the first premolars, like the wisdom teeth, are usually extracted for orthodontic reasons (crowding) among whites. Anterior wear will suggest habits such as pipe smoking or nail biting. Fractured upper incisors are very useful not only in visual identification and photographic comparisons but also in bite-mark analysis. The jaws can show evidence of previous injuries as well as past or present disease. In discussing these and other aspects of the case with a forensic dentist, investigators must be sure that they understand any distinctions made between scientific fact and investigative opinion.

Dental records are hard to obtain, and searches for them are not always productive because (1) many individuals under the age of 30 have had no dental decay and (2) individuals with decayed or missing teeth may never have sought treatment. In either case, there are no records of antemortem dental restorations that can be compared with the postmortem dental features of a victim. For these reasons, "smiling-photograph" comparisons have become important in making dental identifications (see photos below). The technique is quick and cost effective, but depends on having a reasonably

## Dental Comparison

Left photo shows upper and lower jaws of an unknown white male. Some bone loss (pyorrhea) and tobacco staining are evident. There were no fillings, decay, or missing teeth and no evidence of any dental treatment. Right photo is enhancement and enlargement of the victim, pictured at his son's birthday party. His kidnappers/killers were sentenced to life terms.

(Courtesy Dr. Richard R. Souviron, D.D.S., ABFO, Chief Forensic Odontologist, Dade County Medical Examiner Department, Miami, Florida)

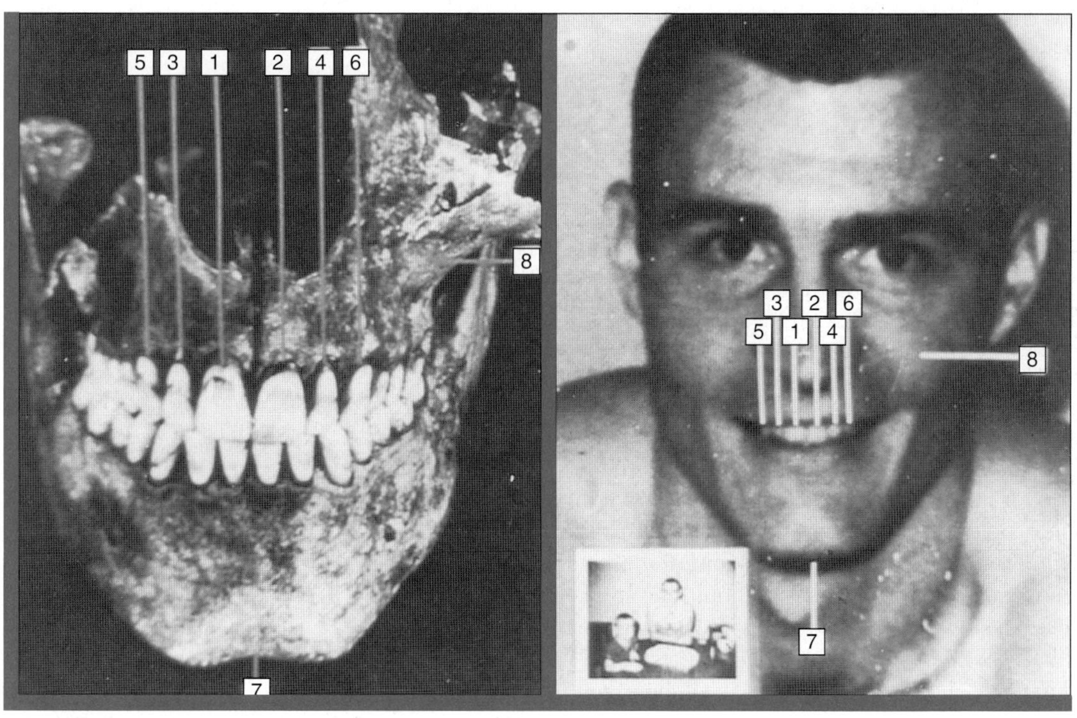

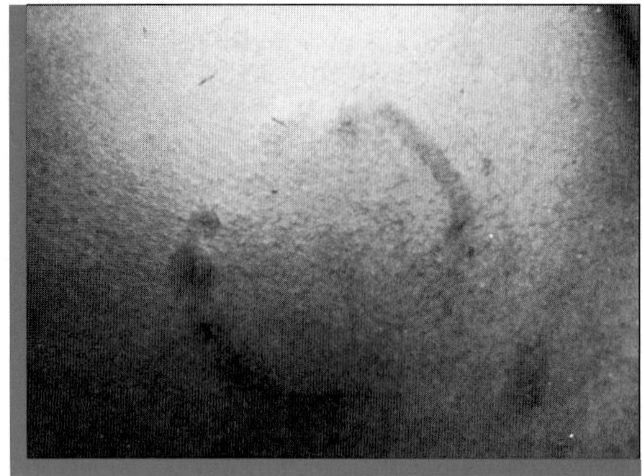

### Lack of Detail in Bite Mark

Bite mark on shoulder of rape victim. The lack of detail is due to the bite's having been made through clothing. The bite mark may become clearer in the next day or so, however, the wound should be rephotographed a day or two later if possible.

(Courtesy Dr. Richard Souviron, D.D.S., ABFO, Chief Forensic Odontologist, Dade County Medical Examiner Department, Miami, Florida)

good photograph of the front teeth. Several such photographs showing the front teeth will enhance the weight of the evidence. However, comparison with dental records such as X-rays and dentagrams is far more accurate.

## BITE-MARK EVIDENCE

Investigators must be particularly alert to the possibility that **bite-mark evidence** exists whenever they are working violent-crime and child-abuse cases. Aggressive bites are left by attackers, and defensive bites are by victims. While some bite marks are fairly obvious, others are less so. Sometimes bites are less distinct, as in the photo above, because they were made through clothing. Occasionally, what appears to be a bite mark is actually a pseudo, or false, bite mark. The injuries shown in the photo below right, for example, were caused by striking the victim with the open end of a pipe.

All suspected or actual bites should be photographed, using both black-and-white and color film if feasible. A color scale should always be included in color photographs because it will be of use in determining the approximate time the victim was bitten. A ruler should be placed next to the bite area (see photo on page 95). This documentation helps the forensic dentist make an exact replica of the bite, which can later be compared with that of a suspect. The ideal ruler to use is the ABFO scale, which corrects for curvature of the skin surface. The first set of photographs should be taken before the wound is cleaned. Qualified medical personnel should then swab the bites and save each swab for laboratory analysis of any saliva or blood. Each time a new bite area is swabbed, a new swab should be used. As with other types of evidence, swabs should be packaged individually to avoid cross-contamination. After this procedure is complete, a second set of photgraphs should be taken. If feasible, follow-up photographs should be taken in 12 to 24 hours. Photographs of bites on live victims may actually be clearer when photographed several days later, as blood seeping into the wound will have lessened. If the victim is dead, embalming will bleach out the color of the wound and make photographs of it less instructive. Bite marks should also be documented by lifting them like latent prints and by making a cast of them using some suitable material, such as silicone.

### False Bite Marks

Pseudo, or false, bite marks on the stomach of a victim. Although thought at first to resemble human bite marks, closer examination revealed that the injuries were caused by the end of a pipe.

(Courtesy Dr. Richard Souviron, D.D.S., ABFO, Chief Forensic Odontologist, Dade County Medical Examiner Department, Miami, Florida)

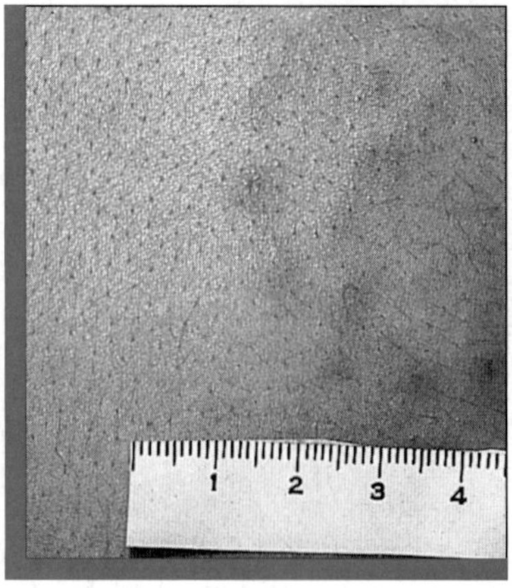

The records needed from the suspect for comparison are photographs and impressions of the teeth, wax bite records, X-rays, and saliva and blood samples. All may be obtained quickly and with little or no discomfort to the suspect. Duplicates of everything should be taken to safeguard against loss or breakage. A suspect may voluntarily bite into a Styrofoam cup or into a block of beeswax. From this "impression," a duplicate or cast can quickly be made of the biting, or incisal, edges of the suspect's teeth. This can be extremely helpful in eliminating multiple suspects. However, care should be taken that a suspect is not forced to bite into an object but does so with his or her full consent. It is best that the forensic dentist making the comparisons get the evidence from the victim and the records from the suspect. Teeth can be altered, broken off, or removed by a suspect. If a suspect does this before dental impressions are taken, the bite-mark comparison becomes more difficult or even impossible to make. Therefore, bite-mark evidence should not be publicized.

If the suspect does not give informed consent, the courts provide two methods of obtaining these records from the suspect—a court order or a search warrant. A court order is often used, but it has the disadvantage of informing the suspect, and in some cases his or her attorney, of the pending examination and permits sufficient time for the teeth to be altered. Thus, a search warrant is a safer method if the alteration of teeth is a distinct possibility. In this way, the suspect is prevented from knowing of the impending examination ahead of time. It is important that the dentist taking these records have a signed copy of the court order or search warrant before he or she examines the suspect. Proceeding on any other basis will jeopardize the admissibility of any evidence obtained. The presence of the prosecutor or his or her representative is desirable but is not a requirement.

**Hand Abrasion**

Abrasion caused by striking victim in the mouth.

(Courtesy Dr. Richard Souviron, D.D.S., ABFO, Chief Forensic Odontologist, Dade County Medical Examiner Department, Miami, Florida)

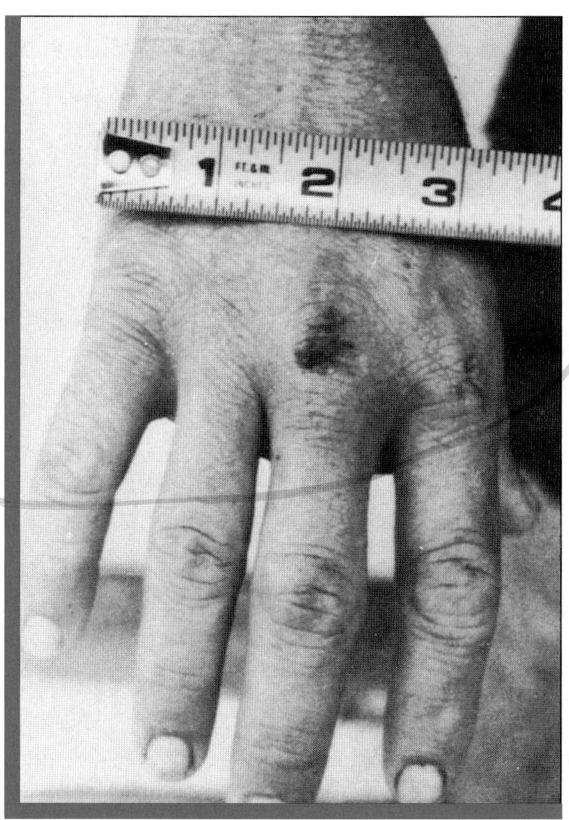

## HAIR

An initial step in the forensic examination of hair is to determine whether or not it is of human origin. Human hair has unique characteristics, and ordinarily this determination is not difficult unless the hair has been subject to gross destruction. When the hair is not human, it is possible to establish the species involved, such as dog, cat, or horse.[53]

Human hair evidence is most frequently found in violent crimes. If the hair root is attached, it may be possible to establish individuality.

Even when there are no roots attached to the hair, precluding a DNA identification,[54] there are a number of useful conclusions that can be established:

1. The area of the body from which the hair came, as well as the race of the donor.[55]
2. The manner in which the hair was removed, such as having been cut or forcibly pulled out.
3. Differentiations between hair samples, based on shampoo residues.[56]
4. Whether the hair has been bleached or dyed.[57]

5. What contaminants are in the hair, such as gunshot residues,[58] blood, semen, soil, paint, pet hair, or fibers.
6. Whether the hair has been subject to force, such as burning or blunt-instrument trauma.
7. What drugs, if any, were ingested, as well as how long ago they were taken.[59]
8. Whether the person is a smoker or nonsmoker.[60]

Although distinctions between the hair of infants and adults can be made, examiners cannot conclusively determine the age of a hair donor. Even when the condition of hair evidence is not sufficiently good to permit all these determinations to be made, the remaining conclusions that can be reached may be of considerable assistance in eliminating suspects or focusing the investigation. Additionally, these conclusions may have more than their ordinary value when combined with other evidence, or they may be useful in destroying an alibi. To illustrate, a rape suspect maintained that he had never had contact with the victim, and his mother stated that he was watching television with her when the crime occurred. An eyewitness maintained that she had seen the victim and the suspect in the parking lot of a mall. The suspect maintained that the eyewitness was mistaken. However, the suspect confessed when confronted with the fact that hairs consistent with the victim's were found in his car, as well as fibers consistent with the victim's sweater and skirt.

Hair recovered at the scene of the crime should be carefully gathered, using a pair of tweezers. Samples recovered at different locations, as in the case of other types of evidence, should be individually packaged. Hair evidence may be placed in a pillbox that is fully sealed with tape or placed in a folded piece of paper that is also fully taped shut. Some laboratories, such as the FBI's, request that hair evidence not be packaged in an envelope. In all cases the container used should be marked with the appropriate identifying information.

Because most examinations of hair are comparative in nature, a collection of standards from both the victim and the suspect, where the latter is known, is critical. The collection of hair standards is a function for medical personnel. When hair standards are collected from a deceased victim, representative samples should be obtained from throughout the body areas that are pertinent to the investigation; ordinarily, the collection of approximately 30 to 40 hairs from each area is sufficient, taking care to package the samples from each body area separately. If hair surrounds wounds on the body of a victim, special notation should be made of this point on the container in which the hair is placed.

In collecting hair samples, combing is used to gather hair left on the victim by the suspect or on the suspect by the victim.[61] For comparison purposes, standard hair samples must be plucked from the individual to ensure that the hair was indeed attached to that person. If this proves to be too painful, then the hair needed may be cut, but the person doing the cutting must be able to substantiate that the hair was attached to the person. The hair should be cut as close to the skin as possible. Approximately 25 hairs from each area of concern are sufficient for a standard hair sample from a living donor.

It is desirable that the investigator be present at the time the hair samples are obtained by medical personnel. If the latter are unfamiliar with investigative procedures, they might fail to clean the tweezers, comb, or scissors after each area is sampled, thereby introducing contamination.

## BLOOD

An adult's body contains, on average, about 5 to 6 quarts of blood, and even small cuts can produce a lot of blood. At crime scenes, blood may be encountered in amounts ranging from small drops to large pools, in states ranging from fresh to dried and in almost any place, including on floors, walls, ceilings, clothes, weapons, the suspect's and victim's bodies, and the exterior and interior of vehicles.

Because of the frequency with which blood is encountered and the fact that DNA analysis can provide individual identification (see Table 3–1), officers need to be alert to locating and protecting this type of evidence. Moreover, they should wear appropriate PPE and take the other kinds of protective measures discussed in Chapter 2.

### THE APPEARANCE OF BLOODSTAINS

If blood at the crime scene is fresh and relatively uncontaminated, identifying it as blood is not difficult. If it is in some other condition, identifying

Hemident = test for blood



blood merely by "eyeballing it" becomes increasingly difficult. Blood may appear as a rust-colored stain or have gray, black, green, or blue tints. It may also be mixed with earth, grease, paint, or other substances, making it difficult to see. One way of locating blood evidence is to do a preliminary or presumptive field test using, for example, Hemident (see Figure 3–4), which does not interfere with subsequent serology tests. Hemident, depending on which chemical reagent is used, may produce a vivid pink or blue-green color and reacts both to human and animal blood. As is the case with all presumptive tests, the quick results gained through testing in the field must be confirmed by more elaborate procedures in the laboratory to have legal significance.

The drying time of blood depends on a number of factors, including whether it is on a porous or nonporous surface, its size and thickness, and the presence or absence of a fan or breeze. Higher temperatures hasten the drying time of blood, while increase humidity decreases it. Drying first appears at the edges of a bloodstain and works toward its center. A dried bloodstain will begin to pucker and crack from the edges inward upon further drying. Thus, it is difficult to accurately estimate the age of bloodstains.

## USING BLOODSTAINS TO RECONSTRUCT THE CRIME

Bloodstains may take many forms at a crime scene. These forms are not random, but are produced by factors such as the type, location, and number of wounds inflicted; the type of weapon involved; movements by the victim while trying to escape, defend himself or herself, or attack the offender; changes in the location of the victim's body due to its being moved by the offender or someone; and continuing postmortem violence to the body by the offender, suggesting that the killer was in a state of rage and possibly knew the victim.

**Table 3-1** Sources of DNA Evidence

| Evidence | Possible Location of DNA on the Evidence | Source of DNA |
|---|---|---|
| Baseball bat or similar weapon | Handle, end | Sweat, skin, blood, tissue |
| Hat, bandanna, or mask | Inside | Sweat, hair, dandruff |
| Eyeglasses | Nose or ear pieces, lens | Sweat, skin |
| Facial tissue or cotton swab | Surface area | Mucus, blood, sweat, semen, earwax |
| Dirty laundry | Surface area | Blood, sweat, semen, vomit |
| Toothpick | Tips | Saliva |
| Used cigarette | Cigarette butt | Saliva |
| Stamp or envelope | Licked area | Saliva |
| Tape or ligature | Inside or outside surface | Skin, sweat |
| Bottle, can, or glass | Sides, mouthpiece | Saliva, sweat |
| Used condom | Inside or outside surface | Semen, vaginal or rectal cells |
| Blanket, pillow, or sheet | Surface area | Sweat, hair, semen, urine, saliva, dandruff |
| "Through and through" bullet | Outside surface | Blood, tissue |
| Bite mark | Person's skin or clothing | Saliva |
| Fingernail or partial fingernail | Scrapings | Blood, sweat, tissue |

**Source:** "What Every Law Enforcement Officer Should Know about DNA Evidence." National Commission on the Future of DNA Evidence (Washington, DC: National Institute of Justice, 1999), pp. 3–4.

**Figure 3-4** Hemident

The use of Hemident in a presumptive or preliminary field test for blood.

(Courtesy Lightning Powder Company, Salem, Oregon)

1. Wear protective gloves. Rub the stain with a clean cotton swab.

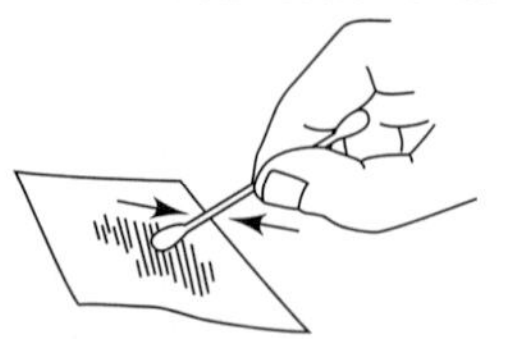

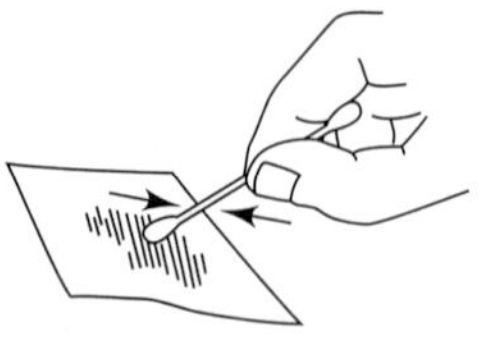

2. Insert the swab into the test unit and break off the excess handle.

3. Put the cap back on the tube and break the bottom ampoule.

4. Tap the tube to make sure the swab is wet. Wait about 20 to 30 seconds.

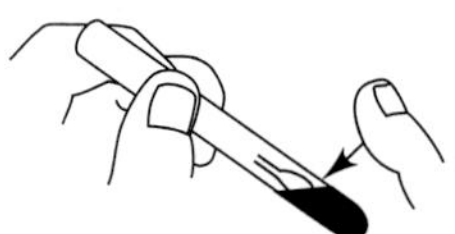

5. Break the top ampoule in the lid.

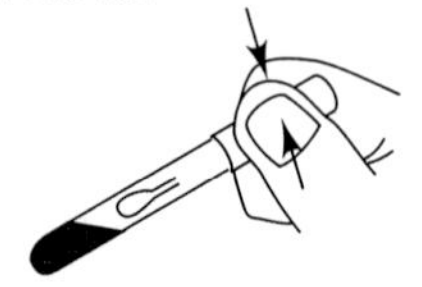

6. Observe the color change on the point where the swab has the suspect stain.

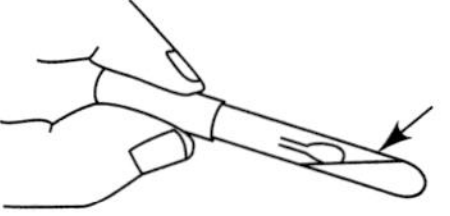

By studying bloodstains evidence, the investigator can learn significant facts that facilitate reconstruction of the crime. These facts include:

1. Direction in which blood droplets were traveling when they were deposited on the surface (see Figure 3–5).
2. Distance from the source of blood to the surface on which droplets were found (see Figure 3–6).
3. Angle at which the droplets impacted (see Figure 3–7).
4. Direction and relative speed of blood trails.
5. Nature of the object used as a weapon.
6. Number of blows struck.
7. Relative locations of other person, surfaces, and objects having droplets on them.
8. Sequence of events, if multiple events are involved.
9. Interpretation of blood-contact or blood-transfer patterns.
10. Estimation of the elapsed time for the event and the volume of bloodshed.[62]

## LOCATING BLOOD EVIDENCE

The places at which the investigator will find blood stains are virtually unlimited. For example, if a criminal homicide occurred indoors, blood might be found not only on the floor but perhaps on the walls or even the ceiling. Ordinarily when perpetrators of violent crimes get blood on their bodies or clothing, they will attempt to rid themselves of it immediately. In some instances, they may be so repelled by the sight of blood on their hands that they will impulsively wipe it on a piece of furniture, such as a stuffed chair; if the fabric is multicolored or sufficiently dark, the stain may escape detection by the unobservant investigator. They may also attempt to clean bloodied hands before leaving the scene by using such surfaces as the reverse side of a small throw rug or the undersides of cushions on a couch. Occasionally, in a criminal homicide that occurs indoors, the perpetrator will remove the body to an outdoor area to avoid discovery and then will return to the scene and attempt to eliminate all traces of the crime. Typically, this involves washing hands and scrubbing or mopping the floor on which the body had lain. A case illustrates these types of behaviors and the actions required by the investigator:

AN aggravated assault occurred between two friends who mutually agreed to misrepresent the crime and claim the cutting was an accident. When the victim appeared at the local hospital for treatment, the police were summoned due to the nature of the wounds and

**Figure 3-5** Directionality of Blood Droplet

To visualize or demonstrate directionality in a droplet, the analyst simply drays a line down the long axis of the stain, splitting it into two equal parts. This line is oriented to the scallops, spines, or satellite stains.

**Source:** Tom Bevel and Ross M. Gardner, *Bloodstain Pattern Analysis with an Introduction to Crime Scene Reconstruction,* 2nd ed. (Boca Raton, FL: CRC Press, 2002), p. 146. Used by permission.

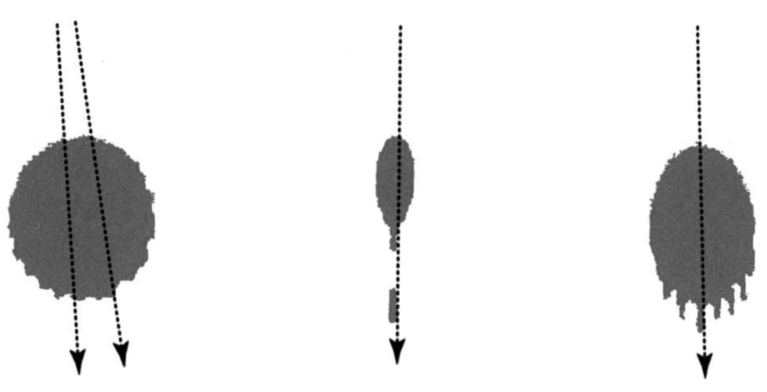


**Figure 3-6** Distance between Bloodstain and Source

Increasing diameter of bloodstains as a function of increasing distance fallen by single drops of blood from fingertips onto smooth cardboard.

**Source:** Stuart H. James and William G. Eckert, *Interpretation of Bloodstain Evidence at Crime Scenes,* 2nd ed. (Boca Raton, FL: CRC Press, 1998), p. 21. Used by permission.

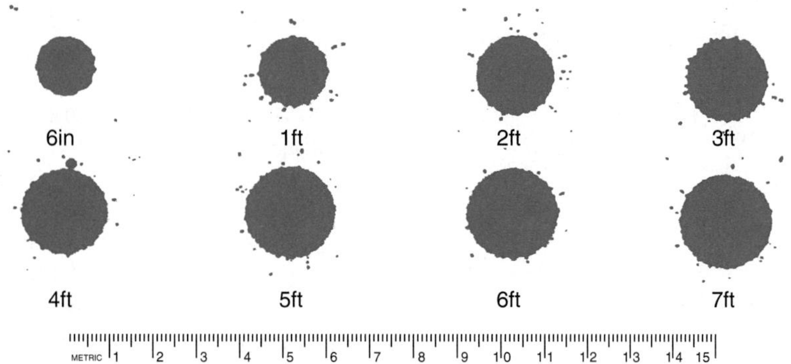


their locations, which suggested to the doctor that they were not accidentally inflicted. Subsequent examination of the scene revealed blood traces under the faucet handles in the kitchen, where the perpetrator had turned on the water to wash his hands, and in the trap of the sink; and although the perpetrator had washed portions of his shirt on which the victim's blood had fallen, he had done so in hot water, which merely set the stain, making it fairly readily observable to the naked eye. Additionally, although the floor at the scene had been mopped, traces of the same-type blood as the victim's were also recovered. The location of the blood evidence was particularly pertinent because the people involved alleged that the accident had happened outside the house while they were barbecuing and that they had gone directly to the hospital.

The investigator must also be alert to the fact that even if there are no apparent bloodstains, laboratory examinations may be able to detect their existence. For example, blood from a victim may be on the perpetrator's clothes. A suspect may initially attempt to wipe the blood away with a washcloth and then later wash both it and his or her clothes. The retention of bloodstains on cloth after washing is variable; it is dependent on several factors, such as the type of fiber and the conditions under which the cloth was washed.[63]

At bloody scenes it is not uncommon for the suspect to have left a shoeprint on some hard, smooth surface. In turn, it is likely that some of the blood may be found in the cracks and crevices of the suspect's shoe soles. This is important evidence because it can tie the suspect to the scene with great certainty.

Very fine drops of blood can be located by viewing the surfaces concerned at an oblique angle close to the plane of the surfaces. If the light is not strong or if the scene is dark, viewing the surfaces will be enhanced by shining a flashlight beam at the same oblique angle.

## HANDLING BLOOD EVIDENCE

Before handling any blood evidence, its location and physical state (e.g., fresh) must be documented by some combination of notes, diagrams, videotapes, and photographs. Other details may be pertinent to record as well, such as the temperature, humidity, or existence of multiple severe wounds but little blood. The latter condition suggests that the person was killed somewhere else or that an attempt was made to clean the victim and/or scene, an action possibly indicating that the perpetrator had an attachment to the victim.

### Blood Samples from a Known Source

Only qualified medical personnel should collect blood samples from a person. The following guidelines apply:

1. Draw two 5-milliliter samples of blood in purple-stoppered tubes, the insides of which are coated with **EDTA,** a preservative used to prevent coagulation.
2. If drug or alcohol testing is to be done, collect a 10-milliliter sample in a grey-stoppered tube, which has a sodium fluoride/potassium oxalate preservative.
3. Identify each tube with the date, time, collector's name, case number, subject's name, location at which drawn, and evidence number.
4. Do not freeze blood samples. Refrigerate them, and use cold packs, not dry ice, to pack them for shipment to the laboratory.
5. Pack the blood tubes in special bubble packs, or wrap them in the same type of material.
6. After sealing the outer container or box, label it "Keep in a Cool Dry Place," "Refrigerate on Arrival," and "Biohazard."
7. Submit the samples to the laboratory as soon as possible.[64]

### Fresh or Dried Blood on a Person

If there is fresh blood, absorb it on a clean cotton cloth or swab. If the blood is clotting or has dried, use distilled water to moisten a cotton cloth or swab and then absorb the blood with the moist surface. Leave a portion of the cloth or swab unstained as a control or blank sample. Let the cloth or swab air-dry naturally. Do not place it in direct sunlight or next to a heat source, and do not use a hair dryer on it. These actions could cause the evidence to begin decomposing, thus reducing or eliminating its evidentiary value. Wrap the evidence in clean, dry paper, or place it in an envelope with sealed corners; plastic or airtight containers should not be used.

### Fresh Blood on Surfaces or in Snow or Water

The procedure for collecting fresh blood from most surfaces is the same as that described above for blood on a person. However, when blood is in a filled bathtub or some other body of water or when it is on snow, a different approach is required. For blood in water, draw the sample from the thickest concentrations of blood whenever possible. When gathering blood from snow, eliminate as much snow as possible from the sample. Freeze it in a

**Figure 3-7** Impact Angle and Stain Shape

The range of droplet shapes that result from the varying impact angles. The more elliptical the stain, the more acute the angle of impact. Round stains indicate the impact angle was closer to 90 degrees.

**Source:** Tom Bevel and Ross M. Gardner, *Bloodstain Pattern Analysis with an Introduction to Crime Scene Reconstruction,* 2nd ed. (Boca Raton, FL: CRC Press, 2002), Color Figure 2.

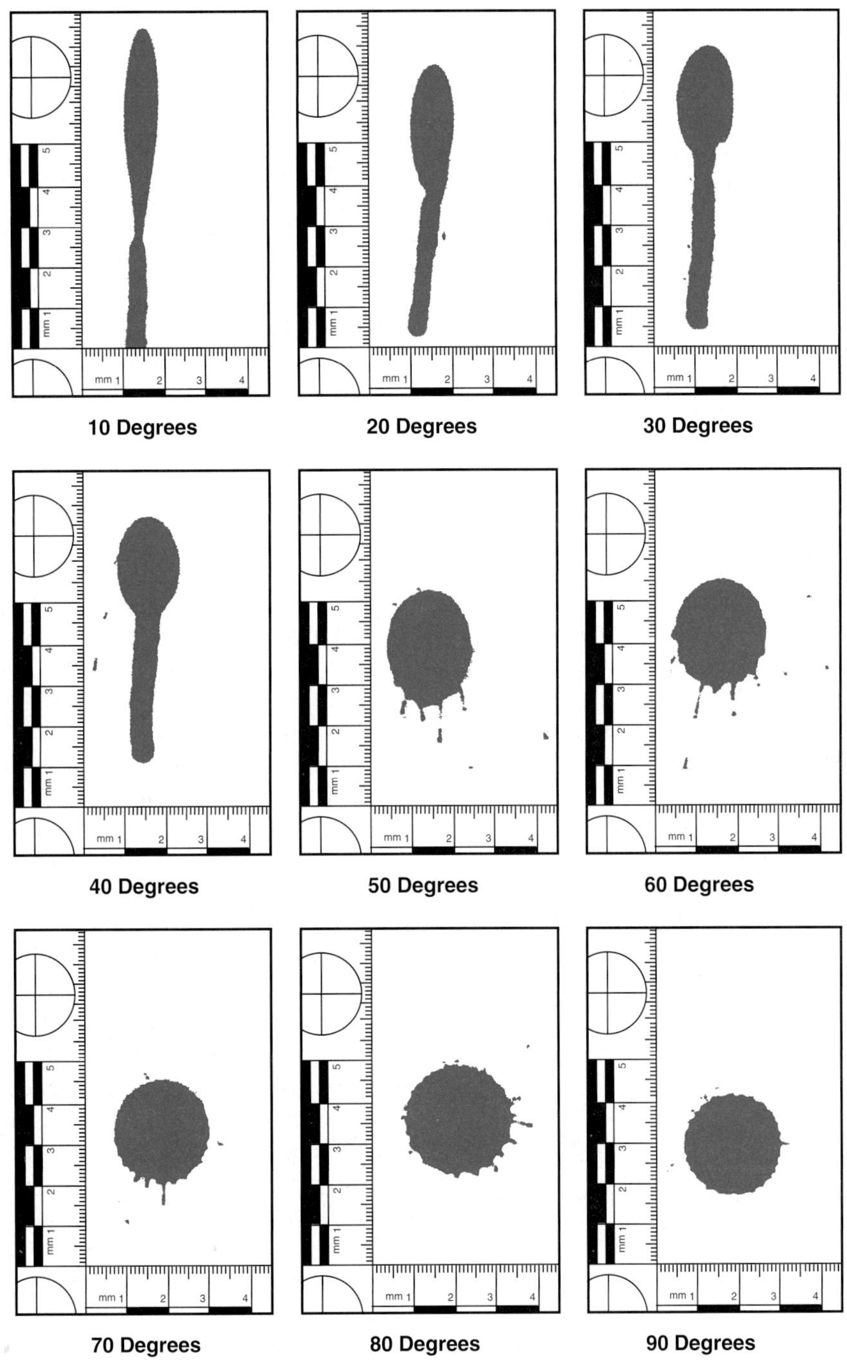

clean, airtight container, and submit the sample to the laboratory as rapidly as possible.

### Fresh or Dried Bloodstains on Garments and Objects

You should allow fresh bloodstains on garments to air-dry naturally; then fold the clothing with the crusts intact. Do not fold clothing in a way that creases bloodstains as the creases may cause them to become dislodged. As you fold the clothing, place clean paper between each layer. Usually, bloodstained garments are found at the crime scene or retrieved from a hospital's emergency room.

Fresh bloodstains on a small movable item, such as a weapon, lamp, or door, should also be allowed to air-dry naturally. The item is then submitted to the laboratory for processing; pack the item in clean paper in such a way that the paper does not rub against the bloodstains, as rubbing could alter or eradicate the bloodstain pattern. When bloodstains are on a large immovable object, they can be collected, if fresh, by using the cotton cloth or swab technique or by cutting a large sample from a dried stain. If there are multiple stains on the object, use a new cloth or swab each time you switch from one stain to another; likewise, thoroughly clean the scalpel, razor blade, or knife you are using to cut dried samples when you switch from one collection area to another. In some cases, it may be necessary to cut a section out of the immovable object and transport it to the laboratory; do not forget the need for a control or blank sample.

### Other Considerations in Handling Blood Evidence

During warm weather, especially during daylight hours, blood evidence should not be locked in car interiors or trunks because heat could rapidly degrade the evidence. If dried-blood evidence is not submitted to the laboratory within 24 hours, the garments, objects, or samples taken should be refrigerated.

## LABORATORY DETERMINATIONS

Under ordinary conditions laboratory examination of blood evidence can determine the following about the source of the blood:

1. The species (human, dog, horse, etc.).
2. The sex.
3. The blood type and the DNA profile.
4. Whether drugs or alcohol have been used by the source of the blood.
5. The presence of certain types of illnesses (e.g., venereal disease).
6. The presence of carbon monoxide.
7. Whether the source was a smoker.

The importance of such determinations was highlighted when labor leader Jimmy Hoffa disappeared. It was thought that a person close to him may have betrayed him because of bloodstains found in that person's car. However, laboratory examination confirmed the person's statement that the bloodstains were from fish he was taking home.

# LIP COSMETICS AND LIP PRINTS

Lip cosmetics include products such as lipsticks, glosses, balms, liners, and lipstick sealants. Many lipsticks will fluoresce under forensic lighting, making it possible to detect trace amounts. Laboratories can differentiate between types of lipstick; in one forensic study, 117 common types of lipstick from 15 different manufacturers were all separately identified.[65] When a case involves a custom lip gloss, such evidence may achieve even greater significance.

In a missing-person case, there may come a point at which it is important to have a DNA profile of the person. Excellent sources of DNA in such cases are lip cosmetics; examination of these personal effects may prove DNA in nearly 80 percent of the cases.[66] Lipstick evidence is occasionally encountered in a variety of offenses, but it is often not appreciated for the contributions it can make to an investigation, particularly its potential to connect the offender with the scene and/or victim and to help evaluate a suspect's alibi. For example, lipstick may be transferred from the victim to her assailant's clothing during rape. If a suspect is stopped in the general area shortly thereafter with lipstick on the collar or shoulder of his shirt, he may claim that it is that of his girlfriend. Comparisons of the victim's lipstick, the lipstick on the suspect's clothing, and the lipstick of the girlfriend could reveal that only the victim's lipstick and that on the suspect's clothing are consistent. Other types of crimes in which lipstick may be encountered as evidence include ritualistic slayings, armed robberies, and other crimes of violence. Even in property offenses, where there has been no victim-suspect contact, obscene messages may be left, with lipstick used to write on mirrors, walls, or other places.

Lipstick evidence should be photographed before disturbing it. When it is on clothing, the entire garment should be submitted to the laboratory, and care should be taken to pack it in such a fashion that the affected area is well protected. Where there are sufficient quantities on other surfaces, a sample should be collected with a clean razor blade or similar instrument and placed in a clean pillbox. Lipstick evidence encountered at several different locations of a crime scene should be collected and packaged separately. Dry cotton should not be used to protect lipstick evidence because it creates problems in handling the evidence in the laboratory. Nor should lipstick evidence be allowed to sit in the sun or remain in the trunk of a car, where it may be subject to extreme heat. In all cases a generous sample of the victim's or other donor's lipstick should also be obtained.

Lip prints are found under many of the same circumstances as is lipstick evidence. Every individual has unique lip prints that do not change with age. As with fingerprints, technicians can lift these prints from objects at the crime scene, such as a glass, and compare them with the suspect's lip pattern. Lip prints are also found elsewhere, such as on the starched collar of a shirt.[67]

## FIREARMS

Firearm evidence is commonly encountered in murder, aggravated-assault, robbery, rape, drug, kidnapping, and suicide cases. Such evidence includes single- and double-action revolvers, semiautomatic handguns, rifles, scopes, shotguns, rim- and center-fire ammunition, bullets, shot pellets and slugs, shell cases, gunshot residues, clips and magazines, firing-pin impressions, and extractor and ejector marks. Moreover, there may be blood, tissue, or fingerprints on firearm evidence, making it even more important to a case. Police officers must acquire a broad, working knowledge of firearm evidence for three primary reasons: (1) the frequency with which they will encounter it; (2) the value of such knowledge in a combat situation, and (3) the personal safety of other personnel when an officer is handling firearms at a crime scene. Never assume that a firearm in unloaded, no matter who brings or hands it to you; that assumption could get you or someone else killed.

IT was late on the evening watch in a detective division and three investigators were sitting around talking. Two detectives brought a man in, who was not handcuffed, and told him to sit down in front of a desk. One of them laid a revolver on the desk and said, "We're charging this guy with murder; watch him until we get back." In about 10 minutes, the suspect stood up, picked up the revolver, and killed himself in front of the three investigators.

The laboratory examination of firearm evidence may be able to provide answers to the questions discussed below.

***Was This Bullet Fired from This Weapon?*** Shotguns are **smooth-bore** weapons, while pistols and rifles have **rifling.** The **caliber** is the diameter of a bullet, whereas the **bore** (see Figure 3–8) is the diameter of the barrel's interior between its

**Figure 3-8** Rifled Barrel

Important features of a rifled firearm's barrel.

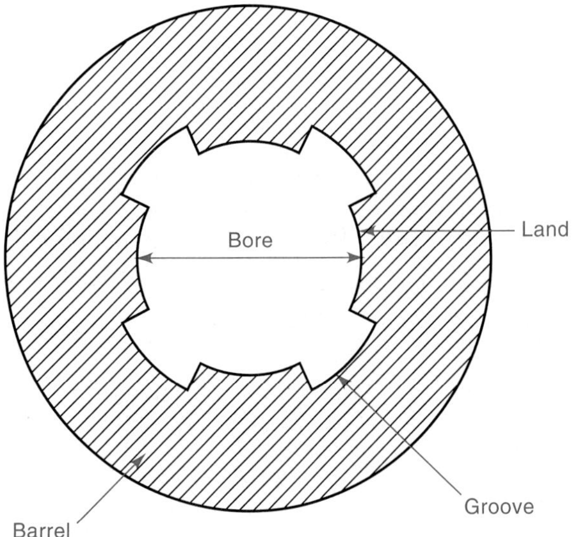

opposing high sides, or **lands.** The low sides of the barrel's interior are called **grooves.** When a cartridge is fired, its bullet portion separates and passes through the barrel. Because the bullet's caliber is somewhat larger than the bore, the rifling grips the bullet, causing it to rotate, usually in a right-hand direction. The rotation increases the range and accuracy of the bullet.

This rotation also creates striations on the bullet. These distinctive scratches can be compared to those on bullets fired through the weapon in question (see photo below). Identification, however, is affected by the condition of the gun and that of the bullet or fragments. While it is ideal to have the firearm, bullets themselves can yield important data. By matching striations on bullets recovered at different crime scenes, investigators can tie together information from several cases; the combined data may produce new leads and result in the clearance of the case.

In some cases, the striations on a bullet recovered from a decomposed body may have been negatively affected by the interaction between the bullet material and the body tissue.[68] Conversely, an older revolver whose cylinders do not properly align may sheer off a portion of the bullet when fired, creating distinctive markings. Other aspects of how individual-class firearm evidence is produced are discussed later in this section.

***What Else Can Be Learned from the Bullet?*** A fired bullet yields evidence of the class characteristics of the weapon that fired it with respect to the number of lands and grooves and their height, depth, and width. The class characteristics of a firearm are the design specifications to which it was manufactured; weapons of a given make and model will have the same class characteristics. The individual characteristics of the bore are found in the striae along the fired bullet. Examination of a fired bullet will suggest the type of weapon from which it was fired, whether the bullet is a hard-nose or soft-nose projectile, and the pitch and direction of twist within the barrel. Additionally, if the fired bullet is recovered in sufficient size, it may be possible, through weighing and measurement, to determine its caliber. Since bullets are often recovered as fragments, the caliber may only be implied; for instance, the weight may rule out smaller calibers. While it is possible to determine the caliber of the bullet, some caution must be taken with respect to determining the bore of the weapon from which it

**Bullet Comparison**

A drug user murdered his supplier in order to "cancel" his debt and obtain additional drugs. Photomicrograph of the bullet recovered from the body (*left*) compared to the bullet fired from the murder gun (*right*) after the revolver was recovered from a river by police divers.

(Courtesy Royal Canadian Mounted Police)

Bullet is slightly bigger than the bore



was fired, as a smaller-caliber bullet can be fired through a larger-bore weapon.

Fired bullets ordinarily experience some damage upon impact. In some cases it will be possible to see fabric impressions on the bullet's nose that were made as the bullet passed through the victim's outer garment. Additionally, there may be minute traces of blood, tissue, bone, or other such materials. Great care must be taken by the investigator not to destroy or in any way alter such evidence. When the fired bullet is to be recovered from the victim, the investigator should alert the attending medical personnel, if there is any doubt about their familiarity with proper handling procedure, as to the irreparable damage that can be wrought by the careless application of forceps or other such instruments in removing the bullet.

It should be noted that it is ordinarily not possible to make a positive identification as to whether pellets were fired from a particular shotgun. However, in extraordinarily rare circumstances involving smooth-bore firearms, it may be possible to make an individual identification on the basis of gross defects in the barrel.[69]

***What Determinations Can be Made from Cartridge Cases?*** In contrast to a bullet, which is typically acted on only by the barrel, a cartridge case is subject to a number of different forces that make marks on it, any of which can produce individual-class evidence. Such marks include:

1. Marks made on the cartridge case as it is loaded into the chamber for firing, which may be caused by the magazine or by the slide action of the firearm (see photo on page 106).
2. A pin impression made on the base of the cartridge case, which is caused by the firing of the weapon (see photo below).
3. Striations made when expanding gases force the cartridge case against the chamber wall and marks left by the same gases when they force the cartridge case back against the breach face of the weapon.
4. Extractor marks made when the case is pulled out of the chamber and ejector marks made when the case is "kicked out," both of which are associated with semiautomatic and automatic weapons.

**Firing Pin Impressions**

Photomicrograph showing comparison of questioned and known firing-pin impressions on a .22-caliber rim-fire cartridge case.

(Courtesy Regional Criminalistics Laboratory, Metropolitan Kansas City, Missouri)

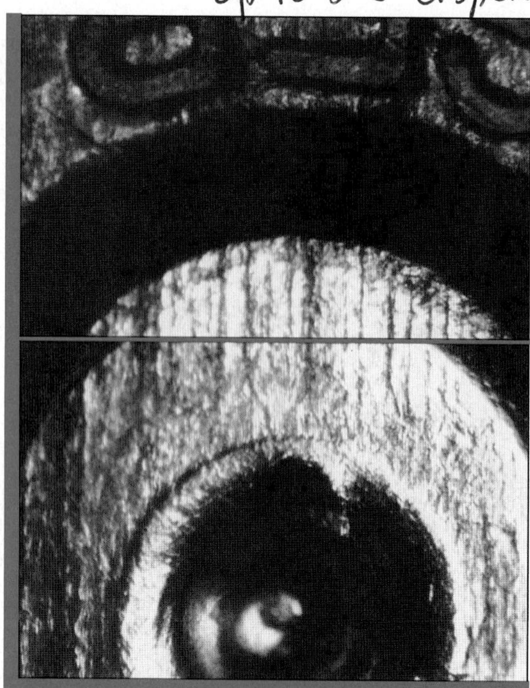

**Breach-Face Markings**

Photomicrograph of the breach-face markings on two Winchester 9-mm cartridge cases that were recovered at different locations at the scene of a murder. The victim was scheduled to testify in the trial of a drug dealer the next day. The murder is unsolved and under active investigation.

(Courtesy Tennessee Bureau of Investigation)

***What Miscellaneous Determinations Can Be Made by Examination of Firearms Evidence?*** If a firearm is received at a crime laboratory, its general mechanical condition can be assessed, and the findings can lend credence to or discredit claims that the shooting was accidental. For example, if the trigger pull on a weapon is of the "hair" nature, requiring only the slightest pressure to pull it, this would indicate that an accidental shooting was possible. Laboratory examination might reveal that a firearm is constructed—or malfunctioning—in such a way that it could discharge if dropped on its hammer, thereby giving more credibility to a claim that a shooting was accidental. Furthermore, even though invisible to the naked eye, obliterated serial numbers can sometimes be restored by the laboratory, thus providing an additional investigative lead. Proximity of the gun to the victim at the time of discharge may be established by an examination of powder residues on the victim's clothing or skin. A shot from 6 inches with black powder produces burning on the surface; a distinctive powder deposit is created at a range of 12 inches; and dispersed grains of powder may be found even when the weapon was fired at a distance of up to 3 feet.[70] The absence or presence of powder residues might be an important factor in assessing whether a shooting was a criminal homicide or a suicide.[71] Additionally, even if there is no apparent presence of powder residues, the victim's clothing should be processed by the laboratory. Finally, by assessing the amount of dust or other debris inside the barrel of a seized weapon, the expert can estimate how recently the weapon was fired. This can also be done, more accurately, through laboratory tests.[72]

## COLLECTING FIREARM EVIDENCE

A cardinal rule in handling weapons at the scene of a crime is that they should never be picked up or moved until they have been photographed and measurements made for the crime scene sketch. As in the case of many rules for criminal investigations, there are several exceptions: First, if the weapon is found outdoors and there is any likelihood that inclement weather may destroy the possibility of obtaining latent fingerprints, it should be immediately removed to a protected area. Second, at the scenes of aggravated assaults and murders, feelings run high and there is a danger that an emotionally charged person may suddenly attempt to pick up the weapon and shoot another party. Third, there may be some compelling safety need, such as uncocking the weapon. Ordinarily, however, the first handling of a weapon should be to process it for fingerprints. The investigator must pick up a firearm with great care, despite familiarity with weapons, as many weapons have individual peculiarities that may produce an accidental discharge through careless or indiscriminate handling.

In no case should a pencil or similar object be placed into the barrel of the gun to pick it up; this can dislodge evidence that may be in the barrel, such as tissue, blood, hair, or other trace evidence, and it can contaminate the barrel, thereby confusing the laboratory examiner. The proper method of

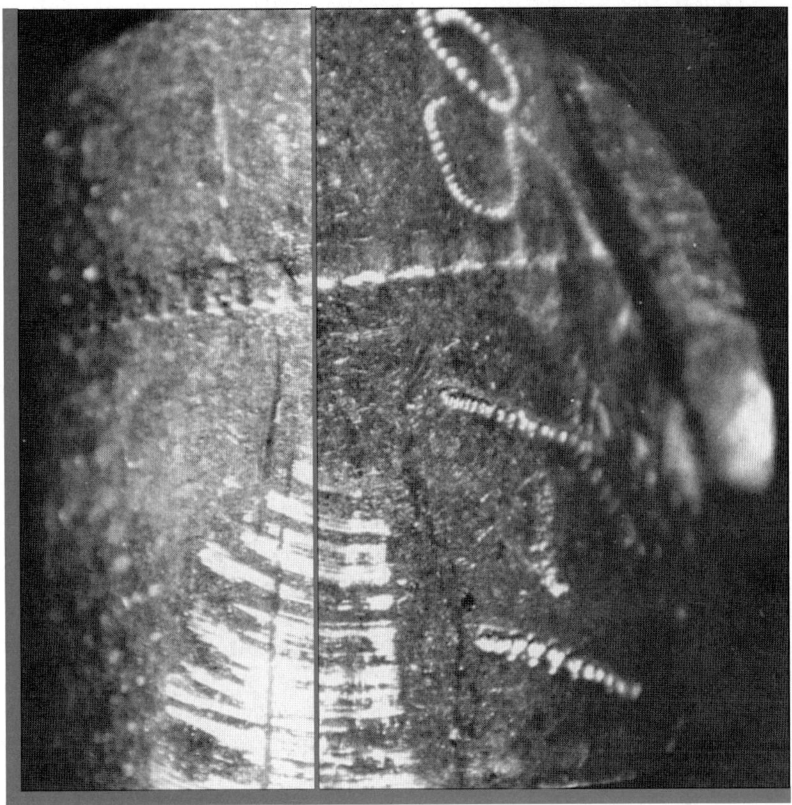

**Striations Made by Slide Action**
Photomicrograph of striated marks made on questioned and known cartridge cases. The marks were made as a slide acted on the mouths of cartridge cases in a Colt .45-caliber semiautomatic pistol.
(Courtesy Regional Criminalistics Laboratory, Metropolitan Kansas City, Missouri)

packaging a handgun—once unloaded—is to suspend it in a small box by a ring that passes through the trigger guard. As bullets, cartridge cases, and related firearm evidence are gathered, they should be packaged separately. The practice of putting a handgun in a coat or pants pocket until transferred to an evidence envelope at some later time should be strictly avoided.

### MARKING FIREARM EVIDENCE

For identification purposes, the FBI does not recommend marking directly on cartridges, shell cases, bullets and fragments, shotgun shells and cases, firearms, magazines, clips, and related materials. Doing so would run the risk of disturbing latent fingerprints, bloodstains, or other evidence. Smaller types of firearm evidence should be surrounded in tissue paper and placed in a suitable rigid container to which an evidence sticker with the appropriate case information is attached. Larger items, such as handguns and long guns, should have a completed evidence tag affixed to them. For obvious reasons, loaded weapons should not be sent to the laboratory.

In all cases involving firearms, the number of shells or rounds remaining in a weapon should be noted, as should any misfeeds or other blockages to the proper functioning of the gun. Additionally, with revolvers there is the possibility of a mixture of unfired bullets, cartridge cases of fired rounds, and empty chambers. The numbers and locations of all these should be noted. The proper procedure is to designate the chamber aligned with the barrel as "1" and to continue numbering the chambers in a clockwise manner until all of them are accounted for. Afterward, each round should be placed in a rigid container.

## TOOL MARKS

For forensic purposes, a **tool mark** is any impression, cut, gouge, or abrasion made when a tool comes into contact with another object.[73] Most often tool marks are found at the scenes of burglaries because the perpetrators have forced their way into a building and then forced open such things as locked filing cabinets and safes. To illustrate, a pry bar may be used to force a door open, leaving an indented impression of the tool action on the doorframe. In the process, the pry bar may also scrape across the door, its hinges, its screws, its edge, or the doorframe, cutting tiny furrows called **striae** (see photo below).[74] As different types of tools are used in burglaries, other marks of investigative interest may also be produced, such as the action of pliers (see top left photo on page 109) or channel locks on a doorknob. As burglars force their way into buildings and their contents, they may break tools. When a broken tool part is recovered at the scene of a burglary, it is possible to align it with a broken tool in the perpetrator's possession; the alignment is called a fracture match (see bottom right photo on page 109).

The examination of a tool mark may yield a great deal of useful information, such as the type and size of the tool and the action employed when the instrument was operated. For example, a clear impression may suggest the use of a hammer or punch, whereas scrape marks may indicate the use of a flat-bladed tool such as a crowbar or screwdriver. A shearing instrument—whose blades pass one another, as with scissors and tin snips—may be suggested, or a pinching-type tool—whose blades butt against each other, as with wire cutters—may seem to have been used.

Additionally, by examining the manner in which the tool was employed, it is often possible to make a fairly reliable determination with respect to the skill of the perpetrator. Perhaps most important in the examination of a tool mark is whether it offers sufficient characteristics to allow for individual identification should a tool be located in a suspect's possession.

In instances where a tool is found in a suspect's possession, the examination of it may yield foreign deposits, such as paint or metal, that may have either class or individual characteristics. The comparison of the tool with the tool mark may establish

**Screwdriver Marks**

Photomicrograph on left depicts microscopic striae left on the head of a woodscrew by a burglar attacking a door. The right side is a known or test impression made by the laboratory examiner using the screwdriver seized in the suspect's custody.

**Plier Marks**
Photomicrograph on left reveals striae left by a burglar using pliers to attack a doorknob. At right is a test impression made with the suspect's pliers in the laboratory.

whether they have consistent class characteristics and, if sufficient microscopic marks are present, whether there are enough individual characteristics to say with certainty that this particular tool made this particular mark.

In collecting evidence of tool marks, every effort should be made to obtain and submit the actual area for direct comparison. When this is not possible, a cast should be made. There are several good choices for casting tool marks, including Mikrosil. While tool marks should be photographed to establish their locations, the images have no forensic identification value. In no event should the investigator place a tool against a tool mark for size evalation, as doing so could lead to accidental cross-contamination or result in the accidental destruction of evidence. When a tool is to be submitted to the crime laboratory for examination, the actual tool should be submitted; the making of test impressions or cuts is a function of qualified technicians in the laboratory. The importance of this last point is illustrated by the fact that under test conditions in the laboratory it was found that when there was more than a 15-degree difference between the vertical angle at which a screwdriver was actually used and the comparison mark made in the laboratory, an improper finding of no identity from the same tool could result.[75]

## QUESTIONED DOCUMENTS

There are numerous illustrations of **questioned documents**: Pensioners sued a corporation, alleging that $21 million was missing due to forged signatures[76]; a check made payable to the "IRS" can be altered to "MRS" followed by a name for whom the forger has false identification;[77] six "newly discovered" piano sonatas by the famous composer Haydn turned out to be complete forgeries;[78] and counterfeiters have made bogus items such as automobile inspection stickers, coupons, ski-lift tickets, driver's licenses, gift certificates, baseball cards, and car and real estate titles (see illustrations on pages 110 and 111).[79]

Loosely defined, a **document** is anything on which a mark is made for the purpose of transmitting a message. A disputed or questioned document is one whose source or authenticity is in doubt (see

**Fracture-Match Tool**
Fracture match of claws of hammer, found at the scene of a burglary, with remainder of tool.

**Certified Copy of Record of Marriage**

}ss.

License No. 93-471
Date issued May 23, 1993
Date filed May 13, 1993

I, CLARA HARTLEY WOODARD, County Clerk hereby certify that:
Mr. Robert M. Webster
of 110 Pine Street in the County of Dade
and State of Florida of the age of 34 years, and
Miss Elizabeth Thomas
of 201 Willow Lane in the County of Dade
and State of Florida of the age of 22 years
were united in Marriage
on the 3rd day of March A.D. 1993
in said County, at Dade County Baptist Church
by Stevenson Edwards a Minister

Witnesses:
Sandra Williams
Louis Hobbs

I do hereby certify that the foregoing is a true and correct copy of the License and Certificate of Marriage as the same appears of record in my office.

IN TESTIMONY WHEREOF, I have set my hand and affixed my Official Seal, this 23rd day of May A.D. 19 93.

Clara Hartley Woodard
COUNTY CLERK

SEAL

By Marianne E. Ayers
Deputy.

## A Counterfeit Marriage License

Note the differences between the "M" in "Robert M. Webster" and the "M" in "May," "March," and "Minister." Also, notice the differences between the "3"and "4" in Webster's age and the same numbers elsewhere in the document. The differences in the type fonts as well as the gaps in the lines under the changed letters, left by whiting out the original entry, indicate a counterfeit document.

(Courtesy Immigration and Naturalization Service, Forensic Document Laboratory)

photo on page 112).[80] Examples of questions that document examiners may help answer are these: Is this the deceased's handwriting on the suicide note? Did the suspect handwrite or print this holdup note or harassing letter? Is the signature on this collector's item, credit application, jail release order, or other document genuine? Was the typewriter seized from the suspect's apartment used to prepare this letter?

Because of the important contributions that can be made, investigators must have a basic familiarity with the different types of document examination.

## DOCUMENT EXAMINATION

### Handwriting and Handprinting Examinations

Because handwriting identification is based on the characteristics found in a person's normal writing, writers of a document can often be positively and reliably identified.[81] However, it is not always possible to reach a definite conclusion. Some of the reasons for inconclusive results are a limited amount of the writing in question and/or an inadequate sample from a known source, disguised handwriting, and insufficient identifying characteristics. There are three types of forgery:

1. A **traced forgery** is created by tracing over a genuine signature. A forgery of this type can be tied to the original, or master, signature if the original signature can be located.
2. A **simulated forgery** is produced by a writer who learns to mimic a genuine signature. It may or may not be possible to identify the forger, depending on the extent to which the suspect's normal handwriting characteristics remain in the signature.
3. A **freehand forgery** is written in the forger's normal handwriting, with no attempt to mimic the style of the genuine signature.

In addition, it is possible under certain conditions for offenders to lift an actual signature made with certain types of erasable pens for about 1 hour after the signature was affixed to the paper. The lift is done using a Scotch frosted tape; the tape is then laid back down on the signature block of a contract or other document and photocopied. The signature on the actual document remains intact, and the signature on the forged document looks right. This procedure can be detected by document examiners.

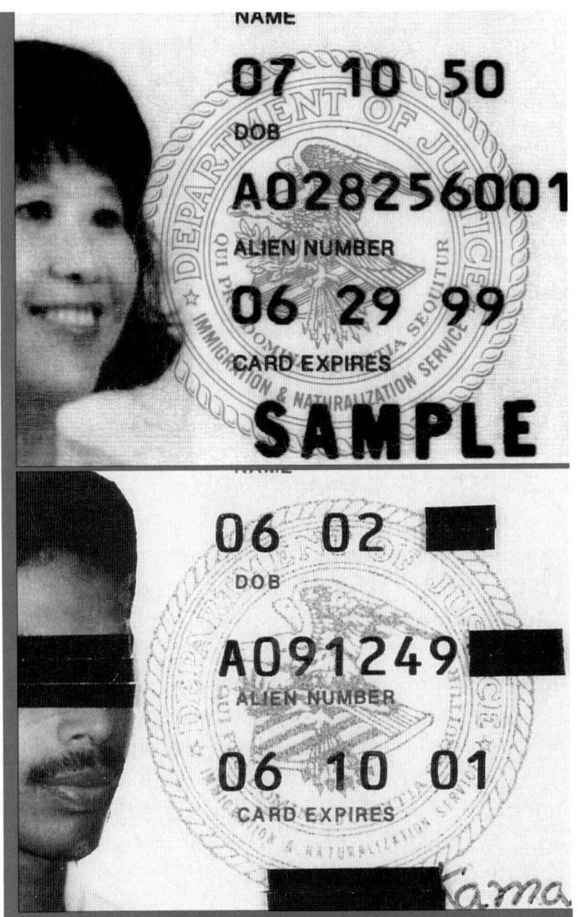


**A Genuine Alien Registration Card (*top*) and a Counterfeit One (*bottom*)**
A comparison of these two photographs illustrates a basic principle: In general, the difference between a genuine and a counterfeit document is found in the quality of the printing, especially in the area with the most fine detail. In this figure that area is the INS seal.
(Courtesy Immigration and Naturalization Service, Forensic Documents Laboratory)

In obtaining a handwriting sample from a known source, such as a suspect, the following guidelines should be followed:

1. Provide the person with the same type of paper and writing instrument as were used in the questioned document.
2. Direct the person to use the same writing style—cursive or printed—as was used in the questioned document, to write the same words, and to execute the same signature.
3. Remove each page of writing from the person's sight as soon as it is completed.
4. Provide no instructions as to format, spelling, or punctuation.
5. If the writing in question is short—such as a forged check—have the person repeat it 10 to 20 times; for longer documents—such as death threats—dictate the entire text word for word and get at least three full copies.
6. In forgery cases, get at least 10 samples of the victim's signature.
7. If the person does not appear to be writing normally, have him or her speed up, slow down, or alter the slant of the writing. Another technique is to have the person provide some writing with the other hand.
8. Obtain samples of nondictated writing from employment records or correspondence.
9. At the end of the session have the writer and a witness initial and date each page.

## Photocopier Examinations

Two documents can be photocopied and then spliced together to create a totally new and illegitimate, but legal-appearing, document. This method can be detected by the appearance of faint lines where the documents were joined, as well as by slight variations in font size, typeface, and line spacing. It is possible to link a photocopied docu-

**A Counterfeit Social Security Card**
Notice the lack of sharpness in areas of fine detail.
(Courtesy Immigration and Naturalization Service, Forensic Documents Laboratory)

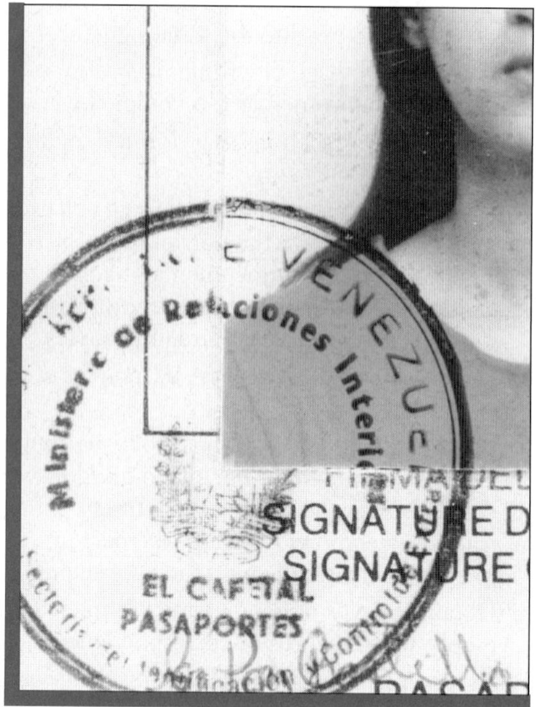


**Forged Passport**

The original photograph on this Venezuelan passport was removed, and the photograph of a different person was substituted for it. Examine the lower left-hand corner of the person's photograph. A counterfeit stamp was used to mark the substituted photograph. Note that the stamp print is misaligned, the stamp print is much sharper on the substituted photograph, and there are inconsistencies in the thickness of stamp lines where the substituted photograph meets the genuine stamp lines on the passport itself.

(Courtesy Immigration and Naturalization Service, Forensic Documents Laboratory)

ment with the machine that produced it if the document whose source is questioned and the samples taken from the machine are made relatively contemporaneously.[82] In collecting samples, the following actions are recommended: (1) Make 10 copies of a paper with some writing or typewriting on it; (2) with the cover up and no documents on the glass, make 10 "copies"; and (3) with no paper on the glass, and the cover down, make another 10 "copies." For laboratory purposes it is important to record the machine's make, model, serial number, and features. When a questioned photocopy is examined, it may be possible to determine the brand or manufacturer of the photocopier. Among the conditions that can help link a copy to a machine are striations on the glass, distinctive indentation marks on the paper from passing over rollers, and "trash marks"—the spots that can appear on a copied document.[83]

## Paper Examinations

This type of examination can yield several different results. It is possible to positively match the torn edges of paper.[84] For example, if a single paper match is found at a crime scene, it can be tied to the stub from which it originated in the matchbook recovered from a suspect. If there is a watermark on paper, the manufacturer can be determined; in addition, some watermarks include information indicating the date the paper was made. Paper can also be examined for indented writing impressions. It is important to realize that indentations not visible to the eye can be made readable by qualified examiners. Investigators should not attempt to develop any page that may have indented writing on it. The paper should not be folded or handled, and caution must be exercised so that additional indentations are not accidentally created by writing on a page that is on top of the evidence.

## Age of Documents

The age of a document is often difficult to establish. It may, however, be possible to determine the earliest date at which a document could have been prepared through examination of watermarks, indented writing, printing, and typewriting.[85] Chemical analysis of the writing ink used may yield some useful information, as inks vary by manufacturer and even production lots.[86] A genuine document could not have been prepared any earlier than the date on which the ink was available. Examiners may also conclude that documents were treated in some manner, such as baking, to make them look older than they actually are.[87] The trash marks produced on copied documents may also be useful in determining the age of a document. By examining months or even years of documents copied and on file in a business, examiners may be able to conclude that a questioned document was produced during a certain time frame on the basis of the similarity between its trash marks and the trash marks of file documents.

Photocopier EXAMINATIONS = 10 copies of a document
10 copies with cover up + no document
10 copies w/cover down " "

## Burned or Charred Paper

Illegal gambling operations, like other businesses, must maintain records. In order to prevent these records from falling into the hands of investigators, they may be chemically treated so that they will burn instantly when touched with a lighted cigarette or match in the event of a raid. Burned and charred documents are also encountered in other types of investigations. For example, a person who has committed a simulated forgery on a check may have attempted to burn the pages on which he or she practiced mimicking the genuine signature in order to destroy evidence related to the crime. Also, a kidnapper may have prepared several drafts of a written ransom demand and tried to destroy unused versions of the note by burning them. Entries on such burned and charred evidence may be revealed when examined. The handling of this type of evidence should be kept to an absolute minimum to avoid its crumbling. It is desirable to ship burned and charred evidence to the laboratory in the container in which it was burned, such as an ashtray.[88]

## Altered or Obliterated Writing

Many types of documents are easily altered. For example, bank deposit slips commonly have a line "less cash received." A dishonest teller could raise the figure in this line, pocket the difference, and still be in balance. Ways to obliterate an entry include the use of crayons, correction fluid, ink, and mechanical or chemical erasures. All of these are detectable under laboratory examination by such means as alternative light sources.

## Writing Instruments

The ink used to write a message involved in a crime can be compared with the ink in a pen recovered from a suspect. This type of examination cannot identify a specific pen but can determine whether or not the inks are of the same formulation.

## Mechanical-Impression Examination

A questioned document that is produced by mechanical impression can be compared with genuine printed documents to determine if it is counterfeit.[89] Two or more printed documents can be associated with the same printing source. It is possible to match a printed document with the source printing paraphernalia, such as negatives and plates. The examination of a checkwriter impression can determine the brand of the checkwriter that produced it, and this type of impression can then be matched with the individual checkwriter that produced it. If it is not possible to send a checkwriter to the laboratory for examination, make at least five copies of the questioned numbers and submit these instead. Both rubber stamps and embossers or seal impressions can be matched with the instruments that produced them. When seized as evidence, an embosser or seal or a rubber stamp should be sent to the laboratory for testing without cleaning or altering it in any way.

## Typewriting

The first commercially successful typewriter was made by Remington in 1873, and there has been a slow but steady improvement in that technology since then. Despite the availability of personal computers, many agencies and people prefer or have a need for a typewriter. The possible brands or manufacturers may be determined from a typewritten document. It is also possible to identify the individual typewriter that produced a questioned document. The following are guidelines investigators should follow in collecting this type of evidence:

1. The ribbon should be removed and submitted to the laboratory, as the text of the material in question may be on it; the correction tape should also be included.
2. All samples of printing should be prepared with a fresh ribbon.
3. The entire text of the questioned document should be reproduced unless it is unusually long, in which case a representative sample will be sufficient.
4. After the ribbon is removed or the machine is placed in the stencil position, samples of each character should be obtained by typing through carbon paper onto a piece of white bond paper.
5. It is usually not necessary to submit the machine to the laboratory, although the document examiner may subsequently request it if comparisons of the questioned and known documents reveal questions about

matters such as alignment, which can be satisfactorily determined only by examining the machine itself.

6. The dates of the machine's last cleaning, maintenance, and repair must be determined, as these procedures could affect the examiner's conclusion. Whenever possible, the machine should be maintained in its current condition until the document examiner submits his or her findings since the machine may have to be sent to the laboratory.
7. All specimens obtained by the investigator should include the machine's make, model, and serial number in addition to the investigator's usual identifying marks.[90]

## COMPUTER PRINTERS AND FAX MACHINES

Instead of printing an image in one stroke, a dot-matrix printer produces an image formed by many individual dots created by pins. The fewer pins in a printer, the easier the dots are to see. Some dot-matrix machines have an option for using a colored ribbon. Ink-jet printers fire droplets of ink at a page to make the dots that form the characters. Laser printers produce dots by shining light against a spinning mirror that flashes light to a rotating drum. The printer toner adheres electrostatically to the charged areas of the drum and is then fused to the paper, creating the characters. Color lasers are also available. The market for wax-jets is declining, with fewer units shipped each year. Thermal dye printers produce outstanding colors by holding a ribbon against the paper and applying heat, which transfers the dyes in the ribbon to a paper with polyester coating. While there is still a market for stand-alone fax machines, faxing is increasingly being bundled with printing, duplicating, and scanning capabilities in multifunction printers for personal computers.

Technological changes in printers are racing ahead, and some manufacturers closely guard information about their printers because it is proprietary. Moreover, great precision is required for manufacturing printers and this reduces variances that would be helpful with the identification process. Thus, printer identification is a difficult task. Although it may be possible to identify the make and model of a printer and to identify a page as having come from a specific printer, most often this cannot be done. Identifying faxes from multifunction printers is fraught with similar difficulties.

## Key Terms

**Adobe Photoshop**
**amido black**
**Automated Fingerprint Identification System (AFIS)**
**basic yellow 40**
**bite-mark evidence**
**bore**
**caliber**
**class characteristics**
**concentric fractures**
**contaminated/visible prints**
**cross-contamination**
**crystal violet**
**dental identification**
**dental stone**
**DFO (diazafluren-9-one)**
**document**
**EDTA**
**fingerprint classification**
**fingerprint patterns**
**fingerprints**
**fluorescent powders**
**footwear impressions**
**footwear prints**
**forensic dentistry**
**fracture match**
**freehand forgery**
**fuming wand**
**grooves**
**Hemident**
**individual characteristics**
**iodine**
**known samples**
**lands**
**laser illumination**
**latent/invisible prints**
**lifters**
**minutiae**
**ninhydrin**
**plastic prints**
**questioned document**
**radial fractures**
**reflected ultraviolet imaging system (RUVIS)**
**rhodamine 6G**
**rifling**
**Shoeprint Image Capture and Retrieval System (SICAR)**
**simulated forgery**
**small-particle reagent (SPR)**

**smooth bore**
**Snow Print Wax**
**striae**
**superglue fuming**
**tool mark**
**traced forgery**
**traditional powders**
**unknown or questioned samples**

## Review Questions

1. What are class and individual characteristics?
2. How are unknown or questioned samples and known samples alike or different?
3. What is the value of soil evidence?
4. How would you recover shoe prints?
5. What is the most common fingerprint pattern?
6. Identify and discuss the three broad categories of latent fingerprints.
7. When would you use amido black?
8. What three factors account for the rapid acceptance of superglue fuming?
9. How is superglue fuming done?
10. Describe the functioning of RUVIS.
11. Why do you use a software package like Adobe Photoshop with images of latent prints?
12. How do you collect bite-mark evidence?
13. Why would you use Hemident?
14. It may be possible to reconstruct a crime on the basis of an analysis of bloodstains. Identify six determinations which may be made from this type of analysis.
15. How do you collect fresh and dried blood from a person?
16. You collect a shirt with wet bloodstains on it at the crime scene. What do you do with it?
17. What determinations can a laboratory make after examining a blood sample?
18. Mrs. Johnson has been missing for seven weeks. A decapitated body, with the hands and feet also missing, is found by hunters. How might you be able to determine if this is her?
19. What can a laboratory determine from examining a cartridge case?
20. Identify and discuss the three types of handwritten forgery.

## Internet Activities

1. Learn more about the forensic examination of questioned documents at the Forensic Document Examination Services website at www.fdeservices.com. Next, go to www.qdewill.com and read the article under the subheading "Theory." What is the physiology of handwriting? Why is it difficult to simulate the handwriting of others? How is handwriting classified by class and individual characteristics?
2. Check out the Introduction to Forensic Firearms Identification website as www.firearmsid.com/index.html. This site covers firearm forensic topics such as firearm function testing, distance determinations, an introduction to ballistics, and new technologies in firearm identification.

## Notes

1. Richard Saferstein, *Criminalistics,* 7th ed. (Upper Saddle River, NJ: Prentice-Hall, 2001), p. 65.
2. Ibid., p. 64
3. Federal Bureau of Investigation, *Handbook of Forensic Science* (Washington, DC: Government Printing Office, 1978), p. 2.
4. Technical Working Group on Crime Scene Investigation, *Crime Scene Investigation: A Guide for Law Enforcement* (Washington, DC: U.S. Department of Justice, 2000), pp. 41–42.
5. Ibid., pp. 42–43.
6. Collen Wade, ed., *Handbook of Forensic Services* (Washington, DC: Federal Bureau of Investigation, 1999), p. 92.
7. Ibid.
8. Ibid.

9. Raymond Murray and John Tedrow, *Forensic Geology* (New Brunswick, NJ: Rutgers University Press, 1975), pp. 17–19.
10. Ibid., p. 23.
11. M. Horrocks and K. J. Walsh, "Pollen on Grass Clippings: Putting the Suspect at the Scene," *Journal of Forensic Sciences,* 2001, Vol. 46, No. 4, pp. 947–949.
12. Murray and Tedrow, *Forensic Geology,* p. 25.
13. Wade, *Handbook of Forensic Services,* pp. 92–93.
14. Barry A. J. Fisher, *Techniques of Crime Scene Investigation,* 6th ed. (Boca Raton, FL, CRC Press, 2000), p. 251.
15. Ibid.
16. Wade, *Handbook of Forensic Services,* pp. 85–86.
17. Fisher, *Techniques of Crime Scene Investigation,* p. 254.
18. Wade, *Handbook of Forensic Services,* p 87.
19. Ibid.
20. Fisher, *Techniques of Crime Scene Investigation,* p. 254.
21. Wade, *Handbook of Forensic Services,* p. 91.
22. Ibid.
23. Mike Byrd, *Crime Scene Evidence: A Guide to the Recovery and Collection of Physical Evidence* (Temecula, CA: Staggs Publishing, 2001), p. 70.
24. Ibid.
25. Fisher, *Techniques of Crime Scene Investigation,* p. 171.
26. Wade, *Handbook of Forensic Services,* p. 60.
27. Fisher, *Techniques of Crime Scene Investigation,* p. 173.
28. R. Koons and J. Buscaglia, "The Forensic Significance of Glass Composition and Refractive Index Measurements," *Journal of Forensic Sciences,* 1999, Vol. 44, No. 3, pp. 496–503.
28. F. Brewster, J. Thorpe, G. Gettinby, and B. Caddy, "The Retention of Glass Particles in Woven Fabrics," *Journal of Forensic Sciences,* 1985, Vol. 30, No. 3, pp. 798–805.
29. Zug Standing Bear, "Glass Examinations in Old and New Reflections," paper presented at the 1983 meeting of the American Academy of Forensic Sciences. Occasionally a defect in the glass itself may create unusual characteristics; see B. Burnette, "A Shot through the Window," *Journal of Forensic Sciences,* 2001, Vol. 46, No. 2, pp. 379–385.
30. Wade, *Handbook of Forensic Services,* p. 49.
31. Ibid.
32. Ibid.
33. Ibid.
34. Ibid.
35. Ibid.
36. Ibid.
37. For information on the laboratory approach to comparing such evidence, see K. Wiggins, "Recognition, Identification, and Comparison of Rope and Twine," *Science and Justice,* 1995, Vol. 35, No. 1, pp. 53–58.
38. Fisher, *Techniques of Crime Scene Investigation,* p. 100. For detailed technical information on the subject of developing latent prints, refer to T. A. Trozzi, R. L. Schwart, and M. L. Hollars, *Processing Guide for Developing Latent Prints* (Washington, DC: Federal Bureau of Investigation, 2000), p. 70.
39. Although the fingerprints of twins may have a high degree of similarity, variations still occur that permit their differentiation. See C. H. Lin, J. H. Liu, J. W. Osterburg, and J. D. Nicol, "Fingerprint Comparison I: Similarity of Fingerprints," *Journal of Forensic Sciences,* 1982, Vol. 27, No. 2, pp. 290–304.
40. Fisher, *Techniques of Crime Scene Investigation,* pp. 103–104.
41. Saferstein, *Criminalistics,* p. 397.
42. Ibid., p. 401.
43. Ibid., p. 117.
44. A. J. Brooks, "The Search for Latent Prints When an Offender Wears Gloves," *Fingerprint and Identification Magazine,* 1972, Vol. 53, No. 12, pp. 3–7, 15–16.
45. Fisher, *Techniques of Crime Scene Investigation,* pp. 105–106.
46. J. E. Watkin and A. H. Misner, "Fluorescence and Crime Scenes in the 90s," *RCMP Gazette,* 1990, Vol. 52, No. 9, p. 1.
47. James Osterburg and Richard H. Ward, *Criminal Investigation* (Cincinnati, OH: Anderson Publishing, 1992), p. 109. For general information on the subject, see S. Clark, "Chemical-Detection of Latent Fingerprints," *Journal of Chemical Education,* July 1993, Vol. 70, No. 7, pp. 593–595.
48. Richard Saferstein, *Criminalistics,* 4th ed. (Englewood Cliffs, NJ: Prentice-Hall, 1990), p. 378.
49. Osterberg and Ward, *Criminal Investigation,* p. 110.
50. E. Roland Menzel, "Applications of Laser Technology in Latent Print Enhancement," in Henry C. Lee and R. E. Gaensslen, *Advances in Fingerprint Technology* (Boca Raton, FL: CRC Press, 1994), p. 136.

51. This section is drawn from Ivan Ross Futrell, "Hidden Evidence: Latent Prints on Human Skin," *FBI Law Enforcement Bulletin*, April 1996, pp. 21–24.
52. The author of this section on dental evidence is Dr. Richard R. Souviron, Chief Forensic Odontologist, Dade County Medical Examiner Department, One Bob Hope Road, Miami, FL 33136-1133, (305-545-2400). His private practice number is 305-445-4956. Dr. Souviron graciously submitted more material than could be used in this book. His portion of the manuscript was, therefore, subject to editing. Any editing that may have unintentionally changed the meaning intended by him is the responsibility of the present authors.
53. Wade, *Handbook of Forensic Services*, p. 49.
54. C. A. Linch, S. Smith, and J. A. Prahlow, "Evaluation of Human Hair Root for DNA Typing Subsequent to Microscopic Comparison," *Journal of Forensic Sciences*, Vol. 43, No. 2, pp. 305–314.
55. Henry C. Lee, Timothy Palmbach, and Marilyn T. Miller, *Crime Scene Handbook* (San Diego: Academic Press, 2001), p. 151.
56. J. Andrasko and B. Stocklassa, "Shampoo Residue Profiles in Human Head Hair," *Journal of Forensic Sciences*, May 1990, Vol. 35, No. 3, pp. 569–579.
57. N. Tanada, S. Kashimura, M. Kageura, and K. Hara, "Practical GC/MS Analysis of Oxidation Dye Components in Hair Fiber as a Forensic Investigative Procedure," *Journal of Forensic Sciences*, 1999, Vol. 44, No. 2, pp. 292–296.
58. S. Kage, K. Kudo, A. Kaizoji, J. Ryumoto, H. Ikeda, and N. Ikeda, "A Simple Method for Detection of Gunshot Residue Particles from Hands, Hair, Face, and Clothing Using Scanning Electron Microscopy/Wave Length Dispersive X-Ray," *Journal of Forensic Sciences*, 2001, Vol. 46, No. 4, pp. 830–834.
59. This determination is possible across a range of drugs. For example, see C. Moore, D. Deitermann, D. Lewis, B. Feeley, and R. Niedbala, "The Detection of Cocaine in Hair Specimens Using Micro-Plate Immunoassay," *Journal of Forensic Sciences*, 1999, Vol. 44, No. 3, p. 609–612.
60. P. Kintz, B. Ludes, and P. Mangin, "Evaluation of Nicotine and Cotinine in Human Hair," *Journal of Forensic Sciences*, 1992, Vol. 37, No. 1, pp. 72–76.
61. D. Exline, F. P. Smith, and S. Drexler, "The Frequency of Pubic Hair Transfer during Sexual Intercourse," *Journal of Forensic Sciences*, 1998, Vol. 43, No. 3, pp. 505–508. This study concluded that pubic-hair transfers occur 17.3 percent of the time. However, it was based on a relatively small sample of consenting heterosexual couples and may not be representative of forcible rapes.
62. Lee, Palmbach, and Miller, *Crime Scene Handbook*, p. 282.
63. M. Cox, "Effect of Fabric Washing on the Presumptive Identification of Bloodstains," *Journal of Forensic Sciences*, November 1990, Vol. 35, No. 6, pp. 1335–1341.
64. Wade, *Handbook of Forensic Services*, pp. 26–30, with additional commentary by the authors.
65. J. Andrasko, "Forensic Analysis of Lipsticks," *Forensic Science International*, 1981, Vol. 17, No. 3, pp. 235–251.
66. L. G. Webb, S. E. Egan, and G. R. Turbett, "Recovery of DNA for Forensic Analysis from Lip Cosmetics," *Journal of Forensic Sciences*, 2001, Vol. 46, No. 6, pp. 1474–1479.
67. Mary Lee Schnuth, "Focus on Forensics: Lip Prints," *FBI Law Enforcement Bulletin*, November 1992, Vol. 61, No. 11, pp. 18–19.
68. O. C. Smith, L. Jantz, H. E. Berryman, and S. A. Symes, "Effects of Human Decomposition on Striations," *Journal of Forensic Sciences*, 1993, Vol. 38, No. 3, pp. 593–598.
69. See R. Thomas, "Contribution to the Identification of Smooth Bore Firearms," *International Criminal Police Review*, 1974, Vol. 28, No. 280, pp. 190–193.
70. Saferstein, *Criminalistics*, pp. 432–433.
71. There are some unique exceptions to determining proximity by gunpowder residues. At one time a compressed-air explosive-propellant .22 caliber was commercially available and used caseless ammunition; as no nitrates were present in the discharge residues, this method was voided. See H. L. MacDonell and V. J. Fusco, "An Unusual Firearm Suicide Case," *Canadian Society of Forensic Science Journal*, 1975, Vol. 8, No. 2, pp. 53–55.
72. J. Andrasko and S. Stahling, "Time Since Discharge of Rifles," *Journal of Forensic Sciences*, Vol. 45, No. 6, pp. 1250–1255.
73. Saferstein, *Criminalistics*, p. 441.
74. Ibid.
75. H. S. Maheshwari, "Influence of Vertical Angle of a Tool on Its Tool Mark," *Forensic Science International*, 1981, Vol. 18, No. 1, pp. 5–12.
76. Michael Davis, "Pensioners Suing Texas Gas Claim Signatures Faked," *Houston Post*, May 8, 1994, p. D1.
77. "Tax Report: Warning," *Wall Street Journal*, May 25, 1994, p. A1. Reprinted by permission of Dow Jones,

Inc., via Copyright Clearance Center, Inc. © 1994 Dow Jones and Company, Inc. All rights reserved worldwide.

78. Michael Beckerman, "All Right, So Maybe Haydn Didn't Write Them. So What?" *New York Times*, May 15, 1994, p. 33.

79. See Ethan Michaeli, "Cops Put End to Fake ID Operation," *Chicago Defender*, January 28, 1993, p. 3; "Business Bulletin: Cunning Copiers," *Wall Street Journal*, Dec. 31, 1992, p. A1; Alexandra Peers, "Your Money Matters: Forgeries Are Coming to Bat More Often as Sports Memorabilia Prices Hit Homer," *Wall Street Journal*, Aug. 14, 1992, p. C1; Beth Potter, "2 Brothers Arrested in Lift-Ticket Forgeries," *Denver Post*, Feb. 20, 1992, p. B1; Michael A. Smith, "Bogus Auto Inspection Stickers Increase," *Houston Post*, Jan. 3, 1992, p. A14; Peter Mantius, "High-Tech Forgeries Easy, Hard to Detect," *Atlanta Journal and Constitution*, Nov. 26, 1993, p. D8.

80. Saferstein, *Criminalistics*, p. 453.

81. Wade, *Handbook of Forensic Services*, pp. 69–75, is the source of information in this section.

82. Ibid., p. 73.

83. F. J. Gerhart, "Identification of Photocopiers from Fusing Roller Defects," *Journal of Forensic Sciences*, January 1992, Vol. 37, No. 1, pp. 130–139.

84. Wade, *Handbook of Forensic Services*, p. 74.

85. Ibid.

86. A. Lofgren and J. Andrasko, "HPLC Analysis of Printing Inks," *Journal of Forensic Sciences*, May 1993, Vol. 38, No. 5, pp. 1151–1160.

87. L. F. Stewart, "Artificial Aging of Documents," *Journal of Forensic Sciences*, February 1982, Vol. 27, No. 2, pp. 450–453.

88. Wade, *Handbook of Forensic Services*, p. 74.

89. Ibid., pp. 74–75.

90. Federal Bureau of Investigation, *Handbook of Forensic Science* (Washington, DC: Government Printing Office, 1992), pp. 76–77.

# FOUR

# Interviewing and Interrogation

*When they respond to domestic violence calls, partners often interview spouses separately—as the two officers are doing here—and compare notes later. (Courtesy Donna Ferrato, Domestic Abuse Awareness Project)*

## CHAPTER OUTLINE



## CHAPTER OBJECTIVES

1. Understand the differences and similarities between interviews and interrogation.
2. Outline the steps in preparing for an interview and an interrogation.
3. Assess the challenges in relying on eyewitness identification.
4. Explain the role of hypnosis in criminal investigation.
5. Describe Neuro-Linguistic Programming.
6. Identify interviewing processes and techniques.
7. Explain the impact of *Miranda* v. *Arizona* and other landmark Supreme Court cases on police interrogation.
8. Identify interrogation processes and techniques.
9. Understand the methods and importance of documenting an interview and interrogation.
10. Explain the importance of listening during an interview and interrogation.

# INTRODUCTION

The business of the police is people. While police rely on people to report and help solve crimes, every facet of police work is concerned with the problems of people. The job of the criminal investigator is no exception. People and the information they supply help accomplish investigative tasks; collecting information is the key investigative task of police work. Roughly 90 percent of an investigator's activity involves gathering, sorting, compiling, and evaluating information. The investigator cannot function without information, and information cannot be obtained without help from people. In short, people are the most valuable resource in any criminal investigation.

In every criminal investigation process, interviewing and interrogation are the most important means of obtaining needed information about a crime. Both require a combination of artistry and skill that must be cultivated and practiced. Not all people who possess information needed by the investigator are willing to share it. This is true in both interviews and interrogations. Witnesses may have various motivations and perceptions, for example, that could influence their responses during an interview. The motivations and perceptions may be based on either conscious choices or subconscious stimuli. In addition, gaining information from specific demographic groups such as the elderly and children requires unique skills on the part of the investigator. Situational characteristics such as the time and place of the interview or interrogation may also create challenges to eliciting information about a particular case. Each of these conditions must be effectively addressed in both interview and interrogation settings. The successful interviewer or interrogator must fully understand the techniques of interviewing and interrogation and be able to evaluate the psychological reasons why people are willing or reluctant to impart information.

The interviewer or interrogator must recognize his or her own capabilities and limitations. Personality and the manner in which interpersonal communications are handled can greatly influence the quality and quantity of information obtained. He or she must be able to convey various emotions at appropriate times but must always remain objective and keep an open mind. Above all, the successful interviewer or interrogator must have an insatiable curiosity.

## OBJECTIVES OF INTERVIEWING

Interviews are conducted in criminal cases for the purpose of gathering information from people who have or may have knowledge needed in the investigation. The information may come from a victim or from a person who has no other relationship to the criminal activity other than being where he or she was. But interviewing is not a haphazard process consisting of a list of questions. It is a planned conversation with a specific goal.

The job of the investigator-interviewer is to extract from the witness information actually perceived through one or more of the witness's five senses—sight, hearing, smell, taste, and touch. In any given case, any or all of a witness's senses may be involved. For example, in a case involving a drug-related killing, a witness may see the perpetrator pull the trigger, hear the victim scream, smell the pungent odor of marijuana burning, taste the white powdery substance later identified as heroin, and touch the victim to feel for a pulse.

Because witnesses report perceptions based on their own interests, priorities, and biases, extracting information from witnesses is not as easy as it may first appear. Investigators must always be sensitive to any and all psychological influences and motivations affecting witness perceptions, the specifics of which are discussed in the next section.

At the outset of the interview, the person to be interviewed must satisfy three requirements of being a witness: presence, consciousness, and attentiveness to what was happening.[1] Presence and consciousness are relatively easy to establish in the interview process; attentiveness is more difficult. Yet all three elements are important to establishing the accuracy of a witness's perception.

## OBJECTIVES OF INTERROGATION

As part of an investigation, interviewing is the process of obtaining information from people who possess knowledge about a particular offense. Interrogation is designed to match acquired information to a particular suspect to secure a confession. Another way to describe this difference is that interviewing is primarily for the purpose of gaining information, whereas interrogation is the process of testing that information and its application to a particular suspect.

There are four commonly recognized objectives in the interrogation process. They are:

1. To obtain valuable facts.
2. To eliminate the innocent.
3. To identify the guilty.
4. To obtain a confession.

As the investigator moves from the preliminary task of gathering valuable facts to the concluding task of obtaining a confession, there is an increase in the difficulty of acquiring information. That difficulty, however, is rewarded by an increase in the value of the information. Figure 4–1 illustrates these relationships. In attempting to obtain a confession from a suspect, the interrogator also gains information about the facts and circumstances surrounding the commission of an offense. In seeking such information, the investigator must be concerned with asking the basic questions that apply to all aspects of the investigative process: Who? What? Where? When? How? With what? Why? With whom? How much?

## INTERVIEWS AND INTERROGATIONS: SIMILARITIES AND DIFFERENCES

As in interviewing, the success of an interrogation depends on a number of personal characteristics and commitments of the investigator. Planning for and controlling the events surrounding both interviews and interrogations are important but are generally viewed as more critical to the success of an interrogation. Establishing rapport, asking good questions, listening carefully, and keeping proper documentation are elements common to both forms of obtaining information. Table 4–1 illustrates the similarities between interviews and interrogations.

Besides the difference in purpose between interviewing and interrogation, many other distinctions exist. Of paramount importance are the myriad of legal requirements that pertain to interrogations but are absent in interviews. Because of the criticality of confessions and their use in obtaining convictions, it is not surprising that numerous legal guidelines and

**Figure 4-1** Objectives of Interrogation

**Source:** John Fay, unpublished notebook, American Society for Industrial Security, Workshop in Criminal Interrogation (Jacksonville, FL: ASIS, 1981), p. A2-1.

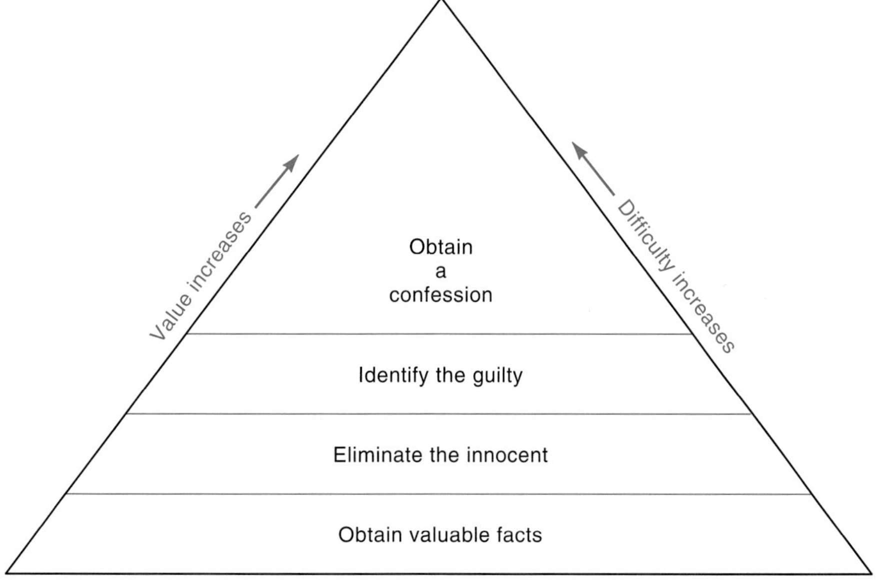

Table 4-1 Similarities between Interviews and Interrogations

| Interviews | Interrogations |
|---|---|
| Planning important | Planning critical |
| Controlling surroundings important | Controlling surroundings critical |
| Privacy or semiprivacy desirable | Absolute privacy essential |
| Establishing rapport important | Establishing rapport important |
| Asking good questions important | Asking good questions important |
| Careful listening | Careful listening |
| Proper documentation | Proper documentation |

standards apply in interrogations that would not be needed in interviewing witnesses or victims. Of course, it is more likely that a hostile and adversary relationship will exist between an interrogator and a suspect than between an interviewer and a victim or witness. The differences between interviews and interrogations are noted in Table 4–2.

## QUALIFICATIONS OF INTERVIEWERS AND INTERROGATORS

The effective interviewer or interrogator must be knowledgeable in the art and science of criminal investigation and know how to use psychology, salesmanship, and dramatics. Persuasiveness and perseverance are essential to success. The interviewer or interrogator must make himself or herself easy to talk to. By the appropriate use of vocal inflection, modulation, and emphasis, even the *Miranda* warnings can be presented to a suspect in a manner that does not cause the suspect to immediately assume a defensive posture. The words can be spoken without creating an adversarial atmosphere. The interviewer or interrogator must have a flexible personality and must be able to convey empathy, sympathy, anger, fear, and joy at appropriate times, but he or she must always remain objective. It is important that the interviewer or interrogator keep an open mind and be receptive to all information, regardless of its nature.

A positive, firm approach, an ability to inspire confidence, and knowledge of a broad range of topics of general interest all help establish dominance or control in an interview:

Table 4-2 Differences between Interviews and Interrogations

| Interviews | Interrogations |
|---|---|
| Purpose is to obtain information | Purpose is to test information already obtained |
| Minimal or no preinterview legal requirements; no rights warning | Extensive preinterrogation legal requirements; rights warning required |
| Cooperative relationship between interviewer and subject likely | Adversarial or hostile relationship between interrogator and suspect likely |
| No guilt or guilt uncertain | Guilt suggested or likely |
| Moderate planning or preparation | Extensive planning and preparation |
| Private or semiprivate environment desirable | Absolute privacy essential |

**Source:** John Fay, unpublished notebook, American Society for Industrial Security, Workshop in Criminal Interrogation (Jacksonville, FL: ASIS, 1981), p. A1-1.

**BEHAVIOR** not words, determines dominance. Good interviewers know that an air of confidence and ease typifies the behavior of truly dominant people; they are inclined to do as they please without asking permission and rarely offend others while doing so. On the other hand, arrogance and pomposity, characteristics often intended to pass for dominance, do not create dominance. They sometimes provide amusement, but more often than not, anger the people subjected to such behavior.[2]

In an interrogation, the investigator must carefully evaluate each development during the interrogation while studiously avoiding the pitfall of underestimating the capabilities of the subject being interrogated. Screaming or shouting, belittling the subject or the information, sneering, and other such unplanned and uncontrolled reactions most often adversely affect the interrogation. The investigator must at all times maintain control of the interrogation without being openly domineering, by being a good active listener, by being serious, by being patient, and, most importantly, by being persistent and persuasive.[3] An ability to categorize the psychological and emotional traits being manifested by the suspect helps the investigator react in a manner that increases the possibility of conducting a successful interrogation, for it is the job of the interrogator to make it easy for a suspect to confess.

## PREPARATION FOR THE INTERVIEW OR INTERROGATION

The success of the interviewer or interrogator and of the interview or interrogation will often be determined by the time and dedication committed to preparing for the conversation. The interviewer must become familiar with the facts of the case under investigation and with the victim. To carry out the four objectives listed earlier in the chapter, the interrogator must learn as much as possible about the offense, the victim(s), and the suspect through the process of collecting, assessing, and analyzing data and theorizing about the motivations and thought processes of the suspect. This begins the formulation of a profile that will then dictate the initial approach the interrogator will take upon first contacting the suspect.

### A WITNESS

If the interview is to be conducted with a **witness** other than the victim, the interviewer should find out as much about the witness as possible before the interview. This includes learning about the witness's motivations and perceptions and any barriers that might exist.

### THE OFFENSE

It is necessary that the interviewer know specifically what crime or crimes were allegedly committed. This knowledge includes a working familiarity with the elements of each offense and some understanding of the kind of information necessary to prove each. Accurate information on the date, time, place, and method of the crime—including tools used, points of entry and exit, method of travel to and from the scene, complete description of any property involved, weapons used, modus operandi, and physical evidence recovered—is essential. The interviewer should also obtain a full description of the crime scene and the surrounding area. Any and all possible motives should be identified.

### THE VICTIM

If the **victim** is a person, the interviewer should learn as much as possible about his or her background, the nature of the injury or loss, attitudes toward the investigation, and any other useful information, such as the existence of insurance in a property crime case. If the victim is an organization or business, a determination of any practices that would make the organization a criminal target could be extremely valuable. In addition, the interviewer should determine whether the business is insured against losses, if relevant.

### THE SUSPECT

The interrogator must evaluate himself or herself and the circumstances surrounding the conduct of the interrogation and must begin to evaluate the **suspect.** An effective interrogator will understand that a successful interrogation cannot be organized and compartmentalized into a neat, orderly, step-by-step package. Rather, it is a combination of personality, behavior, and interpersonal communication skills between the interrogator and suspect. It is made up of verbal processes and the way they are communicated, nonverbal actions including body language, and personality characteristics that together might be characterized as a psychological profile.[4] Only by understanding the interaction of all these variables can the interrogator effectively evaluate the interrogation process as it will be initiated and as it will be modified during the interrogation.[5] To begin the preparation, the interrogator should review the offense report, statement of witnesses, laboratory reports, all file information pertaining to the suspect, and other related data. It is also essential that the interrogator know all the elements of the offense involved. Failure to possess this information may preclude obtaining a complete confession, which, by definition, must contain admissions by the suspect to the commission of each and every element of the crime.

The investigation should reveal as much personal background information on the suspect as can be obtained. This should include aliases, Social Security number, date and place of birth, education, marital status, employment history, financial history and current circumstances, prior offenses, past and present physical and mental health, any drug or alcohol abuse or addiction, relationship to the victim or crime scene, possible motive, biases and prejudices, home environment, sexual interests (if relevant), and hobbies. Additionally, the investigation and preparation for an interrogation should determine whether the suspect had the capability and opportunity to commit the offense and should confirm or disprove an alibi.

The interrogator should also obtain as much information as possible from other people involved to determine the suspect's attitude. This will enable the interrogator to anticipate levels of hostility or cooperativeness during the interrogation. Figure 4–2 can serve as a review and checklist for the investigator's planning and interrogation.

## WITNESSES: MOTIVATIONS, PERCEPTIONS, AND BARRIERS

There are many types of witnesses, and each has different motivations and perceptions that influence his or her responses during an interview. The motivations and perceptions may be based on either conscious choices or subconscious stimuli. The interviewer must learn to recognize, overcome, and compensate for these factors.

There is no way to categorize all personalities, attitudes, and other character traits. The variables are too numerous and individualized; the combinations are as complex as the human mind. Nevertheless, there are some basic groupings that can be mentioned:

- Some witnesses may be honest and cooperative and desire to impart information in their possession to the investigator. Despite these admirable qualities, however, the information may still be affected by other factors that influence all witnesses, such as age, physical characteristics, and emotions. It may be wise in most circumstances to interview this type of witness first to obtain basic information that can then be compared with later-acquired stories.
- Some witnesses may desire not to give any information in an interview regardless of what they know. Some of these witnesses simply may not want to get involved, others may fear any contact with a law enforcement agency, some may not understand the significance of information they have, and others may not want to do anything that would aide the police.
- Some witnesses may be reluctant to cooperate or be suspicious of the motives of the interviewer until a rapport is established and the investigator can assure the witness of his or her good intentions.

Because there are witnesses who may be deceitful and provide incorrect information, it is a basic principle that an investigator should never take a witness's explanation totally at face value but, rather, should obtain supporting information or evidence.

There may be other barriers that must be overcome in order to successfully interview someone who has knowledge of the circumstances under which a crime was committed. Language barriers, which may not initially be recognized as significant, may prevent the interviewer from obtaining any useful information; on the other hand, some people may be so talkative and provide so much information

**Figure 4-2** Preinterrogation Checklist

**Source:** John Fay, unpublished notebook, American Society for Industrial Security, Workshop in Criminal Interrogation (Jacksonville, FL: ASIS, 1981), p. A4-1.

| Do You Have These Facts Regarding the Crime? | | Check Here |
|---|---|---|
| 1 | The legal description of the offense | |
| 2 | The value and nature of loss | |
| 3 | Time, date, and place of occurrence | |
| 4 | Description of crime scene and surrounding area | |
| 5 | Physical evidence collected | |
| 6 | Weather conditions at time of offense | |
| 7 | Specific entry/exit points of perpetrator | |
| 8 | Approach and departure routes of perpetrator | |
| 9 | Methods of travel to and from scene | |
| 10 | The modus operandi of the perpetrator | |
| 11 | The tools or weapons used | |
| 12 | Names of persons having knowledge | |
| 13 | Possible motive | |
| 14 | Details from other case files that<br>a. point to particular suspects | |
| | b. show matching modi operandi | |
| | c. suggest a pattern of criminality | |

that their motives should be questioned, along with the information they provide. A potential witness who may be under the influence of alcohol or drugs may or may not have information that could be used at trial, but the condition of the witness is a major factor to be considered in assessing the value of any information obtained.

## JUVENILES

In evaluating information provided by juveniles, consideration needs to be given not only to chronological age but also to the level of schooling. In preschool juveniles, generally under 5 or 6 years of age, verbal ability is still being developed as the primary means of communication and recall ability tends to be underdeveloped. Hence, accounts of an event may be rambling and disjointed as well as accompanied by poor distinction between relevant and irrelevant data and by a limited ability to comprehend abstract concepts. A child at this age generally can focus only on one thought at a time and cannot combine thoughts into an integrated whole. The child may have a short attention span, occasional problems in differentiating between what was seen and what was heard, and difficulty distinguishing between fact and fantasy.

Verbal ability improves with the growth of vocabulary and is strongly influenced by peer groups.

These are, of course, products (or byproducts) of schooling affecting juveniles between 6 and 18 years of age. Abstract concepts are learned through trial-and-error evaluations rather than an understanding of cause-and-effect relationships. Recall ability improves with age and maturity but develops differently for males and females. For example, males can recall the make and model of an automobile more accurately, while females can generally recall colors and clothing more accurately. (For a more detailed discussion of interviewing children, see Chapter 11, "Crimes against Children.")

The emotional characteristics exhibited by children are another factor that can affect the content and quality of information gleaned. Some children are expressive; they are outgoing and verbal. Other children are controlled and are timid and nonverbal. Expressive children often speak with ease on a range of topics and may, at times, be too talkative. Controlled children are generally quiet and do not show their feelings. They frequently avoid eye contact and keep their heads or bodies turned away from interviewers.[6] (See photo below)

### Interviewing Juveniles

The investigator is showing a boy a photograph of a suspect, hoping that he will recognize him and be able to say where the suspect lives, hangs out, or "runs" with. Although information provided by juveniles can be problematic, it can sometimes be crucial to solving a case.

(Courtesy New York City Police Department)

## SENIOR CITIZENS

Interviewing an older person may also present a unique set of challenges. The interviewer must have knowledge of and appreciation for the physical changes that may occur with aging and be able to effectively respond to those changes when conducting an interview.[7]

### Vision

Changes in vision that are related to aging vary widely from person to person. These changes are not strictly dependent on chronological age or general health. The eye is so constructed that excellent vision without glasses is sometimes maintained even in extreme old age. However, this is an exception. About three-fourths of all older women and over half of all older men experience moderate to severe changes in visual functions. Those 65 or older account for half of all legally blind persons in the United States. The simple statistical probabilities are that an older person will have vision difficulties of one kind or another.

There are many ways in which investigators can help people with poor vision. In any written communications—letters, memos, or signs—large lettering should be used, and the focus should be on conveying important information rather than including too many details.

Farsightedness is a condition that facilitates the ability to see distant objects clearly but makes it more difficult to focus on objects at close range. Because of farsightedness problems, the identification of a purse snatcher, for example, may be a problem, since the only opportunity the elderly person may have to recognize the suspect occurs when the thief is at a very close proximity. In contrast, when the elderly are nearsighted, they may need to hold objects closely to see them clearly.

Older persons are twice as likely as the rest of the population to wear glasses to facilitate reading. However, the fact that an older person is wearing glasses does not necessarily mean that he or she has adequately compensated for vision changes. For example, the eyeglass prescription may be outdated, or dirty glasses may be interfering with clear vision. Therefore, when an investigator is assisting an older person who is nearsighted or farsighted, positioning is important. The most suitable distance will vary from individual to individual.

## Hearing

Hearing loss resulting in a distortion of sounds generally is caused by changes in the inner ear. A person who suffers from a hearing loss must take advantage of every opportunity to use other skills in communicating, such as speech reading. Speech reading, often thought of as "lip reading," is the process of visually receiving cues from all lip movements, facial expressions, body posture, gestures, and the environment. Speech reading is a skill everyone has to a certain degree. It is only when hearing becomes impaired that this skill becomes important.

Interviewers will be able to communicate most effectively and patiently with hearing-impaired people by following these suggestions:

- *Gain attention:* The investigator should wait until he or she is visible to the older person before speaking. The investigator should attract the older person's attention by facing the person and looking straight into his or her eyes or by touching the person's hands or shoulders lightly. The environment should be arranged so that the speaker's face and body can be seen easily and clearly. Good lighting on the speaker's face is important. Facial expressions, gestures, and lip and body movements serve to illustrate the verbal message. Chewing, eating, or covering the mouth with a hand or a piece of paper minimizes effective communication.
- *Be at the right distance:* When speaking to an older person, the investigator should be between 3 and 6 feet from the person.
- *Speak clearly:* The investigator should carefully monitor his or her speaking voice for volume, pitch, pace, and enunciation and should speak slightly louder than normal if necessary. A low-pitched voice is often easier to hear; older persons may have difficulty understanding the higher-pitched voices of women and children. The investigator should speak at a moderate pace, but if there is to be a change in subject, a new name, a number, or an unusual word, it should be communicated at a slower rate. Sounds should not be exaggerated when speaking because this tends to distort the message and makes visual cues from the face difficult to understand.
- *Reinforce and rephrase:* Whenever possible, the investigator should give a clue about the topic of the conversation. If the older person does not appear to understand what is being said, the statement should be rephrased in short, simple sentences. The investigator should not repeat the whole sentence. Some persons with hearing loss are unduly sensitive about the handicap and pretend to understand when they do not. An investigator who detects this situation should tactfully repeat the communication using different words until he or she is certain the person understood. The investigator should use gestures and objects to reinforce messages.
- *Control noises:* Communication with a hearing-impaired older person is much more difficult when there is a great deal of environmental noise.
- *Encourage participation:* The older person should be encouraged to communicate. Because a hearing-impaired person takes longer to respond, the investigator should allow an appropriate amount of time for the person to answer a question.

In many ways a hearing loss can have a greater impact than a loss of vision. Many people seem to have less patience and sympathy for those who cannot hear well than they do for those with vision impairments. Because of this, people with hearing losses may pretend to understand. Hearing loss is very strongly related to feelings of depression and suspicion. The isolation that can result from a declining ability to communicate detracts from the quality of life. By using the skills that help offset hearing impairments, an investigator can communicate more effectively with anyone who needs to understand and be understood.

Because a witness's information also must be evaluated in light of its potential value in court, the interviewer must evaluate the witness's competency and credibility. (These concepts are treated in more detail in Chapter 21, "The Investigator and the Legal System.")

## COMPETENCY OF A WITNESS

The term **competency** refers to a witness's personal qualifications for testifying in court. It must be determined before he or she is permitted to give any testimony. The witness's personal qualification depends on circumstances that affect his or her legal ability to function as a sworn witness in court. Competency has nothing to do with the believability of a witness's information.

Among the factors an investigator must evaluate in determining the competency of a witness are age, level of intelligence, mental state, relationship to individuals involved in the case, and background characteristics that might preclude the testimony of the witness from being heard in court. For example, in many jurisdictions, a young child cannot be a witness unless it can be shown that the child knows the difference between truth and imagination and understands the importance of telling the truth. Chronological age is not the determining factor. Similarly, any person whose intelligence or mental state prevents him or her from understanding the obligation of telling the truth is not permitted to testify, regardless of the information he or she may possess.

Relationships among individuals involved in a case may also affect a witness's competency. Husbands and wives need not testify against each other, nor may attorneys testify against clients, doctors against patients, or ministers against penitents. Privileges vary by state (see Chapter 21, "The Investigator and the Legal System"). Background characteristics also may preclude a witness's testimony from being accepted in court. For example, some state laws forbid a convicted perjurer from testifying in court.

Possibilities like those described in the preceding paragraphs mean that the investigator must learn as much as possible about the witness before and during the interview.

## CREDIBILITY

**Credibility** is distinguished from competency in that the latter is based on the assumption that a witness is qualified and will be permitted to testify. Credibility relates to that quality of a witness that renders his or her testimony worthy of belief. Credibility in this sense is the same as weight or believability. The credibility of a witness is established in terms of presence, consciousness, and attentiveness during the interviewing process. An investigator must examine each of these requirements carefully and in detail. Among the questions to which the interviewer must receive satisfactory answers in evaluating the credibility of a witness are:

- Was the witness conscious at the time of the event?
- Was the witness under the influence of alcohol or drugs?
- How did the witness happen to be in a position of seeing, hearing, or otherwise perceiving the crime?
- Where was the witness coming from or going to?
- What was the witness doing at the exact moment that the crime occurred?
- What else was going on at the time that might have distracted the witness's attention?

The rules of evidence, which guide the admissibility and use of witnesses and their testimony in court, also guide the impeachment or attack by the opposing side on cross-examination of a witness's testimony (see Chapter 21, "The Investigator and the Legal System"). The investigator-interviewer must be aware of these factors to prevent the witnesses who appear for the state from being impeached. To do this, the investigator must ascertain the truth of the following:

- Does the witness have any particular bias, prejudice, or personal interest in the case?
- Does the witness have any physical or mental impairments that may affect his or her ability to observe, recollect, or recount the events? (Does the witness normally wear glasses? Was the witness wearing them at the time? Does the witness have a hearing problem?)
- What physical conditions, such as weather, lighting, and visibility, existed at the crime scene?
- What is the witness's reputation for being a truthful person?

The effective interviewer cannot accept any witness's account at face value. The interviewer must question and requestion, check and recheck. The investigator must recognize and gauge the effects that physical and emotional characteristics, external influences, and attitudinal and behavioral factors have on the witness's perception and on the reliability of the information possessed.

## EYEWITNESS IDENTIFICATION

### RELIABILITY OF EYEWITNESS IDENTIFICATION

**Eyewitness identification** and other information provided by eyewitnesses to a criminal event are relied on heavily by both the police and courts in the investigative and adjudication stages of our system of justice,[8] yet research indicates that eyewitness testimony may be unreliable.[9] (See photo on page 132.)

> EYEWITNESS identification and description is regarded as the most unreliable form of evidence and causes more miscarriages of justice than any other method of proof.[10]

> RESEARCH and courtroom experience provide ample evidence that an eyewitness to a crime is being asked to be something and do something that a normal human being was not created to be or do. Human perception is sloppy and uneven.[11]

> EXISTING research does not permit precise conclusions about the overall accuracy of the eyewitness identifications that are a common feature of criminal prosecutions, but research does lead us to conclude that identification errors are not infrequent.[12]

The point raised in the final quote above has been borne out by case studies in which the use of DNA evidence exonerated people who had been convicted on the basis of eyewitness identification.[13]

Many factors influence an individual's ability to accurately recognize and identify persons, and all of them depend on the circumstances under which the information is initially perceived and encoded, stored, and retrieved.[14] Eyewitness identifications take place in a social context[15] in which the witness's own personality and characteristics, along with those of the target observed, are as critical as factors relating to the situation or environment in which the action takes place.

The gender, age, expectations, intelligence, race, and facial recognition skills of the witness are factors that individually may or may not influence the eyewitness identification process but collectively or in combination with other variables are likely to have a bearing.[16] Facial attractiveness and distinctiveness, disguises, facial transformations, and the gender and race of the target (the person identified) are factors likely to influence identification.[17] Situational factors include such things as the presence of a weapon, exposure duration, and significance of the event in relation to all surrounding circumstances.[18]

Thus, human perception and memory are selective and constructive functions, not exact copiers of the event perceived—constructive in that gaps will be filled to produce a logical and complete sequence of events:

> PERCEPTION and memory are decision-making processes affected by the totality of a person's abilities, background, attitudes, motives, and beliefs, by the environment and the way his recollection is eventually tested. The observer is an active rather than a passive perceiver and recorder; he reaches conclusions on what he has seen by evaluating fragments of information and reconstructing them. He is motivated by a desire to be accurate as he imposes meaning on the overabundance of information that impinges on his senses, but also by a desire to live up to the expectations of other people and to stay in their good graces. The eye, the ear, and other sense organs are, therefore, social organs as well as physical ones.[19]

Agreeing with this theory of eyewitness perception, one observer notes:

> STUDIES of memory for sentences and pictures indicate that when we experience an event, we do not simply file a memory, and then on some later occasion retrieve it and read off what we've stored. Rather, at the time of recall or recognition we reconstruct the event, using information from many sources. These include both the original perception of the event and inferences drawn later, after the fact. Over a period of time, information from these sources may integrate, so that a witness becomes unable to say how he knows a specific detail. He has only a single unified memory.[20]

Experts distinguish a number of factors that limit a person's ability to give a complete account of events or to identify people accurately. The following are among those factors:

- *The significance or insignificance of the event:* When an insignificant event occurs in the presence of an individual, it does not generally motivate the individual to bring fully into play the selective process of attention.
- *The length of the period of observation:* If ample opportunity is not provided for observation, the capability of the memory to record that which is perceived is decreased.
- *Lack of ideal conditions:* In situations where ideal conditions for observation are absent, the ability of the witness to perceive details is significantly decreased. Distance, poor lighting, fast movement, or the presence of a crowd may significantly interfere with the efficient working of the attention process.
- *Psychological factors internal to the witness:* A witness under stress at the time of observation may find this to be a major source of unreliability in his or her observations.
- *The physical condition of the witness.*
- *Expectancy:* Research has shown that memory recall and judgment are often based on what psychologists term expectancy. This concept means that an individual perceives things in the manner in which he or she expects them to appear. For example, a right-handed eyewitness to a homicide might, in answer to a question and without positive knowledge, state that the assailant held the gun in his right hand, while a left-handed person might say the opposite. Biases or prejudices are also illustrated by the expectancy theory, as is the classic problem associated with stereotyping.[21]

In addition, there can be significant error even when two or more eyewitnesses provide similar descriptions:

> ONE might expect that two eyewitnesses—or ten or one hundred—who agree are better than one. Similarity of judgment is a two-edged sword, however; people can agree in error as easily as in truth. A large body of research results demonstrates that an observer can be persuaded to conform to the majority opinion even when the majority is completely wrong.[22]

In one test, people were asked to describe a mock crime they had viewed earlier. They first gave individual responses then met as a group. The group descriptions were more complete and in greater detail than those reported by individual subjects,

## Look-Alikes

Mistaken identifications led to the arrests of two innocent men: Lawrence Berson (*left*) for several rapes and George Morales (*right*) for a robbery. Both men were picked out of police lineups by victims of the crime. Berson was cleared when Richard Carbone (*center*) was arrested and implicated in the rapes. Carbone was convicted. Later he confessed to the robbery, clearing Morales.

**Source:** *Scientific American,* 1974, Vol. 231, No. 6, Reprinted by permission.

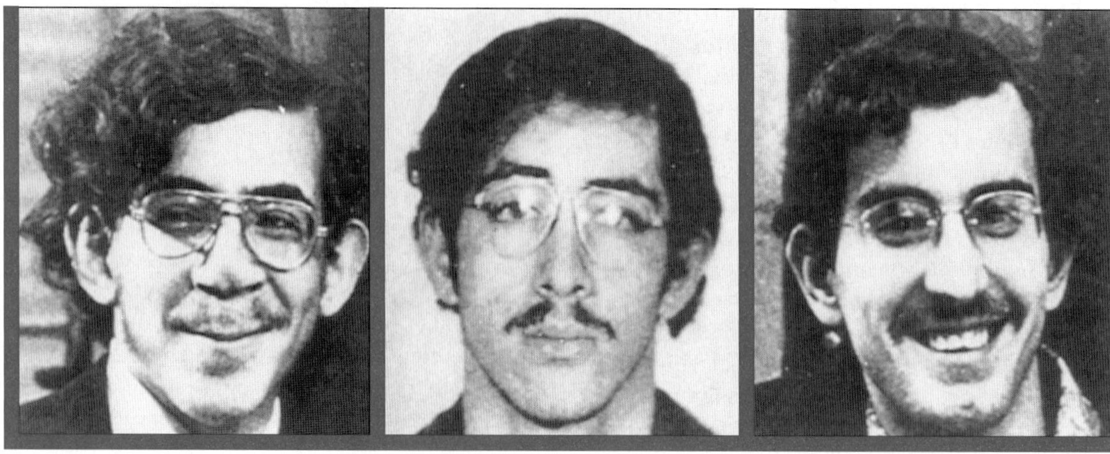

but the group descriptions also gave rise to significantly more errors as well as an assortment of incorrect and stereotyped details.[23]

An eyewitness's conduct can be influenced by expectations and inferences, which in turn can be influenced by the verbal and nonverbal behavior of investigators, the structure of the identification process, and the environment in which the identification takes place.[24] Much research has been conducted of lineups, showups, and photographic identifications, with a vast array of results indicating that such processes, by their nature, are suggestive, irrespective of whether the police intended them to be so or not.[25] For example, taking a victim or witness from one place to another to observe a person who has been arrested may be suggestive enough to produce a false identification. The fact that the police spend time putting together a photographic lineup may suggest that they have identified a perpetrator whose picture will be among those presented, regardless of whether such suggestiveness is intended by the police or not. The police may not even have a suspect.[26]

In summary, the problems associated with eyewitness identification can result in errors. Mistaken identifications of people, things, places, times, events, and other facts can result in miscarriages of justice. In some instances, these errors can be corrected.

Addressing the problem of eyewitness fallibility, in 1999 the National Institute of Justice issued protocols to be followed by law enforcement personnel in the effort to ensure the highest level of integrity in the eyewitness identification process. While the institute recognizes that accuracy cannot be guaranteed, its guidelines are designed to eliminate even inadvertent suggestibility from the eyewitness identification techniques employed by law enforcers. They cover a broad range of situations, including receiving a 911 call; initially arriving at the scene; conducting a follow-up investigation; reviewing mug books; developing composite drawings (by an artist or with a kit or a computer imaging system); returning a suspect to a scene for a showup; and conducting photographic and live lineups.[27]

The guidelines also briefly address some areas for future consideration. For example, scientific research indicates that identification procedures such as lineups and photo arrays produce more reliable evidence when the individual lineup members or photographs are shown to the witness one at a time, rather than simultaneously. (Thus, in the case illustrated by the photos on page 132, would identification have been more accurate if the photographs of all three men could have been shown to the individual victims sequentially? Even if the photos had been shown simultaneously, the results would have been interesting.[28]

Another area for future study involves unintentional cues. Psychology researchers point out that an investigator might provide an unintentional cue by body language, tone of voice, or other actions that would be suggestive to a witness. They believe that this could be avoided if lineups, showups, photo array, and the like, were conducted under "blind" conditions; that is, the identification procedure would be conducted by someone who does not know who the suspect is and therefore cannot do or say anything that would promote suggestibility.[29]

## THE LEGAL PERSPECTIVE OF EYEWITNESS IDENTIFICATION

Because eyewitness identification is so critical in obtaining a conviction in a criminal case and because of the problems associated with potential unreliability, there is no absence of judicial pronouncements on this issue. The problems were addressed by the U.S. Supreme Court in the 1960s and 1970s. In *Stoval* v. *Denno* (1967), the Court said that the police must follow recommended procedures to guarantee impartiality before, during, and after a lineup.[30]

In the 1972 case of *Neil* v. *Biggers,* the Supreme Court listed five factors to be used in determining the reliability of eyewitness identification, particularly in situations where identification is delayed rather than made immediately at the crime scene. These factors are:

- The opportunity of the witness to view the act at the time of the crime.
- The degree of attention paid by the witness.
- The accuracy of the witness's prior description of the criminal.
- The level of certainty of identification demonstrated by the witness at the confrontation.
- The length of time between the crime and the confrontation.[31]

*Manson* v. *Brathwaite,* decided in 1977, dealt with the corrupting effect of a suggestive eyewitness identification procedure.[32] The case produced the **Biggers-Brathwaite Factors Test,** which balances the five factors of *Biggers* with the "corrupting" effect of any suggestive procedures. As a result, if a police officer or an investigator accidentally does something that jeopardizes the fairness or impartiality of a procedure, the identification can still be used in court if the reliability of the eyewitness identification is strong.[33]

## HYPNOSIS AS AN INVESTIGATIVE TOOL

The use of **hypnosis** as a means of aiding witnesses in recalling facts buried in the subconscious is often thought to overcome many of the difficulties experienced in seeking accurate human memory. Although hypnosis can elicit many repressed and forgotten memories from witnesses to and victims of crimes, its use is not without problems. Theories suggesting that the human brain is like a videotape recorder—a machine that stores all experiences accurately and, when the right buttons are pushed, can be made to recall an "exact" copy of a prior event—are seriously challenged through research.[34] Moreover, both legal and scientific questions have been raised surrounding the reliability of hypnotically refreshed memory. The problems tend to focus on hypersuggestibility, hypercompliance, and confabulation.[35]

Hypnosis is often erroneously believed to be a form of sleep. In fact, it is the opposite. It is best described as a state of heightened awareness in which the subconscious is somewhat surfaced and the conscious is somewhat repressed. In this altered state of consciousness, the subject of hypnosis has a heightened degree of suggestibility, or **hypersuggestibility.** This raises perhaps the greatest concern about the admissibility of hypnosis evidence: The hypnotist has the potential to influence the subject; whether by design or not, he or she can suggest that the subject give false information or can mislead the subject into doing so.[36] There is virtual agreement among hypnosis experts that this can occur unless extreme caution is exercised. Subjects may come to believe such false information after hypnosis, and this could affect the truthfulness and reliability of any subsequent testimony given in court. Thus, many states refuse to admit testimony developed under hypnosis on the theory that even the witness may not know the truth after being subjected to suggestive influences while hypnotized.

The technique most frequently used in hypnosis is to suggest to the subject that he or she is reliving the event at issue but is doing so in a detached manner, as if watching it on a mental television screen. This is done to avoid a firsthand reinvolvement in a potentially traumatic experience. Nevertheless, a hypnotist may inadvertently suggest a response. Some studies conducted on suggestibility involve cases in which the subject was encouraged to picture a license plate and describe its numbers when, in fact, the witness had never seen the car;[37] a witness was asked to describe a suspect's facial features when, in actuality, those features had not been seen;[38] and the subject confessed to a crime he had not committed.[39]

**Hypercompliance,** closely related to hypersuggestibility, is a desire on the part of the hypnotized subject to please the hypnotist or others who have supported the hypnosis effort. Thus, the hypnotized subject may provide information or "facts" that are designed to please the listener and do not reflect the subject's actual memory of the event.[40]

The third major area of concern about reliability of hypnotically enhanced memory is **confabulation.** This is the process of artificially filling in the gaps when the actual memory is not as complete as the subject desires it to be. Thus, a witness who admits to being uncertain about his or her recollections when questioned about a matter before hypnosis may, in fact, become thoroughly convinced of the accuracy of those recollections after hypnosis. The recollections, however, may have been brought about by hypersuggestibility, hypercompliance, and confabulation, resulting in false memories.[41]

As a result of these concerns, U.S. courts have taken various positions on the subject of admissibility of hypnotically refreshed testimony.

### THE ADMISSIBILITY OF HYPNOSIS EVIDENCE

The forensic use of hypnosis gained popularity in the 1960s, yet courts addressing the issue of admissibility have continually disagreed on whether such testimony should be admissible and, if so, what standards and guidelines should be followed. There are a variety of judicial positions on the issue of admissibility among the states and the federal judicial circuits that have decided on this matter. In a minority of jurisdictions, hypnotically refreshed testimony is not admissible under any circumstances. Many jurisdictions have allowed the admissibility of prehypnosis testimony as long as that testimony is based on independent recall rather than solely on the product of a hypnosis session. Posthypnotic evidence is not admissible unless it agrees with the prehypnotic statements given by the witness.

Still other jurisdictions allow the admissibility of hypnosis evidence provided there are sufficient safeguards and standards, under the law, to ensure that the hypnotically produced testimony was obtained objectively and without a great deal of suggestivity. As research continues to reveal that suggestivity is highly probable and almost impossible to avoid,[42] the legal position of these jurisdictions is becoming more and more questionable. Some jurisdictions admit posthypnotic testimony and allow juries to weigh the evidence and determine its credibility.

### THE HYPNOTIST: LAW ENFORCEMENT OR MENTAL HEALTH PROFESSIONAL

One of the controversies still in existence is whether a hypnotist should be a mental health professional (preferably a psychiatrist or psychologist) with special training in the use of hypnosis or a trained law enforcement investigator, also with special training in the use of hypnosis. Those who argue for the latter position assume that the trained investigator will best know what questions need to be asked and can best evaluate the information obtained from hypnosis in the context of an ongoing criminal investigation. On the other hand, mental health professionals believe that law enforcement personnel cannot be trained regarding how to handle a mental health crisis that may occur during a hypnotic session.

As a consequence of all the research, many law enforcement jurisdictions are resorting to the use of hypnosis only as an investigative tool, without seeking to have the results be admissible in court.[43] As an investigative tool, hypnosis has proved to be most effective in many cases and continues to be supported.

## TIME, PLACE, AND SETTING OF THE INTERVIEW

Police officers conduct interviews in a number of situations. The most common is the on-the-scene interview. Whether it is a routine traffic accident investigation or a major felony case, officers who respond to the scene should, at the earliest possible moment, seek out and identify individuals who may have knowledge of the event and whose information may contribute to the investigation. Such individuals, of course, include victims and other participants as well as uninvolved witnesses. Once witnesses have been identified, they should be separated from one another and, as much as possible, isolated from other people who may be loitering in the area. This prevents the witnesses from seeing or hearing irrelevant matters that may taint their actual knowledge. All witnesses should be interviewed as soon as practical, while their memory is still fresh, but this rule must be applied with discretion to take into account all circumstances.

The physical circumstances under which the interview takes place can be critical to the value of the information obtained. Immediacy may have to be sacrificed in some instances due to lack of privacy, inconvenience, or physical discomfort of the witness. Conditions that tend to decrease the ability or desire of the witness to give full attention to the interview should be avoided. If such conditions exist, investigators may wisely choose to seek only basic preliminary information at the scene, followed by a more detailed interview at a more convenient time and place (see photo on page 136).

Although convenience of the witness is important to a successful interview, the interviewer need not relinquish the psychological advantage in selecting the time and place of the interview. It is not a good practice, for example, to rouse a witness from bed in the middle of the night. However, there are certain psychological advantages to questioning a witness at police headquarters rather than in the witness's own home or office. A witness may feel in a better position to control the interview in familiar surroundings. The investigator cannot let this happen; he or she must be fair but always be in command of the situation.

After taking into account the factors of immediacy, privacy, convenience, and control, and weighing

**Inside Interview**
The investigator wraps up an inside interview, giving the witness her card. On the desk is a mug book that the witness has been examining to see if he recognizes the suspect.
(Courtesy New York City Police Department)

the importance of each in the context of the total circumstances, it may be best to interview witnesses at their homes or places of business. As a matter of courtesy, the investigator should attempt to make an appointment to ensure convenience, particularly for professional and businesspeople. Others, such as salespeople, office workers, and laborers, may be interviewed during working hours with approval of their supervisors.

Privacy is of the utmost importance in conducting interviews. Distractions, whether in the home, office, or police station, tend to have an adverse effect on the interview and its results. The interviewer should insist on as much privacy as possible, but the circumstances of on-the-scene interviews often have to be recognized as a fact of life for the investigator, who can be expected to perform only to the best of his or her ability in the given case. Similarly, investigators are often called on to canvas neighborhoods and interview residents. In these instances, investigators often are in no position to influence the conditions under which the interview takes place. Noisy children, blaring television sets, nosy neighbors, and similar factors must be accepted.

The physical and emotional states of the witnesses are important in conducting or in determining whether to conduct an interview. "Cold, sleepy, hungry, or physically uncomfortable people generally prove to be unsatisfactory witnesses."[44] Similarly, persons suffering noticeable emotional problems can give, at the most, highly questionable information. Most investigators can recognize this state and wisely prefer to wait until the witness becomes lucid before conducting the interview.

Particular caution must be exercised in interviewing juveniles. In many jurisdictions parents must be notified of the purpose of the interview and the nature of the information sought from the juvenile. In other jurisdictions, notification may be recommended but not required. In some instances the presence of the parent during the interview is required or possibly desirable. Even when their presence is required, parents should not be allowed to distract or in any way influence the juvenile's responses. Local law should be consulted.

Reinterviewing witnesses should be avoided if the reinterview is likely to produce nothing beyond the information given in the initial statement. Reinterviewing tends to become less and less convenient for witnesses, even though they may be friendly and cooperative. There may also be a tendency for reinterviewed witnesses to feel that the investigator does not know his or her job or was not prepared during the initial interview. To avoid this problem, the investigator should first tell the witness that the purpose of the interview is not to rehash old information and should then explain what new information is being sought. The investigator should ask for the information in a manner that does not elicit a repetition of the previous interview. But investigators should not hesitate to conduct follow-up interviews when necessary, whether because there was lack of skill in obtaining an initial statement, new information has developed, or the time or setting of the initial interview did not elicit the full attention of the witness.

## TIME, PLACE, AND SETTING OF THE INTERROGATION

Unlike the interview, which may take place in any number of different locations and at various

**Traditional Interrogation Room**

The traditional interrogation room is typically bleak, with minimal furniture and nothing on the wall or anywhere else that a subject can use to divert the questioning. The very nature of the room communicates seriousness of the situation and the control the police have over a subject.

(Courtesy Dallas Police Department)

times—which may or may not be advantageous to the investigator—interrogation is a controlled process, controlled by the interrogator. The interrogator is in command of the setting. The interrogator governs the number and kinds of interruptions. The most critical factor in controlling the interrogation is to ensure privacy. Privacy guarantees that any distractions, planned or otherwise, are controlled by the interrogator. In addition, privacy may be used as a psychological tool; the suspect may feel more willing to unload the burden of guilt in front of only one person.

The traditional interrogation room should be sparsely furnished, usually with only two chairs. There should be no physical barriers, such as tables or desks, between the investigator and the suspect. From the officer's standpoint, such barriers may create an unwanted feeling of psychological well-being on the part of the suspect.

Notice the arrangement of the table and chairs in the photo above. They are corner to corner rather than on opposite sides. This arrangement permits the interrogator to move both chairs away from the table and eliminate the barrier.[45]

The two-way mirror, although still a useful tool for allowing others to observe the interrogation, is widely known and may cause some subjects to refuse to cooperate in the interrogation. If a two-way mirror is to be used, it should be small and unobstrusive. As a standard practice, the interrogation room should be equipped with a microphone connected to a recording device located somewhere nearby, unless prohibited by state law.

Although the traditional interrogation room just described is designed to ensure control and domination over the interrogation because of its privacy, security, and aura of authority, this approach does not impress the habitual or experienced offender, who understands the rules and standards of conduct of the classical interrogation room. If the offender is skilled and intelligent, he or she not only can cope with the psychological influences such a setting is designed to foster but perhaps can become the dominant force, or at least be on the same psychological level as the interrogator.

The national trend is to stick with the classical approach. Some experts, though, are attempting to overcome the "orientation" of the experienced offender by using a nontraditional interrogation room. This room is decorated like a fairly plush office or lounge. It is carpeted, paneled, and pleasantly furnished, and it has lighting fixtures capable of being controlled by rheostat for more or less intestity (see photo below).

The room is "off the beaten path," so that the subject is not led through a larger office where

**Nontraditional Interrogation Room**

The nontraditional interrogation room is very different from a traditional one. Here a couch, several seats, and a potted plant are seen. Wall colors and music that are calming, are selected for nontraditional interrogation rooms to relax suspects and to ease them into the questioning in a nonthreatening way.

(Courtesy Detective Thomas Streed, San Diego County Sheriff's Department)

The MOST CRITICAL FACTOR IN CONTROLLING THE INTERROGATION IS TO ENSURE PRIVACY

everyone is staring. Soft background music may be piped in and the room may be painted a color that either has a relaxing or calming effect or can increase blood pressure, respiration, perspiration, and brain-wave activity. The temperature in the room should be comfortable.

Interrogations of habitual offenders in settings like this have been successful because such a room is totally unexpected and the interrogation has already begun well before the subject realizes what is happening and before there is an opoprtunity for the subject's defense mechanisms to take hold and the deception to begin.[46]

## NEURO-LINGUISTIC PROGRAMMING

At the outset of any interview or interrogation, the investigator must establish **rapport.** If any useful information is to be forthcoming, the person being interviewed or interrogated must begin to identify with and trust the interviewer or interrogator and common grounds of communication must be established. In fact, the word rapport refers to a relationship or communication characterized by harmony.[47] Communication can be enhanced if the words and actions of the interviewer and interviewee are similar; thus, if the investigator "mirrors" the words and actions of the witness or suspect, rapport is more easily established.[48]

**Neuro-linguistic programming (NLP)** embraces three simple concepts. First, behavior orginates from neurological processes involving the five sense—seeing, hearing, smelling, tasting, and feeling. It is through these senses that we experience life. Then we communicate our life experiences through language, the linguistic element. Programming refers to how we organize our ideas and actions to produce results.[49]

An interviewer or interrogator who undestands these concepts and can get in sync with the witness or suspect by mirroring, or matching, mannerisms, actions, and words can make communication barriers disappear, foster trust, and create the flow of desired information. To achieve these results, the investigator should **mirror** the interviewee's kinesics, language, and paralanguage.

The term **kinesics** refers to body language, including gestures, posture, and movement of hands, feet, arms, and legs. The investigator must be cautious that the mirroring of behavior does not appear to be mimicry. The matching must be done subtly; otherwise, the interviewee might be offended, and the entire effort will be counterproductive.

Language used to relate experiences may take any of three forms: visual, auditory, or kinesthetic (feeling). Generally, one of these will be a person's dominant method of communicating. The dominant form appears readily in an interview setting. A person who answers a question with "It looks good to me" is predominantly visual; thus, he or she might respond better to a question phrased in visual terms, such as "Picture this, John was sitting. . . ." In contrast, someone who is auditory may say, "Sounds good to me"; in this case, the question might be worded "If you heard that John. . . ." A feeling or *kinesthetic* person might say, "How do you think I feel?" The investigator might phrase the question, "How would you feel if what happened to John . . . ?"[50]

A person's dominant mode can often be determined by watching his or her eyes. Generally speaking, left-brained individuals—about 90 percent of the population—display the following eye movements when searching their memories: Visually oriented people look up and to the left at a 45-degree angle; people with an auditory dominant mode look directly left; and kinesthetics look down and to the right at a 45-degree angle. People in the other 10 percent of the population are right-brained and will display a mirror image of their left-brained counterparts.51 (See Figure 4–3.)

**Paralanguage** involves how a person says something, along with the rate of speaking and the volume, pitch, tone, and tempo of the voice. Matching those characteristics can help build trust and can cause the interviewee to bond with the interviewer. This fosters communication and that flow will often provide the investigator with needed information.[52]

## INTERVIEWING: PROCESSES AND TECHNIQUES

Regardless of the time, place, or setting of the interview, or ultimately the type of witness or victim

**Figure 4-3** The Eyes Have It

**Source:** After David E. Zulawski and Douglas E. Wicklander, *Practical Aspects of Interview and Interrogation* (New York: Elsevier, 1992), p. 154.

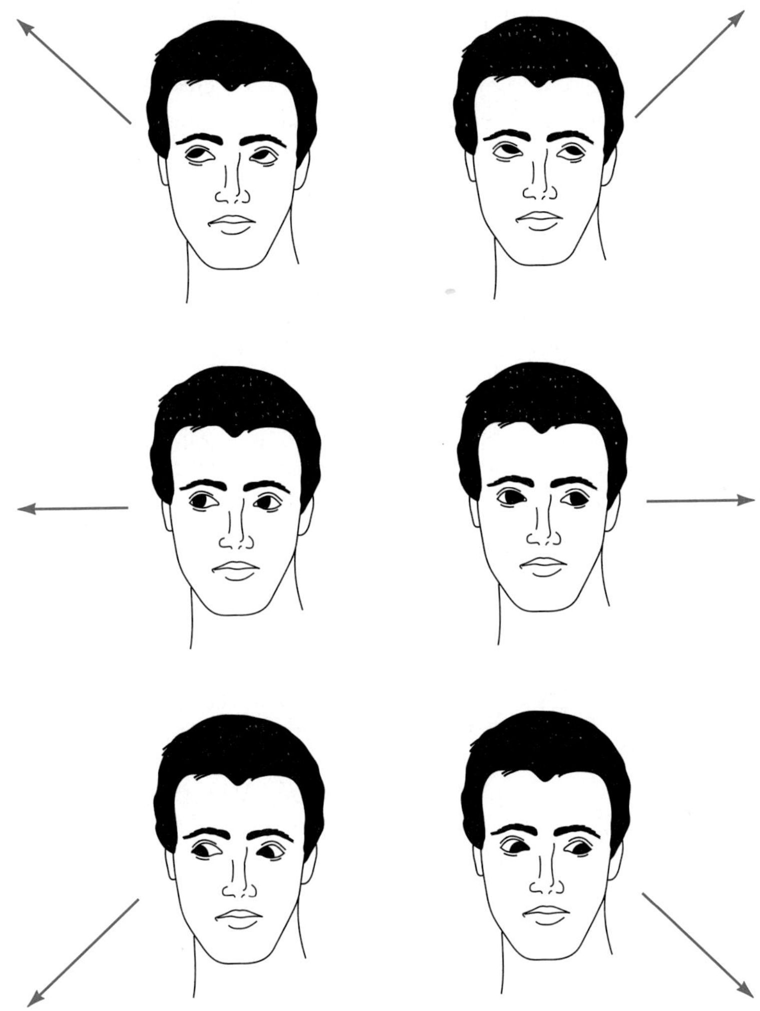

interviewed, there exists some standardization in technique. "An interview . . . has a beginning, a middle—its main segment—and an end."[53] The beginning is the warm-up period, the time when the interviewer must establish rapport. The main segment is devoted to acquiring the desired information. The end occurs when the investigator has accomplished certain goals and shows appreciation to the witness.

The investigator must remember that the mission is to gather all relevant information possessed by the witness about a particular occurrence. Regardless of the attitude of the witness, the interviewer must establish rapport. The warm-up period allows the interviewer to provide identification, state the purpose of the interview, and put the witness at ease with small talk. Matters of common interest may be discussed, such as children, sports, military service, or membership in civic organizations. Friendly conversation can convey interest in the witness, get the witness talking, and provide the interviewer with an opportunity to evaluate the witness.

Although topics of mutual interest do not guarantee rapport, the purpose of the warm-up period is to attempt to reduce anxiety on the part of the person being interviewed. Sometimes flattery may also work to accomplish this objective.[54] Now the investigator can determine the type of witness being interviewed, the appropriate NLP techniques and approaches to use, and, in general, the tone to be taken in the interview. The length of the warm-up period depends on a number of variables, including the attitude of the witness, the level of cooperation, and the degree to which the witness can be motivated to provide useful information. The warm-up is time well spent if it helps to ensure a successful interview.

When leading into the main body of the interview, the investigator should remember that his or her role is to direct the flow of the interview and to do so in a nonsuggestive manner. That is, care should be taken not to lead the witness by asking questions that imply the answer.

Questions should always be phrased positively so that the response is also positive. Questions such as "You don't really believe that, do you?" imply that anything other than a negative answer will be unacceptable. "Do you believe that?" allows the witness more feedom to respond.

Studies substantiate that the exact manner in which interview questions are asked is critical to the response. The choice of a single word and it use in a sentence can dramatically affect the nature of a response. In laboratory studies in which subjects were shown a film of a traffic accident, portions of the study group were later asked if they had seen *the* broken headlight; others were asked if they had seen *a* broken headlight. The group presented with the question containing "the" said yes significantly more often than did the group presented with the question using "a." These results were consistent whether witnesses had or had not seen a broken headlight. The significance of this illustration is that use of "the" by the questioner implies the existence of a broken headlight, causing the witness to assume its existence and potentially influencing the answer given by the witness.

Further studies attempted to determine if word substitutions could affect quantitative judgments as well as a simple yes or no answer. Seven films of traffic accidents were shown to a group of subjects. Later, they were all asked *substantially* the same question: "About how fast were the cars going when they hit each other?" The only difference was in the verb used in the question. When various subjects were asked the question, the words "smashed," "collided," "bumped," or "contacted" were substituted for "hit." Although any of the words could be used properly in the question, each tends to imply a difference in speed and force of impact. Results showed that estimates of the speed of vehicles involved tended to increase as a more forceful verb was used in the question.[55]

To avoid such problems, interviewers should begin by asking witnesses to relate in their own words the events of which they have knowledge. Witnesses should be allowed to continue this narrative uninterrupted, unless the amount of superfluous or irrelevant material becomes excessive. Interviewers must remain attentive to what is and is not said and must prepare questions that separate facts from inferences and implications.

When beginning the questioning process, investigators should recall that their objective is to gather information so that they may picture the occurrence with the same clarity and in the same order as the witness. Questions should be asked in systematic and chronological order. They should be stated simply and clearly so that the witness understands them. Concise questions should be asked one at a time. Long, complex questions must be avoided, because they tend to produce disorganized and confused answers. For example, take the question, "Was the man you saw with the scar on his face walking south from where you saw the other man lying near the curb, or did he have the gun in his hand, and was he going the other way, toward the hill, and about how old would you say he was?" This question certainly looks ridiculous on paper. But many people utter questions like these—run-on, complicated, and disorganized.

In developing the chronology of events through questioning, the interviewer should first establish where the witness was positioned and related facts. The interviewer must keep the witness talking and discourage digressions as much as possible. Perhaps the most successful technique for keeping the witness talking is the use of open-ended, nondirectional questions, such as "What happened next?" They are designed to compel the witness to elaborate on the issue rather than merely respond in a yes-or-no fashion.

The interviewer should always permit witnesses to save face if errors in their statements become apparent. Provided the interviewer is satisfied that the mistake is an honest one and not the result of deliberate misrepresentations, he or she should attempt to assist the witness in clarifying the statement without seeming judgmental.

Often, what the interviewee said was not what the interviewer heard, and when such differences arise in a courtroom situation much later, the discrepancy can be embarrassing for the investigator. Consequently, it is always advisable to verify the information presented by the witness. To do this, interviewers should simply rephrase what they think they have heard and ask the witness to verify its accuracy. Although this is often not done, it can overcome a major stumbling block to proceeding with an effective investigation and a successful prosecution, where warranted. Also, verifying what was heard can cause the witness to recall additional information that was not told during the basic part of the interview.[56]

Occasionally the interviewer misses or fails to ask questions on some points simply because there was a lack of information that would have caused a question to be asked. Therefore, it is also advisable for the interviewer to ask a final "catch-all" question, such as "Is there anything I have not asked that you think I should have asked?" This way, if there were any gaps in the questioning, the witness has the opportunity to provide the missing information to the investigator. This method ensures that if a relevant issue crops up later, the investigator will not have to ask, "Why didn't you tell me this during the interview," only to have the witness reply, "You didn't ask."[57]

The complexity of the case and the amount of information possessed by the witness are critical variables in the amount of time required for the interview. When satisfied that all relevant information has been obtained, the interviewer has reached the primary goal and may terminate the interview, preferably with a thank-you and a short statement of appreciation for the witness's time and efforts in cooperating with the police in the investigation.

## THE COGNITIVE INTERVIEW TECHNIQUE

To this point we have discovered that eyewitness reports of crime are known to be incomplete, often unreliable, and at least partially incorrect. During the normal police interview an "eyewitness" is generally asked what happened. After a 10- or 15 minute narrative by the witness, the interviewer then asks specific questions to clarify certain points. None of this improves the memory of the witness, largely because many eyewitnesses are so preoccupied with the shocking reality of the event that has occurred that they don't have time to learn or memorize details about the suspect or about the crime. In a typical situation the event occurs so rapidly and is so emotionally charged that the eyewitness has trouble concentrating on things that should be remembered, even if the eyewitness is a trained observer, such as an off-duty police officer.[58] On the other hand, the concern about the inherent unreliability of the hypnosis interview and the legal questions it raises for the purposes of determining admissibility in court makes its use in many cases less than desirable.

The inherent problems of these two types of interviews are further complicated by the traditional type of questioning used by police investigators to ascertain who, what, where, when, why, and how. This process hardly encourages careful disclosure of the facts. The **cognitive interview technique** was developed in the hope of improving the completeness and accuracy of eyewitness accounts while avoiding some of the legal pitfalls that surround the use of hypnosis.

The cognitive interview technique is deceptively simple. At first glance it does not appear to be unique or particularly useful. However, the four general methods for jogging memory, used along with several specific techniques, become a very powerful and effective means of obtaining a complete and accurate picture of the events recalled.[59] The four techniques used to elicit information are explained to the witness beforehand and are designed to allow the witness to approach memory recall and retrieval from several different avenues.

The first step is to ask the witness to reconstruct the general circumstances surrounding the incident. The witness is asked to think about and recall what the surrounding environment looked like at the scene: rooms, arrangement of furniture, lighting, the presence of vehicles, weather conditions, smells, nearby objects or people, and any other details. In addition, the witness is asked how he or she was feeling at the time and what his or her reaction was to the incident. The purpose of this line of inquiry is to return the witness deeply into the scene.

Second, the investigator asks the witness to report everything remembered about the incident and all surrounding circimstances. The investigator explains that some people hold back information they don't think is relevant or important. The witness is asked not to edit any information or make any determination as to the importance of the material. In addition to the possibility that a tidbit of information may be of extreme importance, the mere act of relaying all information may cause the witness to remember something that had been forgotten.

An example of how obtaining all the details can work occurred when federal drug agents were debriefing an informant who had been to Central America about what he had seen at a remote airstrip used by drug smugglers. The informant recalled that there were mango trees around the airstrip and that he had eaten one of the mangoes. The answers given by the informant when he was asked to relive the experience of eating the mango and describe the taste, the smell, and the reactions of his other senses elicited some other memories of important details that enabled the drug agents to identify and locate the airstrip.[60]

Step three is to have the witness recall the events in a different order. For example, the witness may be asked to begin with the thing that most impressed him or her and work backward and forward from that point. Too often a witness asked to begin at the beginning will fill in gaps and tell a "complete" and logical story that makes sense but may not be entirely accurate. Starting at a different point forces the witness to recall events that actually occurred.

The fourth step is to have the witness change perspectives. The witness is asked to look at the incident from a different point of view or to put himself or herself in the position of some other person who was present and describe the incident from that other person's point of view.

Several other specific techniques may be used by an investigator to help strengthen the ability of the witness to retrieve stored memory. For example, in an attempt to obtain a physical description, the investigator may ask if the suspect reminded the witness of anyone. If so, who? Or why? Did anything about the person's appearance or clothing bring back any memories? How about names? Go through the alphabet to try to recall the first letter of a name. Did the person's voice remind the witness of anyone else's voice? Were any unusual words used? Any accent?

Many parts of the cognitive interview technique have been used for years. The parts are old, but using them together in a systematic method seems to be proving successful. Investigators can be trained in the technique easily, and, from the studies and experiments conducted thus far, it appears to be efficient and effective as a workable memory enhancement technique.[61]

## PREINTERROGATION LEGAL REQUIREMENTS

Before delving into the specifics of interrogations, it is important to discuss the legal requirements. This issue became of critical concern during the 1960s; as a result, the Supreme Court handed down a landmark decision that has dramatically affected the conditions under which interrogations take place. The issue revolved around the Fifth Amendment protection against self-incrimination and the Sixth Amendment guarantee of the right to counsel, both as made applicable to the states through the due process clause of the Fourteenth Amendment.

### *Miranda* V. *Arizona*

In ***Miranda* v. *Arizona*** the Supreme Court, in a five-to-four decision, spelled out the requirements and procedures to be followed by officers when conducting an in-custody interrogation of a suspect.

In March 1963, Ernest Miranda was arrested for kidnapping and rape. After being identified by the victim, he was questioned by police for several hours and signed a confession that included a statement indicating that the confession was given voluntarily. The confession was admitted into evidence over the objections of Miranda's defense counsel, and the jury found him guilty. The Supreme Court of Arizona affirmed the conviction and held that Miranda's constitutional rights had not been violated in obtaining the conviction because following the ruling from *Escobedo* v. *Illinois*,[62] the year before, in which Escobedo's confession was ruled to have been improperly admitted because he asked to see his lawyer but was denied that right, Miranda had not specifically requested counsel. The U.S. Supreme Court, in reversing the decision, attempted to clarify its intent in the *Escobedo* case by spelling out specific guidelines to be followed by police before they interrogate persons in custody and attempt to use their statements as evidence. In clarifying the requirements of *Escobedo*, the Court felt compelled to include the Fifth Amendment requirements against self-incrimination in the decision. The guidelines require that after a person is taken into custody for an offense and before any questioning by law enforcement officers, if there is any intent to use a suspect's statements in court, the person must first be advised of certain rights. (See Figure 4–4.) These rights include:

1. The right to remain silent.
2. The right to be told that anything said can and will be used in court.
3. The right to consult with an attorney prior to answering any questions and the right to have an attorney present during interrogation.
4. The right to counsel. If the suspect cannot afford an attorney, the court will appoint one.[63]

## SUSPECT'S RESPONSE: WAIVER AND ALTERNATIVES

It is common practice for the officer to ask the suspect if he or she understands the rights as they have been explained. If the answer is yes, then the officer may ask if the subject wants to talk with the officer. At this point, four alternatives are open to the suspect:

1. *The suspect may choose to remain silent,* not wanting even to respond to the officer's question. The courts have held that choosing to remain silent does not imply consent to be interrogated.
2. *The suspect may request counsel.* At that point, the investigator must not undertake any questioning of the suspect, for anything said will not be admissible in court. In *Edwards* v. *Arizona* in 1981, the Supreme Court held that no police-initiated interrogation may lawfully take place once

**Figure 4-4** Warning-Rights Card in English and Spanish

(Courtesy Los Angeles County Sheriff's Department)

THE EXPLANATION OF THE ADMONITION AND USE OR WAIVER OF YOUR RIGHTS

1) You have the right to remain silent—you do not have to talk.
2) What you say can be used, and shall be used against you in a court of law.
3) You have the right to talk with an attorney before you talk with us, and you have the right to have the attorney present during the time we are talking to you.
4) If you do not have the funds to employ an attorney, one shall be appointed to represent you free of charge.
5) Do you understand these rights as I have explained them to you, yes or no?
6) Do you want to talk to us about your case now, yes or no?
7) Do you want an attorney present during the time we are talking to you, yes or no?

LA EXPLICACION DEL AVISO Y EL USO O NO DE TUS DERECHOS

1) Tienes el derecho de quedar en silencio—no tienes que hablar.
2) Lo que digas se puede usar y se usará en contra de ti en la corte de ley.
3) Tienes el derecho de hablar con un abogado antes de hablar con nosotros, y tienes el derecho de tener el abogado presente durante el tiempo que nosotros estamos hablando contigo.
4) Si no tienes el dinero para emplear un abogado, uno sere fijado para que te represente, sin pagar.
5) ¿Comprendes estos derechos como te los expliqué, si o no?
6) ¿Quieres hablar con nosotros de tu caso ahora, si o no?
7) ¿Quieres un abogado presente durante el tiempo que estamos hablando contigo, si o no?

the suspect has invoked the right to counsel unless and until an attorney has been provided or unless the defendant voluntarily begins to talk with the officers.[64] In *Minnick* v. *Mississippi* in 1990, the Supreme Court held that once counsel is requested, interrogation must cease; officials may not reinitiate interrogation without counsel being present, whether or not the accused has consulted with his or her attorney. The requirement that counsel be made available to the accused refers not to the opportunity to consult with a lawyer outside the interrogation room but to the right to have the attorney present during custodial interrogation. This rule is necessary to remove suspects from the coercive pressure of officials who may try to persuade them to waive their rights. The rule also provides a clear and unequivocal guideline to the law enforcement profession.[65] In the 1988 case of *Patterson* v. *Illinois,* the Supreme Court said that a defendant who was indicted but unrepresented could waive the right to counsel after having been given the *Miranda* warnings. No more elaborate warning was required, and it was not deemed necessary that authorities refrain from interrogation until counsel was made available.[66]

3. *The suspect may waive his or her rights and agree to talk with police without the benefit of counsel.* The waiver of rights is a sensitive topic for police, as it is the responsibility of the police and the prosecutor to prove in court that the waiver was validly obtained. A valid waiver must be voluntarily, knowingly, and intelligently given by the suspect. The burden is on the prosecution to prove that the suspect was properly advised of his or her rights, that those rights were understood, and that the suspect voluntarily, knowingly, and intelligently waived those rights before the court will allow the introduction of any incriminating testimony in the form of a confession. The waiver cannot be presumed or inferred. It must be successfully proved by the prosecution. Therefore, it is preferable for the investigator who secures a waiver of rights from a suspect to attempt to get the waiver in writing with sufficient witnesses to substantiate its voluntariness. Figure 4–5 is a sample waiver form. One additional fact should remain under consideration: Even the suspect who has waived his or her rights is free to withdraw that waiver at any time. If this occurs during questioning, the investigator is under a legal obligation to cease the interrogation at that point and either comply with the suspect's request for representation or simply cease the interrogation if the suspect refuses to talk.

4. *The suspect may indicate a desire not to talk with the investigators.* At this point, the police have no choice other than to refrain from attempting to interrogate the suspect concerning the events of the crime for which he or she has been arrested. In this event, the case must be based on independent evidence, which may or may not be sufficient to warrant prosecution. The U.S. Supreme Court's emphatic position on terminating interrogation once a suspect has invoked the right to remain silent was announced in 1975 in the case of *Michigan* v. *Mosley.*[67]

Since the responsibility is on the prosecution, supported by evidence provided by the investigators, to substantiate the voluntariness of the waiver and the propriety of the warnings given to the suspect, many police agencies provide printed cards with the exact wording of the required warnings. They further recommend or require that when warnings are given they be read verbatim from the printed card. In this manner the officer, when testifying in court, can positively state the exact words used in advising the suspect of his or her constitutional rights. Such a procedure avoids any confrontation with the defense as to the exact wording and contents of the *Miranda* requirements. But in 1989 in *Duckworth* v. *Eagen,* the Supreme Court held that it was not necessary that the warnings be given in the exact form described in the *Miranda* decision, provided that the warnings as a whole fully informed the suspect of his or her rights.[68]

A person being subjected to in-custody interrogation often chooses not to answer any questions posed by the police—or at least not until an attorney is present. When counsel is made available to the suspect before or during interrogation, it is

**Figure 4-5** Rights Waiver Form

(Courtesy Geauga County, Ohio, Sheriff's Department)

YOUR RIGHTS

Date______________________________

Time______________________________

WARNING

Before we ask you any questions, you must understand your rights.

You have the right to remain silent.

Anything you say can and will be used against you in court.

You have the right to talk to a lawyer for advice before we ask you any question and to have him with you during questioning.

If you cannot afford a lawyer, one will be appointed for you.

Geauga County has a Public Defender. Before answering any questions, you have a right to talk with the Public Defender.

If you decide to answer questions now, without a lawyer present, you will still have the right to stop answering at any time. You also have the right to stop answering at any time until you talk to a lawyer.

Do you understand these rights? ______________________________

Signed: ______________________________

Witnesses:

______________________________

______________________________

WAIVER OF RIGHTS

I have read this statement of my rights and I understand what my rights are. I am willing to make a statement and answer questions. I do not want a lawyer at this time. I understand and know what I am doing. No promises or threats have been made to me and no pressure or coercion of any kind has been used against me.

Signed: ______________________________

Witnesses:

______________________________

______________________________

Date: ______________________________

Time: ______________________________

almost universal practice for the attorney to advise the client not to say anything to the police. Therefore, the effect of the *Miranda* decision has been to reduce significantly the number of valid interrogations by police agencies in this country today. For the most part, however, confessions obtained in compliance with prescribed rules are of better quality and are more likely to be admissible in court.

It must be impressed on investigators that the failure to properly advise a suspect of the rights required by *Miranda* does not invalidate an otherwise valid arrest, nor does it necessarily mean that a case cannot be successfully prosecuted. Even in light of the line of court decisions indicating that *Miranda* warnings may not be required in all interrogation situations, good practice or departmental policy may require that all suspects in custody be advised of their rights.

## WHY PEOPLE CONFESS

It is human nature to talk. Most people cannot keep a secret. It has been estimated that 80 percent of all people will confess to a crime. There are two basic categories of people who tend to confess to crimes: (1) guilty parties who psychologically need to "get if off their chest," and (2) persons who are not guilty but who act under some urge to confess. It is to protect the latter category of people that some procedural safeguards are provided. For example, a conviction cannot be based solely on a confession. There must be some other independent corroborating evidence to support the conviction.

The psychological and physiological pressures that build in a person who has committed a crime or who suffers from guilt feelings concerning any other type of conduct are best alleviated by communicating. Talking is the best means of communicating. Therefore, in spite of having been advised of certain protections guaranteed by the Constitution, some people feel a need to confess. Even most confirmed criminals suffer from the same pangs of conscience as first-time offenders. However, fear of the potential punishments that await them contributes to their silence. Those who confess rarely regret it, for doing so gives them peace of mind. It permits them to look at themselves and life differently and to live with themselves. Most guilty individuals who confess are, from the outset, looking for the proper opening during an interrogation to communicate their guilt to the interrogator. The good interrogator will seek out and be able to recognize individuals who desire to confess and will approach the interrogation in such a way as to provide the accused with the proper opening and reason for the relief of the psychological and physiological pressures that have built up.[69] If it is human nature to talk and if people cannot generally keep secrets, then the job of the interrogator is to make it easy for a suspect to confess.

# IN-CUSTODY INTERROGATION

For investigators to understand the proper application of the *Miranda* requirements, it is essential that they understand the meaning of **in-custody interrogation.** The *Miranda* case involved simultaneous custody and interrogation. Subsequent police actions revealed that all cases were not so nicely defined and that the meanings of "in custody" and "interrogation" required clarification. Although it may be difficult to separate the custody from the interrogation in certain factual situations, the two concepts must be considered separately. The cases cited in the following paragraphs should be examined from the standpoint of the subheading under which each is included.

## CUSTODY

Analyses of case decisions show that there is not yet a universally accepted definition of custody. Rather, case-by-case analysis is used to determine the applicability of the *Miranda* requirements.

In *Beckwith* v. *United States,* agents of the Internal Revenue Service interrogated the defendant, who was the subject of a tax fraud investigation. The defendant was not under arrest at the time but was advised of all the *Miranda* warnings except the right to a court-appointed attorney. He waived his rights, subsequently furnished incriminating evidence, and was convicted. On appeal, the defendant claimed that the complete warnings had not been given and therefore that incriminating statements should not have been admitted. On appeal, the Supreme Court held that the agents were not required to apply *Miranda* in those circumstances. *Miranda* application depends on custodial police interrogation, involving questioning in a coercive, police-dominated atmosphere. Those conditions did not exist in this case.[70]

In a 1977 case, the Court again emphasized that something more than suspicion or focus of an investigation is necessary before *Miranda* applies. In *Oregon* v. *Mathiason,* the defendant was asked to come to the state patrol office to be interviewed about a burglary. Mathiason was told that he was not under arrest but was informed that the police believed he had participated in the burglary. No *Miranda* warnings were given. He confessed, was convicted, and appealed. The

Oregon Supreme Court reversed the conviction, finding that the defendant was interviewed in a "coercive environment" and that *Miranda* applied.[71] The U.S. Supreme Court disagreed with the state court, pointing out that the defendant had not been formally arrested and his freedom of locomotion had not been restrained in any significant way and that, without the presence of either of these factors, *Miranda* does not apply. The Court said:

> ANY interview of one suspected of a crime by a police officer will have coercive aspects to it simply by virtue of the fact that the police officer is part of a law enforcement system which may ultimately cause the suspect to be charged with a crime. But police officers are not required to administer *Miranda* warnings to everyone whom they question. Nor is the requirement of warnings to be imposed simply because the questioning takes place in the station house, or because the questioned person is one whom the police suspect. *Miranda* warnings are required only where there has been such a restriction on a person's freedom as to render him "in custody." It was that sort of coercive environment to which *Miranda* by its terms was made applicable, and to which it is limited.[72]

In 1983, the Supreme Court again addressed the *Miranda* custody issue. In *California* v. *Beheler*, the defendant and several others had attempted to steal a quantity of hashish from the victim, who was selling the drug in the parking lot of a liquor store. While resisting the robbery, the victim was killed by one of the perpetrators. Shortly afterward, Beheler called the police and told them who had killed the victim. Later the same day, Beheler voluntarily agreed to accompany police to the police station and was specifically told he was not under arrest. During the 30-minute interview, he told police what had happened. He was not advised of his rights under the *Miranda* decision. After the interview, Beheler was permitted to return home. Five days later he was arrested for aiding and abetting first-degree murder. He was advised of his rights, which he waived, and confessed. Both confessions were used against him in his conviction. The California Court of Appeals reversed the decision, holding that the first interview was "in-custody" because it took place in the station, Beheler was a suspect at the time, and the interview was designed to elicit incriminating information.

The U.S. Supreme Court reversed the California appellate court decision and, following its previous holding in *Oregon* v. *Mathiason,* held that in determining whether custody exists for purposes of *Miranda,* the inquiry is simply whether there is a formal arrest or restraint on freedom of movement as usually associated with a formal arrest. Finding that no such restraint existed in this case, the Court added that the amount of information possessed by the police concerning the person to be questioned and the length of time between the commission of the crime and the time of questioning are not relevant to the issue of whether custody exists for purposes of applying *Miranda.*[73]

All interviews do not have to take place in a police station to have a coercive effect. In *Orozco* v. *Texas,* the Court held inadmissible a confession given after the defendant was questioned in his bed in the middle of the night by four police officers. The Court concluded in this 1969 case that the defendant had been deprived of his freedom in a significant way.[74]

Similarly, the defendant in *United States* v. *Lee* was questioned by two federal agents in a government car parked in front of his home. The questioning concerned the death of Lee's wife. Lee agreed to answer questions and was told he was free at any time to terminate the interview and leave. The conversation lasted between and hour and an hour and a half, during which time the agents advised Lee of the incriminating evidence they possessed. Lee finally confessed to killing his wife but was not arrested until the next day, when he voluntarily appeared at the police station for further questioning. At no time was he advised of his rights. Using a test called the **totality of the circumstances,** a federal appeals court in 1982 upheld the trial court's decision to exclude the statements on the basis that Lee was in custody and was not free to decline the interview under the circumstances, even though he had not been formally arrested.[75]

Other courts using the totality-of-circumstances test have come to conclusions different from those in the *Lee* case, but perhaps because of different factual conditions. In *United States* v. *Dockery,* a 24-year-old bank employee was questioned by FBI agents concerning the theft of bank funds. She was questioned for just over 15 minutes in a small vacant room in the bank. Dockery was told at the outset that she did not have to answer any questions, that she was not under arrest nor was she going to be arrested, and that she was free to leave at any time. Dockery denied any involvement in the thefts. After the interview ended, Dockery was asked to wait outside the interview room. A few minutes later, she asked to see the agents, who again advised her that she did not have to talk to them and that she was free to leave whenever she desired. Shortly thereafter, Dockery gave a signed statement implicating herself in the thefts. In 1984, the federal appellate court reviewing the conviction ruled that Dockery was not in custody during the interviews and therefore that her confession was properly admitted at her trial.[76]

To fully comprehend the definition of custody, it is necessary to explore additional case decisions. For example, in *Mathis* v. *United States,* the defendant was convicted of filing false claims against the government. Part of the evidence used to convict consisted of statements made by the defendant to a federal agent while the defendant was in prison serving a state sentence. At the time of questioning, the government agent did not advise the defendant of his rights. On appeal of the conviction to the Supreme Court, the defendant argued that the statements used against him had been obtained in violation of *Miranda.* The government countered with the argument that *Miranda* did not apply because the defendant had not been put in jail by the agents questioning him but was there for a very different offense. The Court, in reversing the decision, held in this 1968 case that it was immaterial why a person had been arrested or by whom. It is the coercive aspect of the custody itself, coupled with the police interrogation, that triggers the application of *Miranda.*[77]

But in the 1990 case of *Illinois* v. *Perkins,* an undercover officer was placed in a cell with the defendant, who was in jail on other, unrelated charges. The Supreme Court said, "Conversations between suspects and undercover agents do not implicate the concerns underlying *Miranda,*" which "forbids coercion, not mere strategic deception by taking advantage of a suspect's misplaced trust in one he supposes to be a fellow prisoner.[78]

A 1984 decision of the Supreme Court for the first time recognized a "public safety" exception to *Miranda.* The facts in the case of *New York* v. *Quarles* involved an officer who entered a supermarket looking for an alleged rapist who was supposed to be armed. The officer spotted the suspect, Quarles, who, upon seeing the officer, ran toward the rear of the store with the officer in pursuit. The officer lost sight of Quarles for a few seconds. Upon regaining sight of the suspect, the officer ordered him to stop. While frisking Quarles, the officer discovered an empty shoulder holster. After handcuffing him, the officer asked Quarles where the gun was. Quarles nodded in the direction of some empty cartons and stated, "The gun is over there."

After retrieving the gun, the officer formally placed Quarles under arrest and advised him of his rights. Quarles waived his rights and, in answer to questions, admitted ownership of the gun and stated where he had obtained it. In the prosecution for the criminal possession of the weapon, the trial court suppressed all the statements about the location or ownership of the gun and suppressed evidence of the gun on the grounds that the officer had failed to initially advise the suspect of his constitutional rights and that the information acquired after the arrest and subsequent *Miranda* warnings was tainted by the first omission.

In reversing the decision, the Supreme Court agreed that Quarles was subjected to custodial interrogation without proper advisement and waiver of his rights. However, the Court ruled that the

**Ernesto Miranda with his Lawyer**
(© UPI/Corbis)

statements concerning the location of the gun and the gun itself were admissible under a public safety exception to the *Miranda* rule. The Court said that the need for answers to questions in a situation posing a threat to the public safety outweighs the need for protecting the subject's Fifth Amendment privilege against self-incrimination. The Court conceded that this exception lessened the clarity of the *Miranda* rule but held that it also would keep police officers from the untenable position of having to consider, often in a matter of seconds, whether it best serves society for them to ask questions without providing the *Miranda* warnings and chance having the evidence excluded or to give the warnings and chance not getting the evidence at all.

The Court further indicated it had confidence that law enforcement officials could easily determine the applicability of the public safety exception, but it cautioned that the burden is on the police later to articulate the specific facts and circumstances justifying the need for questioning, without the warnings, in order to protect themselves, other officers, or the public. Furthermore, because this is a very narrow exception to the *Miranda* rule, once the reason for the public safety exception ends, any further questioning should be preceded by the warnings and waiver.[79]

The question of whether *Miranda* applies to misdemeanor arrests was the subject of controversy for many years. In 1984, the Supreme Court settled this issue. The Court ruled in *Berkemer* v. *McCarty* that *Miranda* applies to the interrogation of an arrested person regardless of whether the offense is a felony or a misdemeanor. The justices found that to make a distinction would cause confusion because many times it is not certain whether the person taken into custody is to be charged with a felony or a misdemeanor.[80]

In 1968, the Supreme Court ruled in the case of *Terry* v. *Ohio* that law enforcement officers may constitutionally detain persons against their will for short periods of time and in a reasonable manner to investigate and resolve suspicious circumstances indicating that a crime has been or is about to be committed. Such "Terry stops" or "stop-and-frisk" situations often require questioning the person detained, because that is often the most effective method of resolving suspicious activities quickly and reasonably.[81] The question has long been asked whether such questioning may be conducted without meeting the requirements of *Miranda*.

*Berkemer* v. *McCarty* squarely addressed that issue. In this case, a state trooper observed McCarty's car weaving in and out of traffic. The vehicle was stopped and, upon getting out of the car, McCarty had difficulty standing. McCarty was asked to take a "balancing test," which he was unable to complete without falling. His speech was slurred. The trooper asked if he had been using any intoxicants. McCarty replied that he had had two beers and had smoked several marijuana joints. At that point, McCarty was arrested and transported to the police station, where he was administered a test that showed no alcohol in the blood. Upon further questioning by the trooper, who was seeking information to complete his report, McCarty again admitted that he had been drinking and also indicated in writing that the marijuana he had smoked did not contain angel dust (PCP). He was then charged with operating a motor vehicle while under the influence of alcohol and/or drugs. At no time was McCarty advised of his rights. At trial, McCarty moved to have his incriminating statements excluded as violation of the *Miranda* requirements. The trial court refused. After his conviction and a series of appeals, McCarty's case was heard by the Supreme Court. Two issues were presented. The first was described earlier, in which the court held that *Miranda* applies to misdemeanor arrests as well as to felonies. The second question concerned the application of *Miranda* to roadside questioning. The Court ruled that an investigative detention does not constitute custody if it meets the test of reasonableness. Therefore, *Miranda* does not apply.[82] This decision continues to be followed, as confirmed by the Supreme Court in the 1988 case of *Pennsylvania* v. *Bruder*.[83]

In *United States* v. *J.H.H.*, the Eighth Circuit held that the questioning of a juvenile that occurred in an unlocked room, where the juvenile was told he was not under arrest and was free to leave at any time—and, in fact, he was not arrested after questioning—did not constitute "in custody" for purposes of using these statements against the juvenile in a later proceeding.[84]

A 10-year-old girl disappeared from a playground in California in 1982. Early the next morning, about 10 miles away, a man observed a large man emerge from a turquoise American sedan and throw something into a nearby flood-control channel. He called the police, who later discovered the girl's body in the channel. There was evidence that the girl had been raped and asphyxiated by a blunt-force trauma to the head. A detective learned that the girl had talked to two ice-cream-truck drivers in the hours before her disappearance. One of the drivers was the defendant. The detective's suspicions focused on the other driver. However, at 11 p.m. one evening, four uniformed officers arrived at the defendant's mobile home and asked him if he would accompany them to the police station to answer some questions. He agreed and rode in the front seat of the police car. At the police station, the detective questioned him about his whereabouts on the evening the girl had been abducted. Nothing was out of the ordinary until the defendant mentioned that he had left his mobile home about midnight in his housemate's turquoise American-made car. This aroused the detective's suspicion. He terminated the interview, and another officer advised the defendant of this *Miranda* rights. The defendant refused to make any further statements, requested an attorney, and was taken into custody. A motion to suppress the evidence was denied. He was subsequently convicted of first-degree murder and other crimes. The California Supreme Court affirmed the conviction. The case was heard by the U.S. Supreme Court to determine whether the defendant was in custody at the time he made the statements and thus was entitled to wave the statements suppressed. The Court said that in deciding whether the defendant was in custody, the totality of the circumstances is relevant and no one factor alone disposes of the question. The Court went on to say that the most important considerations include where the investigation took place, whether the investigation had focused on the subject, whether the objective bases for making an arrest are present, and the length of questioning. The Court, in reversing the decision, said the California Supreme Court was wrong in considering whether the investigation had focused on the subject to determine the custody issue, primarily because the officers never communicated their feelings so that the defendant was made aware that he was now a suspect in the case. Because the officers did not manifest this view, it could have no bearing on the question of whether the suspect was in custody at the time. The state subsequently acknowledged that the officer's subjective, undisclosed suspicions had no bearing on the question of whether the defendant was in custody for the purposes of *Miranda* during the questioning that occurred in the police station. The state, however, argued that the objective facts and records supported a finding that the defendant was not in custody until the arrest. The defendant, on the other hand, asserted that the objective circumstances showed that he was in custody during the entire time he was questioned. The U.S. Supreme Court reversed and remanded the case back to the California Supreme Court and told the state to consider this question because it had not been considered before.[85]

The cases cited clearly show that the statement offered in the beginning of this section is still correct. There are no universally accepted definitions of custody, and with as much direction as the courts are trying to provide, many decisions are still subject to case-by-case scrutiny.

## INTERROGATION

For many years following the *Miranda* ruling, there was considerable confusion over what constituted questioning or interrogation. For example, in a 1977 case the Supreme Court found that an impermissible interrogation occurred when a detective delivered what has been called the "Christian burial speech" to a man suspected of murdering a young girl. While the suspect was being transported between cities, the detective told the suspect to think about how the weather was turning cold and snow was likely. He pointed out how difficult it would be to find the body later. The detective went on to say that the girl's parents were entitled to have a Christian burial for the little girl, who had been taken from them on Christmas Eve and murdered. Subsequent to this little speech, the suspect led the detectives to the spot where he had disposed of the body. The Supreme Court held this to be an interrogation within the scope of *Miranda*, even though direct questions had not been asked of the suspect.[86]

The Supreme Court faced the question of what constitutes interrogation for the first time in the 1980 case of *Rhode Island* v. *Innis*. In that instance a robbery suspect was arrested after the victim had identified him from photographs. The prisoner was advised several times of his constitutional rights and was being transported by three officers who had been specifically ordered not to question the suspect. During the trip, two of the officers were having a conversation about the case, and one commented how terrible it would be if some unsuspecting child found the missing shotgun (used in the robbery) and got hurt. The conversation was not directed at the suspect, nor did the officers expect a response from the suspect. However, the suspect interrupted the conversation and, after again being advised of his rights, led the officers to the shotgun. The Supreme Court stated the rule regarding interrogation as follows:

> We conclude that *Miranda* safeguards come into play whenever a person in custody is subjected to either express questioning or its functional equivalent. That is to say, the term "interrogation" under *Miranda* refers not only to express questioning, but also to any words or actions on the part of the police (other than those normally attendant to arrest and custody) that the police should know are reasonably likely to elicit an incriminating response from the suspect. The latter portion of this definition focuses primarily upon the perceptions of the suspect, rather than the intent of the police. This focus reflects the fact that the *Miranda* safeguards were designed to vest a suspect in custody with an added measure of protection against coercive police practices, without regard to objective proof of the underlying intent of the police.[87]

Interrogation, as defined by *Innis,* was found by one federal circuit to have been conducted when officers questioned the defendant about a homicide and showed him physical evidence linking him to the crime.[88] By applying this rule to the facts of the case, the Court held that the conversation between the officers did not amount to an interrogation and was properly admissible. Consequently, the current rules appear to be that if a suspect is in custody or otherwise deprived of freedom in a significant way, and if the suspect is to be asked pertinent questions, or if an officer uses words or acts in such a way that the officer should know would be reasonably likely to elicit incriminating responses from the suspect, the warnings must be given.[89] It is also fairly clear that volunteered statements, such as those given when a person walks into a police station and confesses to a crime, and general on-the-scene questioning by an investigator—such as "What happened?"—do not fall within the scope of *Miranda* requirements.[90]

The Court's position in the *Innis* case was again supported seven years later in *Arizona* v. *Mauro,* in which the police allowed the defendant's wife to talk with him after he had invoked his right to counsel. The conversation was conducted in the presence of a police officer, who was present for security purposes only, and it was also openly being recorded. The officer asked no questions. Incriminating statements made by the defendant were held to be properly admissible.[91]

As a general rule, *Miranda* warnings need not precede routine booking questions that are asked in order to obtain personal-history data necessary to complete the booking process. As long as the questions are for that purpose and not a pretext to obtain incriminating information, *Miranda* warnings need not be given.[92]

# THE INTERROGATION PROCESS

Effective interrogators, like interviewers, must be skilled in psychology, persuasiveness, and acting. Good interrogators must also be good seducers; they must be able to make others do what they want them to do. They must be capable of giving the appearance of empathy, sympathy, and objectivity when those characteristics are most appropriate to accomplishing their objectives. The character one assumes as an interrogator must be determined from the reactions of the suspect and the approach that will obtain the best response. A successful interrogation requires that the investigator sell himself or herself to the subject.

## BEGINNING THE INTERROGATION

Just as in interviewing, it is important in interrogating to establish rapport with the person to be questioned, and neuro-linguistic programming techniques can help accomplish this. Rapport can be established by showing a sincere interest in the person and his or her personal problems. Complimenting the suspect on some outstanding trait or characteristic often gets the suspect talking, and getting the suspect to talk is, of course, a prime objective. Small talk can often accomplish the same objective. Once conversation has started, the objective is to keep the suspect talking—about anything.

It is essential that the interrogator be in complete command of the interrogation and that this be made absolutely clear to the suspect at the outset. The interrogator must project competence and self-confidence in making a first impression on the suspect. As an example, if the interrogator perceives that the suspect considers himself or herself superior to the interrogator, the suspect may be addressed by last name only, instructed to sit, instructed not to smoke, and manipulated in other ways.

At this stage, it is important for the interrogator, using personal observations and known facts about the suspect, to evaluate the mental capacity of the suspect. Intelligence is an important aspect of this process. Generally speaking, physiological changes in the suspect's body will be stronger in persons of higher intelligence. This is not always true, however, and often such changes will not be immediately visible. On the other hand, an individual of very low intelligence may be less likely to experience physiological changes due to a lack of understanding of the danger he or she confronts or the inability of the interrogator to communicate the extent of that danger through the conversation. Emotional stability or instability is also important to evaluate. However, caution must be exercised. The emotionally unstable person can often produce reactions completely opposite from those which might be expected. Such unpredictable reactions can make it difficult to assess the emotional stability of the suspect.[93]

In evaluating the suspect, the interrogator also must consider the suspect's cultural and ethnic background. Often, behavioral signals have cultural roots. What might appear to be a deceptiveness signal may, in fact, be quite the opposite. For example, it is not uncommon for Hispanic males to look down when in the presence of a person of authority, rather than looking directly at that person. Drugs or alcohol can also cause a suspect to produce a deceptive reaction, such as delaying answering a question.[94]

Often, an interrogator bombards a suspect with a series of questions, hoping to get satisfactory answers. The interrogator believes that he or she has conducted an interrogation when, in fact, all the interrogator did was try to cross-examine the suspect, which rarely produces a confession. As has been pointed out, a guilty person needs to have an acceptable reason to tell the truth. This does not mean that the interrogator should be noncommittal or anything but firm. It is suggested that at the outset of an interrogation, the interrogator should tell the suspect the exact purpose of the interrogation. Doing so may require initially coming out and accusing the suspect of committing the crime. If the interrogator is confident that the suspect is the offender, showing confidence in that position often weakens any defenses that the suspect may try to raise and puts the interrogation on a firm footing of understanding in regard to what is to be accomplished. For example, the interrogator might say, "I know that you have committed this offense, but we need to get beyond that and start talking about why you committed the offense," or "I know there are two sides to every story, and the purpose of this discussion is to find out your version of the truth so that we can get this truth working for you rather than against you.[95]

## COMPOSING AND ASKING QUESTIONS

There are certain basic rules an interrogator should keep in mind when composing and asking questions.

Questions should not be complex, because they will be difficult to understand; they should be short, direct, and confined to one topic. They must be clear and easily understood. Only words that the suspect can understand should be used. Questions should avoid legal terms—larceny, homicide—and, unless intended, accusatory questions should be avoided. Leading questions (those asked in a manner that suggests the answer desired, e.g., "You don't mean to tell me that you're actually denying pulling the trigger?") should be avoided unless necessary to facilitate the questioning process. Adherence to these basic rules ensures that both interrogator and suspect understand what each is talking about. As in most processes in criminal investigation, interrogation questions should initially focus on a wide base of general information and then narrow the focus continually to more specific issues.

Before an interrogator can decide on specific questions to be asked or interrogation techniques and approaches to use, the evaluation process must continue. This includes the ability to recognize and cope with deception.

## RECOGNIZING AND COPING WITH DECEPTION

Deception is not always easy to detect, but, in general, there are both verbal and nonverbal cues that can be examined to determine whether a suspect is telling the truth or is being deceptive. In addition, statements can be written or recorded and analyzed to aid in this determination. Human behavior is diverse, and therefore there is no single nonverbal symptom or verbal cue that proves a person is being truthful or deceptive. To believe otherwise is foolish.[96]

To be effective in detecting when a suspect is being deceptive, the investigator who has thoroughly prepared should have some idea of the suspect's personality type. All the factors that are learned about the case and the suspect go into forming some opinion on how to approach the interrogation. In modern terms, this might be a type of "profiling." The interrogator will alter and modify the approaches and techniques used as the interrogation progresses and as he or she learns more about what is being said, how it is being said, and whether or not there are detectable signs of deception.

Neuro-linguistic programming, discussed earlier, can help the investigator not only in establishing rapport but also in detecting deception. Through the use of NLP, the interrogator can learn the suspect's dominant paralanguage pattern; identify his or her dominant visual, auditory, and kinesthetic speech patterns; and learn whether the suspect is left-brained or right-brained. By gaining these insights during the warm-up phase of an interrogation, the investigator will be in a better position to recognize deception.

### Verbal Signals

Verbal signals are generally easier for a deceptive subject to control than nonverbal signals. Verbal signals may take the form of changes in voice quality as well as specific statements. Stuttering or slurring words may be an indication of deception, as may a change in the speed of talking. Rapid speech may indicate nervousness, while abnormally slow speech may suggest careful planning of each word to avoid incriminating statements. An unusually high pitch or cracking of the voice may indicate deception.

Religious statements such as "Honest to God" and qualified answers beginning with such phrases as "to be perfectly honest" are potential indicators of deception and should be pursued by the attentive interrogator.

The content of speech is also important. Guilty suspects often go through a progression of negative responses that include anger, then depression, followed by denial, bargaining, and finally, acceptance.[97] The responses and methods of conducting the interrogation for each one of these states of mind are discussed later in the section on interrogation techniques.

### Nonverbal Signals: Body Language

There are generally far more nonverbal signals and behaviors than there are verbal. The primary reason for this is that suspects are generally not as able to control **body language** as they are to conceal verbal signals. Individually, nonverbal signals are not as significant as an individual verbal signal. However, when body-language signals appear in clusters, they are generally much larger and much more symptomatic of deception. Body language is best considered as a means of confirming the symptoms and information that are being generated through the questions and answers during the interrogation. Deception is generally taking place, particularly when the verbal cues are inconsistent with the nonverbal cues.[98]

The body of a person who is being deceptive—lying—may experience certain physiological and psychological changes. The changes occur because of an inherent fear of detection. In many cases, the deceptive person's fears tend to intensify when questions focus on those investigative details posing the greatest threat to the suspect's personal welfare. Thus, the body language indicating deception tends to become more pronounced the closer the interrogator's questions come to incriminating the suspect. Often the deceptive person who attempts to disguise body language and to create an impression of nonconcern produces the opposite result. When this occurs, the body language is accentuated and more easily interpreted as signs of deception. Although not all persons who act deceptively are in fact deceptive, body language can supplement common sense, experience, and hunches for the investigator who wants to distinguish truth from deception.

Everyone experiences and participates in nonverbal communications with others every day. Most people are capable of making general interpretations of this body language, but the skillful interrogator looks for more—specifically, for signs of deception. The qualified interrogator understands that what may seem to be a sign of deception may in fact be nothing more than natural nervousness or may indicate an emotional illness unrelated to the topic of the interrogation.

Among the more common symptoms that may appear as a result of pressure produced by lying are an increase in sweating; changes of color in the skin; a dry mouth, shown when the subject frequently swallows, wets the lips, or constantly indicates thirst; an increase in the pulse rate; an observable change in the breathing rate; a significant increase in the eye-blink rate; and eyes open wider than normal.[99] A good investigator is constantly alert for the manifestation of such symptoms and is able to use them to advantage. Such manifestations should be pointed out to the suspect as indications of lying. The interrogator should never allow a suspect to lie and get away with it. If this occurs, the suspect will be in control of the interrogation, an intolerable condition.

Body language is extremely difficult to control. One's body reacts naturally to a situation, and the reactions cannot be fabricated without a great deal of training. Body language indicating deception can be a reaction to a verbal statement, question, remark, photograph, or the sight of evidence. It can occur in response to a body-language message sent by the interrogator. The entire body or any part or parts of the body can be involved in body language—the arms, legs, shoulders, lips, eyes, nose, the entire face, posture, and gestures. To illustrate, the sitting posture of a deceptive individual may differ significantly from that of a nondeceptive one. The deceptive individual often slouches rather than sitting upright, sits rigidly instead of relaxedly, does not face the interrogator but looks to the side, sits with arms or legs crossed, and shifts sitting positions often and in a very jerky manner. Gestures indicating tension include wringing the hands, popping knuckles, chewing nails, picking lint from clothes, and clearing the throat, to name but a few. Facial expressions can display fear, anger, confusion, pleasure, and a myriad of other emotions.[100]

Many qualified interrogators have been using body language as part of interviewing and interrogation processes for years. "Body language" may be the current term used to refer to this technique, but its concepts are not new and have been closely studied over the years. Some experts claim that it would take two years to teach a trained social scientist the skills needed to properly evaluate body language.[101]

**Proximity** in an interrogation can also be important. For years, experts have favored the "knee-to-knee" approach in interrogation: subject and interrogator are close enough to touch without being too close and without having any object such as a chair or desk between them. "It seems, for example, that around 27 inches is the limit of proximity for white American middle-class males. . . . If you move closer, people become uncomfortable . . . further away than 27 inches, you can't read a person's face well."[102]

Detecting deception, obviously, is not a science; hence, the phrase "may indicate deception" is frequently used. Behavioral actions and reactions must be interpreted in the social and psychological context of a specific situation, which can at times be misleading to even the most skillful interrogator.[103]

Recent research studies, although not conducted in the real-life law enforcement environment, reveal that many of the beliefs about reading body language can be misinterpreted. For example, vocal pitch may actually decrease during deception. Hand, leg, foot, and other "indicators" of nervousness may decrease, and eye contact may increase during deception.[104]

Often when the deceiver fails to adequately plan and rehearse the deception beforehand, emotional responses to a skilled interrogation will result in uncontrolled body-language responses, which can be and often are properly interpreted as deceit. Emotional reaction is the key factor. Three emotions closely related to the act of deception are worthy of explanation. The first emotion is the fear of being caught lying. The extent of the fear—mild, moderate, heavy—will, of course, influence the suspect's reaction. A number of determinants will influence the extent of apprehension, including the suspect's belief (or knowledge) about the skill of the interrogator in detecting deception. The greater the interrogator's skills are, or are believed to be, the greater the apprehension on the part of the suspect. In actuality, the interrogator must be able to distinguish between the guilty person's fear of getting caught and the innocent person's fear of not being believed.

Other determinants controlling the degree of apprehension include the level of experiences and successes the suspect has had in deceiving people in the past, the level of fear about the punishment for being detected, and the "acting ability" of the suspect (is he or she a good or bad liar?)[105]

The second emotion caused by deception is guilt about lying as distinguished from any feelings about the content of the lie. The greater the guilt about lying, the greater will be the emotional reaction irrespective of the existence or degree of guilt about the criminal act itself.[106]

The third emotion, about which there is not much research, is the positive feeling that can accompany lying. Some subjects experience excitement at the challenge of being deceptive or at successfully deceiving the interrogator, especially if the interrogator has a reputation for being hard to deceive.[107]

When a suspect is being deceptive, her or his emotional reactions produce physiological changes. These changes may be observed in a suspect as changes of the position of the head; changes in facial color and in facial expression, including facial tics; changes that occur in the nose, the mouth, and the behavior of lips; changes in smoking behavior; changes in the eyes, including pupillary responses and blinking; changes in the arms, shoulders, and elbows, including the manner and behavior of crossing arms; changes in the use and positioning of the hands; changes in the positioning and movement of the legs, knees, and feet; and changes in sitting postures.[108]

The relationship between emotional triggers and physiological changes can be summarized as follows:

> FEAR is the major activator of [these] physical change[s]. The penalty for being caught in a criminal activity is reasonably clear. The threats of imprisonment, financial loss, or personal embarrassment are sufficiently obvious [to the interviewee] so that no life-long conditioning process is necessary to explain the fear response. While fear is the emotion most likely to [surface] during deception . . . conflict and guilt can also alter the physical state of the individual. . . . Conflict causes tension or anxiety that, like guilt and fear, activates the body processes. During interviews, culpable people tend to have more tension and related physiological changes such as blushing, sweating palms, and other reflections of internal turmoil. . . . The autonomic nervous system causes certain behavioral changes which may be evident to the observant investigator as possible signals of deception.
>
> Fear and conflict are inherent responses, but what a person reacts to is learned. Guilt, on the other hand, is a learned response that had its beginnings in early childhood. Parents, church, and important people in a child's life teach a specific set of values, attitudes, and morals. These teachings are begun early and taught so thoroughly that they become very firmly ingrained within the person. Every time he goes against their teachings, he punishes himself through guilt until he, like most people, functions within the bounds of his conscience.[109]

## STATEMENT ANALYSIS

Aside from the issues of how to properly document an interrogation, particularly as it relates to obtaining a confession that will later be used in court, a story told by the suspect while being interrogated is more than just facts. How the person says something may reveal far more than what is said. If possible, an experienced interrogator will attempt to have the suspect's statement reduced to a verbatim transcript, which will give the interrogator the opportunity to examine the statement thoroughly. This process is know as **statement analysis.** This transcript often provides additional insights into what the suspect intended to convey. For example, honest persons rarely talk about themselves in the third person, but dishonest persons often do so.

Pronoun usage offers a great opportunity for gaining insight into the suspect's thinking. The absence of the word "I" in the later portion of a statement, when questions are more specific about the suspect's involvement in the offense, suggest that the suspect is unwilling to acknowledge involvement. Refusal to use that personal pronoun shows

Logical Approach = works best w/ males with criminal records, educated people and mature adults



an extremely impersonal approach to the topic about which questions are being asked. However, if the word "I" changes to "we" during the interrogation, the switch often suggests an attempt by the suspect to dilute his or her own responsibility and to imply the involvement of others—in other words, trying to spread the blame.

Verb tense can also be important. Normally when an individual recalls a past event, he or she describes it in the past tense. That is because, when remembering, the mind sees what has occurred. However, if there is no memory, because the event never occurred, the mind must create the occurrence as it goes along. Hence, a suspect who is being deceptive may often use descriptive terms in the present tense. When this occurs, there is most likely some deception.

Balance is also a common element of speech. A story usually consists of an introduction, a body, and a closing. A deceptive person will sometimes spend just a short time talking about the important issues concerning the offense and spend a great deal of time describing extraneous information or trivia.[110]

## INTERROGATION TECHNIQUES AND APPROACHES

Identical techniques do not work for all interrogations. Approaches and questions differ with the type of suspect being questioned. Questioning a suspect whose guilt is certain requires a different approach from that used in questioning a suspect whose guilt is uncertain. Similarly, different approaches are used to interrogate unemotional and emotional suspects. All these techniques assume either a logical approach or an emotional approach. The **logical approach** is based on common sense and sound reasoning. It tends to work better with males with past criminal records, educated people, and mature adults. The **emotional approach** appeals to the suspect's sense of honor, morals, righteousness, fair play, justice, family pride, religion, decency, and restitution. This approach tends to work better with women and first-time offenders.

When a suspect's guilt is certain, the interrogator should display confidence in this fact, perhaps by asking the suspect *why* rather than *if* he or she committed the crime, by pointing out the futility of telling lies, and by asking the suspect, "Aren't you sorry to have become involved in this mess?" Warning the suspect to tell the truth and pointing out some of the circumstantial evidence of guilt are also techniques to be used when guilt is certain. Calling attention to psychological and/or physiological symptoms of guilt can also work.

A sympathetic approach that gives the suspect a way out of a predicament can often be successful, and because the suspect is offered the opportunity to save face, confessions are sometimes forthcoming. Three mechanisms—rationalization, projection, and minimization, collectively called RPM—may be used. Rationalization offers the suspect a plausible way to explain his or her actions in a positive light. Projection excuses an act by placing the blame on someone or something else. Minimizing the offense or the suspect's role in its commission may provide psychological satisfaction that might cause the suspect to acknowledge participation in the crime.[111]

When a suspect's guilt is uncertain, the interrogator should begin with an indirect approach, assuming that the interrogator already possesses all necessary facts. By using all physical evidence, photographs, and sketches and challenging all lies, the interrogator may make this method extremely productive.

With the emotional suspect, the interrogator may call attention to physiological and psychological symptoms indicating guilt while pointing to the futility of resistance and appealing to the suspect's pride.

The "Mutt-and-Jeff," or good-guy/bad-guy, approach to interrogation works in some cases. One partner plays the bad guy, who rejects and refuses to believe all explanations put forth by the suspect. When that partner finally leaves the room, the good guy makes an emotional appeal and offers friendly assistance so that the suspect will not have to be confronted again by the bad guy.

Playing one person against the other sometimes works when there are at least two suspects, both of whom swear they are telling the truth during separate interrogations. The interrogator asks the first suspect to write on a piece of paper, "I swear I am telling the truth," and sign it. The interrogator then shows the paper to the second suspect, telling this

Emotional Approach = works best w/ woman and 1st time offenders suspect that the first suspect just told the whole story but, that, before the interrogator totally accepts the story, he or she would like to hear the true story from this suspect.

Thus, trickery and deceit are often used in interrogation. The U.S. Supreme Court has not disapproved of these methods as long as they are not forcefully used to encourage an innocent person to incriminate himself or herself.

For suspects who are undergoing the negative reactions of anger, depression, denial, and bargaining before acceptance is achieved, as discussed earlier, there are causes and symptoms that an experienced interrogator can identify and use to prepare appropriate questions and responses. For example, anger exemplifies frustration of the suspect. The interrogator should not get caught up in the anger but, rather, should allow the anger to burn itself out. If it is not encouraged and the interrogator does not respond to the display of anger, it will generally disintegrate in short time.

Depression is aggression directed internally rather than externally, as in the case of anger. There may be both verbal and nonverbal symptoms of depression that are fairly obvious, such as a bowed head, downcast eyes, slumped or hunched shoulders, crying, and remarks about being depressed. The interrogator must be able to distinguish between clinical depression, which will clearly indicate that the interrogation will not produce helpful results; feigned depression, in which the interrogator should bargain with the suspect to attempt to overcome the depression; and stress-related depression, which can be caused by the interrogation process. Stress-related depression should be encouraged by the interrogator, as it can result in the suspect's use of additional defensive reserves and thus reduce the energy levels needed to continue resisting the interrogator.

When a suspect whose guilt is certain enters a state of denial, the interrogator must go on the attack. This is an appropriate time to affirmatively accuse the suspect of the commission of the crime and to begin letting the suspect know that there already exists an assumption that he or she committed the crime and that it is time to move on to other issues.

When a suspect enters the state of bargaining, this indicates that the suspect accepts the reality of his or her involvement, but only to a limited extent. Normally, the suspect will still want to share responsibility. This is a good time to use techniques that will make it easier for the suspect to live with his or her involvement without expecting the suspect to accept full responsibility.

When the state of acceptance is reached, it is a positive state in which a confession is most likely to occur.[112]

## TECHNOLOGICAL AIDE

In 1996, instructors who teach interviewing and interrogation at the FBI Academy met with representatives from the Applied Physics Laboratory at Johns Hopkins University. Their goal was to determine if the laboratory could create a computer program that would simulate a human personality. The Applied Physics Laboratory delivered such a program in 1998. Since then, the FBI has been using a software program that enables students to practice interviewing and interrogation techniques with a computerized subject that simulates a human personality. The "interviewee personality" emulates the many different types of individuals that investigators encounter in interview and interrogation situations. The user-friendly, self-paced learning package is interesting enough to make students want to use but is designed so that students cannot "beat the system" by learning a pattern of questions to ask.[113]

The subject character, Mike, has a "brain" designed with both logical and emotional components. The computer randomly selects fluctuations of Mike's emotional state so that his mood and his answers change each time the user conducts an interview or interrogation. Thus, the student-user never knows how Mike will respond from one interview to the next.[114]

A manual is provided with the CD software. Users review a case study and then select a category of questions from choices covering different parts of Mike's life, such as his personal habits, work relationships, or possible involvement in the crime. The user conducts the interview by selecting questions from a long list of possibilities. As Mike responds (or does not respond), the computer provides new questions and eliminates those that are no longer relevant. Mike's emotional responses also include body language that affects the line of questioning the user might take. At any time during the interview, the user can replay and review the interview. When the user decides to end the interview, he or she must determine whether Mike was truthful or deceptive. At the conclusion, the user is given a score. The program can be used repeatedly for practice purposes; as the user becomes more proficient, he or she can progress through four levels of increasing difficulty.[115]

At the FBI Academy, the software appears to be improving the interviewing and interrogating skills of those who are using it. The FBI will provide the software free to state and local law enforcement agencies.[116]

### THE IMPORTANCE OF LISTENING

Regardless of the amount of their preparation and experience, investigators can conduct a fully successful interview or interrogation only if they are good listeners. There never was and never will be a completely successful interview or interrogation if the investigator *hears* but does not *listen*. Hearing without listening, without concentrating, without comprehending that which is being communicated by the other party, provides little useful information.

Listening is as valuable in interviewing and interrogation as is questioning. Investigators should first listen to witnesses' full stories and then ask specific questions triggered by that careful listening. The resulting information is likely to be complete and accurate.

Being a good listener is not easy. To be effective, one must be an active listener too. It has been estimated that 65 percent of communication is nonverbal. Active listening requires that listeners be conscious of their own body movements, eye contact, hand gestures, facial expressions, head nodding, and tones of voice. All these nonverbal forms of communication must convey interest in a witness or suspect and in what he or she is saying. Even a slight movement, such as leaning toward the person while listening, conveys interest and enthusiasm. Discouraging nonverbal messages may adversely affect an interview and cause an otherwise cooperative person to become evasive or defensive. In such an instance, a witness might wonder, "Why should I try to help if this investigator isn't interested enough to care what I'm saying?"

Another tactic in good listening is to repeat or paraphrase witnesses' or suspects' stories. This tactic, known as verification, provides the opportunity to check the stories and ensure the quality of communication in the interview.

Every communication has two components—the verbal, which consists of the content, and the nonverbal, which is the emotional or attitudinal element. Both are critical to listening and, hence, to effective communication.

Notes or other means of documenting the interview should, when possible, reflect the emotional as well as factual components of the interview.[117]

Active listening is of utmost importance in an interrogation. In addition to being attuned to the body language of the suspect, the interrogator must listen to the verbal component of a communication in a two-dimensional manner. On the one hand, the content per se is an important outcome of the interrogation. On the other hand, and equally important, is the necessity of understanding the intention and meaning of what is being said. To effectively listen to and evaluate the communication in these two dimensions, it is necessary for the interrogator to follow the basic rule of being a good active listener: Be quiet!

## DOCUMENTING THE INTERVIEW

In the majority of routine cases involving interviews, handwritten notes made by the investigator during and immediately following the interview generally serve as sufficient documentation. Investigators should not rely on memory for the storage of investigative information. The human mind can absorb and recount only a limited amount of information at one time, and most of the information is soon lost if notes are not taken.

Note taking during the interview raises two primary concerns for the interviewer. First, it may occasionally be distracting or suspicious to a witness; witnesses may be reluctant to give information knowing that it is being documented. Consequently, the investigator should tell witnesses that notes will prevent the need for subsequent interviews due to lapses of the investigator's memory. This will usually ease the reluctance of the witness. Second, the interviewer should avoid becoming preoccupied with taking notes, for this creates the appearance of inattentiveness. As important as notes may be, the interviewer should treat them as less important than conversation with the witness. Note taking during the interview should be kept to a minimum, recording only salient details. As soon as possible after the interview, the investigator should complete the notes, before memory wanes.

In some instances, it is desirable for witnesses to write or sign statements concerning the events of which they have knowledge. Statements generally are not necessary in routine cases. However, in important cases, if there is likelihood that the witness may change statements in the courtroom or may not be available to testify, a signed statement in the witness's handwriting can be extremely valuable.

The best form of documentation is a sound recording or a sound-and-visual recording of the interview. Visual recordings are generally not practical when the interview is held anywhere other than a police station, where equipment can be permanently situated. Cassette tape recorders, however, are inexpensive, portable, and helpful in the majority of cases. The recorded interview has many significant advantages: All information is recorded in the witness's own words, details are not left to be recalled by human memory, concerns about detracting from the interview by note taking are absent, interviewers may listen to the verbatim conversations over and over at a later time to be sure that they have understood completely and accurately, and the taped interview might avoid unnecessary reinterviews. The advantages and disadvantages of each type of documentation are shown in Table 4–3.

At the conclusion of an interview, it is wise for investigators to review and evaluate their performance. The checklist in Table 4–4 can serve as a good review and basis for self-evaluation. Such a self-critique can serve as an excellent learning tool for improving one's ability as an interviewer. Experience is the best teacher only if you learn from your mistakes.[118]

## DOCUMENTING THE INTERROGATION

Documenting an interrogation consists of three main phases: note taking, recording, and obtaining written statements. All three of these phases

**Table 4-3** Comparison of Types of Interview Documentation

| Type | Advantages | Disadvantages |
|---|---|---|
| Memory | Quick and easy | Limited absorption and recall<br>Most information lost shortly afterward |
| Note taking by interviewer | Sufficient in most cases<br>Captures salient details<br>Prevents need for reinterviewing | May distract or offend witness<br>May preoccupy interviewer, creating appearance of inattentiveness<br>May cause interviewer to miss nonverbal messages |
| Handwritten or signed statements by witness | Useful if witness cannot testify<br>Can be used to impeach if witness changes story in court | Request may be offensive to witness<br>Not necessary in routine cases |
| Sound or sound-and-visual recordings | Relatively inexpensive<br>Some equipment portable<br>All information recorded in witnesses' own words<br>Does not rely on inaccuracies of memory or another's notes<br>Does not distract<br>Prevents unnecessary reinterviews | Not necessary except in the most important cases<br>Generally not practical |

**Table 4-4** Postinterview Self-Evaluation Checklist

| WITH THIS WITNESS, DID I: |
|---|
| 1. Conduct the interview as quickly, privately, yet conveniently as possible? |
| 2. Establish good rapport with the witness? |
| 3. Listen? |
| 4. Ask good questions? |
| 5. Control the interview? |
| 6. Establish the witness's presence, consciousness, and attentiveness? |
| 7. Determine any factors that now would affect the witness's competency in court? |
| 8. Evaluate the witness's potential credibility in court? |
| 9. Use the right approach in seeking information? |
| 10. Get complete and accurate information? |
| 11. Document the interview well? |

are geared to accomplishing two basic functions: retaining information for the benefit of the interrogator and the continued investigation and securing of a written statement or confession from the accused for later use as evidence in court.

The three most widely accepted means of keeping notes during an interrogation are mental notes, written notes, and notes taken by a third party. There are advantages and disadvantages to each. The advantages of making mental notes are (1) the subject is able to communicate with the interrogator without being constantly interrupted while the interrogator makes notes and the note keeping is not distracting to the suspect. The disadvantage is apparent: If the interrogation continues for any period of time, details that might have proved to be of considerable importance are likely to be lost in the maze of information.

Written notes are more advantageous in that they permit the interrogator to document salient information. However, even a well-trained interrogator can record only a certain amount of information during an interrogation, and there is a tendency to concentrate on the major points while disregarding minute but salient details. In addition, making written notes requires thought and concentration. The interrogator may not fully concentrate on what the suspect is saying and thus may miss something important. Note taking may also distract the subject, who may be hesitant to convey the truth, knowing that the information is being taken down.

Although having a trained third party, such as a stenographer, take notes during an interrogation can provide the most extensive documentation of information, including the suspect's own words (useful for statement analysis), the person's presence can be a distraction to the subject. The subject may not want to communicate openly knowing that a third party is present and that complete notes are being taken.

The situation dictates which, if any, of these methods are to be used. The interrogator should keep in mind that the primary objective is to communicate with the subject. If note taking will hinder that function, the advantages and disadvantages must be weighed.

Recording an interrogation is the best means of documentation. Audio, video, or a combination of both may be used, but, because of the absence of case law to serve as a legal guide, local requirements should be checked.

Police use of audio-video technology to document interrogations became widespread in the 1990s. During that period, the Christopher Commission recommended video technology to the Los Angeles Police Department as a means of reducing police brutality and protecting officers from unfair accusations of using excessive force. One year later, the Kolts Commission criticized the Los Angeles County Sheriff's Department for failing to tape-record statements by witnesses and officers involved in police shootings. A citizen's videotape of

Rodney King's beating illustrates the power video technology can have on judges and juries.[119]

In the early 1990s, one out of every six law enforcement agencies used videotaping in at least some interrogations situations; in larger jurisdictions, about one third did so. In most jurisdictions the videotaping was used for the most serious crimes; as the severity of the offense lessened, so did the use of videotaping in interrogations.[120]

Videotaping interrogations offers many advantages. Videotapes force investigators to better prepare for conducting interrogations; clarify whether an interrogator missed something that requires further questioning; give prosecutors a better understanding of cases, thereby fostering better charging decisions, plea-bargaining options, and case preparation; minimize challenges by defense attorneys about the accuracy of audiotapes and the completeness of written confessions; reduce doubts about the voluntariness of confessions; and jog investigators' memories when they are testifying. In addition, tapes can be reviewed and used as training aids for interrogators and other investigators.[121]

Nearly all agencies videotape openly, rather than covertly, and tell suspects that they are being taped. Often, the camera and microphone are visible during the session. There seems to be no significant difference between the number of confessions from videotaped suspects and that from nonvideotaped suspects. Some offenders may be less likely to incriminate themselves on tape, but others take advantage of the opportunity to either put on a show or "get if off their chest." As noted earlier, state and local law should be consulted in regard to videotaping interrogations and the subsequent admissibility of videotaped confessions in court. Federal constitutional law should not be a bar, since a suspect would be hard-pressed to prove that he or she had a "reasonable expectation of privacy" in an interrogation room, in a law enforcement agency, and after having been advised of his or her *Miranda* rights.[122]

Because the law is constantly evolving concerning the use and admissibility of videotaping, many courts allowing its use require testimony of a qualified technician or operator as a condition of admissibility. The technician must be sufficiently knowledgeable and experienced with the equipment and process of videotaping to assure the court that all the equipment was in working order, that the tape was not edited, and that a proper chain of custody was maintained. Despite every effort to ensure fairness and accuracy in the taping process, a court may find other reasons to suppress a tape. Therefore, it has been suggested that, when possible, it is best to obtain a statement first and then have it repeated on tape. Then if the tape is suppressed, the confession may still be admissible.

Quality equipment and tapes should be used to ensure a quality product. It should be remembered that the purpose behind this effort is to convince a jury. The higher the quality, the more convincing it will be. Interrogators and technicians must be aware that little things can affect the message on the tape. For example, it is important to select a location for taping that exudes an atmosphere of fairness and nonhostility. A background filled with handcuffs, firearms, wanted posters, and sounds of blaring sirens is not likely to portray the kind of impression to the jury that the law enforcement agency or prosecutor desires.

Audio documentation is the second-best method for recording. Its introduction in court necessitates establishing the identity of the people involved in the interrogation and what each had to say. One disadvantage arises if the subject does not know that the interrogation is being recorded. The individual is likely to point out things or make statements that an interrogator can see but no one else will be able to identify from the audio recording. For example, the suspect may hold up a knife and say, "I held it like this." The interrogator knows what is meant, but to a third party listening to the recording later, the words may be meaningless.

Documenting information incriminating the accused may take a number of forms. All of them are generally admissible, but the weight they carry with the jury is likely to vary. The most convincing means that can be used is an audiovisual recording of a confession or admission given by a suspect during an interrogation. Barring the use of such recordings, the next-best form is a signed statement written in the first person by the suspect in his or her handwriting. Frequently, however, it is not possible to convince a suspect to prepare such a statement. Or perhaps the suspect cannot write.

Other forms in which statements may be admitted into evidence, listed in descending order of the credibility that they are likely to have with a jury, are a typed or handwritten statement by someone else that is signed in the accused's own hand; a typed or otherwise prepared statement that the accused does not sign but that is acknowledged in front of witnesses; and the oral testimony of a person who was present and overheard the subject give a confession or admission. In the last case, even though admissible, the testimony is likely to carry little weight with the jury. Table 4–5 lists the types of documentation in descending order of preference and the advantages and disadvantages of each.

The distinction between confessions and admissions is important. A **confession** is defined as an acknowledgment by an accused that he or she has committed a crime. It includes an acknowledgment of the commission of all the elements of the crime and the individual's involvement in their commission. The burden is on the prosecution to prove that a confession was obtained freely and voluntarily. An **admission** is an acknowledgment by the accused of certain facts that tend to incriminate him or her with respect to a particular crime but that are not sufficiently complete to constitute a confession. The burden of proving that an admission was obtained involuntarily is on the defense, should they seek to have it suppressed.

The form and content of a written statement should include a heading, which incorporates the data identifying the circumstances under which the statement was taken; the body of the statement; and a verification. The statement should open with an indication of the place where it was taken; the date, time, city, county, and state; and an identification of the person giving the statement by name, address, and age. The heading must also include a definite statement to the effect that the subject is giving the statement freely and voluntarily after having been appropriately advised of his or her constitutional rights.

The body of the statement, which acknowledges the subject's involvement in the crime under investigation, should, if possible, be phrased in the first person, allowing the suspect to include his or her own ideas in a free-flowing manner. However, if this is not possible or practical, then the question-

**Table 4-5** Comparison of Types of Confession Documentation (in descending order of believability to juries)

| Type | Advantages | Disadvantages |
|---|---|---|
| 1. Video-audiotape or movie | Shows all, including fairness, procedures, and treatment<br>Easy to do<br>Can be relatively inexpensive | May be legal constraints<br>Quality equipment may be costly |
| 2. Audio recording | Can hear conversations<br>Can infer fairness | Some words or descriptions may be meaningless without pictorial support<br>Necessitates identifying people and things involved |
| 3. Statement written and signed in suspect's own handwriting | Can be identified as coming directly from suspect | Can't see demeanor or hear voice inflections<br>Suspect may not agree to procedure |
| 4. Typed statement signed by suspect | Signature indicates knowledge of and agreement with contents of statement | Less convincing than methods described above |
| 5. Typed unsigned statement acknowledged by suspect | Contents of confession or admission are present<br>Acknowledgment helps show voluntariness | Reduced believability of voluntariness and accuracy of contents |
| 6. Testimony of someone who heard confession or admission given | Contents admissible | Carries little weight with juries |

and-answer format is permissible. The terminology used should include the words, grammar, idioms, and style of the person making the statement. The body of the statement should be arranged so that its content follows the chronological order of the subject's involvement in the case under investigation.

As the end, the statement should indicate that the subject has read the statement or has had it read to him or her, that its contents and implications are understood, and that the subject attests to its accuracy.

Other suggestions for the interrogator to keep in mind include:

- Each page of the statement should be numbered consecutively with an indication that it is page _____ of _____ pages. If the pages get separated, they can later be easily restored to order.
- The interrogator should ensure that each page is initialed by the subject. If the subject is unwilling to sign, the statement should be acknowledged by him or her. In instances when the subject cannot write, another identifying mark may be used.
- On occasion an interrogator may encounter someone who says, "I'll tell you what I've done, but I'm not writing anything and I'm not signing anything." In such circumstances the interrogator can explain that the suspect just confessed and that the interrogator or some other person who heard the confession can go into court and testify about it. By preparing or signing a statement, the suspect protects himself or herself against the interrogator's testifying to something more damaging by changing the story in court.
- If the suspect cannot read, the statement must be read to him or her, and the interrogator must ensure that the suspect understands its contents before the suspect is allowed to attest to its accuracy.
- All errors in the statement should be corrected on the final copy and initialed by the suspect. The interrogator may accommodate the suspect by allowing small errors if this will help obtain the suspect's initials on each page of the statement.
- The interrogator should make sure that the suspect understands all the words used in the statement. If some words are confusing, their meanings should be explained to the subject and the subject should be required to explain them back in front of witnesses in order to establish understanding.
- During the process of drafting and attesting to a statement derived through interrogation, there should be at least one additional witness who can testify to the authenticity of the statement and the circumstances under which it was obtained. After the suspect signs the statement in ink, the witnesses should sign their names, addresses, and positions.[123]

## ADMISSIBILITY OF CONFESSIONS AND ADMISSIONS

Prior to 1936 the only test for the validity and admissibility of a confession or admission was its voluntariness. However, the determination as to whether it was given voluntarily by the suspect was subject to very loose interpretation. There were no rules restricting the method by which police obtained "voluntary" statements. Physical violence, psychological coercion, empty promises, and meaningless guarantees of rewards were not considered objectionable procedures.

### THE FREE-AND-VOLUNTARY RULE

The first notable incidence of Supreme Court intervention into interrogation practices came about in *Brown* v. *Mississippi*.[124] In this 1936 case, the Supreme Court held that under no circumstances could a confession be considered freely and voluntarily given when it was obtained as a result of physical brutality and violence inflicted by law enforcement officials on the accused. The reaction to this decision by police was not unexpected. Many threw up their hands and claimed that they could no longer function effectively because "handcuffs had been put on the police." However, as was true with many other decisions placing procedural restrictions on law enforcement agencies, the police found that they were able to compensate by conducting thorough criminal investigations.

Subsequent to the *Brown* decision, the Supreme Court, in a succession of cases, has continued to reinforce its position that any kind of coercion, whether physical or psychological, would be grounds for making a confession inadmissible as being in violation of the **free-and-voluntary rule.** This includes such conduct as threatening bodily harm to the suspect or members of the suspect's family,[125] using psychological coerecion,[126] engaging in trickery or deceit, or holding a suspect incommunicado. Investigators are also cautioned about making promises to the suspect that cannot be kept. All these practices were condemned in *Miranda* v. *Arizona.*[127] Despite the appearance that *Miranda* has eliminated all coercive techniques previously used in interrogations, this is not actually the case. What *Miranda* seeks is to abolish techniques that would prompt *untrue* incriminatory statements by a suspect. Thus, unlike physical coercion, psychological coercion, threats, duress, and some promises, the use of trickery, fraud, falsehood, or similar techniques are not absolutely forbidden. If such methods are not likely to cause an individual to make self-incriminating statements or to admit to falsehoods in order to avoid threatened harm, confessions or admissions so obtained are admissible.[128]

## THE DELAY-IN-ARRAIGNMENT RULE

In 1943, the Supreme Court delivered another decision concerning the admissibility of confessions. Even though the free-and-voluntary rule was in effect in both the federal and state courts, another series of statutes seemed to have gone unheeded. Every state and the federal government had legal provisions requiring that after arrest a person must be taken before a committing magistrate "without unnecessary delay." Before 1943, if there was an unnecessary delay in producing the accused before a committing magistrate, the delay was merely one of a number of factors that the courts were required to take into consideration in determining whether the confession was freely and voluntarily given.

The facts of *McNabb* v. *United States* reveal that McNabb and several members of his family were involved in bootlegging. They were arrested after the murder of federal officers who were investigating their operation in Tennessee. McNabb was held incommunicado for several days before he was taken before a committing magistrate. He subsequently confessed, and the confession was admitted into evidence at his trial. He was convicted, but on appeal to the Supreme Court the conviction was reversed. The Court held that the failure of federal officers to take the prisoner before a committing officer without unnecessary delay automatically rendered his confession inadmissible. The significance of this case is that for the first time the Court indicated that failure to comply with this procedural requirement would render a confession inadmissible regardless of whether it was obtained freely and voluntarily. Thus, instead of examining the facts of the case to determine the voluntariness of the confession, the Court ruled, as a matter of law, that the procedural violation also rendered the confession inadmissible.[129] The holding in the *McNabb* case was emphatically reaffirmed in 1957 by the Supreme Court in *Mallory* v. *United States.*[130]

As the mandate of the Supreme Court in the *McNabb* and *Mallory* cases had applicability only to federal prosecutions, the states were free to interpret their own statutes on unnecessary delay as they saw fit. Few chose to follow the *McNabb-Mallory* **delay-in-arraignment rule:** the majority have continued to require that there must be a connection between the failure of police to produce the accused before a committing magistrate without unnecessary delay and the securing of a confession.

## Key Terms

**admission**
**Biggers-Brathwaite Factors Test**
**body language**
**cognitive interview technique**
**competency (of a witness)**
**confabulation**
**confession**
**credibility (of a witness)**
**delay-in-arraignment rule**
**emotional approach**
**eyewitness identification**

**free-and-voluntary rule**
**hypercompliance**
**hypersuggestibility**
**hypnosis**
**in-custody interrogation**
**interrogation**
**interviewing**
**kinesics**
**logical approach**
***Miranda* v. *Arizona***
**mirror**
**neuro-linguistic programming (NLP)**
**paralanguage**
**proximity**
**rapport**
**statement analysis**
**suspect**
**totality of the circumstances**
**victim**
**witness**

## Review Questions

1. What is the importance of information to the criminal investigator? How is information obtained?
2. How do the purposes of interviewing and interrogation differ?
3. What are the qualities of an effective interviewer or interrogator?
4. How does an investigator prepare for an interview or interrogation? Are there differences?
5. What factors motivate witnesses to give or withhold information?
6. What special concerns must an interviewer be aware of when interviewing an elderly person?
7. What criteria will affect the competency of a witness?
8. In evaluating the credibility of a witness, with what factors must the investigator be concerned?
9. Despite the amount of reliance placed on information supplied by eyewitnesses, how reliable is it? Why?
10. What role can hypnosis play in a criminal investigation? What are its pitfalls?
11. If the setting for an interview is not ideal, what conditions should be established for conducting the interview?
12. Describe the steps in the interview process.
13. What is neuro-linguistic programming?
14. Describe the cognitive interview technique.
15. What requirements are imposed on law enforcement personnel by *Miranda* v. *Arizona*?
16. Why do some people confess?
17. What is the significance of understanding the meaning of "in-custody interrogation"?
18. How does an interrogator evaluate and thus control a suspect?
19. Describe the conditions under which an interrogation should take place.
20. Of what significance is the interrogator's ability to compose proper questions?
21. Why is an understanding of behavioral and psychological principles important for a successful interrogation?
22. How can statement analysis be of use to an interrogator?
23. Why is listening so important in interviews and interrogations?
24. How can the investigator best document an interview? An interrogation?
25. Why is it important to number the pages in a statement?
26. What is the evidentiary test for admissibility of confessions and admissions?

## Internet Activities

1. Much debate surrounds the fairness and effectiveness of eyewitness identification in police lineups. Go to www.eyewitness.utep.edu/consult05.html and read the summary of the white paper regarding evaluating lineup fairness. What two aspects of lineup fairness should investigators consider? How similar to one another should the members of the lineup be?
2. Learn more about the practice and legal implications of testimony developed under hypnosis by logging on to www.crimelibrary.com/

forensics/hypnosis/3.htm. When was hypnosis first used in court? What are the legal implications and potential problems with the use of hypnosis? What is the current status of forensic hypnosis?

## Notes


1. Marshall Houts, *From Evidence to Proof* (Springfield, IL: Charles C. Thomas, 1956), pp. 10–11.
2. John E. Hess, *Interviewing and Interrogation for Law Enforcement* (Cincinnati: Anderson, 1997), pp. 33.
3. John E. Hess, *Interviewing and Interrogation for Law Enforcement* (Cincinnati: Anderson, 1997), pp. 81–84; Charles L. Yeshke, *The Art of Investigative Interviewing* (Boston: Butterworth-Heinesmann, 1997), pp. 56–68.
4. Stan B. Walters, *Principles of Kenesic Interview and Interrogation* (New York: CRC Press, 1996), p. 1.
5. Yeschke, *The Art of Investigative Interviewing,* pp. 25–40, 113–134.
6. David Gullo, "Child Abuse: Interviewing Possible Victims," *FBI Law Enforcement Bulletin,* January 1994, p. 20.
7. New York City Police Department, *Student's Guide—Social Science 1998,* pp. 4–7. This discussion of the process of aging was provided by the New York City Police Department.
8. Brian L. Cutler and Steven D. Penrod, *Mistaken Identification: The Eyewitness, Psychology, and the Law* (New York: Cambridge University Press, 1995) p. 6.
9. Ibid, p. 7.
10. Robert L Donigan, Edward C. Fisher, et al., *The Evidence Handbook,* 4th ed. (Evanston, IL: Traffic Institute, Northwestern University, 1980), p. 205.
11. Robert Buckhout, "Eyewitness Testimony," *Scientific American,* December 1974, Vol. 231, No. 6, p. 23. Also see Elizabeth F. Loftus, Edith L. Greene, and James M. Doyle, "The Psychology of Eyewitness Testimony," in *Psychological Methods in Criminal Investigation and Evidence,* David C. Raskin, ed. (New York: Springer, 1989), pp. 3–45; Hunter A. McAllister, Robert H. I. Dale, and Cynthia E. Hunt, "Effects of Lineup Modality on Witness Creditability," *Journal of Social Psychology,* June 1993, Vol. 133, No. 3, p. 365.
12. Cutler and Penrod, *Mistaken Identification,* p.112.
13. Janet Reno, Message from the Attorney General," Introduction in National Institute of Justice, Office of Justice Programs, *Eyewitness Evidence: A Guide of Law Enforcement* (Washington, DC: U.S. Department of Justice, October 1999), p. iii.
14. Siegried Ludwig Sporer, Roy S. Malpass, and Guenter Koehnken, *Psychological Issues in Eyewitness Identification* (Mahwah, NJ: Lawrence Erlbaum, 1996), p. 23.
15. Cutler and Penrod, *Mistaken Identification,* p. 113.
16. Sporer, Malpass, and Koehnken, *Psychological Issues,* pp. 26–29.
17. Ibid., pp. 34–35.
18. Ibid., pp. 36–39.
19. Buckhout, "Eyewitness Testimony," p. 24.
20. Elizabeth Loftus, "Incredible Eyewitness," *Psychology Today,* December 1974, Vol. 8, No. 7, p. 118.
21. Buckhout, "Eyewitness Testimony," pp. 24–26.
22. Ibid., p. 28.
23. Ibid.
24. Cutler and Penrod, *Mistaken Identification,* p. 113.
25. Ibid., p. 135. See also Gary L. Wells, et al., "Eyewitness Identification Procedures for Lineups and Photospreads," www.unl.edu/ap-ls/whiteeye.html.
26. Cutler and Penrod, *Mistaken Identification,* p. 113.
27. Technical Working Group for Eyewitness Evidence, Office of Justice Programs, National Institute of Justice, *Eyewitness Evidence: A Guide for Law Enforcement* (Washington, DC: U.S. Department of Justice, October 1999).
28. Ibid.
29. Ibid.
30. 388 U.S. 293, 87 S.Ct. 1967, 18 L.Ed.2d 1199 (1967).
31. 409 U.S. 188, 93 S.Ct. 375, 34 L.Ed.2d 401 (1972).
32. 432 U.S. 98, 97 S.Ct. 2243, 53 L.Ed.2d 140 (1977).
33. "Identification, Bail, Asset Forfeiture, and Other Pretrial Procedures,"
34. Bill Putnam, "Some Precautions Regarding the Use of Hypnosis in Criminal Investigations," *Police Chief,* May 1979, p. 62. Also see G. D. Burrow, "Forensic Aspects of Hypnosis," *Australian Journal*

of *Forensic Sciences,* 1981, Vol. 13, no. 4, pp. 120–125.

35. Kimberly A. Kingston, "Admissibility of Post-Hypnotic Testimony," *FBI Law Enforcement Bulletin,* April 1986, pp. 23–24.
36. Ibid., p. 23.
37. Fred Graham, "Should Our Courts Reject Hypnosis?" *Parade Magazine,* Oct. 25, 1981, p. 10.
38. Ibid.
39. Ephram Margolin, "Hypnosis Enhanced Testimony: Valid Evidence or Prosecutor's Tool?" *Trial,* 1981, Vol. 17, No. 110, p. 43.
40. Kingston, "Admissibility of Post-Hypnotic Testimony," p. 23.
41. Ibid., p. 24.
42. Kevin M. McConkey and Peter W. Sheehan, *Hypnosis, Memory and Behavior in Criminal Investigation* (New York: Guilford, 1995), pp. 4–6.
43. John E. Hess, *Interviewing and Interrogation for Law Enforcement* (Cincinnati: Anderson, 1997), p. 19.
44. Paul B. Weston and Kenneth M. Wells, *Criminal Investigation: Basic Perspectives* (Englewood Cliffs, NJ: Prentice-Hall, 1970), p. 151.
45. Hess, *Interviewing and Interrogation,* p. 84.
46. Thomas Streed, "The Psychology of Interviewing and Interrogation," unpublished document, copyright by Thomas Streed, 1986, pp. 21–22, and used with permission of the author. Portions of this material were obtained in a telephone interview with Detective Thomas Streed, San Diego, California, County Sheriff's Department, October and November 1990.
47. Vincent A. Sandoval and Susan H. Adams, "Subtle Skills for Building Rapport: Using Neuro-Linguistic Programming in the Interview Room," *FBI Law Enforcement Bulletin,* August 2001, p. 1.
48. Law Enforcement Communications Unit, *Interviewing and Interrogation,* unpublished manuscript, FBI Academy, Quantico, VA, p. 14.
49. Sandoval and Adams, "Subtle Skills for Building Rapport," p. 2.
50. Ibid., p. 3.
51. Law Enforcement Communications Unit, *Interviewing and Interrogation,* pp. 16–17.
52. Sandoval and Adams, "Subtle Skills for Building Rapport," pp. 4–5.
53. Charles C. Vanderbosch, *Criminal Investigation* (Washington, DC: International Association of Chiefs of Police, 1968), p. 196.
54. Hess, *Interviewing and Interrogation,* pp. 13–14.
55. Loftus, "Incredible Eyewitness," p. 119.
56. Hess, *Interviewing and Interrogation,* pp. 24–25.
57. Ibid., p. 25.
58. R. Edward Geiselman and Ronald P. Fisher, "Interviewing Victims and Witnesses of Crime," National Institute of Justice, *Research in Brief,* December 1985, p. 1. See also Ronald P. Fisher and Edward Geiselman, *Memory Enhancing Techniques for Investigative Interviewing: The Cognitive Interview* (Springfield, IL: Charles C. Thomas, 1992).
59. Irwin W. Fisk, "Hypnotic Transition," *Police,* June 1990, p. 94; Geiselman and Fisher, "Interviewing Victims and Witnesses," p. 2.
60. Geiselman and Fisher, "Interviewing Victims and Witnesses," p. 2.
61. Ibid., p. 3. For an exhaustive treatment of the cognitive interview technique and experiments that have been conducted, see R. Edward Geiselman and Ronald P. Fisher, "The Cognitive Interview Technique for Victims and Witnesses of Crime," in David C. Raskin (ed.), *Psychological Methods in Criminal Investigation and Evidence* (New York: Springer Publishing, 1989), pp. 191–215.
62. *Escobedo* v. *Illinois,* 378 U.S. 478 (1964).
63. *Miranda* v. *Arizona,* 384 U.S. 436 (1966).
64. 451 U.S. 477, 101 S.Ct. 1880 (1981).
65. 498 U.S. 146 (1990).
66. 108 S.Ct. 2389 (1988).
67. 423 U.S. 96, 96 S.Ct. 321 (1975).
68. 492 U.S. 195, 109 S.Ct. 2875 (1989).
69. Fred E. Inbau and John E. Reid, *Criminal Interrogation and Confessions* (Baltimore: Williams & Wilkins, 1962), p. 1.
70. 425 U.S. 341 (1976).
71. 429 U.S. 492 (1977).
72. 429 U.S. 492, 495 (1977).
73. 103 S.Ct. 3517 (1983).
74. 89 S.Ct. 1095 (1969).
75. 699 F.2d. 466 (9th Cir. 1982)
76. 736 F.2d. 1232 (8th Cir. 1984).
77. 391 U.S. 1 (1968).
78. 110 S.Ct. 2394 (1990).
79. 104 S.Ct. 2626, 81 L. Ed. 550 (1984).
80. 82 L. Ed. 317 (1984).

81. 392 U.S. 1 (1968). For additional references, see C. E. Riley III, "Finetuning Miranda Policies," *FBI Law Enforcement Bulletin,* January 1985, pp. 23–31; R. Jacobs, "The State of *Miranda,*" *Trial,* January 1985, pp. 45–48.
82. 468 U.S. 420, 104 S.Ct. 3138, 82 L. Ed. 317 (1984). See also *Pennsylvania* v. *Bruder,* 109 S.Ct. 205 (1988).
83. 109 S.Ct. 205 (1988).
84. *United States* v. *J.H.H.,* 22 F.3d 821 (8th Cir. 1994).
85. *Stansbury* v. *California,* 511 U.S. 318 (1994).
86. 430 U.S. 387 (1977).
87. 446 U.S. 291, 100 S.Ct. 1682 (1980).
88. *Pope* v, *Zenon,* 69 F.3d 1018 (9th Cir. 1995).
89. John C. Klotter and Jacqueline R. Kanovitz, *Constitutional Law,* 4th ed. (Cincinnati: Anderson Publishing, 1981), p. 343.
90. Robert L. Donigan, Edward C. Fisher, David H. Hugel, Robert H. Reeder, and Richard N. Williams, *The Evidence Handbook,* 4th ed. (Evanston, IL: Traffic Institute, Northwestern University, 1980), p. 44.
91. 107 S.Ct. 1931 (1987).
92. *United States* v. *Clark,* 982 F.2d 965, at 968 (6th Cir. 1993).
93. Paul Eckman and Maureen O'Sullivan, "Hazards in Detecting Deceit," in Raskin, *Psychological Methods,* p. 297.
94. John Fay, unpublished notebook from a Workshop in Criminal Interrogation, November 17–18, 1981, sponsored by the Jacksonville, Florida, Chapter, American Society for Industrial Security, pp. A5-1–A5-2.
95. Hess, *Interviewing and Interrogation,* pp. 66–69.
96. Walters, *Principles of Kenesic Interview and Interrogation,* p. 9.
97. Yeschke, *The Art of Investigative Interviewing,* pp. 13–14.
98. Walters, *Principles of Kenesic Interview and Interrogation,* p. 73.
99. Charles G. Brougham, "Nonverbal Communication: Can What They Don't Say Give Them Away?" *FBI Law Enforcement Bulletin,* July 1992, pp. 15–18.
100. See Daniel Goleman, "People Who Read People," *Psychology Today,* July 1979. See also Daniel Goleman, "The 7000 Faces of Dr. Ekman," *Psychology Today,* February 1981, p. 43; John Leo, "The Fine Art of Catching Liars," *Time,* Apr. 22, 1985, p. 59.
101. Forest E. Kay, Jr., "Detecting Deceptions during the Criminal Interview," *Police Chief,* May 1979, p. 57.
102. William Hart, "The Subtle Art of Persuasion," *Police Magazine,* January 1981, p. 10.
103. Eckman and O'Sullivan, "Hazards in Detecting Deceit," p. 297.
104. Ibid., pp. 297-299.
105. Ibid., pp. 302–306.
106. Ibid., pp. 306–310.
107. Ibid., pp. 310–312.
108. Stan B. Walters, *Principles of Kenesic Interview and Interrogation,* pp. 73–138.
109. Stanley A. Abrams, *Polygraph Handbook for Attorneys* (Lexington, MA: Lexington Books, 1977), as reported in Yeschke, *The Art of Investigative Interviewing,* pp. 16–17.
110. Hess, *Interviewing and Interrogation,* pp. 59–64.
111. Michael R. Napier and Susan H. Adams, "Magic Words to Obtain Confessions," *FBI Law Enforcement Bulletin,* October 1998, pp. 11–15.
112. Walters, *Principles of Kenesic Interview and Interrogation,* pp. 141–158.
113. Owen Einspahr, "The Interview Challenge: Mike Simmen versus the FBI," *FBI Law Enforcement Bulletin,* April 2000, p. 17.
114. Ibid.
115. Ibid., pp. 17–20.
116. Ibid., p. 16.
117. Edgar M. Miner, "The Importance of Listening in the Interview and Interrogation Process," *FBI Law Enforcement Bulletin,* June 1984, pp. 12–16.
118. Hess, *Interviewing and Interrogation,* p. 26.
119. William A. Geller, "Videotaping Interrogations and Confessions," *Research in Brief,* Office of Justice Programs, National Institute of Justice, (Washington, DC: U.S. Department of Justice, March 1993), p. 1.
120. Ibid., pp. 1–3.
121. Ibid., pp. 5-7.
122. Ibid., p. 4.
123. See Timothy T. Burke, "Documenting and Reporting a Confession: A Guide for Law Enforcement," *FBI Law Enforcement Bulletin,* February 2001, Vol. 70, No. 2, pp. 17–21.
124. 297 U.S. 278 (1936).
125. *Payne* v. *Arkansas,* 356 U.S. 560 (1958).
126. *Miranda* v. *Arizona,* 384 U.S. 436 (1966).

127. Ibid.
128. Donigan et al., *The Evidence Handbook,* pp. 47–48. See also *Frazier* v. *Cupp* 394 U.S. 731 (1969); *Oregon* v. *Mathiason,* 429 U.S. 492 (1977).
129. 318 U.S. 332 (1943).
130. 354 U.S. 449 (1957).

# FIVE

# Field Notes and Investigative Reporting

*Police sergeant checking the identity of a person at an automobile service center. If the interview begins to yield useful information, the sergeant will begin taking field notes. (Courtesy Georgetown, South Carolina, Police Department)*

## CHAPTER OUTLINE



## CHAPTER OBJECTIVES

1. Understand the importance of field notes.
2. Distinguish between basic and primary investigative questions.
3. List the six primary investigative questions.
4. Understand formats for basic incident reports.
5. Discuss aids to information gathering.
6. Summarize the report approval and disposition processes.
7. List elements common to incident reports.
8. Explain techniques involved in writing effective reports.

## INTRODUCTION

Field notes play a significant role in every criminal investigation. They provide a short written record of events, times, places, suspects, witnesses, and other information and are used as the basis of incident/offense reports. The importance of taking effective and complete notes in every investigation, regardless of the offense, should not be underestimated. Because field notes are more reliable than a person's memory, they can be used as a source of specific facts and details that otherwise might be forgotten. Detailed field notes also reduce the need to recontact victims and witnesses regarding information that was overlooked or questions that were not asked in the initial contact. Finally, it is not uncommon for officers to testify in court several months or years later regarding a particular investigation. Comprehensive field notes not only can help refresh the investigator's memory but also can strengthen his or her court testimony.

This chapter examines several aspects of the field-note and report-writing processes. After discussing field notes and the basic and primary questions that need to be asked in an investigation, it addresses the importance of completing well-prepared incident/offense reports. Incident-report formats vary among law enforcement agencies. Despite the variation, however, there are common elements that should be included in all reports. Investigators should gain as much information as possible when arriving at the crime scene. Even facts and details that seem unnecessary at first may later prove to be highly valuable to the investigation.

Aids to information gathering are also discussed in this chapter. Investigators will often interview witnesses and victims who may be unable to provide or articulate important details. Visual and descriptive aids such as suspect description forms and photographs of weapons can improve the information-gathering process. After presenting a brief overview on the growing use of mobile data terminals and other computerized tools that facilitate the report-writing process, the chapter concludes with a discussion on writing effective reports.

## FIELD NOTES

The subject of field notes was introduced in Chapter 2. There it was explained that **field notes** are the shorthand written record made by a police officer from the time she or he arrives at the scene until the assignment is completed. The factors discussed below explain the importance of field notes.[1]

*Field notes are more reliable than an officer's memory.* It is probably easy to remember what you had for breakfast this morning, but what about your lunch five months ago?[2] Often an officer "shags" several calls before he or she has time to write an incident/offense report on an earlier call. Even during that short period of time, some important details can be forgotten. The only way to prevent the possibility of lost information is to prepare thorough field notes.

*Field notes are the primary information source for the incident/offense report.* Because the first-responding officer is usually the person who writes any incident report required by the situation, field notes are important as they contain the information that forms the content of the incident report. Moreover, other officers who also responded may have taken actions or seen and heard things that are of investigative significance and for which there needs to be an investigative record. They will rely on their own field notes to write reports that supplement the incident report. Well-taken, detailed field notes are the wellspring for good incident reports.

*Detailed field notes may reduce the need to recontact the parties involved.* Once in a while, victims and witnesses get annoyed and even angry when they are recontacted by an officer who obviously didn't take good field notes when he or she talked to them earlier and therefore cannot complete the incident report without additional information. Comments such as "Weren't you listening to me?" or "You couldn't be very interested in my case or you would have asked about this when you talked to me the first time" can be avoided by thorough note taking. The follow-up investigator faces the possibility of similar comments when recontacting victims and witnesses: "Didn't you talk to the officer who took the report?" "With you guys, it looks like the left hand doesn't know what the right one is doing." Although follow-up investigators may be required by departmental policy to make such contacts, sometimes they may have to do so because of shortcomings in the incident report. (For more on this point, see Chapter 6, "Follow-Up Investigation."

*Field notes can be used to defend the integrity of the incident/offense report.* When an officer is testifying in a case for which he or she wrote the incident report, the officer can refer to field notes for assistance in recollecting the events. Most often, cases come to trial months after the incident report is written, so it would be rare for a testifying officer to remember everything about the event and all its details. In court, field notes are an indication of an officer's thoroughness as an investigator. Moreover, if at trial an officer is asked what sources of information were relied on in preparing the incident report, the notes add to the credibility of the report.

### GUIDELINES FOR NOTE TAKING

There are six main guidelines that should be followed when taking notes:

1. Listen attentively, without interrupting the person who is speaking.
2. Intervene if the speaker is losing focus; bring the person back to the topic as gently as possible.
3. Review all specifics in your notes with the person providing the information.
4. Allow time for the person to consider the information you have stated and to verify it, correct it, or add information.
5. Add and/or correct information as needed.
6. Verify all changes in your notes with the speaker.[3]

## Equipment

Officers typically use small loose-leaf and spiral-bound notebooks for their field notes. Through experience they learn which sizes and types best suit the way they work.[4] Most officers use a ballpoint pen to write their notes. If you are going to write on the front and back of pages, do not use a heavy ink, as it "bleeds" through to the other side of a page and you will not be able to use that side for note taking. Number the pages separately for each case, and use some kind of case identifier, such as the case number, on each page so that the pages can be put back in place if they are accidentally separated.

Officers should place a departmental business card, or duplicate its information, on the inside of the notebook used for field notes. In no event should an officer's home address or telephone number be recorded in the notebook, as this information provides an easy opportunity for harassment if the notebook is lost.

Entries in the notebook should be made on a chronological basis. If you are using a loose-leaf notebook, remove the pages when they are filled, place them in a sealed envelope with the covered time period noted on the outside, and insert new blank pages. If you are using a spiral-bound notebook, place the entire notebook in a sealed envelope and start with a new one. Unless departmental policy dictates otherwise, most officers keep their notes in their lockers.

## Basic and Primary Questions

The basic questions the first-responding officer to a crime scene needs to ask are those that will elicit the information needed on the face of an incident report. Typically this information includes the type of crime, who the victims and witnesses are and how to contact them, the specifics associated with the crime, and descriptions of the suspect, any associated vehicles, and any stolen property. Some officers make their notes on a copy of an incident report so that they are less likely to overlook any basic information.

Numerous other questions must also be asked. Although no single set of questions can meet the investigative needs in all types of crime, six primary questions have long been recognized in the field as being very useful. These questions are summarized as follows:

1. What
   - crime was committed?
   - actions did the suspect take?
   - methods did the suspect use?
   - do witnesses know about the crime?
   - evidence is there?
   - tools or weapons were used?
   - actions did you take?
   - further action is needed?
   - knowledge, skills, or strength was needed?
   - other units or agencies are involved or need to be notified?
2. When
   - were you dispatched, and when did you arrive?
   - was the crime discovered?
   - was the crime committed?
   - was the victim last seen?
   - did help arrive, and what type was it?
   - was the suspect arrested?
   - did the suspect decide to commit the crime?
3. Where
   - was the crime discovered?
   - was the crime committed?
   - were any tools, evidence, or recovered property found?
   - was the victim when the crime was committed?
   - is the victim now?
   - were the witnesses?
   - did the suspect go?

- does the suspect frequent, live, and work?
- is the suspect now?
- was the suspect arrested?
- was the evidence marked?
- is the evidence stored?
- might other witnesses be located?

4. Who
- was the victim?
- discovered the crime?
- reported the crime?
- took the victim to his or her present location?
- does the suspect associate with?
- was last seen with the victim?
- last saw the victim?
- may be with the suspect when he or she is arrested?
- are the witnesses connected with or related to?
- had a motive and the means of committing the crime?
- completed the crime scene entry and other logs?
- processed the scene?
- took what evidence where?
- else may have heard, smelled, touched, or seen anything of investigative value?

5. How
- was the crime committed?
- did the suspect get to and from the scene?
- did the suspect get the information needed to commit the crime?
- were tools and weapons obtained?
- was the arrest made?
- much injury was done to the victim?
- much damage was there to any premises involved?
- much money and valuables of what type were taken?
- difficult was it to carry off the property that was stolen?
- much information may victims and witnesses be withholding?
- much does the victim claim was stolen?
- well does the victim's account of the event match that of any witnesses, the appearance of the scene, and the physical evidence?
- much information and evidence of what types do you need to clear the crime?
- is the suspect described by the victim and witnesses?
- closely do the descriptions of victims and witnesses match and diverge?

6. Why
- was the crime committed?
- were particular tools or weapons used?
- was the crime reported?
- is there a delay in reporting the crime?
- was the victim or witnesses reluctant to talk?
- was the victim or witnesses so quick to identify the suspect?
- am I uncomfortable with the victim's account and description of the suspect?

## INCIDENT REPORTS

The two most fundamental truths about police departments are (1) they are labor intensive, with as much as 80 percent of the operating budget going to personnel costs, and (2) they are information driven. Despite the fact that **incident reports** are a crucial source of investigative information, writing them is often not a popular duty. More than a few excellent investigations have been undone by an officer's failure to fully document what was done and not done. The case history that follows indicates the importance of recording all aspects of an investigation:

A burglary in progress was reported at a one-story doctor's office. As two officers moved to cover the building, a suspect was seen leaping from an office window carrying a small flight bag. The suspect ran from the scene, followed by one of the officers. He attempted to scale a fence. In the ensuing struggle, the suspect fell on the far side of the fence, breaking his arm. During treatment at a hospital, the suspect told the officer, in front of medical personnel, that he was going to claim his arm had been broken during questioning. He further indicated this would be an attempt to discredit the police, as he had only recently been released from the state prison and feared that such an immediate second violation would cause the court to invoke a stringent sentence upon conviction. Because many arrested people state that they are going to claim the police violated their civil rights, the officer regarded it as little more than a commonplace occurrence. Even though they did not relate directly to the investigation, the suspect's remarks and the identity of persons witnessing them were included in the report as a matter of thoroughness. Subsequently, when the FBI investigated the matter of a possible violation of the suspect's rights, the allegation was easily refuted by corroborating statements from the medical personnel identified in the police officer's report.

A well-prepared incident report based on a thorough investigation of an offense also promotes the rapid apprehension of the suspect, thus preventing further crimes and making the recovery of property more likely. The report also serves as the official memory of the department. Offenses may be placed in an inactive status, receiving no further investigative treatment for some time. If an officer resigns from the force, retires, or gets transferred to other duties, resulting in the assignment of another investigator to the case, the incident report ensures that complete information will be readily available at future dates to people who may not have been involved in the case originally.

Incomplete or improperly prepared incident reports may, ironically, be associated with complaints that officers often voice about prosecutors and judges. Inadequate reports may contribute to such practices as refusal to prosecute, a weakening of the prosecutor's plea-bargaining position, and lenient sentences. Prosecutors and police agencies serving the same jurisdictions sometimes jointly develop a list of key questions that can be used by the police and the prosecutor as a checklist for investigating and preparing criminal cases.

Incident reports serve important operational and administrative purposes. When their data are combined, useful crime analysis reports can be produced, personnel assignments in the department can be properly aligned with the actual workloads, and geographic information system (GIS) data can produce informative maps showing, for example, where robberies with certain types of characteristics are being committed. Moreover, by reviewing the reports written by subordinates, supervisors get a current picture of the quality of their officers' investigative efforts and report-writing skills. On the basis of such information, supervisors can give constructive feedback to subordinates, as well as make appropriate performance evaluations.

## FORMATS FOR INCIDENT REPORTS

While the exact layout for incident reports varies from one jurisdiction to another, they all have a "face" with blank spaces that must be filled in by the officer conducting the preliminary investigation. He or she enters basic case information in the blanks, such as information about the type of crime committed; the complainant, victim, witnesses, and offenders; and other details. Figure 5–1 is a basic incident report.

The virtue of the face of an incident report is that a great amount of information can be recorded on just one page. However, the information may not be available, as is the case with a dismembered body, partial skeletal remains, or a fire that was set to conceal some other crime.

Almost always, there is more information to document than can fit on the face of an incident report. The additional information is entered chronologically in **narrative style.** This narrative is the officer's recorded account of events from the time he or she was dispatched to the scene until the completion of the preliminary investigation. The account is written in the blank space on the reverse of the report's face or on a page referred to as "continuation," "investigative narrative," or "supplemental" (see Figure 5–2, a case that started as a missing-person report and turned into a criminal homicide investigation). Less commonly, the procedures of an agency may require that the narrative be written in

**Figure 5-1** Basic Incident Report

(**Source:** Courtesy Athens-Clarke County, Georgia, Police Department)

CRN 01-____-____-_______

**Athens-Clarke County Police**
INCIDENT REPORT

Page 1 of ___
ORI - GA0290100
Revised 0900

Press Hard - Multiple Copies

Press Hard - Multiple Copies

From Date | From Time | To Date | To Time | ☐ Complainant ☐ Victim No. ___ ☐ Witness No. ___ Desires Personal Information Not Be Released

Department Title Most Serious Criminal / Traffic / Ordinance Offense. See Table. | Zone | ☐ Downtown ☐ AHA

Incident Location - Common Name | Address: No., Dir., St., Suffix, Apt. | ☐ Athens ☐ Winterville ☐ Bogart

**Premise Type**
☐ 1. Highway
☐ 2. Serv. Station
☐ 3. Conv. Store
☐ 4. Bank
☐ 5. Commercial
☐ 6. Residence
☐ 7. School/Campus
☐ 8. All Other

**Case Status**
☐ Active
☐ Inactive
☐ Arrest -Adult
☐ Arrest-Juv.
☐ Ex. Cleared
☐ Unfounded
**Status Date**

☐ Alcohol Related ☐ Drug Related ☐ Unknown

**Type Of Drug(s)** ☐ Amphetamine ☐ Barbiturate ☐ Cocaine ☐ Hallucinogen ☐ Heroin ☐ Marijuana ☐ Opium ☐ Methamphetamine ☐ Synthetic Narcotic ☐ Unknown ☐ Form: ________________

**Solvability Factors:** ☐ M.O. Present ☐ Physical Evidence ☐ Property Traceable ☐ Witness

**Suspect Can Be:** ☐ Named ☐ ID ☐ Located ☐ Described ☐ Vehicle ID

**Complainant Information** ☐ Juvenile ☐ Victim
Last | First
Middle | Suffix
Address: No., Dir., St., Suffix, Apt
City, State ☐ Athens, GA | Zip Code
Phone: Home | Work
Race ☐ M ☐ F | DOB

**Victim Information** ☐ Juvenile ☐ State Of GA ☐ A.C.C.
Last
First
Middle | Suffix
Address: No., Dir., St., Suffix, Apt
City, State ☐ Athens, GA | Zip Code
Home | Work | Cell/Pager
Race ☐ M ☐ F | DOB
Alias/Street Name
Employer | Occupation
☐ County Resident ☐ Student | School
☐ Can ID Suspect ☐ Will File Charges ☐ Medical Treatment
Hospital
**Type / Extent Of Injury:** ☐ Fatal Injury ☐ Broken Bones ☐ Gun/Knife ☐ Superficial Injury ☐ Sexual Abuse ☐ Other ☐ Property Damage/Loss ☐ Mental Abuse ☐ Threats

**Witness 1 Information** ☐ Juvenile
Last, First, Middle, Suffix
Address: No., Dir., St., Suffix, Apt
City, State ☐ Athens, GA | Zip Code
Phone: Home | Work
Race ☐ M ☐ F | DOB

**Witness 2 Information** ☐ Juvenile
Last, First, Middle, Suffix
Address: No., Dir., St., Suffix, Apt
City, State ☐ Athens, GA | Zip Code
Phone: Home | Work
Race ☐ M ☐ F | DOB

**Offender 1 Information** ☐ Juvenile
Last
First
Middle | Suffix
Address: No., Dir., St., Suffix, Apt
City, State ☐ Athens, GA | Zip Code
Home | Work | Cell/Pager
Race ☐ M ☐ F | DOB
Alias/Street Name
Employer | Occupation
☐ County Resident ☐ Student | School
OLN | State
Height | Weight | **Stranger To Stranger?** ☐ Yes ☐ No
**Eye Color:** ☐ Black ☐ Brown ☐ Blue ☐ Green ☐ Hazel ☐ Gray ☐ Other________
**Hair Color:** ☐ Blonde ☐ Brown ☐ Black ☐ Red ☐ Gray ☐ Salt&Pepper ☐ Other________
Offender's Vehicle Description ☐ Vehicle Searched
Tag | Year | State
Veh. Year | Make
Model | Style
Color-Top | Color-Bottom

☐ **Incident Recorded** ☐ Hand cuffed
Tape No. ☐ D. L. ☐ B. B.

**Burglary Factors** For Incident/Offense No.______
**Forced Entry?** ☐ Yes ☐ No ☐ Unknown | ☐ Kicked ☐ Pushed ☐ Pry Tool | ☐ Heavy Object ☐ Lock Tamper ☐ Cutting Tool
**Point Of Entry?** ☐ Door ☐ Window ☐ Roof ☐ Wall ☐ Attic ☐ Other ☐ Unk | ☐ Front ☐ Rear ☐ Side ☐ Basement ☐ Move A/C
**Point Of Exit?** ☐ Same As Entry ☐ Other ________________
**Structure Was:** ☐ Occupied ☐ Unoccupied

**Attached Documents:**
☐ **Incident/Offense Continuation**
☐ **Persons Form** ☐ **Juvenile Complaint**
☐ **Domestic Violence** ☐ **Property / Vehicle**
☐ **GCIC** ☐ **ABR** ☐ **Victim Notification**

**Incident /Offense 1** Code Section
☐ Attempted ☐ Committed
Title
**Assault Factors** ☐ Assault ☐ Theft ☐ DV ☐ Sexual ☐ Mental Subject ☐ Hate Crime ☐ Unknown
**Weapon Type** ☐ Gun ☐ Other ☐ Knife/Cutting Tool ☐ Hands/Fists/Etc.
Weapon Description
**Offense Status** ☐ Active ☐ Inactive ☐ Unfounded ☐ Arrest ☐ Ex. Cleared
Involved Suspect No.(s)______ Victim No. (s)______
Murder Circumstance

**Incident /Offense 2** Code Section
☐ Attempted ☐ Committed
Title
**Assault Factors** ☐ Assault ☐ Theft ☐ DV ☐ Sexual ☐ Mental Subject ☐ Hate Crime ☐ Unknown
**Weapon Type** ☐ Gun ☐ Other ☐ Knife/Cutting Tool ☐ Hands/Fists/Etc.
Weapon Description
**Offense Status** ☐ Active ☐ Inactive ☐ Unfounded ☐ Arrest ☐ Ex. Cleared
Involved Suspect No.(s)______ Victim No. (s)______
Murder Circumstance

**Incident /Offense 3** Code Section
☐ Attempted ☐ Committed
Title
**Assault Factors** ☐ Assault ☐ Theft ☐ DV ☐ Sexual ☐ Mental Subject ☐ Hate Crime ☐ Unknown
**Weapon Type** ☐ Gun ☐ Other ☐ Knife/Cutting Tool ☐ Hands/Fists/Etc.
Weapon Description
**Offense Status** ☐ Active ☐ Inactive ☐ Unfounded ☐ Arrest ☐ Ex. Cleared
Involved Suspect No.(s)______ Victim No. (s)______
Murder Circumstance

**Incident /Offense 4** Code Section
☐ Attempted ☐ Committed
Title
**Assault Factors** ☐ Assault ☐ Theft ☐ DV ☐ Sexual ☐ Mental Subject ☐ Hate Crime ☐ Unknown
**Weapon Type** ☐ Gun ☐ Other ☐ Knife/Cutting Tool ☐ Hands/Fists/Etc.
Weapon Description
**Offense Status** ☐ Active ☐ Inactive ☐ Unfounded ☐ Arrest ☐ Ex. Cleared
Involved Suspect No.(s)______ Victim No. (s)______
Murder Circumstance

| Reporting Officer | Emp. No. | Report Date | Approving Supervisor | Emp. No. |
|---|---|---|---|---|
| | | | | |

**Figure 5-2** Portion of an Investigative Narrative

Incident # 2002710051 Report Date: Wednesday, September 27, 2000
THERESA ANDREWS 23 YOA...5'7 BROWNISH RED HAIR 9 MONTHS PREGNANT.
COP ENTRY SENT OUT AT 16:51. 17:19 TELETYPE OHALLTERM SENT OUT. RIVERS WAS CALLED AT 17:57

We received a call to go to 207 W. Riddle Ave. reference a missing person. Circumstances as stated by dispatch was that a female adult was missing from the home. It was reported that the husband came home from work, found the door open, his wife's belongings such as purse, keys, and cell phone at the residence. It was also reported that a person was to take a test ride in a vehicle for sale this morning.

Based on information given by dispatch I asked Detective Francis to accompany myself and Ptl. Wlimington to the residence. Upon arrival we were met my Mr. Andrews who was in the front lawn talking on a cell phone. He appeared to be upset but not frantic.

Upon speaking to him he stated that his wife paged him at work around 9:00 am this morning and told him that a lady was coming by to take a look and test drive their jeep that was for sale. The Pr stated that they have the jeep listed in trading times and were trying to sell the car. He stated that he tried to call back around noon or so and could not get an answer. He stated that he told her not to go with anyone, just get their driver's license and let them take a drive. Pr stated that upon arriving home he found the front door wide open. He stated that his wife's purse, house keys, and cell phone were in the house but she was gone as was the jeep.

The Pr described his wife as being 8 1/2 months pregnant and not feeling well. He stated that she has to be helped in and out of bed and that she had not been feeling well. Pr stated he had checked the hospital and was trying to phone the doctor to see if something had happened with the baby. The jeep was described as all black 1999 with soft top and Ohio Reg. CAB4351 and is a Wrangler type.

Ptl. Wilmington, Det. Francis and myself checked the interior of the house as well as the yard and garage area. No one was located. The house appeared to be very tidy with no signs of foul play or struggle. I instructed dispatch to place a COPS teletype, administrative teletype, and radio broadcast with the information. I also advised dispatch to enter Mrs. Andrews as missing as well as the vehicle.

a particular format with the following types of headings and content:

1. *Additional information about suspects,* such as foreign languages used, regional accents, lisps, notable mannerisms, names they referred to each other by, and weapons displayed.
2. *Information from witnesses,* including their descriptions of events and things as they experienced them through hearing, smelling, touching, and seeing. For example, in addition to giving a basic description of the suspect's vehicle, a witness might be able to make statements about hearing its loud muffler, smelling the car "burn rubber" (who else's attention might this sound also have attracted, and what might they have seen?), and seeing large, fluffy white dice hanging from the rearview mirror.

***Evidence*** The evidence seized, how it was marked, the chain of custody, and the numbers assigned by the property or evidence control room are recorded. If a diagram is made, reference is usually made to it at this point. Original diagrams are placed into the property or evidence control room in the same manner as physical articles seized at the scene. Information pertaining to photographs is also included under this category, as well as other types of evidence, such as latent fingerprints.

***Interviews*** All persons with whom the investigator talked during the course of the inquiry should be identified, even if they could not provide information at the initial contact. On occasion the perpetrator may remain near the scene, usually in property crimes where no witnesses are involved, in an attempt to determine what the police have established. More rarely, the perpetrator or an accomplice will deliberately provide false information in order to misdirect the investigation. The identification of all witnesses is helpful in ferreting out the rare instances of such occurrences. Moreover, people who have actually seen something of value to the inquiry may be reluctant to discuss it with the police at the scene, but will readily reveal it during a follow-up contact.

***Investigation*** A short description of the crime scene may be given to permit a basic conceptualization of it by persons to whom it is unfamiliar. This element requires the documentation of all actions taken by the investigator at the scene regardless of whether they yield useful information.

***Reconstruction*** The **reconstruction** is a narration of the probable manner in which the crime was committed, based on statements made by the suspect (if in custody and cooperating), interviews of witnesses, the examination of the crime scene, and physical evidence.

### NIBRS-Compliant Incident Reports

For roughly a decade, a voluntary program has been moving police departments away from the basic incident-report format and toward a detailed format that documents much more data about an offense. This program, the **National Incident-Based Reporting System (NIBRS),** is administered by the FBI and is in use in over 4,000 small and medium-size local law enforcement agencies throughout the country, as well as a growing number of jurisdictions with populations in excess of 250,000. A large number of departments are working toward becoming NIBRS-compliant.

National crime reporting in this country dates back roughly 70 years, to the time when the FBI began collecting and publishing annual "counts" of offenses in its **Uniform Crime Reports (UCRs).** Over the past 20 years, the desire for detailed, descriptive data about criminal offenses for crime analysis and other uses has necessitated a shift in incident-report formats. With this shift, which is still in progress, police agencies have started accumulating data about the relationship between victims and offenders, the role of drugs and alcohol in offending, and other factors. The availability of NIBRS data means that law enforcement officials can more effectively allocate their resources to combat crime. Figure 5–3 reveals the level of detail in an NIBRS-compliant report, the last page of which is a continuation sheet for the chronological narrative.

The next section of this chapter discusses computer-generated and handwritten incident reports. Such reports may or may not be NIBRS compliant.

## AIDS TO INFORMATION GATHERING FOR INCIDENT REPORTS

Whenever there are witnesses to a crime, even the most conscientious investigator may fail to elicit all information available. Certain aids, however, can be of critical importance in preventing this. One tool, shown in Figure 5–4, is a **suspect description form** for collecting personal-description information about the suspect.

One of the most frustrating experiences for investigators occurs when trying to obtain a description of a firearm, as the victim or witnesses are often injured, unfamiliar with firearms, or visibly shaken by their experience. One helpful device in such situations is photographs of some commonly encountered firearms, as shown in Figure 5–5 (a similar sheet is available for long guns). Very frequently even emotionally upset victims or witnesses can make an identification or at least give a good description of the weapon when these are viewed.

## COMPUTER-GENERATED REPORTS

Since the 1980s, many police cars have been equipped with **mobile data terminals (MDTs).** Although the terminals initially had limited capabilities and occasional reliability problems, MDTs have reduced demands on the overcrowded voice channels and enhanced officer safety. Technological advances continue to create new options and possibilities for the use of wireless systems in police cars. Depending on the system and software used, current MDTs can do the following

1. Provide consistently secure communications between 911 and police units and among police units.

Figure 5-3 NIBRS-Compliant Incident Report

(**Source:** Courtesy Sterling Heights, Michigan, Police Department)

# STERLING HEIGHTS POLICE DEPARTMENT

**ADMINISTRATION**

| OFFICER / #: | DATE: | TIME(S) OF INCIDENT: / | DATE(S) OF INCIDENT: / | INCIDENT #: |
|---|---|---|---|---|
| LOCATION OF INCIDENT: (Address or Block No.) | | ARRIVAL TIME AND DATE: | AREA/SECTION | RELATED INCIDENT #: |
| REPORTEE: (Last, First, Middle) | DOB | | PHONE (Home): ( ) | |
| ADDRESS: (Street, City, State, Zip) | | | PHONE (Business): ( ) | |

**OFFENSE**

OFFENSE:
1. 2. 3.

OFFENSE STATUS: (Check only one per offense)
1.A ❑ ATTEMPTED C ❑ COMPLETED
2.A ❑ ATTEMPTED C ❑ COMPLETED
3.A ❑ ATTEMPTED C ❑ COMPLETED

Assist Agency

SUSPECT(S) USED: (Check as many as apply)
A ❑ ALCOHOL
C ❑ COMPUTER EQUIP.
D ❑ DRUGS
N ❑ NOT APPLICABLE

(For Burglary Only)
NUMBER OF PREMISES ENTERED: ________
METHOD OF ENTRY:
F ❑ FORCEABLE N ❑ NO FORCE

LOCATION OF OFFENSE: (Check Only One) (Enter Code Number for Offense #2 ________ #3 ________ )
01 ❑ AIR/BUS/TRAIN TERMINAL
02 ❑ BANK/SAVINGS & LOAN
03 ❑ BAR/NIGHT CLUB
04 ❑ CHURCH/SYNAGOGUE/TEMPLE
05 ❑ COMMERCIAL/OFFICE BUILDING
06 ❑ CONSTRUCTION SITE
07 ❑ CONVENIENCE STORE
08 ❑ DEPARTMENT/DISCOUNT STORE
09 ❑ DRUG STORE/DR'S OFFICE/HOSPITAL
10 ❑ FIELD/WOODS
11 ❑ GOVERNMENT/PUBLIC BUILDINGS
12 ❑ GROCERY/SUPERMARKET
13 ❑ HIGHWAY/ROAD/ALLEY
14 ❑ HOTEL/MOTEL/ETC.
15 ❑ JAIL/PRISON
16 ❑ LAKE/WATER
17 ❑ LIQUOR STORE
18 ❑ PARKING LOT/GARAGE
19 ❑ RENTAL/STORAGE FACILITY
20 ❑ RESIDENCE/HOME
21 ❑ RESTAURANT
23 ❑ SERVICE/GAS STATION
24 ❑ SPECIALTY STORE (TV, FUR, ETC.)
31 ❑ SCHOOL
32 ❑ COLLEGE
33 ❑ REST AREA/ROADSIDE PARK
34 ❑ SCALE
88 ❑ OTHER
99 ❑ UNKNOWN

TYPE CRIMINAL ACTIVITY: (Check Up To Three)
B ❑ BUYING/RECEIVING
C ❑ CULTIVATING/MANUFACTURING/PUBLISHING
D ❑ DISTRIBUTING/SELLING
E ❑ EXPLOITING CHILDREN
O ❑ OPERATING/PROMOTING/ASSISTING
P ❑ POSSESSING/CONCEALING
T ❑ TRANSPORTING/TRANSMITTING/IMPORTING
U ❑ USING/CONSUMING

TYPE WEAPON/FORCE INVOLVED: (Check Up To Three) (Enter A in Box if Automatic)
11 ❑ FIREARM (type not stated)
12 ❑ HANDGUN
13 ❑ RIFLE
14 ❑ SHOTGUN
15 ❑ OTHER FIREARM
20 ❑ KNIFE/CUTTING INSTRUMENT
30 ❑ BLUNT OBJECT
35 ❑ MOTOR VEHICLE
40 ❑ PERSONAL WEAPONS
50 ❑ POISON
60 ❑ EXPLOSIVES
65 ❑ FIRE/INCENDIARY
70 ❑ NARCOTICS/DRUGS
85 ❑ ASPHYXIATION
88 ❑ OTHER
99 ❑ UNKNOWN
00 ❑ NONE

**ARRESTEE / SUSPECT**

❑ ARRESTEE ❑ SUSPECT SUSPECT CONNECTED TO OFFENSE NUMBER: 1. ❑ 2. ❑ 3. ❑

#1: (Last, First, Middle) | ADDRESS: (Street, City, State, Zip)

DOB: | M ❑ MALE F ❑ FEMALE U ❑ UNKNOWN | W ❑ WHITE B ❑ BLACK I ❑ INDIAN A ❑ ASIAN U ❑ UNKNOWN | PHONE (Home): | PHONE (Business):

ARRESTEE WAS ARMED WITH: (Check Up To Two) (Enter A in Box if Automatic)
01 ❑ UNARMED
11 ❑ FIREARM, (type not stated)
12 ❑ HANDGUN
13 ❑ RIFLE
14 ❑ SHOTGUN
15 ❑ OTHER FIREARM
20 ❑ LETHAL CUTTING INSTRUMENT (e.g. Switchblade, Knife, etc.)
30 ❑ CLUB/BLACKJACK/BRASS KNUCKLES

TYPE OF ARREST:
O ❑ ON-VIEW
S ❑ SUMMONED/CITED
T ❑ TAKEN INTO CUSTODY

ARREST CHARGE:

| HEIGHT: | WEIGHT: | EYES: | HAIR: |
|---|---|---|---|
| __'__" | | | |

❑ ARRESTEE ❑ SUSPECT SUSPECT CONNECTED TO OFFENSE NUMBER: 1. ❑ 2. ❑ 3. ❑

#2: (Last, First, Middle) | ADDRESS: (Street, City, State, Zip)

DOB: | M ❑ MALE F ❑ FEMALE U ❑ UNKNOWN | W ❑ WHITE B ❑ BLACK I ❑ INDIAN A ❑ ASIAN U ❑ UNKNOWN | PHONE (Home): | PHONE (Business):

ARRESTEE WAS ARMED WITH: (Check Up To Two) (Enter A in Box if Automatic)
01 ❑ UNARMED
11 ❑ FIREARM, (type not stated)
12 ❑ HANDGUN
13 ❑ RIFLE
14 ❑ SHOTGUN
15 ❑ OTHER FIREARM
20 ❑ LETHAL CUTTING INSTRUMENT (e.g. Switchblade, Knife, etc.)
30 ❑ CLUB/BLACKJACK/BRASS KNUCKLES

TYPE OF ARREST:
O ❑ ON-VIEW
S ❑ SUMMONED/CITED
T ❑ TAKEN INTO CUSTODY

ARREST CHARGE:

| HEIGHT: | WEIGHT: | EYES: | HAIR: |
|---|---|---|---|
| __'__" | | | |

❑ ARRESTEE ❑ SUSPECT SUSPECT CONNECTED TO OFFENSE NUMBER: 1. ❑ 2. ❑ 3. ❑

#3: (Last, First, Middle) | ADDRESS: (Street, City, State, Zip)

DOB: | M ❑ MALE F ❑ FEMALE U ❑ UNKNOWN | W ❑ WHITE B ❑ BLACK I ❑ INDIAN A ❑ ASIAN U ❑ UNKNOWN | PHONE (Home): | PHONE (Business):

ARRESTEE WAS ARMED WITH: (Check Up To Two) (Enter A in Box if Automatic)
01 ❑ UNARMED
11 ❑ FIREARM, (type not stated)
12 ❑ HANDGUN
13 ❑ RIFLE
14 ❑ SHOTGUN
15 ❑ OTHER FIREARM
20 ❑ LETHAL CUTTING INSTRUMENT (e.g. Switchblade, Knife, etc.)
30 ❑ CLUB/BLACKJACK/BRASS KNUCKLES

TYPE OF ARREST:
O ❑ ON-VIEW
S ❑ SUMMONED/CITED
T ❑ TAKEN INTO CUSTODY

ARREST CHARGE:

| HEIGHT: | WEIGHT: | EYES: | HAIR: |
|---|---|---|---|
| __'__" | | | |

**VEH.**

| IMPOUND Y OR NO | MAKE | MODEL | YEAR | COLOR | V.I.N. | LIC. ST. | LIC. YR. | LICENSE NO. |
|---|---|---|---|---|---|---|---|---|
| | | | | | | | | |

**Figure 5-3** NIBRS-Compliant Incident Report, *continued*

(**Source:** Courtesy Sterling Heights, Michigan, Police Department)

# STERLING HEIGHTS POLICE DEPARTMENT - Part Two

| OFFICER / #: | DATE: | SUPERVISOR / #: | DATE: | INCIDENT #: |
|---|---|---|---|---|
| | | | | |

## VICTIM

| VICTIM #1: (Last, First, Middle) | PHONE (Home): | PHONE (Business): |
|---|---|---|
| | | |

| ADDRESS: (Street, City, State, Zip) | DOB: | M ❑ MALE<br>F ❑ FEMALE<br>U ❑ UNKNOWN | W ❑ WHITE<br>B ❑ BLACK<br>I ❑ INDIAN | A ❑ ASIAN<br>U ❑ UNKNOWN |
|---|---|---|---|---|
| | | | | |

AGGRAVATED ASSAULT/HOMICIDE CIRCUMSTANCES:

01 ❑ ARGUMENT
02 ❑ ASSAULT ON LAW OFFICER
03 ❑ DRUG DEALING
04 ❑ GANGLAND
05 ❑ JUVENILE GANG
06 ❑ LOVERS' QUARREL
07 ❑ MERCY KILLING
08 ❑ OTHER FELONY INVOLVED
09 ❑ OTHER CIRCUMSTANCES
10 ❑ UNKNOWN CIRCUMSTANCES
20 ❑ CRIMINAL KILLED BY PRIVATE CITIZEN
21 ❑ CRIMINAL KILLED BY POLICE OFFICER
30 ❑ CHILD PLAYING WITH WEAPON
31 ❑ GUN-CLEANING ACCIDENT
32 ❑ HUNTING ACCIDENT
33 ❑ OTHER NEGLIGENT WEAPON HANDLING
34 ❑ OTHER NEGLIGENT KILLINGS

TYPE OF VICTIM: (Check Only One)

I ❑ INDIVIDUAL
B ❑ BUSINESS
F ❑ FINANCIAL
P ❑ POLICE OFFICER
O ❑ OTHER
G ❑ GOVERNMENT
R ❑ RELIGIOUS
S ❑ SOCIETY/PUBLIC
U ❑ UNKNOWN

JUSTIFIABLE HOMICIDE CIRCUMSTANCE:

01 ❑ Criminal Attacked Police Officer and that Officer Killed the Criminal
02 ❑ Criminal Attacked Police Officer and Criminal Killed by Another Police Officer
03 ❑ Criminal Attacked a Civilian
04 ❑ Criminal Attempted Flight from a Crime
05 ❑ Criminal Killed in Commission of a Crime
06 ❑ Criminal Resisted Arrest
09 ❑ Unable to Determine/Not Enough Information

VICTIM CONNECTED TO OFFENSE NUMBER

1. ❑
2. ❑
3. ❑

INJURY TYPE:

N ❑ NONE
B ❑ BROKEN BONES
I ❑ POSS. INT. INJURIES
L ❑ SEVERE LACERATION
F ❑ FATAL
M ❑ MINOR INJURY
O ❑ MAJOR INJURY
T ❑ LOSS OF TEETH
U ❑ UNCONSCIOUSNESS

RELATIONSHIP OF VICTIM TO SUSPECT: (For multiple suspect relationships enter suspect number(s) in space before box)

01 ❑ SPOUSE
02 ❑ COMMON-LAW
03 ❑ PARENT
04 ❑ SIBLING
05 ❑ CHILD
06 ❑ GRANDPARENT
07 ❑ GRANDCHILD
08 ❑ IN-LAW
09 ❑ STEPPARENT
10 ❑ STEPCHILD
11 ❑ STEP-SIBLING
12 ❑ OTHER FAMILY
20 ❑ ACQUAINTANCE
21 ❑ FRIEND
22 ❑ NEIGHBOR
23 ❑ BABYSITTEE (baby)
24 ❑ BOY/GIRLFRIEND
25 ❑ CHILD OF "BG" ABOVE
26 ❑ HOMOSEXUAL REL.
27 ❑ EX-SPOUSE
28 ❑ EMPLOYEE
29 ❑ EMPLOYER
30 ❑ OTHERWISE
31 ❑ VICTIM WAS SUSPECT
98 ❑ STRANGER
99 ❑ RELATIONSHIP UNKNOWN

Victim Residence

R ❑ Resident of the Community
C ❑ Resides in the County
S ❑ Resides in the State
O ❑ Out of state
U ❑ Unknown

## WITNESS

| NAME (Last, First, Middle): | ADDRESS (Street, City, State, Zip): | DOB | RESIDENTIAL PHONE: | BUSINESS PHONE: |
|---|---|---|---|---|
| | | | | |
| | | | | |
| | | | | |
| | | | | |

## PROPERTY

| TYPE/ CODE | QTY | DRUGS | PROPERTY DESCRIPTION - INCLUDE MAKE, MODEL, SIZE, TYPE, SERIAL #, ETC. DRUGS - INCLUDE TYPE, QUANTITY, MEASUREMENT | VALUE | DATE RECOVERED Month/Day/Year |
|---|---|---|---|---|---|
| / | | | | | |
| / | | | | | |
| / | | | | | |
| / | | | | | |
| / | | | | | |
| / | | | | | |
| / | | | | | |

TYPE PROPERTY LOSS/ETC.

0 NONE
1 STOLEN/ RECOVERED
2 BURNED
3 COUNTERFEITED/ FORGED
4 DAMAGED/ DESTROYED
5 RECOVERED
6 SEIZED
7 STOLEN
8 UNKNOWN

PROPERTY DESCRIPTION CODE TABLE: (Enter Number in Code Column Above)

01 AIRCRAFT
02 ALCOHOL
03 AUTOMOBILES
04 BICYCLES
05 BUSES
06 CLOTHES/FURS
07 COMPUTER HARDWARE/ SOFTWARE
08 CONSUMABLE GOODS
09 CREDIT/DEBIT CARDS
10 DRUGS/NARCOTICS
11 DRUG/NARCOTIC EQUIPMENT
12 FARM EQUIPMENT
13 FIREARMS
14 GAMBLING EQUIP.
15 HEAVY CONSTRUCTION/ INDUSTRIAL EQUIPMENT
16 HOUSEHOLD GOODS
17 JEWELRY/PRECIOUS METALS
18 LIVESTOCK
19 MERCHANDISE
20 MONEY
21 NEGOTIABLE INSTRUMENTS
22 NON- NEGOTIABLE INSTRUMENTS
23 OFFICE-TYPE EQUIPMENT
24 OTHER MOTOR VEHICLES
25 PURSES/HANDBAGS/WALLETS
26 RADIOS/TVs/VCRs
27 RECORDINGS-AUDIO/VISUAL
28 RECREATIONAL VEHICLES
29 STRUCTURES-SINGLE FAMILY
30 STRUCTURES-OTHER DWELLINGS
31 STRUCTURES-OTHER COMMERCIAL BUSINESS
32 STRUCTURES-INDUSTRIAL/MANUFACTURING
33 STRUCTURES - PUBLIC/COMMUNITY
34 STRUCTURES - STORAGE
35 STRUCTURES - OTHER
36 TOOLS - POWER/HAND
37 TRUCKS
38 VEHICLE PARTS/ACCESSORIES
39 WATERCRAFT
77 PENDING INVENTORY
88 OTHER
99 SPECIAL

TYPE DRUG

01 = "Crack" Cocaine
02 = Cocaine
03 = Hashish
04 = Heroin
05 = Marijuana
06 = Morphine
07 = Opium
08 = Other Narcotics
09 = LSD
10 = PCP
11 = Other Halucinogens
12 = Amphetamines/ Methamphetamines
13 = Other Stimulants
14 = Barbiturates
15 = Other Depressants
16 = Other Drugs
17 = Over 3 Drug Types
99 = Unknown

MEASUREMENT

WEIGHT

GM = Gram
KG = Kilogram
OZ = Ounce
LB = Pound

CAPACITY

ML = Millimeter
LT = Liter
FO = Fluid Ounce
GL = Gallon

UNITS

DU = Dosage Units/Items
NP = Number of Plants
XX = Not Reported

| BIAS | Y❑ N❑ | #1 | | | #2 | | | #3 | | |
|---|---|---|---|---|---|---|---|---|---|---|

**Figure 5-3** NIBRS-Compliant Incident Report, *concluded*

(**Source:** Courtesy Sterling Heights, Michigan, Police Department)

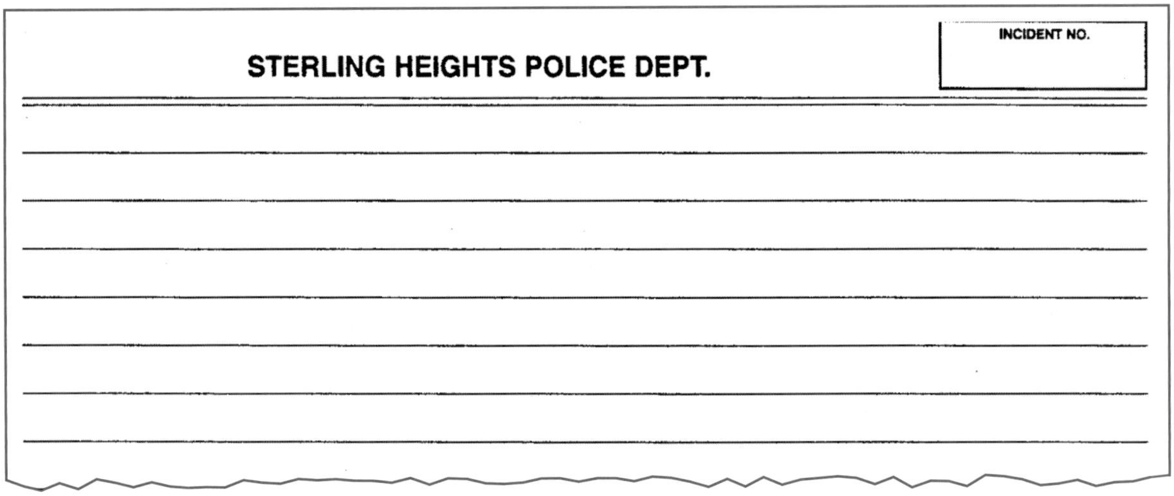

**STERLING HEIGHTS POLICE DEPT.**

INCIDENT NO.

2. Allow officers to directly check important databases (rather than going through a dispatcher and waiting for a reply. They can access the National Crime Information Center (NCIC), as well as state and local systems. Officers can also receive information about newly wanted persons, including a facial composite likeness or mug shot. Outstanding warrants, court orders, stolen property inquiries, criminal and driving records, mug-shot files, crime analysis reports, and GIS maps of crimes and other incidents may all be directly available to the officer.
3. Perform many computing functions via touch screens or penlights.
4. Have e-mail and Internet capabilities.
5. Enable officers in the field to write incident reports electronically, with full access to spelling- and grammar-checking tools. In modest systems, the reports are saved to a disk, from which they are printed at the station. After supervisory review and approval, the reports go to the records unit. In advanced systems, reports are sent wirelessly to the supervisor. If the supervisor declines a report, it is sent back, with comments, to the officer, who resubmits it after addressing the comments. Once a report is approved, the supervisor sends it from his or her MDT to the records unit. (See Figure 5–6 on page 184.)

In addition to using MDTs, some agencies are using **personal digital assistants (PDAs).** These small, handheld units are particularly useful in traffic enforcement. The PDA prints a hard copy of the citation for the violator and sends a digital copy to the station.

Agencies using wireless technologies have experienced significant productivity gains as the systems reduce the amount of time officers must spend on paperwork. In general, the time gained per officer ranges from 2.5 to 4 hours per day.

## HANDWRITTEN REPORTS

Despite the widespread use of MDTs, many officers still write all their reports by hand because their jurisdictions cannot afford MDT technology, have not made its acquisition a priority item in their budgets, or feel that the technology's cost outweighs its benefits. In actuality, when the formats of handwritten and MDT-generated reports are compared, the differences can be so slight that it is difficult to distinguish between the two.

Handwriting reports is slower, and officers do not have the advantages provided by spelling and grammar checkers. Moreover, if officers make mistakes, sometimes the only solution is to rewrite the page up

**Figure 5-4** Suspect Description Form

# IN CASE OF CRIME

Try to remain calm and aware of everything around you. Observe the suspect as closely as possible. Try not to focus on any weapon. Call police only when it is safe to do so, identify your situation, location, name, phone number and wait for them to arrive. Utilize this sheet to record the incident as best you can.

| SEX | SPEECH PATTERN | SCARS | WEAPONS | BAIT MONEY SERIAL NO. |
|---|---|---|---|---|
| | | | | |

| | |
|---|---|
| HAIR | CLOTHING WORN |
| EYES | HAT |
| RACE | FACIAL HAIR |
| AGE | COAT |
| HEIGHT | PANTS |
| WEIGHT | SHOES |

| AUTO DESCRIPTION | WHAT ROBBER SAID | AUTO LICENSE NUMBER |
|---|---|---|
| | | |

| ADDITIONAL REMARKS |
|---|
| |

This form is designed to assist you in remembering the appearance of a suspect. Complete it as soon as possible after the incident. Start at the suspect's head and use the diagram to guide you. Use the reverse of worksheet if additional space is needed. Complete it alone. Do not discuss what you remember with others. The idea is to record what you remember, not to form an agreement with other witnesses.

suspectws.pdf

Philadelphia Police Department
One Franklin Square
Philadelphia, PA 19106

**Figure 5-5** Assorted Handguns

**Source:** *A Visual Aid for Firearms Identification,* Federal Bureau of Investigation.

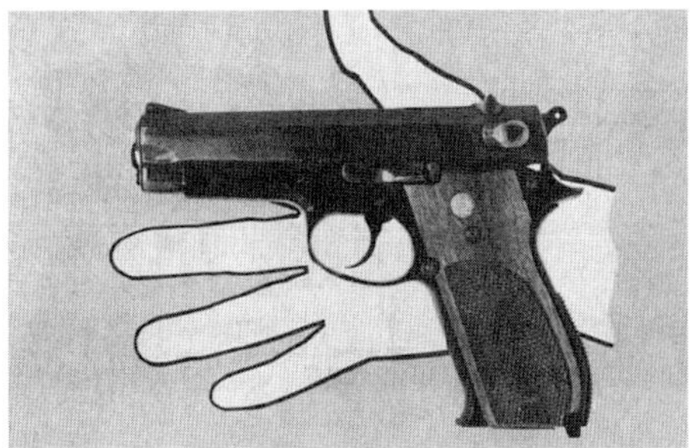

9-mm Smith & Wesson Semiautomatic

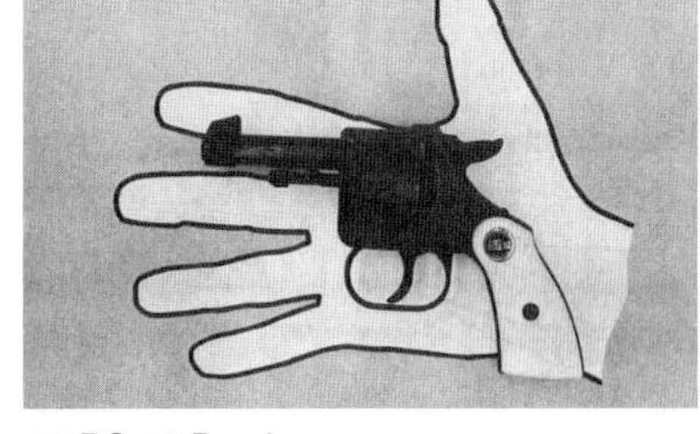

.22 RG-10 Revolver

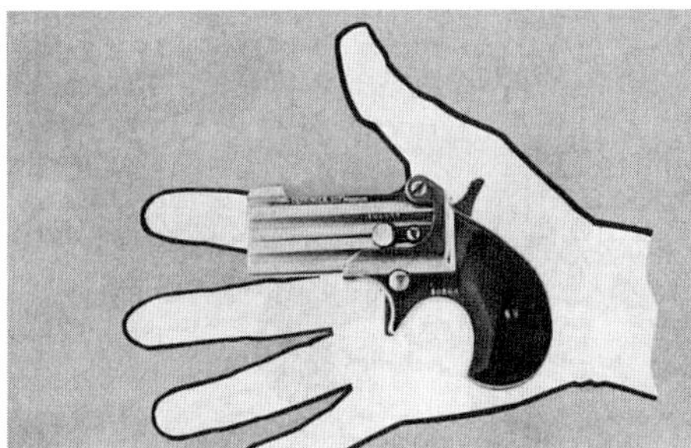

.357 Herter's Derringer

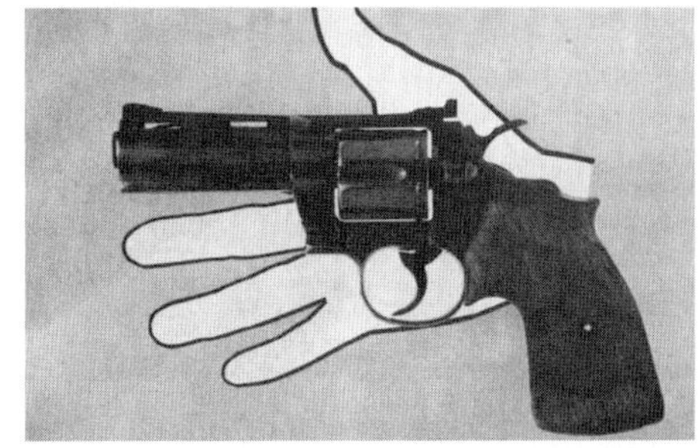

.357 Colt Python Revolver

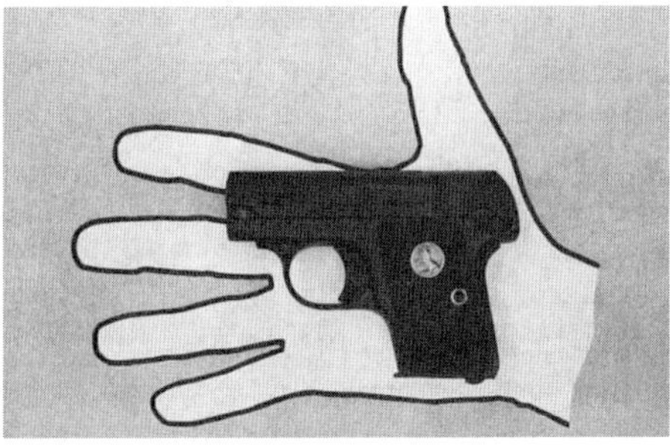

.25 Colt Semiautomatic

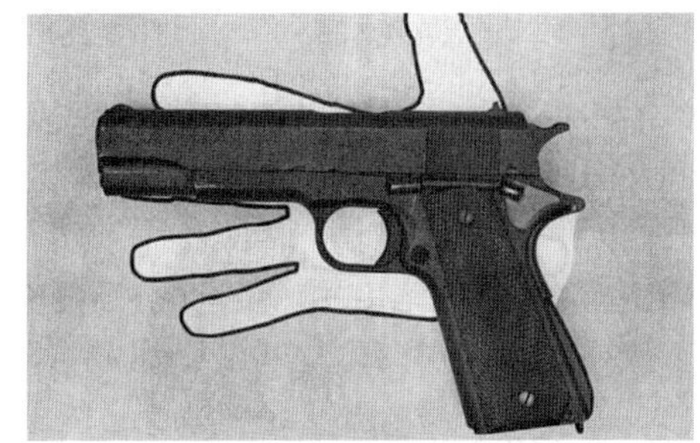

.45 U.S. Semiautomatic

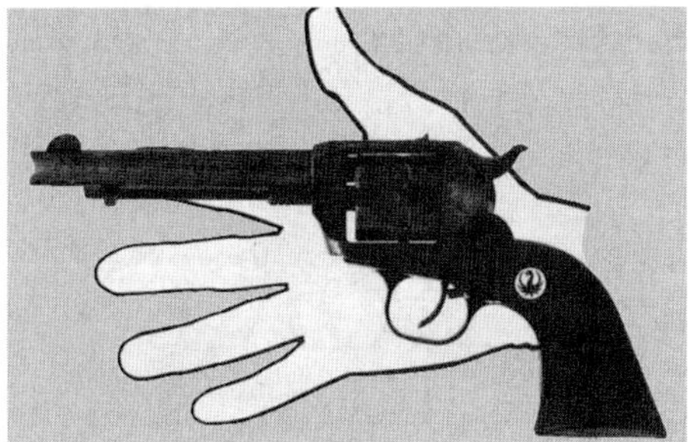

.22 Ruger Revolver

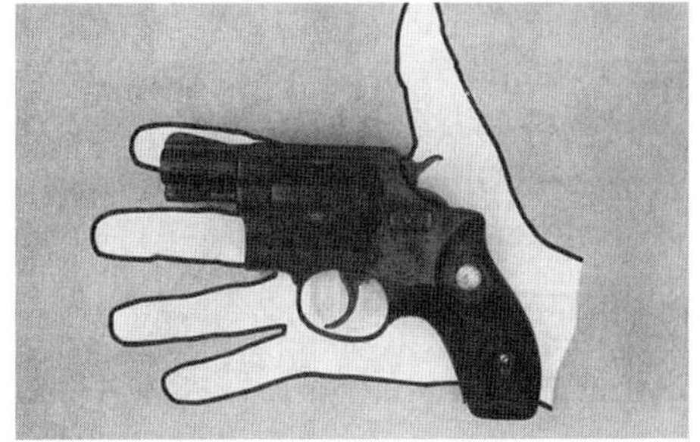

.38 Smith & Wesson Chief's Special Revolver

**Figure 5-6** Screen of an MMDT

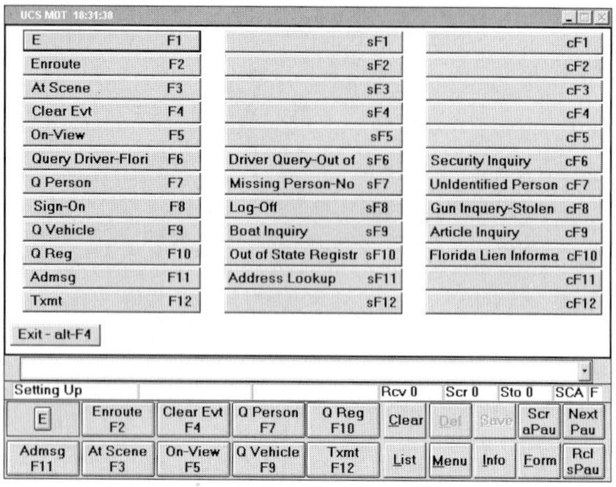

UCS MDT 18:31:38

| | | |
|---|---|---|
| E F1 | sF1 | cF1 |
| Enroute F2 | sF2 | cF2 |
| At Scene F3 | sF3 | cF3 |
| Clear Evt F4 | sF4 | cF4 |
| On-View F5 | sF5 | cF5 |
| Query Driver-Flori F6 | Driver Query-Out of sF6 | Security Inquiry cF6 |
| Q Person F7 | Missing Person-No sF7 | UnIdentified Person cF7 |
| Sign-On F8 | Log-Off sF8 | Gun Inquery-Stolen cF8 |
| Q Vehicle F9 | Boat Inquiry sF9 | Article Inquiry cF9 |
| Q Reg F10 | Out of State Registr sF10 | Florida Lien Informa cF10 |
| Admsg F11 | Address Lookup sF11 | cF11 |
| Txmt F12 | sF12 | cF12 |

Exit - alt-F4

Setting Up Rcv 0 Scr 0 Sto 0 SCA F

| | | | | | | | | | |
|---|---|---|---|---|---|---|---|---|---|
| E | Enroute F2 | Clear Evt F4 | Q Person F7 | Q Reg F10 | Clear | Del | Save | Scr aPau | Next Pau |
| Admsg F11 | At Scene F3 | On-View F5 | Q Vehicle F9 | Txmt F12 | List | Menu | Info | Form | Rcl sPau |

to the point of the error and then continue with the correct information. While officers writing incident reports electronically also make mistakes, recovery is much easier because it is a simple matter to insert additional words, sentences, and paragraphs.

The approval process for handwritten incident reports is much like that described for MDT-generated reports. Several times during the shift the officer's supervisor will call to meet with him or her to review any completed incident reports. If a report is accepted, the supervisor makes a disposition, signs the report, and takes it to the station for processing by the records unit (see Figure 5–7). The original incident report is kept in records, and copies are made and distributed as required by the supervisor's disposition. For example, if the case is referred for follow-up investigation, a copy is sent to the appropriate supervisor, who reviews the report and then assigns the case on the basis of workloads, the level of skill required, and the amount of "heat" and media attention the crime may create.

## SUPERVISORY DISPOSITION OF INCIDENT REPORTS

After approving an incident report, the supervisor must make a **disposition** of it. As depicted in Figure 5–7, any of the following dispositions may be made:

1. The case may be retained for further investigation by uniformed officers.
2. It may be unfounded (i.e., the complaint is false).
3. The case may be inactivated due to the lack of leads.
4. It may be referred to plainclothes investigators.

To some extent, a department's situation and policies affect the supervisor's decision of which dispositions to use. If the Uniform Division is seriously understaffed and officers have been reduced to being "report takers" because they do not have time to conduct thorough preliminary investigations, rarely will a case be retained for further investigation. By policy or the strong will of the investigations commander, the authority to unfound a case may be reserved for an investigation supervisor. In addition, because copies of incident reports may be routinely routed to an investigations supervisor, a uniformed supervisor who has inactivated cases only to have an investigations supervisor reactivate them may be slow about doing anything other than referring them to the investigations division, especially if the reactivations have at least occasionally resulted in the cases being successfully cleared.

## COMMON ELEMENTS OF INCIDENT REPORTS

Incident-report contents vary, ranging from the essential data in a basic incident report to the more extensive information in an NIBRS-compliant report. However, certain elements are common to most reports. Each of these is discussed below.

### Name

The full names of complainants, witnesses, and other parties must always be obtained. In recording proper names, the first time an individual is referred to in a report the sequence of names should be last, first, middle. When a person mentioned in the report is commonly known to acquaintances by some name other than the proper name or an apparent derivation, the nickname should also be provided.

### Race or Ethnicity and Sex

Race or ethnic extraction should never be documented in such a manner as to cast aspersion on a

**Figure 5-7** Report Approval and Disposition Process

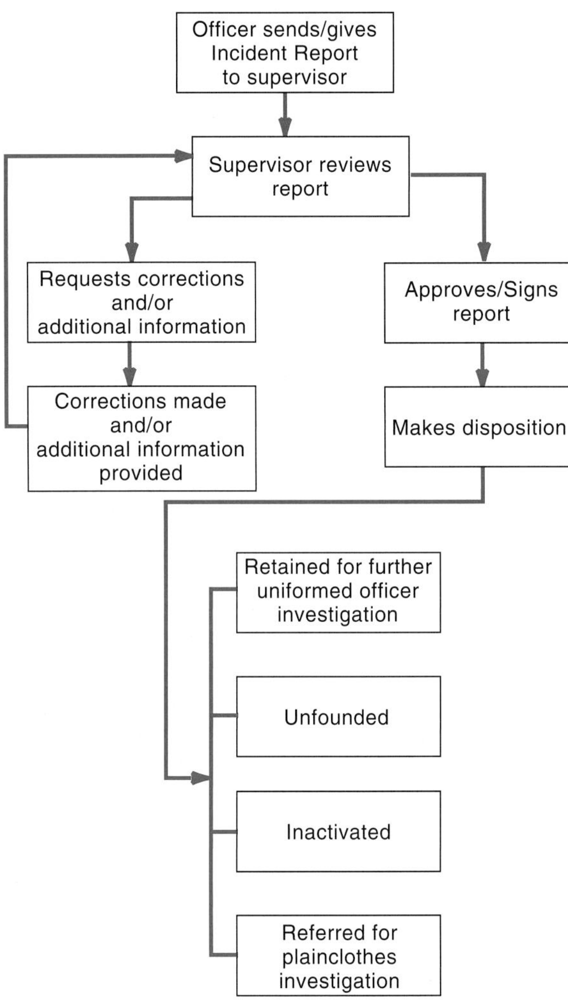


person. Ordinarily race is indicated by use of one of the following abbreviations:[5]

| Race | Abbreviation |
|---|---|
| White | W |
| Black | B |
| Hispanic | H |
| Asian or Pacific Islander | A |
| American Indian or Native Alaskan | I |
| Unknown | U |

Sex is always designated by "F" for female and "M" for male. The proper sequence is race/sex, for example, "W/F."

## Age

On entries requiring only a person's age, it should be indicated as of the last birthday. However, the first reference to the individual in the narrative portion of the report should give the exact date of birth, if known. Birth dates are recorded in an eight-digit sequence of month/day/year: January 10, 1965, would be recorded as "01/10/1965." For certain parties, such as an unidentified deceased person or a suspect whose identity has not been established, age may be approximated or given in a narrow span of years, for example, "approximately 32 years" or "approximately 31–33 years."

## Physical and E-Mail Addresses

This information is particularly important because it helps investigators find people for additional interviews or related procedures. Each residence and business address should show the street number and, when applicable, the apartment, suite, or room number. If this is not immediately ascertainable, the general location should be described in sufficient detail to make its whereabouts known. When military personnel are involved, the location information should include serial numbers, unit designations, and ship or installation, if applicable. If a person is only visiting a location, both temporary and permanent addresses should be obtained. E-mail addresses have become so prevalent that they should be included in the report.

## Telephone, Cell-Phone, and Pager Numbers

The telephone numbers of an individual should always be obtained, including area code, residence number, business number, and any extension number. Additionally, officers should inquire about and record any cell-phone or pager numbers.

## Personal Description

A model form for recording personal descriptions of suspects was shown in Figure 5–4. Minimally, the following points should be included: sex, race, age, complexion, hair and eye color, physical defects, scars, marks, tattoos, build, and the nature and color of clothing worn.

## Property Description

Elements useful in describing property are make, model, serial number, color, and type of material from which constructed. Other types of information may also be pertinent. Using the case of a stolen car as an example, the presence of stickers, cracked windows, articles hanging from the mirror, or loud engine noise would be additional information useful in locating the vehicle.

## Occupation

The occupation of a person may be of some importance to an investigation. In the case of a suspect it may establish familiarity with the use of certain types of equipment or procedures associated with a particular function, such as banking. It may also lend further credibility to the statement of a witness:

> A man exited from a restaurant as two suspects ran about 15 feet from the bank they had just robbed, entered a vehicle, and rapidly drove around the corner. Despite being presented with only a brief view of the car, the witness was able to give the police a fairly detailed description of it. At the trial the defense was unsuccessful in casting doubt on the accuracy of the description, as the witness operated an automobile repair service.

Occupation is also useful in suggesting times when a person might be successfully and conveniently contacted by the investigator. An unemployed individual's ordinary line of work is to be given along with the notation "currently unemployed." Certain categories of people may be unemployed but not seeking a position in the compensated labor market; in such instances it is more appropriate to give the person's exact status, for example, "college student" or "homemaker." If the individual is employed, the occupation given in a report should be as specific as possible, for example, "brick mason" as opposed to "manual laborer."

## Value

The value of property stolen may determine whether the offense is a felony or misdemeanor. For articles subject to depreciation, the fair market value should be used, unless the property is new or almost new, in which case the replacement cost should be used. On goods stolen from retail establishments, the merchant's wholesale cost, which constitutes the actual dollar loss, is the proper value to use. The value placed on nonnegotiable instruments such as traveler's checks or money orders should be the cost of replacing them; negotiable instruments, including bonds payable to the bearer, are valued at the market price at the time of the theft.

When the stolen property is subject to appreciation from the time of its acquisition by the owner—for example, limited-edition prints—the current fair market value is to be indicated.

The value of recovered stolen property ordinarily equals the valuation placed on it at the time of theft unless damaged, in which case it is to be established by the fair market value. In cases where the value of the stolen article is not readily ascertainable, the conservative estimate of the owner may be used.

## Date

As a result of the Y2K problem, police departments abandoned the use of the six-digit format to record dates (MM/DD/YY, e.g., 10/22/98) and adopted an eight-digit format (MM/DD/YYYY, i.e., 10/22/1998) for the same purpose. Many officers continue to use the familiar six-digit format in handwritten reports, but the records unit recodes such entries into the eight-digit format. Birth and other dates should be recorded using the longer format.

## Time

For all official business, excluding general public and related information, most police agencies use the military system, or 24-hour clock, of hundred hours. Time runs from 0001 hours (12:01 A.M.) through 2400 hours (12 A.M.).

# WRITING EFFECTIVE REPORTS

If incident reports are going to serve the many uses to which they can be put, they must meet certain standards. Among the standards most usually cited are proper classification; complete, accurate, concise, objective, and fair information; and timely submission.[6] Keep the following guidelines in mind when you are preparing incident and investigative reports:

1. *Fill in all the blanks* on the incident report unless the information is not available or it is withheld, in which case this should be

explained in the report. As discussed earlier, it is easier to get the necessary information at the scene than to try to recontact complainants and witnesses.

2. *Write the report in the first person,* using "I arrived at the scene at 1645 hours" as opposed to "Officer Morales arrived at the scene at 1645 hours." The reader of the report knows that Officer Morales wrote the report, and the officer's constant reference to himself or herself in the third person (Officer Morales) is awkward. Although some departments require the use of the third person in reports, the trend in report writing is to move away from it.
3. *Avoid unnecessary technical or legalistic jargon* such as "hereinafter," "point of fact," or "thereof," because you may convey a meaning that you do not intend or do not fully understand. Such jargon is a means by which your credibility can be attacked. Avoid writing statements of your own whose meaning you cannot fully explain. Certainly, if a suspect tells you, "I was abducted by aliens who implanted a control box in my head and they sent me commands to rob the pharmacy," you must faithfully record the statement even if you can't explain it—but, the words are not your own.
4. *Write short sentences* because they are less likely to be confusing to or misunderstood by readers, such as the prosecutor. A concise, "punchy" presentation of the facts makes it easier for the reader to "find the beef."
5. *Use short paragraphs* for the same reasons as those for writing short sentences.
6. *Support any conclusions you express with details,* because others who read the report, such as the prosecutor, need to know what facts shaped your thinking. Also, when a trial begins weeks, months, or even years later, you will have forgotten many facts. If you included them in the report, you will be able to refresh your recollection and provide convincing testimony.
7. *Don't repeat facts more than once,* unless doing so is required by your department's reporting format or policies. Duplication of entries wastes your time, and it creates the possibility that when you are distracted, tired, or in a hurry, your entries may conflict in some way with one another, calling your credibility into question.
8. *Check your spelling.* People who don't know you will form opinions of your capabilities on the basis of the reports you write and they read. Also, you are representing your department, so its reputation is on the line because defense attorneys, judges, members of the news media, juries drawn from the community, and prosecutors read police reports. Misspelled words can change the meaning of a sentence or cause the meaning to be lost. Spell-checker software is an aid to accuracy, but it does not catch words that are spelled correctly but used inappropriately (e.g., "E. Wazolewski took a write turn").
9. *Edit what you write.* Don't miss an opportunity to catch and correct your own errors. Many people do this best when they read slowly and out loud, but you may find a system that works better for you. Taking the time to edit your own report is more important than the system you use. If you are using a computer, editing is far easier than writing several successive handwritten drafts of a report. Moreover, the software includes a spell checker, thesaurus, and grammar checker.[7]

Officers also have their own rules, such as putting the most effort into reports for important cases and writing other reports—such as those needed solely to make a minor insurance claim—just good enough to be accepted. When all is said and done, there are two indispensable elements of reports: (1) accuracy and (2) clear communication of the meaning that the writer intended.

Not infrequently a new investigator will, if only at the subconscious level, attempt to impress those who will be reading the incident report by writing in an elaborate manner in order to display mastery of the English language. However, persons reading the report will learn much, or perhaps all, they will ever know about the investigation from what has been written. Therefore, it is essential to write in a clear and uncluttered style; the report must be written not only so that it can be understood but, more importantly, so that it cannot be misunderstood.

The report must be completely accurate. No detail should be added or deleted; the potential or actual consequences of such deviations, however innocent the motivation, are considerable. For example, at the scene of an armed robbery, a young investigator was conducting interviews necessary to prepare the original report. One of the questions he asked the victim was, "Have you ever seen the perpetrator before this happened?" The response was, "Yes, he works on the loading platform of the grocery on Sixth Avenue." Out of a desire to provide as much detail as possible, the investigator supplemented this statement with information from the telephone directory, writing a portion of the interview in the following manner:

THE victim told the undersigned officer that the suspect works at Blake's Grocery Wholesale, located at 1425 Sixth Avenue, telephone number (813) 223-3291.

Later, the following exchange took place between the officer and the defense attorney in court:

Q–Defense Attorney: Officer, do you recognize this report?

A–Officer: Yes, I do.

Q–Defense Attorney: Did you prepare it?

A–Officer: Yes, sir, I did.

Q–Defense Attorney: Would it be fair to say that it represents your investigation?

A–Officer: That is correct, sir.

Q–Defense Attorney: Then, having conducted the investigation and having prepared the report, your testimony would be that it accurately and completely portrays your actions and what you learned?

A–Officer: Yes, sir.

Q–Defense Attorney: Would you read from page 2 of this report?

A–Officer: "The victim told the undersigned officer that the suspect works at Blake's Grocery Wholesale, located at 1425 Sixth Avenue, telephone number (813) 223-3291."

Q–Defense Attorney: Officer, the complainant in this case has already testified to the effect that she did not, in fact, tell you this. Why are you prejudiced toward the defendant in this case, and what else have you added to the report or subtracted from it in order to strengthen the state's case?

Thus, a seemingly innocuous addition to a report reduced the credibility of the entire investigation. Clear communication and accuracy are the mainstays of effective reports. The absence of one diminishes the other.

## THE FOLLOW-UP INVESTIGATION AND SUPPLEMENTAL REPORTS

Periodically during the follow-up investigation supplemental reports must be initiated. Ordinarily, supplemental, or follow-up, reports should be written no less frequently than every 10 days, and the continuance of a particular investigation beyond 28 days should require supervisory approval to ensure proper use of an investigator's time. The purpose of writing follow-up reports is to keep the file current as new or corrected information is gathered. Additionally, specific acts or accomplishments might require individual supplemental reports, such as the activation or cancellation of a pickup order or BOLO, the issuance of a search warrant, the arrest of a suspect, the complainant's discovery that additional property was stolen that was not noticed as missing at the time the incident report was made, the recovery of all or part of the property taken, or a change in the title of the offense due to improper classification on the original report, for example, a strong-arm robbery reclassified as a purse snatch.

Other circumstances under which supplemental reports are required include (1) when the offense is unfounded; (2) when it is exceptionally cleared, meaning that the police know who the perpetrator is but are unable to pursue the case further due to circumstances beyond their control, such as the death of the only witness; and (3) when the case is inactivated. If the supervisor reviewing the incident report inactivates it due to insufficient leads to warrant follow-up investigation, then a supplemental report is not required. However, if some follow-up work is done, no promising leads are developed, and the case is then inactivated, the person assigned responsibility for it must complete a supplemental report to substantiate the basis for inactivation.

As a general concluding note, case files inactivated may in later months or years receive further investigative work that is productive. Therefore, it is of considerable importance that at each stage of report writing care is exercised in presenting all available information.

## Key Terms

**disposition (of incident report)**
**field notes**
**incident reports**
**mobile data terminal (MDT)**
**narrative style**
**National Incident-Based Reporting System (NIBRS)**
**personal digital assistant (PDA)**
**reconstruction (of crime)**
**suspect description form**
**Uniform Crime Reports (UCRs)**

## Review Questions

1. Identify and briefly discuss four reasons why field notes are important.
2. What is the difference between a basic question and a primary question?
3. What are the six primary investigative questions?
4. Briefly discuss the operational and administrative uses of incident reports.
5. How would you characterize the difference between basic incident reports and those that are NIBRS compliant? (Check the Internet for additional information on how these reports differ.)
6. How are MDTs and PDAs being used in law enforcement?
7. After a uniformed supervisor accepts a report, he or she must make a disposition of it. What are four dispositions that might be made?

## Internet Activities

1. Learn more about NIBRS at www.search.org/nibrs. Find out if your state has recently received any NIBRS grants. Read the brief report entitled, "Effects of NIBRS on Crime Statistics." How do NIBRS statistics differ from UCR data? What impact does NIBRS have on crime statistics? What factors need to be considered when comparing summary UCR statistics and NIBRS data?
2. Log onto your local, county, or state law enforcement agency website and find out if the agency uses mobile data terminals. If it does, in what capacity are they used? Are all patrol vehicles equipped with MDTs? Does the site provide any information on other data technology used by officers (PDAs, etc.)? If so, what?

## Notes

1. California Commission on Peace Officer Standards and Training, Basic Course Workbook Series, *Investigative Report Writing* (Sacramento: Office of State Publishing, 1999), p. 2-1, with some additions to and restatement of the discussion of these points by the authors.
2. Michael Biggs, *Just the Facts: Investigative Report Writing* (Upper Saddle River, NJ: Prentice Hall, 2001), p. 16. Like citation 1 above, this is an excellent source of information on field notes and report writing.
3. California Commission, *Investigative Report Writing*, p. 2-12, is the source of several of these points.
4. Biggs, *Just the Facts*, pp. 16–19, with some restatement by the authors.
5. U.S. Equal Employment Opportunity Commission, Standard Form 100, Rev. 3-97, "Employer Information Report EEO-1, 100-118," *Instruction Book*, www.eeoc.gov/stats/jobpat/e-1instruct.html, Nov. 14, 2001.
6. Allen Z. Gammage, *Basic Report Writing* (Springfield, IL: Charles C. Thomas, 1966), pp. 13–14. These points remain valid even today; for example, see California Commission, *Investigative Report Writing*, p. 4-21.
7. These points are drawn from Paul L. Godwin, "Painless Report Writing," *Law and Order*, February 1993, pp. 38–40, with some additions by the authors.

SIX

# The Follow-Up Investigation

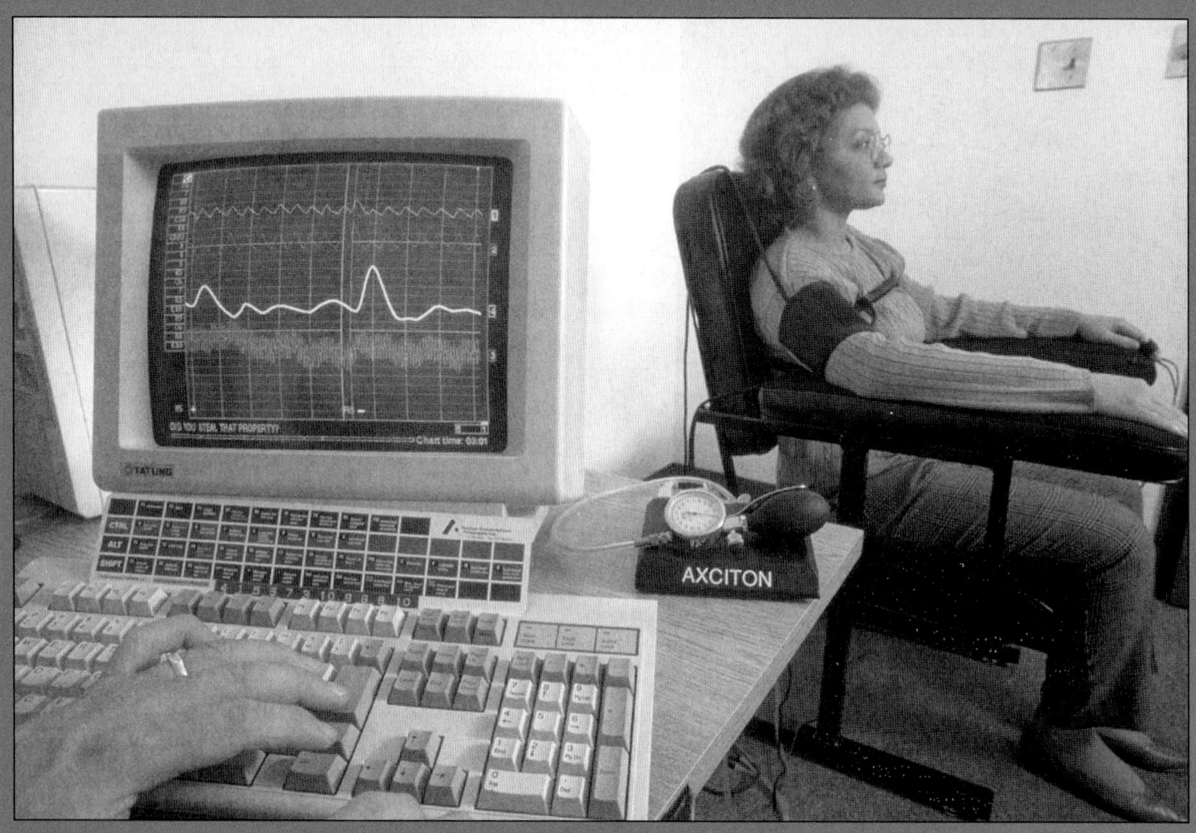


*The polygraph or "lie detector" is one of many investigative tools that may be used in follow-up investigations. Today's polygraphs are often computerized, like this one from the Montgomery County Police Department. (© Richard T. Nowtiz/Corbis)*

## CHAPTER OUTLINE



## CHAPTER OBJECTIVES

1. Summarize the factors used to determine whether a follow-up investigation is needed.
2. Outline common internal and external sources of case information.
3. Explain the techniques used in neighborhood and vehicle canvasses.
4. Discuss the role and use of informants.
5. Understand the purpose and objectives of surveillance.
6. Be familiar with the practice of polygraph and psychological-stress evaluators.
7. Describe the methods for conducting photo and live lineups.
8. Explain the guidelines for recording identification results.

# INTRODUCTION

One of the most important decisions a criminal investigator makes is determining whether a follow-up investigation for a particular case is needed. While a follow-up investigation is inherently necessary in some cases (i.e., rapes, homicides, suicides), factors such as the solvability of the crime, departmental policy, and availability of personnel and other resources dictate the protocol for follow-ups in other cases. Typically, follow-ups are conducted for the most serious offenses and those with potential for conclusive results. If a follow-up is needed, various sources of information from both inside and outside the department can be helpful. Internal sources such as incident and supplemental reports, jail booking reports, inventories of impounded vehicles, traffic citations, and intelligence files may provide some answers to questions that have not been addressed or were missed in the initial investigation. External sources such as Internet investigations, criminal profiling, and financial analysis can also assist the follow-up process.

This chapter explains the methods used in conducting an effective follow-up investigation. In addition to existing internal and external reports and documents, neighborhood and vehicle canvasses in the immediate vicinity of the crime are essential. For various reasons, witnesses and other parties who may have valuable information do not always initiate contact with the police.

Conducting a thorough neighborhood canvass may not only uncover necessary information but, in some instances, lead to identification of a suspect.

Surveillance, another issue discussed in this chapter, can be an effective tool for gaining extra information for a follow-up and/or for other aspects of criminal investigation. Obtaining probable cause for a search warrant, identifying a violator's associates, establishing informant reliability, and preventing crime are just a few of the many functions of surveillance operations.

The chapter concludes with a discussion of the use and implications of polygraph and psychological-stress evaluations and live and photo lineups.

## THE DECISION TO INITIATE A FOLLOW-UP INVESTIGATION

A **follow-up investigation** is the police effort to gather information after the initiation of the original report and until the case is ready for prosecution. After a uniformed officer initiates a report, his or her immediate supervisor makes an initial disposition. Certain crimes, such as homicides, rapes, and suicides, invariably receive follow-up work. Other offenses receive follow-up investigations on the basis of department policy. Ordinarily only the most serious offenses and those with potential for conclusive results receive investigative effort beyond that necessary to generate the original report.

### INVESTIGATIVE SOLVABILITY FACTORS

The following are some questions that investigative supervisors should answer in determining whether or not to move forward with a follow-up investigation:

- Can the identity of the suspect be established through (1) the discovery of usable fingerprints, (2) the finding of significant physical evidence, (3) victim, witness, or informant information, and/or (4) the license number or a useful description of the vehicle known to have been used in the offense?
- Is there serious physical harm or threat of serious physical harm to the victim? (Generally bomb threats and obscene phone calls would not be assigned for follow-up. However, aggravated circumstances may cause the offense to be so assigned.)
- Did the suspect use a deadly weapon or dangerous ordinance?
- Is there a significant method of operation that will aid in the solution of the offense?
- Is it a sex offense in which the victim and suspect had physical contact?
- Can a suspect be named?
- Can a suspect be identified?
- Can a suspect be described?
- Is there another reason that leads you to believe that the offense should be assigned for a follow-up investigation (e.g., hazardous or dangerous materials stolen or an offense that would raise community concern)?[1]

### DECISION MODELS

Some police departments have attempted to develop decision models that are more objective and remove some of the discretion from personnel who decide whether or not to go forward with a follow-up investigation. Figures 6–1 and 6–2 provide examples of two of these models.

## THE FOLLOW-UP INVESTIGATION PROCESS

When working a case, follow-up investigators have many sources of information within the department that can be checked for related information. These sources are discussed below.

**Figure 6-1** Burglary Screening Decision Model

| *Weight* (circle) | *Information Element* | |
|---|---|---|
| | 1. Suspect Information | |
| 10 | A. Positive Identification | |
| 8 | B. Tentative Identification | |
| 6 | C. Poor Identification | |
| | 2. Vehicle Information | |
| 10 | A. Positive Identification (tag and/or other) | |
| 8 | B. Definitive Description | |
| 6 | C. Poor Description | |
| | 3. Estimate Time Between Incident - Report | |
| 4 | A. Less than one hour | |
| 3 | B. One to twelve hours | |
| 2 | C. Twelve hours and over | |
| | 4. Method of Reporting | |
| 2 | A. Witness and/or victim | |
| 1 | B. Officer on-view | |
| | 5. Information Received → | SECTION 5 TO BE USED *ONLY* IF INFORMATION AVAILABLE AT CODING *OR* TO ACTIVATE AN INACTIVE CASE |
| | A. Confidential Informant and/or victim | |
| 10 | 1. Definitive information | |
| 8 | 2. Possible information | |
| 6 | 3. Poor information | |
| | B. Information shared from other investigator and/or agency | |
| 10 | 1. Definitive information | |
| 8 | 2. Possible information | |
| 6 | 3. Poor information | |
| | 6. Modus Operandi | |
| 5 | A. Definitive pattern | |
| 4 | B. Possible pattern | |
| 3 | C. Poor pattern | |
| | 7. Fingerprints | |
| 10 | A. Identified with suspect | |
| 1 | B. Without suspect | |
| ______ | TOTAL CUT POINT FOR CASE ACTIVATION IS 10 | |

Case: Active
Inactive (circle)

Other factors not listed which cause the case to be active.

(Specify) ____________________________

NOTE: *This scale is to be used as a guideline only and is not intended to override nor interfere with the good judgment of a superior in assigning cases where there may be considerations not included in the scale.*

CASE NUMBER__________ INVESTIGATOR__________

DATE__________ SCREENER__________

## Incident and Supplemental Reports

The preliminary investigation report, typically referred to as an incident, offense, or crime report, has the answers to many of the basic questions that follow-up investigators need to ask (e.g., What was the offense? Is there a suspect in custody? Were there witnesses? If so, what did they report seeing and where can they be contacted?). There may also

**Figure 6-2** Theft-from-Auto Screening Decision Model

POLICE DEPARTMENT

| DATE OF OFFENSE | NAME OF SCREENING OFFICER | CLASS | DIST. NO. | CENTRAL COMPLAINT NO. |
|---|---|---|---|---|
| | | | | |

| INFORMATION ELEMENT | WEIGHTING FACTOR |
|---|---|
| Can complainant or witness identify the offender by name? | 10 |
| Is the stolen property traceable, serial number, etc. ? | 7 |
| Can complainant or witness provide registration of auto used? | 7 |
| Will complainant sign a complaint in court if offender is apprehended? | 3 |
| Estimate range of time of occurrence | |
| Less than 1 hour | 5 |
| 1 to12 hours | 1 |
| 12 to 24 hours | 0.3 |
| more than 24 hours | 0 |
| Witness's report of offense | 7 |
| On-view report of offense | 1 |
| Usable fingerprints | 7 |

**INSTRUCTIONS**

(1) Circle the weighting factor for each information element that is present in the Incident Report

(2) Total the circled factors.

(3) If the sum is seven (7) or more, the case is assigned for investigation.

(4) If the sum is less than seven (7), suspend the case.

**TOTAL SCORE:** ____________

**DECISION MODEL RULE RECOMMENDATION**

____________ ASSIGN CASE ____________ OVERRIDE DO NOT ASSIGN CASE ____________

**EXPLAIN OVERRIDE:**

SIGNATURE OF SCREEN OFFICER ____________

DATE ____________

**DETECTIVE ASSIGNMENT**

CASE ASSIGNED TO: ____________ DETECTIVE SUSPENSE DATE: ____________

UNIT SUPERVISOR: ____________

**CASE STATUS**

____________ ARREST MADE ____________ PENDING ____________ INACTIVE OTHER ____________

DATE ____________ SIGNATURE OF CODING OFFICER: ____________

be other reports or forms attached to the incident report. For example, assume that the suspect has been shot while fleeing from a bank robbery. An officer must be in the ambulance with the suspect during the ride to the hospital. This officer will file a supplemental report on what was done and said in the ambulance.

Reviewing old incident reports on crimes for which the suspects were previously convicted may reveal a pattern—such as a propensity to steal certain kinds of property (e.g., stamp and coin collections) or a preference for certain types of targets (e.g., pharmacies)—that may be helpful in the current case.

## Physical Evidence Seized

The physical evidence seized at the scene, as well as any evidence seized, for instance, by an ambulance officer (such as some orange-dye-stained bills), is placed in the evidence room. When the evidence is submitted, each officer is given a written receipt with the date and time on it. In our example, the officer conducting the preliminary investigation attaches the receipt to the incident report, and the ambulance officer appends his evidence receipt to his supplemental report.

## Jail Booking Reports

Depending on the local situation, the **jail booking report** may or may not be an internal document of the agency conducting the investigation. As a result of the growth of regional jails and the desire of many jurisdictions to be free of the liability of maintaining their own jails, many suspects are now housed for a fee in facilities that are not operated by the investigating agency. The booking report contains complete personal information about the suspect, including his or her medical condition and any treatment that was required. A current photograph and fingerprints are included, as well as a record of any combativeness or the need to place the suspect in isolation. The report also contains an inventory of the suspect's personal property, which may include telephone numbers, matchbooks, various keys, tobacco products, business cards, photographs, and identity cards for the suspect that show different names. Such items may reveal places the suspect frequents, the names of associates, personal habits, aliases, and other information of investigative value.

## Field Interview Information Reports

A **field interview/information report (FIR)** is shown in Figure 6–3. Such reports are filled out when patrolling officers identify persons or vehicles that are suspicious to them but are not connected with any particular offense. These cards can establish whether a suspect was in the immediate area of a crime, how he or she was dressed at the time, what vehicle the suspect had access to, and who else was in the vehicle. On rare occasions, FIR cards have proved to be the suspect's best alibi witness.

## Inventories of Impounded Vehicles

If a suspect is arrested while driving a vehicle, the vehicle is inventoried and towed to an impoundment lot. Articles that appear on the inventory may or may not have a relationship to the case. Moreover, the impounding officer may not recognize their significance, as can be the case with common tools that have been modified for use in burglaries. Thus, the impounding report should be carefully read. Under most circumstances, a follow-up investigator cannot search a car after it has been impounded without a search warrant issued on a showing of probable cause.

## Traffic Citations

As with FIR cards, traffic citations can link suspects to the vehicles they register and drive, as well as those to which they may have access. Access to the vehicles of others usually denotes a special relationship and may help identify girlfriends or boyfriends, criminal associates, relatives, or operators of particular kinds of businesses, such as used-car and scrap-metal firms. Traffic citations can also pinpoint where the operator was at a particular date and time. Occasionally, FIR cards are written during traffic stops, so these two sources of information are immediately associated.

## Crime Laboratory Reports

The larger the size of the agency, the more likely it is that laboratory reports are an internal source of information. Crime laboratory reports have the potential to answer the following types of questions: Did the paint embedded in the pedestrian's arm come from the vehicle operated by the suspect? Does the tip of the screwdriver found at the burglary scene match the broken screwdriver found in the suspect's garage? Could the gun found at the scene have fired the fatal shot? Are the fibers found on the victim's underclothes consistent with the fibers from the suspect's couch? Was the forged copy duplicated on the machine in the suspect's business? Is the marriage license a counterfeit? Is the soil found on the victim's back consistent with the soil at the location where the body was found?

Laboratory reports are of great significance, and often they are the most compelling evidence in a case. When tied to other evidence, such as the statements of victims, witnesses, and suspects, they may assume additional importance as they move

**Figure 6-3** Field Interview/Information Card

(**Source:** Courtesy Springfield, Missouri, Police Department)

FRONT

**SPRINGFIELD POLICE DEPARTMENT FIELD INFORMATION**

Data:__________ Time: __________ FIR #: __________

Stopped/Seen at: ______________________________ Beat: __________

Subject #1:

Name: ____________________ Address: ____________________

Sex:____ Race:____ Age:____ DOB:____ Hgt:____ Wgt:____ Hair:____ Eyes:____

Tattoos/Misc Description: ______________________________

Subject #2:

Name: ____________________ Address: ____________________

Sex:____ Race:____ Age:____ DOB:____ Hgt:____ Wgt:____ Hair:____ Eyes:____

Tattoos/Misc Description: ______________________________

Subject #3:

Name: ____________________ Address: ____________________

Sex:____ Race:____ Age:____ DOB:____ Hgt:____ Wgt:____ Hair:____ Eyes:____

Tattoos/Misc Description: ______________________________

BACK

Vehicle Color (top/bottom): ____________________ Year: __________

Make: ______________ Model: ______________ Style: __________

License Number ______________ License Year: __________ State: ______

Misc. Description: ______________________________

Reason for stop: ______________________________

List Suspicious Activity/Admitted or Known Criminal History/Gang Activity:

______________________________

______________________________

______________________________

______________________________

______________________________

______________________________

______________________________

Officer/ DSN: ____________________ Supervisor: ____________________
Signature Initial

the investigation from one direction to another and confirm or disconfirm alibis.

## Neighborhood and Vehicle Canvasses

A fundamental aspect of most investigations is the **neighborhood canvass** of residents, merchants, and others who may have been in the immediate vicinity of a crime and have useful information (see Figure 6–4). It is estimated that a systematic neighborhood canvass soon after the commission of an offense results in information of investigative value in approximately 20 percent of all cases. The extent of the canvass depends on variables such as the type of offense, time of day, and characteristics of the crime scene. The timing of a neighborhood canvass is an important consideration. People not only move randomly through areas but also ebb and flow on a variety of schedules. To mistime a neighborhood canvass by 30 minutes, for example, may mean eliminating the possibility of locating persons who regularly catch a bus at a particular time and who, on the day of an offense, might have seen something of considerable investigative value.

Before a neighborhood canvass, investigators should be given all information relating to the offense, including a full description of the suspect, any injuries sustained by the suspect, and the type of property taken. The possession of these facts is absolutely essential for two major reasons. First, investigators can then question witnesses intelligently, increasing the probability that all available information will be elicited. Second, the investigator is protected from unknowingly encountering the suspect and thus being placed in jeopardy.

Interviews should be conducted first at businesses or dwellings with a clear view of the crime scene and at the suspect's avenues of approach and flight. When there are substantial numbers of locations involved, several teams of officers canvassing simultaneously are helpful. If merchants or residents are not on site during the canvass, a later contact is necessary. Even when persons interviewed do not provide any useful information, investigators must record the fact that no information was obtained in order to eliminate the possibility of duplicating effort later on. Another reason for recording that no positive information has been provided is shown in the following case study:

ON a Sunday morning, a residential burglary of $3,800 in rare coins was reported. The uniformed officer making the original investigation received permission to conduct the neighborhood canvass. Usually the follow-up investigator did the canvass, but the uniformed officer had extra time that day. The victim's home was situated on a cul-de-sac along with four other homes with some view of the victimized premises. There were no homes to the rear of the victim's residence. After interviewing residents of the four neighboring homes, including a teenage boy, the uniformed officer recorded the identities and statements of those with whom he had talked in his report. All indicated they had seen nothing. Because of the value of the property taken, the case was referred for follow-up investigation.

The detective assigned to the case recently had been transferred from the Youth Services Bureau to the Burglary Bureau and recognized the name of the youth identified in the interview section of the uniformed officer's report as an individual with an extensive juvenile record for breaking and entering. Investigation revealed that the youth had committed the offense, and all coins taken were recovered.

Admittedly, this is an unusual case. Although luck played some part, the neighborhood canvass and adherence to sound reporting procedures not only avoided duplication of effort but cleared the case so quickly that the perpetrator had no opportunity to dispose of the stolen property.

Like the neighborhood canvass, the **vehicle canvass** should be conducted as soon as there is sufficient information to do so. As Figure 6–5 indicates, the address or location of each vehicle must be recorded, as well as its description and plate or tag number. Anything unusual about a vehicle should be noted, such as bullet holes, blood, odd appearance of the interior, recent damage, noteworthy stickers, unusual articles, items hanging from the rearview mirror, whether the car is hot, warm, cold, muddy, or clean. For vehicles that seem to be possibly related to the case, the types and condition of the tires should also be noted. If a suspect feels that an investigation is tightening around him or her and there is a possibility of tying tire marks to the scene, the suspect may buy new tires. If so, the vehicle canvass notes will reveal this

**Figure 6-4** Building/Neighborhood Canvass

(**Source:** Courtesy Imprimus Forensic Services, LLC)

## BUILDING / NEIGHBORHOOD CANVASS

AGENCY: ____________________ INCIDENT#: ____________________

INSTRUCTIONS: Document whether or not all occupants of the residence were interviewed. Document locations where no persons were contacted. if available, list pager and / or cellphone numbers in the remarks column. Use the back side of this sheet for notes.

MULTIPLE UNIT OCCUPANCY: Address ____________________ Number of Units ____________________

*(List only unit numbers below)*

| ADDRESS (indicate residence, business, etc.) | | PERSON CONTACTED | DOB | HOME TX# | WORK TX# | REMARKS (pager / cell phone) |
|---|---|---|---|---|---|---|
| | # OF OCC. | | | | | FOLLOW-UP RQ'D ☐ NOTES ON BACK ☐ |
| | # OF OCC. | | | | | FOLLOW-UP RQ'D ☐ NOTES ON BACK ☐ |
| | # OF OCC. | | | | | FOLLOW-UP RQ'D ☐ NOTES ON BACK ☐ |
| | # OF OCC. | | | | | FOLLOW-UP RQ'D ☐ NOTES ON BACK ☐ |
| | # OF OCC. | | | | | FOLLOW-UP RQ'D ☐ NOTES ON BACK ☐ |
| | # OF OCC. | | | | | FOLLOW-UP RQ'D ☐ NOTES ON BACK ☐ |
| | # OF OCC. | | | | | FOLLOW-UP RQ'D ☐ NOTES ON BACK ☐ |
| | # OF OCC. | | | | | FOLLOW-UP RQ'D ☐ NOTES ON BACK ☐ |
| | # OF OCC. | | | | | FOLLOW-UP RQ'D ☐ NOTES ON BACK ☐ |
| | # OF OCC. | | | | | FOLLOW-UP RQ'D ☐ NOTES ON BACK ☐ |
| | # OF OCC. | | | | | FOLLOW-UP RQ'D ☐ NOTES ON BACK ☐ |
| | # OF OCC. | | | | | FOLLOW-UP RQ'D ☐ NOTES ON BACK ☐ |
| | # OF OCC. | | | | | FOLLOW-UP RQ'D ☐ NOTES ON BACK ☐ |
| | # OF OCC. | | | | | FOLLOW-UP RQ'D ☐ NOTES ON BACK ☐ |
| | # OF OCC. | | | | | FOLLOW-UP RQ'D ☐ NOTES ON BACK ☐ |
| | # OF OCC. | | | | | FOLLOW-UP RQ'D ☐ NOTES ON BACK ☐ |
| | # OF OCC. | | | | | FOLLOW-UP RQ'D ☐ NOTES ON BACK ☐ |

CANVASSING OFFICER (Print): ____________________ INITIALS: ________ DATE: ________ START TIME ________ TIME END: ________

Figure 6-5 Vehicle Information Canvass

(**Source:** Courtesy Imprimus Forensic Services, LLC)

AGENCY: ____________________ INCIDENT#: ____________________

INSTRUCTIONS: Document all vehicles in the area you have been assigned. Include vehicles parked in the streets, driveways, alleyways and yards. Under "Remarks" list anything unusual noted about the vehicle (manner of parking, warm engine, fresh damage, etc.)

For vehicles without license plates, enter the VIN in the "Remarks" column.

| ADDRESS (indicate alley, driveway, street, etc.) | MAKE | MODEL | COLOR | PLATE | REMARKS (VIN) |
|---|---|---|---|---|---|
| | | | | | |
| | | | | | |
| | | | | | |
| | | | | | |
| | | | | | |
| | | | | | |
| | | | | | |
| | | | | | |
| | | | | | |
| | | | | | |
| | | | | | |
| | | | | | |
| | | | | | |
| | | | | | |
| | | | | | |
| | | | | | |
| | | | | | |

CANVASSING OFFICER (Print): ____________________ INITIALS: ________ DATE: ________ START TIME ________ TIME END: ________

change, and it may be possible to locate the old tires at the dealership where the new tires were bought.

The level of detail recorded for each vehicle varies according to the judgment of the investigator making the vehicle canvass. However, if any error is to be made on the amount of information, it is always better, without being wasteful of resources, to have too much detail than not enough.

## Intelligence Files

The criminal intelligence function is discussed fully in Chapter 8, "Investigative Resources." However, some discussion of it here is appropriate for an understanding of the importance and use of intelligence. "Intelligence consists of pieces of raw information that when collected, evaluated, collated, and analyzed form meaningful and useful judgments that are both timely and accurate.[2] Two ways of thinking about intelligence files are as categories of intelligence and as specific types of files.

In terms of categories of intelligence, there are at least four different types:

- **Indicative intelligence,** which focuses on emerging and new criminal developments. It may include both fragmentary and impossible-to-immediately-substantiate information, as well as hard facts. Examples are plans to manufacture a new and more potent illicit drug, reports of an unnamed criminal ring that is seeking inside information on armored-car schedules, and anonymous reports that a mysterious group is accumulating explosives.
- **Tactical intelligence,** which implies immediate action and can lead to arrests and the collection of additional information. Tactical intelligence is illustrated by information derived from electronic or physical surveillance, as well as that provided by confidential informants. It may also be derived from intelligence analysis techniques (such as those described in Chapter 8). It should be noted that surveillance and analysis are intelligence tools rather than a type of intelligence.
- **Strategic intelligence,** which is gathered and analyzed over time and usually confirms new or newly discovered patterns of criminal activity. Some strategic intelligence accumulates from indicative and tactical intelligence. For instance, there may be rumors on the street of a new major fencing operation (indicative intelligence), and a burglary suspect may subsequently be arrested who trades information about the fence for favorable sentencing (tactical information). The resultant investigation produces strategic intelligence, which may then lead to an arrest of the fence and the possibility of rolling up those with whom the fence does business.
- **Evidential intelligence,** which consists of factual, precise information that can be presented in court. Its use is determined by the needs of the investigative unit, not the intelligence unit. Evidential intelligence can be used in preparing tactical and strategic assessments, as well as in deciding which investigative techniques can best be employed.[3]

The specific types of files maintained by an agency are largely determined by the agency's mission and resources. In turn, this determination affects the nature of the information available to the investigator. Among the common types of files in intelligence units are modus operandi (MO), moniker or nickname, threat assessment, and violator file summary, or target identification, files. The latter file is a summary of all available data on a suspected or known violator. If the resources of the agency allow such files to be current, an investigator can learn a great deal about a suspect fairly quickly because these files include the following data:

- Name
- Physical description
- Date of birth
- Place of birth
- AKA ("also known as") names
- Social Security number
- FBI number
- Vehicles registered to
- Telephone number
- Real estate owned
- Associates
- History

## Automated Criminal Intelligence Screen

Technological advances have greatly aided the criminal investigative process in recent years. While police agencies have traditionally maintained detailed manual data filing systems, today's computers allow vast amounts of criminal intelligence information to be stored and easily retrieved. Automated criminal intelligence files are a valuable tool for many follow-up investigations.

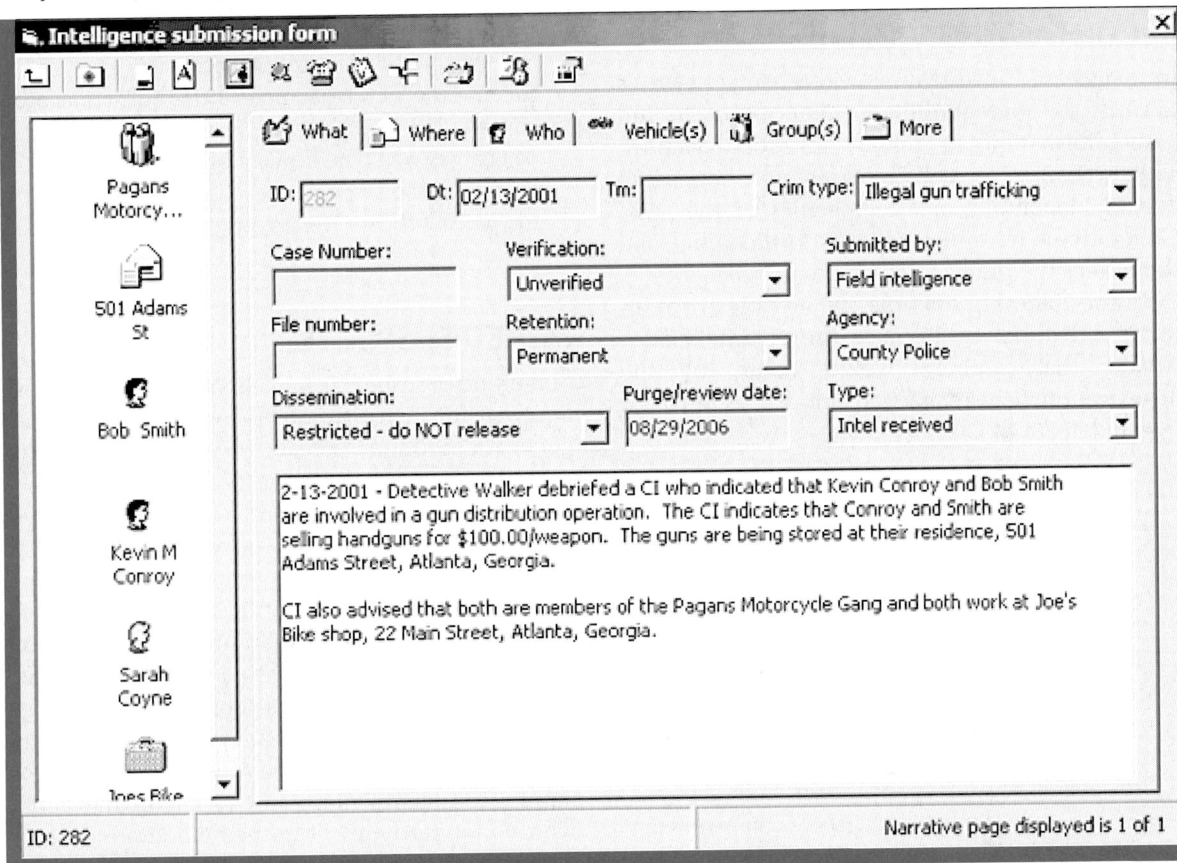


- Methods of operation
- Geographic area
- Interested agencies
- Supporting documentation
- Driver's license number
- State Bureau of Criminal Identification number
- Miscellaneous criminal number
- Last known address
- Employer or business
- Utilities paid
- Photographs
- Criminal activity involved in
- Violence potential and patterns
- Other interested agencies[4]

## EXTERNAL SOURCES OF CASE INFORMATION

Beyond the investigator's internal sources of case information are external capabilities and information systems. Many departments do not have the resources for maintaining expertise in such areas as criminal profiling, geoprofiling, forensic financial analysis, and Internet investigations. Moreover, there are numerous local, regional, state, and federal information systems (such as those noted in

Chapter 1, Table 1–1). Chapter 8, "Investigative Resources," explores these capabilities and information systems, particularly the systems maintained by the federal government.

## RECONTACTING VICTIMS

In many cases, investigators will recontact victims to verify the content of the incident report, to find new information, or merely to satisfy victims. These recontacts may be made by telephone or in person, depending on the specifics of the case. Generally, no new information is forthcoming, and sometimes the public relation attempts backfire.

In the following example the investigator reinterviewed a victim. Because the victim had assumed that nothing would come of the investigation, he was annoyed at being recontacted by the detective:

AN investigator visited the victim of a burglary. Earlier that week the victim's home had been broken into and several hundred dollars' worth of electronic entertainment and citizen-band radio equipment was stolen. The victim expressed surprise at the appearance of the investigator and stated that he had given the patrol officer all the information. The interview of the victim took approximately 20 minutes, provided no new information, and confirmed the lack of substantial leads. The victim seemed bothered by the amount of time the interview was taking. Finally, taking his cue from the victim, the investigator left, having acquired no new leads.

The next example illustrates a case in which recontacting the victim and searching for possible witnesses were unsuccessful but did uncover the fact that the victim had not been truthful with the officer who initiated the incident report.

AN investigator checking the address of a strong-arm robbery victim found that he lived in a halfway house for juvenile delinquents. At the victim's residence, the investigator was introduced to the victim by the adult supervisor. The investigator asked the victim to explain in greater detail than was in the incident report the circumstances of the robbery. After some hesitation, the victim stated that the suspect was known to him, but not by name, and that the victim and suspect had gone to the location of the incident together. After further inquiries, the victim admitted that he had wanted to purchase some marijuana from the suspect but the suspect had beaten him and taken his money. The victim had not told this fact to the patrol officer, because the victim had been afraid to incriminate himself. The investigator assured the victim that no charges would be brought against him and confirmed the suspect's description as obtained by the patrol officer. The investigator then continued pursuing the case.

## NAMED SUSPECTS

Sometimes a suspect is named in an incident report assigned for investigation. Investigators then may check department arrest records to see if the named suspect has a criminal record. Since the suspect may not have any record, because he or she either has never been involved with the particular agency or is a juvenile, this activity may not always be useful. Indeed, the identification of a suspect in an incident report is no guarantee that the person committed or had anything to do with the offense.

Although a named suspect sometimes can be arrested and charged, the testimony of victims and witnesses often leaves much to be desired. For example, the victim may only be theorizing about who committed the offense. Sometimes victims and witnesses see someone they know in the vicinity of an offense, but no other evidence links the suspect to the offense. Thus a named suspect or a description in an incident report may provide valuable leads, but they often do not make the investigation easy or guarantee a solution. The following example illustrates this point:

WHILE conducting a follow-up investigation to a burglary, an investigator found a juvenile suspect listed in the patrol report. The suspect had been named by the victim, who claimed to have seen the suspect near her house shortly after it was broken into. The suspect's parents were contacted by phone and an appointment was made for the next day at the suspect's home. At that time, the investigator interviewed the suspect and discussed the case with his parents in their living room. The suspect claimed not to be involved but was aware of the incident; he also claimed that he could name the people who had committed the burglary. The suspect provided the name of another person who he said could verify that he was not involved. The investigator was aware of the activities (not directly related to the offense under consideration) of some of the people named by the juvenile and felt that this suspect probably had had little or nothing to do with the burglary. After warning the juvenile to stay away from some of his associates because of their links to known offenders, the investigator left. The investigator believed that although the suspect might not have been completely innocent, he certainly was not deeply involved in the offense, and his parents seemed to be the type to keep him in line.

## LEADS

The amount of effort required to follow up a good or bad lead is seldom mentioned in research or investigative work. However, as the following example shows, even when good leads are available, the investigation is not a simple matter of arresting suspects:

A burglary victim called an investigator to explain that she thought the offenders were two employees of a firm that the apartment complex had hired to do some work in her apartment. The described suspects, names unknown, had been given a key to her apartment in order to perform the necessary work. The burglary had been committed eight days later, and there had been no forced entry. The apartment manager, when contacted by the investigator, denied that the suspects could have committed the burglary but provided the name of the firm that employed them. The owner of the firm testified to the suspects' good employment records and reliability. A message was left for the suspects to contact the investigator. The suspects called back about a half-hour later and gave the investigator their full names, dates of birth, and past criminal histories and described the work done on the victim's apartment. The investigator used this information to check his own department's records and also requested a record check on the suspects from a neighboring jurisdiction. The investigator concluded after following up these leads that the suspects were not likely to have been the offenders and closed the investigation.

This example demonstrates that even when apparently good leads are available, additional work is required to check them out, and even then the case still may not be solved.

Although information about a suspect may not be present in an incident report, there may be enough evidence to lead to the identification of a suspect. In the following example, the incident report included a few tenuous leads that proved very useful. Of particular interest is the fact that at every step of this investigation, the likelihood of identifying the suspect was small:

AN incident report of a robbery included the name and address of a juvenile witness but failed to indicate the nature of the information she might have. The investigator visited the address listed on the incident report; it was the address of the witness's grandmother. Although the witness had been living there at the time of the robbery, she had just moved back with her parents. The investigator drove to the address provided by the grandmother and interviewed the witness in the company of her parents. The witness thought she recognized the suspect and provided what she thought was the suspect's name. She also stated that she would recognize the suspect if she saw him again.

The investigator returned to the police station and began checking for the suspect's name in department records. Several variations of the name were tried without success. The investigator discussed the case with a youth officer, who suggested a different variation on the suspect's name. A recheck of department records provided a photo, description, name, address, and prior record of a suspect who matched the descriptions given by the victim and witness. Furthermore, and as important to the investigator, the suspect had a prior record of assaults and drug offenses.

The investigator then put together a photo lineup of five color photographs of similar-looking people plus the suspect's photo. When the investigator returned to the witness's home, she easily identified the photo of the suspect. Armed with this information, the investigator drove by the suspect's home but did not stop. He then called the dispatcher and asked that a particular patrol officer meet him nearby. When the officer arrived, the investigator gave the information about the suspect to the officer and directed him to arrest the suspect on sight. Shortly thereafter the suspect was arrested by the officer.

Major cases, such as the murder of a community leader or a robbery with a large "score," typically require the combined efforts of a number of investigators, who report to the supervisor responsible for the case. A key responsibility of the case supervisor is coordination of information, especially with respect to making sure that leads are prioritized and worked and that the results are disseminated to all team members. One way that this can be done, by hand or on a computer, is by using a lead-assignment sheet log (see Figure 6–6).

## INFORMANTS

Information provided by **informants** often plays a vital role in making an investigation successful. Such information may provide evidence of an unreported crime or constitute the basis for a legal search or an arrest. Whatever the value of information provided by informants, the reality—depending on the motivation of the individual informant involved—is that the informant-investigator transaction is often sordid business. Although relationships with certain informants may approach the genteel, they frequently involve an investigator's finding a point of leverage in the potential informant's values or personal history and applying pressure, ranging from veiled threats to outright coercion.

Not all informants have committed crimes. They come from all walks of life. In dealing with them, investigators often find it useful to determine their motivations. The list of informant types discussed here is not exhaustive, nor are the categories mutually exclusive.

Mercenary informants provide information to the police for financial reward. Foreign police systems, such as the system in France, historically have placed great reliance on paid informants, but the practice is less common in the United States. It is, nonetheless, not an uncommon occurrence. From time to time, individuals who themselves are engaged in illegal activities may want to eliminate a competitor. The rival informant provides information to establish control over the activity in question, using the police to achieve legally what he or she cannot do alone. An individual arrested for a crime may know of criminal activities by others and, in exchange for telling the police, the plea-bargaining informant seeks reduced charges or a lenient sentence. Frequently, police departments receive anonymous information either by telephone or in writing. Because the identity of the anonymous informant is unknown, the motivations are not identifiable. Anonymous information should not be discarded but should be pursued, as long as it may be fruitful. Many law-abiding citizens have information about crimes that they will share with the police. In a strict sense, such persons are not informers. But they are designated legitimate informers to distinguish them from other types.

The self-aggrandizing informant has many contacts in criminal circles and feels important by giving information to the police. When investigators identify this motivation, they should give ample praise each time information is supplied. Otherwise such informants may not continue the relationship. A comparative rarity is the false informant, who intentionally provides misleading information to direct attention away from himself or herself, friends, or relatives. Fearful informants worry that they will be endangered by the criminal activities of an associate. Fearing for their own well-being, they supply information.

Swap shops and pawnshops, however properly operated, occasionally are places where stolen property is recovered. Shop operators may share information about criminal activities with the police to build credit and reduce the likelihood that they will be formally charged if stolen property is found in their possession.

### Dealing with Informants

Investigators must observe certain rules in dealing with informants. Breaking these rules prevents investigators from cultivating and retaining informants and creates a negative image of the police department, thereby reducing the potential flow of information. The following are some of the rules for dealing with informants:

- Investigators must never make promises they cannot or do not intend to keep.
- When talking with a plea-bargaining informant, investigators cannot promise a

**Figure 6-6** Lead-Assignment Sheet

(**Source:** Imprimus Forensic Services, LLC, copyright 2001. This form may be reproduced for law enforcement purposes only.)

INVESTIGATION SUPERVISOR'S

**LEAD ASSIGNMENT SHEET**

Incident#:

Check When Lead Is Cleared

| LEADS | DATE REC'D | DATE ASSIGNED | INVESTIGATOR | TASK / COMMENTS | X | Add'l LEAD # |
|---|---|---|---|---|---|---|
| | | | | | | |
| | | | | | | |
| | | | | | | |
| | | | | | | |
| | | | | | | |
| | | | | | | |

lenient sentence or reduced charge; they can promise only support in seeking it.

- Meetings with informants should be held not in police facilities but in places where informants will not be identified as having an association with an investigator.
- Investigators should never meet informants by themselves. This can put them in a disadvantageous position, since the informant can allege that promises and threats were made when in fact they were not.
- Investigators should corroborate all information provided by informants.
- Investigators should never socialize with informants. This is especially true in regard to female informants. Many a police officer has lost an assignment or a job as a result of having become intimate with a confidential informant. In addition, confidential informants should not be given the officer's home phone number.
- Investigators should never pay an informant without obtaining a witnessed signed statement. If possible, how much the informant will be paid should be set up in advance and in writing.
- Whenever possible, expenses such as meals and rooms should be reimbursed only on presentation of a receipt or within limits agreed on by the investigator and the informant.
- Regardless of his or her reliability, no informant should receive payment until the reliability of the information has been verified.
- The proper names of informants should never be used in investigative reports. Instead, informants should be identified by codes, such as "A273." The identity should be revealed only to persons designated by the police department, such as investigators and immediate supervisors.
- Access to an informant's file should be limited to the fewest persons possible and be permitted only on a need-to-know basis.
- Regardless of informants' value and reliability, they should never be permitted to act illegally.
- Informants should be fully told the circumstances that constitute entrapment and be advised to avoid them scrupulously.

## SURVEILLANCE

**Surveillance** is defined as the secretive and continuous observation of persons, places, and things to obtain information concerning the activities and identity of individuals. Surveillance, as practiced by law enforcement, is a hidden or secret activity typically designed to be carried on without the subject's knowledge. It is the requirement of secrecy that makes a successful surveillance particularly difficult.[5]

A special jargon, or terminology, is used by surveillance officers. Some of the more common terms are:

*Subject* or *hare:* The person being observed.

*Surveillant:* The officer or investigator doing the observing.

*Burn:* Recognition of the surveillant by the subject.

*Covert:* Secret or hidden.

*Overt:* The opposite of covert—an apparent, readily observable surveillance.

*Tail:* Synonymous with "surveillant."

*Visual* or *eyeball:* Term indicating that the officer or investigator can see the subject.

*Loose surveillance:* Surveillance at a discreet distance from the subject, so that the surveillant avoids being burned.

*Tight surveillance:* Surveillance at a minimum distance from the subject to avoid losing the subject; the risk of being burned is thus high.

## Uses of Surveillance

Surveillance is used for a number of reasons and in varying situations. Primarily, it is used to obtain information. It is used when other information-gathering methods fail or when information previously obtained needs to be verified and expanded.

In addition to its primary use as an information-gathering method, surveillance is used as a means of preventing crime. An example of this is the open and continuous surveillance of an active criminal by police to discourage any criminal activity. It is also used as a means of apprehending criminals in the act of committing crimes and of providing protection for investigators working under cover.

The methods used to accomplish a surveillance are as varied as the circumstances and imagination will allow. It is accomplished on foot, by vehicle, by aircraft, by boat, and from stationary positions. Binoculars, high-power telescopes, radios, cameras, sophisticated mechanical and electronic tracking and listening devices, and ultraviolet light are used to aid the surveillance officer.

## Objectives of Surveillance

A surveillance is initiated when an investigator wants to accomplish a particular investigative objective. For example, the investigator may need to learn a subject's routine in order to make an appropriate undercover approach, to corroborate information given by an informant, or to determine a subject's activities with reference to a conspiracy investigation. The objectives may be single or multiple, or they may change as the surveillance progresses. Whatever the objective, it is important that all surveillants understand what information is being sought.

Surveillance often proves very effective in situations such as those discussed below.

***Establishing the Existence of a Violation*** Term indicating that frequently information is received or an allegation is made that an individual is violating the law. Intelligence concerning the individual's activities might establish that the information or allegation is true or at least has some basis. Surveillance is one of the more practical approaches in proceeding with the investigation in such situations, and in many cases it is the only approach available.

***Obtaining Probable Cause for a Search Warrant*** If a violation has been established but insufficient probable cause exists for either a search warrant or an arrest warrant, surveillance may be used to find probable cause. Enough probable cause may be obtained after several hours of observation, or several months of prolonged surveillance may be needed to accomplish this objective. The intelligence gained in this manner will not only produce the probable cause needed but may be used as evidence in any subsequent prosecution of the subject.

***Apprehending Violators in the Commission of Illegal Acts*** Surveillance is especially effective in identifying violators at the scene of a criminal activity and often establishes how each violator is involved. A violation that occurs at a particular location and is repeated over a period of time, such as street-level narcotic sales, is very vulnerable to surveillance.

***Identifying Violator Associates*** As an investigation develops, the investigator is sometimes surprised at how extensive the violation is and soon realizes that the initial principal has one or more associates in the criminal venture. Surveillance can be the most efficient means of identifying these associates and determining how they are involved with the principal.

***Establishing Informant Reliability*** Often information received from an informant needs to be expanded or corroborated in order to obtain sufficient probable cause for definite action against the subject of the investigation. Informant reliability, the all-important factor in dealing with informants, can be determined by surveillance. That is, preliminary information may be verified, and this helps establish that a first-time informant's information is reliable even if his or her credibility cannot be established. The informant may even become the subject of a surveillance if the investigator suspects that the informant is using the investigator to entrap a second individual.

***Providing Protection for an Undercover Investigator or Informant*** At particularly sensitive points in an investigation, both undercover officers and informants may require backup in the form of investigators in the immediate vicinity to furnish help if needed. This type of security is supplied by surveillance in a very discreet manner. The surveillance investigators must be careful not to reveal their presence to the subject of the investigation; otherwise, the undercover investigator or informant may be compromised. This in turn could jeopardize both the investigators and the success of their investigation.

***Locating Persons, Places, or Things*** Wanted persons can be located by surveillance when other approaches will not work. If enough information is obtained about the subject's background, a surveillance employed in conjunction with the background information usually will produce results. For example, a surveillance of a person or residence that is closely connected with the subject will likely produce positive results in locating a wanted subject. The locations of contraband stashes and manufacturing sites of illegal products frequently are found through the use of well-executed surveillances.

***Preventing Crime*** In some situations, law enforcement agencies purposely alert a subject that they are aware of his or her presence in their city, or they make it known to him or her that they are in the subject's area. The U.S. Secret Service, on some protection assignments, will place a high-security risk under a tight surveillance with the object being to keep the subject under continuous observation. The surveillance is conducted so tightly that it may evolve from a covert to an overt surveillance, depending on the situation. Its primary objective, however, is to prevent the subject from taking any aggressive action against the protectee. This same type of surveillance has been employed by city and state police when known criminals visit their locality for some illegal purpose. The subject usually is confronted by detectives who establish his or her identity and ask the reason for the visit. Then an almost open surveillance is maintained on the subject for as long as he or she remains in the area. This has the effect of discouraging any criminal activity by that subject.

***Gathering Intelligence on Individuals and Premises before the Execution of a Search Warrant*** The more current information an agency has about a subject and his or her residence before the execution of a search warrant, the more intelligently the act can be planned and safely accomplished. Executing a search warrant with insufficient intelligence about a residence and its occupants is dangerous and foolhardy. Observations of the target of a search warrant should be standard procedure, and surveillance should be carried out over a period of several days and just before the execution of the warrant, if possible.

***Gathering Intelligence on Illegal Groups' Activities*** Militant groups and outlaw gangs present the investigator with unique problems that lend themselves to solution only after sufficient intelligence is gathered. Undercover work is very effective in penetrating these groups, and surveillance is used as a preliminary approach to gain information to determine the jurisdiction of the criminal activity. Once the area of jurisdiction is learned, surveillance is used either to aid in the placing of an undercover agent in the group or to keep the group's activity under observation for intelligence in order to more effectively take enforcement action when needed.

## Facial Recognition Software

**Facial recognition software** compares video images with mug shots of known offenders for the purpose of identifying and apprehending wanted persons.[6] The video cameras may be mounted at the entrances to sports arenas, at airports, in bus and train stations along tourist strips,[7] in hotel lobbies, and at other places. With this technology it is possible to scan up to 1 million faces per second in a moving crowd. (See photos below and on page 209.)

Facial recognition software is based on principles similar to those in anthropometry (see Chapter 1). After scanning a face, it measures the distance between a person's nose and 80 different points on his or her face to produce an identification. The program is able to account for the growth or absence of facial hair, the use of eyeglasses, and similar means of disguise. During Super Bowl XXXV, in Tampa, one type of facial recognition software was tested, and it resulted in the identification of 19 persons for whom there were outstanding warrants.

Facial recognition software is being used by a number of local police agencies, as well as U.S. Customs, the Central Intelligence Agency, the Drug Enforcement Administration, the Federal Bureau of Investigation, and Scotland Yard. This technology offers great potential for thwarting terrorist attacks, particularly as intelligence services from a number of countries are sharing the images and data in their files.

**Facial-Recognition-System Public Notice**

Signs in a heavily traveled tourist section in Tampa, Florida, warn people of video monitoring cameras in the area. The use of video surveillance camera systems in public places has become more common in the United States. Such systems may be used to deter crime as well as to gather evidence of a crime after the offense has been committed. The surveillance system shown in the picture compares faces of persons walking the streets of this location to faces of known criminals suspected to be in this area of Florida.

(Courtesy © Scott Iskowitz and Tampa Tribune)

## THE POLYGRAPH AND THE PSYCHOLOGICAL-STRESS EVALUATOR

The **polygraph** (see photo on page 212) can be an important adjunct to the criminal investigation process, but its findings cannot stand in place of other evidence. Use of the polygraph is not a substitute for a proper investigation. Agency policies stipulate that only certified polygraphists or interns operating under their guidance may administer an investigative polygraph examination. Such examinations are used to:

- Verify, corroborate, or refute statements made by victims, witnesses, and suspects.
- Obtain additional investigative leads.
- Narrow or focus investigations.
- Eliminate suspects.[8]

A polygraph measures and records three types of physiological changes that may occur in a subject's body while she or he is being questioned:

1. *Blood pressure and heart rate*—obtained by using a blood-pressure cuff.
2. *Respiratory rate*—obtained by stretching two rubber tubes filled with air across the subject's abdomen and chest to measure air displacement.
3. *Amount of sweat on the fingertips* (also called galvanic skin resistance [GSR] and

electrodermal activity)—measured by attaching special cups to several of the subject's fingertips.

These measurements are compared to normal readings obtained when the subject is asked innocuous, nonstressful questions. Any deviations indicate deception, but the results are subject to the examiner's interpretation.

The psychological-stress evaluator (PSE) and computerized voice-stress analyzer (CVSA) measure fluctuations in a person's voice that indicate stress and can reveal deception. People's voices change in pitch under stress, usually getting higher or somewhat squeaky. Some fluctuations may not be audible to the human ear but are detectable with PSE-type equipment. There are many advantages to such equipment, including the fact that direct contact with the subject is not necessary since the equipment can be used with recordings of telephone conversations.

The Fifth Amendment to the U.S. Constitution stipulates that people cannot be compelled to be witnesses against themselves. Thus, submission to a polygraph or PSE-type examination must be voluntary and may be terminated by the subject at any time. The Supreme Court has not directly ruled on

### Facial-Recognition-System Monitor

Thirty-six cameras are monitored from a room the size of a closet. It is hidden behind a door along one of the main tourist streets in Tampa, Florida. Ten monitors overseen by an operator relay features, and the system triggers an alarm when it might have found a criminal. The surveillance systems shown in the picture compares faces of persons walking the streets of this location ot faces of known criminals suspected to be in this area of Florida.

(Courtesy Scott Iskowitz and Tampa Tribune)

the admissibility of polygraph and PSE-type evidence; thus, the rules on this issue vary among the circuits of the federal court system. Additionally, states use different standards for the admissibility of this type of evidence, further contributing to differences in practices. The federal Employee Polygraph Protection Act (EPPA), enacted in 1988, imposes limitations on most public employers regarding the use of polygraphs.

Research indicates that the accuracy of polygraphs runs from 62 to 98 percent, with most findings being at the higher end of that range. The variation in findings is accounted for by differences in the natures and sizes of the populations studied, in research definitions and protocols, and in the polygraphs themselves. Advances in recent generations of digital polygraphs have helped achieve a higher level of accuracy. Findings on the accuracy of CVSAs also vary. In a study conducted by the Department of Defense Polygraph Institute, the accuracy of the CVSA significantly trailed that of the polygraph.[9] However, it is possible that the research design did not produce enough stress in study participants; this factor would significantly affect the findings.

On the near horizon is the use of thermal imaging to detect persons who lie. Liars get "hot" around the eyes, a bodily change that can be observed with this type of imaging system. Among the advantages of thermal imaging are that its digital technology facilitates fast results, it can be used without subjects' being aware of it (e.g., when people are being verbally screened at airport security checkpoints), and it can detect heat loss from heads caused by disguises such as makeup and wigs. In the early testing of thermal-imaging deception equipment, the results have been fairly accurate.[10]

**Posed Polygraph Test**

The findings of a polygraph test can be very useful in a follow-up investigation to obtain additional investigative leads, narrow the focus of an investigation, or eliminate suspects, among other things. Only certified, well-trained polygraph examiners should be used.

(Courtesy Lafayette Instrument)

## GUIDELINES FOR CONDUCTING PHOTO AND LIVE LINEUPS

Juries attach great significance to lineup identification of suspects by witnesses. Yet every investigator and anyone who reads the newspaper knows that such identifications have led to miscarriages of justice. Because of the importance and perils of lineup identifications, investigators must carefully observe appropriate guidelines. Sometimes, as the following case history shows, this requires some inventiveness:

A cab driver reported to the police that he had been robbed by one of his passengers. The cab driver made the report immediately after the suspect had fled on foot with the money. The driver reported that the suspect was a black male, approximately 25 years old, 6 feet 6 inches tall, 285 pounds, armed with a large chrome-plated semiautomatic pistol. The man was wearing an orange silk shirt, blue jeans, and a cowboy hat. Exactly $52 in cash had been taken. Approximately 1 hour after the crime was reported, the suspect was observed in the vicinity of the robbery by the same two officers who had taken the original report. The suspect was arrested by the police officers. A search produced a chrome-plated .45-caliber semiautomatic pistol and $52.12.

In their effort to conduct a lineup, the officers realized that they could not possibly find five people who approximated the suspect in size, race, age, attire, and so forth. The officers decided to use a photo lineup instead of a live lineup. They had a black-and-white photo taken of the suspect, minus the cowboy hat, and incorporated it into a packet of five other photos of similar black males. The cab driver was able to positively identify the photo of the suspect, who subsequently confessed to the crime.

**Lineups** may be conducted in a variety of ways, such as by showing witnesses individual photos sequentially or having them view all photos simultaneously. Likewise, live lineups participants may appear sequentially or may all appear simultaneously. The trend in recent years has been to use photo lineups rather than live lineups due to the problems inherent in the latter; but if a department does use live lineups, the guidelines, procedures, and forms below will work though they are not a substitute for local legal advice.[11]

Following these guidelines will enhance the possibility of a successful prosecution; conversely, shortcomings could cause lineup identification evidence to be ruled as inadmissible.

## CONDUCTING THE IDENTIFICATION PROCEDURE

The purpose of the identification procedure is to conduct the lineup in a consistent manner in order to ensure accuracy, reliability, fairness, and objectivity in the witness's identification. To do so, the person administering the process:

1. Must receive confirmation from the witness that he or she understands the process.
2. Must avoid doing or saying anything that might influence the witness.
3. Must not say anything about the witness's selection before obtaining the witness's statement of certainty (see Figure 6–7).
4. Should encourage the witness to carefully consider his or her comments before responding to media contacts for the witness's own safety and to avoid the possibility that spontaneous or poorly thought-out statements will impede the prosecution.

**Figure 6-7** Witness Lineup-Identification Form

(**Source:** Courtesy St. Petersburg, Florida, Police Department)

[ ] Offense Number

TO WITNESS: PLEASE READ THESE INSTRUCTIONS CAREFULLY.

The position of the persons in the line-up will be numbered left to right, beginning with the number one (1) on your left. Take as much time as you wish to view the line-up. Examine each of the line-up participants carefully. You will be viewing the line-up in a manner which will enable you to see the participants while they will be unable to see you. PLEASE DO NOT DISCUSS any aspect of the case or line-up with any other witness who may be present.

1. If you can identify any of the persons in the line-up as having participated in the criminal offense to which you were a witness, place a "X" in the appropriate square corresponding to the number of the person in the line-up.
2. If none, place a "X" in the square marked NONE.

[1] [2] [3] [4] [5] [6]

[NONE]

3. Then sign your name and fill in the date and time.
4. When completed, hand this sheet to the officer conducting the line-up.

| | |
|---|---|
| OFFICER CONDUCTING LINE-UP | WITNESS' SIGNATURE |
| ATTORNEY FOR THE STATE | DATE TIME |
| LINE-UP ATTORNEY FOR DEFENDANT | |

## GENERAL GUIDELINES FOR PHOTO AND LIVE LINEUPS

1. Care must be taken to ensure that the suspect does not unduly stand out, but complete uniformity of features is not required.
2. Whenever possible, the primary investigator should not be the person conducting the lineup, since he or she might give inadvertent verbal or body-language cues.
3. Witnesses should be instructed before the lineup that the suspect may not be in the lineup, and they should not feel compelled to make an identification.

## Procedures for Photo Lineups

1. Include only one suspect in each identification procedure.
2. Select "fillers" (nonsuspects) who generally match the witness's description of the perpetrator. If the witness has provided a limited or "inadequate" description or if the description of the perpetrator differs significantly from the appearance of the suspect, fillers should resemble the suspect in significant features.
3. If multiple photos of the suspect are available, use the one made closest to the time that the crime was committed.

**Figure 6-8** Police Lineup Worksheet

(**Source:** Courtesy St. Petersburg, Florida, Police Department)

Offense Number ____________

| SUBJECT # | 1 | 2 | 3 | 4 | 5 | 6 |
|---|---|---|---|---|---|---|
| NAME | | | | | | |
| RACE | | | | | | |
| AGE | | | | | | |
| HEIGHT | | | | | | |
| WEIGHT | | | | | | |
| SHIRT | | | | | | |
| PANTS | | | | | | |
| SHOES | | | | | | |

| WITNESS PRESENT AT LINE-UP: | | | SUSPECT IDENTIFIED | | |
|---|---|---|---|---|---|
| NAME | ADDRESS | PHONE | YES | NO | TIME ALLOWED |
| | | | | | |
| | | | | | |
| | | | | | |
| | | | | | |
| | | | | | |
| | | | | | |
| | | | | | |

Did suspect waive right to counsel at line-up? YES_______ NO_______

NAME OF ATTORNEY PRESENT:

ADDRESS: ______________________ PHONE: ______________

OFFICER(S) CONDUCTING LINE-UP: ______________________

DATE: __________ TIME BEGAN: __________ TIME ENDED: __________ CHARGE: __________

NOTE: All subjects in LINE-UP are numbered from left to right, facing interviewing office. Officer conducting interview shall fill in description of subjects PRIOR TO LINE-UP BEING CONDUCTED.

REMARKS: ______________________

______________________

4. Lineups should include a minimum of five fillers.
5. If there are multiple witnesses, consider placing the suspect in a different position each time a lineup is shown to a witness.
6. If a new suspect is developed, avoid using fillers who were used in a previous lineup for the same witness.
7. Make sure that no writing or information about the suspect's previous criminal history can be seen by the witness.
8. Before the witness views the lineup, check again to make sure that the suspect does not unduly stand out.
9. Record the presentation order of the lineup and handle the original photographs as evidence.
10. Write a supplemental report that chronologically describes what happened; include the identification of all lineup participants, the names of all persons at the lineup, and the date and time it was conducted (See Figure 6–8).

## Procedures for Live Lineups

1. Apply the procedures listed above, which are not photo-lineup specific.
2. Use a minimum of four fillers.

### Automated Photo-Lineup File

The Investigative Search program has an automated photo-lineup module, in addition to other capabilities. This file shows all the images captured for one person in the database. Photo lineups that are automated by computer are very useful in follow-up investigations. After witness descriptions have been entered, the computer searches the database of suspects and persons with similar physical characteristics. Large numbers of photos can be stored and easily retrieved in order to expedite investigative efforts.

(Courtesy of TFP, Inc.)

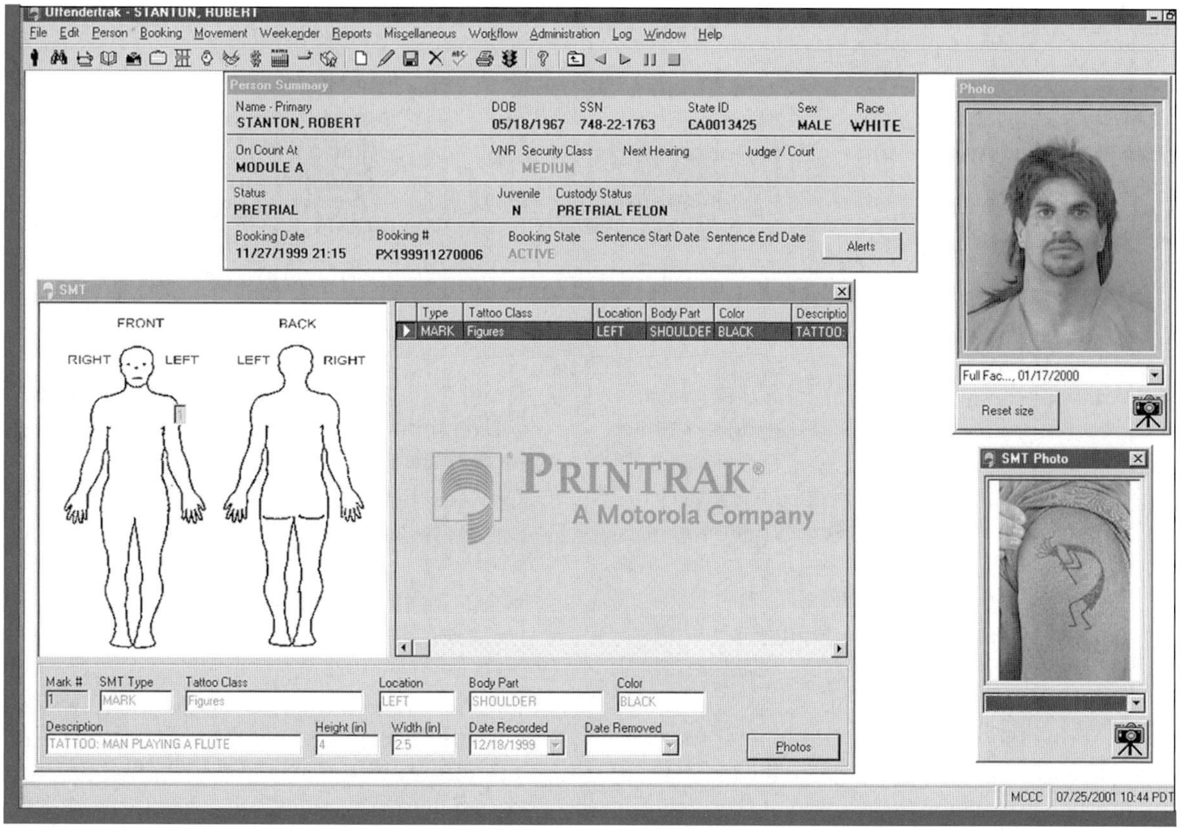

3. Document the lineup by photo or video, and handle this record as evidence.

## Recording Identification Results

Some information about documenting lineup procedures was discussed earlier in this section. In addition, the following steps should be taken:

1. Check to make sure that all signatures needed on the various forms are complete.
2. Collect the information needed for completing standard forms before conducting the lineup.
3. If another witness will have contact with any photographs or forms, make sure that the previous witness has not put any marks or comments on them.
4. Include in the supplemental report a record of both identification and nonidentification results, as well as any statements about how sure or unsure the witnesses are.

## Automated Photo Lineups

Photo lineups that are automated by computer must comply with the guidelines presented throughout this section. Once the witness's description has been entered, the computer searches the database of suspects and persons to locate those with similar features, scars, birthmarks, tattoos, ages, weights, and other characteristics (see photo on page 213). When the selection of the lineup is complete, it can be displayed in color or black and white on the screen for the witness to view or can be printed on paper for the witness. Automated lineup systems automatically generate much of the information needed for record keeping.[12]

## Key Terms

**evidential intelligence**
**facial recognition software**
**field interview/information report (FIR)**
**Follow-up investigation**
**indicative intelligence**
**informant**
**jail booking report**
**lineup**
**neighborhood canvass**
**polygraph**
**strategic intelligence**
**tactical intelligence**
**vehicle canvass**
**surveillance**

## Review Questions

1. What are the questions that should be considered before a follow-up investigation is done on a crime?
2. What were some of the internal investigative information sources outlined in this chapter?
3. What were the external investigative sources of information provided in this chapter?
4. What type of information should an investigator have before beginning the neighborhood canvass?
5. Describe the major categories of informants.
6. For which situations has surveillance often proved very effective?
7. How are video cameras used in conjunction with computer programs as it relates to wanted individuals?
8. Discuss the various principles on which the polygraph and psychological stress evaluator work.
9. What are the major legal factors that must be considered when employing any mechanical lie-detection test?
10. Discuss some important steps that can be taken by law enforcement agencies to enhance and ensure victim and witness cooperation in criminal investigations.

## Internet Activities

1. Search several local newspaper and/or media sources on the Web for a recent and highly publicized crime in your area. From the facts presented, how would you as an investigator conduct a follow-up investigation? What motives of the crime would you explore? Would you conduct a neighborhood and/or vehicle canvass? Would you conduct any type of surveillance? If so, where and for what purpose? What potential witnesses, victims, and suspects would you contact? Make a list of questions that you would ask each of these parties.
2. Learn more about the legal requirements for conducting electronic surveillance by logging on to the FBI's Law Enforcement Bulletin website at www.fbi.gov/publications/leb/leb.htm. Read the February 2000 article, "Electronic Surveillance: A Matter of Necessity." Under what conditions is a warrant needed to conduct electronic surveillance?

## Notes

1. The listing of investigative solvability factors was obtained from the Cincinnati Police Department, Cincinnati, Ohio, and the Greensboro Police Department, Greensboro, North Carolina.
2. Marilyn B. Peterson, Bob Morehouse, and Richard Wright, *Intelligence 2000* (Law Enforcement Intelligence Unit and International Association of Law Enforcement Intelligence Analysts, 2000), p. 7.
3. Chandler, Arizona, Police Department, General Order D-23, "Criminal Intelligence," Aug. 7, 2001, pp. 2–3.
4. California Department of Justice, *The Bureau of Investigation Intelligence Operations Manual* (Sacramento, CA: Division of Law Enforcement, 1993), pp. 14–16.
5. This discussion of surveillance was adapted from materials provided by the Department of Treasury, Federal Law Enforcement Training Center, Glynco, Georgia, 1989.
6. Two companies that manufacture facial recognition software are Visionics Corporation (Face It) and Visage Technology (Face Finder).
7. Geoff Dutton, "Eye on Ybor," *Tampa Tribune*, June 30, 2001, pp. 1, 4.
8. This information is drawn from material that appears on the IQM Inc. website and is derived from Bureau of Justice Assistance Grant No. 93-DD-CX-K009 (1993) and work by the International Association of Chiefs of Police and the American Polygraph association. See www.viptx.net/polygraph/IACP.htm.
9. For example, see V. L. Cestaro, *A Comparison between Decision Accuracy Rates Obtained Using the Polygraph Instrument and the Computer Voice Stress Analyzer (CVSA),* Report No. DoPI195-R-002 (Fort McClellan, AL: Department of Defense Polygraph Institute, 1995).
10. See Helen Pearson, "Liars Caught Red-Faced," Nature News Service, www.nature.com/nsu/020101/020101-3.html, January 16, 2002, pp. 1–2.
11. These guidelines are drawn, with restatement, from John J. Farmer, Jr., "Attorney General Guidelines for Preparing and Conducting Photo and Live Identification Procedures," April 18, 2001, pp. 1–7.
12. See information on Investigative Search at www.tf-pinc.com/isearch.html. This information was obtained from that website on January 16, 2002.

# SEVEN

# The Crime Laboratory

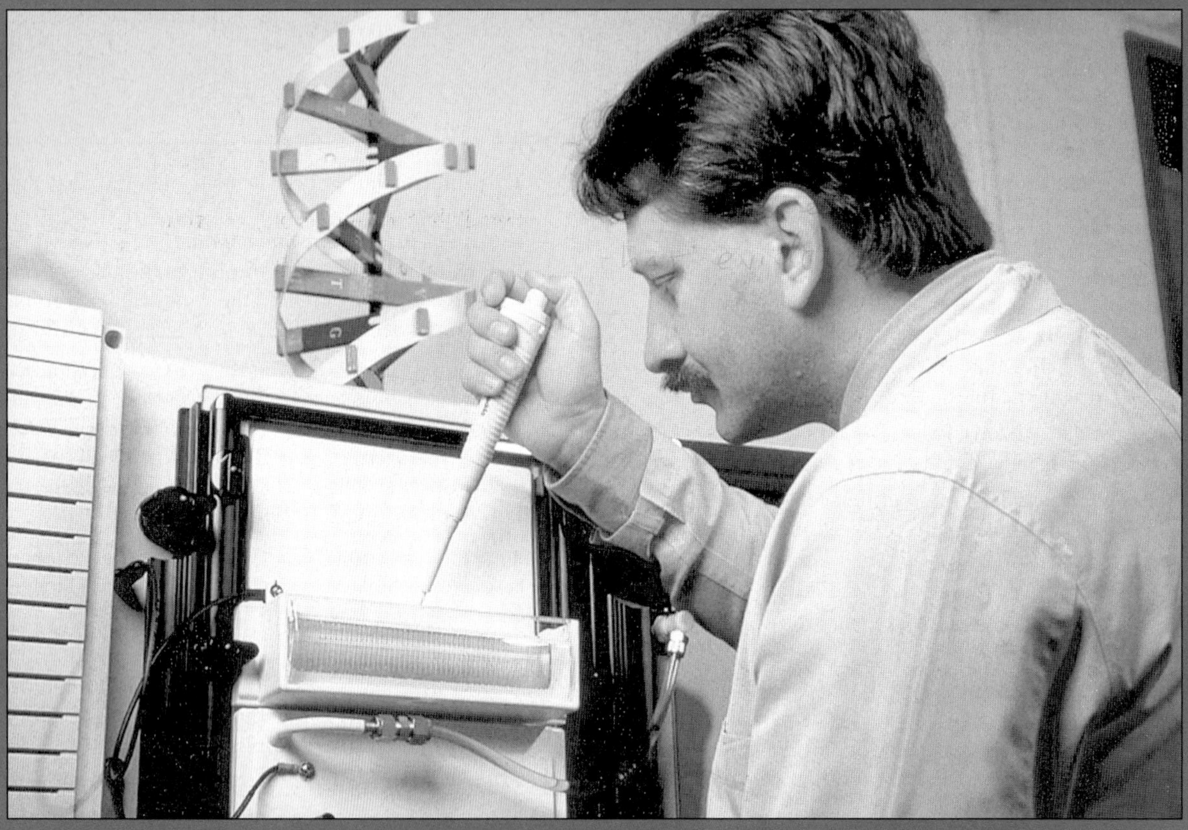

*The FBI crime laboratory is recognized as one of the most comprehensive and prestigious crime labs in the world. Since its inception in 1932, the FBI crime lab has provided valuable services for law enforcement agencies at the state, county and municipal level free of charge.*
*(© R. Crandall (The Image Works))*

## CHAPTER OUTLINE



## CHAPTER OBJECTIVES

1. Define and distinguish forensic science and criminalistics.
2. Understand the importance of an investigator's understanding of crime laboratory capabilities.
3. Describe the three measures of effectiveness of crime laboratories.
4. Distinguish the *Frye* test from the *Daubert* test regarding the admissibility of scientific evidence.
5. Explain the role and importance of DNA analysis in criminal investigation.
6. Identify the latest technologies in DNA evidence investigation and data banking.
7. Highlight the process of fingerprint identification and comparison.
8. Describe AFIS and IAFIS.
9. Describe NIBIN.
10. Briefly explain the techniques and methods used by both the ATF and FBI crime laboratories to examine evidence.

# INTRODUCTION

A crime laboratory is a scientific organization with a dedicated mission of aiding the process of criminal justice. It provides this aid by answering, or helping to answer, the vital questions of whether a crime was committed, how and when it was committed, who committed it, and who could not have committed it. The criminal laboratory seeks answers to questions such as these through scientific analysis of material collected primarily from the scenes of crimes or from suspects.[1] While there are hundreds of federal, state, and local crime laboratories throughout the country, the range of services and personnel expertise within the laboratories varies among the organizations.

To understand the role of crime laboratories, one must understand their relationship to the scientific community and to the functions of the criminal justice system. There are two distinct activities involved in laboratory work. One is the gathering of evidence at the scene of a crime, which is done by evidence technicians or investigators. The second function is the scientific analysis of evidence, which occurs in the laboratory. The effectiveness of the latter activity often depends on the efficiency with which the first operation is performed.

An important issue addressed in this chapter is an investigator's expectations regarding the function and responsibilities of a crime laboratory. While the laboratory is one of the most valuable tools for a criminal investigator, he or she must be aware of its capabilities and limitations. It is not uncommon, for example, for an investigator to send evidence to a laboratory and delay the investigation until the laboratory results are received. Crime laboratories are not intended to replace field investigations. In addition, investigators are often not familiar with the types of evidence that are subject to laboratory analysis. Even the most minute and seemingly insignificant pieces of evidence may be subject to laboratory examination. If investigators are not aware of a laboratory's capabilities, critical pieces of evidence can go uncollected, unprocessed, and unused in substantiating guilt or innocence. Because the analysis of evidence is no better than the samples submitted, investigators themselves play an important role in the success of scientific analysis.

The terms "forensic science" and "criminalistics" are often used interchangeably. **Forensic science** is that part of science applied to answering legal questions. It is the examination, evaluation, and explanation of physical evidence in law. Forensic science encompasses pathology, toxicology, physical anthropology, odontology (dental structure, development, and diseases), psychiatry, questioned documents, firearms, tool-mark comparison, and serology, among other fields. Recent technological advances have added molecular biology and genetics to this list.

One of the branches of forensic science, **criminalistics,** deals with the study of physical evidence related to a crime. From such a study, a crime may be reconstructed. Criminalistics too is interdisciplinary, drawing on mathematics, physics, chemistry, biology, anthropology, and many other scientific endeavors. The late Paul L. Kirk, a leader in the criminalistics movement in the United States, once remarked, "Criminalistics is an occupation that has all of the responsibilities of medicine, the intricacy of the law, and the universality of science."[2]

## CRIME LABORATORIES

There are more than 350 federal, state, and local **crime laboratories** in this country. The oldest crime laboratory in the United States was established in 1923. Fifty-five percent of the labs were established between 1968 and 1978, just after Supreme Court decisions limited police interrogations and while funds were available from the now defunct Law Enforcement Assistance Administration. Seventy-nine percent of the laboratories are within public safety and law enforcement agencies; the remainder are distributed in medical examiners' offices, prosecutors' offices, scientific and health agencies, and other private and public institutions.[3]

Most crime laboratories have developed in response to a particular need in a community or region. The areas of scientific concentration in particular laboratories are based on those needs and also on the interests and skills of the people available:

> Not all crime laboratories have the same capabilities. Some can do much more than others. Laboratories also tend to emphasize and build up expertise in particular areas. The manner of collection of some types of physical evidence . . . will vary according to the type of test procedures the laboratory applies. Therefore, it is important that police investigators familiarize themselves with the capabilities of the crime laboratories supporting their jurisdictions, as well as with

the requirements of the national forensic science laboratories.[4]

As can be expected, almost all laboratories originated or were expanded to examine drugs (and, more recently, DNA), but the percentage of crime laboratories with the capability to examine other categories of physical evidence varies from 5 to 81 percent. In an effort to overcome some of the problems caused by varying specializations and concerns, and because of the absence of agreement on what should be the purpose, function, and services of crime laboratories, the **American Society of Crime Laboratory Directors (ASCLD)** was formed. This organization is a nonprofit professional society of more than 400 crime laboratory directors, managers, and supervisors from the United States and 17 other countries, who have backgrounds as biologists, chemists, document examiners, physicists, toxicologists, and law enforcement officers. The ASCLD is devoted to the improvement of crime laboratory operations through sound management practices. Its purpose is to foster common professional interests, management practices, information, and communication among its members and to promote, encourage, and maintain the highest standards of practice for crime laboratories. To carry out its purpose, ASCLD has established two additional entities.[5]

ASCLD/LAB, the crime laboratory accreditation program, is a voluntary program in which any crime laboratory may participate to demonstrate that its management, operations, personnel, procedures, instruments, physical plant, security, and personnel safety procedures meet certain standards. At the federal level, the ATF laboratory system was the first to be accredited, and, the FBI laboratory, perhaps the most comprehensive crime laboratory in the world, received its accreditation a few years ago. This is not to imply that a laboratory is inadequate or untrustworthy if it chooses not to undertake this voluntary accreditation process.[6] Accreditation can be very time consuming and expensive.

The National Forensic Science Technology Center (NFSTC) was established by ASCLD in 1995 and began operating in 1996. Its two primary functions are to help crime laboratories prepare for accreditation, especially laboratories whose primary focus is on DNA analysis, and to offer continuing education programs for crime laboratory personnel, including the support of college and university degree programs.[7]

## THE MORGUE

One type of crime lab often forgotten is the morgue. A **morgue** is not just a place that houses the bodies of deceased persons; it is critical on the forensic scene as the place where cause of death is determined. Experienced forensic pathologists conduct autopsies and analyze body fluids, tissues, and organs to produce information useful in an investigation when cause of death is questionable or when death has been caused by something other than a known disease.

## EXPECTATIONS

It is not unusual to find situations in which investigators not acquainted with the services of the crime laboratory expect too much from scientific analysis. Some expect the crime laboratory to be able to provide a solution in every criminal case. When investigators do not receive answers to the questions they pose through the submission of physical evidence, they are not only disappointed but more than occasionally reluctant to use the technical assistance of the laboratory again.

To some extent, investigators must be selective in collecting and preserving evidence that they believe can be profitably submitted for scientific analysis to a crime laboratory. It should always be kept in mind that the laboratory was never intended to replace a complete field investigation. The function of the laboratory is to support the investigator and the primary line units of the police agency. The laboratory is sometimes capable of lightening the burden of the investigator, but it can never completely assume that burden. Too often personnel collect evidence at the scene, send it to the laboratory, and then allow the investigation to stall until the laboratory report is received, expecting the laboratory to come up with some magical solution. This is an unrealistic expectation and largely results because the investigator does not understand what is and is not evidence subject to laboratory examination. The analysis of evidence can be no better than the samples submitted. The investigator therefore has a vital role to play in the success of laboratory examinations. James Osterburg, another criminalistics leader, summarizes why there is underutilization or total neglect of crime laboratories. What he said in 1968 is still largely true:

1. Lack of knowledge about how the laboratory can aid the criminal investigator.
2. Unfamiliarity with the more esoteric varieties of clue material, resulting in evidence not being preserved for examination.
3. Failure to collect physical evidence. This may be caused by a fear of cross-examination on some technical, legal, or scientific requirement that may be overlooked. It may be due to inadequate training or experience or to the overcautiousness of field investigators and the fear of destroying evidence.
4. Overrepresentation of laboratory capabilities.
5. Inconvenience to the investigator when there is no local laboratory available or backlogs are so great as to prohibit timely reports of laboratory results.[8]

This list is accurate and complete. The second and fourth points are especially important. If investigators do not know how the most minute or insignificant-looking item can be processed at a properly equipped laboratory, critical pieces of material go uncollected, unprocessed, and unused in substantiating guilt or innocence. In addition, if the capabilities of a crime laboratory are overrepresented so that investigators, uniformed officers, prosecutors, and judges all believe it can produce results that it, in fact, cannot produce, these people eventually will underuse the laboratory. Too often scientists fail to keep justice personnel informed of the state of the art in forensic work.[9]

The laboratory can be an extremely valuable investigative tool if the field investigator uses it intelligently and understands its capabilities and limitations. The investigator must also assume responsibility for providing the laboratory with evidence that is properly collected, marked, and preserved so that laboratory analysis, to the effective limits of present technology, can be successful.[10]

## MEASURES OF CRIME LABORATORY EFFECTIVENESS

The effectiveness of crime laboratory services can be measured in terms of three criteria: quality, proximity, and timeliness.[11]

### QUALITY

Quality is judged largely on the technical capabilities of the laboratory and the abilities of the personnel who staff the laboratory.

The technical capabilities of the scientific community affect how fully laboratories answer the questions posed by investigators. Although technical advances are developing rapidly, there are still limits on what science can do in analyzing and individualizing evidence. Unfortunately, because of these inherent technological limitations, crime laboratories may not receive the needed resources to expand or even deliver basic services.

Budget considerations largely determine the level of services that a crime laboratory can deliver. A lack of understanding of the extent to which efficient crime laboratory programs can contribute to the effectiveness of a law enforcement agency has led many administrators to channel financial resources into more traditional kinds of law enforcement operations.

"The most important resource in any crime laboratory is the scientific staff. Without an adequately trained, competent staff, the best organized and equipped laboratory will not be efficient."[12] Historically, there has been a shortage of qualified personnel with scientific backgrounds interested in working in a criminalistics laboratory. Many who are qualified shun police laboratory work, particularly on a local level, because private industry can offer much more attractive salaries.[13] (See photo on page 221.)

### PROXIMITY

It is understood, if not accepted, that most law enforcement agencies cannot afford to staff and maintain a crime laboratory. In light of this fact, however, police agencies that desire and will use the facilities of a crime laboratory should not be denied the opportunity to have such services at their

### Laboratory Personnel at Work

Modern police crime labs are typically equipped to scientifically examine a wide variety of physical evidence submitted by investigators. The scientists working in these labs usually have college degrees in chemistry, biology, or other physical sciences and are often called upon to testify regarding the evidence they have examined in criminal trials.

(Courtesy New Jersey State Police)

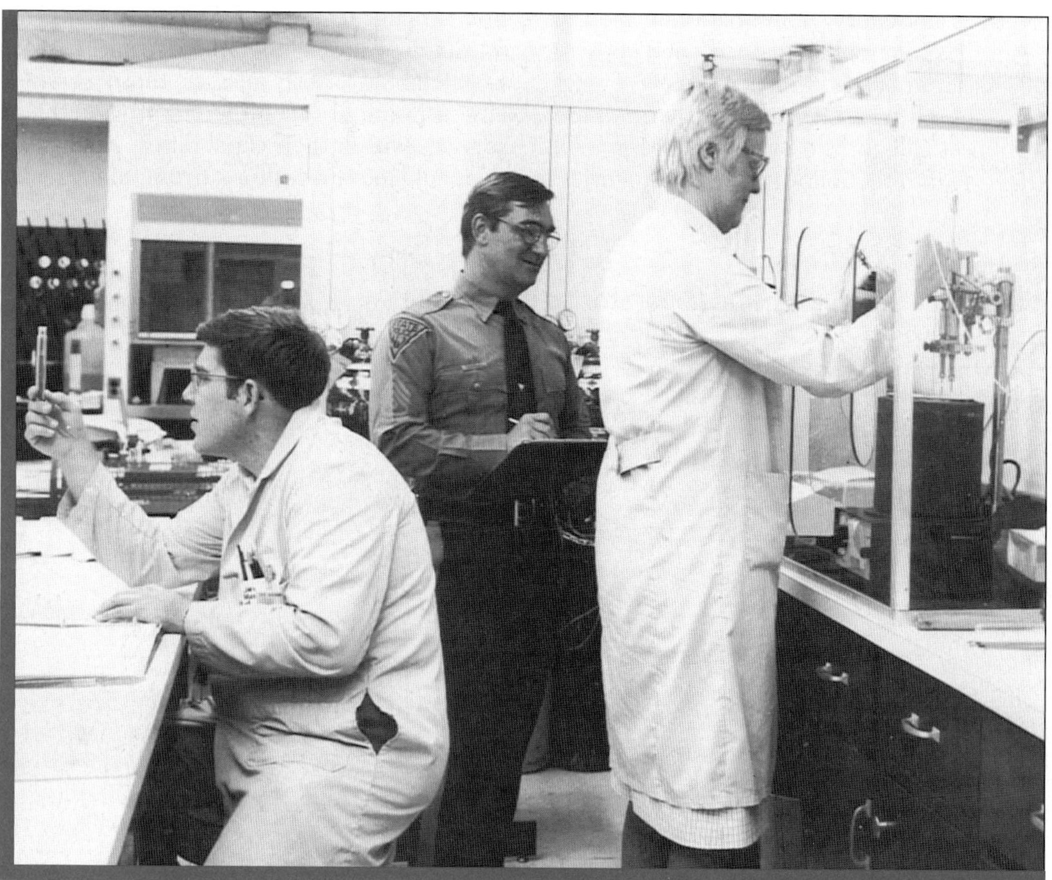

disposal. Past experience indicates that police investigators rarely seek laboratory assistance when the facility is inconvenient. There are areas where the technician or investigator must travel an unreasonable distance to obtain laboratory services. Studies have shown that evidence submission decreased sharply as the distance from the crime scene to the laboratory increased.[14] The solution to this dilemma lies in adequate planning on the state level to provide needed laboratory services.

Studies have indicated that a unified state system can best serve the needs of the law enforcement community by providing a parent, or core, laboratory on the state level capable of delivering most laboratory services and strategically located regional laboratories that respond to immediate, less sophisticated analytical needs and funnel evidence when more sophisticated analysis is required. Texas, for example, has its headquarters laboratory located under the auspices of the Texas Department of Public Safety in Austin, with field laboratories in Dallas, Tyler, Houston, Corpus Christi, Midland, El Paso, Lubbock, and Waco. The Division of Consolidated Laboratory Services in Richmond, Virginia, serves as a parent laboratory with regional facilities located in Norfolk, Roanoke, and Fairfax. Other states adopting the regionalized concept include Alabama, California, Florida,

Georgia, and Illinois. Figure 7–1 shows the location of Florida's regional crime laboratories and state-subsidized local laboratories joined into a regional network.

Several studies have addressed the issue of proximity of crime labs. One recommended that a regional crime laboratory should be established to serve each population group of 500,000 to 1,000,000 in an area where at least 5,000 Part I crimes are committed each year. (Part I crimes are serious offenses categorized by the FBI's *Uniform Crime Reports* into the following eight categories: murder, forcible rape, robbery, aggravated assault, burglary, larceny, arson, and auto theft.) Another study recommended that regional laboratories be located within a 20-mile radius of 90 percent of the law enforcement agencies' sworn personnel who would use the facilities. A third recommendation is that a regional laboratory be located within 50 miles of any agency that it routinely serves.[15] Local laboratories, such as those serving large cities or counties, continue to provide the level of services within their capabilities and also serve as regional laboratories for surrounding agencies.

**Figure 7-1** Location of Crime Laboratories in Florida

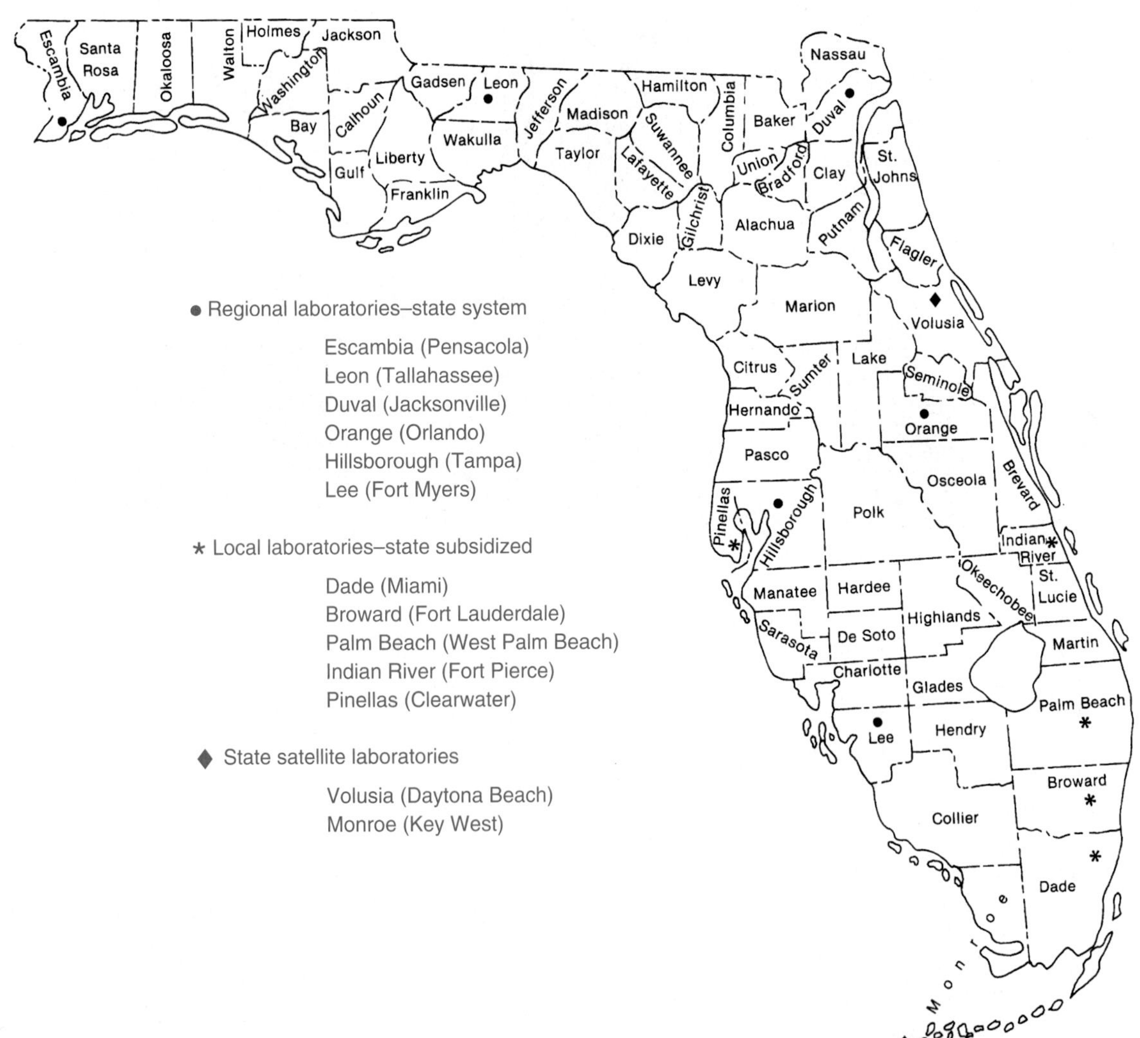

Even in law enforcement agencies that have a crime laboratory, the organization of the lab and its placement within the organizational structure may reveal much about the importance and priority the criminalistics function carries within the agency. In turn, that decision affects budget considerations and the quality of services provided. It is highly unlikely that an administrator who has fought for and was instrumental in establishing a crime lab would give it anything other than high priority and provide for adequate funding. But what about the next administrator? Or the one after that? Priorities in a law enforcement agency, just as in any other organization, can and do change.

If the crime lab or forensic science program has any importance to the chief executive, that function will not be buried within the organization; rather, it will be accessible to the operation functions and "within sight" of the administration in case assistance is needed. The committed chief executive will ensure that the supervisory chain of command understands and appreciates the scientific roles and responsibilities of the laboratory. In fact, it is in the agency's and the laboratory's best interests for the entire supervising and command staff of the laboratory to be scientists who happen to have supervisory or command capabilities. In this manner, when resource allocation and criticality-of-function issues arise in the agency, the people representing the laboratory are knowledgeable about the scientific mission.

## TIMELINESS

Timeliness, also extremely important to the investigator, is the third measure of effectiveness of a crime laboratory. A major portion of the caseload of most laboratories today results from investigators' requests for analysis of suspected or known samples of narcotics or dangerous drugs[16] and DNA evidence. Regarding narcotics and dangerous drugs, even in areas where officers carry and are trained to use presumptive test kits that are available on the commercial market, the results of laboratory analysis provide conclusive evidence necessary to the success of cases. Unlike the case with many other articles or items submitted to a laboratory for examination, which only corroborate evidence possessed by the investigator, the analysis of suspected narcotics or dangerous drugs can be the key to a successful prosecution. Their identification can significantly affect early stages of the judicial proceedings, such as the probable-cause hearing; and very often this is an essential piece of corpus delicti evidence. Hence, it is necessary that the results of laboratory examinations be made available to the investigator as quickly as possible. Such a prompt turnaround requires an appropriate allocation of money and personnel to the process by those who control the purse strings and make the decisions.

Timeliness is occasionally affected by the length of the examination or the processing time necessary for accurate and reliable test results. Early DNA analysis, for example, took weeks before conclusions could be properly drawn. This lack of timeliness, in large measure, caused further research that has resulted in faster, easier, and more reliable DNA testing methods.

## ADMISSIBILITY OF EXAMINATION RESULTS

In 1923, a federal court rendered a decision in the case of ***Frye v. United States*** that ruled inadmissible the results of a "deception test," an early version of the polygraph. The decision established a standard which provided that, for the results of a scientific technique to be admissible, the technique must be sufficiently established to have gained general acceptance in its particular field.[17]

Half a century later, the federal **rules of evidence** were adopted, which provide that if scientific, technical, or other specialized knowledge will help the trier of fact understand the evidence or determine a fact in issue, such evidence is admissible. The federal rules of evidence do not apply to the states, and several circuits continued to follow *Frye* rather than the federal rules. In 1993, the U.S. Supreme Court decided the case of ***Daubert v. Merrell Dow Pharmaceuticals, Inc.*** In that case, the Court said that the "general-acceptance" test of *Frye* is not part of the federal rules and, in fact, was superceded by the rules' adoption. The Court went on to say that the trial judge must make a preliminary assessment of whether the testimony of an expert provides an underlying reasoning or methodology that is scientifically valid and can properly be applied to the facts of the case. Many considerations will bear on the inquiry, including whether the theory or technique in question can be (and has been) tested, whether it has been subjected to peer review and publication, its known or potential error rate, the existence and maintenance of standards controlling its operation, and whether it has attracted widespread acceptance within a relevant scientific community. The Court went on to say that the inquiry is a flexible one and that its focus must be solely on principles and methodology, not on conclusions that they generate.[18]

Although *Daubert* applies only to cases in federal courts, a number of states have adopted the *Daubert* standard. Consequently, the application of *Daubert*, and its aftermath, has presented a challenge to crime laboratories to ensure that the standards imposed by the Court are followed in forensic examinations so that expert testimony and the results of examinations by crime laboratory personnel will be admissible, in both state and federal courts.

## TECHNOLOGIES

The speed at which technological advances with forensic applications are developing, expanding, and evolving makes their description immediately obsolete. Computerization has increased speed and reliability of many of the processes formerly manually performed. Computer software is available to identify and track serial killers; produce aging progression, facial imaging, and other data to aid in the search for missing children; analyze hair to improve the detection of drug abuse, particularly after a long period of time has elapsed since the use of specified drugs; highlight fingerprints with laser technology that were previously unrecognizable or undetectable on smooth surfaces; and digitally enhance photographs.

The critical role that investigative and forensic sciences play in the U.S. justice system, as well as the attorney general's interest in the rightful conviction of criminals and the exoneration of innocent persons, prompted a significant investment in improving efforts in these areas. This has been accomplished through management efforts of the Investigative and Forensic Sciences Division of the National Institute of Justice (NIJ) within the Office of Justice Programs (OJB) in the U.S. Department of Justice. The work has been coordinated with other bureaus in OJB and with the Federal Bureau

**"Sniffing" Robot**

Advancing technology is rapidly changing the field of criminal investigation. For example, robots like this are being developed and used to locate explosives or drugs as well as to collect physical evidence at crime scenes.

(Courtesy Nashville Police Department)

of Investigation, the Drug Enforcement Agency, the Bureau of Alcohol, Tobacco and Firearms, the U.S. Secret Service, and the Departments of Defense, Commerce, and Energy.[19]

The National Institute of Justice has demonstrated the use of teleforensic technology as a means for communicating knowledge from forensic scientists in a crime laboratory to investigators at a crime scene. This joint project with NASA and the New York State Police has explored the use of NASA space technology and other remote sensing technologies for remote crime scene imaging. The institute is developing a robot that can identify explosives and drugs and can be used to collect evidence at a crime scene. It is also developing a fluorescent imaging tool that will enable investigators to identify fingerprints or biological evidence under natural lighting conditions.[20] Private companies are developing numerous state-of-the-art tools to aid crime scene investigators and crime laboratories, including strong laser-directed light sources that will enhance the investigator's ability to detect and identify evidence.

Among the other forensic science projects in which the NIJ is involved are research to validate a procedure for determining the postmortem interval (the time between death and discovery of a body) by means of entomology; the development and validation of a ballistics-matching technology that uses three-dimensional images of bullets and cartridge cases; and a project with the Royal Canadian Mounted Police that will create a comprehensive firearms identification system database to be made available to law enforcement agencies on CD-ROM. In addition, the institute is funding development of a computer-assisted procedure for handwriting analysis and comparison and is supporting a project for developing and validating a linguistic method of distinguishing authors of electronically created documents.[21]

The NIJ is heavily involved in many projects that aim to establish standards and protocols for DNA analysis, develop newer, faster, more accurate DNA testing methods, and ensure that only accurate results are used as evidence in criminal trials.

## DNA ANALYSIS

Advances in technology have helped DNA testing to become an established part of criminal justice procedure. Despite early controversies and challenges by defense attorneys, the admissibility of DNA test results in the courtroom has become routine. In 1997 crime laboratories in the United States received DNA samples from about 21,000 known- or unknown-subject cases.[22] In a 1996 survey, almost half of the more than 2,300 prosecuting officers who participated indicated that they had used DNA evidence either in plea bargaining or in the trial of felony cases. It was primarily used in

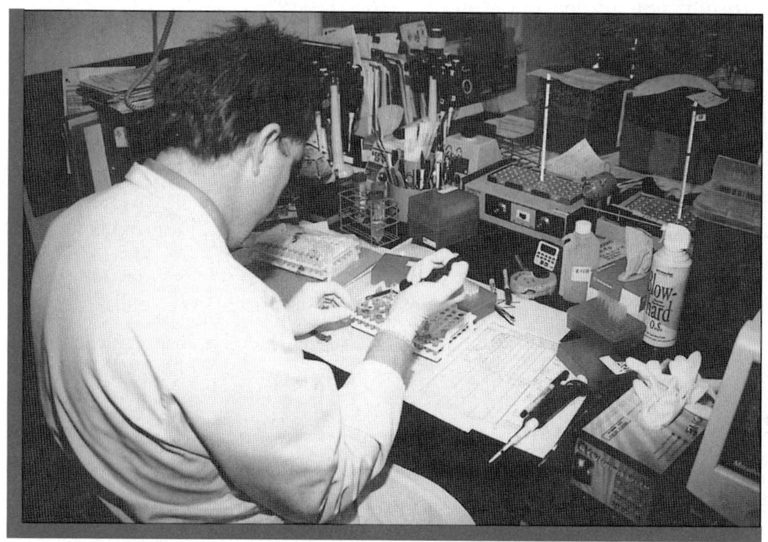

**DNA Evidence Being Processed in a Laboratory**
Today, DNA testing is a widely accepted procedure used in the criminal justice system. Due to a series of technological advances, questions about the validity and reliability of DNA test methods have been addressed. The fact that DNA is known to be present in all body tissues and fluids has important implications for the physical evidence collected in criminal investigations.

(Courtesy: San Bernardino County, California, Sheriff's Department)

cases involving sex offenses, followed by a lesser number of murder and manslaughter cases and aggravated-assault cases.[23]

Questions about the validity and reliability of forensic DNA test methods have been addressed, and for the most part validity and reliability are established. As a result of DNA testing, traditional blood testing and saliva testing have been rendered obsolete because DNA is found in these substances and, in fact, is found in all body tissues and fluids.

**Deoxyribonucleic acid (DNA)** consists of molecules that carry the body's genetic information and establish each person as separate and distinct. Until recently, DNA was found primarily within the nuclei of cells in the chromosomes. DNA can now be extracted and processed from blood, tissue, spermatozoa, bone marrow, hair (with or without roots), saliva, skin cells, bone, teeth, urine, feces, and a host of other biological specimens, all of which may be found at crime scenes. DNA has been recovered from fingerprints, cigarette butts, drinking cups, and hatbands and other articles of clothing (e.g., Monica Lewinsky's dress).

Because of recent developments, there are two places in a cell where DNA is found. They are used for different crime detection purposes. **Nuclear DNA** is found in the nucleus, and **mitochondrial DNA (mtDNA)** is found in the mitochondria, which are in the body of the cell. Nuclear DNA is the product of the DNA of a person's mother and father. When a sperm and an egg join at conception, the new individual gets half of his or her nuclear genetic information from each parent. Conversely, mitochondrial DNA is inherited only from the mother. At conception, all of the new person's mitochondria come from the mother. Since mitochondrial DNA is passed directly through maternal relatives, it serves as a perfect identity marker for those relatives.[24]

## Identifying and Collecting DNA at a Crime Scene

DNA evidence may be found and collected from virtually everywhere at a crime scene, and only a few cells can be sufficient to obtain useful DNA information. Table 7–1 lists some common types of evidence,

**Table 7-1** Sources of DNA Evidence at Crime Scenes

| Evidence | Possible Location of DNA on the Evidence | Source of DNA |
|---|---|---|
| Baseball bat or similar weapon | Handle, end | Sweat, skin, blood, tissue |
| Hat, bandanna, or mask | Inside | Sweat, hair, dandruff |
| Eyeglasses | Nose or ear pieces, lens | Sweat, skin |
| Facial tissue, cotton swab | Surface area | Mucus, blood, sweat, semen, ear wax |
| Dirty laundry | Surface area | Blood, sweat, semen |
| Toothpick | Tips | Saliva |
| Used cigarette | Cigarette butt | Saliva |
| Stamp or envelope | Licked area | Saliva |
| Tape or ligature | Inside or outside surface | Skin, sweat |
| Bottle, can, or glass | Sides, mouthpiece | Saliva, sweat |
| Used condom | Inside or outside surface | Semen, vaginal or rectal cells |
| Blanket, pillow, sheet | Surface area | Sweat, hair, semen, urine, saliva |
| "Through and through" bullet | Outside surface | Blood, tissue |
| Bite mark | Person's skin or clothing | Saliva |
| Fingernail, partial fingernail | Scrapings | Blood, sweat, tissue |

**Source:** National Commission on the Future of DNA Evidence, National Institute of Justice, "What Every Law Enforcement Officer Should Know about DNA Evidence," pamphlet (Washington, DC: U.S. Department of Justice).

the possible location of DNA on the evidence, and the biological source containing the cells. DNA does more than just identify the source of the sample; it can place a specific person at a crime scene, refute a claim of self-defense, disprove a claimed alibi, and put a weapon in a suspect's hand. Consequently, the more an investigator knows about how DNA can be used, the more powerful a tool it becomes.[25]

Because samples of DNA are easily contaminated, extreme care should be taken while collecting samples. Suggested precautions include:

- Wear gloves and change them often.
- Use disposable instruments, or clean instruments thoroughly before and after handling each sample.
- Avoid touching any area where it is believed DNA may exist.
- Avoid talking, sneezing, or coughing over evidence.
- Avoid touching your face, nose, and mouth when collecting and packaging evidence.
- Air-dry evidence thoroughly before packaging evidence.
- Put evidence into new paper bags or envelopes. Do not use plastic bags, and do not use staples to seal bags or envelopes.[26]

## Some Successes

Even though DNA may be collected from a crime scene, it may not be submitted to a laboratory for a variety of reasons. Something may prevent further investigation on the case, or the DNA may not be needed to resolve the case. Of the 21,000 cases for which crime labs received samples in 1997, the laboratories analyzed samples from about 14,000 cases and were running a backlog of 6,800 cases at the end of that year.[27] However, there have been some successes in both identifying offenders and clearing those who had been suspects. A woman informed the FBI that she had overheard a man talking on a pay phone. The man said that he had killed a woman and buried her in the woods of a local park reserve. The local police were notified, and they located the badly decomposed skeletal remains of a person but could not find the victim's teeth. Since the medical examiner could not visually identify the person or use dental records for identification, she sent the remains to the FBI laboratory, where examiners removed DNA from the victim's bones and performed mitochondrial DNA analysis. The results were compared to the DNA of missing persons in a national database. Law enforcement authorities were able to identify the victim and later convicted her killer—the man on the pay phone (see, e.g., the **positive match** in Figure 7–2).[28] Another example involved a threatening letter that was sent to a newspaper editor. The FBI swabbed the envelope flap and recovered some saliva cells, which were then typed using a DNA marker. The result was compared to a known suspect and was found to match.[29]

DNA can be extracted and analyzed from specimens that may be years or even decades old. In a case involving Kirk Bloodworth, who was found guilty of sexually assaulting and murdering a young girl, the verdict was based on an anonymous tip, identification from a police artist's sketch, eyewitness statements, and other evidence. He was later retried and again found guilty. But in 1993, more than eight years after his arrest, prosecutors compared DNA evidence from the victim's clothing to Bloodworth's DNA and found that the two did not match. He was subsequently released and then pardoned (see, e.g., the **negative match** in Figure 7–2).[30]

## DNA Technologies

In 1985, Alec Jeffreys and his colleagues in England first used DNA in a criminal case. Shortly thereafter, DNA evidence began making appearances in trials in the United States. Initially, DNA analysis required a fairly large sample, and the manual processing technique, called Restriction Fragment Length Polymorphism (RFLP), took up to 14 weeks, on average, to produce results. The RFLP system is slow, but produces good results. Technological advancements have led to a polymerase chain reaction (PCR), which takes small samples of DNA and reproduces as many copies as are needed for adequate analysis. Short tandem repeats (STRs), which are even smaller pieces of the DNA helix (ladder), can be reproduced using PCR to generate multiple copies in an instrument called a thermocycle. With the PCR-STR process, it takes about 24 hours to extract DNA from an evidentiary sample and only 2 to 3 hours to type the DNA using automation. It works well on degraded samples and on analysis of old cases.[31]

**Figure 7-2** Forensic Identity Test

(**Source.** Courtesy Lifecodes Corporation, Tarrytown, New York)

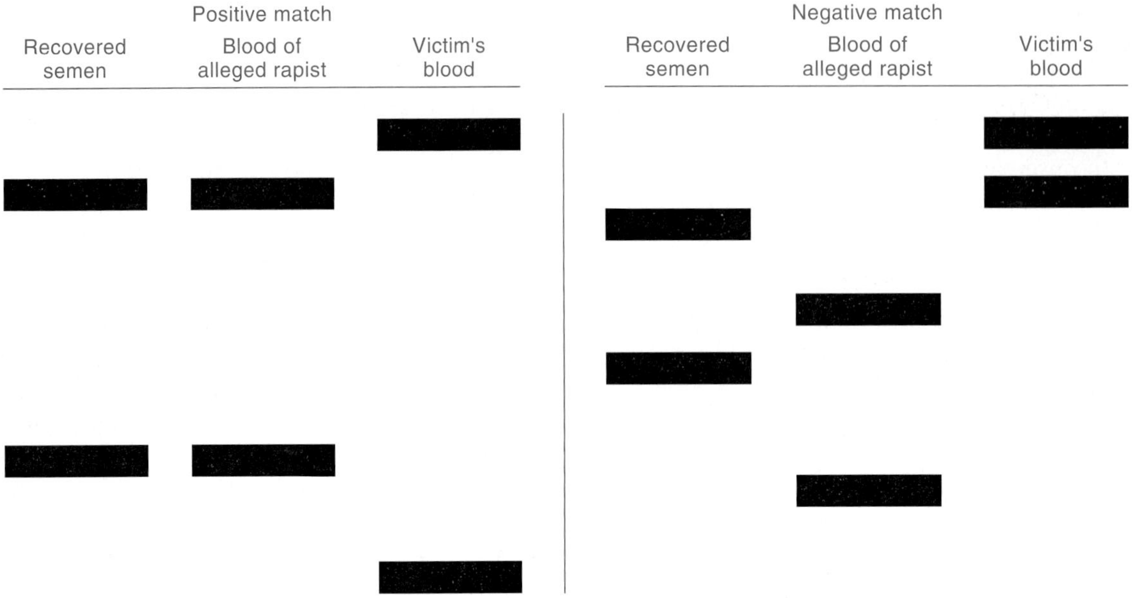

## Contamination

Just as contamination is an issue in the collection and packaging of evidence containing DNA, it is a very big issue in the handling of DNA during extraction and examination. It is also an issue that can affect the admissibility of and credibility given to DNA evidence in court. Coughing or sneezing while handling DNA evidence can cause contamination.

## Population-Genetics Statistics

The effectiveness of DNA evidence in court depends on the ability of a witness to explain the probability that no other person, except an identical twin, has the same DNA type as that discovered on a crime scene sample that identically matches the DNA type of the defendant. Thus, the question is, Is it possible to individualize the identity of a person on the basis of an analysis of his or her DNA? The answer is yes and maybe. While there are a number of ways geneticists can calculate the probability that no other person has the same genetic "footprint" as the defendant, the question often arises as to what database of individuals is being used to calculate the probability. For example, if a Hispanic person is the defendant, would the probability that there would be another person with the same DNA sequence be any greater if the database used to compare DNA consisted of only Hispanics? Is this the fair way to determine probability? This is a simplified example of some of the issues that are being examined. In the end, the statistical probability derived by any method of calculation is an estimate.

## Data Banking and CODIS

Today, all U.S. jurisdictions have legislation requiring the data banking of DNA evidence of convicted offenders. In some jurisdictions, DNA can be collected only from offenders convicted of sex-related crimes and homicides. In others, legislation has been expanded to allow for the collection of DNA specimens from all convicted offenders. This has dramatically increased the workload of laboratories that are processing the material to establish the data banks. At the end of 1997, crime labs had a backlog of 287,000 convicted-offender cases; 116,000 offender samples had been received during that year.[32] And the numbers keep growing.

In addition to individual-jurisdiction data banking, there is a national investigation support database, developed by the FBI, called the **Combined**

**DNA Index System (CODIS).** CODIS is used in the national, state, and local index-system networks to link typing results from unresolved crimes with cases in multiple jurisdictions or persons convicted of offenses specified in the data-banking laws passed by the jurisdictions. By alerting investigators to similarities among unsolved crimes, CODIS can aid in apprehending perpetrators who commit a series of crimes. The database contains over 553,000 convicted-offender profiles and more than 24,000 forensic known and unknown profiles. Florida has taken a leading role by collecting, analyzing, and contributing 90,000 of the half-million offender profiles. As of April 2001, there had been 791 offender "hits" in 24 states, 519 forensic hits in 25 states, and 1,659 investigations aided in 25 states.[33]

## Standards, Testing, Research, and Development

Laboratory accreditation by the American Society of Crime Laboratory Directors' accreditation board in all areas of forensic science requires that quality-assurance measures be in place at the laboratory. Quality-assurance standards have been developed for DNA analysis by the FBI's DNA Advisory Board. The National Institute of Standards and Technology has tested these performance standards for the various analysis techniques discussed earlier. The National Institute of Justice supported the development of criteria for external DNA proficiency training.

The NIJ is also supporting a five-year effort to fund research on and technological enhancements to the use of DNA in the criminal justice system. Projects include DNA chip technology that will make it possible to have portable DNA analysis equipment for use at crime scenes; mass spectrometry that offers great improvements in sample processing speed and throughput; and statistical modeling that facilitates producing acceptable statistical probabilities for use in court.[34]

## Human Genome Project

The Human Genome Project is a $20 billion international effort to map the 50,000 to 100,000 genes found in the human body. The project is supposed to be finished by 2005, but some claim that they have already completed it. In the long run, the mapping should lead to many medical and forensic breakthroughs.[35] It is anticipated that, within a decade, genetics laboratories will be able to determine an individual's personalized DNA sequence from a blood sample. From that data, a physician will be able to ascertain if a person has any of roughly 5,000 known genetic diseases and will be able to evaluate the patient's probability of contracting any number of specific diseases, perhaps months, years, or decades in advance.

## Postconviction DNA Testing

The contemporary issue in the DNA field is postconviction cases. Because the speed and accuracy of testing have improved and because of stories about convicted people who were exonerated as a result of DNA tests, many inmates now want to be tested if there is any evidence from which DNA can be extracted. They have nothing to lose and everything to gain. Some of the requests may have a legitimate basis, as in cases where earlier DNA tests with older, less accurate analysis were inconclusive and current technology might clear an innocent person. Not all the situations are this clear-cut. There are many cases in the gray area that should be addressed. The National Commission on the Future of DNA Evidence has produced a manual containing recommendations for handling requests.[36]

# AUTOMATED FINGERPRINT IDENTIFICATION SYSTEM

In the mid-1970s, in San Francisco, Miriam Slamovich, a concentration camp survivor, was shot point-blank in the face. She died a month later. On the bedroom window, her killer left a full, perfect fingerprint that became the object of thousands of hours of manual fingerprint comparisons over a 10-year period. When San Francisco installed an **Automated Fingerprint Identification System (AFIS),** the latent print from the Slamovich case was the first search made, and a hit was recorded in less than 6 minutes. The killer was in custody the same day.[37]

In August 1991, two pieces of paper allegedly handled by an unknown suspect in a Jacksonville, Florida, sexual-assault case were submitted to the Florida Department of Law Enforcement regional crime lab for analysis. A number of latent prints were developed on the paper and searched in the Automated Fingerprint Identification System without success. The unidentified latent prints were entered into the AFIS Unsolved Latent Fingerprint

File (ULF) so that they could be searched against incoming fingerprint cards from current arrests throughout the state. In April 1994, an individual was arrested for auto theft and released. The fingerprint card taken at the time of the arrest was submitted to the department and searched against the ULF. On May 16, 1994, as a result of the reverse search (current fingerprint cards searched against the ULF), an identification was made. The offender was eventually located in New York and extradited to Florida. As a result of the AFIS search, blood was drawn from the suspect for comparison with semen samples obtained from the victim at the time of the offense almost three years earlier. There was a DNA match. In April 1995, the offender pled guilty to the sexual assault and was sentenced to 10 years in prison.[38]

Traditionally, fingerprints have been classified, filed, and searched according to the Henry Classification System. Technical searches of newly fingerprinted persons, conducted to determine if they have any prior criminal record, are labor-intensive but have been fairly productive. On the other hand, searches of latent fingerprints collected from crime scenes against a Henry system file have been so labor-intensive and unproductive that some jurisdictions don't even attempt them. Certainly, the larger the agency, the greater the problem.

In the early 1970s, the FBI and the National Bureau of Standards conducted feasibility research for establishing an automated fingerprint identification process. After a successful pilot study, the computers hit the market and one of the most beneficial high-tech tools for law enforcement use in this century became a reality.[39] (See photo on right.)

AFIS allows law enforcement agencies to conduct comparisons of applicant and suspect fingerprints with literally thousands or millions of file prints in a matter of minutes. A manual search of this nature would take hundreds of hours with little hope for and less chance of success. The heart of AFIS technology is the ability of the computer equipment to scan and digitize fingerprints by reading spacing and ridge patterns and translating them into the appropriate computer language coding. The computer is capable of making extremely fine distinctions among prints, lending further accuracy and reliability to the system.

The computer can map 90 or more minutia points (ridge endings, bifurcations, directions, and contours) for each finger. This is a number high enough to individualize a fingerprint and distinguish it from all others. Latent prints normally do not have 90 minutia points, but matches usually can be made with as few as 15 or 20 minutia points. One agency reported a hit on 8 minutia points.

Technicians can computer-enhance fingerprints when preparing them for a search. This process enables an experienced technician to fill in missing or blurred portions of print fragments or to correct for breaks in patterns or ridges caused by burns or scars.

As noted, the computer translates patterns into mathematical computer codes. Thus, the computer is not comparing images of a suspect's prints against images of known prints; rather, it is conducting a mathematical search that can compare a subject print against file prints at a rate of up to 600 prints per second. Search time will vary depending on such factors as preparation time, demographic data that are entered to limit the prints required to be searched, the size of the file, and the number of

**AFIS Workstation**

One of the major technological innovations developed over the last three decades has been the Automated Fingerprint Identification System (AFIS). Prior to this development, fingerprints collected at crime scenes had to be manually compared to fingerprints in police data files—a very slow and labor-intensive procedure. AFIS allows law enforcement agencies to compare suspect fingerprints to thousands (or in some cases millions) of file prints in a matter of minutes.

(Courtesy St. Louis Police Department)

key factors, or matchers, being used to seek a match. A latent print can be searched against a file of 500,000 prints in about half an hour.

Although the accuracy of the AFIS system is 98 to 100 percent, this does not mean that the computer makes positive matches that percentage of the time. In fact, the system never makes a final decision on identity. The system produces a list of possibles, called a candidate list. It is from this list that further determinations are made by a qualified fingerprint examiner.

The computer uses a scoring system that assigns points to each criterion used in the match. The technician sets a threshold score above which a hit is fairly well assured. The technician also sets the size of the candidate list. If any of the scores are high above the threshold, a hit may be likely. If all the scores on the candidate list are low, a hit is unlikely. Policy of the agency may dictate the placement of the threshold, thus limiting or enlarging the number of candidates. Time constraints and resources may be controlling factors in these determinations.

AFIS makes no final decisions on identity. A technician must make the final verification as to whether the system has obtained a hit. The computer assists but does not replace the fingerprint expert.

AFIS has two major duties. First is performing the functions of classifying, searching, and matching prints. Second is the storage and retrieval of fingerprint data. Data are stored on optical disks, thereby permitting side-by-side comparisons of search prints and file prints. Such comparisons are useful for verifying the data found in an AFIS search (see Figure 7–3).[40]

In July 1999, law enforcement agencies began to have access to the FBI's **Integrated Automated Fingerprint Identification System (IAFIS),** a national online fingerprint and criminal-history database with identification and response capabilities. IAFIS consists of three integrated segments: AFIS, the Interstate Identification Index (III), and Identification Tasking and Networking (ITN).

Here is how IAFIS works: A local agency must have a live-scan fingerprint terminal. If it does, it can scan the prints of a person who is arrested and electronically transmit the prints and mug shots, along with personal information about the arrestee, to the state's law enforcement network for a fingerprint check. The same electronic prints and personal information are transmitted to the FBI fingerprint repository maintained by the Criminal Justice Information System (CJIS) Division in Clarksburg, West Virginia. The system was designed to support a daily traffic load of more than 62,000

**Figure 7-3**

### AFIS Fingerprint Comparison

This is an actual AFIS print. On the left is a file print several years old. On the right is a latent print left at the scene of a burglary. Even though a new scar is seen on the fingerprint on the right, AFIS was still able to match the prints.

(Courtesy Dallas Police Department)

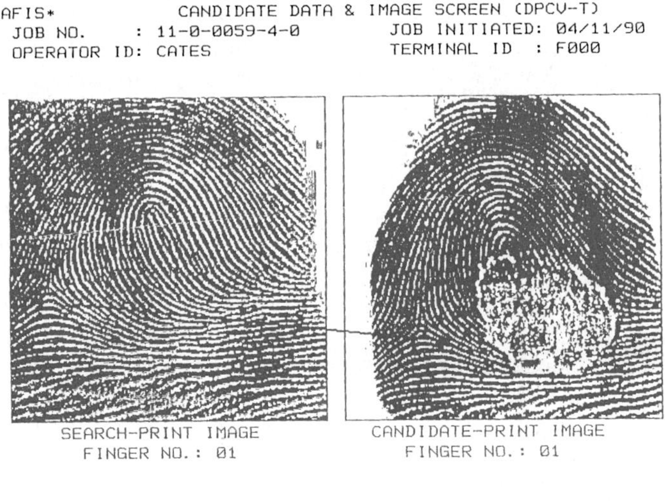

fingerprint-package transmissions and hundreds of thousands of other transactions. After going through several quality-control checks, the information is run against an automated system, housing "rap sheets" on about 35 million offenders. If a match is found, it is verified by an examiner who manually compares the prints. If no match is found in the rap-sheet file, the prints are run against the FBI's AFIS system, which houses 35 million 10-print digitized files. The system can examine 3 million fingerprints per second. A potential match is manually examined to ensure accuracy. If no match is found in either the subject search or the fingerprint search, the record is added to the appropriate databases, an FBI identification number is assigned, and the submitting agency is notified of the search results and the assigned number.[41]

## NATIONAL INTEGRATED BALLISTIC INFORMATION NETWORK PROGRAM

A joint program of the Bureau of Alcohol, Tobacco and Firearms (ATF) and the FBI, the **National Integrated Ballistic Information Network (NIBIN)** integrates all the elements of Ceasefire and Brasscatcher (both former ATF programs) and Drugfire (an FBI program).

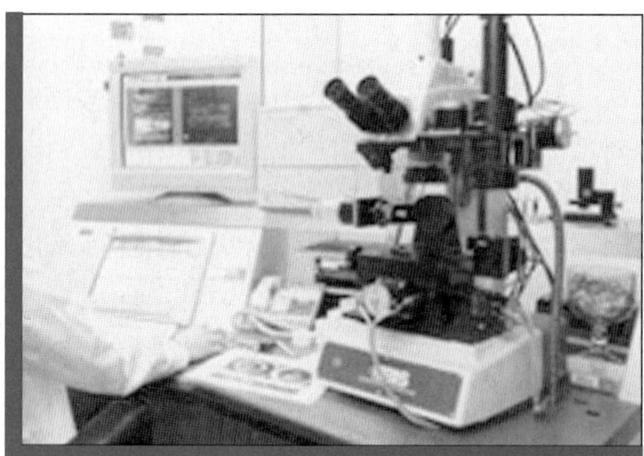

**NIBIN System**

Just as individual fingerprints differ, each firearm leaves different, unique characteristics on expended ammuntion. The National Integrated Ballistic Information System Network, developed by ATF and the FBI, compares images of ballistic evidence obtained at crime scenes to recovered firearms. Matches or "hits" are confirmed by a firearms examiner in the lab.

(Courtesy Iowa Criminalistic Laboratory, Department of Public Safety)

Just as each fingerprint is different, so a firearm leaves unique identifiable characteristics on expended ammunition. NIBIN compares images of ballistic evidence, both projectiles and casings, obtained from crime scenes and recovered firearms. As new images are entered, the system searches the existing database for possible matches. Hits are confirmed by a firearm examiner. (See photo on left.)

The system has amassed a large ballistic-image database filled with crime gun data submitted by local, state, and federal agencies throughout the country, and the intelligence information is available to all law enforcement agencies. Since the inception of the system, partner agencies have achieved over 2,200 hits.[42]

# HANDLING EVIDENCE IN THE LABORATORY

## HUMAN FACTORS

In handling evidentiary materials, laboratory personnel—scientists and technicians alike—have always been cautious not to disturb or ruin the viability of the materials for any possible examination that would later prove to be useful. Today, because of concerns over the transmission of hepatitis and the AIDS virus, the handling of evidence is of even greater concern.

Although a few laboratories may autoclave specimens, such sterilization with heat may tend to decrease the usefulness of the specimen for analysis purposes. Most laboratories, including the FBI, are merely extra careful in handling evidence involving tissue or body fluids. The procedure followed normally is to ask the agency sending the specimen for any factual information available on the subject so that a determination can be made as to whether the evidence was obtained from a person who may have been infected. In addition, scientists and technicians are instructed to keep their work areas clean, to clean those areas between conducting examinations, and to change and clean lab coats and gloves frequently.

## INSTRUMENTAL ANALYSIS

The kinds of evidence subject to laboratory examinations are many and varied. For laboratory purposes, examinations generally fall into the following categories: chemical examinations, biological examinations, physical examinations, personal identification, firearm identification, documentary examinations, and photography.

In a textbook of this nature it is not practical to present a detailed discussion of the technical intricacies of various scientific instruments. However, it is appropriate to acquaint readers with some of the capabilities of instruments used in scientific analysis of evidence.

The first, and perhaps most important, instrument that needs to be mentioned is the computer. The advances that have been made in laboratory analyses can largely be credited to computerization and its continued refinement. A majority of the instruments discussed in this section and many others used in laboratories depend on computers for rapid and accurate analysis.

## Emission Spectrograph

Each element, such as tin, iron, and copper, when properly burned, will give off light that is characteristic of itself and different from the light produced by all other elements. Emission spectrography is capable of identifying elements from the light that is produced. Its uses include rapid analysis of all metallic constituents in an unknown substance; detection of traces of metallic impurities in residues such as oils, ashes, glasses, or metals; testing the purity of a substance; detection of rare metals; and examination of paint specimens. Emission spectrography has the advantage of allowing a complete analysis of metallic elements in an unknown substance through one operation. In addition, analysis requires only a relatively small sample, and it provides positive identification of the elements present in the substance.[43]

## Mass Spectrometer

This instrument is used in analyzing a wide range of forensic specimens, including drugs, poisons, accelerants, explosive residues, and biological samples, by breaking the samples down into chemical "building blocks" and creating profiles of the molecules. As noted earlier, this is the instrument being studied for use in expediting DNA analysis.

## Visible Spectrophotometer

This instrument is used for studying color and coloring agents such as dyes and pigments. For example, all the colors of the rainbow are paraded through a dye in solution. The instrument records the percentages of each color that pass through the solution. The variation in the amount of each color that can pass through the solution is characteristic of the dye. The instrument can also be used to measure the amount of each color reflected from a colored surface. The visible spectrophotometer is often used in comparing dyes and coloring agents in materials such as cloth, paint, and glass. The instrumental analysis of colors can eliminate personal error in color comparisons. Small samples can be examined and studied and the instrumentation provides a rapid analysis.

## Infrared Spectrophotometer

This instrument passes a narrow beam of infrared energy through a thin film of the substance being studied. As the wavelengths change, the amount of energy transmitted by the specimen is measured and recorded on a chart. The chart is a "fingerprint" of the material being subjected to study. Infrared spectrophotometry is a primary means for the identification and comparisons of plastics, rubber, paint, and other organic compounds, as well as for inorganic minerals. It has the advantage of being able to detect slight differences in composition and molecular arrangements of minute amounts of material.

## Atomic Absorption Spectrophotometer

Atomic absorption spectroscopy is a quantitative technique whereby elements in a sample are placed in a vapor state, which allows them to be analyzed by means of a flame. It is used to determine concentrations of specific elements in a sample. This procedure is used not for a survey-type analysis to establish which elements may be present but, rather, for determining the proportional concentration of each known element in the sample. The advantage of atomic absorption spectroscopy is that it is a very accurate and sensitive method of determining elemental concentration, especially when many samples are involved and when a sample can be readily placed in solution. It also provides a relatively economical and normally rapid procedure for determining the concentrations of elements.

## Gas Chromatograph

Essentially used as an analytical instrument for separation and identification of gases or liquids from complex mixtures or solutions, the gas chromatograph can analyze organic material such as narcotics, explosives, paints, plastics, inks, or petroleum products (see photo at right). Since the crime laboratory rarely receives evidence of a chemical nature that is pure, separation methods are essential to the proper identification of constituent components, liquids, or gases. The gas chromatograph can separate and indicate the composition by retention time and relative amounts of components. It can also be used for solving a wide variety of analytical tasks through the analysis of volatile solids, high-boiling liquids, or gases. The recording and evaluation of the analytical results of the testing are not time-consuming. The gas chromatograph frequently is used in conjunction with the mass spectrometer.

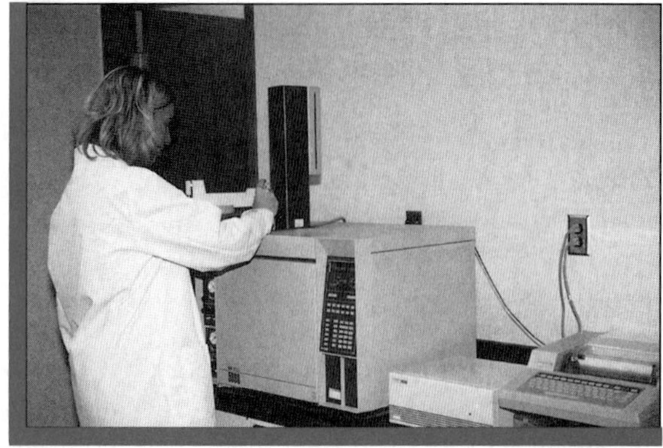

**Gas Chromatograph**

The Gas Chromatograph is used to separate and identify gasses or fluids from complex mixtures or solutions. In criminal investigations, it is often used to analyze organic materials such as narcotics, explosives, and paints.
(Courtesy Indiana State Police)

### X-Ray Diffraction Spectrophotometer

This instrument is used to identify and compare unknown crystalline substances. Crystals that differ in chemical composition also differ in size and shape and will diffract X-rays differently, thus permitting the identification of crystalline material in comparison with known standards. Only small samples are required, and the sample is not consumed in using this technique.

This discussion has explained some of the more sophisticated equipment currently being used in full-service crime laboratories. It excludes the more obvious or technical examination methods, such as many chemical analyses, fingerprint identification, firearm identification, physical and chemical documentary examinations, photographic techniques and equipment, microscopy, and DNA analysis; some of these methods were discussed earlier.

## ATF FORENSIC SCIENCE LABORATORIES

The Bureau of Alcohol, Tobacco and Firearms (ATF) of the U.S. Department of the Treasury maintains five forensic science laboratories. The ATF National Laboratory was created by Congress in 1886. The ATF laboratories, in addition to analyzing alcohol and tobacco samples, conduct forensic examinations in support of the bureau's explosives, bombing and arson, and illegal-firearm-trafficking investigations, along with major case investigations of state and local authorities. In 2000 the ATF laboratories analyzed 8,631 new alcohol product applications, processed 2,878 forensic cases, and spent 213 days providing expert testimony in courts, 215 days at crime scenes, and 334 days training federal, state, and local investigators and examiners.[44]

The laboratories hold the distinction of being the first federal laboratory system accredited by the ASCLD.[45] The majority of the examinations conducted by the laboratories involve chemical and physical examinations of explosives, firearms, and arson evidence, as well as the document, tool-mark, and latent-fingerprint examinations associated with those investigations.

The forensic laboratories are staffed by over 130 employees, most of whom are chemists, physical scientists, document analysts, latent-print specialists, and firearm and tool-mark examiners. The remainder are evidence technicians and clerical personnel.

Evidence collected at crime scenes of suspected arsons is examined to identify accelerants, incendiaries, and incendiary-device components. Evidence collected at explosion scenes is examined to identify explosives used, blasting caps, leg wires, fuses, timing mechanisms, energy sources, containers, wires, tapes, and various other component parts used to make the bomb. The laboratory system maintains liaison with explosive manufacturers, who provide exemplars of new explosives products on the market.

Comparative trace-evidence examinations are conducted on materials including tapes, wires, glass, metals, soil, hair, paint, fibers, ink, paper, and wood to determine whether the materials could have a common origin and thereby associate a suspect with a crime.

Questioned-document examinations are conducted to identify handwriting on firearm transaction forms. In addition, examinations are performed to identify typewriters, copy machines, and cigarette tax stamps. Attempts are also made to decipher indented and obliterated writings.

The laboratories also perform a full range of fingerprint, firearm, and tool-mark examinations in support of agency investigations.

Firearm examinations involve primarily serial-number restoration, determination of the operability of weapons, comparison of metals in sawed-off barrels, and determination of the possible common origin of silencers seized from different suspects or locations. Gunshot-residue tests are conducted in shootings that involve law enforcement officers. In addition, special tests to evaluate the performance of ammunition and weapons are occasionally done.

Tool-mark examinations generally involve evidence associated with bombings and arson. This includes examination of cut wires, torn tapes, drill holes, pipe wrench marks, saw marks on wood and metal, and numerous other marks made by tools.

The bureau has four National Response Teams that respond to major bombings and arson disasters, nationally and internationally. The teams consist of highly trained investigators, forensic chemists, and explosives technology experts. The teams respond within 24 hours, collect evidence, and complete most laboratory examinations before leaving the crime scene.[46]

## THE FBI CRIME LABORATORY

The **FBI Crime Laboratory** is one of the largest and most comprehensive forensic laboratories, and it is the only full-service forensic laboratory. It was established in 1932. Of importance to the investigator is the fact that the facilities of the FBI laboratory are available without charge to all state, county, and municipal law enforcement agencies in the United States.[47] There are, however, some provisos concerning the submission of evidence for examination to the laboratory. The laboratory will not make examinations if any evidence in the case has been or will be subjected to the same type of technical examination by another laboratory or other experts. This policy is designed to eliminate duplication of effort and to ensure that evidence is received in its original condition, thereby allowing laboratory personnel to interpret their findings properly and ensure meaningful testimony and presentation of evidence in subsequent court cases.

In order to more effectively and efficiently use its current resources, the FBI laboratory has a policy not to accept cases from other crime laboratories that have the capability of conducting the requested examination. If such cases are submitted by other crime laboratories and there are no special circumstances to warrant the submissions, the cases will be returned unopened and unexamined. This policy should not be construed as lessening the FBI laboratory's continuing commitment to the scientific training of state and local crime laboratory personnel, and it does not limit the laboratory's acceptance of cases from other crime laboratories when special circumstances prevail.

Also, the FBI laboratory no longer accepts evidence from state and local law enforcement agencies regarding property crime investigations unless the cases involve personal injury or the offenses were designed to cause personal injury.

In addition to doing analysis, the FBI furnishes the experts necessary to testify in connection with the results of its examination in either state or federal courts. Again, there is no charge to local law enforcement agencies for this service.

The laboratory provides a comprehensive array of forensic services. Laboratory personnel conduct microscopic examinations of hair and fiber, fabric, tape, rope, and wool (see top left photo on page 236). Chemical examinations are conducted on many substances, often to supplement examinations conducted by other sections. Examinations are conducted on poisons (toxicology), paint, ink, tear gas, dyes, and flash and water-soluble paper, among others.

Mineralogy examinations are conducted on soils and combinations of mineral substances such as safe insulation, concrete, plaster, mortar, glass, ore, abrasives, gems, industrial dusts, and building materials.

Firearm examiners may be asked to determine if firearms are operating properly or to conduct gunpowder shot–pattern tests (see bottom right photo on page 236). Using the same basic principles of firearm examination, the identification of telltale marks left at crime scenes by punches, hammers, axes, pliers, screwdrivers, chisels, wrenches, and other objects can be made. The explosives specialist can analyze fragments of explosives to determine

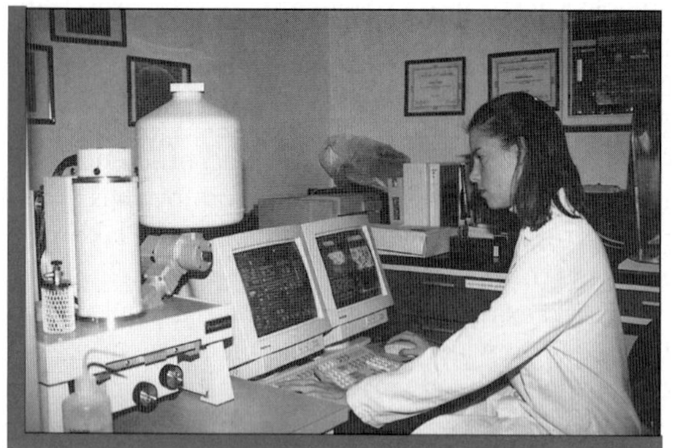

**Forensic Examiner Conducting Examination with a Scanning Electron Microscope**
One of the standard instruments in today's crime labs is the electron microscope. Typically, evidence such as hair, fiber, fabric, and rope will undergo microscopic examination in the crime lab. Many criminal investigations have been solved by lab personnel, with the help of an electron microscope, matching these types of physical evidence to materials found in the possession of a suspect.
(Courtesy Indiana State Police)

their original composition and possible sources of raw materials.

The metallurgy unit is called on to restore obliterated or altered numbers on such things as firearms, sewing machines, watches, outboard motors, slot machines, automobiles, tools, and other metallic items. Tests can show whether two or more pieces of metal are related, the possible cause of metal separation, and whether production specifications for metals have been met.

Handwriting examiners agree that no two individuals write exactly alike. Even though there may be superficial resemblances in the writing of two or more persons as a result of similar training, the complexity of writing is such that individual peculiarities and characteristics appear. These characteristics can be detected by a document expert, who then can arrive at a scientific opinion.

The FBI laboratory has also developed the ability to conduct forensic examinations on chemical, biological, and nuclear hazards. In 1996, the Hazardous Materials Response Unit was established in response to the threat of terrorism involving chemical, biological, and nuclear weapons and to an expanding caseload of environmental crimes. The laboratory has also developed the Computer Analysis and Response Team (CART) program, capable of conducting examinations in which information is extracted from magnetic, optical, and similar storage media and converted into a form usable to investigators or prosecutors. The FBI's laboratory is leading the research and development efforts to improve and expedite DNA analysis methods and is one of the few laboratories conducting mitochondrial DNA testing.

## REFERENCE FILES

To aid examiners in their work, the FBI laboratory in 1932 established what is now one of the largest reference collections for helping solve cases. These files are of two types: standard reference files and collections, which contain known samples of items, generally of manufactured products, and reference files of questioned materials, which are composed

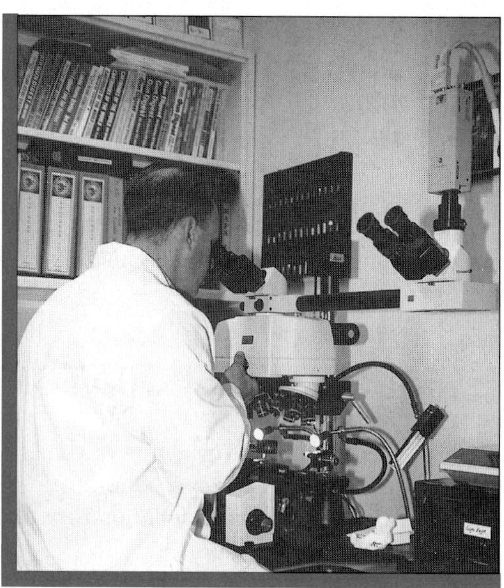

**Forensic Examiner Conducting Firearm Examination**
In serious violent crimes such as armed robbery or homicide where a handgun is used, the crime lab firearms examiner will often play a major role. Frequently, he/she will be called upon to examine firearms recovered as evidence as well as to conduct gunpowder shot-powder images in an effort to link suspects or their handguns to a particular crime.
(Courtesy Indiana State Police)

of items actually arising from cases worked and which may form the basis for subsequent identification of individuals or their method of operation (MO). Many of these collections and reference files have been computerized to provide better and faster analyses and comparisons.

The Standard Ammunition File contains over 13,000 specimens of domestic and foreign manufacturers' samples. The Firearms Reference Collection contains over 2,900 handguns and 1,600 shoulder weapons and is used for identifying gun parts and locating serial numbers. The Reference Fired Specimen File contains test bullets and cartridge cases from weapons that have been in the laboratory.

The National Automobile Altered Numbers File is composed of selected specimens, including replica plastic impressions of altered vehicle identification numbers (VINs) found on stolen cars, trucks, and heavy equipment. The file helps investigators identify recovered stolen cars and link them with commercialized theft rings nationwide or other FBI-investigated cases. The National Vehicle Identification Number Standard File maintains standards of VIN plates from each factory of the major manufacturers of American automobiles. The file enables laboratory personnel to determine if a submitted VIN plate is authentic. In the event that bogus VIN plates are being prepared in an automobile factory, the factory as well as the particular machine used can be identified.

The Typewriter Standards File consists of original samples of typewriting from numerous styles of type made in this country as well as in foreign countries. The file permits classification of questioned typewriting on the basis of make and model. The Watermark Standards File is an index of watermarks and brands used by paper manufacturers and aids in tracing the source or origin of paper. Original samples of safety paper used for checks are the contents of the Safety Paper Standards File. These can be used to determine manufacturers. The Checkwriter Standards File is a collection of original checkwriter impressions and permits classification of questioned checkwriter impressions as to make and model. As an aid in determining the manufacturers of office copying machines (either photocopy or duplicator), the laboratory maintains the Office Copier Standards File.

The Shoe Print File contains photographs of designs used in soles and heels made by major U.S. manufacturers. The Tire Tread File, including wheelbase and tire-stance information, is now in a database against which comparisons can be made. This replaces the blueprints, drawings, and photographs of tire-tread patterns, furnished by tire manufacturers, that used to form the basis of the reference file.

The National Motor Vehicle Certificate of Title File consists of original state motor vehicle certificates of title, manufacturers' certificates of origin, and vehicle-emission stickers. This file also contains photographic copies of fraudulent titles, statements, and stickers. The National Fraudulent Check File contains over 100,000 samples of checks, writings, and other documents. More than half of all checks examined are identified with other material in this file. The Anonymous Letter File consists of photographic copies of kidnap notes and extortion and threatening letters. The Bank Robbery Note File contains photocopies of writings of known bank robbers and holdup notes. The Pornographic Materials File includes pornographic materials submitted to the laboratory; it assists in determining the production and distribution sources of the materials. The Explosive Reference Files contain technical data, known standards of explosive items, and bomb components of commercial and military explosives and improvised explosive devices or homemade bombs.

Other files maintained by the FBI are the Automotive Paint File (which can identify makes and models involved in hit-and-run cases), the Hair and Fiber File, the National Stolen Coin File, Blood Serum Files, Safe Insulation Files, and the National Stolen Art File.

## Key Terms

**American Society of Crime Laboratory Directors (ASCLD)**
**Automated Fingerprint Identification System (AFIS)**
**Combined DNA Index System (CODIS)**
**crime laboratory**

**criminalistics**
***Daubert v. Merrell Dow Pharmaceuticals, Inc.***
**deoxyribonucleic acid (DNA)**
**FBI Crime Laboratory**
**forensic science**
***Frye v. United States***
**Integrated Automated Fingerprint Identification System (IAFIS)**
**mitochondrial DNA (mtDNA)**
**morgue**
**National Integrated Ballistic Information Network Program (NIBIN)**
**negative match**
**nuclear DNA**
**positive match**
**rules of evidence**

## Review Questions

1. Define *forensic science.*
2. What difficulties are caused by an investigator's not understanding the capabilities and limitations of crime laboratories?
3. Define *criminalistics.*
4. Describe the most important resource in a crime laboratory.
5. Describe the measures of effectiveness of crime laboratories.
6. Describe the role and importance of DNA analysis in criminal investigation.
7. Describe AFIS.
8. How are body fluids that are submitted for analysis handled in a laboratory, in light of concerns about the transmittal of hepatitis and AIDS?
9. What are the main areas of responsibility of the ATF laboratories?
10. What limitations are placed on the submission of evidence to the FBI laboratory?
11. Describe NIBIN.
12. Describe IAFIS.
13. Describe CODIS.
14. What are the primary DNA analysis techniques that have been used since 1985?
15. Distinguish the *Frye* test from the *Daubert* test regarding the admissibility of scientific evidence.
16. Briefly describe the forensic activities that occur at a morgue.

## Internet Activities

1. Search the Web and find several state-operated crime laboratories in your state. How many employees do these organizations have? What types of services do they provide? If you were a criminal investigator in your city, what would be the closest laboratory to your location? Next, search for local crime laboratories. What is the total number of employees in these laboratories? Do their services differ from those provided by the state-operated labs?
2. Go to www.crimelynx.com and search for information about postconviction DNA cases under "Crime Policy Links." What is the most recent estimate of the number of convicted offenders who have been exonerated due to DNA testing? According to the proposed S. 486 Innocence Protection Act of 2001, under what conditions can an offender request DNA testing? Who pays for the testing? What occurs if the DNA tests are inconclusive? In your opinion, will the increasing popularity of postconviction DNA testing affect the nature of criminal investigations?

## Notes

1. Florida Bureau of Law Enforcement, *Crime Laboratory,* unpublished document, p. 2.
2. Paul L. Kirk, "The Ontogeny of Criminalistics," *Journal of Criminology and Police Science,* 1963, Vol. 54, p. 238.
3. Joseph L. Peterson, Steven Mihajlovic, and Joanne L. Bedrosian, "The Capabilities, Uses, and Effects of the Nation's Criminalistics Laboratories," *Journal of Forensic Sciences,* 1985, Vol. 30, No. 1, p. 11.

4. Richard Fox and Carl L. Cunningham, *Crime Scene Search and Physical Evidence Handbook* (Washington, DC: U.S. Department of Justice, 1985), p. 1.
5. Statement of Kevin L. Lothridge, president, American Society of Crime Laboratory Directors, National Forensic Science Technology Center, before the House Judiciary Committee, Subcommittee on Crime, May 13, 1997.
6. Ibid.
7. www.nfstc.org/aboutus.htm (graciously supplied by NFSTC).
8. James W. Osterburg, *The Crime Laboratory* (Bloomington: Indiana University Press, 1968), p. 3.
9. Marc H. Caplan and Joe Holt Anderson, *Forensics: When Science Bears Witness*, National Institute of Justice (Washington, DC: Government Printing Office, October 1984), p. 2.
10. For a discussion of working relationships between police investigators and crime laboratory personnel, see Joseph L. Peterson, *The Utilization of Criminalistics Services by the Police, An Analysis of the Physical Evidence Recovery Process*, Law Enforcement Assistance Administration, National Institute of Law Enforcement and Criminal Justice (Washington, DC: Government Printing Office, March 1974).
11. The President's Commission on Law Enforcement and the Administration of Justice, Task Force Report: *The Police* (Washington, DC: Government Printing Office, 1967), p. 90.
12. National Advisory Commission on Criminal Justice Standards and Goals, *Police* (Washington, DC: Government Printing Office, 1973), p. 303.
13. See Kenneth S. Field, Oliver Schroeder, Jr., Ina J. Curtis, Ellen L. Fabricant, and Beth Ann Lipskin, *Assessment of the Forensic Sciences Profession: Assessment of the Personnel of the Forensic Sciences Profession*, Vol. II, National Institute of Law Enforcement and Criminal Justice, Law Enforcement Assistance Administration, U.S. Department of Justice (Washington, DC: Government Printing Office, March 1977), pp. I-4–I-9.
14. National Advisory Commission, *Police*, p. 302.
15. Ibid.
16. Peterson, *Utilization of Criminalistics Services*, p. 6.
17. 293 Fed. 1013 (D.C. Cir. 1923).
18. 507 U.S. 904 (1993).
19. Office of Justice Programs and Office of Community Orientated Policing Services, National Institute of Justice, *A Resource Guide to Law Enforcement, Corrections, and Forensic Technologies* (Washington, DC: U.S. Department of Justice, May 2001), www.ncjrs.org, p. 53.
20. Ibid, p. 57.
21. Ibid, pp. 57–58.
22. Bureau of Justice Statistics, National Institute of Justice, "Survey of DNA Crime Laboratories, 1998" (Washington DC: U.S. Department of Justice, February 2000), p. 1.
23. *Prosecutors in State Courts, 1996* (Washington, DC: U.S. Department of Justice, 1996), p. 6.
24. www.fbi.gov/kids/dna/dna.htm, July 17, 1998.
25. National Commission on the Future of DNA Evidence, National Institute of Justice, "What Every Law Enforcement Officer Should Know about DNA Evidence," pamphlet (Washington, DC: U.S. Department of Justice, no publication date).
26. Ibid.
27. Bureau of Justice Statistics, "Survey of DNA Crime Laboratories, 1998," p. 1.
28. www.fbi.gov/kids/dna/dnastory.htm, July 17, 1998.
29. Ibid.
30. Office of Justice Programs, *National Institute of Justice Journal* (Washington, DC: U.S. Department of Justice, December 1997), pp. 17–19.
31. Notes from the seminar "Supporting Your Case Using DNA Evidence," Altamonte Springs, Florida, August 23–24, 2001.
32. Bureau of Justice Statistics, "Survey of DNA Crime Laboratories, 1998," p. 1.
33. Notes from the seminar "Supporting Your Case Using DNA Evidence."
34. Office of Justice Programs and Office of Community Orientated Policing Services, *A Resource Guide*, pp. 56–57.
35. *Solutions* (publication for policyholders, General American Life Insurance Company), Spring–Summer 1998, Vol. 5, No. 1, pp. 5–7.
36. National Commission on the Future of DNA Evidence, National Institute of Justice, *Post Conviction DNA Testing: Recommendations for Handling Requests* (Washington, DC: U.S. Department of Justice, September 1999).
37. Thomas F. Wilson, "Automated Fingerprint Identification Systems," *Law Enforcement Technology*, August–September 1986, p. 17.
38. Florida Department of Law Enforcement, *Criminal Justice Information Systems Newsletter*, May 1995, p. 1.
39. Kenneth R. Moses, "A Consumer's Guide to Fingerprint Computers," *Identification News*, June 1986, p. 6.
40. Much of the material in this section is drawn from Thomas F. Wilson and Paul L. Woodward, *Auto-*

*mated Fingerprint Identification Systems: Technology and Policy Issues* (Washington, DC: U.S. Department of Justice, 1987).

41. Federal Bureau of Investigation, *CJIS* (a newsletter for the criminal justice community), 1999, vol. 3, no. 2, pp. 1–3.
42. www.atf.treas.gov/statistics/NIBIN, updated November 2001.
43. Federal Bureau of Investigation, *Handbook of Forensic Science,* rev. ed. (Washington, DC: Government Printing Office, October 1978). This discussion of the equipment used by crime laboratories was taken with permission from pp. 63–64 of this source.
44. www.atf.treas.gov/labs/index.htm.
45. www.atf.treas.gov/cor/explarson.htm.
46. www.atf.treas.gov/cor/labs/hist.htm.
47. www.fbi.gov/lab/report/labhome.htm.

# EIGHT

# Investigative Resources

*Today, law enforcement agencies make use of state-of-the-art technology to assist in criminal investigations. For example, software is now available to use eyewitness description information to produce reasonable likenesses of potential suspects, like this one, made with EFIT. (Courtesy of Royal Canadian Mounted Police (RCMP))*

## CHAPTER OUTLINE



## CHAPTER OBJECTIVES

1. Outline the intelligence/analytical cycle.
2. Understand various components of crime analysis.
3. Assess criminal profiling and its criticisms.
4. Discuss the organized/disorganized offender model.
5. Explain the practice of investigative psychology.
6. Describe behavioral evidence analysis.
7. Discuss the practice of geoprofiling.
8. Recognize financial difficulty indicators used in financial analysis.
9. Identify three major components of NCAVC and the services they provide.
10. Describe the functions of NCIC and CODIS.

## INTRODUCTION

Given the continuous advancement in computer technology and information system availability, many police departments across the country are developing or enhancing criminal intelligence/analytical units. These units may include a crime analysis function, or that function may be structured as a separate entity within the organization. The intelligence/analytical cycle begins and ends with planning and direction and involves the collection of raw data, followed by processing and analysis and production. The completed cycle results in finished and usable products for clients. A supervisor of a sexual-assault unit, for example, may request assistance from the intelligence/analytical unit to find a pattern among several rapes that have occurred in the area. In addition to a discussion on the intelligence/analytical process, this chapter provides information about an array of analytical and investigative tools available to investigators.

Crime analysis, time-event charting, and telephone record analysis, can all be useful in establishing offense trends and patterns and tracking specific crimes or suspects for investigative purposes. Criminal profiling has proved to be a popular and successful method of understanding what types of offenders commit particular crimes. The practice of creating profiles of organized/disorganized offenders and employing investigative psychology and behavioral evidence analysis is increasing in the criminal investigation field. An overview of geoprofiling, an investigative strategy that uses the locations of a series of crimes to determine the most probable area of the offender's residence, and the use of financial analysis is included in this chapter. The remainder of the chapter focuses on federal law enforcement programs, such as the National Center for the Analysis of Violent Crime, the National Crime Information Center, and CODIS, and includes a discussion on the ways that police agencies are using the Internet as an investigative tool.

You will find these subjects referred to in a number of other chapters and occasionally you may find it useful to return to this chapter and freshen your understanding of them. This chapter cannot provide the depth of attention that many of its topics deserve. You should come away from this chapter, however, with an understanding of some of the more specialized concepts and tools available to investigators.

## CRIMINAL INTELLIGENCE UNITS

Police agencies are increasingly turning toward an intelligence-led model,[1] which can be used to support any type of philosophy, such as respond-to-incident (R2I) or community policing. In order to implement an intelligence-led capability, criminal intelligence units are being "beefed up" or separate analytical units are being established. Roughly speaking, agencies that have an established analytical capability employ 3 to 12 analysts.[2] The International Association of Law Enforcement Intelligence Analysts (IALEIA) suggests that there should be 1 analyst for every 12 investigators or even 1 for every 5 investigators when they are dealing with sophisticated specialized crimes, as in the case of financial investigations, for example.[3]

Whether law enforcement executives choose the beefing-up or separate-analytical-unit model depends on the agency's history and mission, along with the preference of the person making the decision. For example, if the intelligence unit has been tainted by a recent scandal, the chief or sheriff could put an analytical unit into it, an approach to be seen as part of its reformation, or decide to put it elsewhere in the structure to avoid immediate cries that the department's analytical data come from an unreliable source.

Agencies have so many analytical needs that even in those with a centralized intelligence/analytical capability, various types of analysis are carried on throughout the department, although the analyses often lack the sophistication that can be achieved by a trained and experienced analyst. Where to place the crime analysis function is a question that comes up when there is an intelligence unit. It may be folded into the intelligence unit, or it may be placed elsewhere in the organization's structure. For the purposes of this chapter, analytical capabilities are discussed without reference to their placement in the organization.

## THE INTELLIGENCE/ANALYTICAL CYCLE

The **intelligence/analytical cycle** is driven by the needs of the client or end-user, who, for purposes of illustration, may be the commander of a task force working a serial-murder case or the supervisor of an investigation unit trying to find a pattern in a string of violent convenience-store robberies (see Figure 8–1). It is the end-user who specifies the types of information he or she wants, and it is the responsibility of the intelligence unit to make sure that the end-user understands both the possibilities and the limitations of the intelligence process and its techniques. As depicted in Figure 8–2, the backbone of

**Figure 8-1** The Intelligence Cycle

(**Source:** Marilyn B. Peterson, Bob Morehouse, and Richard Wright, eds., *Intelligence 2000: Revising the Basic Elements* (New Jersey: International Association of Law Enforcement Analysts, 2000), p. 8.)

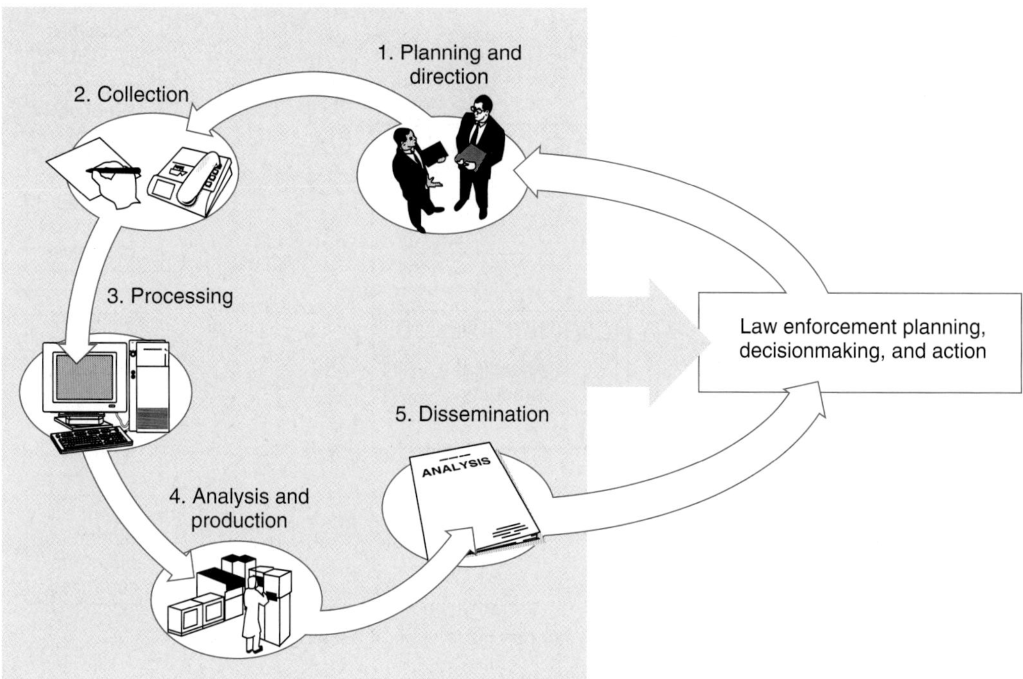


the intelligence/analytical cycle is a continuous five-step process,[4] which is discussed below.

## 1. PLANNING AND DIRECTION

The intelligence/analytical process must be managed throughout, from identifying the focus of the intelligence effort to delivering the finished product to the police unit requesting it.[5] Planning and direction are both the beginning and the end of the intelligence cycle. They are the beginning because they involve identifying a focus and specific data collection procedures, processing, analysis, and dissemination requirements. They are also the end, because when finished intelligence products are accepted, the cycle can be said to be completed. As a practical matter, finished intelligence often creates new questions, which start the process all over again.

## 2. COLLECTION

Collection is the gathering and managing of raw data, which is then analyzed to produce the finished product.[6] To be effective, collection must be planned, focused, and directed. There are many sources of information, including law enforcement and open-source records. Included in agency-generated sources are incident and supplemental investigations, field interview cards, traffic citations, undercover and informant records, criminal and driving histories, neighborhood- and vehicle-canvass results, photographic files, facial composites of suspects, previously prepared analytical reports, and files on known and active offenders. Similar types of data are accessible from other departments and available regionally and nationally through various types of databases, including that of the National Crime Information Center. It is useful to think of such sources as being *restricted,* since they are generally not for use outside law enforcement.

Another broad category of information sources is called open sources, which means anyone can access them, either for free or for a fee. Included in this category are public records such as births, deaths, divorces, credit histories, news media reports, many

**Figure 8-2** The Product Model

(**Source:** Marilyn B. Peterson, Bob Morehouse, and Richard Wright, eds., *Intelligence 2000: Revising the Basic Elements* (New Jersey: International Association of Law Enforcement Analysts, 2000), p. 20.)

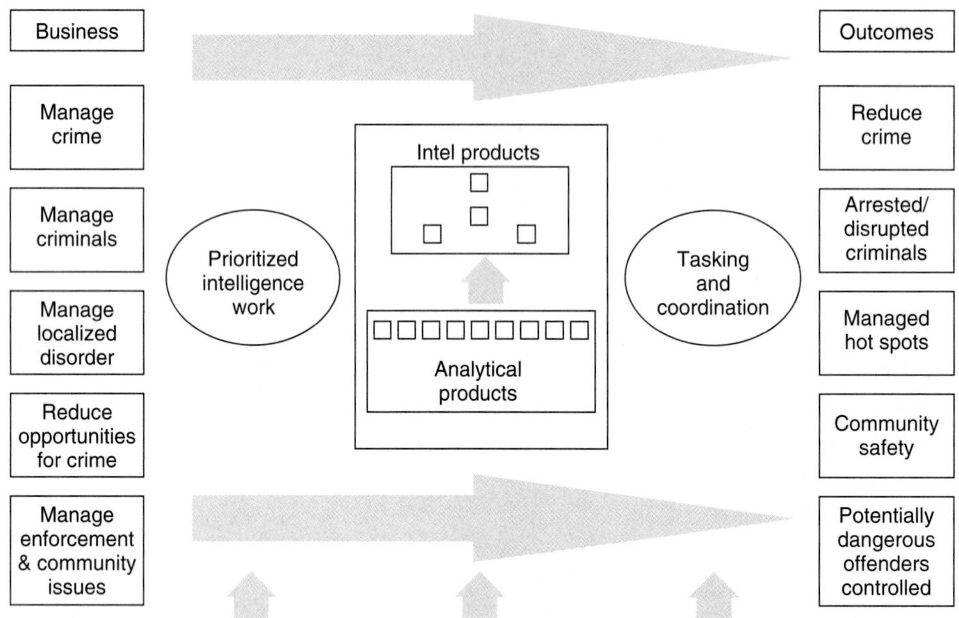


periodicals and books, government reports, and annual corporate filings that state where a business is located and who occupies which leadership positions in it. The value of open-source information is indicated by the fact that the FBI made a budget request of $4.5 million for it in 2000.[7]

Accessing some sources of information, such as bank, hotel, taxicab, e-mail, travel agency, public utility, and student records, may require some type of legal process.

## 3. PROCESSING

In processing, raw information from all sources is converted into a form that can be used by analysts.[8] This is accomplished by information management, which is the indexing, sorting, and organizing of raw data into files for rapid retrieval. It includes entering the data into a computer, checking the entries for accuracy, and collating paper files. One of the key considerations in processing is ensuring that the data-processing methods fit the analytical techniques that will be used.

## 4. ANALYSIS AND PRODUCTION

In the analysis and production step, the data that have been processed are translated into a finished intelligence product.[9] This includes integrating, collating, evaluating, and analyzing all the data, some of which may be fragmented and contradictory. Through analysis of the data, the value of intelligence work increases. Analysts, who are subject-matter specialists (e.g., organized crime, gangs, or terrorists), carefully scrutinize the data for timeliness, reliability, validity, and relevance. The role of the analyst is to combine the data and his or her analysis and judgment into a finished intelligence product that informs the end-user of the analyst's assessment of events and the implications of that assessment. Methods of analysis are discussed later in this chapter.

## 5. DISSEMINATION

The last element in the five-step cycle is the dissemination of the finished intelligence report to the end-user who requested it.[10] The end-user can then make decisions or take actions on the basis of

**Laptop Computer in Police Cruiser**
Police officer Peter Rehmann of Helena, Montana, accesses the Criminal Justice Information Network via the new laptop computer in his police cruiser. One of the more popular technological innovations in law enforcement agencies has been the placement of computers in police cars, which allows officers on the street access to a variety of investigative and/or intelligence data without returning to their desks. In many departments, such data includes hot spots information, suspect descriptions, stolen property descriptions, and the status of arrest warrants. (AP/Wide World Photos)

the intelligence provided. It is crucial that the end-user provide feedback about the value of the intelligence so that there can be an ongoing cycle of improvement. Moreover, the finished intelligence report itself, the decisions made, and the actions taken all have the potential to create new questions that lead back to the first element, planning and direction, thus beginning a new intelligence/analytical cycle.

## ANALYTICAL AND INVESTIGATIVE TOOLS

To some extent, distinctions between crime, intelligence, and investigative analyses are artificial for three reasons: (1) All three share some common analytical techniques; (2) "intelligence" is simply information that has been processed; and (3) by concentrating on their differences, their commonalities are obscured.[11] Therefore, this section deals with a number of analytical techniques employed in police departments without pigeonholing them into one type of analysis or another.

### CRIME ANALYSIS

**Crime analysis** is the process of using systematic analytical methods to acquire timely and pertinent information on crime patterns and trend correlations.[12] The three general types of crime analysis are summarized in Table 8–1. Discussed below are some of the specific elements analysts focus on to link crimes:[13]

- *Trends:* **Trends** are general tendencies in the occurrence of crime across large geographic areas over extended periods of time. They arise when areas become, for any number of reasons, more conducive or less conducive to a particular crime or crimes. Trends can be associated with shifts in demography; for example, as a neighborhood ages, its residents are seen as soft targets for muggings and home-invasion robberies. Trends can also stem from the creation of new targets; for instance, the presence of a new shopping mall increases the opportunities for shoplifting and thefts from and of vehicles. Although the same locations or victims may be repeatedly selected in a trend, there are usually multiple perpetrators.

- *Patterns:* In a **pattern,** the same crime is committed repeatedly over a short period of time, sometimes, but not always, by the same offender. For example, outside a five-star restaurant, female patrons who are leaving have their purses snatched; or, as students return to campus in the fall, the theft of laptops from dormitories rises.
- *Series:* In a **series,** the same type of crime is committed over a short period of time, probably by the same offender. For instance, in an affluent, gated residential community of 73 houses, six burglaries occur in nine days; two days later, a rape-burglary occurs when the victim enters her home while the perpetrator is still inside; and three days after that, there is an aggravated assault–burglary when the victim awakes and discovers the offender leaving with his valuable coin collection.
- *Sprees:* In a **spree,** the same type of offense is committed at almost the same time by the same offender(s). An example is the vandalizing of cars by a group of kids who spray-paint the license plates while walking through a neighborhood.
- *Hot spots:* A **hot spot** is a location where various crimes are committed on a regular basis, usually by different perpetrators. An example is a bar where underage drinkers are served, there are numerous fights, user-level drug sales take place, prostitution flourishes, and patrons are occasionally mugged, robbed, or carjacked in the parking lot.
- *Crimogens:* A **crimogen** is either an individually known offender who is responsible for a large number of crimes or one victim who reports a large number of crimes. Examples include a career criminal and a convenience-store operator who reports gas drive-offs, shoplifting, robberies, assaults, and even thefts of entire ATM machines.

## Crime Bulletins

One method by which crime analysts can disseminate general-interest information is through the publication of a series of **crime bulletins.** The frequency and extent of such bulletins are a function of how much time and other resources the analyst can devote to them. Among the types of bulletins most frequently published are those dealing with:

1. Person crimes
2. Property crimes
3. Arrest information
4. Warrant information
5. Probation and parole information
6. Most active criminals

**Table 8-1** Types of Crime Analysis

| Type | Description |
|---|---|
| Tactical | Provides analytical information used to assist operations and investigative personnel in identifying specific, present crime trends, thereby giving them an informed basis for making rapid, effective responses to field problems (e.g., a series of pharmacy robberies). |
| Strategic | Involves analyzing long-range problems and making projections about likely increases or decreases in crime rates and trends; also includes preparing crime statistic reports and providing data for use in allocation of personnel. |
| Administrative | Focuses on providing economic, social, geographic, and other information to administrators; includes doing feasibility studies, special research projects, grant proposals, and reports to county commissions or city councils (e.g., in answer to the question, Why is crime decreasing?). |

**Source:** Steven Goettlieb, Sheldon Arenberg, and Raj Singh, *Crime Analysis from First Report to Final Arrest* (Montclair, CA: Alpha Publishing, 1994), pp. 13–24.

7. Most wanted persons
8. Stolen autos
9. Crime series and trends
10. Suspicious activity
11. Field interviews
12. Sex offenders[14]

Crime bulletins may be printed, but they are increasingly appearing on the Internet if their information is of interest to members of the community (see Figure 8–3). More sensitive information is available to all officers in a department through their own information system.

## TIME-EVENT CHARTING

One of the most useful and quickly learned techniques for analyzing crime is creating a **time-event chart (TEC),** which displays events in chronological order. A simple time-event chart is shown in Figure 8–4; it depicts the major events involving an offender paroled from the state prison. For seven months he made his regularly scheduled meetings with his parole officer. Three months later, an informant described him as a frequent crack user. Three weeks after that, the parolee robbed a tourist. Over the next 30 days, he committed three more robberies, each time progressing upward to a more lucrative target. The choice of a pharmacy as a target gave him both money and drugs, which are the same as money on the streets. If he is selling drugs, informants may know of it. The interval between robberies is growing shorter, and the parolee has become violent. It is possible that he is pulling jobs while high and the potential for further violence is great.

## TELEPHONE RECORD ANALYSIS

The most requested type of intelligence/analytical products is telephone toll analysis.[15] "**Telephone record analysis** is the compilation and review of telephone company, long-distance service and/or dialed-number recorder information to show the strength and patterns of relationships between the subscriber and the numbers called."[16] It is particularly useful in conspiracy, drug, and organized-crime investigations, although it is routinely applied in many other types of investigations. Telephone record analysis consists of the following steps:

**Figure 8-3** Sex Offender Bulletin

**Madison Police Department**

**Criminal Intelligence Section**

**Madison Police Department**

**SEX OFFENDER INFORMATION BULLETIN**

February 19, 2002

The Madison Police Department is releasing the following information pursuant to Wisconsin State Statute 301.46(2m) which authorizes law enforcement agencies to inform the public of a sex offender's release when; in the discretion of the agency, the release of information will enhance public safety, awareness and protection. The individual who appears on this notification has been convicted of a sex offense. *Further, his criminal history places him in a classification level which reflects the potential to re-offend.*

This sex offender *has served* the sentence imposed on him by the courts. **He is NOT wanted by the police at this time.** *This notification is not intended to increase fear, rather, it is our belief that an informed public is a safer public.*

Sex offenders **have always** lived in our communities; but it was not until Act 440 was enacted that law enforcement is able to share this information with the community. **Citizen abuse of this information to *threaten, intimidate or harass* registered sex offenders will NOT be tolerated.**

**Leslie A. Johnson** is registered with the Sex Offender Registry, and upon his release from prison, will be escorted directly to the Madison Police Department where a face-to-face registration with law enforcement will take place. If **Leslie Johnson** violates any of these rules or conditions of his parole, he will be taken into custody and placed in confinement pending review of possible revocation proceedings. Witnessed violations should be reported to the Madison Police Department.

Name: **Leslie A. Johnson**
DOB: **10-27-57**
Age: **44**
Race: **White**
Sex: **Male**
Height: **5'10"**
Weight: **170**
Hair: **Grey**
Eyes: **Brown**

**Leslie A. Johnson** will be residing in a supervised facility on Odana Rd., Madison. He was convicted in 1990 of 1st Degree Sexual Assault of a Child and for Enticing a Child for Immoral Purpose. He had been previously convicted in 1980 on a amended charge of First Degree Sexual Assault. The victims in both cases were 5-year-old girls who were not acquainted with **Mr. Johnson**. One girl was assaulted after **Johnson** used a cat to lure her into an alleyway. The other victim was assaulted after she was enticed into an abandoned automobile.

**Mr. Johnson** will be under 24-hour electronic monitoring and will be supervised by agents specializing in intensive supervision. He will need to comply with all rules and is a registrant of the Wisconsin Sex Offender Registration Program.

**Additional Sex Offender Information:**

As of the date of this bulletin, there are over 11,000 sex offenders who have registered as required in the State of Wisconsin. There are over 5,400 sex offenders on probation or parole throughout the State. Approximately 465 of these are registered to Dane County Addresses, with over half of those registered to addresses within the city limits of Madison. 75% of these offenders are on probation, having served no time in a prison.

Back to MPD Home Page

Back to Sex Offender Information

1. Collect the data to be analyzed from the targeted subscriber, including local and long-distance calls on home, business, car, and cell telephones, collect calls, and third-party calls (i.e., credit card or other calls billed to the

**Figure 8-4** Time-Event Chart

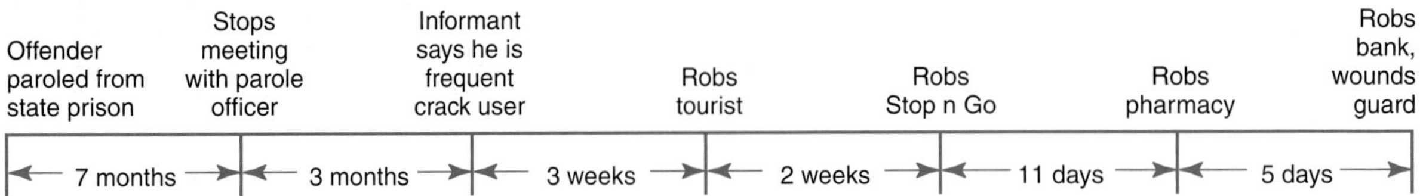


subscriber in which the subscriber is neither the number called to nor the number called from). With the approval of a court, a pen register/dialed-number recorder (DNR) can be used to gather additional information, such as the date a call is made, the time the call is made, the number called, and the duration of the call. For local calls, this information is usually not available from service providers, but cellular and digital companies make a record of such calls. Obtaining the records, however, requires a subpoena or some other type of legal sanction, and this increases the danger that the subscriber will learn of the investigative interest in him or her.

2. Determine the scope of the calls, including the dates they were made, the number of calls, and the dates between which the calls were made.
3. Establish the frequency of calls by date, day of week, and time made.
4. Count the frequency of calls to each number.
5. Add up the total amount of time spent on calls to each number.
6. Develop a primary listing of calls on the basis of the frequency determined in steps 3 and 4.
7. Analyze frequently-called numbers for patterns (e.g., to particular countries). A number called at regular intervals and times may suggest that a subordinate is reporting to a superior or that illegal commodities, such as drugs, are being ordered from a supplier.
8. Prepare a report on the findings, including any recommendations for further investigative efforts.[17]

Assume that a known and reliable confidential informant tells the investigator that someone known to her only as "Crazy Joe" is putting together "a big drug deal." In the nickname files, there are records on 11 Crazy Joes. Eight of them are currently in prison, two of them are small-time felons, and the last one, Joseph "Crazy Joe" Barnes, has one conviction for drug trafficking. Subsequently, the informant picks Crazy Joe out of a photo lineup. An investigation is launched that includes getting the telephone records for the residence of Joseph Barnes, also known as (AKA) Crazy Joe.

Figure 8–5 is a link record for Crazy Joe's home telephone, 520-318-4475. It reveals that a total of 19 calls were made between March 16 and April 9, 2002. Of these, 17 were from 520-318-4475 or were made to that number by collect calls, establishing it as the central node. The 011 prefix identifies all 19 calls as being placed internationally. One interpretation of the pattern is that it indicates a period of negotiation between the central node and 011-90232-558-6413. The deal, which may be about a commodity exchange, appears to have been finalized on April 9, 2002. With minimal additional effort, the data shown in Table 8–2 are produced, providing numerous other leads to be investigated.

## CRIMINAL PROFILING

"The process of inferring distinctive personality characteristics of individuals responsible for committing crimes has commonly been referred to as **criminal profiling.**"[18] It is also known as behavioral, crime scene, criminal-personality, offender, and psychological profiling.[19] "There is currently a general lack of . . . uniformity or agreement on the application of these terms to any one profiling method."[20] In general, profilers should, at a minimum, be well educated in logic and argument, sociology, psychology, criminalistics, and medico-legal death investigation.[21]

### Criticisms of Profiling

Despite its successes, profiling as a field is not without criticisms. Included in these criticisms are

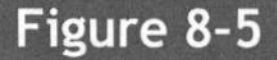


Single-Subscriber Link Diagram

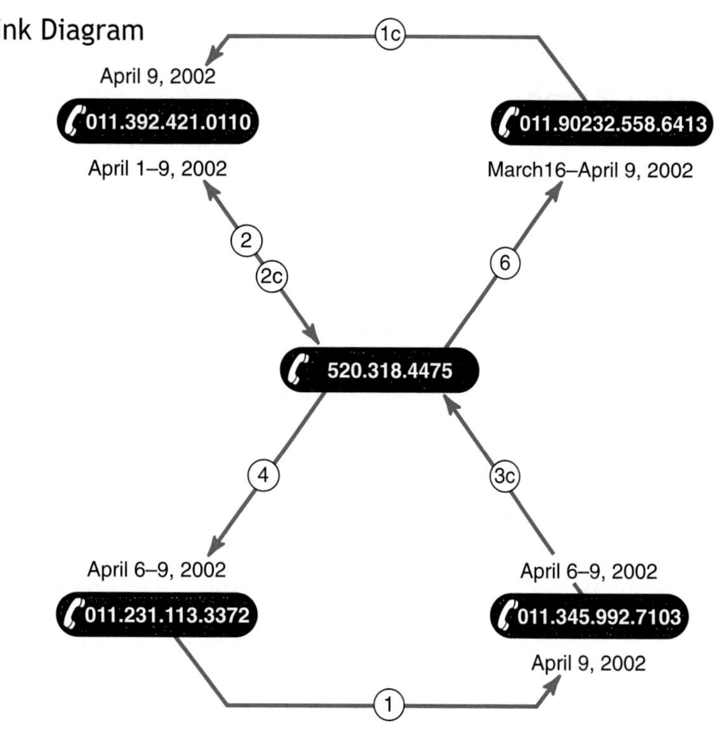


Table 8-2 Telephone Record Matrix

| | CALLS FROM:* | | | | |
|---|---|---|---|---|---|
| **Calls to:** | **Barnes** | **Mystic** | **Castle** | **Stanic** | **Fuentes** |
| 520-318-4475<br>Joseph Barnes residence, Tucson, Arizona | 0 | 0 | 2 c | 0 | 3 c |
| 011-90232-558-6413<br>Mystic Imports and Exports, Izmir, Turkey | 6 | 0 | 0 | 0 | 0 |
| 011-392-421-0110<br>Castle Virgin Oil Distributors, Milan, Italy | 2 | 1 c | 0 | 0 | 0 |
| 011-231-113-3372<br>Stanic Charter, Bogota, Columbia | 4 | 0 | 0 | 0 | 0 |
| 011-345-992-7103<br>John Fuentes residence, Cayman Islands | 0 | 0 | 0 | 1 | 0 |
| Total | 12 | 1 c | 2 c | 1 | 3 c |

***c = collect.**

claims of using untrained or inadequately trained profilers, promising too much and delivering too little, relying on inadequate or dated databases, overstating the meaning of physical evidence, and engaging in racial profiling. Such criticism should be taken as a natural component of a discipline that is evolving and as an important means for learning and making improvements. Any criticism should be evaluated with respect to the model to which it refers, the time period in which it was made, who the profiler was and his or her stage of development, and any possible motivations of the critic.

## The Mad Bomber

Roughly speaking, criminal profiling has a history of about 50 years, with its most important milestones coming in the past quarter-century. Noteworthy among early events is the work of New York City criminal psychiatrist James Brussels on the "Mad Bomber" case. Between 1940 and 1956, with a "patriotic pause" during the years of World War II, the Mad Bomber left over 30 bombs in phone booths, public libraries, movie theaters, and other places.[22] Alarmed at the serious injuries created by a 1956 theater bombing, the police turned in desperation to Dr. Brussels for help. After reviewing all available information, including the Mad Bomber's letters to the newspapers, police, cinemas, and an electric company, Brussels produced the following profile:

> The mad bomber is male, middle-aged, meticulous, largely self-educated, Slavic, Roman Catholic, had an Oedipal Complex and lived in Connecticut . . . he worked for Consolidated Edison or one of its subsidiaries . . . . The police would have to publicize the profile if the Mad Bomber was to be drawn out. When apprehended he will be wearing a buttoned double-breasted suit.[23]

The more publicity the Mad Bomber got, the more antagonized and arrogant he became. He eventually gave himself away through a published letter in which he revealed details about his grievance against his former employer, Consolidated Edison.[24] When George P. Metesky was arrested in Waterbury, Connecticut, in 1957, he was wearing a buttoned double-breasted suit, and the other details in Brussels's profile were also eerily accurate.

## Methods of Profiling

Because it was regarded as unconventional and its documented successes were isolated events, profiling did not make much progress for roughly 20 years after the apprehension of the Mad Bomber. However, during the 1970s, events began to unfold that led to the development of three approaches to criminal profiling: the organized/disorganized-offender model, investigative psychology, and behavioral evidence analysis.[25]

### *The Organized/Disorganized-Offender Model*

The **organized/disorganized-offender model** was developed by the FBI. The bureau's initial efforts in profiling rest on the work of Agents Howard Teten and Pat Mullany, who in the late 1970s and early 1980s developed an applied criminology course that was taught throughout the country to state and local police officers.[26] The goal of the course was to promote a better understanding of criminal behavior in order to identify, arrest, and convict offenders.

After Teten left the Behavioral Science Unit (BSU), John Douglass and Robert Ressler were assigned to it in 1979. Over the next four years these two and other agents undertook a large study that

**The Mad Bomber**

Criminal profiling is the process of inferring distinctive personality characteristics of individuals responsible for committing crimes. One of the earliest and most noteworthy cases involving criminal profiling was the successful identification of the "mad bomber" who had terrorized New York City between 1940 and 1956. Criminal psychiatrist James Brussels used the technique successfully to lead to the arrest of George P. Metesky (shown here), arrested in 1957.

(© Corbis)

involved visiting prisons, interviewing offenders about their backgrounds and their crimes, and studying court records, including psychiatric reports. The data they collected and the conclusions they reached formed the basis of the organized/ disorganized-offender model, a profiling method that is still used in many jurisdictions.[27] The organized/disorganized-offender dichotomy (see Table 8–3) has a strong crime scene focus (see Table 8–4). The model includes the six stages discussed below:

- *Stage 1: Collecting inputs:* Inputs are essential for accurate profiling.[28] The required information includes incident and supplemental reports, as well as detailed information about the crime scene, with any factors that may be relevant, such as weather conditions. Complete background data on the victim should cover domestic setting, employment, reputation, criminal history, habits, hobbies, physical condition, social conduct, and family relationships.[29] Complete forensic information is likewise needed, including the autopsy report (with toxicology and serology results), photographs of the wounds and the cleansed wounds,[30] and the medical examiner's conclusions and impressions about time of death, sequence of wounds, cause of death, and weapon used.[31]
- *Stage 2: Using decision process models:* This is the process of organizing and arranging the inputs into meaningful patterns.[32] It entails consideration of seven factors: homicide type and style, primary purpose of the murder (e.g., criminal enterprise or sexual?), victim risk (such as slight physical stature), offender risk (e.g., was the victim seized from a crowded street at midday or plucked from a bar's nearly empty parking lot at 4 A.M.?),

**Table 8-3** Profile Characteristics of Organized and Disorganized Murderers

| Organized | Disorganized |
|---|---|
| Average or above-average IQ | Below-average IQ |
| Socially adept | Socially inadequate, often never married, fearful of people, may have developed well-defined delusional system |
| Skilled-occupation employment history, but uneven work history, sometimes has jobs below abilities | Poor work history |
| Sexually competent | Sexually incompetent, may never have achieved sexual intimacy |
| High birth order in family, often first son | Low birth order in family |
| Father's work generally stable | Father's work history unstable |
| Parental discipline perceived by offender as inconsistent | Harsh parental discipline |
| May feel angry or depressed at time of crime, but reports himself as calm during it | Recurring obsessional and/or primitive thoughts, at time of crime is confused and distressed, acts impulsively under stress |
| May use alcohol prior to crime | Limited use of alcohol |
| Precipitating situational stress, e.g., financial, marital, relationships with females, and employment problems | Minimal situational stress |
| Usually living with partner | Lives alone or with parental figure |
| Likely to have car in good condition | Usually finds victims in his geographic area, lives in close proximity to scene |
| Follows crime in newspapers, clippings about crimes committed often found at offender's home, may take souvenirs from victim or scene | Little interest in news media |

**Source:** Robert Ressler, Ann W. Burgess, and John E. Douglas, *Sexual Homicides: Patterns and Motives* (New York: Free Press, 1992), pp. 121–122, 130.

**Table 8-4** Crime Scene Differences between Organized and Disorganized Sexual Homicides

| Organized | Disorganized |
|---|---|
| Offense planned; semblance of order before, during, and after the crime suggests aim of avoiding detection | Spontaneous offense, appears to be no plan to avoid detection |
| Victim frequently a targeted stranger in a location staked out by offender, to some extent victim a target of opportunity; serial victims may share common characteristics, and offender may spend considerable time waiting for "right" victim | May know victim or select randomly, often familiar with location of crime |
| Personalizes victim | Depersonalizes victim; specific areas of the body may be selected for extreme violence; overkill or excessive force to face is often attempt to dehumanize victim |
| Offender may strike up conversation with victim as attempt to gain her confidence in order to capture victim without resorting to physical force | Minimal conversation aside from orders and directions |
| Scene reflects overall control | Scene random and sloppy, in great disarray |
| Demands submissive and compliant victim; may require certain reactions, e.g., fear and passivity during sexual activity | Sudden, overpowering violence to victim; offender uses a surprise blitz-style attack |
| Restraints used, e.g., ropes, chains, handcuffs, chemicals, belts, gags, blindfolds | Minimal use of restraints; victim killed quickly to avoid victim's getting the upper hand |
| Aggressive acts prior to death, weapon displayed, victim's life threatened | Any sexually sadistic acts follow death, e.g., mutilation of face, breasts, and genitals |
| Body hidden | Body left in view, often left in position killed |
| Weapons and evidence absent | Evidence and weapons often present, normally much physical evidence available |
| Transports victim or body, often using his or her vehicle | Body left at death scene |

**Source:** Robert Ressler, Ann W. Burgess, and John E. Douglas, *Sexual Homicide: Patterns and Motives* (New York: Free Press, 1992), pp. 121–124, 131.

potential for escalation of violence, time factors (e.g., how long did it take to kill the victim), and location (where the victim was first approached and similar data).[33]

- *Stage 3: Making the crime assessment:* This is the reconstruction of the sequence of events and of the behavior of both the victim and the offender.
- *Stage 4: Developing the criminal profile:* This process addresses the type of person who committed the crime and his or her behavioral organization in relation to the crime. Among the factors considered are background information, physical characteristics, habits, beliefs, values, preoffense behavior leading to the crime, and postoffense behavior.[34] Recommendations may be made with respect to investigating, identifying, interrogating, and apprehending the offender.[35]
- *Stage 5: Adjusting the profile:* While the investigation continues, the profiler makes adjustments in the profile if fresh information warrants them. He or she is available on an as-needed basis to discuss the case with persons assigned to it.[36]
- *Stage 6: Reviewing and following up:* After the apprehension, the profiler conducts a review to determine the amount of agreement between the outcome and the profile; various stages of the profiling process are examined.

At an appropriate time it is important that the profiler interview the offender in detail to check the validity of the profiling process.[37]

***Mixed Organized-Disorganized Homicides*** While many offenders fit neatly into the organized or disorganized pattern, some crimes reflect aspects of both patterns. A number of factors can lead to a mixed organized-disorganized crime: multiple offenders with different behaviors may be involved; a planned crime may deteriorate as unanticipated events unfold, such as being unable to control the victim; or the original motive may have been solely rape, but the victim's resistance (which sometimes leads to escape) or the offender's changed emotional state may lead to murder. Youthful offenders or the offender's use of drugs and alcohol can also lead to a mixed scene.[38]

***Investigative Psychology*** Although more than a few psychologists and psychiatrists are involved in profiling, **investigative psychology** is associated with the work of Englishman David Canter, an environmental psychologist, who was asked by New Scotland Yard in 1985 to integrate investigative and psychological concepts.[39] The model he developed rests on five factors:[40]

1. *Interpersonal coherence* assumes that offenders will deal with their victims in a manner similar to the way they treat people in their day-to-day lives. Victims may represent significant people from the offender's noncrime life. For example, many of serial killer Ted Bundy's victims resembled his ex-girlfriend. Variations in criminal activity may relate to changes in how the offender treats people generally.
2. The *significance of time and place* may provide analysts with clues about the offender's mobility and even his or her residence. Because the offender picks the time and place of the attack, these factors may also be clues about his or her work, off time, and perhaps even employer.
3. *Criminal characteristics* are used by researchers and analysts to place offenders into broad categories, from which subcategories can be selected or developed. This information can then be passed along to investigators.
4. The *criminal-career* assessment determines whether the offender may have engaged in criminal activity before and, if so, what type of activity it most likely was.
5. *Forensic awareness* draws in part on item 4, above. It is an assessment of the scene and evidence to determine if the offender has any special knowledge of evidence-gathering procedures used by the police. Positive indications–or indications that the suspect has knowledge of evidence-gathering procedures–include such measures as the offender's wearing gloves and removing items contaminated with his or her body fluids.

***Behavioral Evidence Analysis*** A leading proponent of **behavioral evidence analysis (BEA)** is Brent Turvey, a private profiler and forensic scientist.[41] A deductive criminal-profiling method, BEA is based on the assumptions listed in Figure 8–6. In operation, BEA is a four-step process that involves the following:[42]

1. *Equivocal forensic analysis:* "Equivocal" is a term applied to something that can be interpreted in more than one way or to an interpretation that can be questioned.[43] Thus, equivocal forensic analysis is a physical-evidence review that questions all assumptions and conclusions.[44] The "inputs" that are reviewed include all documents and reports; crime scene videos, photographs, sketches, and access logs; neighborhood and vehicle canvasses; the medical examiner's or coroner's report and autopsy videos and photographs; and written and taped statements from witnesses and victims.[45] A central aspect of this analysis is establishing what behaviors occurred on the part of the offender and the victim, such as the type of resistance used by the victim.[46]
2. *Victimology:* Victimology is the thorough study and analysis of the victim's characteristics.[47] Establishing this information can be useful in making inferences about the offender's behavior, modus operandi, and signature behaviors, as well as the victim's lifestyle.[48] Signature behaviors are actions that are not necessary to commit the crime

**Figure 8-6** Behavioral Evidence Analysis: Fundamental Assumptions

(**Source:** Brent Turvey, *Criminal Profiling: An Introduction to Behavioral Evidence Analysis* (London: Academic Press, 1999), p. 30.)

1. No offender acts without motivation, though sometimes only he or she knows what the motivation is.
2. Every offense should be investigated as its own unique motivational and behavioral event.
3. Different offenders exhibit the same or similar behavior for completely different reasons.
4. Given the nature of human behavior, human interaction, and environmental influences, no two cases are ever completely alike.
5. Human behavior develops uniquely, over time, in response to environmental and biological factors.
6. Criminal MO behavior can evolve over time and over the commission of multiple offenses.
7. A single offender is capable of multiple motives over the commission of multiple offenses or even during the commission of a single offense.
8. Statistical generalizations and theorizing, while sometimes initially helpful, can mislead an investigation if they cause us to think we have all the answers in a case or cause us not to collect evidence that does not fit those answers.

but are taken by the offender to satisfy his or her psychological or emotional need.[49] Examples are placing a pillowcase over a deceased victim's face, positioning the body in a particular way, or urinating on the floor. Not all crime scenes include signatures.

3. *Crime scene characteristics:* These characteristics may include, among many other things, methods of approach, of attack, and of controlling the victim; location, nature, type, and sequence of sexual acts; materials used; verbal statements; and precautionary acts taken by the offender,[50] such as cutting telephone lines, bringing duct tape to bind the victim, wearing a mask, taking the victim's clothing, or setting a fire to destroy evidence. The crime scene characteristics are derived from the equivocal forensic analysis and victimology. Because identifying them depends on evidence, not all crime scene characteristics can be determined all the time.[51]
4. *Offender characteristics:* The first three steps are, for the most part, based on the scientific tenets of crime scene reconstruction and established forensic sciences. However, while relying on their inputs, the fourth step is more artful and therefore a matter of expertise rather than science.[52] Offender characteristics fall into two categories: "hard" and "soft." Examples of hard characteristics are age, sex, DNA and blood, secretor status, fingerprints, race (which may be a soft characteristic in some instances), and marital, medical, military, and incarceration histories, as well as property and vehicle ownership.[53] Hard characteristics are verifiable. Soft characteristics are demonstrated or suggested by the physical or behavioral evidence or by the victim's and witnesses' statements; they are potentially alterable, are affected by time, and/or are subject to interpretation.[54] The following are some of the many types of soft characteristics: offender's relationship history, grooming habits, physical characteristics (including dress), hobbies, criminal versatility, glibness or superficial charm, skill levels, aggressiveness, motive or fantasy, and impulsivity.[55]

The final report covers all the major elements above, as well as numerous subcategories which are not appropriate to detail in a general investigative text. It must be crafted with integrity, be devoid of bias, exaggeration, and preconceived ideas, recognize everyone's contributions, and be consistent with the evidence in the case.[56]

## GEOGRAPHIC PROFILING

Geographic information system (GIS) software provides the capability to superimpose different types of data onto a map. For example, by entering the pertinent data into a GIS, analysts can see where traffic citations are being issued versus where traffic accidents are happening. If these data points do not correspond, the reasonable conclusion is that the traffic enforcement effort is not properly focused and that officers are writing citations where it is easy to do so. Maps generated by GIS are very potent ways to present data visually because what is being shown is usually immediately understood.

The growth of GIS applications in police departments has spawned a specialized field, geographic information analysis (GIA). One of its techniques is **geographic profiling** or **geoprofiling (GP)** the "father" of which is Dr. Kim Rossmo, formerly an inspector with the Vancouver, Canada, Police Department. He developed the concept of criminal geographic targeting (CGT) while working on his doctorate.[57] Not the least bit coincidentally, Rossmo headed the first geoprofiling unit, which was in the Vancouver Police Department.

Geoprofiling is an investigative strategy that uses the locations of a series of crimes to determine the most probable area of the offender's residence. It is usually used in cases of serial murder, rape, arson, and robbery, although it can also be used in investigating single crimes such as auto theft, burglary, and bombing, which typically involve primary and secondary scenes.[58] The distinctive feature of GP is determining where the offender lives, as opposed to where the next crime will take place. Using complex mathematical formulas, GP software processes the data inputted and then presents the results in the form of two- or three-dimensional surface maps called "jeopardies," one of which shows the probable location of the offender's residence (see geoprofiling probability map).[59] Geographic profiling typically involves the following steps:

1. A thorough perusal of the case file, including investigative reports, witness statements, autopsy reports, and the criminal profile, if available.
2. A detailed examination of the crime scene and area profiles.
3. Interviews with lead investigators and crime analysts.
4. Visits to each crime scene, if possible.
5. A review of the relevant neighborhoods and their characteristics (e.g., from where was the victim abducted and where was she or he left).
6. A study of street, land-use, and transit maps.
7. Analysis.
8. Report preparation.[60]

The information gathered by GP analysts is used to answer a series of questions, such as the following: Why did the offender pick victims from a particular neighborhood? Why did he dump the victim where he did? What route must he have used, and when did he use it? Is the route generally available to other people? Why was this route attractive to him? Are there escape routes? Are there geographic patterns? Was the area to which the victim was taken appropriate for predatory activities? Was the victim attacked in the same place the offender encountered her? If there was a vehicle involved, was it dumped?[61]

A key component of geoprofiling is the concept of a mental map: "This is a cognitive map of one's surroundings which is developed through experiences, travel routes, reference points, and centers of activity; it also includes the places where we feel safe and what we take for granted. These concepts also hold true for offenders."[62] If offenders are geographically stable, they tend to stay in a certain area or region. Transient offenders, such as serial killer Ted Bundy, travel more widely; in Bundy's career he committed murders in 10 states from the Pacific Northwest to Florida.[63] Whether offenders are stable or transient depends on their experience with travel, their means for getting from one place to another, their sense of personal security, and their predatory motivations.[64] An offender's mental map may be dependent on his or her geographic style because the type of approach made toward a victim is related to a killer's "home base."[65] In GP terms, predatory criminals can be classified according to how they acquire victims:

- *Hunters,* who search for victims, often using their own residences as home base.
- *Poachers,* who travel away from home, including to other cities, to hunt.
- *Trollers,* who, while engaged in other activities, have opportunistic encounters with their victims.
- *Trappers,* whose strategy is to draw the victims to them.[66]

Predatory offenders attack their victims in different ways. Raptors attack their victims when they encounter them; stalkers follow and then attack

### Geoprofiling Probability Map

Geographic Information System (GIS) software has many uses in police work. One application is geographic profiling, an investigative strategy that uses the location of a series of crimes to determine the probable area of the offender's residence. It is most often used in cases of serial murder, rape, arson, or robbery.

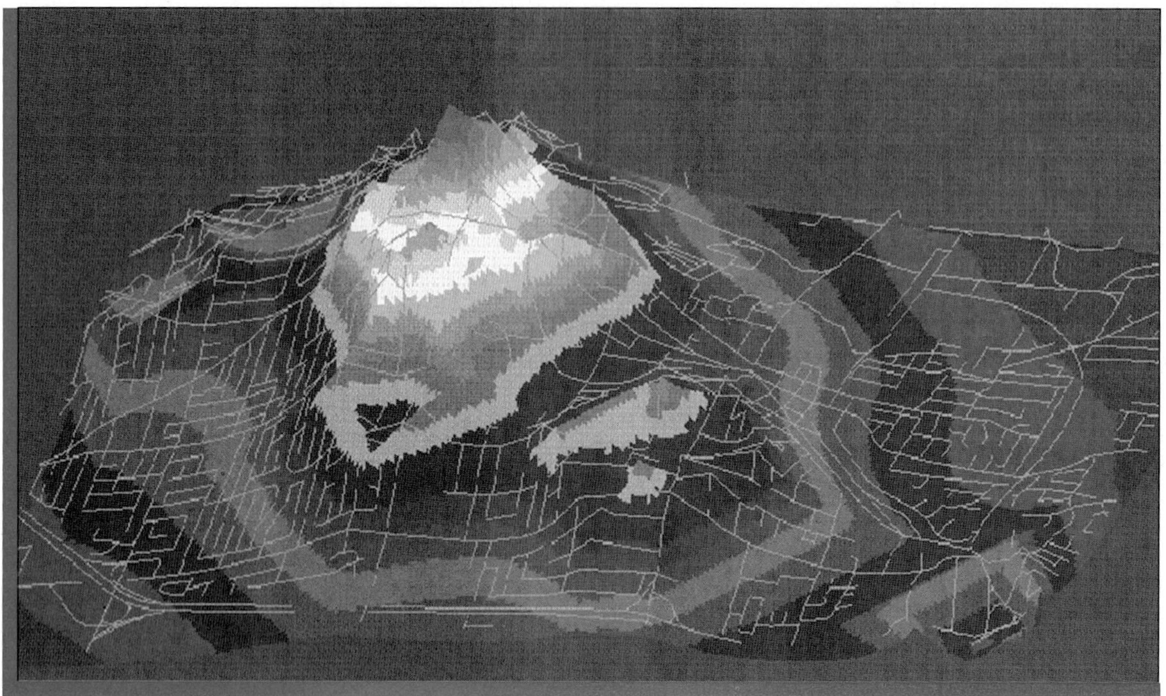

those they prey on; and ambushers entice their victims to places they control and in which they feel comfortable, such as the offender's home, and then spring their attacks.[67]

GP does not solve crimes; it prioritizes suspects and their likely addresses, thereby allowing investigators to focus their resources and strategies (e.g., saturation patrol, surveillance, and neighborhood canvasses) where they have the highest probability of being successful. The following case illustrates the value of geoprofiling:

ONTARIO, Canada, Provincial Police (OPP) were investigating a series of over 80 burglaries in a cottage community near Midland. Using geoprofiling, police were able to focus their investigative effort on a small geographic area. Subsequently, an offender was arrested, 50 burglaries were solved, and stolen property was recovered. GP had indicated that the most likely place the offender lived was a particular area less than 100 meters by 100 meters. As it turned out, the person who was arrested lived in that small area.[68]

## FINANCIAL ANALYSIS

Financial investigations can be relatively modest, for crimes such as a credit card fraud involving two transactions and a total of $50, or very complex, as in the case of money-laundering schemes involving multiple corporate shells and banks in a dozen countries throughout the world. Fortunately, state and federal investigative agencies can assist with the more complicated cases. The Federal Law Enforcement Training Centers (FLETCs), state police academies, and other providers offer excellent instruction in financial investigations.

Nonspecialists in this area should be alert for the possibility of a financial motive, particularly in murder and arson cases. Among the indicators of financial difficulty are the following:[69]

### Business Indicators of Financial Difficulty

- Decreasing revenue.
- Increasing production costs (e.g., labor and material).
- Increased competition; better products available.
- Costly rental and lease agreements.
- Failure to record depreciations.
- Numerous product defects, spoilage.
- Double payment of bills.
- Numerous bank accounts.
- Low or overdrawn bank balances.
- Increased borrowing.
- Large or frequent cash transactions.
- Bounced checks.
- Overinsured or hypothetical assets.
- Liens on assets.
- Credit limits imposed by suppliers or lenders; credit refused.
- Numerous overdue accounts.
- Delinquent loan payments.
- Frequent COD purchases.
- Inability to pay current utility bills.
- Delinquent or tardy tax accounts.
- Litigation against business and/or owners.
- Inventory reduced before fire.
- Overstocked because of overproduction or low demand for products.
- Duplicate sales receipts.
- Slow-moving items; obsolete inventory.
- Two sets of books maintained.
- Loans to or from corporate officers and employees.
- Bankruptcy proceedings.
- Losses in prior years.
- Duplicate insurance claims.
- Alleged renovations.
- Frequent change of ownership before fire.
- Bills paid by cashier's checks, certified checks, or money orders.
- Use of photocopies of records instead of original sources.

### Personal Indicators of Financial Difficulty

- Bounced checks.
- Costly rental and lease agreements.
- Inability to pay current bills (e.g., utilities).
- Lenders impose or refuse loans or credit.
- Payment of bills by cashier's checks, certified checks, or money orders.

There are also personal life situations that may suggest personal financial difficulty. Such situations include marital discord; loss of overtime or job; substance, child, or spouse abuse; a recent divorce; and inability or refusal to make child support and/or alimony payments.

### Financial Crimes Enforcement Network

The **Financial Crimes Enforcement Network (FinCen),** located within the U.S. Department of the Treasury, is one of the primary agencies responsible for preventing and detecting money laundering by arms dealers, terrorists, drug dealers, criminal enterprises, and others. It serves as a link among law enforcement, financial institutions, and regulatory agencies. Annually, in addition to its own investigative efforts, FinCen serves 165 different law enforcement agencies by providing approximately 6,500 analytical reports involving nearly 33,000 subjects. The value of FinCen for state and local law enforcement is the agency's expertise and its access to highly specialized databases, trained analysts using advanced technology, and worldwide sources of information.[70]

## NATIONAL CENTER FOR THE ANALYSIS OF VIOLENT CRIME

Operated by the FBI, the **National Center for the Analysis of Violent Crime (NCAVC)** is organized into three components, discussed below.

The Behavioral Analysis Unit (BAU) provides behavior-based investigative and operational support for complex and time-sensitive cases typically involving threats and acts of violence. Its program areas include crimes against children, crimes against adults, communicated threats, corruption, bombing, and arson. The unit provides criminal-profiling services to federal, state, and local agencies if, after it screens a case, the offense and available data appear to be amenable to this technique. Figure 8–7 is a release from NCAVC that provides a linguistic and behavioral assessment of the person responsible for mailing anthrax letters to Tom Brokaw, the New York Post, and Senator Daschle.

The Child Abduction and Serial Murder Investigative Resources Center (CASMIRC) was mandated by Congress in 1998. As its name indicates, this unit focuses on children and provides agencies with advanced capabilities and expertise in dealing with abductions, mysterious disappearances, child homicides, and serial murders. (CASMIRC is also discussed in Chapter 11, "Crimes against Children.")

The Violent Criminal Apprehension Program (VICAP) facilitates cooperation, coordination, and communication among enforcement agencies in support of their efforts to investigate, identify, track, apprehend, and prosecute violent serial offenders.[71] (VICAP is discussed in detail in Chapter 9, "Injury and Death Investigations.")

## NATIONAL CRIME INFORMATION CENTER

Since its inception in 1967, the **National Crime Information Center (NCIC)** has repeatedly demonstrated its value to federal, state, and local agencies. In 1968, NCIC identified 1,200 possible suspects in the slaying of Reverend Martin Luther King, Jr., and examiners later determined that the latent fingerprints lifted from the murder weapon belonged to one of them, James Earl Ray.[72] Twenty-seven years later, federal agents investigating the Oklahoma City bombing ran Timothy McVeigh's name through NCIC and learned that a state trooper had stopped him approximately an hour after the bombing 88 miles away and McVeigh was still in police custody.[73] Sandwiched in between these events are numerous other success stories in which the online services of NCIC were a crucial determinant of investigative success.

As time passes and new technologies and capabilities become available, it is essential that information systems take advantage of them and be responsive to new client needs. Thus it was that in mid-1999 the newest version of the FBI's system, NCIC 2000, went online. The databases provided by its predecessor, the "legacy system," as well as NCIC 2000's capabilities, are summarized in Figure 8–8. The broad scope of the additional NCIC 2000 services can be seen in the following examples:

- An officer notices a man, with a small child in the front passenger's seat, driving his car too rapidly and weaving through traffic, causing other drivers to slam on their brakes. The officer stops the vehicle and checks on the driver through NCIC 2000. It is learned from the Convicted Sexual Offender Registry and the Convicted Persons on Supervised Release Database that the subject is a registered sexual offender who should not be with a young child, is on parole in another state, and should not have left it.[74]
- Investigators working the fugitive detail got a tip that a person wanted on a rape warrant is in the Blue Light Lounge. This turned out not to be the case, but as soon as they went into the bar, they noticed a man nervously glancing over his shoulder at them as he made a beeline to the rest-room area. When he does not come back, they locate him in the stall of the ladies room and ask him why he is so nervous. He gives them several different stories and names, but has no identification. After using the single-print scanner in their unmarked vehicle, the investigators electronically send his print to NCIC 2000. In minutes they learn the identity of the subject, as well as the fact that he is wanted for a double homicide two states away.
- A patrolling officer sees a pickup pulling a sailboat. The brake lights for the trailer are either not working or not hooked up. The officer stops the truck with the intent of getting this potentially dangerous deficiency corrected. The driver nervously hands over his license when requested to do so. The officer notices a second driver's license on the dashboard of the pickup. Both photographs match the driver, but there are different names and birth dates

**Figure 8-7** NCAVC Release

**November 9, 2001**
**Amerithrax Press Briefing**

**Linguistic/Behavioral Analysis of Anthrax Letters**
**Critical Incident Response Group**
**National Center for the Analysis of Violent Crime**

Today the FBI is releasing linguistic and behavioral assessments of the person responsible for mailing anthrax-laden letters on September 18 and October 9, 2001. We ask the American public to study these assessments and reflect on whether someone of their acquaintance might fit the profile. The safety of the American people is at stake. If you have credible information that might help identify this person, please contact the FBI immediately at 1-800-CRIMETV (274-6388), at www.ifccfbi.gov, or by calling your local FBI field office.

**EVIDENCE DESCRIPTION**

**Letter 1**
One page, hand-printed letter
Transmittal envelope, also similarly hand printed
Addressed to "NBC TV–Tom Brokaw"–No return address
Postmarked Trenton, NJ 09/18/2001 (Tues.)

**Letter 2**
One page, hand-printed letter
Transmittal envelope, also similarly hand printed
Addressed to "NY Post"_No return address
Postmarked Trenton, NJ 09/18/2001 (Tues.)

**Letter 3**
One page, hand-printed letter
Transmittal envelope, also similarly hand printed
Addressed to "Senator Daschle–509 Hart Senate Office Building"
Return address–"4th Grade, Greendale School Franklin Park, NJ"
Return address zip code – "08852"
Postmarked Trenton, NJ 10/09/2001 (Tues.)

**LINGUISTIC ASSESSMENT**

It is highly probable, bordering on certainty, that all three letters were authored by the same person. Letters 1 and 2 are identical copies. Letter 3, however, contains a somewhat different message than the other letters. The Anthrax utilized in Letter 3 was much more refined, more potent, and more easily disbursed than Letters 1 and 2.

In the past, the public has helped the FBI solve high profile investigations that involved writings by coming forward to identify the author, either by how he wrote or by what he wrote. We are asking for the public's help here again in the same way.

While the text in these letters is limited, there are certain distinctive characteristics in the author's writing style. These same characteristics may be evident in other letters, greeting cards, or envelopes this person has written. We hope someone has received correspondence from this person and will recognize some of these characteristics.

The characteristics include:

1. The author uses dashes ("-") in the writing of the date "09-11-01." Many people use the slash ("/") to separate the day/month/year.
2. In writing the number one, the author chooses to use a formalized, more detailed version. He writes it as "1" instead of the simple vertical line.
3. The author uses the words "can not," when many people prefer to spell it as one word, "cannot."

**Figure 8-7** NCAVC Release, *continued*

4. The author writes in all upper case block-style letters. However, the first letter of the first word of each sentence is written in slightly larger upper case lettering. Also, the first letter of all proper nouns (like names) is slightly larger. The is apparently the author's way of indicating a word should be capitalized in upper case letters. For whatever reason, he may not be comfortable or practiced in writing in lower case lettering.
5. The names and address on each envelope are noticeably tilted on a downward slant from left to right. This may be a characteristic seen on other envelopes he has sent.
6. The envelopes are of the pre-stamped variety, the stamps denoting 34 cents, which are normally available directly from the post office. They are not the traditional business size envelopes, but the smaller size measuring approximately 6¼ x 3 ½.

**BEHAVIORAL ASSESSMENT**

Based on the selection of Anthrax as the "weapon" of choice by this individual, the offender:

- Is likely an adult male.
- If employed, is likely to be in a position requiring little contact with the public, or other employees. He may work in a laboratory. He is apparently comfortable working with an extremely hazardous material. He probably has a scientific background to some extent, or at least a strong interest in science.
- Has likely taken appropriate protective steps to ensure his own safety, which may include the use of an Anthrax vaccination or antibiotics.
- Has access to a source of Anthrax and possesses knowledge and expertise to refine it.
- Possesses or has access to some laboratory equipment; i.e., microscope, glassware, centrifuge, etc.
- Has exhibited an organized, rational thought process in furtherance of his criminal behavior.
- Has a familiarity, direct or indirect with the Trenton, NJ, metropolitan area; however, this does not necessarily mean he currently lives in the Trenton, NJ, area He is comfortable traveling in and around this locale.
- Did not select victims randomly. He made an effort to identify the correct address, including zip code, of each victim and use sufficient postage to ensure proper delivery of the letters. The offender deliberately "selected" NBC News, the New York Post, and the office of Senator Tom Daschle as the targeted victims (and possibly AMI in Florida). These targets are probably very important to the offender. They may have been the focus of previous expressions of contempt which may have been communicated to others, or observed by others.
- Is a non-confrontational person, at least in his public life. He lacks the personal skills necessary to confront others. He chooses to confront his problems "long distance" and not face-to-face. He may hold grudges for a long time, vowing that he will get even with "them" one day. There are probably other, earlier examples of this type of behavior. While these earlier incidents were not actual Anthrax mailings, he may have chosen to anonymously harass other individuals or entities that he perceived as having wronged him. He may also have chosen to utilize the mail on those occasions.
- Prefers being by himself more often than not. If he is involved in a personal relationship it will likely be of a self-serving nature.

**Pre-Offense Behavior**

Following the events of September 11, 2001, this person may have become mission-oriented in this desire to undertake these Anthrax mailings. He may have become more secretive and exhibited an unusual pattern of activity. Additionally, he may have displayed a passive disinterest in the events which otherwise captivated the Nation. He also may have started taking antibiotics unexpectedly.

**Post-Offense Behavior**

He may have exhibited significant behavioral changes at various critical periods of time throughout the course of the Anthrax mailings and related media coverage. These may include the following;

1. Altered physical appearance.
2. Pronounced anxiety.
3. Atypical media interest.
4. Noticeable mood swings.
5. More withdrawn.
6. Unusual level of preoccupation.
7. Unusual absenteeism.
8. Altered sleeping and/or eating habits.

These post-offense behaviors would have been most noticeable during critical times, including but not limited to: the mailing of the letters (09/18/01 and 10/09/01), the death of the first Anthrax victim, media reports of each anthrax incident, and especially the deaths and illnesses of non-targeted victims.

on them. An NCIC 2000 check reveals that both names are aliases used by a man with a criminal history who is wanted in connection with a series of boat thefts. In his patrol car, the officer receives a mug shot, the suspect's real name, and a photograph of his tattoo, as well as photographs of and other data on the stolen boats, one of which is attached to the suspect's truck.

- A 9-year-old boy is molested by a man. Prior to the incident, a witness happened to see the two of them walking near an abandoned building in the neighborhood. The victim's statement and physical evidence in the building confirm that this is where the victimization took place. Using NCIC 2000, investigators conduct a search based on the zip code for the building. The Convicted Sexual Offender Registry establishes that a paroled sexual offender lives in the same zip code. Subsequently, the witness picks the parolee out of a photo lineup, the offender is arrested, and he confesses to the crime.

## COMBINED DNA INDEX SYSTEM

It was immediately apparent that without DNA databases, a counterpart to fingerprint files, the full potential of DNA evidence in investigations would not be realized. States began enacting DNA database laws that mandated the collection of DNA samples from certain categories of offenders, such as those convicted of murder, rape, and child abuse. By 1998, the FBI's Combined DNA Index System (CODIS) was fully operational, electronically linking local, state, and federal DNA files.

**Figure 8-8** NCIC 2000 Databases

(**Source:** Louis Freeh (director of the FBI), NCIC 2000 press release, July 15, 1999, p. 2.)

| Databases Continued from NCIC | Additional NCIC 2000 Services |
|---|---|
| Stolen Articles | Enhanced name search (searches all derivatives of names, such as Jeff, Geoff, Jeffrey) |
| Foreign Fugitives | Search of right-index-finger prints |
| Stolen Guns | Mug shots |
| Criminal History Queries | Other identifying images (such as scars, tattoos, and images of vehicles (e.g., Ford Mustang) |
| Stolen License Plates | Convicted Sexual Offender Registry |
| Deported Felons | Convicted Persons on Supervised Release Database |
| Missing Persons | Persons Incarcerated in Federal Prisons |
| Criminal Justice Agency Identifier | User manuals available online |
| Stolen Securities | Information linking (all information related to a case will be returned on a single inquiry; e.g., if guns are in a stolen vehicle, a query on the vehicle will return information on the stolen guns as well) |
| Stolen Boats | Improved data quality |
| Gang and Terrorist Members | Online ad hoc searches to support criminal investigations |
| Unidentified Persons | Maintains five days of system inquiries to allow agencies to be notified if they are looking for information on the same individual or stolen property |
| U.S. Secret Service Protective File | |
| Stolen Vehicles | |
| Persons Subject to Protection Orders | |
| Wanted Persons | |
| Canadian Police Information Center | |

**NCIC in Action**

Established in 1967, the National Crime and Information Center (NCIC) is a computerized link among federal, state, and local law enforcement officials in the United States. Examples of databases in the NCIC system available to the police agencies include: stolen articles, fugititves, criminal histories, and missing persons. The FBI has now implemented the NCIC 2000 system which has even greater capabilities, including the following databases: mug shots, enhanced name searches, and right-index fingerprint searches.

This cooperative effort of the three levels of government is consistently providing results:

IN 1995, an unidentified woman's body was found on an off-ramp along an interstate highway in Iowa. After identifying the victim and considering the location where the body was found, the police investigation focused on the possibility that the offender was a truck driver. Biological evidence from the scene was sent to the FBI for DNA analysis. Five years after the offender's DNA profile was developed, it was uploaded to CODIS, where a match was made with a man incarcerated for a sexual offense in Florida. It was also learned that he had a commercial driver's license, validating the police belief that the offender was a truck driver.[75]

## THE INTERNET

The Internet has transformed how people communicate and how often they communicate. All types of organizations have been quick to use the power and versatility of the Net, from the American Red Cross to pornographers. The possibilities of the Internet have not escaped the police, who have been quick to use it for investigative, administrative, and public information purposes. For investigative purposes, the police use the Internet in many ways, such as:

1. Appealing to the public for information about specific crimes, often through "crime-stopper" programs.
2. Requesting information about missing children and adults.

**Figure 8-9** FBI Internet Terrorist Bulletin

**MURDER OF U.S. NATIONALS OUTSIDE THE UNITED STATES; CONSPIRACY TO MURDER U.S. NATIONALS OUTSIDE THE UNITED STATES; ATTACK ON A FEDERAL FACILITY RESULTING IN DEATH**

# USAMA BIN LADEN

**Aliases:** Usama Bin Muhammad Bin Ladin, Shaykh Usama Bin Ladin, the Prince, the Emir, Abu Abdallah, Mujahid Shaykh, Hajj, the Director

## DESCRIPTION

| | | | |
|---|---|---|---|
| **Date of Birth Used:** | 1957 | **Hair:** | Brown |
| **Place of Birth:** | Saudi Arabia | **Eyes:** | Brown |
| **Height:** | 6'4" to 6'6" | **Sex:** | Male |
| **Weight:** | Approximately 160 pounds | **Complexion:** | Olive |
| **Build:** | Thin | **Citizenship:** | Saudi Arabian |
| **Language:** | Arabic (probably Pashtu) | | |
| **Scars and Marks:** | None known | | |
| **Remarks:** | Bin Laden is believed to be in Afghanistan. He is left-handed and walks with a cane. | | |

## CAUTION

Usama Bin Laden is wanted in connection with the August 7, 1998, bombings of the United States Embassies in Dar es Salaam, Tanzania, and Nairobi, Kenya. These attacks killed over 200 people. In addition, Bin Laden is a suspect in other terrorist attacks throughout the world.

## REWARD

The Rewards For Justice Program, United States Department of State, is offering a reward of up to $25 million for information leading directly to the apprehension or conviction of Usama Bin Laden. An additional $2 million is being offered through a program developed and funded by the Airline Pilots Association and the Air Transport Association.

**SHOULD BE CONSIDERED ARMED AND DANGEROUS**

**IF YOU HAVE ANY INFORMATION CONCERNING THIS PERSON, PLEASE CONTACT YOUR LOCAL FBI OFFICE OR THE NEAREST AMERICAN EMBASSY OR CONSULATE.**

[ New York Field Office ] [ Most Wanted Terrorists ]
[ FBI Home Page ] [ FBI Field Offices ]

Figure 8-10 FBI Internet Fugitive Bulletin

**Hobbs Act - Armored Carrier Robbery**

## UNKNOWN SUSPECTS

**DESCRIPTION -- SUSPECT #1**

| | | | |
|---|---|---|---|
| **Age:** | 30 to 35 | **Build:** | Heavy |
| **Sex:** | Male | **Hair:** | Dark |
| **Height:** | 5'9" to 5'10" | **Eyes:** | Unknown |
| **Weight:** | Approximately 200 pounds | **Race:** | White |

**DESCRIPTION -- SUSPECT #2**

| | | | |
|---|---|---|---|
| **Age:** | 30 to 35 | **Build:** | Heavy |
| **Sex:** | Male | **Hair:** | Medium to dark |
| **Height:** | 6'2" | **Eyes:** | Unknown |
| **Weight:** | Over 300 pounds | **Race:** | White |

**CAUTION**

On September 21, 1999, two unknown white males robbed a Brinks Armored Car Service messenger in Birmingham, Alabama. The same two men have allegedly committed five other armored car robberies that took place from 1992 to 1998 in Knoxville, Tennessee, Lexington, Kentucky, and Florence, Kentucky.

In the September robbery, the suspects approached the Brinks messenger as he exited the bank with his cash pick-up. The 1st suspect drew a gun from a shopping bag and, as the messenger tried to draw his own gun, the 2nd suspect dissuaded him. The 1st suspect then disarmed the messenger at gunpoint while the 2nd suspect carried away the money. The two suspects got into a dark green Toyota or similar imported car that was parked in a nearby lot and drove away.

The first suspect wore a dark-colored, short-sleeved polo shirt, dark-colored, Bermuda shorts, and sunglasses. He had dark hair and a small goatee beard. He was armed with a blue-steel revolver and drove the getaway car.

The second suspect was wearing a light-colored plaid shirt, dark pants, and sunglasses. He had medium to dark hair. The suspect was armed with a dark-colored, semi-automatic pistol.

**SHOULD BE CONSIDERED ARMED AND DANGEROUS**

**IF YOU HAVE ANY INFORMATION CONCERNING THIS PERSON, PLEASE CONTACT YOUR LOCAL FBI OFFICE OR THE NEAREST AMERICAN EMBASSY OR CONSULATE.**

DIRECTOR
FEDERAL BUREAU OF INVESTIGATION
UNITED STATES DEPARTMENT OF JUSTICE
WASHINGTON, D.C. 20535
TELEPHONE: (202) 324-3000

[ Birmingham Field Office ] [ Knoxville Field Office ] [ Louisville Field Office ]
[ Unknown Suspects ] [ FBI Home Page ] [ FBI Field Offices ]

3. Posting federal, state, and local most-wanted lists. These lists may be limited to the "top 10," or there may be separate most-wanted lists, such as a list for the most-wanted violent felons or terrorists (see Figure 8–9).
4. Publicizing individuals who are wanted as fugitives, as well as fugitives who have been located.
5. Alerting the public about jail and prison escapees and requesting information if they are sighted.
6. Requesting information about the identities of unknown subjects ("unsubs"; see Figure 8–10) and victims.
7. Showing photographs of recovered stolen property so that the owners can identify and claim it.
8. Providing beatwide and citywide crime-mapping capabilities so that investigators can approach their work with better information.
9. Conducting various types of electronic covert investigations.

Item 9 is well illustrated by an operation undertaken by the Lake County Sheriff's Office, in Illinois. Members of the office's Child Exploitation Unit go online posing as youngsters in their early to mid-teens in order to apprehend child pornographers and pedophiles.[76] The detectives visit chat rooms that have sexually suggestive names, where they have been "hit on" as quickly as 5 seconds to six months after they began electronically talking to someone. This type of Internet investigation is a delicate dance in which the detectives must get sexual predators to make revealing remarks about themselves—without giving them any hint that they are actually talking to police officers. If a suspect asks for a photograph of the "boy" or "girl," he is talking to, a high school photograph of the detective working the case is sent. The police can arrest an individual once he or she agrees to meet with the "boy" or "girl," as this shows that the person has the intent to commit a crime. The detectives call these predators "travelers" because they come from neighboring cities and states to meet their victims.

The Internet is also increasingly being relied on by computer-savvy investigators. Among the resources they tap into are websites providing "people-locator" search engines and reverse phone, address, and e-mail directories. The Library of Congress maintains an extensive listing of Internet search engines from which investigators can select the sites most helpful to them.

**Law Enforcement Online (LEO)** is a secure intranet system created and maintained by the FBI as a tool for communicating, obtaining mission-critical information, providing or participating in online educational programs, and participating in professional-interest or topically focused dialogs. Access to LEO is free to qualified enforcement officers; on a daily basis 23,000 users take advantage of it. Through LEO's e-mail service, users can stay in contact with colleagues, make contact with experts, share information about unique MOs, request help with unsolved crimes, conduct research, participate in special-interest groups (LEOSIGs), and use the links to numerous websites including those of the International Association of Auto Theft Investigators, Asset Forfeiture Program, NCAVC, National Drug Intelligence Center, and FBI Bomb Center.[77]

## Key Terms

**behavioral evidence analysis (BEA)**
**crime analysis**
**crime bulletins**
**criminal profiling**
**crimogen**
**Financial Crimes Enforcement Network (FinCen)**
**geographic profiling or geoprofiling (GP)**
**hot spot (crime)**
**intelligence/analytical cycle**
**investigative psychology**
**Law Enforcement Online (LEO)**
**National Center for the Analysis of Violent Crime (NCAVC)**
**National Crime Information Center (NCIC)**
**organized/disorganized-offender model**
**pattern (crime)**
**series (crime)**
**spree (crime)**
**telephone record analysis**
**time-event charting (TEC)**
**trend (crime)**

## Review Questions

1. Identify and briefly discuss all the major elements in the intelligence/analytical cycle.
2. What are the three general types of crime analysis, and what are they used for?
3. Prepare a time-event chart for the major events in the class.
4. Look again at Table 8-2, the "Telephone Record Matrix." State at least four things you would like to know or investigate if you were assigned to the case and just received the matrix.
5. In terms of at least five factors, differentiate between the characteristics of organized and disorganized offenders.
6. What are mixed organized-disorganized homicides?
7. Identify the steps in Turvey's BEA, and explain each one in no more than two sentences.
8. With respect to geoprofiling, what is a mental map?
9. What are the three major components of the NCAVC, and what services does each provide?
10. Which of NCIC 2000's capabilities impresses you the most, and why?
11. Why is CODIS important?
12. Log on to the Internet, and using any standard search engine (e.g., google.com), do a search for "unsolved murders." What kinds of information have you retrieved, and from where?
13. A large amount of software is available to automate intelligence and analytical processes. Log on to the Internet and see what types of software are available. What capabilities do the programs offer?

## Internet Activities

1. *Crime Times*, an online national newsletter, contains numerous articles on research that links areas such as neurochemical imbalances, drugs, toxic environment, genetic factors, psychological dysfunction, and behavior to crime. Go to www.crime-times.org and find several articles that you believe could be useful to criminal profiling for serious crimes such as rape, arson, and homicide.
2. Check out the National Institute of Justice's Crime Mapping Research Center at www.ojp.usdoj.gov/cmrc. This site provides research and information on geographic information systems and crime analysis. Read the article "The Use of Computerized Crime Mapping by Law Enforcement: Survey Results," which reports findings on law enforcement agencies that use crime mapping and on the effectiveness of and obstacles to crime mapping.

## Notes

1. International Association of Law Enforcement Intelligence Analysts, *Starting an Analytical Unit for Intelligence Led Policing* (Lawrenceville, NJ: IALEIA, July 2001), p. 1.
2. Ibid., p. 2.
3. Ibid.
4. There is nothing magical about five steps. Some authorities say there are four steps and others as many as seven.
5. This paragraph is drawn, with restatement, from Russell M. Porter, "The Intelligence Production Cycle," Iowa Department of Public Safety, www.state.ia.us/government/dps/intellcycle.htm, Nov. 19, 2001, p. 2.
6. Ibid., pp. 2–3, with additions by the authors.
7. Louis Freeh (director of the FBI), "President's Fiscal Year Budget 2000," statement made before the House Committee on Appropriations, Subcommittee on the Departments of Commerce, Justice, and State, the Judiciary, and Related Agencies, May 17, 1999, p. 4.
8. Porter, "The Intelligence Production Cycle," p. 3.
9. Ibid.

10. Ibid.
11. These points came up during a November 21, 2001, telephone conversation with Marilyn Peterson, a widely recognized expert and author in the field of intelligence matters. She is director of training for the International Association of Law Enforcement Intelligence Analysts (IALEIA), which was founded in 1981.
12. Steven Gottlieb, Sheldon Arenberg, and Raj Singh, *Crime Analysis from First Report* (Montclair, CA: Alpha Publishing, 1994), pp. 13–24. (To obtain information abut the purchase of this excellent book, contact Mr. Gottlieb, P.O. Box 8, Montclair, CA 91763 or telephone 909-989-4366.) Also see Victor Goldsmith, ed., *Analyzing Crime Patterns: Frontiers of Practice* (Thousand Oaks, CA: Sage, 2000), and Karim H. Vellani and Joel Nahoun, *Applied Crime Analysis* (Boston: Butterworth-Heinemann, 2001).
13. Massachusetts Association of Crime Analysts, "Crime Analysis," www/macrimeanalysts.com/aboutca.html, Oct. 18, 2001.
14. Susan Wernicke, "What Is a Crime Bulletin?" International Association of Crime Analysts, www.iaca.net/resources/articles/bulletins.html, Nov. 19, 2001.
15. Marilyn B. Peterson, "Telephone Record Analysis," in Paul B. Andrews and Marilyn B. Peterson, eds., *Criminal Intelligence Analysis* (Loomis, CA: Palmer Enterprises, 1990), p. 200.
16. Ibid.
17. Ibid., pp. 200–201.
18. Brent Turvey, *Criminal Profiling: An Introduction to Behavioral Evidence Analysis* (San Diego: Academic Press, 1999), p. 1. A second edition of this book is in progress.
19. Ibid.
20. Ibid.
21. Ibid., p. xxvii.
22. "New York's Mad Bomber," njnj.essortment.com/madbomber_rwid.htm, Dec. 3, 2001, p. 1.
23. Ibid., pp. 1–2.
24. Ibid., pp. 2–3.
25. In a series of excellent articles, Wayne Petherick identifies and critiques various aspects of criminal profiling. See Wayne Petherick, "Criminal Profiling: Fact, Fiction, Fantasy, and Fallacy," www.crimelibrary.com/serial4/criminalprofiling/index.html, Dec. 4, 2001. The authors have adopted his structure of organized/disorganized offenders, investigative psychology, and behavioral evidence analysis. Wayne Petherick teaches at Bond University, Australia, and is an affiliate member of the Academy of Behavioral Profiling.
26. Petherick, "Criminal Profiling: How It Got Started and How It Is Used," www.crimelibrary.com/criminology/criminalprofiling2/3.htm, Dec. 7, 2001, p. 1.
27. Ibid.
28. Robert K. Ressler, Ann W. Burgess, and John E. Douglas, *Sexual Homicides: Patterns and Motives* (New York: Free Press, 1992), p. 136.
29. Ibid.
30. Ibid.
31. Ibid.
32. Ibid, p. 138.
33. Ibid, pp. 138–142.
34. Ibid., p. 145.
35. Ibid.
36. Ibid.
37. Ibid., pp. 145–146.
38. John E. Douglas, Ann W. Burgess, and Robert K. Ressler, *Crime Classification Manual* (San Francisco: Jossey-Bass, 1992), pp. 133–134.
39. Petherick, "Criminal Profiling: How It Got Started," Dec. 4, 2001, p. 1.
40. Ibid., pp. 1–2.
41. Brent Turvey can be contacted at the Academy of Behavioral Profiling, BTurvey@profiling.org. The academy publishes the Internet-only *Journal of Behavioral Profiling*, which is accessible on a subscription basis.
42. Ibid., pp. 28–31.
43. Ibid., p. 57.
44. Ibid.
45. Ibid., pp. 63–64, with additions by the authors.
46. Ibid., p. 29.
47. Ibid.
48. Ibid.
49. Ibid., p. 69.
50. Ibid., p. 29.
51. Ibid.
52. Ibid., p. 31.
53. Ibid., p. 184
54. Ibid., p. 185.
55. Ibid.
56. Daniel B. Kennedy, "Ethical Guidelines for Professional Conduct," Academy of Behavioral Profiling, www.profiling.org/abp_conduct.html, Aug. 21, 2001.

57. For more detailed information, see Kim Rossmo, *Geographic Profiling* (Boca Raton, FL: CRC Press, 2000).
58. Environmental Criminology Research, "What Is Geographic Profiling?" www.ecricanada.com/geopro/index/html, Nov. 21, 2001, p. 1.
59. Environmental Criminology Research, Inc., "What Is Regel," www.ecricanada.com/rigel/index.html/, Nov. 21, 2001, p. 1.
60. Environmental Criminology Research, Inc., "Requesting a Geographical Profile," www.ecricanada.com/geopro/ref_request.html, Nov. 21, 2001, p. 1.
61. Katherine Ramsland, "Geographic Profiling: The Components of a Geographical Profile," www.crimelibrary.com/forensics/geog/4.html, 2000, p. 1.
62. Ibid., p. 2.
63. Ibid.
64. Ibid.
65. Ibid.
66. Ibid.
67. Ibid.
68. Environmental Criminology Research, Inc., "Case Studies," www.ecricanada.com/geopro/cs.html, Nov. 21, 2001, p. 1.
69. Douglas, Burgess, and Ressler, Crime Classification Manual, pp. 327–328. For detailed information about sources of information in financial investigations, see Bureau of Alcohol, Tobacco and Firearms, Audit Services Division, "Financial Investigation Sources of Information," interfire.org/res_file/Fin-Srcs.htm.
70. Financial Crimes Enforcement Network, "Law Enforcement/Direct Case Support," www.ustreas.gov/fincen/le_directcasesupp.html, Dec. 7, 2001, p. 1.
71. This information is drawn from Federal Bureau of Investigation, "Critical Incident Support Group," http://www.fbi.gov/hq/isd/crg/ncavc.htm.
72. Stephanie L. Hitt, "NCIC 2000," *FBI Law Enforcement Bulletin*, July 2000, Vol. 69, No. 7, p. 12.
73. Ibid.
74. Ibid., p. 14.
75. www.fbi.gov/hq/codis/stories.htm, Nov. 23, 2001, p. 1.
76. Russell Lissau, "Police Hook Pedophiles on Web in Five Seconds," cnn.com/2000/local/westcentral/07/24/ahd.police.web/, July 24, 2000, pp. 1–4.
77. "Law Enforcement Online (LEO) Promotes Law Enforcement Information Sharing," *FBI Law Enforcement Bulletin*, August 2000, Vol. 69, No. 8, p. 21.

# NINE

# Injury and Death Investigations

*The investigation of deaths, whether by accidental or felonious cause, can often be aided by modern technology. For example, the underwater search for missing bodies can be facilitated by sonar tracking devices such as the one shown in the photo from Hennepin County, Minnesota, where deputies are using a side scan sonar unit to attempt to locate a body. (© AP/Wide World Photos)*

## CHAPTER OUTLINE



## CHAPTER OBJECTIVES

1. Describe the four motivational models for classification of homicide.
2. Identify the investigator's responsibilities when responding to the scene of a suspected homicide or assault.
3. Comprehend the importance of personal identification of a victim in a homicide investigation.
4. Outline the major elements in a search for buried bodies.
5. Understand the individual observations used collectively to determine the time of death.
6. Discuss the five most common types of wounds encountered in injury and death investigations.
7. Assess information used by investigators to distinguish between a homicide and a suicide.
8. Outline facts that need to be determined in the investigation of fire deaths.
9. Define stalking, and identify common categories of stalking.
10. Describe what items are needed for a psychological profile.

# INTRODUCTION

The investigation of felonious injuries and criminal homicides can be the most important, yet difficult, responsibility assigned to a police investigator. First, these crimes are viewed as being among the most serious offenses committed in our society. The seriousness is reflected in all state statutes, which impose severe penalties for acts resulting in the grave bodily injury or death of a human being. Second, in the beginning stages of some homicide investigations, the inability to identify the decedent greatly complicates the investigative process and prevents it from moving forward. In all homicides, questions such as "Who were the victim's enemies?" and "Who would benefit most from the victim's death?" must be answered before any significant progress can be made in the investigation. Estimating the time of death also needs to be done early in the investigation.

Third, the interview and interrogation process for the investigator in both felony assaults and homicides can be very difficult. For felony assaults, the victim may be unwilling to cooperate because he or she wants to settle the dispute personally, believes he or she deserved the assault and does not want the perpetrator to be punished, or fears reprisal. Witnesses and other parties who have valuable information about criminal homicides may also fear revenge from the suspect, may fear implicating themselves in the crime, or for other reasons simply may "not want to get involved." Furthermore, once a suspect has been identified, given the gravity of the offense and the punishment that he or she faces, obtaining a confession or at least enough information for an arrest and prosecution can be a formidable task. Finally, criminal homicides, in particular, can generate a lot of media attention and public scrutiny for the department. Pressure to solve the crime from both inside and outside the police agency creates added strain on the criminal investigator.

For these cases, in particular, investigators may need to call on the assistance of experts in the scientific and medical fields. Investigators should create working relationships with specialists such as forensic pathologists, toxicologists, entomologists, and botanists, who can all provide useful assistance to the case. In short, the severity of these crimes warrants that investigators use all available resources in their investigations.

## THE LAW

The various state statutes contain different names for **felonious assaults**—such as aggravated assault, assault with intent to commit murder, and felonious battery—but all have one common legal element, namely, that the assault was committed for the purpose of inflicting severe bodily harm or death. In most such assaults, a deadly weapon is employed.

Police officials and members of the public often use the terms "homicide" and "murder" interchangeably. In fact, murder is only a part of the broad category of homicide, and **homicide,** defined as the killing of a human being by another human being, is divided into two broad classifications: nonfelonious homicides and felonious homicides.

### NONFELONIOUS HOMICIDES

**Nonfelonious homicides** may be justifiable or excusable. **Justifiable homicide** is the necessary killing of another person in performance of a legal duty or the exercise of a legal right when the slayer was not at fault.

**Excusable homicide** differs from justifiable homicide in that one who commits an excusable homicide is to some degree at fault but the degree of fault is not enough to constitute a criminal homicide. There are two fundamental types of excusable homicide. The first involves death that results from misadventure. This is similar to what may be termed "accidental" death at the hands of another. **Misadventure** is death occurring during the commission of a lawful or an unlawful act when the slayer has no intent to hurt and there is no criminal negligence. An example of misadventure is the death of a person who runs in front of a moving automobile whose driver is unable to avoid the collision.

The second type of excusable homicide involves death that results from self-defense when the slayer is not totally without fault, such as someone who gets in a sudden brawl and has to kill to preserve his or her life.[1]

### FELONIOUS HOMICIDES

**Felonious homicides** are treated and punished as crimes and typically fall into two categories: murder and manslaughter. **Murder** is defined by common law as the killing of any human being by another with malice aforethought. Most states now provide for varying degrees of murder. **Manslaughter** is a criminal homicide committed under circumstances not severe enough to constitute murder, yet it cannot be classified as either justifiable or excusable homicide.[2]

## MOTIVATIONAL MODELS FOR CLASSIFICATION OF HOMICIDE

The identification of a criminal's motives has both legal and investigative implications. By identifying the motive for a crime, investigators can begin to focus investigative efforts in a specific direction. If a motive cannot be identified, the range of possible suspects is broad and the investigation therefore more difficult.

In the late 1980s the agents from the Investigative Support Unit at the FBI Academy joined with the Behavioral Science Unit to begin working on the *Crime Classification Manual* (CCM). In the CCM,[3] classification of homicide by motive includes four major categories: the criminal enterprise, the personal cause, the sexual homicide, and the group cause.[4]

### CRIMINAL-ENTERPRISE HOMICIDE

Criminal-enterprise homicide entails murder committed for material gain. The material gain takes many forms, for example, money, goods, territory, or favors. This category has eight subcategories: contract killing (third party), gang-motivated murder, criminal competition, kidnap murder, product tampering, drug murder, insurance-motivated murder (individual profit or commercial profit), and felony murder (indiscriminate or situational).

### PERSONAL-CAUSE HOMICIDE

Personal-cause homicide is motivated by a personal cause and ensues from interpersonal aggression; the slayer and the victim(s) may not be known to each other. This type of homicide is not motivated by material gain or sex and is not sanctioned by a group. It is the result of an underlying emotional conflict that propels the offender to kill. The victim targeted is very often a person with high mass-media visibility of local, national, or international scope, but victims also include superiors at work or even complete strangers. The victim is almost always perceived by the offender as someone of higher status. Personal-cause homicide has 11 subcategories: erotomania-motivated killing, domestic killing (spontaneous or staged), argument murder, conflict murder, authority killing, revenge killing, nonspecific-motive killing, extremist murder (political, religious, or socioeconomic), mercy killing, hero killing, and hostage murder.

### SEXUAL HOMICIDE

In sexual homicide, a sexual element (activity) is the basis for the sequence of acts leading to death. Performance and meaning of the sexual element vary with the offender. The act may range from actual rape involving penetration (either before or after death) to a symbolic sexual assault, such as insertion of foreign objects into a victim's body orifices. Sexual homicide has four subcategories: organized crime scene murder, disorganized crime scene murder, mixed crime scene murder, and sadistic murder.

### GROUP-CAUSE HOMICIDE

In group-cause homicide, two or more people with a common ideology sanction an act, committed by one or more of the group's members, that results in death. This category has three subcategories: cult murder, extremist (political, religious, or socioeconomic) murder (paramilitary or hostage), and group-excitement murder.

## RESPONDING TO THE SCENE

In responding to the scene of a suspected homicide or assault, fundamental rules must be followed. The officer should proceed with deliberate but not reckless speed. As the officer approaches the scene, he or she should be observant for a suspect fleeing either on foot or by vehicle. The dispatcher may have been able to obtain and relate specific details to the responding officer about the offense and suspect. If not, the officer has to rely on discriminating observations, training, and past experience. The officer should be suspicious of a vehicle being driven away from the crime scene at a high rate of speed or in an erratic manner, an individual who attempts to hide from view, or a person whose clothing indicates recent involvement in a struggle.

# ARRIVING AT THE HOMICIDE SCENE

When the investigator arrives at the scene, formal contact should be established with other official agency representatives. The investigator must identify the first respondent to ascertain if any artifacts or contamination may have been introduced to the death scene. The investigator must work with all people to ensure the scene's safety before entering the scene. The investigator must take the initiative to introduce himself or herself, identify essential personnel, and establish rapport. Before entering the scene, the investigator should identify other essential officials at the scene (e.g., fire, EMS, social or child protective services), explain his or her role in the investigation, and identify and document the identity of the first essential official(s) to the scene (first "professional" arrival at the scene for investigative follow-up).

## DETERMINE SCENE SAFETY

Determining scene safety for all investigative personnel is essential to the investigative process. The risk of environmental and physical injury must be removed prior to initiating a scene investigation. Risks can include hostile crowds, collapsing structures, traffic, and environmental and chemical threats. To prevent injury or loss of life, the investigator must attempt to establish scene safety before entering the scene and should contact appropriate agencies for assistance with particular scene-safety issues.

Upon arrival at the scene the investigator should assess and/or establish physical boundaries; secure his or her vehicle and park as safely as possible; use personal safety devices (physical, biochemical safety); arrange for removal of animals or secure them, if present and if possible; and obtain clearance/authorization at the scene from the individual responsible for scene safety (e.g., fire marshall, disaster coordinator).

While exercising scene safety, the investigator must protect the integrity of the scene and evidence, to the extent possible, from contamination by people, animals, and the elements. Due to the potential scene hazards, the body may have to be removed before the scene investigation can continue.

## CONFIRM OR PRONOUNCE DEATH

Appropriate medically trained personnel must make a determination of death prior to the initiation of the death investigation. The confirmation or pronouncement of death determines jurisdictional responsibilities. The investigator must be certain that appropriate personnel have viewed the body and that death has been confirmed. The investigator should also identify and document the name and organizational affiliation of the individual who made the official determination of death, as well as the time of determination.

Once death has been determined and rescue/resuscitative efforts have ceased, medical and legal jurisdiction can be established.

## PARTICIPATE IN SCENE BRIEFING WITH ATTENDING AGENCY REPRESENTATIVES

Scene investigators must recognize the varying jurisdictional and statutory responsibilities that apply to individual agency representatives (e.g., law enforcement, fire, EMT, judicial, legal). Determining each agency's responsibility at the scene is essential in planning the scope and depth of each scene investigation and the release of information to the public. Investigators must identify specific responsibilities, share appropriate preliminary information, and establish investigative goals with each agency that is present at the scene. When participating in the scene briefing, the investigator should locate the staging area (entry point to the scene, command post, etc.), document the scene location (address, mile marker, building name), determine the nature and scope of the investigation by obtaining preliminary investigative results (e.g., suspicious versus nonsuspicious death), and ensure that initial accounts have been obtained from the first witness(es).

## CONDUCT A SCENE WALK-THROUGH

Conducting a scene **walk-through** provides the investigator with an overview of the entire scene. The walk-through is the investigator's first opportunity to locate and view the body, identify valuable and/or fragile evidence, and determine the initial investigative procedures for a systematic examination and documentation of the scene and body. The investigator can also conduct a scene walk-through to establish pertinency and perimeters. Upon arrival at the scene the investigator should reassess scene boundaries and adjust as appropriate; establish a path of entry and exit; identify visible physical and fragile evidence; document and photograph fragile evidence immediately and collect it, if appropriate; and locate and view the body. An initial scene walk-through is essential for minimizing scene disturbance and preventing the loss and/or contamination of physical and fragile evidence.

# ESTABLISHING A CHAIN OF CUSTODY

Ensuring the integrity of the evidence by establishing and maintaining a chain of custody is vital to the investigation. This will save the investigator from subsequent allegations of tampering, theft, planting, and contamination of evidence. Before the removal of any evidence the custodian(s) of evidence should be designated and should generate and maintain a chain of custody for all evidence collected. Throughout the investigation those responsible for preserving the chain of custody should document the location of the scene and the time of the death investigator's arrival at the scene; determine the custodian(s) of evidence, determine which agencies are responsible for the collection of specific types of evidence, and determine evidence-collection priority; identify, secure, and preserve evidence, using proper containers, labels, and preservatives; document the collection of evidence by recording its location at the scene, time of collection, and time and location of disposition; and develop personnel lists, witness lists, and documentation of times of arrival and departure of personnel. It is essential to maintain a proper chain of custody for evidence. Through proper documentation, collection, and preservation, the integrity of the evidence can be ensured. A properly maintained chain of custody and prompt transport of the evidence will reduce the likelihood of a challenge to the integrity of the evidence.

# INVESTIGATIVE TOOLS AND EQUIPMENT

Following are the tools and equipment necessary for conducting an appropriate crime scene investigation in homicide cases: gloves; writing implements (pens, pencils, markers); body bags; communication equipment (cell phone, pager, radio); flashlight; body ID tags; camera (35 millimeter, video, Polaroid), with extra batteries, film, tapes, etc.; investigative notebook (for scene notes, etc.); measurement instruments (tape measure, ruler, rolling measuring tape, etc.); official identification (for yourself); watch; paper bags (for hands, feet, etc); specimen containers (for evidence items and toxicology specimens); disinfectant; departmental scene forms; blood collection tubes (syringes and needles); inventory lists (clothes, drugs, etc.); paper envelopes; clean white linen sheet (stored in plastic bag); evidence tape; business cards or office cards with phone numbers; foul-weather gear (raincoat, umbrella, etc.); medical equipment kit (scissors, forceps, tweezers, exposure suit, scalpel handle, blades, disposable syringe, large-gauge needles, cotton-tipped swabs, etc); phone listing (important phone numbers); tape or rubber bands; disposable (paper) jumpsuits, hair covers, face shield, etc.; evidence seal (use with body bags and locks); pocketknife; shoe covers; trace-evidence kit (tape, etc.); waterless hand wash; thermometer; crime scene tape; first-aid kit; latent-print kit; local maps; plastic trash bags; gunshot-residue analysis kits; boots (for wet conditions, construction sites, etc.); hand lens (magnifying glass); portable electric area lighting; barrier sheeting (to shield body or a specific area from public view); purification mask (disposable); reflective vest; tape recorder; basic hand tools (bolt cutter, screwdrivers, hammer, shovel, trowel, paintbrushes, etc.); body-bag locks (to secure body inside bag); personal comfort supplies (insect spray, sunscreen, hat, etc.); and presumptive blood test kit.[5]

## THE MEDICO-LEGAL EXAMINATION

The medico-legal examination brings medical skill to bear upon injury and death investigations. The medical specialist frequently called upon to assist in such cases is the forensic pathologist. **Forensic pathology,** a subspecialty of pathology, is the study of how and why people die. To become a forensic pathologist, a physician first attends an approved pathology residency program and then attends three years in a strictly anatomic program or five years in a combined anatomic and clinical program. One or two additional years are devoted to studying the pathology of sudden, unexpected, natural death, as well as violent death, in an approved forensic fellowship training program (there are approximately 30 throughout the country). Most programs are centered in major cities that have a large number of deaths from various causes. The most important area of study for a forensic pathologist is death investigation, but some forensic pathology programs also include examination of the living to determine physical and sexual abuse. Physicians specializing in forensic pathology are ordinarily employed by some unit of government and are not in private practice.[6]

## THE AUTOPSY

All violent and suspicious deaths require an **autopsy** to determine the time and precise cause of death.[7] The autopsy may also answer the following questions:

- What type of weapon was employed?
- If multiple wounds were inflicted, which wound was fatal?
- How long did the victim live after the injury?
- What position was the victim in at the time of the assault?
- From what direction was the force applied?
- Is there any evidence of a struggle or self-defense?
- Is there any evidence of rape or other sex-related acts?
- Was the deceased under the influence of alcohol or any type of drug?[8] (The actual analysis will be done by the toxicologist.)

Answers to all or even some of these questions increase the possibility of bringing the death investigation to a successful conclusion.

If any of the victim's clothing is damaged, the investigator should determine whether the damage

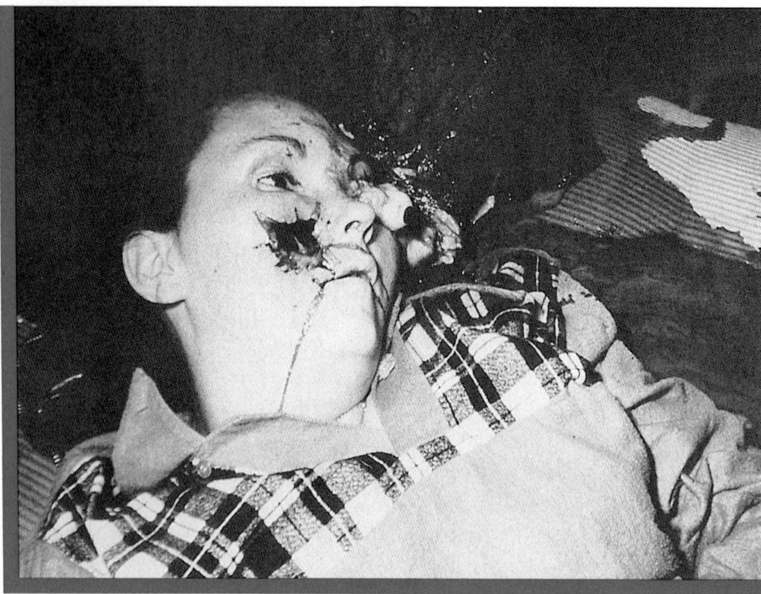

**Photographing the Homicide Scene**
One of the key steps in processing the scene of a criminal homicide is taking photgraphs of the scene and the body. These photographs are important documents in the investigative process and will be critical if a suspect is arrested and eventually brought to trial.

was related to the assault or was caused by hospital or emergency personnel giving emergency treatment. When a determination is made of the cause of the damage, it should be recorded in the investigation report.

The victim should be fingerprinted, even if there is positive proof of identification. If circumstances dictate, palm prints and footprints should also be obtained. They may prove useful if matching prints are later found in the suspect's home, business, car, or some other location. In instances of possible physical contact by the victim with the assailant or contact with some object employed in the attack by the assailant, standard specimens of hair should be removed by medical personnel from the victim's head, eyebrows, pubic area, anus, armpits, legs, and chest.

## IDENTIFICATION OF THE DEAD PERSON

Personal identification is one of the most important functions of an investigation. The inability to identify a deceased person greatly complicates the investigative process. The major problem attending the failure to identify a deceased person is the difficulty in focusing the investigation toward, for example, the victim's enemies or those who would most stand to gain from the death. These and other important questions cannot be answered until the victim's identity is established.

A number of elements contribute to establishing a deceased person's identity, including fingerprinting, forensic odontology, DNA, physical description, surgical history, viewing by possible identifiers, occupational trademarks, and personal belongings. On any unidentified body, fingerprints should be obtained if the hands are in a condition to yield diagnostic prints.[9]

Identification based on examination of teeth, fillings, inlays, crowns, bridgework, and dentures is valuable inasmuch as the teeth are probably the most durable part of the human body.[10] Physical-description data—sex, age, weight, height, build, color of hair, color of eyes, race, amputations, deformities, birthmarks, or tattoos—help in the checking of missing-person reports in an effort to locate individuals who fit the description of the victim.

The medical examiner should search for the presence of evidence of surgery on the victim. In some cases, scars are readily visible, as in the case of an appendix operation. However, in other instances, surgical scars may be completely internal. The medical examiner should also note the surgical removal of any internal organs.

Visual inspection leaves much to be desired for two reasons. First, if the victim has sustained severe facial injuries, they may cause gross distortion of the face. This is also true if decomposition has begun and the face is swollen. Second, this method of identification results in a certain amount of psychological trauma for relatives and friends called on to view the body. Sometimes there is no choice but to use this method, but if other options are available, they should be used.

Valuable indicators may be obtained by close examination of the victim's body, especially the hands. For example, the occupational trademarks of a bricklayer's hands will be distinctly different from those of a clerk. Also, one frequently finds that an auto mechanic has hard-to-remove grease stains under the fingernails. An examination of personal belongings may prove to be of value in establishing where they were purchased or, in the case of clothing, where they were dry cleaned. If the victim was wearing a watch, the internal portion of the watch may possess the unique markings left by the watchmaker who repaired it. In some instances, the victim's jewelry, such as rings or watches, may be inscribed with the victim's initials or personal inscriptions.[11]

### PERSONALITY RECONSTRUCTION FROM UNIDENTIFIED REMAINS

The identification of deceased persons takes on additional difficulty when the body is badly decomposed. However, remarkable work has been done in recent years by scientists in identifying such victims. The following case, investigated by an East Coast police department, provides an excellent example of the state of the art:

THE badly decomposed remains of a human were found in an isolated wooded area adjacent to an industrial park. The crime scene investigation disclosed that the skeletal remains had been dragged a few feet from the location, and it was suspected that this dislocation of the remains resulted from animal activities. An intensive search produced only a few strands of hair, a medium-size sweater, and a few pieces of women's jewelry. The physical remains were taken to the medical examiner's office, where the time of death was estimated to be three to six weeks prior to the discovery of the body. A subsequent review of missing-person reports for the pertinent time period produced no additional clues.

With the question of the victim's identity still unresolved, the remains were forwarded to the curator of physical anthropology at the Smithsonian Institution in Washington, D.C. Based on an examination of the skeletal remains (see photo), it was concluded that the skeleton was that of a white female, approximately 17 to 22 years of age, who was of less-than-average stature. She had broader-than-average shoulders and hips and was believed to be right-handed. Her head and face were long, the nose was high-bridged. Also noted was the subcartilage damage to the right hip joint, a condition that had probably caused occasional pain and suggested occupational stress. An irregularity of the left clavicle (collarbone) revealed a healed childhood fracture.

Local police officials then began a social and personality profile of the deceased based on an analysis of the physical evidence obtained through the crime scene search and related photographs, medical examiner's reports, and reports from the FBI laboratory. In addition, aided by a physical anthropologist from the Smithsonian Institution, a police artist was able to provide a sketch (see photo on page 281). The sketch was then published in a local newspaper, and police officials immediately received calls from three different readers who all supplied the same name of a female whom they all knew. They advised that she resembled the sketch, and they further advised that she had been missing for approximately four months.

A search of the local police files disclosed that the individual with this name had been previously photographed (see photo on page 281) and fingerprinted. These prints were compared with the badly decomposed prints from one of the victim's fingers, and a positive identification was made.

Further investigation by the police determined that the victim was 20 years of age. Associates related that when she had worked as a nightclub dancer, she occasionally had favored one leg. It was further determined that she had suffered a fracture of the left clavicle at age 6.[12]

The lessons learned from this case have significantly contributed to forensic anthropology and crime scene technology. When police investigate a crime scene where skeletal remains are located, extreme caution should be exercised in the search. Because animals may have disturbed parts of the body, the search should be conducted over a fairly large area. It may be significant to know that dogs, coyotes, and hogs consume bones and that rodents gnaw or nibble on skeletal remains. Although murderers may scatter or burn parts of victims, enough bone fragments may survive to be useful for identification. A victim's facial features, however, can be reconstructed only when the skull is virtually complete, with lower jaw and teeth.

Depending on the composition of the ground beneath the remains, there may be an outline of the body. If so, this area should be recorded with precise measurements and photographs, and if possible, plaster casts of the site should be considered.

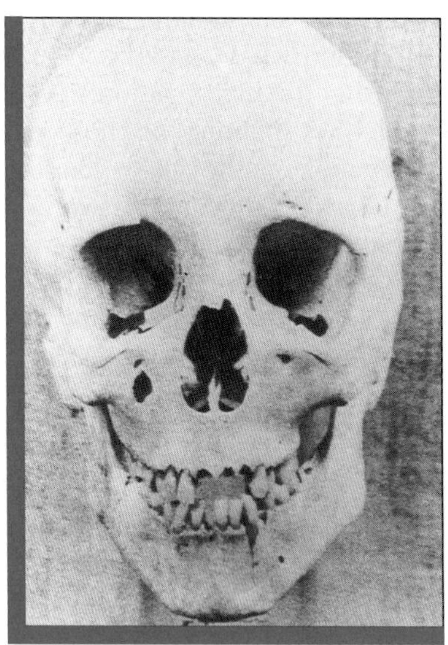

**Skull of Murder Victim**

There are times when the only remains of a dead person are body parts such as the skull. Identifying the actual victim from a human skull may require investigatrors to tap into the talents of physical anthropologists or other scientists. At times, physical anthropologists have provided assistance to police departments in developing sketches of victims for release to the general public to aid in possible identification.

(Courtesy Federal Bureau of Investigation)

### Police Artist Sketch Based on Information Provided by the Physical Anthropologist

The sketch shown here was drawn by a police artist assisted by a physical anthropologist. The physical anthropologist's careful examination of an unidentified human skull was the basis of the sketch.

(Courtesy Federal Bureau of Investigation)

### Police Photograph of Victim

Once the police artist's sketch was released to the media, several people called the police and supplied them the name of a female who had been missing. A search of police files led to a picture and set of fingerprints of the female, which matched with a fingerprint taken from one of the fingers of the badly decomposed body.

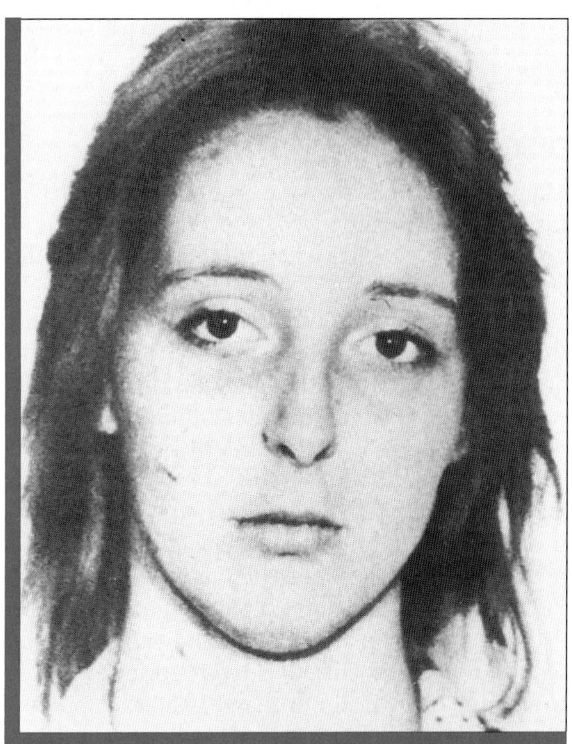

Through the use of such techniques, valuable clues to tissue thickness may be found, indicating whether the deceased was heavy or thin. Clothing sizes are helpful, too. If a skeleton is situated on an incline, a very careful search should be conducted downhill from the original site because the action of rain, wind, animals, and even gravity may have caused some parts to separate from the main skeleton.

The skeletal remains themselves must, of course, be carefully measured and photographed. After the bones have been recovered, the ground under them should be sifted for additional bits of evidence.

The artistic team, having made a thorough analysis of all physical evidence, must then strive to re-create a living likeness.

The case presented above provides an excellent example of what can be accomplished when the police artist, scientist, and investigator pool their talents to reconstruct a face, lifestyle, and personal history—a personality—from skeletal remains.

## THE SEARCH FOR BURIED BODIES

The multitude of problems an investigator faces at the scene of a murder case is compounded when the victim has been buried.[13] Such cases are not common, but they are common enough to warrant training in their proper handling.

### PREPLANNING

One important facet of major case investigations is administrative preplanning, an area that is frequently and unfortunately neglected.

The case supervisor usually is confronted with a series of problems in the initial stage of the investigation, most of them requiring immediate decisions and actions. Often the result is confusion, which can hinder the successful completion of an investigation. However, on-scene confusion can be avoided by good planning of details, from how to run a command post in a wooded area to establishing written policy dealing with written confessions.

## DISCOVERY

Many buried bodies come to light accidentally. Occasionally, information is received that a body is buried at a particular location; these cases will be considered later.

The first duty of an officer responsible for such a case is to establish a list of priority items, despite pressures from both within and outside the department. Officers should not allow themselves to be rushed or misdirected from orderly procedures. On notification of a body's discovery, efforts should be made to safeguard the entire scene before the arrival of law enforcement officials. Generally, a hunter, passerby, or construction worker will find the buried body and notify a police agency. The entire area should be cordoned off, as with any crime scene, and access refused to *anyone* prior to the arrival of the investigator in charge, who can appraise the situation before any damage is done.

If the body has already been removed from the burial site, an archaeologist as well as a forensic pathologist and evidence technician should be called to the scene. This example of preplanning is critical: these experts should have been contacted previously and contingency plans formulated so that they are on call when the need arises. Generally, they are enthusiastic about such an opportunity, especially when the crime scene remains undisturbed.

The archaeologist is proficient in the careful and systematic excavation of a burial site. Most of the excavation phase of the investigation should be left to the archaeologist's direction, while others of the team assist as necessary.[14]

Forensic pathologists are the experts most familiar to law enforcement officers, and their work is becoming more prevalent throughout the country as a replacement for that of the coroner. They can provide valuable and impartial expertise when investigating the various forms of death.

Unless some extremely unusual circumstances exist, there is generally no need to hurry at this stage. If, for example, the weather is inclement, guards should be posted about the area until the weather improves. If there is need for immediate excavation, the erection of a tent over the site should be adequate. (This item should be included in preplanning equipment.) The same rule would apply during hours of darkness. Nothing is to be gained, and all may be lost, by a premature excavation. After the area is secured, all team members are assembled, and plans have been completed, the actual work may commence. The golden rule of homicide investigation is never move, touch, or alter anything until it has been noted, sketched, and photographed. This is especially applicable in this type of case.

Prior to a thorough search and processing of the area, the entire site should be mapped. Then the search may continue, both visually and with mechanical assistance (metal detectors and the like), and any items noted, sketched, and photographed.

Photographs should be taken of the entire area, including aerial views if possible. The team can then move in slowly to the actual site. Photographs, both black-and-white and color, are to be taken at intervals up to and including the actual burial site. If possible, as with any discovered body, determine the path taken to the site by the finding party, mark it, and then use *only* this way in for the initial investigation in order to preserve as much of the general area as possible. The photographer should be accompanied by the crime scene technician or investigator, who can note and preserve any item of evidentiary nature on the way to the site—tire tracks, articles of clothing, possible weapons, or anything that might possibly be connected to the crime.

Photographs should not include any persons standing around the scene or any items not originally located there. At the same time, any item of evidence that has been moved, even accidentally, must never be replaced for purposes of photographing. It can never be put back exactly as found, and the fact that it was moved and replaced for photographing could be damaging in subsequent court testimony. Items should be photographed with and without identifying numbers, a scale, and an arrow pointing to magnetic north.

The definition of site is important in the buried-body case. When a grave is dug and the excavated soil is placed near the grave, the surface of the soil is disturbed, so the grave site is considered to be the entire disturbed area. If an average-size body had been buried, the entire site of grave and disturbed section would easily measure 6 feet wide and 8 feet long. The depth of the excavation generally depends on soil composition and the amount of time the subject spent burying the body.

When the excavated soil is placed on the surface, vegetation may be compressed or broken off. When the grave is refilled, some of this surface vegetation goes back into the grave (see Figure 9–1a and b). Here another expert may be of value—a botanist, who can estimate when the vegetation was damaged by observing the height, distribution, and depth of root systems. If a botanist is not available, measurements and samples should be taken for later study. Damage done by digging and refilling a grave may be visible and measurable for years. If any dead insects are recovered from the grave, an entomologist may give information about them. (An expanded discussion of the role of the entomologist is presented later in this chapter.)

## EXCAVATION

The surface of the grave should now be carefully cleared of extraneous material with a flat-bladed spade or hand trowel so that the boundary of the actual grave may be visible. Then the dimensions should be recorded on the map and excavation begun.

Extreme care should be taken to preserve the exact limits of the original grave or the undisturbed remains, if part of the site has been damaged during the discovery. When the soil was originally removed and then thrown back into the grave, the various layers and compositions of soil and vegetation may have become mixed or mottled. Slow and careful removal of this material may reveal the tool marks made on the outside edges; it may even show the type of blade involved, whether curved or straight, with enough definitions to make tool-mark identification later on.

Before actual excavation and after the photographs have been taken of the burial site in its original condition, additional maps should be made of the site to show both plane and elevation views of the grave and to tie in items found both by horizontal location and depth (see Figures 9–2 and 9–3). Expert help may be available through a county or state highway department engineer or surveyor, who would have the tools necessary to do the job properly. (Items such as a compass, plumb bob, string, protractor, and string level are necessities.)

The soil should be removed in even layers of 4 to 6 inches and all material sifted through two screens. The first screen should have ¼-inch mesh;

**Figure 9-1a** Excavation Site

(**Source:** Courtesy Federal Bureau of Investigation)

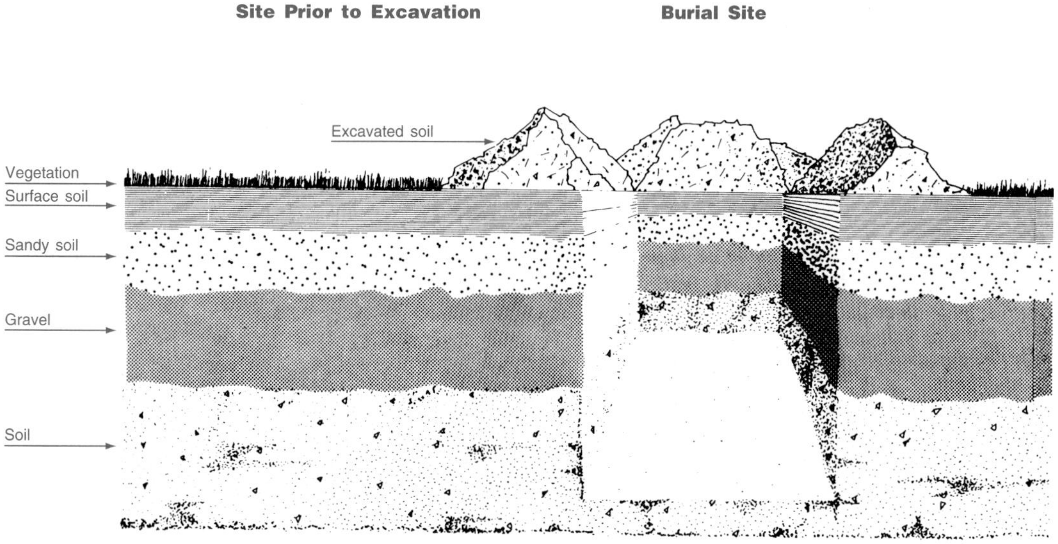

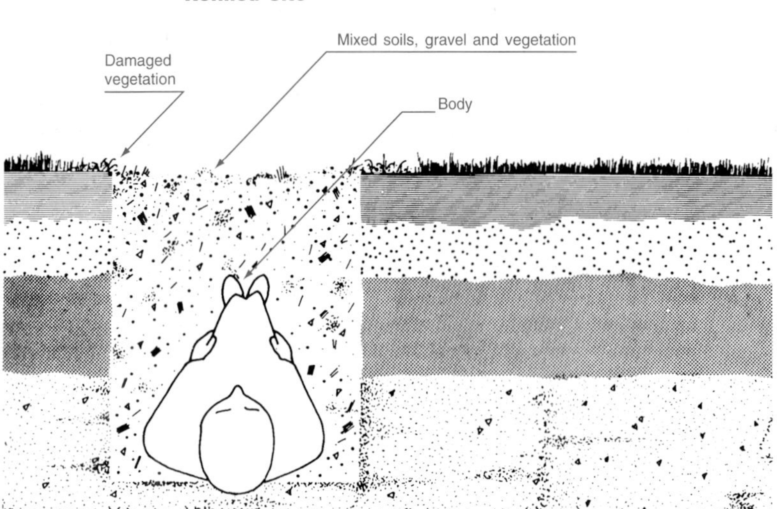


Figure 9-1b Excavation Site

(**Source:** Courtesy Federal Bureau of Investigation)

the second should be standard window screen. As items are located and recovered, they should be plotted on the elevation or side view of the drawings. The completed drawing then accurately reflects the various vertical levels of items in the grave, and the plane view indicates their horizontal distances apart. For comparison, soil samples should be taken where each item is recovered, and each should be accurately documented. Recovered items may still bear latent fingerprints.

## THE BODY

When the body is uncovered and has tissue remaining on it, the forensic pathologist may make an on-scene cursory examination. When this examination is completed and photographs taken, a freshly laundered or new sheet should be available and the remains carefully placed in it to preserve any evidence that is not immediately visible but might be lost in transit. Next, the sheet's edges should be folded over and placed with the remains in a body bag or container for removal to a proper place of autopsy. The sheet and physical evidence should be separately marked for identification and carefully packaged.

After removal of the body, the grave should again be photographed and the area under the body carefully searched and excavated to a depth of several more inches. A metal detector is useful if bullets were fired into the body after it was placed in the grave or to find other metal objects.

## SEARCHING A SUSPECTED AREA

In some cases, information is received through an informant, a citizen, or a confession that a body has been buried, and an approximate location is given. The grave site may be identified precisely or as in an area as small as a city lot or as large as several hundred acres. In all cases, it is critical to establish security quickly around the entire suspected area to prevent access by unauthorized persons.

Good planning is vital. The more that is known about the circumstances of the crime and burial, the greater the chances for locating the site. For example, if it is known or believed that the victim was killed and then buried elsewhere, the grave may not be too far from a road. However, if the killing was alleged to have taken place at the site, then the victim could have been made to walk a considerable distance. The time since the killing affects vegetation around the site and the grave itself; the grave may have sunk, or the surplus dirt may still be in a mound. A botanist can give approximations on damaged plant life that started growing again. Areas of sparse vegetation offer little to go on. Buried insects may be useful. When the surface has been cultivated, the only remaining visual indicator of a grave may be a depression in the surface.

An aircraft, especially a helicopter, may be used before a foot search to spot soil or vegetation disturbance. Thermal infrared photography may be of help. Infrared film detects heat, and a decomposing body emits heat. However, heat ceases to be generated very soon after a body has been buried, and nothing will show on infrared film. Aerial photographs should be taken of the area before a search and, if the search is successful, after it.

When it is necessary to conduct a foot search in a suspected area, mechanical aids are essential, especially if a visual search has been negative. Probing is the first step. Before probing begins, the coordinator of the search must formulate the plans carefully by having a map of the area, making a grid overlay tied into known landmarks, and preparing lanes with stakes and string for the searchers. In areas of woods or heavy underbrush, the establishing of grids is more difficult, and the case coordinator will have to be especially watchful to ensure that locations are checked properly. The area should be probed in not more than 2-foot squares and in a staggered pattern. Coordinators must also keep their maps posted on areas where the search has

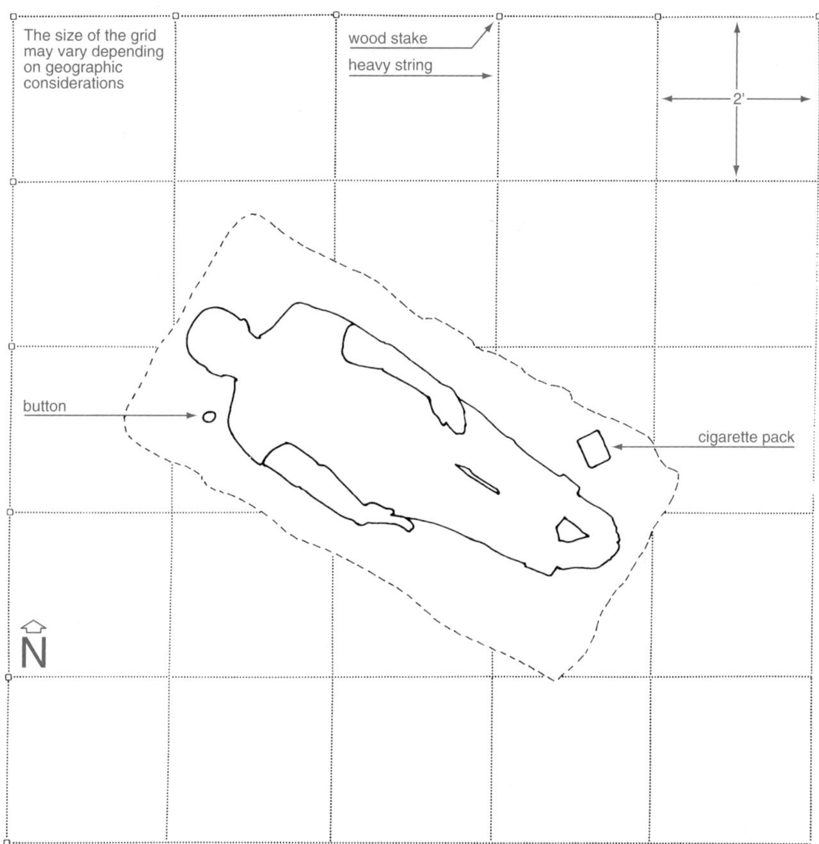


**Figure 9-2**

**Plane View of Site**
Illustration of lanes laid out in north-south direction. Then a cross-grid is laid out when the body is located. Smaller grids may be used when small objects are found in the grave.
(**Source:** Courtesy Federal Bureau of Investigation)

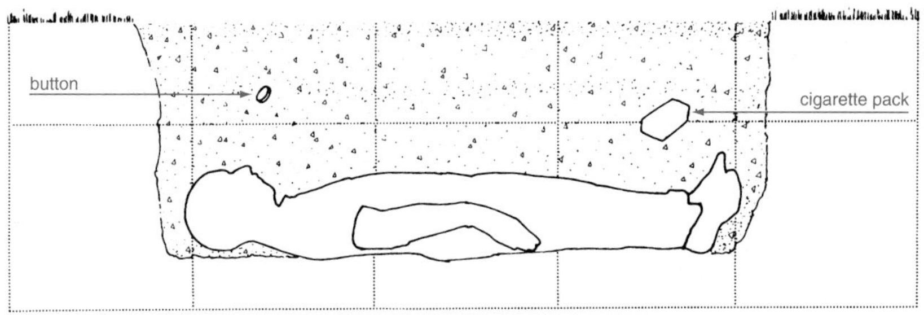


**Figure 9-3**

**Elevation View of Site**
Photograph items of evidence with ruler and north indicator.
(**Source:** Courtesy Federal Bureau of Investigation)

been completed. As probing is difficult and requires the use of generally unused muscles, care should be taken to plan for shifts of searchers and frequent rest periods.

Probing is done with a steel rod, preferably stainless steel, approximately 5⁄16 inch in diameter and 4½ to 5 feet long. A "tee" handle is welded to one end; the other end is sharply pointed. Probing works by detecting differences in disturbed and undisturbed subsurface soil. Investigators need to practice in the immediate area to get a feel for the soil.

When a soft spot is located, indicating a possible grave, the probe should be left in the ground and no further probing done to the area. At that point a second mechanical aid is employed, an instrument to verify the presence of a body without the need of excavating. One such instrument uses methane gas as a primary source of verification. Gases are formed by a decomposing body. The gas formation is minimal at low temperatures, 32° to 35°F, but at these low temperatures the ground also would likely be frozen, and probing would not be attempted. At warmer temperatures, gas forms.

After a suspected site is located, a temperature-sensing probe is inserted and a reading is taken to adjust the gas instrument to the correct sensitivity. Gases from a buried body penetrate the soil upward in a V shape, with the greatest concentration directly over the body. A probe inserted beside a body or too deeply could therefore miss the gas area. Consequently, several probings are made at different depths to ensure complete coverage (see Figure 9–4). This probe can be an invaluable aid in checking suspected areas without an excavation at each one. It can also be used to check under concrete—roadways, patios, floors—after a small hole is drilled through the concrete. This instrument or one like it should be a part of a crime lab's equipment, especially where rural areas are included in the jurisdiction.

## USE OF CADAVER DOGS

Dogs have been used in a variety of forensic contexts because of their superior sense of smell.[15] It is estimated that their ability to smell some scents, particularly fatty acids, is as much as a million times more sensitive than that of humans. Around 1985, a number of police departments in the United States started using specially trained **cadaver dogs** to assist in locating bodies that were either buried in the ground or submerged in water. These dogs, which

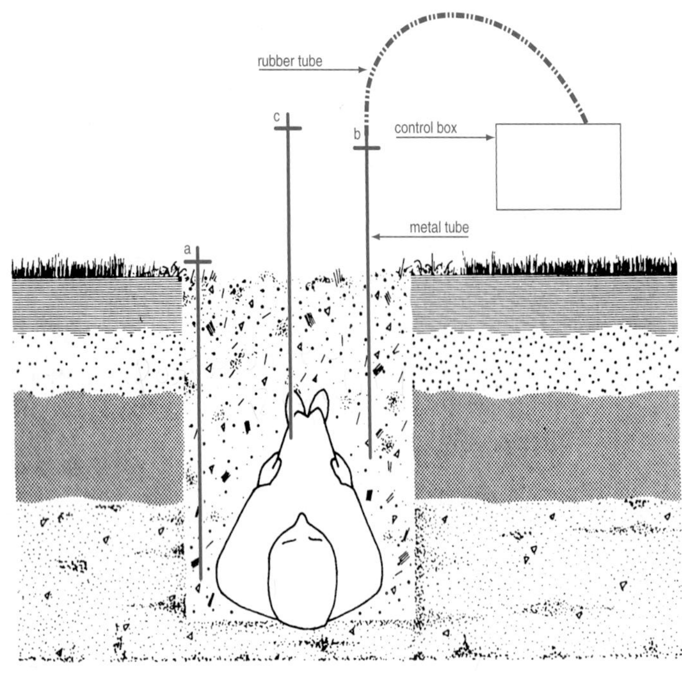


**Figure 9-4** Vapor Detector

(*a*) Missed vapors—too deep. (*b*) Not directly over body, but shallow vapors. (c) Directly over body—strongest vapors.

(**Source:** Courtesy Federal Bureau of Investigation)

are also often used as canine patrol dogs, are trained to become sensitive to the odor of decomposing human remains. There are typically two methods employed to train the dogs. One method is exposing the dogs to decomposing human tissues and bones. Specimens of decomposing human flesh and bone are usually provided by the local medical examiner's office. A second method is exposing the dogs to artificial chemical combinations that mimic the scent well enough for training purposes.[16] Once a geographic area has been identified where a body might be either buried in the ground or submerged in water, the dogs are brought into the area to begin tracking. If the body is submerged in water, a dog is typically placed at the bow of a small boat while the handler sets up a systematic search pattern in order to cover the water area where the body is most likely to be submerged (see photo). Even though the body may be submerged in many feet of water, the gases from the decomposing tissue will still come to the surface, and it is these gases that the dogs detect. When these gases are detected, whether on land or in the water, the dogs will signal by barking, scratching at the surface, or doing a combination of both. Once a suspicious area has been located on the water surface, divers can be called in to search for the body. Officers who have used cadaver dogs for water searches report that such searches are easier to conduct in freshwater than in salty tidal water. However, in spite of this, dogs have been successful in locating bodies in both types of water.

## ESTIMATING TIME OF DEATH

Determination of the time of death or the interval between the time of death and the time that a body is found (i.e., the **postmortem interval**) can be difficult. A forensic pathologist attempts to determine the time of death as accurately as possible, realizing, however, that such a determination is only a best estimate. Unless a death is witnessed, or a watch breaks during a traumatic incident, the exact time of death cannot be determined. The longer the time since death, the greater the chance for error in determining the postmortem interval. There are numerous individual observations that, when used together, provide the best estimate of the time of death. These include body temperature, rigor mortis, livor mortis, decompositional changes, and stomach contents. A thorough scene investigation must also be performed, and environmental conditions should be documented. The environment is

**Use of a Cadaver Dog**

Cadaver dog with two law enforcement officers searching a lake for a missing child. These dogs are specifically trained to assist in locating bodies that were either buried or submerged in water. Even when a body is submerged, the dog can detect gasses from the decomposing tissues rising to the surface of the water.

(Courtesy Bob Westenhouser *Tampa Tribune*)

the most important factor in determining the postmortem interval.[17]

## ALGOR MORTIS

After death, the body cools from its normal internal temperature of 98.6°F to the surrounding environmental temperature. Many studies have examined this decrease in body temperature, called **algor mortis,** to determine formulas that could predict its consistency. Unfortunately, because of numerous variables, body cooling is an inaccurate method of determining the postmortem interval. In general, however, evaluating a decrease in body temperature is most helpful within the first 10 hours after death. During this time, with a normal body temperature and at an ideal environmental temperature of 70° to 75°F, the body cools at approximately 1.5°F per hour.

However, the problem with using the 1.5°F-per-hour calculation is the assumptions that the internal temperature is 98.6°F and the environmental temperature is 70° to 75°F. If a decedent's body temperature is higher than normal because of infection or physical exercise, the body temperature of 98.6°F cannot be used. Furthermore, the outside environment is rarely in the 70° to 75°F range. For example, a body may actually gain heat if an individual expires outdoors during the summer, when temperatures may be greater than 100°F. Conversely, if a person expires in a 25°F environment, rapid cooling will take place.

Nonetheless, if body temperature is measured at a scene, it should be taken by the attending physician on at least two separate occasions before the body is moved. A rectal or liver temperature is the most accurate measurement. The environmental temperature should also be recorded. If these relatively simple procedures are followed, a very crude estimate of the postmortem interval can be made.[18]

## RIGOR MORTIS

After death, the muscles of the body initially become flaccid. Within 1 to 3 hours they become increasingly rigid and the joints freeze—a condition called **rigor mortis** (or postmortem rigidity or rigor).

Rigor mortis is affected by body temperature and metabolic rate: the higher the body temperature, the more lactic acid produced and rigor occurs sooner. For example, a person dying with pneumonia and a fever will develop rigor sooner than a person with normal body temperature. Similarly, if a person's muscles were involved in strenuous physical activity just before death, rigor develops much more quickly. The process is also retarded in cooler environmental temperatures and accelerated in warmer ones.

All muscles of the body begin to stiffen at the same time after death. Muscle groups appear to stiffen at different rates because of their different sizes. For example, stiffness is apparent sooner in the jaw than in the knees. Thus, an examiner must check to see if joints are movable in the jaws, arms, and legs.

A body is said to be in complete rigor when the jaw, elbow, and knee joints are immovable. This takes approximately 10 to 15 hours at an environmental temperature of 70° to 75°F. A body remains rigid for 24 to 36 hours before the muscles begin to loosen, apparently in the same order they stiffened.

A body remains rigid until rigor passes or until a joint is physically moved and rigor is broken. Consequently, in addition to indicating an approximate time of death, body position in full rigor can indicate whether or not a body has been moved after death.[19]

## LIVOR MORTIS

A purplish color that appears under the skin on the portions of the body that are closest to the ground denotes **livor mortis.** The discoloration is caused by the settling of the blood. It may begin as early as a half-hour after death and is pronounced 4 hours after death. The officer who is unfamiliar with this condition could erroneously conclude that the discoloration resulted from an assault. However, there are certain differences between the discoloration caused by lividity and that caused by bruising: A bruise may have swelling or abrasions around the wound, whereas lividity does not; the coloring of bruises may vary, being black, blue, yellowish green, and so forth, but lividity color remains uniform; and bruises may appear on numerous parts of the body, while lividity appears only on the portions of the body closest to the ground, unless the body was removed before the blood completely clotted.

Livor mortis is extremely important for three reasons:

1. When considered with other factors, it may help estimate the time of death.
2. Because the skin must be relaxed and not lying flush against any surface, object, or even clothing folds for the lividity coloration to develop, it may indicate whether the body has been moved or even slightly disturbed after death. It is for this reason that exact measurements, sketches, and photographs must be made at the scene before and while a body is being recovered.
3. The actual coloration of the skin may indicate the cause of death, as in the case of carbon monoxide poisoning, certain forms of cyanide poisoning, or extreme cold, when the color of the lividity is not purplish but a cherry red color.[20]

The following case illustrates that in some instances livor mortis and rigor mortis can provide valuable clues in determining if a body has been moved after death:

A young woman failed to report to work one morning, and a female coworker and close friend became concerned after telephoning the victim's home and receiving no answer. The friend left work and went directly to the victim's apartment. She knocked on the door several times, and when no one answered she tried the doorknob and discovered that the door was unlocked. She entered the apartment and went through the living room and into the bedroom, where she discovered the victim clad in her nightgown lying in bed on her back. She tried to wake the victim but could not. She then called for the police and an ambulance. When the medical personnel arrived, they examined the victim and pronounced her dead. There were no signs of foul play, but the police did discover some barbiturates on the nightstand and suspected, quite correctly as it turned out, that the victim had died of an overdose of drugs. There was a small amount of blood approximately 2 inches in diameter on the front of the victim's nightgown in the pubic area, and as would later be determined, it was blood from her menstrual period.

The body was removed and taken to the morgue, where a visual examination revealed the presence of livor mortis on both the front and back of the victim's body. In addition, rigor mortis had begun and the victim's left foot was extending straight out (see photo). The position of the foot was not consistent with the rigor mortis patterns that would normally result when someone was lying on her back but rather would be consistent with someone who was lying on her stomach. These inconsistencies, along with the presence of the menstrual blood on the front of the victim's nightgown rather than on the back, strongly suggested that the victim had likely been lying

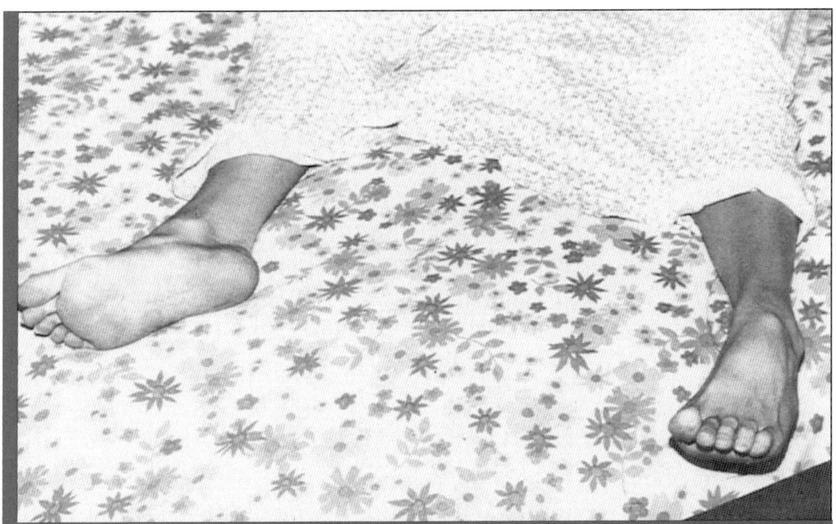

**Rigor Mortis Clues**

Rigor mortis pattern in left foot not consistent with the position of the body when discovered.

(Courtesy Leon County Sheriff's Department, Tallahassee, Florida)

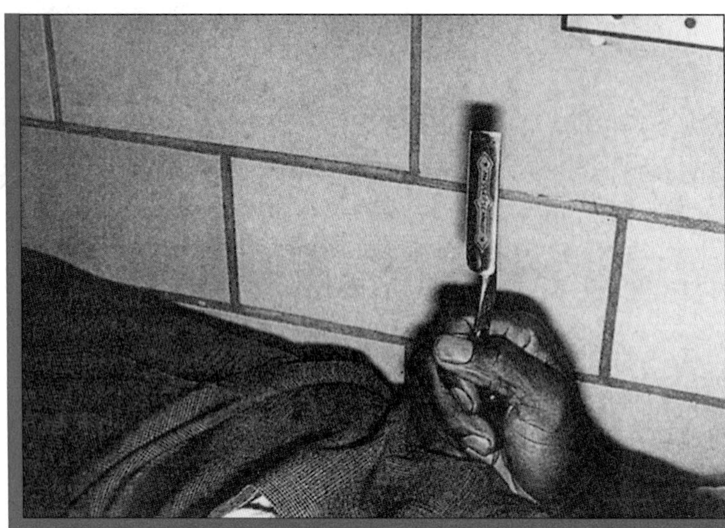

**Cadaveric Spasm**

Cadaveric spasm is a term used to describe the instantaneous tightening of a hand or other body part at the time of death. The literature describes a decedent's hand tightly clutching the weapon at the time of death. However, few actual cases of cadaveric spasm have been documented.

(Dominic J. DiMaio and Vincent J. M. DiMaio, *Forensic Pathology*, copyright 1989, reproduced with permission of copyright owner, CRC Press, Boca Raton, Florida)

face down for several hours after death and that someone had moved the body.

The autopsy revealed no signs of foul play; however, semen was found in the victim's vagina. The cause of death was determined to be from an overdose of drugs used in combination with liquor.

The subsequent investigation and interviews of her friends revealed that the victim was last seen alive in a nearby bar the evening before. She was drinking quite heavily and was also taking some barbiturates. During the course of the evening she met a man who bought her several drinks. Around midnight she left the bar with the male companion. The witnesses who were at the bar were able to provide the police with the name and address of the man. The male companion, who was married and from out of town, provided the police with the following information.

After leaving the bar, he and the woman had gone directly to her apartment. They went to her bedroom, disrobed, and had sexual intercourse in her bed. The man fell asleep and was awakened when the alarm clock went off at 7:30 A.M. When he woke up, the woman was lying face down on the floor next to the bed in her nightgown. He picked her up and put her back in bed. When he realized that she was dead, he became frightened about having to explain what he was doing there, got dressed, and left the apartment.

The fact that this woman's body was moved is really inconsequential in this specific case, but in other instances the knowledge that a body was moved, especially from one location to another, can be profoundly important. This is so because important physical evidence available at the first location may be totally absent from the second location. On occasion, postmortem conditions may provide important clues for determining if in fact the body was moved after death.

## CADAVERIC SPASM

Although firm statements are frequently made concerning the instantaneous tightening of an extremity or other part of the body at the time of death—a **cadaveric spasm,** commonly called a "death grip"—there seems to be a general failure to explain its mechanism. The literature typically describes a decedent's hand tightly clutching a weapon, usually a gun, knife, or razor at the moment of death (see photo). However, the actual cases of cadaveric spasm are few and far between. To date, the precise physiological mechanism of cadaveric spasm remains unknown.[21]

## DECOMPOSITION

In general, as rigor passes, skin first turns green at the abdomen. As discoloration spreads to the rest of the trunk, the body begins to swell due to bacterial methane-gas formation. The bacteria are normal inhabitants of the body. They proliferate after death, and their overgrowth is promoted in warm weather and retarded in cold weather.

The different rates and types of decomposition a body undergoes depend on the environment. Bodies buried in earth, submerged in water, left in the hot sun, or placed in a cool basement appear different after the same postmortem interval. When a body is bloated, epidermal sloughing and hemoglobin degradation begin. Moreover, as bloating continues, hair is forced from the skin. The increased internal pressure, caused by bacterial gas production, forces decomposed blood and body fluids out of body orifices by a process called purging. As the body undergoes skeletonization, the rate of tissue deterioration is dependent on environmental temperature. For example, a body exposed to a 100°F environmental temperature may completely decompose to a skeleton within a few weeks. In contrast, a body in a temperature of 65°F may not skeletonize for many months. In general, a body decomposing above ground for a week looks similar to a body that has been under water for two weeks or has been buried for six weeks. This generalization should serve as a reminder that an uncovered or naked body decomposes more rapidly than a covered or clothed one.

After a body is found, it is usually refrigerated until an autopsy is performed or a final disposition is made. Decomposition slows down or ceases if a body is refrigerated. When the body is exposed to room temperature, decomposition occurs rapidly. Recognition of this accelerated decomposition is particularly important if a person dies in a cold environment and is then moved to a warmer one.

Decomposition may not occur evenly throughout the body. For example, decomposition occurs more rapidly in injured areas. If a person is struck on the head and bleeding occurs only in that area, decomposition may be much more advanced on the head than on the remainder of the body. Fly larvae proliferate during summer, spring, and fall in warm, moist areas of the body such as the eyes, nose, and mouth. Larvae are attracted to injured areas, where they feed on exposed blood proteins and cause accelerated decomposition. Due to the uneven decomposition, it is common to see skeletonization in only part of the body.[22]

## CARRION INSECTS

The forensic entomologist can help in estimating the time of death by examining the various carrion insects, because different carrion insects successfully attack the body at various stages of decomposition and under certain environmental conditions.[23]

The following case illustrates how a qualified entomologist can assist investigations in death cases:

DR. Bernard Greenberg, of the University of Illinois (Chicago), helped solve a double murder that had occurred in the basement of an apartment house. The only evidence he had to work with was a photograph of the bodies at the scene. He examined the photograph, which clearly depicted the advanced pupae (the developmental stage immediately before full maturity) of flies, under a microscope. He then obtained National Weather Service information for the period when the murders took place and determined how long it would have taken the flies to develop to the stage shown in the photograph. His estimate of

### Decomposition

This white female was a victim of suicide by an overdose of drugs. She was dead for approximately one week in an unventilated hot room before her body was discovered. Note that her skin has turned black, there is thickening of the features, liquid and gas blisters appear on the skin, and body fluids have been secreted through the body cavities.

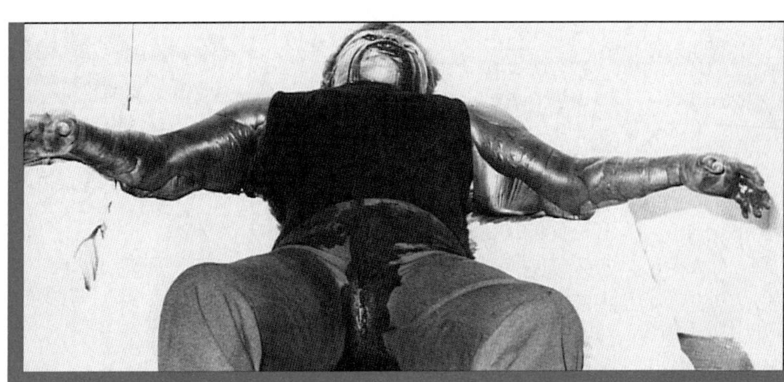

the time of death came within two days of the actual murders, and this evidence linked the suspect to the murders. The suspect was eventually convicted.

## Collection of Carrion Insects from a Clothed and Decomposing Body

When an entomologist is to assist, the investigator must, before examining the body, take several photographs of the body, including close-ups of the areas of insect activity. Then the investigator should record the present air temperature, relative humidity, and environmental setting (shaded wooded area, open field, and the like).

Collection of the insects should begin in the facial area of the decomposing body, because it is the first to undergo degradation by insects. Only an open wound attracts insects more readily. The investigator must be sure to collect as many different insect forms as possible and all life stages (egg, larvae, pupae, and adult).

If time or other complications limit insect collection, the investigator should collect at least fly larvae. With fly larvae the largest specimens should be obtained, because they represent the earliest attacking insects. Examination of the folds in the clothing and underlying soil for pupating larvae or pupae cases is very important. If there is no evidence of hatched pupae cases, one may assume that the fly larvae collected represent the first life cycle.

Collected insect specimens should be placed in a container of preservative solution of 85 percent alcohol. Duplicate samples should be placed in aerated containers with small amounts of soil. Each specimen container should be labeled with the date, time, and area of the body from which it was collected.

As the clothing is removed from the body, many more insects are observable. Efforts should be made to collect samples from within the folds of the clothing. If the decomposed body has been placed in a disaster bag and transported to a morgue, insects still can be easily collected. Some insects drop off the body before it is placed in the disaster bag, but most continue feeding on the body. On opening the disaster bag, the investigator will observe many beetle forms. The darkness in the disaster bag causes the fly larvae to migrate into the various body orifices and the beetles to surface from the clothing and body orifices. The same procedure as described above for collecting insects should be followed after the body is removed from the disaster bag. (See Figure 9–5 for areas of the body from which to collect insects.)

After a complete examination of the body, collected insects should be taken immediately to an entomologist for identification and determination of how long the insects have been feeding on the human remains.

## Collection of Carrion Insects from Human Skeletal Remains

As a body decomposes, it is attacked by many insect forms. Most belong to the insect orders Diptera (flies) and Coleoptera (beetles). These insects feed on decomposing tissue or on other carrion insects.

Some of the carrion insects that attack a body shortly after death themselves die after laying eggs or after being caught in the viscous and putrefying liquids of the decaying corpse. The remains (exoskeletons) of these insects, however, stay intact for long periods in the many skeletal

**Figure 9-5** Body Areas from Which to Collect Insects

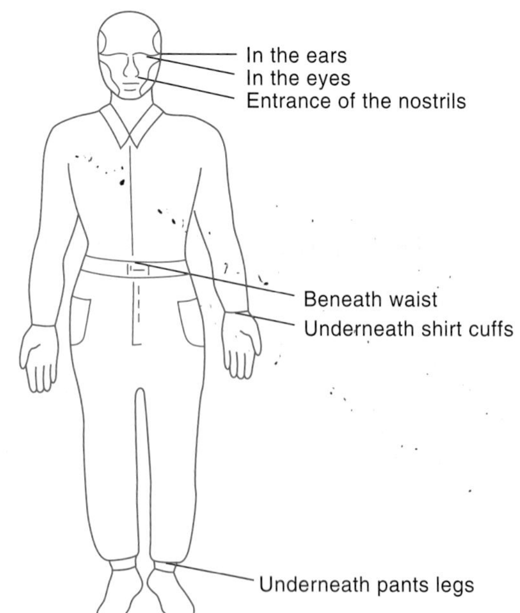


FACIAL AREA IS THE 1ST TO UNDERGO DEGRADASION BY INSECTS

cavities or underlying soil. Close examination of the cavities of a skeleton (before it is removed from the crime scene) usually produces numerous insect remains.

The best area in which to find these remains is the skull, particularly inside the cranial vault (see Figure 9–6). The examination can begin when the skull is placed carefully on a white sheet or on a large piece of paper. Then with forceps and a penlight, the investigator probes the eye orbits, nasal opening, and external auditory meatus for insect remains. The remains most commonly belong to carrion and rove beetles and blowflies. Sometimes the remains are obscured by mud or dried debris within the skull. In this case, the skull should be carefully placed into a plastic bag to avoid the loss of any insect remains. Later the skull should be removed from the bag and washed over a fine screen tray. The mud and debris along with the insect remains will become separated and caught on the screen. After recovery of the insect remains, they should be air-dried, placed in cotton in a small container, and taken to an entomologist for identification. The entomologist can also provide information on the developmental timing of the insects, from which can be inferred a fairly accurate estimation of time since death.

In certain instances, when a consulting entomologist is not available, an investigator must rely on taxonomic and entomological texts for identification of the insect remains. Many states publish entomological bulletins with good information on seasonality, developmental rates, and geographic ranges.

Entomologists may also be able to assist investigators in other types of criminal investigations. The following case illustrates this:

In a case referred to as the "Cocklebur Caper," a woman was raped near her apartment by a man wearing a ski mask. Investigators found such a mask in the apartment of a suspect, who said he had not worn it since the previous winter. A small cocklebur was embedded in the mask, and inside it was a beetle. It was determined that a beetle larva in the cocklebur could not possibly have survived from the previous winter, and therefore the mask had been worn outside during the current summer. The cocklebur was of the same species as others found near the rape scene. The suspect was ultimately convicted of the rape.

## DETERMINING SUBMERSION INTERVAL

Although potentially valuable, the use of aquatic insects in determining submersion intervals at death scene investigations has not been exploited. Aquatic

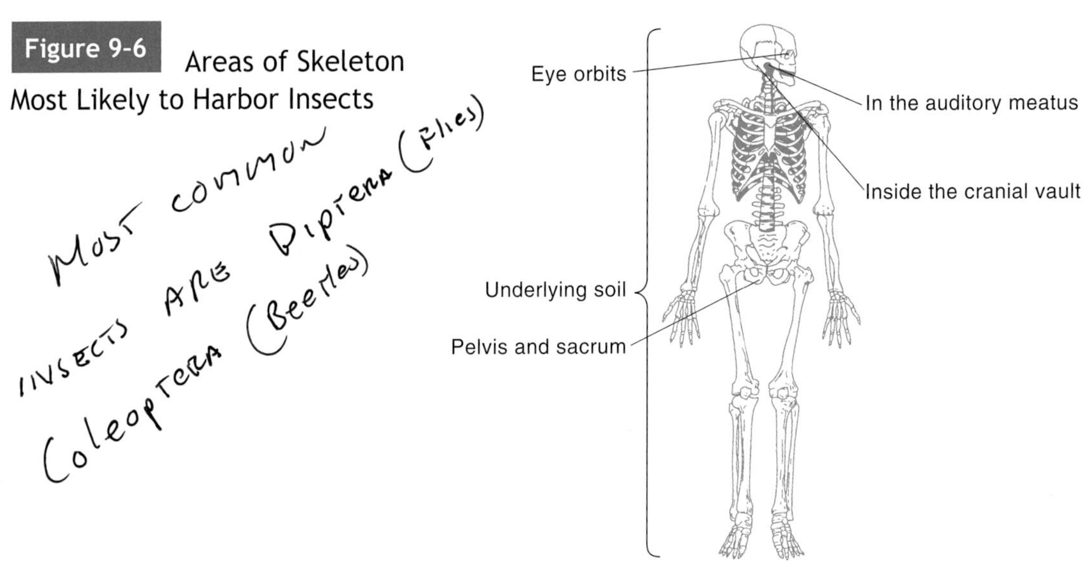


**Figure 9-6** Areas of Skeleton Most Likely to Harbor Insects

environments have no known true specific indicator species, as do terrestrial habitats. The aquatic environment is a new frontier for forensic entomology. The primary problem in aquatic environments, however, is that there are no purely sarcophagous aquatic insects to compare with the common terrestrial indicator species such as blowflies or carrion beetles. Aquatic insects feed primarily on algae, decaying plant matter, and other insects. They do not commonly have access to submerged carrion of large animals; therefore, aquatic insect species have no specialized sarcophagous feeding habits.

In spite of lack of specific indicator species in the aquatic environment, there is tremendous potential for determining the submersion interval for a human body. Some factors that may help determine submersion intervals are progression and development, on the corpse, of algae and aquatic insect "communities"; deposition of silt; presence of specific life stages of aquatic insects; presence of specific structures built by aquatic insects; and presence of species known to inhabit certain microhabitats. The majority of these factors, however, will involve some speculation. The development of an aquatic insect community on a corpse is highly dependent on available colonizers, location of introduced colonizers, geographic location, seasonality, temperature, and current speed. It is recommended that if a body is recovered from the water and some insect colonization is found, the forensic entomologist be called on for assistance.[24]

## EVIDENCE FROM WOUNDS

A basic knowledge of wounds is of great assistance to officers who are responsible for injury and death investigations. It helps them reach preliminary conclusions. The five most common types of wounds encountered by police officers in injury and death investigations are firearm wounds, incised wounds, stab wounds, puncture wounds, and lacerations.

### FIREARM WOUNDS

When a bullet strikes a body, the skin is first pushed in and then perforated while in the stretched state. After the bullet has passed, the skin partially returns to its original position, and the entry opening is drawn together and is thus smaller than the diameter of the bullet. The slower the speed of the bullet, the smaller the entry opening. The bullet passing through the stretched skin forms a so-called contusion ring around the entrance opening as the bullet slips against the skin that is pressed inward and scrapes the external epithelial layers. (See Figure 9–7.) The skin itself, in the contusion ring, becomes conspicuous by drying after some hours. In a favorable case, rifling marks on the bullet leave such a distinct mark in the contusion ring that the number of grooves in the rifling can be counted. The combined section of the contusion ring and entrance opening corresponds to the caliber of the bullet or exceeds it slightly. When a bullet strikes the body squarely, the contusion ring is round; when a bullet strikes at an angle, the ring is oval.

Along with the contusion ring there is another black-colored ring, the "smudge ring," which often entirely covers the contusion ring (see Figure 9–8). It does not contain any powder residues or contamination from the bore of the firearm but consists

**Figure 9-7** A Bullet Penetrating the Skin

Representation of a bullet penetrating the skin. The skin is pressed inward, stretched, and perforated in the stretched condition, after which it returns to its original position. The entry opening is smaller than the diameter of the bullet. Immediately around the opening is the contusion ring, caused by the bullet's rubbing against this part of the skin and scraping off the external layer of epithelial cells.

(Source: Barry A. J. Fisher, *Techniques of Crime Scene Investigation*, copyright 1992, reproduced with permission of copyright owner, CRC Press, Boca Raton, Florida)

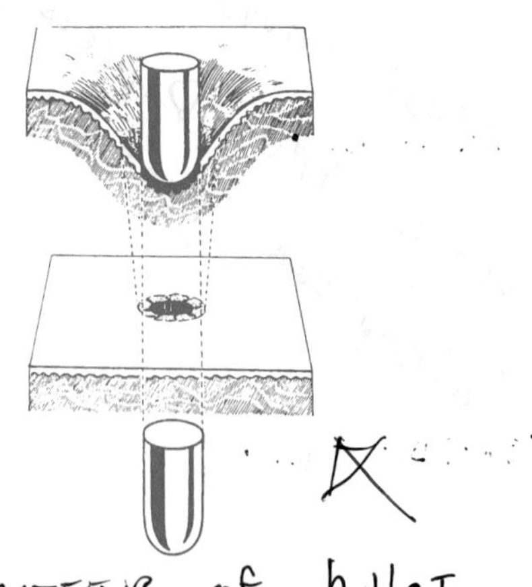

wholly of small particles originating from the surface of the bullet. The smudge ring may be absent in the case of clean-jacketed bullets or a bullet that has passed through clothing.

A bullet passing through the body forms a track that is usually straight but can also be bent at an angle in an unpredictable manner if the bullet meets or passes through a bone. Thus it is not possible to determine with certainty, from observation of the entrance and exit openings, the direction of the weapon when the shot was fired. The direction must be calculated by the pathologist from the results of the autopsy. The velocity of the bullet has a great influence on the appearance of the track: straight tracks indicate a high velocity, and bent or angular ones indicate a low velocity.

In gunshot injuries in soft parts of the body, especially in the brain, the bullet can produce a considerable explosive effect, which is greatest with unjacketed or soft-nosed bullets from large-caliber firearms. Such a bullet may split into several parts, each of which forms its own track, and thus there may be several exit wounds. When such a bullet strikes the head, large parts of the cranium can be blown away and the brain scattered around. A soft-nosed bullet that, before hitting the body, is split by striking against a tree branch can produce a number of regular entrance holes.

A shot through the head is not always fatal. To be immediately fatal, the bullet must either produce a bursting effect or injure an artery of the brain or a vital brain center. A shot through the brain that is not immediately fatal does not always produce unconsciousness. Even when the heart has been perforated by a bullet, it occasionally happens that the injured person lives for several hours retaining some capacity for movement.

It is often difficult to distinguish the exit wound from the entrance wound, especially from a shot at long range with a metal-jacketed bullet, assuming, of course, that the bullet passes through the body intact. In a favorable case, the exit wound may have a ragged appearance with flaps directed outward. To determine the direction of the shot with certainty in such a case, an autopsy is necessary. If the bullet was damaged by its passage through the body or if there was a bursting effect, it is generally easy to determine the exit wound, which is then considerably larger than the entrance wound and shows a star-shaped, ragged character, with flaps

**Figure 9-8** Marks Around an Entry Opening of a Bullet Wound

A diagram showing the marks that may be found around the entry opening of a bullet in a close shot: (*a*) contusion ring, (*b*) smudge ring, (*c*) grains of powder, and (*d*) deposit of powder residue.

(Source: Barry A. J. Fisher, *Techniques of Crime Scene Investigation*, copyright 1992, reproduced with permission of copyright owner, CRC Press, Boca Raton, Florida)

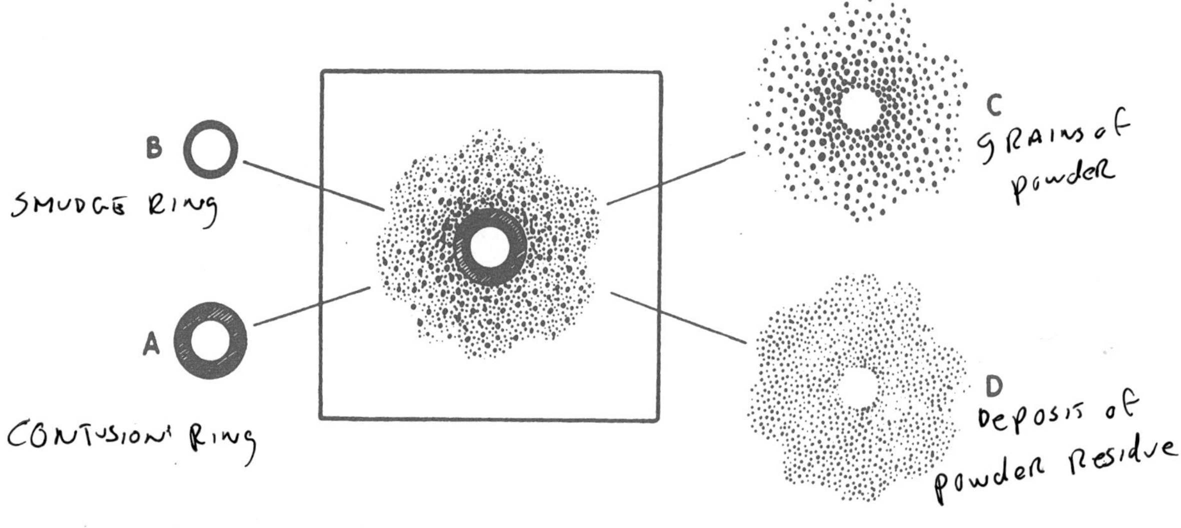

directed outward. Note, however, that in contact shots the entrance wound may be ragged and star-shaped. A bullet that ricochets may strike with its side or obliquely and produce a large and characteristic entrance wound.

## Close and Distant Shots

It is very important to be able to estimate the distance from which a shot was fired. In many cases this fact is the only evidence available that can distinguish between suicide, a self-defense killing, manslaughter, or murder.

In practice, a distinction is made among contact, close, and distant shots. A contact shot is one in which the muzzle of the weapon is pressed against the body when the shot is fired. In a close shot, the distance of the muzzle is less than about 18 inches from the body, whereas a distant shot is one fired at a distance greater than 18 inches.

In the case of a contact shot against an exposed part of the body, soot, metallic particles, and powder residues are driven into the body and can be found there during the autopsy. Blackening, caused by soot and powder, around the entry opening is often absent. A contact shot against a part of the body protected by clothing often produces a powder zone on the skin or in the clothes, and soot, powder residue, and fragments of clothing are driven into the track. In a contact discharge, the entrance wound differs considerably from an entrance wound in a close shot or distant shot. When a contact shot is fired, the gases of the explosion are driven into the track but they are forced out again and produce a bursting effect on the skin and clothes. The entrance wound is often star-shaped with flaps directed outward (see photos on pages 297 and 298). It is also possible, in a contact shot, for the muzzle of the weapon to mark the skin, causing an impression that reproduces the shape of the muzzle of the weapon.

A close shot produces a zone of blackening around the entrance wound of the track, either on the skin or on the clothes. Sometimes the flame from the muzzle has a singeing action around this opening, with hair and textile fibers curled up. The zone of blackening is formed of substances carried along with the explosion gases. When a cartridge is fired, the bullet is forced through the barrel of the weapon by the explosion gases. Only a small amount of the gas passes in front of the bullet. The combustion of the powder is never complete, even with smokeless powder and still less with black powder, and the explosion gases therefore carry with them incompletely burned powder residues, the amount of which decreases as the distance increases. Thus, in a close shot, a considerable amount of incompletely burned powder residue is found on the target. In addition to carrying this residue, the gases also carry along impurities from the inside of the barrel, consisting of rust (iron), oil, and particles rubbed off the bullet. Metallic residues from the percussion cap and cartridge case also occur in the gases of the explosion. If the shot is fired at a right angle to the body, the zone of blackening is practically circular; if fired obliquely, the zone is oval. The extent of the zone of blackening is often difficult to determine by direct observation, and it is often better to photograph it, using infrared-sensitive material, which intensifies the zone of blackening so that its extent is more easily determined. The zone of blackening gives valuable information for determining the distance from which a shot was fired, which may be an important factor in deciding between murder and suicide. It is important that comparative test shots be fired with the same weapon and same type of ammunition as those used in the actual crime.

Close shots with black powder show marks of burning up to a distance of 4 to 6 inches and a distinct deposit of powder smoke up to 10 or 12 inches. Dispersed grains of powder embedded in the target may be detected even at a distance of 3 feet. In distant shots, none of the characteristics of a close shot can be detected.

Powder residues occur on the object fired at in the form of incompletely and completely burned particles. A careful microscopic examination should precede any chemical examination, as it is often possible to establish in this way the shape and color of unburned powder particles and to distinguish many kinds of powder (see Figures 9–9 and 9–10).

Black powder, which consists of potassium nitrate, sulfur, and charcoal, is identified by the presence of potassium and nitrate in the entrance wound. Smokeless powder consists chiefly of nitrocellulose or of nitrocellulose with nitroglycerine and is identified by the presence of nitrite, which can be detected by various microreactions. The grains of smokeless powder are generally coated with graphite and occur in many forms (e.g., round or angular discs, pellets, and cylinders).[25]

### Contact Bullet Wound

Homicidal contact bullet wound of forehead. Notice the charring of the edges and the star-shaped tears of the skin due to undermining of the scalp. In the case of a contact shot against an exposed part of the body (in this case the head), soot, metallic particles, and powder residues are driven into the body and can be found during the autopsy.

(Courtesy Santa Ana, California, Police Department)

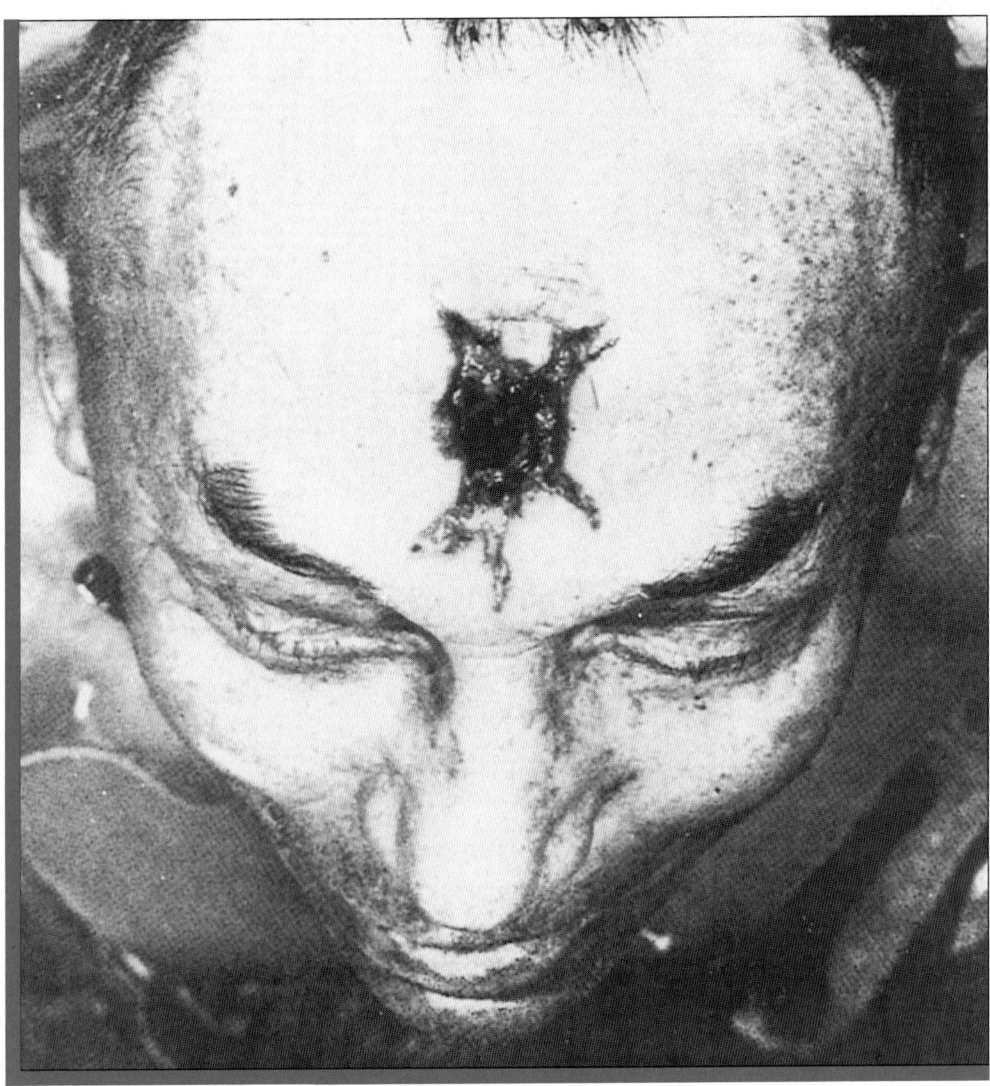

## Shotgun Wounds

A shotgun is a smooth-bore, shoulder-fired firearm and is usually used to fire multiple pellets, rather than a single slug. The most common gauges with their corresponding bore diameters are:[26]

The pellets fired range in size from 0.08 inch for No. 9 shot to 0.33 inch for 00 Buck. A "wad," which may be either paper or plastic, lies between the shot pellets and the powder. Most modern shells use plastic wads. A shotgun shell can contain anywhere from a couple of hundred pellets to nine for 00 Buck, to one large lead slug.

***Entrance Wounds*** From contact to 12 inches, there is a single round entrance 0.75 to 1 inch in

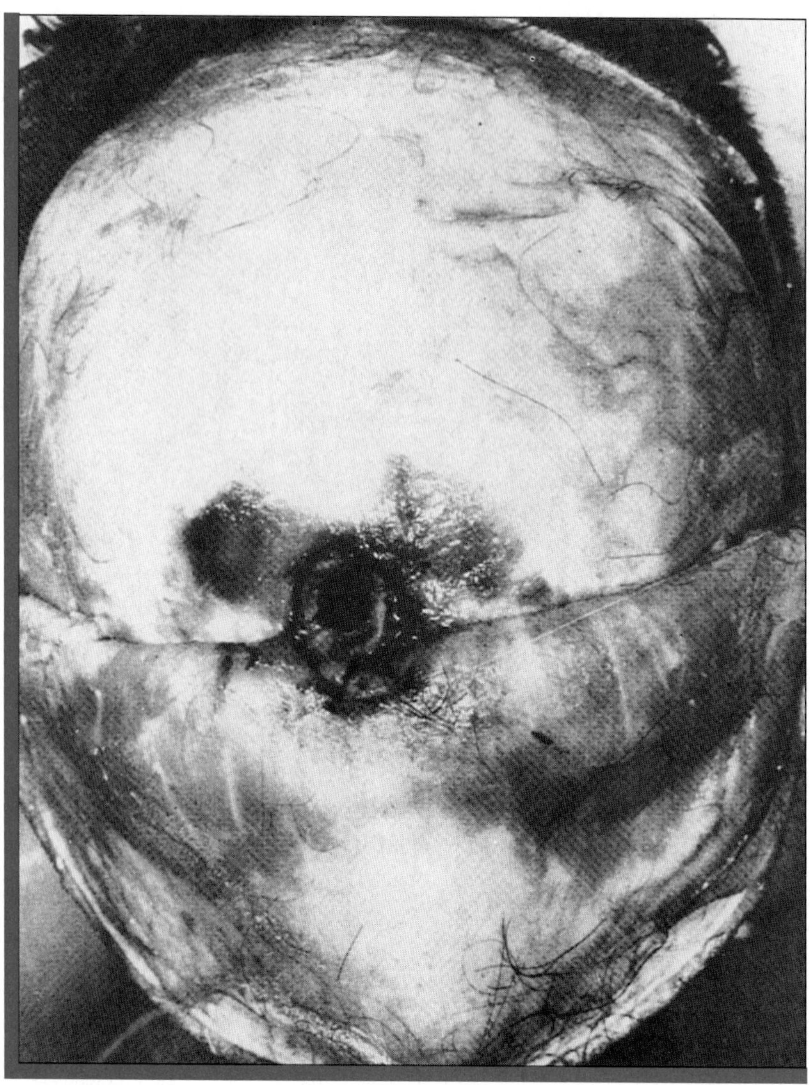

**Contact Bullet Wound Damage to Underlying Scalp Tissue and Skull**
The same bullet wound shown in the photo on page 297, but with the scalp reflected forward over the face. Notice how the blast has undermined the scalp, singeing and blackening the surface of the skull.
(Courtesy Santa Ana, California, Police Department)

diameter. The edge of the wound shows an abrasion ring. As the distance between muzzle and skin increases, powder tattooing appears. Powder blackening is most prominent at less than 12 inches. Powder tattooing is considerably less dense than it is in pistol wounds (see photo on page 300).

When pellets are discharged at between 3 and 6 feet of range, the single entrance wound widens to 1.5 to 2 inches in diameter and shows "scalloping" of the edges. At about 6 feet, the pellets begin to separate from the main mass of pellets. Beyond 10 to 12 feet, there is great variation in the spread of the pellets.

***The Wad*** At close ranges, the wad will be propelled into the body through the large single entrance wound. Beyond 10 to 15 feet, the wad will have separated from the pellets and will not enter. However, it may mark the body. The gauge of the shotgun and the size of the pellets can be obtained from the wad and pellets, respectively. On occasion, a plastic wad may be marked by the choke or irregularities at the end of the barrel, making ballistic comparison possible.

***Range Determination*** Range determinations can be made later if the size of the shotgun pattern

**Figure 9-9** Firearm Discharged at Close Range

Close shot, short distance. The diagram shows both incompletely burned powder grains and smoke deposits in the zone of blackening. The powder grains are concentrated immediately around the entrance hole.

(Barry A. J. Fisher, *Techniques of Crime Scene Investigation*, copyright 1992, reproduced with permission of copyright owner, CRC Press, Boca Raton, Florida.)

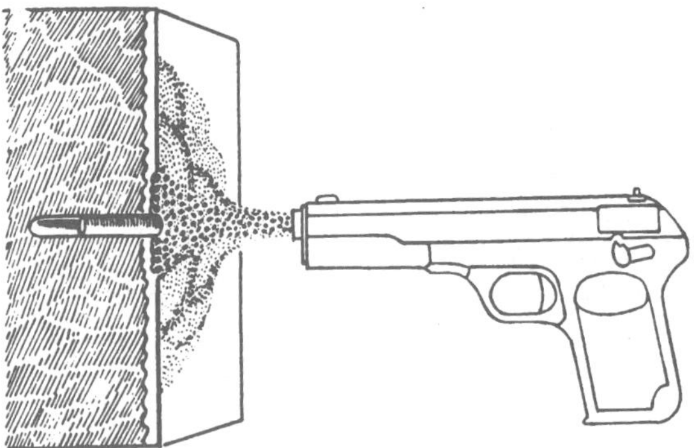

was described at autopsy and duplicated on paper. The same weapon with the same type of ammunition must be used in duplication of the pattern if accurate results are desired. Range formulas do *not* work.

X-ray patterns of the shot in the body are useless for range determinations, as are patterns on the body in which the shot first struck the target.

**Figure 9-10** Firearm Discharged from a Distance

Close shot, greater distance than in Figure 9–9. The diagram shows unburned powder grains, but no smoke deposits, in the zone of blackening.

(Barry A. J. Fisher, *Techniques of Crime Scene Investigation*, copyright 1992, reproduced with permission of copyright owner, CRC Press, Boca Raton, Florida.)

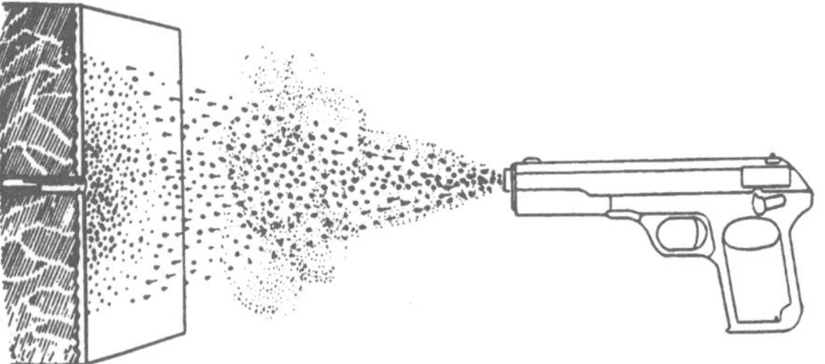

The size of the shot pattern on the body depends primarily on the choke of the gun. The type of ammunition and barrel length are secondary factors. The size of the pellet pattern is independent of the gauge of the shotgun, and an increase in gauge just increases the density of the pattern.

***Exit Wounds*** Shotgun pellets very rarely exit except when used as instruments of suicide in the region of the head.

## Firearm Residues

Detecting firearm residues on the hands of an individual may be of great importance in evaluating deaths due to gunshot wounds. Detection of such residues on the hands of a deceased individual is often confirmatory evidence of a suspected suicide.[27]

One of the earliest methods of determining whether an individual discharged a weapon, the paraffin test or dermal nitrate test, was based on the detection of nitrates on the surfaces of the hands. Paraffin was employed for the removal of powder residues from the hands. Diphenylamine was the reagent used to detect the nitrates picked up by the paraffin. This test is no longer considered valid, because no distinction can be made between nitrates of gunpowder origin and those from other sources, which are quite commonly encountered in day-to-day living.

Several years ago, a series of chemical spot tests for detection of metallic components of firearm discharge residues was developed. Such metallic substances originate mainly from the primer, though they can also come from the bullet or cartridge case. Spot tests were developed for the presence of antimony, barium, and lead, substances found in most primers. These tests are inconclusive because they are essentially qualitative rather than quantitative.[28]

The concept of detecting metallic primer components led to more sophisticated approaches now in general use. Compounds of antimony, barium, and lead are used in modern noncorrosive primers. When a handgun is discharged, discrete particulate matter containing these elements is deposited on the thumb, forefinger, and connecting web (the back of the hand holding the weapon). The metallic compounds are removed from the hand, either with paraffin or, more commonly, with cotton swabs saturated with a dilute solution of acid. This material is then submitted for analysis.

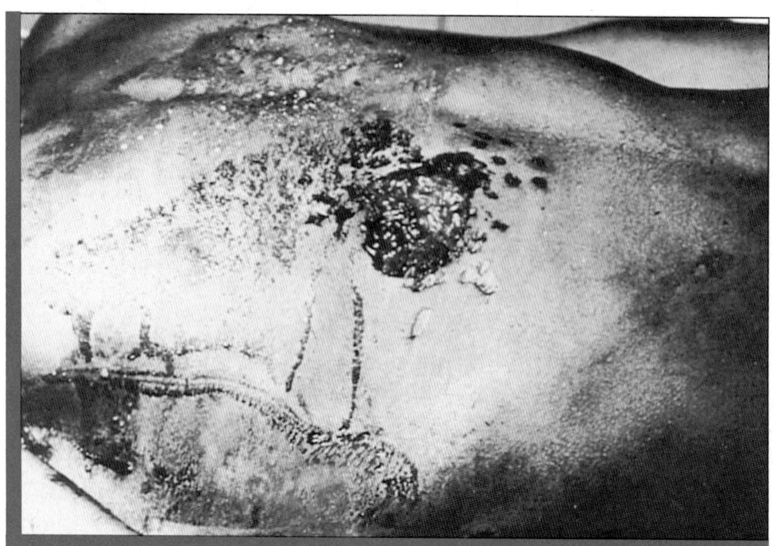

**Close-Range Wound from a 12-Gauge Shotgun**

In shotgun entrance wounds, the characteristics of the wound vary based upon the distance between the muzzle and the skin. For example, from contact to 12 inches, the edge of the wound shows an abraion ring. As the distance increases, powder tattooing appears. This photo shows that powder tattooing is considerably less dense than it is in pistol wounds.

***Atomic Absorption Analysis and Neutron Activation Analysis*** The two methods for the detection of firearm discharge residue that have received the greatest attention in recent years are atomic absorption analysis and neutron activation analysis. However, atomic absorption analysis has emerged as the test of choice, in part because the necessary equipment is less expensive. Most modern crime laboratories now offer atomic absorption analysis. Both methods of analysis have been employed to detect the trace elements of antimony and barium deposited on the hands when a gun is discharged. Atomic absorption analysis, however, is also able to detect lead deposits in gunshot residue, thus giving it one more advantage over neutron activation analysis.[29]

***Removal of Gunshot Residue*** Whatever the system of analysis to which the pathologist has access, the procedures for removal of firearm discharge residues from the hand are the same. The solution most commonly used is of dilute acid. Four cotton swabs are used to remove the firearm discharge residues from the hands. Two swabs are used on each hand; one for the palm, the other for the "back" of the hand. The swabs of the nonfiring hand and the palm of the hand suspected of discharging the weapon act as controls. A control swab dipped in the acid also should be submitted as a blank. Cotton swabs with plastic shafts should be used. Those with wood shafts should not be used because the wood may be contaminated with metallic elements. Because wood shows great variation in the concentration of such elements, no blank can be used.

If a person has discharged the handgun, firearm discharge residues should appear only on the back of the hand that fired the weapon, not on the palm of that hand or on the other hand. Some people, because of their occupations, may have high levels of barium, antimony, or lead on their hands. Thus if the back of the hand were the only area submitted for examination, a misleadingly positive report would come back. If analysis reveals firearm discharge residues only on the palms, it strongly suggests that the individual's hands were around the weapon at the time of the discharge or were trying to ward off the weapon. However, in suicide, high levels of residue often show up on the nonfiring palm when that hand is used to steady the weapon by grasping the barrel and receiving the muzzle or cylinder discharge.

It must be realized that determining whether an individual fired a gun cannot be based on absolute quantities of primer residue on the hands. Rather, it is based on contrast of the levels of these compounds from right to left and from palm to back.

## INCISED AND STAB WOUNDS

The **incised wound**—more commonly referred to as the "cutting wound"—is inflicted with a sharp-edged instrument such as a knife or razor.

The weapon typically employed in inflicting both incised and stab wounds is a pocketknife, although kitchen knives are also common. In comparison with shootings, fewer cutting assaults result in death, largely because the perpetrator's intention was to injure or disfigure rather than kill the victim. Cutting wounds are often found on the arms, face, and legs. Even in these "friendly" cuttings, as they are sometimes referred to, death may occur. When the victim does die from a cutting wound, it generally is found around the throat. The severity of most incised wounds is directly related to the shape and sharpness of the weapon, the part of the body being cut, and the amount of force used in striking the victim. The incised wound is typically narrow at the edges and gaping at the center, with considerable bleeding (see photo). The inexperienced investigator may conclude that a gaping incised wound was inflicted by a large cutting instrument. However, a small knife with a honed blade is capable of causing very severe wounds.

Most frequently, death is caused after a stab results in severe damage to a vital organ, internal bleeding, shock, or secondary infections that develop several days after the attack. Any of these factors may itself be fatal; they often occur in combination. The shape, size, and keenness of the blade all determine a wound's shape and depth, as does the manner in which the knife is thrust into and pulled out of the body. One noticeable aspect of multiple stab wounds is their different shapes when made with the same knife. The proximity of the wounds in a multiple-stabbing assault may be helpful in determining the actions of the victim prior to death. If the wounds are concentrated within a small region of the body, then there is a good possibility that the victim was immobilized at the time of the assault, that is, held down, asleep, or intoxicated.

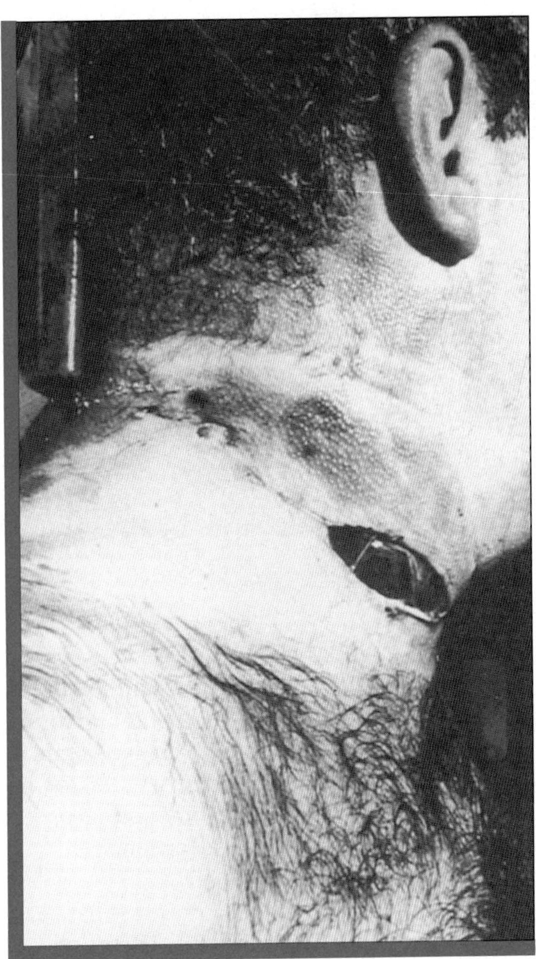

**Incised Wound Inflicted with a Knife**
Note the wound is narrow at the edges and gaping in the middle. Such wounds also typically bleed a lot. Incised wounds are often inflicted with a sharp-edged instrument, such as a knife or razor. These wounds are often found on the arms, face, and legs.
(Courtesy Federal Bureau of Investigation)

## PUNCTURE WOUNDS

The weapon most frequently used in assaults resulting in **puncture wounds** once was the ice pick. It is less common today. Leather punches and screwdrivers also are capable of producing puncture wounds, which are normally small and have little or no bleeding (see photo on page 302). Such wounds can be easily overlooked, particularly if they are in hairy parts of the body. Infliction of a puncture wound produces death in the same way as do stab wounds.

## LACERATIONS

When used in an assault, clubs, pipes, pistols, or other such blunt objects can produce open, irregularly shaped wounds termed **lacerations.** Such wounds bleed freely and characteristically are accompanied by bruising around the edges. There is no necessary relationship between the shape of the wound and that of the weapon employed. Occasionally, such force will be used in an attack that an impression of the weapon is left on the victim's

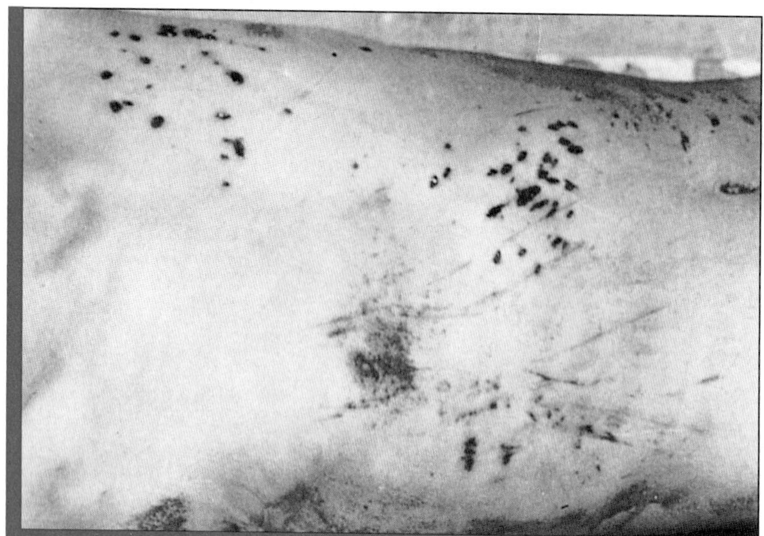

**Puncture Wound**
This victim received multiple ice-pick stab wounds. Leather punches and screwdrivers are all capable of producing puncture wounds. As there is often little bleeding, this wound can easily be overlooked, particularly if it is on a hairy part of the body.

skin. Most frequently, when death results from an assault in which lacerations were inflicted, the cause is severe head injuries. Laceration wounds may be inflicted accidentally, as in the case of an intoxicated person who falls and strikes his or her head against a curb or step. In some instances, circumstances may appear more suspicious:

**CHECKING** the back doors of businesses at about 9:30 P.M., an officer found the proprietor of a jewelry store dead at the open rear entrance to his store. He had sustained a large laceration on his forehead and had bled considerably. It appeared that a murder had taken place during a robbery or burglary. Careful processing of the scene yielded traces of blood and one small skin fragment from the brick wall near the rear entrance.

Nothing was established as missing from the business. The medical examiner found the cause of death to be a heart attack. The head laceration contained minute traces of brick. Thus a reconstruction of events showed that as the owner was closing his business, he suffered a heart attack and convulsions, striking his head against the brick wall. The lacerations he suffered made it look as though he had suffered a fatal head wound.

The severity, extent, and appearance of injuries due to blunt trauma depend on the amount of force delivered to the body, the amount of time over which the force is delivered, the region struck, the amount (extent) of body surface over which the force is delivered, and the nature of the weapon. If a weapon deforms and/or breaks on impacting the body, less energy is delivered to the body to produce injury, since some of the energy is used to deform and/or break the weapon. Thus, the resultant injury is less severe than would have been the case if the weapon did not deform and/or break. If the body moves with the blow, this increases the period of time over which the energy is delivered and decreases the severity of the injury.[30]

For any given amount of force, the greater the area over which it is delivered, the less severe the wound, because the force is dissipated. The size of the area affected by a blow depends on the nature of the weapon and the region of the body. For a weapon with a flat surface, such as a board, there is a diffusion of the energy and a less severe injury than that due to a narrow object, for example, a steel rod, delivered with the same amount of energy. If an object projects from the surface of the weapon, then all the force will be delivered to the end of the projection and a much more severe wound will be produced. If a blow is delivered to a rounded portion of the body, such as the top of the head, the wound will be much more severe than would be the case if the same force is delivered to a flat portion of the body, such as the back, where there will be a greater area of contact and more dispersion of force.[31]

## DEFENSE WOUNDS

**Defense wounds** are suffered by victims attempting to protect themselves from an assault, often by a knife or club. These wounds are commonly found on the palms of the hands, the fingers, or the forearms (see photo). In the most aggravated form, the defense wound may sever one or more fingers.

## STRANGULATION WOUNDS

### Ligature Strangulation

In **ligature strangulation,** the pressure on the neck is applied by a constricting band that is tightened by a force other than the body weight. Virtually all cases of ligature strangulation are homicides. Females predominate as victims. Suicides and accidents are rare. The mechanism of death is the same as in hanging, occlusion of the vessels that supply blood and thus oxygen to the brain. Consciousness is lost in 10 to 15 seconds.[32]

Ligatures used range from electric cords, neckties, ropes, and telephone cords to sheets, hose, and undergarments (see photos on page 304). The appearance of a ligature mark on the neck is subject to considerable variation, depending on the nature of the ligature, the amount of resistance offered by the victim, and the amount of force used by the assailant. The ligature mark may be faint, barely visible, or absent in young children or incapacitated adults, especially if the ligature is soft (e.g., a towel) and removed immediately after death. If a thin ligature is used, there will be a very prominent deep mark encircling the neck. Initially, it has a yellow parchmentlike appearance that later turns dark brown.

In ligature strangulation, in contrast to hangings, the ligature mark usually encircles the neck in a horizontal plane often overlying the larynx or upper trachea. When a wire or cord is used, it often completely encircles the neck. There may be a break in the furrow, however, usually at the back of the neck, where a hand has grasped the ligature and tightened it at that point. Aside from the ligature mark, abrasions and contusions of the skin of the neck are usually not present. They may occur, however, if the assailant places his or her hands beneath and around the ligature and twists it, tightening it around the neck, or if the victim claws at the neck in an attempt to remove the ligature or relieve the pressure. If there is more than one loop of the ligature around the neck, there may be bruising of the skin if the ligature pinches the skin between two loops.

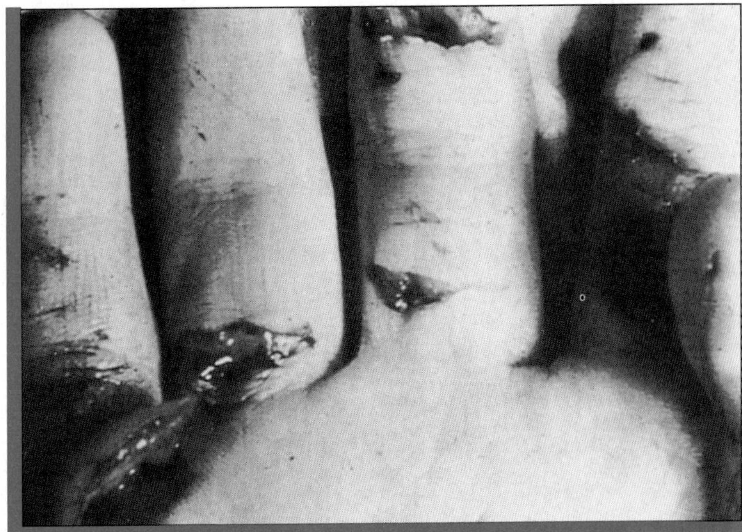

**Defense Wounds**
This victim received severe defense knife wounds on the hands while trying to stop his assailant from stabbing him to death.

### Death by Ligature Strangulation

Victim strangled with (*a*) telephone cord and (*b*) boot lace. The face is congested with numerous petechiae. A horizontally oriented ligature mark overlies the larynx, encircling the neck.

(Source: Dominic J. DiMaio and Vincent J. M. DiMaio, *Forensic Pathology,* copyright 1989, reproduced with permission of copyright owner, CRC Press, Boca Raton, Florida.)

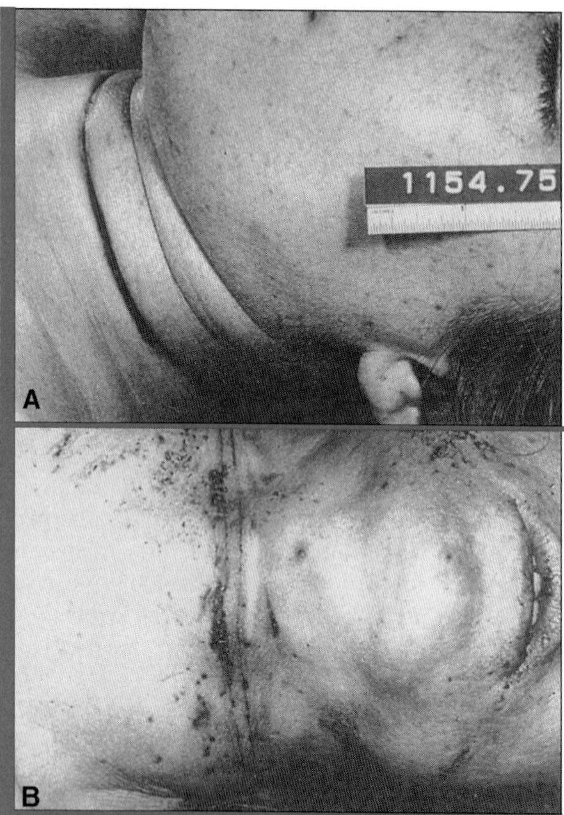


## Manual Strangulation

**Manual strangulation** is produced by pressure of the hand, forearm, or other limb against the neck, compressing the internal structures of the neck. The mechanism of death is occlusion of the blood vessels that supply blood to the brain. Occlusion of the airway probably plays a minor, if any, role in causing death.

Virtually all manual strangulations are homicides. One cannot commit suicide by manual strangulation since as soon as consciousness is lost, pressure would be released and consciousness would be regained.

In most cases of manual strangulation, the assailant uses more force than is necessary to subdue and kill the victim. Hence, marks of violence are frequently present on the skin of the neck. Usually, there are abrasions, contusions, and fingernail marks on the skin (see photos on page 305).

While in most manual strangulations, there is evidence of both external and internal injury to the neck, in some cases there is no injury, either externally or internally. For example, one medical examiner reports seeing three women in a three-month period who had been manually strangled. The first woman showed absolutely no evidence either externally or internally; the second showed congestion of the face with fine petechiae of the conjunctivae and skin of the face, but no evidence of injury to the neck, either externally or internally;

### Death by Ligature Strangulation

(*a*) Ligature strangulation with cloth band; ligature marks on anterior and lateral aspects of neck. (*b*) Close-up showing vertically oriented pattern to cloth.

(Source: Dominic J. DiMaio and Vincent J. M. DiMaio, *Forensic Pathology,* copyright 1989, reproduced with permission of copyright owner, CRC Press, Boca Raton, Florida.)

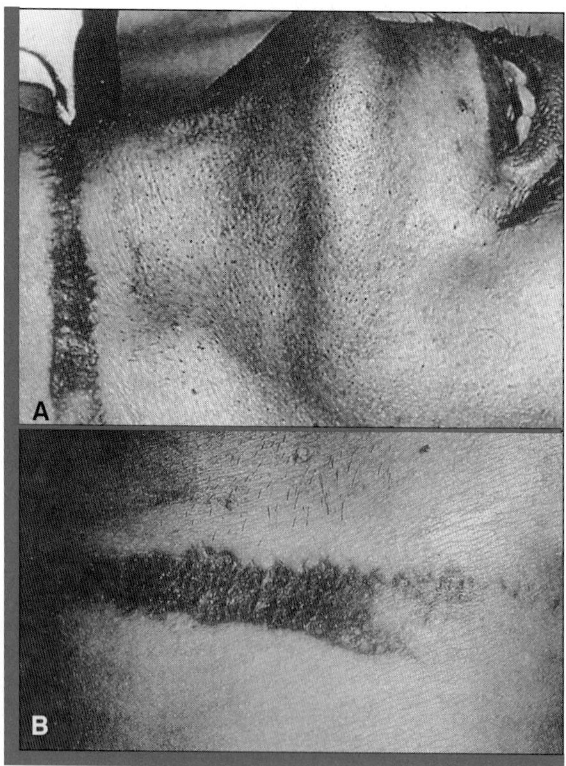

and the third victim showed the classic evidence of injury: abrasions and scratches of the skin with extensive hemorrhage into the muscles of the neck. All three women were killed by the same individual. All three had blood alcohol levels above 0.30. The modus operandi of the perpetrator was to meet a woman in a bar, buy her liquor until she was extremely intoxicated, and then go off with her and have intercourse. He would then strangle her. At the time he strangled them, the women were unconscious due to acute alcohol intoxication, so a very minimal amount of pressure was necessary. He would place his hand over their necks and push downward, compressing the vessels of the neck. In the last case, the individual regained consciousness and struggled, with the resultant injuries. The perpetrator admitted having killed a number of other women in the same way over past years in a number of states.

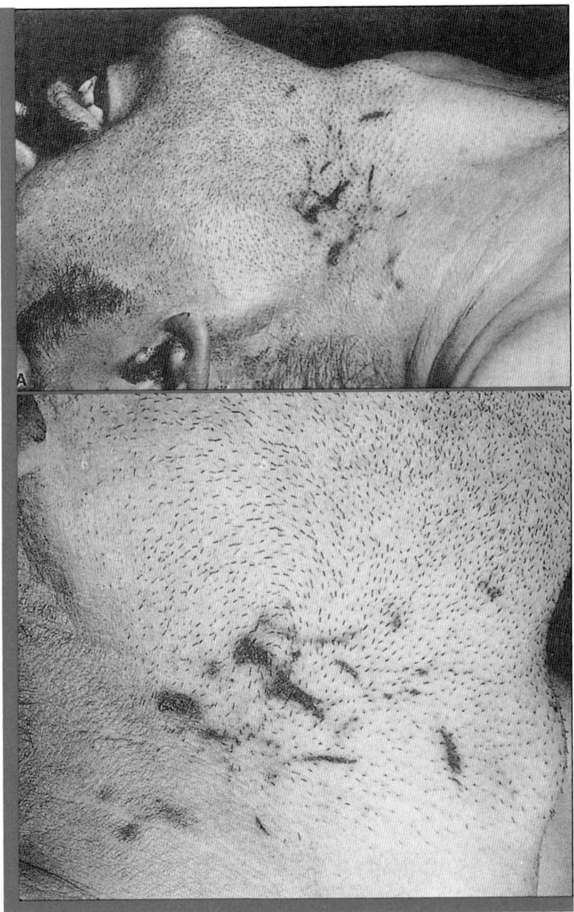

**Death by Manual Strangulation**

(*a* and *b*) Manual strangulation with fingernail marks and scratches on side of neck. Manual strangulation is caused by pressure of the hand, forearm, or other limb against the neck, compressing the internal structure of the neck. Virtually all manual strangulations are homicides.

(Source: Dominic J. DiMaio and Vincent J. M. DiMaio, *Forensic Pathology*, copyright 1989, reproduced with permission of copyright owner, CRC Press, Boca Raton, Florida.)

In manual strangulation, the victims are usually female. When they are male, they are often highly intoxicated. It is suggested that in all manual strangulations, a complete toxicological screen be performed.

## THE UNCOOPERATIVE VICTIM

Officers sometimes find victims uncooperative in identifying assailants and in providing details about offenses. If a victim is uncooperative, the reason is often one of the following:

- The assailant is a husband or boyfriend, wife or girlfriend, whose arrest would undo an arrangement from which the victim benefits.
- The victim wants to settle the dispute personally.
- The victim believes that he or she deserved the assault and therefore does not want the assailant punished.
- The victim fears revenge if charges are pursued.

The uncooperative victim creates both legal and investigative difficulties. All states consider felony assaults to be crimes against the people of the state; thus the state is legally considered the aggrieved party. Technically, the victim has no legal right to decide whether the offense will or will not be prosecuted. This decision is the prosecutor's. However, many prosecutors are reluctant to pursue the prosecution of a felony assault when the victim is going to be uncooperative, especially when the victim's injuries are not critical and when the parties involved are related. Because victims often do not know that the usual practice is not to prosecute such cases, they may be uncooperative or even fabricate a story about how the offense occurred. The officer's concern is to get the uncooperative victim to provide facts about the crime.

**Figure 9-11** Common Types of Wounds

| Type of Wound | Characteristics |
|---|---|
| Firearm: | |
| Contact (muzzle against body) | No blackening around entry; star-shaped, often with flaps directed outward |
| Close (less than 18 inches) | Blackening around entry; grains of powder and deposits of powder residue |
| Distant (18 inches or more) | None of above characteristics appear |
| Incised | Cutting wound inflicted with sharp-edged instrument, wound typically narrow at ends and gaping in middle with a great deal of blood |
| Stab | As above; manner in which knife is thrust into and pulled out of body can result in wounds of different shapes made with same knife |
| Puncture | Can be caused by ice picks, leather punches, and screwdrivers; result in small wounds with little or no blood |
| Lacerations | Open, irregularly shaped wounds, caused by clubs, pipes, pistols and other blunt instrument wounds accompanied by bruising and bleeding |
| Defense | Commonly found on palms of hands, fingers, and forearms |
| Strangulation: | |
| Ligature | Mark encircling neck in a horizontal plane overlying larynx or upper trachea; sometimes broken at back of neck where hand grasped ligature; abrasions and contusions of skin not usually present |
| Manual | Abrasions, contusions and fingernail marks on skin |

There are a number of ways in which this may be done, but they generally revolve around convincing the victim that no legal action will be taken against the assailant. The laws vary from state to state, but in some jurisdictions informal arrangements have been worked out between the prosecutor's office or the courts and the police department, and under carefully controlled conditions the police may be given authority to have the victim sign a complaint-withdrawal affidavit, which includes the following:

- The name of the assailant.
- The victim's total satisfaction with the investigation by the police department.
- The victim's desire not to have the state pursue prosecution.

There are people who object to these practices because they believe such approaches tend to encourage assault offenses. They base their objection on the assumption that persons who commit assaults and are not punished will be encouraged to commit other assaults. Nevertheless, overcrowded court dockets and the difficulties associated with prosecuting cases with reluctant victims obviate any benefits that might derive from the full prosecution of such cases.

Many state and local governments have statutes and ordinances that make it unlawful either to withhold information relating to a crime intentionally or to provide false and misleading information about it. The victim who is uncooperative or who is suspected of not being completely truthful should be advised of such laws and of the penalties associated with them.

Incapacity may also be the cause of noncooperation. If the victim is intoxicated at the time of the initial interview, then it may be necessary to wait until he or she is sober before continuing. Naturally, if the severity of the injury makes any delay in interviewing unwise, then the investigator must proceed with the interview, while recognizing the inherent limitations.

## SUICIDE

For the investigator, a major concern in an apparent suicide case is to make certain that the death was self-induced and not the result of a homicide.

In some cases, the investigator finds overwhelming evidence to this effect at the scene. In other cases, important information about the victim's behavior before death can be obtained from relatives, friends, coworkers, and employers. Suicide is often committed for the following reasons:

- Ill health or considerable pain.
- Severe marital strife.
- A recent emotionally damaging experience, such as an unhappy love affair, separation, or divorce.
- Financial difficulties, including the threat of a much lower standard of living or failure to meet some significant and past-due financial commitments.
- Perceived or actual humiliation.
- Remorse over the loss of a loved one or over an act of one's own.
- Revenge, a frequent motive for adolescents who have serious difficulties with parents and for spurned lovers.[33]

These factors are far from all-inclusive, but the investigator will find a significant number of suicides associated with them. Conversely, if there is an apparent suicide and thorough scrutiny fails to produce a solid motive, then the investigator's suspicion should be aroused. Thus, in all apparent suicides the possibility of a criminal homicide should never be lightly discarded.

## METHODS AND EVIDENCE OF SUICIDE

Nine methods are most commonly employed in suicides: shooting, hanging, ingesting sleeping pills and other pharmaceuticals, drowning, cutting and piercing, ingesting of poisons, inhaling gases, jumping from high places, and intentionally crashing an automobile.[34] These methods are summarized in Table 9–1.

Although all of these can be simulated in the commission of murders, there are important differences in physical evidence that distinguish suicides from murders.

### Gunshot Wounds

It is sometimes difficult to determine whether a gunshot wound was self-inflicted or resulted from the actions of an assailant. However, there are certain indicators that may be helpful in reaching a conclusion. One of these is the location of the wound and the trajectory of the projectile on entering the body. The most common method of committing suicide with a firearm involves the victim's placing a handgun to the temple and firing a shot into his or her head. Frequently, there is no exit wound, and it will be impossible for the investigator to determine the precise angle at which the projectile entered. This information is obtained during the autopsy, but it may be several days before this is performed. The investigator must therefore make some preliminary determination. The following case illustrates some of the points discussed thus far:

#### Suicide by Hanging

Suicide investigations can be very time consuming for investigators. The first major task is to ensure that what appears to be a self-induced death is not a homicide. If overwhelming evidence is not present at the scene, the investigator must gather information about the victim's behavior before death in order to discover possible motives for the apparent suicide.

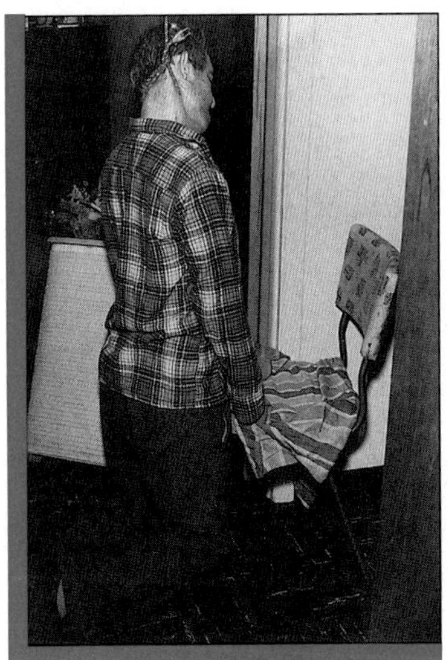

A man telephoned the police hysterically, reporting that his wife had just shot and killed herself. When the police and an ambulance arrived, the victim was dead of a bullet wound in

## Table 9-1 Types of Suicide

| Method | Evidence and Procedure |
| --- | --- |
| Shooting | Most commonly a gunshot to the temple; frequently no exit wound; investigators look for blood spatter, gunshot residue, and hammer-spur impressions on decedent's hands |
| Hanging | Neck is rarely broken; feet or knees are often touching the ground—only when unconsciousness occurs is full weight of body applied to noose, resulting in cutoff of all oxygen to the brain and thus death; petechial hemorrhaging in eyes common |
| Ingesting pharmaceuticals | Interviews with relatives, friends, neighbors can help determine whether death is accidental or suicidal; especially difficult because of possible unexpected interactions among drugs |
| Drowning | Chest cavity and lungs distended and soggy; heart flabby, with right side dilated and filled with dark red fluid; hemorrhaged mastoid cells in ear; water in stomach and duodenum; algae in body; parts of lips, ears, and nose often eaten away |
| Cutting | Investigators look for hesitation marks—series of lesser wounds in general region of fatal wound; self-inflicted throat wounds deep at point of entry, shallow at terminus; not unusual to see a series of cuts on different parts of the body |
| Ingesting poison | May be signs of vomiting & severe damage to lips, tongue, and mouth; victims may employ second means of suicide because death does not occur rapidly; search for poison container critical; details under "Pharmaceuticals," above, also apply |
| Inhaling gas | Carbon monoxide, most common, causes skin to turn bright red |
| Jumping | Witness interviews and assessment of victim's predisposition to suicide critical |
| Intentionally crashing automobile | Usually a single occupant speeding into an off-road obstacle; lack of skid marks; shoe-sole imprints from gas and brake pedals sometimes useful |

her upper left temple. The husband was holding the gun with which he alleged his wife had shot herself. He stated that he had arrived home from work just before the incident but that neither his wife nor their three pre-school-age children had been there. His wife had arrived home a short while later, and she had been drinking heavily. When he questioned her about the whereabouts of their three children, she had told him they were at his mother's home. A heated argument then followed about her neglect of their children, her drinking, and her seeing other men. According to the husband, his wife then slapped him in his face, and he slapped her back. At that point, she walked over to a nearby desk drawer, where he kept a revolver. She removed the revolver from the desk drawer, placed the barrel against her head, fired a single shot, and fell to the floor. No one else was home at the time this incident occurred.

The following set of facts was revealed by the medical examiner's autopsy report:

- The bullet entered the upper left portion of the head, traveled downward through the brain, and continued downward through the victim's body, coming to rest in her chest.
- There were no powder burns present around the gunshot wound.
- Death occurred immediately.
- If the wound had been self-inflicted, the victim would have been holding the weapon in her left hand, at least 2 feet from her head, and would have used her thumb to pull the trigger.

The relatives of both the victim and her husband provided the police with the following information:

- To their knowledge, the victim had not been despondent, nor had she ever previously attempted or discussed suicide.
- The victim and her husband had been having serious domestic difficulties because she was seeing other men, spending the house money

on liquor, and not properly caring for their three young children.

- Both parties were known to have assaulted each other in domestic disputes in the past.

These facts tended to indicate that the victim's death was perhaps not a suicide but a criminal homicide. An interrogation of the husband established what the facts suggested. The husband related that he had been truthful about the events leading up to the argument but that after his wife slapped him, he had angrily knocked her to the floor, removed the revolver from the desk drawer, and gone back to his wife, who was now on her knees. Standing over her, he fired a single shot into her head. After shooting her, he became frightened and fabricated the story of his wife's suicide.

This case demonstrates the importance of two factors in the investigation of an alleged suicide. The first is the importance of the location of the wound on the body and its trajectory on entering the body. Second is the presence or absence of evidence indicating that the victim was predisposed to committing suicide.

In certain rare instances there may be more than one self-inflicted gunshot wound in the body. In an investigation conducted by one police department, a suicide victim was found with three gunshot wounds in the right temple, but the handgun reviewed at the scene had only two spent shells. Although there was considerable physical evidence at the scene, along with supporting historical data to suggest that the death was a suicide, the presence of the three wounds was an apparent contradiction of this evidence. The medical examiner's autopsy report revealed that two of the wounds were gunshot entrance wounds and that one wound was a gunshot exit wound. After establishing the nature of the three wounds, the medical examiner concluded that the victim first fired a single shot into his right temple. The bullet had failed to penetrate the skull, but instead slid under the scalp for a distance of approximately 2 inches and then exited. The victim's second shot into his head penetrated the skull and lodged in the brain. Death resulted as soon as the second shot was fired. The medical examiner hypothesized that the first shot did not penetrate the skull because of the angle at which the victim was holding the gun (see photo at top of page 310).

Hammer-spur impressions can provide important physical evidence, as was the case several years ago when a homicide investigator and a police officer from the Identification Section of the Fairfax County, Virginia, Police Department were dispatched to an alleged suicide scene. On arriving, they were met by a patrol officer, who was conducting the preliminary investigation. The victim was a white male, 61 years of age, who had apparently died of a self-inflicted gunshot wound to the head; the weapon was still in the decedent's right hand. The victim's daughter, who discovered the body when she returned home from work, advised the investigating officer that her father had given her no indication that he was contemplating suicide.[35]

The decedent, found in the master bedroom, was clad in pajamas, lying on his back on the right side of the bed. There was a penetrating gunshot wound to the right side of the head; a 9-millimeter Walther pistol was located in the deceased's right hand. The hammer was cocked, with a 9-millimeter Winchester Western cartridge chambered. On the right thumb of the deceased was a hammer-spur impression that contained class characteristics similar to the hammer spur on the pistol.

The impression was photographed and cast. The impression of the hammer spur of the pistol was found only to be similar in size and shape to the contours of the weapon's hammer. Yet it was one more piece of evidence supplied to the medical examiner to aid in determining whether the cause of the man's death was a self-inflicted gunshot wound (see photo at bottom of page 310).

While examining the scene, investigators look for the usual physical evidence associated with gunshots to be present on the deceased. This includes a contact entrance wound, blood spattered on the hand or hands, and gunshot residue on the hand that held the gun. An item of physical evidence often overlooked is the presence of a hammer-spur impression on the decedent's finger or fingers; this enhances the probability that death was caused by a self-inflicted gunshot wound. Such impressions often are obliterated and subsequently overlooked when inked fingerprint impressions are taken for comparison and identification purposes.

The hammer-spur impression is caused when the firearm is cocked in the single-action phase, causing the principal identifying features of the

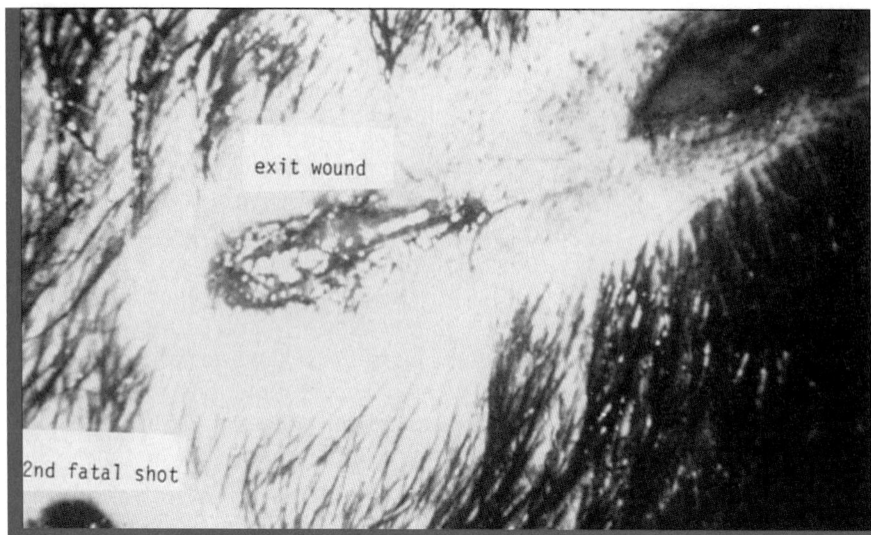


### Self-Inflicted Gunshot Wounds

The medical examiner's autopsy revealed that the wound in the upper right portion of the head was the first gunshot entrance wound. The wound in the center was an exit wound resulting from the first gunshot, and the entry in the lower left portion of the photograph represents the second and fatal self-inflicted wound.

hammer—for example, machine marks, outline of the hammer size and shape, and contours formed through wear and accidental damage—to be impressed into the skin of the finger. If blood circulation stops soon after the fatal wound is inflicted, some or all of the characteristics revealed in the impression may remain for several hours after death on the finger that cocked the weapon.

## Hanging

Certain misconceptions associated with suicidal hangings can lead to erroneous conclusions. The first is that the victim's neck gets broken; the second, that the feet are off the floor. Although both of these conditions *may* occur, they are exceptions rather than the rule. The first misconception is related to the circumstances of legal executions by hanging. In legal executions the procedures involved in inflicting death are intended to result in the neck being broken. This is accomplished by the use of a specific type of noose and a gallows with a trap door through which the person will drop some distance before being abruptly stopped. However, in a suicidal hanging, even when the feet are suspended, the neck is rarely broken, because the fall is not long enough to cause the jolt necessary to break the neck.

It is also common in suicidal hangings for the victim's feet or even the knees to be touching the ground. Occasionally, the victim is found in a sitting position (see Figure 9–12). Finding victims in these positions often creates suspicion because it is difficult for inexperienced investigators to understand how anyone could remain in these positions while slowly choking to death. They might improperly conclude that the victim first was rendered unconscious or was killed and placed in the hanging position. It is more likely, however, that the victim did not slowly choke to death, but rather first tied the

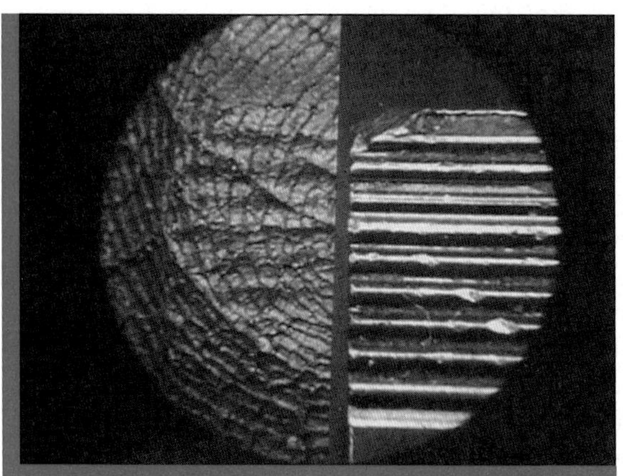

### Comparison Microscope Used in a Suicide Investigation

Comparison-microscope photograph of a hammer-spur impression and the actual hammer spur. Hammer-spur iimpressions can provide important physical evidence in determining whether a death is the result of a homicide or suicide. Hammer-spur impressions found on the thumb of a deceased person can be compared to the hammer spur on a pistol by the use of a microscope.

(Courtesy Federal Bureau of Investigation)

rope around some supporting device and then around his or her neck. Pressure was then applied by the victim either by crouching down, if in a standing position, or leaning forward, if in a sitting position. This initial pressure painlessly cuts off the flow of blood to the brain, which results in unconsciousness. When unconsciousness does occur, the full weight of the body is then applied to the noose, whereupon all oxygen is cut off to the brain and death follows. There is very little physical pain associated with suicides of this type. If one considers that many suicidal hangings occur in victims' homes, then it is logical to expect the feet not to be suspended above the floor because few household objects are strong enough to hold the weight of a fully suspended body or one that has fallen several feet from a chair or table.

Livor mortis is most pronounced in the lower portion of the arms and legs and around the face, lips, and jaw. There may be some variations in the location of the discoloration, depending on the position of the body. When death occurs in this manner, one frequently finds petechial hemorrhaging in the eyes, caused when small blood vessels in the eye bleed because blood pressure increases in response to compression around the neck (see photo on page 312).

Occasionally, hangings are accidental, not suicidal. The individual may have himself in a modified hanging position while masturbating and accidentally fall, slip, and knock over the object on which he is standing, resulting in an accidental death, known as autoerotic death or sexual asphyxia; the intent is sexual rather than suicidal. In these cases, the genitals are exposed and semen may be present. (Chapter 10, "Sex-Related Offenses," provides an in-depth explanation of autoerotic death.) The presence of feces and urine is common because of the total relaxation of the bladder and bowel muscles at the time of death.

**Figure 9-12**

**Various Positions in Hanging**

(Arne Svensson and Otto Wendel, *Techniques of Crime Scene Investigation* (New York: Elsevier-North Holland, 1973) p. 352. Reprinted by permission of the publisher.)

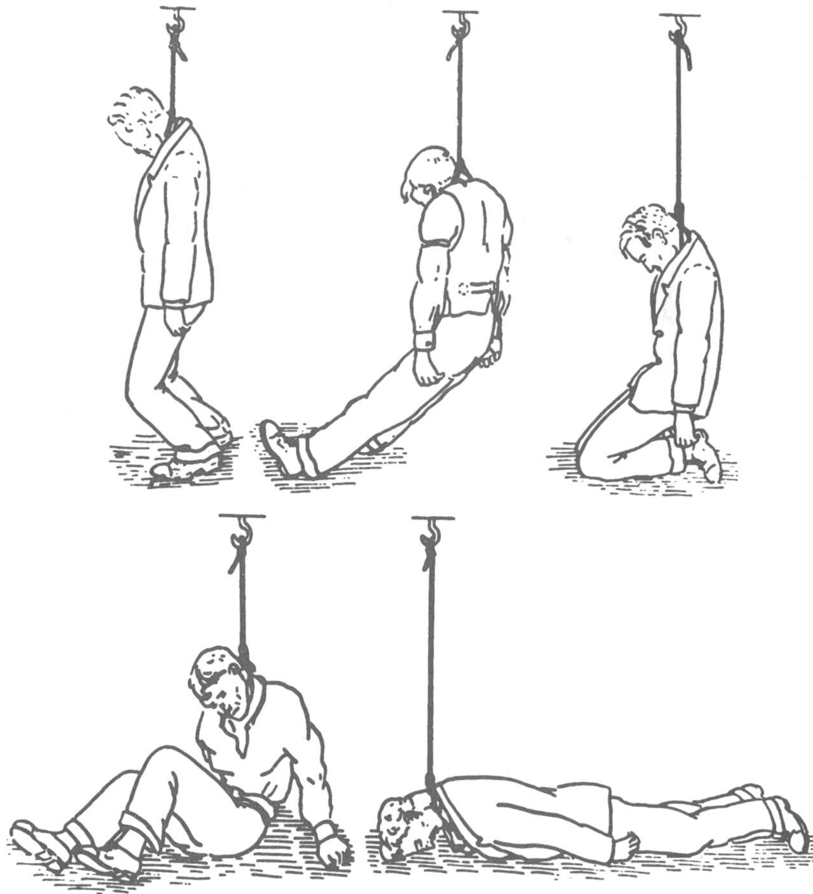

**Petechial Hemorrhaging in the Eye**
Victim of suicidal hanging. In suicidal hangings, investigators often find what is referred to as a petechial hemorraging in the eyes of the deceased. This is a result of the small vessels in the eye bleeding due to an increase in blood pressure caused by the compression around the neck.

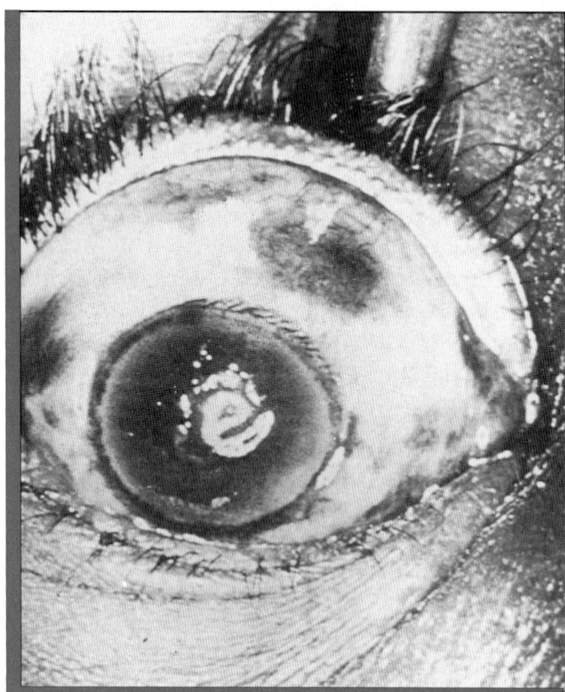

## Sleeping Pills and Other Pharmaceuticals

Sleeping pills and other pharmaceuticals have for many years been a common means of committing suicide. However, some deaths resulting from the ingestion of sleeping pills or tranquilizing drugs may be accidental, not suicidal. The investigator has an obligation to determine whether the death was accidental or suicidal. Certain types of medication, such as barbiturates, when mixed with alcohol have a synergistic effect, which increases the potency of the drug beyond its normal strength. One should not be too quick to decide that the death is a suicide until the investigation is completed and some evidence is available to support this conclusion. In such cases, the investigator should seize as evidence any remaining medication and its container. Frequently, the container identifies the medication, the drugstore dispensing it, and the physician prescribing it. There is always the possibility that the medication was purchased or obtained illegally, thus complicating the investigative process. As in all apparent suicides, the investigator should conduct interviews of relatives, friends, or neighbors who may be able to provide background information about the victim.

## Drowning

The majority of drowning incidents are either accidental or suicidal, but some are homicidal. Three questions must be answered in apparent drowning cases before any final conclusions can be reached: Was the cause of death drowning, or was the victim first killed and then placed in the water? If the cause of death was drowning, did it take place in the water where the body was recovered, or was the victim drowned elsewhere and then placed in the water where found? Was the victim conscious when placed in the water? Answers to these questions can be obtained by external examination of the body by the investigator. External signs to indicate that the victim was alive and conscious when entering the water include:

- Objects clutched in the hand, such as grass or bottom soil commonly found in water.
- Fingernail marks on the palms of the hands.
- White, pink, or red foam extruding from the nose and open mouth.
- Livor mortis most marked in the head and neck because the body settled with these parts in a dependent position.[36]

An internal examination by a physician serves to establish whether death occurred by drowning. The following may be found in drowning cases:

- The chest cavity and the lungs are distended and soggy, with fine foam in the trachea and bronchi.
- The heart is flabby, with its right side dilated and filled with dark red fluid. The blood is unclotted and usually hemolyzed due to the absorption of the drowning fluid into the system.
- The mastoid cells of the ear have hemorrhaged.

- Air embolisms may have formed in the blood in deep-water drownings.
- There may be water in the stomach and duodenum.
- Algae and other marine particles may be found in the stomach and adhering to the sides of the air passages.

In removing the body from the water, the investigator may notice considerable damage to portions of the victim's body, especially around the head and face. This should not cause the investigator to conclude prematurely that the victim was the object of foul play. Some bodies of water contain many rocks and shells; a free-floating body that is subject to strong currents can be repeatedly slammed into and dragged across such objects, causing severe damage, especially to the forehead, knees, tops of the feet, and backs of the hands. In addition, if the water is rich with fish, crabs, and other marine life, these too can cause damage. It is not unusual for the lips, ears, and nose to be at least partially eaten away (see photo). The extent of damage from objects or marine life in the water varies; understanding what can result from their presence minimizes the possibility of premature conclusions. But the investigator must not prematurely conclude, either, that all damage resulted after the body was placed in the water. The medical examiner can help draw conclusions about the actual nature of wounds.

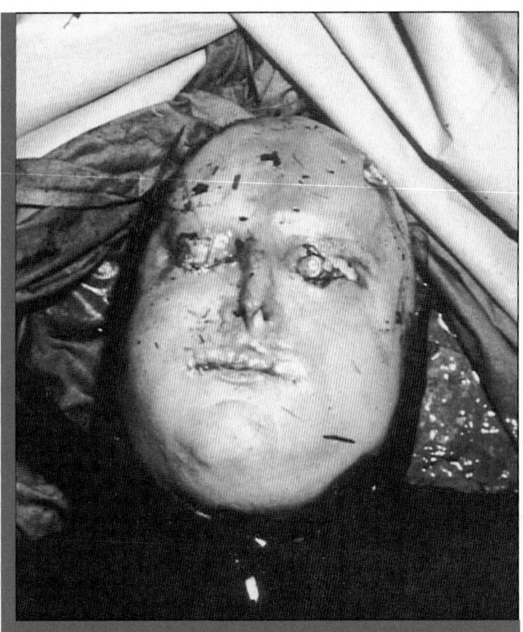

**Decomposition and Marine Life Damage to an Immersed Body**
Damage sustained by the victim in this photograph occurred while immersed in water. Note that the ears and eyelids are completely missing and there is extensive damage to the nostrils and lips. These are areas that are among the first attacked by marine life.

## Cutting and Piercing Instruments

The instruments ordinarily employed in suicides by cutting are razor blades, knives, and occasionally glass. One of the common characteristics of suicides inflicted by these instruments is the presence of hesitation marks. Hesitation marks are a series of lesser wounds inflicted by the victim in the general region of the fatal wound, often the wrists, forearms, or throat. In certain throat cuttings, it may be possible to reach a conclusion about whether the injury was self-inflicted or resulted from an assault. If a wound is self-inflicted, it tends to be deep at the point of entry and to shallow out at its terminus, which is near, or slightly past, the midline of the throat. In homicidal throat cutting, the wound appears deep from the start to the terminus. It is not unusual for a victim to inflict a series of severe cuts on different parts of the body to ensure death. The reasons vary, sometimes involving the influence of alcohol or hallucinogenic drugs. The ingestion of drugs may have been a planned prelude to the act of self-destruction. Self-inflicted wounds can be surprisingly brutal and tend to make people disbelieve that they were self-imposed, particularly when mutilation of the sexual parts is involved. In one case, a 28-year-old man used a single-edged razor blade to cut off his penis. When questioned by paramedics, the man said: "It's just been eating away at me for so long and when I thought about it, I heard voices saying 'Do it, do it.' I was just angry at myself. I had it all planned out and I did it."[37]

## Poisons

The ingestion of liquid poisons is sometimes clear from outward signs on the body. Powerful caustic lyes or acids may produce vomiting once the liquid reaches the digestive tract. There is considerable damage to lips, tongue, and mouth, and there may

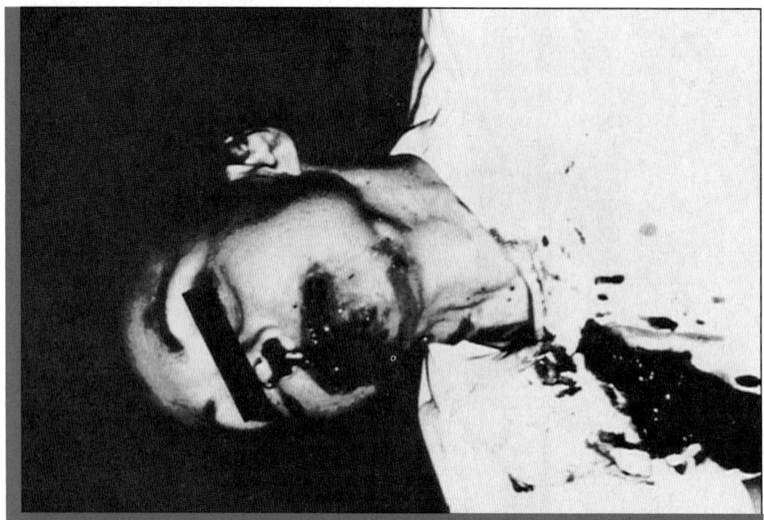

**Ingestion of a Caustic Drain Cleaner**

This victim committed suicide by ingesting a strong caustic drain cleaner. On ingestion, vomiting was induced, thereby causing severe burns to the nose, chin, and chest area.

be blood in the vomitus, along with pieces of the esophagus and stomach (see photo). Usually, death does not occur rapidly, and victims may employ another means of suicide to stop the excruciating pain.

Cases of suspected poisoning frequently pose very difficult problems to the police investigator and to the medical examiner. Many poisons produce symptoms similar to those of certain diseases, a fact that can complicate determination of whether a crime has been committed. However, if there is any reason to suspect poisoning, the investigation must proceed along the lines of a possible homicide, suicide, or accidental death until death due to natural causes is established.[38] To compound the problem, suicides and accidental deaths by poisoning are sometimes very difficult to distinguish from homicide. Alcohol, when consumed with certain medications, may result in an accidental (possibly suicidal) death by respiratory failure. An example is the combination of barbiturates and alcohol. When the alcohol level in the blood reaches about half the lethal dose, most individuals lose consciousness and thus stop drinking. But with the addition of a stimulant, such as an amphetamine, this effect may not occur, and individuals may drink a lethal dose of alcohol before they fall into a coma.

Actually, poisoning is now rarely used in homicides because modern laboratory techniques can readily detect most poisons, thus unmasking an intended homicide. But when it is the method, a wide variety of poisons may be used.

Even though the crime scene investigators seldom can identify the chemical compound that caused the death, they should be alert to the general range of possibilities and the potentially hazardous environmental factors that may be connected with a poisoning.

Regardless of the nature of the incident—homicide, suicide, or accident—the symptoms of death by poison are the same. The field investigator should attempt to determine if the victim had any of the symptoms—vomiting, convulsions, diarrhea, paralysis, rapid or slow breathing, contracted or dilated pupils, changes in skin color, or difficulty in swallowing—just prior to death. These symptoms are general manifestations of systemic poisoning. They do not provide proof of poisoning but can be meaningful in relation to other evidence. Someone who observed the victim just before death provides the best source of information concerning his or her symptoms. If no witness is available, the investigator must rely all the more on physical evidence from the crime scene. Table 9–2 lists common poisons and their associated physical manifestations.

The investigator should collect all available information concerning the activities of the victim during the last three days of life. Information on what types of medication were taken, when the last meal was eaten, and where it was eaten can be very important in determining the type of poison involved.

Table 9-2 Poisons and Associated Physical Manifestations

| Type of Poison | Symptom or Evidence |
|---|---|
| Caustic poison (lye) | Characteristic burns around lips and mouth of victim |
| Carbon monoxide | Victim's skin takes on an abnormally bright cherry-red color |
| Sulfuric acid | Black vomit |
| Hydrochloric acid | Greenish-brown vomit |
| Nitric acid | Yellow vomit |
| Silver salts | White vomit turning black in daylight |
| Copper sulfate | Blue-green vomit |
| Phosphorus | Coffee-brown vomit, onion or garlic odor |
| Cyanide | Burnt almond odor in air, cherry-red lividity color |
| Ammonia, vinegar, Lysol, etc. | Characteristic odors |
| Arsenic, mercury, lead salts | Pronounced diarrhea |
| Methyl (wood) alcohol, isopropyl (rubbing) alcohol | Nausea and vomiting, unconsciousness, possibly blindness |

**Source:** Richard H. Fox and Carl L. Cunningham, *Crime Scene Search and Physical Evidence Handbook* (Washington, DC: Government Printing Office, 1985), p. 126.

Medical history may indicate that death was due to natural causes.

The **toxicologist** is concerned with the identification and recognition of poisons, with their physiological effects on humans and animals, and with their antidotes. Crime laboratories usually provide some toxicological support but vary considerably in the amount and type that they can furnish. However, full toxicological support is always available through a combination of hospital, medical examiner's, coroner's, and criminalistics laboratories. Crime laboratories can direct police to local facilities.

If the investigator suspects that poison was ingested, a diligent search should be conducted for the container. In suicides and accidental poisonings, the container frequently is close at hand. Even though a container appears empty, it should be processed for fingerprints, packaged, marked, and forwarded to the laboratory for examination. Additionally, any other object that could reasonably relate to the poisoning should be collected, such as unwashed dishes and glasses, wastebasket contents, envelopes, and medicine containers.

## Gases

The gas most frequently involved in medico-legal investigations is carbon monoxide. When a death does result from this gas, it is generally accidental or suicidal. Carbon monoxide is found in automobile exhaust fumes and improperly ventilated space heaters in homes. In a death caused by auto emissions, the individual may have started the engine of the vehicle in the garage after closing the garage door or may have extended a flexible hose from the exhaust pipe into the vehicle and then closed the windows.

When death occurs from carbon monoxide poisoning, the victim's skin takes on an abnormally bright cherry-red color because of the reaction of the red blood cells to the gas. The red blood cells have a very high affinity for carbon monoxide molecules (approximately 210 times greater than for oxygen), absorbing them rapidly, thereby making the red blood cells incapable of absorbing oxygen and rendering them dysfunctional in the life-sustaining process. Death generally occurs when the red blood cells have reached a saturation level usually above 40 percent, although this varies; the level sometimes goes higher before death results if the victim is asleep, due to the body's reduced oxygen needs.

## Jumping from High Places

The major question to be answered in death resulting from jumping is whether the victim voluntarily leaped or was thrown or pushed. Often, there are witnesses who can provide this information, suicide notes, or background information that indicates previous suicide attempts or a predisposition toward suicide.

## Vehicle Suicide

The motor vehicle as a means of suicide, although not as common as the means previously discussed, is one that police officers should be sensitive to. Usually a vehicle suicide entails a single occupant speeding into an off-road obstacle. Physical evidence to look for in these accidents includes a lack of skid marks, indications that the person did not attempt to stop or avoid the obstacle, and shoe-sole imprints.

Shoe-sole imprints can provide information regarding the position of a driver's feet and thus his or her action. Most imprints are found on soft-soled shoes, but some are found on hard leather soles. These shoe imprints are clear and indisputable impressions; they are not simply dust marks that may be easily erased by rubbing the sole with a finger or cloth. A word of caution to police officers: These marks are evidence and must be handled properly. For laboratory personnel to properly examine the sole imprint, control pedals from the car need to be removed. Routinely officers should examine the brake, clutch, and accelerator. These pedals, as well as other floor-mounted controls such as the dimmer switch, should be collected as evidence. The photo shows an accelerator pattern imprinted on a tennis-shoe sole. The driver and only occupant committed suicide by crashing the motor vehicle against a concrete support next to a highway. The imprint comparison provided evidence that the act had been a suicide, and follow-up investigation revealed the suicidal tendencies of the deceased.

All of the deceased's clothing should be retained as evidence. Officers need to alert the personnel in the hospital emergency room that the person's clothing must not be discarded, regardless of its condition. Additionally, officers at the crash scene must find any shoes that may have been torn off during the force of the crash and strewn about the area. At the laboratory, the clothing is examined. Marks on shoe soles are compared with patterns on the control pedals.

It is only after painstaking investigation that a death is determined to be a suicide. By recognizing some of the important evidence of self-inflicted wounds, investigators contribute to the successful solution of the death investigation.[39]

**Accelerator Pattern Clearly Imprinted on Tennis-Shoe Sole**

The driver and only occupant successfully committed suicide by crashing her motor vehicle against a concrete support of an elevated highway.

(Courtesy *Journal of Police Science and Administration*)

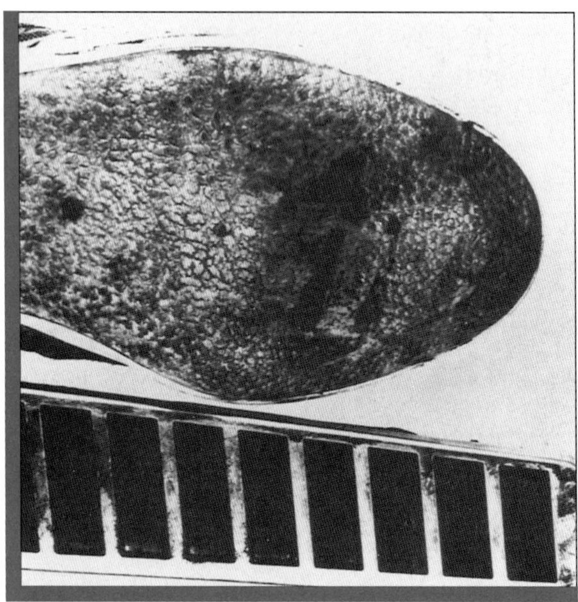

## THE SUICIDE NOTE

Research indicates that suicide notes are not left in most suicides. One study revealed certain facts about persons who do and do not leave notes. Generally there are no differences between the two groups in age, race, sex, employment, marital status, history of mental illness, place of suicide, reported causes or unusual circumstances preceding the act, medical care and supervision, or history of previous suicide attempts or threats. However, the note writers differed from the non-note writers in the methods used to kill themselves. The note writers used poisons, firearms, and hanging more often as a means of death than did the non-note writers.[40]

## GENDER DIFFERENCES IN SUICIDAL BEHAVIOR

Studies of suicide in the United States indicate that the suicide rate is higher for men than for women, whereas the attempted suicide rate is higher for women than men. Some evidence suggests that there are differences between men and women in the methods employed to commit suicide: women prefer barbiturates and poisons; if women do use a firearm, the fatal wound is frequently in the body rather than the head. It has been suggested that these methods are used because they are not disfiguring and because women are often more concerned about their appearance after death than are men. It is not uncommon for a female to leave a note to her female friends or relatives specifying in detail the clothes she wants to be buried in, along with details relating to facial cosmetics.[41]

In contrast, some males kill themselves where their bodies will not be discovered by family members, such as in the woods. These types of suicides can create investigative problems, especially if a note is not written. For example, if a passerby is tempted to steal a gun and valuables from a suicide victim, the police may think that the death was a murder and robbery rather than suicide.

## SUICIDE INSURANCE SCHEMES

Sometimes individuals take their own lives and try to convey the impression that the death was accidental or even homicidal. Generally, they try to create this impression because they have invested in insurance policies that will not pay out money to the beneficiary if a death is self-inflicted. The following case illustrates such an instance:

SEVERAL years ago an Armenian man from Iran died in the Marina del Rey area of Los Angeles, California, when a bomb blew up his car. At first investigators believed that the incident might have been a terrorist killing. However, after a long investigation, they concluded that the man had killed himself in a way that looked like a terrorist attack to allow his father to collect more than $1 million from newly secured insurance policies.

Victor R. Galustian, 42, had lived in Los Angeles since 1950, when his father returned to Iran. His father had sent him money illegally from Iran for safekeeping against the day when the father would come to the United States. Galustian used the money to entertain acquaintances at lavish restaurant dinners, passing himself off as a real estate businessman or sometimes an engineer.

Because the money entered this country illegally, it is impossible to know just how much Galustian received, but investigators estimate that he spent at least $600,000 of the money his father had sent. Desperate when he learned that his father was planning to return to this country, Galustian began planning how to regain the money he had spent. He took out numerous insurance policies shortly before he died, with his father as beneficiary. All the policies had double-indemnity clauses, which double the benefits if the policyholder dies an unnatural death. The policies prohibit payoff if the policyholder commits suicide.

Early one morning, Galustian was driving his car near his apartment when a powerful explosive under his front seat went off, propelling Galustian's body 25 feet from the demolished auto and spewing debris for 600 feet. The explosion occurred after an outbreak of violence involving local Armenian and Iranian families. Authorities initially believed that the explosion, too, might be political. A few days before his death, Galustian had told a security guard in his apartment building that he had found a bomb in his car. That and other clues, including his lack of political activity in the Armenian community, convinced investigators that Galustian's death was not the result of a political attack. It took investigators several months to piece everything together, but they eventually concluded that the death was a suicide.[42]

# VEHICLE HOMICIDES

Few drivers in fatal hit-and-run accidents intended the accident to occur. The driver generally fails to stop for one or more of the following reasons:

- The driver had been drinking.
- The vehicle was stolen.
- The driver had a suspended or revoked operator's license.
- There was someone in the car whose presence, if discovered, could cause additional problems (e.g., someone else's spouse).
- The driver had no liability insurance.
- The driver or a passenger was injured, thus requiring a trip to the nearest emergency room.

- The driver did not realize that he or she had hit anyone.
- The driver had committed a crime before the accident and still had evidence of it in the vehicle.

## PHYSICAL EVIDENCE FROM HIT-AND-RUN ACCIDENTS

The physical evidence created by hit-and-run accidents is located at the scene, on the victim's body, and on the hit-and-run vehicle. The physical evidence left by the vehicle typically is broken glass from headlights, paint fragments, and underbody debris. (Chapter 3, "Physical Evidence," provides an in-depth explanation of the potential of these items as physical evidence.) The investigator may also find broken equipment, which can provide extremely valuable clues in identifying the make, model, and year of the hit-and-run vehicle, especially if the equipment was manufactured for a specific model. Broken equipment at the scene can often be matched to parts on the hit-and-run vehicle.

Tire marks typically are found in mud, clay, dirt, snow, warm tar, and sometimes on the body of the victim (see photo). If a good negative impression is left and the hit-and-run vehicle is recovered, it can often lead to a positive identification. As with all other physical evidence, the tire prints should be protected, photographed, and measured before any efforts are made to make a cast.

Skid marks, unlike tire marks, provide clues regarding direction of travel before the accident and the estimated speed of the vehicle. The absence of skid marks at the point of impact suggests a variety of things. The driver may not have seen the victim ahead of time, possibly because the driver fell asleep at the wheel or was intoxicated or because visibility was poor. This would also be the case if the skid marks appear only after the point of impact. If there are no skid marks at all, the investigator should consider the possibility of planned vehicular assault. However, most modern vehicles are equipped with an antiskid braking system, which is another possibility to consider in the absence of skid marks.

The investigator is looking for complementary physical evidence between the hit-and-run vehicle and the victim. Because the physical evidence may be quite small, such as paint fragments or a few fibers from the victim's clothing, the investigator must take painstaking efforts in searching for, collecting, and preserving such evidence. If the accident involved a pedestrian, his or her clothing may be of value in two ways. First, fibers from the victim's clothing may adhere to the vehicle, and these can be compared and matched. They are likely to be found on or near the part of the vehicle first striking the victim. If the victim was rolled under the vehicle, pieces of cloth, blood, hair, and skin may adhere to the undercarriage. Second, fiber marks from the victim's clothing may be embedded in the paint of the hit-and-run vehicle.

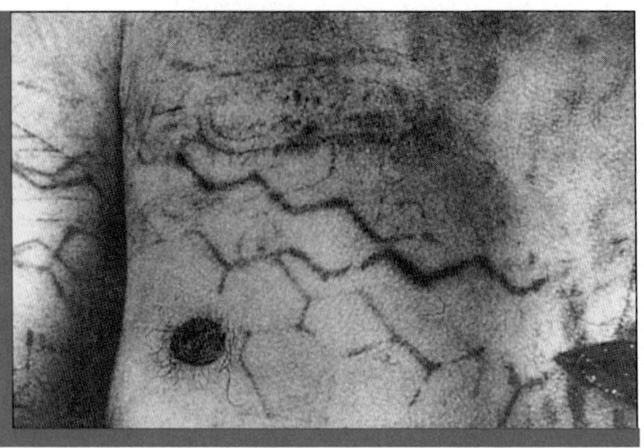

**Hit-and-Run Victim**
Tire tread marks across arm and chest on a 42-year-old man who, while asleep in a parking lot, was run over by a truck.
(Dominic J. DiMaio and Vincent J. DiMaio, *Forensic Pathology* [New York: Elsevier, 1990].)

The medical examiner should obtain blood samples from the victim for possible comparison with blood found on the hit-and-run vehicle. In addition, the victim's blood should be analyzed for the presence of alcohol or drugs, because the victim's condition at the time of the accident may have contributed to the accident.

On occasion, it may be important to determine if the headlights of a hit-and-run vehicle were on or off at the time of the accident. For example, a driver suspected of being involved in a nighttime hit-and-run collision claimed that the damage to his car was done in a previous daytime accident. Examination of the damaged headlight showed that the headlights were on at the time of the collision. This finding by the investigator suggested that the damage to the suspect's vehicle was done during the evening hours and not during the daytime, as stated by the driver.

Determining whether a vehicle's headlights were on or off at the time of impact is done by examining the filament. The effect of a crack on a filament is quite different when the filament is incandescent and when it is cold. This fact gives two bases for judging whether the lamp was on or off. First, if the glass breaks and air replaces the nitrogen surrounding the filament, oxygen in the air has no effect on a cold filament but quickly blackens an incandescent one. Second, if the glass does not break, collision shock may sharply fracture a cold, brittle filament but it will stretch out and uncoil an incandescent filament, which is quite elastic in this condition.[43] Investigators therefore should be certain to preserve not only the external glass lens of the lamp but its internal components as well, especially when there is a question of whether the headlights were on or off at the time of the accident.

### SEARCH FOR THE VEHICLE

The steps to be taken in searching for a hit-and-run vehicle depend mainly on information provided by witnesses and the victim and by physical evidence located at the scene. In the absence of eyewitnesses or physical evidence that readily identifies the suspect or the vehicle, the investigator may have to use logic and deductive reasoning. For example, the investigator may often safely assume that the driver of the vehicle was at the scene of the accident because the driver was coming from someplace and going to another place by apparently the best route. But in some cases drivers are lost or otherwise unaware of where they are and what they are doing. These cases are exceptions.

Three significant facts should be determined by the investigator in seeking to discover the driver's objective: first, the time of the accident; second, the direction of travel; and third, if it can be learned, the direction of travel after the accident.[44] Every area has certain features that investigators must consider in making tentative assumptions. For example, let us assume that a hit-and-run vehicle was described by witnesses as a flashy sports car driven by a man approximately 20 years old. The accident occurred on a weekday at 9 A.M. Before the accident, the vehicle was traveling in the direction of a nearby college. In the absence of other evidence, the investigator might assume that the vehicle was being driven by a student to the college. Of course, this assumption could be totally erroneous; but when there are no solid leads, then the only initial course of action may be to apply logic and deductive reasoning.

If the investigator can locate physical evidence or a witness who can identify the make, model, year, and color of the vehicle, a detailed notice should be sent out to area repair shops, garages, and parts stores. If the damage to the vehicle is severe, the driver generally does one of several things. First, the driver may try to keep the car concealed in a private garage. Second, the driver may take the vehicle to a repair shop. Third, the driver may try to purchase the replacement parts from a dealer or junkyard.

In some situations, investigators ask for help from the news media and, through them, help from the public. They may do so when existing clues are sparse.

## FIRE DEATHS

Frequently, human remains are found at the scene of a fire. Properly examined, these remains may provide important data to the investigator about the facts surrounding the fire and the cause of death. Investigators should ask these questions:

- Was the decedent accidentally killed by the fire (whether or not the fire was caused by arson)?
- Was the decedent deliberately killed by the fire?
- Was the decedent already dead when the fire occurred?

To answer these questions, investigators should determine certain facts. These facts are outlined in the remainder of this section.[45]

### COORDINATION AND COOPERATION

Coordination of and cooperation between police and fire investigators are of paramount importance in the successful investigation of any questioned fire. As with other forms of physical evidence at a fire scene, a body should never be moved until fully examined at the scene unless there is some possibility that the person is still alive or there is danger of further destruction of the body if it remains where it is. Also, because a dead human being is probably the most complex and rapidly changing type of physical evidence at a crime scene, cooperation between medical personnel (preferably forensic pathologists) and investigators is essential. This coordination should extend from the scene of the fire to the medical facility where the postmortem examination is conducted.

## DEGREES OF BURNING

Burns are medically classified into four types. The extent of burns may provide information about the proximity of the body to the point of origin of the fire, the length of time the body was exposed to the fire, and the intensity of the fire.

First-degree burns are superficial and limited to the outer layers of skin. Although the burned area is red and swollen, blisters do not form and peeling may follow. Second-degree burns involve blistering and the destruction of the upper layers of skin. They occasionally cause scarring in living victims. With third-degree burns, the entire thickness of the skin (epidermis and dermis) is destroyed. In living victims with third-degree burns, pain is usually absent as nerve endings are destroyed; scarring results and skin grafting is usually necessary. Fourth-degree burns completely destroy (char) the skin and underlying tissue.

The degree of incineration of the body should be considered in comparison with other facts and circumstances of the fire. Are the burns of the decedent consistent with the nature of the fire and other burned areas? Body mass should be considered, keeping in mind that faster and greater destruction occurs to smaller, lighter bodies. Less destruction may be expected in ordinary house fires (usually of 1,200°F or less) than in fires accelerated, for example, by certain chemicals. Complete incineration of a body, as in cremation, usually takes 1½ hours at temperatures of 1,600° to 1,800°F, resulting in an ash weight of 2 to 3 pounds for an adult.

## IDENTIFICATION OF REMAINS

Because fire destroys human tissue, identification of the remains may be especially difficult. Yet because identification of a decedent is a key factor in any questioned death investigation, an orderly, sequential approach must be used in the identification process. The six means that follow should be considered in sequence, from the "best" identification tools to the "worst":

- *Fingerprints:* Although considered the best means of identification because of centralized files of fingerprints, fingerprint identification may not be possible in fire death cases due to the destruction of the skin.
- *Dentition:* Being the hardest substance in the human body, teeth are frequently the best form of identification for fire victims. The only drawback is that in order to make a dental comparison, one must have something to compare the decedent's teeth with. The investigator must have some idea of who the decedent was.
- *DNA printing:* Following recent advances, DNA printing (described in Chapter 3, "Physical Evidence") has emerged as a viable tool for identifying fire death victims. As with dental records, the investigator must have some indication of the identity of the deceased before DNA printing can yield results.
- *Scars, marks, or tattoos on the exterior of the body:* These abnormalities on the skin, like fingerprints, are frequently obscured or destroyed by fire.
- *Scars, marks, abnormalities, or appliances inside the body:* Bone abnormalities, surgical appliances, or operative scars may be helpful, but the investigator must have some idea of who the victim was so that appropriate medical records can be examined.
- *Identification, jewelry, and clothing on the body:* This least-desirable means is a last resort due to the possibility of substitution. Indeed, in some arson and/or murder cases, the body is disguised to look like someone else.

## SCENE CONSIDERATIONS

As with any physical evidence, burned bodies must be sketched, measured, and photographed in place and in relation to other evidence at the scene of the fire. The actual location of the body may be crucial to the investigation. Determination as to whether the decedent was a smoker is important for establishing what caused the fire and whether he or she was alive at the time of the fire.

## EXAMINATION OF THE EXTERNAL BODY

The body of the deceased should be examined in detail both at the scene and again at the morgue. Significant areas for examination include those discussed below.

***Signs of Trauma*** Any sign of injury to the external body should be carefully noted, sketched, and photographed. The use of a five-power magnifying glass (as a minimum) is required, because fire obscures signs of injury.

***Skull Fracture*** Another factor that may be misconstrued is the discovery that the victim's skull is fractured. Care must be taken to determine whether the fracture is implosive or explosive. An implosive fracture may have been caused by a fall, may be evidence of a prior felonious assault or homicide, or may result from a collapsed structural member. The exact cause will be determined at autopsy and evaluated during the follow-up investigation. An explosive fracture, however, is usually a natural consequence of fire. The extreme heat may cause the fluids in and around the brain to boil and expand. The resulting steam produces pressure sufficient to cause an explosive (pressure-release) reaction. The fracture(s) that result usually follow the natural suture lines of the skull. In extreme cases, the cranium may burst, causing the expelled brain and skull matter to form a circular pattern around the head. This is more common in children than in adults: the fontanel, or membrane-covered opening between the uncompleted parietal bones, is the weakest point in a fetal or young skull. The resulting circular pattern (0 to 12 inches from the skull) is significant when compared with the type of splattering that might result from a shotgun blast or high-order explosion.[46]

***Blistering and Splitting Skin*** The inexperienced investigator may be somewhat apprehensive in attempting to evaluate the effects of heat and flame on the skin of the victim. The medical investigator is in the best position to render a judgment in this area.

The formation of blisters (vesicles) is part of the body's natural defense system. The exact distinction between antemortem and postmortem blistering can be made only at autopsy. There are, however, certain signs that a medical investigator can use in developing a hypothesis. Postmortem blisters are generally limited in size and may contain only air or air mixed with a small amount of body fluid. Antemortem blisters are larger in size and contain a complex mix of body fluids. The precise determination of the fluids requires microscopic analysis. A blister surrounded by a pink or red ring can be considered to have occurred before death; the reddish ring is the result of an antemortem inflammatory reaction.

In some instances, temperatures may not have been sufficiently high to produce blistering. Likewise, if the skin is burned off or otherwise heavily damaged, blistering will not be evident.

The heat and flames of the fire also cause the skin to shrink or tighten and ultimately split. The splitting or lesions may be seen on the arms, legs, and torso. At first glance this condition, coupled with pugilistic attitude, could be misinterpreted as indicating defense wounds.

In some cases, a seriously burned person survives the fire and is removed to a burn center. In an effort to save the person, the medical staff at the center may attempt to duplicate the natural splitting of the skin with a surgical technique known as an escharotomy. This technique is used to help foster circulation and to prevent the onset of gangrene. Should the burn victim die some time after the fire, these splits should not be misinterpreted as fire induced.[47]

***Noncranial Fractures*** If enough heat is applied, bones shrink, warp, and fracture. Determining whether fractures were caused by a trauma or heat requires painstaking examination.

***Pugilistic Attitude*** The so-called pugilistic attitude of the body is a natural result of the dehydrating effect caused by the heat from the fire and is not related to the cause or manner of death. The arms and legs will be drawn into a posture resembling that of a boxer (see photo on page 322).

More often than not in fire deaths, a forensic pathologist who is an expert on burned bodies may have to be summoned.

## EXAMINATION OF THE INTERNAL BODY

After the body has been closely examined, sketched, and photographed, an internal examination of the

### Pugilistic Attitude

The heat of the fire can result in the arms and legs of a body being drawn up into a posture resembling that of a boxer.

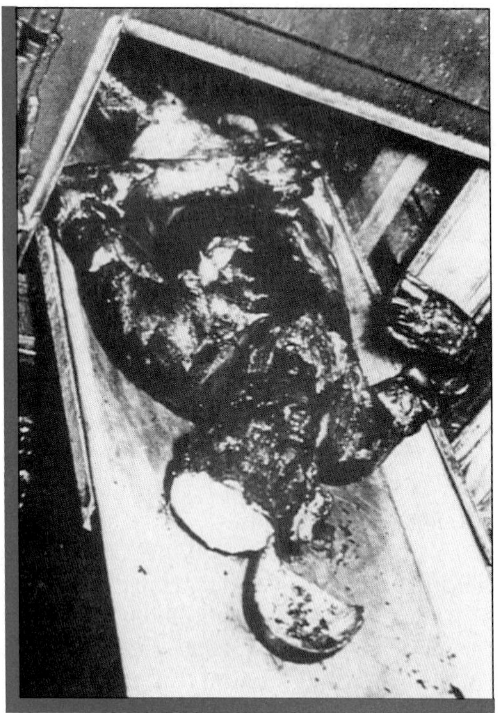

body should be conducted by a forensic pathologist. Investigators should attend this procedure to get information about the facts, to correct discrepancies in data (such as measurements), and to recover evidence from the body. Significant areas for examination are as follows:

***Soot, Other Debris, or Burning in the Air Passages*** These findings may indicate that the decedent was breathing while the fire was burning.

***Pulmonary Edema*** A frothy substance in the lungs may result from irritants breathed in during a fire.

***Epidural Hemorrhages*** Hemorrhages above the tough membrane covering the brain (the dura mater) and under the skull may occur at the rear of the head due to heat. These hemorrhages should not be mistaken for the hemorrhages associated with blunt-force injuries.[48]

***Internal Injuries*** All internal injuries should be closely examined, measured, and photographed, with samples taken by the pathologist for later microscopic examination.

***Foreign Objects*** Any foreign objects found in the body, such as bullets, should be recovered as evidence by the investigator. Because these objects are frequently small and difficult to locate, X-ray examination of the body before internal examination is recommended.

## TOXICOLOGIC EXAMINATION

The pathologist should take samples for later examination by a toxicologist. Toxicologic results may be of extreme importance to the investigation.

***Alcohol*** Alcohol in blood indicates whether the decedent was incapacitated at the time of the fire and thus unable to escape. A finding of high levels of alcohol raises questions for the investigator about the decedent's habits.

***Other Drugs*** Indications of other possibly incapacitating drugs may provide new leads. The possibility of drug interactions—barbiturates with alcohol, for example—should also be considered.

***Carboxyhemoglobin*** Carbon monoxide (CO) is an odorless, colorless gas present at hazardous levels in all structural fires. Carbon monoxide asphyxiation (usually about 40 percent saturation) is probably the most common cause of death in fires. As previously discussed, CO causes the cherry-red color of postmortem lividity (as well as that of internal organs and muscle tissue).

At autopsy, the pathologist will test the victim's blood for the level of carboxyhemoglobin-carbon monoxide present in the pigment of the red blood cells. The concentration of carbon monoxide in the blood is a very important element in determining whether the victim was alive before and during the fire. Its concentration is quantified in terms of a percentage of saturation. Because carbon monoxide in the blood is generally due to the inhalation of CO during the fire, the absence of CO in the red blood cells (less than a 10 percent saturation) would be rather conclusive evidence that the victim was dead before the fire.[49]

***Presence of Other Chemicals*** Chemicals given off by burning materials may indicate the accelerant of the fire, as well as that the decedent was breathing them in at the time of the fire. Hydrogen cyanide or hydrogen sulfide found in the blood may contribute to death. Nitrous oxides may indicate the presence of nitrogen-containing fuels; acrolein may indicate the destructive distillation of fats and oils. Refrigerants and other chemicals such as ammonia, Freon, or methyl chloride may indicate the nature of the fire.

## HISTOLOGIC EXAMINATION

Microscopic examination of tissues is also an important part of the postmortem examination and is carried out by the pathologist after selected tissues from the victim have been placed in a fixative, usually for 10 to 14 days. Frequently, injury sites are microscopically examined for signs of white blood cells at the injury. White blood cells may indicate that the injury was inflicted at least several hours before death.

## "FLASH" FIRES

Concentrated burns in one area of a body may indicate the nature and cause of death. Examples include a spray of burning fuel, as in a motorcycle accident, or the application of a device such as a blowtorch to a particular area of the body (face or hands) to obscure identification.

## MOTIVES IN FIRE DEATHS

In fire deaths, the following motives should be kept in mind by investigators:

- Destruction or mutilation of the body to conceal the identity of the decedent.
- Destruction or mutilation of the body to conceal the true cause or manner of death.
- Incineration of the body with homicidal intent.
- Incineration of the body to collect on an insurance policy. For example, a decedent may have committed suicide but have an insurance policy prohibiting collection after death by suicide. Beneficiaries may burn the body to indicate accidental death by fire.
- Suicide with an accelerant.
- An attempt by a suicide victim to hide the cause of death.
- A victim trapped in a building burned by an arsonist or by accident.

## RECORDING THE SCENE

Photographs of the body in its original position and of the room or area in which it is found will prove to be very valuable later in the investigation. These photographs, along with investigative notes and any rough sketches prepared at the scene, serve the following purposes:

- To provide an overview of the body and its surroundings so that its relative position can later be established.
- To provide close-up photographs (including a ruler for true size comparison) of any evidence that indicates the identity of the victim; a circumvented alarm or fire-suppression system; point(s) of forced entry or exit; another (underlying) crime or signs of a struggle; the presence of gas cans, trailers, plants, and so on.
- To clarify the condition of the body regarding the extent of burning or cremation; the flow of fire patterns on the body and whether they are consistent with the extent of damages to the surroundings (e.g., was a victim who died on the second floor found buried in an ash-filled basement because of the collapse of interior structural members?); whether the body was found face up or face down, and the degree to which it insulated the floor below it (or failed to do so).
- To identify furnishings (e.g., bed, coffee table, desk) in the area where the body was found.
- To indicate the relative position of the body in relation to the point(s) of origin.
- To identify any other factors of importance to technical or forensic procedures.

In some cases, especially when the victim is found quite a distance from the point of origin of the fire, it is necessary to trace the connection between the fire and the resultant death. The connection may seem obvious when the investigator is at the scene, but when she or he is on the witness stand 12 or 15 months later, the connection may not be as clear. The following case, concerning a fire that occurred in the Bronx, New York, several years ago, illustrates this problem:

AT 5 A.M., a fire started in the basement of an abandoned five-story walkup. The adjoining buildings were fully occupied and were evacuated by the responding fire units. One of the evacuees was a 9-year-old, mentally retarded boy. During the ensuing confusion, the boy was separated from his parents; apparently frightened by the crowd, he reentered his residence to seek the safety of his room. The boy's father, searching for his son, found him under his bed. The boy had died from carbon monoxide asphyxiation.

The fire damage to the abandoned building was extensive, but the fire did not extend to the adjoining buildings. The boy's body was found one building away and four stories above the source of the carbon monoxide that caused his death. The investigators involved in the case traced and (wisely) photographically documented the path that the billowing smoke and gases took between the source and the boy's room.

On occasion, the medical examiner will, after autopsy, refer a case to the police for further investigation. The autopsy may have revealed insufficient and/or contradictory data or may have raised additional questions that the medical examiner wants to have clarified before signing a death certificate. Such a case is referred to as a **CUPPI,** which stands for "circumstances undetermined pending police investigation." If the crime scene was processed and recorded accurately, the investigator, in many cases, should be able to review the crime scene data and provide the medical examiner with satisfactory answers.[50]

## FAMILY OR DOMESTIC VIOLENCE

Family or domestic violence is unquestionably underreported, even by victimization studies. It often happens in private, and many victims are reluctant to report it because they are ashamed, they are afraid of reprisals if they do speak out,[51] they suffer from such low self-esteem that they think they "deserve what they got," or they were raised in violent families where abuse was "normal." As discussed in Chapter 2, acts constituting domestic or family violence are exceptions in most states to the general rule that an officer must personally view the commission of a misdemeanor in order to make an arrest. And because the bulk of these crimes do not rise to the level of felonious acts, in years past officers could only tell the victim to take out a warrant. However, as can be seen by the following laws from one state, not only is it possible for officers to now take immediate action in nonfelony situations, but there are specific requirements as to what investigative actions must be taken:

**19-13-1 "Family Violence"**..."means the occurrence of one or more of the following acts between past or present spouses, persons who are parents of the same child, parents and children, stepparents and stepchildren, foster parents and foster children, or other persons living or formerly living in the same household:

(1) any felony; or

(2) commission of offenses of battery, simple battery, simple assault, assault, stalking, criminal damage to property, unlawful restraint, or criminal trespass."

As used in 19-13-1, the term "family violence" does not include reasonable discipline administered by a parent to a child in the form of corporal punishment, restraint, or detention.[52]

**17-4-20 "Arrest by Law Enforcement Officers Generally"** provides that "an arrest for a crime may be made by a law enforcement officer either under a warrant or without a warrant if the offense is committed in his presence or within his immediate knowledge; if the offender is endeavoring to escape; if the officer has probable cause to believe that an act of family violence, as defined in Code Section 19-13-1, has been committed; or for other cause if there is likely to be a failure of justice for want of a judicial officer to issue a warrant."[53]

**17-4-20.1 "Investigation of Family Violence"** imposes the following requirements for law enforcement officers conducting an investigation into an act of family violence:

1. an officer may not base a decision of whether to arrest and charge a person on the specific consent of the victim or on a request

by the victim solely or on consideration of the relationship of the parties;

2. no officer investigating an incident of family violence shall threaten, suggest, or otherwise indicate the arrest of all parties for the purpose of discouraging requests for law enforcement intervention;

3. when family violence complaints are received from two or more opposing parties, the officer shall evaluate each complaint separately to attempt to determine who was the primary aggressor. If the officer determines that one of the parties was the primary physical aggressor, the officer shall not be required to arrest any other person believed to have committed an act of family violence during the incident. In determining whether a person is a primary physical aggressor, an officer shall consider:

a) prior family violence involving either party;
b) the relative severity of the injuries inflicted on each person;
c) the potential for future injury; and
d) whether one of the parties acted in self-defense.

If the officer concludes that an act of family violence has occurred, regardless if an arrest is made, the officer must prepare a Family Violence offense or incident report and address the following matters:

a) names of the parties;
b) relationship of the parties;
c) sex of the parties;
d) time, date, and place of the incident;
e) whether children were involved or whether the incident was committed in the presence of children;
f) type and extent of the alleged abuse;
g) existence of substance abuse;
h) number and types of weapons involved;
i) existence of any prior court orders;
j) number of complaints involving persons who have previously filed complaints;
k) type of police action taken to dispose of the case, the reasons for the officer's determination that one party was the primary physical aggressor, and mitigating circumstances if an arrest is not made;
l) whether the victim was advised of available remedies and services; and
m) any other pertinent information.[54]

## STALKING

**Stalking** is harassing or threatening behavior that an individual engages in repeatedly, such as following a person, appearing at a person's home or place of business, making harassing phone calls, leaving written messages or objects, or vandalizing a person's property. These actions may or may not be accompanied by a credible threat of serious harm, and they may or may not be precursors to an assault or murder.[55]

Legal definitions of stalking vary widely from state to state. Though most states define stalking as the willful, malicious, and repeated following and harassing of another person, some states include in their definition such activities as lying in wait, surveillance, nonconsensual communication, telephone harassment, and vandalism.[56] While most states require that the alleged stalker engage in a course of conduct showing that the crime was not an isolated event, some states specify how many acts (usually two or more) must occur before the conduct can be considered stalking.[57] State stalking laws also vary in their threat and fear requirements. Most stalking laws require that to be deemed a stalker the perpetrator must make a credible threat of violence against the victim; others include in their requirements threats against the victim's immediate family; and still others require only that the alleged stalker's course of conduct constitute an implied threat.[58]

The definition of stalking used in the National Violence against Women (NVAW) survey closely resembles the definition used in the model antistalking code developed for states by the National Institute of Justice.[59] The survey defines stalking as "a course of conduct directed at a specific person that involves repeated visual or physical proximity, non-consensual communication, or verbal, written or implied threats, or a combination thereof, that would cause a reasonable person fear," with "repeated" meaning two or more occasions. The model antistalking code does not require, as a criterion of stalking, that stalkers make a credible threat of violence against victims, but it does require that victims feel a high level of fear ("fear of bodily harm"). Similarly, the definition of stalking used in the NVAW survey does not require that stalkers make a credible threat against victims, but it does require that victims feel a high level of fear.[60]

## CHARACTERISTICS OF STALKERS

Stalking is a gender-neutral crime, with both male and female perpetrators and victims. However, most stalkers are men: statistics indicate that 75 to 80 percent of all stalking cases involve men stalking women. Most stalkers are young to middle-aged and have above-average intelligence. Stalkers come from every walk of life and socioeconomic background. Virtually anyone can be a stalker, just as anyone can be a stalking victim.[61]

Forensic psychologists (those who study criminal behavior) are just beginning to examine the minds and motives of stalkers. Discussed below are the most common types of stalkers and stalking behavior.

### Love-Obsession Stalkers

A love-obsession stalker develops a romantic obsession with or fixation on another person with whom he or she has no personal relationship. The target may be only a casual acquaintance or even a complete stranger. About 20 to 25 percent of all stalking cases involve love-obsession stalkers. People who stalk celebrities, such as David Letterman, and movie stars, such as Jodie Foster and Madonna, are love obsessionists; however, this category also includes those who develop fixations on regular, ordinary people, such as coworkers, instructors, casual acquaintances, or people they pass in the street.

The vast majority of love-obsession stalkers suffer from a mental disorder—often schizophrenia or paranoia. Regardless of the specific disorder, nearly all display some delusional thought patterns and behaviors. Since most are unable to develop normal personal relationships through more conventional and socially acceptable means, they retreat to a life of fantasy relationships with persons they barely know or with strangers. They invent fictional stories, complete with what are to them real-life scripts, that cast their unwilling victims in the lead role as their own love interests. They then attempt to act out their fictional plots in the real world.

Love-obsession stalkers not only attempt to live out their fantasies but expect their victims to play their assigned roles as well. They believe they can make the objects of their affection love them. They desperately want to establish a positive personal relationship with their victims. When a victim refuses to follow the script or does not respond as the stalker hopes, the stalker may attempt to force the victim to comply by use of threats and intimidation. When threats and intimidation fail, some stalkers turn to violence. Some decide that if they cannot be a positive part of the victim's life, they will be a negative part. Some even go so far as to murder their victims in a twisted attempt to romantically link themselves to their victims forever. This was the case with the man who shot and killed Rebecca Schaffer, the young actress and star of the television show *My Sister Sam*.

**Jerry Lewis Stalker**

Convicted stalker, Gary Randolf Benson leaves the courtroom after comedian Jerry Lewis asked the Clark County Justice Court to extend a protective order against Benson. Stalking is a harassing or threatening behavior that an individual engages in repeatedly. The vast majority of stalkers are men—young to middle-age—and of above-average intelligence. Stalkers come from every walk of life and every socioeconomic background.

(© Reuters NewMedia, Inc./Corbis)

## Simple-Obsession Stalkers

A simple-obsession stalker develops a fixation on someone he or she had a personal or romantic relationship with before the stalking behavior began. Stalkers in this category account for 70 to 80 percent of all stalking cases. The stalkers in virtually all domestic violence cases involving stalking are simple obsessionists, as are the stalkers in casual dating relationships (commonly referred to as "fatal attraction" cases, after the popular movie with that title).

While simple-obsession stalkers may or may not have psychological disorders, all clearly have personality disorders. One forensic psychologist has attempted to identify some of the common personality traits and behavioral characteristics of simple obsessionists. Such stalkers are characterized as individuals who are:

- Socially maladjusted and inept.
- Emotionally immature.
- Often subject to feelings of powerlessness.
- Unable to succeed in relationships by socially acceptable means.
- Jealous, bordering on paranoid.
- Extremely insecure about themselves and suffering from low self-esteem.

The self-esteem of simple-obsession stalkers is often closely tied to their relationships with their partners. In many cases, the stalkers bolster their own self-esteem by dominating and intimidating their mates. Exercising dominance over another gives them a sense of power in a world where they would otherwise feel powerless. In extreme cases, such a personality attempts to control every aspect of the partner's life.

Since the victim literally becomes the stalker's primary source of self-esteem, the stalker's greatest fear is that he or she will lose the victim. The stalker's self-worth is so closely tied to the victim that when the stalker is deprived of that person, he or she may feel that life is without worth. It is this dynamic that makes simple-obsession stalkers so dangerous. In the most acute cases, the stalker will literally stop at nothing to regain his or her "lost possession"—the victim—and, in so doing, regain his or her self-esteem.

Just as in most domestic violence cases, a simple-obsession stalker is the most dangerous when first deprived of his or her source of power and self-esteem, that is, when the victim determines to physically remove herself or himself from the offender's presence on a permanent basis by leaving the relationship. Indeed, stalking cases that emerge from domestic violence situations constitute the most common and potentially lethal class of stalking cases. Domestic violence victims who leave abusive relationships run a 75 percent higher risk of being murdered by their partners than that run by those who remain in such relationships.

## Cyberstalkers

The term **cyberstalking** refers to the practice of harassing victims by means of the Internet, using various modes of contact such as e-mail, chat rooms, newsgroups, and the World Wide Web. Cyberstalkers pose a serious threat because they are often able to obtain personal information about their victims, such as phone numbers, school names, workplaces, and home addresses. They may trick people into revealing such information, or they may simply ask for it. Either way, once the information is attained, the stalker has easy access to the individual's private life. The cyberstalker may even use the information as a means of meeting the victim in person.

One researcher has developed a psychological profile of cyberstalkers based on six case studies. Cyberstalkers, as a group, tend to be sophisticated perpetrators (e.g., they are computer literate and financially able to support subscriptions to online services). The individual cyberstalker is typically an emotionally troubled loner who searches for companionship and attention in cyberspace, often becoming fixated on someone he or she meets in a chat room. The pursuit by a cyberstalker tends to have an obsessional, angry component, which usually results from rejection.

Cyberstalking is a new type of stalking that needs to be explored empirically. The anonymous quality and lack of social constraints tied to cyberstalking enable the offender to feel less social anxiety. One implication of this aspect of stalking on the Internet is that aggressive behavior, which is typically inhibited by social anxiety, is not restricted.[62]

## Stalking Behavior Patterns and Cycles

Stalking behavior is as diverse as the stalkers themselves. Yet behavioral experts are beginning to identify patterns in the cycle of violence displayed by simple-obsession stalkers. The stalking behavior patterns closely mirror those common in many domestic violence cases.

The pattern is usually triggered when the stalker's advances toward the victim are frustrated—regardless of whether the stalker is seeking to establish a personal relationship or continue a previously established relationship contrary to the wishes of the victim. The stalker may try to woo the victim into a relationship by sending flowers, candy, and love letters, in an attempt to prove his or her love. However, when the victim spurns the unwelcome advances, the stalker often turns to intimidation. Attempts at intimidation often begin in the form of an unjustified, jealous, and inappropriate intrusion into the victim's life. Often such contacts recur, becoming more numerous and intrusive over time, until they constitute a persistent pattern of harassment.

Many times, the harassing behavior escalates to threatening behavior. The threats may be direct or indirect and may be communicated explicitly or implicitly by the stalker's conduct. Unfortunately, cases that reach this level of seriousness too often end in violence and/or murder. Stalkers, unable to establish or reestablish a relationship that gives them power and control over their victims, turn to violence as a means of reasserting their domination. In some cases, the stalker is even willing to kill the victim and himself or herself in a last, desperate attempt to dominate the victim. Such a stalker's thought pattern progresses from "If I can just prove to you how much I love you" to "I can make you love me" to "If I can't have you, nobody else will."

While this progression in behavior is common, no stalking case is completely predictable. Some stalkers may never escalate past the first stage. Others jump from the first stage to the last stage with little warning. Still others regress to previous stages before advancing to the next. It is not uncommon to see stalkers intersperse episodes of threats and violence with flowers and love letters. As difficult as it is to predict what a stalker will do, it is at least as difficult to predict when he or she will do it. In some cases, stalkers progress to later stages over only a few weeks or even days. In other cases, stalkers who have engaged in some of the most serious stalking behaviors go months or even years without attempting a subsequent contact.

## PROTECTIVE ORDERS

Most states have laws authorizing civil orders of protection in domestic abuse cases.[63] Such statutes limit in some way the eligibility for protection under such orders; in some states the applicant must be or have been married to the person against whom the protective order is sought.[64] There is a need for each state to review its protective-order statutes to determine if under the present provisions such orders are available to all stalking victims.[65]

**Protective orders** can serve as the first line of defense against stalkers: such orders put them on notice that their behavior is unwanted and that future acts will be dealt with more severely; in most states investigators can immediately make a warrantless arrest if they have probable cause to believe an order was violated.[66] All states allow temporary protective orders to be issued on an emergency basis and without the defendant's being present.[67] If an emergency or temporary order is issued, then a hearing on a permanent order is subsequently held. Among the things that protective orders prohibit a defendant from doing is communicating with the victim and entering the residence, workplace, school, or property of the victim, as well as any place frequented by the victim.[68] In some cases, mental illness and use of drugs or alcohol may be major factors in the behavior of a stalker; officers should be alert to documenting this possibility when conducting their investigation and coordinate with appropriate officials so that judges can incorporate mental health and substance-abuse counseling and monitoring into restraining orders.[69]

To be effective, protective orders must be rigorously enforced and violators dealt with in a manner that ensures their strict accountability. This requires that victims promptly report all violations. While victims may initially be satisfied with the response of the police to their original complaint, they are often disappointed with the lack of responsiveness to later complaints of a violation of the protective order.[70] Investigators must rapidly respond to such complaints and take enforcement action whenever the defendant's conduct warrants it. To do otherwise may make a defendant bolder and can result in serious injury or death.

## PSYCHOLOGICAL AND SOCIAL CONSEQUENCES OF STALKING

The NVAW survey produced strong confirmation of the negative mental health impact of stalking. Of the respondents, about one-third of the women

**Serial Killer, Robert Lee Yates, Jr.**
Confessed serial killer, Robert Lee Yates, Jr., the Spokane serial killer responsible for seven women's deaths since late summer of 1997, stands emotionless as he is sentenced to a 408-year prison term.
(© Reuters NewMedia, Inc./Corbis)

(30 percent) and one-fifth of the men (20 percent) said they sought psychological counseling as a result of their stalking victimization. In addition, stalking victims were significantly more likely than nonstalking victims to be very concerned about their personal safety and about being stalked, to carry something on their person to defend themselves, and to think personal safety for men and women had gotten worse in recent years.

Over one-quarter (26 percent) of the stalking victims said their victimization caused them to lose time from work. While the survey did not query victims about why they lost time from work, it can be assumed they missed work for a variety of reasons—to attend court hearings, to meet with a psychologist or other mental health professional, to avoid contact with their assailants, and to consult with an attorney. On average, victims who lost time from and returned to work missed 11 days.

Stalking victims were asked whether they took any measures (other than reporting their victimization to the police or obtaining a protective order) to protect themselves from their stalkers. Fifty-six percent of the women and 51 percent of the men reported taking some type of self-protective measure.[71]

## SERIAL MURDER

Serial murder was originally described, in early 1980, as "lust murder."[72] The term "serial murder" was first used in 1982 or 1983; no one knows for sure who coined the term, but it has been with us ever since.

For the law enforcement community, **serial murder** comprises a series of sexual attacks and resulting deaths of a minimum of three or four individuals and is committed by a killer who tends to follow a distinct physical or psychological pattern. There are seven major components that may serve as flags to alert investigators to the possibility that a serial murderer is operating in their jurisdiction:

- One or more individuals (in most cases, males) commit a second murder and/or subsequent murders.
- There is generally no prior relationship between victim and attacker (if there is a relationship, it will be one that places the victim in a subjugated position relative to the killer).
- Subsequent murders occur at different times and have no apparent connection to the initial murder.
- Subsequent murders are usually committed in a different geographic location.
- The motive is not for material gain; it is for the murderer's desire to have power or dominance over his or her victims.
- Victims may have a symbolic value for the murderer, and/or they may be perceived as lacking prestige, being unable to defend themselves or alert others to their plight, or being powerless given their situation in time, place, or status within their immediate surroundings.
- Victims typically include vagrants, the homeless, prostitutes, migrant workers, homosexuals, missing children, single women

(out by themselves), elderly women, college students, and hospital patients.

Much of the early research on serial murder focused on the sexual component of the crime to explain the killer's motivation. Psychologists have referred to the sexual component in a number of ways, describing serial killers as those "who suffer from a deviation or perversion of the sexual impulse"[73] or who "kill because of an underlying basis of sexual conflicts."[74] "They [serial killers] usually have few normal social and sexual relationships. In fact, they often have had no experience of normal sexual intercourse."[75] Some criminologists have stated, "The serial killer is motivated by sex and sadism . . . favors immediate gratification, regardless of the consequences."[76]

Other researchers disagree, arguing that the sexual component either is overstated or is simply an instrument of the killer, not the motivating factor behind the act. For these researchers, the focus of study is on the power relationships or the issue of control. The motivation is thus the enhancement of the killer's sense of control and domination over the victims. The motivational dynamics of serial murder seem to be consistent with research on the nature of rape, which is considered to be a power and dominance crime.[77] This similarity becomes even more evident when one considers that it may take only a small increase in the fury of the rapist or the struggle of the victim to change a violent rape into a murder.

Many social science researchers have found trauma, abuse, and neglect in the childhoods of serial killers.[78] The social and psychological deprivation consistently identified in the childhoods of serial killers would certainly indicate a strong correlation between such a childhood and serial killing. However, such childhoods can also be identified in many people who do not go on to become serial killers. Correlation does not equal causation. Indeed, if such a correlation were revealed to be the central causal factor of the serial murderer, the United States would have thousands of serial killers, given the current disturbing statistics on child abuse and neglect in this country. A terrible childhood may contribute to the serial killer's makeup, but it is apparently only one factor in the etiology of serial killing.

Research on serial murder has focused on finding similarities among murders. The victims of serial killers have largely been ignored. Serial killers seem to prey on people who are vulnerable or easy to lure and dominate, but little else is known about the victims of serial murders except that they are almost always strangers to the murderer. They appear to be selected because they happen to cross the path of the serial murderer or because their physical appearance holds some symbolic significance for the killer. Vulnerable victims may simply happen to be in the area where the killer is hunting, their appearance may trigger the selection, or the opportunity and the victim's availability in a specific location may contribute to the fatal selection.

The high-risk lifestyles of some victims (such as some cult members, released mental patients, skid-row alcoholics, and prostitutes) certainly contribute to their victimization. Serial killers seem to pick victims whom they can dominate. They do not care about their victims or have any feelings of remorse.

## SERIAL MURDER AND THE NCAVC

If a serial murderer confines his or her activities to a single community or a small region, local police are in a good position to see emerging patterns. But because many serial murderers cover many miles in a short period of time, the FBI has developed the National Center for the Analysis of Violent Crime (NCAVC). It is designed to form a partnership among federal, state, and local law enforcement agencies in the investigation of potentially related, unsolved violent crimes. NCAVC combines law enforcement techniques, behavioral science principles, and data processing to help any law enforcement agency confronted with unusual, bizarre, particularly vicious, or repetitive crimes.

The following are the types of offenses and incidents that are reported to NCAVC for analysis:

- Sexually oriented murder or assault by mutilation or torture, dismemberment, violent sexual trauma, or asphyxiation.
- Spree murder (a series of indiscriminate murders or assaults, all committed within hours or days; e.g., a series of sniper murders or the Chicago cyanide murders).
- Mass murder (four or more murders in a single incident).
- Robbery murder and nonfatal robbery with extreme violence.

- Murder committed during the commission of another felony.
- Kidnapping: fatal, with injury, or for ransom.
- Murder of a hostage.
- Murder for hire, contract murder, syndicate execution.
- Murder of a law enforcement officer.
- Political or other assassination.
- Terrorist or nationalistic murder.
- Drug-related murder.
- Gang murder.
- Missing person with evidence of foul play.
- Unidentified dead body when the manner of death is classified as a homicide.[79]

NCAVC can analyze every unsolved murder in the United States, identify the existence of serial patterns, and link cases together. It then notifies the individual local agencies that have similar murders, and they in turn may establish investigative contact among themselves. NCAVC emphasizes that the primary responsibility for investigating cases lies with the state and local authorities.

NCAVC also conducts research in violent crimes and trains local officers in analytic techniques. It is located at the FBI Academy in Quantico, Virginia, where it is administered by the Behavioral Science Unit. The FBI Academy was chosen as the site because it is a national law enforcement training center with vast resources for research and many capabilities for providing investigative support.

## VICAP CRIME REPORT

When a violent crime remains unsolved for a period of time, the local law enforcement agency provides details about it on a special violent-criminal apprehension program (VICAP) reporting form.[80] This form is submitted to the nearest FBI field office, which reviews and forwards it to NCAVC.

Information flow in the VICAP process is outlined in the following hypothetical case:

JANUARY—Los Angeles County: The body of a young female is found near Interstate 10 east of La Puente. The victim has blunt-force skull fractures and a number of mutilation knife wounds, several of which are unique. Two days later, the Los Angeles homicide detectives forward a VICAP offense report to VICAP. This report includes coroner protocol information and the identity of the victim, a 14-year-old runaway from a small northern California town. All information is entered into the VICAP computer and analyzed to compare MO and physical-evidence characteristics with those in other reported homicides. Los Angeles detectives are advised that the VICAP search reveals no similar-pattern cases on file.

February—San Bernardino, California: Detectives respond to a "found body" call on the southern edge of the city. The victim is a 16-year-old female from Hollywood. Injuries are similar to those of the January homicide in Los Angeles County. Regardless of the proximity of the two departments and the cooperation that exists between the detectives, a VICAP analysis confirms that a similar pattern does exist, and both agencies are notified.

April—Marshall, Texas: Detectives forward VICAP information of the mutilation murder of a 19-year-old female college student whose vehicle, with a flat tire, was located on I-20 east of Dallas. After a pattern analysis, VICAP alerts Los Angeles, San Bernardino, and Marshall detectives that MO and physical evidence in the three murder cases are similar. It is also apparent that the killer is traveling east on the I-10, I-20 interstate system.

VICAP, after a request from the three police departments, prepares and transmits an information all-points bulletin (APB) directed to the special attention of all law enforcement agencies on or near the I-10, I-20 route. The APB requests that any department with information related in any way to the MO of the three murders contact the VICAP center. The following day, the police in Las Cruces, New Mexico, respond. In March, in that city, a 15-year-old female, hitchhiking to a friend's house, escaped after being assaulted by a male subject who had identified himself as a juvenile officer "working runaway cases." A description of the suspect, suspect vehicle, and MO of the assault is forwarded to VICAP. VICAP alerts the departments working on the three murder cases. VICAP is asked to transmit an APB of the suspect and vehicle description.

The VICAP center also conducts a computer search on its known-offender (profile and MO) file using the MO, physical evidence, and victim information from the murders in California and Texas and the assault MO and suspect description from New Mexico. Two possible names are produced. VICAP alerts the case investigators, who send for and receive mug photos from two state prisons.

One subject is positively identified by the Las Cruces victim. Arrest warrants are issued, and a supplemental APB is transmitted. Two days later the suspect, a parolee from a northwestern state, is arrested after picking up a young hitchhiker in Jackson, Mississippi.[81]

The VICAP form has been organized into the following categories:

- *Part I: Administration*
  Case administration
  Crime classification
  Date and time parameters
- *Part II: Victim information*
  Victim status
  Victim identification
  Physical description
  Scars and /or birthmarks
  Tattoos
  Outstanding physical features
  Clothing of victim
  Miscellaneous
- *Part III: Offender information*
  Offender defined
  Offender status
  Offender identification
  Physical description
  Scars and/or birthmarks
  Tattoos
  Outstanding physical features
- *Part IV: Identified-offender information*
  Offender background
  Property of others
  Offender admissions
- *Part V: Vehicle description*
  Vehicles used in the incident
  Offender's approach to the victim at time of incident
  Exact geographic location
  Location of events, body recovery site
  Site of offender's initial contact with victim
  Victim's last-known location
  Events at assault site
  Offender's writing or carving on body of victim
  Offender's writing or drawing at the scene
  Symbolic artifacts at crime scene
  Offender's communications
  Body disposition
  Restraints used on victim
  Clothing and property of victim
- *Part VI: Cause of death and/or trauma*
  Cause of death
  Bite marks on victim
  Elements of torture or unusual assault
  Sexual assault
- *Part VII: Forensic evidence*
  Weapons
  Blood
- *Part VIII: Request for profile*
- *Part IX: Other related cases*
- *Part X: Narrative summary*

## Key Terms

**algor mortis**
**autopsy**
**cadaver dogs**
**cadaveric spasm**
**CUPPI**
**cyberstalking**
**defense wounds**
**excusable homicide**
**felonious assaults**
**felonious homicides**
**forensic pathology**
**homicide**
**incised wounds**
**justifiable homicide**
**lacerations**
**ligature strangulation**
**livor mortis**
**manslaughter**

**manual strangulation**
**misadventure**
**murder**
**nonfelonious homicides**
**postmortem interval**
**protective order**
**puncture wounds**
**rigor mortis**
**serial murder**
**stalking**
**toxicologist**
**walk-through (of crime scene)**

## Review Questions

1. Briefly discuss the differences between felonious and nonfelonious homicides.
2. What are the four major categories of homicide set forth in the *Crime Classification Manual*?
3. What should the investigator do when responding to a death scene?
4. What are the purposes of an autopsy?
5. Why is the personal identification of a victim so important in homicide investigation?
6. What roles can be played by archaeologists, forensic pathologists, entomologists, and botanists in the search for and discovery of buried bodies?
7. What two methods are typically employed to train cadaver dogs to become sensitive to the smell of decomposing human remains?
8. What role can be played by entomologists in estimating time of death?
9. Briefly describe the typical entrance and exit gunshot wound.
10. What are the basic differences between neutron activation analysis and atomic absorption analysis in testing for firearm residues?
11. Describe an incised wound, stab wound, and laceration.
12. What are defense wounds, and where are they most commonly found?
13. What are the mechanisms of death in ligature strangulation?
14. How is death produced by manual strangulation?
15. Which misconceptions are associated with suicidal hangings?
16. Why are poisons rarely used in homicides?
17. Discuss the differences in suicidal behavior between men and women.
18. What are the most common reasons that hit-and-run drivers fail to stop?
19. In regard to human remains at a fire, what three broad questions should investigators keep in mind?
20. What are the common motives in fire deaths?
21. In determining whether a person is a primary physical aggressor in a family violence complaint, an officer should consider certain factors. What are these factors?
22. What is stalking?
23. What are some of the major characteristics of the simple-obsession stalker?
24. What is cyberstalking?
25. What types of offenses and incidents are reported to the National Center for the Analysis of Violent Crime for analysis?
26. What items are necessary for a psychological profile?

## Internet Activities

1. Within the last decade, several states have revised their statutes relating to domestic violence. Find out if your state has a specific statute on domestic violence. Does the statute outline under what conditions arrests can be made? Is there a mandatory-arrest law? Are there guidelines for officers to follow when addressing domestic violence incidents? How does your state's statute affect the investigation of domestic violence? Legal resource websites such as www.megalaw.com and www.crimelynx.com are a good place to start.

2. Find out more information about the prevalence of stalking by checking out the website www.soshelp.org/. What are the chances of a woman's being stalked in her lifetime? What percent of stalking victims report their victimization to the police? What percent of restraining orders against stalkers are violated? How does the nature of stalking affect a criminal investigation? How might an investigator approach the investigation of this crime differently from that of other crimes?

## Notes

1. Neil C. Chamelin and Kenneth R. Evans, *Criminal Law for Policemen* (Englewood Cliffs, NJ: Prentice Hall, 1995), pp. 116–130.
2. Ibid.
3. John E. Douglas, W. Burgess, Allen G. Burgess, and Robert K. Ressler, *Crime Classification Manual* (New York: Lexington Books, 1992), pp. 22–123.
4. Readers interested in the topic should refer to the most recent *Crime Classification Manual* for a more detailed treatment of the subject.
5. Steven C. Clark, *National Guidelines for Death Investigation* (Washington, DC: U.S. Department of Justice, December 1997), pp. 13–20.
6. Jay Dix and Robert Calaluce, *Guide to Forensic Pathology* (Columbia: University of Missouri, 1998), p. 3.
7. Wisconsin Crime Laboratory, *Criminal Investigation and Physical Evidence Handbook* (Madison: Department of Justice, State of Wisconsin, 1968), p. 10.
8. John J. Horgan, *Criminal Investigation* (New York: McGraw-Hill, 1974), p. 292.
9. Lemoyne Snyder, *Homicide Investigation* (Springfield, IL: Charles C. Thomas, 1973), p. 62.
10. Horgan, *Criminal Investigation,* p. 294.
11. Wisconsin Crime Laboratory, *Criminal Investigation and Physical Evidence Handbook,* p. 11.
12. Donald G. Cherry and J. Lawrence Angel, "Personality Reconstruction from Unidentified Remains," *FBI Law Enforcement Bulletin,* 1977, Vol. 46, No. 48, pp. 12–15. Much of the information dealing with personality reconstruction was obtained from this article.
13. R. M. Boyd, "Buried Bodies," *FBI Law Enforcement Bulletin,* 1979, Vol. 48, No. 2, pp. 1–7. Much of the information dealing with the search for buried bodies was obtained from this article.
14. William M. Bass and Walter H. Birkby, "Exhumation: The Method Could Make the Difference," *FBI Law Enforcement Bulletin,* 1978, Vol. 47, No. 7, pp. 6–11.
15. Marcella H. Sorg, Edward David, and Andrew J. Rebmann, "Cadaver Dogs, Taphonmy, and Post-Mortem Interval in the Northeast," in Kathleen J. Reichs, ed., *Forensic Osteology* (Springfield, IL: Charles C. Thomas, 1998), p. 121.
16. J. S. Sachs, "Fake Smell of Death," *Discover: The World of Science,* 1996, Vol. 17, No. 3, pp. 87–94.
17. Dix and Calaluce, *Guide to Forensic Pathology,* p. 32.
18. Ibid., pp. 35–36.
19. Ibid., pp. 33–34.
20. Francis E. Camps, ed., *Gradwohl's Legal Medicine,* 3rd ed. (Bristol: Wright and Sons, 1976), p. 83.
21. There is no mention of cadaveric spasm in the voluminous and comprehensive work of Werner V. Spitz and Russell S. Fisher, eds., *Medicolegal Investigation of Death,* 2nd ed. (Springfield, IL: Charles C. Thomas, 1980).
22. Dix and Calaluce, *Guide to Forensic Pathology,* pp. 38–40.
23. W. C. Rodriguez and William C. Bass, *Determination of Time of Death by Means of Carrion Insects,* paper presented at the 35th annual meeting of the American Academy of Forensic Sciences, Cincinnati, Ohio, Feb. 15–19, 1983. This discussion and accompanying figures were taken, with modification, from pp. 1–6.
24. N. H. Haskell, David G. McShaffrey, D. A. Hawley, R. E. Williams, and J. E. Pless, "Use of Aquatic Insects in Determining Submersion Interval," *Journal of Forensic Sciences,* May 1989, Vol. 34, No. 3, pp. 622, 623.
25. Barry A. J. Fisher, *Techniques of Crime Scene Investigation* (New York: Elsevier, 1992), pp. 452–458. This discussion was adapted with permission from this source.
26. The information on shotgun wounds was obtained from material developed by Vincent J. M. DiMaio, M.D., medical examiner, Dallas County, Texas.
27. The information on firearm residue included in this chapter was developed by the Southwestern Institute of Forensic Sciences at Dallas, Texas.

28. R. C. Harrison and R. Gilroy, "Firearms Discharge Residues," *Journal of Forensic Sciences,* 1959, No. 4, pp. 184–199.
29. S. S. Krishman, K. A. Gillespie, and E. J. Anderson, "Rapid Detection of Firearm Discharge Residues by Atomic Absorption and Neutron Activation Analysis," *Journal of Forensic Sciences,* 1977, No. 16, pp. 144–151. Also see I. C. Stone and C. S. Petty, "Examination of Gunshot Residues," *Journal of Forensic Sciences,* 1974, No. 19, pp. 784–788.
30. Dominic J. DiMaio and Vincent J. M. DiMaio, *Forensic Pathology* (New York: Elsevier, 1989), p. 87.
31. Ibid.
32. Ibid., pp. 231–243.
33. Jacques Charon, *Suicide* (New York: Scribner's, 1972), p. 56.
34. Ibid., p. 39.
35. Andrew P. Johnson, "Hammer Spur Impressions: Physical Evidence in Suicides," *FBI Law Enforcement Bulletin,* September 1988, pp. 11–14. This discussion was adapted from this article.
36. Lemoyne Snyder, *Homicide Investigation* (Springfield, IL: Charles C. Thomas, 1973), p. 228.
37. Donna Newson, "Doctors Perform Rare Surgery," *Tampa Tribune,* July 25, 1980, pp. A1, A10.
38. Richard H. Fox and Carl L. Cunningham, *Crime Scene Search and Physical Evidence Handbook* (Washington, DC: Government Printing Office, 1973), pp. 124, 126. This discussion of poisons was taken from this source.
39. *Suicide Investigation, Part II: Training Key 196* (Gaithersburg, MD: International Association of Chiefs of Police, 1973), pp. 4–5.
40. J. Tuckman et al., "Credibility of Suicide Notes," *American Journal of Psychiatry,* June 1960, No. 65, pp. 1104–1106.
41. David Lester, *Why People Kill Themselves* (Springfield, IL: Charles C. Thomas, 1972), p. 36.
42. D. Hastings, "Long Investigation Uncovers Suicide Scheme," *Tampa Tribune-Times,* Jan. 22, 1984, p. A24.
43. J. Stannard Baker and Thomas Lindquist, *Lamp Examination for On or Off in Traffic Accidents,* 3rd ed. (Evanston, IL.: Traffic Institute, Northwestern University, 1983).
44. *Hit and Run Investigation: Training Key 7* (Washington, DC: International Association of Chiefs of Police, 1967), pp. 2–3.
45. Z. G. Standing Bear, *The Investigation of Questioned Deaths and Injuries—Conference Notes and Outline* (Valdosta, GA: Valdosta State College Press, 1988), pp. 78–82.
46. John J. O'Conner, *Practical Fire and Arson Investigation* (Boca Raton, FL: CRC Press, 1993), pp. 160–161.
47. Ibid.
48. Camps, *Gradwohl's Legal Medicine,* p. 358; Lester Adelson, *The Pathology of Homicide* (Springfield, IL: Charles C. Thomas, 1974), p. 610; Richard Lindenberg, "Mechanical Injuries of the Brain and Meninges," in Spitz and Fisher, *Medicolegal Investigation of Death,* pp. 447–456.
49. O'Conner, *Practical Fire and Arson Investigation,* pp. 165–166.
50. Ibid., pp. 152–153. This discussion is taken with permission from this source.
51. Ronet Bachman, *Violence against Women,* National Institute of Justice (Washington, DC: U.S. Department of Justice, 1994), p. 6.
52. *Official Code of Georgia Annotated,* Vol. 16 Cumulative Supplement (Charlottesville, VA: Michie Company, 1994), p. 89.
53. *Official Code of Georgia Annotated,* Vol. 15 Cumulative Supplement (Charlottesville, VA: Michie Company, 1994), p. 8.
54. Ibid., pp. 11–12.
55. Patricia Tjaden and Nancy Thoennes, *Stalking in America: Findings from the National Violence against Women Survey,* National Institute of Justice, Center for Disease Control and Prevention, U.S. Department of Justice (Washington, D.C.: Government Printing Office, April 1998), pp. 1–3.
56. Kenneth R. Thomas, "How to Stop the Stalker: State Anti-Stalking Laws," *Criminal Law Bulletin,* Vol. 29, No. 2, pp. 124–136.
57. "Stalking Laws," *State Legislative Report,* Denver, Col., National Conference of State Legislatures, Vol. 17, No. 19, October 1992, pp. 1–6.
58. National Institute of Justice, *Domestic Violence, Stalking and Anti-Stalking Legislation: An Annual Report to Congress under the Violence against Women Act* (Washington, DC: U.S. Department of Justice, April 1996).
59. Ibid.
60. National Criminal Justice Association, *Project to Develop a Model Anti-Stalking Code for States* (Washington, DC: U.S. Department of Justice, October 1993).
61. National Victim Center, www.ojp.usdoj.gov/ovc/help/stalk/info43.htm, Apr. 19, 2001, pp. 1–4. This discussion of stalking was adapted from this source.
62. J. M. Deirmenjian, "Stalking in Cyberspace," *Journal of American Academic Psychiatry and Law,* 1999, Vol. 27, No. 3, pp. 407–413.

63. National Criminal Justice Association, National Institute of Justice, *Project to Develop a Model Anti-Stalking Code for States* (Washington, DC: U.S. Department of Justice, 1993), p. 75.
64. Ibid., p. 76.
65. Ibid., p. 75.
66. Ibid.
67. Ibid., p. 76.
68. Ibid.
69. Ibid.
70. Ibid., p. 77.
71. Tjaden and Thoennes, *Stalking in America,* p. 11.
72. A. Egger, *The Killers among Us* (Upper Saddle River, NJ: 2002), pp. 4–7, 11; R. Hazlewood and J. Douglas, (1980, April). "The Lust Murderer," *FBI Law Enforcement Bulletin,* April 1980, pp. 1–5.
73. J. de River, *Crime and the Sexual Psychopath* (Springfield, IL: Charles C. Thomas, 1958), p. 99.
74. E. Revitch and L. Schlesinger, *Psychopathology of Homicide* (Springfield, IL: Charles C. Thomas, 1981); M. Reynolds, *Dead Ends* (New York: Warner Books, 1992), p. 281.
75. D. Lunde, *Murder and Madness* (Stanford, CA: Stanford Alumni Association, 1976), p. 53.
76. J. Levin and J. Fox, *Mass Murder* (New York: Plenum, 1985), p. 225.
77. S. Egger, *Serial Murder and the Law Enforcement Response,* unpublished dissertation, College Of Criminal Justice, Sam Houston State University, Huntsville, Texas.
78. A. Ellis and J. Gullo, *Murder and Assassination* (New York: Lyle Stuart, 1971); R. Hazlewood and J. Douglas, "The Lust Murderer," *FBI Law Enforcement Bulletin,* April 1980, pp. 1–5; J. Reinhardt, *The Psychology of a Strange Killer* (Springfield, IL: Charles C. Thomas, 1962).
79. National Center for the Analysis of Violent Crime, Behavioral Science Unit, FBI Academy (Quantico, VA: 1985), p. 5.
80. VICAP Crime Analysis Report Form used by the FBI for profiling, 1999.
81. National Center for the Analysis of Violent Crime, p. 7.

# TEN

# Sex-Related Offenses

*Jennifer W., rape victim, is consoled by her fiance during the sentencing of Timothy Mobly in Reno, Nevada. The investigation of sex-related offenses is one of the most sensitive matters undertaken by the police and is given high priority because these offenses involve not only physical but also psychological injury to the victim. (© AP/Wide World Photos)*

## CHAPTER OUTLINE



## CHAPTER OBJECTIVES

1. List and explain the classifications of sex offenses.
2. List and explain the four types of sexual murder.
3. Discuss interview procedures and investigative questions for sexual assault cases.
4. Explain why women do not report rape to the police and the motivations for false rape allegations.
5. Outline the types of physical evidence collected in rape and sexual assault cases.
6. Discuss the important of condom trace evidence.
7. Identify the use and effects of Rohypnol and GHB.
8. Assess investigative and evidence collection techniques for drug-facilitated sexual assaults.
9. Recognize common characteristics of sexual asphyxia, or autoerotic death.
10. Describe a psychological autopsy.

# INTRODUCTION

The term "sex-related offenses" covers a broad category of specific acts against adults, children, males, and females. Rape or sexual battery is legally defined as the crime of a person's having sexual relations with another person under the following circumstances: (1) against the person's consent, (2) while the person is unconscious, (3) while the person is under the influence of alcohol or drugs, (4) if the person is feeble-minded or insane, and (5) if the person is a child who is under the age of consent as fixed by statute. This chapter focuses primarily on sexual assaults that are typically directed toward postpubescent and adult females.

Sex offenses in general are classified into several categories, such as serious, nuisance, and mutual consent. Various types of sexual murders including their dynamics, homicidal patterns, and suspect profiles, are also discussed in this chapter. In addition, the chapter provides very specific recommendations on how to conduct criminal investigations that are sexual in nature. The investigation and interview of a sexual assault victim can be one of the most delicate and challenging tasks for the criminal investigator. The investigator must obtain all the necessary information yet, at the same time, do so with respect and concern for the traumatic event the victim has just experienced. It is absolutely imperative that the investigator does not in any way pass judgment on the victim that results in revictimization. The chapter also outlines and discusses the considerable amount of physical evidence that is often available when sex crimes are committed.

Recently, the issue of drug-facilitated sexual assault, particularly the use of Rohypnol and GHB, has received much attention. Investigating this type of sexual assault is unique in that the drugs can be slipped into drinks of unsuspecting victims, the victim often experiences a loss of consciousness and therefore cannot recall the assault, and the drugs are only traceable in a person's blood or urine for a limited amount of time. The effects of these drugs and the investigative procedures used for this type of sexual assault are addressed. The chapter concludes with a discussion of sexual asphyxia, or autoerotic death, and a description of psychological autopsies.

## CLASSIFICATION OF SEX OFFENSES

There are three classifications of **sex offenses:** serious, nuisance, and mutual consent. With the exception of murder, few crimes generate greater public concern and interest than serious sex offenses.

### SERIOUS SEX OFFENSES

The term "serious" is used because not all sex offenses are a significant threat to the individual or to the public. Sex offenses of this type, such as rape or sexual battery as it is also called, are high-priority offenses because they constitute the greatest physical and psychological injury to the victim.

In this chapter, the focus is primarily on the crime of rape and the physical evidence associated with this crime.

### NUISANCE SEX OFFENSES

Included in this classification are such acts as voyeurism and exhibitionism. Usually such acts present no personal danger to anyone except the offender, who may fall prey to an angry father, husband, or boyfriend. Few perpetrators of nuisance sex offenses physically injure anyone. But such instances do sometimes occur:

THE police were called to an apartment complex by tenants who had become concerned after not having seen their next-door neighbor for two days. The neighbor was an attractive 25-year-old woman. The police entered the apartment of the woman and discovered her dismembered body stuffed in a clothes trunk in her bedroom.

The investigation resulted in the arrest of a suspect. He stated that a few days before the murder, he had seen the victim hanging some undergarments on a clothesline. The suspect returned a few hours later, at dark, and stole two of the victim's panties and bras off the clothesline.

The victim mentioned the incident to a neighbor but not to the police. Later, the suspect returned to the victim's home and saw her, through a bedroom window, disrobe and put on a nightgown. He became sexually aroused and entered the house through an unlocked, rear kitchen door. He picked up a knife from a table in the kitchen and went directly to the victim's bedroom. When she saw him, she became frightened. The perpetrator told her not to scream or he would kill her. He ordered her to take off her nightgown and get into bed. He got into bed with her, still clutching the knife. While having sexual intercourse with her, for some reason he could not explain, he started choking her. When she started to resist, he plunged the knife into her heart, killing her instantly. He then dressed the victim in undergarments and a dress, propped her in a chair in the bedroom, and talked to the deceased victim for approximately 45 minutes. Then he disrobed and dismembered the body and stuffed it into the clothes trunk. The suspect admitted to the police that he had acted as a voyeur on other occasions but had never before assaulted any woman.

## SEX OFFENSES INVOLVING MUTUAL CONSENT

Sex offenses of this nature involve consenting adults whose behavior is deemed illegal by various state and local laws; examples include adultery, fornication, prostitution, and certain homosexual activities. Except for commercial prostitution and public solicitation by homosexuals, many police agencies assign these acts low investigative priority. When enforcement action is taken, it is generally because of a citizen complaint or because the act was performed in a public place and observed by the police or a private citizen.

## RAPE-MURDER

Several years ago Robert D. Keppel and Richard Walter developed a classification model for understanding **rape-murder.**[1] By examining the behaviors, homicidal patterns, and suspect profiles of convicted sexual murderers, they came up with four classifications:

- Power assertive
- Power reassurance
- Anger retaliatory
- Anger excitation

Each category is discussed in detail below. See Table 10–1 for a comparison of the dynamics of the four categories.

### Power-Assertive Rape-Murder

***Dynamics*** The power-assertive rape-murder is a series of acts in which the rape is planned but the murder is an unplanned response of increasing aggression to ensure control of the victim. The acts within the rape assault are characterized by forceful aggression and intimidation. Specific to the expression of virility, mastery, and dominance, a direct and overpowering assault is necessary and often results in multiple antemortem rapes of the victim.

***Homicidal Pattern*** The homicidal pattern in the power-assertive murder is characterized by the sating of power needs through sexual assault and murder. Once the perpetrator has decided to commit either the initial or a repeat rape-murder, the methods for victim selection and acting out will be determined by previous experience, the stress of internal pressures, and opportunity. Accordingly, in selecting the victim, the perpetrator may choose on the basis of opportunity and surprise. Often, the victim is a stranger who is available by surprise on the street or through a breaking and entering into a home. If the rape assault occurs in a home and the husband is present, he may be required to watch the assault or participate.

***Suspect Profile*** The power-assertive type of killer is usually in his early twenties and somewhat emotionally primitive. He is primarily preoccupied with projecting a macho image and orients his life accordingly. Despite a wide range of physical characteristics and types, the power-assertive offender is sensitive to his characteristics of masculinity. Therefore, he often is a bodybuilder and portrays a muscular image and/or displays tattoos for a show of machismo and power. In addition to displaying a confident body posture, the offender cruises in his well-attended car, carries weapons, and shows an arrogant and condescending attitude to others. Alcohol and drugs may be used heavily to bolster the offender's courage and power, but he does not abuse these substances to the point of blacking out.

Although the offender may associate with people, he is not seen as a team player. Socially, he may not be a hermit, but because of his level of frustration with social contacts, he at times lives on the edge of being a loner. Although he may have an active interest in sports, it is generally limited to individual-contact events such as wrestling, judo, and karate. For the most part, he seeks to gain power and displays a winner-take-all attitude. Although he may have a history of multiple marriages and relationships, he does not view them as successful.

In demonstrating his potential for power, he has a history of perpetrating crimes such as burglary, theft, and robbery. Unless the criminal history has

**Table 10-1** Rape-Murder Classifications: Comparison of Dynamics

| Power Assertive | Power Reassurance | Anger Retaliatory | Anger Excitation |
|---|---|---|---|
| Rape is planned; murder is not planned | Rape is planned; murder is not planned | Rape and murder are planned | Rape and murder are planned |
| Power interest | Power interest | Anger driven | Anger driven |
| Killer's increasing aggression toward the victim ensures control | Killer acts out fantasy and seeks reassurance from the victim | Killer seeks revenge for anger toward another person by attacking a symbolic victim | Killer engages in prolonged torture, exploitation, and/or mutilation, thereby energizing his fantasy life |

**Source:** Robert D. Keppel and Richard Walter, "Profiling Killers: A Revised Classification Model for Understanding Sexual Murder," *International Journal of Offender Therapy and Comparative Criminology,* 1999, Vol. 43, No. 4, p. 420.

resulted in a mental health referral, he may have had no contact with mental health workers.

Educationally, he is typically a school dropout. Based on the limits of the masculine image, his sexual preferences will not accommodate the variety of materials contained in hard-core pornographic literature. He is especially conflicted over unconventional sexual interest and may display a strong antihomosexual attitude. For the most part, if he reads magazines, they will likely be of the *Playboy* and *Penthouse* type.

Although he may have served in the Marines or the Navy, his service record is generally poor, and he may have terminated his service prematurely. He is generally viewed as antisocial.

## Power-Reassurance Rape-Murder

***Dynamics*** In the power-reassurance rape-homicide, a planned, single rape attack is followed by an unplanned overkill of the victim. Motivated by an idealized seduction and conquest fantasy, the killer focuses on acting out a fantasy and seeks verbal reassurance of his sexual adequacy. When the victim does not yield to the killer's planned seduction scenario, a sense of failure and panic thrusts him into a murder assault. In the murder assault, he gains control and lessens the threat over the situation in which the victim was not compliant. After killing his unrequited lover, the murderer may act out his sexual fantasies through exploratory postmortem mutilation.

The power-reassurance type tries to express his sexual competence through seduction. When that fails, the subsequent killing permits him to reintroduce the fantasy system for further sexual exploration that he was not allowed to do prior to the killing. The quest for sexual competency and personal adequacy dominates any fantasy drawings he may do.

***Homicidal Pattern*** In planning the rape, the power-reassurance perpetrator selects and watches a female victim, often 10 or 15 years older or younger than the perpetrator. He may choose a casual acquaintance, neighbor, or stranger. No matter which, he applies his fantasies to that victim. In the power-reassurance rape-homicide, the murder occurs after the attempted rape has failed and the perpetrator feels a need for emotional catharsis and victim control. Although the offender has no intent of harming or degrading the victim, the failure of the rape assault and the rejection from the victim panics him into a homicide overkill. Believing that he can act out sexual fantasy and reality, he prepares a scenario of misbeliefs designed to seduce the victim into validating his sexual competence. When the victim does not follow his plan, he feels threatened and attacks the victim.

The power-reassurance offender uses threats and intimidation to gain initial control and sometimes enters the crime scene with a weapon. Usually the first time he attacks, a weapon is not preselected and brought to the scene. The second time, he may bring a gun and display it but will not fire it due to the noise. The third time, the weapon may be a knife.

After the initial attack on the victim, the offender tries to act out the preprogrammed fantasy. In this respect, he has been called the polite and gentleman rapist due to the verbal dialogue that he tries to carry on with the victim. During the assault, he may ask the victim to remove her clothing and be quite polite with other such requests. While assuring her that he is not going to hurt her, he seeks reassurances of his sexual competency from her. Typically, he may ask, "Is this nice? Do you like this? Is this pleasing to you? Am I better than . . . ?"

When the killer finds his sexual competence threatened through ridicule, challenge, and counterattack, he loses control of the situation and kills the victim through pummeling and manual strangulation. Because he fears the revelation of his failure at sex, he initiates the homicidal attack to control the victim and protect his self-image.

Because the incomplete sexual assault does not validate his sexual competency, he will often explore the mysteries and curiosities of sex on the postmortem body. Consequently, there is sometimes mutilation of the body coupled with evidence of ritualism. Because his fantasies have been shunted by the unsuccessful rape, there often is no evidence of sperm at the murder crime scene.

***Suspect Profile*** The general acting-out age of the power-reassurance murderer is the midtwenties. Of course, the age can vary and may depend on circumstances such as the incarceration of the offender for other crimes during his midtwenties. Although intellectually and educationally equal to most other types of offenders, the murderer relies excessively on fantasies that allow opposing ideas to come in close proximity. This often makes the offender appear dull and somewhat emotionally scattered. He prefers to satisfy his needs through certain fantasies rather than risk rejection. As a consequence, he is often plagued by an inadequate sex life and uses sexual fantasies and relationships to overcome the dysfunction and pain of reality.

In developing his extensive repertoire of rape fantasies, he borrows notions from erotic pornography and a long history of substitutions for sexual activity such as window peeping, fondling of clothing, and obsessive daydreaming. Developmentally, the onset of absorbing fantasies may have started in the early juvenile years. Because his fantasies have taken him into a private world, he is generally viewed as socially isolated, with no male or female friends. He is viewed as a loner and a weirdo. Generally, he is an unmarried person without a history of normal sexual activities.

Due to the dominating influence of fantasy activities, he tends to be an immature person who views life as a spectator, not as a participant. In other words, he lacks the confidence to participate. He feels inferior and cannot tolerate criticism of team members. Again, because his activities are dominated by compressed and edited illusions, he often bypasses the social intermediate steps in developing normal social-sexual interactions.

Given the excessive energies directed toward his own self-stimulation, the offender may live at home and try to subsist on little income. If income is not available, he may perform menial labor to support basic needs. Accordingly, he often lives, works, and plays in a neighborhood familiar to him. A common form of transport is walking. However, if he does have a car, it is most likely an older model in need of repair.

## Anger-Retaliatory Rape-Murder

***Dynamics*** In the anger-retaliatory rape-murder, the rape is planned and the initial murder involves overkill. It is an anger-venting act that expresses symbolic revenge on a female victim. Nettled by poor relationships with women, the aggressor distills his anguish and contempt into an act of explosive revenge on the victim. Although the assault is not predicated on a fantasy system, it is often precipitated by a criticism or scolding from a woman with power over him. In the attempt to express revenge and retaliation for being disciplined, the aggressive killer either directs his anger at that woman or redirects his anger to a substitute woman. Because the latter scapegoating retaliation does not eliminate the direct source of hate, it is likely that it will be episodically repeated to relieve internal stresses. Dynamically, the rape-homicide is committed in a stylized violent outburst for the purposes of retaliating, getting even, and taking revenge on women.

***Homidical Pattern*** The homicidal pattern is characterized by a violent sexual assault and overkill of a victim. Inasmuch as the actual source of the killer's anger is a woman who belittles, humiliates, and rejects him, the fatal hostility may not be directed at a mother, wife, or female supervisor but at an unsuspecting substitute victim whom the killer has sought out. In such instances, the victim is likely to be in the killer's age group or older. Often, the substitute victim comes from areas in which the aggressor lives or works. That is, while conducting routine, everyday living, the aggressor may find a potential victim who reminds him of his mother or girlfriend. A chance meeting could occur at a local store, or the killer could find the victim by cruising a neighborhood. When a potential victim is selected, he will keep in mind her location and living circumstances.

Alternatively, the aggressor tends to act out against the actual victim directly, rather than through a substitute, when the actual (targeted) victim is a younger person. This type of victim, for example, may be a dismissive female clerk who says "no" or a child who threatens to expose inappropriate sexual behaviors. The victims are from familiar areas, and the aggressor is intent on sating.

In approaching the crime scene, the killer usually walks. However, if necessary, he may drive to the crime scene area and approach the last 200 feet on foot. The anger-retaliatory killer may have some type of ruse to get inside the victim's home, but once the victim is isolated, he confronts her.

Armed with a barrage of accusations, he responds to the victim's denial of him by hitting her in the mouth and about the face. As the assault becomes more combative, the aggressor may use weapons of opportunity (knives, statuary, etc.) to brutalize the victim. Depending on the aggressor's age, experience, and internal stresses, the rape assault may be incomplete because of an inability to get an erection. Therefore, semen may not be found at the crime scene. In either case, the aggressor is intent on sating his anger through percussive acts of assault with fists, blunt objects, or a knife.

Regardless of whether the victim is alive or dead, the assault continues until the perpetrator is emotionally satisfied. As his anger begins to cool, he puts the body in a submissive position by placing it on its side away from the door or face down, putting an artifact or cloth across the eyes, or placing the body in a closet with the door closed. Generally, after the intense expression of anger, the killer tends to leave a disorganized crime scene, and the improvised murder weapon may be found within 15 feet of the body. Just before leaving the crime scene, the perpetrator often takes a small trinket or souvenir.

***Suspect Profile*** The anger-retaliatory offender is usually in his mid- to late twenties and somewhat younger than his victims. He is seen as an explosive personality who is impulsive, quick-tempered, and self-centered. In dealing with people, he is not reclusive but is a loner in the midst of a crowd. Generally, his social relations are superficial and limited to many drinking buddies. Socially, he is a person whom no one really knows. Although a sportsman, he prefers playing team-contact sports.

Conflicted over his relationship with women, he may often feel dependent on and aggressively

**Lawrence Singleton**

Lawrence Singleton stands motionless as the jury in his first-degree murder trial hands down a guilty verdict Friday afternoon, February 20, 1998, at the Hillsborough County Courthouse in Tampa, Florida. Singleton was found guilty of stabbing a prostitute during an argument. He is most noted for being released early from prison after being convicted in 1978 of raping and cutting the arms off a California teen.

(© AP/Wide World Photos)

resistant to them. When challenged by women, he may use various forms of aggression to get even and degrade them. If he has been married, his marital relationship may have been ill-fated or may be in some phase of estrangement. The marriage is generally characterized by a history of spousal abuse. Rather than dealing with the problems in the marriage, he will often avoid them by seeking extramarital liaisons. For the most part, these relationships are unsatisfactory.

Sexually, he is frustrated and may be impotent. Often, he links eroticized anger with sexual competence. Although he may look at *Playboy* and similar types of magazines out of curiosity, he does not use pornographic materials for stimulation.

When his aggressive feelings toward women are linked with impulsive behavior, he may develop a history of committing crimes such as assault and battery, wife beating, felonious assault, and reckless driving. Humiliated by disciplinary violations, he is usually a school dropout who has not lived up to his potential. If he joined the military, his unsettled behavior often results in a discharge from service. Consistent with this behavioral pattern, his free-floating anger is the cause of many difficulties with authority. His unpredictable behavior may have resulted in his being referred to a mental health worker.

## Anger-Excitation Rape-Murder

***Dynamics*** The anger-excitation rape-murder is designed to inflict pain and terror on the victim for the gratification of the perpetrator. The prolonged torture of the victim energizes the killer's fantasies and temporarily satisfies a lust for domination and control. Precipitated by highly specialized fantasies, the perpetrator selects the victim, male or female, and escalates violence through various acquired and learned incremental levels of ritualistic carnage. Dynamically, the approach of the victim, exploitation of naivete, torture, and mutilation all serve to appease the perpetrator's insatiable appetite for the process of killing.

Unlike the case with other murderers, the satisfaction of the sadist is found in the art and process of killing, not in the death. In some instances, the actual death may be anticlimactic. However, in the execution of crimes, the excitement is heightened by the realization of a rehearsed scenario of eroticized anger and power that has been building in his fantasy life until he steps across the line into the reality of murder. Again, sadistic murder is comprised of a series of recognizable deviancies that coalesce into a ritualistic satisfaction. Inasmuch as the development of the process requires an investment of acquired skills, energy, and time, the intent becomes one of indulgent luxury rather than the end goal of a dead body.

***Homicidal Pattern*** In the anger-excitation rape-murder, the homicidal pattern is characterized by a prolonged, bizarre, ritualistic assault on the victim. Sponsored by a plan of action, the fantasy of the assault is put into action with an equipped murder kit. Often, the victim may be a stranger who fits the perpetrator's needs for a symbol, such as a nurse, a prostitute, a child, a student, or a matriarch. Also, he may be attracted to victims who meet certain criteria, such as long blond hair, specialized shoes, or a tramp image. When preparing to encounter the victim, the organized offender can invoke a disarmingly charming manner and dispel most immediate fears from the victim.

Once the victim is isolated, the offender will drop the mask. At that time, he will begin to display vacillating mood shifts that confuse the victim. He may tell her, in a very matter-of-fact, monotone voice, "I'm going to kill you," just to watch the look of terror on the victim's face. When he sees the victim becoming terrorized, he goes into a fantasy, and a methodical love for torture is demonstrated through acts of sexual ritual and experimentation. While showing variant forms of dependency, dread, and degradation, the offender is limited only by imagination. Most commonly, bondage and domination play a significant role in the killing process.

In addition, there may be evidence of antemortem cuttings, bruises, and various forms of incomplete strangulation, body washing, shaving, and burns. Although some offenders may attempt perimortem sex, the evidence of ejaculate in the body is not likely at this stage. After the victim has been bludgeoned and strangled, the likelihood for postmortem experimental sexuality increases. At this stage, evidence of secondary sexual mechanisms is most likely. The evidence of sexual exploration is revealed by localized brutalization, skin tears, and objects inserted into the body. In addition, the killer may leave the body in a bizarre state of undress after possibly cutting the clothing off. In some cases, the clothing may be fetish items that he takes as souvenirs. In other cases, the perpetrator may leave clothing neatly folded alongside the body. In still others, he may harvest parts of the body.

***Suspect Profile*** The age range of the anger-excitation murderer, is considered somewhat variable. Although the perpetrator usually commits his first homicide by the age of 35, it is possible that a late bloomer could do so at an older age. Characteristically, the organized offender is often a well-appearing person who is bright and socially facile with others. On the basis of his ability to appear conventional and law abiding, he can cunningly deceive others. Because he is able to separate his general lifestyle from his criminal interest, he may have a good marriage in which he may perform as a dutiful and conventional husband. Financially, he is identified as an adequate provider. His work history may be tumultuous until he finds a position with minimum supervision. Sometimes, he may show a penchant for mechanical interests and working with his hands. If so, he may seek employment in the semiskilled trades, such as auto mechanics, carpentry, or specialty factory work. In his daily habits, he is often compulsive and structurally organized. Educationally, he may have two years of college and/or may have graduated. If he served in the military, he will have done well and may have been identified as "good officer material."

Because of his exceptional ability to organize, he can successfully segment his criminal interest into a private world of protected ritualisms. Often, his ritual paraphernalia and souvenirs are contained in a private chamber of horrors, which may be a dark closet, a room, a basement, or a hole in the ground or an abandoned barn, cabin, or garage. Inside this special area, he will keep the victim's souvenirs, his murder kit, and favored pornographic materials. Characteristically, the pornographic materials will depict terror and scantily dressed victims; most often, the literature shows bondage and sadism. Because the special area is designed to help the perpetrator manufacture and refine his fantasies, it may contain a wide range of masochistic and sadistic clues. Although alcohol is not indicated, it is possible that the perpetrator will use chemical drugs to fuel his fantasies.

**Michael P. Nickerson**

Convicted child rapist Michael P. Nickerson listens during a hearing to revoke his probation in Brockton Superior Court in Brockton, Massachusetts, on charges he had violated his parole by carrying a knife and hanging around with teenagers. Nickerson, soon after his release from prison, was found in the company of two teenage boys, ages 13 and 15, in the woods, according to the Plymouth County District Attorney prosecutor, who said the former assistant Boy Scout troop leader was also in possession of weapons.

(© AP/Wide World Photos)

## SEX-RELATED INVESTIGATIONS

**Rape,** or **sexual battery,** is a legal term defining the crime of a person having sexual relations with another person under the following circumstances: (1) against the person's consent, (2) while the person is unconscious, (3) while the person is under the influence of alcohol or drugs, (4) if the person is feeble-minded or insane, and (5) if the person is a child who is under the age of consent as fixed by statute. Rape is generally considered a woman-centered issue, but growing awareness has led to a rise in reports of male rape. Keep in mind that society places greater stigma on male rape victimization. Fear, shame and this stigmatization still prevent a large number of male victims from reporting their experience. Whether the victims are male or female, the offenders are overwhelmingly male but it is certainly possible for a female to perpetrate rape.[2]

When police and medical examiners are confronted with a dead body, they are obviously not able to interview the deceased victim to obtain an explanation for what has occurred. Investigators must rely on their initial impression of the scene, such as the state of the victim's clothing, positioning of the body, items found, and the presence or absence of injuries related to sexual activity (e.g., bite marks, hickeys, direct genital or oral injury), in deciding whether sexual activity or attempted sexual activity was related to the cause of death. The investigator must be mindful, however, in weighing the significance of the presence of sexual evidence. Although the victim may have engaged in sexual activity with another person before death, the intercourse might not be related to the cause of death.

In the case of a homicide involving a female victim, it is a frequent and ordinary occurrence for investigators to question whether a rape has taken place. However, it is imperative that the question of rape also arise when the victim of a homicide is male. This is especially true when a male child is involved. Currently, the U.S. Department of Justice estimates that about 1 out of every 10 rape victims over the age of 12 is male and that fully half of all underage sexual-abuse victims are male.[3] Sex is a major motivator and modifier of human behavior. Therefore, a determination of sexual activity may be of great value not only in a rape-murder case but also in natural, suicidal, or accidental deaths. Careful observation of the scene and the body may indicate a need for a rape investigation. Even if sexual intercourse does not seem to have any direct bearing on the cause of death, it may explain motives or timing of death or simply provide a check on the veracity of a suspect or witness. The following cases illustrate these points:

A 53-year-old businessman was found dead in a motel room. There was no evidence of foul play. The bed was in slight disarray, with one of the pillows on the floor. The bed covers were bunched in an unusual position. The body on the floor was dressed in a shirt, loosened tie, trousers, underclothes, and socks. Shoes were neatly laid out next to a chair, and a jacket was on the back of a chair. Examination of the contents of the deceased's trouser pockets revealed the usual items, except for a pair of female panties. Autopsy revealed a massive heart attack and no vaginal cells on the penis. A logical reconstruction of the events preceding death suggested sexual foreplay with a female, in the course of which a wrestling match ensued during which the man took the woman's panties and then suffered a heart attack.

Although establishing the absence of sexual intercourse in this case did not significantly add to the medical solution of the problem, it did explain why the victim was found at a motel when he was supposedly having lunch.

A furnace repairman was found dead, slumped over the front seat of his van. There was no evidence of foul play, and the medical examiner was not called to the scene. Observation at the morgue revealed that there were peculiar parallel linear abrasions over the victim's knees, tearing of the overalls at the same region, and no underwear. His boots were reversed and loosely laced. Penile washings were positive for vaginal cells. Further investigation disclosed that he had visited a woman at 7 in the morning under the pretext of cleaning her furnace and had been stricken by a heart attack during intercourse. The woman hastily dressed him and dragged him across the back alley to his truck, not realizing that his underwear was neatly tucked under her bed.

A 15-year-old girl's body was found in a vacant lot. The absence of clothing on the lower body suggested sexual intercourse immediately before or at the time of death. Faint abrasions were present on the back of the neck, and marked hemorrhages were present in the eye. The medical examiner believed that this was a case of rape-murder. Autopsy confirmed recent sexual intercourse. The scratch on the back of the neck, however, proved to be superficial, and there were no deeper injuries. Reconstruction of the events immediately preceding death confirmed that the girl had had sexual intercourse with her boyfriend (who lived nearby), in the course of which (according to the boyfriend's testimony) the girl started making choking noises. She reported pain in her chest but said that it was going away. The boyfriend resumed intercourse. The girl started making even more violent noises. He assumed these to be related to orgasm. After intercourse, he noticed that the girl was motionless and unresponsive. After a few minutes, he decided that she was dead and became very scared. He escaped from the scene and told investigators that he had not seen his girlfriend on the night of her death.

THE body of a missing preadolescent boy was found in the woods, face down, with his hands tied behind his back by laces removed from his sneakers and his belt. His trousers and jockey shorts were pulled down below the buttocks. The ligature on the hands consisted of laces removed from the boy's sneakers and the boy's own belt. He had been tied around the neck with a torn piece of his shirt. The scene suggested homosexual rape-murder. However, the investigation revealed no evidence of sexual assault. Although there was a depressed groove under the ligature, no subcutaneous hemorrhages were associated with it. A contusion on the back of the neck was associated with deep hemorrhages in the muscles and around the base of the skull and cervical spine. Reconstruction of the case directed suspicion to the boy's stepfather, who had discovered the body. The subsequent investigation revealed that after finding the boy, who frequently played hooky from school, wandering through the woods, the stepfather had hit him with a karate chop to the neck, killing him. The stepfather then tied and disrobed the child to convey the impression of homosexual assault.

**Mary Vincent**

Mary Vincent, who was raped and mutilated by Lawrence Singleton in 1978 in California, testifies in Hillsborough County Court in the penalty phase of Singleton's murder trial. Singleton was charged with first degree murder in the death of Roxanne Hayes. Hayes's body was found in Singleton's home stabbed to death. Singleton, who was convicted for Hayes's death, had served prison time in California for chopping off the arms of then teenage hitchhiker Mary Vincent.

(AP Photo/Tampa Tribune, David Kadlubowski)

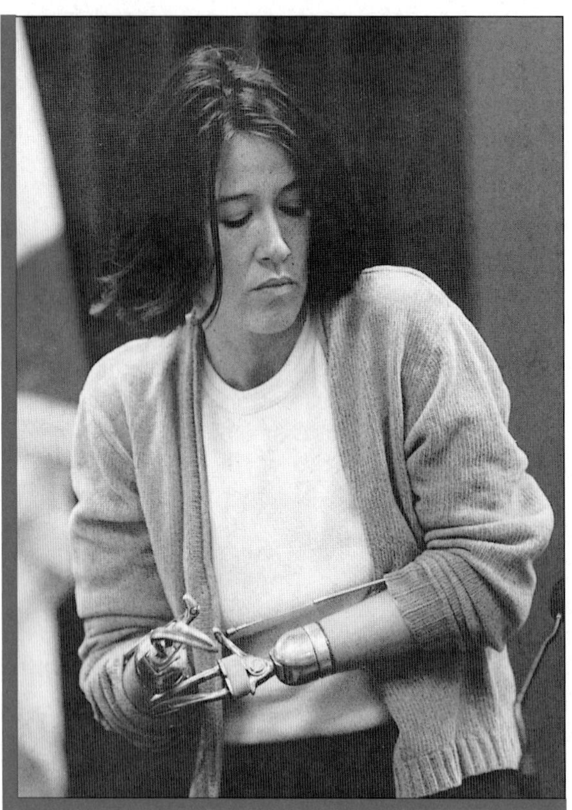

## INTERVIEW OF THE RAPE VICTIM

The interview requires intimate communication between a police officer and a victim who has been physically and psychologically assaulted. As such, the investigative nature of the interview represents only one dimension of the officer's responsibility. By conducting the interview tactfully and compassionately, the officer can avoid intensifying emotional suffering. At the same time, the cooperation of the victim is gained and the investigative process is thereby made easier.

It is absolutely crucial that the investigator does not in any way pass judgment on the victim. The rape investigation is only the beginning of a long judicial-legal process often referred to as "the second rape" by victims and rape counselors.[4] Statements such as "She was *where* at *what time* that night?!" or "With that outfit, she was practically begging for it!" transfer blame from the perpetrator to the victim and leave the victim feeling just as helpless and abused emotionally as she was physically during the attack. There is no place for judgmental attitudes or predispositions such as these in a rape investigation.[5]

While they may at first numb themselves to the trauma and try to go on as if nothing had happened, nearly all women who have been raped experience emotional or psychological disturbance to some degree. Victims generally at some time experience fear, insecurity, anger, depression, aversion to sexual contact, and feelings of loss of control. These feelings may last for months or even years after the assault.[6]

Rape victims frequently exhibit signs of posttraumatic stress disorder (formerly referred to as the rape trauma syndrome) and, as a consequence, may experience alternating periods of feeling rage and helplessness. Flashbacks may leave victims overwhelmed and unable to function in mind and body.[7]

The investigator must be sensitive to the psychological state of the victim. Insensitivity can have two bad effects. First, from a practical standpoint, it might diminish the ability or the willingness of the victim to cooperate in the investigation. Second, it might cause serious psychological aftereffects. Certain steps make the interview less painful for the victim and more effective for the investigator.[8]

## INTERVIEW PROCEDURES AND INVESTIGATIVE QUESTIONS

The attitude of the officer is extremely important and makes a lasting impression on the victim. The initial interview of the victim should not be excessively thorough. It is frequently best to obtain only a brief account of events and a description of the perpetrator for the pickup order. Rapid placement of the pickup order is essential. Unless the circumstances of the offense make it unwise to delay the investigation, the detailed interview should be conducted the following day, when the victim has calmed down. When threats have been made against the victim, protection should be provided. The interview should be conducted in a comfortable environment with absolute privacy from everyone, including husbands, boyfriends, parents, children, friends, or anyone else personally associated with the victim. Without privacy the victim's reluctance to discuss the details may be magnified greatly.[9]

There is some question about whether the investigator interviewing the victim should be male or female. Some argue that a female victim feels more at ease in discussing the details of the assault with another woman. Others argue that an understanding male may help the victim to overcome a possibly aversive reaction to men, especially if the victim is relatively young or sexually inexperienced. The major criterion, regardless of whether the investigator is male or female, is that the person have the ability to elicit trust and confidence from the victim, while possessing considerable investigative ability. Many police departments have moved toward male-female teams in rape investigation.[10]

In interviewing the victim, the investigator may find that the victim uses slang terms to describe the sex act or parts of the body. This may be done because the victim does not know the proper terminology. It is possible that at some point the investigator may find it necessary to use slang terms to interview the victim; however, in today's world investigators must protect themselves from allegations of insensitivity or professional misconduct. Delicately employed proper terms can be used immediately after a victim's slang usage. This in no way demeans the victim's intellect but, rather, conveys an image of professionalism to which most victims respond positively.

When the victim has had an opportunity to compose herself, the investigator should make inquiries into the following areas.

### Type and Sequence of Sexual Acts during an Assault

To determine the motivation behind a rape, it is imperative to ascertain the type and sequence of sexual acts during the assault.[11] This task may be made difficult because of the victim's reluctance to discuss certain aspects of the crime out of fear, shame, or humiliation. Often, however, investigators can overcome victims' reluctance with a professional and empathic approach. It has been found that although interviewers are likely to ask about vaginal, oral, and anal acts, they often do not ask about kissing, fondling, use of foreign objects, digital manipulation of the vagina or anus, fetishism, voyeurism, or exhibitionism by the offender.[12] In a sample of 115 adult, teenage, and child rape victims, researchers reported vaginal sex as the most frequent act, but they also reported 18 other sexual acts. Repetition and sequence of acts are infrequently reported. Most reports state, "The victim was raped," "vaginally assaulted," or "raped repeatedly."

By analyzing the sequence of acts during the assault, the investigator may determine whether the offender was acting out a fantasy, experimenting, or committing the sexual acts to punish or degrade the victim. For example, if anal sex was followed by fellatio (oral sex—mouth to penis), the motivation to punish and degrade would be strongly suggested. In acting out a fantasy, the offender normally engages in kissing, fondling, or cunnilingus (oral sex—mouth to female genitals). If fellatio occurs, it generally precedes anal sex. If a rapist is experimenting sexually, he is moderately forceful and verbally profane and derogatory. Fellatio may precede or follow anal sex.[13]

## Verbal Activity of Rapist

A rapist reveals a good deal about himself and the motivation behind the assault through what he says to the victim. For this reason, it is important to elicit from the victim everything the rapist said and the tone and attitude in which he said it.

A study of 115 rape victims revealed several themes in rapists' conversations, including "threats, orders, confidence lines, personal inquiries of the victim, personal revelations by the rapist, obscene names and racial epithets, inquiries about the victim's sexual 'enjoyment,' soft-sell departures, sexual put-downs, possession of women, and taking property from another male."[14]

Preciseness is important. For example, a rapist who states, "I'm going to hurt you if you don't do what I say," has threatened the victim, whereas the rapist who says, "Do what I say, and I won't hurt you," may be trying to reassure the victim and gain her compliance without force. A rapist who states, "I want to make love to you," has used a passive and affectionate phrase and may not want to harm the victim physically. But a statement such as "I'm going to fuck you" is much more aggressive, hostile, and angry. Compliments to the victim, politeness, expressions of concern, apologies, and discussions of the offender's personal life, whether fact or fiction, indicate low self-esteem in the offender. In contrast, derogatory, profane, threatening, or abusive language suggests anger and the use of sex to punish or degrade the victim.

When analyzing a rape victim's statement, the interviewer is advised to write down an adjective that accurately describes each of the offender's statements. For example, the interviewer might record, "You're a beautiful person" (complimentary); "Shut up, bitch" (hostility); "Am I hurting you?" (concern). The interviewer then has better insight into the offender's motivation and personality.

## Verbal Activity of the Victim

The rapist may make the victim say certain words or phrases that enhance the rape for him. By determining what, if anything, the victim was forced to say, the interviewer learns about the rapist's motivation and about what gratifies him. For example, a rapist who demands such phrases as "I love you," "Make love to me," or "You're better than my husband" suggests the need for affection or ego-building. One who demands that the victim plead or scream suggests sadism and a need for total domination. If the victim is forced to demean herself, the offender may be motivated by anger and hostility.

## Sudden Change in Rapist's Attitude during Attack

The victim should be specifically asked whether she observed any change in the attitude of the rapist during the time he was with her. She should be asked whether he became angry, contrite, physically abusive, or apologetic and whether this was a departure from his previous attitude. If the victim reports such a change, she should be asked to recall what immediately preceded the change. A sudden behavioral change may reflect weakness or fear. Factors that may cause such sudden behavioral changes include a rapist's sexual dysfunction, external disruptions (a phone ringing, noise, or a knock on the door), the victim's resistance or lack of fear, ridicule or scorn, or even completion of the rape. An attitudinal change may be signaled verbally, physically, or sexually. Because the rape is stressful for the rapist, how he reacts to stress may become important in future interrogations, and knowing what caused the change can be a valuable psychological tool for the investigator.

In attempting to determine the experience of the rapist, the investigator should ask the victim what actions the offender took to protect his identity, remove physical or trace evidence, or facilitate his escape. It may be possible to conclude from the offender's actions whether he is a novice or an experienced offender who may have been arrested previously for rape or similar offenses. Most rapists take some action, such as wearing a mask or telling the victim not to look at them, to protect their identity. But some go to great lengths to protect themselves from future prosecution. As in any criminal act, the more rapes a person commits, the more proficient he becomes in eluding detection. If a person is arrested because of a mistake and later repeats the crime, he is not likely to repeat the same costly mistake.

The offender's experience level can sometimes be determined from the protective actions he takes. Novice rapists are not familiar with modern medical or police technology and take minimal actions to protect their identity. Some wear a ski mask and gloves, change their voice, affect an accent, or blindfold and bind their victims. The experienced rapist's modus operandi can indicate a more than common knowledge of police and medical developments. The rapist may walk through the victim's residence or prepare an escape route prior to the sexual assault, disable the victim's telephone, order the victim to shower or douche, bring bindings or gags rather than using those available at the scene, wear surgical gloves during the assault, or take or force the victim to wash items the rapist touched or ejaculated on, such as bedding and the victim's clothing.

## Theft during Rape

Almost without exception, police record the theft of items from rape victims. All too often, however, investigators fail to probe the matter unless it involves articles of value. But knowing about the items stolen may provide information about the criminal and aid in the investigative process. In some cases, the victim initially may not realize that something has been taken. For this reason, the victim should be asked to inventory items.

Missing items fall into one of three categories: evidentiary, valuables, and personal. The rapist who takes evidentiary items—those he has touched or ejaculated on—suggests prior rape experience or an arrest history. One who takes items of value may be unemployed or working at a job providing little income. The type of missing items may also provide a clue as to the age of the rapist. Younger rapists have been noted to steal items such as stereos or televisions; older rapists tend to take jewelry or items more easily concealed and transported. Personal items taken sometimes include photographs of the victim, lingerie, driver's licenses, and the like. These items have no intrinsic value but remind the rapist of the rape and the victim. A final factor to consider is whether the offender later returns the items to the victim, and if so, why. Some do so to maintain power over the victim by intimidation. Others want to convince the victim that they meant her no harm and want to convince themselves that they are not bad people.

Rapists often target their victims beforehand. A series of rapes involving victims who were either alone or in the company of small children is a strong indication that the offender had engaged in peeping or surveillance. He may have entered the residence or communicated with the victim earlier. For this reason, the investigator should determine whether the victim or her neighbors experienced any of the following before the rape:

1. Calls or notes from unidentified persons.
2. Residential or automobile break-in.
3. Prowlers or peeping toms.
4. Feelings of being watched or followed.

Frequently, rapists who target their victims have prior arrests for breaking and entering, prowling, peeping, or theft of women's clothing.

## Delayed Reporting

If the victim has delayed making a complaint, the investigator should establish the reason. It may be that the victim was frightened, confused, or apprehensive. However, delays of several weeks or several months reduce the likelihood of apprehending the suspect and tend to weaken the state's case should a trial be held. Nevertheless, such a complaint must be investigated in the same way as all other similar complaints, until or unless it is substantiated or considered unfounded. An unfounded case does not go forward for prosecution because of reasons such as lack of medical evidence, delay in reporting, intoxication of the victim, or previous relationships between victim and offender or because the victim is too embarrassed or too upset to cooperate.[15]

## WHY WOMEN DO NOT REPORT RAPE TO THE POLICE

Studies have shown that there is considerable reluctance on the part of many women to report rape to their local police. Victims do not report the crime because of:

- Lack of belief in the ability of the police to apprehend the suspect.
- Worries about unsympathetic treatment from police and discomforting procedures.
- Apprehension, a result of television programs or newspaper reports, of being further victimized by court proceedings.
- Embarrassment about publicity, however limited.
- Fear of reprisal by the rapist.[16]

Unfortunately, some complaints about the criminal justice system's treatment of rape victims are justified. In many jurisdictions, efforts are being made to correct deficiencies. Many corrections have come about through legislative changes.[17] In other instances, women's groups have worked with local police departments to educate the public, especially women, about the crime of rape and to correct much of the misinformation that may be transmitted via television programs and other news media.

The failure of victims to report rapes has serious implications, because without such information, the effectiveness of the police in protecting other women is considerably diminished. A case in point occurred a few years ago in San Francisco:

A young woman who was raped turned first to her friends for help and comfort, then sought aid from a local Women Against Rape group. No one encouraged her to make a police report; she was indecisive and did nothing. Several days later, she read a news account describing a rape similar to her own. She immediately notified the police and learned that the rapist had attacked three other women. With the additional information that she provided, the police located and arrested the rapist by the end of the day.[18]

## FALSE RAPE ALLEGATIONS

During the past several years, police agencies have been more selective in assigning personnel to rape investigations. They are now more sensitive to the emotional trauma experienced by victims. However, although the vast majority of rape complaints are legitimate, investigators must remain alert to the possibility of false rape complaints.

In the rape investigation, officers have a responsibility both to the legitimate victims of rape and to men who are falsely accused of rape. There are no hard-and-fast rules to guide the investigator to the truth, but experienced investigators generally find it by carefully questioning all parties involved and scrutinizing the circumstantial and physical evidence. Investigators should conduct a complete check on the background of the victim and all suspects. If the victim is a prostitute or promiscuous, these facts should be considered in the search for the truth. But once it is evident that the legal elements for rape are present, the victim's character should be disregarded. The following case shows the importance of the victim's background in rape complaints:

AN 18-year-old woman reported that she had been walking past a vacant house at night when three young men whom she knew casually leaped from behind some bushes and dragged her, kicking and screaming, into the house. She claimed that she resisted. But while two men held her down, each of the three had sexual intercourse with her. When the last one had finished, they fled. She went to a nearby store and called the police.

The officer assigned to the case had reservations about the validity of the victim's complaint for the following reasons:

- The occupant of the house next to the vacant house said that he had heard no scream even though his house was only 20 feet away and his windows were open.

- Sand examined in the area where the men supposedly had leaped from behind the bushes was undisturbed, although there were a number of shoe impressions in the sandy patch leading into the house.
- The woman's clothing showed no indications of struggle.
- The interior of the house was examined, and a large piece of cardboard was found on the floor in a back room. The woman stated that she had been forced to lie on this while the men raped her. There was a considerable amount of dirt in the room and near the cardboard, but, except for some shoe impressions, there were no tracks that would indicate that a person had been dragged through the house and to the cardboard.
- Physical examination indicated that the victim had recently had sexual intercourse, but there were no injuries or other traumas. The investigator assigned to the case went to the suspects' hangout, a pool hall. The pool hall manager reported that the victim had voluntarily left the pool hall with the three suspects earlier in the evening.

The manager said that the girl frequently came into the pool hall to pick up men; he said that he had been told by patrons that she was a prostitute who took her customers to an abandoned house nearby to have sexual intercourse. The manager was asked to call the police if any of the men returned. The following day one of the young men, who had heard that the police were looking for him, voluntarily came to police headquarters. He said that he and two other young men had agreed to pay the girl $1 each for her sexual services, to which she agreed. They were directed by her to a nearby abandoned house, and each had sexual intercourse with her. When they finished, they refused to pay her and one of the men stole her brand-new shoes to give to his girlfriend. The victim was reinterviewed and admitted that she had lied to the police because she was angry with the men for cheating her out of the money they had agreed to pay her and because they also had stolen her shoes.

Had the victim actually been sexually assaulted, her background would have been immaterial.

Occasionally women will report that they have been raped as an attention-getting device. The following case illustrates this point:

A woman whose husband was a long-distance truck driver and frequently away from home reported to police that a house painter, who had responded to her home to apply for a painting job she had advertised in a local paper, had raped her. Because of the detailed information she gave the police, they were able to arrest the man. A lineup was conducted at police headquarters, and she positively identified the painter as the man who raped her. He was then charged with rape and bound over to the local district court. He spent three days in jail before being bonded out. Several days later the woman had second thoughts, contacted the prosecutors, and confessed that she had fabricated the rape story in order to get her husband to stay home and pay more attention to her. She was subsequently charged with and convicted of perjury.

She was sentenced to 180 days in jail and two years' probation. Further, she was ordered by the court to apologize to the man in the local newspaper and in radio advertisements. The man who was arrested lost his job and had to employ a lawyer; his children in school were confronted by other children who said, "Your dad's a rapist." His wife was too embarrassed to go to town, and his 18-year-old daughter quit high school because of the way she was treated. The accused man was also fired from his primary job as a driver after being arrested. Even though he had been cleared of the charges, there was still a stigma associated with his arrest.[19]

Some inexperienced investigators are not suspicious of false allegations because of the victim's age. This complacency is an error, as the following case illustrates:

A 65-year-old great-grandmother reported that a 19-year-old neighbor had raped and robbed her in her home. The woman advised police that she had invited the young man over for a cup of coffee. After a while, he told her that he wanted to have sexual intercourse with her. She refused his request, whereupon he slapped her in the face and told her he would kill her great-grandson, who was asleep in a nearby bedroom, unless she had sexual intercourse with him. The woman said she agreed because of her concern for her great-grandson's safety. She went into her bedroom, disrobed, and had sexual intercourse with the man. When they were finished, he demanded that she give him some money and again threatened to injure the child if she failed to comply with his wishes. She gave him money, and he left.

The police pickup order was broadcast for the man. The woman was questioned and admitted that she had invited the young man to her home and had suggested that they have sexual intercourse; he had agreed. When they were finished, he demanded money from her. She refused, and he threatened her great-grandson. The woman said that she became frightened and gave the man the rent money. Because she now had to explain to her husband why the rent money was gone, she made up the rape complaint. Although the rape complaint was unfounded, a robbery had occurred.

While there is always the possibility that a rape accusation is false, it is also crucial for an investigator to keep in mind the fact that, according to the FBI's Uniform Crime Report, in 47 percent of all forcible-rape cases in the year 2000 sufficient evidence was present to make an arrest.[20] These are simply the cases in which evidence conclusively points to a particular offender. There are a large number of cases where a rape has clearly occurred but no specific offender can be determined from the evidence. Furthermore, there are cases in which police investigators simply find no evidence that a crime has taken place. Even in these cases (which police often dismiss) there is still the possibility that in fact a rape has occurred. The following story illustrates this point:

ON arriving home late one evening and before going to bed, a 30-year-old woman living alone checked all the windows and doors to be certain that they were locked. After checking them, she went to bed. Shortly thereafter she was awakened by a man in her bed; he held a knife to her throat and warned her not to make any noise or attempt to resist or he would kill her. The man then proceeded to rape the woman. After raping her, he ordered her to go to the bathroom and to douche. After douching, she was instructed to flush the toilet. The suspect then fled by the front door. When the police arrived, they could find no signs of forced entry into the home. When the woman was examined at the hospital, there was no evidence of sexual intercourse or the presence of semen. The police thought the woman had fabricated the incident because of the absence of forcible entry into the home or any physical evidence of sexual intercourse. Two months later the man was arrested for another rape in the same general area where this first rape had occurred. The police found in his possession a number of keys; with the cooperation of his family members, it was determined that one of the keys was for a home the family had been renting several months before. This was the same home in which the first victim had been raped. The owners of the home had failed to rekey the lock after the family moved out and the new tenant moved in. The rapist merely retained the key and used it to enter through the front door, whereupon he committed the rape.

## THE VICTIM AND PHYSICAL EVIDENCE

Rape investigations usually begin when the victim either places a call to report the rape or takes herself to a hospital. The report may be filed moments after the incident occurred, or it may be days or weeks later. In either case, it is important to remember that the victim is a walking crime scene. Certain investigative procedures must be followed to ensure that physical evidence is not lost or accidentally destroyed.[21]

### INSTRUCTIONS TO THE VICTIM

The officer responding to a reported sexual assault should make a great effort to ensure that any evidence that may be on the victim is secure. Once evidence is destroyed, there is no getting it back. Attending to the victim's well-being is unquestionably the primary concern; if she is in immediate

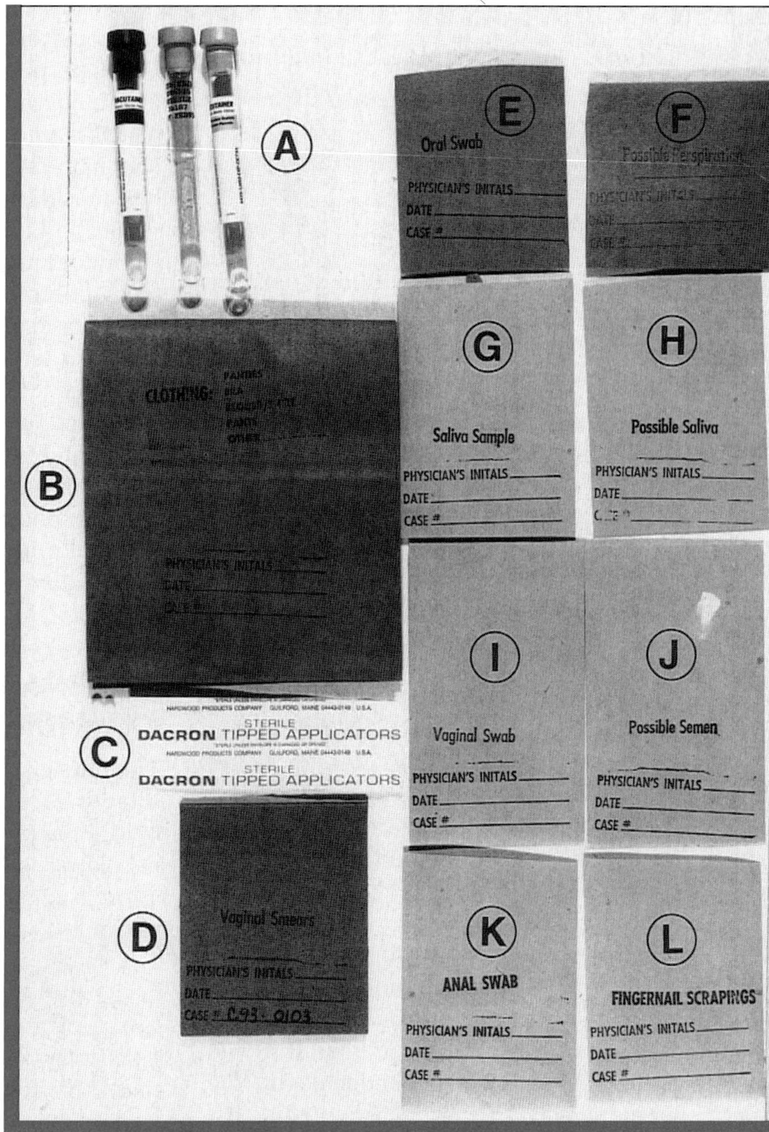


## Sexual-Battery Examination Kit

Partial contents of a sexual-battery examination kit. (A) Blood vials: left vial, which has a red top, is used for collecting blood from the victim for blood typing; center vial, which has a purple top, is used for collecting blood from the victim that is used in the DNA typing; right vial, which has a gray top, is used for collecting blood from the victim for drug screening. (B) Paper bag used to collect victim's panties, bra, blouse, pants, and other items. (C) Sterile Dacron-tipped applicators used in obtaining oral swabs, vaginal swabs, and anal swabs. (D) Holder for glass slide containing vaginal smears. (E) Envelope for holding oral swabs. (F) Envelope for holding possible perspiration. (G) Envelope for holding saliva samples. (H) Envelope for holding possible saliva. (I) Envelope for holding vaginal swabs. (J) Envelope for holding possible semen. (K) Envelope for holding anal swab. (L) Envelope for holding fingernail scrapings.

(Courtesy Pinellas County, Florida, Public Health Unit, Sexual Assault Victim Examination Program)

need of medical attention, attending to that need is the officer's first responsibility. However, a well-trained officer will tactfully find a way to meet the victim's physical and psychological needs while preserving potentially useful and incriminating evidence. For instance, the officer should encourage the victim not to shower or douche (assuming she has not already done so) and should urge her not to change clothes. These actions cause the loss of hair and body fluids such as blood or semen that could be analyzed at the crime lab and used to corroborate the victim's testimony.

The victim should also be advised not to alter the scene of the crime. Even the placement and shape of body fluids and hairs can be telling, and such routine actions as flushing the toilet may mean a loss of crucial evidence (e.g., in cases where the perpetrator used a condom and dropped it into the toilet.)[22]

## SEMEN AND HAIR AS EVIDENCE

As was discussed in considerable detail in Chapter 3, "Physical Evidence," semen that contains sperm and hair that has the root attached can now be identified, through DNA typing, as coming from a specific individual. Thus, it is absolutely essential that appropriate samples of both be collected and preserved from both the victim and the suspect. It should be noted that the presence of semen is not evidence that a rape occurred, nor does its absence mean that a rape did not occur. For example, because rapists sometimes experience sexual dysfunction, the examining physician may find no semen during the pelvic examination. In interviews of 133 convicted rapists, 50 (37 percent) admitted some sexual dysfunction. Of the rapists, 23 stated that they were unable to achieve an orgasm during the sex act; 22 experienced difficulty in achieving and sustaining an erection (impotency); and 5 experienced premature ejaculation.[23]

It must be pointed out that the terms "semen" and "sperm" are not synonymous. **Semen** is a grayish-white fluid, produced in the male reproductive organs, ejaculated during orgasm. In liquid form, it has a chlorinelike odor; when dried, it has a starchlike consistency. **Sperm** are the tadpolelike organisms that are contained in and travel through semen to fertilize the female egg. This distinction is important because the laboratory examinations and tests that are employed to search for each are quite different. Thus, if a rape was committed by a male who is sterile (having no sperm in his ejaculate), then semen but not sperm may be present. It should be noted that DNA typing is conducted on the sperm, not the semen. The physician examining the victim for sperm in the vagina therefore aspirates the vagina—removes fluids with a suction device—and microscopically examines them for sperm. The motility of sperm in the vagina is short, measured in hours rather than days; motility decreases to zero in about 3 hours. Menstruation may prolong motility to 4 hours. If large numbers of highly motile sperm are aspirated from the vagina, one may conclude that sexual intercourse had occurred 1 to 2 hours before the examination. If a few motile sperm remain, one may conclude that sexual intercourse had occurred within 3 hours of the examination. Nonmotile sperm may be found in a living female in small numbers up to 48 hours after sexual intercourse. Nonmotile sperm have been found in dead bodies for up to several hours after death.[24]

When sperm cannot be found, a second test may be employed to identify the presence of acid phosphatase. Acid phosphatase, an enzyme, is a component in the liquid portion of semen. The test should be conducted by experienced crime laboratory personnel and interpreted with care. Routine hospital laboratory techniques are not applicable to this type of examination and may be erroneously interpreted as significant. Only strong reactions should be considered evidence of semen, as mild positive reactions have been noted with vegetable matter, feces, and many other types of organic substances. Experiments have been conducted to determine the persistence of a significantly positive reaction to the acid phosphatase test over variable lengths of time following sexual intercourse. In the living, acid phosphatase may be lost from the vagina after 12 to 40 hours.

## INFORMATION FOR THE EXAMINING PHYSICIAN

The physician responsible for examining the victim should be provided with all the available facts before the physical examination. Frequently, a gynecologist is called in to examine a living victim; a forensic pathologist should examine a deceased victim.

Usually certain hospitals in a community are designated as the ones to which rape victims are taken for a physical examination. These hospitals frequently have both specially trained staffs and the necessary technical facilities. Under no circumstances should a male investigator be present in the hospital room when a female victim is being physically examined. If a male investigator believes that some physical evidence may be adhering to the victim's body, he should instruct the examining physician to collect such evidence and turn it over to him. The collection of physical evidence in this manner must conform to all guidelines for preserving the chain of custody.

## COLLECTION OF THE VICTIM'S CLOTHING

The victim's clothing should be collected as soon as possible. If she is still wearing the clothes worn during the incident, she should undress over a clean cloth or large paper mat so that any evidence that may be dislodged from her clothes is not lost. Even if the victim was forced to disrobe before the sexual attack, it is possible that hair, semen, or fibers from the suspect's clothing have been deposited on her clothing. Each article of clothing should be placed in a separate container, properly labeled, and stored for later analysis. The victim may then be photographed before redressing to document any evidence of physical abuse.[25] Underpants should not be the only item of a victim's clothing recovered, because they often offer only limited physical evidence and are likely to be contaminated with other stains, such as vaginal secretions or urine, that interfere with the laboratory examination. Other garments, such as the dress, slip, or coat, may be of greater value in providing physical evidence. The evidence most frequently obtained from the victim's clothing is fibers from a suspect's clothing and loose pubic hairs. If the assault occurred in a wooded or grassy area, there will often be soil, seeds, weeds, and other vegetation adhering to the victim's clothing.[26]

The following actual case, which occurred before the advent of DNA typing, illustrates the importance of a careful search for physical evidence:

THE partly dressed body of a 16-year-old female was discovered by two young boys traveling through a wooded area. The victim's slacks and underpants were pulled down around her ankles, and her brassiere was pulled up around her head. A check of the missing-persons file revealed that a female fitting her description had been reported missing by her parents 18 hours earlier. The body was later identified as the missing female.

The victim's body was removed from the scene in a clean white sheet and transported to a local hospital. The medical examination of the victim revealed that she had died from brain damage after being struck repeatedly with a blunt object. In addition, she had a large bruise on her right cheek, also caused by a blow from a blunt object, possibly a fist. The examination of the deceased's person and clothing yielded the following:

- Her clothing.
- Pubic-hair samples.
- Blood samples for typing.
- Grease stains on the inside of her thighs. The grease was initially deposited on the suspect's hands after he used an automobile master cylinder that had been on the floorboard of his car to batter the victim unconscious.
- A single human hair clutched in her hand, mixed with considerable dirt, leaves, twigs, and so forth.
- No semen either in or on her body, clothing, or the immediate area.

Physical evidence also was obtained from the crime scene:

- Tire impressions.
- Samples of soil, leaves, weeds, and other vegetation.

A suspect who had been the last person seen with the victim and who also had an arrest record for a similar offense was taken into custody and his vehicle was impounded. The vehicle's entire interior, including steering wheel, dashboard, door panels, seats, floor mats, and visor, was removed, as were all four wheels. These items were transported to the FBI laboratory along with all the evidence collected from the victim and the crime scene. A pair of blood-stained trousers and hair samples were obtained from the suspect. The results of the laboratory examination revealed the following:

- The victim's brassiere had several fibers caught in the hooks, which were identical to those of the terrycloth seat covers in the suspect's car.
- The grease stain on the victim's thighs was compared with the grease found under the dashboard and near the ignition switch in the suspect's vehicle and found to be identical. An examination of the ignition switch revealed that the car could be started only if someone reached under the dash and crossed the ignition wires; thus when the suspect tried to start his car, he deposited grease from the master cylinder onto the ignition switch.
- The single hair found in the victim's hand was similar in all characteristics to that of the suspect.

- Samples collected from the victim's hair at the morgue were similar to those recovered from the floorboard of the suspect's vehicle.
- Fibers from the victim's underpants were identical to fibers recovered from the suspect's vehicle.
- A tire impression at the scene matched a tire on the suspect's vehicle.
- Debris collected from the scene matched debris recovered from the interior of the suspect's car and dirt extracted from the rims of the wheels of the suspect's car.
- Human blood was found on the steering wheel of the suspect's car, but the presence of various contaminants prevented the blood from being typed accurately.
- Because the suspect had soaked his trousers in cold water overnight, blood typing was impossible.

The suspect confessed to murdering the victim after abducting her from a teenage dance, although his confession was not needed in view of the physical evidence. As previously indicated, he identified the murder weapon as an automobile master cylinder, which he had disposed of after the crime. It was never located. He killed the victim after she had violently resisted his efforts to assault her sexually.

Examination of most hair, fiber, debris, and tire or shoe prints at the scene can narrow the field. Analysis of these materials, however, will most often yield evidence characteristic of class (discussed in considerable detail in Chapter 3), not individualized results. However, the preponderance of class-characteristic evidence, coupled with the particulars of the case, made a compelling argument against the suspect.

## THE ROLE OF THE INVESTIGATOR IN SECURING THE RAPE SCENE

It is the criminal investigator's job to collect, catalog, and store physical evidence for later analysis in the laboratory. As soon as possible, the investigative unit should take photographs of the scene of the crime, including the specific area where the rape is believed to have occurred, the area around the rape, and the areas around the entrances, exits, and general perimeter of the facility where the rape occurred (if it occurred indoors). After this is done, various methods may be used to gather evidence for laboratory testing. Evidence recovery methods may include naked-eye searches, the use of oblique light to spot hair and fiber on the surface of furniture or other surfaces, the use of ultraviolet light to illuminate fibers, careful vacuuming of selected small areas, adhesive lifts, combing or brushing, scraping under the fingernails and certain other surfaces, the use of blue light to detect semen, and the use of lasers.[27]

## INCIDENCE OF ERRORS IN THE COLLECTION OF EVIDENCE

Physical evidence in a case is often the decisive factor in determining guilt or innocence. Developments in DNA technology within the past five years have added a new dimension to rape investigation. Currently, DNA analysis combined with careful hair and fiber analysis can "describe the clothes worn by the criminal, give an idea of his stature, age, hair color, or similar information," and thereby significantly limit the officers search for a suspect.[28] With the exception of identical twins, no two persons have the same DNA structure. A good DNA sample can now be analyzed to identify with forensic and legal certainty any individual whose DNA structure is known.[29]

However, DNA testing is only as good as the investigative techniques used to gather the evidence. As items are collected, the investigator must carefully label the items and store them in such a way that they are preserved intact and uncompromised for later laboratory analysis. Current laboratory technology is accurate to such a degree that defense lawyers have little to challenge other than the chain of custody of the evidence and any possible contamination. Keeping careful records of the chain of custody of the evidence and protecting the evidence from contamination are crucial both for preserving the sample itself so that it *can* be analyzed and for ensuring that conclusions drawn from the analysis of the sample cannot be challenged in court.[30]

In spite of the importance of proper handling, evidence still continues to be mishandled. The FBI Crime Laboratory indicates a number of common errors in collecting physical evidence. It cites the failure to:

- Obtain fingernail scrapings from the victim.
- Obtain all the victim's and suspect's clothing worn at the time of the offense.
- Obtain samples of soil and other vegetation at the crime scene.
- Mark each item of evidence properly for future identification purposes.
- Obtain saliva and blood samples.
- Remove obvious, visible hair and package it properly when the location of the hair may be germane to the investigation.
- Obtain hair samples from the suspect and the victim. Hair samples are extremely important because in rape-murder cases the victim is soon buried and obtaining samples after the burial presents serious problems.[31]

The FBI also cites faulty handling and packaging of evidence, which results in contamination during shipment.

### SEXUAL-BATTERY EXAMINATION

Most hospitals or crisis centers responsible for the collection of evidence from sex-offense victims have developed sexual-battery examination kits. Such kits generally include the following components:

1. A large envelope containing all the appropriate forms and specific items needed for the collection of evidence. This envelope is also used for the storage of evidence once it is collected. It is then forwarded to the crime laboratory for analysis.
2. Sexual-assault victim examination consent form, sexual-assault victim exam summary for the patient, and victim confidential evaluation.
3. Blood vials used for collecting blood from the victim for blood typing; paper bag used to collect victim's panties, bra, blouse, pants, and other items; sterile Dacron-tipped applicator used in obtaining oral swabs, vaginal swabs, and anal swabs; holder for glass slide containing vaginal smears; envelope for holding oral swabs; envelope for holding possible perspiration; envelope for holding possible saliva samples; envelope for holding vaginal swabs; envelope for holding possible semen; envelope for holding anal swab; and envelope for holding fingernail scrapings.
4. Tissue paper for collecting hair samples; envelope for storage of pubic-hair pluckings; envelope for storage of pubic-hair cuttings; envelope for storage of scalp-hair cuttings; and envelope for storage of scalp-hair pluckings.

## CONDOM TRACE EVIDENCE

Manufacturers produce condoms using a variety of materials, both natural and synthetic. Each manufacturer has its own formula, which may vary even among its different brands.[32] Some condoms are made from lamb membranes, and one manufacturer recently introduced a model made from polyurethane plastic. Still, latex rubber condoms have, by far, the largest share of the market, perhaps because they cost considerably less. In addition to the basic materials they use to produce condoms, manufacturers also add other substances, known as **exchangeable traces** that comprise particulates, lubricants, and spermicide.

### EXCHANGEABLE TRACES

#### Particulates

Condom manufacturers add finely powdered particulates to prevent a rolled-up latex condom from sticking to itself. Particulates found in different brands include cornstarch, potato starch, and lycopodium (a powder found in plants), as well as amorphous silica, talc, or other minerals. In the laboratory, forensic scientists use several different techniques to characterize these particles and compare them with those obtained from other condom brands.

#### Lubricants

Sexual assailants prefer lubricated condoms, probably for the same reason they use petroleum jelly, that is, to facilitate their crimes.[33] Many condom brands contain a liquid lubricant, which may be classified as either "wet" or "dry." Both types of condom lubricant have an oil-like consistency, but wet lubricants are water-based and/or water-soluble, while dry lubricants are not. Although many different manufacturers use the same dry lubricant, the viscosity grades sometimes differ. The forensic laboratory can recover these silicone oils easily from items of evidence and possibly associate them with a condom manufacturer. Wet lubricants may contain either polyethylene glycol or a gel made from a combination of ingredients similar to those found in vaginal lubricants. Despite similarities to other products on the market, forensic examination can associate specific formulations with particular condom brands.

### Spermicide

Both wet- and dry-lubricated condoms also may contain the spermicide nonoxynol-9. Its recovery and detection, along with lubricant ingredients and particulates, can help show condom use and indicate the specific brand.

## THE VALUE OF CONDOM TRACE EVIDENCE

Condom trace evidence can assist investigators in several ways. It can help prove corpus delicti, provide evidence of penetration, produce associative evidence, and link the acts of serial rapists.

***In Proving Corpus Delicti*** Traces associated with condoms can help prove corpus delicti, the fact that a crime has occurred. This evidence can support the claims of either the victim or the accused. For example, the U.S. military can prosecute personnel diagnosed as HIV-positive for aggravated assault if they engage in unprotected sex, even if it is consensual. If servicemen accused of aggravated assault claim that they did in fact wear a condom but it broke or slipped off, condom trace evidence can support that claim.

***In Providing Evidence of Penetration*** Condom traces found inside a victim can provide evidence of penetration. In many jurisdictions, this evidence raises the charge to a higher degree of sexual assault.

***In Producing Associative Evidence*** Recovered condom traces may correspond to those found in a certain brand or used by a certain manufacturer. An empty packet of this particular brand found near the crime scene, especially if it bears the suspect's fingerprints, provides a strong association between the suspect and the crime. Unopened condom packages of the same brand found on the suspect, in his car, or at his residence also would help tie the suspect to the crime.

***In Linking the Acts of Serial Rapists*** People tend to be creatures of habit, and sexual criminals are no exception. A serial rapist likely will use the same brand of condom to commit repeated acts. Moreover, repeat offenders whose DNA profiles have been stored in a computer data bank may be likely to use a condom when committing subsequent crimes. Along with other aspects of his modus operandi, traces from the same condom brand or manufacturer found during several different investigations can help connect a suspect to an entire series of assaults.

## GUIDELINES FOR EVIDENCE COLLECTION

Investigators need not make any drastic changes in their usual procedures in order to include the possibility of condom trace evidence. The following guidelines will assist criminal investigators and medical examiners in collecting this valuable evidence.[34]

### At the Crime Scene

First and foremost, investigators must wear powder-free gloves to protect themselves from blood-borne pathogens and to avoid leaving particulates that may be similar to those contained in some condom brands. After collecting the evidence, they should package the gloves separately and submit them with the evidence so that the forensic laboratory can verify that the gloves did not leave behind any particulates.

At the crime scene, investigators should make every effort to locate any used condom and its foil package. If a condom is recovered, the traces from the victim on the outside and the seminal fluids from the assailant on the inside will have the greatest evidentiary value.

If investigators find an empty packet, they first should try to recover any latent prints from the outside. The inside of the package will probably not contain prints, but it may contain lubricant, spermicide, and particulate residues. Investigators should wipe the inside with a clean cotton swab. The traces on this swab will serve as a standard for comparison with traces recovered from the victim and the suspect.

### With the Victim

In addition to providing general information about the crime, victims may be able to supply valuable details about the condom and its wrapper. They may recall the brand itself or other important details, including the condom's color, shape, texture, odor, taste, and lubrication.

After obtaining facts about the condom, investigators should ask victims about their sexual and hygienic habits, which might account for traces not attributable to the crime. A comprehensive interview would include the following questions:

- Has the victim recently engaged in consensual sex?
- If so, was a condom used? A vaginal lubricant? What brand?
- Does the victim use any external or internal vaginal products (anti-itch medications, deodorants, douches, suppositories, etc.)?
- If so, what brands?

These questions assume an adult female victim. Investigators must modify the interview to accommodate male or child sexual-assault victims.

### With the Suspect(s)

Investigators also should question the suspect about the condom. A cooperative suspect will reveal the brand, tell where he purchased it, and describe how and where he disposed of both the condom and the empty packet. An uncooperative or deceitful suspect may claim he does not know or cannot remember, or he may name a popular brand but be unable to describe the condom or the packet in detail.

### Legal Considerations

When investigators know or suspect that a sexual offender used a condom, they must remember to list condoms on the warrant obtained to search the suspect's possessions. The search of a suspect's home may reveal intact condom packets, but if investigators have not listed condoms on the search warrant, they will not be able to seize this valuable evidence.

## RECORD OF INJURIES

A careful record should be made of the victim's injuries and be included in the report. Photographs of the victim's injuries serve two purposes. First, if a suspect is arrested and tried for the offense, the photographs tend to corroborate the victim's account of the attack. Second, the injuries may be of an unusual nature—bite marks, scratches, or burns from cigarettes—and may provide data valuable for developing the suspect's MO. In some cases, the injuries are readily visible to the investigator. In other cases, the injuries are concealed by the victim's clothing. The examining physician can provide details of injuries not readily noticeable. Color photographs should be taken if the victim has sustained visible severe injuries. If the injuries are in a location that requires the victim to disrobe partially or completely to be photographed, then it is essential that a female nurse, female police officer, or some other female officially associated with the police department or the hospital be present. If possible, a female police photographer should photograph the victim.

## DRUG-FACILITATED SEXUAL ASSAULT

The U.S. Department of Justice has estimated that over 430,000 people in this country are victimized by sexual assault each year and that three out of four victims are acquainted with their attackers. Many of the women who report being raped by an acquaintance also report unusual symptoms such as blacking out and having hazy or no memories about the attack. Sexual offenders' increasing use of **date-rape drugs,** such as Rohypnol, as tools of submission accounts for much of the complexity surrounding these cases.

Congress has responded to the growing use of date-rape drugs by passing the Drug-Induced Rape Prevention and Punishment Act of 1996, an amendment of the Controlled Substance Act. The law imposes a prison term of up to 20 years on anyone convicted of giving any controlled substance to another person without his or her knowledge, with the intention of committing a sexual assault. The law also requires that the U.S. Drug Enforcement Administration consider reclassifying Rohypnol from a Schedule IV to a Schedule I controlled substance to provide for closer control, and it instructs the U.S. attorney general to create educational materials for law enforcement.

Law enforcement personnel can contribute to the successful prosecution of drug-facilitated sexual-assault cases by recognizing the symptoms of drugging, the availability and toxicology of widely used substances, and the range of delivery methods.[35]

## DRUGS OF CHOICE

The two drugs that are most commonly used by sex offenders to facilitate their crimes are Rohypnol and gamma hydroxybutyrate.

### Rohypnol

**Rohypnol,** also known as flunitrazepam, belongs to a class of drugs called benzodiazepines. It produces a spectrum of effects similar to those of diazepam (Valium), including skeletal muscle relaxation, sedation, and a reduction in anxiety. Of these effects, the sedative and hypnotic effects are the most important. Flunitrazepam is considered to be approximately 8 to 10 times more potent than Valium. The effect or "high" may last from 7 to 12 hours or longer after the dose. With pills or "hits" readily available for prices ranging from $2 to $5, Rohypnol is extremely sought after. Street names include "roofies," "R-2's," "roach-2's," "trip & fall," and "mind erasers." (See photos on this and next page.)

This fast-acting drug can be ground into a powder and easily slipped into food or drink. It can take effect within 30 minutes and symptoms may persist for up to 8 hours.[36] Symptoms of Rohypnol intoxication include sedation, dizziness, visual disturbances, memory impairment, and loss of consciousness and motor coordination.[37] These effects may be compounded, and made potentially lethal, by alcohol. It is traceable in a person's urine for only 48 to 96 hours after ingestion and in blood for only 12 hours.

The drug is easily obtained on the black market, through the Internet, and in other countries. A significant amount of Rohypnol makes its way to the United States from Mexico and Colombia. The recent notoriety of Rohypnol as a date-rape drug has prompted manufacturers to create a tablet that is more difficult to dissolve in liquid and that will turn a drink blue. Unfortunately, the original colorless, dissolvable tablets are still widely available.

Many victims of drug-induced sexual assault are targeted at parties, clubs, and bars. Members of the high school- and college-age populations are especially vulnerable to perpetrators of drug-induced sexual assault. The following case, which occurred in Prince William County, Virginia, several years ago, illustrates this point:

TWO 15-year-old girls were forcibly raped after unknowingly ingesting Rohypnol. During the trial, prosecutors dubbed this drug the "new stealth weapon" on the basis of its odorless and tasteless properties. Commonly known as the "date-rape drug," it dissolves rapidly when placed in a carbonated drink, making it virtually impossible for unsuspecting victims to detect. Once in the victim's system, it quickly produces physical as well as mental incapacitation. Ten times stronger than Valium, Rohypnol's sedative effect occurs 20 to 30 minutes after ingestion. The main side effect is amnesia, but it also produces an intoxicated appearance, impaired judgment, impaired motor skills, drowsiness, dizziness, and confusion.

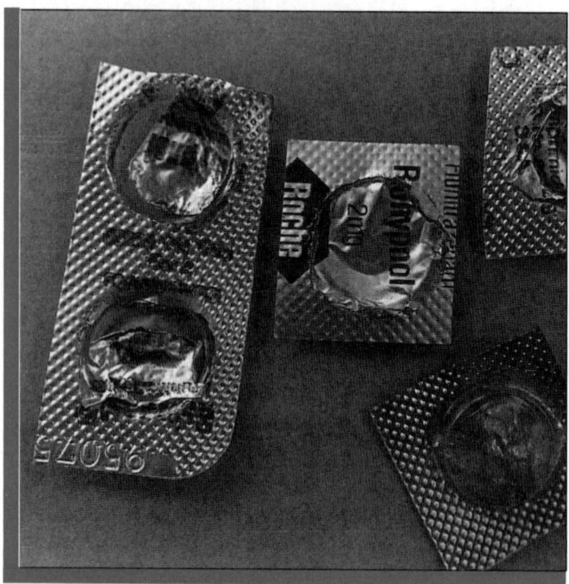


**Rohypnol Packaging**

The drug Rohypnol is commonly used by sex offenders to facilitate their crime. It produces effects such as skeletal muscle relaxation, sedation, and a reduction in anxiety. The drug can be easily slipped into food or drink and can take effect in 30 seconds. This drug is often found to be present in cases of date rape.

(Courtesy Sergeant Christopher McKissick and Detective Tyler Parks, Port Orange, Florida, Police Department)

The Prince William County's investigation revealed that in the late afternoon, the two young girls were taken willingly to an adult's apartment, having been reassured that they would be returned home after they saw the apartment. Once at the apartment, they were offered a soft drink. They both drank a Mountain Dew and started to feel "weird," as one victim put it, within about 30 minutes. Neither victim could remember what occurred over the next 9 hours.

The first victim woke up, disoriented, on the couch in the early morning hours. She went to the bathroom and noticed "hickeys" on her neck that had not been present the day before. She could not remember having sexual contact with anyone. She then went to look for the second victim, whom she found asleep on a pull-out bed. Once awakened, she too was disoriented. The second victim noticed a "hickey" on her inner thigh but did not remember engaging in any sexual contact. During the subsequent interviews, the men present in the apartment admitted having sexual intercourse with the victims but said it was consensual.

Three white tablets, marked "RH" were recovered from one of the men. These tested positive for Rohypnol. Both victims were seen by a sexual-assault nurse examiner. The internal genital findings were consistent with nonconsensual sexual assault.

After a jury trial, the defendant was found guilty of rape, distribution of a Schedule IV drug to a minor, and contributing to the delinquency of a minor. The codefendant was found guilty of contributing to the delinquency of a minor.[38]

## Gamma Hydroxybutyrate

**Gamma hydroxybutyrate** or **GHB** (also known as "gamma-OH," "liquid ecstasy," "georgia home boy," and "goop") is another central nervous system depressant that is used to perpetrate sexual assaults. It is a clear liquid, slightly thicker than water, and can easily be mixed into food or drinks. As with Rohypnol, ingestion of GHB can lead to a variety of symptoms, such as an intense feeling of relaxation, seizures, loss of consciousness, coma, and even death.[39] The drug is traceable in a person's blood for only 4 to 8 hours and in urine for 12 to 15 hours.

It is often marketed as an antidepressant and a bodybuilding and weight control supplement. In addition, the Internet abounds with recipes for homemade GHB. The drug's intoxicating effects have led to its increasing popularity at parties and nightclubs,[40] where in some cases it becomes the tool of sexual offenders:

### Rohypnol

The drug Rohypnol is known on the streets as "roofies," "R-2's," "roach-2's," "trip and fall," and "mind erasers." This drug is often used by perpetrators who target their victims at parties, clubs, or bars where drinking is a common occurrence. The victims often cannot remember what happened to them while under the influence of Rohypnol.

(Courtesy Sergeant Christopher McKissick and Detective Tyler Parks, Port Orange, Florida, Police Department)

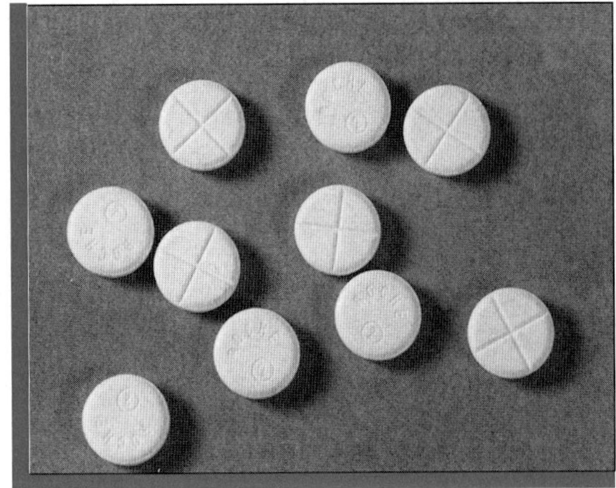

AT a party several years ago in Detroit, three men slipped GHB into a 15-year-old female's soft drink with the intention of raping her. She lapsed into a coma and died the next day. The three men were convicted of involuntary manslaughter in connection with her death.

OVER a two-year period several years ago, two men had been drugging women with GHB at "raves" and nightclubs. After the Los Angeles Sheriff's Department received complaints and had sufficient evidence to obtain a search warrant, officers uncovered more than 2,000 photographs of unconscious, naked women being assaulted and in sexually explicit poses. Many of the victims were unaware that they had been violated until they identified themselves in the photographs, and many of the women in the photographs have yet to be identified. The men were convicted of over 50 counts of rape and sexual assault. One of the men received a 77-year sentence while the other was sentenced to 19 years.

## OTHER DATE-RAPE DRUGS

Rohypnol and GHB are only two substances used to facilitate rape. A host of other depressants and benzodiazapines can debilitate sexual-assault victims. Valium, Ambien, Temazepam, Flexeril, Xanax, and Benadryl are all drugs that may be legitimately obtained but then appropriated for illicit purposes. Five teenage girls who were raped at a party went to the authorities with strong suspicions that they had been drugged. Each victim tested positive for Valium. Two men were later convicted on five counts of rape in connection with the incident.[41]

## EVIDENCE COLLECTION AND PROCESSING

Because victims may be unaware, or may only suspect, that an assault has occurred, law enforcement personnel have the critical task of gathering as much physical evidence as they can as quickly as possible. Dispatchers or call takers should be trained to recognize the signs and symptoms of drug-facilitated rapes. Call takers should be prepared to handle calls in which victims are confused, incoherent, or unclear about what may have happened, and they should keep victims on the phone until an officer arrives. In addition to the standard instruction that the victim should not bathe or discard the clothes she was wearing, it is imperative to advise the victim not to urinate until she has been transported to a medical facility for an examination and there has been a proper collection of her urine. Because many drugs exit the system within hours, a urine sample should be the first order of business as soon as a sexual assault is suspected. Treating all sexual assaults as possibly drug-induced ensures consistent evidence collection of urine in every case. However, it is important to get a victim's consent before drug screening is conducted.

Many laboratories are not equipped to do proper screening for the types of drugs used in sexual assaults. For an adequate drug screen, the laboratory test should include a screen for benzodiazapines, muscle relaxants, sleep aids, antihistamines, cocaine, marijuana, ketamine, opiates, and other substances that can depress the central nervous system. However, even though a laboratory might have the capacity to test for all these substances, its tests may not be sensitive enough to detect the minute amounts that can trigger criminal prosecution. For instance, most laboratories can detect 50 to 200 nanograms of Rohypnol per milliliter of urine, but even 10 nanograms per milliliter is sufficient for the purposes of an investigation; and it is recommended that GHB should be detected as low as 1 microgram per milliliter.[42]

## THE INVESTIGATION

Law enforcement officers cannot rely on forensic toxicology reports alone because the drugs may already have left the victim's system by the time evidence collection is initiated. The victim may delay contacting police because of embarrassment, guilt, or lack of knowledge regarding the incident. In many cases, it may take a victim time to piece together the events that led to the blackout period. The investigator should remain objective and open-minded when interviewing the victim. A victim's inability to offer a clear and detailed account of the assault may be quite frustrating for the investigating officer, but he or she should always remember that the "not knowing" is even more frustrating and traumatic for the victim. It is quite normal for a victim of drug-induced sexual assault to have significant gaps in her memory and incomplete facts regarding the incident.

Accounts from any people at the scene of the suspected drugging can be very valuable for corroborating any unusual behavior or identifying possible suspects. These witnesses may also be useful in determining who escorted the victim from that location and what statements the suspect made about the victim. They may also provide leads to more evidence.

Inquiring about the victim's level of alcohol consumption before the incident and ascertaining the victim's typical reactions to alcohol may help clarify whether the symptoms resulted from drugging or from "normal" intoxication. Parents, roommates, or other persons residing with the victim can assist in establishing the victim's state of mind and behavior after the incident and in piecing together a time line of events.

## EVIDENCE

When the investigation reaches the point at which a search warrant can be obtained for a suspect's residence, car, or place of work, the following items should be included in the search warrant:

- Packages of Rohypnol and other drugs.
- Bubble envelopes and other types of packaging that indicate receipt of a drug shipment.
- Cooking utensils.
- Precursors and reagents.
- Prescriptions (from the United States and other countries), especially for sleeping aids, muscle relaxants, and sedatives.
- Liquor bottles, mixers, and punch bowls (in which drugs may have been mixed with liquor).
- Glasses, soda cans, bottles, and any other containers that might contain drug residue.
- Video and photo camera equipment.
- Photographs or videotapes of the victim.
- Pornographic literature.
- Internet information on Rohypnol and GHB recipes.
- Computers and computer disks.

# AUTOEROTIC DEATHS

Death from accidental asphyxiation occasionally occurs as a result of masochistic activities of the deceased. This manner of death has been described as **autoerotic death,** or sexual asphyxia.

Typically, a white male is found partially suspended and nude, dressed in women's clothing or women's undergarments (see photo on page 366), or with his penis exposed. A ligature, suspended from a point within his reach, is affixed to his neck; it is padded to prevent bruising and visible evidence of his activity. There is no indication of suicidal intent, and the death surprises friends, relatives, and associates. Usually, the deceased has no history of mental or sexual disorder.[43]

Unfortunately, this dangerous practice has gained popularity in some homosexual communities. Individuals "hang" each other while orally copulating the potential victim. According to participants, the ligature reduces oxygen to the brain and heightens orgasm. Accidental slippage sometimes occurs as the willing partner becomes comatose due to oxygen starvation. The practice is commonly called "scarfing," after the thin, often silk, sash or scarf used as a ligature.

The death is attributable to asphyxia. The most common method is neck compression; more exotic forms involve chest compression, airway obstruction, and oxygen exclusion with gas or chemical replacement. Neck compression is illustrated in the first and chest compression in the second of the cases that follow:

A 33-year-old government employee was found in a rented motel room. He was in an upright position, and his feet were resting on the floor. A T-shirt around his neck suspended him from a room divider. He was attired in a skirt, sweater, brassiere padded with socks, panties, panty hose, and high heels. In the room were two suitcases. One contained men's trousers, shirts, socks, and undergarments. The second contained a knit sweater, skirt, slip, panties, bra, panty hose, and high heels. Investigators determined that he was married, had two preschool children, had recently been promoted in his job, and was well thought of by his associates.

THE victim was a 40-year-old commercial airline pilot who was married and the father of two small children. On his day off, he left home, telling his wife that he was going to target practice. A fisherman discovered him a short time later, crushed against the left rear fender of his 1968 Volkswagen in a large turnaround area at the end of a secluded road. The left door was open and the motor was running. The steering wheel was fixed in an extreme left-turn position and the automatic transmission was in low gear. Tire tracks indicated that the automobile had been moving in concentric circles. The body was held against the car by a heavy link chain and was totally nude except for a chain harness. The harness had a moderately tight loop around the neck and was bolted in front. The chain passed down the sternum and abdomen and around the waist to form a second loop. From the waist loop, strands of chain passed on each side of the testicles and into the gluteal fold and were secured to the waist loop in the small of the back. A 10-foot length of chain was attached from the waist loop to the rear bumper and had become wound around the rear axle five times. It is not known whether he jogged behind the car or was dragged; however, when he tired of the exercise, he approached the car intending to turn off the motor. In doing so, the chain became slack and the back tire rolled over it, causing the chain to become wound onto the rear axle. The trunk of the car contained his clothing and a zippered bag holding locks, bolts, chains, and wrenches. A lock and key were on the ground beside the body and another lock was found 20 feet from the body.[44]

Airway obstruction is illustrated in the following case:

THE The victim, a middle-aged male, was discovered dead in his apartment. He was totally nude and held to a pole that had been fitted into his apartment floor. Several black leather belts had been permanently affixed to the pole. These belts supported the victim from the neck, waist, and legs. Leg irons connected his ankles, handcuffs dangled from one wrist, and a gag was over his mouth. The belt around his neck was so tightly buckled that it lacerated his neck. On removal of the gag, it was found that he had placed so much paper in his mouth that he had been asphyxiated. Evidence of masturbation was also present.

The following is a case of oxygen exclusion with gas replacement:

A 50-year-old dentist was discovered dead in his office by an assistant. He was lying on his stomach, and over his face was a mask that he used to administer nitrous oxide to his patients. The mask was connected to a nitrous oxide container and was operational. His pants were unzipped, and he was thought to have been fondling himself while inhaling the gas.

Each of these cases was ruled accidental, and each occurred while the victim was involved in autoerotic activities. Although the motivation for such activity is not completely understood, asphyxia appears to be the cardinal feature of the act: "A disruption of the arterial blood supply resulting in a diminished oxygenation of the brain . . . will heighten sensations

**Autoerotic Death**
Note the female undergarments being worn by the male victim with oranges stuffed into the cups of the brassiere. A towel was wrapped around the rope to keep it from bruising his neck.

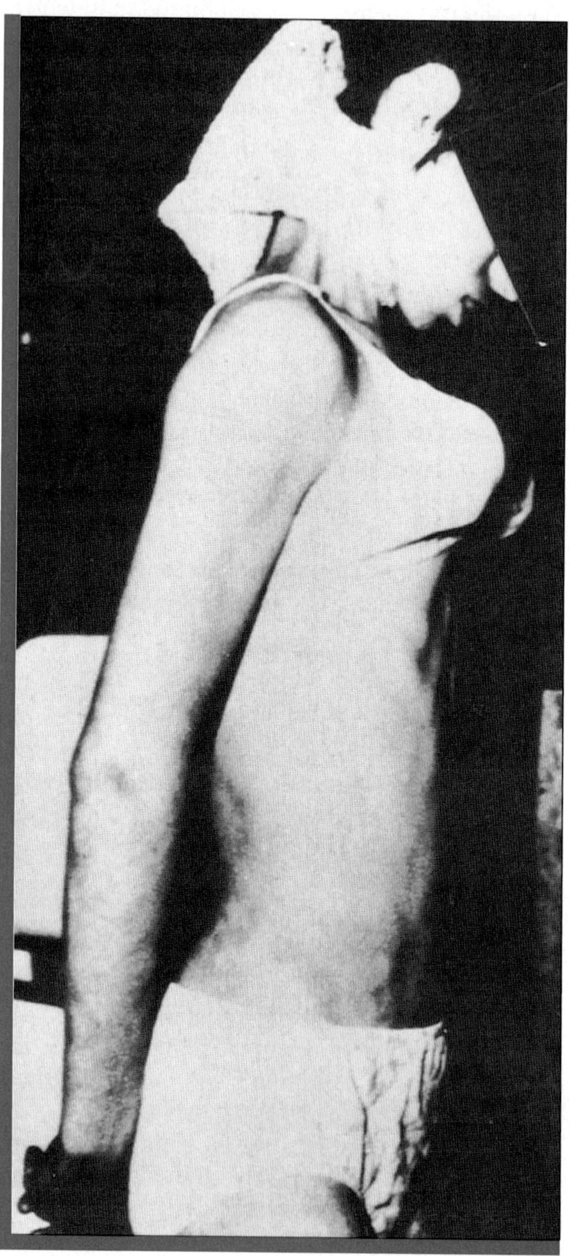

through diminished ego controls that will be subjectively perceived as giddiness, light-headedness, and exhilaration. This reinforces masturbatory sensations."[45] In autoerotic deaths, there does not appear to be a conscious intent to die, although the danger of death may well play a role. The masochistic aspect of this activity is evidenced by the elaborate bondage employed. Another masochistic practice associated with sexual asphyxia is the practice of infibulation, or masochism involving the genitals. The fantasies of the individuals who engage in sexual asphyxiation are heavily masochistic, involving such thoughts as one's own "penis being skewered with pins; being tied up in an initiation rite; being the leader of an imperiled group; and being raped by cowboys."[46] Evidence of the fantasy involvement may be found in the form of diaries, erotic literature, pornography, films or photographs of the individual's activities, or other such paraphernalia.

It appears that this phenomenon is quite rare among females, but the following case illustrates that it certainly does occur.[47]

THIS case involved a 35-year-old woman, a divorcée with a 9-year-old daughter. The mother was found deceased by the daughter in the morning after the child arose from a night's sleep in an adjoining room.

The child had gone to bed at 10 P.M. the night before and on awakening noticed a strange humming noise coming from her mother's room. After entering the room, she found her mother hanging dead in a small closet off the bedroom.

The victim was found completely nude lying on a small shelved space at the rear of the closet. Her feet were against the wall and her body was extended in a prone position, head downward, thus placing her legs and thighs in a horizontal position, resting on the shelved area from her feet to her waist. There was a folded quilt placed on the front portion of the shelf that was immediately under her abdomen and upper thighs. Behind the quilt and toward the rear of the shelf area was a broken cardboard box containing numerous books and other personal or family items. Her lower legs and feet were lying on these boxes, causing them to be at a slight upward angle from her waist.

It was estimated that the victim had been dead 10 to 12 hours, as there was evidence of scattered livor mortis on the body. She died of strangulation. An electric vibrator connected to an extension cord was found running. The vibrator was positioned between her thighs with the hard rubber massaging head in contact with the victim's vulva. There was a string-type clothespin on the nipple of her right breast, compressing the nipple, and another clothespin of the same type was found in a basket, immediately below her left breast.

In front of the shelved area, on the floor of the closet, was a laundry basket containing dirty clothes, and another quilt was folded and placed on top of the dirty clothes. The victim's hands were resting on this folded quilt in an arms-down position. The palms were facing upward. Over the place where the body was lying on this shelved area was a small narrow shelf 66 inches above the floor. This was attached to the wall by two steel brackets, and the one closest to the shelved area had a nylon hose tied around it that formed a long loop. The victim had placed her head in the loop and placed a hand towel between her neck and the nylon hose. Her face was turned toward the wall and lying against it.

The investigating officer made several important observations based on the body's position and condition at the time of discovery:

1. Because of the position of the clothespin on the nipple of her right breast and the depressed or flattened nipple on the left breast, it appeared that this second clothespin had fallen off and dropped into the basket.
2. It was felt that the hand towel beneath the nylon stocking served as a padding to prevent injury to the neck. The padding in the form of the quilt on the shelved area in the closet was probably placed there to make the deceased more comfortable.
3. The victim placed herself in this position, placed clothespins on her nipples to cause discomfort, and used the electric vibrator for additional sexual gratification. The victim intended to support part of her weight with her arms, as in a push-up, but passed out. This relaxed her arms, and the full weight of her body then came to rest on the nylon stocking around her neck, causing the strangulation.[48]

## THE PSYCHOLOGICAL AUTOPSY

Occasionally the medical examiner or police investigator is confronted with a death that may be the result of autoerotic or suicidal intent on the part of the deceased. For resolving questions about the death, there is a technique employed called the **psychological autopsy,** described as follows:

> Resolution of unexplained death has long been of concern within law enforcement activities and for the past quarter century, an object of inquiry within the mental health specialties. The term "autopsy" is usually associated with postmortem examination of human remains to determine the cause of death. The psychological autopsy is an analytical statement prepared by a mental health professional based upon the deceased's thoughts, feelings, and behavior.
>
> Its specific purpose, therefore, is to form a logical understanding of death from tangible physical evidence, documented life events, and intangible, often illusive, emotional factors. To accomplish its purpose, the psychological autopsy is structured to address three questions: What was the deceased like? What occurred in his/her life that could have been stressful? What were his/her reactions to those stresses? To accomplish this, structured interviews are conducted with friends, relatives, and associates of the deceased in the hope of developing psychological motivation for the death and pinpointing patterns of life-threatening behavior.[49]

## Key Terms

**autoerotic death**
**date-rape drugs**
**exchangeable traces**
**gamma hydroxybutyrate (GHB)**
**psychological autopsy**
**rape-murder**
**rape or sexual battery**
**Rohypnol**
**semen**
**sex offenses**
**sperm**

## Review Questions

1. What are the major characteristics of the four classifications of rape-murders?
2. What is sexual sadism?
3. Briefly discuss the major factors that should be considered in interviewing rape victims.
4. What are some of the major reasons that women do not report rape?
5. Why do women sometimes make false rape allegations?
6. Why is the discovery of semen, sperm, and hair valuable in rape investigations?
7. Why is the absence of semen fairly common in rape cases?
8. What errors are most commonly made in collecting evidence on rape investigations?
9. What are condom exchangeable traces composed of?
10. How can condom trace evidence be of value in linking acts of serial rapists?
11. What are the effects of Rohypnol?
12. When laboratories conduct drug screening tests in order to identify drugs that might have been used in sexual assaults, which types of drugs should they screen for?
13. In the investigation of a possible drug-facilitated sexual assault, what kinds of evidence should be collected?
14. What factors should indicate to the investigator that a death may have resulted from accidental sexual asphyxiation?
15. What is a psychological autopsy?

## Internet Activities

1. Check out the Rape Victim Advocates website at www.rapevictimadvocates.org. This site provides a discussion on the phases and concerns experienced by victims of rape trauma syndrome. In addition, it presents an overview of males as rape survivors—a topic not frequently addressed.
2. Go to the website of the Office of National Drug Control Policy (ONDCP) at www.whitehousedrugpolicy.gov and read the fact sheet on Rohypnol. According to the report, what are the characteristics of this drug's users? What regions of the United States have reported the most frequent use of Rohypnol?

## Notes


1. Robert D. Keppel and Richard Walter, "Profiling Killers: A Revised Classification Model for Understanding Murder," *International Journal of Offender Therapy and Comparative Criminology,* 1999, Vol. 43, No. 4, pp. 417–439. This discussion was adapted from this article with permission.
2. Bureau of Justice Statistics, "Number of Victimizations and Victimization Rates for Persons Age 12 and Older, by Type of Crime and Gender of Victim," www.ojp.usdoj.gov/bjs/pub/pdf/cvus9901.pdf, 1999.
3. Ibid.
4. Robert Spaulding and David Bigbee, "Physical Evidence in Sexual Assault Investigations," in Robert Hazlewood and Wolbert Burgess, eds., *Practical Aspects of Rape Investigation: A Multidisciplinary Approach,* 3rd ed. (New York: CRC Press, 2001), pp. 261–277.
5. Rebecca Campbell and Sheela Raja, "Secondary Victimization of Rape Victims: Insights from Mental Health Professionals Who Treat Survivors of Violence," *Violence and Victims,* 1999, Vol. 14, No. 3.
6. Karen Carlson, Stephanie Eisenstat, and Terra Ziporyn, "Rape," in *The Harvard Guide to Women's Health* (Cambridge, MA: Harvard University Press, 1996), pp. 526–527.
7. Karen Carlson, Stephanie Eisenstat, and Terra Ziporyn, "Posttraumatic Stress Disorder," in ibid., pp. 495–496.
8. *Interviewing the Rape Victim: Training Key 210* (Gaithersburg, MD: International Association of Chiefs of Police, 1974), p. 1.
9. Ibid.
10. Morton Bard and Katherine Ellison, "Crisis Intervention and Investigation of Forcible Rape," *Police Chief,* May 1974, Vol. 41, No. 5, pp. 68–74.
11. This discussion and accompanying references came from R. R. Hazelwood, "The Behavior-Oriented Interview of Rape Victims: The Key to Profiling," *FBI Law Enforcement Bulletin,* September 1983, pp. 13–15.
12. L. L. Holmstrom and A. W. Burgess, "Sexual Behavior of Assailants during Rape," *Archives of Sexual Behavior,* 1980, Vol. 9, No. 5, p. 437.
13. Ibid., p. 427.
14. L. L. Holmstrom and A. W. Burgess, "Rapist's Talk: Linguistic Strategies to Control the Victim," *Deviant Behavior,* 1979, Vol. 1, p. 101.
15. C. LeGrande, "Rape and Rape Laws: Sexism in Society and Law," *California Law Review,* 1973, p. 929.
16. Queens Bench Foundation, *Rape Victimization Study* (San Francisco, 1975), pp. 81–87; E. L. Willoughby and James A. Inciardi, "Estimating the Incidence of Crime," *Police Chief,* 1975, Vol. 42, No. 8, pp. 69–70; President's Commission on Law Enforcement and the Administration of Justice, *Task Force Report: Crime and Its Impact* (Washington, DC: Government Printing Office, 1967), p. 80; Eugene J. Kanin, "False Rape Allegations," *Archives of Sexual Behavior,* 1994, Vol. 23, No. 1, pp. 81–90.
17. The state of Florida repealed its previous statute, Forcible Rape and Carnal Knowledge 794, replacing it with a new statute, titled Sexual Battery 794. The new law provides for various penalties for sexual battery depending on the amount of force used and the injuries sustained by the victim. In addition, the statute provides that specific instances of prior sexual activity between the victim and any person other than the defendant cannot be admitted into evidence.
18. Queens Bench Foundation, *Rape Victimization Study,* p. 86.
19. "Vicious Lies and Apologies," *St. Petersburg Times,* July 30, 1990, pp. A1, A4.
20. "Crime in the United States: 2000 Uniform Crime Reports," www.fbi.gov/ucr/cius_00/00crime3.pdf.

21. Spaulding and Bigbee, "Physical Evidence in Sexual Assault Investigations."
22. Ibid.
23. A. N. Groth and A. W. Burgess, *Rape, A Sexual Deviation,* paper presented to the American Psychological Association Meeting, Washington, DC, Sept. 5, 1976, p. 4.
24. J. H. Davis, "Examination of Victims of Sexual Assault and Murder," material developed for a homicide seminar offered by the Florida Institute for Law Enforcement, St. Petersburg, Florida, 1965.
25. Ibid.
26. Arne Svensson and Otto Wendel, *Techniques of Crime Scene Investigation* (New York: American Elsevier, 1973).
27. William Watson, "Forensic Serology and DNA Analysis," lecture given at the University of North Texas, 2001.
28. Joe Nickell and Jolm Fischer, *Crime Science: Methods of Forensic Detection* (Lexington: University Press of Kentucky, 1999).
29. Watson, "Forensic Serology and DNA Analysis."
30. Spaulding and Bigbee, "Physical Evidence in Sexual Assault Investigations."
31. FBI National Academy, *Collection of Physical Evidence in Sex Crimes* (Quantico, VA: 1975), p. 2.
32. Robert D. Blackledge, "Condom Trace Evidence: A New Factor in Sexual Assault Investigations," *FBI Bulletin,* May 1996, pp. 12–16. This discussion was adapted from this article.
33. R. D. Blackledge and L. R. Cabiness, "Examination for Petroleum Based Lubricants in Evidence from Rapes and Sodomies," *Journal of Forensic Sciences,* 1983, Vol. 28, pp. 451–462.
34. R. D. Blackledge, "Collection and Identification Guidelines for Traces from Latex Condoms in Sexual Assault Cases," *Crime Laboratory Digest,* 1994, Vol. 21, pp. 57–61.
35. Tamantha Chapman, "Drug-Facilitated Sexual Assault, *Police Chief,* June 2000, pp. 38–39.
36. Bureau of Justice Statistics, *Violence against Women: Estimates from the Designed Survey* (Washington, DC: U.S. Department of Justice, August 1995).
37. Hoffman-LaRoche, Inc., "Rohypnol Fact Sheet"; Drug Enforcement Administration, "Intelligence Report (Rohypnol)," July 1995.
38. A. G. Gardiner, Jr., "Rohypnol: The New Stealth Weapon," *Police Chief,* April 1998, p. 37.
39. Drug Enforcement Administration, "Fact Sheet (GHB)," August 1998; Food and Drug Administration, "Training Bulletin," Office of Criminal Investigations, San Diego, CA.
40. Executive Office of the President's Office of National Drug Control Policy, "Gamma Hydroxybutyrate (GHB) Fact Sheet," October 1998.
41. Chapman, "Drug-Facilitated Sexual Assault," p. 41.
42. American Prosecutors Research Institute, *The Prosecution of Rohypnol and GHB Related Sexual Assaults* (Alexandria, VA: APRI, 1999).
43. R. R. Hazelwood, *Autoerotic Deaths* (Quantico, VA: Behavioral Science Unit, FBI Academy, 1984.)
44. J. Rupp, "The Love Bug," *Journal of Forensic Science,* 1973, pp. 259–262.
45. H. L. P. Resnick, "Eroticized Repetitive Hangings: A Form of Self-Destructive Behavior," *American Journal of Psychotherapy,* January 1972, p. 10.
46. R. Litman and C. Swearingen, "Bondage and Suicide," *Archives of General Psychiatry,* July 1972, Vol. 27, p. 82.
47. R. D. Henry, *Medical Legal Bulletin,* Office of the Chief Medical Examiner, Department of Health, State of Virginia, 1971, Vol. 20, No. 2, Bulletin 214.
48. E. A. Sass, "Sexual Asphyxia in the Female," *Journal of Forensic Science,* 1975, pp. 182–184.
49. N. Hibbler, "The Psychological Autopsy," *Forensic Science Digest,* September 1978, Vol. 5, pp. 42–44.

# ELEVEN

# Crimes against Children

*Stefan Jahn shown entering a coutroom. Jahn was convicted of kidnapping a 12-year-old girl from the eastern German town of Eberswalde, abusing her, and then strangling her.* (© Reuters NewMedia Inc./Corbis)

## CHAPTER OUTLINE



## CHAPTER OBJECTIVES

1. Recognize types and patterns of burn injuries found in child abuse.
2. Define and discuss shaken-baby syndrome.
3. Explain Munchausen syndrome by proxy.
4. Identify types of child molesters, and explain investigative and interview techniques for cases of child molestation.
5. Outline types of child pornography.
6. Define *incest* and outline profiles of incestuous fathers.
7. Describe the profile of the infant abductor.
8. Outline the assessments and investigative procedures used to determine whether a child has run away or has been abducted.
9. Discuss sex-offender registration and community notification laws.
10. Recognize threat assessment factors and levels of risk in committing school crime.

# INTRODUCTION

Probably no other crimes are more emotionally laden than those involving children as victims. Police officers and investigators often speak of the intense emotion associated with viewing innocent children as victims of crime. Unfortunately, incidents of crime against children have increased dramatically during the past decade. Today, their prevalence seems to have reached epidemic proportions. It takes little effort to find reports of child abuse and assault in newspapers, on television, and from other media sources. As a result, increasing numbers of police departments have investigators who are assigned exclusively to the investigation of crimes against children. For this reason, this chapter focuses on issues of child abuse and assault, including some of the techniques and problems associated with investigating these crimes.

Crimes perpetrated against children can appear in many forms and contexts. Children may experience abuse, for example, that results in burn injuries, yet deliberate burning often goes unrecognized. It is especially important in such cases that investigators establish good rapport with hospital workers and, particularly, emergency medical technicians, who will probably be the first persons to see the child's injuries. After discussing burn injuries, the chapter explains shaken-baby syndrome and Munchausen syndrome by proxy, two crimes that have recently received much societal attention. Next, the chapter addresses the investigation of sexual crimes against children, such as molestation and incest. This investigation is one of the saddest experiences in any officer's career, and few officers are able to complete it without some feeling of anger and remorse, particularly since in many cases these crimes are committed against children by their own parents or guardians.

Also discussed in this chapter is infant abduction, another crime that is on the rise. In regard to older missing children, strategies are provided for use by investigators in determining whether a child has been abducted or has run away. Next, child pornography, a crime that is rapidly increasing due to facilitation by the Internet, is discussed. The chapter concludes with sections on sex-offender registration and on crimes in schools, including overviews on threat assessments and on personality traits and behaviors of troubled children who commit crimes in schools.

## ASSAULTS AGAINST CHILDREN

The most common cause of children's death is physical abuse, often by their own parents. The clinical term commonly used to describe physically abused children is the **battered-child syndrome**. This possibility should be considered in any child exhibiting evidence of bone fracture, subdermal hematoma, failure to thrive, soft-tissue swelling, or skin bruising; in any child who dies suddenly; or in any child when the degree and type of injury are at variance with the history given regarding the occurrence of the trauma.[1]

Abuse of children takes various forms, from minor assaults to flagrant physical torture. Many times these injuries cannot or will not be explained by the parents or the story seems inconsistent with the injuries received. For example, bruises in various stages of healing generally vary in color. Thus, one should be suspicious of an explanation of such injuries as being caused by a fall from a bike. Intentional injuries tend to occur most frequently on the face, back, ribs, buttocks, genitals, palms, or soles of the feet. Although abusers use a wide variety of instruments, the two most common are the belt (see photo) and electric cord.

### Boy Beaten with the Buckle End of a Belt

One of the most common instruments used to physically abuse children is the belt. While the leather end of a belt can inflict significant pain, the buckle end can cause even more serious injuries to young children, as is depicted in this photo.

**(Courtesy Tampa Police Department)**

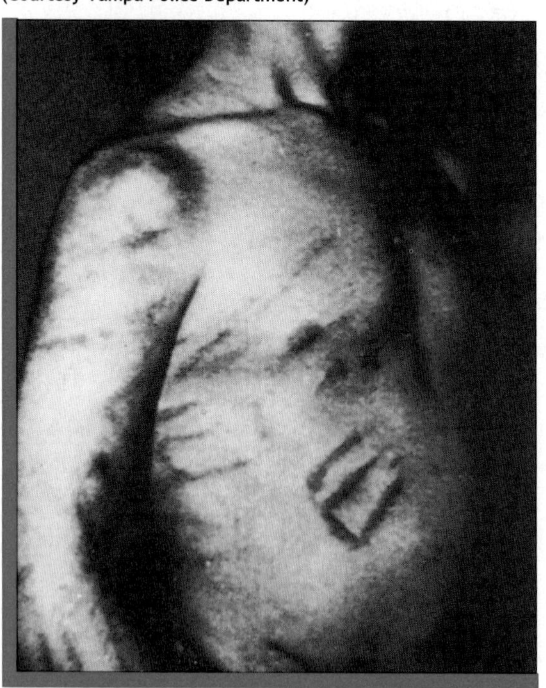

## BURN INJURIES AND CHILD ABUSE

Although general awareness of the magnitude of child abuse is increasing, deliberate injury by burning is often unrecognized. Burn injuries make up about 10 percent of all child-abuse cases, and about 10 percent of hospital admissions of children to burn units are the result of child abuse. In comparison with accidentally burned children, abused children are significantly younger and have longer hospital stays and higher mortality rates. Child burn victims are almost always under the age of 10, with the majority under the age of 2.[2]

Children are burned for different reasons. Immersion burns may occur during toilet training, with the perpetrator immersing the child in scalding water for cleaning or as punishment. Hands may be immersed in pots of water as punishment for playing near the stove. A person may place a child in a hot oven as punishment or with homicidal intentions.

Inflicted burns often leave characteristic patterns of injury that fortunately cannot be concealed. Along with the history of the burn incident, these patterns are primary indicators of inflicted burns versus accidental ones. Findings in response to the following questions can raise or lower the index of suspicion, as well as help to determine whether a burn was deliberately inflicted:

- Is the explanation of what happened consistent with the injury? Are there contradictory or varying accounts of the method or time of the "accident" or other discrepancies in the witnesses' descriptions of what happened?
- Does the injury have a clean line of demarcation, parts within or immediately around the injured area that are not burned, a burn pattern inconsistent with the injury account, or any other typical characteristics of an inflicted burn? Are the burns located on the buttocks, the area between the child's legs, or the ankles, wrists, palms, or soles?
- Are other injuries present, such as fractures, healed burns, or bruises?
- Are the child's age and level of development compatible with the caretaker's and witnesses' account of the injury?
- Was there a delay in seeking medical attention? Less serious burns may have been treated at home.
- Does the caretaker insist there were no witnesses to the injury incident, including the caretaker?
- Do those who were present seem to be angry or resentful toward the child or each other?

A detailed history, including previous trauma, presence of recent illnesses, immunization status, and the status of routine medical care, is critical, as is careful documentation of the scene of the injury, including photographs and drawings. To investigate a burn injury, the investigator should do the following:

- Stay focused on the facts, and proceed slowly and methodically.
- Ask questions, be objective, and reenact the incident.
- Treat each case individually.

The incidence of further injury and death is so high in deliberate burn cases that it is critical for all concerned persons to be aware of the indicators of this form of child abuse.

## TYPOLOGIES OF BURNS

Children may incur various types of burn injuries. A burn may be classified by how severe or "deep" it is or by how the injury occurred. It is essential to have an understanding of the different grades of burn severity and to recognize the cause of a burn by observing the patterns that are evident when a child's skin comes into direct contact with hot objects or liquid. An informed analysis of burn cause and severity is fundamental in ascertaining whether a child's injury is deliberate or accidental.

## MEDICAL CLASSIFICATION OF BURN SEVERITY

Physicians primarily categorize burns as having either partial thickness or full thickness (see Table 11–1). Only an experienced medical practitioner can determine how deeply a burn has penetrated the skin, but there are some features of partial- and full-thickness burns that can be observed immediately after the incident:

**Table 11-1** Classification of Burns

| Classification | Characteristics |
|---|---|
| First degree | Partial-thickness burns:<br>• Erythema (localized redness)<br>• Sunburnlike<br>• Not included when calculating burn size<br>• Usually heal by themselves |
| Second degree | Partial-thickness burns:<br>• Part of skin damaged<br>• Have blisters containing clear fluid<br>• Pink underlying tissue<br>• Often heal by themselves |
| Third degree | Full-thickness burns:<br>• Full skin destroyed<br>• Deep red tissue underlying blister<br>• Presence of bloody blister fluid<br>• Muscle and bone possibly destroyed<br>• Require professional treatment |
| Fourth degree | Full-thickness burns:<br>• Penetrate deep tissue to fat, muscle, bone<br>• Require immediate professional treatment |

- Patches of reddened skin that blanch with fingertip pressure and then refill are shallow partial-thickness burns. Blisters usually indicate deeper partial-thickness burning, especially if the blisters increase in size just after the burn occurs.
- A leathery or dry surface with a color of white, tan, brown, red, or black indicates a full-thickness burn. The child feels no pain because the nerve endings have been destroyed. Small blisters may be present but will not increase in size.

It is essential for investigators to develop good rapport with medical personnel, including both the hospital staff workers involved with the case and emergency medical technicians (EMTs). The EMTs, especially, can provide a wealth of information due to the fact that they were probably the first persons to see the child's injuries. Also, an experienced social service investigator can provide valuable information regarding family history and any observed patterns of abuse.

Several factors affect the severity of a burn. A child's age plays a part in how severely the child is injured by a particular incident. For example, an adult will experience a significant injury of the skin after 1 minute of exposure to water at 127°F, 30 seconds of exposure at 130°F, and 2 seconds of exposure at 150°F. A child, however, will suffer a more severe burn in less time than an adult because children have thinner skin than adults. A young child's skin will be severely harmed even more rapidly and by less heat than will an older child's skin.

Furthermore, certain parts of the body have thinner skin, including the front of the trunk, inner thighs, bottom of forearms, and inner-arm area. Thicker-skinned areas include the palms, soles, back, scalp, and back of the neck. Given the same cause, burns incurred in thinner-skin areas tend to be more severe than burns incurred in areas protected by thicker skin.

## CAUSES OF BURN INJURIES

The severity of a burn is also directly influenced by the circumstances that caused the burn:

- Scald burns occur when the child comes into contact with hot liquid.
- Contact burns occur when the child encounters a hot solid object or flame.

### Scald Burns

**Scald burns** are the most common type of burn injury to a child. They are caused by hot liquids—hot tap water, boiling water, hot drinks such as tea or coffee, and thicker liquids such as soup or grease. Scald burns may occur in the form of spill/splash injuries or as immersion burns. Most deliberate burns are scald burns caused by immersion in hot tap water.

***Spill/Splash Injuries*** **Spill/splash injuries** occur when a hot liquid falls from a height onto the victim. The burn pattern is characterized by irregular margins and nonuniform depth. Ascertaining the area of the skin where the scalding liquid first struck the victim is the key to determining whether a burn is accidental or nonaccidental. Water travels downward and cools as it moves away from the initial contact point. When a pan of water is spilled or thrown on a person's chest, the initial contact point shows a splash pattern. The area below this point tapers down, creating what is called an "arrow-down" pattern. This pattern is more commonly seen in assaults on adults than in assaults on children.

If the child was wearing clothing at the time of injury, the pattern may be altered. This is why it is important to determine whether clothing was worn and, if possible, to retain the actual clothing. Depending on the material, the water may have been against the skin longer, which would result in a deeper injury and pattern. A fleece sleeper, for instance, will change the course of the water and hold the temperature longer in one area as opposed to a thin, cotton T-shirt.

Questions to ask in a scalding-injury investigation include the following:

- Where were the caretakers at the time of the accident?
- How many persons were home at the time?
- How tall is the child? How far can he or she reach?
- Can the child walk, and are the child's coordination and development consistent with his or her age?
- How much water was in the pan, and how much does it weigh?
- What is the height to the handle of the pan when the pan is on the stove (or counter or table)?
- Was the oven on at the time (thus making it unlikely that the child could have climbed onto the stove)?
- Does the child habitually play in the kitchen or near the stove? Does the child usually climb on the cabinets or table?
- Has the child been scolded for playing in the kitchen? For touching the stove?

It is unusual for a child to incur an accidental scald burn on his or her back, but it has happened. As in all burn investigations, factors other than location of the burn must be considered before concluding that the injury was nonaccidental. Deliberate burning by throwing a hot liquid on a child is usually done either as punishment for playing near a hot object or in anger. However, the child may have been caught in the crossfire between two fighting adults and then been accused of having spilled the liquid accidentally.

***Immersion Burns*** When a child falls or is placed into a tub or other container of hot liquid, **immersion burns** result. In a deliberate immersion burn, the depth of the burn is uniform. The wound borders are very distinct, sharply defined "waterlines" with little tapering of depth at the edges, and there is little evidence that the child thrashed about during the immersion, indicating that the child was held in place. Occasionally there may be bruising in the area of the soft tissue where the child was being forcibly held.

Only children with deliberate immersion burns sustain deep burns of the buttocks and/or the area between the anus and the genitals. The motivation for this type of injury generally involves punishment for failing to toilet train or for soiling of clothing. Dirty diapers or soiled clothing may be found in the bathroom. The water in the bathtub may be deeper than what is normal for bathing an infant or child and may be so hot that the first responding adult at the scene is unable to immerse his or her own hand in it.

Several key variables must be observed in investigating immersion burns:

- *The temperature of the water:* Variables that must be taken into account include the temperature of the water heater, the ease with which it can be reset, and recent prior usage of water.
- *The time of exposure:* This is an unknown that can sometimes be estimated from the burn pattern and its depth.
- *The depth of the burn:* Several days may need to pass before the true depth of the burn can be determined.
- *The occurrence of "sparing":* There may be areas within or immediately around the burn site that were not burned.

When a child's hand is forced into hot water, the child will make a fist, thus "sparing" the palm and discounting the statement that the child reached into the pan of hot water for something. A child whose body is immersed in hot water will attempt to fold up, and there will be sparing in creases in the abdomen. Curling up the toes when the foot is forced into a hot liquid will spare part of the soles of the feet or the area between the toes. The area where the child was held by the perpetrator will also be spared. These flexing actions prevent burning within the body's creases, causing a striped configuration of burned and unburned zones, or a "zebra" pattern.

Deliberate immersion burns can often be recognized by one of the following characteristic patterns:

- *Doughnut pattern in the buttocks:* When a child falls or steps into a hot liquid, the immediate reaction is to thrash about, try to get out, and jump up and down. When a child is held in scalding hot bathwater, the buttocks are pressed against the bottom of the tub so forcibly that the water will not come into contact with the center of the buttocks, sparing this part of the buttocks and causing the burn injury to have a doughnut pattern.
- *Sparing the soles of the feet:* Another instance of sparing occurs in a child whose buttocks and feet are burned but whose soles have been spared. If a caretaker's account is that the child was left in the bathroom and told not to get into the tub, and that the caretaker then heard screaming and returned to find the child jumping up and down in the water, the absence of burns on the soles of the child's feet is evidence that the account is not true. A child cannot jump up and down in hot water without burning the bottoms of the feet.
- *Stocking- or glove-pattern burns:* Stocking and glove patterns are seen when feet or hands are held in the water. The line of demarcation is possible evidence that the injury was not accidental.
- *Waterlines:* A sharp line on the lower back or in some cases the legs indicates that the child was held still in the water. A child falling into the water would show splash and irregular-line patterns. The waterline on a child's torso indicates how deep the water was. (See top photo on page 379.)

## Contact Burns

**Contact burns** occur when a child's skin comes into contact with a flame or a hot solid object. A contact-burn injury may be caused by a curling iron, steam iron, cigarette or lighter, fireplace, stovetop burner, outdoor grill, or some other hot implement. When a hot solid object touches a child, the child's skin is "branded" with a mirror image of the object. Flame burns are a much less common cause of deliberate injury. When they do occur, they are characterized by extreme depth and are relatively well-defined as compared with accidental flame burns.

When a child accidently touches a hot object or the object falls on the child, there is usually a lack of pattern in the burn injury, since the child quickly moves away from the object. However, even brief accidental contact, such as falling against a hot radiator or grate, can cause a second-degree-burn imprint of the pattern of the object.

***Distinguishing Nonaccidental from Accidental Contact Burns*** Nonaccidental burns caused by a hot solid object are the most difficult to distinguish from accidental injuries. Cigarette and iron burns are the most frequent types of these injuries (see bottom photo on page 379). Cigarette burns, especially multiple burns on the child's feet, back, or buttocks, are unlikely to have been caused by an accident; therefore, they are more suspect than indi-

## Wet Burn

A child forcibly immersed in a tub of hot water. Note the end of the immersion line near the knees. In this case, the child's legs were placed in water hot enough to cause significant blistering. The motivation for this kind of crime is often punishment of the child.

(Courtesy Tampa Police Department)

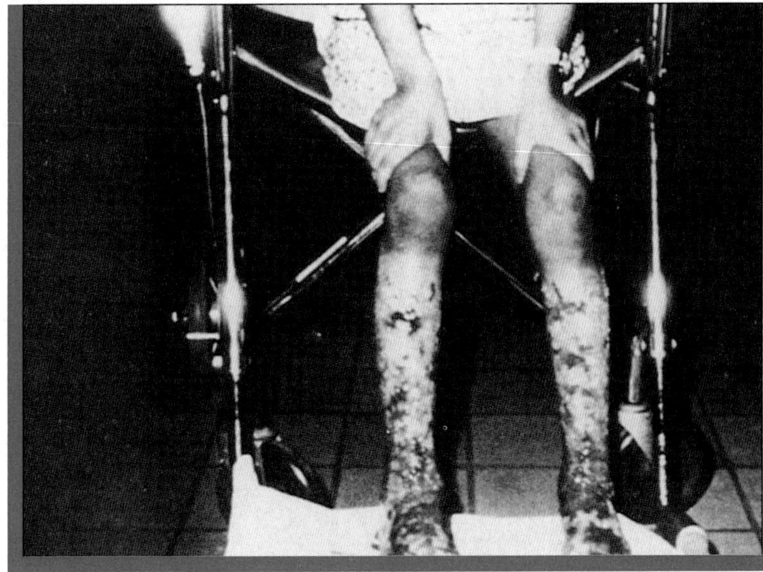

vidual burns in the area of the child's face and eyes, which can occur accidentally if the child walks or runs into an adult's lit cigarette held at waist height. Accidental burns are usually more shallow, irregular, and less well defined than deliberate burns.

Purposely inflicted "branding" injuries usually mirror the objects that caused the burn (such as cigarette lighters and curling irons) and are much deeper than the superficial and random burns caused by accidentally touching these objects. Most accidental injuries with hot steam or curling irons occur when the hot item is grasped or falls. These are usually second-degree injuries that are randomly placed, as might be the case when a hot iron strikes the skin in multiple places as it falls. It is important to know where the iron was—for example, was it on an ironing board or a coffee table at the child's height?

Another source of accidental burns is contact with items that have been exposed for prolonged periods to hot sun. Pavement in hot sun, which can reach a temperature of 176°F, can burn a child's bare feet; however, such burns are not likely to be deep. A child placed in a carseat that has been in a car in the sun can receive second- and even third-degree burns. Full-thickness burns have also resulted from contact with a hot seat-belt buckle.

The following key questions will help in determining whether contact burns are accidental or nonaccidental:

- Where is the burn injury, and could the child reach the area unassisted?
- Does the child normally have access to the item (such as a cigarette lighter) that caused the injury?
- How heavy is the item, and how strong is the child? For instance, is the steam iron a

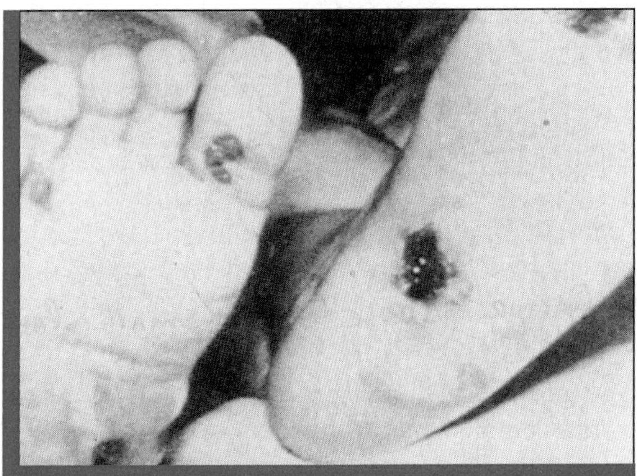

## Cigarette Burns

Burn injuries inflicted to the soles of this child's feet by use of a lit cigarette. Cigarette burns, especially ones like those in the picture, are unlikely to have been caused by an accident. Investigators are highly suspicious of burns such as those on the bottoms of feet and immediately look for other signs of physical abuse.

(Courtesy Milwaukee County Department of Social Service)

compact, travel-size one that a small child could lift or a full-size home model that might be too heavy?

- Is there any sparing that would be significant to the injury?
- How was the item heated, and how long did it take for the item to become hot enough to cause the injury?
- Is the injury clean and crisp, with the distinctive pattern of the object, or is it shallow or irregular, as from a glancing blow? Several cleanly defined injuries, especially on an older child, could indicate that the child was held motionless by a second perpetrator while the first perpetrator carefully branded the child.
- Are there multiple burns or other healed burns?
- Has the child been punished before for playing with or being too close to the hot object?

## SHAKEN-BABY SYNDROME

The phrase "shaken-baby syndrome" was coined to explain instances in which severe intracranial trauma occurs in the absence of signs of external head trauma. **Shaken-baby syndrome (SBS)** is the severe intentional application of violent force (shaking), in one or more episodes, that results in intracranial injuries to the child. Physical abuse of children by shaking usually is not an isolated event. Many shaken infants show evidence of previous trauma. Frequently, the shaking has been preceeded by other types of abuse.[3]

### MECHANISM OF INJURY

The mechanism of injury in SBS is thought to result from a combination of physical factors, including the proportionately large cranial size of infants, the laxity of their neck muscles, and the vulnerability of their intracranial bridging veins. However, the primary factor is the proportionately large size of the adult relative to the child. Shaking by admitted assailants has produced remarkably similar injury patterns:

- The infant is held by the chest, facing the assailant, and is shaken violently back and forth.
- The shaking causes the infant's head to whip forward and backward from chest to the back.
- The infant's chest is compressed, and the arms and legs move about with a whiplash action.
- At the completion of the assault, the infant may be limp and either not breathing or breathing shallowly.
- During the assault, the infant's head may strike a solid object.
- After the shaking, the infant may be dropped, thrown, or slammed onto a solid surface.

The last two events likely explain the many cases of blunt injury, including skull fractures, found in shaken infants. However, although blunt injury may be seen at autopsy in shaken infants, research data suggest that shaking in and of itself is often sufficient to cause serious intracranial injury or death.

### INDICATORS AND SYMPTOMS

Crying has come under increasing scrutiny as a stimulus for abusive activity. Because shaking is generally a response to crying, a previous illness causing irritability may increase the likelihood that the infant will be shaken. The occurrence of infant abuse is a product of a delicate balance between the frequency of the stimulus of crying and the threshold for violent action by potential abusers. The effects of drugs, alcohol, and environmental conditions may trigger this interaction.

The average age of infants abused by shaking is 6 months. The physical alterations characteristic of SBS are uncommon in children older than 1 year. Many symptomatic shaken infants have seizures, are lethargic, or are in a coma. Many are resuscitated at home or en route to the hospital and arrive there in serious condition. Some children have milder changes in consciousness or a history of choking, vomiting, or poor feeding. Although gross evidence of trauma is usually absent, careful inspection may reveal sites of bruising.

Most infants in whom shaking has been documented have retinal hemorrhaging (bleeding along the back inside layer of the eyeball). Other intracranial injuries ascribed to shaking trauma are fluid between the skull and brain, tearing of brain tissue, and swelling of the brain.

## INVESTIGATIVE GUIDELINES

- The use of MRI has helped detect old and new intracranial injuries and has aided recognition of subtle instances of repetitive shaking.
- Repetitive abuse has important legal and clinical implications. If abuse is repetitive, the child is at high risk for further injury unless legal action is taken. Establishing that there has been a pattern of abuse can also help in identifying potential perpetrators and may lead to increased legal penalties.
- The fact that shaken children, and possibly their siblings, often have been previously abused should dispel the notion that shaking is an isolated and somewhat "unintentional" event.
- From the perspective of the protection of the child or the criminal prosecution of the abuser, it is not as important to distinguish the precise mechanism of injury as it is to be certain that the event was nonaccidental.
- Pediatricians should not be deterred from testifying when the cause of the nonaccidental injury is not entirely clear.
- Shaking a child creates an imminent risk for an acute injury.
- Injuries that appear to be caused by shaking create a high index of suspicion of child abuse and should be followed by intensive efforts (e.g., skeletal survey, CT scan, and MRI) to identify concurrent and previous abuse of the patient and any siblings.
- If an infant's injuries are fatal, an autopsy should be performed by a forensic pathologist. Autopsies of all infants who die of causes other than known natural illness should include thorough skeletal imaging.

## THE ROLE OF THE PHYSICIAN IN CHILD-ABUSE CASES

The problem the investigator often encounters is that the victim is either too young to explain what has occurred or too intimidated to cooperate. In injuries or deaths of young children, investigators find radiologists (physicians who specialize in the interpretation of X-rays) especially helpful. It is common for abused children to be brought to the hospital emergency room by their parents or relatives, who tell hospital personnel that the child was injured in a fall or some other accident. When there is a discrepancy between the characteristics of the injury and the explanation, X-rays can be useful in determining whether the injuries were accidental. X-rays of the entire body reveal not only the presence of fractures and other injuries to joints and bones but also the existence of older injuries in various stages of healing.

Careful questioning of the persons bringing the child to the hospital may be sufficient to confirm the need for a complete investigation. The following facts about child abuse are helpful in such questioning:

- In many cases, only one of a number of children in the family is chosen as the target of abuse, and frequently that child was conceived or born extramaritally or premaritally.
- The marital partner tends to protect the abusive parent through denial of the facts.
- Occasionally, an abusing father also assaults his wife, but more frequently he restricts the gross abuse to a child.
- In over half the cases in which child abuse results in hospitalization, there was a preceding incident of abuse of equal severity.
- Not infrequently the battered child is taken to a different hospital after each abuse in order to conceal the recurrence of injuries.[4]

The families of battered children range across the entire socioeconomic spectrum. The investigator cannot assume that an injured child who comes from what appears to be a "good home" is not the victim of child abuse.

In cases where medical examination is inconclusive but abuse is strongly suspected, interviewing becomes even more significant. The rule is to leave no source unexamined. To fail to do so places the abused child back into a defenseless position in which further injury or death could occur. The interviewing of baby-sitters, neighbors, teachers, and others must be conducted sensibly and sensitively. The aim is not to "get the person who did it," because there may not in fact have been an abuse incident. The primary objective is to get the information so that if there has been abuse, the child can be protected.

## MUNCHAUSEN SYNDROME BY PROXY

Munchausen syndrome is a psychological disorder in which the person fabricates the symptoms of disease or injury in order to undergo medical tests, hospitalization, or even medical or surgical treatment. To command medical attention, individuals with Munchausen syndrome may intentionally injure themselves or induce illness in themselves. In cases of **Munchausen syndrome by proxy (MSBP),** a parent or caretaker suffering from Munchausen syndrome attempts to elicit medical attention to himself or herself by injuring or inducing illness in a child. The parent then may try to resuscitate the child or to have paramedics or hospital personnel save the child.[5] The following actual cases are examples of MSBP:

M.A., a 9-month-old boy, had been repeatedly admitted to Children's Hospital because of recurrent life-threatening apnea (cessation of breathing). At 7 weeks of age, he experienced his first apneic event, and his mother administered mouth-to-mouth ventilation. Spontaneous respiration returned, and M.A. was hospitalized, treated, and discharged with a home monitor.

During the next 9 months, M.A. experienced 10 similar events and 7 more hospitalizations. Eight of the events required mouth-to-mouth ventilation. All of these episodes occurred while mother and child were alone, so only M.A.'s mother witnessed the actual events. Two episodes occurred in the hospital.

Unfortunately, despite many tests and surgical procedures, M.A.'s apnea persisted and his growth slowed. Because of his persistent apnea and failure to thrive, M.A. received home nursing care. During these home visits, several nurses observed that M.A. would refuse to eat in his mother's presence. If she left the room, however, he would eat.

In time, both medical and nursing staffs became increasingly suspicious that Mrs. A. was somehow responsible for her child's apnea. To better observe mother-child interaction, M.A. was moved to a hospital room equipped for covert audiovisual surveillance.

On the sixth day, the video clearly recorded Mrs. A. bringing on the apnea by forcing the child against her chest, which caused him to lose consciousness. M.A. became limp and experienced a falling heart rate. Mrs. A. then placed the baby back on the bed, called for help, and began mouth-to-mouth resuscitation.

The hospital immediately informed child protection services and police authorities, who reviewed the recording. Shortly thereafter, a team consisting of a physician, nurse, social worker, and police officer confronted her. At first, Mrs. A. expressed disbelief at the suggestion that she had smothered M.A., but when she was informed of the video, she made no comment. She was then arrested.

Mrs. A. was a 36-year-old occupational therapist and the mother of three boys. Late into her pregnancy with M.A., she worked in an early intervention program for developmentally delayed children. During many of M.A.'s hospitalizations, she appeared caring and concerned but emotionally distant. Clearly, Mrs. A. was the dominant parent, who made all decisions regarding medical treatment.

Mrs. A. subsequently pled guilty to felonious, third-degree assault. At the time, she stated: "The only time I ever caused M.A. to stop breathing was in the hospital." She received three years' probation, during which she was to receive psychotherapy. If she successfully completed psychotherapy, the felony charge would be reduced to a misdemeanor. She also had to live apart from her children and could visit them only in the presence of two other adults.

M.A. had no further apnea, and at 24 months of age he appeared vigorous, healthy, and normal. Eventually, the family was reunited.

C.B., a 10-month-old girl, was admitted to a hospital because of recurrent life-threatening apnea. C.B. had been born in another state and had been sexually assaulted at the age of 3 months by an acquaintance of her father. After the assault, local child protection services closely monitored the family.

At 6 months of age, C.B. experienced her first apneic episode. Her father shook her vigorously, and then administered mouth-to-mouth ventilation. She was subsequently admitted to a local hospital. After examination and treatment, she was discharged with a home monitor. During the next two months, C.B. experienced six apneic events and three hospitalizations. The family then moved to Minnesota.

During her first month in Minnesota, C.B. experienced four apneic episodes and three more hospitalizations. All required vigorous stimulations to restore spontaneous breathing. Other family members observed the child immediately after the events. However, only C.B.'s father had witnessed all the actual events. C.B. was eventually referred to Children's Hospital.

While in the hospital, C.B. had no clinical apnea or monitor alarms. Most of the time, she appeared happy and playful. However, when anyone attempted to touch her face, she became hysterical and combative. Over time, both the medical and nursing staffs began to suspect that C.B.'s parents were responsible for her apnea.

Local police and child protection services were notified, and C.B. was placed in a room with covert audiovisual surveillance. On the third day of monitoring, the video recording clearly showed C.B.'s father producing an apneic event by smothering her. Mr. B. was seen picking up the sleeping child, placing her prone on the bed, and forcing her face into the mattress. C.B. awoke and struggled to escape, wildly kicking her legs. Mr. B. continued until C.B.'s struggling stopped and she appeared limp and unconscious. Then he repositioned her on the bed and called for help. A nurse entered the room, stimulated her, and administered supplemental oxygen.

C.B.'s parents were confronted by a physician, nurse, and police officer. Mr. B. adamantly denied smothering C.B. He was subsequently arrested and removed from the hospital.

Mr. B. was a 27-year-old, unemployed, semiliterate laborer in good health. He was actively involved in C.B.'s day-to-day medical care and was clearly the dominant parent. He also became very knowledgeable about the mechanics of the various county and hospital welfare systems. Officials described him as "demanding and manipulative." During C.B.'s hospitalizations, the family lived in a hotel adjacent to the hospital with room, board, and radio pagers provided by the hospital. Throughout C.B.'s hospitalization, Mrs. B. was passive and deferred all medical decisions to her husband.

When they first arrived in Minnesota, the family had received emergency financial assistance and was closely monitored by local social service agencies. Four years earlier, Mrs. B. had allegedly been assaulted and raped. Two months prior to C.B.'s monitored episode, Mrs. B. was evaluated at a local emergency room for a "hysterical conversion reaction."

Following the incident at Children's Hospital, Mr. B. was taken to the county jail, and upon viewing the video, he admitted smothering C.B. He was charged with felonious, third-degree assault. The judge ordered a psychiatric examination. Mr. B. received a 10-month sentence in a local workhouse and 5 years' probation. Also, he was to have no contact with his daughter and no unsupervised contact with any child in the future.

J.C., a 2 1/2-year-old boy, suffered from asthma, severe pneumonia, mysterious infections, and sudden fevers. He was hospitalized 20 times during an 18-month period. Doctors were even concerned that he might have AIDS. However, they soon began to suspect that the mother may have caused the child's problems. Finally, when the boy complained to his mother's friend that his thigh was sore because "mommy gave me shots," the authorities were called.

On searching the residence, investigators seized medical charts and information and hypodermic needles. It was believed that material had also entered the boy through a catheter doctors surgically inserted in the arteries near his heart to give him constant medication.

J.C.'s mother was a 24-year-old homemaker and part-time worker in a fast-food restaurant. When the mother was 7 years old, an older sister had died of a brain tumor at Children's Hospital. During her sister's prolonged illness, J.C.'s mother, of necessity, spent long periods of time at the hospital. Although this had occurred long ago, J.C.'s mother remembered the experience vividly.

During J.C.'s many hospitalizations, the mother seemed almost obsessively involved in medical matters and hospital routines. She spent hours in the hospital library reading medical texts. She had few friends outside the hospital, and the medical and nursing staff described her as an isolated person.

J.C.'s father was a 24-year-old church janitor afflicted with many health problems, the most notable being severe insulin-dependent diabetes. During J.C.'s many hospitalizations, his father appeared distant and only marginally involved. J.C.'s 7-year-old sister was in good health and was named after her mother's deceased sister.

Since J.C. was removed from his home, he has been healthy. As in previous cases, only Mrs. C. was present when the boy became ill, and until investigators showed evidence linking her to her child's illnesses, she denied any wrongdoing. Assault charges were filed, and Mrs. C.'s case is pending.[6]

### INVESTIGATIVE GUIDELINES

- Consult with all experts possible, including psychologists.
- Exhaust every possible explanation of the cause of the child's illness or death.
- Find out who had exclusive control over the child when the symptoms of the illness began or at the time of the child's death.
- Find out if there is a history of abusive conduct toward the child.
- Find out if the nature of the child's illness or injury allows medical professionals to express an opinion that the child's illness or death was neither accidental nor the result of a natural cause or disease.
- In cases of hospitalization, use covert video surveillance to monitor the suspect.
- Determine whether the caretaker had any medical training or a history of seeking medical treatment needlessly. MSBP is often a multigenerational condition.

## CHILD MOLESTATION

For purposes of discussion, Kenneth V. Lanning, supervisory special agent of the Federal Bureau of Investigation, divides child molesters into two categories, namely, situational and preferential.[7]

### SITUATIONAL CHILD MOLESTERS

The **situational child molester** does not have a true sexual preference for children but engages in sex with children for varied and sometimes complex reasons. For such a child molester, sex with children may range from a once-in-a-lifetime act to a long-term pattern of behavior. The more long term the pattern is, the harder it is to distinguish from preferential molesting. The situational child molester usually has fewer numbers of different child victims. Other vulnerable individuals, such as the elderly, sick, or disabled, may also be at risk of sexual victimization by him or her. For example, the situational child molester who sexually abuses children in a day care center might leave that job and begin to sexually abuse elderly people in a nursing home. The number of situational child molesters is larger and increasing faster than that of preferential child molesters. Members of lower socioeconomic groups tend to be overrepresented among situational child molesters. Within this category the following four major patterns of behavior emerge: regressed, morally indiscriminate, sexually- indiscriminate, and inadequate (see Table 11–2).

#### Regressed

A regressed offender usually has low self-esteem and poor coping skills; he turns to children as a sexual substitute for the preferred peer sex partner. Precipitating stress may play a bigger role in his molesting behavior. His main victim criterion seems to be availability, which is why many of such offenders molest their own children. His principal method of operation is to coerce the child into having sex. This type of situational child molester may or may not collect child or adult pornography. If he does have child pornography, it will usually be the best kind of evidence from an investigative point of view and will often include homemade photographs or videos of the child he is molesting.

#### Morally Indiscriminate

The morally indiscriminate pattern characterizes an increasing number of child molesters. For such an individual, the sexual abuse of children is simply part of a general pattern of abuse in his life. He is a user and abuser of people. He abuses his wife, friends, and coworkers. He lies, cheats, or steals whenever he thinks he can get away with it. His primary victim criteria are vulnerability and opportunity. He has the urge, a child is there, and so he acts. He typically uses force, lures, or manipulation to obtain his victims. He may violently or nonviolently abduct his victims. Although his victims frequently are strangers or acquaintances, they can

Table 11-2 Situational Child Molesters

| | Regressed | Morally Indiscriminate | Sexually Indiscriminate | Inadequate |
|---|---|---|---|---|
| **Basic characteristics** | Poor coping skills | User of people | Sexual experimentation | Social misfit |
| **Motivation** | Substitution | Why not? | Boredom | Insecurity and curiosity |
| **Victim criteria** | Availability | Vulnerability and opportunity | New and different | Nonthreatening |
| **Method of operation** | Coercion | Lure, force, or manipulation | Involve in existing activity | Exploits size, advantage |
| **Pornography collection** | Possible | Sadomasochistic; detective magazines | Highly likely; varied nature | Likely |

**Source:** Kenneth V. Lanning, *Child Molesters: A Behavioral Analysis for Law Enforcement Officers Investigating Cases of Child Sexual Exploitation,* 3rd ed. (Arlington: VA: National Center for Missing and Exploited Children, 1992), p. 10. Reprinted with permission of the National Center for Missing and Exploited Children (NCMEC). 

also be his own children. The incestuous father (or mother) might be a morally indiscriminate offender. He frequently collects detective magazines or adult pornography of a sadomasochistic nature. He may collect some child pornography, especially that which depicts pubescent children. Because he is an impulsive person who lacks conscience, there is an especially high risk that he will molest pubescent children.

## Sexually Indiscriminate

The sexually indiscriminate pattern of behavior is the most difficult to define. Although the previously described morally indiscriminate offender often is a sexual experimenter, the sexually indiscriminate individual differs in that he appears to be discriminating in his behavior except when it comes to sex. He is the "try-sexual"—willing to try anything sexual. Much of his behavior is similar to and most often confused with that of the preferential child molester. While he may have clearly defined sexual preferences—such as bondage or sadomasochism, he has no real sexual preference for children. His basic motivation is sexual experimentation, and he appears to have sex with children out of boredom. His main criteria for his victims are that they be new and different, and he involves children in previously existing sexual activity. Again, it is important to realize that these children may be his own. Although much of his sexual activity with adults may not be criminal, such an individual may also provide his children to other adults as part of group sex, spouse-swapping activity, or even some bizarre ritual. Of all situational child molesters, he is by far the most likely to have multiple victims, be from a higher socioeconomic background, and collect pornography and erotica. Child pornography will be only a small portion of his potentially large and varied collection, however.

## Inadequate

The inadequate pattern of behavior includes persons suffering from psychoses, eccentric personality disorders, mental retardation, and senility. In layperson's terms, the inadequate individual is the social misfit, the withdrawn, the unusual. He might be the shy teenager who has no friends of his own age or the eccentric loner who still lives with his parents. Although most loners are harmless, some can be child molesters and, in a few cases, even child killers. This offender seems to become sexually involved with children out of insecurity or curiosity. He finds children to be nonthreatening objects with whom he can explore his sexual fantasies. The child victim could be someone he knows or could be a random stranger. In some cases the victim might be a specific "stranger" selected as a substitute for a specific adult (possibly a relative of the child) whom the offender is afraid of approaching directly. Often his sexual activity with children is the result of built-up impulses. Some of these individuals find it difficult to express anger and hostility,

**Convicted Murderer Pleads for Life**
This photo shows Jesse Timmendequas, a convicted child murderer, at the penalty phase of his trial. At this point in the trial, he apologized for his actions and begged to have his life spared.
(© AP/Wide World Photos)

which then builds until it explodes—possibly against their child victims. Because of mental or emotional problems, some might take out their frustration in cruel sexual torture. The inadequate molester's victims, however, could be elderly persons as well as children—anyone who appears helpless at first sight. He might collect pornography, but it will most likely be of adults.

## PREFERENTIAL CHILD MOLESTERS

**Preferential child molesters** have a definite sexual preference for children. Their sexual fantasies and erotic imagery focus on children. They have sex with children not because of some situational stress or insecurity but because they are sexually attracted to and prefer children. Although they can possess a wide variety of character traits, they engage in highly predictable sexual behavior. Their sexual behavior patterns are called sexual rituals and are frequently engaged in even when they are counterproductive to getting away with the criminal activity. Although preferential offenders may be fewer in number than situational child molesters, they have the potential to molest large numbers of victims. For many of them, their problem is not only the nature of the sex drive (attraction to children) but also the quantity (need for frequent and repeated sex with children). They usually have age and gender preferences for their victims. Members of higher socioeconomic groups tend to be overrepresented among preferential child molesters. More preferential child molesters seem to prefer boys rather than girls. Within this category at least three major patterns of behavior emerge: seduction, introverted, and sadistic (see Table 11–3).

## Seduction

The seduction pattern characterizes the offender who engages children in sexual activity by "seducing" them—courting them with attention, affection, and gifts. Just as one adult courts another, the pedophile seduces children over a period of time by gradually lowering their sexual inhibitions. Frequently his victims arrive at the point where they are willing to trade sex for the attention, affection, and other benefits they receive from the offender. Many seduction offenders are simultaneously involved with multiple victims, operating what has come to be called a child sex ring. This may include a group of children in the same class at school, in the same scout troop, or in the same neighborhood. The characteristic that seems to make the seduction molester a master seducer of children is his ability to identify with them. He knows how to talk to children—but, more importantly, he knows how to listen to them. His adult status and authority are also an important part of the seduction process. In addition, he frequently selects as targets children who are victims of emotional or physical neglect. The biggest problem for this child molester is not how to obtain child victims but how to get them to leave after they are too old. This must be done without the disclosure of the "secret." Victim disclosure often occurs when the offender is attempting to terminate the relationship. This child molester is most likely to use threats and physical violence to avoid identification and disclosure or to prevent a victim from leaving before he is ready to "dump" the victim.

## Introverted

The introverted pattern of behavior characterizes the offender who has a preference for children but lacks the interpersonal skills necessary to seduce them. Therefore, he typically engages in a minimal amount of verbal communication with his victims and usually molests strangers or very young children. He is like the old stereotype of the child molester in that he is more likely to hang around playgrounds and other areas where children congregate, watching them or engaging them in brief sexual encounters. He may expose himself to children or make obscene phone calls to them. He may use the services of a child prostitute. Unable to figure out any other way to gain access to a child, he might even marry a woman and have his own children, very likely molesting them from the time they are infants. He is similar to the inadequate situational child molester, except that he has a definite sexual preference for children and his selection of only children as victims is more predictable.

## Sadistic

The sadistic pattern of behavior characterizes the offender who has a sexual preference for children but who, in order to be aroused or gratified, must inflict psychological or physical pain or suffering on

**Table 11-3** Preferential Child Molester

| | Seduction | Introverted | Sadistic |
|---|---|---|---|
| **Common characteristics** | Sexual preference for children; child pornography or erotica | Sexual preference for children; child pornography or erotica | Sexual preference for children; child pornography or erotica |
| **Motivation** | Identification | Fear of communication | Need to inflict pain |
| **Victim criteria** | Age and gender preferences | Strangers or very young | Age and gender preferences |
| **Method of operation** | Seduction process | Nonverbal sexual contact | Lure or force |

**Source:** Kenneth V. Lanning, *Child Molesters: A Behavioral Analysis for Law Enforcement Officers Investigating Cases of Child Sexual Exploitation,* 3rd ed. (Arlington: VA.: National Center for Missing and Exploited Children, 1992), p. 10. Reprinted with permission of the National Center for Missing and Exploited Children (NCMEC). 

the child victim. He is aroused by his victim's response to the infliction of pain or suffering. Sadistic molesters typically use lures or force to gain access to their victims. They are more likely than other preferential child molesters to abduct and even murder their victims. There have been some cases where seduction molesters have become sadistic molesters. It is not known whether the need to perform sadistic acts developed late or was always there and surfaced late for some reason. In any case, it is fortunate that sadistic child molesters do not appear to be large in number.[8]

## INTERVIEWING MOLESTED CHILDREN

Common sense and formal research agree that children are not merely miniature adults. We know, for example, that children develop in stages during which they acquire capacities for new functions and understanding. We do not, generally speaking, read Shakespeare to 2-year-olds, nor do we expect adult commentary on political issues from them. Adults, for the most part, attempt to speak to and treat children in accordance with their capabilities. We do not ordinarily expect children to understand or function on a par with adults.[9]

When children become victims or witnesses of violence or sexual abuse, however, they are thrust into an adult system that traditionally does not differentiate between children and adults. As one attorney has said:

> Child victims of crime are specially handicapped. First, the criminal justice system distrusts them and puts special barriers in the path of prosecuting their claims to justice. Second, the criminal justice system seems indifferent to the legitimate special needs that arise from their participation.[10]

What are some of the reasons for the problems that arise when children are called to participate in criminal proceedings? The first reason is the children's immaturity with regard to physical, cognitive, and emotional development. The second reason involves unique attributes of the offense of child sexual abuse, particularly when the perpetrator is a parent, parent substitute, or other adult having a trusting or loving relationship with the child. The third reason is our limited understanding of children's capabilities as witnesses. These three factors affect children's ability to comply with the expectations of our judicial system and inform our entire discussion of interviewing molested children.

### Developmental Issues

Three developmental issues are important when allegations of sexual abuse arise.[11]

First is the child's developmental level relative to other children in his or her age group. Knowing this information will dictate the nature of questioning to which the child can reasonably be expected to respond. It will also help place the child's observable reactions to victimization in an appropriate context.

Second is the child's developmental level with regard to sexuality. Normal preschoolers, for example, express curiosity about the origin of babies and mild interest in physical differences between the sexes. While it is not unusual for young children to engage in self-stimulatory behavior or exhibitionism, intercourse or other adult sexual behaviors are quite rare.[12]

Third is the child's ability to respond adequately to interviews and to testify in court. Those who work with young children should be aware of the following:

- Children think in concrete terms.
- Children do not organize their thoughts logically. They often include extraneous information, and they have trouble generalizing to new situations.
- Children have limited understanding of space, distance, and time. A child may not be able to say at "what time" or in "what month" something occurred but may be able to say whether it was before or after school, what was on television, or whether there was snow on the ground.
- Children have a complex understanding of truth and lying.
- Children see the world egocentrically. Because they believe that adults are omniscient, they may expect to be understood even when they have answered questions only partially.[13]
- Children have a limited attention span.
- Children may have varying degrees of comfort with strangers.

These kinds of cognitive limitations are common among young children.

Older children tend to exhibit different, yet equally challenging, developmental patterns.[14] For example, although preadolescents have fairly sophisticated language capabilities, they may use words or phrases they do not fully understand. The emergence of sexuality and concern with sexual identities during preadolescence make these youngsters particularly vulnerable to disruption when they are sexually abused. As they enter adolescence, they tend to become very self-centered and have strong needs for privacy and secrecy. It is common for preteens and teenagers to express their feelings through the arts or physical activity or by acting out in inappropriate or socially unacceptable ways.

Some researchers have specifically explored developmental aspects of children's understanding of the legal system.[15] Not surprisingly, they have found that older children have more accurate and complete knowledge of legal terminology (e.g., court, lawyer, jury, judge, and witness) as well as a better grasp of certain basic concepts of American justice. The researchers caution that children's understanding of the legal system is not only limited but sometimes faulty, so child witnesses may behave in ways that appear counterintuitive or inappropriate to the context.

For example, an interview with a child may begin by requesting identifying information: name, age, school, grade, home address. But young children may misinterpret these initial questions as meaning they are under suspicion or arrest.[16] Also, because they do not understand the different roles and obligations of all the people who interview them, children do not understand why they must tell their stories for police, social workers, doctors, prosecutors, and, ultimately, the court. While this repetition may be simply exasperating for some children, others may relive the traumatic event each time, and still others may assume the story is already known and omit important details in subsequent interviews. Some children may feel protected by the presence of the judge, but others may be intimidated by the big stranger in the dark, scary robe who yells at people in the courtroom and sits towering above the witness stand. One therapist tells of a child witness who was afraid that the judge would hit her with the gavel, which she referred to as a hammer. Children perceive the judge's power to punish and may not understand that they are not the potential object of that punishment.

To correct these problems, researchers recommend that attorneys, judges, and investigators choose their words with care when questioning child witnesses.[17] Some believe that targeted instruction for children who may serve as witnesses, possibly in the form of a "court school," would be helpful as well.[18] Many prosecutors and victim advocates take children for a tour of the courtroom and introduce them to some of the key players before their scheduled court date. Critics contend, however, that such precautions may induce unnecessary apprehension for children who ultimately are not called to testify. At a minimum, interviewers would be wise to explain thoroughly the nature and purpose of each interview or court appearance before the child is questioned.

A further problem in interviewing children who may be victims of sexual molestation centers on the delicate issue of body parts and techniques for achieving accurate communication. The two major techniques involve the use of anatomically detailed dolls and the alternative method of asking children to create their own drawings.

## Anatomically Detailed Dolls

When anatomically detailed dolls (male and female dolls with all body parts, including genitals; see photo on page 390) were first introduced in the late 1970s,[19] they were widely hailed and almost universally adopted by child-serving professionals as an important advance in techniques for communicating with troubled children. Congress (in the Victims of Child Abuse Act of 1990) and eight states[20] have enacted legislation expressly permitting children to use anatomically detailed dolls as demonstrative aids when they testify in court, and many appellate courts have upheld the use of such dolls.[21] The actual use of dolls at trial appears limited, however: courtroom observations of child sexual-abuse trials in eight jurisdictions revealed only one use of dolls per jurisdiction over the course of a year, with one exception where dolls were used in three of the four cases observed.[22]

Yet even as the dolls' value as demonstrative aids in court has gained widespread acceptance, their use in investigative interviews to arrive at a finding, or "diagnosis," of sexual abuse that is later presented in court as expert opinion has been sharply criticized. At the core of the controversy is the extent to which anatomically detailed dolls may suggest sexual behaviors even among children with no history of abuse. Improper use of the dolls, and unsupported inferences about children's behavior with them, can imperil the search for truth.

## Anatomically Detailed Dolls

Interviewing children who either have been sexually abused or have witnessed sexual abuse creates challenges for investigators. One tool that often assists investigators is the use of an anatomically detailed doll with all body parts, including genitals, present. While there is some disagreement among experts as to the overall usefulness of these dolls, many law enforcement agencies still use them.

(Courtesy Eymann Anatomically Correct Dolls, Sacramento, California)

Proponents of anatomically detailed dolls maintain that, when properly used, the dolls can facilitate and enhance interviews with children.[23] Dolls can help in the following ways:

- They can help establish rapport and reduce stress. Most children relate well to dolls. The dolls can have a calming effect and make the interview room appear less formal and more child oriented.
- They can reduce vocabulary problems. Interviewers can use the dolls to learn a child's sexual vocabulary before questioning the child about the alleged abuse.
- They allow the child to show what may be difficult or embarrassing to say. Anatomically detailed dolls can be an invaluable aid to children who are unable or unwilling to verbalize what happened to them.
- They can enhance the quality of information. Dolls may help interviewers gather information without resorting to leading or protracted questioning to overcome children's reluctance to describe sexual acts.
- They can establish competency. Interviewers can use the dolls in a general way to demonstrate the child's mental capacity and ability to communicate.

Many critics fear, however, that anatomically detailed dolls could have adverse effects, whether by provoking horror or alarm at the sight of genitalia or by eliciting apparently sexualized responses, even among children who have not been sexually abused. Even some appellate courts have raised the issue that interviewing children with anatomically detailed dolls may contaminate their memory.[24] Research offers little support for these contentions, however. For example, one study of "nonreferred" children (i.e., children with no history or current allegation of sexual abuse) found that although they did play more with undressed dolls than with dressed dolls, the children's primary activity was, in fact, dressing the dolls.[25] Others report that nonreferred children do examine the genitalia and orifices of anatomically detailed dolls but only rarely do they enact sexual behaviors.[26] It should be recognized, of course, that some proportion of nonreferred children may have experienced some form of undetected sexual abuse.

Related to this controversy is the fact that professionals in this field have yet to reach consensus on "proper" use of anatomically detailed dolls. A number of questions remain unanswered:[27]

- How "correct" in their appearance must the dolls be? Some respondents to a survey by Boat and Everson[28] revealed using Barbie dolls, Cabbage Patch dolls, and homemade stuffed dolls with varying degrees of accuracy in their representation of genitalia. Does the presence or absence of certain details influence children's behavior with the dolls? Must the dolls also be matched by age and racial features to the child and alleged perpetrator?

- When and how should the dolls be used to assist an investigation? Should the dolls be available to children at the start of the interview, or should they be introduced only after the child falters in responding to traditional questioning? Who should undress the dolls, and how should this activity be incorporated into the interview?
- How many sessions with a child are necessary before drawing conclusions about the child's behavior with the dolls?
- Should other adults be present during the interview?
- How many dolls should be available?

The answers to these questions vary with the professional orientations of the people who are asked. Clinicians' responses are more likely to reflect concerns for the children's well-being; legal professionals, on the other hand, express concern for the potential effects of certain practices when revealed in court. From the courts' perspective, it is probably least objectionable to:

- Introduce the dolls only after the child has verbally disclosed, or as a last resort to assist reluctant children.[29]
- Allow children to choose from a variety of dolls (rather than present only two to represent child and perpetrator).[30]
- Offer the child minimal or no instruction in use of the dolls.
- Incorporate information gathered from doll interviews with other data to provide a complete assessment.[31]

Similar recommendations would apply to use of other props, such as puppets or artwork.

## Drawing Interviews

One alternative that is being used by some police agencies either in connection with or instead of anatomically detailed dolls is to have the child draw his or her own picture. It is believed by investigators using this technique that in many cases using the child's own drawings rather than the dolls will provide a more productive interview with the child-abuse victim.[32]

The drawing interview should begin with the interviewer asking the victim to write or print his or her name on a sheet of paper, which, depending on the victim's age, is either lined or unlined and colored. This step of the interview will provide the police officer with some idea of the educational and developmental stages of the victim.

The second step is to ask the child to draw a picture of himself or herself. Children may object at this point, telling the interviewer that they can't draw, but they should simply be encouraged to do the best they can.

When the child has finished the drawing, the interviewer can use it to go over the child's name and locations of the different body parts. The interviewer should begin this portion of the interview by asking the child to color the hair on the drawing and to locate the eyes, the mouth, body parts, and so on. The last question asked should be the location and names of the sexual body parts. In some cases, the interviewer may want to have the child label the body-part locations on the drawing. It is important to realize that children often have their own terms for body parts; the interviewer should learn what their words are and use them. For example, in Figure 11–1, the drawing was done by a 14-year-old boy who had been anally and orally sodomized by his stepfather for over six years.

**Figure 11-1** "Draw Yourself"

Drawing completed by a 14-year-old boy who had been anally and orally sodomized by his stepfather for over six years.

(**Source:** Courtesy Robert Hugh Farley, Cook County, Illinois, Sheriff's Department)

When questioned by the investigators about the object depicted in his mouth, the boy said that it was a "wanger." Further questioning established that the wanger was the stepfather's penis.

In the third step, the child should be provided with another sheet of paper and asked to draw a picture of the "family." This step is important; it may provide the interviewer with information concerning an outsider, such as a boyfriend or grandfather, who is living in the family residence or has daily access to the family. When the family drawing is completed, the child is asked to label all the people in the drawing, including the family pet. The interviewer can ask such questions as where the various people sleep in the house, which person the child likes the least or the best, and so forth. For example, in Figure 11–2, a 10-year-old girl who was asked to draw all members of the family depicted two friends between Mom and stepdad. When later questioned by the interviewer, she identified them as Mom's two boyfriends, who visit the house when stepdad is out driving his truck on the road.

In the final step of the drawing interview, the child is provided with another sheet of paper and asked to "draw what happened." When the drawing is completed, the child is asked to explain the circumstances of the abuse portrayed in the picture, to label the name of the abuser and victim, and in cases of physical abuse to identify the instrument of abuse and where it was stored. For example, in Figure 11–3 the drawing was done by an 8-year-old boy who had suffered a history of physical abuse from his stepfather. In the drawing, the boy had knocked over a bag of feed in the basement of the family's home. The boy's 6-foot-5-inch stepfather grabbed him by the neck and, while holding him in the air, choked the breath out of him. Going over the drawing with the interviewer, the boy explained that the shading on his face was from when he had turned red and the tear was from when he was crying. Note the heavy black mouth depicting the anger on the stepfather's face.

As the child completes each drawing, the interviewer must take the time to go over it in detail with the child. The interviewer who observes some portion of the drawing that is unusual, exaggerated, or overemphasized, such as the mouth in Figure 11–3, should ask the child for an explanation rather than making assumptions of any kind. Of course the police officer–interviewer, who is typically untrained in art therapy, must remember not to fall into the trap of playing amateur psychologist and attempt to analyze the drawings. This job must be left to professional art therapists.

## Asking Leading Questions

Professionals who interview children who are suspected of having been sexually abused are caught

**Figure 11-2**

**"Draw Your Family"**

Drawing by a 10-year-old girl identifying members of her family unit. The two "friends" were her mother's boyfriends, who visited the house when her stepfather was away.

(**Source:** Courtesy Robert Hugh Farley, Cook County, Illinois, Sheriff's Department)

**Figure 11-3**

**"Draw What Happened"**
This drawing was done by an 8-year-old boy who had suffered a history of physical abuse from his stepfather.
(**Source:** Courtesy Robert Hugh Farley, Cook County, Illinois, Sheriff's Department)

in a perilous dilemma. In the words of two well-known clinicians:

> In the best of all possible worlds, it would be advisable not to ask children leading questions. . . . But in the best of all possible worlds, children are not sexually assaulted in secrecy, and then bribed, threatened, or intimidated not to talk about it. In the real world, where such things do happen, leading questions may sometimes be necessary.[33]

As with the anatomical dolls, leading questions are widely used as a courtroom technique to assist child witnesses,[34] but they are seriously challenged when used in investigative interviews. There is, however, a grain of truth to the argument that children can be led, coached, or even "brainwashed" by the interview process, and interviewers would be wise to reexamine their methods in light of our growing experience in the courts.

Briefly, the defense argument rests on the social psychological theory of social influence. In essence, as it applies to child sexual-abuse cases, this theory holds that children's responses to questioning are heavily influenced by the perceived authority or power of the adult interviewers. When they are praised or otherwise "rewarded" for disclosing elements of abuse, children learn what the interviewers want to hear. In other words, children answer to please adults.[35]

Furthermore, to continue this argument, the effect of social influence is magnified in child sexual-abuse cases because the children are typically interviewed repeatedly by several different adults, each of whom contributes to the child's expanding story by infusing—and reinforcing—new information. Ultimately, according to one of the leading defense experts,

> In situations where a child will eventually testify, the memory will consist of a combination of recall and reconstruction influenced by all of the interrogations, conversations, and sexual abuse therapy that have occurred during the delay. The longer the delay, the greater the possibility of social influence and the more the memory may consist of reconstruction rather than recall.[36]

Challenges based on this theory have successfully undermined prosecution of several highly publicized cases, including the well-known McMartin Preschool case.

In one study, 72 children age 5 to 7 underwent physical examinations. Half received external examinations of their genital and anal areas; the other half were examined for scoliosis (curvature of the spine).

Within one month of the exam, the children were interviewed about the event using open-ended questions, anatomically detailed dolls, and specific and misleading questions. The results of this study were both illuminating and provocative. Specifically:

- The majority of children who experienced genital and anal touching did not report it, either in response to open-ended questions or when asked to demonstrate with the dolls.
- All but 5 (of 36) disclosed touching in response to specific questions (e.g., "Did the doctor touch you here?").
- Only 3 (of 36) girls who received scoliosis examinations incorrectly reported genital or anal touching; only 1 of those provided additional (incorrect) details.

In sum, based on the total number of questions asked, "When all of the chances to reveal genital/anal contact were considered, children failed to disclose it 64 percent of the time, whereas the chance of obtaining a false report of genital/anal touching was only 8 percent, even when leading questions were asked.[37]

## CHILDREN'S REACTIONS TO VICTIMIZATION

There are few in our society who would argue that child sexual abuse does not cause serious problems for its victims. The burgeoning research on this subject suggests that the effects of victimization on children can be far-reaching, negative, and complex. In a review of the literature, researchers found seven "clusters" of effects on children:[38]

- *Affective problems:* guilt, shame, anxiety, fear, depression, anger.
- *Physical effects:* genital injuries, pregnancy, sexually transmitted diseases, somatic complaints (e.g., headaches, stomachaches, bed-wetting, hypochondria), changes in appetite or sleep patterns.
- *Cognitive effects:* concentration problems, short attention spans.
- *Behavioral symptoms:* acting out (hostile-aggressive behaviors, antisocial behaviors, delinquency, stealing, tantrums, substance abuse), withdrawal, repetition of the abusive relationship.
- *Self-destructive behaviors:* self-mutilation, suicidal thoughts and attempts.
- *Psychopathology:* neuroses, character disorders, multiple personalities, psychotic features.
- *Sexualized behavior:* excessive masturbation, repetition of sexual acts with others, atypical sexual knowledge.

Other commonly cited effects were low self-esteem and problems with interpersonal relationships.

Many of the early studies in this area were flawed because they relied on populations of clinical samples of sexually abused children or on retrospective findings from adults who had been sexually abused as children. Neither approach allows comparisons to "normal" populations. But in one study that compared 369 sexually abused children to 318 nonabused children, eight factors emerged to distinguish the two groups.[39] The sexually abused children were significantly more likely to demonstrate the following:

- Poor self-esteem
- Aggressive behaviors
- Fearfulness
- Concentration problems
- Withdrawal
- Acting out
- Need to please others

Another study compared sexually abused children to two groups of nonabused children: one from a psychiatric outpatient clinic and the other from a well-child clinic. The researchers found that the sexually abused children were more similar to the psychiatric outpatients than to the normal children.[40] Sexually abused children displayed significantly more behavior problems (particularly sexual behaviors) and fewer social competencies than did normal children.

### Sexually Abused Child Syndrome

Early attempts to describe a "sexually abused child syndrome" were quickly discarded as lacking a foundation in empirical research. Today, however, some of the leading researchers and clinicians in this field are moving toward consensus on behavioral indicators of child sexual abuse. The results of a nationwide survey of professionals experienced in evaluating suspected child sexual abuse revealed high levels of agreement concerning the following factors:[41]

- The child possesses age-inappropriate sexual knowledge.
- The child engages in sexualized play.
- The child displays precocious behavior.
- The child engages in excessive masturbation.
- The child is preoccupied with his or her genitals.
- There are indications that pressure or coercion was exerted on the child.
- The child's story remains consistent over time.
- The child's report indicates an escalating progression of sexual abuse over time.
- The child describes idiosyncratic details of the abuse.
- There is physical evidence of abuse.

It is important to recognize, however, that these indicators represent a broad constellation of behaviors that are frequently seen among sexually abused children as a group. Due to the many forms sexual abuse may take and the variations in individual coping methods and personalities, every child will exhibit a different set of behaviors subsequent to abuse. Thus, a child who experienced a single abusive incident may well be consistent with her story over time. Conversely, a child who experienced several years of abuse by a close relative may seem to contradict his or her story over time, depending on the attitudes expressed by family members or the manner in which he or she is questioned. In other words, there is no single array of behavioral indicators that will definitively identify a sexually abused child.

## THE RISK OF FALSE ALLEGATIONS

A recent spate of highly publicized sexual-abuse allegations has caused the public to recoil and question the limits of credulity. These allegations tend to fall into two categories: alleged sexual abuse of preschool children in day care facilities, sometimes including bizarre and ritualistic elements; and sexual abuse allegations arising in the context of divorce and custody or visitation disputes. Such cases have caused many observers to question the veracity of child-sexual-abuse reports.[42]

Researchers have attempted to determine the percentage of unsubstantiated cases that can actually be attributed to false reports. The most comprehensive of these studies analyzed all reports of suspected sexual abuse filed with the Denver Department of Social Services (DSS) several years ago. All 576 reports had been investigated by the DSS Sexual Abuse Team and designated either "founded" (53 percent) or "unfounded" (47 percent). With the assistance of DSS caseworkers, the researchers applied clinical judgments to the case files and reclassified these reports, using the following categories:

- *Founded cases:*
  Reliable accounts
  Recantations of reliable accounts
- *Unfounded cases:*
  Unsubstantiated suspicions
  Insufficient information
  Fictitious reports by adults
  Fictitious reports by children

The latter two categories, "fictitious reports by adults" and "fictitious reports by children," included deliberate falsifications, misperceptions, confused interpretations of nonsexual events, and children who had been coached by adults. On reclassification by the researchers, 6 percent of the total cases (34 allegations) were found to be fictitious. Of those, only 8 allegations had been made by five children, four of whom had been substantiated victims of abuse in the past.[43]

In a second phase of this study, the researchers examined 21 fictitious cases that had been referred to a sexual-abuse clinic for evaluation over a 5-year period. Of these allegations, 5 had been initiated by the child and 9 by an adult; in 7 cases the researchers could not determine who had initiated the charge. Custody or visitation disputes were ongoing in 15 of these cases: in 1 child-initiated case, in 7 adult-initiated cases, and in all the "mixed" cases.[44]

Another study examined 162 consecutive sexual-abuse cases seen at a children's hospital over a 10-month period. Twenty-five of those cases involved allegations against a parent, and seven of those (28 percent) involved a custody or visitation dispute. The disputed cases were less likely to be substantiated than cases without such conflict, but they were nevertheless substantiated more than half the time.[45]

Other studies have approached the relationship between custody disputes and false allegations from a different perspective, beginning with cases that are referred to clinicians for custody evaluations (rather than sexual-abuse diagnosis). These studies have found that a relatively high proportion of custody disputes involve false sexual-abuse allegations.[46] It is important to note, however, that these studies depend on clinical populations (i.e., troublesome cases that had been referred to a specialist for evaluation or diagnosis). Findings are based on a small number of cases, and, furthermore, the decision to label a report "fictitious" is based on clinical judgment: there is no objective, definitive measure of "truth." Because of these limitations, such studies cannot generalize to a conclusion that sexual-abuse allegations associated with custody disputes are necessarily false.[47]

In fact, sexual-abuse allegations arising from divorce and custody disputes appear to be quite rare. One study that attempted to quantify this phenomenon found that in most courts, about 2 to 10 percent of all family court cases involving custody and/or visitation disputes also involved a charge of sexual abuse. As an alternative way of framing the magnitude of this problem, sexual-abuse allegations occurred in the range of approximately 2 to 15 per 1,000 divorce filings among the courts that were studied. Based on data from seven jurisdictions, 105 of 6,100 cases (or less than 2 percent) of custody or visitation disputes involved sexual-abuse allegations.[48]

Research also suggests that sexual abuse in day care is no more common than it is within families. Extrapolating from 270 substantiated cases in 35 states over a three-year period, researchers estimated that 500 to 550 actual cases occurred in that period, involving more than 2,500 children. On the basis of the total of 7 million children attending day care facilities nationwide, the researchers calculated that 5.5 of every 10,000 children enrolled in day care are sexually abused. This compares to an estimated 8.9 of every 10,000 children who are sexually abused in their homes. The conclusion: The apparently

**Accused Pedophile Awaits the Start of Trial**

Eric Franklin Rosser, who had been on the FBI's 10-most-wanted list, is shown here after his arrest. He is being prosecuted for his alleged involvement in child prostitution and pedophilia. He was arrested in Bangkok, Thailand.

(© Reuters NewMedia Inc./Corbis)

large number of sexual-abuse cases reported in day care "is simply a reflection of the large number of children in day care and the relatively high risk of sexual abuse to children everywhere."[49]

## EMOTIONAL REACTION TO THE PEDOPHILE

Because many investigators are parents, they react strongly to the pedophile. However, for legal and pragmatic reasons, such feelings must never be translated into physical or verbal abuse. Physical abuse by police is unlawful and should result in criminal and civil charges. Verbal abuse or open expressions of revulsion minimize the possibility of obtaining the suspect's cooperation and, perhaps, of obtaining a much-needed voluntary statement. The following case illustrates this point:

A 5-year-old girl told her mother that the man next door had taken her into his home, removed her underpants, placed his penis between her legs, and rubbed her vagina with it. After putting her underpants back on, he had sent her home. The mother called the police, but when they arrived the child was very hesitant to repeat the story.

Careful handling of the interview by the officer provided enough information to justify probable cause for an arrest, although the suspect denied the offense. Supplementing the child's statements were those of neighbors who had seen the man taking the child into his house, where she had remained for about 10 minutes.

The child was taken to the hospital and given an examination. The examining physician could find no injuries, semen, or pubic hair. The victim's clothing was normal in appearance. The situation at this juncture was a shy young child who probably would not be a good witness, an absence of physical evidence, a suspect who denied the charges, and witnesses who saw the child enter the suspect's house but saw no molestation. A voluntary statement was imperative if a successful prosecution was to result.

The suspect was interrogated and at first denied the charges. But when confronted with the child's and the neighbors' statements, he admitted molesting the child in the manner she described. He said that he had been drinking heavily at the time and attributed his actions to intoxication. The suspect agreed to give a full statement under oath to the state prosecutor.

Before the suspect was sworn in, the prosecutor was advised, outside the presence of the suspect, of the facts in the case. The prosecutor requested that the suspect be brought into his office. In an angry voice, he told the suspect, "If that had been my little girl, you son of a bitch, I would have broken your goddamned neck." The prosecutor then asked the suspect if he would like to make a statement. The suspect replied, "I have nothing to say to you." Subsequently, he pleaded guilty to contributing to the delinquency of a minor, a misdemeanor.

The reason for this misdemeanor rather than the felony charge was insufficient evidence. The prosecutor was not new to this job, and he had an excellent reputation. Unfortunately, what he had done was identify the victim with his own daughter, who was about the same age as the molested child.

# CHILD PORNOGRAPHY

Kenneth V. Lanning, supervisory special agent of the Federal Bureau of Investigation, divides what the pedophile collects into two categories: child pornography and child erotica.[50] **Child pornography** can be behaviorally (not legally) defined as the sexually explicit reproduction of a child's image and includes sexually explicit photographs, negatives, slides, magazines, movies, videotapes, and computer disks. In essence, it is the permanent record of the sexual abuse or exploitation of an actual child. In order to legally be child pornography, it must be a visual depiction (not the written word) of a minor (as defined by statute) that is sexually explicit (not necessarily obscene, unless required by state law). Child pornography can be divided into two subcategories: commercial and homemade.

Child erotica is a broader and more encompassing term than child pornography. It can be defined as any material, relating to children, that serves a sexual purpose for a given individual. Some of the more common types of child erotica include toys, games, drawings, fantasy writings, diaries, souvenirs, sexual aids, manuals, letters, books about children, psychological books on pedophilia, and ordinary photographs of children. Child erotica might also be referred to as pedophile paraphernalia. Generally, possession and distribution of these items does not constitute a violation of the law.

For investigative purposes, child erotica can be divided into the categories below.

***Published Material Relating to Children*** Examples of this include books, magazines, articles, or videotapes dealing with any of the following areas:

- Child development
- Sex education
- Child photography
- Sexual abuse of children
- Sexual disorders
- Pedophilia
- Man-boy love
- Personal ads
- Incest
- Child prostitution
- Missing children
- Investigative techniques
- Legal aspects
- Access to children
- Detective magazines
- "Men's" magazines
- Nudism
- Erotic novels
- Catalogs
- Brochures

Listing of foreign sex tours, guides to nude beaches, and material on sponsoring orphans or needy children provide them with information about access to children. Detective magazines saved by pedophiles usually contain stories about crimes against children. The "men's" magazines collected may have articles about sexual abuse of children. The use of adult pornography to lower inhibitions is discussed elsewhere in this book. Although the possession of information on missing children should be carefully investigated to determine possible involvement in abduction, most pedophiles collect this material to help rationalize their behavior as child "lovers," not abductors. Personal ads include those in "swinger" magazines, video magazines, and newspapers, and may mention "family fun," "family activity," "European material," "youth training," "unusual and bizarre," "better life," and so on. Erotic novels may contain stories about sex with children but without sexually explicit photographs. They may contain sketches or drawings. Materials concerning current or proposed laws dealing with sex abuse; arrested, convicted or acquitted child molesters; or investigative techniques used by law enforcement are common.

***Unpublished Material Relating to Children*** Examples include items such as the following:

- Personal letters
- Audiotapes
- Diaries
- Fantasy writings
- Manuscripts
- Telephone and address books
- Pedophile manuals
- Newsletters and bulletins
- Directories
- Adult pornography
- Financial records

## COMMERCIAL CHILD PORNOGRAPHY

Commercial child pornography is pornography that is produced and intended for commercial sale. Because of strict federal and state laws today, there is no place in the United States where commercial "child" pornography is knowingly openly sold. In the United States it is primarily a cottage industry run by pedophiles and child molesters. The commercial child pornography still being distributed in the United States is smuggled in from foreign countries—primarily by pedophiles. The risks are usually too high for the strictly commercial dealer. Because of their sexual and personal interests, however, pedophiles are more willing to take those risks. Their motive goes beyond just profit. Commercial child pornography is still assembled and is much more readily available in foreign countries. United States citizens, however, seem to be the main customers for this material. Some offenders collect their commercial child pornography in ways that make it appear to be homemade child pornography (e.g., by taking photographs of pictures in magazines; cutting up pictures and mounting them in photo albums, with names and descriptive information written below; or putting homemade labels on commercial videotapes). If necessary, highly experienced investigators and forensic laboratories can be of assistance in making distinctions between homemade and commercially produced child pornography.

## HOMEMADE CHILD PORNOGRAPHY

Contrary to what its name implies, the quality of homemade child pornography can be as good as, if not better than, the quality of any commercial pornography. The pedophile has a personal interest in the product. "Homemade" simply means it was not originally produced primarily for commercial sale. Although commercial child pornography is not openly sold anywhere in this country, homemade child pornography is continually produced, swapped, and traded in almost every community in the United States. While rarely found in "adult" bookstores, child pornography is frequently found in the homes and offices of doctors, lawyers, teachers, ministers, and other apparent pillars of the community. There is, however, a connection between commercial and homemade child pornography. Sometimes homemade child pornography is sold or winds up in commercial child pornography magazines, movies, or videos. The same pictures are reproduced and circulated again and again. With rapidly increasing frequency, more and more of both commercial and homemade child pornography is in video format. This actually increases the odds of finding child pornography in any investigation.

It is important for the law enforcement investigator to realize that most of the children in prepubescent child pornography were not abducted into sexual slavery. They were seduced into posing for these pictures or videos by a pedophile they probably know. They were never missing children. The children in child pornography are frequently smiling or have neutral expressions on their faces because they have been seduced into the activity after having had their inhibitions lowered by clever offenders. In some cases their own parents took the pictures or made them available for others to take the pictures. Children in pubescent or technical child pornography, however, are more likely to be missing children—especially runaways or thrownaways being exploited by morally indiscriminate pimps or profiteers. In contrast to adult pornography, but consistent with the gender preference of most preferential child molesters, there are more boys than girls in child pornography.

In understanding the nature of child pornography, the law enforcement officer must recognize the distinction between technical and simulated child pornography. The Child Protection Act of 1984 defines a **child** as anyone under the age of 18. Therefore, a sexually explicit photograph of a 15-, 16-, or 17-year-old girl or boy is technical child pornography. Technical child pornography does not look like child pornography, but it is. The production, distribution, and, in some cases, possession of this child pornography could and should be investigated under appropriate child pornography statutes. Technical child pornography is an exception to much of what we say about child pornography. It often is produced, distributed, and consumed by individuals who are not child molesters or pedophiles; it is openly sold around the United States; and it more often portrays females than males. Because it looks like adult pornography, it is more like adult pornography.

On the other hand, sexually explicit photographs of 18-year-old or older males or females are not legally child pornography. But if the person portrayed in such material is young looking, dressed youthfully, or made up to look young, the material could be of interest to pedophiles. This is simulated child pornography. Simulated child pornography looks like child pornography, but it is not. It is designed to appeal to the pedophile but it is not legally child pornography because the individuals portrayed are over 18. This illustrates the importance and sometimes the difficulty in proving the age of the child in the photographs or videotapes. Particularly difficult is pornography portraying underage children pretending to be overage models pretending to be underage children.

## USES OF CHILD PORNOGRAPHY COLLECTIONS

Although the reasons why pedophiles collect child pornography and erotica are conjecture, we can be more certain as to how this material is used. Study and police investigations have identified certain criminal uses of the material.

Child pornography and child erotica are used for the sexual arousal and gratification of pedophiles. They use child pornography the same way other people use adult pornography—to feed sexual fantasies. Some pedophiles only collect and fantasize about the material without acting out the fantasies, but in most cases the arousal and fantasy fueled by the pornography is only a prelude to actual sexual activity with children.

A second use of child pornography and erotica is to lower children's inhibitions. A child who is reluctant to engage in sexual activity with an adult or to pose for sexually explicit photos can sometimes be convinced by viewing other children having "fun" participating in the activity. Peer pressure can have a tremendous effect on children; if other children are involved, the child might be led to believe that the activity is acceptable. When the pornography is used to lower inhibitions, the children portrayed will usually *appear* to be having a good time.

Books on human sexuality, books on sex education, and sex manuals are also used to lower inhibitions. Children accept what they see in books, and many pedophiles have used sex education books to prove to children that such sexual behavior is acceptable. Adult pornography is also used, particularly with adolescent boy victims, to arouse them or to lower inhibitions.

A third major use of child pornography collections is blackmail. If a pedophile already has a relationship with a child, seducing the child into sexual activity is only part of the plan. The pedophile must also ensure that the child keeps the secret. Children are most afraid of pictures being shown to their friends. Pedophiles use many techniques to blackmail; one of them is through photographs taken of the child. If the child threatens to tell his or her parents or the authorities, the existence of sexually explicit photographs can be an effective silencer.

A fourth use of child pornography and erotica is as a medium of exchange. Some pedophiles exchange photographs of children for access to or phone numbers of other children. The quality and theme of the material determine its value as an exchange medium. Rather than paying cash for access to a child, the pedophile may exchange a small part (usually duplicates) of his collection. The younger the child and the more bizarre the acts, the greater the value of the pornography.

A fifth use of the collected material is profit. Some people involved in the sale and distribution of child pornography are not pedophiles; they are profiteers. In contrast, most pedophiles seem to collect child erotica and pornography for reasons other than profit. Some pedophiles may begin nonprofit trading, which they pursue until they accumulate certain amounts or types of photographs, which are then sold to commercial dealers for reproduction in commercial child pornography magazines. Others combine their pedophiliac interest with their profit motive. Some collectors even have their own photographic reproduction equipment. Thus, the photograph of a child taken with or without parental knowledge by a neighborhood pedophile in any U.S. community can wind up in a commercial child pornography magazine with worldwide distribution.

## USE OF THE COMPUTER AND THE INTERNET IN CHILD PORNOGRAPHY

Computers have become a pervasive part of daily life. Unfortunately, the ubiquity of the computer, and by extension the Internet, is an asset to the child pornographer. Child pornographers use personal computers to create, distribute, and catalog pornographic depictions of children and to widen their net of victimization.

Many child pornographers are compulsive record keepers, and for them the computer as a cataloging tool is electronic gold. While stable people might use computers to track a bank balance or store family vacation photos, law enforcement investigations have determined that child pornographers use computers to organize and store photographs and movies that graphically depict scenes of sexual exploitation of children.

Child pornographers can acquire additional material through instant contact with other pedophiles. Chat rooms, bulletin boards, newsgroups, instant messaging, and e-mail are just some of the means child pornographers currently use to communicate with other pedophiles. Once he has made contact with willing cohorts, a pedophile can electronically exchange photographs, movies, and other depictions of child pornography. In a matter of seconds, a child pornographer may send or receive child pornography to or from almost anywhere in the world. Web cams have even made it possible to broadcast and receive live, real-time images of child molestation and pornography.

In addition, the home computer provides tools that make it easy to store and retrieve names and addresses of accessible victims. This library of victims can be developed with great ease and efficiency by way of referral from the pedophile's perverse network of colleagues.

Also, pedophiles can use computers to directly establish a rapport with children. Adolescent boys who spend a great amount of their time online are at particularly high risk of this type of contact. Again, using chat rooms, e-mail, and instant messaging, the pedophile may pose as an adolescent to gain the trust of the child. He may then indirectly victimize the child by sharing with him or her sexually explicit information or material. He may further attempt to obtain the child's phone number or whereabouts in order to engage in face-to-face contact and direct sexual victimization.

Desktop publishing holds unique possibilities for child pornographers. Like any other small publisher, pedophiles who use child pornography as a profit-making business can produce high-quality prints with relative ease. They can collect, record, "publish," and distribute pornographic material either as hard copy or as an electronic file. They can also create false or doctored graphic images of children in pornographic positions. The question arises, then: Are such false images punishable by law?

In the United States, Title 18, Section 2252, of the U.S. code, more commonly known as the Child Pornography Prevention Act (CPPA), deals with this aspect of child pornography and the Internet. The CPPA makes it a crime to sell, possess with intent to sell, download, or produce child pornography or any visual depiction that is intended to *represent or resemble* child pornography. This includes material "transported, by any means, including by computer, if (i) the producing of such visual depiction involves the use of a minor engaging in sexually explicit conduct; and (ii) such *visual depiction* is of such conduct."[51]

It is important to reiterate that there does not have to be an actual child involved in the making of such pornography in order for it to be legally punishable; there must be merely the presence of the "visual depiction" of a child. This stipulation assumes that there are harmful secondary effects associated with virtual child pornography, namely, as mentioned earlier, that pedophiles may use graphic depictions of child pornography to seduce children to join in the "fun."[52]

The movie *Traffic* contains a scene in which an underage character enacts having sex with a drug dealer. Under the CPPA, this scene would, in legal terms, be viewed as child pornography. For this reason, the Free Speech Coalition, an adult trade organization, has challenged the CPPA claiming that it is overly vague and violates First Amendment free speech rights.[53] A federal district court ruled against the Free Speech Coalition in 1997, but the 9th Circuit reversed that decision in late 2001, and the reversal was upheld by the Supreme Court in Spring 2002.[54] (See Figure 11–4.)

Unfortunately, due to the anonymous nature of the Internet and the sheer volume of Internet activity, transactions involving child pornography are often difficult for government agencies to track. As discussed in Chapter 16, "Computer Crime," however, some investigators are taking advantage of the anonymity of the Net by posing as minors in order to identify pedophiles. Once a pedophile has been discovered, his records of his computer activities can frequently be used as incriminating evidence. Furthermore, under strictly regulated circumstances, investigators may be able to track the Internet activity of pedophiles with the watchdog program "DCS 100."[55]

Child pornography is often found in computer files on hard drives. Whenever such a condition may exist, it is important to remember the special techniques of investigating technologically based crime and retrieving digital images as evidence. For a more thorough discussion of digital forensics and the investigation of child pornography involving computers, refer to Chapter 16, "Computer Crime."

Currently, 50 percent of Internet child pornography cases call for investigation abroad.[56] The recent upsurge in worldwide child pornography prevention and detention agencies lends credence to the notion that child pornography on the Internet cannot be tackled by one country alone but has to be dealt with globally.[57]

# INCEST

## DEFINITIONS OF INCEST

Almost every state has some mention of incest in its statutes. However, the focus of these statutes varies broadly. Many states describe the biological relationship and the kind of sexual contact prohibited (e.g., intercourse); other states refer only to the prohibition of marriage between biologically related persons, with no mention of sexual activity with a

580 4/979

minor child. These statutes appear to have two purposes: to prevent marriage and sexual relations between people who are too closely related and to protect children from sexual abuse by adult relatives. Some state laws do not recognize stepparents, foster parents, or adoptive parents in their incest statutes and handle these cases of sexual abuse under their sexual-assault or rape statutes.[58]

In this chapter we define **incest** broadly, to include any sexual abuse of a minor child by an adult perceived by the child to be a family member. The sexual behaviors include genital fondling, indecent exposure, oral and anal sexual contact, finger insertion, and intercourse. The perpetrator may be a biological parent, stepparent, foster parent, adoptive parent, mother's boyfriend, other parent surrogate, or relative in a caretaking relationship with the child, including extended family members such as grandparents or uncles. Sibling relationships are included when there is exploitation, assault, or a large age gap between parties. We do not discuss incest between consenting adults.

Because the most frequently reported form of sexual abuse is between father and daughter, we use the pronouns "he" to refer to the perpetrator and "she" to the victim. However, it is important to be aware that the child may be male and the adult, female.

## CHARACTERISTICS OF INCESTUOUS FAMILIES

What kinds of families are involved in incest? All kinds. There are many kinds of incestuous families, and there is much discussion in the professional literature about how the family members got the way they are. In this section, we briefly describe some of the common behavior and attitudes of incestuous families.

The incestuous family is often reclusive. The child victim lives in a secretive home environment and frequently cannot have friends in, especially as overnight guests. Further, she is discouraged from mingling with neighbors, developing close relationships, or taking part in outside activities or events. The family may be zealously religious. There may be heavy dependency on the closeness of the family relationships, with extreme authority residing in the father figure. The family may have strong beliefs about right and wrong, good and evil, and these beliefs may be imposed on the children by the authoritarian parent. Fear is often used to control the child's behavior.

Overt incest is an example of tension-reducing acting out in a dysfunctional family. Yet the family maintains a facade to outsiders. Many factors can contribute to the incest: family breakdown due to some sort of stress, such as unemployment, alcoholism, or the physical or mental illness of one parent; an emotionally immature parent or parents; and a lack of understanding of adult nurturing roles within the family. The parents may come from poor family backgrounds.

Serious disorganization in family roles often occurs before the beginning of the incestuous relationship. Usually the mother becomes passive or absent. The victimized daughter becomes the mother substitute, supporting the mother in her housework but giving in to the father, whom she perceives as having been turned away by her own mother. In turn, the father, unrelieved in his sexual drives, turns to the daughter to maintain the family unit. The incest may be reported only after some outsider notes evidence of it or of other maltreatment of the children in the family.

It is not uncommon for more than one child to be sexually exploited in the same family. When several of children are being abused, disclosure may occur when the oldest child becomes aware that her younger siblings are also being victimized. In one such case, the eldest daughter had kept her own abuse a secret in exchange for her father's promise that he would not touch her younger sisters. When she discovered that they, too, were being abused, she reported her father to the authorities out of her desire to protect them.

## PROFILE OF INCESTUOUS FATHERS

David Finkelhor and Linda Meyer Williams, sociologists at the Family Research Laboratory of the University of New Hampshire, have recently completed the most thorough study to date of men who have sexually abused their daughters. The sample consisted of 118 incestuous fathers—55 men in the U.S. Navy and 63 civilians from treatment centers around the country—and a carefully matched control group of nonincestuous fathers.[59]

In this landmark study on the characteristics of incest offenders, Finkelhor and Williams set out to determine whether men are socialized to see all

**Figure 11-4** Timeline: *Ashcroft v. Free Speech Coalition*

(**Source:** Copyright© 2001, First Amendment Center, www.freedomforum.org/fac/2001-02/ashcroft_time.htm.)

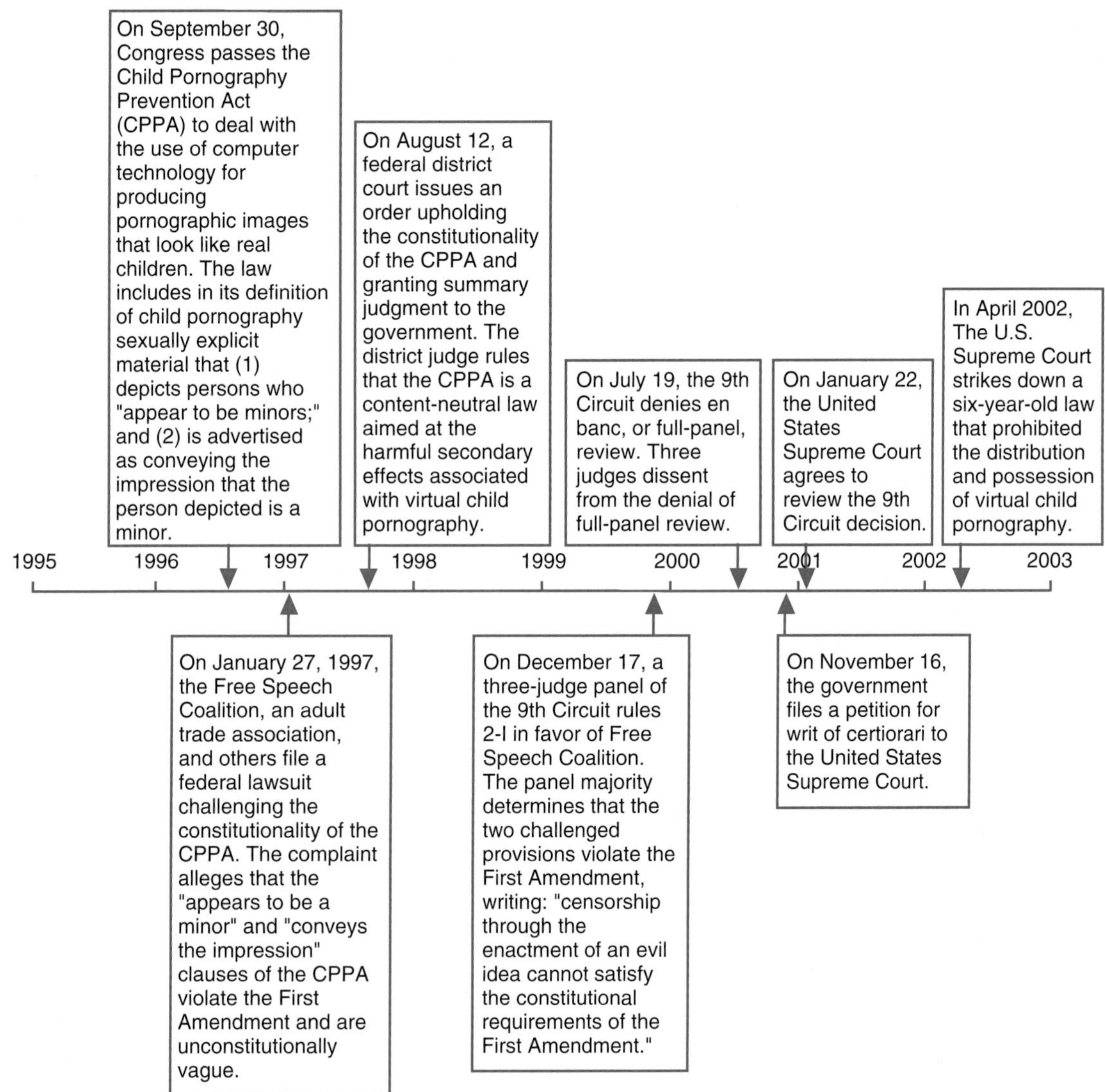


intimacy and dominance as sexual, whether fathers separated from their daughters for long periods soon after birth are more likely to molest them than fathers who have not been absent, and whether incestuous men were more likely than nonoffenders to have been abused as children. The researchers also sought to learn each man's feelings about his daughter, his outlook on sex, and his attitudes toward incest.

Many theories have been posited about why fathers molest their daughters. Everything from alcoholism to a frigid wife has been blamed. With this study, Finkelhor and Williams have shed new light on the subject and produced much new insight. They have established, for example, that there are distinct differences in the onset of abuse: daughters ranged in age from 4 weeks to 15 years old when the incest began. "Fathers were more likely to start abuse when their daughter was four to six years old or ten to twelve years old," the study reveals, "than to initiate abuse when she was seven, eight, or nine years old." Men reported various behaviors leading up to the abuse: the father had masturbated while thinking of his daughter, the father had exposed himself to the daughter; or the father had made her touch his genitals before he began touching hers. A substantial percentage of the men—63 percent—had been sexually attracted to their daughters for a period of years before the abuse began. Most significantly, the findings reveal that there are many paths to incestuous behavior and that there is not just one type of man who commits such abuse.

Each man was interviewed for at least 6 hours and was asked hundreds of questions. The results dispel some common myths and prompt the following typology:

- *Type 1—The sexually preoccupied:* Twenty-six percent of the fathers studied fell into this category. These men had "a clear and conscious (often obsessive) sexual interest in their daughters." When they told what attracted them to their daughters, they talked in detail about physical qualities—the feel of the girl's skin, for example, or the smell of her body.
- *Type 1 subcategory—Early sexualizers:* Among the sexually preoccupied fathers, many regarded their daughters as sex objects almost from birth. "One father reported that he had been stimulated by the sight of his daughter nursing and that he could never remember a time when he did not have sexual feelings for her. . . . He began sexually abusing her when she was four weeks old." Many of the offenders had themselves been sexually abused as children. "These men are so sexualized that they may simply project their sexual needs onto everybody and everything. . . . The children may be those who are most easily manipulated to satisfy the preoccupations."
- *Type 2—Adolescent regressives:* About one-third of the fathers—33 percent—became sexually interested in their daughters when the girls entered puberty. They said they were "transfixed" by the changes in the daughter's body. For some the attraction began when the daughter started to act more grown up, but before her body changed. Some of the fathers in this group became aroused by a daughter after having been away from her for a long time. Her new maturity and developing body caught them by surprise. Sometimes the fathers let the attraction build for years, masturbating to fantasies of the daughter, before they acted. These men acted and sounded like young adolescents themselves when they talked about their daughters. One said, "I started to wonder what it would be like to touch her breasts and touch between her legs and wondered how she would react if I did." "The father-adult in me shut down," said another offender, "and I was like a kid again."
- *Type 3—Instrumental self-gratifiers:* These fathers accounted for 20 percent of the sample. They described their daughters in terms that were nonerotic. When they abused the daughter, they thought about someone else—the wife, even the daughter as an adult. In contrast to the sexually preoccupied and adolescent-regressive fathers who focused on their daughters, the instrumental self-gratifiers blocked what they were doing from their minds: "They used their daughter's body as a receptacle." The fact that they were abusing a daughter or that a daughter was so young was actually "a distracting element" that these fathers had to work to ignore. While one man was giving his 7-year-old a bath, she rubbed against his penis. "I realized that I could take advantage of the situation," he said. "She wasn't a person to me." Another man said, "I abused her from behind so I wouldn't see her face." Instrumental self-gratifiers abused sporadically, worried about the harm they were causing, and felt great guilt. To alleviate the guilt, some convinced themselves that the daughter was aroused.
- *Type 4—The emotionally dependent:* Just over 10 percent of the sample fit this category. These fathers were emotionally needy, lonely, depressed. They thought of themselves as failures and looked to their daughters for "close, exclusive, emotionally dependent relationships," including sexual gratification, which they linked to intimacy and not to the daughter's real or imagined sexual qualities. One man, separated from his wife, saw his 5-

year-old daughter only on weekends. "It was companionship," he said. "I had been alone for six months. We slept together and would fondle each other. The closeness was very good and loving. Then oral sex began." The average age of the daughters when the incest began was 6 to 7 years. But it happened with older daughters as well. The fathers of older daughters described the girls as their "best friends," and the relationships had a more romantic quality: the men described their daughters as they might have described an adult lover.

- *Type 5—Angry retaliators:* About 10 percent of the men were in this category. These fathers were the most likely to have criminal histories of assault and rape. They abused a daughter out of anger at her or, more often, at her mother for neglecting or deserting them. Some denied any sexual feelings for the daughter. One father of a 3-year-old said, "My daughter has no sex appeal for me at all. What I did was just an opportunity to get back at my daughter for being the center of my wife's life. There was no room for me." Sometimes the daughter was abused because she resembled her mother, sometimes because of the father's desire to desecrate her or to possess her out of an angry sense of entitlement. Some angry retaliators tied up, gagged, beat, and raped their daughters and were aroused by the violence.

While 33 percent of the men reported being under the influence of alcohol when the abuse occurred, and 10 percent reported that they were using drugs, only 9 percent held alcohol or drugs responsible. "Preliminary analysis indicates that the incestuous fathers are not more likely than the comparison fathers to have drug or alcohol abuse problems, although they may use alcohol or drugs to lower their inhibitions to abuse."

Forty-three percent of the men felt that their relationship with their wives was part of the reason for the incest. "However, the wife was rarely the only factor mentioned. . . . Different men probably come to incestuous acts as a result of different needs, motives, and impairments."

Significantly, 70 percent of the men said that they themselves had been sexually abused in their childhood. Half were physically abused by their fathers and almost half—44 percent—had been physically abused by their mothers. "Although not all who are abused go on to become perpetrators, it is critical that we learn more about how child sexual victimization affects male sexual development and male sexual socialization."

Considering the "intergenerational transmission of sexual abuse," Finkelhor and Williams suggest that men be given more opportunities for positive fathering—including paternity leave and more liberal visitation in cases of divorce or separation. They also suggest that males be encouraged to be intimate in nonsexual ways, beginning in boyhood. The study argues that, based on the evidence, it is very likely that people can become more aware of the precursory signs of incest. "It is conceivable," Finkelhor and Williams conclude, "that the sequence of events that leads to abuse can be interrupted."

## THE MOTHER'S ROLE

The role of the mother in incestuous families has been a controversial subject. Mothers have been accused of setting up opportunities for the incest to occur and of working against authorities attempting to end it. For effective intervention to occur, it is important for investigators to realize the difficulties a woman confronts when she must cope with these behaviors in her family. It is very easy to judge a mother's lack of support for the child victim as indicating a lack of love or caring. However, this judgmental attitude merely alienates the mother further from helping systems. It is important to recognize that the mother is often emotionally and financially dependent on the abuser. She fears public disclosure and embarrassment, loss of economic support, loss of partnership, disruption of the family, and incarceration of her partner or spouse.

Even when a mother reports the abuse, she will have ambivalent feelings, and her support for the child may waver over time. It is helpful to have some understanding of what precipitated the mother's report. It may surface that she made the report in the heat of anger without considering the consequences. It is possible that she had been aware of the sexual abuse for some time and reported it out of anger because of other events in the relationship. It is also possible that she genuinely had no idea that abuse was taking place. She may start out very supportive of the child, and yet, as her anger dissipates, her support may waver.

Often the mother experiences the disclosure of the information as a reflection on her adequacy as a wife, sexual partner, and mother. She may feel guilty, ashamed, and inadequate. She may begin to place pressure on the child to drop the charges or may give overt or covert messages to the child until the child decides on her own to end cooperation with the authorities. In some cases, mothers have taken extreme measures to avoid cooperation with authorities, including taking the child out of the state, providing negative information about the child to discredit her statements, or expressing a willingness to testify against the child.

## THE POLICE OFFICER'S ROLE

A police officer and protective service worker may interview a child jointly. In such an interview, the role of the police officer is to investigate the suspected incest and to compile evidence for a case against the abuser. The role of the protective service worker is to assess the validity of the abuse complaint and the needs of the family. It is also important to be aware that people working on cases of childhood sexual abuse often have strong feelings about the information they receive from the children. Many express anger, discomfort, and embarrassment when they first encounter sexual abuse. To intervene effectively in these cases, they must be aware of their feelings and keep them in check during the interview.

Before the interview with the child, it is important to obtain answers to the following questions: Who reported it? What is that person's relationship to the child? How did he or she come to know? Information about the child's personality is helpful. Is this child very verbal and expressive, readily showing her feelings, or is she controlled and closed? It is an advantage when a child makes a self-report, because it indicates that she looks at the police officer as a helping resource and that she has decided to take action to end the sexual abuse. Other children may interpret the presence of a police officer to mean that they are the ones who are in trouble. The police should reassure the child that telling about the abuse, in the long run, will do good for her and her family.

Because it is extremely important not to make the child confront the abuser during the interview, it is best if the social worker and police officer can interview the child alone, in a place that is comfortable for her. Tape-recording the interview can be a very efficient way of gathering information without distracting the child. If a child has first gone to a trusted person, such as a school counselor or pastor, she may request that person's presence during the initial interview to allay her fears and provide emotional support. A child who is extremely frightened and fearful of strangers may be unwilling to communicate without such support.

The earlier section "Child Molestation" addresses in depth the topic of interviewing molested children. Since incest is a special instance of child molestation, the reader is referred back to that section for guidelines in conducting such an interview. But there are also two further considerations to bear in mind when interviewing a victim of incest.

First, it is important to be aware of how the child may be viewing the sexual experience(s) and her interview. Some children have no idea that the behavior was wrong or inappropriate. Consequently, it is important not to convey, by attitude or words, negative judgments about what happened. The incestuous activity may have been the only affection the child has known, and she may have very strong positive feelings about the abuser.

Second, if the incest has been undetected for a long time, the child may have built up catastrophic expectations about what will happen when she tells. The interviewer can find out what she has been told will happen to her if she tells. Frequently children have been threatened with physical harm or harm to their family. They may have been told that telling will destroy the family, put Daddy in jail, cause Mother to have a nervous breakdown, and send the children to a foster home. They also may have been bribed to keep silent through special favors, presents, or money. For other children, the authority of the adult involved, plus assurances that there is nothing wrong with the sexual behavior, may have been enough to have ensured the child's silence.

# SUDDEN INFANT DEATH SYNDROME

Although **sudden infant death syndrome (SIDS)** is a medical phenomenon, not a crime, a lack of knowledge about its elements can cause individuals involved in its investigation to erroneously conclude they have a criminal homicide.

Health professionals in the past had limited contact with SIDS families because SIDS rarely occurs outside the home. A few babies have died of SIDS while hospitalized, but the usual case involves a baby who is brought to the hospital emergency room and is pronounced dead on arrival. As a result, many physicians and nurses have had little knowledge of SIDS.[60]

## WHAT IS SUDDEN INFANT DEATH SYNDROME?

Simply defined, SIDS is the sudden and unexpected death of an apparently healthy infant that remains unexplained after the performance of a complete autopsy. On the average, 2 of every 1,000 infants born alive succumb to SIDS, and it is the leading cause of death among infants 1 week to 1 year of age.

In the majority of instances, the baby is apparently in good health prior to death and feeds without difficulty. Although there may be evidence of a slight cold or stuffy nose, there is usually no history of serious upper respiratory infection. In most cases, the infant is placed in a crib to sleep and is found dead several hours later.

Most SIDS deaths occur between November and March. Sudden changes in temperature may trigger SIDS. The risk of SIDS appears to be highest in crowded dwellings; in infants of young mothers; in males; in nonwhites regardless of socioeconomic status; in families of lower socioeconomic status regardless of race; and in premature infants. Twins have an increased risk of SIDS, which is likely a consequence of their low birthweight and premature birth. SIDS occurs in both breast-fed and bottle-fed babies. Most victims are between the ages of 1 and 6 months, with the highest frequency of occurrence between 2 and 4 months.

### Characteristics of SIDS Victims' Appearance

- Usually normal state of nutrition and hydration.
- Blood-tinged, frothy fluids around mouth and nostrils, indicative of pulmonary edema.
- Vomitus on the face.
- Diaper wet and full of stool.
- Bruiselike marks on head or body limbs (postmortem pooling or settling of blood in dependent body parts).

### Autopsy Findings

- Some congestion and edema of the lungs.
- Petechial hemorrhages in thymus, heart, and lungs.
- Minor evidence of respiratory tract inflammation.

## MISCONCEPTIONS ABOUT SIDS

*Aspiration, choking:* The babies do not inhale or choke on their feeding.

*Unsuspected illness:* Particularly if the baby had a cold, the parents may feel guilty about not having taken the child to the doctor. If the baby was checked by the doctor, the parents (and the doctor) may wonder what the doctor missed. In any case, neither is at fault.

*Freezing:* Although the body may be cold when discovered, this is a postmortem change.

*Accidental injury, neglect, or abuse:* Law enforcement officers should not jump to the wrong conclusions because of the appearance of the infant. The results of accusations of wrongdoing have been tragic. A few innocent and grief-stricken parents have been accused of murdering their babies and put in jail. Appearances can be deceiving.

## SIDS RESEARCH

Currently, the most widely recognized theory about the mechanism of SIDS is spontaneous, protracted apnea, or cessation of breathing. Considerable progress in understanding SIDS has been made by the SIDS Institute at the University of Maryland. In comprehensive tests of 1,000 babies, it was found that fully 10 percent stopped breathing for periods longer than 15 to 20 seconds or their heart rate dropped below 80 beats per minute. Detected in time, such infants are considered at risk for SIDS and are monitored with an electronic device that sets off an alarm if the child's breathing or heart rate drops below a certain level (see photo on page 408).

Perhaps the most significant research supporting the apnea theory is the work of Dr. Richard Naeye of the Pennsylvania State University College of Medicine. Dr. Naeye began to look for structural changes in the infant's body at autopsy that would indicate chronic lack of oxygen attributable to repeated and

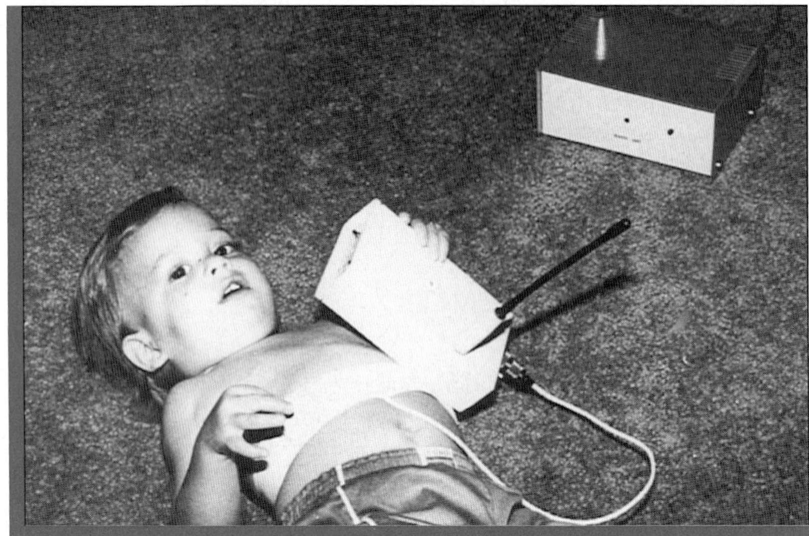

### Electronic Monitoring Device Used to Prevent SIDS

The electronic device attached to this child is used to monitor the heart and respiration rates. If the heart rate drops below 80 beats per minute or the child stops breathing for 15 to 20 seconds, a red light comes on and an audible alarm is sounded by the monitor depicted in the upper right corner of the figure.

(Courtesy Joseph and Karin Venero)

relatively long periods of apnea. He found the following changes in a large group of SIDS victims:

1. The walls of the small arteries in the lungs were thicker than normal.
2. The wall of the right ventricle of the heart was thicker than normal.
3. The relative retention of brown fat around the adrenal gland was greater than normal.
4. There was abnormal retention of fetal capacity for the production of red blood cells in the liver.

Dr. Marie Valdes-Dapena, of the University of Miami School of Medicine, has confirmed Naeye's observations with respect to the two latter changes and is currently working on the first two.

In a study conducted several years ago and reported in the New England Journal of Medicine, it was found that infants who usually slept in the face-down position had a significantly higher risk of SIDS than those who slept on their backs.[61] Respiratory obstruction in relation to the position of infants has also been studied.[62] It was concluded that the air passage of an infant is impaired when the body is placed face down on any type of mattress or pillow. Another study described 25 infants with SIDS who were discovered face-down on polystyrene cushions.[63] Studies in animals have suggested that the accidental suffocation results from the rebreathing of carbon dioxide.[64]

## THE POLICE OFFICER'S ROLE

The law enforcement officer serves a key role in the SIDS case and is often the first person to encounter the shock, grief, and guilt experienced by the parents.

It may be an experience such as this: The officer responds to a call, entering a house where an infant has just died. The mother is hysterical, incoherent, and unable to clarify what happened. The father is dazed yet tearless; he is confused and responding evasively. As the officer proceeds, the mother continues to sob, blaming herself. The infant is in the cradle, its head covered with a blanket. When the blanket is removed, the officer notes a small amount of blood-tinged fluid in and around the mouth and nose and bruiselike marks on the body where the blood settled after death.

Was the death a result of illness, abuse, neglect, or unexplained causes? The officer will make a preliminary assessment based on the information obtained at the scene.

If the circumstances are unclear, an autopsy may establish the need for criminal investigation. If the death is unexplainable, the officer can do a great service to the family by telling them that their baby was possibly a victim of SIDS. The officer can explain that it is the leading cause of death in infants after the first month of life and can tell them that there are organizations to provide them with information and assistance. By knowing about this disease and being able to provide sympathy and information to parents, the law enforcement officer serves a key role in the management of a SIDS case.

### CRIMINAL HOMICIDE AS A POSSIBILITY

Nevertheless, in spite of the findings just discussed, the police must be sensitive to the possibility of an intentional suffocation. Some recent studies raise the specter that in recent years there may have been cases in which children had actually been murdered but the deaths were incorrectly classified as SIDS. Every year in the United States more than 3,000 infant deaths are listed as SIDS, while 300 or more are identified as infanticides. Now two scientific studies suggest that some of the deaths in the first category belong in the second:

- Dr. David Southall of City General Hospital in Stoke-on-Trent, England, set up video cameras in the hospital rooms of children brought in after parents reported that the children had stopped breathing and nearly died. The cameras captured 39 instances of mothers trying to smother their babies. Fully one-third of these "near-miss-SIDS" cases, it is estimated, are actually cases of Munchausen syndrome by proxy. Overall, Dr. Southall concludes that 5 to 10 percent of SIDS deaths are in fact infanticides.[65]
- In an unpublished study, Dr. Thomas Truman concluded that as many as one-third of the repeated near-SIDS cases at what may be the most prestigious SIDS center in the United States may be cases of Munchausen syndrome by proxy. While serving a fellowship at Massachusetts General Hospital from 1993 to 1996, Truman analyzed the medical records of 155 children treated at the hospital. In 56 of these cases the child's chart contained circumstantial evidence of possible abuse. One baby suffered repeated breathing crises at home, turning blue and limp, but only when the mother and no one else was present. Another one had no breathing problems during the six months he spent in a local hospital, but the day he went home alone with his mother he had a life-threatening breathing emergency. The authorities were alerted to the possibility of the case, but no action was taken. The child died 1 year after being sent home.[66]

It should be noted that if death has been induced by intentional suffocation, there may be petechial hemorrhaging of the eyes and surrounding areas. (See Chapter 9, "Injury and Death Investigation," for a more detailed discussion of this condition.)

## INFANT ABDUCTION

**Infant abduction** is the taking of a child less than 1 year old by a nonfamily member. Although the FBI classifies such cases as kidnappings, infant abductions occur, by definition, for reasons not typically associated with kidnappings. For the most part, infant abductions do not appear to be motivated by a desire for money, sex, revenge, or custody, which are considered traditional motives in kidnapping cases.[67]

Since 1987, an average of 14 infants have been abducted annually. These abductions had no boundaries in terms of location or size of the hospital or of race, sex, or socioeconomic background of the infant.

### PROFILE OF THE ABDUCTOR

The data from infant abduction indicate certain offender characteristics. Investigators can use these traits to profile and apprehend suspects.

By way of general background, infant abductors usually are women, who account for 141 of the 145 cases analyzed. Offenders whose ages were verified ranged from 14 to 48 years old, with an average age of 28. Race was determined in 142 cases: 63 offenders were white, 54 were black, and 25 were Hispanic. The typical abductor may not have a criminal record. If a criminal record does exist, it likely will consist of nonviolent offenses, such as check fraud or shoplifting. To gain further insight into infant abductors and the crimes they commit, members of the FBI's National Center for the Analysis of Violent Crime (NCAVC) interviewed 16 abductors.[68] Offenders included whites, blacks, and Hispanics and ranged in age (at the time of the abduction) from 19 to 42. They had abducted infants in 10 different states. Nine of the abductors targeted hospitals directly; five approached the infant's residence; and two chose other locations. Although none had committed a violent crime before, four killed the infant's mother before stealing her baby.

Five of the abductors were single, seven were married, and four were either separated or divorced. Ten had no children. Though 13 offenders said they were involved in a significant relationship at the time of the abduction, many described it as "rocky," stressful, and lacking in communication.

## Motivation

Although little research exists on the topic of infant abductors' motivation, the cases outlined here illustrate that the need to present their partners with a baby often drives the female offender. Ten of the women interviewed admitted they had faked pregnancy. One of them recalled crying in the parking lot of a hospital, wondering if she should tell her husband she was not pregnant. Though she knew in her heart that she should tell him the truth, she thought he would leave her if she did. She chose to remain silent. Later, she followed a mother home and stole her baby.

Another woman had feigned pregnancy successfully with her husband before they were married, but her second attempt proved unsuccessful. After her conviction for infant abduction, her husband admitted that he would not have married her had he known she was not pregnant.

Five other women claimed to have miscarried without telling their partners, although no evidence existed to confirm their pregnancies. One said she had miscarried four months into her pregnancy but had continued living the lie, rationalizing that the stress placed on her by her husband's desire to have a baby had prompted her to deceive him.

Thus, as these cases illustrate, the infant abductor frequently attempts to prevent her husband or boyfriend from deserting her or tries to win back his affection by claiming pregnancy and, later, the birth of a child.[69] She may view a baby as the only way to salvage the relationship with her partner.[70]

According to the National Center for Missing and Exploited Children (NCMEC), sometimes the infant abductor is driven by a desire to experience vicariously the birth of a child she is "unable to conceive" or carry to term.[71] She is desperate to "bask in the rapture of baby love—to feel adored and needed.[72] Just as many expectant mothers tell others the "good news," the typical infant abductor truly believes that "she is about to give birth, and she fully expects everyone to accept the reality she has attempted to create.[73]

## Planning

Some of the interviewed abductors spent a great deal of time planning their crimes; others apparently acted on impulse. Their efforts ranged from a few hours to over nine months before the abduction. Eleven of the abductors interviewed gained weight prior to the abduction: one gained 61 pounds. Eleven purchased baby goods, and 12 told others they were pregnant. Then, when it came time to "deliver," the abductors employed such tactics as surveilling hospitals, monitoring birth announcements in the newspaper, following mothers home, and posing as hospital employees, baby-sitters, or social workers.

One abductor drove over 300 miles to steal an infant from an area where she had once resided. She also admitted to "checking out the security" of at least two area hospitals. While her actions appear premeditated, when asked to explain them, she responded, "I knew I was going somewhere, but I didn't know where. It was like I escaped into this little dream."

In fact, though most women planned events leading up to the abduction, many seemed to have not prepared for the act itself. They also could not, or would not, recall the mechanics of how they had carried out the abduction. One woman, who had entered a residence and murdered the mother before stealing her baby, remembered, "I had no plan of action, you know, it just was whatever happened, happened." The same woman had visited at least three hospitals, while wearing maternity clothes, prior to committing her crime.

After the abduction, 14 of the 16 offenders openly displayed the stolen infant to others. Six claimed to have given birth in an area hospital; four, out of town; and two, at home. Only three of the abductors altered the baby's appearance. According to one abductor, she cut the baby's hair to make him look younger.

# THE SCENE OF THE CRIME

## Location

Traditionally, the hospital setting has been the primary target for infant abductions. In the analysis discussed above, 83 of the 145 infants were taken from within a hospital: 49 from the mother's room, 14 from the nursery, 13 from pediatric hospital rooms, and 7 from other hospital locations.

Bolder criminals try nonhospital locations. Three babies were stolen from a clinic or doctor's office; two from day care centers. One quick-thinking abductor snatched a baby from the hospital curb. Forty brazen abductors targeted the residence of the infant or of a baby-sitter.

### Time of Day

Even in these emotion-driven crimes, the perpetrators showed signs of logic. In the majority of these cases the abductors chose to act during normal business hours: of the 145 cases, 121 occurred on a weekday, and in the 124 cases where the time of the abduction was recorded, 95 occurred between 8 A.M. and 6 P.M. The reason for this appears to be ease of movement. That is, in a hospital during normal working hours, abductors could disguise themselves as employees and slip in and out virtually undetected. Similarly, at a residence, there would be less likelihood of confronting a spouse during the workday.

### Month

From January 1983 through December 1994, abductions occurred more frequently between May and October and less frequently between November and April, with the exception of December. More infant abductions occurred in December (20 total) and May (19 total) than in any other months. Historically, November has shown the lowest number of abductions (a total of 8). Although a pattern seems to exist here, it simply could be coincidence: most of the 16 abductors interviewed had feigned pregnancy;. they had to "deliver" a baby 9 months later, regardless of the time of year.

### Method

Whether they steal babies from a hospital or from another location, abductors usually gain access through a con or ruse, as did 101 of the 145 subjects studied. Methods vary but have included posing as hospital employees, baby-sitters, or social workers. Some abductors have asked to use the telephone to get into the victim's home.

While cons help abductors gain access, they do not always make the abduction itself easier. As a result, abductors have used force either alone or in combination with a con in 16 cases, leading to the deaths of seven mothers and one father. Of these forcible abductions, 10 occurred in the victim's home, and the abductors used guns in 11 cases.

Abductions away from the hospital pose access difficulties for the offender and may account for the need to exercise force. In these cases, the degree of force ranged from threatening or binding the mother to shooting and stabbing the parents. In one of the most gruesome cases, the abductor strangled the mother and removed her unborn child from her womb, performing a crude caesarean section with car keys. Miraculously, the infant survived. Unfortunately, the mother did not. In 25 cases, the abductor stole the infant without having direct contact with another person at the moment of abduction.

## INVESTIGATIVE STRATEGIES

Successful resolution of any case depends on several factors, including the efforts of law enforcement. In 135 of the 136 resolved cases, the amount of time the infants remained missing ranged from mere hours to just over 300 days. Ninety-three of the babies were recovered in two days or less. Overall, law enforcement has a 94 percent rate of resolution.

One of the primary investigative strategies in infant abduction cases has been using the media to activate community awareness. Friends, relatives, and/or neighbors identified the abductor after media reports in approximately 53 out of 129 cases where researchers knew how the crime was solved. Anonymous phone tips resulted in the capture of 20 abductors after media exposure of the 16 abductors interviewed by researchers; four admitted to following the media reports, but none altered her plans on the basis of the coverage. In short, the media played a significant role in identifying the offenders but did not affect their actions. Accordingly, investigators probably need not fear that publicizing a case will bring harm to the infant.

# USE OF AGE-PROGRESSION TECHNOLOGY TO SEARCH FOR MISSING CHILDREN

One of the serious difficulties encountered by authorities in attempting to locate children who have been missing for a number of years is that their appearances can be dramatically changed during the

**Table 11-4** Investigative Guide for Assaults Against Children

| Type of Assault | Clues and Questions |
|---|---|
| Burn injuries (scald burns and contact burns) | Consistent story and explanation? Are there conflicting and/or various accounts of the injury? Clean lines at burn site? Is the burn on the buttocks, legs, ankles, wrist, palms, or soles? Are other injuries present, such as fractures or bruises? Are there other burn scars? Is the child's age compatible with the explanation of the burns? Are there any witnesses to the incident, including a caretaker? Why or why not? Do the caretakers seem angry or resentful toward the child or each other? |
| Shaken-baby syndrome | Has a skeletal survey, CT scan, and/or MRI been conducted to detect old or new intracranial injuries? Any other incidents of abuse? Repetitive abuse places the child at a higher risk of further injury. Have other children or siblings shown signs of past abuse? If the injuries are fatal, has an autopsy been performed with a thorough skeletal imaging scan? |
| Munchausen syndrome by proxy | Consult with an expert, including a psychologist or psychiatrist. Is there a history of abuse? Discuss the case with the medical professional involved. Did the caretaker have any medical training or desire for medical education? Remember, MSBP is often multigenerational. |
| Child molestation | When interviewing the victim, remember that children think egocentrically, in concrete terms; they often include extraneous information, have limited understanding of space, distance, and time, and have limited attention spans. Use anatomically correct dolls to help the victim explain what happened. Be sensitive to the child's victimization and trauma. |
| Child pornography | Is the material professional quality or homemade? Are the children depicted prepubescent? Is the material technical or simulated child pornography? What is the motive of the suspect: Sexual arousal? Lowering of other children's inhibitions? Blackmail? Exchange for other material? Profit? Is the material foreign or domestic? Does the suspect use a computer or the Internet for child pornography? Consult a digital forensics expert to retrieve evidence from the computer. |
| Incest | Is the family reclusive? Are there signs of serious disorganization in the family? Is more than one child a victim? Can the father be profiled? Remember the unique conditions for interviewing children. |
| Sudden infant death syndrome | Are there signs of abuse? What is the emotional state of the parents? Be sensitive to the needs of the parents. |
| Infant and child abduction | What was the location of the abduction? Time of day? Month? Method of abduction? Use the media to activate community awareness. Contact the National Center for Missing and Exploited Children for assistance. Use computer technology to search for missing children. Determine whether the incident is an abduction or the child has run away. |

normal aging process.[74] However, in recent years, computer technology has been used to age-enhance photographs of missing children. The Sony Corporation of America and QMA Corporation of Reston, Virginia, recently collaborated with the National Center for Missing and Exploited Children to assist in searching for missing and unidentified youths. Through their collective efforts, they installed a Video Imaging Laboratory at the NCMEC headquarters in Arlington, Virginia. The system was built using the expertise and techniques of the Federal Bureau of Investigation and experienced police artists, and this technology will help breathe new life into cases of abducted children who have remained missing for long periods of time. NCMEC's Video Imaging Laboratory represents a potentially dramatic breakthrough in law enforcement technology, speeding the process by which pictures are enhanced.

The process is accomplished by collecting information on the missing child, including full frontal photographs of the child; videotapes of the child, if available; and any information regarding identifying marks, hair color and style, and traditional information. Photographs of the parents and siblings at the comparable age of enhancement are also valuable. Computerized records of these photographs and details are then created and stored (see photos below).

Dissemination of photographs of missing children has proved to be a successful tool in their location, but in long-term cases the age enhancement of the photograph plays a vital role in the search for the child as he or she might currently look.

# RUNAWAY OR ABDUCTION?

The assessment made by the first officer responding to a report of a missing child will have a great impact on the outcome of the case.[75] The attitude of approach that officers take in the initial response to a missing-child call actually may determine whether the child is recovered and returned home safely, remains missing, or is found dead.[76]

To assess a missing-child report accurately, responding officers must explore the missing child's lifestyle and behaviors. Officers must have the motivation and the resources necessary to take the extra time needed for such an evaluation and to form an assessment as to whether a voluntary departure proves consistent with the child's behavior patterns.

## THE PARENTAL INTERVIEW

It is critical that parents be interviewed separately from each other and from other family members and reporting parties. Responding officers may feel reluctant to conduct separate interviews of the parents because of their emotionally escalated state. Conversely, if the parents do not appear particularly concerned about the child's absence, the officers may not view separate interviews as necessary. While they cannot determine what a parent's "normal" reaction to missing child would

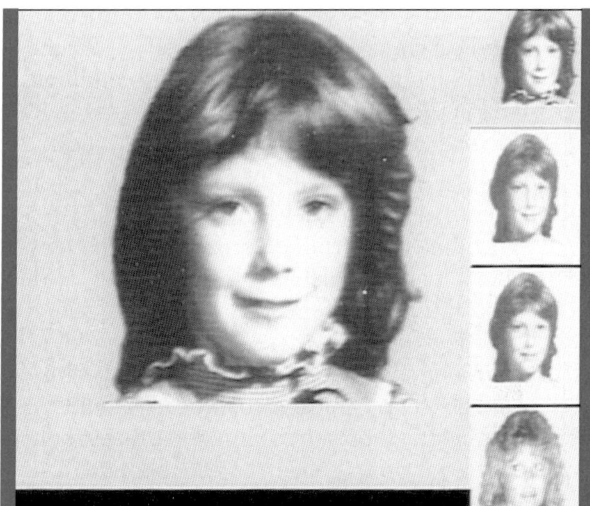

**Missing Child: 8 Years Old**

A photograph of Marjorie C. (Christy) Luna at 8 years of age. A facial image was stretched for merging with her sister's photograph, which appears in the insert, lower right corner.

(Courtesy National Center for Missing and Exploited Children)

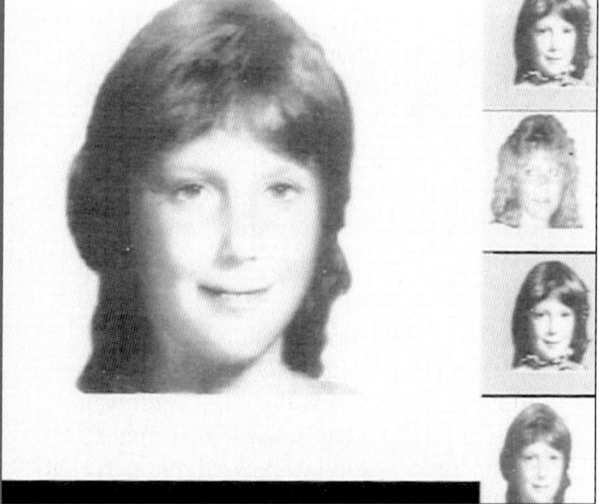

**Missing Child: Age Progression to 14 Years Old**

Completed age progression of Marjorie C. Luna. Her age has been progressed from 8 to 14 years of age.

(Courtesy National Center for Missing and Exploited Children)

be, officers must remain objective and realize that a family member may later become a suspect if the child has been abducted. They must balance this objectivity with empathy and support if the parents are in a state of emotional crisis. Most important, officers must ensure that they interview parents individually, preserve potential evidence, and document each parent's demeanor and attitude throughout the interview.

During the parental interview, officers should quickly compile accurate physical characteristics of the child, such as his or her appearance, age, and clothing, and should obtain recent photographs and videotapes. Officers should attempt to include full criminal- and psychiatric-history checks of all family members who had access to the child, as well as acquire a local agency history of any prior abuse or neglect calls to the home. In separate interviews of family members, responding officers should question whether the child's absence shows a significant deviation from established patterns of behavior.[77] However, further exploration into the victimology of the missing child can answer this question.

## VICTIMOLOGY

To understand whether the child's absence is consistent with established patterns of behavior, officers first must understand the child's normal actions before the disappearance. Officers should use the following guidelines for assessing the missing child's personality.[78]

- Develop and verify a detailed timeline of the child's last known activities up to the time the child was last seen or reported missing.
- Determine habits, hobbies, interests, and favorite activities.
- Identify normal activity patterns, and determine the victim's known comfort zone. Officers should assess the child's survival skills, ability to adapt to new or strange circumstances, and intellectual maturity. Did the child frequently travel alone? Did the child have a routine where independent travel occurred on a regular basis (e.g., riding a bike to school)? What fears and phobias did the child exhibit? For example, if the child was afraid of the dark, the probability of leaving voluntarily at night is low. Similarly, if the missing child was afraid to travel without a favorite item, such as a toy or security blanket, and the item remains in the house after the disappearance, the child may not have left voluntarily.
- Note any recent changes in behavior or activity patterns and any unusual events and stressors. Officers should explore any motivations for leaving. How does the child normally deal with stressful situations? Have any recent traumatic or stressful events caused such a prompt departure? Have any abuses occurred within the residence or family? Officers also should determine whether there were any recent changes in sleeping and eating patterns that would indicate stress.
- Identify and separately interview family members, close friends, schoolmates, teachers, coworkers, and other significant individuals. The FBI's National Center for the Analysis of Violent Crime has created a general assessment form for distribution to family members and associates that can assist in police officers' efforts to understand the child's personality.[79]
- Determine any history of alcohol and other drug use. Does the child have any particular medical conditions or allergies? If so, are the child's medications for the existing conditions still in the house? The presence of medications that the child needs may indicate an involuntary departure.
- Identify and interview boyfriends and/or girlfriends; determine normal dating patterns, including sexual activity. If the missing child is a postpubescent female, are there pregnancy and abortion issues? If so, officers should consider contacting local pregnancy, health, and abortion clinics. Also, officers should familiarize themselves with department policy and legal issues concerning confidentiality if they find the missing child at such a clinic.
- Obtain and review any personal writings, diaries, drawings, and schoolwork, including any entries into a personal computer or interaction with online systems or services. A critical item often overlooked in the missing-child call is the presence or absence of journals or diaries. Besides the obvious

insights that diaries may provide into the child's state of mind, the presence or absence of any written communication can prove relevant. A child who consistently and regularly has expressed thoughts and feelings in writing might not depart voluntarily without leaving some form of written communication for people left behind.[80] Similarly, calendars or schedules indicating planned events may provide insight into the child's possible motivation for staying or leaving.

- Determine any history of running away, discontent with home life, or suicidal ideations. Has the child disappeared voluntarily on prior occasions? If so, officers should note the last time the child ran away and the length of time spent away. Did the child go to friends, other family members, or a runaway shelter? Officers should determine what enabled the child to run away successfully or, conversely, what prevented the child from sustaining a long-term absence. What happened that prompted the child's departure in prior absences? Officers should determine whether the child exhibited any runaway gestures (e.g., staying out all night), threats to leave, or other behaviors that violated clear directives from parents or caregivers. Officers also should determine the existence of any prior suicide attempts or gestures by the child and consider the possibility that the child has disappeared as a result of a self-inflicted injury.

These observations will assist officers in crafting the child's victimology, which will indicate whether the child had the motivation and capability of leaving voluntarily. If the victim assessment suggests that these two factors do not exist, officers must consider the possibility that an abduction has occurred.

## RESOURCES

To successfully sustain a voluntary long-term absence, the runaway child must have access to resources that will satisfy basic needs, such as food, shelter, and transportation:

*Money:* Does the child have access to money or credit cards? Officers should verify whether the child recently accessed bank accounts through ATM withdrawals or other means. Is money missing from parents or siblings? Officers should also determine whether the child possesses adequate skills to obtain employment and, therefore, additional money.

*Transportation:* Does the missing child have access to a vehicle? If so, is that vehicle present or absent? Officers should determine whether the child is familiar with public transportation, such as a bus or train system, and conduct appropriate follow-up contacts with local transportation providers. Friends or family members unwittingly may have helped the child run away by providing some form of transportation.

*Clothing and toiletries:* Does evidence suggest that the child has packed any clothing or toiletries? Remembering the possibility that a crime scene may exist within the child's residence, officers should attempt to verify what items, if any, are no longer present in the child's room. Missing clothes, toiletries, makeup, medications, or other items of personal significance often may indicate predeparture preparations.

## SCENE ASSESSMENT

In a survey of police agencies, approximately 93 percent of law enforcement officers responding to missing-child calls stated that they usually interview the parents or guardian in person, However, only 41 percent would routinely search the child's home.[81] A search of the missing child's residence can serve as a preliminary assessment and provide officers with information. Upon arriving at the child's residence or last known location, officers must remember that the entire house may be a potential crime scene; they should take all necessary steps to prevent the destruction of evidence. Officers can make some important observations. They can note the presence or absence of obvious signs of disruption, such as forced entry. How did the offender and the victim enter and exit the house? If the house appears disorderly or in disarray, officers should determine whether the child's personal living space is in a similar condition. They should note any dramatic changes in the child's room that coincide with the departure, as these may indicate predeparture preparation or an attempt by an abductor to conceal evidence. Officers should attempt to verify whether any of the child's clothing or toiletries are missing since this could indicate packing or preparation. If officers or family members cannot find any items missing or evidence of packing, officers must consider the possibility that the child may have been abducted.

In addition to examining the child's room, responding officers should consider examining the parents' room or other areas of the house. If no items appear missing from the child's room, are items missing from other areas of the house that may provide additional resources?

Has the child left any communication for discovery by parents or guardians? This includes written letters, voice-mail messages, and computer messages. Law enforcement officers should consider all modes of communication available to the missing child, including access to online chat rooms and communication with others via the Internet.

Officers should attempt to compile and examine a list of known associates or family members from whom the child would most likely seek assistance. If those individuals are unaware of the child's whereabouts, this is an indication of the child's lack of available resources. Thus, officers must contemplate the possibility that someone has abducted the child.

### TIME FACTORS

How long does a runaway child typically stay away from home, and how does the passage of time influence the classification of a missing-child case? The California Department of Justice's Missing/Unidentified Persons Unit has reported the following trends in runaway returns:

| Time Frame | Runaways Returned |
|---|---|
| Within 7 days | 50% |
| 7–14 days | 30 |
| 14–30 days | 17 |
| More than 30 days | 3 |

These statistics indicate that the majority of the runaway children cannot sustain an absence for more than 2 weeks. In general, the longer the absence, the greater the likelihood that an individual has abducted the child or that the child has fallen victim to a violent crime. If the child has a history of running away, officers should determine the length of time the child remained missing during previous absences. If the time length of the current absence grossly exceeds that of previous absences, officers should consider the current disappearance a deviation from normal behavior patterns.

Responding officers should note the amount of time that transpired between when the child was last seen and when the parents or guardian alerted authorities. While 24 hours or more may indicate apathy or neglect, this time frame also may reflect the common misconception that an individual must be missing for 24 hours before law enforcement can respond. The responding officers should construct a timeline identifying the parents' activities during this interval. The timeline highlights family dynamics and clarifies the parents' potential role in the child's disappearance.[82]

## SEX-OFFENDER REGISTRATION

In October 1989, 11-year-old Jacob Wetterling was abducted less than a 10-minute bike ride from his St. Joseph, Minnesota, home as he, his 10-year-old brother, and their 11-year-old friend rode home from the local video store.[83] Although law enforcement officers never found Jacob or his abductor, they did discover a number of halfway houses in their county boarded convicted sex offenders from another county.[84]

Ten months after Jacob's disappearance, Pam Lychner, a Houston, Texas, real estate agent, entered a vacant home to prepare to show it to a prospective buyer. She was brutally assaulted by a twice-convicted felon. Her husband saved her life when he interrupted the beating.[85]

In July 1994, 7-year-old Megan Kanka went to a neighbor's home to see his new puppy. The twice-convicted sex offender—who lived across the street from Megan's Hamilton Township, New Jersey, home—raped and murdered Megan and dumped her body in a nearby park.[86]

These tragic events spurred the Wetterlings, the Lychners, and the Kankas to push for legislation that would protect the lives of others. Their efforts spawned sex-offender registration and notification laws, which require that states maintain registries of sex offenders and release information about these offenders to the public.

## THE LAWS

In 1994, Congress passed the **Jacob Wetterling Crimes against Children and Sexually Violent Offender Registration Act**.[87] The act required that states create sex-offender registries within three years or lose 10 percent of their funding under the Edward Byrne Memorial program.[88] Offenders who commit a criminal sexual act against a minor or commit any sexually violent offense must register for a period of 10 years from the date of their release from custody or supervision. All 50 states have sex-offender registration.[89]

The Jacob Wetterling act gave states the option of releasing information about registered sex offenders to the public but did not require that they do so. This changed in 1996 when Congress amended the act to require that states disclose information about registered sex offenders for public safety purposes. This legislation became known as **Megan's law**, in memory of Megan Kanka.[90] U.S. Department of Justice guidelines allow states considerable discretion in determining the extent and manner of notification when warning the public about sex offenders living in the community. At least 44 states have passed community notification laws since 1990.[91]

The Pam Lychner Sexual Offender Tracking and Identification Act of 1996[92] mandated the establishment of a national sex-offender database, which the FBI maintains.[93] This national tracking system gives law enforcement authorities access to sex-offender registration data from all participating states. The Lychner act also requires that the FBI register, and verify the addresses of, sex offenders in states that have not met the minimum compliance standards set forth by the Jacob Wetterling act, although this may change.[94]

## REGISTRATION REQUIREMENTS

Although sex-offender registration requirements vary according to state laws, some common features exist in registries throughout the country. In most states, the state criminal justice agency or board (e.g., the state police or state bureau of investigation) maintains the state's registry. Sex offenders, both juveniles and adults, register at local law enforcement or corrections agencies, which then forward the information to the state's central registry. Registry information typically includes the offender's name, address, date of birth, Social Security number, and physical description, as well as fingerprints and a photograph. In addition, Iowa requires information about the sex-offense conviction that triggered the registration, and at least eight states collect samples for DNA identification.[95]

Most state laws require that offenders register only if their convictions occurred after the law's effective date, although some states, such as Minnesota, require that offenders register after they are *charged* with a sexual offense.[96] Offenders receive notice of the registration requirement from the court or registry agency. In Iowa, offenders can contest the registration requirement by filing an application for determination with the state Department of Public Safety.

Usually, offenders must register by a certain number of days after their release from custody or placement on supervision. The types of offenses requiring registration vary according to state law but must comply with the Jacob Wetterling act, which mandates registration for sex crimes against minors and for violent sex crimes. For example, in Iowa, the qualifying offenses are criminal sexual offenses against minors; sexually violent offenses; sexual exploitation; aggravated offenses, including murder, nonparental kidnapping, and false imprisonment; manslaughter; and burglary, if sexual abuse or attempted sexual abuse occurred during the commission of the crime; as well as other relevant offenses, such as indecent exposure.

The registration requirement lasts at least 10 years. Some states require lifetime registration for all or some offenses, and some states allow offenders to petition the court for a reduction.[97] Iowa law requires lifetime registration for offenders deemed "sexual predators" by the courts and for any registered offenders who are convicted of a subsequent sexual offense. In most states it is a criminal offense to knowingly fail to register or to report subsequent changes in information, such as the registrant's name or address. In Iowa, public officials verify annually the addresses of all registrants.

## NOTIFICATION FEATURES

The most basic form of notification, sometimes referred to as passive notification, allows citizens to access registry information at their local law enforcement agencies. In Iowa, citizens must complete a request form at their local police or sheriff's department and provide the name of the person being checked *and* one of three identifiers: address, date of birth, or Social Security number. If the agency finds the person's name on the registry, it can release certain information about the offender; however, federal guidelines prohibit states from releasing the identities of victims. Employers also may check potential employees. Since Iowa's law took effect in 1995, members of the public have made 14,973 requests for registry information.[98]

Several states provide a toll-free number that citizens can call to obtain information. California and New York operate 900-number services for inquiries.[99] Many states allow public access to sex-offender registry information through Internet sites maintained by criminal justice agencies. This information usually includes offenders' photographs, their biographical data, and information about their previous sex offenses.

In addition to allowing passive notification, a number of states allow government agencies to disseminate information about registered sex offenders to vulnerable individuals and organizations. Using this process, known as active notification, officials may choose to notify prior victims, landlords, neighbors, public and private schools, child care facilities, religious and youth organizations, and other relevant individuals or agencies. Most officials reserve community-wide notification for only the most dangerous sex offenders. Community-wide notification usually involves using the media and public forums such as neighborhood associations and other community meetings.

States have various methods for determining which offenders qualify for active notification. In Florida and Montana, state courts determine which sex offenders pose the greatest threat to the community and target them for active notification.[100] A number of states, including Iowa, allow criminal justice officials or state registry review boards to assess the offender's level of risk, and then law enforcement officials, prosecuting attorneys, or corrections personnel typically make the notification. Louisiana requires that registered sex offenders themselves notify neighbors within 1 square block in the city or a 3-mile radius in rural areas.[101]

## CRIME IN SCHOOLS

Forty years ago, surveys of public school teachers indicated that the most pressing classroom problems were tardiness, talkative students, and gum chewing.[102] Far more serious complaints are currently heard from teachers, administrators, and students—about the presence of drugs, gangs, and weapons on campus and the threat of assault, robbery, theft, vandalism, and rape.[103] According to the popular media, such as *Time* magazine and *U.S. News and World Report,* the problems in our nation's schools may be paralyzing the system.[104] In an effort to develop a systematic procedure for threat assessment and intervention in school violence cases, the FBI's National Center for the Analysis of Violent Crime (NCAVC) conducted an in-depth review of 18 school shootings. Because of confidentiality issues, the shooting cases studied were not identified. The study analyzed the shootings from a behavioral perspective and resulted in the development of the threat assessment intervention model. The model outlines a procedure for evaluating a threat and the person making the threat so that an accurate assessment can be made of the likelihood that the threat will be carried out.

### THREAT ASSESSMENT

A threat is an expression of the intent to do harm or act out violently against someone or something. A threat can be spoken, written, or symbolic—for example, motioning with one's hands as though shooting at another person.

**Threat assessment** rests on two critical principles: (1) that all threats and all threateners are not equal, and (2) that most threateners are unlikely to carry out their threats. However, all threats must be taken seriously and evaluated.

In NCAVC's experience, most threats are made anonymously or under a false name. Because threat assessment relies heavily on evaluating the threatener's background, personality, lifestyle, and resources, identifying the threatener is necessary so that an informed assessment can be made—and so that charges can be brought if the threat is serious enough to warrant prosecution. If the threatener's identity cannot be determined, the evaluation will

**Students and Faculty Flee from School after Shooting**

Recently, a number of the nation's high schools have experienced situations in which students have brought guns to school and killed or wounded many people. The FBI's National Center for the Analysis of Violent Crime (NCAVC) has conducted an in-depth review of 18 school shootings. From this analysis, they have developed a threat assessment model to help prevent school violence.

(© AFP/Corbis)

have to be based on the threat alone. That assessment may change if the threatener is eventually identified: a threat that was considered low risk may be rated as more serious if new information suggests the threatener is dangerous; conversely, an assessment of high risk may be scaled down if the threatener is identified and found not to have the intent, ability, means, or motive to carry out the threat.

## Motivation

Threats are made for a variety of reasons. A threat may be a warning signal, a reaction to fear of punishment or some other anxiety, or a demand for attention. It may be intended to taunt; to intimidate; to assert power or control; to punish; to manipulate or coerce; to frighten; to terrorize; to compel someone to do something; to strike back for an injury, injustice, or insult; to disrupt someone's or some institution's life; to test authority , or to protect oneself. The emotions that underlie a threat can be love, hate, fear, rage, or desire for attention, revenge, excitement, or recognition.

Motivation can never be known with complete certainty, but understanding motive to the extent possible is a key element in evaluating a threat. A threat reflects the threatener's mental and emotional state at the time the threat is made, but it is important to remember that a state of mind can be temporarily but strongly influenced by alcohol or drugs or by a precipitating factor such as a romantic breakup, failing grades, or conflict with a parent. After a person has absorbed an emotional setback and calmed down, or when the effects of alcohol or drugs have worn off, his or her motivation to act on a violent threat may also diminish.

## Signposts

In general, people do not switch instantly from nonviolence to violence. Nonviolent people do not "snap" or decide on the spur of the moment to meet a problem by using violence. Instead, the path toward violence is an evolutionary one, with signposts along the way. A threat is one observable behavior; another may be brooding about frustration or disappointment or fantasizing about destruction or revenge in conversations, writings, drawings, and the like.

## Level of Risk

A low-level threat poses a minimal risk to the victim and public safety:

- The threat is vague and indirect.
- The information contained in the threat is inconsistent or implausible or lacks detail.
- The threat lacks realism.
- The content of the threat suggests that the threatener is unlikely to carry it out.

A medium-level threat is one that could be carried out but may not seem entirely realistic:

- The threat is more direct and more concrete than a low-level threat.
- The wording in the threat suggests that the threatener has given some thought to how the act will be carried out.
- There may be a general indication of a possible place and time (but the signs still fall well short of a detailed plan).
- There is no strong indication that the threatener has taken preparatory steps, although there may be some veiled reference or ambiguous or inconclusive evidence pointing to that possibility (e.g., an allusion to a book or movie that shows the planning of a violent act, or a vague, general statement about the availability of weapons).
- There may be a specific statement seeking to convey that the threat is not empty: "I'm serious!" or "I really mean this!"

A high-level threat poses an imminent and serious danger to the safety of others:

- The threat is direct, specific, and plausible.
- The threat suggests that concrete steps have been taken toward carrying it out (e.g., statements indicating that the threatener has acquired or practiced with a weapon or has had the victim under surveillance).

## Factors in Threat Assessment

Specific, plausible details are a critical factor in evaluating a threat. Details can include the identity of the victim or victims; the reason for making the threat; the means, weapon, and method by which it is to be carried out; the date, time, and place that the threatened act will occur; and concrete information about plans or preparations that have already been made.

Specific details can indicate that substantial thought, planning, and preparatory steps have already been taken, suggesting a higher risk that the threatener will follow through on the threat. Similarly, a lack of detail suggests that the threatener may not have thought through all the contingencies, has not actually taken steps to carry out the threat, and may not seriously intend violence. He or she may merely be "blowing off steam" over some frustration or be trying to frighten or intimidate a particular victim or disrupt a school's events or routine.

Details that are specific but not logical or plausible may indicate a less serious threat. For example, a high school student writes that he intends to detonate hundreds of pounds of plutonium in the school's auditorium the following day at lunchtime. The threat is detailed, stating a specific time, place, and weapon, but the details are unpersuasive. Plutonium is almost impossible to obtain, legally or on the black market. It is expensive, hard to transport, and very dangerous to handle, and a complex high-explosive detonation is required to set off a nuclear reaction. No high school student is likely to have any plutonium at all, much less hundreds of pounds, nor would a student have the knowledge or complex equipment required to detonate it. A threat this unrealistic is obviously unlikely to be carried out.

The emotional content of a threat can be an important clue to the threatener's mental state. Emotions are conveyed by melodramatic words and unusual punctuation—"I hate you!!!!!" "You have ruined my life!!!!" "May God have mercy on your soul!!!!"—or in excited, incoherent passages that may refer to God or other religious beings or may deliver an ultimatum.

Though emotionally charged threats can tell the assessor something about the temperament of the threatener, they are not a measure of danger. They may sound frightening, but no correlation has been established between the emotional intensity in a threat and the risk that it will be carried out.

Precipitating stressors are incidents, circumstances, reactions, or situations that can trigger a threat. The precipitating event may seem insignificant and have no direct relevance to the threat, but nonetheless it becomes a catalyst. For example, a student has a fight with his mother before going to school. The argument may be a minor one over an issue that has nothing to do with school, but it sets off an emotional chain reaction that leads the student to threaten another student at school that day—possibly something he has thought about doing in the past.

The impact of a precipitating event obviously depends on predisposing factors: underlying personality traits, characteristics, and temperament that predispose an adolescent to fantasize about violence or act violently. Accordingly, information about a temporary "trigger" must be considered together with broader information about underlying factors, such as a student's vulnerability to loss and depression.

## Personality Traits and Behavior

- *Leakage*: "Leakage" occurs when a student intentionally or unintentionally reveals clues to feelings, thoughts, fantasies, attitudes, or intentions that may signal an impending violent act. These clues can take the form of subtle threats, boasts, innuendos, predictions, or ultimatums. They may be spoken or conveyed in stories, diary entries, essays, poems, letters, songs, drawings, doodles, tattoos, or videos.[105] Leakage can also occur when a student tries, at times deceptively, to get unwitting friends or classmates to help with preparations for a violent act (e.g., the student asks a friend to obtain ammunition for her because she is "going hunting").
- *Low tolerance for frustration*: The student is easily bruised, insulted, angered, and hurt by real or perceived injustices done to him or her by others and has great difficulty tolerating frustration.
- *Poor coping skills:* The student has little, if any, ability to deal with frustration, criticism, disappointment, failure, rejection, or humiliation. His or her response is typically inappropriate, exaggerated, immature, or disproportionate.
- *Lack of resiliency:* The student lacks resiliency and is unable to bounce back even when some time has elapsed since a frustrating or disappointing experience, a setback, or a put-down.
- *Failed love relationship:* The student may feel rejected or humiliated after the end of a love relationship and cannot accept or come to terms with the rejection.
- *"Injustice collector":* The student nurses resentment over real or perceived injustices. No matter how much time has passed, the "injustice collector" neither forgets nor forgives the wrongs the people he or she believes are responsible. The student may keep a hit list with the names of people who have wronged him or her.
- *Signs of depression:* The student shows symptoms of depression such as lethargy, physical fatigue, a morose or dark outlook on life, a sense of malaise, and loss of interest in activities that he or she once enjoyed.
- *Narcissism:* The student is self-centered, lacks insight into others' needs and/or feelings, and blames others for failures and disappointments. The narcissistic student may embrace the role of a victim to elicit sympathy and to feel temporarily superior to others. He or she displays signs of paranoia and assumes an attitude of self-importance or grandiosity that masks feelings of unworthiness.[106] A narcissistic student may be either very thin-skinned or very thick-skinned in responding to criticism.
- *Alienation:* The student consistently behaves as though he feels different or estranged from others. This sense of separateness reflects more than just being a loner. It can involve feelings of isolation, sadness, loneliness, not belonging, and not fitting in.
- *Dehumanization of others:* The student consistently fails to see others as fellow

humans. He or she characteristically views other people as "nonpersons" or objects to be thwarted. This attitude may appear in the student's writings and artwork, in interactions with others, or in comments during conversation.

- *Lack of empathy:* The student shows an inability to understand the feelings of others and seems unconcerned about anyone else's feelings. When others show emotion, the student may ridicule them as being weak or stupid.
- *Exaggerated sense of entitlement:* The student constantly expects special treatment and consideration and reacts negatively if he or she doesn't get that treatment.
- *Attitude of superiority:* The student has a sense of being superior and presents himself or herself as smarter, more creative, more talented, more experienced, and more worldly than others.
- *Exaggerated need for attention:* The student shows an exaggerated, even pathological, need for attention, whether positive or negative, no matter what the circumstances.
- *Externalization of blame:* The student consistently refuses to take responsibility for his or her own actions and typically faults other people, events, or situations for any failings or shortcomings. In placing blame, the student frequently seems impervious to rational argument and common sense.
- *Masking of low self-esteem:* Although the student may display an arrogant, self-glorifying attitude, his or her conduct often seems to veil underlying low self-esteem. The student avoids high visibility or involvement in school activities, and other students may consider him or her a nonentity.
- *Anger-management problems:* Rather than expressing anger in appropriate ways and circumstances, the student consistently tends to burst out in temper tantrums or melodramatic displays or to brood in sulky, seething silence. The anger may be noticeably out of proportion to the cause or may be redirected toward people who had nothing to do with the original incident. The anger may come in unpredictable and uncontrollable outbursts, and it may be accompanied by expressions of unfounded prejudice, dislike, or even hatred toward individuals or groups.
- *Intolerance:* The student often expresses racial or religious prejudice or intolerant attitudes toward minorities or displays slogans or symbols of intolerance through such means as tattoos, jewelry, clothing, bumper stickers, or book covers.
- *Inappropriate humor:* The student's humor is consistently inappropriate. Jokes or humorous comments tend to be macabre, insulting, belittling, or mean.
- *Manipulation of others:* The student consistently attempts to con and manipulate others and win their trust so that they will rationalize any signs of his or her aberrant or threatening behavior.
- *Lack of trust:* The student is untrusting and chronically suspicious of others' motives and intentions. This lack of trust may approach a clinically paranoid state. The student may express the belief that society has no trustworthy institution or mechanism for achieving justice or resolving conflict and that if something bothersome occurs, he or she has to settle it in his or her own way.
- *Closed social group:* The student appears introverted. He or she has acquaintances rather than friends or associates only with a single small group that seems to exclude everyone else. Students who threaten or carry out violent acts are not necessarily loners in the classic sense, and the composition and qualities of peer groups can be important pieces of information in assessing the danger that a threat will be acted on.
- *Change of behavior:* The student's behavior changes dramatically. His or her academic performance may decline, or the student may show a reckless disregard for school rules, schedules, dress codes, and other regulations.
- *Rigid and opinionated outlook:* The student appears rigid, judgmental, and cynical, voices strong opinions on subjects about which he or she has little knowledge, and disregards facts, logic, and reasoning that might challenge these opinions.
- *Unusual interest in sensational violence:* The student demonstrates an unusual interest in

school shootings and other heavily publicized acts of violence. He or she may declare his admiration for those who committed the acts or may criticize them for "incompetence" or failing to kill enough people. The student may explicitly express a desire to carry out a similar act in his or her own school, possibly as an act of "justice."

- *Fascination with violence-filled entertainment:* The student has an unusual fascination with movies, TV shows, computer games, music videos, or printed materials that focus intensively on themes of violence, hatred, control, power, death, and destruction. He or she may repeatedly watch one movie or read one book with violent content, perhaps involving school violence. Themes of hatred, violence, weapons, and mass destruction recur in virtually all the student's activities, hobbies, and pastimes. The student spends inordinate amounts of time playing video games with violent themes and seems more interested in the violent images than in the game itself. On the Internet, the student regularly searches for websites involving violence, weapons, and other disturbing subjects. There is evidence that the student has downloaded and kept material from these sites.
- *Negative role models:* The student may be drawn to negative, inappropriate role models such as Hitler, Satan, or others associated with violence and destruction.
- *Behavior relevant to carrying out a threat:* The student appears to be increasingly occupied with activities that could be related to carrying out a threat (e.g., spending unusual amounts of time practicing with firearms or visiting violent websites). The time spent on these activities has noticeably begun to exclude normal everyday pursuits such as doing homework, attending classes, going to work, and spending time with friends.

## CLASSIFICATION OF THREATS

### Types of Threats

Threats can be classified into four categories:

- A direct threat identifies a specific act against a specific target and is delivered in a straightforward, clear, and explicit manner: "I am going to place a bomb in the school's gym."
- An indirect threat tends to be vague, unclear, and ambiguous. The plan, the intended victim, the motivation, and other aspects of the threat are masked or equivocal: "If I wanted to, I could kill everyone at this school!" While violence is implied, the threat is phrased tentatively—"If I wanted to"—and suggests that a violent act *could* occur, not that it *will* occur.
- A veiled threat is one that strongly implies but does not explicitly threaten violence: "We would be better off without you around anymore." Such a statement clearly hints at a possible violent act but leaves it to the potential victim to interpret the message and give a definite meaning to the threat.
- A conditional threat warns that a violent act will happen unless certain demands or terms are met: "If you don't pay me one million dollars, I will place a bomb in the school." This type of threat is often used in extortion cases.

## THE ROLE OF LAW ENFORCEMENT

In the vast majority of cases, whether to involve law enforcement will hinge on the seriousness of the threat: low, medium, or high.[107]

*Low level:* A threat that has been evaluated as low level poses little danger to public safety and in most cases would not necessitate law enforcement investigation for a possible criminal offense. (However, law enforcement agencies may be asked for information in connection with a threat of any level.) Appropriate intervention in a low-level case would involve, at a minimum, interviews with the student and his or her parents. If the threat was aimed at a specific person, that person should be asked about his or her relationship with the threatener and the circumstances that led up to the threat. The response—disciplinary action and perhaps a referral for counseling or some other form of intervention—should be determined according to school policies and the judgment of the responsible school administrators.

*Medium level:* When a threat is rated as medium level, the response should in most cases include contacting the appropriate law enforcement agency, as well as other sources, to obtain additional information (and possibly reclassify the threat into the high or low category). A medium-level threat will sometimes, though not necessarily, warrant investigation as a possible criminal offense.

*High level:* Almost always, if a threat is evaluated as high level, the school should immediately inform the appropriate law enforcement agency. A response plan, which should have been designed ahead of time and rehearsed by both school and law enforcement personnel, should be implemented, and law enforcement should be informed and involved in whatever subsequent actions are taken in response to the threat. A high-level threat is highly likely to result in criminal prosecution.

## Investigating School Violence

Law enforcement efforts regarding school violence and crime generally center on early detection and prevention. A recent study conducted by George Mason University revealed that 69 percent of U.S. police chiefs support the creation of more after-school programs and educational child care arrangements, seeing this as the most effective method of reducing juvenile crime. Among police chiefs, 30 percent cited prosecuting juveniles as adults and hiring more juvenile investigators as their first choices for reducing youth crime. Only 1 percent of the chiefs believed that installing more metal detectors

**Weapon detection program**
A successful, but labor-intensive, weapon detection program at a New York City high school. Given the frequency with which handguns and other weapons have been discovered on school grounds, some school districts have gone to considerable expense to install metal detectors at entry points. In addition, security officers must be present at these sites to further review suspicious circumstances.

(Courtesy Chester A. Higgins, Jr., and the U.S. Department of Justice, Office of Justice Programs, National Institute of Justice)

and surveillance devices in schools would be the most effective method of reducing crime.[108]

When investigating threats of violence in schools, it is important to listen carefully to witnesses in order to correctly identify the level of the threat and subsequently take appropriate action. Key questions include:

- Who made the threat?
- To whom was the threat made?
- Under what circumstances was the threat made?
- Exactly what words were said?
- How often were threats made?[109]

On some occasions, undercover juvenile informants can be used by police to gain insight in a school where threats have been received or plots of violence are suspected.[110] However, this practice is usually discouraged, since it places juveniles in a very precarious and potentially dangerous position. Some jurisdictions forbid the practice; others have developed very sophisticated guidelines regulating the use of a confidential informant who is under 16 years of age.

Ascertaining who made the threat or committed the act is often the least difficult part of the investigation due to the fact that juvenile perpetrators frequently use their crimes as a way of getting attention. Also, a young criminal often lacks the experience, sophistication, and self-control needed to adequately avoid detection.

Clearly, most of the police effort is on prevention, focusing on the development of programs that emphasize "team" efforts among school administrators, the police, and the community at large. When an incident does occur, specially trained teams of police intervention officers lead the investigation in an attempt to not only apprehend the suspect but also quell growing fear that might arise from recent high-profile incidents of school violence. Some departments are now using **rapid response deployment** or **quick action deployment (QUAD)**. This approach focuses on training patrol officers in the principles and tactics of rapid deployment for responding to critical incidents, especially incidents of school violence. In theory the concept has merit: immediately responding officers are able to enter buildings where life-threatening situations are in progress or where loss of victims' lives is imminent. Proponents of the concept argue that such intervention cannot wait until the SWAT team responds and therefore that police action must be taken immediately. While there is no doubt that such a condition has presented itself, the vast majority of incidents (including school shootings) are deescalated by time. We suggest that the best approach for patrol officers responding to a critical and violent incident at a school, especially one involving potential hostages, is to take action only when appropriate and that their primary mission is to control and contain the scene. They should let specially trained hostage negotiation and critical-incident teams handle any protracted incident of school violence. Once the scene has been secured, detectives should then investigate the crime as they would any other homicide, assault, or threat.

## Key Terms

**battered-child syndrome**
**child**
**child pornography**
**contact burns**
**immersion burns**
**incest**
**infant abduction**
**Jacob Wetterling Crimes against Children and Sexually Violent Offender Registration Act**
**Megan's law**
**Munchausen syndrome by proxy (MSBP)**
**preferential child molester**
**rapid response deployment or quick action deployment (QUAD)**
**scald burns**
**shaken-baby syndrome (SBS)**
**situational child molester**
**spill/splash injuries**
**sudden infant death syndrome (SIDS)**
**threat**
**threat assessment**

## Review Questions

1. What are the two most common instruments used in child abuse?
2. What are some of the ways that intentional immersion burns are distinguished from accidental immersion burns?
3. Why was the phrase "shaken-baby syndrome" coined?
4. What is the mechanism of injuries in shaken-baby syndrome?
5. What role does the physician play in child-abuse cases?
6. What is Munchausen syndrome by proxy (MSBP)?
7. What are some of the major behavioral characteristics of situational and preferential child molesters?
8. Identify the three developmental issues that are important when allegations of sexual abuse arise.
9. What are some of the benefits of using an anatomically detailed doll in interviewing children?
10. How is child pornography behaviorally defined?
11. What are the five categories of incestuous fathers?
12. Describe the appearance of a SIDS victim.
13. What motivations are typically *not* involved in infant abduction?
14. What appears to be the major motivating factor that drives female offenders to abduct infants?
15. How is the process of age progression technologically accomplished?
16. What resources must a runaway child have to successfully sustain a voluntary long-term absence?
17. What are the major features of the Jacob Wetterling against Children and Sexually Violent Offender Registration Act?
18. Threats in school violence can be classified into four categories; what are they?

## Internet Activities

1. Check out the Office of Juvenile and Delinquency Prevention's "Battered Child Syndrome: Investigating Physical Abuse and Homicide" at www.ncjrs.org/html/ojjdp/portable_guides/bcs/contents.html. This guide focuses on investigative procedures for battered-child syndrome, shaken-baby syndrome, Munchausen syndrome by proxy, and sudden infant death syndrome.
2. For a comprehensive site on information, news, statistics, and other issues regarding sexual abuse against children, check out www.prevent-abuse-now.com. Find out if sex-offender registration or community notification laws apply in your state and community. If they do, what are the conditions of the registration? Is the community actively or passively notified of convicted sex offenders? If information about your state and community is not provided at this site, check your local and state law enforcement sites.

## Notes

1. C. J. Flammang, *The Police and the Unprotected Child* (Springfield, IL: Charles C. Thomas, 1970), p. 90; Harold E. Simmons, *Protective Services for Children* (Sacramento, CA: General Welfare Publications, 1968), p. 45.
2. Phylip J. Peltier, Gary Purdue, and Jack R. Shepherd, *Burn Injuries in Child Abuse* (Washington, DC: U.S. Department of Justice, 1997), pp. 1–9.
3. Randell Alexander and K. Kleinmann, *Diagnostic Imaging of Child Abuse* (Washington, DC: U.S. Department of Justice, 1996), pp. 6–9.
4. James D. Regis, "The Battered Child," *Police Work*, April 1980, pp. 41–42.
5. Rob Parrish, *Battered Child Syndrome: Investigating Physical Abuse* (Washington, DC: U.S. Department of Justice, 1996), pp. 9–10.

6. Stephen J. Boros and Larry C. Brubaker, "Munchausen Syndrome by Proxy: Case Accounts," *FBI Law Enforcement Bulletin,* 1992, Vol. 61, No. 6, pp. 16–20. These case reports were taken from this article.
7. Kenneth V. Lanning, *Child Molesters: A Behavioral Analysis for Law Enforcement Officers Investigating Cases of Child Sexual Exploitation,* 3rd ed. (Arlington, VA: National Center for Missing and Exploited Children, 1992), pp. 6–10. This entire discussion of child molesters has been reproduced (with minor changes) with permission. No part of this may be reproduced without the express written permission of the National Center for Missing and Exploited Children, 1-800-843-5678.
8. Ibid.
9. Debra Whitcomb, *When the Victim Is a Child* (Washington DC: National Institute of Justice, 1992), pp. 15–20.
10. D. Floyd, testimony before President's Task Force on Victims of Crime, Final Report, December 1982, p. 51.
11. J. Waterman, "Development Considerations," in K. MacFarlane and J. Waterman, eds., *Sexual Abuse of Young Children* (New York: Guilford Press, 1986), pp. 15–29.
12. W. M. Friedrich, J. Fischer, D. Broughton, D. Houston, and C. R. Shafran, "Normative Sexual Behavior in Children: A Contemporary Sample," *Pediatrics,* Vol. 101, No. 4, April P.E. 9.
13. A. Warren-Leubecker et al., "What Do Children Know about the Legal System and When Do They Know It? First Steps Down a Less-Traveled Path in Child Witness Research," in, S. J. Ceci, D. F. Ross, and M. P. Toglia, eds., *Perspectives on Children's Testimony* (New York: Springer-Verlag, 1989), pp. 158–183.
14. M. A. Young, "Working with Victims Who Are Children or Adolescents: Using the Lessons of Child Development with Young Trauma Victims," *NOVA Newsletter,* 1989, Vol. 13.
15. Warren-Leubecker et al., "What Do Children Know about the Legal System"; K. J. Saywitz, "Children's Conceptions of the Legal System: 'Court Is a Place to Play Basketball,' " in Ceci et al., *Perspectives on Children's Testimony,* pp. 131–157. Also see S. P. Limber, G. B. Melton, and S. J. Rahe, "Legal Knowledge, Attitudes, and Reasoning Abilities of Witnesses," paper presented at AP-LS Division 41 Biennial Convention, Williamsburg, Virginia, March 1990.
16. R. Pynoos and S. Eth, "The Child Witness to Homicide," *Journal of Social Issues,* 1984, Vol. 40, p. 98.
17. K. J. Saywitz and C. Jaenicke, "Children's Understanding of Legal Terms: A Preliminary Report of Grade-Related Trends," paper presented at the Society for Research on Child Development Biennial Meeting, Baltimore, Maryland, April 1987.
18. A. Warren-Leubecker et al., "What Do Children Know about the Legal System."
19. Whitcomb, *When the Victim Is a Child,* pp. 33–38. This discussion was adapted from this source.
20. Alabama, Connecticut, Michigan, New Jersey, New York, Pennsylvania, West Virginia, and Wyoming.
21. See, for example, *Cleveland v. State,* 490 N.R. 2nd 1140 (Ind. App. 1986); *People v. Garvie,* 148 Mich. App. 444, 384 N.W. 2d 796 (1986); *State v. Jenkins,* 326 N.W. 2d 67 (N.D. 1982).
22. E. Gray, "Children as Witnesses in Child Sexual Abuse Cases Study," Final Report submitted to the National Center on Child Abuse and Neglect under Grant No. 90-CA-1273, by the National Council of Jewish Women, New York, New York, 1990, p. 51. (Henceforth referred to as NCJW Study.)
23. K. R. Freemand and T. Estrada-Mullany, "Using Dolls to Interview Child Victims: Legal Concerns and Interview Procedures," *Research in Action,* National Institute of Justice, January/February 1988, p. 2.
24. White, pp. 472–473.
25. S. White and G. Santilli, "A Review of Clinical Practices and Research Data on Anatomical Dolls," *Journal of Interpersonal Violence,* December 1988, Vol. 3, pp. 437–439.
26. L. Berliner, "Anatomical Dolls," *Journal of Interpersonal Violence,* December 1988, Vol. 3, pp. 468–470; also see B. W. Boat and M. D. Everson, "Normative Data: How Non-Referred Young Children Interact with Anatomical Dolls," paper presented at the Symposium of Interviewing Children, cited in Berliner, "Anatomical Dolls," p. 469.
27. White and Santilli, "A Review of Clinical Practices," p. 431.
28. B. Boat and M. Everson, "Use of Anatomical Dolls among Professionals in Sexual Abuse Evaluations," *Child Abuse and Neglect,* 1988, Vol. 12, pp. 171–179.
29. K. MacFarlane and S. Krebs, "Techniques for Interviewing and Evidence Gathering," in MacFarlane and Waterman, *Sexual Abuse of Young Children,* pp. 74–75.
30. Ibid.

31. White and Santilli, "A Review of Clinical Practices," pp. 439–440.
32. Robert H. Farley, "Drawing Interviews: An Alternative Technique," *Police Chief,* 1987, pp. 37–38. Copyright held by the International Association of Chiefs of Police, Inc., 1110 North Glebe Road, Suite 200, Arlington, VA 22201. Further reproduction without express written permission from the IACP is strictly prohibited.
33. MacFarlane and Krebs, "Techniques for Interviewing and Evidence Gathering," p. 87.
34. NCJW Study, pp. 439–440.
35. S. J. Ceci, D. Ross, and M. Toglia, "Age Differences in Suggestibility: Narrowing the Uncertainties," in S. J. Ceci, M. P. Toglia, and D. F. Ross, eds., *Children's Eyewitness Memory* (New York: Springer-Verlag, 1987), pp. 79–91.
36. H. Wakefield and R. Underwager, "Techniques for Interviewing Children in Sexual Abuse Cases," *VOCAL Perspective,* Summer 1989, pp. 7–15.
37. K. Saywitz et al., "Children's Memories of Genital Examinations: Implications for Cases of Child Sexual Assault," paper presented at the Society for Research in Child Development Meetings, Kansas City, Missouri, 1989.
38. R. Lusk and J. Waterman, "Effects of Sexual Abuse on Children," in MacFarlane and Waterman, *Sexual Abuse of Young Children,* pp. 15–29. Also see A. Browne and D. Finkelhor, "Initial and Long-Term Effects: A Review of the Research," in D. Finkelhor et al., eds., *A Sourcebook on Child Sexual Abuse* (Beverly Hills: Sage, 1986), pp. 143–152.
39. J. R. Conte and J. R. Schuerman, "The Effects of Sexual Abuse on Children: A Multidimensional View," *Journal of Interpersonal Violence,* December 1987, Vol. 2, pp. 380–390.
40. W. N. Freidrich, R. L. Beilke, and A. J. Urquiza, "Children from Sexually Abusive Families: A Behavioral Comparison," *Journal of Interpersonal Violence,* December 1987, Vol. 2, pp. 391–402.
41. J. Conte et al., "Evaluating Children's Report of Sexual Abuse: Results from a Survey of Professionals," unpublished manuscript, University of Chicago, undated, cited in J. E. B. Myers et al., "Expert Testimony in Child Sexual Abuse Litigation," *Nebraska Law Review,* 1989, Vol. 68, p. 75.
42. Whitcomb, *When the Victim Is a Child,* pp. 6–11.
43. D. Jones and J. McGraw, "Reliable and Fictitious Accounts of Sexual Abuse to Children," *Journal of Interpersonal Violence,* March 1987, Vol. 2, pp. 27–45.
44. Ibid.
45. J. Paradise, A. Rostain, and M. Nathanson, "Substantiation of Sexual Abuse Charges When Parents Dispute Custody or Visitation," *Pediatrics,* June 1988, Vol. 81, pp. 835–839.
46. See, for example, E. P. Benedek and D. H. Schetky, "Allegations of Sexual Abuse in Child Custody and Visitation Disputes," in D. H. Schetky and E. P. Benedek, eds., *Emerging Issues in Child Psychiatry and the Law* (New York: Brunner/Mazel, 1985), pp. 145–158; A. H. Green, "True and False Allegations of Sexual Abuse in Child Custody Disputes," *Journal of the American Academy of Child Psychiatry,* 1986, Vol. 25, pp. 449–456.
47. For an excellent summary of the drawbacks of such studies, see D. Corwin et al., "Child Sexual Abuse and Custody Disputes: No Easy Answers," *Journal of Interpersonal Violence,* March 1987, Vol. 2, pp. 91–105; also see L. Berliner, "Deciding Whether a Child Has Been Sexually Abused," in E. B. Nicholson, ed., *Sexual Abuse Allegations in Custody and Visitation Cases* (Washington, DC: American Bar Association, 1988), pp. 48–69.
48. N. Thoennes and J. Pearson, "Summary of Findings from the Sexual Abuse Allegations Project," in Nicholson, *Sexual Abuse Allegations,* pp. 1–21.
49. D. Finkelhor, L. M. Williams, and N. Burns, *Nursery Crimes: Sexual Abuse in Day Care* (Newbury Park, CA: Sage, 1988).
50. Kenneth V. Lanning, *Child Molesters: A Behavioral Analysis for Law Enforcement Officers Investigating Cases of Child Sexual Exploitation,* 3rd ed. (Arlington, VA: National Center for Missing and Exploited Children, 1992), pp. 24–31. This entire discussion of child pornography has been reproduced (with minor changes) with permission. No part of this may be reproduced without the express written permission of the National Center for Missing and Exploited Children, 1-800-843-5678.
51. The Child Pornography Prevention Act, U.S. Code Title 18, Section 2252: Certain Activities Relating to Material Involving the Sexual Exploitation of Minors.
52. U.S. Code, Title 18, Section 2251: Sexual Exploitation of Children.
53. *In the Supreme Court of the United States John D. Ashcroft, Attorney General of the United States, et al., Petitioners, v. The Free Speech Coalition, et al.,* http:/www.usdoj.gov/osg/briefs/2000/3mer/2mer/2000-0795.mer.aa.html.
54. Supreme Court of the United States, www.supremecourtus.gov/index.html.

55. Donald M. Kerr, "Internet and Data Interception Capabilities Developed by the FBI," Statement for the Record, U.S. House of Representatives, Committee on the Judiciary, Subcommittee on the Constitution, www.cdt.org/security/carnivor/000724 fbi.shtml, July 24, 2000.

56. Holger, Kind, "Combating Child Pornography on the Internet by the German Federal Criminal Police Office (BKA),"

57. "14 Nations Join to Bust Huge Internet Child Porn Ring," www.cnn.com/WORLD/europe/9809/02/internet.porn.02/.

58. Marianne Ewig, Lynne Ketchum, and Carolyn Kott Washburne, "Incest," *Police Work,* April 1980, pp. 11–18. The discussion was taken with modifications from this source.

59. Heidi Vanderbilt, "Incest—A Chilling Report," *Lear's,* February 1992, pp. 49–64. For a more detailed discussion of the results of this study, see David Finkelhor and Linda Meyer Williams, University of New Hampshire, Family Research Laboratory, Durham, New Hampshire, 1992.

60. *A Resource Handbook: Sudden Infant Death Syndrome* (Tallahassee, FL: Department of Health and Rehabilitative Services, 1978), pp. 1–2. Much of the information dealing with SIDS was taken from this source.

61. Ann L. Ponsonby, Terrence Dwyer, Laura E. Gibbons, Jennifer A. Cochrane, and You-gan Wang, "Factors Potentiating the Risk of Sudden Infant Death Syndrome Associated with the Prone Position," *New England Journal of Medicine,* August 1993, Vol. 329, No. 6, p. 378. The scientists conducting this study analyzed data from a case-controlled study (58 infants with SIDS and 120 control infants) and perspective cohort study (22 infants with SIDS and 233 control infants) in Tasmania. Interactions were examined and math analyses done with a multiplicative model of interaction.

62. J. L. Emery and J. A. Thornton, "Affects of Obstruction to Respiration in Infants with Particular Reference to Mattresses, Pillows, and Their Coverings," *BMJ,* 1968, Vol. 3, pp. 309–313.

63. J. S. Kemp and B. T. Thach, "Sudden Infant Deaths in Sleeping on Polystyrene Filled Cushions," *New England Journal of Medicine,* 1991, Vol. 324, pp. 1858–1864.

64. J. A. Corbyn and P. Matthews, *Environmental Causes of Sudden Infant Death* (Freemantle, Australia: Western Technical Press, 1992); E. L. Ryan, "Distribution of Expired Air in Carrying Cots—A Possible Explanation for Some Sudden Infant Deaths," *Australias Phys. Eng. Sci. Med.,* 1991, Vol. 14, pp. 112–118.

65. David P. Southall, "Covert Video Recording of Life-Threatening Child Abuse: Lessons for Child Protection," *Pediatrics,* November 1997, Vol. 100, No. 5, pp. 735–760; Sharon Begley, "The Nursery's Littlest Victim," *Newsweek,* Sept. 22, 1997, p. 72.

66. Begley, "The Nursery's Littlest Victim."

67. L. G. Ankrom and C. J. Lent, "Cradle Robbers: A Study of the Infant Abductor," *FBI Law Enforcement Bulletin,* September 1995, pp. 12–17.

68. These interviews were conducted with funds provided by Interagency Agreement #91–MC-004, issued through the cooperation of the Office of Juvenile Justice and Delinquency Prevention.

69. P. Beachy and J. Deacon, "Preventing Neonatal Kidnapping," *Journal of GN,* 1991, Vol. 21, No. 1, pp. 11–16.

70. Ibid.

71. Ibid.

72. R. Grant, "The New Babysnatchers, *Redbook,* May 1990, p. 153.

73. Ibid., p. 152.

74. This discussion of age progression technology was adapted from a news release distributed by the National Center for Missing and Exploited Children, June 18, 1990.

75. Andre B. Simons and Jeannie Willie, "Runaway or Abduction? Assessment Tools for the First Responder," *FBI Law Enforcement Bulletin,* November 2000, pp. 1–7. This discussion was adapted from this source.

76. National Center for Missing and Exploited Children, *Investigator's Guide to Missing Child Cases* (Alexandria, VA: 1987), p. 2.

77. K. Hanfland, R. Keppel, and J. Weis, "Case Management for Missing Children: Homicide Investigation," Washington State Attorney General's Office, 1997.

78. Adapted from Federal Bureau of Investigation, *Child Abduction Response Plan,* Critical Incident Response Group, National Center for the Analysis of Violent Crime (Quantico, VA:), pp. 15–16.

79. For more information, agencies can contact the NCAVC coordinator at their local FBI field office.

80. Interview with Supervisory Special Agent Mark Hilts, Federal Bureau of Investigation, NCAVC, Mar. 2, 1999.

81. Office of Juvenile Justice and Delinquency Prevention, *National Incidence Studies of Missing, Abducted, Runaway, and Throwaway Children in America* (Washington, DC, U.S. Department of Justice, 1990) p. 63. (Law enforcement officers should consult with their departments' legal advisors to ensure that any search of a residence is legal.)
82. Federal Bureau of Investigation, *Child Abduction Response Plan,* p. 17.
83. Alan D. Scholle, "Sex Offender Registration," *FBI Law Enforcement Bulletin,* July 2000, pp. 17–24. This discussion was adapted from this source.
84. Patte Wetterling, "The Jacob Wetterling Story," speech, in Bureau of Justice Statistics, *National Conference on Sex Offender Registries: Proceedings of a BJS/SEARCH Conference,* NCJ 168965, Office of Justice Programs, Washington, DC, U.S. Department of Justice, April 1998, pp. 3–7.
85. Ibid., p. vii.
86. Ibid., pp. 3–7.
87. 42 U.S.C. §14071; National Criminal Justice Association, *Sex Offender Community Notification Policy Report* (Washington, DC: October 1997), p. 5.
88. The Edward Byrne Memorial State and Local Law Enforcement Assistance Program provides grants to states to "improve the functioning of the criminal justice system, with emphasis on violent crimes and serious offenders." Available from www.ojp.usdoj.gov/BJA/html/byrnef.htm, accessed Feb. 22, 2000.
89. Scott Matson and Roxanne Lieb, *Sex Offender Registration: A Review of State Laws* (Olympia: Washington State Institute for Public Policy, July 1996), p. 5.
90. 104. P.L. 145, 100 Stat. 1345; Wetterling, "The Jacob Wetterling Story," p. 8.
91. Wetterling, ibid., p. 1.
92. 42 U.S.C §14072; Wetterling, ibid., pp. 8–9. Congress named the act after Lychner when she and her two daughters died in the TWA Flight 800 explosion off the coast of Long Island in July 1996.
93. The National Sex Offender Registry (NSOR), which became operational in 1997, initially served as a pointer system for a convicted sex offender's record in the Interstate Identification Index. The permanent registry—part of NCIC (National Crime Information Center ) 2000—went online in 1999, replacing the earlier version. The NSOR flags sex offenders when agencies request authorized, fingerprint-based, criminal-history checks. Information provided by the Crimes against Children Unit, Criminal Investigative Division, FBI Headquarters, Washington, DC, Feb. 24, 2000.
94. The U.S. attorney general has set October 2001 as the date that the Department of Justice (DOJ) will determine whether states have met the compliance standards. To help states develop sex-offender registries, the DOJ provides funding, while the FBI's Criminal Justice Information Services Division assists with the technical aspects of the program. Information provided by the Crimes against Children Unit, Criminal Investigative Division, FBI Headquarters, Washington, DC, Feb. 24, 2000.
95. Edward Byrne Memorial, p. 1.
96. Ibid.
97. Elizabeth Rahmberg Walsh, "Megan's Laws: Sex Offender Registration and Notification Statutes and Constitutional Challenges," in *The Sex Offender,* Vol. 2 (Kingston, NJ: Civic Research Institute, 1997), p. 3.
98. Iowa Department of Public Safety, sex offender registry statistics, Apr. 28, 2000.
99. Scott Matson and Roxanne Lieb, *Sex Offender Community Notification: A Review of Laws in 32 States* (Olympia: Washington State Institute for Public Policy, July 1996), p. 3
100. Ibid., 2.
101. Peter Finn, *Sex Offender Community Notification* (Research in Brief), U.S. Department of Justice, Office of Justice Programs, National Institute of Justice (Washington, DC: February 1997), p. 3.
102. National Institute of Education, *Violent Schools—Safe Schools: The Safe School Study Report to the Congress,* Washington, DC: U.S. Department of Education, 1978.
103. National School Safety Center, "School Crime: Annual Statistical Snapshot," *School Safety* (Winter 1989).
104. Hall, J., "The Knife in the Book Bag." *Time* (May 22, 1993); Toch, T., T. Guest, and M. Guttman, "Violence in Schools: When Killers Come Home," *U.S. News and World Report* (Nov. 8, 1993).
105. The School Shooter: A Threat Assessment Perspective. National Center for the Analysis of Violent Crime, FBI National Academy, Quantico, VA, 2000, pp. 2–9. (Much of this discussion on crime in school was adapted from this source.)
106. C. Malmquist, Homicidal Violence, malq001@atlas.socsci.umn.edu.

107. Op cit., pp. 16–21.

108. Associated Press, "Police Chiefs Back After-School Programs," www.apbonline.com/cjprofessionals/behindthebadge/1991/11/01chiefs_children1101_01, Nov. 1, 1999.

109. Glenn Stutzky, "How to Battle the School Bully," an interview with *ABC News,* www.abcnews.go.com/sections/community/DailyNews/chat_bullying11298.html, Nov. 29, 2001.

110. James Blair, "The Ethics of Using Juvenile Informants: Murder in California Prompts New Bill, Raises Questions about Whether Minors Should Be Operatives," *Christian Science Monitor,* www.csmonitor.com/durable/1998/04/14/p3s1.htm, Apr. 14, 1998.

# TWELVE

# Robbery

*In recent years, convenience store clerks, taxicab drivers, pizza delivery persons, and the like have all been targeted in armed robberies. In an attempt to forestall such robberies, many of these kinds of businesses now display "warning" signs like the one pictured above alerting would-be robbers to the fact that minimal cash is on hand or accessible. (© Joel Gordon)*

## CHAPTER OUTLINE



## CHAPTER OBJECTIVES

1. Identify and explain the elements of robbery.
2. Describe the three styles of robberies based on the amount of planning involved.
3. Be familiar with the various types of robberies.
4. Discuss three explanations for the increase in carjackings.
5. Explain police response to the robbery scene and tactical situations at the scene.
6. Explain officers' responsibilities in the original robbery investigation and follow-up investigation.
7. Describe action, physical, and situational stereotyping.
8. Define and give examples of robbery preventive measures, anticipatory strategies, and reactive measures.

## INTRODUCTION

The importance of robbery resides in its economics, its frequency, its resistance to investigative efforts, the fear it creates, and the potential for violence that accompanies it. Robbery can occur in several contexts including visible street robberies, carjackings, home invasions, truck hijackings, and automatic-teller-machine robberies. Further, taxicab drivers and convenience-store personnel in particular are easy targets for robbery because they often work alone at all hours of the day and night, with minimal or no protection from robbers, and a large part of the business they conduct is on a cash basis. Similar to their variation by place, robberies also vary in terms of the amount of time spent on their planning: Some robberies occur without any planning; others involve considerable premeditation.

Because of the face-to-face confrontation between perpetrator and victim, the potential for violence is always present in a robbery. When violence does occur, it may range from minor injury to loss of life. Due to its personal and often violent nature, robbery is one of the crimes most feared by the public, a fear that may be heightened by perceptions of police inability to deal effectively with robberies. However, witnesses are often upset and may have seen the perpetrator only briefly—factors that sometimes limit how much they can assist the investigative process. This, coupled with the fact that most offenders operate alone, can make robbery investigations extremely difficult. Mitigating the investigative challenge are recent identification technologies that make is possible to quickly generate and distribute a likeness of a suspect. When security cameras are present and operating, they can also be of major assistance in providing leads.

In coping with a heightened sense of fear and alarm, robbery victims often seek guidance and advice to help prevent repeat victimization. Along with arresting suspects and recovering the victim's property, investigators and their departments can serve in a crime prevention role. Providing the public with tips on what to do before, during, and after a robbery cannot only help prevent robberies but also help lessen the chance of repeat victimizations.

## ELEMENTS OF THE CRIME

In order for a crime to be considered **robbery** it should consist of the following elements: the (1) taking and (2) carrying away of (3) personal property of (4) another, with (5) the intent to deprive permanently, by (6) the use of force, fear, or threat of force.

### TAKING

The property taken in a robbery must be taken illegally by the robber. Someone who has the right to take such property cannot properly be convicted of robbery. This illegal taking is called **trespassory.** The property must be taken from the custody, control, or possession of the victim and, as will be seen later, from the victim's presence. This element of the crime is satisfied once the robber has possession of the property; until possession has occurred, only an attempt has taken place.

### CARRYING AWAY

Once the element of taking has been satisfied, the robber must then carry away the property. As is true in the crime of larceny, this element can be satisfied simply by showing that the accused totally removed the article from the position that it formerly occupied. It is not necessary to show that any great distance was involved in the carrying away.

### PERSONAL PROPERTY

The object of the robbery must be personal property as opposed to real estate or things attached to the land. Again as in larceny, any tangible property and some forms of intangible property represented by tangible items, such as stocks and bonds, gas, electricity, minerals, and other such commodities, can be objects of robbery.

### ANOTHER

The property taken must belong to another, not to the accused. This again relates to the first element of taking. If the taking is trespassory—illegal—then the property must be the rightful property of someone other than the robber.

### THE INTENT TO DEPRIVE PERMANENTLY

Robbery is a crime of specific intent and requires that the prosecution establish, in court, that the defendant, at the time of taking the property by force or threat of force from the victim or the victim's presence, did, in fact, intend to deprive the victim of the use and enjoyment of that property permanently. In most cases this can be concluded from the facts and circumstances surrounding the case, but in specific-intent crime cases juries are not permitted to assume this particular fact. Thus, the police officer's investigation must be geared to establishing this as an essential element of the crime. The fact that force or the threat of force was used to secure the property from the victim is often enough to convince a jury of the accused's intent to deprive permanently.

## THE USE OF FORCE, FEAR, OR THREAT OF FORCE

This element of the crime requires that the force or threat of force be directed against the physical safety of the victim rather than his or her social well-being. Thus, threats to expose the victim as a homosexual or an embezzler do not satisfy this element of the crime. Proof that force was used or, at the very least, that threats were made such that the victim feared imminent bodily harm is essential for successful prosecutions of robbery cases. The taking of property without force is simply a theft. However, the force used to separate the victim from his or her property in robbery need not be great.

When the victim of a robbery is seriously injured, there is usually little difficulty in convincing the investigator or the jury that force was used. However, difficulties may arise in the case of a victim who claims to have been robbed under the threat of force when no actual injury occurred. In this case, the skill of the investigator in determining the facts of the case becomes crucial to successful prosecution.

There are also more subtle situations in which the investigator must know legal requirements as well as investigative techniques. The typical purse-snatching case is an illustration. Often, the force element of the crime of robbery can be satisfied only by determining whether the victim attempted to resist the force used and, if so, the extent of that resistance. It is generally accepted by courts that a woman who puts her purse next to her on the seat of a bus without keeping her hand on it or loosely holds it in her hand is not the victim of robbery if someone quickly grabs the purse and runs. In these cases, the woman has not resisted. However, if she were clutching the bag tightly and someone managed to grab it from her after even a slight struggle, sufficient force and resistance would have occurred to constitute robbery. A good rule for the investigator to follow in cases of uncertainty is that the removal of an article without more force than is absolutely necessary to remove it from its original resting place constitutes larceny. If any additional force, no matter how slight, is used, it is then robbery, provided the object is taken from the presence or person of the victim. The property does not have to be held by the victim physically or be on his or her person. It merely has to be under the victim's control. "Control" in this sense means the right or privilege to use the property as the victim sees fit. Neither is it necessary or essential that the property be visible to the victim when the crime is committed.

The force or threat of force must precede or accompany the taking. Force applied after the taking does not constitute robbery. Thus a victim who realizes that his or her property has been stolen and attempts to recover that property, at which time force ensues, is not the victim of a robbery if the property was originally taken surreptitiously and without force.

When force is not used but a threat to the physical well-being of the victim is indeed made, it is not necessary that the victim actually be frightened to the point of panic. It is enough that the victim is reasonably apprehensive and aware of the potential for injury.

# OVERVIEW: THE OFFENSE, THE VICTIM, AND THE OFFENDER

When generalizing about offenses, victims, and offenders, certain limitations must be acknowledged. Research findings are occasionally inconclusive and conflicting. A variety of factors account for this. For example, a study of the various aspects of robbery in one city has limited generalization power because, while cities may share certain characteristics, such factors are not precisely duplicated from city to city or perhaps not even in the same city over time. If we attempt to compensate for this factor by using national data, a general picture emerges and individual differences disappear. If we use an intensive scrutiny of a smaller number of cases, their profile may not be like that of other intensive studies or the general profile. Additionally, a limitation common to most studies of criminals is that we are focusing on those who "failed," that is, those who were caught and whose resemblance to those not apprehended is a matter of conjecture. Despite such issues, information concerning offenses, victims, and offenders is useful in providing a qualified frame of reference.

Robbery is essentially a problem of large cities. In metropolitan areas the robbery rate per 100,000 people is 180.[1] However, in cities outside of metro areas the robbery rate is only 67 and in rural areas it is 15.[2] Regionally, the most populous southern states registered 37 percent of all reported robberies.[3] Table 12–1 indicates the settings of reported robberies nationally.

In terms of weapons used, a firearm is used in 40 percent of the incidents, a knife or other cutting instrument in 8 percent of the cases, and "some other weapon" in another 10 percent of reported robberies; the remaining 42 percent of the incidents are "strong-armed," meaning no weapon was used.[4] An illustration of the use of "some other weapon" is the robbery of a convenience store by a man using a hypodermic needle filled with what he claimed was AIDS-contaminated blood. Together these data reveal that approximately 6 of every 10 robberies are armed and the balance are strong-armed. Armed robbers often carry two or more weapons. Because of this, officers must continue to exercise great caution when approaching a suspect who has thrown a weapon down.

About one-third of all robberies result in a physical injury to the victim.[5] Females are about 10 percent more likely to be injured than are males, while Caucasians and African Americans face nearly the same prospects for being injured.[6] Robbery is basically a stranger-to-stranger crime: 71 percent of the time the robber and victim do not know each other.[7] About 60 percent of all robberies are committed by a single offender.[8] This factor tends to make robbery investigations more difficult: if the sole offender can keep his or her mouth shut, does not attract attention to himself/herself or run with other criminals, and does not get a bad break, the offender can be hard to catch. Although a small number of victims fight back in some way, in 82 percent of robberies it is the offender who initiates violence.[9]

The objective of the confrontation between robber and victim is to get the victim's immediate compliance. In most situations, the mere showing of a gun will accomplish this. One offender reports, "Sometimes I don't even touch them; I just point the gun right in front of their face. I don't even have to say nothing half the time. When they see that pistol, they know what time it is."[10] A victim who hesitates or is seen as uncooperative may or may not get a warning:

**Table 12-1** Settings of Robberies as Reported Nationally

| Setting | Percentage of Total |
|---|---|
| Street or highway | 48.3% |
| Commercial house | 13.8 |
| Gas or service station | 2.2 |
| Convenience store | 6.0 |
| Residence | 12.2 |
| Bank | 2.0 |
| Miscellaneous | 15.8 |
| Total | 100.0 |

**Source:** Federal Bureau of Investigation, *Crime in the United States–1999* (Washington, DC: Government Printing Office, 2000), p. 28.

> If I run up to you with a revolver like this and then you hesitate, I'm gonna cock it back and that will be your warning right there.[11]
>
> If they think I'm bullshitting, I'll smack them up in the M____ F____ head. You'd be surprised how cooperative a person will be once he has been smashed across the face with a .357 Magnum.[12]

Other robbers are less "tolerant," and when faced with uncooperative victims, they will shoot them in the leg or foot. However, for some offenders injuring the victim is part of the thrill, the "kick" of "pulling a job." What type of violence is used and when it is used may form part of an identifiable modus operandi. Such an MO can tie together several robberies, and the combined information from various investigations often produces significant investigative leads.

There is not a great deal of variation in robberies by month, although December has the highest.[13] Forty-four percent of robberies take place between 6 A.M. and 6 P.M. and another 40 percent between 6 P.M. and midnight.[14] The average dollar loss nationally per robbery is $1,131, with an average loss of $620 for convenience stores and $4,552 for banks.[15]

There is no question that being under the influence and committing robberies are intimately related. Victims believe that 28 percent of those robbing them are high on drugs and/or alcohol.[16] Some offenders use alcohol to lessen their apprehension about getting caught:

> When you get it in your head to do a stickup and you get high, you ain't gonna care no more about getting caught . . . that's why me and my partners get high so much. We get high and stupid . . . whatever happens, happens . . . you don't care at the time.[17]

Robbery is basically an intraracial crime; in one study, blacks said that they were robbed by blacks 80 percent of the time, and whites said that they were robbed by whites 75 percent of the time.[18] Nationally, among those apprehended for robbery, 90 percent are males, 54 percent are blacks, and 19 percent are under 25 years of age.[19]

Although no robbery is routine to victims, many cases are fairly straightforward to investigators. Some robberies, however, stand out because of unusual circumstances, as the following incidents illustrate:

A lone robber held up a bank and made off with $600. As police were chasing him, the robber crashed the stolen Chevrolet Suburban he was driving. It burst into flames and the money burned up. Now being pursued on foot by a police officer, the robber tossed off his plaid jacket and escaped. The police found a napkin with a name and telephone number in the jacket. With the bank's surveillance photos in hand, the police confronted the man identified on the napkin. In turn, he identified the robber as someone whom he had been letting sleep on his couch. An arrest was subsequently made in the case.[20]

TWO thugs were cruising in a residential area looking for someone to rob. They spotted two men playing pool in an open garage. Blissfully unaware that the two men were off-duty police officers, the thugs approached them and placed a gun to one officer's head and the officer began to struggle. The second officer pulled a weapon and shot both offenders.[21]

A teenage boy robbed a convenience store at knifepoint around 1:30 in the morning, taking money and merchandise and fleeing on foot. The police solved the case by following the offender's shoeprints in the freshly fallen snow straight to his home.[22]

A Marathon gas station clerk reported that she was held up by two men. On the basis of this information, the police notified area businesses of the crime and the descriptions of the two "suspects." Within a week, the clerk admitted she had stolen the money and made up the robbery story. Not knowing that the police had already "solved" the Marathon robbery, a worker at a nearby Pappa John's Pizzeria reported that he was also robbed by the two men who had done the Marathon robbery. When police explained the facts of the Marathon case, the worker admitted to fabricating the robbery story to conceal his theft of money from the store.[23]

Despite such variations, three styles of robberies—the ambush, the selective raid, and the planned operation—can be classified according to the amount of planning conducted by the perpetrators. The **ambush** involves virtually no planning and depends almost entirely on the element of surprise. A prime example is robberies in which victims are physically overpowered by sudden, crude force and in which "scores" are generally small.[24] The lack of planning does not mean, however, that there is no premeditation, a distinction made by one offender:

> I never really did any planning, as you see it. I pulled robberies at random . . . without disguises or anything. . . . But you must understand one thing, just because I didn't do "planning" as you describe it doesn't mean I didn't think about crime a lot. I had to get myself mentally ready to do crimes. This doesn't mean I planned . . . but . . . I was thinking and preparing for crime constantly; I simply waited for the right circumstances to occur. When I saw the time was right, I would pull the job.[25]

The **selective raid** is characterized by a minimal amount of casual planning. Sites are tentatively selected and very briefly cased, and possible routes of approach and flight are formulated. Scores vary from low to moderate, and several robberies may be committed in rapid succession:

> When I get ready to fall in for one, I visit the place a couple of times in one day. I want to

> see how it's laid out, how to get away as quick as possible and what kind of people work there . . . women are bad to rob because they get all emotional . . . if the man there looks hard, I might not even mess with the place. You can tell what people are like by the way they present themselves. . . . I wouldn't want to just blow a family man away, but if it's me or him, that's business. I like to do pharmacies because besides the money, there's drugs and on the streets that's the same as cash. You can't even worry about being caught because that is negative thinking. . . . I don't mess with no disguises, I just go to someplace like about 25 or 30 miles away where nobody knows me and do it, sometimes a couple real quick if I'm on a roll. Before I go out to do one, I try to relax and fish or make love a lot. You want your head to be right because it could be your life or someone else's. I don't do no pills or drink until after the work for the same reason . . . but if I need the money and have been doing some of that shit, I'll just go ahead and pull one, but working that way is dangerous.[26]

The **planned operation** is characterized by larger "scores," no planned use of force, less likelihood of apprehension, and careful planning:

> The reason I was never apprehended in five years was because I never had any partners, I worked alone, kept my own counsel, I wasn't on an ego trip—I wasn't shooting my mouth off to the girls I went around with, I changed my name like I changed my socks. I had four different aliases during that period—legitimate aliases where I would go down and get a driver's license in a different name and tell them that I was retired military or had just gotten discharged after thirteen years and didn't have a current license, and the only license I had was a military license. With the driver's license, I opened up savings accounts, checking accounts, and so forth. As far as the friends I had at the time, I never knew a thief in my life. Not even when I was robbing banks. I never knew a thief until I went to prison.
>
> I would go into the bank well dressed—suit and so forth, dyed hair and moustache, a couple of sweatshirts under the suit to make me look heavier, a hat to make me look taller . . . never sunglasses . . . and an attaché case and so forth. And I would go into the manager's outer office where his secretary was by saying I had an appointment or something like this. To make an impression on her, I [would show her my pistol]. I wanted [the manager] to call his chief teller or whoever he considered the most reliable and tell him to take my attaché case into the vault and come out with all the larger bills—no ones, fives, or tens—which, incidentally, led to my downfall, that little old line, because I may just as well have signed my name to every bank I ever robbed. So the guy would go out and bring the money back, and then I would have him open the attaché [so I could check it and see] how much money was in it. If it looked like a considerable sum of money, then I had transacted my business. Very rarely was anyone in the bank aware of what was going on. I wanted to be in and out of there in three minutes flat.
>
> The way I left the bank is—I never stole a car in my life—I'd buy a clunker for a few hundred dollars two weeks before I robbed the bank. This guy advertised in the paper, and you go, give him the money, sign the slip, and that's all there is to it. You never reregister it; you use it two times—driving it from where you bought it and the next time when you rob the bank. Then you ditch it within one minute, however far you can get. I used to pick a shopping center within a mile or whatever of the bank, and there I'd have my other car, and I'd switch cars. And I would be wearing these dishwashing type gloves so there would be no fingerprints. Sometimes I'd let the car be running with the key in it, hoping some kid would steal it. I'd be tickled to death if he'd run off with it! And then of course I would change clothes and sometimes take the old clothes and throw them in a convenient garbage can, Goodwill box, or whatever. Then I'd take cover, more or less, whether it be a local hotel, motel, crowded part of town, and I'd just stay inside.[27]

## TYPOLOGY OF ROBBERIES

In addition to knowing the broad profile of the offense, the investigator must also be familiar with various types of robberies.

## VISIBLE STREET ROBBERIES

Approximately 5 of every 10 robberies happen on the street.[28] In 93 percent of the cases, the victim is alone[29] and typically on the way to or from a leisure activity within 5 miles of his or her home,[30] such as patronizing a nightclub or restaurant:[31]

> I'd watch people in bars and follow them. One time, I followed this guy and grabbed his tie and swung it down to the ground. And, uh, he hit his head and that's when I took the money and ran.[32]

The victim is three times more likely to be confronted by a single perpetrator than by multiple perpetrators.[33] Youthful robbers are particularly likely to commit **strong-armed robberies**—also referred to as **muggings**—in which no weapons are involved and in which they suddenly physically attack and beat the victim, taking cash, jewelry, wallets, purses, and other valuables. Purse snatching may or may not be a robbery. If a woman is carrying a purse loosely on her open fingers and someone grabs it and runs and she then experiences fear, robbery is not an appropriate charge because the fear did not precede the taking. But if the same woman sees or hears someone running toward her and in fear clutches her purse, which is then ripped from her by the perpetrator, a robbery has occurred.

Street robberies usually involve little or no planning by the perpetrators. They may have been waiting in one place for a potential victim to appear, or they may walk around looking for someone to rob on the spur of the moment:

> You know, we knew we was going . . . to stick somebody up, but we wasn't gonna be like, let's rob her . . . we just did it, just you know, whoever we saw.[34]

Another perpetrator expressed a similar view about the amount of planning he did prior to a robbery:

> Well, once the gun was bought you might say it was planned, but, you know as far as who or where, no. That was kind of spontaneous. You have to have an eye open for that type of thing.[35]

Because street robberies happen so quickly and often occur at night in areas that are not well lighted, victims often have difficulty providing anything more than a basic physical description. The description may be even more limited if the victim is injured either by a weapon or by a beating in a sudden, overpowering mugging.

Spontaneous street robbers may "graduate" to jobs that involve a certain amount of planning. For example, they may stake out automatic teller machines (ATMs) or banks. In the case of ATMs, they may have decided that they are going to rob the first "soft-looking" person who is alone and driving an expensive car. In the case of banks, they may rob someone on the street whom they have watched long enough to know that the person is going to the bank to make a cash deposit or to use the night depository. Although people sometimes commit robberies for excitement or to be "one of the guys," for the most part they do it to get the money, which often goes to pay for drugs:

> When I first started it was for fun. I was 15. I wanted to be down with the group. We'd just take things . . . chains, jewelry, stuff like that. Now, it is to take care of my habit. It is money for drugs.[36]

## CARJACKINGS

During the 1960s, many cars were stolen as temporary transportation by youthful offenders who used them for "joyriding" and then abandoned them. In many states the criminal statutes recognized both a felony auto theft and a misdemeanor joyriding charge. Around 1970, there was a shift to stealing cars for their parts and an increase in stealing cars for resale here and abroad, after they had been "repapered," meaning that the vehicles were given new, false identities.

In conventional auto thefts, the car is removed surreptitiously and there is no contact between the thief and the vehicle's owner. Before 1990, if an offender used a weapon to confront an owner and steal the person's car, the crime was simply classified as a robbery. But in 1990, with the number of such incidents increasing, the term **carjacking** was coined in Detroit to describe the growing numbers of this potentially violent type of confrontation between offender and victim.[37]

In 1992, "carjacking" became a household word nationwide when two men carjacked Pamela Basu's BMW at a stop sign. Entangled in her seat belt, Basu was dragged for more than 1 mile and died of her injuries. Her 22-month-old daughter, strapped in a car seat, survived after being thrown from the vehicle a few blocks from where the BMW had been seized.[38] As a result of the Basu and other highly publicized incidents, some jurisdictions enacted laws making carjacking a felony with stiff penalties. Although state statutes vary, the elements of the crime of carjacking are (1) the taking of a motor vehicle from the person or the immediate presence (2) of the motorist or passenger, (3) by use of force, fear, or threat of force, (4) with the intent to temporarily or permanently deprive the owner of its use.

One explanation for the increase in carjackings is that such crimes are the result of too much success in the antitheft-device market, including tracking devices such as Lojack, the Club, computer chips in ignition keys, and motion sensors. A second explanation is that there is a widespread supply of potential victims, no skill is required, no inside information is needed, and the need for planning is minimal. Also, publicity about this crime may create some incentive to "do one." For example, shortly after a San Diego newspaper ran a front-page story about carjacking, the number of such incidents leaped from 10 to 22 per month.[39]

The thought of being carjacked frightens people in two major ways: (1) the possibility of being injured or killed by the perpetrator and (2) the realization that cars are no longer "bubbles of safety," that simply going to or from one's car can be dangerous.[40]

There are about 49,000 nonfatal carjackings annually and about 27 fatal auto thefts.[41] Eight out of 10 carjackings are completed with a weapon, and overwhelmingly the weapon of choice is a gun.[42] Ninety-seven percent of offenders are male; typically a carjacking involves two or more offenders, who are perceived to be black, and 64 percent of the time they strike between 6 A.M. and 6 P.M. when many people are leaving for or returning from work.[43] Injuries occur in 16 percent of carjackings; serious injuries, such as gunshot or knife wounds, broken bones, and loss of consciousness, take place in 4 percent of such offenses.[44]

In terms of location, 44 percent of carjackings occur at the victim's home or within 1 mile of the victim's home; 85 percent happen within 5 miles of the victim's home. [45] Often this offense is committed at gas stations, ATMs, car washes, parking decks, shopping-center parking lots, and convenience stores; at restaurant, bar, office, train station, apartment, and public transportation parking lots; and at traffic control signs and signals.[46] In 70 percent of the cases at least some of the victim's property is returned.[47]

Carjackers tend to operate in small groups of two to five perpetrators. The modus operandi used is to quickly separate the person from the car. In some instances, doing so may be as quick and violent as using a brick to shatter the driver-side window of an occupied car and manhandling the occupant out of the vehicle. Mothers with children

**Abandoned Vehicle from Carjacking**

Since the 1990s, offenders using weapons to confront owners and steal their cars has become commonplace. The term associated with this crime is carjacking. Carjackers tend to operate in small groups of two to five perpetrators and often strip cars for parts and abandon them, as shown here.

(© Joseph Sohm, ChromoSohm Inc./Corbis)

are particularly vulnerable when confronted by offenders who threaten to harm the children if the keys to the car are not given up immediately. One method of carjacking involves accidentally bumping the victim's car from the rear; when the driver gets out to investigate, one perpetrator pulls a gun, takes control of the victim's car, and flees, followed by his or her accomplices in the "bumper car." Another tactic is to use several cars to "box in" the target vehicle and then slow down gradually until it is stopped and the victim can be dealt with. Some carjackers target victims who drive into high-crime areas to buy drugs; some watch expensive cars in parking lots and then carjack them because they believe the victims are more likely to have jewelry and cash that can also be taken.

According to the FBI, the primary motives for carjacking are to acquire transportation away from the crime scene after robbing the driver, to get to and from another crime, such as another robbery or a drive-by shooting, to sell the car for cash, to trade it for drugs,[48] and to acquire temporary transportation. Whenever a carjacking takes place, the potential for a more serious crime exists:

A woman had taken the rail from downtown to a heavily used suburban stop where her husband was waiting for her in their car. As she left the train, she heard gunshots and rushed to the street, where she found her husband dying of wounds inflicted by carjackers. When later arrested, the offenders said they were waiting to take the rail into the city, but decided to carjack the car so they could drive downtown instead.

Carjacking may also be a tool used by perpetrators to execute other crimes, which can lead to murder. A woman was carjacked and then forced into another car by the offenders. She was taken to a different location and raped. Later, she was forced to make several ATM withdrawals. Over the next several days, she was further abused and then executed by being slowly strangled with a coat hanger by one of the perpetrators while the others taunted her and cheered the executioner.

## HOME-INVASION ROBBERIES

Robberies in which one or more perpetrators actually enter the home make up about 12 percent of reported robberies.[49] Although deliberate **home invasion robberies (HIRs)** are thought to be a recent development, their roots can be traced to the "cocaine cowboys" operating in South Florida in the late 1970s and early 1980s.[50] Rival drug dealers and drug bandits saw HIRs as a quick and effective means of obtaining large amounts of drugs and cash.[51] Subsequently, this very violent modus operandi was copied by other criminals.

Home invaders typically target the person, rather than the residence, often selecting women, and senior citizens.[52] Invaders often follow potential targets from shopping centers to their homes. They may enter the residence through an unlocked door or window, talk an unsuspecting victim into opening the door, or simply force the door open:

THREE men wearing rubber gloves and face masks forced their way into a home. They tied the victims up with cords cut from the home's venetian blinds, placed guns to their heads, and demanded jewelry, cash, and the keys to a Ford Explorer in the driveway. Two hours after the suspects had fled, one of the victims was able to free himself and called the police. During the investigation the victims related that when the incident started, the robbers parked an older-model blue Cadillac in their driveway and walked to the door and that they had also seen the same car drive by earlier in the day.[53]

Occasionally targets turn out to be much more difficult than the offenders could possibly imagine: Two intruders got more than they bargained for when, after knocking a farmhouse door down, they were attacked by the couple living there. The woman threw scalding water on them, giving the husband time to start his chain saw.[54] When the police arrived, one invader was laying on the lawn bleeding profusely and the other one was apprehended nearby.

In some cases, the targets are "fingered," or identified, by others who pass information on to the invaders for drugs or money. Such offenders will also use deceit to gain entry into a residence. Home invaders pose as police officers, water department employees, florists delivering bouquets, motorists who have "just struck your parked car," natural gas and electric company representatives, and "supervisors checking on your newspaper delivery service," to name just a few, to get people to initially open their doors:

> **TWO** men knocked on the door of a home and asked to use the telephone. After gaining entry by this ruse and casing the place, they decided the home was worth robbing. They returned that afternoon, forced their way in, severely beat the couple—who were in their late seventies—and left with valuables and the victims' pickup truck.[55]

Invaders tend to work in "crews" of two to seven men who may work in a single city or travel nationally to commit their crimes. In some instances, these crews are ethnically based, such as Asians, who specialize on preying on those who share their heritage. Whatever their composition, the gangs carry firearms, handcuffs, tape, masks, and clubs, which they employ to strike terror in their victims and to achieve maximum control over the victims. Gangs burst into houses shouting and striking people, often forcing them to lay face-down on the floor. In addition to making family members easier to control, this tactic also makes it harder for victims to give good descriptions of the invaders to the police. The offenders may also threaten to shoot children and may strip and fondle females, break plates over victims' heads, and fire warning shots, all of which are intended to ensure swift and total compliance to their commands.[56] In some cities juvenile invaders have quickly struck a room or two at a motel and then vanished back into the security of their neighborhoods, knowing that the victims are usually from out of town—a circumstance that will hinder prosecutorial efforts if gang members are apprehended.

## AUTOMATIC-TELLER-MACHINE ROBBERIES

Automatic teller machines were introduced in the early 1970s, and their use has grown at a staggering rate since then. Today, there are approximately 12 billion ATM transactions annually.[57] At one point robberies at these locations were so publicized that critics referred to ATMs as "magnets for crime." However, the ATM robbery rate has dropped from 1 robbery per 1 million transactions during the 1990s to its present 1 per 3.5 million transactions.[58] A combination of factors account for this drop, including locating ATMs where customers has high visibility of their surroundings, using landscaping of 24 inches or less in height, and keeping the ATM areas well-lit at night.[59] In addition, customers are becoming knowledgeable about self-protection measures and are adopting them. Despite such realities, public fear of being victimized at or near an ATM is substantial.

The ATM robbery victim is typically a lone woman who is using the machine between 8 P.M. and midnight.[60] To minimize the time spent with

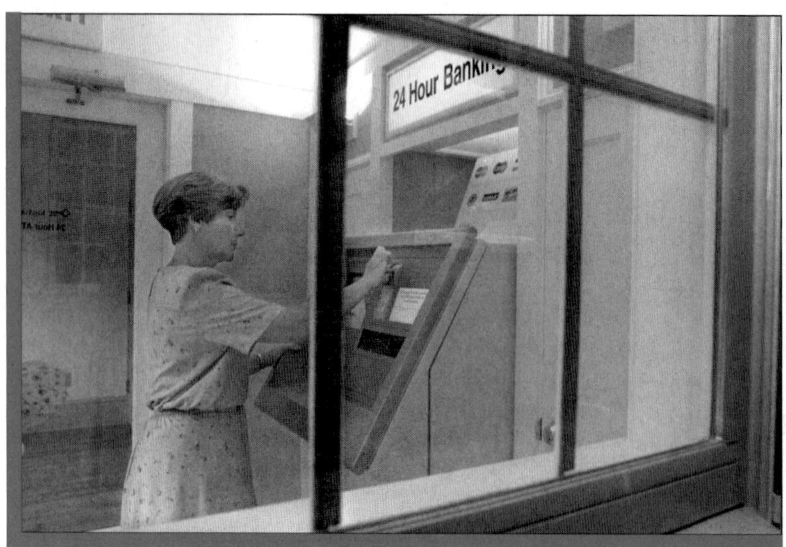


**Automatic Teller Machines: A Natural Target for Robberies**
Automatic teller machines are very popluar today as a means of obtaining on-the-spot cash. At one point, robberies at these locations were so frequent that critics referred to ATMs as "magnets for crime." Placing ATMs in highly visible areas and improving surrounding lighting has led to a decrease in this form of robbery over the last few years.
(© Syracuse Newspapers/The Image Works)

the victim and to avoid having to pressure the victim to make a withdrawal, many offenders simply wait until the transaction is completed before they pounce. Others confront the victim before the transaction, forcing her or him to make large withdrawals. Many victims report that they never saw the robber coming.

Offenders are most likely to work alone and are typically armed. They are usually about 25 years of age and tend to position themselves near an ATM, waiting for a likely victim to appear.[61] In addition to taking the cash and any valuables the victim has, offenders may carjack the victim's vehicle to flee the scene.

ATM service teams, which bring cash to the machines, are also subject to being robbed. Offenders who target them need inside information and have to recruit "associates"; they also must conduct a thorough reconnaissance of areas where the target could be approached, develop a workable plan, have several vehicles not traceable to them, acquire appropriate weapons, and have a place where they can "go to ground" for several days afterward. In short, they are most likely to be professionals who have records and are willing to use violence.

## TAXICAB ROBBERIES

Taxicab drivers are easy targets because they work alone, are available at all times of the day and night, do business on a cash basis, and can be called or directed to locations that favor the aims of offenders. As a result cab drivers have a higher criminal homicide victimization rate than any other occupational group in the United States.[62] Knowing this, cabbies take precautions and a few even have miraculous escapes:

> **TWO** armed robbers sat in the backseat of a taxi. One placed a gun to the driver's head and pulled the trigger. The shooter's gun either misfired or wasn't loaded. As the gunman fiddled with his weapon, the cabbie slammed the taxi into reverse and floored it. Alarmed at being jostled around, the two robbers "bailed out" and the driver escaped unharmed.[63]

Robberies of taxicabs frequently occur during the evening hours. Perpetrators are typically armed and have set out with the intent to do a robbery. The reasons given by offenders range from "I needed money to pay my bills" to "I wanted to get some money to party." When perpetrators have been drinking and/or doing drugs, the opportunity for violence is increased. In a common method of operation for this type of robbery, the perpetrator hails a taxi on the street or calls one to meet him or her at a particular intersection. The robber climbs inside the cab and asks to be driven to a particular location. At any point during the ride, the "fare" tells the driver to stop and then robs the driver. The robbery may take place when the cab is in a relatively secluded area or at the heart of a busy intersection where the offender can simply meld into the crowd. Calling a cab implies that the robber doesn't have his or her own transportation. Sometimes, however, the robbery occurs near a place where an accomplice is waiting with a getaway car.

In Houston, Washington, DC, and other cities, digital cameras have been installed in taxis, taking a picture when the doors are opened, when the meter is activated, and at unspecified intervals during the ride. Offenders are being apprehended and successfully prosecuted on the basis of photographs that were taken.[64]

## CONVENIENCE-STORE ROBBERIES

Although spectacular robberies, such as the $1 million robbery of a Las Vegas jewelry store by a lone gunman,[65] capture the interest of the media and public, investigators are more likely to work commercial robberies where far less is taken, such as the losses incurred by convenience stores.

As shown in Table 12–1, convenience stores account for about 6 percent of all reported robberies. These stores do a great deal of business in cash, are often open 24 hours a day, have numerous locations, typically offer no or minimal protection from robbers, and may have only one person on duty (see photo on page 444). Inasmuch as some of these characteristics also apply to taxicabs, it is not surprising that convenience-store workers, like cab drivers, are among the occupational groups having the highest risk for workplace violence.[66]

A study of 1,835 convenience-store robberies showed that 59 percent of them happened at night, between 9 P.M. and 3 A.M., and that the offender was armed with a firearm in 63 percent of the cases.[67] Employees were more likely to be injured

**Robbery of a Convenience Store**

Working as a pair, one robber takes the cash from the till while his accomplice controls the clerk by using physical force and holding a weapon in the clerk's back.

(Courtesy Phoenix, Arizona, Police Department)

when the offender used a blunt object, as opposed to a firearm, although all worker deaths were by firearms. Among the factors that contribute to lowering the probability of employee injury are the presence of a customer in the store, the store's having previously been robbed multiple times, and the robber's getting some money as opposed to getting none.

When robbers are choosing a store to rob, the factors that are most important to them are the amount of money they can get, a good escape route, inadequate police coverage, an unarmed clerk, a lone employee, no video surveillance cameras, and the absence of customers.[68]

There is some evidence that certain measures are associated with lower rates of being robbed. These include locating the cash registers in the center of the convenience store, having good visibility into the store from outside of it, installing bright parking-lot lighting, having two workers on duty, not counting money in the open, and posting signs noting that there is only a limited amount of money, e.g., $100, in the till.[69]

## TRUCK-HIJACKING ROBBERIES

In the United States, cargo theft may be responsible for losses of $10 billion to $12 billion a year.[70] If so, the only crime category with a higher dollar loss is health care fraud. The estimate for cargo-theft losses includes both cargo theft and truck hijacking. It is believed that hijacking accounts for a significant percentage of total cargo-theft losses, but because crime statistics on it are not kept, no one knows what the percentage really is. As cargo theft through hijacking has increasingly been recognized as a significant crime problem, there have been calls to gather statistics for it in the National Incident Based Reporting System (NIBRS). The FBI office in Long Beach, California, estimates that cargo-theft losses in that region are $1 million per day.[71] It should also be noted that truck hijacking is not a uniquely American problem. For example, in Argentina, truck hijackers are referred to as *piratas del asfalto,* which means "asphalt pirates."

The fact that accurate statistics are needed has not discouraged law enforcement agencies from making important moves to combat this crime problem. Large agencies, such as the New Jersey State Police, have created Cargo Theft and Robbery Investigative Units, while others have adopted the use of multiagency task forces and Cargo Criminal Apprehension Teams (Cargo CATs). Additionally, specialized law enforcement groups, such as the Western States Cargo Theft Association, exist to supply training and to exchange information on this subject.

Truck hijacking is committed by experienced armed robbers acting on inside information. Because transporting goods by truck generates a substantial written record, there are many points at which insiders can learn the nature of a cargo and when it will be moved. Many truck hijackings happen in or near large cities because it is easy to dispose of the goods there. If there is a seaport, the goods taken may also be quickly on their way to a foreign country within hours. The contents of some hijacked trucks are off-loaded to another truck or several smaller trucks and may be in several other states by the time the investigation is getting started. Hijackers take what is valuable, with a preference for cargoes that are easy to dispose of and hard to trace. Examples include loads of clothing and high-tech equipment components, which may each have a value of $500,000 or more:

A driver for Serve-All Air had just made a pickup of computer equipment and drove for a while before he pulled over to the side of the road to catch up on his paperwork. A man in his thirties approached the truck and asked for directions. The driver consulted his map and gave directions to the man. The "lost" person appeared to be having difficulty understanding the directions, so the driver stepped out of the truck to help him. Someone approached the driver from the rear and grabbed him in a bear hug, while another person put a blindfold over the driver's eyes and tied him up. He was forced into another vehicle and driven around. Eventually he was taken back to his truck, which was now in another location after being relived of its cargo. He was placed in the back of the looted truck, and the door was closed. After about 30 minutes he was able to free himself and call 911.[72]

In another case, several conspirators bungled the hijacking of a UPS truck carrying expensive computer equipment, despite the fact that they had inside knowledge of its route.[73] According to their plan, one car would block the path of the UPS truck, and then several armed men would leap from the car and abduct the driver at gunpoint. The driver would be blindfolded and bound with rope or duct tape and taken away in a van. A member of the hijacking team, dressed in a UPS uniform, would drive the truck to another point, where the cargo would be quickly off-loaded, and then the driver would be released at another location. The robbery was rehearsed several times. On the day of the hijacking the gang successfully blocked the road the UPS truck was traveling on with a Toyota Corolla, forcing the truck to stop. However, seeing a car approach, the perpetrators fled before completing the hijacking. Subsequently, one of the conspirators was arrested on another charge, and ultimately all the conspirators to the UPS-truck hijacking were identified and convicted of conspiracy to rob it.

A number of truck hijackings involve collusion on the part of the driver with those committing this specialized form of robbery. The driver may be bribed or given some portion of the cargo for his or her personal use. In a variation of this, hijackers give drugs to drivers and provide them with women and then coerce the drivers into cooperating by threatening to cut off their supply of drugs and women, give a spouse photographs of the driver's liaisons with other women, or expose the driver's use of drugs to employers.

Drivers of rigs may be confronted at roadblocks or "detours" set up by hijackers. They may be forced from the road or accosted by the hijackers as they enter or leave truck rest stops. Some drivers have been tricked into stopping to help a "disabled" motorist. In more brazen moves, hijackers may invade truck parks, seize or kill security personnel, and take the trucks that they have targeted.

## ARREST PROBABILITIES

Robbery bears a comparatively low clearance rate, only 29 percent.[74] The reasons for this are several: Physical evidence may not be found; the time that perpetrators are at the scene is limited; and witnesses are usually upset, so their information runs from minimal to completely erroneous. Physical descriptions are the most common evidence.

# INVESTIGATIVE TECHNIQUES

The police response to the report of a robbery has these components: responding to the scene, tactical situations at the scene, the original investigation, and the latent or follow-up investigation.

## RESPONDING TO THE SCENE

In route to the scene of a robbery call, the officer must ensure that all information available from the dispatcher has been obtained, including the answers to the following questions: What is the exact location of the offense, including the type of business? Is the offense in progress? How many suspects are involved? What type of and how many weapons were displayed? What description of the suspect is available? By what method and in what direction did the suspect flee? What is the description of the means of transportation used by the suspect?

In approaching the scene, the officer must be alert for several possibilities:

- The dispatcher may provide information on the suspects' escape, such as their direction in fleeing from the scene and whether they were on foot or in a vehicle.
- If the dispatcher cannot supply any information other than the nature of the call, information about the target, MO, suspects, vehicles, weapons used, and other factors in recent robberies may help the responding officer recognize the suspects if they are moving away from the scene on the street along which the officer approaches.
- The fleeing suspects may, as the officer approaches them on the way to the scene, abruptly turn off, fire at the officer, or otherwise suddenly reveal themselves.

The primary tactical objectives of officers responding to a robbery call are public safety, officer protection, and tactical control of the scene. Secondary objectives include conducting the preliminary investigation, apprehending perpetrators, and recovering property. Arriving at the scene unobserved by the suspects facilitates the achievement of both primary and secondary objectives. It also allows tactical control and the element of surprise to pass from the robbers to the police. Units assigned to a robbery call should plan and coordinate the actions to be taken at the scene. Because the perpetrators may have police scanners, care should be taken with respect to radio transmissions. Arriving officers should not give away their exact positions and should refer to buildings by prearranged letter designations (e.g., "the A building").[75] They can never assume that the robber(s) have left the scene; for example, robbers have been known to hide near or at the scene, seeking to escape detection. Responding units should approach separately on streets parallel to that on which the robbery occurred or is occurring, using emergency lights but not sirens. The use of emergency lights permits more rapid progress through traffic. The reason for not using a siren is that the sound may panic suspects near or at the scene, triggering violence or hostage taking. It is believed that 9 out of 10 hostage situations that develop out of robberies occur because of a too visible first-responding officer.[76] At a distance of three to five blocks from the scene in an urban area and much farther in rural settings,[77] the emergency lights should be turned off to avoid possible detection by a lookout. The police officer should begin to smoothly decelerate, thus avoiding engine noise, squealing tires, or "emergency" stops that could give away the police car's arrival.

The first officer on the scene must quickly "size up" the area to gather any possible intelligence, including location of the robbers, **lookouts,** and escape vehicles. The locations of the perpetrators are particularly important given the fact that such criminals may have automatic and other weapons—which they are willing to use. Actually identifying the lookouts may be difficult; two officers in New York were killed by a lookout disguised as a nun.[78] The officer should leave his or her car quietly and move—unobserved—to a protected position to watch, where possible, two sides (e.g., north and east) of the building. One of these sides should be the exit most likely to be used by the robbers. Moving unobserved does not necessarily imply moving quickly. Running into position may invite passersby to "rubberneck," giving away the officer's position.[79] Before moving to any position, the officer should make sure that the background of that position, when viewed from the perpetrators' positions, does not silhouette him or her.[80]

The officer in the second unit should take the same precautions as the first in moving into position. The second officer's responsibility is to cover the two remaining sides (e.g., the south and west).

Both officers should keep their vehicles and portable radios at low volume to avoid being detected. The primary and backup officers should be sure that their positions in the lines of fire do not endanger each other.

It is also of particular importance when moving into their respective unobserved positions that officers not get inside of, that is, between, any possible lookouts and the robbery scene. Such a position would leave them vulnerable to fire from several sides.

Both in approaching the scene and at the scene, officers should avoid action, physical, or situational stereotyping.[81]

## Action Stereotyping

**Action stereotyping** occurs when the officer's expectations are so set to see one thing that he or she fails to perceive the event accurately. For example, the responding officer may expect the suspect to come rushing out of the store, hop into a car, and speed away. Although this may be the case, there are also other possible behaviors:

TWO robbers who confessed to over 20 "quick mart" robberies had been apprehended during a police surveillance. While being interrogated, the pair revealed that they had come close to being caught on several occasions when responding units arrived at the scene very quickly. They said they had escaped apprehension at those times by simply walking away in a normal manner. This proved to be an embarrassment for one officer who remembered the pair walking past his car. This officer said that they just appeared to be "normal" citizens and that there was nothing extraordinary about them.[82]

IN Wilkes-Barre, Pennsylvania, a man walked into one of the busiest branch banks and grabbed a deposit bag from a woman. The bag reportedly contained money from one of the bank's overnight deposit boxes. Running from the bank, the young bandit hopped on a silver performance bike and pedaled rapidly away from the scene.[83]

OFFICERS responding to a robbery call arrived at the scene as several people ran out of the business involved. When the people ignored orders to halt, one officer shot and killed one of them and injured several others. All of them were witnesses or victims running to escape from the robber, who was still inside.

A silent alarm was triggered, and officers were dispatched to the scene of a possible robbery in progress. As the officers got out of their cars, a man calmly walked out and waved at them, stating that the alarm had accidentally been set off. The officers left. Later it was found that the robber had killed a pharmacist and shot a clerk, who survived to identify the robber-murderer as the man who had greeted the police.

## Physical Stereotyping

**Physical stereotyping** is an officer's expectations that the robber will be of a particular description. Such stereotypes may allow the suspect to escape or be fatal to officers:

AN officer entered a convenience store in response to an alarm; his gun was drawn, but he started to put it away when he didn't see anything out of the ordinary. As he approached the two clerks behind the counter, the younger one yelled a warning: the other "clerk" was an armed robber whose appearance—he was 60 years old—did not fit with the officer's stereotype of a robber.[84]

Another aspect of physical stereotyping is that investigators may have difficulty believing witnesses' descriptions. For example, we expect bank robbers to be relatively young adults and vigorous. However, in northern Colorado nearly a decade ago, an 82-year-old man known as the "salt-and-pepper bandit" was arrested for a string of bank robberies; in another case, a 105-pound woman just 12 years younger donned a black plastic bag as a disguise and robbed a bank, declaring, "There's a bomb here; give me the money, no bells, no sirens."[85]

## Situational Stereotyping

In **situational stereotyping,** the officers' previous experience with and knowledge of a particular location increases their vulnerability:

A silent alarm went off at a bar; the call was dispatched and as the assigned unit drove toward the bar, the two partners joked about the inability of the owner to set the alarm properly as he was continuously tripping it accidentally, creating frequent false alarms. The officer operating the police car parked it in front of the bar, and as the two officers began to saunter casually up to the front door of the bar, two suspects burst out with guns in hand and began shooting. Miraculously, neither officer was hit. One of the suspects was wounded and arrested at the scene; the other one escaped and was not apprehended until several weeks later.

Returning to some earlier points, although the suspects may be observed fleeing the scene or may reveal themselves in some manner to the officer assigned to respond to the call, such encounters do not take place with any regularity. In addition, deviating from the assignment to become engaged in a "pursuit," instead of proceeding directly to the call, will often be unproductive. In such instances the "suspect," especially one driving an automobile, may merely be acting in a suspicious manner because he or she may have committed some minor traffic violation and is fearful that the officer is going to write a traffic citation. The officer actually assigned to the robbery call should not normally deviate from the assignment without significant reason; the officer's responsibility is to get to the scene and to get accurate, detailed information for the preliminary pickup order or BOLO as rapidly as possible. By doing so, more resources are then brought to bear on the offense, and the likelihood is reduced that other officers may unknowingly stop armed suspects for what they think is only a traffic violation.

If not assigned to the call as the primary or backup unit, other officers should not respond to the scene. Instead, they should patrol along a likely escape route such as entrances to expressways. They should avoid transmitting routine messages, as the primary unit will need to transmit temporary pickup orders or BOLOs concerning the offense.

If available, helicopters have the potential of being helpful in robbery investigations when a good description of the vehicle in which the robbers fled is included in the BOLO. Helicopters can cover territory rapidly. Flying at 500 feet, a helicopter provides observers accompanying the pilot with an excellent observation platform. Approximately 75 percent of all pursuits aided by a helicopter are successful.[86] If ground units are in pursuit of a vehicle containing bandits fleeing the scene, the helicopter can:

1. Direct other units into the area to seal off likely avenues of travel.
2. Make the occupants aware of its presence and induce them to stop and surrender.
3. Keep the bandits' car illuminated at night and—if they stop it and "bail out"—keep one or more of the suspects spotlighted. It can also use its infrared heat-sensing system to locate suspects hiding in yards or fields.[87]
4. Light the road ahead of the vehicle if its lights are turned off, thereby lessening the danger to other motorists.
5. Inform pursuing police units of traffic conditions or special hazards—such as construction equipment actively working on the highway, rush-hour traffic, bridges raised for ships, spectators leaving a sports stadium at the end of an event, and railroad cars blocking an intersection—so that pursuing units can turn off emergency equipment and slow down if necessary to protect the public.
6. Warn ground units if the suspects are setting up ambushes.

## TACTICAL SITUATIONS AT THE SCENE

Having arrived undetected at the scene, the first responding officer must make a crucial assessment: Have the suspects fled the scene, or are they still inside the building? The officer's best course of action is to have the dispatcher call the business and have the owner, operator, or an employee come out of the building and approach the officer. When this happens, unless the officer recognizes the person as being connected with the business, the person should be asked to raise both hands above the head, halt 30 feet away in a position not near cover, raise his or her coat if the person is wearing one (so the officer can check for weapons), approach to 15 feet and toss some identification toward the officer, and remain standing there, hands above the head, while the officer examines the identification and shares the information with the dispatcher. In doing so, the officer must be alert to what is going on at the business, what the subject is doing, and movement on the street generally. It is crucial that the officer not leave protected cover until fully satisfied. An officer who has any suspicions at any time during this process should require the subject to kneel with hands raised above the head and request assistance. Even if the officer recognizes the person who exits the business, he or she must continue to exercise caution. Consider a husband and wife who operate a small neighborhood grocery. A subject in that grocery may have spotted the officer moving into position and ordered the husband out of the store, telling him, "Get rid of the cop or get him in here or your wife is dead."

Thus, any person who comes out of the building should be asked how many people are on the premises. These people should be asked to exit the building individually on the command of the officer, and they should be also checked for weapons. Still, the officer should enter the building with great care only after he or she has appropriate backup in the proper position. Such tactics may occasionally upset the businessperson who has just been robbed if the suspects have already left the scene, but their use is justified by reasons previously noted in this chapter. Moreover, experience has shown that most victims will readily accept their use when given an explanation. While the policy of some departments limits the use of invisible response tactics to robbery-in-progress calls, others use it for all robbery calls, a position that is reflected here.

If a suspect is immediately observed, the investigator should determine the person's most likely avenue of flight and possible locations of any accomplices. If the investigator is fired upon by the perpetrator, he or she should not return the fire unless able to do so without needlessly endangering the victim or passersby. The dispatcher should immediately be advised of all gunshots so that arriving units will not unknowingly be placed in jeopardy. It is far better to allow the escape of the perpetrator than to kill an innocent person by the premature or careless discharge of a weapon. With a suspect who is not attempting to flee or take aggressive action but who refuses to drop his or her weapon when so directed, the investigator is not authorized to open fire. Instead, the officer should remain alert for some sign that the suspect intends to discharge the weapon or flee. Assistance will arrive rapidly, and at that time the suspect can be disarmed by standard cover-and-disarm techniques. Deadly force must be used only as a last resort.

When the subject is barricaded or holding hostages, the officer assigned to the call should immediately advise the dispatcher of this and proceed as provided by departmental policy. Usually this entails dispatching a supervisor and special tactical units and sealing off and evacuating the area.

## THE ORIGINAL INVESTIGATION

Although a robbery may produce a great variety of physical evidence—hair samples, blood, fingernail scrapings, fibers, buttons, notes, and similar materials—such evidence may be discovered only through diligent effort. Therefore, the investigator must always conduct a thorough crime scene search. The most common type of evidence is produced by careful interviews of victims and witnesses. It usually includes a description of the perpetrator and the weapon, directions given in committing the offense, the direction of approach and flight, and, less frequently, a description of the means of fleeing the scene. Thus, the interview phase of a robbery investigation is critical to a successful conclusion.

Because of the availability and importance of this type of evidence in robbery cases, the investigator must be thoroughly familiar with principles of witness perception and identification. The investigator must remember that identifications are made by human beings who perceive things differently. The whole approach to the investigation must be directed toward securing the most accurate identifications and descriptions humanly possible, because no less is acceptable in the courtroom. A number of departments use a checklist for obtaining personal descriptions, such as the one in Chapter 5, "Field Notes and Investigative Reporting." Even experienced investigators will, on occasion, inadvertently fail to obtain a full description, resulting in lost information and a consequent reduction in opportunity for apprehension. A description report also offers the possibility of computerizing the information so that, by means of periodic searches and the correlation of information from offenses involving similar descriptions, the probability of apprehension can be increased.

Typically, robbers approach the scene with care. After the robbery, however, they may flee recklessly (see photo on page 450 for an exception to this rule, however). The investigator should take great care to establish and check the avenues of flight and approach to locate dropped articles that might help in the identification of the suspect. The immediate

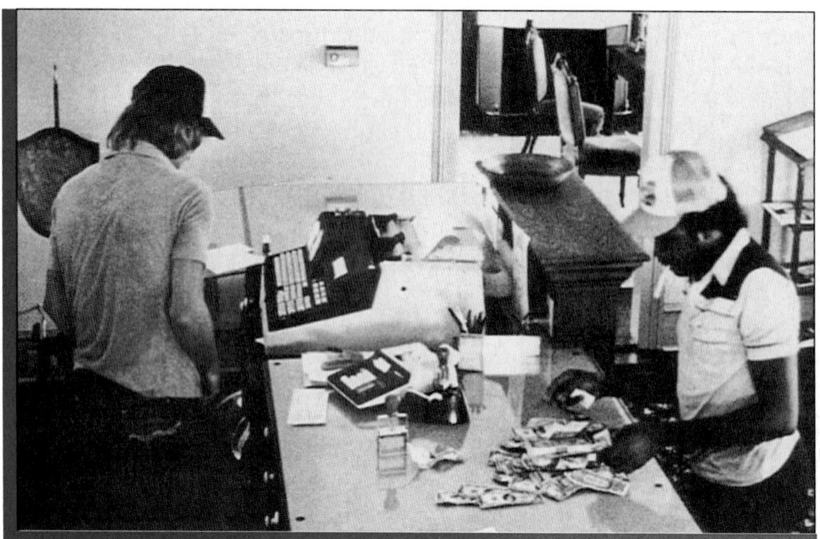

**Robbers at the Scene**
Here is an illustration of an exception to the notion that robbers approach the crime scene with care and flee with abandon: Two robbers are calmly counting their "take" while still on the premises. Off camera, two accomplices are standing guard over employees.

(Courtesy Austin, Texas, Police Department)

area should be canvassed through a neighborhood check to locate witnesses to the offense or to the flight of the perpetrator. In the latter case the investigator is occasionally able to locate persons who observed an individual matching the suspect's description enter a vehicle about which they can provide considerable information.

In addition to obtaining a description of the offense and offender, the interview of the victim should elicit information concerning the exact words spoken by the offender, which may constitute an identifiable MO; the physical condition of the perpetrator, including anything that would suggest the use of alcohol or drugs; the possibility that a disguise was used (see photo on page 451); any nervous mannerisms of the perpetrator, such as tics or stutters; and the possibility that the perpetrator had recently visited the victimized premises and said, done, or worn something that would assist in identification. Another aspect of an MO is any written note used by bandits to communicate with victims. The threats and demands made, the vocabulary and punctuation used, the manner in which the note was created (e.g., hand printed, letters cut from newspaper, typewritten, type of printer, use of color, or cursive writing) may all be elements of an MO. A classic example of a robbery note as an MO involved a man dubbed the "note bandit," who robbed 23 businesses in 33 days *using the same laminated note.*[88] Whenever possible, the note should be recovered and checked for prints.

## Generating a Likeness of the Suspect

A likeness of the suspect should be created and distributed as rapidly as possible. Although some departments continue to have artists prepare the likeness, others use a manual or computerized **facial identification system** to prepare a composite likeness.

A national survey of 163 law enforcement agencies revealed that investigators were more satisfied, by only a very slight margin, with the results of sketches prepared by artists as compared to likenesses prepared by other methods.[89] Given the small number of respondents to this survey, this finding may or may not be confirmed by a larger study.

Many police agencies use Smith & Wesson's manual identification kit, Identi-Kit, which includes hundred of transparencies of different features—such as facial shape, nose, ears, head gear, lips, chin, facial hair, glasses, and so forth—that can be "sandwiched" together to form a likeness of the offender (see photos on page 452). An experienced Identi-Kit operator can prepare a suspect likeness in as little as 20 minutes.

There are a number of software programs that can be used to generate a suspect likeness, including Identi-Kit 2000, Electronic Facial Identification Technique (EFIT), Faces (see photo on page 453), Compusketch (see photos on page 454), ComPhotofit, and Crime Reduction Image Man-

**Disguises**

The dress of these two bank robbers is intended to hamper the original investigation: the wig, hat, and masks can be readily discarded. Wearing an overcoat, which can also be easily discarded, allows the robber to more easily get weapons into the bank; it also makes it more difficult for witnesses to describe the physical build of the robber.

(Courtesy Atlanta Police Department)

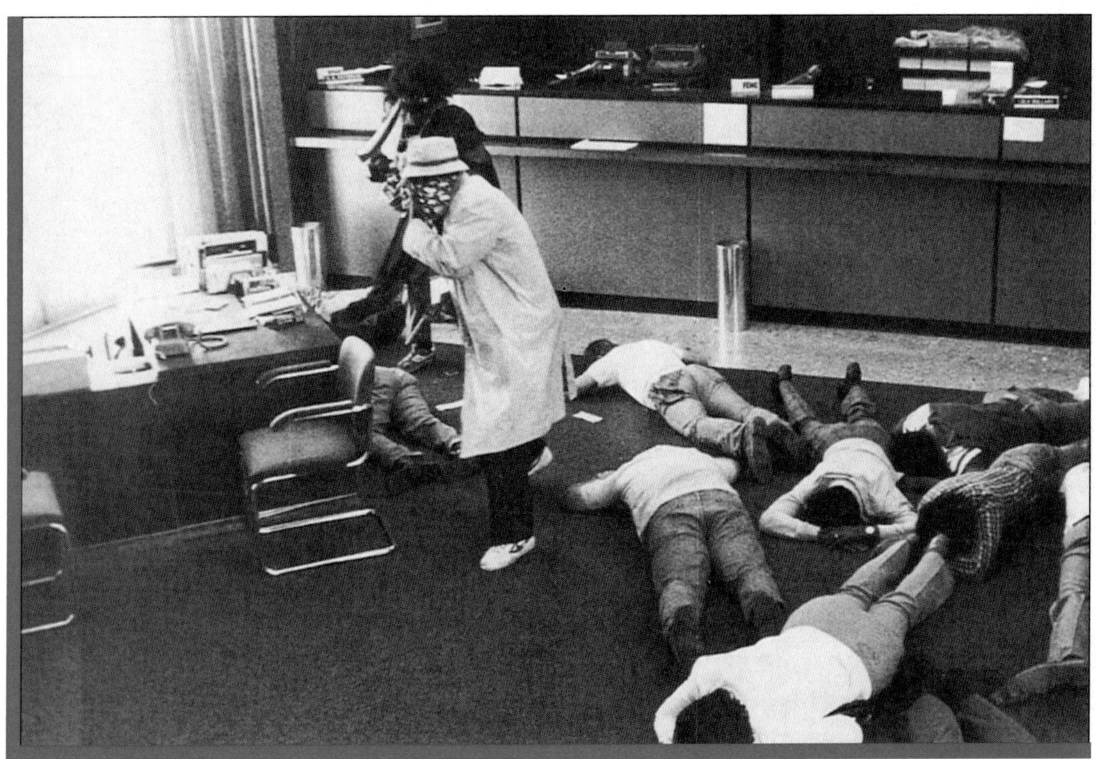

agement and Enhancement System (C.R.I.M.E.S.). Typically these systems are also able to search for similar composites previously generated by the system and to search existing digital mug-shot databases. In addition to being used by federal, state, and local agencies, these software programs are used throughout the world in several different languages.

The Identi-Kit 2000 software is organized—like its manual counterpart—around features, such as eyes, nose, lips, chin, hair, age lines, facial tones, head gear, glasses, and face hair, all of which can be quickly changed. The "paint brush" command allows the operator to add scars, moles, and other distinguishing features. "Blend brush" provides the capacity to move the hairline back to reduce the height of the suspect's hair. "Reverse" allows the victim to immediately see what the robber would look like if his or her hair was parted on the opposite side. A notepad function allows the operator to add notes to the file automatically if the witness makes important statements about the suspect while working with the operator. Several different versions of the suspect's likeness can be saved at the bottom of the screen, so the witness can later pick the one that is most like the suspect. All numbers of the specific features that make up the suspect's likeness are automatically generated and saved, so they can be transmitted by any means. More commonly, the likenesses produced are faxed. The feature-numbering systems in both the manual and the computerized Identi-Kits are the same.

In using Compusketch, the process begins with an on-screen interactive interview that includes

**Identi-Kit**
Manual Identi-Kit likeness of suspect (*left*) versus photograph of one of two suspects later arrested for the robbery. Many police agencies use Identi-Kit–which includes hundreds of transparencies of different facial and head features that can be "sandwiched" together–to form a likeness of the offender. An experienced Identi-Kit operator can complete a suspect's composite in as little as 20 minutes.
(Courtesy Clark County Sheriff's Office, Vancouver, Washington)

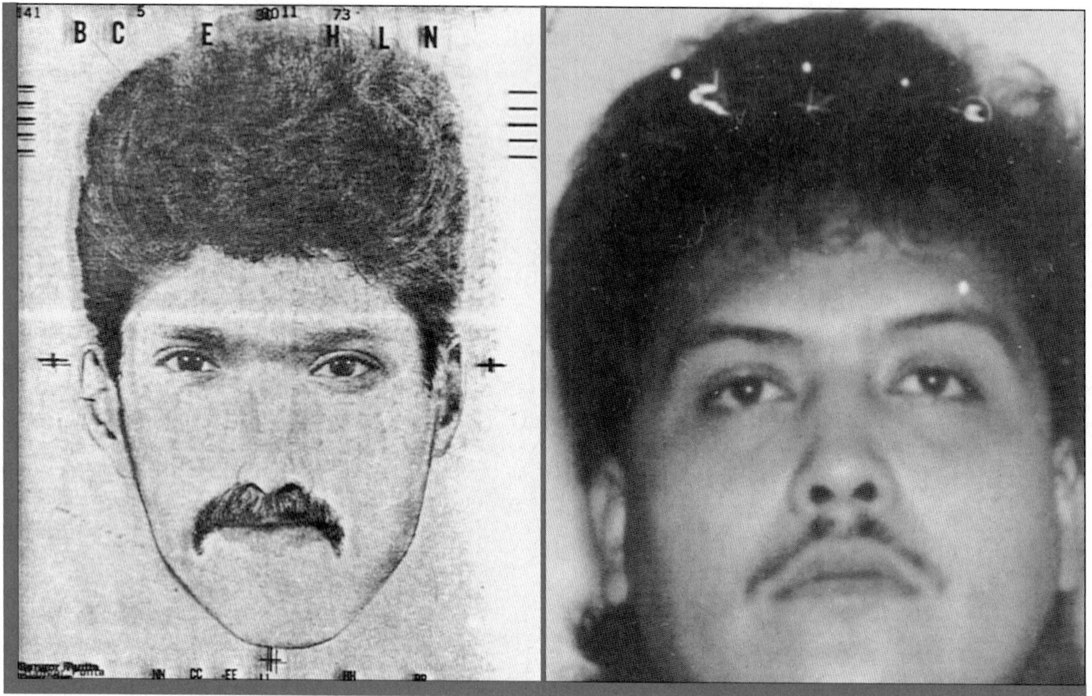

both multiple-choice and open-ended questions. Upon the completion of the interview, a sketch is automatically assembled from a comprehensive image library of over 40,000 features. This initial sketch can then be further modified to portray unique facial characteristics on the basis of witnesses' reactions. Compusketch can create images of virtually any race, gender, or age beyond approximately 12 years. Compusketch can be used, following an 8-hour course, with appropriately configured Apple or IBM-compatible personal computers. The left photo on page 454 shows the results obtained from the use of Compusketch in one case.

## THE FOLLOW-UP INVESTIGATION

The follow-up investigator should review a copy of the original offense report to become familiar with the case. The investigator should consider facts that suggest an MO, such as the target of the robbery, weapons, the type of property taken, the exact words spoken by the perpetrator, the number of suspects and the tasks they performed, needless or vicious force, and similar elements. All physical evidence should be personally examined by the officer assigned to the follow-up investigation. A file check should be made of the victim's name in case the person has a history of making crime reports. For instance, certain types of businesses—such as economy gasoline stations—may not conduct even a minimal background investigation of employees. Given the availability of cash and long periods of isolation during the night hours, an untrustworthy employee occasionally pockets the cash for personal gain and covers its absence by claiming a robbery was committed. A file check on the complaining witness may suggest such a pattern.

The investigator should reinterview the victim if there are reasons to believe that a robbery did not actually take place:

TWO teenage clerks were shot in a robbery at a Quik-Mart convenience store. Despite the clerks' wounds, investigators were suspicious about the incident. Upon further questioning by the police, both "victims" admitted they made up the story about being robbed to conceal their theft of $400 and shot each other to make it look more convincing.[90]

A woman told officers that a laughing man put a gun against her 2-year-old daughter's head and robbed her at an ATM. The victim also reported that no one else was around the ATM when the incident happened at 7:52 A.M. Investigators initially thought it was highly unlikely that nobody else was at that ATM around the time of the alleged robbery. They checked the transactions at the ATM and found that a man had used the ATM just 4 minutes before the robbery and did not see anyone matching the robber's description. Moreover, the man did not immediately leave the ATM after he had finished his transaction. Based on this evidence, it was established that the woman had made up the story because she wanted some attention.[91]

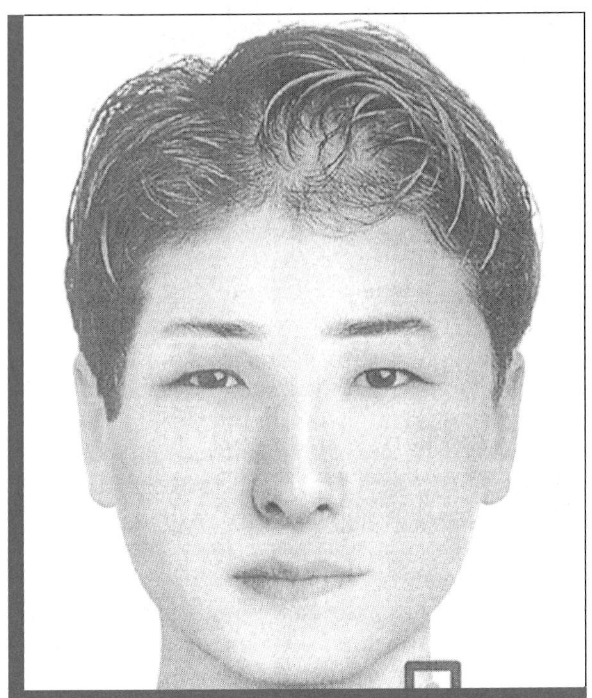

**Faces**

A Faces-generated composite of one of three Chinese-speaking Asian males who invaded the home of a local restaurant owner of Asian descent and robbed him at gunpoint.

(Courtesy Lt. Jim Peterson, Santa Barbara County, California, Sheriff's Department)

There have been several nationally publicized cases in which black males have been falsely accused of crimes. One of these was discussed in Chapter 2; another was the South Carolina case in which Susan Smith subsequently confessed to drowning her two small sons. In this less noted ATM case, the "laughing man" was also invented as a black male by the "victim."

The investigator should also reinterview the victim and witnesses if it appears that there may be information that was not obtained due to incomplete questioning or insufficient recall of the event. Occasionally witnesses will remember some detail and not go to the "trouble" of looking up the police department's listing. Therefore, the investigator should leave a card with his name and departmental phone number. If a likeness of the suspect has not been made, this should be done immediately. Additionally, the victim and witnesses should review the mugshot file of known and active robbery perpetrators. The investigator should return to the crime scene at exactly the same time of day that the offense was committed and attempt to locate additional witnesses; at the same time, the neighborhood check should be reconducted. An attempt should be made to tie the offense to other robberies, as the combined information from several offense reports may result in sufficient detail to identify a perpetrator. Reliable informants should be contacted by the investigator. However, this should be done judiciously, as they should not be called on to provide information on every open case regardless of its importance.

## THE CRIME SCENE TECHNICIAN AND THE LABORATORY

In many departments, the uniformed officer is responsible for processing the crime scene. Other departments are fortunate enough to have the services of a crime scene technician trained in procuring

### Compusketch

Compusketch of suspect (*left*) versus photograph of the person subsequently convicted. Today, software programs such as Compusketch greatly assist investigators in trying to create a suspect likeness. Such programs are also able to search for similar composites previously generated by the software and to search existing digital mugshot databases. These systems are used by all levels of law enforcement in the United States and throughout the world.

(Courtesy Idaho Bureau of Investigation)

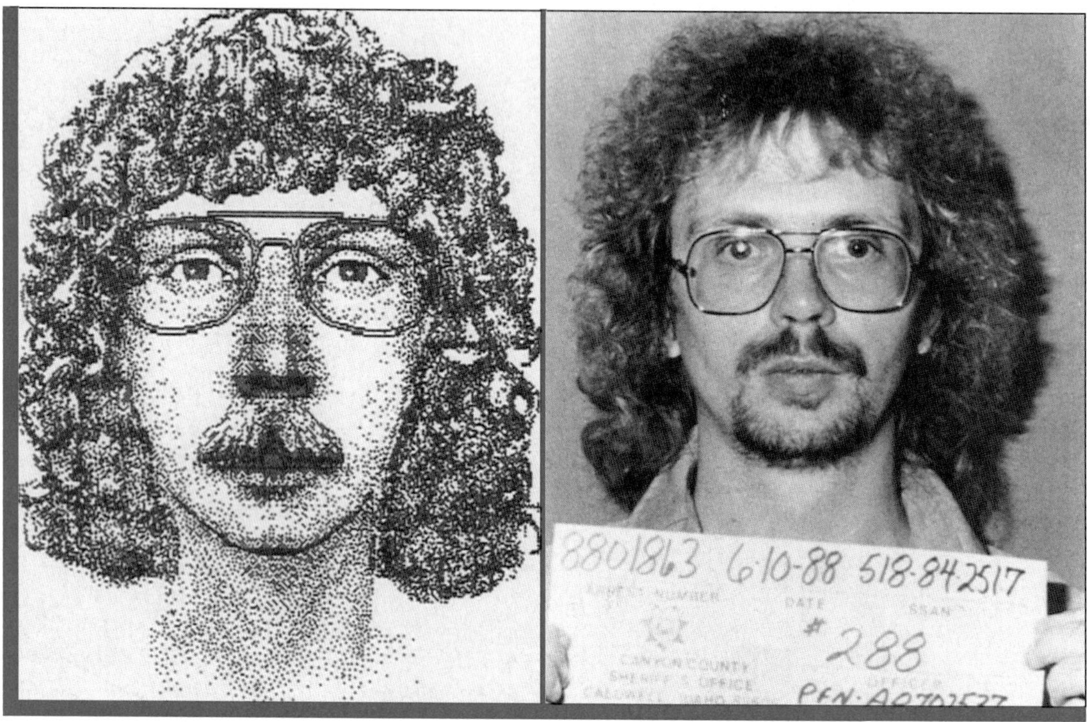


evidence at the crime scene. It must be borne in mind that such technicians are not miracle workers—they cannot develop evidence that simply does not exist. Likewise, laboratory personnel can contribute little if they have not been given something substantive with which to work. Evidence must be collected, preserved, and identified according to established procedures for the laboratory to process it and for it to be usable in a court proceeding. To ensure the admissibility of physical evidence, responsibility must be firmly fixed for maintaining the chain of custody of each item with a view toward accurate and appropriate identification of the item in court.

## FORENSIC PHOTOGRAPH ANALYSIS

Security surveillance cameras are commonplace. We see them in banks, motels, convenience stores, and other types of businesses. As a result, it is not uncommon to have photographs of an actual robbery. In one case, a police department received reports that police officers were shaking down drug dealers. A "drug den," staffed by undercover investigators, was established. Subsequently, three officers were arrested after they were videotaped breaking into the apartment, beating the undercover investigators, searching for drugs, and stealing cash.[92] In some banks, the number of photographs may be as high as 800 to 1,000, although fewer than a dozen ordinarily yield information of investigative significance. When the robber has not worn a mask, it is possible, through **forensic photograph analysis,** to compare the forensic (surveillance) photograph with file pictures of suspects. The comparison may involve doing a simple visual check or laying a photographic transparency over the file pictures to compare the size, shape, and symmetry of the eyes, eyebrows, nose, mouth, ears, facial creases, scars, marks, and head shape.

Even when robbers wear a mask, the analysis of forensic photographs may yield useful information, such as the height of the suspect and defects in clothing. Despite the fact that analysis of forensic photographs has already demonstrated their utility on a number of occasions, it is a field from which additional determinations can be expected as the quality of forensic photographs improves and as new methods of analysis are applied.

## THREE-STRIKES LAWS

In response to the public's demand to "get tough on crime," 24 states and the federal government adopted **three-strikes laws** during the mid-1990s which require that persons convicted repeatedly of serious crimes be sentenced to lengthy incarceration or to imprisonment without parole.[93] These laws can be used to remove robbery offenders from the street without having to wait until they can be convicted of yet another robbery.

Most, if not all, states prohibit felons from owning or possessing guns. Such acts are typically felonies in and of themselves. Because weapons are taken in many crimes, criminals carrying them may be tied to and charged with those crimes. They may have also opened themselves to possession of stolen property or probation- or parole-violation charges. Criminals have a propensity to carry firearms. Fourteen percent of arrestees report that they carry guns most or all of the time.[94] Juveniles do so 20 percent of the time, and for gang members the figure rises to 31 percent.[95] Investigators can legitimately target violent predatory criminals for investigation and use a variety of techniques, including surveillance and sweeps of hot spots, to make arrests of them on firearm and related charges.

## THE INVESTIGATOR'S EDUCATIVE RESPONSIBILITY

Investigators and their departments, in addition to arresting suspects and recovering victims' property, must be prepared to provide robbery prevention tips to lessen the chance that victims will be victimized again. This section focuses on preventing small-business robberies. Although crime prevention is a specialty, investigators may be able to make a few suggestions at the scene, such as (1) calling attention to the department's robbery prevention website; (2) recommending that the store's risk management personnel or insurer evaluate procedures, employee training, and environmental factors, such as location and lighting; (3) helping the business make arrangements for one of the department's crime prevention or threat assessment officers to come and make an assessment; (4) recommending attendance at a department-sponsored seminar on robbery prevention; and (5) leaving appropriate literature.

Most robbery prevention information concentrates on three different, but related, categories of information: preventive measures (what to do before a robbery), anticipatory strategies (what to do during a robbery), and reactive strategies (what to do after a robbery).[96]

### PREVENTIVE MEASURES: WHAT TO DO BEFORE A ROBBERY

1. Post signs reporting that you keep less than $50 on hand.
2. Limit entrances and exits.
3. Never open the safe when you can be observed; if robbers know you have the combination, they can force you to open the safe.
4. Count cash and prepare bank deposits out of sight.
5. If possible, have two people make bank deposits; vary the times and routes for each deposit; make deposits several times a day to limit the amount of cash on hand; make deposits during daylight hours when more people are around; do not leave bank deposits in the car while you run an errand; do not place deposits in an observable area of your car when driving to the bank. Before going to make a deposit, remove name tags and shirts with your company's name or logo. Be alert to the possibility that you may be followed, and keep your car doors locked going to and returning from the bank.
6. Make sure that the interior and exterior of the store, rear area, and parking lot are all well lit.

7. Post signs that report your state's law on robberies (e.g., "Robbery of these premises will result in a 5-year mandatory prison sentence).
8. Use surveillance cameras, and do not obstruct their views by merchandise displays. Publicize the use of these cameras by posting signs.
9. Make sure that from the outside of the store there is a clear, unobstructed view of the cash registers.
10. Remove any advertisements or signs that block the view into the store.
11. Ask customers for exact change or the smallest-denomination bill that will cover the purchase.
12. Keep "bait" money"—currency whose serial numbers you have recorded.
13. Write money orders from customers only after you have received the amount and put it in a drop safe.
14. Make sure that emergency alarms are periodically serviced and operating well.
15. Report all suspicious people and circumstances to the police. Complete (if available in your jurisdiction) an authorization form—sometimes referred to as a trespass authorization—that gives the police standing authority to talk to anyone who is loitering at your store.
16. Post all emergency numbers next to the telephone.
17. Place dye packs in stacks of currency. However, even when an offender is splattered with a dye, it does not automatically follow that people will call the police when they see it:

A man drove his personal car to a branch bank and robbed it. As he was entering his car after the robbery, a dye pack exploded, covering him and his car with bright orange paint. A witness heard him say, "Oh damn!" The suspect drove back to his place of employment, a large manufacturing plant, and went back to work. When the police arrested the man at work a few hours later, they asked his supervisor if he thought it at all odd that the man was covered with bright orange paint. After thinking for a moment, the supervisor replied, "No, a lot of strange people work here."

## ANTICIPATORY STRATEGIES: WHAT TO DO DURING A ROBBERY

1. Robbers are usually desperate and tense; they may be on drugs and/or alcohol. Tell the robber you will comply with his or her directions. Once a robbery starts, your job is to safely survive it.
2. Follow the robber's directions; your life is more important than cash. There are some situations, however, in which this may not be the correct action; for example, if a robber tries to force you into a bathroom, he or she may have the intention of shooting you there, where your body would not be immediately evident.
3. Stay calm.
4. Covertly study the robber. Even if there is more than one offender, concentrate on only one. If there is more than one person on duty for a shift, prearrange the zones in which each of you will study offenders.
5. Try to observe the offender's direction and method of flight, noting descriptive elements (e.g., "He ran out of the store, started a green motorcycle, and went west on State Street.")

## REACTIVE STRATEGIES: WHAT TO DO AFTER THE ROBBERY

1. Do not attempt to follow the robber out of the store.
2. Hit the alarm, and call 911 immediately.
3. Ask witnesses to stay; instruct them not to discuss what they saw. Try to get the names and address of any witnesses who cannot await the arrival of the police.
4. Lock the door, and do not conduct any further business.
5. Protect the crime scene.
6. Immediately write down what you remember about the approach of the robber, the exact words spoken, the type of weapon(s), a description of the offender, the direction and method of flight, and a description of any vehicle used.

## Key Terms

**action stereotyping**
**ambush**
**carjacking**
**facial identification systems**
**forensic photograph analysis**
**home-invasion robbery (HIR)**
**lookouts**
**mugging**
**physical stereotyping**
**planned operation**
**robbery**
**selective raid**
**situational stereotyping**
**strong-armed robbery**
**three-strikes laws**

## Review Questions

1. What are the elements of the crime of robbery?
2. On the basis of the amount of planning involved, describe three robbery styles.
3. Give a profile of visible street robberies.
4. When is purse snatching a robbery?
5. Give three explanations for the increase in carjackings.
6. Discuss how home invaders operate.
7. What are the two occupations in which a person has the greatest danger of being the victim of a violent crime on the job?
8. How are drivers confronted in truck-hijacking robberies?
9. Explain action, physical, and situational stereotyping.
10. What considerations are essential as an officer approaches the scene of a robbery?
11. Why is it important to determine the exact words spoken by a robber?
12. What actions must the officer assigned to do the follow-up investigation take?
13. Define and give examples of robbery preventive measures, anticipatory strategies, and reactive measures.

## Internet Activities

1. Most large police agencies in the United States have robbery investigation units. Find several such agencies in your region. What is the total number of officers assigned to these units? What are the units' functions and responsibilities? Is there information concerning the numbers of robberies that are investigated and/or cleared? Is any robbery prevention information provided? Websites such as www.officer.com provide information to both local and international police agencies.
2. Go to the website www.forensicartist.com, and learn more about how forensic artists generate the likenesses of people through age composition, composite drawing, and facial reconstruction.

## Notes

1. Federal Bureau of Investigation, *Crime in the United States—1999* (Washington, DC: Government Printing Office, 2000), p. 28.
2. Ibid.
3. Ibid.
4. Ibid., p. 29.
5. Bureau of Justice Statistics, *Criminal Victimization in the United States—1999* (Washington, DC: Bureau of Justice Statistics, 2000), p. 79, table 75.
6. Ibid., p. 80.
7. Ibid., p. 27, table 27.
8. Ibid., p. 39, table 37.
9. Ibid., p. 71, table 67.
10. Jody Miller, "Up It Up: Gender and the Accomplishment of Street Robbery," *Criminology*, 1998, Vol. 36, No. 1, p. 48.
11. Ibid., p. 49

12. Ibid.
13. FBI, *Crime in the United States.*
14. Bureau of Justice Statistics, *Criminal Victimization in the United States*, p. 63, table 59. When the remaining robberies are committed is not known.
15. FBI, *Crime in the United States.*
16. Bureau of Justice Statistics, *Criminal Victimization in the United States*, p. 32, table 32.
17. Richard T. Wright and Scott Decker, *Armed Robbers in Action* (Boston: Northeastern University Press, 1997).
18. Bureau of Justice Statistics, *Criminal Victimization in the United States*, p. 41, table 43.
19. FBI, *Crime in the United States*, p. 29.
20. Matt Nelson, "Note, Tipster Help in Search for Bank Robber," *Duluth News-Tribune* (Minnesota), Mar. 1, 2000.
21. "Two Plead Guilty in Robbery Try," *Las Vegas Review-Journal*, May 25, 2001.
22. "Deer River," *Duluth News-Tribute* (Minnesota), Feb. 21, 2001.
23. Ben Schmitt and Dan Shine, "Macomb and Pointes Today," *Detroit Free Press*, Aug. 27, 2001.
24. See Werner J. Einstadter, "The Social Organization of Armed Robbery," *Social Problems*, 1969, Vol. 17, No. 1, p. 76. The broad categories are those identified by Einstadter; some of the content has been extended by the authors.
25. Joan Petersilia, Peter W. Greenwood, and Marvin Lavin, *Criminal Careers of Habitual Felons* (Washington, DC: Government Printing Office, 1978), p. 61.
26. Interview by Charles Swanson with convicted armed robber, Jan. 19, 1983, Clarke County, Georgia, Jail.
27. Petersilia, Greenwood, and Lavin, *Criminal Careers of Habitual Felons*, pp. 60-61.
28. FBI, *Crime in the United States*, p. 28.
29. Bureau of Justice Statistics, *Criminal Victimization in the United States*, p. 38, table 36.
30. Ibid., p. 68, table 64.
31. Ibid., p. 69, table 65.
32. Ira Sommers and Deborah R. Baskin, "The Violent Context of Violent Female Offending," *Journal of Research in Crime and Delinquency*, May 1993, Vol. 30, No. 2, p. 147.
33. Bureau of Justice Statistics, *Criminal Victimization in the United States*, p. 39, table 37.
34. Sommers and Baskin, "The Violent Context of Violent Female Offending," p. 146.
35. Ibid.
36. Ibid., p. 144.
37. Tod W. Burke and Charles O'Rear, "Armed Carjacking: A Violent Problem in Need of a Solution," *Police Chief*, January 1993, Vol. 60, No. 1, p. 18.
38. Burke and O'Rear, "Armed Carjacking.
39. Federal Bureau of Investigation, *An Analysis of Carjacking in the United States* (Washington DC: Government Printing Office, 1992), p. 25.
40. Don Terry, quoting Lawrence W. Sherman, "Carjacking: New Name for an Old Crime," *New York Times*, Dec. 9, 1992, p. A18.
41. Patsy Klauss, *Carjackings in the United States, 1992–1996* (Washington, DC: Bureau of Justice Statistics, March 1999), p. 1.
42. Ibid.
43. Ibid. p. 43.
44. Ibid. p. 2.
45. Ibid. p. 3.
46. Ibid., p. 3. On this point also see Burke and O'Rear, "Armed Carjacking," p. 18, whose illustrations of places where people have been carjacked have been drawn on here.
47. Ibid., p. 3.
48. FBI, *An Analysis of Carjackings*, p. 3.
49. FBI, *Crime in the United States*, p. 29.
50. James T. Hurley, "Violent Crime Hits Home," *FBI Law Enforcement Bulletin*, June 1995, p. 11.
51. Ibid.
52. Ibid., p. 10.
53. "Three Tied Up, Robbed in Pawtucket House," *Providence Journal* (Rhode Island), June 16, 2001.
54. Ron Walton, "Tulsa World on Line," TULSAWORLD.com, Dec. 8, 1998.
55. Padilla, Howie, "Two Men Beat Up Couple in Their Home," *Star Tribune* (Minneapolis, MN), September 6, 2001.
56. Tod W. Burke, "Home Invaders: Gangs of the Future," *Police Chief*, November 1990, Vol. 57, No. 11, p. 23.
57. Office of Banks and Real Estate, State of Illinois, "ATM Report," www.obre.state.il.usa/agency/atmrpt.htm, 1999, p. 1.
58. Ibid., p. 1.
59. Ibid., pp. 4–5.

60. Ibid., p. 4.
61. Ibid.
62. Eric F. Sygnatur and Guy A. Toscano, "Work-Related Homicides: The Facts," *Compensation and Working Conditions*, Spring 2000, Vol. 5, No. 1, p. 4.
63. Mike Brassfield, "Taxicab Driver Survives Robbery," *St. Petersburg Times* (Florida), Aug. 11. 2001.
64. Tom Jackman and Leef Smith, "Taxi Camera Develops Its First Lead for Police," *Washington Post*, Aug. 22, 2001.
65. J. M. Kalil, "Bellagio Robber Flees with $1 Million in Jewelry," *Las Vegas Review-Journal*, July 11, 2001.
66. National Institute for Occupational Safety and Health, "Update: Risk Factors for Injury in Robberies of Convenience Stores Examined in NIOSH Study," May 1997, p. 1.
67. The information in this paragraph is drawn from H. E. Amandus et al., "Convenience Store Robberies in Selected Metropolitan Areas," *Journal of Occupational and Environmental Safety*, Vol. 39, No. 5, May 1997, pp. 442–447.
68. School of Criminal Justice, State University of New Jersey, Rutgers, "Preventing Convenience Store Robbery through Environmental Design," crimeprevention.Rutgers.edu/case_studies/cpted/cpted_cs2htm, Sept. 22, 2001, p. 1.
69. Ibid., p. 1.
70. "Fighting Cargo Theft," *Transportation Topics, Trucking's Electronic Newsletter*, Sept. 8, 1999, p. 4.
71. Ibid.
72. Sam Scott, "Suspects Jack Truck, Steal High-Tech Equipment," *Sun* (Sunnyvale, California), May 31, 2000.
73. *United States of America* v. *Carlos Albverto Prieto*, 11th Circuit Court of Appeals, D.C. Docket No. 96-00565-CR-LCN, Nov. 6, 2000, p. 2.
74. FBI, *Crime in the United States*, p. 29.
75. Charles Remsberg, *The Tactical Edge: Surviving High Risk Patrol* (Northbrook, IL: Calibre Press, 1986), p. 251. This publication continues to provide content for Calibre Press's street survival seminars.
76. Ibid.
77. Ibid., p. 248.
78. Ibid., p. 253.
79. Ibid., p. 252.
80. Ibid.
81. The distinction between these types of stereotyping is taken from Jerry W. Baker and Carl P. Florez, "Robbery Response," *Police Chief*, October 1980, Vol. 47, No. 10, pp. 46-47.
82. Ibid., p. 47.
83. Andy Mehalshick, "Bicycle Bank Robber Strikes Busy Branch," WBRE-TV, www.wbre.com, Sep. 25, 1998.
84. Baker and Florez, "Robbery Response," p. 47.
85. Coleman Cornelius, "Police Bag Bank Heist Suspect," *Denver Post*, Dec. 4, 1998.
86. Geoffrey P. Alpert, *Helicopters in Pursuit Operations* (Washington, DC: National Institute of Justice, 1998), p. 3, with some additions by the authors.
87. Elizabeth Fitzsimmons, "Suspect Can't Elude Copters's Heat Sensor," *San Diego Union-Tribune*, Apr. 4, 2001.
88. Erin Emery, "Note Bandit Suspect Arrested, 23 Businesses Robbed in 33 Days," *Denver Post*, Nov. 4, 1998.
89. Dawn E. McQuiston and Roy S. Malpass, "Use of Facial Composite Systems in U.S. Law Enforcement Agencies," paper presented at the American Law Society Meeting, New Orleans, Louisiana, March 2000.
90. Kevin B. O'Leary, "Robbery 'Hoax': Shootings Real," *Boston Globe*, Nov. 19, 1993, p. 1.
91. Richard Perez-Pena, "Teller Machine Robbery Was a Hoax, Police Say," *New York Times*, Feb. 19, 1994, p. A25.
92. Clifford Krauss, "3 Officers Held in New York Police Sting after Robbery Is Taped," *New York Times*, Mar. 19, 1994, p. A1.
93. Jeremy Travis, *Three Strikes and You're Out: A Review of National Legislation* (Washington, DC: National Institute of Justice, 1997), pp. 1, 3.
94. Jeremy Travis, *Illegal Firearms: Access and Use by Arrestees* (Washington, DC: National Institute of Justice, 1997), p. 3.
95. Ibid.
96. The information in this section was obtained on October 6, 2001, from the following websites: Riverside (California) Police Department, "Information Bulletin: Robbery Prevention," police2.ucr.edu/unetbulletin-1.html; Houston Police Online, "Robbery Prevention for Businesses, www.ci.houston.tx/departme/police/busprev.htm; Eugene (Oregon) Police Department, "Robbery Prevention Tips," www.ci.eugene.or.us/DPS/police/crime%20prevention/robbery.htm.

# THIRTEEN

# Burglary

*During the course of a burglary investigation, often after a burglar is arrested, stolen property is recovered. This property—which is also considered evidence—must be safely stored in a police property/evidence room such as the one pictured. (© Bonnie Kamin)*

## CHAPTER OUTLINE



## CHAPTER OBJECTIVES

1. Be familiar with different types of burglars.
2. Describe appropriate responses to burglaries in progress.
3. Recognize burglary tools.
4. Explain several methods of attacking safes.
5. Identify types of evidence to be collected in safe burglaries.
6. Describe the characteristics of residential burglaries.
7. Understand the investigator's burglary prevention role.
8. Outline strategies for investigating criminal fences and other stolen-property outlets.
9. Describe techniques for reducing the risk of commercial burglary.

## INTRODUCTION

Two important aspects of burglary are its frequency and its economic impact. Nationally, if reported burglaries were distributed evenly over time, one would occur every 15.4 seconds.[1] Residential burglaries account for two-thirds of this category of crime, with the rest being attacks on various types of commercial establishments.[2] In terms of sheer numbers, there are more residential than commercial burglaries. Businesses have a greater risk of being victimized, however, because there are far fewer of them. The average loss in residential offenses is $1,381; in nonresidential offenses it is $1,615.[3]

Nationally, among reported burglaries, 64 percent involve a forcible entry in which an instrument such as a pry bar, screwdriver, or axe is employed; 30 percent of the cases involve an entry without the use of force, such as by using a master key, opening an unlocked door, or picking a lock; the remaining offenses consist of attempted entries.[4] Most burglaries are characterized by entry through a door rather than a window. In general, commercial establishments are entered at the rear, whereas entry for residences tends to be at the front. Attempting to gain entry at the front of a house during the day has a certain logic to it. Neighbors who remain at home are used to seeing salespeople or political workers approach front doors, so seeing any pedestrian approaching a front door is not likely to be considered an abnormal occurrence. In addition, front doors are often recessed, thereby limiting entry way visibility, and many doors can be compromised quickly, further reducing the possibility of detection.

Although national data for reported burglaries vary by month, with July and August having the most burglaries and February the fewest, there is little seasonal fluctuation.[5] Residential burglaries most often occur during working hours on a weekday, when many homes are not occupied; most commercial burglaries are committed on weeknights, when the absence of people can be predicted accurately.

Burglary has a low clearance rate: 13 percent.[6] As a rule of thumb, burglaries resulting in very low or very high property losses are associated with a greater clearance rate than are those that result in midrange losses. Although midrange-loss burglaries are reported more frequently than others, low-loss, petty burglaries are committed by less-sophisticated offenders who are more easily identified and high-loss burglaries receive more attention than do burglaries with midrange losses.

## OFFENDERS

From the time people began using even primitive structures, there were thieves who committed the crime that is now called burglary. The elaborate tombs of the Egyptian pharaohs, designed to send the rulers into the next world in splendor, contained magnificent treasures. They also contained elaborate security features to protect those riches. Yet they were often plundered by thieves of that time.

The nature of burglary has stayed the same over time, but *how* it is committed changes, largely as an influence of technological advances and architectural design. For example, now virtually extinct in the United States are such specialized methods of burglary as entry through coal chutes—because people in this country heat mainly with electricity, natural gas, and even solar power. As municipalities began requiring the use of fire escapes, they were appended to the outside of apartment buildings. This created a new method of burglary—the "step-over." Although people would place bars or other barriers over apartment windows by the fire escape, they would neglect to protect other windows. The step-over artist would go up a fire escape to the apartment to be hit and then step over from the fire escape to the ledge of a window that was unprotected. As interior fire escapes became more common, the opportunities to be a step-over artist gradually declined, although they certainly still exist. A slight variation on the step-over method is still in practice: parents send children as young as 5 years old to do the step-over and then open the apartment door from the inside to let in the parents, who plunder the premises. In the last 10 years a method of burglary that has gained in popularity is one in which the offenders steal a car and drive it through the front door of a gun, a jewelry, or another type of store. Once inside, they grab what they can in 30 to 45 seconds, exit, get picked up by a confederate (who is often operating another just-stolen car), flee the scene, and then abandon the stolen car. This method is essentially an aggravated case of the well-known "smash-and-grab," in which a perpetrator throws a brick or concrete block through the plate-glass window of a jewelry store, seizes what can immediately be reached, and then gets away from the scene as quickly as possible.

Some targets selected for burglaries require more than just crude force; they demand a high level of skill and daring. A former Army paratrooper who stole some $6 million in cash, jewelry, and credit cards was dubbed "Spiderman" by investigators because he specialized in burglarizing high-rise apartments—a total of 132 of them—before he was apprehended. To reach his targets, Spiderman would climb as many as 30 stories on the outside of the buildings—without any climbing equipment.[7] Initially, investigators had difficulty even considering this method of approaching the target because its use seemed too improbable. Some burglaries

 BURGLARY = 13% CLEARANCE RATE

require careful planning and coordination. Thieves stole merchandise from parked Susquehanna Railroad freight cars four times in three months, netting as much as $100,000. The men used 30-inch bolt cutters to force entry into the cars. Once inside, the merchandise was "selected" and walkie-talkies were used to summon gang members driving gutted vans, which were used to haul the loot off. To stay ahead of the police, the ring monitored a police scanner. After surveillance of the tracks failed to produce any results, officers were pulled off of that assignment and the burglars went back to work. However, a man walking his dog at 9:30 P.M. spotted the men on top of the freight cars and alerted police, who were able to make arrests at the scene.[8]

The purposes and functioning of gangs, ethnically based crime organizations, and crime groups are all well understood by law enforcement agencies. The "players" and the criminal orientation of these entities change over time, and occasionally a major new crime group—such as the YACs (Yugoslavian, Croatian, Serbian)—emerges.

New York City is the center for YACs. Although they operate heavily along the East Coast, YACs have been active as far west as California and into southeastern states as well. This crime group specializes in burglarizing ATMs, especially those in supermarkets and malls and outside banks, which may have as much as $100,000 in them.[9] They also attack safes in businesses believed to have cash on hand, such as restaurants and bars. For example, in a two-month period YACs hit 20 restaurants in New York City, steadily bringing in $4,000 to $8,000 per job.

Because YACs operated in different states and most of the burglaries were unsolved, their activity was not understood in the early 1990s. However, as investigators began to develop and share MOs across agencies, states, and regions, a pattern began to emerge. Supermarket operators would arrive to open their stores and find telephone lines slashed to disable the alarms and holes chopped in roofs—through which the burglars entered and attacked the ATMs. At about the same time, the international association for supermarket corporations—the Food Marketing Institute (FMI)—began to meet with law enforcement officials to advance claims that literally hundreds of supermarket ATM burglaries were likely to have been committed by YACs suspects. This, and the growing number of such suspects being arrested for the burglaries, gave investigators a new investigative avenue to pursue.

In response, the FBI created the YACs Crime Group (YCG) and went to work. FMI security managers developed a partnership with the FBI and began reporting all suspected YAC activities to it within 24 hours of all incidents. The New York field office was selected to lead the investigation because the YAC center was located there. One early initiative was to hold conferences in the areas where YACs had been most active, to alert potential targets to the problems. Many corporations examined their security measures and upgraded to "harden" their stores. Some elected to take special measures whereby slashed telephone lines would register as "telecommunication failures" at central monitoring stations—which meant that armed security guards or the police would be dispatched to investigate.

All available records on known YACs were scrutinized for information, and YACs were covertly surveilled to gain additional information. As intelligence piled up, there was a corresponding increase in understanding YAC operations. YACs operated in groups of four to six. Initially, a YAC would be a member of one or more groups; with increased experience, he could become a leader of his own group. Members of a group were selected only hours before going out on a job.

YACs often carried false identification and had a prearranged number to call if they were arrested and needed to be bailed out of jail. This meant that many suspects were released before their true identities were known. Additionally, YACs often supplied other false information when questioned, so written police records were not reliable. All information, including photographs, was centralized by the FBI, and true identities for suspects began to emerge. Armed with this information, investigators and prosecutors were able to arrest many YACs who were fugitives and to demand higher bails for them because they were likely to flee again.

Many YACs were also caught in the act of burglary because intelligence about their organization, members, and tactics was sufficiently sound to allow investigators to take the offensive. Continuous surveillance of YACs across several state boundaries led to their arrest at burglary scenes; in other instances, arrests were made by covering probable targets more closely.

The YACs have been hurt by law enforcement, but they continue to operate, perhaps changing the types of crimes they commit or devising new ways to commit them. The significance of this case history, however, is that it highlights the importance of cooperation and information sharing between enforcement agencies and private industry in an era of highly mobile and sophisticated offenders.

Most burglars are poor and have attained only modest educations. Despite this broad profile, the fact remains that there are many people in well-respected professions who are also burglars:

A former police officer pleaded guilty to 16 felony counts involving a string of residential and commercial burglaries he committed while on duty. Just a month before entering his plea, the 18-year law enforcement veteran was granted a disability pension after experts testified at his retirement hearing that he suffered from an obsessive-compulsive disorder that led to his pathological gambling.[10]

A former church organist was arrested for committing three burglaries of churches and synagogues in which religious items of gold and silver valued at $25,000 were stolen. Following his arrest, the suspect confessed to having burglarized 500 such places, taking articles worth $2.5 million. There was little hope that any of the stolen property would ever be recovered, as it was believed to have been melted down and sold. Police were led to the suspect when a drifter was arrested for disorderly conduct. In the drifter's duffel bag, religious articles were found. He admitted having stolen them from the suspect, who had provided him with shelter for the night.[11]

Because so few burglaries are cleared, it is difficult to make sweeping generalizations, but on the basis of arrest statistics, burglary is overwhelmingly a male endeavor involving multiple perpetrators, with females representing only about 13 percent of those arrested for this offense.[12] Of those arrested for burglary, 64 percent are under 25 years old, 69 percent are Caucasian, and 28 percent are black.[13]

While burglars may be classified according to a number of variables, such as preferences for premises to be attacked and types of property that they will, or will not, take, the most useful classification is skill. Conceived as a continuum, the two extremes would be the amateur and the professional. The largest number of burglars would be clustered toward the less-skilled end of the continuum, with progressively fewer toward the skilled end.

**Professional burglars** may commit only a few offenses per year, going for the bigger "scores":

IN 2001, the FBI, working with Brazilian police officials, recovered three Norman Rockwell paintings valued at over $1 million. Nearly 25 years ago, they were stolen from the Elayne Galleries in St. Louis Park, Minnesota. No one knows how the Rockwells ended up in Brazil. The thieves have never been caught.[14]

SPACE Coast Credit Union employees came to work on a Monday morning to find a hole in the roof over the vault and more than $100,000 missing. The police had responded to the alarm that went off at 12:30 and 1:30 Sunday morning, but they could not see the roof from the parking lot or the highway, nor could they find anyone with a key to the premises so that they could check inside. Several months before, a bank was successfully attacked using the same method of operation. In that case, the burglary was described as "the biggest financial loss in our city."[15]

On the other hand, professional burglars can also be quite active, committing a large number of offenses:

MEMBERS of a burglary ring were arrested for committing some 1,000 burglaries over a three-year period. They selected shops, businesses, and fast-food restaurants that would have anywhere from several thousand to $75,000 on hand. The targets included McDonald's, Pizza Hut, Burger King, and Dunkin Donuts.[16]

While many professional burglars may commit only a few offenses a year, they are of considerable interest to investigators because of the large value of cash or property taken and their intimate knowledge of sophisticated fencing systems, which are often detected, and therefore investigated, only following the apprehension of a professional. In addition to the big score, the hallmark of the professional is the thorough planning that precedes each burglary. Professionals refuse to place themselves in jeopardy for anything other than sizable gains and do so only after weeks or even months of painstaking study of the target selected. Knowing exactly what they want in advance, professionals do not ransack premises. Thus, if they have employed surreptitious methods of entry, articles taken may not be missed for some time. Working nationally, or at the very highest professional level, internationally, this type of burglar often operates for long periods of time without being arrested. When arrested, such burglars are often released without being charged due to a lack of physical evidence, coupled with their own adroitness in responding to the questions of investigators. When operating in elegant hotels or apartment buildings, the professional will use a businesslike appearance and manners to talk his way out of a situation. Should an occupant return unexpectedly, the burglar may pull out forged credentials identifying him as the building's security officer and say he found the door ajar and was just beginning his investigation. Or he may pretend to be drunk, ask for directions to some similarly numbered room, and stagger away acting very confused.

However, if these or similar ploys fail or if the burglar's real intent is apparent, the professional will employ violence if necessary to escape:

A well-known cardiologist was shot to death when he walked into the burglary of his home in a fashionable section of Washington, DC. The police arrested a man who was alleged to be a "superthief" for the crimes. Upon searching the suspect's swank suburban home, the police found some $4 million worth of allegedly stolen property. It took the police 472 man-hours and 400 legal-size pages to count, tag, and describe the property. The 18-foot truck in which the seized property was transported away contained 51 large boxes and two smelters that were believed to have been used to melt down precious metals.[17]

**Amateur burglars** often operate on the basis of impulse or react to suddenly presented opportunities. Such burglars tend to work not only in one city but often in a relatively small segment of it. Amateurs may cruise in cars looking for businesses to victimize, prowl hotels seeking unlocked doors, or try to locate doors whose locks can be easily slipped using a credit card. While amateurs may occasionally enjoy a relatively big score, it is the absence of preplanning that sharply differentiates them from professionals. If they are narcotics addicts, amateurs must often work four or more days per week, committing several offenses each day, in order to support their habits; even if they are not addicts, this may still be necessary to support their lifestyles. Frequently using sheer force to enter, amateurs crudely ransack businesses or residences to find anything of value. Occasionally, unlike their discerning professional counterparts, they take costume jewelry in the belief that they have found something of considerable value. When confronted by an unexpectedly returning business owner or occupant of a residence, amateurs may become immediately violent, and secondary crimes, such as murder or rape, unintended in the original concept of the offense, will occur. Finally, amateur burglars often have lengthy records and are frequently in and out of jail.

## THE LAW

The crime of **burglary** generally consists of the following elements: (1) breaking and (2) entering (3) a dwelling house or other building (4) belonging to another, (5) with the intent to commit a crime therein. The common-law crime of burglary necessitates that the act be committed in the nighttime. This element has been deleted in a number of state statutes.

Burglary and related offenses are classified as crimes against the habitation, dwelling, or building itself; no force need be directed against a person. The breaking element may be satisfied through acts that constitute a breaking into, a breaking out of, or a breaking within. Generally, the slightest force used to remove or put aside something material that makes up a part of the building and is relied on to prevent intrusion, for example, doors or windows, constitutes breaking. This element can be satisfied whether accomplished at the hands of the perpetrator, through the use of some inanimate object like a brick, or by the participation of an innocent third party. Similarly, the element of entry is satisfied once the slightest intrusion has taken place by the perpetrator, an inanimate object, an animal, or an innocent third person.

The character of the building at which the breaking and entering takes place will largely determine the type of offense committed. The most serious offense is breaking and entering of a dwelling house, that is, a place used by another person as a residence. The nature of the dwelling itself is not determinative but, rather, the manner in which it is used. Hence, a hotel room can be considered a dwelling house.

The other major ingredient controlling the nature of the crime is the intent with which the perpetrator unlawfully breaks and enters the building. The more serious the crime intended to be committed after entry, the more serious becomes the breaking and entering itself. Thus, the most serious breaking-and-entering offense is that which is done with the intent to commit a felony.

## APPROACHING THE SCENE AND INITIAL ACTIONS

When responding to a burglary-in-progress call, uniformed officers should drive rapidly while avoiding excessive noise, such as the dramatic but unnecessary use of the siren. The last several blocks to the scene should be driven at lower speeds for two reasons. Doing so eliminates the possibility that the squealing tires of the police vehicle will give the perpetrators, if still on the scene, the advantage of crucial seconds of warning. Additionally, lower speeds allow opportunity for observation. A vehicle driving away from the vicinity of the scene may be seen and its description and license plate number noted as a possible investigative lead. Under such conditions, late-model, expensive cars, such as Cadillacs or Lincolns, should not be discounted. Burglars often select these, not only because of the large amounts of equipment and stolen property such cars can hold but also because they recognize the fact that the police often act with deference to the occupants of these vehicles because of the implied social status.

When dispatched to a burglary-in-progress call, the uniformed officer working alone should attempt to coordinate his or her arrival time and position with the backup unit. This will enable the officers to secure the building immediately. One unit can arrive positioned so that it can watch two sides of the building, for example, the north and east sides, while the other unit can observe the west and south sides. When a two-officer unit is dispatched to a burglary-in-progress call, the operator of the police vehicle should drop his or her partner off in a position to view two sides of the building and position the vehicle to allow observation of the remaining two sides. When working alone, if it is necessary to begin checking the building immediately, the uniformed officer should drive around the building to determine whether there is a readily observable break. If this is not possible, the officer should check rapidly, but cautiously, on foot. When a flashlight is used during the hours of darkness, it should be held away from the body, as the suspect is most likely to aim at the light source if firing at the officer. If a point of entry is established, under no circumstances should an officer attempt to enter, as entering would needlessly expose him or her to extreme danger. Most burglars prefer to be unarmed because, in many states, breaking and entering while armed is a more serious offense than an unarmed breaking and entering. However, occasionally burglars are armed and willing to use their weapons to avoid apprehension:

A woman whose home overlooked the back of a shopping center saw two people break into a dress shop through the rear door. She called 911, who gave the call out as a burglary in progress, subjects on the premises. A motorcycle officer who was returning to the station at the end of his shift heard the call, which was assigned to a patrol unit, and swung by to back them up because he was close to the scene. The woman, still connected to 911, gave a running account of what happened. The motorcycle officer pulled up and pointed his lights at the rear door. Instead of maintaining his position and waiting for assistance, he walked up to the door—fully silhouetted by his own lights. As he stood in the doorway, he was shot three times and collapsed. As the officer lay dying, one of the perpetrators stood over him and emptied his pistol into him. This death should not have occurred. It was caused because the officer used a tactically unsound procedure and because he encountered armed subjects willing to shoot it out with the police. Both subjects were arrested at the scene. Follow-up investigation revealed that they had a major incentive to use deadly force against the police—they were wanted on murder charges in two other states.

The fact that no point of entry is determined by riding or walking around the building does not mean that a forcible entry has not occurred. Whenever possible, the roof should be checked, particularly vents and skylights.

Even if there is an alarm sounding, there may not be a burglary. Alarms frequently malfunction, particularly during inclement weather. However, officers must never become complacent about checking premises with a reputation for false alarms. If a breaking and entering has occurred, additional cars, if available, should be brought into the general area. Burglars often park their vehicles some blocks from the building to be attacked, and the perpetrator may not yet have had time to flee the area. "Lovers" parked in the general area should not go overlooked by the police. Burglars often use couples as lookouts or have their girlfriends remain in the car while they commit the offense. The perpetrator may have reached the car but have been unable to flee the immediate area; the use of a "just parked lovers" story may allow him to escape detection.

If a burglary has been committed and the police department has a canine unit, the uniformed officer at the scene should request its presence before entering the building. The alarm servicing company will ordinarily have a representative at the scene fairly rapidly to provide officers with access to the building. If there is no alarm, then the owner must be contacted either from information usually posted on the door or from other sources. Before beginning the crime scene search, officers must thoroughly check the building to ensure that the burglar is not hiding on the premises. In order to achieve the proper degree of caution, the building check should be conducted as though it were known that the burglar was still there.

## INVESTIGATIVE CONSIDERATIONS AT THE SCENE

Caution must be exercised to avoid the accidental destruction of physical evidence while attempting to make a determination of whether the burglar is still in the building. Officers should be sensitive to the possible presence of physical evidence but not act in a manner that might jeopardize the most important thing—the officer's safety. If gross physical force has been used in gaining entry, the point of attack is easily established. However, one cannot assume that it is also the point of exit. Often burglars will break into a building at a particular point and then leave by opening a door. Where gross physical force is used, the point of attack is of particular importance because it may yield the types of physical evidence discussed in Chapter 3, "Physical Evidence." In combination, the determination of the points of attack and exit will suggest the avenues of approach and flight traveled by the perpetrator, which also must be explored for the possible presence of physical evidence.

Officers must be particularly attentive for unusual signs that may be of investigative value. Juvenile burglars commonly commit destructive acts of vandalism. Also, age may be suggested from the choices of what is taken and what is left behind:

> When I started hustling . . . didn't know much, like what crap be really worth and how to get bills for it . . . at first alotta stuff I just leave back . . . just grabbed things for me . . . like a nice coat or small crap you can just walk with and sell quick for cash . . . like a gun . . . main thing for me was getting some bills so I could high-cat around and get stuff . . . Nike shoes. I couldn't walk around with no stereo or tv . . . had to leave the big stuff.

The sudden removal of trophies or other prized possessions by their owner from a business or residence, followed by a burglary for the purpose of committing an arson, should raise certain questions in the investigator's mind. Further, the weight or dimensions of property taken in a burglary may suggest, if only roughly, the number of people involved in the offense. Articles or tools left behind, combined with other specifics of the crime, may be useful in the identification of an MO.

Many commercial establishments keep check imprinters on their premises. A not uncommon occurrence is for a burglar to gain entry to a commercial building, tear several checks from the company checkbook, imprint them, and cash them the next day. Thus, it is of particular importance to have the

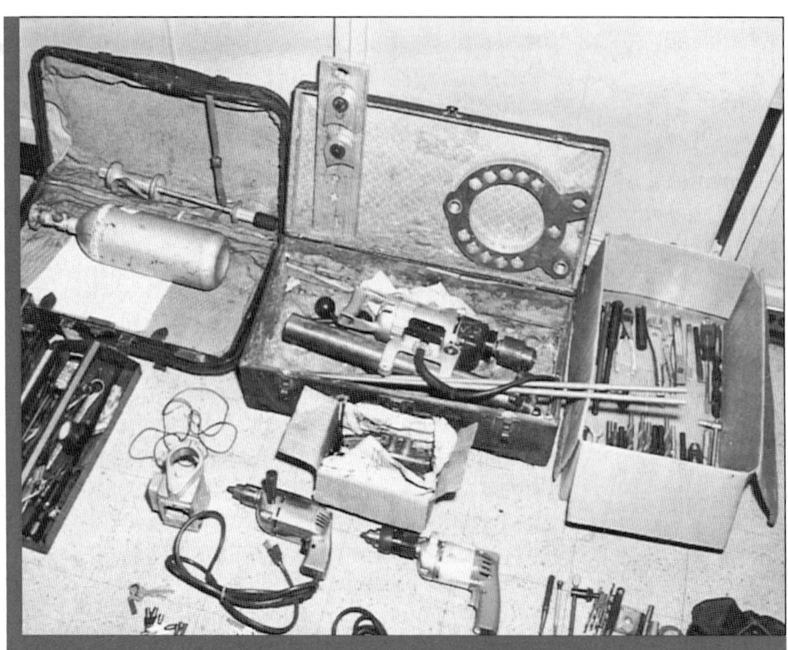

### Burglary Tools

An array of tools commonly employed by a burglar who specialized in attacking safes. Many of these tools are similar to those found in a typical household. For example, screwdrivers or crowbars may be sharpened to be effective in attacking doors and windows.

proprietor ensure that no checks have been taken. Normally, when a burglar employs this practice the checks will be taken from the very rear of the book or from several different series in order to lessen the likelihood of detection.

## RECOGNITION OF BURGLARY TOOLS

Most often when tools used in the commission of a burglary are recovered at the scene, they are not very different from those found in many house-

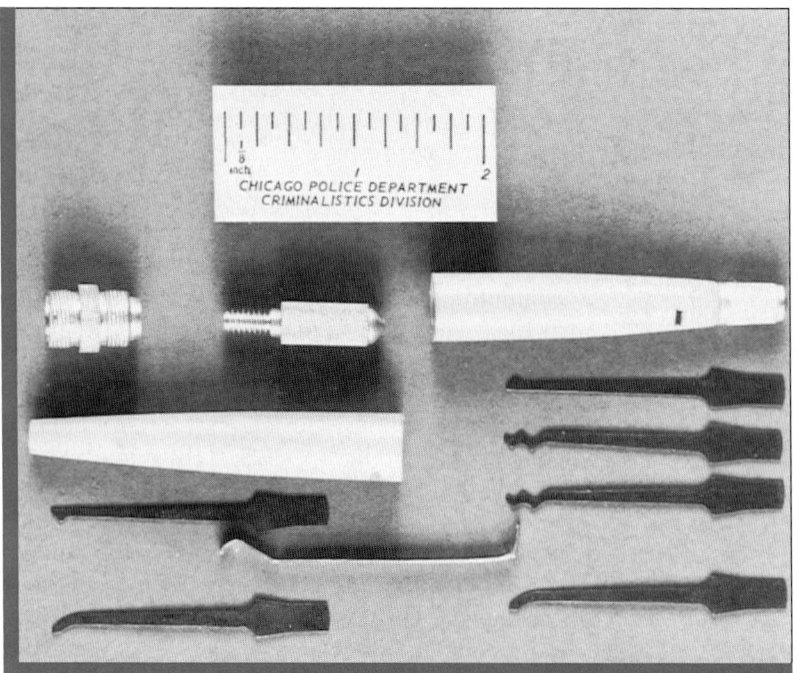


### A "Ball-Point-Pen" Container for Concealing Lock Picks

Apprehension of a suspect not in the act of a burglary but in possession of lock picks—specifically modified tools or standard tools that can be used in burglaries—may permit a felony charge of possession of burglary tools. Professional burglars often try to hide their specialized tools in common carrying cases such as the ball-point-pen container shown here.

### Lock Picks Concealed in an Eyeglass-Type Case

Another example of the craftiness of professional burglars is shown in this photo, where an eyeglass-type case is used to conceal various burglary tools. Some states require that a person found in possession of burglary tools must have a prior conviction before a felony charge of possession of burglary tools can be placed against him.

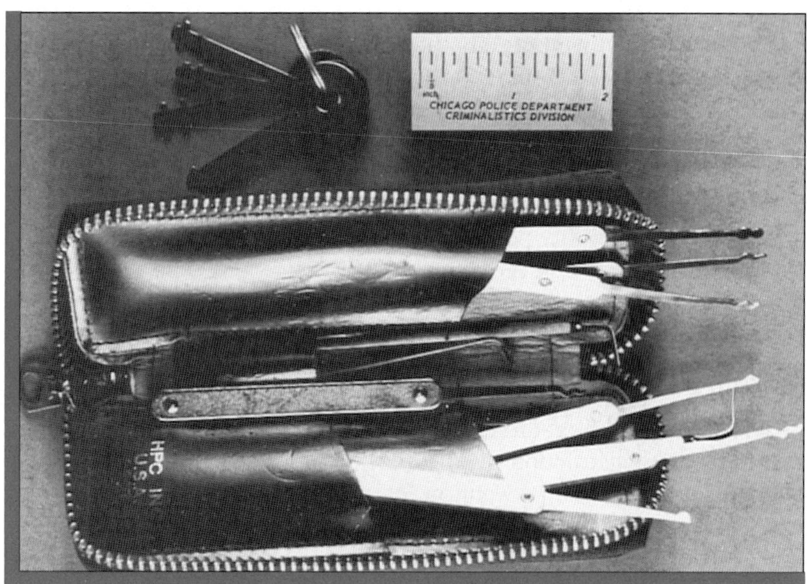


holds. A partial list of **burglary tools** includes knives, screwdrivers, crowbars, tire irons, pipe wrenches, chisels, sledgehammers, hacksaws, hydraulic jacks, bolt cutters, vise grips, axes, and glass cutters. In the crude smash-and-grab burglary, where the display window of a jewelry store is broken and articles immediately available are taken, the "tool" may be as unsophisticated as a brick in a paper sack. However, tools left at the scene may have been subject to certain adaptations to facilitate their use in a burglary (see photo). Screwdrivers or crowbars may be carefully sharpened or shaped to increase their effectiveness in attacking doors and windows; nippers can be transformed into lock pullers if they are honed in a manner that permits firmer biting ability on exposed lock edges. Burglars will also apply masking tape in the shape of a cone to the end of a flashlight so that it emits only a very thin light beam.

Apprehension of a suspect not in the act of burglary but in possession of lock picks (see photos on page 468 and above), specially modified tools, or standard tools that can be used in burglaries may permit a felony charge of possession of burglary tools. Some states require that a person have a prior conviction for burglary in order for this charge to be placed. Even where this requirement does not exist, proof of intent to commit burglary is essential for conviction.

## SURREPTITIOUS ENTRIES

Occasionally, the investigation of a burglary cannot establish a point of entry or exit. What happens in such instances is in large measure determined by the knowledge and thoroughness of the investigator, who may initiate a report indicating "entrance by unexplained means," decline to take a report due to lack of evidence, or take a report knowing that due to departmental policy it will subsequently be designated "unfounded." Complaints of this nature frequently involve **surreptitious entries;** that is, a burglary has occurred, but there was no apparent force used. Excluding the case of closed but unlocked doors, the most common explanations are that the door was "loided," the lock was picked, or the premises were victimized by someone who has an unauthorized possession of a key.

**Loiding** is the act of slipping or shimming, by using a strip of celluloid, a spring-bolt lock that does not have an antishim device. Technically, a spring bolt without an antishim device should be considered a privacy, rather than a security, device. Simply stated, **picking** is a process of manipulating a lock into an unlocked position using picks rather than a key. When picking is suspected as the means used to gain entry, the lock should be submitted to the laboratory for examination. By examining the lock, the laboratory will be able to determine whether or not the lock was picked. From the marks alone on a lock, the laboratory cannot state the type of picking device used, except in general terms. If, however, a pick is seized as evidence, it is possible to make an individual identification by comparing the marks on the lock with test marks made by the seized pick. To facilitate the reassembly of the lock after its examination by laboratory personnel, the key should also be submitted. The laboratory cannot determine whether a lock was loided, due to the lack of physical evidence associated with this technique.

Officers must be familiar with privacy and security devices, as this increases their investigative effectiveness and the credibility of their testimony, assists in the construction of MO files, generates data to support crime prevention legislation, and allows them to talk knowledgeably before community groups.

## IMPORTANCE OF THE TIME FACTOR

An important aspect of taking burglary reports is attempting to determine when the offense took place. Typically, burglaries are reported from several hours to a number of days after they are committed. Late reporting is largely attributable to the circumstances of businesses being closed for the weekend and home owners being away for short trips or extended vacations. Summer communities, populated by people living some distance away who visit their mountain or lakefront vacation homes only intermittently, represent a large problem for the police. Such residences are particularly vulnerable to burglars, who may take all the furniture and dispose of it several months before the offense is even detected. In such instances, the estimate of the time frame in which the offense occurred will of necessity be very broad. Frequently, however, it is possible to identify a range of time during which the perpetrator attacked the premises; the range can then be correlated with other data to provide investigative leads and to include or exclude certain persons as suspects. For example, a person known to employ an MO similar to the one used in a particular offense would be a suspect. If, however, a field interrogation report was initiated on him some

**Figure 13-1** Typical Fire-Resistant Safe

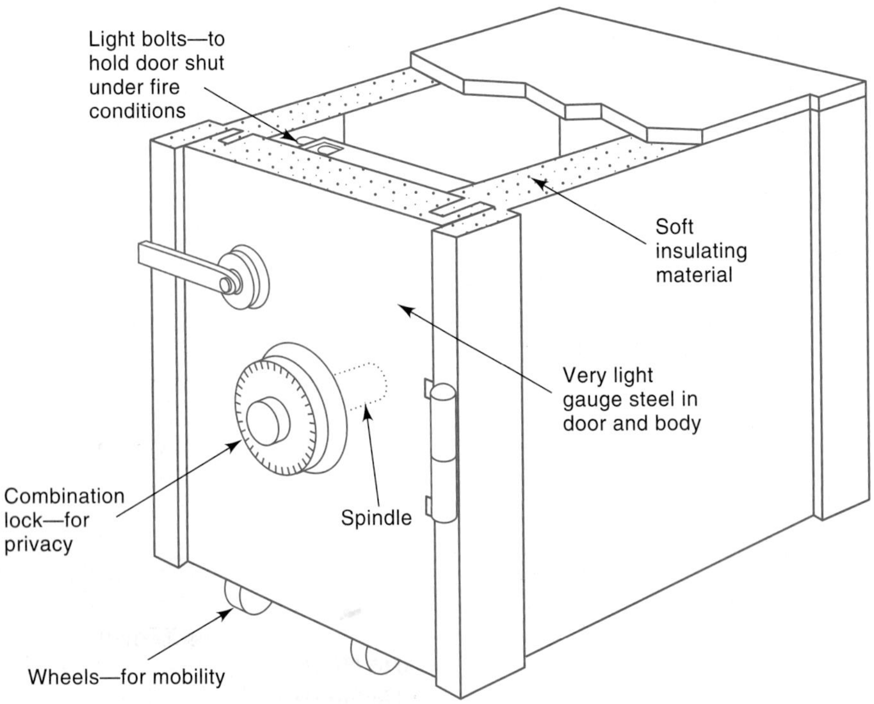

Figure 13-2 Money Chest

The money chest is a burglary-resistant safe; note the round door.

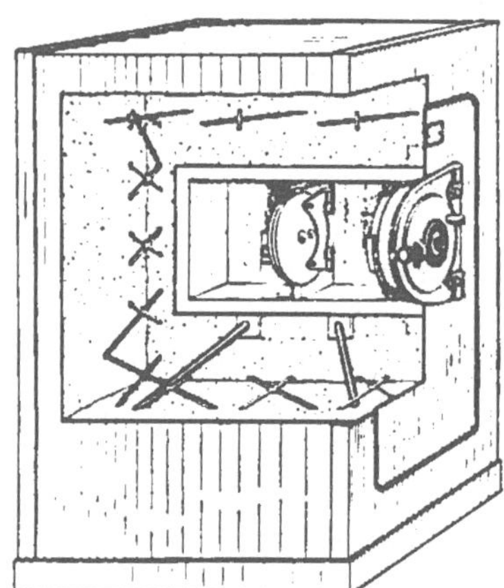

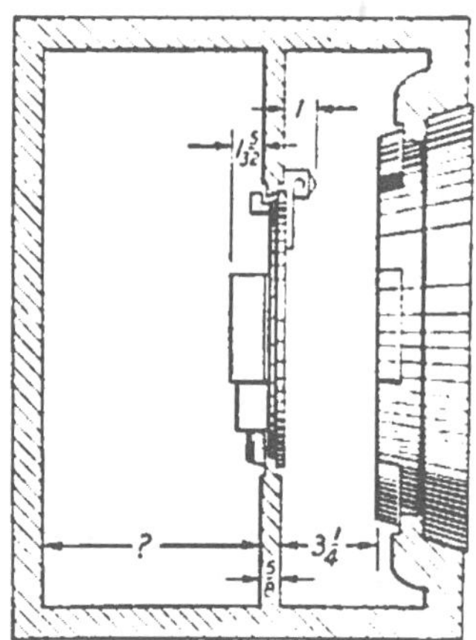

distance away from the scene at about the same time that the offense occurred, his presence there would have been virtually impossible, thus excluding him as a suspect. While this example is an unusual occurrence, its essence is important. As the time range in which the offense could have taken place narrows, other information becomes more useful.

## SAFE BURGLARIES

### TYPES OF SAFES

Safe burglaries do not occur with any great frequency. Improved designs of commercial buildings have created harder targets, the use of credit and debit cards limits the amount of cash on hand, sophisticated alarm systems are more readily affordable, more stringent employee screening has reduced the flow of information from tipsters, newer safe designs are increasingly "harder nuts to crack," and private police patrols have increased the chances of detection. All of these factors have contributed to the decline of this type of crime over the past several decades. Yet it is still important to provide some information on safe burglaries so that officers can be well-rounded in their knowledge and avoid destroying special types of evidence. Moreover, without such knowledge, officers might take uninformed actions at safe-burglary scenes, some of which could be fatal to them.

The term **safe** is often used with little appreciation of the difference between fire-resistant safes and those intended to be burglar resistant. Victimized business owners will lament, "How could this happen to me; how could they have gotten into my safe?" In fact, what has been compromised is a fire-resistant safe, the construction of which is intended to protect the contents from heat, with a lock system intended for privacy, rather then security.

To the uninitiated, most safes look very much alike: they are relatively large, have combination locks, and seem heavy. Safes, however, can be divided into two distinct classes: the fire-resistant safe and the money chest, which is intended to be burglar resistant. In general, fire-resistant safes have square or rectangular doors, while money chests have round ones (see Figures 13–1 and 13–2). There are, however, a few money chests with square or rectangular doors; a check of the manufacturer's label, which is attached to the inside of the door, will resolve any confusion in classifying the safe. The walls of the fire-resistant safe are of comparatively light metal with a thick insulation between the inner and outer walls to protect the contents from heat. The money chest has thick walls and a strong door. Fire-resistant safes are graded by the period of time they can protect their contents from a particular level of heat. In contrast, money chests are classified by the amount of time they can protect their contents from attack by an expert burglar using common hand tools, mechanical tools, torches, and explosives. The fire-resistant safe provides protection from fire but only a minimum amount of security. Security and reasonably good protection from fire are given by the money chest. There are also dual-purpose units, often configured as an outer fire-resistant safe with an inner round-door money chest.

### ATTACK METHODS FOR SAFES

Knowledge of methods of safe attack is important because it allows the investigator to make judgments about the skill and knowledge of the perpetrator and thus narrow the focus of the investigation. The methods of safe attack include the punch, pulling, the peel, the rip, blasting, drilling, burning, manipulation, the pry, and the carry-off. Some of these methods are encountered infrequently, but they are included here because in the few instances when they are used, investigators must be prepared to respond properly. The methods of safe attack are summarized in Table 13–1.

### SAFE-BURGLARY EVIDENCE

The scenes of safe burglaries are usually rich with physical evidence. Broken parts of screwdrivers, pry bars, drill bits, and other equipment offer the possibility of making a fracture match with the remaining portion in the suspect's possession. If a drill and bit are seized from a suspect, marks on drill-bit shavings recovered at the scene can be compared to those made by the equipment seized. Drilling is noisy, so safe crackers may make special sound-deadening boxes in which to place their drills. The materials used have the potential to be matched with the remaining material in the suspect's possession. Bolt cutters recovered from the suspect's home can be tested in the laboratory to see whether the striae made match those on chains, padlock hasps, or fences at the burglary site. Slag seized at the scene of a burning job can be analyzed for consistency with samples obtained from the suspect's car or home. At some burglaries opportunities to locate DNA evidence exist: offenders may have left hats with dandruff in the sweatbands; may have cut themselves accidentally when using equipment, leaving blood; may have left their saliva on water or other bottles they brought to or used at the scene; or may have used the bathroom but forgot to flush, leaving urine. They may have used company telephones to make calls, providing investigative leads, and one cannot ignore the possibility of finding latent prints and impressions.

Whenever an attack on a safe has exposed the safe insulation, samples should be collected as evidence. Depending on circumstances, particles of insulation may be found on perpetrators' tools, adhering to their clothing; under their fingernails; in their shoes, pants cuffs, or pockets; on the floormat of their car; or embedded in their shoes. In a number of cases safe insulation has been found in the nail holes of shoe heels several weeks after the commission of the offense.

It is the variation among insulations that makes them valuable as class evidence. Many safes made before 1930 contain an insulation of natural cement made by burning to a powder certain claylike limestones, used without gravel or cement only as safe insulation. A number of more recently made safes use an insulation of diatomaceous earth, portland cement, and vermiculite mica, a combination used only in safe insulation. Many brands of safes contain distinctive insulation, samples of which are kept in the FBI laboratory files. It is, therefore, possible to compare insulation found on a suspect's tools or person with those in the file and name the make of safe from which it came. Some safe manufacturers use material for insulation, such as gypsum mixed with wood chips, which is not peculiar to safe insulation. In such instances, however, laboratory examination can establish consistency, or the lack thereof, between insulation samples from the scene and from the suspect.

As a final note on the value of safe insulation as evidence, establishing intent is important in charging a person with possession of burglary tools. Tools found with what can be conclusively established as safe insulation on them may be the basis for providing that intent.

## RESIDENTIAL BURGLARY

Earlier in this chapter it was noted that residential burglaries were primarily committed during the day, with the front door being the point of attack.

**Table 13-1** Methods of Safe Attack

| Method | Execution | Comments |
|---|---|---|
| Punch or punching | The attacker knocks off the combination dial, either by swinging a heavy hammer down from above or by placing a cold chisel at the top center of the dial and striking its end sharply with a hammer. The attacker places a punch on the exposed head of the spindle and forcefully strikes the end of the punch. Hammering sounds are masked by deadening all to-be-struck surfaces with a piece of inner tube or cloth. The safe's locking mechanism is defeated by the force of the spindle's being driven into it. | The spindle is the axle on which the combination dial rotates the safe's tumblers or locking wheels.<br>The punch requires little skill and little knowledge of the safe's construction.<br>This method is most successful in attacking older fire-resistant safes; it does not work with safes that have tapered spindles because they cannot be driven into the locking mechanism, nor does it work with money chests.<br>The principle disadvantage of this method is the amount of noise made. |
| Pulling, drag, or come-along | The attacker places a wheel-puller over the combination dial, flat against the safe's face, and uses the wheel-puller to extract the spindle. | Whereas the punch forces the spindle inward, this method forcibly moves it in the opposite direction.<br>This method is rarely seen due to improved types of safe construction.<br>It will work with some older fire-resistant safes but not with money chests. |
| Peel | The attacker makes a small hole in the safe's outer metal skin, often at the upper left-hand corner of the face of the safe. A large pry bar is then used to peel the metal skin off the face. This exposes the locking bolts and locking mechanisms, which are then compromised. | This is the common method of attack on fire-resistant safes, often after a failed attempt at punching the safe.<br>Moderate knowledge of safe construction is required.<br>The more skill the perpetrator has, the less the damage done to the safe.<br>If efforts to start the peel have failed at several locations, a less-experienced "safe cracker" is suggested.<br>This method creates a lot of noise and physical evidence.<br>The peel works on some fire-resistant safes but not on money chests.<br>Inexperienced peelers will simply beat on the safe with sledgehammers until crude force creates the initial opening. |
| Rip or rip job | Crude physical force is used to make a hole in the safe. The hole is expanded until it is big enough to allow a hand to fit inside the safe. The attacker then reaches inside and takes whatever is in the safe. | Sometimes the "chop" is thought of as a separate method of safe attack. Technically, the chop is a rip applied to what is sometimes the weakest portion of the safe, its bottom. Often an axe is used to execute a chop.<br>This method is very noisy and creates a large amount of physical evidence.<br>The rip is successful with a number of fire-resistant safes but not with money chests. |

*(continued on next page)*

**Table 13-1** Methods of Safe Attack, *continued*

| Method | Execution | Comments |
|---|---|---|
| Blasting or soup job | Explosives are applied to the safe. They are set off, and the safe's contents are taken. | This method, which can be effective with all types of safes, has virtually disappeared because of the stiffer state penalties associated with carrying explosives during a burglary and federal laws regulating the sale and use of explosives.<br>If you encounter explosives, know how to protect yourself and others: Don't touch them; call the ordinance team. In the room where the explosives are located and in adjacent rooms, do not turn lights on or off, do not change settings on thermostats or equipment, open windows and doors, and do not take photographs using flash attachments. Evacuate the building; do not transmit on your radio within 300 feet or allow the use of mobile radios within 500 feet. |
| Drilling | The perpetrator precisely marks off where the drilling will be done. The drill may be mounted on a jig to promote stability and accuracy when drilling to compromise the safe. | Expert knowledge of safe construction is necessary, and the perpetrator must be a skilled driller.<br>Drilling easily defeats fire-resistant safes and is the most successful method of attacking money chests.<br>A variant of precision drilling is using a core drill to remove a plug from the safe, usually on its sides or bottom, and then reaching in and taking the safe's contents. If a core drill is not available, the attacker may accomplish the same thing by repeatedly drilling in the same area.<br>Diamond and carbide-tipped bits and a high-torque drill are required. |
| Burning or torch job | The attacker places the oxygen and acetylene tanks near the safe and hooks up the cutting "torch." He or she precisely marks off where the cutting will be done, lights the torch, and makes the cuts. | This method is successful with fire-resistant safes and money chests, although its use on the former indicates inexperience because it is a much more advanced technique than is required to get the job done.<br>Characteristically, an experienced cutter makes smooth, clean cuts, while a novice makes jagged lines that are often connected by round holes where he or she paused too long.<br>Smaller, portable oxygen and acetylene tanks are preferred.<br>Although cutters often wear gloves, they may roll their sleeves up to be cooler and may have unexplained burns, possibly caused by molten slag.<br>Offenders may have committed one or more burglaries to get the equipment they need to do the job. |

*(continued)*

**Table 13-1 Methods of Safe Attack,** *concluded*

| Method | Execution | Comments |
|---|---|---|
| Combination manipulation | The combination dial is worked back and forth so that the tumblers can be heard falling into position. Using those numbers, attacker opens the safe. | Genuine manipulation is a rarity, but it is possible on old, worn-out safes. Look for some other explanation (e.g., insider information or the combination numbers left in an obvious place. Attackers who are given the combination numbers may attempt to conceal this fact by doing damage to the safe. If the force applied would not have opened the safe, it's likely the perpetrator was given the numbers by an insider or former employee. |
| Pry or prying | For a fire-resistant safe, a large pry bar is used, usually on the top front edge of the safe, to separate the door from the rest of the safe. Occasionally, a logging chain attached to a hydraulic jack is used for the same purpose. | This is an amateurish method and will not compromise money chests. |
| Carry-off | Strictly speaking, the carry-off is not a method of attacking safes. The safe is simply removed from the premises and then attacked elsewhere using any of the above methods. | Often the safe will be taken to an isolated location, such as the woods, a barn, a warehouse, or an abandoned building. |

Black home owners are victimized at a higher rate than any other group.[18] The younger the head of a household is, the more likely that the residence will be burglarized.[19] As shown in Table 13–2, the losses associated with residential burglaries are not intrinsically significant. However, to many households even relatively small losses are devastating. Moreover, when you consider the residual feelings of the victims, there is another type of loss: Victims feel as though their privacy has been violated. They often struggle psychologically afterward to regain a sense of security in their own homes.

Many burglars are amateurs in the sense that even though they may commit the crime numerous times, they often act on impulse, driven by the need to have money:

> Usually when I get in my car and drive around I'm thinking, I don't have any money, so what is my means for money? All of a sudden I'll just take a glance and say, there it is, there's the house! . . . Then I get the feelin', that very moment that I'm moving then.[20]

Some burglars report that "legitimate" financial emergencies are the only reason they resort to breaking in:

> Usually what I'll do is a burglary [or a couple of them] if I have to . . . helps get me over the rough spot until I can get it straightened out. Once I get it straightened out, I just go with the flow until I hit a rough spot where I need the money again . . . The only time I would go and commit a burglary is if I needed money at that point in time. That would be strictly to pay light bill, gas bill, rent.[21]

While there are clearly such cases, burglaries are more often committed for other reasons:

> I might find somebody with some good crack . . . while I'm high I say damn I want me some more of that good shit. Go knock a place off, make some more money, go buy some more dope.[22]

> I use the burglary money for gifts for young ladies—flowers or negligee or somethin'. Some

**Table 13-2** Home-Burglary Victimizations by Amount of Loss

| Amount of Loss | Percentage of Burglaries |
|---|---|
| No loss | 3.1% |
| Less than $50 | 13.8 |
| $50–$99 | 7.8 |
| $100–$249 | 19.1 |
| $250–$499 | 12.0 |
| $500–$999 | 8.5 |
| $1,000 or more | 21.3 |
| Not known/not available | 14.5 |

**Source:** Bureau of Justice Statistics, *Criminal Victimization in the United States–1999* (Washington, DC: U.S. Department of Justice, 2001) p. 75, table 83.

> shoes . . . put them shoes on, them pumps . . . then watch 'em dance nude.[23]

> See I go steal money and go buy me some clothes . . . See, I like to look good. I likes to dress . . . own only one pair of blue jeans 'cause I like to dress [well].[24]

> Burglary is excitin' . . . it's just a thrill to going in undetected and walking out with all their shit . . . like going on a treasure hunt.[25]

From these quotes, it can be seen that burglars tend to commit their crimes for four broad reasons: (1) keeping themselves and their families fed, clothed, and sheltered, (2) keeping the party going, (3) keeping up appearances so that they can look better off financially than they are, and (4) keeping adventure in their lives.[26]

While amateur burglars act on impulse, the more professional burglars are, the less likely they are to take such chances. They develop information on their own or pay tipsters for it. They may simply cruise well-to-do neighborhoods looking for opportunities or follow expensive cars to their homes. Once they have identified a preliminary target, they begin a "workup," watching the house until they have become familiar with the people who live there, their daily routines, the absence or presence of alarms and dogs, views of possible attack points from other homes in the area, and frequency of private and public police patrols. One way of developing information on their own is simply to read the newspapers. Wedding announcements often reveal that a couple will honeymoon in another city or country and then reside in whatever community. With a little effort, burglars can often find out the actual address and burglarize the home, stealing wedding gifts and other items, while the victimized couple are blissfully enjoying their honeymoon. Other types of announcements that might provide similar opportunities include funeral arrangements and gala charity events or parties, which many wealthy people can be expected to attend. Butlers and maids can get lists of the people attending such events. Tipsters—sometimes called "spotters," "fingermen," "noses," or "setup people"—are another source of information that can be used in selecting homes for burglaries. For example, insiders at cruise ship operations can provide passenger lists. Medical personnel know when patients will be in their offices for appointments. Workers in various occupations enter numerous homes legitimately, such as telephone installers and flower delivery workers, and have the chance to size up opportunities. Coworkers know when their bosses are going on vacation. Insurance office personnel know which homes' contents have been heavily insured and which may have special riders attached for silverware or other valuables. Armed with such information, professional burglars reduce the risk of apprehension and increase the probability of "making a nice haul."

Homes are burglarized during the day because that's when the occupants are most likely to be gone—working, attending school, or running errands. The same generally holds true with many neighbors, who might otherwise witness the attack. Burglars do not want to attract attention to themselves, but they also do not want a confrontation with an occupant. If they have learned the home's telephone number, they will call to see if anyone is there. While an answering machine encourages some burglars, it makes others leery of going ahead, fearing that someone is home and using the machine to screen the calls. Alarms and dead-bolt locks are a deterrent to amateur burglars but not to more professional ones. Residential burglars usually do not have to carry an assortment of tools because so many targets are "soft." Often they carry little other than workman's gloves and a large screwdriver or small pry bar. If they cannot easily effect entry at the front door, they will try to enter through the garage—which is ideal because they are out of sight—or a rear window. Most home burglars go straight to the bedroom because that's where most people keep small valuables, such as jewelry, cash, furs, and guns. The master bathroom is also where most people keep their prescription drugs. As their experience builds up, burglars will begin to check the "clever" places where people hide their valuables, including in freezer compartments and behind towels in linen closets. If they have an accomplice, they will call him or her to bring the vehicle into which televisions, VCRs, stereo systems, tools, and other valuables are loaded. Table 13–3 shows the seven types of property most commonly taken in burglaries.

**Table 13-3** Property Most Frequently Taken from Residences

| Type of Property | Percentage of Burglaries |
|---|---|
| Cash | 6.5% |
| Purse, wallet, credit cards | 2.6 |
| Vehicles or parts (including bicycles) | 4.5 |
| Household furnishings | 10.5 |
| Portable electronics, photography gear, jewelry, clothing | 28.0 |
| Firearms | 2.1 |
| Tools, machinery | 7.9 |
| Total | 62.1% |

**Source:** Bureau of Justice Statistics, *Criminal Victimization in the United States—1999* (Washington, DC: U.S. Department of Justice, 2001) p. 89, table 84.

## INVESTIGATING CRIMINAL FENCES AND OTHER OUTLETS FOR STOLEN PROPERTY

Criminal **fences** or **receivers** are persons who knowingly purchase stolen property at a fraction of its cost and then resell it at a considerable profit but still at a "really good deal" price to the consumer. Fences usually buy at 10 to 20 percent of an item's actual cost or may simply set a flat price for the goods, for example, $700 for a particular year, make, and model of car. How "hot" the goods are and how quickly they can be safely resold are also factors in setting the price.

When confronted with someone who bought property that later turned out to be stolen, officers must determine whether the purchaser acted in good or bad faith. Among the indicators of a buyer's lack of good faith are:

1. Paying a price below that of a "good bargain."
2. Purchasing from persons who are not known to them.
3. Buying from persons whom they don't know how to recontact.
4. Accepting items without a receipt.
5. Buying property that bears an obliterated identification number or from which the number has been removed.
6. Purchasing articles that have unusual property control numbers on them, such as those identifying the owner as a state agency.
7. Having a past history of receiving stolen property.

The most basic notion of a fence is that after committing a burglary or another crime (e.g., hijacking a truckload of clothing), the thief takes the merchandise (e.g., a television) to the fence and says, "How much will you give me for it?" While this approach is still used, fencing has become considerably more complicated, and there are numerous types of fences,[27] as shown by these examples:

- *Amateurs*, who usually do fencing intermittently, have limited resources, and may buy stolen goods for resale to friends, as gifts to girlfriends, or for their own personal use.
- *Store owners and individuals*, who often buy only the goods for which they have placed an order with the thief or only from a thief who works for them relatively full time. Such thieves may also work as freelancers or as members of gangs, some of which are ethnically based, in multistate areas.

THEFT of luxury clothing items, such as leather coats and upscale designer-label clothing, is a growth industry. The property may be stolen in burglaries or some other type of crime, including "mopping," another term for shoplifting. The clothing is then sold to fences or underground boutiques. Inside one drab family residence in Queens, police uncovered over $500,000 in stolen clothes. Said one detective, "The inside of this place looks like Macy's."[28]

PAKISTANI owners of a convenience store also led a three-state ring of thieves. They recruited 200 professional shoplifters and illegal Pakistani immigrants with promises of a better life and plenty of money to send home. Members of this group stole over-the-counter cosmetics, computers, DVD players, jet skis, apples, ziti, pharmaceuticals, and anything else they could get their hands on. The merchandise was taken to a warehouse where it was repackaged and sent to coconspirators in two different states and in Pakistan. Competition to "bring in the most" was intense. One thief, enraged that another thief had brought in more than he had, hired thugs to beat up the higher-performing member of the gang. Gang cohesion was also reduced when some members "skimmed" some items for themselves, reducing the "take" for the rest of them. As investigators "rolled" individual gang members, the investigation snowballed, resulting in the eventual recovery of $450,000 in cash and $1.6 million in stolen goods.[29]

- *Professionals,* who have substantial bankrolls, do business with a select clientele known by them or reliably referred to them, may work for long periods without being caught, and usually have several locations at which to store their purchases.
- *Occasional or opportunistic fences,* who normally conduct their businesses legally (e.g., as garages or pawnshops) but who from time to time "turn a deal."
- *Providers of illicit goods and services,* such as those who trade drugs and access to prostitutes for stolen merchandise.
- *Technology-proficient fences,* who do their business on the Internet. Some of these "fences" are the thieves themselves:

TWO career thieves who may have committed as many as 100 burglaries in Massachusetts and New Hampshire sold approximately $30,000 worth of their booty on eBay. They had another $70,000 in stolen property that they also planned to sell there when police arrested them.[30]

Many fences can operate for long periods of time without being detected because they are often "invisible" until some situation creates the need for police to take a closer look at individuals and/or locations. Outlets for stolen property include swap meets, flea markets, for-sale advertisements in local newspapers, secondhand furniture stores, the Internet, and overseas venues, often in third-world countries. In some instances knowledge about fencing operations comes to the police under more unusual circumstances:

TWO men approached a police sergeant with an offer of a $25,000 cash bribe in return for destroying physical evidence that tied them to a robbery. They were given some items and appeared satisfied with having bought themselves a cop. However, the officer was actually working the two men with the knowledge and support of his department and the local FBI field office. Ultimately, the two men and their associates were linked to warehouse burglaries and container thefts that totaled more than $3 million in stolen goods, and they had acted as fences for stolen laptop computers.[31]

From a policy viewpoint, the police know that the more the receiver markets can be disrupted or eliminated, the greater the likelihood that there will be some reduction in burglary and other offenses, whose profits depend on the availability of these illicit markets. Plainclothes officers quietly visit swap meets, flea markets, and other likely outlets, looking for known burglars or their associates offering merchandise for trade or sell. Such locations may be good candidates for the use of facial recognition software. Articles being offered are examined for possible signs of being stolen, such as missing or newly attached serial numbers. Arrested burglary offenders are always asked, "What did you do with the stuff you took?" When squeezed between facing almost certain prison time and giving their fences up, some will barter the information for a more lenient sentence. Because drug users usually steal to support their habits, whenever they are arrested, they are going to be asked, "What can you give me?" Their answers to this question may help identify drug dealers, fences, and other types of offenders.

Once in a great while, such questioning may yield a professional, big-time fence, but more frequently this is not the case. Professional fences usually screen their customers carefully and have worked with them over a period of years. Moreover, an arrested offender knows that by giving up a big-time fence, he or she will risk getting "wacked" for talking. Thus, the more usual case is that offenders try to get away with giving up "little fish."

Once a suspected fence is detected, officers work the case, investigating to confirm or disconfirm the fencing operation. When this is accomplished, officers attempt to broaden the case and apprehend more than just the offenders in front of them. This often entails both physical and electronic surveillance to identify the places fences frequent and who their associates are. An undercover officer may then be assigned to begin frequenting these places, covertly gathering additional information and/or attempting to develop a relationship with the fence and his or her associates. This method is also used when active burglars are targeted for arrest and surveillance is initiated. At some point, arrest and search warrants will be issued. When multiple locations and perpetrators are involved, raids executing the warrants should be conducted simultaneously to prevent offenders from slipping away.

As an industry, pawnshops suffer a continuing image problem from the illegal conduct of some operators. When the illegality was perceived as a serious problem, state statutes and local ordinances were enacted to regulate their shops' conduct, and this has reduced the number of pawnshops acting as fences. Usually these laws require that the

**Pawn Shops: Legitimate Businesses or Fencing Operations?**

Fences are persons who knowingly purchase stolen property for a fraction of its cost then resell it at a considerable profit. Pawnshops suffer a continuing image problem from the illegal conduct of fencing by some of its operators. Many locations have enacted statutes and ordinances in an effort to regulate operators and to reduce the number of pawnshops acting as fences.

(© D. Boone/Corbis)

pawnshops provide the names and addresses, and in some instances fingerprints, or persons pawning property, along with a full description of the property. In some locations, all secondhand dealers of property must provide the same type of information. In both instances, this must ordinarily be done within 24 hours of each transaction. Because of the temptations created by the high profits that can be gained by buying and selling stolen property, pawn and other secondhand dealers are closely scrutinized. State investigative agencies and many individual agencies maintain **pawnshop databases** to monitor secondhand-merchandise transactions:

WHILE entering information in the database, an officer working with the burglary squad noticed that a subject had sold an expensive loose diamond to a local used-jewelry store. She further noticed that the subject had also previously sold expensive jewelry to the same business. In the sale that had attracted the officer's attention, the subject had received $10,400 for the diamond. On the transaction slip from the jewelry store, it was noted that the seller lived in a nearby jurisdiction and worked as a plumber, so the officer contacted the police department there to find out if any high-priced jewelry thefts had occurred. She was not successful there, but ultimately she found a department in the area where investigators had noted a pattern in which the subject did plumbing jobs and subsequently there would be missing jewelry from the homes he had worked in. Eventually, the diamond, actually valued at $63,000, was matched with a victim's ring from which the plumber had pried it.[32]

IN another case, the same officer noted that the home of one of the department's employees had been burglarized, resulting in the loss of a camera, zoom lens, and credit card. While processing transaction slips, she found a pawnshop that had taken in the camera and zoom lens, along with a diamond ring and bracelet, which had been purchased with the stolen credit card. Investigation revealed that the subject selling the articles to the pawnshop had an extensive criminal background and lived within a few blocks of the employee. On the basis of this and other evidence, he was arrested and the property recovered.[33]

Police **sting operations** are an effective means of combating fences, identifying active criminals, penetrating criminal organizations, and recovering property. In a typical sting, officers set up a legitimate-appearing "front" business in which they slowly develop a reputation as being fences. As all transactions are videotaped, a great deal of intelligence is gathered that can be used in their current investigation or in collateral ones. Alternatively, the officers may do business in a different type of setting and use a warehouse located elsewhere to store the stolen property:

AN FBI agent, a cooperating witness, and participating local departments ran a fencing operation out of a Brooklyn social club. The "drop" for the merchandise was a warehouse they had rented at another location. This undercover operation resulted in the indictments of 39 individuals on charges of selling stolen property, drug trafficking, gun dealing, and loan-sharking. Over $5 million in property was recovered, including a hijacked truckload of design gowns valued at more than $1 million.[34]

In Chapter 8, "Investigative Resources," the enhanced capabilities of NCIC 2000 were discussed. The NCIC databases are of great importance for investigators, particularly since images of stolen property have been added. This new capability enhances the opportunity to recover stolen property.

## THE INVESTIGATOR'S CRIME PREVENTION ROLE

While at the scene of a burglary, investigators should tell the victims the precautions they can take to decrease the likelihood of their being "hit" again.

### REDUCING THE RISK OF RESIDENTIAL BURGLARY

To protect their residences, occupants should do the following things when they are on vacation or otherwise away:

1. Stop delivery of mail and newspapers, or arrange for a neighbor to pick them up daily.
2. Arrange for a special watch on their premises by patrol officers.
3. Use timers to turn on lights and radios at various times to make it look like the residence is occupied.
4. Ask reliable neighbors to immediately report any suspicious activity to the police.
5. Ask a trusted neighbor to come over occasionally and change the position of drapes, blinds, and other things.
6. Put up "Beware of Dog" signs, or if they really have a dog, ask someone to take care of it in the home whenever feasible.

For day-to-day security, occupants can take other actions that will help them avoid being burglary victims or, if they are victimized, will help reduce their losses:

1. Create an uninviting target: use motion-sensor lights, purchase an alarm system, use dead-bolt locks on solid doors mounted in steel frames, and place locks on windows.
2. If possible, avoid placing valuables where they can be seen through windows.
3. Cut plants low around doors and windows so that burglars can't conceal themselves while breaking in.
4. Grow thorny plants around places where someone might attempt to force an entry.
5. Don't leave ladders or tools laying around in the yard or clothes on an outside line—a thief who initially may have thought of just taking them will see the greater opportunity they create.
6. Don't tell strangers about your comings and goings.
7. Don't allow strangers to use your telephone, and don't give your correct number to anyone who alleges calling by mistake; instead, ask the caller whom he or she was trying to reach at what number. Baby-sitters and children should be instructed to do the same thing.
8. Don't keep spare keys in the usual places—under the mat, over the door, and in flower pots. Burglars know these places.
9. Don't go out to run a quick errand without locking all doors, including garage doors.
10. Engrave valuables with special identifying numbers. Alternatively, mark them with small translucent decals that have your special identification data on them. These microdots are about the size of a speck of pepper and virtually invisible to the naked eye.
11. Keep strong control over your keys. It may be helpful to leave them for service workers or give them to maids, but at the cost of greater risk exposure.
12. Don't leave notes on the door saying where you have gone or when you will be back.
13. Get to know your neighbors; they'll be more likely to respond faithfully to requests to "watch my place while I'm gone."
14. When new snow is on the ground, back out of your driveway and pull back in several times; do the same walking in and out of your door. This makes it harder for burglars to figure out if you are home.
15. To enhance recovery of your property if you are victimized, take pictures of valuables and record makes, models, and serial numbers of your property.

## REDUCING THE RISK OF COMMERCIAL BURGLARY

Many of the suggestions for preventing residential burglaries also apply to businesses. Operators of businesses should be told to prevent easy access to their roofs by securing all vents and roof openings; to use security-providing locks, frames, and doors properly; to light the exterior of the building; to use, if feasible, an alarm system and surveillance camera; to use a money chest rather than a fire-resistant safe; and to set the safe in concrete in open view at a place that can be lighted at night. Completion of the office security checklist in Figure 13–3 will serve two purposes: It will provide the owners with useful information about how to improve their security, and it may provide important investigative leads, particularly if a surreptitious entry is involved.

**Figure 13-3** Sample Office Security Checklist

(**Source:** Courtesy Bolen Industries, Hackensack, New Jersey, with modification)

| | Yes | No |
|---|---|---|
| 1. Do you restrict office keys to persons who actually need them? | ☐ | ☐ |
| 2. Do you keep complete, up-to-date records of the disposition of all office keys? | ☐ | ☐ |
| 3. Do you have adequate procedures for collecting keys from terminated employees? | ☐ | ☐ |
| 4. Do you restrict duplication of office keys, except for those specifically ordered by you in writing? | ☐ | ☐ |
| 5. Do you require that all keys be marked "Do not duplicate" to prevent legitimate locksmiths from making copies without your knowledge? | ☐ | ☐ |
| 6. Have you established a rule that keys must not be left unguarded on desks or cabinets, and do you enforce that rule? | ☐ | ☐ |
| 7. Do you require that filing-cabinet keys be removed from locks and placed in a secure location after opening cabinets in the morning? | ☐ | ☐ |
| 8. Do you have procedures that prevent unauthorized personnel from reporting a "lost key" and receiving a "replacement"? | ☐ | ☐ |
| 9. Do you have some responsible person in charge of issuing all keys? | ☐ | ☐ |
| 10. Are all keys systematically stored in a secured wall cabinet either of your own design or from a commercial key-control system? | ☐ | ☐ |
| 11. Do you keep a record showing issuance and return of every key, including name of person, date, and time? | ☐ | ☐ |
| 12. Do you use telephone locks or access codes to prevent unauthorized calls when the office is unattended? | ☐ | ☐ |
| 13. Do you provide at least one lockable drawer in every secretary's desk to protect personal effects? | ☐ | ☐ |
| 14. Do you have at least one filing cabinet secured with an auxiliary locking bar so that you can keep business secrets under better protection? | ☐ | ☐ |
| 15. Do you leave a night light on? | ☐ | ☐ |
| 16. Do you record all equipment serial numbers and file them in a safe place to maintain correct identification in the event of theft or destruction by fire? | ☐ | ☐ |
| 17. Do you shred all important papers before discarding them in wastebaskets? | ☐ | ☐ |
| 18. Do you lock briefcases and attaché cases containing important papers in closets or lockers when not in use? | ☐ | ☐ |
| 19. Do you insist on identification from repair people who come to do work in your office? | ☐ | ☐ |
| 20. Do you deposit incoming checks and cash each day so that you do not keep large sums in the office overnight? | ☐ | ☐ |
| 21. Do you clear all desks of important papers every night and place them in locked fireproof safes or cabinets? | ☐ | ☐ |
| 22. Do you frequently change the combination of your safe to prevent anyone from memorizing it or passing it on to a confederate? | ☐ | ☐ |
| 23. When working alone in the office at night, do you set the front-door lock to prevent anyone else from getting in? | ☐ | ☐ |
| 24. Do you have the police and fire department telephone numbers posted and handy? | ☐ | ☐ |
| 25. Do you check to see that no one remains in hiding behind you at night if you are the last to leave the office? | ☐ | ☐ |
| 26. Are all windows, transoms, and ventilators properly protected? | ☐ | ☐ |
| 27. Do you double check to see that all windows and doors are securely locked before you leave? | ☐ | ☐ |
| 28. Are all doors leading to the office secured by heavy-duty, double-cylinder, dead bolt locks? | ☐ | ☐ |
| 29. If your office is equipped with a burglar alarm system or protected by a guard service, do you make sure the alarm equipment is set properly each night? | ☐ | ☐ |
| 30. Do you have a periodic security review by a qualified security expert or locksmith? | ☐ | ☐ |
| 31. Are computer access codes and/or selected files password-protected on a need-to-know basis? | ☐ | ☐ |
| 32. Are all computer disks and tapes containing sensitive, client, or secret information maintained under controlled conditions during the day and locked securely at night? | ☐ | ☐ |

## Key Terms

**amateur burglars**
**burglary**
**burglary tools**
**fences or receivers**
**loiding (of a lock)**
**pawnshop databases**
**picking (of a lock)**
**professional burglars**
**safes**
**sting operation**
**surreptitious entries**

## Review Questions

1. Describe the dimensions of the crime of burglary.
2. What is the profile of persons arrested for burglary?
3. How are professional and amateur burglars distinguished?
4. What are the elements of the crime of burglary?
5. What considerations are important in approaching the scene of a burglary?
6. The text noted that black home owners and younger people are victimized more frequently than others. What are some possible explanations for this?
7. How are fire-resistant safes and money chests differentiated?
8. What special actions are required if there are explosives at a burglary scene?
9. How do burglars get their information?
10. With respect to the possible illegal receiving of stolen property, what are some indicators of the absence of good-faith purchasing?
11. Explain two investigative approaches to locating fences.
12. What measures can home owners and business operators take to lessen their chances of being burglarized?

## Internet Activities

1. For a comprehensive source of facts and information about burglary, check out the *Sourcebook of Criminal Justice Statistics* at www.albany.edu/sourcebook/1995/ind/BURGLARY.ind.html. Information on arrests by demographic variables and location, court statistics, sentencing, juveniles, and victimization can be found at this site.
2. To learn how some police agencies across the country have applied community policing principles to burglary, log on to the Community Oriented Policing Services (COPS) website at www.usdoj.gov/cops/home.htm. Go to the site map and click on "Community Policing Resources." Read the brief summaries of strategies in Newport News, Virginia; St. Louis, Missouri; and St. Petersburg, Florida.

## Notes

1. Federal Bureau of Investigation, *Crime in the United States, 2000* (Washington, DC: Government Printing Office, 2001), p. 4.
2. Ibid., p. 42.
3. Ibid.
4. Ibid.
5. Ibid.
6. Ibid., p. 45.
7. Mildrade Cherfils, "Jury Convicts 'Spiderman,'" Associated Press, www.canoe.ca/TopStories/Spiderman_dec8.html, Dec. 8, 1998.
8. Paulo Lima, staff writer, *"The Bergen Record Online,"* www.bergen.com/bse/trainrob199811281.htm, Nov. 28, 1998.
9. Richard A. Ballezza, "YACs Crime Groups," *FBI Law Enforcement Bulletin,* November 1998, Vol. 67,

No. 11, pp. 7–12, is the source of information for this section on YACs.

10. Sandra Gonzales, "Ex-Cop Admits Burglary Charges," *San Jose Mercury News,* Dec. 8, 1998.
11. Marvine Howe, "Anger Mixed with Sorrow for Organist Suspected in Church Burglaries," *New York Times,* Jan. 6, 1992, p. B4.
12. FBI, *Crime in the United States,* p. 45.
13. Ibid. For additional information on burglary offenders, see Richard T. Wright and Scott Decker, *Burglars on the Job* (Boston: Northeastern University Press, 1994).
14. "FBI Recovers Normal Rockwell Paintings Stolen from Twin Cities Gallery," *Minneapolis Star Tribune,* Dec. 13, 2001.
15. Marilyn Meyer, "Burglars Hit Titusville Bank," Florida Today.com, www.flatoday/!newsroom/localstorya1264A.htm, Dec. 12, 2001, pp. 1–2.
16. Richard Perez-Pena, "3 Arrests Hit Burglary Ring in Manhattan," *New York Times,* Nov. 14, 1992, pp. 21–22.
17. "Loot Jams Va. Home of Alleged Superthief," *Atlanta Constitution,* Dec. 16, 1980, p. 20D.
18. Bureau of Justice Statistics, *Criminal Victimization in the United States—1999* (Washington, DC: National Institute of Justice, 2001), p. 17, Table 16.
19. Ibid., p. 20, Table 19.
20. Wright and Decker, *Burglars on the Job,* p. 36.
21. Ibid., p. 37.
22. Ibid., p. 39.
23. Ibid., pp. 41–42.
24. Ibid., p. 43.
25. Ibid., p. 58.
26. Ibid., pp. 38, 58, with some restatement.
27. For example, see P. F. Cromwell, J. N. Olson, and D. W. Avary, "Who Buys Stolen Property? A New Look at Criminal Receiving," *Journal of Crime and Justice,* 1993, Vol. 16, No. 1, pp. 75–96.
28. Guy Trebay, "Shoplifting on a Grand Scale: Luxury Wear Stolen to Order," *New York Times,* Aug. 8, 2000, p. 8.
29. Federal Bureau of Investigation, "Operation American Dream," www.fbi.gov/majcases/dream/dream.htm, Aug. 28, 2001, 2 pp.
30. Richard Zitrin, "Two Accused of Fencing Loot Online," APB News.com, www.apbnews.com/newscetern/breakingnews/2000/06/02/burglaries0602 _01.html, June 2, 2000, p. 1.
31. Alexis Muellner, "Good Cop, Bad Cop Played in Miami Cargo Theft Sting," southflorida.bcentral.com/southflorida/stores/1999/11/15/newscolumn3.html. *South Florida Business Journal,* Nov. 12, 1999, pp. 1–2.
32. Fort Lauderdale Police Department, "Investigative News," ci.ftlaud.fl.us/police/cid1200.html, Dec 2000, p. 8.
33. Ibid., p. 6.
34. Federal Bureau of Investigation, untitled news release, www.geocities.com/pentagon/9719/129117.txt, Jan. 23, 1997. 2 pp.

FOURTEEN

# Larceny and Fraud

*One of the most common forms of larceny/theft is shoplifting. Shoplifters come from all walks of life and cost retail businesses millions of dollars per year in lawsuits. (© Bonnie Kamin)*

## CHAPTER OUTLINE



## CHAPTER OBJECTIVES

1. Explain the four categories of credit card fraud.
2. Be familiar with check-fraud schemes and organizations.
3. Understand the process of cellular-phone cloning.
4. Describe the classifications of shoplifters and the patterns of professional shoplifting groups.
5. Explain the most common types of confidence games.
6. Identify several forms of mail fraud.
7. Outline various techniques for laundering money.
8. Describe identity theft.
9. Discuss the looting of archaeological sites.

# INTRODUCTION

The legal definition of **larceny** contains five essential elements: (1) taking and (2) carrying away (3) personal property (4) of another (5) with the intent to deprive permanently.[1] Many criminal offenses may be classified under the general heading of larceny. This chapter discusses some of the most frequently encountered types of larceny: fraud by credit card and check, cellular-phone cloning, shoplifting, confidence games, mail fraud, Ponzi schemes, and money laundering. The chapter also includes a discussion on identity theft, a more calculated form of fraud. Identity theft can result from thieves rummaging through garbage, stealing and redirecting mail, using internal access of databases, and surfing the Internet for personal information. The chapter concludes by examining a type of larceny which many law enforcement agencies are unaware of but which is increasing in frequency: the looting of archaeological sites.

The information age has changed the ways thieves commit crimes. Easily accessible personal information in the networked world translates into more opportunities for perpetrators to steal valuable data that give them knowledge about people and businesses. However, investigating crimes that have been committed through the Internet, such as identity theft, can be an extremely daunting task. Many criminal investigators are not well trained in identifying and recognizing the sophisticated means by which thieves secure personal information from the Web. In a similar vein, many departments do not have the resources, or personnel, to conduct such investigations on their own. These challenges highlight how important it is for investigators to contact other available resources for help in investigating Internet fraud.

A look at the FBI Uniform Crime Reports quickly shows that larceny comprises the largest volume of offenses reported by local law enforcement agencies to the FBI. The dollar loss suffered by the American public from larceny is enormous, and frequently this loss is directed back to consumers in the form of higher prices. Larcenies such as the fraudulent use of checks and credit cards, confidence games, and identity theft can also create much personal anguish for victims. Yet except for cases that involve large sums of money or items of substantial value, larceny tends to generate less public interest than do certain other crimes.

## INVESTIGATIVE PROCEDURE

For theft to occur, two elements must be present: opportunity and desire. Investigative procedure depends on the facts of each case. Thus, the theft of an item from a home—possibly by a guest—would be handled differently from business thefts by employees. However, certain inquiries are common to most theft cases:

- At what time, as accurately as possible, did the theft occur? This information is valuable in identifying individuals who were in the area when it occurred and had the opportunity to commit the crime and in eliminating suspects.
- Who had access to the item, and if the item was not readily visible, who knew its location?
- If the stolen item was not readily visible, did the perpetrator go directly to the item or was a general search made of the area? Thieves who have prior knowledge of where an item is hidden because of a personal or professional relationship with the victim may intentionally disrupt drawers, closets, and so forth, in order to convey the impression that the item was discovered during a general search and thereby cast suspicion away from themselves.
- Who discovered the theft? Is discovery by this person usual or unusual?
- Is anyone with access to the item having financial difficulties? Checks of credit and local pawnshop files might provide indications.
- Has anyone expressed a strong interest in the item lately?
- Is the stolen item likely to have been retained by a suspect, pawned, sold, or given to someone as a gift?
- Has the victim reported similar thefts to the police in the past?
- Was the item insured? If so, was the dollar amount of the policy sufficient to cover the total value of the item, or will the owner lose a considerable amount of money as a result of the theft?
- Do any circumstances about the case suggest that the victim is making a false or misleading report?

The following case illustrates one example of a suspected misleading report:

A coin dealer reported that he and his wife had been participating in a dealers' show at a local hotel. At the conclusion of the show the coin dealer placed his rare coins, valued at $5,000, in the trunk of his car and drove to a nearby supermarket. He told the police that he took the coins in an attaché case into the supermarket with him. His wife accompanied him into the supermarket.

When they returned to their car, they were confronted by three armed men. One ordered the coin dealer to surrender the attaché case, which he did. The three men then got into a vehicle parked nearby and sped away. The police were called and the coin dealer related what had happened.

The coins were insured for their full value, but a clause in the insurance policy nullified the coverage if the coins were stolen from an unattended vehicle. This information came to light only when the insurance policy was carefully reviewed by the investigator assigned to the case.

The supermarket cashier and the boy who bagged the groceries reported to the investigator that they were certain that neither the coin dealer nor his wife had been carrying an attaché case in the store. Therefore, there was reason to suspect that the coins had been left unattended in the car and were stolen from it—although there was no indication of forced entry into the vehicle—or that the coins had been stolen while unattended at some other location, or that the dealer had sold the coins, or that he was concealing them.

The coin dealer was requested to submit to a polygraph examination in order to corroborate his report. He refused. Upon his refusal, the initial pickup order on the three alleged suspects and the vehicle was canceled. A copy of the police report was forwarded to the insurance company.

There are many ramifications to a case like this one. The first consequence, of course, is that a police investigation and pickup order were sent in a completely erroneous direction, wasting time and presenting the specter of arresting innocent people. Criminal fraud also was attempted by the complainant, and so further investigation was required. Hence, if there is some serious doubt about the legitimacy of a complaint, every effort should be made to investigate thoroughly.

## CREDIT CARD FRAUD

Companies issuing credit cards are secure from losses due to counterfeit account numbers because of a sophisticated electronic information system that provides approval of credit card transactions in advance of purchase. However, this system is defenseless if the card being used has a valid account number but was stolen.[2] Valid account numbers can be obtained in a variety of ways, but, according to MasterCard, "lost and stolen credit cards remain the biggest problems, accounting for 67 percent of the association's fraud."[3]

### TYPES OF CREDIT CARD FRAUD

Credit card fraud can be divided into four categories: stolen cards, counterfeit cards, shave-and-paste schemes, and fraudulent applications.

#### Stolen Cards

Credit cards can be stolen in a variety of ways, such as muggings, purse snatchings, and office and health club thefts. However, one of the simplest ways to obtain bank card account information is through postal theft. Numerous Nigerian fraud rings run sophisticated theft operations throughout the eastern and southern regions of the United States. Having illegally obtained legitimate bank cards or account information, the group then creates portfolios of fictitious identification, including driver's licenses, Social Security cards, and other materials, to support the purchasing power behind those cards. At the direction of group leaders, "runners" purchase merchandise from a variety of sources until the legitimate owners report the cards stolen or confiscated.[4]

These organizations also take advantage of contacts within the various credit bureaus to obtain legitimate bank card account information for counterfeiting or telephone order purchasing. The groups commonly mail stolen cards and information via overnight courier to other factions located throughout the country. For this reason, the U.S. Postal Inspection Service has implemented the Express Mail Label Profiling Program to identify packages likely to contain contraband. The profile flags suspicious packages on the basis of mail quantity, delivery, delivery frequency, destination, label and packaging-material characteristics, and so on. The profile was developed initially to identify packages containing drugs. Postal inspectors in the drug unit forward profiles to the credit card–fraud unit if they believe that nondrug criminal activity is occurring.[5]

#### Counterfeit Credit Cards

Counterfeit cards vary in quality from those made on embossing machines stolen from companies that produce cards to those of obviously poor quality. There are nine points merchants should check when examining credit cards:

1. Always check the credit card's expiration date to make sure the card has not expired. Expiration dates are frequently altered to give new life to an expired card.
2. Carefully feel the credit card. Does the card feel too heavy or too light? Does the card feel too lumpy or rough on the surface or edge? Any card possessing these abnormalities could be a counterfeit.

3. Examine the signature. Beware of any irregularities in the lettering or spacing of the name.
4. Be certain the printed and embossed issuing-bank identification number (BIN) both match, and check to be certain the printed BIN above the embossed account number is not missing.
5. Examine the card for embossed characters that are uneven, faded, or have "ghost" images from a previously embossed number.
6. Look for crooked lines in the embossing or characters that do not line up with others on the same line of type.
7. Be alert for chipped or scratched printed surfaces.
8. Examine the card for silver or gold paint used to blend in the hologram or touch up the embossed numbers after they have been embossed.
9. Look for a missing, painted-on, or "blank" magnetic strip on the back of the card. Magnetic strips are occasionally erased accidentally, but counterfeit cards often omit the information entirely. When the strip is coded properly, the information contained there should match that on the front of the card exactly.[6] Figure 14–1 provides specific information on both Visa and MasterCard security features.

### Shave-and-Paste Schemes

Account numbers are shaved off one or more legitimate credit cards and replaced by new numbers. The individuals using the altered card hope the forged account number will be a current, valid account number.

### Fraudulent Application

Individuals apply to several credit card companies, hoping that one or more will issue them credit cards. The cards are then used as often as possible and as fast as possible. Information provided on the application is false.

Banks and credit card companies have attempted to counter the rise in credit card fraud in many ways. Some issue credit cards with the cardholder's photo on it. The banks use a computer imaging system to produce cards in-house.[7]

The biggest advance in the war on credit card fraud has been the development of the Issuers Clearinghouse Service (ICS). The ICS helps identify fraudulent applications by matching various information requested of the applicant with a large national database of consumer information. The service matches names, birth dates, addresses, telephone numbers, and Social Security numbers. If the information on the application does not match the information in the database, the application may well be fraudulent.[8]

## PREVENTING CREDIT CARD FRAUD

Investigators are often asked how people and businesses can prevent credit card fraud. They can make a number of suggestions. Merchants should be cautioned to follow the guidelines given above. Furthermore, certain types of behavior by the person presenting the card suggest a potential fraud.

Most stores set a limit on the amount of charge purchases a clerk may accept without authorization from a supervisor or manager. A purchase by credit card or check that is above the clerk's authorization limit must be brought to the attention of the manager. Therefore, the cardholder may split the purchase between charge cards to circumvent the need for authorization. The cardholder may attempt to explain this by saying that he or she is close to the credit limit and would prefer not to suffer the embarrassment of being turned down. A parallel tactic is for the cardholder to move through the store, making multiple charges for purchases with the credit card, but doing them separately so that they remain under the amount that requires authorization by the issuer.

The best way to avoid credit card fraud is for the individual consumer to protect his or her account number. Many merchants ask for two forms of identification when a customer pays with a check. Do not write your credit card account number on the back of a check, using it as a form of identification. Do not put your address and phone number on charge slips, even if requested to do so by the merchant. Do not write your account number on your checks when remitting payment, even if requested to do so by the credit card company.

The director of credit card–fraud control at Citibank MasterCard/Visa discourages people from

Figure 14-1 Visa and MasterCard Security Features

(**Source:** Courtesy Federal Bureau of Investigation)

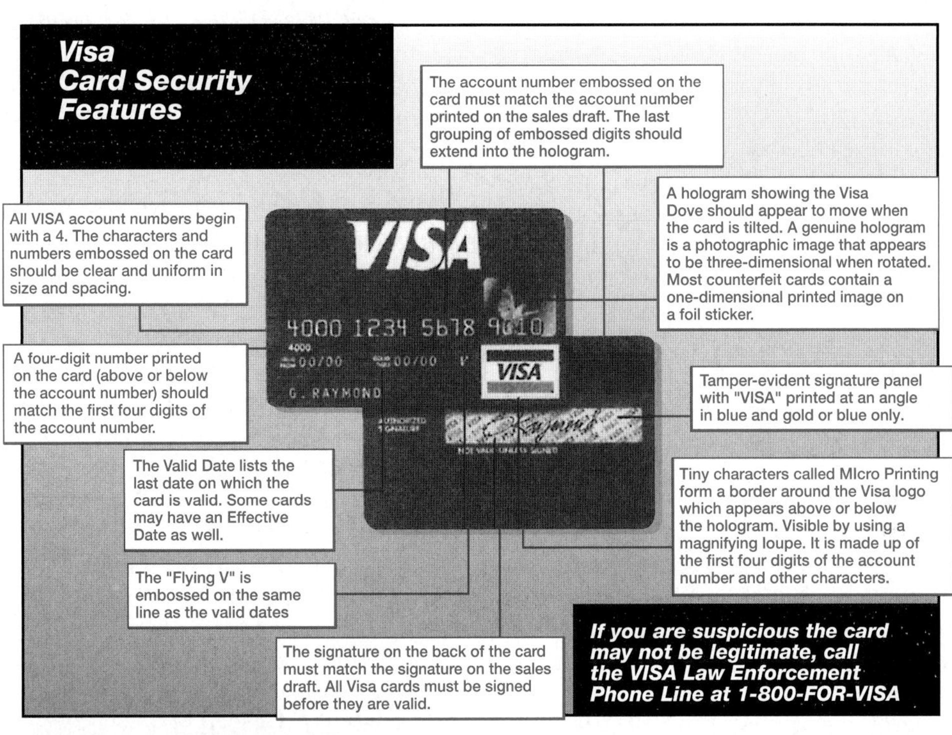


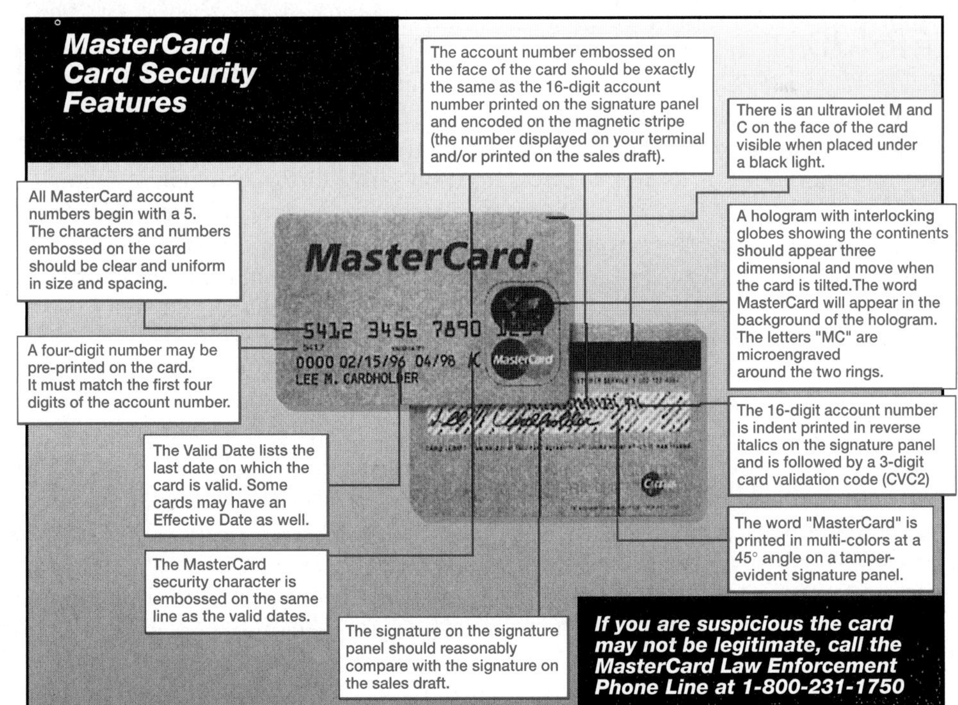

writing their account numbers on checks, "since that check goes through a lot of hands. With that information, someone could pose as you and contact your bank to get other information."[9] The director also advises against putting your telephone number and address on credit slips. A credit card–fraud specialist of Visa USA states that the practice is forbidden by major card issuers.[10] Moreover, according to the Bankcard Holders of America, writing your credit card number on a check serves no purpose because "Visa and MasterCard operating rules strictly prohibit merchants from charging a credit card to cover a bounced check."[11]

Finally, cardholders should not give their credit card account numbers to any individual who telephones them stating that they have won a valuable prize or trip and that their credit card account numbers are required for verification. Old credit slips and carbons should be destroyed. Billing statements should be checked closely. Lost or stolen credit cards must be reported immediately to reduce the potential for loss. When consumers report a lost or stolen credit card before it is used, they are not liable for any unauthorized charges.

# CHECK FRAUD

Before the 1980s, bank-fraud schemes generally involved only a few transactions perpetrated by a single individual or small group. Losses averaged less than $100,000 to the victim institution, and law enforcement investigations were fairly routine in nature.[12]

After the deregulation of the savings and loan industry in 1982 and the initiation of more speculative, risky ventures by those in charge of these institutions, a new wave of fraud emerged. During the late 1980s and early 1990s, large-scale frauds perpetrated by institution insiders and by persons held in trust within the banking industry became prevalent. Law enforcement agencies used massive, task-force-oriented investigations to calm the surge of these frauds. As a result, the banking industry as a whole has stabilized and continues to insulate itself from insider abuse.

Conversely, the number of frauds perpetrated by outsiders, especially organized ethnic groups, has risen dramatically in the last decade. Outsider fraud now accounts for more than 60 percent of all fraud against financial institutions.[13] The most prevalent problem in the industry, by far, centers on **check fraud,** but also involves other counterfeit negotiable instruments, such as traveler's checks, credit cards, certified bank checks, money orders, and currency.

## CHECK-FRAUD ORGANIZATIONS

Worldwide, 80 billion checks exchange hands annually; 60 billion of them are written in the United States.[14] As anyone who has mailed a check to a mortgage company three days before payday can attest, Americans have become enamored with writing checks and taking advantage of the "float" period, the time required for the check-clearing process. Criminal elements within numerous immigrant groups in the United States have analyzed American banking, noting the system's deficiencies and the fact that it affords opportunities for fraud. Presently, organized ethnic enterprises conduct a sizable portion of the annual check-fraud activity throughout the country.

### The Major Groups

The principal ethnic groups involved in check-fraud schemes include Nigerians, Asians (particularly Vietnamese), Russians, Armenians, and Mexicans. The majority of the Vietnamese, Armenian, and Mexican organizations base their operations in California, especially in the Orange County, San Francisco, and Sacramento areas. However, they have networked their operations throughout the country, with a number of connections in Chicago, Houston, and Washington, DC.

The Nigerian and Russian groups, with bases in the northern and eastern areas of the country, exhibit more nomadic tendencies. They roam throughout the United States, stop to pass stolen or counterfeit checks, and then move on to new locations. The Russian groups initially established themselves in New York but have extended their activities to Chicago and the West Coast.

Nigerian groups often solicit legitimate identification and account information to further their check fraud schemes. Recently, law enforcement authorities have noted their interaction with Vietnamese organizations in the Chicago and Houston regions. In the Northeast, Nigerian rings have opened numerous investment accounts within various brokerage houses and deposited large sums of money using stolen and counterfeit corporate checks.

Most West Coast Asian gangs began to organize their bank-fraud activities during the 1980s and have continued to expand and develop these sometimes-sophisticated operations. Many such groups originated in Taiwan, Hong Kong, and Vietnam, among them the Viet Ching, Big Circle Boys, V-Boyz, Wo Hop To, Wah Ching, and Red Door gangs.[15] Within the Asian gangs, known as triads, the group leader usually holds the title of "master" and oversees all organizational operations.

Current investigations indicate that some Asian groups have been dealing with Russian counterparts, especially to negotiate (deposit or cash) counterfeit currency through the banking system. Recently, members of the Russian Mafia obtained such currency, which was printed in Montreal, Canada, sold to several West Coast Vietnamese factions, and distributed throughout California.

Notably, each of these groups commits a myriad of white-collar, drug, and violent crimes. The groups perceive check fraud—unlike drug trafficking, extortion, or murder—as a "safe" crime, since it carries minimal penalties and a low risk of apprehension.

### The Players

Regardless of ethnic origin, groups involved in check fraud maintain certain universal characteristics. Unlike traditional, tight-knit, organized criminal groups, such as La Cosa Nostra, these groups, which may embody several hundred members, usually are loosely organized. Members often network among several organizations. Despite the lack of a rigid hierarchy, members typically fall into one of several roles: leader, check procurer, counterfeiter, information broker, or check passer.

***Leaders*** Leaders of an organization generally have an extensive criminal history and possess above-average intelligence. Often, they have a degree in business and/or law. These individuals provide the overall direction of the group, as well as expertise in understanding U.S. business and the banking system.

***Check Procurers*** Check procurers obtain authentic checks, usually by stealing them while employed within a financial institution. Group members then sell or negotiate the stolen checks as is, or they duplicate the checks for future use.

***Counterfeiters*** Counterfeiters duplicate corporate and payroll checks, traveler's checks, credit cards, certified bank checks, money orders, currency, and other negotiable instruments, as well as personal identification documents. They usually are well versed in the use of personal computers, especially in the field of desktop publishing.

***Information Brokers*** Information brokers gather personal and financial information on legitimate individuals. Using this credible information, associates open new bank accounts, pass counterfeit checks, and secure loans, which they fail to repay.

***Check Passers*** Check passers actually negotiate stolen and counterfeit checks through the banking system and collect the proceeds to distribute to the group. They often travel throughout the country, opening new accounts and transporting their illicit proceeds. Typically, they negotiate only about 10 percent of a group's illicit checks; the group sells the rest of the checks to other individuals and organizations. Check passers maintain little contact or status within the hierarchy and often are the only members whose ethnic backgrounds differ from those of the core-group members.

Ethnic organizations tend to distrust anyone not of their own heritage, making it difficult for law enforcement to infiltrate them. Even though police frequently arrest check passers throughout the country, these street-level criminals generally possess little information concerning upper-echelon group members.

## TYPES OF CHECK-FRAUD SCHEMES

The variety of check-fraud schemes perpetrated throughout the country ranges from depositing single stolen checks to counterfeiting thousands of negotiable instruments and processing them through hundreds of bank accounts. Although it is impossible to summarize all the check-fraud schemes currently operating, three schemes in particular—large-scale counterfeiting, identity assumption, and payroll-check fraud—typify frauds being tracked by bank

CHEMICAL TECHNIQUES + COMPUTERS = 2 PRIMARY MEANS of ALTERING CHECKS



security officials and law enforcement authorities throughout the nation.

## Large-Scale Counterfeiting

The most notorious groups engaged in large-scale counterfeiting operations are the Vietnamese triads operating out of Orange County, California. Members routinely get jobs within local financial institutions in order to collect master original bank checks, money orders, and corporate or payroll checks for counterfeiting. The triad masters, who often are counterfeit experts with a host of duplication devices, manage the group's criminal activities.

The groups exchange their counterfeit instruments for cash in a variety of ways. Check passers directly negotiate a portion of the counterfeit documents through financial institutions. They deposit the fraudulent checks, often into new accounts, and withdraw the funds before the bank can complete the check-clearing process and discover the fraud. The transient check passers open accounts in different institutions throughout the country; however, group members within the organizational hierarchy ultimately control their activities from a home base.

In order to minimize their exposure to law enforcement, the counterfeiters sell the majority of their phony goods to third parties for negotiation or further resale. They create most counterfeit checks in $2,000 to $5,000 increments and sell them to black-market customers at 5 to 25 percent of their face value, depending on quality and appearance.

## Identity Assumption

Seen in various metropolitan areas, identity-assumption schemes often involve Nigerian and Vietnamese criminal organizations. Group members obtain employment with or develop sources in local banks and credit agencies so that they can acquire otherwise-confidential information on bona fide bank customers. The groups then create counterfeit identification, including driver's licenses, Social Security cards, and credit cards, to assume the innocent persons' identities. Under the assumed identities, the criminals open new bank accounts, which they use for depositing fraudulent checks and subsequently withdrawing the funds, as well as for securing personal loans and lines of credit.

Once bank accounts have been established, the financial institutions become vulnerable to a variety of frauds. Before depositing fraudulent checks and withdrawing the proceeds, the "customer" is likely to obtain a credit card account with a substantial credit line. The perpetrator withdraws funds against the credit line and distributes the money within the criminal organization, along with any bogus loan money he or she has procured. After withdrawing funds on the basis of deposit of fraudulent checks, the "customer" leaves town, and the bank sustains a substantial loss.

Such schemes hurt more than just the banks, however. The innocent people whose identities were assumed suffer from ruined credit histories, which may inhibit their future financial activity.

## Payroll-Check Fraud

A variation of the identity-assumption scheme involves placing group members within payroll-check-processing companies. These firms compile and distribute payroll checks on behalf of their corporate clients.

The miscreant employees print duplicate payroll checks for various client recipients. They then steal the checks from the premises, and the group duplicates them for negotiation. Concurrently, the group obtains full background identifying data on the client's regular employees, which can be used in future schemes.

# METHODS OF ALTERATION

New technologies give check-fraud perpetrators a wide variety of schemes and devices for committing their crimes. Chemical techniques and computers are the primary means by which criminals manipulate and counterfeit checks.

## Chemical Techniques

Legitimate personal checks can be changed by chemical means. Similarly, someone well versed in manipulation techniques can modify corporate checks, traveler's checks, bank checks, and U.S. government checks with minimal effort.

Chemical alteration is commonly referred to as **check washing.** Check washers use a variety of acid-based chemical solutions to erase amount and payee information while maintaining the integrity of the preprinted information. They then dry the check and inscribe a new payee and a significantly higher dollar amount before presenting the check to a bank for payment.

One acid-based solution even allows criminals to revise a check and subsequently destroy the evidence. In this instance, the check washers must move quickly because the chemical solution causes the paper to disintegrate within 24 hours, leaving no supporting evidence of the transaction.

### Technology

Today's computer technology makes it relatively simple to counterfeit checks. A counterfeiting operation requires only a laser scanner to capture the image of an original check, a personal computer to make changes, and a quality laser printer to produce the bogus check. The necessary equipment can be obtained for less than $5,000.

Once an original check has been scanned, its data can be manipulated and reprinted with ease. Still, the counterfeiter faces the tough challenges of matching the paper stock used by the check manufacturer; correlating complex color schemes, such as those used on U.S. government and traveler's checks; and overcoming some of the counterfeiting safeguards currently used by legitimate check printers.

Yet counterfeiters can overcome even these hurdles without much difficulty. A number of unscrupulous printers throughout the country offer preprinted checks containing whatever information the customer desires, without bank confirmation or concurrence. Further, today's computers can come very close to duplicating even the most complex color schemes and check safeguards. A counterfeiter's success hinges on knowing that most checks will not be scrutinized closely enough to detect the fraud until they have been cashed and cleared through the banking system.

## CHECK-FRAUD PREVENTION

In order to prevent fraud, check-printing companies offer a variety of counterfeiting safeguards.[16] All such features make attempted alteration detectable in one way or another. Yet these enhancements are not foolproof and often prove cost-prohibitive to the purchaser. In response, financial institutions have begun to implement a type of biometric fingerprint identifier as a more cost-effective approach.

The Bank of America (BOA) in Las Vegas, Nevada, was the first financial institution to use fingerprinting technology to deter check fraud.[17] At BOA, when customers who are not account holders present checks for payment, they must place an inkless fingerprint next to their endorsement. When bank officials identify an attempted fraud, the fingerprinting system provides law enforcement with evidence and background information never before attainable at the onset of an investigation. This pilot project has garnered impressive results. BOA officials report that the biometric identification system has nearly eliminated check-fraud schemes perpetrated by outsiders. It also has reduced the bank's overall fraud problem by 40 percent.

BOA's success in Nevada spurred the Arizona Bankers Association to lead a campaign with member financial institutions to adopt a similar program. A core group of Arizona-based banks implemented this technology in the fall of 1995. Moreover, BOA officials plan to extend fingerprinting operations to their branches in Texas and New Mexico. A number of financial institutions have expressed a desire to expand the program to new customer accounts, another hotbed for fraudulent checking activities.[18]

During this implementation process, the banks involved have become cognizant of the sociological and privacy concerns underlying such an identification system. Some customers fear the improper use of identifying information. Bank officials stress, however, that no central database of fingerprint information will be maintained and that fingerprint records will be furnished to law enforcement only in the event of suspected criminal conduct.

# CELLULAR-PHONE CLONING

**Cloning** is defined as the unauthorized and illegal programming of cellular phones with the access codes of legitimate cellular customers. It has allowed criminals to obtain cheap, mobile communications that are untraceable through traditional law enforcement methods. These crooks—or "bandits"—also have apparent anonymity in their communications and the ability to quickly migrate to a new number in a few minutes.[19]

But their calls can also help police build a solid case against them. Under federal law, Title 18 of the U.S. Code, Section 1029, it is a violation to possess, use, or traffic in altered cellular phones or devices used to alter phones, including computers, software, and scanners, with intent to defraud. Under Section 1029, the U.S. Secret Service has federal jurisdiction over cellular crimes. Most states have similar laws making it a felony to obtain telecommunication services through fraud. Applicable Canadian law is found under Sections 326 and 328 C.C.C., relating to theft of telecommunication service, as well as Section 380 C.C.C., relating to fraud, and Sections 362 and 403 C.C.C., dealing with false pretense/false statement and impersonation, respectively.

Investigators need to understand the logistics of cloning. To begin with, a cellular access code includes the customer's 10-digit phone number or mobile identification number (MIN) and the phone's electronic serial number (ESN). When a cellular phone places a call, it transmits the MIN and ESN so that the cellular system can verify whether the caller is a legitimate customer. As with credit card validation, the cellular system compares the transmitted MIN/ESN to a database of valid access codes. However, as in the case of the banking industry validation of counterfeit credit cards, the cellular validation system cannot differentiate between an access code transmitted by the true customer's phone and the same code transmitted by a counterfeit or clone phone.

The actual cloning process is completed using an IBM-compatible computer—usually a laptop—or a custom device called a cloning "black box" (see photo). Both systems allow portable and easily concealed methods of illegal cloning operations. Such operations are run from homes, offices, or even moving cars. In each case, the MIN/ESN originally programmed into the phone is overwritten with a stolen MIN/ESN of a legitimate customer.

When a computer is used, the process requires specialized cables that are fabricated to plug into the phone, connecting it with a parallel port of the computer. Black-market cloning software, stored either on the computer's hard drive or on a diskette, runs the cloning process. The cloning software is user-friendly, allowing an amateur to become a cloning expert in a matter of minutes. Programming a cloned MIN/ESN into a phone takes only about 5 minutes.

Custom cloning computers, also known as black boxes, are fabricated on the black market for sale to street-level cloning operators. They contain specialized computer chips that store the cloning program. These chips are believed to be made in the Far East (Hong Kong, Taiwan) and smuggled into the United States and Canada, where the boxes are assembled.

Once a cloner obtains cloning equipment, a source of MIN/ESN combinations is required in order to program the codes into customer phones.

**Cloning Box**

A cloning box (also known as a "black box") with Motorola-brand "Flip and Brick"–style phones. This box can clone either of these types of Motorola phones.

(Courtesy Police Magazine)

Until 1994, the most common source of MIN/ESN codes was insiders, persons working for a cellular carrier or the carrier's distribution chain. But the need for insiders is less common now, as cloners have become more self-sufficient through the use of ESN readers. An ESN reader is a radio scanner and decoder, which is able to monitor the radio signal of a cellular phone and intercept the phone's transmission of the MIN/ESN. These devices were originally developed for use by cellular technicians as testing units for phones. However, a gray market has developed for the devices because of their ability to "suck MINs/ESNs out of the air."

The use of cloned service is proliferating rapidly—especially in metropolitan areas—because of the big profits and declining prices for equipment and service. An average cloner may activate (or, in street jargon, "hook up," "air up," "chip," or "charge up") 20 to 40 phones per week, generating revenues of $1,500 to $5,000 weekly ($80,000 to $260,000 annually). Cloning software and the necessary cables (to connect a computer to the cloned phone) currently sell for as little as $500 to $800. If a computer is included, the street price of a cloning package may be $2,500 to $3,000. Prices for cloning black boxes range from $3,000 to $6,000, depending on the city and the type of black box.

Street prices for cloned service range from $50 to $125 for 30 days' "guaranteed" service (assuming the customer provides his or her own phone). Lower prices apply in larger cities such as New York, Los Angeles, and Miami. If the cloner provides the phone, the price increases by $100 to $200. Cloners usually guarantee their service by agreeing to reprogram the customer's phone with a new cloned number within 30 days. Cloners stimulate return business and maximize revenues by programming the same number into many customers' phones. The combined usage of a particular MIN/ESN usually generates enough fraudulent calls to guarantee that the carrier will detect the fraud and shut the number off within 30 days. When the number is shut off, each clone customer using that number must "resubscribe" for service. The multiple-clone approach also allows the cloner to activate many customers' phones—receiving activation fees from each—even if he or she has a limited supply of access codes (MIN/ESN combinations).

## A POWERFUL INVESTIGATIVE TOOL

Cloning can provide law enforcement with a powerful investigative tool against major criminal enterprises. In the Los Angeles area, for instance, cellular cloning and major credit card–fraud rings operate hand in hand.

Let us assume that a law enforcement agency is trying to arrest a major drug trafficker and that the individual's phone records are needed but there is no way of finding the cellular number. Often, the wanted person's pager number is known or can be determined through undercover sources or informants. In such cases the procedure outlined below is the best course of action to be taken.

First, page the wanted person to a prearranged cold-line phone number. Second, record the date and time the call is returned. Finally, prepare a search warrant for each of the cellular carriers in your city requesting "automated message accounting (AMA) call records for any cellular telephone that placed a call to [your cold-line telephone number] on [date and time the page was returned]." Also, specify in the warrant that "the carrier must provide detailed call [AMA] records for any mobile number(s) identified by this search, together with the cell site and sector of origin for such calls for the following period: [insert time period of interest for crook's calling activity]." The carrier is also instructed to provide the investigating agency with "the address(es) of cell sites where such calls originate as requested by such agency."

If the wanted person does use a cell phone to return a call, the carrier should be able to identify the cellular number used (in response to the search warrant). As a result, the investigator will be able to obtain the cellular number used by the wanted person, the person's call records, and an indicator of where the person is calling from on the basis of the cell-site information requested in the warrant.

Cellular phones are commonly used by kidnappers, terrorists, and extremists to place ransom demands, make threats, or plan their intended actions. Each call generates an AMA call record, which identifies the cellular number used and the cell-site location from which the call originates. Cellular service also offers capabilities similar to those of land-line telephone service for establishing wiretaps: call traps and dialed-number recorders.

A few other high-tech approaches are also available to law enforcement through the service of carrier personnel or private consultants. These experts can assist with radio direction finding or other electronic and analytical measures to establish numbers being used by criminals. They also help generate other evidence against suspects using cellular phones.

A strong rapport with local cellular carriers can be invaluable when their support is needed during an investigation. It is always a good idea to know which of the local carriers' personnel are responsible for fraud investigations and law enforcement support.

## SHOPLIFTING

Ironically, most shoplifters who are apprehended do not need to steal and have the means available to them to pay for the merchandise stolen. "There are many people . . . who don't need to steal. Eighty percent of the shoplifters who get caught have the cash or credit cards in their pocket to pay for what they stole."[20]

Shoplifters can be classified into two groups: **commercial shoplifters,** or **boosters,** who steal merchandise for resale, and **pilferers,** who take merchandise for private use.

There are two patterns emerging in shoplifting: Many more people are shoplifting, and the vast majority, as many as 92 percent, are amateurs. Many have no real personal need for the merchandise.[21]

As might be suspected, professional shoplifters not only are apprehended less frequently than amateurs but also steal more at each theft. Many professional shoplifters work in teams. For example, several years ago local, state, and federal officials arrested six men who were involved in a series of shoplifting thefts in the Alexandria, Virginia, area. These men were all part of what has been characterized by police as South American theft groups. The men had managed to steal $150,000 worth of merchandise from four northern Virginia malls in just a few days. These men were part of only one of a growing number of such operations around the country. Many of the shoplifting teams consisted of Central and South American immigrants.[22]

In addition, these Hispanic groups appear to be affiliated with a loose-knit organization, based out of New York, Los Angeles, and possibly Philadelphia, that fences the stolen property through makeshift apartment clothing "stores" or through flea-market-type setups in the Flushing and Corona areas of Queens, New York, and the "Bad Lands" and Franklin Mills sections of Philadelphia, Pennsylvania.

**Shoplifting Booster Bag**

Detective Irwin Ellman displays a shoplifting "booster bag" and other paraphernalia seized during a search warrant execution in Alexandria, Virginia.

(Courtesy Detective Joseph Morrash, Alexandria, Virginia, Police Department)

These particular groups' criminal activity involves the theft of large quantities of clothing from major malls and retail stores along the East Coast. The groups usually operate in teams of two to six people and generally follow the criminal pattern outlined here:

- The shoplifter uses a **booster bag** specifically designed and constructed to defeat electronic security sensor devices routinely placed on clothing in major retail stores as a loss prevention tool. These booster bags are always made of a large department-store shopping bag lined with an inner bag made of tin foil and duct tape (see photo above). Several such bags have been recovered in Alexandria and Fairfax County, Virginia, and most recently in Nassau County, New York, and Howard County, Maryland, as a result of arrests and execution of search warrants. Also, specific tools are used to remove sensor devices.

- The groups use the U.S. Mail, United Parcel Service (UPS), and/or Federal Express (FedEx) to ship the stolen clothing to specific addresses in New York, Los Angeles, and, during the initial phase of this investigation, Annandale, Virginia. Once the stolen property is received it is distributed through stores, set up specifically to market and sell the stolen merchandise; it is sold "on the street," or it is shipped to specific countries in South America, particularly Chile.
- The respective groups have been documented as routinely stealing between $25,000 and $40,000 worth of clothing (retail value) over a two- to three-day period, before shipping the stolen merchandise and moving on to their next target malls or stores. The groups particularly like to steal blue jeans, women's apparel and lingerie, and men's suits.
- Individual subjects routinely provide false information and identification at the time of their arrests on local charges in any respective jurisdiction, and they are known to have an elaborate system for securing their release through the utilization of specific and apparently legitimate bonding companies that are backed by legitimate insurance companies based in Los Angeles, California, Miami, Florida, and Fairfax County, Virginia, among other places as yet unidentified.
- Subject groups routinely use local motels as a base of operation to inventory, store, and package stolen merchandise prior to shipping, (see photo). A group usually rents one or several rooms in the same motel for periods of several days to a week.

It is conservatively estimated that such groups, operating in the Washington, DC, metropolitan area, are responsible for retail losses in excess of $1 million per month. Splinter groups, which have been documented to operate in the Washington metropolitan area and who arrive from Los Angeles, New York, and Philadelphia, are believed to account for conservatively estimated retail losses in excess of $10 million per month.

Additionally, it was documented that the group originating out of Los Angeles was also involved in travel agency burglaries throughout the country, several of which were confirmed in Fairfax County and Richmond, Virginia, respectively, as well as in Los Angeles, New York, Dallas, and Houston. During the commission of these burglaries, the group stole blank airline tickets and plates so as to manufacture, market, sell, and use the tickets throughout the United States and all over the world. Losses to the airlines as a result of theft, manufacturing, and use of stolen and counterfeited airline tickets, as reported by the Airline Reporting Corporation and confirmed by the FBI's New York Division, are conservatively estimated at well in excess of $1 billion.

**Recovered Stolen Property**

Stolen property piled up inside a motel room, found during a raid in Alexandria, Virginia. In this particular case, the shoplifting group used local motels as their base of operations. The motel rooms served as holding facilities for stolen property until the property could be fenced.

(Courtesy Detective Joseph Morrash, Alexandria, Virginia, Police Department)

## REDUCING SHOPLIFTING LOSSES

The retailing industry is increasingly taking steps to reduce shoplifting losses, with techniques running from the simple to the sophisticated. The new anti-shoplifting techniques are designed to combine greater efficiency with unobtrusiveness.

The Kroger food chain in Dallas, Texas, and Cub Foods in Colorado Springs, Colorado, have installed "scarecrooks" in high-theft areas of their stores. Six-foot cardboard cutouts of police officers in uniforms bear an apt slogan: "Shoplifting is a crime."[23]

In Denver, Colorado, a mannequin repairman has given birth to "Anne Droid," a female mannequin equipped with a video camera in her eye and a microphone in her nose—price: $1,150. The camera has automatic iris control and automatic focus within a range of light and distance. The microphone has a range of about 10 feet, with quality of sound dependent on background noise levels.[24]

The Marshall Field Company has developed its Trojan Horse, "an enclosed structure covered with one-way glass that hides a lone detective."[25] The system can be moved from one location to another as needed, and it may or may not contain a security officer.

Electronic measures include the Sensormatic TellTag, a device that beeps whenever someone tampers with it or tries to walk out of the store with the tagged item. Knogo Corporation makes Chameleon, a micromagnetic thread that is hidden on the price label or bar-code sticker. Color-Tag, Inc., provides a tag that has a dye-filled capsule. When it is removed incorrectly, the capsule ruptures and releases a liquid staining agent, which stains the article as well as the individual.[26]

Customers are often recipients of subliminal messages while in a store or mall. The music broadcast in many stores subliminally says to the consumer: "I am an honest person; stealing is dishonest." Or the message may be merely a sound—the clanging of a prison door shutting.[27]

However well these devices work, many stores remain convinced that the greatest deterrent to shoplifting is a helpful, courteous, and watchful sales staff. "Shoplifters hate customer service."[28]

Local police usually become involved in shoplifting cases either to organize crime prevention programs for merchants or to respond to businesses that have been victimized or that have a violator in custody. The greatest security deterrents are often accomplished through security education programs for employees:

> Staff should be trained to look for the incongruous—someone wearing a raincoat on a sunny day, a wheelchair shopper with worn soles on his or her sneakers, a baby stroller with too many blankets on it, people trying on clothes that is not their size. Salespeople [should] know about diversionary techniques—the heart attacks or marital squabbles faked by shoplifting teams.[29]

Other deterrents are the use of basic display controls relating to the type of merchandise displayed and its physical location, and the use of highly trained security personnel both in civilian clothes and in uniform.

Recently, merchants have gained another weapon to combat shoplifting. In order to help merchants recoup their losses from shoplifting, many states have legislated civil remedies for those who suffer at the hands of shoplifters. As of 1988, 30 states had enacted such legislation. Though the civil process and the amount of recoverable damages vary from state to state, the general procedures are common throughout.

The store calculates the damages it incurred due to the loss and mails the shoplifter a demand letter and a copy of the state's civil recoveries law. The shoplifter must pay the requested amount within a certain time. If payment is not received within the specified time, a second letter is sent to the shoplifter. This letter informs the shoplifter that nonpayment may result in a civil court action. If the second letter is ignored, the merchant may seek redress of his or her grievance in civil court. Estimates of the recovery of damages by means of the two letters vary from 50 to 60 percent, both for in-house collection activities and for contract collection agencies.[30]

# CONFIDENCE GAMES

The **confidence artist** is a recurring figure in history and in fiction, police annals, and the literature of criminology. The confidence artist steals by guile in a person-to-person relationship. Most confidence artists have insight into human nature and its frailties, not least among which is the desire to get something for nothing or for a bargain.

Many people who read the details of some of the confidence games below will find them hard to believe. How, they will ask, can anyone be so easily "conned"? But the police reports speak for themselves. The monetary loss and the number of confidence games very likely exceed the recorded figures because many victims are too embarrassed to make a police report.[31]

## PIGEON DROP

This swindle is operated by two people. A lone victim, usually elderly, is approached on the street by one of the swindlers, who strikes up a conversation. A wallet, envelope, or other item that could contain cash is planted nearby. The second swindler walks past, picking up the wallet or envelope within full view of the pair. The swindler approaches the partner and victim, saying that he or she has found a large sum of money and is willing to divide it with them. But first the two must produce a large sum of money to show good faith. The victim is given no time to ponder and is urged to withdraw money from a savings account to show good faith. After withdrawing the money, the victim places it in an envelope provided by the first swindler. It is then shown to the second swindler, who, by sleight of hand, switches envelopes, returning an identical envelope filled with paper slips to the victim. Both swindlers then depart. The victim does not become aware of the con until he or she goes to deposit the newfound "money."[32]

## BANK EXAMINER SCHEME

The bank examiner scheme is one of the more sophisticated con games and requires knowledge of the target bank. The con artist, usually a man, calls the victim—let us say an elderly woman—and introduces himself as a federal bank examiner, saying that there has been a computer breakdown at the bank and that he wants to verify when she last deposited or withdrew money and her current balance. If she replies, for example, that there should be a deposit of $8,000 in the account, then the caller indicates that the bank records show a deposit of some lesser amount, perhaps $2,000. The caller then suggests that a dishonest teller may be tampering with the account and asks for help in apprehending the teller. Once the victim agrees, the caller says that a cab will come and bring her to the bank. She is instructed that she should withdraw $7,000. One con man stays near the woman's house and observes her enter the cab. Another waits at the bank to verify the withdrawal and to be certain that bank officials or police are not alerted. After withdrawing the money, the woman gets back into the waiting cab and returns home. One of the con men then telephones her to discuss the next phase of the bank's "investigation." While she is still on the phone, the second man knocks on the door. The man at the front door identifies himself as a bank employee, the woman lets him in, and lets him talk to the "bank examiner" on the telephone. After a short conversation, the con man hands the phone back to the woman. The caller instructs her to give her money to the bank employee so that he can redeposit it with the suspected teller. Victim and money are soon parted—she may even be given a receipt.

## INHERITANCE SCAM

In this scam, the victim's phone rings and, on the other end, a sweet-sounding person says, "You may be the recipient of a huge inheritance. But first some questions must be answered, such as birthday, birthplace, mother's maiden name, Social Security number"—all the information needed to withdraw money from the victim's bank account. When the victim answers the questions, the con artist says that he or she will deposit the inheritance in the victim's bank account. In the morning, a fraudulent check is deposited into the victim's account. In the afternoon, before the fraudulent check can be discovered, a withdrawal is made, and the victim has lost money.[33]

In one variation of the inheritance scam the victim pays an "inheritance tax" before the inheritance is paid. Sometimes the caller tells the victim to mail the inheritance tax. Sometimes a well-dressed, official-looking gentleman collects the inheritance tax in cash before awarding the victim a phony cashier's check.

## THREE-CARD MONTE

This scam is similar to the traditional shell game. The crook, using three "marked" playing cards, shuffles the cards and coaxes the victim to pick the ace, queen of hearts, or whatever. In this case, the hands of the crook are usually quicker than the eyes of the victim. The cards are "marked"—sometimes by feel, such as folded edges—in some way that is recognizable to the shuffler. Initially permitted to win, thus receiving ego strokes, the victim is then cheated out of his or her money.

### C.O.D. SCAM

For this scam, con artists usually pose as delivery employees. In an affluent neighborhood, the con artist spots an empty house and finds the resident's name. After writing a phony mailing label, the con artist goes next door and asks the neighbor to accept a perishable package for the absent neighbor and to pay cash for C.O.D. charges.

In a variation carried out on weekends, the con artist demands that a naive teenage gas station attendant take cash register funds to pay for a package the owner supposedly ordered. Hoping to please the boss, who is off work for the weekend, the young employee pays the money. Of course, the boss ordered nothing, and the money is lost.

### MONEY-MAKING-MACHINE SCAM

In this scam, a couple of con artists visit a local dice game to look for victims. They tell the victim that they have smuggled a secret formula out of Germany (or some other foreign country) that will bleach the ink on $1 bills. Then the blank paper can be pressed against a $100 bill to form another $100 bill. In one case reported in Philadelphia, a victim brought 150 hundred-dollar bills from his bank to a motel room, where the money was washed and stuck in between pieces of tissue paper with "bleached" dollar bills. While the victim went drinking with some of the con artists, one went back to the motel room and took the money. Another promised to look for the thieves and kept the victim from calling the police for a week. When the victim finally did call the police a week later, the suspects were long gone.

## MAIL FRAUD

The use of mail to defraud individuals has been increasing in dramatic fashion in the last few years. The following represents some of the most common types of **mail fraud.**[34]

### CHAIN LETTERS

A chain letter is a "get-rich-quick" scheme that promises the recipients that their mailboxes will soon be stuffed full of cash if they decide to participate. They are told that they can make thousands of dollars every month if they follow the detailed instructions in the letter. A typical chain letter includes the names and addresses of several individuals whom the recipient may or may not know. The recipient is instructed to send a certain amount of money—usually $5—to the person at the top of the list and then eliminate that name and add his or her own to the bottom. The recipient is also instructed to mail copies of the letter to a few more individuals, who hopefully will repeat the entire process. The letter promises that if they follow the same procedure, their names will gradually move to the top of the list and they will receive money—lots of it.

There is at least one problem with chain letters. They are illegal if they request money or other items of value and promise a substantial return to the participants. Chain letters are a form of gambling, and sending them through the mail (or delivering them in person or by computer but mailing money to participate) violates Title 18 of the U.S. Code, Section 1302, the Postal Lottery Statute.

### FREE-PRIZE SCHEME

Every day, thousands of people are notified by mail that they have won a free prize. Usually, the notice is a postcard advising that their prize will be one of four or five "valuable" items—a new car, a vacation, a color television, or a $1,000 savings bond. Major companies sometimes give away expensive items in special promotions, but they usually do not notify winners with a postcard. Typically, the postcard notices are mailed by con artists whose sole purpose is to obtain money from the unwitting victim.

The following examples illustrate this point: A man in San Mateo, California, paid $398 for "shipping charges" to receive a "free" 1988 Pontiac automobile. Needless to say, he got nothing. A Bergen County, New Jersey, resident paid a $69 "shipping and handling charge" to get his "free" $1,000 savings bond (with a maturity of 30 years). He could have bought the same bond from the U.S. government for only $50. Often a prize is never sent. If one is sent, it typically is an inferior, overpriced, or grossly misrepresented piece of merchandise.

## NIGERIAN ADVANCE-FEE SCAM

This scheme, which has been going on at least since the 1980s, is based in Nigeria or another western Africa country where the legal system is either corrupt, inept, or controlled by a dictatorship. The scam works as follows: An unsolicited letter arrives from Nigeria purporting to be from a high government official or an officer of the Nigerian National Oil Company. The sender asks if your company can help him (or them) move tens of millions of dollars, from a contract "overpayment," out of Nigeria. In return for the help, the sender offers to let you keep several million dollars. All you have to do is send the person all your financial information and an advance fee to pay for transfer costs. Needless to say, you will never see your "advance fee" again.

## FOREIGN-LOTTERY SCAM

Most foreign-lottery solicitations sent to addresses in the United States do not come from foreign government agencies or licensees. They come from "bootleggers" who seek exorbitant fees from persons wanting to play the lotteries. The activities of the bootleggers are not controlled or monitored by the government of the country in which they are located. Typically, people who pay the required fees never see any lottery tickets that are issued by the government-operated lottery they are hoping to enter. They are left to rely on various forms of entry "confirmation" issued by the bootleggers.

In general, sending lottery material through the mail is prohibited by federal law. This material includes, among other things, letters or circulars concerning a lottery, tickets or any paper claiming to represent tickets, chances or shares in a lottery, and payments for purchasing any such tickets, chances, or shares.

## FREE-VACATION SCAM

When a postcard or letter is received in the mail and/or an unexpected phone call comes from an unknown company promising a complimentary vacation in an exotic spot, the sender or caller is probably trying to victimize the recipient through the free-vacation scam.

If contact is made by mail, the recipient is asked to call the company to claim his or her vacation. But there is always a catch. In the most common form of this scam, to be eligible for the free vacation, the recipient is required to pay a service charge or to purchase a travel-club membership that may cost as much as $200 to $300. Under no circumstances should the recipient give the company his or her credit card number or even just its expiration date.

## 900-TELEPHONE-NUMBER SCHEMES

In recent years, 900 telephone numbers, which the caller pays a fee per minute for using, have been used by television stations to elicit viewer participation and to offer services such as current weather reports. There are swindlers who lure people to call a 900 number without giving anything in return for their money. Such a call may even result in charges on a phone bill of $30 or more. The swindlers may promise a product or service, such as credit repair or a travel package, but what is actually received is often quite disappointing. People with bad credit hoping to receive a credit card by calling a 900 number might receive a list of banks to which they can apply for such a card. Those who are told to call because they are winners in a sweepstakes receive nothing at all.

In the past, swindlers used toll-free 800 numbers to carry out many of the scams they now promote via 900 numbers. The scams include phony free-prize and free-vacation offers, as well as deceptive credit card promotions. This type of scam often begins when the swindler sends a notification in the mail claiming that the recipient has won something for free or has qualified for credit.

## ADVANCE-FEE LOAN SCHEMES

The advance-fee swindler claims to be able to obtain a loan for a prospective borrower with ease from a legitimate lending institution, such as a bank or a savings and loan association. However, the swindler has no ability to secure a loan. He or she either steals the fee and disappears or remains in the area to bilk other unsuspecting victims while stalling the prospective borrower with various excuses as to why the loan has not been funded.

Advance fee swindlers frequently ask for a percentage of the gross loan amount as their fee. For example, if a 5 percent fee is requested, the borrower would have to pay the swindler $500 to obtain a loan of $10,000.

## CREDIT CARD SCHEMES

The credit card scam starts with a phone call, a postcard, or a letter which claims that for a fee the recipient can obtain a VISA card, MasterCard, or some other major credit card or can establish that he or she is creditworthy enough to obtain one of these cards. Typically, the promoter of the phony offer indicates that the card is preapproved and that it can be obtained without any credit check. The fee charged usually ranges from $35 to $50. When the card arrives in the mail, the recipient finds out that it can be used only to pay for orders from a specific store or catalog. The store or catalog, which is owned by the company that issued the credit card, may not even offer merchandise of interest.

The "single-use credit card" is not a new concept, but recently unwary victims of this type of scam are being sold such credit cards by con artists who misrepresent the cards as being all-purpose bank credit cards. At times, the deception is magnified by the fact that the merchandise in the catalog is either inferior or grossly overpriced.

## CUT-RATE HEALTH INSURANCE FRAUD

Senior citizens, perhaps more so than any other group of people in the United States, are aware of the high cost of medical care. While Medicare does cover many bills, it does not pay for everything. Seniors, who generally live on fixed incomes generated by Social Security, interest, and small pensions, sometimes buy supplemental insurance to pay for medical expenses not covered by Medicare.

There are sources for legitimate supplemental medial insurance. However, some policies offered to seniors through mailed advertisements, and in other ways, are offered by unscrupulous companies and salespeople who will try to sell anything they can, whether there is a need for it or not. Such policies provide inadequate or inappropriate coverage. For example, one 93-year-old woman thought she was purchasing a valuable health insurance policy only to learn that she had bought *maternity* insurance.

To reduce the chances of falling victim to health insurance fraud, recipients should carefully read any sales promotion received in the mail, including the "fine print" in the policy. They should become suspicious if a company requests that they pay premiums in cash, requests premiums in advance, pressures recipients to buy immediately because "it's their last chance," or requests that the recipient sign a blank insurance form.

## OIL AND GAS INVESTMENT FRAUDS

Some oil- and gas-well deals are offered by "boiler rooms," or fly-by-night operations that consist of nothing more than bare office space and a dozen or so desks and telephones. Boiler-room operators employ slick telephone solicitors trained to use high-pressure sales tactics. These con artists make repeated unsolicited telephone calls in which they follow a carefully scripted sales pitch that guarantees high profits. Some swindlers surround themselves with the trappings of legitimacy, including professionally designed color brochures.

In a fraudulent oil and gas scheme, scam artists promoting the investment often offer limited-partnership interest to prospective investors who live outside the state where the well is located and outside the state the scam artists are calling from. This reduces the chances that an investor will visit the site of a well or what may be a nonexistent company headquarters.

## WORK-AT-HOME SCHEMES

Advertised opportunities to earn money by doing work at home are frequently nothing more than fraudulent schemes and, at best, rarely result in any meaningful earnings. The targets of the work-at-home con artists are people who need extra money but who are not able to work outside their homes. Victims typically include mothers at home caring for young children, the unemployed, the elderly, handicapped persons, and people with low incomes.

The ads usually promise a "large income" for working on projects "in great demand." Some promotions stress that "no experience is necessary," while others indicate that "no investment is required." The one characteristic common to all work-at-home schemes is that responders are required to purchase something before they can start work. Typically, the only thing they receive for their

**Police Officer Taking a Report from a Victim of Mail Fraud**
The use of the mail to defraud persons has increased over the last few years. Some frauds advertise opportunities to work at home to make money. These con artists require respondents to purchase something before they can start to work. Elderly, unemployed, and disabled persons are often targeted as victims of these crimes.
(Courtesy Federal Bureau of Investigations. Photographer Kathy L. Morrison)

money is instructions for placing an ad like the one they answered. In effect, this means they must rip off fellow citizens to make any money.

Probably, the most common kind of work-at-home scheme is envelop stuffing. However, modern mailing techniques and equipment have virtually eliminated the need for homeworkers to perform legitimate envelope stuffing, addressing, and mailing services.

## HOME-IMPROVEMENT AND HOME-REPAIR FRAUDS

Because home repairs and improvements are expensive undertakings, con artists and vagabond thieves have entered the industry. A favorite trick of dishonest home-repair firms is to mail a brochure offering to do an expensive job for an unusually low price. Once the contract is signed, the home owner learns why the price was so low. The firm never delivers the service, which was paid for in advance.

Free inspections by con artists turn up plenty of expensive repairs that are not actually needed. Some vagabond thieves may not even mail an offer to do a free inspection. They just show up at the home and try to gain access by posing as utility workers or home insulation inspectors offering a free inspection. They may quickly flash something that looks like an identification card to convince the home owner to let them enter. Some offer to do the work on the spot. However, when they leave, the home owner is left with a large bill and a faulty repair job.

## PHONY-INSURANCE SCAMS

If a notification from an "estate locator" is received in the mail stating that there is an unclaimed inheritance waiting for the recipient, it should be treated with considerable suspicion. Also calling themselves "research specialists," unscrupulous white-collar criminals mail thousands of letters across the nation to targeted people. Thousands of individuals with the same last name receive notification that inheritance funds have been located in their names. Many of these recipients are lured into mailing a fee—sometimes $30 or more—for an estate report, which will supposedly explain where the inheritance is located and how it can be claimed. The promoter may also offer to process the claim for a fee.

### MISSING-PERSONS SCHEMES

The missing-persons scam is one of the more unusual types of fraud schemes. It preys on people whose loved ones have disappeared. For example, postal inspectors once investigated a promoter who was running a "recovery bureau." The bureau attempted to collect $20,000 on the basis of fraudulent claims that it knew the whereabouts of a California man's missing former wife and children.

The Californian traveled to Michigan on the basis of the promoter's promises that he could find and reclaim his family in that state. The man became suspicious when the contact he was sent to see in Michigan demanded a $20,000 payment before he would provide any information about the missing family members. Subsequent investigation by postal inspectors revealed that the ex-wife and children had never been in Michigan. The promoter had no information about the missing family members. In reality, he had only received a routine notice from a private investigator who was seeking assistance in finding the ex-wife and children.

## WHITE-COLLAR CRIME

In 1949 a new type of crime was brought to the attention of law enforcement when Professor Edwin H. Sutherland defined **white-collar crime** as "a crime committed by a person of respectability and high social status in the course of his [or her] occupation."[35] The definition of white-collar crime has since been expanded to include people of lower status. It is an illegal act or series of illegal acts committed by nonphysical means and by concealment or guile to obtain money or property, to avoid the payment or loss of money or property, or to obtain business or personal advantage.[36]

For a successful prosecution, law enforcement officials must show that one or more criminal statutes have been violated. They must prove an illegal activity rather than concentrating on the offender.

It is important, therefore, for officers to understand how white-collar crimes are committed. Knowing the identity of the perpetrator of a fraud is not enough. The law enforcement officer must be able to understand, explain, and show conclusively how and why the activities are illegal. In this section, we look at three types of white-collar crime and demonstrate their complexity and fraudulence: Ponzi, or pyramid, schemes; money laundering; and fraudulent use of Social Security numbers. These are only three examples of the briberies, kickbacks, payoffs, bankruptcy, credit card, check, consumer, and insurance frauds that occur each year.

### PYRAMID, OR PONZI, SCHEMES

**Pyramid,** or **Ponzi, sales schemes,** also known as chain-referral schemes, have mushroomed across the United States and may be operating in other countries. There is no way of calculating the exact amount of money lost by the victims, but it is estimated to be well over half a billion dollars in the United States alone. Some officials contend that pyramid sales schemes are the leading consumer fraud problem today. Despite the scope of the problem, many people still do not know what pyramids are.

A pyramid scheme is a marketing program by which people buy the right to sell others the right to sell a specified product. The promoters select a product, such as household items, cosmetics, or safety devices, and sell large inventories to distributors with the incentive of permitting the distributor to sell new distributorships. The real profit is earned as recruiters develop new recruits. In all this activity, little or no real concern is given to the direct public sale of products or services. Consumer distribution is a sham.[37]

One of the earliest known examples of a pyramid scheme appeared in 1920, in Boston. Charles Ponzi, an Italian immigrant and financial wizard, established the Securities and Exchange Company. The corporation consisted of only Ponzi, who started his company with a few hundred dollars borrowed from two silent partners. The company promised investors substantial returns on their investments in Ponzi's company. Within 45 days investors were promised their original investment plus 50 percent interest; in 90 days, they would double their original investment. By June 1920 Ponzi claimed to be receiving $500,000 and paying out $200,000 a day.

Ponzi explained to doubters that knowing how to take advantage of the varying currency exchange rates in different parts of the world was how he made his profit. He started his company upon receiving a business letter from a conspirator in Spain, who enclosed a reply coupon that, if exchanged at any U.S. Post Office, was worth $0.06. In Spain, the cost of the coupon to a buyer was only $0.01. Ponzi reasoned that by buying the coupon in Spain and redeeming it in the United States, he made a $0.05 profit. Thereafter, Ponzi began operations in nine different countries, with his agents traveling back and forth between these countries and the United States to take advantage of the disparity in currency value.

A *Boston Post* reporter was convinced that Ponzi had never purchased any coupons and that he was taking money from one investor to pay off another. This reporter turned up information that Ponzi, under his real name of Charles Bianchi, had been sentenced to prison in Canada for forgery several years earlier. At the end of 1920, Ponzi's world collapsed, and he was convicted in Massachusetts. Of the $15 million that Ponzi had taken in, there was no accounting for $8 million. Such schemes became known as Ponzi schemes.

In recent years, a pyramid scheme hit the United States in which one needed only a chart and $1,000 in cash (see Figure 14–2). With the $1,000, you could buy a slot on the bottom line. You gave $500 each to the investor above you (position 8) and the one in the 0 position. Pyramid success occurred when all the slots on the player's line were filled and the player progressed up the chart. When an investor finally moved into the zero position, he or she could begin collecting up to $16,000.

At the heart of each pyramid scheme was the expressed or implied representation that a new participant could recoup his or her original investment by simply inducing two or more prospects to make the same investment. Promoters failed to tell participants that this is mathematically impossible, because some people dropped out of the pyramid even before recouping their original investment, and others recouped their original investment and then dropped out. This misrepresentation constitutes the heart of the fraud. If each investor recruits two additional investors and no one drops out, everything works according to plan. If there are 15 investors at the meeting to start a pyramid and one person at the top level, the number of new members doubles each day thereafter until, at the end of two weeks, 262,143 people are involved and, at the end of three weeks, there are 33,554,431 participants. The whole scheme collapses before this. Therefore, the earlier one gets in on the pyramid,

### Charles Ponzi Awaits Court Appearance on Fraud Charges

Pyramid sales schemes are often called Ponzi Schemes. Charles Ponzi, who lived in Boston in the 1920s, was one of the first developers of such schemes. These schemes are marketing programs by which people buy the right to sell others a product such as household items or cosmetics. The real profit is earned as recruiters develop new recruits. Consumer distribution of goods is a sham.

(© Bettmann/Corbis)

Figure 14-2 The Pyramid Scheme

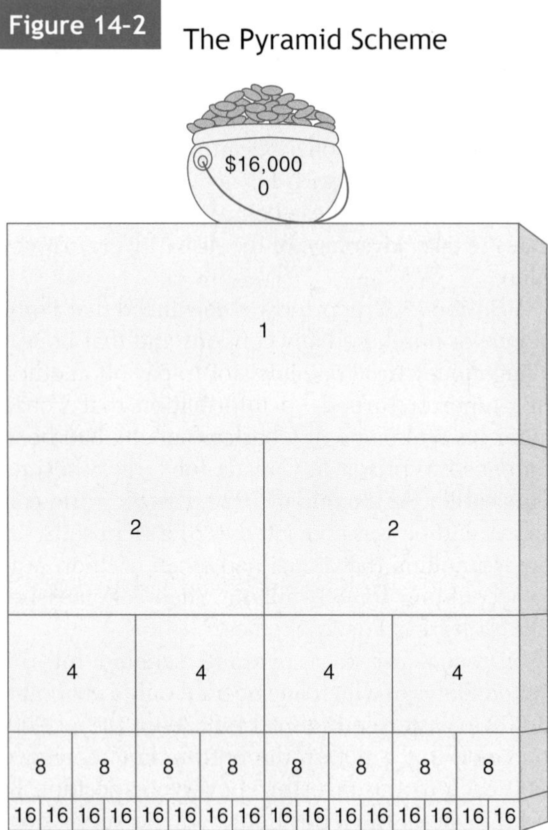


the better the possibility of collecting the $16,000. For everyone to win, an infinite number of investors would have to fill the chart.

## Method of Cash-Flow Analysis

The method of cash-flow analysis in Ponzi schemes is a two-step process. The first step for investigators is to obtain all relevant records—such as checks, deposit slips, and monthly bank statements—from the financial institution(s) in which the suspect placed the victims' money. The second step involves turning over these financial records to a forensic accountant for the cash-flow analysis.[38]

***Step One*** Since most victims make their investments by personal or cashier's check, the Ponzi artist usually deposits these funds (if only temporarily) into a bank account. This makes each investment a traceable transaction. After investigators become confident that they have amassed sufficient probable cause, they can obtain a search warrant and secure the relevant records.

Generally, in an investment-fraud case, courts base the probable cause necessary to obtain a search warrant on multiple factors. Several individuals must have given money to a suspect for purposes of making an investment; these investors relied on the suspect's promise that their funds would be invested for a limited period of time; and the time period has since expired without repayment to the investors or a reasonable explanation from the suspect.

Investigators should be aware that because grand juries possess the authority to subpoena all information relevant to matters under their investigation, financial records may also be obtained through a grand jury subpoena *duces tecum.*[39] However, for a cash-flow analysis, securing a search warrant is generally preferable.

By securing a search warrant, investigators directly receive the relevant bank records, which can then be given to a forensic accountant. If the financial records are obtained through a grand jury subpoena *duces tecum,* auditors must complete the cash-flow analysis while the grand jury hears the case. This may prolong the time required to secure an indictment.

***Step Two*** The second step for investigators in this process is to turn over all the financial records obtained through the search warrant or subpoena to a forensic accountant for the cash-flow analysis. The forensic accountant then analyzes the bank account records and prepares cash-flow compilations of these records in financial statement form. This statement shows all the known receipts of a particular bank account during a specified period of time. Accordingly, this report demonstrates the flow of funds into and out of a Ponzi artist's account.

When completed, the compilation also assists investigators in determining whether the suspect accurately represented the investments to contributors. If investigators determine that a crime may have been committed, the compilation can then be introduced at subsequent court proceedings as demonstrative evidence of theft. The cash-flow analysis compilation allows prosecutors to provide juries with a tangible record of how the suspect committed the crime and spent the victims' money.

***Use of Forensic Accountants*** Investigators traditionally underuse **forensic accountants** in cases of white-collar crime. This is an unfortunate and potentially damaging oversight. In other types of major crime cases, investigators employ such specialists as pathologists, serologists, psychiatrists, fingerprint and document examiners, and criminalists to aid in analyzing evidence. Similarly, in many major cases of white-collar fraud, forensic accountants should be called on to apply their training and expertise to legal matters and to testify in court as expert witnesses.

### Problems for Law Enforcement

When companies promote Ponzi schemes, auditing becomes difficult, expensive, and time consuming. The presence of many promoters in an area makes prosecution impractical. By the time police have all the information they need, most promotions have run their course.

The problem of establishing criminal liability is made more difficult by the need to separate victims from promoters. It is in the victim's best interest to become a promoter and transfer his or her loss to another. For this reason, useful victim testimony is limited. Only victims who invested in the pyramid for reasons other than participation in the chain referral provide useful testimony.

In a Ponzi scheme, investigators also face the arduous task of determining the validity of suspects' claims to victims regarding their investments. In addition, prosecutors must then demonstrate how offenders spent the victims' money. These two elements make Ponzi schemes especially difficult to investigate and prosecute, since Ponzi artists generally "cover their bases" well.

Often, in order to limit victims' inquiries, offenders represent investment opportunities as being highly technical and sophisticated in nature. Further, many victims of white-collar crime hesitate to cooperate with investigators, fearing that if the offender becomes aware of an investigation, they will not be repaid. Or victims may simply be embarrassed because they made a foolish investment.

While victim reluctance to cooperate hampers many investigative techniques used in white-collar crime, it has little effect on the method of cash-flow analysis. Because this approach traces suspected illegal activity through financial records, investigators and prosecutors do not have to base their cases predominately on the testimony of victims.

## MONEY LAUNDERING

Al Capone, the infamous gangster of the 1920s, is said to have amassed a fortune of $20 million in 10 years through bootlegging and gambling. Yet when Capone was sentenced to 11 years in prison in 1931, it was for income tax evasion. The conviction of Capone taught other organized-crime members an important lesson: Money not reported on an income tax return is money that cannot be spent or invested without risk of detection and prosecution.

Because most money collected by organized crime is from illegal sources, such as loan-sharking, prostitution, gambling, and narcotics, criminals are reluctant to report the income or its sources on tax returns. Before spending or otherwise using such funds, they must give the money an aura of legality. This conversion is known as **money laundering.** To combat organized crime successfully, law enforcement officials must understand how money is laundered.[40]

### The Laundering of Money by Organized Crime

At the end of the 1800s, most money earned by the U.S. underworld was gained through extortion, blackmail, and dock racketeering. By the 1920s, most came from bootlegging, and some believe that Prohibition supplied organized crime with the funds and skills to operate multimillion-dollar ventures. "Organized crime is an estimated $100 billion-a-year untaxed business operated by groups ranging from motorcycle gangs, to Asian drug triads, to the Italian Mafia."[41]

### Domestic Laundries

Certain businesses lend themselves to laundering money. For example, the business must be capable of absorbing a large volume of cash income, because most illicit income is received as cash. The purpose of laundering funds is to commingle licit and illicit monies so that they cannot be separated and to prevent the discovery of the introduction of illegal money into the business. Because most checks and credit card receipts are traceable by law enforcement officials, businesses such as restaurants, bars, and massage parlors, which take in a high proportion of cash, tend to be more desirable as laundries than businesses that receive most of their income as checks or other traceable instruments.

Another favorable characteristic for a laundry is expenses that do not vary with sales volume. An example of such a business is a movie theater that shows pornographic films. The expenses of such a business (rent, electricity, wages) are almost constant, regardless of whether the theater is full. Illicit income can be introduced and camouflaged in this type of business quite easily, because the additional sales do not increase expenses. Law enforcement officials who examined the records of such a theater would have trouble proving that the legitimate income generated by the theater was lower than that recorded.

Businesses that experience a high rate of spoilage or other loss of goods may also be used to launder money. Groceries and restaurants are good examples. Money is introduced into the business and recorded in its general income accounts as if it had been received from customers. Fraudulent invoices for produce or other perishable items are issued to these businesses by companies acting as suppliers. The grocery or restaurant issues checks to these "suppliers" or records the transaction as a cash payment and charges it to an expense account, such as cost of goods sold. The undelivered produce or perishable items listed as spoiled and discarded are written off the books (see Figure 14–3). The grocery store or restaurant thus avoids tax liability, and the funds paid to "suppliers" seem legal and may be spent or invested with little risk of discovery. Within a week of the transaction, it is almost impossible for law enforcement officials to disprove the story of the grocer or restaurant owner.

The above techniques have been used to launder funds successfully for a number of years, and large numbers of domestic businesses controlled by organized crime are still being used for this function. In recent years, however, law enforcement officials have adapted new methods, such as sampling, ratio analysis, and flowcharting, to discover laundering operations and to prosecute the people involved in them.

Sampling is a statistical procedure in which the number of customers of an establishment is randomly counted, a conservative estimate is made of the amount of money spent by each customer, and a projection is made of how much money is actually received by an enterprise in the ordinary course of operation. If the projected income is materially smaller than that reported to taxing authorities, it is a good indication that the business is being used to launder funds.

Ratios for evaluating businesses have been used for many years by accountants, investors, and lending institutions. There are four basic types of ratios:

1. *Liquidity ratios,* which indicate the ability of an enterprise to satisfy its immediate (short-term) financial obligations.
2. *Operating ratios,* which indicate the efficiency of the business.
3. *Profitability ratios,* which indicate the effective use of assets and the return of the owner's investment in the business.
4. *Leverage ratios,* which indicate the extent to which the enterprise is financed by debt.

**Nude Bar: A Focus on Money Laundering**
Organized crime groups are always looking for ways to hide money made from illegal activities. The process is known as "money laundering." Businesses such as restaurants and bars take in large amounts of cash on a daily basis. The purpose of laundering funds is to comingle licit and illicit monies so they cannot be separated or traced by law enforcement.
(© Joel Gordon)

Figure 14-3 Laundering of Money from Illicit Sources

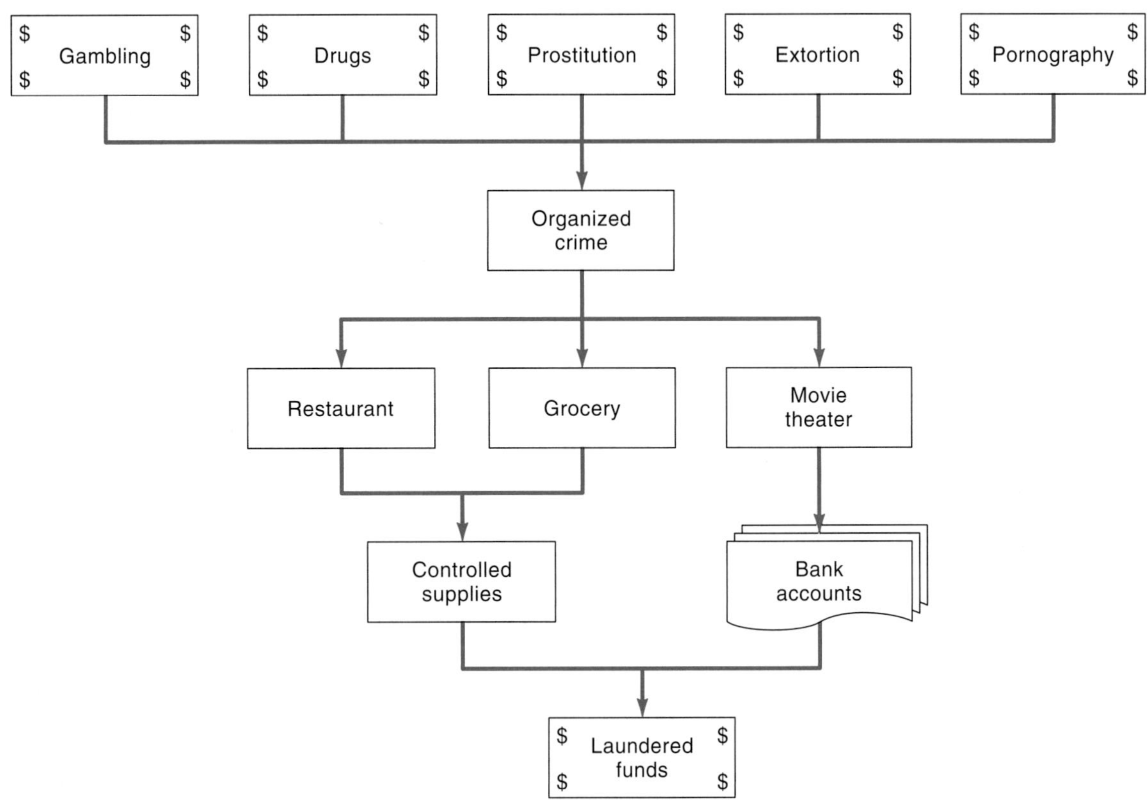


By using ratio analysis, an investigator can compare the past performance of a business with that of the industry in which the business operates. This comparison can be used to spot significant deviations from the norm, and these may indicate the existence of a laundering operation.

Another method used to uncover laundering involves researching the corporate and ownership structures of both the suspected business and all the companies with which it deals. The relationship between the various companies may be illustrated visually by the process of flowcharting, which allows investigators, prosecutors, and juries to grasp more easily the sometimes complex relationships that exist in laundering operations.

Although law enforcement agencies have been relatively successful in exposing domestic laundering operations, underworld leaders have perfected international laundering operations, which have traditionally been immune from exposure. Although international laundries vary greatly in form, organization, and complexity, their object is still to disguise the true nature and origin of illegal funds. International laundering schemes often involve the use of dummy corporations, numbered bank accounts, or financial instruments issued by banks (often referred to as offshore banks) located in countries where banking regulations are lax.

## Foreign Laundries

Much of the money invested by organized crime in legitimate businesses in the United States is first routed through secret numbered bank accounts in countries such as Liechtenstein, Luxembourg, the Channel Islands, Panama, the Bahamas, the Netherlands Antilles, Antigua, Anguilla, Montserrat, the Grand Cayman Islands, Hong Kong, Dubai, the United Arab Emirates, Singapore, Nauru, Vanuatu,

Uruguay, Austria, and Bulgaria.[42] This arrangement is ideal for the racketeer who wants to clean large amounts of cash. Often it involves depositing illicit funds in a secret numbered account and then bringing them back into the United States as a loan from the foreign bank or from a dummy corporation set up under the laws of a foreign country. Not only are the illegal income and its sources hidden from the Internal Revenue Service and law enforcement agencies, but the interest on this supposed loan is often deducted as a business expense on the tax return of the racketeer.

In many cases, organized-crime members have not been content with merely using secret numbered accounts in foreign banks. As early as the 1960s, it was recognized that many banks in Switzerland and the Bahamas had been taken over by Americans known to be associated with organized-crime activities.[43] Not only did the American ownership protect the identity of bank customers and allow for the falsification of bank records, but it also enabled the racketeers to bring apparently legitimate money back into the United States in the form of various financial instruments issued by these banks and by foreign governments. Owners realized that controlled banks could also be used to generate illicit income by issuing fraudulent financial instruments that are used in this country as collateral for loans and in other fraud schemes. Enforcement agents working for the U.S. Comptroller of the Currency have estimated that the volume of phony financial instruments issued by offshore banks is in the hundreds of millions of dollars.[44]

## Use of the Internet to Launder Money

One method of electronic money laundering is to establish a company offering services payable through the Internet.[45] The launderer then "uses" those services and pays for them using credit or debit cards tied to accounts under his control (located perhaps in an offshore area) that contain criminal proceeds. The launderer's company then invoices the credit card company, which, in turn, forwards the payment for the service rendered. The launderer's company may then justify such income payments for services rendered (see Figure 14–4). In this example, the launderer actually controls only the invoiced accounts and the company offering services through the Internet. The credit

**Figure 14-4** Money Laundering

(**Source:** Financial Action Task Force on Money Laundering, "Report on Money Laundering Typology, 2000-2001," Paris, France.)

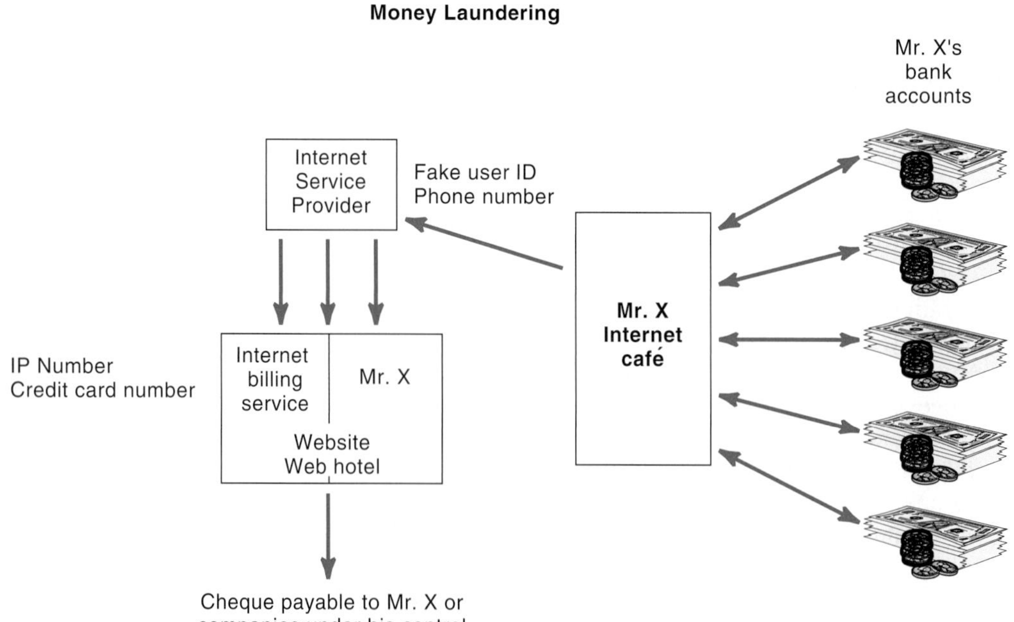

card company, the Internet service provider, the Internet invoicing service, and even the bank from which the illegal proceeds begin this process would likely have no reason to believe there was anything suspicious about the activity, since they each see only one part of it. Indeed, this method is almost the same as that used in many fraud cases, with the difference being that, in the latter, the bank accounts billed belong to innocent third parties rather than to the perpetrator of the scheme (see Figure 14–5).

The problem for the investigator in dealing with such a scheme is being able to follow the links between the various parts of the scheme. The launderer can easily use fictitious identities in setting up his or her presence on the Web. By taking advantage of the easy access to Internet services in other geographic locations to ensure additional distance between the launderer and his or her activities, the launderer can be certain that service providers' lack of uniformity in maintaining online communication records will also work to ensure his anonymity. The fact that the various components of the scheme see only part of the picture means it will be very difficult to determine whether illegal activity is taking place without first obtaining a picture of the whole operation. In short, the criminal using the Internet takes advantage of certain inherent aspects of the system to ensure that the whole picture is not visible to the investigator. To help you understand this better, the subsection below explains how Internet communication is organized.

***The Internet Communication Trail*** All information conveyed via the Internet[46] passes through a series of computer servers. Each connection from a particular server should leave traces (i.e., a record of its Internet protocol, or IP, number; the date and time of connection; etc.) on the servers with which it communicates. This information is available, however, only if the receiving servers at each step have been set up to create "log files." If the log files exist at each step and the user sending the information has a fixed IP address, it is relatively straightforward to trace back from the addressee to the originator. In instances where the user is operating using dial-up access, his or her identity can be discovered through the log files of the Internet service provider (ISP). However, if the log files are not maintained at any step of the way or dial-up user

**Figure 14-5** Internet Fraud: Dial-Up Connection

(**Source:** Financial Action Task Force on Money Laundering, "Report on Money Laundering Typology, 2000-2001," Paris, France.)

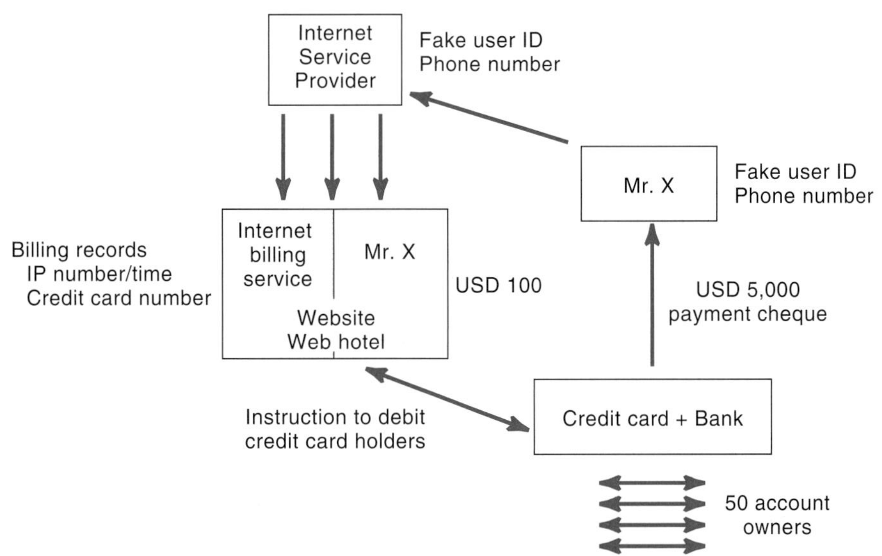

(or subscriber) information is considered to be protected information, then it may be more difficult to determine the ultimate link between an illegal activity and a specific individual.

***Internet Gambling*** Given the above scenario, it seems that Internet gambling might be an ideal Web-based "service" to use as a cover for a money-laundering scheme. There is evidence that criminals are using the Internet gambling industry to commit crime and to launder the proceeds of crime. Despite attempts to deal with the potential problems of Internet gambling by regulating it, requiring licenses for operating it, or banning such services outright, a number of concerns remain in addition to the inability to track the Internet links mentioned above. For example, transactions are primarily performed through credit cards, and the offshore placement of many Internet gambling sites makes locating and prosecuting the relevant parties very difficult, if not impossible. Furthermore, gambling transactions, the records of which might be needed as evidence, are conducted at the gambling site and are software based; this may add to the difficulty of collecting and presenting such evidence.

***Possible Countermeasures*** Several years ago the Financial Action Task Force (FATF) on Money Laundering met to discuss the problem of laundering money on the Internet,[47] and experts offered the following suggestions:

- Require that Internet service providers maintain reliable subscriber registers with appropriate identification programs.
- Require that ISPs establish log files with traffic data relating Internet-protocol numbers to subscribers and to telephone numbers used in the connections.
- Require that this information be maintained for a reasonable period (six months to a year).[48]

## Forensic Examination of Money-Laundering Records

Determining where suspects' cash originates and the means they use to conceal this cash can be exceedingly difficult for investigators, unless they have reliable informants, cooperating witnesses, or undercover agents. In addition, investigators may find it difficult to distinguish cash gained through legitimate businesses from cash gained through illegal means.[49]

For these reasons, circumstantial evidence becomes critical in money-laundering cases. It is often the only evidence available to provide a connection between the funds in question and their original source. In fact, it is this very link, the "specified unlawful activity" (SUA), that is a statutory requirement in federal money-laundering prosecutions.

Today, the **Racketeering Records Analysis Unit (RRAU)** of the FBI laboratory in Washington, DC, can establish this necessary link by examining the records kept by criminals who launder money. Criminals, in order to provide proof to their superiors that they properly channeled all the cash, document the collection and disbursement of all funds. Fortunately, these records also provide critical evidence for investigators, who must prove that the funds were acquired illegally.

This subsection provides information on the operations of the RRAU and explains how the unit can assist investigators and prosecutors in developing money-laundering cases. It also discusses some of the methods criminals commonly use to hide illegal proceeds. Although these methods vary greatly, experts can now identify characteristics unique to such types of organizations. And, while none of these methods are new, what is new is that law enforcement now recognizes the value of forensic examination of business records.

The RRAU uses the clandestine business documents confiscated from organizations believed to be laundering funds to trace the history of the alleged illicit businesses. These documents reveal valuable information as to the amount of money laundered and how the suspects packaged, transported, disguised, and hid these funds. By providing a more complete picture of the roles and behaviors of criminals and their illegal operations, the RRAU expands the scope of money-laundering investigations.

In addition, this information can aid prosecutors in gaining stiffer sentences for individuals found guilty of money laundering. The courts base suspects' sentences on the amounts they laundered, which are determined through their own business records. Current federal sentencing guidelines[50] allow for such sentence adjustments, and at least one federal appeals court has upheld the use of RRAU testimony in connection with related sentencing adjustments in drug matters.[51]

As previously discussed, individuals who launder money use a variety of techniques to avoid detection by law enforcement. Therefore, it is important that law enforcement personnel understand the various techniques and the proof needed to ensure successful prosecution of these cases.

***Secreting Funds*** Criminals often hide illegally obtained funds until they can smuggle the money to another destination. Although hiding funds increases the risk of seizure by authorities or theft by other criminals, it eliminates the need for a professional money launderer, who typically charges a fee ranging from 3 to 5 percent to assist in transferring the money through legitimate financial institutions.

This technique was evident in a New York case in which authorities seized millions of dollars in currency, as well as business records, from an alleged furniture and appliance warehouse. Although officials had kept the warehouse under surveillance for several months, the evidence acquired during that time was largely circumstantial, consisting mainly of investigators' accounts of activity in and around the warehouse. In this case, investigators observed that the subjects frequently used telephone paging devices and made numerous attempts to elude, or otherwise mislead, surveillance units. Investigators also found cocaine residue on a piece of duct tape retrieved from a trash receptacle located outside the warehouse. Finally, they noted that although the warehouse moved little furniture, there still appeared to be a lot of activity inside the building.

When investigators raided the warehouse, they discovered a collection and storage point for drug proceeds, instead of the cocaine "stash house" that they had expected to find. Although they did not confiscate drugs, they did confiscate approximately $18 million in U.S. currency, packaged in cardboard boxes and secreted in a concealed compartment of a truck. In addition, investigators also confiscated numerous handwritten documents from both the warehouse and other search locations, which they then submitted to the RRAU for analysis.

The initial review of the records indicated that they represented transactions involving millions of dollars in cash—recorded as it came into the warehouse—followed by confirmed totals counted by denomination. The suspects assigned the totals to at least 11 accounts before combining the cash into outgoing sums that were packaged in boxes and suitcases and placed in the truck. This method typifies how money launderers hide large sums of cash until they can transport it out of the country.

However, a more detailed analysis of the warehouse documents by the RRAU revealed more damaging evidence to be used at trial. Records showed that the organization had received, through at least 114 exchanges, over $44 million in cash during a three-month period. Individuals in the warehouse had listed the amount of cash received, the date of receipt, the account relating to each transfer of funds, the *alleged* amount at time of delivery, and the *confirmed* count of each amount. The listing of incoming and confirmed accounts, along with counts of the currency by denomination and coded account designations, characterizes money-laundering records.

Of particular interest was an outgoing amount of nearly $7.5 million, listed on one page of the seized documents. The same amount appeared on another page of the documents as the sum of three smaller amounts of cash that the suspects placed in boxes and a suitcase. Further examination of the documents revealed a third page, which indicated that the individuals derived the smaller amounts of money by counting it by currency denominations, that is, $100s, $50s, $20s, and so on. The amount of money seized in the warehouse closely approximated that of the currency listed on an inventory recovered from one of the search locations. By comparing documents, examiners determined that the criminals sorted the cash according to denomination and boxed it for storage, most likely until they could smuggle the money out of the country. Finally, the confiscated records revealed that the suspects had collected the nearly $7.5 million over a period of several days just prior to preparing it for shipment. This evidence served to further strengthen the case for prosecutors.

However, in order to prosecute the suspects under the federal money-laundering statutes, prosecutors needed to provide proof that the suspects had obtained the funds illegally. Therefore, an FBI examiner testified in court concerning notations on two seized documents. These notations showed the purchase/sale of 35 units, at prices of $13,500 and

$14,000 each, between August 24 and October 4. The examiner further testified that there appeared to be a relationship between the units and their corresponding prices: the units were consistent with kilogram prices for cocaine. This type of bookkeeping—partial dates and an informal accounting flow—typifies drug records. It also provided another indication that the suspects had obtained the funds through an illicit drug trade.

It is important to note in this case that even though investigators found the drug documents in one location and the cash documents in another, RRAU experts were still able to establish a circumstantial relationship between the two sets of records. It is this type of evidence that can be so crucial to any such case.

***Disguising the Source of Illicit Funds*** "Operation Polarcap," a joint investigation conducted by the FBI, the Drug Enforcement Administration (DEA), and the U.S. Customs Service, is an excellent example of how business records and paperwork provide critical evidence in money-laundering cases. By examining seized documents, examiners gained valuable insights into how the criminals had disguised the actual source of illegal funds. This undercover investigation, which involved months of surveillance, resulted in the seizure of thousands of documents, many of them found in trash receptacles at various businesses connected to the laundering scheme, including a jewelry store located in Los Angeles.

When RRAU examiners received the confiscated documents, their task was to show, solely on the basis of an analysis of the documents, how the suspects received cash and circulated it through legitimate financial institutions in ways designed to conceal its true origin. Their analysis revealed a laundering network that acquired millions of dollars in cash from sources in New York, Los Angeles, and Houston. A large portion of this cash from these cities was delivered to the Los Angeles jewelry store.

RRAU examiners were able to show that when the suspects received the cash, they noted on bills of lading the total number of packages in a given shipment, as well as individual weights and total dollar values of each package. For example, one of the receipts indicated a delivery of five packages weighing 250 pounds and valued at $1,568,000. A handwritten entry in a seized ledger book showed that same dollar amount under the column heading "$ Received." Finally, a computerized summary of currency transaction reports (CTRs) filed by several Los Angeles area banks at which the jewelry store maintained accounts showed $1,568,000 deposited to an account at one of these banks. A comparison of all these documents confirmed that the numerical notations represented amounts of cash delivered from New York to Los Angeles.

Other evidence indicating that the suspects had attempted to disguise the illicit funds included a dated ledger entry showing that the jewelry store had received $2.8 million on September 2. A scrap of paper bearing the same date showed that this figure was a combination of three smaller amounts labeled "L.A." One of these amounts was $1 million. Other scraps of paper found in the trash at the jewelry store indicated that the $1 million was counted by denomination on September 2. All this evidence pointed toward a possible money-laundering operation.

***Fraudulent Documents*** Money-laundering organizations also produce fraudulent documents, such as sales receipts, designed to conceal the true origin of a business's cash. For example, in the Los Angeles jewelry store case, investigators found a scrap of paper, dated August 10, 1988, which indicated two amounts of collected cash totaling $1,034,000 and designated "L.A." This corresponded with a cash deposit of $1,034,000 made on that date to an account of the business at another Los Angeles bank.

In addition, investigators recovered two consecutively numbered receipts from trash receptacles. These receipts revealed how the suspects broke down this total in an effort to portray the source of the money as cash proceeds from two sales of 24-karat gold to a gold refiner in the amounts of $693,000 and $341,000. Since cash sales that large would be highly unusual in any legitimate business, the suspects produced fraudulent documents designed to conceal the true origin of the business's cash. At trial, the RRAU examiner testified that these types of business practices are inconsistent with normal business activities. Instead, they are associated with money-laundering operations.

Of tremendous importance in this case was the seizure, on an almost daily basis, of many documents from trash discarded at the business. A critical lesson learned from this analysis is that the potential value of garbage in criminal investigations cannot be overestimated.

***Structuring Financial Transactions*** Another method for laundering money involves structuring financial transactions. This type of activity was evident in a case uncovered through a federal investigation in Brooklyn and Manhattan in 1990.

The case involved a residential setting—specifically, four apartments—where suspects collected, counted, and prepared drug funds for conversion to negotiable instruments, such as bank money orders. When investigators raided the apartments, they recovered $1,304,595 in cash, along with money orders worth approximately $73,000, all in amounts of less than $10,000. Investigators also seized hundreds of additional money order receipts and related handwritten documents, which they submitted for examination.

An RRAU analysis of the seized documents disclosed that the operation received cash totaling at least $13,503,441 in 26 deliveries from September 1989 to March 1990. After the suspects received the cash, they listed daily breakdowns that showed, through a series of deductions, how specific amounts were used to purchase money orders at area financial institutions. These purchases totaled a minimum of $11,022,141 during a six-month period, allowing authorities to convict the main defendant for laundering over $10 million in cash.

This evidence resulted in an increase of nine levels in the defendant's sentence under the federal sentencing guidelines. Partly on the basis of a previously negotiated plea bargain, the defendant received a much longer prison sentence than would have resulted had the documents not been carefully examined.[52]

# IDENTITY THEFT

**Identity theft** differs from other forms of less calculated fraud. For example, a juvenile's use of someone else's driver's license to purchase alcohol does not constitute identity theft. Although intentional deception exists, using someone else's license to make a purchase does not result in a loss to the victim.[53]

The Identity Theft and Assumption Deterrence Act of 1998 makes identity theft a federal crime with penalties of up to 15 years' imprisonment and a maximum fine of $250,000. Under this act, a person whose identity is stolen is a true victim. Previously, only credit grantors who suffered monetary losses were considered victims. This legislation enables the Secret Service, the Federal Bureau of Investigation, and other law enforcement agencies to combat identity-theft crime, and it enables victims to seek restitution in cases that result in conviction. It also established the Federal Trade Commission as the central agency that acts as a clearinghouse for complaints (against credit reporting agencies and credit grantors), referrals, and resources for the assistance of victims of identity theft.[54]

## HOW IDENTITY THEFT OCCURS

Identity theft can occur in many ways. Identity thieves scavenge through garbage, steal and redirect mail, use internal access of databases, and surf the Internet searching for personal information. The following represent some of the more common ways that thieves gather other persons' identifying information.

### Dumpster Diving

Individuals or businesses that fail to dispose properly of personal identification information, by shredding or mutilating, are susceptible to a "dumpster diver," who retrieves discarded material while looking for anything of value. Dumpster divers obtain account numbers, addresses, and dates of birth from financial, medical, and personal records—all of which they can use to assume an identity.

One dumpster diver drove around affluent neighborhoods on garbage collection day.[55] He picked up garbage bags left on the curb, took them home, and rummaged through them. The Social Security numbers and preapproved credit card applications he obtained from the garbage, along with the use of rented mailboxes, cloaked him from his crime.[56] Businesses that rent mailboxes for short periods of time make tracing a dumpster diver difficult. These companies do not require a lot of information about the renter, and this aids the individual in remaining mobile and isolated from the crime. Law enforcement agencies should establish mutual agreements with these businesses to facilitate information gathering. Additionally, police may deter dumpster divers by patrolling residential areas more aggressively on garbage collection days and during the tax season, a prosperous time for dumpster divers. Many people dispose of old receipts and financial records carelessly. By encouraging people to shred documents and by enforcing local trespass ordinances with regard to residential and industrial dump sites, law enforcement agencies can prevent thousands of identity-theft cases.

## Mail Theft

Mail theft is another way that criminals obtain personal identification information. Thieves check mailboxes looking for bill or credit card payments that people leave in their boxes for the postal carrier to collect. They use information from these items to obtain credit or to purchase products and services in the victim's name. Mail theft can also occur from mail processing areas, where it is perpetrated by unscrupulous postal employees.

Additionally, some criminals complete change-of-address cards in order to divert victims' mail to a rented mailbox. Police agencies should instruct victims to notify their postal inspector immediately if they suspect that someone has forwarded their mail to another location. Law enforcement departments should urge that people not leave their bill payments in their mailboxes for the carrier to collect but, instead, take their payments to the post office or drop them in a locked mailbox.

## Internal Access

The term internal access refers to an individual's obtaining personal information illegally from a computer connected to a credit reporting bureau or to an employee's accessing a company's database that contains personal identification information. Such an insider will look for names similar to her or his own or for people with good credit, intending to assume their identities and commit credit fraud. Also, the insider may attempt to sell the personal information to another thief. This happened in Fayetteville, California, when a consumer learned that her credit report listed five new accounts issued in her name. An identity thief had charged over $65,000 of unsecured debt using her identity.[57]

The negligence of a company that permits such access in an unmonitored environment contributes to this type of identity theft. One medical office employee illegally obtained a patient's name and Social Security number and then established a credit line, rented an apartment, and earned income in the patient's name.[58]

To reduce the misuse of personal information, police departments with financial or crime prevention units should conduct one- or two-day workshops for businesses that have the threat of internal-access fraud. Law enforcement representatives should work with business security managers to suggest possible restrictions and procedures that would limit access to personal identification information.

## Computerized Information and the Internet

The information age has changed the way thieves commit crimes. With so much personal information obtainable in the networked world, thieves can access information easily. (See Chapter 16, "Computer Crime," for a detailed discussion.) They find personal identifying information through computerized information services, also known as information brokers. These services collect, sort, package, and sell personal information in electronic form to other businesses and individuals. Computerized information services may not safeguard the personal information adequately or screen purchasers of computerized information appropriately, creating the opportunity for an identity thief to commit fraud. Private companies and individuals in some states can purchase driver's license information and photos, traditionally restricted to law enforcement authorities. South Carolina and Florida officials sold millions of digital photos of driver's licenses to private companies—transactions that raised serious questions about personal privacy. Who has access to the information? How will individuals and companies safeguard the data? After a surge of citizen complaints and questions, state officials in Florida and South Carolina halted the sale of digital photographs.[59]

According to one organization, the Internet also provides opportunities for identity theft.[60] Compromised public and private networks endure millions of dollars in losses annually.[61] In one company, a security breach allowed anyone to view thousands of private customer information files, which contained names, addresses, and other personal information, without restrictions.[62] Company officials corrected the problem quickly, but many consumers began to question the guarantees of information confidentiality and realized the vulnerability of information on the Internet.

## HOW TO RESOLVE IDENTITY THEFT

Victims may need months or years to restore their credit and reputation. Law enforcement agencies should advise citizens to report identity theft immediately. Departments should gather as much documented evidence from the victims as possible. After completing the initial report, the agency should provide a copy to the victim, along with the phone number of the fraud investigator assigned to the case. Credit card companies, banks, and insurance companies often require the police report to verify the crime.

After notifying the police, victims should take the necessary steps to mitigate and resolve the damage caused by identity theft. Departments can explain these steps in a booklet or through private investigator-victim consultations, using different procedures for different types of identity theft. Credit theft remains the most common type, but other types of identity theft exist (e.g., theft of cellular phones, driver's licenses, passports, and checks).

Law enforcement agencies should instruct victims to contact their current credit card and loan companies about the theft. Victims should cancel old cards and order new cards with different account numbers. They should also inform all check-monitoring agencies of the theft and alert the fraud departments of the three major credit bureaus in order to place a hold on accounts.

Additionally, each victim should complete a credit-fraud report with a victim statement and submit it to the credit bureaus. The victim statement should explain briefly that an individual has used the victim's identity fraudulently to apply for credit, and it should provide a contact number for verifying credit applications. Victims should request that the credit bureaus provide free monthly credit reports to monitor for evidence of new fraudulent activity. Departments should recommend that victims keep a log of all conversations with police officers and financial institution officials. Agencies should advise victims that no one can remove information from their credit reports and should warn them about credit-repair scams that promise to restore tarnished credit reports. Officers may need to refer traumatized victims to support groups, which can assist and support identity-theft victims as well as help the recovery process.[63]

### Recommendations and Strategies for Preventing Identity Theft

- Patrol residential areas on trash collection days and during the tax season.
- Enforce trespass laws with regard to residential and industrial dump sites.
- Advise citizens to shred documents and drop off mail in a locked mailbox.
- Remind people to be cautious when using automated teller machines.
- Disseminate information to the public on how to mitigate and prevent computer, credit, and cellular-telephone fraud.
- Suggest restrictions to businesses that would reduce internal-access fraud.
- Educate officers about the various methods used to commit identity theft and about the types of fraud that result.[64]

## THE LOOTING OF ARCHAEOLOGICAL SITES

One type of larceny that has existed for centuries is increasingly an issue in the United States. Unfortunately, many enforcement agencies lack awareness of its importance—or even its existence. "**Archaeological looting** is defined as illegal unscientific removal of archaeological resources."[65] This nationwide problem has been studied primarily as it relates to public and tribal lands, but looting also takes place on private land when objects are removed without the permission of the landowner. On federal land (e.g., national parks, areas under the direction of the Bureau of Land Management, and national forests) there were 1,720 documented violations of laws protecting archaeological resources between 1985 and 1987.[66] Because of the difficulty of even detecting the crimes in some areas, it is believed that this figure represents only 25 percent of the actual number of looting cases.[67] The looting of archaeological resources is related to the widespread fascination with our past; the interest of individuals in collecting archaeological materials; the high dollar value for which some archaeological works can be sold; the right to buy, possess, and sell legally obtained specimens; and the frequent difficulty of proving that the archaeological materials were illegally obtained.[68]

Archaeological resources are nonrenewable: when they are looted or vandalized, the information they contain is lost forever. The looting of archaeological sites in the United States is happening on a vast scale. Stated bluntly, part of our history has been, and continues to be, stolen. In the process, thieves have damaged and destroyed the archaeological sites that are the only way to learn about most of the 12,000-year history of humans in North America (see photo). Such looting also means that some private collectors can withhold from the public precious and beautiful objects that they or others have stolen.

This problem is not isolated in one region of the country. It is occurring on public and private lands, in battlefield parks, and in historic cemeteries. Although a certain amount of the looting is done by individuals seeking to enhance their own collections, there is also significant illegal commercial trafficking in artifacts for personal profit.[69] Persons bent on profiting are not the only offenders responsible for the loss of artifacts; the so-called casual looters and vandals also contribute significantly to the problem.[70] Vandalism may be intentional—as in the case of defacement of ancient rock art by graffiti or target shooting—or unintentional, as in accidental site damage from off-road vehicles.[71]

There is a substantial market for Native American artifacts in the United States, as well as in Germany, Japan, and other countries. An ancient pot from the Southwest was sold for $250,000 in Paris; a Mississippi stone ax was offered for sale for $150,000 in New Orleans; and a single rare arrowhead has an appraised value of $20,000.[72] In the Four Corners area alone (the point where Arizona, Colorado, New Mexico, and Utah meet), more than 44,000 known sites have been looted or vandalized in recent years.[73] On the Navajo reservation, the number of archaeological sites victimized increased 900 percent between 1980 and 1987.[74] One of the most spectacular Native American sites is the famous Cliff Palace in Mesa Verde National Park, Colorado. This stone structure was built by the Anasazi (a Navajo word meaning "Ancient Ones") as home for 400 people nearly 900 years ago.[75] The Anasazi were the ancestors of the Pueblo, Hopi, Zuñi, and other tribes. The intricate designs of their pottery and woven baskets are stunning.[76] Today, an unbroken Anasazi mug or bowl crafted or painted not particularly well is worth $150 to $200, a piece of midrange quality is worth $500 to $800, and even a specimen that is just "pretty good" will bring several thousand dollars and up.[77] In Oregon's Deschutes National Forest, a looter was apprehended

**Looted Grave at Chavez Pass, Pueblo, Arizona**
Archaeological looting is defined as illegal, unscientific removal of archaeological resources. The looting of these resources is related to the wide-spread fascination with our past and the high dollar value for which some archaeological works can be sold. This nationwide problem has been studied as it relates to public and tribal lands throughout the United States.

(Courtesy National Park Service)

with a trailer containing 3,000 artifacts, digging equipment, and site maps coded to where artifacts were most plentiful.[78] Other public lands that have suffered losses due to vandalism and theft of Native American artifacts include Pisgah National Forest in North Carolina, Chippewa National Forest in Minnesota, Tongass National Forest in Alaska, and Ocala National Forest in Florida, as well as sites such as Metichawon, an area in New Milford, Connecticut, and Shawnee National Forest, Illinois.

It is not only prehistoric Native American artifacts that are being stolen; another target is historic Euro-American sites such as some of our national parks. In Virginia, park rangers spotted three men entering Richmond National Battlefield Park at 1:30 A.M.[79] With the assistance of local deputy sheriffs, a stakeout was established. Four hours later, as the defendants left the park, they were arrested and charged with federal offenses. In their possession were state-of-the-art metal detectors and Civil War artifacts, including a bayonet, mini balls, grapeshot, a button, and other associated items (see photo). Physical evidence was gathered that connected the three men and the artifacts to freshly dug holes in the park's historic earthworks. A similar incident involving a different defendant occurred in Fredericksburg and Spotsylvania National Military Park.[80] In Uncompahgre National Forest, Colorado, portions of a wooden cabin that was built around 1879 were taken for use as firewood; investigation of the case led to the execution of a search warrant and recovery of portions of the cabin.[81] California's Channel Islands Marine Sanctuary was the scene of underwater looting by scuba divers; the divers took hundreds of relics from the wreck sites of the *Winfield Scott* and the *Golden Horn,* fast sail transport ships that sank in the 1800s.[82]

## LEGAL CONSIDERATIONS

### Federal Provisions

Federal preservation laws date from the late nineteenth century. At that time the primary intent was to document information, to set aside land areas as monuments, and to collect items of importance related to national public figures, historic military events, and ancient cultures.[83] Federal policy to preserve historic and prehistoric sites on federal land was first embodied in the Antiquities Act of 1906.[84] This act authorized a permit system for investigation of archaeological sites on federal and Native American lands and gave the president the power to establish national monuments on federal lands to protect historic landmarks, historic and prehistoric structures, and other objects of historical and scientific interest.[85] This federal law has misdemeanor (but no felony) provisions, and fines of up to $500 and/or 90 days' imprisonment can be imposed on persons "who shall appropriate, excavate, injure, or destroy any historic or prehistoric ruin or monument or any

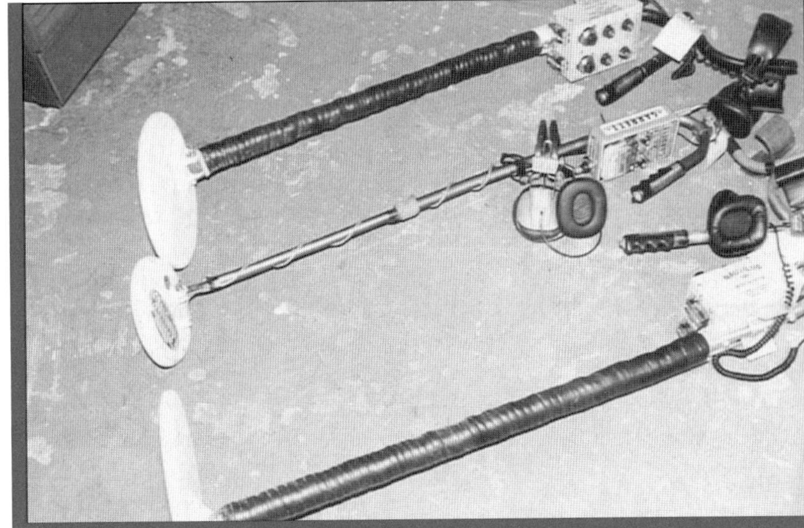

**Metal Detectors Used by Looters**
Metal detectors seized from looters who entered Richmond National Battlefield Park and located and removed a bayonet, bullets, and other objects.
(Courtesy National Park Service)

object of antiquity situated on lands owned or controlled" by the federal government unless they have been issued a permit.[86] Between 1906 and 1979, the overall enforcement impact of the Antiquities Act was very small, totaling only 18 convictions and two 90-day jail sentences.[87] It is important, however, to note that the federal management of prehistoric and historic resources on national and Native American lands has always included the responsibility to protect the resources from violators. A great deal of good was accomplished through this responsibility although it is not reflected in enforcement statistics.

The federal government passed other legislation related to historic sites in the years following 1906, but from an enforcement standpoint, the most far-reaching law was the Archaeological Resources Protection Act (ARPA) of 1979, as amended in 1988.[88] Both felony and misdemeanor charges can be made against persons who violate ARPA, as listed in the following provisions:

1. No person may excavate, remove, damage, or otherwise alter or deface or attempt to excavate, remove, damage, or otherwise alter or deface any archaeological resource located on public lands or Native American lands (without a permit, unless the resource is specifically exempt under law);
2. No person may sell, purchase, exchange, transport, receive, or offer to sell, purchase, or exchange any archaeological resource (in violation of ARPA or any other federal law);
3. No person may sell, purchase, exchange, transport, receive, or offer to sell, purchase, or exchange, in interstate or foreign commerce, any archaeological resource excavated, removed, sold, purchased, exchanged, transported, or received in violation of any provision, rule, regulation, ordinance, or permit in effect under state or local law; and
4. Any person who knowingly violates, or counsels, procures, solicits, or employs any other person to violate any prohibition of the above shall be held accountable under the law.[89]

Archaeological resources that are protected include pottery, basketry, bottles, weapons, weapon projectiles, tools, structures, pit houses, rock paintings and carvings, graves, skeletal materials, organic waste, by-products from manufacture, rock shelters, apparel, shipwrecks, or any part of such items.[90] If the value of the damage to the archaeological resource or the value of the artifact(s) stolen is $500 or more, then the act is a felony and conviction carries a fine of up to $100,000 and/or a term of imprisonment not to exceed five years. Offenders may also be required to pay restitution, which is calculated on the basis of the actual archaeological damage done and is often used to restore the site.[91] When a defendant has a prior ARPA conviction, whether for a misdemeanor or felony, all second and subsequent ARPA violations are treated as felonies regardless of the actual dollar damage or loss.[92]

In contrast to traditional federal criminal legislation, ARPA is part of land-use and conservation legislation and also contains a provision for the forfeiture of equipment, vehicles, and tools used in the attempted or actual taking of protected archaeological resources.[93] Protected resources can be characterized broadly as material remains of past human existence, of archaeological interest, that are over 100 years old.[94] ARPA has several exemptions: paleontological resources (fossils) not located within an archaeological site, arrowheads found on the surface of the ground, and the collection of rocks, bullets, coins, and minerals for private purposes. However, a "savings clause" in ARPA provides that items not protected by ARPA are still subject to protection under other federal laws.[95] In short, materials on federal lands remain federal property and may not be removed without permission.[96] ARPA and the regulations under which it is implemented defer to Native American tribal self-government and require close coordination with any tribe(s) affected when an excavation of potential tribal religious significance is contemplated outside formal Native American lands.[97] A basic provision for permits to excavate on tribal lands is that the applicant must obtain the consent of the Native American tribe owning, or having jurisdiction over, those lands.

## State Laws

As of mid-1990, none of the states had a unified law comprising all statutes protecting archaeological resources.[98] Instead, states tend to categorize laws related to archaeological resources under a variety of headings. These individual statutes may address such subjects as disturbance of marked and unmarked burial sites, the forging of antiquities, vandalism to cemeteries, and grave robbing. As seen in Figure 14–6, about two-thirds of the states have laws—resembling to some extent the federal ARPA—that protect archaeological resources on state property.[99] Eleven states have passed legislation to discourage activities that damage archaeological resources on private land.[100] In addition, several states have statutes providing protection to specific types of areas, such as underwater salvage sites (10 states), caves (4 states), forts (2 states), and ghost towns (Colorado only).[101] States also have statutes that provide for state archaeologists, registers of historic places, requirements for the issuance of permits to conduct field investigations, obligations to report discoveries that may have historic or prehistoric significance, and protection of the confidentiality of site locations.

Under federal law there is no regulation of archaeological resources on private land, and under most state laws the types of "archaeological" activities conducted on private land by landowners or with their permission is largely uncontrolled. Perhaps the most noteworthy example of this issue occurred at the Slack Farm in western Kentucky.[102] Ten "artifact miners" paid the new owner of the farm $10,000 for the right to dig up and remove archaeological resources. It was long known that a Late Mississippian village, dating from around 1450 to 1650, was located on the farm, but it had enjoyed protection from exploitation by the previous owner.[103] This site was of special significance because it covered a period of centuries related to the first European contact with the "New World."[104] Legally empowered by the new owner, the artifact miners rented a tractor and began plowing through the village midden (the term archaeologists use for a refuse heap) and dwellings to

**Figure 14-6** State Archaeological Protection Laws

(**Source:** Courtesy State Historical Society of Iowa)

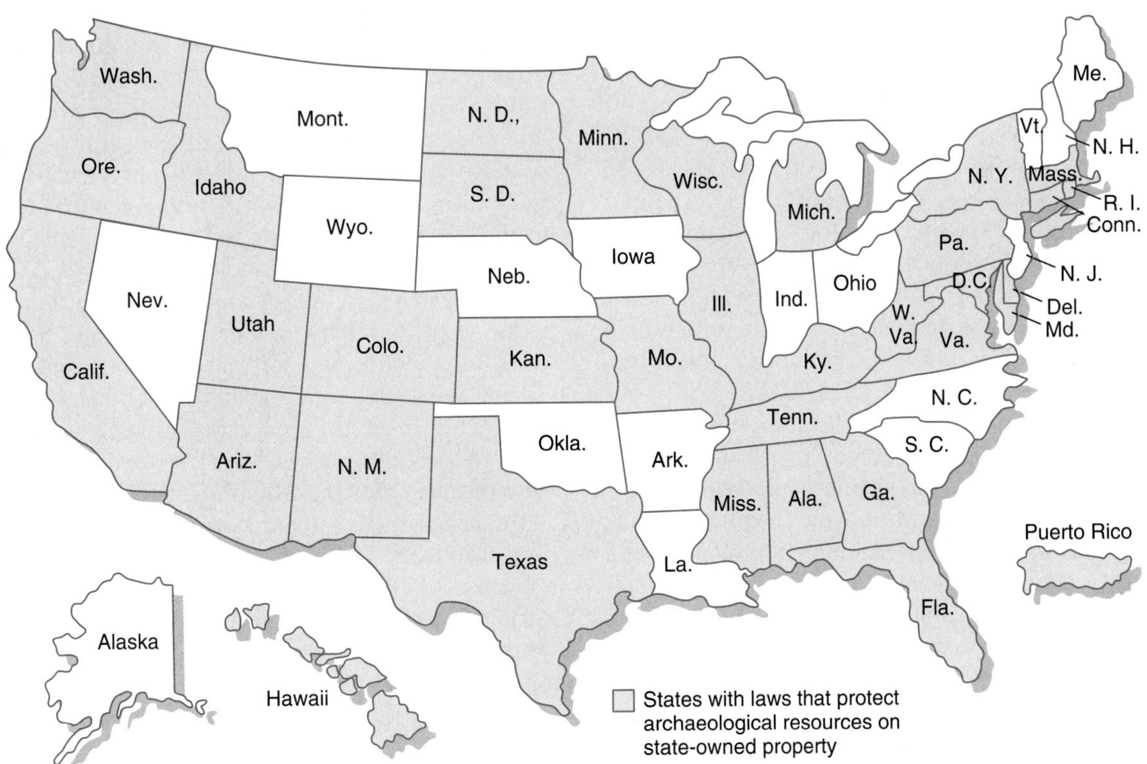

get to graves to locate pottery, stone tools, and weapons.[105] The result was the large-scale destruction of an important site, the loss of invaluable information, and the littering of the field with more than 450 craters, exposed bones, and soft-drink and beer cans.[106] In response, the Kentucky legislature made such treatment of buried remains a felony:

> A person is guilty of desecration of venerated objects in the first degree when, other than authorized by law, he intentionally excavates or disinters human remains for the purpose of commercial sale or exploitation of the remains themselves or of objects buried contemporaneously with the remains.[107]

Note that this Kentucky criminal statute does not distinguish between acts committed on public and private lands. Also, while some state statutes regarding desecration of graves have been interpreted to apply to historic, but not prehistoric sites, the Kentucky law covers both types.

## CONDUCTING ENFORCEMENT INVESTIGATIONS

Archaeological resource protection investigations pose a number of challenges. Different laws apply when the violation occurs on federal land as opposed to state land, and there are relatively few laws applicable to private lands as opposed to the more heavily protected public lands. Moreover, some historic areas are divided in such a manner that one portion is under federal jurisdiction while another section is on state and/or private land. As mentioned earlier, many offenses go undetected for long periods of time because of the difficulty in monitoring sites, which are numerous and often very remote, such as those in Alaska, with over 150,000 archaeological sites. Because of this delay, opportunities to gather crucial physical evidence, which can associate the crime scene with the offenders, may be lost. Moreover, an offender may leave his or her vehicle outside the boundaries of a protected area and claim to be transporting the collection from one point to another or transporting artifacts gathered on private land. Although a law enforcement officer in such circumstances may have some reasonable suspicion, if the subject was not observed entering or leaving the protected area, it is not likely to rise to the level of probable cause. Additional indicators may be found in several areas: Would a claim that a person is transporting his or her personal collection be consistent with artifacts that appear to be freshly dug up? Does the subject claim to have been on private land but have maps of protected lands with site markings on them? Have digging tools been camouflaged to avoid reflecting light? How close was the subject's vehicle stopped in relationship to protected public lands? Does the subject seem unusually nervous? Can the subject's story of being on private land be verified by the owner? Is the subject's version credible if this occurs at 3 A.M.? Are there two or more subjects carrying two-way radios and scanners? Are the subjects known to have committed previous violations of archaeological resource protection or related laws? It is from the totality of the circumstances that reasonable suspicion may rise to the level of probable cause.

Being able to recognize the tools commonly employed by looters is essential. Looters typically have shovels and metal rods up to 5 feet long with a T handle, which they use to probe for human remains, artifacts, and changes in soil density that suggest good places to examine. Offenders often carry pieces of screen through which they sift dirt, leaving artifacts on the screen, or the screen may have a wooden edge built around it for added strength. Other equipment includes trowels, small brushes to clean artifacts, a small handheld metal "claw" to break the soil and with which to dig, lanterns and head lamps (for night work), backpacks in which to carry the stolen artifacts, and motorcycles and all-terrain vehicles (ATVs).[108] In historic battlefield parks, suspects often carry metal detectors. Some small-time looters will appear innocent enough, walking along with a stick or staff in their hand, turning over apparent surface debris. The stick or staff is referred to as a "flipper," and as the subjects find articles of value, they pick them up and keep them.

Initial information about looting comes from a variety of sources. Hikers, farmers, campers, hunters, ranchers, and fishers who see acts of vandalism or looting in progress or discover sites that have been victimized may contact a government agency with the information they have. Routine patrols by employees of the agency that manages the public land also may uncover crimes in progress, as well as those that have been completed. If there is evidence of fresh digging, the site or sites may be placed under surveillance. In examining a site that has been looted, one factor to consider is whether there is any evidence suggesting that the perpetrators may return. For example, has a supply of digging tools and screens been left behind, hidden in some way? Although subjects might have simply left the tools to avoid being seen leaving with them, if there are other significant sites in the immediate area that have not been disturbed, it is likely that the looters are planning to return.

Offenders conduct their looting operations using a variety of techniques. They may have someone drop them off and then pick them up there or at another location at a specified time. Looters frequently operate at night or on holidays, when they are unlikely to encounter other people and enforcement staffing levels are traditionally low, and they may use snow or heavy rain as a cover. In the Four Corners area, one violator used a jet boat to get into and away from a site in the mistaken belief that the method and speed of the approach would make apprehension almost impossible. Offenders may also have dogs with them to warn them when someone approaches.

## CRIME SCENE AND FOLLOW-UP INVESTIGATION

Investigators occasionally come across looting operations in progress. In such situations investigators may let the operation go on so that surveillance photographs of the crime, which make powerful evidence in court, can be taken. Or investigators may approach the subjects and halt the process to prevent large-scale destruction or to prevent a particularly important site from experiencing further damage. In either case, before acting, the investigator must observe long enough to be able to evaluate the situation. How many subjects are there? Where are any lookouts located? What are the probable means and direction of flight if the subjects are approached? Are the subjects armed? Do some offenders in that region have a history of violently resisting arrest? How far away is assistance for the investigator? What law enforcement assets can be pre-positioned along roads that the suspects must travel as they leave the area?

The principles discussed in Chapters 3 and 4 apply to crime scene investigations in looting cases. There are, however, some differences in approach and emphasis that deserve attention here. Violations of federal and state laws related to the protection of archaeological resources should be pursued, beginning with the crime scene investigation, by an archaeologist and an investigator.[109] Because a crime has been committed, the investigator is in charge of the process. However, the archaeologist makes a unique contribution by conducting the damage assessment, without which there is no ARPA case. The archaeologist must demonstrate that there has been damage, determine how the damage was caused, and fix the dollar amount of the damage, which if $500 or more moves the offense from being a misdemeanor to a felony. In addition, the archaeologist's considerable contributions include taking the crime scene photographs, making the crime scene sketch, and identifying, collecting, marking, and preserving physical evidence.[110] The archaeologist can also offer tentative conclusions about the types of tools used by the suspects if they are not recovered at the scene, the amount of time the offenders spent on the site, the level of skill and knowledge of the perpetrators based on the type and amount of damage done to the site and the kinds of artifacts left behind (see photo below), the number of suspects

### "Rejects" Left Behind by Looters

Bold looters simply left their "rejects," a trowel, and an empty beer can at one site in Uwharie National Forest, North Carolina.

(Courtesy U.S. Forest Service)

involved, and whether the act was an opportunistic crime, an amateur's raid, or the work of commercial looters or serious private collectors. Both the archaeologist and the investigator must be alert to the possibility that the offenders were unable to transport all the artifacts and are planning to return later to collect artifacts hidden nearby.

Soil evidence is of particular importance in looting offenses. Although soil is class-characteristic evidence, in some looting cases it has achieved the status of individual-characteristic evidence. A number of factors may interact to allow soil evidence to achieve individual-characteristic status, including layers of soil in unusual combinations, pollen content, pottery shards (fragments) that are unique to particular locations, and the inclusion of material that allows for carbon dating. The careful collection of soil evidence will permit meaningful comparison with samples collected from suspects' clothes, from under their fingernails, from their tools, from artifacts found in their possession, and from the floorboards, trunks, tires, and undersides of their vehicles. Because vegetation can also be highly unusual alone or in combinations and may also be located only in particular areas or elevations, the investigator should also take samples of vegetation found at the scene.

To some extent, where stolen artifacts end up depends on who took them and what was taken. Some people may take an arrowhead from the surface to keep as a memento. The offenders using flippers usually know they are on sites and have personal collections to which they want to add. Commercial looters steal artifacts to sell and may use a variety of channels, including dealer shows, auctions, and middlemen, or they may sell directly to collectors.

In the follow-up investigation the archaeologist can be of particular assistance to the investigator in estimating the amount of time a commercial looter would need to turn artifacts into salable items and in speculating about the markets in which they might appear.[111] Also, when an application for a search warrant is being prepared, archaeologists can be extremely helpful in specifying the shape, types, colors, raw materials from which made, and characteristic production process and appearance of artifacts that are normally associated with the site that has been looted. In this regard, they can make very useful diagrams.

It is essential for investigators to realize that although artifacts are typically stolen from remote, rural, or urban fringe sites, many of them will ultimately be sold in cities. Therefore, there is a considerable need for cooperation with, and coordination among, many types of agencies.

## Key Terms

**archaeological looting**
**booster bag**
**check fraud**
**check washing**
**cloning (of cellular phones)**
**commercial shoplifters or boosters**
**confidence artists**
**forensic accountants**
**identity theft**
**larceny**
**mail fraud**
**money laundering**
**pilferers**
**pyramid, or Ponzi, sales schemes**
**Racketeering Records Analysis Unit (RRAU)**
**white-collar crime**

## Review Questions

1. What two elements must be present for a larceny to occur?
2. What are the ways in which a counterfeit credit card may be recognized?
3. Which groups constitute the principal ethnic enterprise involved in illegal check-fraud schemes, and where are their bases of operation?

4. What is cellular-phone cloning?
5. The greatest deterrent to shoplifting can be a security education program for employees. What are some suggestions for such a program?
6. Describe the techniques employed in the pigeon-drop and bank examiner schemes.
7. What are the major categories of mail fraud that were discussed in this chapter?
8. Describe a pyramid sales scheme.
9. The method of cash-flow analysis in Ponzi schemes is a two-step process. What are these two steps?
10. What is the purpose of laundering money?
11. Why are groceries and restaurants considered good businesses for laundering money?
12. What are some countermeasures for dealing with the use of the Internet to launder money?
13. What type of service can the Racketeering Records Analysis Unit (RRAU) provide in examining money-laundering records?
14. What are the major features of the Identity Theft and Assumption Deterrence Act of 1998?
15. What is dumpster diving?
16. What are some recommendations and strategies for preventing identity theft?
17. How is archaeological looting defined?
18. What are the major provisions of ARPA?
19. Summarize state laws pertaining to the protection of archaeological resources.
20. Describe the respective roles of the investigator and the archaeologist in crime scene and follow-up investigation.

## Internet Activities

1. The National Consumers League sponsors the National Fraud Information Center, a website providing up-to-date alerts and warnings about fraud. Log on to www.fraud.org and find out more about scams against businesses, fraud against the elderly, and the latest fraud alerts. What can police departments and investigators do to help prevent businesses and the elderly from becoming victims of fraud?
2. Learn more about interacting with victims of identity theft by checking out the Privacy Rights Clearinghouse at www.privacyrights.org. Click on "Identity Theft" and read the article "Enhancing Law Enforcement—Identity Theft Communication." What facts about victims of identity theft should an investigator consider when addressing this type of case? In the initial meeting with the victim, what type of information should the investigator obtain? What information should the investigator be prepared to give the victim?

## Notes

1. Neil C. Chamelin and Kenneth R. Evans, *Criminal Law for Policemen*, 5th ed. (Englewood Cliffs, NJ: Prentice Hall, 1991), p. 153.
2. William T. Neumann, "Busting Credit Card Crime Is Tough," *American Banker*, Sept. 18, 1989, Vol. 154, p. 26.
3. Ellen Memmelaar, "MasterCard Saw Fraud Drop in '89," *American Banker*, July 17, 1990, Vol. 155, p. 14.
4. Keith Slotter, "Plastic Payment—Trends in Credit Card Fraud," *FBI Law Enforcement Bulletin*, June 1997, pp. 2–3.
5. *Credit Card Mail Theft Newsletter*, U.S. Postal Inspection Service, Office of Criminal Investigations, November 1995, Vol. 4, No. 1, p. 3; see also Mark T. Langan and Gerald Vajgert, "Profiling Postal Packages," *FBI Law Enforcement Bulletin*, February–March 1996, pp. 17–21.
6. Timothy M. Dees, "Countering Credit Card Fraud," *Police*, March 1994, p. 46.
7. Ellen Braitman, "More Focus on Cards with Photos," *American Banker*, Nov. 1, 1990, Vol. 155, p. 6.
8. Neumann, "Busting Credit Card Crime Is Tough," p. 26.

9. Ellen E. Schultz, "Plastic Explosives: Ways to Defuse Credit-Card Fraud," *Wall Street Journal,* Nov. 16, 1990, p. C1.
10. Ibid.
11. John W. Merline, "Check Fraud," *Consumers' Research Magazine,* December 1989, Vol. 72, p. 2.
12. Keith Slotter, "Check Fraud—A Sophisticated Criminal Enterprise," *FBI Law Enforcement Bulletin,* August 1996, pp. 1–7.
13. "FBI Financial Institution Fraud Criminal Referral Statistics for Fiscal Year 1995," Sept. 30, 1995.
14. Frank W. Abagnale, *Document Verification and Currency Transactions Manual* (Abagnale & Associates, 1994).
15. "Asian Gangs Involved in Credit Card Fraud," *Intelligence Operations Bulletin*, Office of the Attorney General, California Department of Justice, December 1994, Vol. 47.
16. Among the safeguards are embossing, artificial watermarks, laid lines, chemical voiding features, warning bands, high-resolution printing, dual-image numbering, and security number fonts.
17. Steven Marjanovic, "Arizona Group Pushes Fingerprinting as a Ploy to Deter Check Fraud," *American Banker,* July 6, 1995, p. 10.
18. Robert Bird, vice president, Bank of America, San Francisco, California, remarks at meeting of the Bank Fraud Working Group Subgroup on Check and Credit Card Fraud, Washington, DC, July 19, 1995.
19. Todd H. Young, "Wireless Bandits," *Police,* May 1995, pp. 33–35. Todd Young, a nationally recognized expert in cellular fraud, is the director of consulting services for the Guidry Group, which specializes in telecommunication security. For more information on cellular technology and investigative methods or cellular training for law enforcement, contact Todd Young at 206-836-0699.
20. "Shoplifting: Bess Myerson's Arrest Highlights a Multibillion-Dollar Problem That Many Stores Won't Talk About," *Life,* August 1988, Vol. 11, p. 34.
21. Ibid., p. 35.
22. This information on South American theft groups was provided by Detective Joseph Moorash, Alexandria, Virginia, Police Department.
23. "American Notes: Police Presence," *Time,* Jan. 8, 1990, Vol. 135, p. 53.
24. Hassell Bradley, "Meet Miss Annie Droid, the Shoplifter's Nemesis," *Women's Wear Daily,* Feb. 27, 1989, p. 18.
25. "Shoplifting: Bess Myerson's Arrest Highlights a Multibillion-Dollar Problem," p. 34.
26. Dody Tsiantar, "Big Brother at the Mall, Retailers Go High Tech in the War on Shoplifters," *Newsweek,* July 3, 1989, Vol. 114, p. 44.
27. "Shoplifting: Bess Myerson's Arrest Highlights a Multibillion-Dollar Problem," p. 36.
28. Jack Acken Smith, "Shoplifters Hate Customer Service," *Gifts and Decorative Accessories,* October 1989, Vol. 90, p. 56.
29. "Shoplifting: Bess Myerson's Arrest Highlights a Multibillion-Dollar Problem," p. 36.
30. Delaney J. Stinson, "Attention, Retailers: Civil Law Provides Tonic," *Security Management Review,* September 1988, Vol. 32, pp. 131, 132.
31. "Con Men—A Sucker's Sampler of the Games People Play," *Miami Herald,* Apr. 21, 1977, p. 15.
32. Ottie Adkins, "Crime against the Elderly," *Police Chief,* January 1975, Vol. 42, No. 1, p. 40.
33. R. Griffin, "Bunko Schemes—The Art of Flim Flam," *National Centurion,* October 1983. The remainder of this discussion of confidence games, exclusive of telemarketing scams, was obtained from this source, pp. 38–42.
34. This information regarding mail fraud has been provided by the U.S. Postal Inspection Service. For more information see www.usps.gov/websites/depart/inspect/chainlet.htm.
35. Edwin H. Sutherland, *White Collar Crime* (New York: Dryden Press, 1949), p. 9.
36. U.S. Department of Justice, LEAA, *The Nature, Impact, and Prosecution of White-Collar Crime* (Washington, DC: Government Printing Office, 1970), pp. 4–6.
37. Vincent P. Doherty and Monte E. Smith, "Ponzi Schemes and Laundering—How Illicit Funds Are Acquired and Concealed," *FBI Law Enforcement Bulletin,* November 1981, pp. 5–11. This discussion was taken from this source.
38. Tom L. Kitchens, "The Cash Flow Analysis Method: Following the Paper Trail in Ponzi Schemes," *FBI Law Enforcement Bulletin,* August 1993, pp. 10–13. This discussion of methods of cash-flow analysis was obtained, with modification, from this source.
39. This is a writ that requires a party summoned to appear in court to bring along a document or other piece of evidence for examination by the court.
40. Wayne Moquin and Charles Van Doren, *The American Way of Crime—A Documentary History* (New York: Praeger, 1976), p. 68.

41. Richard Behar, "The Underworld Is Their Oyster," *Time*, Sept. 3, 1990, Vol. 136, p. 54.
42. Jonathan Beaty and Richard Hornik, "A Torrent of Dirty Dollars," *Time*, Dec. 18, 1989, Vol. 134, p. 51.
43. James Cook, "The Invisible Enterprise," *Forbes*, Oct. 13, 1980, p. 125.
44. Jim Drinkhall, "Con Men Are Raking in Millions by Setting Up Own Caribbean Banks," *Wall Street Journal*, Mar. 23, 1981, p. 1.
45. Financial Action Task Force, "Report on Money Laundering Typologies, 2000–2001," Paris, France, pp. 4–8. This discussion of money laundering was modified from this source.
46. The Internet is a global "network of networks" that is used for communicating digital information. This communication takes place between servers and services in a system that relies on and thus in some ways overlays the telephone communication infrastructure. Information communicated via the Internet is converted to digital format in what are called "packets." Each packet carries information about its originator and destination, that is, the sending and receiving servers. To ensure that the information packets arrive at their intended destination, every Internet server has a unique "address," an internet protocol (IP) number. There are approximately 4 billion IP numbers in use worldwide. Some of these numbers have been assigned to specific Internet users, who thus have fixed IP addresses. Despite the high number of IP addresses, there are not enough numbers for every Internet user to receive an individual address. Therefore, IP numbers are often assigned to a user on a temporary basis by his or her Internet service provider (ISP). Such users have the IP numbers while connected to the Internet; when a user exits the service, his or her IP number is reassigned to the next active user. Temporarily assigned IP addresses are usually associated with dial-up connections to the Internet.
47. See Financial Action Task Force, "Report on Money Laundering Typologies, 1999–2000," p. 4. The relevant concerns and countermeasures proposed in the 1999–2000 report primarily deal with customer identification issues as related to Internet banking. This year's suggested actions should therefore be viewed as complementing those put forward in the FATF-XI report.
48. There is no agreement yet on exactly how much time would be sufficient. The minimum period suggested by various authorities and the industry itself ranges from six months to one year or more. Some of the FATF experts underscored the need, however, for standardization of this minimum period for retention of log files at ISPs in all jurisdictions.
49. James O. Beasley II, "Forensic Examination of Money Laundering Records," *FBI Law Enforcement Bulletin*, March 1993, pp. 13–17. This discussion of forensic examination of money-laundering records was taken with minor modifications from this source.
50. *Federal Sentencing Guidelines Manual, 1992* (St. Paul, MN: West Publishing, 1991).
51. See *United States* v. *Harris*, 903 F. 2d 770 (10th Cir. 1990).
52. The following are some guidelines for handling and submitting evidence: Submit original evidence (photocopies and facsimiles may be reviewed under limited circumstances, but examiners prefer to use the original documents when preparing a written forensic report); submit evidence as soon as possible after its acquisition; submit all documentary evidence relating to the seizure; contact an RRAU examiner in advance to resolve potential problems regarding large volumes of evidence (in some cases, a field examination may be in order); advise the RRAU of any requested examinations that may necessitate special handling, such as those involving handwriting or latent-fingerprint comparisons; and indicate in a brief cover letter the subject's name, the exact place and date of seizure, any trial date or other reason for expeditious handling, and the name and telephone number of the submitter.
53. Matthew L. Lease and Tod W. Burke, "Identity Theft—A Fast Growing Crime," *FBI Law Enforcement Bulletin*, August 2000, pp. 8–13. This discussion was adapted from this source.
54. For a more detailed discussion regarding the act, see "Identity Theft—Prevention and Survival," www.identitytheft.org/title18.htm.
55. J. Hoffman, *The Art and Science of Dumpster Diving* (Port Townsend, WA: Loompanics Unlimited, 1993).
56. T. Dacolias, "Identity Theft," www.congames.com.identity.html, accessed on Mar. 5, 1999. This site is not longer accessible.
57. B. Horne, "Identity Theft Disrupts Fayetteville Woman's Life," *Fayetteville Observer-Times*, Sept. 21, 1998.
58. State of California, Department of Consumer Affairs, "Credit Identity Theft: Tips to Avoid and

Resolve Problems," Legal Guide P-3, January 1998, p. 1.

59. R. O'Harrow and L. Leyden, "Firm Got Almost $1.5 Million in Federal Aid to Build Driver's License Database," *Dallas Morning News*, Feb. 18, 1999, p. 6A.

60. The Computer Security Institute, established in 1974, is an organization of computer security professionals dedicated to serving and training information, computer, and network professionals. It offers classes in encryption and intrusion management.

61. *Newswire* magazine, "eBay Selects Equifax Secure to Verify Identity of Buyers, Sellers over the Internet," Jan. 15, 1999.

62. T. Hamilton, "Privacy Czar Raps Absence of Online Protection, Commissioner Says Electronic Commerce Will Stagnate until Regulations Establish Trust on the Internet," *Globe and Mail*, Mar. 4, 1999. p. T1.

63. California Public Interest Research Group, "Victims of Identity Theft Action and Support Group," www.igc.apc.org/pirg/calpirg/consumer/privacy/toi/_voit.htm, accessed on Jan. 5, 2000.

64. Identity-theft resources include the Social Security Administration fraud report, 800-269-0271, and the three major credit bureaus: *Transunion*—fraud report, 800-680-7289, credit report, 800-888-4213, cancel preapproved credit card offers, 888-567-8688; *Equifax*—fraud report, 800-525-6285, credit report, 800-685-1111 or 800-997-2493; *Experian*—fraud report, 800-301-7195, credit report, 800-682-7654, cancel preapproved credit card offers, 800-353-0809. For more details on identity theft, visit these websites: www.identitytheft.org, www.privacyrights.org, and www.futurecrime.com.

65. Sherry Hutt, Elwood Jones, and Martin McAllister, *Archeological Resource Protection* (Washington, DC: Government Printing Office, 1991), pp. 6–7.

66. National Park Service, *Listing of Outlaw Treachery: Loot Clearinghouse,* on file, Archeological Assistance Division, 1990.

67. Bennie Keel, Francis P. McManamon, and George S. Smith, *Federal Archeology: The Current Program* (Washington, DC: National Park Service, 1989), pp. 30–31.

68. Hutt, Jones, and McAllister, *Archeological Resource Protection,* p. 5.

69. The information in this paragraph is drawn, with restatement, from National Park Service, *Looting America's Archeological Heritage: An Update* (Washington, DC: U.S. Department of Interior, 1989), p. 1.

70. Robert K. Landers, "Is America Allowing Its Past to Be Stolen?" In Marcus D. Rosenbaum, ed., *Congressional Quarterly's Editorial Research Reports,* Jan. 18, 1991, p. 35.

71. Hutt, Jones, and McAllister, *Archeological Resource Protection,* p. 6.

72. Landers, "Is America Allowing Its Past to Be Stolen?" pp. 35, 37.

73. Hutt, Jones, and McAllister, *Archeological Resource Protection,* p. 2.

74. Landers, "Is America Allowing Its Past to Be Stolen?" p. 37.

75. Ibid.

76. Ibid.

77. Ibid.

78. National Park Service, *Looting America's Archeological Heritage: An Update.*

79. National Park Service, *Summary of Archeological Looting Cases* (Washington, DC: U.S. Department of Interior, 1989); prepared for the Society for American Archeological Anti-Looting Working Conference, Taos, New Mexico, May 7–12, 1989, manuscript unnumbered, but apparently p. 111.

80. Ibid., p. 150.

81. Ibid., p. 70.

82. Ibid., p. 100.

83. Christopher J. Duerksen, *A Handbook of Historic Preservation Law* (Washington, DC: National Center for Preservation Law, 1983), p. 193.

84. National Park Service, *Archeological Assistance Technical Brief No. 11: The Legal Background of Archeological Resources Protection, 1991* (Washington, DC: U.S. Department of Interior), p. 2.

85. Ibid.

86. Ibid.

87. Hutt, Jones, and McAllister, *Archeological Resource Protection,* p. 20.

88. National Park Service, *Archeological Assistance Program Technical Brief No. 11,* pp. 3–4.

89. Hutt, Jones, and McAllister, *Archeological Resource Protection,* pp. 32–33.

90. Ibid., pp. 26, 28, 42, 48.

91. Ibid., p. 48.

92. Ibid.

93. Ibid., p. 42.

94. Ibid., p. 28.

95. Ibid.

96. Ibid.
97. Ibid., p. 26.
98. National Park Service, *Archeological Assistance Program Technical Brief No. 11,* p. 7.
99. Landers, "Is America Allowing Its Past to Be Stolen?" p. 41.
100. National Park Service, *Archeological Assistance Program Technical Brief No. 11,* p. 7.
101. Ibid.
102. This example is from Landers, "Is America Allowing Its Past to Be Stolen?" p. 44.
103. Ibid.
104. Ibid.
105. Ibid.
106. Ibid.
107. Criminal Law of Kentucky, 525.105.
108. Hutt, Jones, and McAllister, *Archeological Resource Protection,* p. 63.
109. Ibid., p. 59.
110. Ibid., p. 60.
111. Ibid., p. 93.

# FIFTEEN

# Vehicle Thefts and Related Offenses

*Today, many vehicles are stolen primarily to be stripped for their parts. Once stripped for parts, such vehicles are abandoned, leaving owners with expensive repair bills. (© Joseph Sohm, ChromoSohm Inc./Corbis)*

## CHAPTER OUTLINE



## CHAPTER OBJECTIVES

1. Identify types of motor vehicle theft.
2. Be familiar with techniques for disposing of stolen motor vehicles.
3. Describe challenges associated with the theft investigation of heavy equipment and farm equipment.
4. Identify major investigative resources.
5. Discuss methods for assisting in the identification of a recovered vehicle.
6. List and explain several vehicle theft fraud indicators.
7. Describe vehicle fire investigation methods.
8. Explain vehicle and equipment theft prevention approaches.
9. Assess title and registration issues related to marine theft.
10. Discuss aircraft and avionics theft and relevant identification and investigative techniques.

# INTRODUCTION

Motor vehicle theft is one of the most significant issues facing law enforcement today. In 2000, there was one motor vehicle theft every 20 seconds. Prior to 2000, the number of thefts had been dropping for about 10 years. With the collapse of communism and the opening of free-market economies in eastern Europe, however, auto theft has become an enormous problem. This, coupled with the increase in fraudulent insurance claims and other factors, has created a real challenge for law enforcement. In addition, investigating motor vehicle thefts can be difficult and in some cases very complex for several reasons.

When investigating vehicle theft, officers must determine the reason for the theft. Vehicles may be stolen temporarily, for example, for use in the commission of other crimes such as robberies or drive-by shootings, after which the vehicles are abandoned. Other reasons for theft can include joyriding, professional theft, or fraudulent schemes.

Professional thieves use a variety of means such as chop shops, stripping, salvage switch, and export to other countries to dispose of stolen vehicles. Once a vehicle has been chopped or stripped, trying to identify particular stolen vehicles and/or parts can be extremely difficult.

However, this seemingly formidable task has been made easier in part by the creation of standardized vehicle identification number systems. Finally, investigators are often faced with situations where the perpetrators are not strangers or professional thieves but the owners themselves.

Given limited law enforcement resources, vehicle theft may not be considered a top priority. Nonetheless, investigators have many major resources and organizations at their disposal. An overview of several of these resources, such as the National Insurance Crime Bureau and the American Association of Motor Vehicle Administrators, and the information they can provide is presented in this chapter. While the issue of motor vehicle theft is the main topic of this chapter, also addressed are theft of other high-value items, such as heavy equipment and farm equipment; commercial vehicle and cargo theft; marine theft; and the theft of aircraft and avionics. Prevention programs that can help minimize the theft of motor vehicles and other items are also discussed in the chapter.

## AUTO THEFT

The number of motor vehicle thefts in the United States, as reported by the FBI, was just under 1,166,000 for 2000, with an estimated national loss of $7.8 billion in vehicle value. Of the total thefts, 74.5 percent were automobiles and 18.7 percent were trucks and buses. Although a large percentage of stolen vehicles are later recovered, only 14.1 percent of the cases are cleared by law enforcement agencies.

Here are more statistics for 2000: There was one theft every 20 seconds; the average value of vehicles stolen was $6,682; and the number of reported thefts increased by 1.2 percent from the previous year.[1] That was the first increase in a number of years. Before 2000, the number of thefts had been dropping for about 10 years.

It is important to note that small increases or decreases in numbers are not significant. They could be caused by changes in reporting procedures, changes in crime classifications at local levels, more or fewer agencies' reporting their statistics for central processing, or a variety of other reasons. Nevertheless, motor vehicle theft remains a problem of national concern.

### MISCELLANEOUS STATISTICS AND NOTES

- It has been estimated that approximately 2 percent of reported thefts are of motorcycles. A substantial portion of the thefts are directed at Harley-Davidsons.
- National and international rings, particularly those in cities near ports, export vehicles to countries all over the developing world where they can be sold for three or more times the price for which they are sold in the United States.
- Since the collapse of communism in eastern Europe, the theft of motor vehicles has skyrocketed. More than 2 million vehicles are stolen annually in Europe. Many are illegally exported to developing countries, particularly in the Middle East.
- The theft of airbags and the resale of stolen salvaged airbags is becoming epidemic. One company that insures about 20 percent of the cars in the United States annually pays out over $10 million because of stolen airbags. Several states have enacted legislation that is

largely ineffective because there is no national system in place to identify and respond to this problem. The National Insurance Crime Bureau (NICB) has been spearheading a drive to develop strategies for attacking this problem.

- Heavy-truck and tractor-trailer thefts are on the increase. The insurance industry annually pays out $18 million because of commercial-vehicle theft, excluding cargo losses. California and Florida have the highest number of tractors stolen, and California, Texas, and Florida are ranked as the top three for trailer theft.

## Auto Theft—Myths

- Auto theft happens to other people, not to me.
- Auto theft is a victimless crime. Insurance companies pay the costs.
- Most of the vehicles stolen are new models, so I don't need to worry if my car is a couple of years old.
- Most stolen vehicles disappear forever because they are either exported or cut up into pieces.
- When an auto thief is caught, punishment is severe.

## Auto Theft—Facts

- It is estimated that in 20 to 30 percent of auto thefts, the operator has left the keys in the car.
- Everyone with comprehensive insurance pays for auto theft and fraud through increased premiums, even if he or she never has a vehicle stolen.
- An estimated 85 percent of stolen vehicles are recovered, indicating that a large percentage of those stolen are probably the object of temporary theft.
- Punishment for auto theft is not swift and sure.
- The theft of older-model cars is prevalent. Year after year, the overwhelming majority of cars stolen are between two and seven years old.
- Everyone's tax dollars pay the cost of fighting auto theft, including the costs of components of the criminal justice system.
- Auto theft is not a victimless crime. Insurance does not pay for the victim's insurance deductible, work loss, inconvenience, emotional trauma, and time loss (estimated to average more than 40 hours, covering making telephone calls; filling out police reports; purchasing a replacement vehicle; completing insurance claim forms; and dealing with licensing and registration problems, vehicle inspection, and repairs, which may take many weeks if parts have to be ordered).[2]

# TYPES OF THEFT

Motor vehicle thefts generally fall into one of four categories: temporary theft, joyriding, professional theft, or fraud.

## Temporary Theft

The term **temporary theft** is used not to imply that the crime is not serious but, rather, to distinguish joyriding from something more ominous. Of growing concern are the thefts of vehicles specifically for use in the commission of other crimes such as robberies or drive-by shootings, after which the vehicles are abandoned. These thefts are on the increase and, when reported, are often recorded only as the underlying crime rather than also as a motor vehicle theft, thereby skewing the actual theft figures.

## Joyriding

**Joyriding** is most often engaged in by teenagers—15 to 19 years old—who steal a car simply to drive and then abandon it. Among the reasons teenage joyriders most often cite for the thefts are that joyriding makes them feel important, powerful, and accepted among peers; it's fun and exciting; they did it on a dare; it relieves boredom and gives an adrenaline rush; they don't feel like walking; they want to impress girls, to make money by stripping cars and selling the parts, to get even with parents, or to escape family problems; it's addictive; it's part of a gang membership or initiation. Since many youngsters are not professionals, they frequently target vehicles that are easy to steal and generally lack any antitheft devices. Perhaps the large number of apprehensions in this age category is accounted for by the arrests of joyriders.

Nationally, in 2000, persons under 18 years of age were involved in 19.8 percent of the cleared motor vehicle thefts, and persons under the age of 25 accounted for 66.5 percent of the 148,225 people arrested for motor vehicle theft. Almost 66 percent of the people arrested for motor vehicle theft were adults, and just under 85 percent of the people arrested were males. Slightly over 55 percent of the arrestees were white and just under 42 percent were black.[3] Nevertheless, no definitive statement is offered that joyriding is the foundation crime for these arrests, for, in fact, many of the thefts committed by or in support of the activities of professional vehicle thieves are accomplished by young people.

## Professional Theft

In **professional theft,** the car thief is motivated by very high profits and generally low risk. The profits to be gained are second only to those from drugs. Anyone who has ever purchased a replacement part for a car is aware that the cost of replacing all the parts of a vehicle is much higher than the original cost of the entire vehicle. The professional can often sell the parts of a stolen car for up to five times the original assembled value. Considering what the thief "paid" for the vehicle, the profit margin is substantial.

However, professionals do have costs in operating their "businesses." It is not infrequent for professional thieves to employ and train youths to steal cars. Often a youth is paid a set amount, several hundred to several thousand dollars, for each theft. The amount varies depending on the make, model, and year of the vehicle. There are even "training schools" in some areas of the country where juveniles and young adults are taught how to steal cars, trucks, motorcycles, and other vehicles.

The professional thief can break into a locked, high-priced car, start it, and drive it away in as little as 20 seconds (see photo below).

## Fraud

Although certain types of theft involve fraud perpetrated on innocent purchasers, the major category of **vehicle fraud** as described here does not actually involve the theft of vehicles by professionals or even strangers. The various types of vehicle fraud are generally committed by the owner or someone acting on behalf of the owner, and the

**Thief Breaks Car Window**

The professional car thief is motivated by high profits and relatively low risk of apprehension. These thieves use a variety of means for entering locked cars, including breaking windows to open locked doors. The professional thief can break into a car, start it, and drive away in as little as twenty seconds.

(© Premium Stock/Corbis)

underlying purpose is to profit at the expense of an insurance company.

The NICB estimates that anywhere from 15 to 25 percent of all reported vehicle thefts involve some type of fraud and that a vast majority of them involve fraudulent insurance claims. Insurance crime is an enormous problem, and its true magnitude is almost impossible to pinpoint.

In addition, some experts on the costs of insurance estimate that between 16 and 35 cents of every dollar in premiums paid by the public for motor vehicle insurance is used to pay fraudulent claims or to fight fraud. The NICB says that if the amount of insurance claim fraud and vehicle theft occurring in the United States represented a corporation, it would rank in the top 25 of the Fortune 500 and be called a growth industry. And insurance fraud is on the rise because it is an easy crime to successfully commit. Insurance companies, even those with highly qualified special investigation units whose function is to investigate suspected cases of fraud, must be concerned about potential liability resulting from lawsuits if someone is wrongly accused or a claim is wrongly denied. The fact that insurance companies are believed to have a great deal of money—deep pockets—makes these companies even more susceptible to civil suits and potential liability and, in turn, even more cautious.

Fraudulent auto-theft claims are not the only type of fraud to which the insurance industry is subjected, but they account for a significant part of the overall fraud. Fully 10 percent of all property and casualty claims are either inflated or outright fraud. Estimates are that fraudulent insurance claim payouts are $100 billion annually. This amount fluctuates, since it is well recognized that fraud increases as the economy worsens.

## METHODS OF OPERATION—THE PROFESSIONAL

To turn a profit, professional thieves use a variety of means to dispose of stolen motor vehicles. Among the most common are chop shops, salvage switches, and exportation.

### Chop Shops

Very simply, a **chop shop** is a place where stolen vehicles are disassembled for resale of their parts. The operators and employees of chop shops cut stolen motor vehicles apart with torches, power saws, and other tools, sometimes in as little as 8 or 9 minutes. They alter or dispose of the parts that are potentially traceable and sell the untraceable parts to repair shops or salvage yards. Sometimes the parts buyers are unsuspecting. Often, the salvage yard or repair shop operator is in collusion with the thief or the chop shop. In fact, a chop shop may well direct the theft of a specific type of motor vehicle in order to "fill an order" for a specific part needed by a repair shop or salvage yard (see photo).

A modification of the typical chop-shop operation is illustrated by the following: Thieves steal a car, disassemble it carefully so that the parts are not damaged, have the remainder conveniently recovered and disposed of through a salvage sale, buy the salvage, reassemble the vehicle with all its original parts, and sell the vehicle, which has already been classed as a recovered theft and is no longer considered stolen.

### Quick Strip

In a **quick strip,** a vehicle is stolen and stripped mainly for valuable accessories such as seats, stereos, car phones, and tires. These items are attractive to

**Interior of a Chop Shop**

A chop shop such as the one pictured here is a place where stolen vehicles are disassembled for resale of their parts. Stolen vehicles are cut apart in as little as eight minutes in these chop shops. Parts are then sold to repair shops or salvage yards. Sometimes the repair shop operator is in collusion with the thief or the chop shop.

(Courtesy National Insurance Crime Bureau)

thieves because they normally do not contain any identifying numbers, thus making them difficult to identify and easy to dispose of.

### Salvage Switch

Generally, a **salvage vehicle** is one that has been damaged or wrecked to such an extent that the cost of repairing it is beyond its fair market value. Thus, its primary value in the legitimate market comes from the sale of its undamaged parts. To the criminal, however, the value of a salvaged vehicle is far greater than its parts. The real profit is made after the criminal buys the salvage, provided it is accompanied by the certificate of title and the vehicle identification number (VIN) plate. Often the offender does not even want the vehicle and will leave it at the salvage yard from which it is purchased or dispose of it elsewhere. The thief then steals a vehicle identical to the wreck, changes the VIN plate, and sells the stolen vehicle, with a matching title, to an innocent purchaser or to a purchaser who is offered such a "good" price that no questions are asked. Through the **salvage switch,** the thief is able to disguise and dispose of stolen vehicles in the legitimate market.

### Export

Vehicles manufactured in the United States are extremely popular in other countries. The sale of American-manufactured vehicles can also be highly profitable. Buyers in foreign nations often pay double the purchase price for quality cars. The NICB estimates that 13 percent of all vehicles stolen in the United States are illegally exported.[4] Mexico and Central and South American countries are among the most popular but certainly not the exclusive destinations for stolen U.S.-manufactured vehicles. It has been estimated that as many as 20,000 stolen or embezzled cars, trucks, buses, motorcycles, and other vehicles are transported into Mexico each year. This amounts to between 6.6 and 10 percent of the estimated number of stolen vehicles exported each year.

Contributing to this problem are the limited, although effective, controls exercised by Mexican customs and the few effective controls exercised by the United States over southbound traffic entering Mexico. The volume of traffic going into Mexico makes it almost impossible to inspect and investigate all vehicles. Many stolen vehicles are also taken to Canada. Some are resold, but many are exported to their final destinations. Exports are accounting for a growing percentage of the unrecovered stolen vehicles, and the rate of growth of this problem is greater in port cities.

With the collapse of communism and the opening of free-market economies in eastern Europe, auto theft has grown to become an enormous problem. In 1997, Jacques De Remer, then president of the International Association of Auto Theft Investigators (IAATI), said:

> With this free market economy came a seemingly insatiable demand for goods that were previously unavailable, and automobiles were at the top of the list. The auto theft and trafficking problem in Europe is far more complex than it is in the United States, as Europe consists of more than forty separate countries, all of which have their own vehicle registration and titling systems, their own documents, their own language, and their own laws. The figures are staggering. In Poland alone, auto theft has gone up more than 400% in the past five years, from 14,691 to 63,527. Recoveries for 1995 were 8.4%, compared to around 50% in the U.S.
>
> Throughout Europe approximately two million cars are stolen each year, with most countries being categorized as "source countries" or "receiving countries." Put simply, the countries that have cars are losing them to the countries that don't.[5]

## FRAUDULENT THEFT SCHEMES

Fraudulent auto theft claim schemes fall into three major categories: false-vehicle claims, in which no vehicle exists or the vehicle is not owned by the criminal; false-theft losses; and inflated-theft losses.

### False-Vehicle Schemes

**False-vehicle schemes** are particularly prevalent where insurance companies are lax or have ineffective programs to verify the existence of a vehicle before issuing an insurance policy. As a general rule, this type of fraud is planned well in advance of obtaining insurance coverage. The criminal will purchase a policy that has a provision covering loss by theft. In fact, the vehicle does not exist except on paper, has already been salvaged, or does not belong to the person who buys the insurance. Most often, the vehicle insured is a recent model. Some time later (generally within three months, to hold down the cost of the insurance coverage purchase) a theft report will be filed with a law enforcement agency, and a claim will be made to the insurance company.

Several modifications of the salvage switch, described earlier, are illustrative of false-vehicle schemes. Once a salvaged vehicle is purchased, insurance coverage will be obtained. After a short time, a theft loss claim will be filed for the vehicle, which, of course, was in "excellent condition."

In some jurisdictions a **salvage title** may be issued. This does not necessarily prevent false-theft claims on salvage; it merely channels the process in a different direction. One way the criminal avoids the problems associated with the issuance of salvage titles is by **washing,** or laundering, the title. This is done by fabricating the sale of the vehicle and transferring the title to an alleged purchaser in another state that does not issue salvage titles or does not carry forward a "brand" on the title issued by another state. The "buyer" then obtains a clean title in that state and transfers it back to the insured either directly or through several other people or businesses to make it appear as a legitimate transaction. Then, with a clean title, the insured files a theft claim.

In another technique, the salvage buyer falsifies the necessary support documentation so that it shows the salvage vehicle as being completely rebuilt or restored and thereby obtains a "clean," or regular, title. The thief may not even bother to get a clean title; upon filing a claim for the alleged theft, he or she may simply contend that the vehicle was rebuilt or restored but was stolen before the insured could file the necessary paperwork to obtain a nonsalvage title.

In still another version of the salvage switch, the VIN plate may be attached to a rented or borrowed car of the same make and model and, along with the certificate of title, may be presented to and inspected by an agent of the company from which coverage is sought. After the policy is issued, the salvage vehicle VIN plate is removed and the vehicle is returned to the person or company from which it was borrowed or rented.

Presenting a counterfeit or stolen certificate of title or manufacturer's certificate of origin (MCO) as the basis for having a policy issued on a **"paper vehicle"** or on a stolen vehicle with a concealed identity is another technique for defrauding insurance companies through the filing of false-vehicle claims. A manufacturer's certificate of origin is the original identification document issued by a vehicle's manufacturer, somewhat like a birth certificate. It accompanies the vehicle through its delivery to a new car dealer until it is first sold to a retail purchaser, after which the MCO is surrendered to the jurisdiction issuing the first certificate of title in the name of the retail purchaser.

A variation on the counterfeit- or blank-title scheme is the altered title, whereby the criminal manages to conceal the existence of a lienholder who may have already repossessed the vehicle because of missed payments. A theft report is then filed along with the fraudulent insurance claim.

It is not uncommon to find the following scenario in a fraudulent claim on a false vehicle: Henry Johnson owns a late-model full-size car. The vehicle is paid for and Johnson has the title in his possession. Johnson decides to sell the car. After he has it advertised for a few days, he receives a satisfactory offer from a person who pays cash and takes the car to another state to have it titled and registered. Johnson signs the title over to the buyer, who takes possession of the vehicle and drives it to his own state of residence. The next day, Johnson, claiming he can't find his car title, applies for a duplicate title in his own state. The title is issued and is branded with the word "duplicate." Although it may take several weeks to receive the duplicate title, the process may still be faster than it takes for the buyer's home state to issue a new title to the buyer and send the original of Johnson's title back to his state for official cancellation. Upon obtaining the duplicate title, Johnson files a theft claim with his insurance company and surrenders the duplicate title to the company in exchange for the theft loss payment. After learning of the scam, the insurance company goes looking for Johnson and finds that all information he provided was false and he has now disappeared not only with the insurance money but with the money he made from selling the vehicle. Normally, the issuance of a duplicate title will render the original or any previously issued duplicate void, but this fact was unknown to the buyer of Johnson's car or to the buyer's home state, where he applied for a title in his own name.

## False-Theft Schemes

As opposed to the many different fraudulent schemes in which no vehicle exists, in a **false-theft scheme,** the vehicle does exist and is in fact owned by the person who has obtained the insurance policy. The primary reason why an owner would file a phony-theft loss is generally either to avoid liability for some conduct that resulted from the use of the vehicle or to reduce or avoid some financial loss. The specific motivation leading to the filing of the fraudulent claim may exist at the time the policy coverage is obtained or may result from circumstances that develop later.

Among the vast number of motivations—and there are as many motivations as there are false claims—for filing false-theft loss claims are the following:

- To cover or avoid personal responsibility for a hit-and-run accident. The owner reports the car stolen (before the police come to question him or her) and subsequently files an insurance claim.
- To replace an old vehicle that just doesn't look good or drive smoothly any longer.
- To replace a "lemon" that can't be sold for a decent price.
- To obtain money for another vehicle that is in need of repair or replacement.
- To avoid loss of the vehicle without receiving any financial gain, for example, through repossession caused by a default of payments or in response to a court order to transfer title to a former spouse after a divorce.
- To end costly car payments or repair bills.
- To avoid the hassle of selling.
- To obtain a more favorable interest rate on a car loan.
- To break a restricting car lease.

As noted at the outset of this chapter, fraud may be committed by the insured acting alone or with another person or other persons. When a vehicle owner conspires with others, the fraud is often referred to as an "owner give-up." Examples of both solo and give-up false-theft schemes include the following:

- The vehicle is abandoned and later reported stolen.
- The vehicle, which may have been previously damaged or had some major mechanical defects, is reported stolen. Shortly afterward it is recovered, and the insured claims that the damage or defects were caused by the theft.
- The vehicle is sold to an out-of-state buyer; then a duplicate certificate of title is applied

**Vehicle Abandoned in False-Theft Scheme**

Vehicle owners have been known to file false theft reports on their cars, often to avoid liability for some conduct associated with the vehicle or to reduce or avoid financial loss. The owner typically attempts to abandon the vehicle in a location beyond the scope of a general search conducted by the police.

(© Chinch Gryniewicz, Ecoscene/Corbis)

for and used to file the claim—just as in the Johnson scenario, reported earlier.

- The vehicle is not stolen but is hidden prior to the theft report and prior to the claim being filed. After the loss is paid, the vehicle can be returned to use, stripped, sold, chopped for parts, taken out of state, or otherwise disposed of.
- The vehicle is dumped in water, a method of causing damage that is increasing in use. This is often referred to as car dunking or vehicle dumping. Such vehicles generally cannot be repaired economically even if recovered.
- Vehicle burying is another way that owners dispose of unwanted vehicles. Consider the following: An employee at the Charlotte/Douglas International Airport in North Carolina was charged with insurance fraud after police unearthed his car from the ground at a remote, wooded edge of the airport. After his attempts to sell the car met with no success, the insured, who worked as a landscaper at the airport, decided to use a backhoe to dig a pit and bury his car inside. He then reported the car stolen in order to collect an insurance settlement.[6]
- Vehicle arson is another form of fraud that is planned beforehand and is motivated by a desire to collect on an insurance policy either to make a profit or to solve a financial problem. Vehicle arson will be covered in more detail later, but it should be noted that all vehicle fires, even though the numbers are increasing annually, are not necessarily arson cases. The first job of any investigator at the scene of a vehicle fire is to ascertain whether natural or accidental causes can be eliminated so that a full-fledged arson investigation can be undertaken. Although manufacturers have made it extremely difficult for vehicles to burn under normal circumstances,[7] it cannot be assumed that, because there was a fire, some accelerant was used and arson has occurred.

## Inflated-Theft-Loss Schemes

As distinguished from the preceding schemes, in the **inflated-theft-loss scheme** the vehicle actually exists, actually belongs to the insured, and actually is stolen. The fraud occurs when the insured makes a false claim concerning the physical or mechanical condition of the vehicle when it was stolen; actually causes some damage or removes some parts on recovery of the vehicle but before it is inspected by the insurance company; claims there were expensive parts on or improvements made to the vehicle before it was stolen; or, if no follow-up inspection is conducted by the insurer, claims certain damage occurred that actually did not happen.

One frequently used scam has the insured enter into a conspiracy with a repair shop, after a stolen vehicle is recovered, to allege that damages were caused during the theft. The damages do not exist. The vehicle is immediately "repaired" before the insurance appraiser has the opportunity to inspect the vehicle, and the repair shop insists that the insurer accept the repair bill, possibly using a photo of a wrecked vehicle of the same make and condition as the vehicle "before repair." A spinoff of this basic scenario has the repair shop show the appraiser an actual wrecked vehicle in its possession of the same make and model as the insured's car.

The inflated-theft-loss claim also extends to vehicle contents. The claimant alleges the vehicle contained valuable clothes, cameras, golf clubs, and other "new" items of considerable value when it was stolen.

## Defrauding the Owner and Insurer

There are times when the owner is not involved in the fraud and both the owner and the insurer become victims, as illustrated in the following example: An individual leases a vehicle from a rental company and, during the rental period, reports the vehicle stolen to both the police and the rental company. Shortly after, the renter again calls the police and reports that the vehicle was recovered, using some excuse like his coworker took it to the store or he forgot where he parked it the night before because he had had too much to drink. Consequently, the police never enter the "stolen" report into the National Crime Information Center (NCIC). Conveniently, the renter fails to notify the rental company, which assumes that the law enforcement agency entered the theft into NCIC. The thief may have several days' or longer use of the vehicle before the victims can put the whole story together.

Some vehicles are exported by owners for the purpose of filing and collecting on fraudulent theft claims.

Another type of export fraud occurs when a vehicle owner makes multiple copies of proof-of-ownership documents to present to U.S. Customs officials and exports his or her vehicle. After the vehicle arrives at its foreign destination, the VIN plate is removed and mailed back to the owner, who steals a car of the same make and model, switches the VIN plate, and, using the additional copies of ownership documents, exports the stolen vehicle.

As illustrated by the examples above, "Insurance thieves are getting smarter each day. As law enforcement agencies put an end to one scheme, criminals conceive another. For example, after the insurance industry established mechanisms to thwart large claims fraud, criminals learned to file multiple small claims to avoid triggering automatic auditing systems."

## THEFT OF HEAVY CONSTRUCTION EQUIPMENT AND FARM EQUIPMENT

Heavy construction equipment (or, simply, **heavy equipment**) and **farm equipment** are commonly referred to as **off-road equipment.** Statistics are not very accurate concerning number of thefts and recoveries because there are no mandatory reporting requirements as exist for on-road motor vehicles. It is fairly accurate that more than 2,500 pieces of construction equipment and more than 4,700 pieces of lawn and farm equipment are stolen each year in the United States.[8] One expert in the field believes that these estimates are at least 30 percent lower than the actual numbers.[9] California, Texas, Florida, Georgia, and North Carolina are the top theft states for heavy construction equipment, and by substituting Alabama for California, they are the top five states for theft of lawn and farm equipment.[10] The value of stolen heavy equipment is estimated at $1 billion annually in the United States and at $2 billion worldwide. An additional $1.7 billion is the estimated loss for farm and lawn equipment. The average value of losses and insurance claims is around $45,000 for construction equipment and $7,500 for farm and lawn machines. Keep in mind that this represents a large amount of stolen small lawn equipment that skews the numbers. Large construction equipment can be valued in excess of $150,000.

It takes experienced tractor thieves approximately 4 minutes to invade a farm, start and load a tractor, and drive away, according to an informant who worked with a theft ring.[11] For pull-type equipment that does not have to be started, the amount of time required for the average theft is less than 2 minutes. Farm and construction equipment thefts are frequently committed by professional operatives who steal for profit. They may steal on order, for stripping, or for export. One offender was caught with a notebook filled with photographs he had taken of machinery on various farms; when interrogated he stated he had roamed the countryside obtaining the photographs in the notebook. The notebook was then used as a "sales catalog" when meeting with prospective buyers and as a means of instructing thieves working with him as to exactly what equipment from a particular location was to be taken. This arrangement made it possible for the equipment to be consigned or sold before it was even stolen, minimizing the amount of time that the equipment was in the thieves' hands and therefore their risk.

The theft of off-road equipment and the investigation of the thefts cause numerous problems for owners, manufacturers, and law enforcement agencies. Title or registration generally is not required for such equipment, and owners have traditionally resisted such requirements for several reasons. They fear that the title and registration records could be used to levy taxes on expensive items of property and that such a financial burden would have to be passed on to their consumers. Further, they believe that registration requirements would impede their ability to move the equipment rapidly and freely around the country.

Owners are also victimized by the problem of inventory control. Construction equipment is often spread over several miles of job site or over several job sites and may be left idle for days or weeks at a time in isolated areas. Thus, when the professional thief is overcome by the irresistible temptation, it is often days before the theft is noticed and reported to the police.

Another issue that compounded the construction equipment theft problem until recently was the fact that off-road equipment, unlike conventional motor vehicles, had no standard, permanently affixed identification number. Historically, each manufacturer had its own system of identification, and the numbering systems could vary from 4 to as many as 15 alphanumeric digits. On January 1, 2000, the 237 manufacturers of heavy equipment throughout the world (including the big four U.S. manufacturers—Case, Caterpillar, Deere, and Ford) began using a standardized 17-character **product information number (PIN)** on all new equipment models.[12] The definition of "new model" will not necessarily change by calendar year. Consequently, it will take a few years before the standardized 17-character PIN becomes uniformly applied.

In at least one instance, the PIN is now more difficult to counterfeit than has been the case in the past. The new PIN plate on Caterpillar equipment is laser-engraved on black anodized aluminum and has a bar code and a microprinted security feature—the PIN number.[13]

Heavy equipment is also easily stolen; a single key may be used to start all models produced by a particular manufacturer, and where key locks are in place, the machinery can be jumped by placing a pocket knife or screwdriver across the electrical posts on the starter. Although manufacturers offer antitheft devices, they are costly items that add substantially to the base price of the equipment.

The unfamiliarity of most law enforcement officers with the nature, identity, and terminology of construction and farm equipment is among the principal problems faced by law enforcement. Few agencies have anyone with the expertise to identify specific machines or to locate and interpret identification numbers (see Table 15–1 and Figure 15–1).

## COMMERCIAL-VEHICLE AND CARGO THEFT

As noted earlier, the insurance industry pays out about $18 million every year because of **commercial-vehicle theft.** It is difficult to convert this figure to the number of vehicles stolen because commercial-vehicle theft data are incorporated into the overall motor vehicle theft statistics. Suffice it to say, the number is significant and rising.

As discussed in Chapter 13, the theft of cargo from or in commercial vehicles—is a rapidly growing criminal enterprise. Although not a separate crime in itself, **cargo theft,** in the United States, is estimated as accounting for as much as $25 billion in direct merchandise losses each year.[14] As an aside, cargo theft is just one aspect of a larger problem called cargo crime, which also includes smuggling, counterfeiting, and product piracy. Total direct merchandise losses from all cargo crime are estimated as approaching $50 billion per year.[15] The products most vulnerable to cargo crime, in general, and cargo theft, in particular, are assembled computers, computer components and software, electronic products, cigarettes, and fashion apparel.[16]

## INVESTIGATIVE TOOLS AND TECHNIQUES

Vehicle theft investigation is a fairly technical and sophisticated specialty. An effective investigator needs experience and expertise. Despite the fact that vehicle theft may not be among the offenses receiving the highest priority for the allocation of limited resources by a law enforcement agency, there are thousands of specialists in the United States and elsewhere whose expertise is available to any investigator needing assistance. Often, these resources are just a telephone call away.

In any specialized investigative field, one is not born an expert and cannot become an expert without extensive training and experience. So it is with vehicle thefts and related crimes. Individuals who possess the expertise, such as highly skilled investigators, cannot assume that uniformed officers with general policing responsibilities have any knowledge about the field beyond their limited exposure in an academy setting. Thus, if investigators are anxious for patrol officers to perform some initial investigative tasks, the investigators should offer to teach those officers how to perform the desired tasks.

### MAJOR INVESTIGATIVE RESOURCES

#### National Insurance Crime Bureau

The National Insurance Crime Bureau (NICB) is not a law enforcement agency that investigates auto thefts and arrests offenders in the traditional sense. Rather, the NICB is an information-gathering and dissemination body and a law enforcement assistance agency. In this regard, its special agents do

**Table 15-1** Construction and Farm Equipment Terminology

| Term | Definition |
|---|---|
| Air compressor | A portable device used to compress air for operating jack hammers, compactors, and other tools and equipment |
| Alternator | Device used to transform mechanical energy to electrical energy |
| Articulation | Vehicle design allowing two segments to bend at or around a middle joint for greater mobility |
| Articulation joint | Large joint around which a machine bends |
| Auger | A rotating screw-threaded drill which carries materials away from the face of the surface |
| Backhoe | Attachment used to remove earth by means of pulling the bucket back toward the operator; generic name for a machine with a backhoe attachment |
| Backhoe loader | Wheeled or tracked vehicle with both a backhoe attachment and a loader attachment |
| Bail | A hinged loop |
| Baler | A wheeled machine (usually pulled behind a tractor) which compacts hay or straw in compact bales, either square or round |
| Body | The load-carrying part of a truck or other vehicle |
| Bogey | An assembly of two or more axles |
| Boom | A maneuverable arm used to extend a piece of equipment |
| Bowl | The load-carrying part of a scraper |
| Bucket | A device attached to backhoes and loaders used to pick up materials |
| Bulldozer | Crawler tractor equipped with a straight front blade designed to move earth by pushing |
| Cab | An enclosure to protect a machine operator from the elements |
| Circle | The rotary table on a motorgrader that supports and regulates the blade |
| Combine | A machine to harvest corn, wheat, beans, etc. |
| Compactor | A machine used to compact materials |
| Cotton picker | A machine that picks or strips cotton, available in two-, three-, or four-row models |
| Crane | A device used to lift materials |
| Crankshaft | Engine component which converts reciprocating piston motion to rotary motion which turns the driveshaft |
| Crawler | Any vehicle, machine, or piece of equipment propelled by tracks; common name for a crawler dozer |
| Crawler dozer | Tracked vehicle designed to move earth with a front blade |
| Crawler loader | Tracked vehicle designed to move earth with a front bucket |
| Crawler tractor | Tracked vehicle with no front attachment |
| Crusher | A machine which reduces rocks to smaller and more uniform sizes |
| Cushion hitch | Mechanism which absorbs shocks, stabilizes machine travel, minimizes bounding, and permits operation of the machine at higher speeds |
| Digger | General term for an excavator or a backhoe |
| Dozer | A blade used to move materials by pushing; may be track or wheel mounted |
| Elevating scraper | Self-contained, self-propelled production unit equipped with a paddle wheel (elevator) and designed to remove earth by scraping; also called pan or pan scraper |
| Elevator | Paddle and roller chain mechanism that pushes material up and into the bowl of a scraper |
| Excavator | Self-propelled wheel or tracked machine equipped with a boom and bucket and designed to remove earth by digging; sometimes called backhoe or hoe |

*(continued)*

**Table 15-1** Construction and Farm Equipment Terminology, *continued*

| Term | Definition |
|---|---|
| Flywheel | A heavy metal disc which attaches to the rear of the crankshaft and maintains its rotation when the engine is not firing |
| Forklift | Device equipped with forks which is used for lifting loads on pallets |
| Front-end loader | A wheel loader |
| Fuel injection pump | Device used to pump fuel to the cylinders of an engine |
| Gooseneck | Curved metal section which fastens a piece of equipment to the hitch of a machine and allows the movement of wheels underneath for steering |
| Grader | Motor grader; vehicle equipped with a blade in the center of the wheels and designed for use in road construction, the maintenance of dirt and gravel roads, and the removal of snow and ice |
| Hoe | Alternate name for an excavator or backhoe |
| Hydraulic pump | Pump which circulates hydraulic fluid |
| Hydrostatic drive | Working off hydraulic pumps and eliminating the use of gears, clutch plates, etc. |
| Injection pump | Fuel injection pump which circulates fuel to the engine cylinders |
| Loader | Attachment designed to lift material; alternate name for wheel loader or backhoe |
| MCO | Manufacturer's certificate of origin; document designed to assist in the establishment of ownership and to provide a paper trail for an off-road vehicle |
| Motor grader | A rubber-tired machine used in road grading, sloping, and finishing (also called maintainers, motor patrols, and blades) |
| Mouldboard | A blade attached to a motorgrader for cutting or leveling |
| Mower | An attachment to a tractor for mowing right-of-way, golf courses, and fields; may be rotary or reel type and is available in widths from 5 feet to 25 feet |
| Nonelevating scraper | An elevating scraper without a paddle wheel |
| Off-highway truck | Heavy truck used in project involving large-scale earthmoving, such as coal mining and ore hauling; also known as a "rock truck" |
| OMM | Operation and maintenance manual; usually contains photographs of the PIN and serial numbers or serial number plate locations |
| Outrigger | Leg-type extensions used on the front or rear of machinery to improve its stability |
| Pan scraper | Alternate name for an elevating or nonelevating scraper |
| PIN | Product identification number; a serial number used to identify a machine or piece of equipment |
| PIN plate | A plate or sticker upon which the product identification number has been embossed or stamped and which is attached to the unit |
| P.T.O. | Power-take-off unit on a tractor used to power implements such as mowers, bush hogs, augers, plows, etc. |
| Push block | Structure at the rear of a scraper which directs the power generated by a push-tractor to the scraper's cutting edge |
| Pusher | A tractor that assists a wheel tractor-scraper in loading |
| Push-pull scraper | Scraper arrangement in which two tractor-scraper units are fitted with hydraulically operated bails and push blocks with hood which allow the two units to hook together—one unit pulls as the other pushes to achieve more rapid loading |
| Ripper | A device pulled behind a crawler tractor or bulldozer which is designed to loosen the earth |
| Roll-Gard | John Deere registered trade name for a rollover protection structure on a piece of equipment |

*(continued on next page)*

**Table 15-1 Construction and Farm Equipment Terminology,** *concluded*

| | |
|---|---|
| ROPS | Rollover protection structure; structure designed to protect the operator of a vehicle in the event that the vehicle overturns |
| Scraper | An elevating or nonelevating scraper used to scrape, level, or move materials |
| Skid-steer loader | A small front loader which steers by applying braking pressure against the wheel; often called a bobcat |
| Tandem-powered | Having two engines |
| Torque converter | A mechanical or hydraulic device for changing the ratio of torque to speed between the input and output shafts of a mechanism |
| Tractor | A gasoline- or diesel-powered machine to which may be attached farm or construction equipment |
| Transaxle | A device which transfers power from the engine to the axle in order to propel the vehicle |
| Transmission case | Housing for the transmission assembly |
| Trencher | A machine used to dig trenches |
| Turbocharger | An exhaust-driven pump which compresses intake air and forces it into the combustion chambers at increased pressures, burning more fuel and increasing the production of horsepower |
| Wheelbase | Distance between the centers of the front and rear wheels |
| Wheel loader | Any wheeled vehicle equipped with a front loader bucket and used for loading materials |
| Wheel loader backhoe | Any wheeled vehicle equipped with a front loader attachment and a rear backhoe attachment; a backhoe loader |
| Wheel tractor | Any vehicle propelled by wheels as opposed to tracks |
| Winch | A motor-driven or hand-powered hoisting machine with a drum around which a rope or chain winds as the load is lifted |

**Source:** National Insurance Crime Bureau, *Commercial Vehicle and Off-Road Equipment Identification Manual,* 7th ed. (Palos Hills, IL: NICB, 2000), pp. 142–147.

investigate professional theft rings and other auto theft cases in conjunction with local, state, and federal law enforcement agencies.

Beginning in 1912 with the efforts of a few individuals, representing different insurance companies, joining forces to disseminate information on stolen motor vehicles, the cooperation gradually spread and evolved into several independent regionalized and, later, national groups. This growth limited communication and interaction. Duplication of efforts and costs, along with the creation of considerable confusion among law enforcement officials in deciding whom to contact for information, led to the initial consolidation of all existing auto theft information agencies and organizations into the National Automobile Theft Bureau (NATB) in 1927. In 1965 the NATB was completely nationalized and centralized.

Late in 1991 a merger took place between the NATB and the Insurance Crime Prevention Institute (ICPI); on January 1, 1992, the National Insurance Crime Bureau was formed. The NICB now has 200 investigative field agents coordinating with another 800 fraud investigators who work for individual insurance companies.

The NICB is not a government organization. It is a nonprofit organization operated by, funded by, affiliated with, and serving approximately 1,000 associated insurance companies nationwide. It conducts and supports engineering and other research and experiments aimed at reducing vehicle theft and fraud and is a recognized national voice for law enforcement and the insurance industry on legislative matters.

The NICB assists in the identification of vehicles and helps educate law enforcement officers in investigative techniques of vehicle identification, fraud, and theft.

In addition to the expertise of its field personnel, the computerized records developed and

**Figure 15-1** Illustrations of Heavy Construction Equipment

BACKHOE, CRAWLER MOUNTED (HYDRAULIC)

BACKHOE/LOADER – WHEEL MOUNTED

CRANES, LIFTING

CRANE, CRAWLER MOUNTED (MECHANICAL)

CRANE, SELF-PROPELLED (HYDRAULIC)

CRANE, TRUCK MOUNTED (MECHANICAL)

CRANE, TRUCK MOUNTED (HYDRAULIC)

DOZER, CRAWLER MOUNTED

GRADERS, MOTOR— SELF-PROPELLED

*(continued on next page)*

**Figure 15-1** Illustrations of Heavy Construction Equipment, *continued*

LOADER, CRAWLER MOUNTED

LOADER – WHEEL MOUNTED

ROLLER, RUBBER TIRED

ROLLER, SELF-PROPELLED PRIME MOVER (WITH SHEEPSFOOT)

ROLLER, STEEL WHEEL – TANDEM

SCRAPER, MOTOR

TRENCHER, CRAWLER MOUNTED LADDER TYPE

established by the NICB, and now maintained and administered by the International Service Organization (ISO), a private company, are invaluable investigative aids. These database services include the following:

- *Theft file:* More than 1,000 insurance companies report stolen vehicles. Theft records from the Canadian Automobile Theft Bureau (CATB) and most European countries are also maintained and include all types of vehicles, off-road machinery, boats, parts, and accessories. The records contain full ownership and insurance information.
- *Salvage file:* Salvage vehicle reports are received from insurance companies on vehicles for which there has been a loss settlement and the company has taken title. These vehicles are generally sold through salvage pools or to salvage buyers. The file contains information on both sellers and buyers of salvage.
- *Export file:* The U.S. Customs Service and others send copies of export declarations for entry into the system. The information aids in the detection of illegal exports and of fraudulent theft reports on exported vehicles in cases where a subsequent stolen vehicle report is filed.
- *NCIC purge file:* Vehicle theft records purged from NCIC since 1972 for a variety of reasons are provided to NICB on a daily basis and are entered into the system as a permanent record. The file is an important and time-saving tool for law enforcement.
- *Information-wanted file:* When a purchaser skips out on payments to a finance company that has purchased physical-damage insurance on the vehicle from one of the NICB sponsoring member companies, the information is made available to law enforcement agencies investigating the vehicle as a suspected stolen unit.
- *Inquiry file:* When a law enforcement agency makes an inquiry on a vehicle for an investigation, any subsequent information received or any inquiry on the same vehicle from another person or agency will be passed on to the original inquirer.
- *Shipping and assembly file:* This file holds the shipping and assembly records for most automobiles; light-, medium-, and heavy-duty trucks; semitrailers; motorcycles; and snowmobiles.
- *Impound file:* An increasing number of states are now collecting and reporting impound records to NICB for entry into this file. The file helps clear many stolen records and is a valuable investigative tool.
- *VINASSIST:* This NICB program edits, evaluates, and corrects vehicle identification numbers, a process that greatly aids law enforcement in positively identifying specific recovered motor vehicles.
- *All-Claims Database:* With this database, claims filed against participating member insurance companies can be compared to detect possible fraudulent claims, including auto theft–related insurance fraud.

The NICB is organized into eight geographic areas, with its headquarters in the Chicago suburb of Palos Hills, Illinois, serving as the Area 1 office. The other offices serving major metropolitan and surrounding locales are in Seattle, Los Angeles, Dallas, Atlanta, Washington, DC, New York, and Cincinnati.

Since 1929, the NICB or its predecessor, the NATB, has annually published the *Passenger Vehicle Identification Manual,* which contains the following:

- Federal motor vehicle theft prevention standards.
- Explanation of vehicle identification numbers.
- VIN plate attachment and location.
- Federal safety certification labels.
- Passenger vehicle and light-duty truck VIN structure.
- Motorcycles and all-terrain vehicle VIN structure.
- General information on snowmobiles and boats.
- Vehicle shipping and assembly record information.[17]

Every five years the NICB also publishes the *Commercial Vehicle and Off-Road Equipment Identification Manual,* which contains the following:

**The Passenger Vehicle Identification Manual**
One of the most important investigative tools used in vehicle theft cases is the Passenger Vehicle Identification Manual. Published by the National Insurance Crime Bureau, this booklet contains useful information including: an explanation of vehicle identification numbers, the federal motor vehicle theft prevention standards, and VIN plate attachment and location.
(© Joel Gordon)

- World manufacturer identification codes.
- Model year identifier.
- Truck-tractor identification.
- Commercial-trailer identification.
- Off-road equipment identification.[18]

## Canadian Insurance Crime Prevention Bureau

The Canadian Insurance Crime Prevention Bureau (ICPB) has been functioning since 1923 but became an independent division within the Insurance Council of Canada on January 1, 1998. It is to Canada what NICB is to the United States. Supported by over 90 percent of private-property and casualty insurers, ICPB employs 130 people, 86 of whom are investigators. Within the organizational structure of ICPB are found the Canadian Automobile Theft Bureau (CATB) and the Canadian Police Information System, the sister organization of NCIC. ICPB is headquartered in Toronto, Ontario. It has five regional offices, located in Burnaby, British Columbia, serving that province; Toronto, which serves all of Ontario; Wesmount, Quebec, serving the Montreal and Quebec region; Halifax, Nova Scotia, which handles cases in Nova Scotia, New Brunswick, Newfoundland, and Prince Edward Island; and Calgary, Alberta, which serves the provinces of Alberta, Saskatchewan, and Manitoba.[19]

## International Association of Auto Theft Investigators

Another resource available to the investigator is the International Association of Auto Theft Investigators (IAATI) and its regional affiliated chapters. With a current membership in excess of 1,500, IAATI was formed in 1952 for the purpose of formulating new methods to attack and control vehicle theft and fraud. Its members represent law enforcement agencies, state registration and titling agencies, insurance companies, car rental companies, the automobile manufacturing industry, and other interested groups. International and regional training seminars are held throughout the year.

## State Organizations

Many states have organizations consisting of auto theft investigators who meet regularly to exchange intelligence information and learn new methods of combating the problems of theft and fraud.

## National Crime Information Center

Another valuable resource for the investigator is the FBI's National Crime Information Center (NCIC). Online inquiries can be made to NCIC's vehicle or license plate files to check on records for stolen vehicles, vehicles wanted in conjunction with felonies, stolen component parts, and stolen license plates. In addition, a request can be made for an off-line search, which is a tool designed to assist an investigator by providing lead information. For example, an investigator attempting to track a stolen vehicle that is known to be traveling across the country can request an off-line search to see if any stolen inquiries had been made within a specific time frame on that vehicle. A hit would identify the time and location from which the inquiry was made, thus providing a lead to locating the vehicle.

The original NCIC system held more than 40 million records in its 17 databases and processed more than 2 million transactions a day, but it was more than 30 years old. An updated, new-generation system, NCIC 2000, was implemented in July 1999. It has all the advantages of the old system plus impressive new capabilities such as image processing, whereby mug shots, other photographs, signatures, and identifying marks can be electronically submitted; single-finger fingerprint matching, including storing and searching for right-index fingerprints; a linkage field, whereby multiple records concerning the same criminal or the same crime can be automatically associated; and several new databases including the Convicted Persons on Supervised Release Database, the Convicted Sexual Offender Registry, and the SENTRY file of persons incarcerated in federal prisons. These can all be accessed through NCIC 2000.[20]

The NCIC databases can be used for many different purposes. For instance, through the linkage function, an inquiry on a gun can also identify a wanted person or a stolen car. Since vehicle information can be included in the Convicted Sexual Offender Registry, a traffic stop with an inquiry on the license plate may identify an individual as a registered sexual offender.[21]

From the implementation date of the new system, all NCIC users have up to three years to switch from NCIC to NCIC 2000. Thus, by July 2002, all users have to be able to transmit and receive messages in the NCIC 2000 format.[22]

## Special Investigative Units

In the mid-1970s, Kemper Insurance Company created the first special investigative unit (SIU) for insurance companies. Its primary purpose was to investigate potentially fraudulent auto theft claims. There are more than 800 SIU investigators employed in the insurance industry working fraud claims. Approximately 80 percent of the insurance companies now have SIUs. The agents and units work with and train insurance adjusters to detect oddities and "red flags" indicating potential fraud. The SIUs also work closely with law enforcement by lending assistance in investigations—providing computer information, claims histories, and statements of insureds made under oath.

## AAMVANET

The **AAMVANET** computerized communication network links state and provincial agencies on matters of highway usage and highway safety. The system was initiated by and for the American Association of Motor Vehicle Administrators (AAMVA). The AAMVANET corporation, a subsidiary of AAMVA, is coordinating the effort to create the **National Motor Vehicle Title Information System (NMVTIS),** being developed in cooperation with NICB. Through NMVTIS any inquiry will receive a complete and up-to-the-minute history of a vehicle, including whether it was reported stolen, salvaged, or exported or is otherwise incapable of being the subject of a new transfer. In addition to inquiry capability, the system will prevent the laundering of titles between states for the purpose of removing brands such as those that appear on salvage, flood-damaged, rebuilt, or unrepairable vehicles. The program is being developed with the help of five pilot states. An ultimate goal of the developers is to provide a system whereby a potential purchaser of a used vehicle will be able to inquire about the status of the vehicle before making a final commitment to purchase.

## Government Agencies

In virtually all state governments, organizations or entities exist that possess information of value to investigators. Specifically, motor vehicle and driver's license offices, insurance fraud investigative units, and fire and arson investigative units may provide valuable information or assistance.

## Manufacturers

Manufacturers are one of the most important resources an investigator can cultivate and turn to for assistance, particularly as it relates to the content and location of numbers on vehicles or parts. Domestic and foreign automobile manufacturers are generally most supportive of an investigator's inquiries, as are the Harley-Davidson Motorcycle Company and the John Deere, Case, and Caterpillar companies, which manufacture construction and farm equipment. This list is not meant to be exhaustive. Help will generally be given by any manufacturer when requested.

## North American Export Committee

In an effort to stem the tide of stolen vehicles being exported from the country, the NICB, U.S. and Canadian Customs, Royal Canadian Mounted Police, Insurance Crime Prevention Bureau in Canada, and Miami-Dade Police Department in Florida, along with other law enforcement agencies, the insurance industry, and other interested parties, established the North American Export Committee in 1995. The committee investigates ways in which the exporting of stolen vehicles could be slowed without impeding commerce at port facilities.

Shipments of vehicles occur in two ways—some vehicles are rolled on and then rolled off a ship, and some are shipped in containers. These are quite different concepts requiring entirely different approaches. U.S. Customs is charged with the responsibility of checking the paperwork on vehicles to be exported, and the paperwork must be received by Customs three days before a vehicle can be shipped. Only limited resources are devoted to this responsibility, however, because Customs is more concerned about property coming into the country and about commodities, other than vehicles, being exported. Nevertheless, Customs, sometimes with the assistance and support of local law enforcement, checks the paperwork, physically examines as many of the vehicles as possible, and enters the VINs into a computer that transmits all those checked to NICB. Overnight, the list is run against the export, stolen, salvage, and VIN verification files. The next morning, an exceptions report is available to the submitting agencies so that the "trouble messages" (problems) can be checked out before the vehicles are shipped. At the Port of Miami, trouble messages occur on approximately 20 percent of the exports.

Containerized vehicles present a different set of problems. There are over 8 million containers exported from the United States in a year. No manifest is going to acknowledge that a container has one or more stolen vehicles. Checking a container, even if it meets a predetermined set of conditions called a profile, is hot, sweaty work—the unloading and reloading take hours—and it interferes with commerce. Stolen vehicles are usually found in the front or middle of a container, with goods packed all around them. To make enforcement more productive, an efficient, effective, and economic method of looking inside containers had to be found. X-ray equipment works, but it is expensive and poses danger to workers subjected to prolonged exposure. And it, too, slows down commerce because the container has to be stopped while the X-ray is taken, thus limiting the number of containers to about 30 that can be checked in one day at one location. Using gasoline-sniffing dogs and drilling holes in containers to insert a hydrocarbon "sniffer" or a camera on a pole have also been tried, with less than satisfactory results.

Science Applications International Corporation has developed a device that examines and photographs the contents of a container as it is passing through a gamma ray. In mid-1998, the corporation, in cooperation with the Miami-Dade County Multi-Agency Auto Theft Task Force and on behalf of the North American Export Committee, tested this equipment for a 90-day period at the Port of Miami in what is called the **Stolen Auto Recovery (STAR) System.** Before the 90 days were up, more than 7,700 containers were scanned in less than 6 seconds each while they continued to move. A total of 630 vehicles were identified and 6 stolen vehicles were recovered, valued at $217,000. There were no false identifications, and the flow of commerce was not impeded. The units cost around $270,000, are very transportable, and are easily installed in one day, and the gamma-ray scan preserves a video image of the contents of the container (see photo on page 553).

Because of the success of the STAR System, Florida has committed to installing the system at 5 additional ports and the NICB is providing support for installation at 50 ports around the country. Canada has also developed a task-force operation at the port in Vancouver, British Columbia, using similar technology, with data transfer to the Canadian Insurance Crime Prevention Bureau. Early results were the recovery of 12 vehicles, all stolen from the province of Ontario.[23]

## National Equipment Register

The scope of the theft of heavy construction equipment has led manufacturers, dealers, and insurers to support the development of a national database of stolen equipment and provide the services of law enforcement specialists in the recovery of stolen equipment. The National Equipment Register (NER) facilitates the identification of lost and stolen

## Gamma-Ray Scan Showing Two Utility Vehicles

Advances in technology have assisted in the discovery of stolen vehicles being exported from the United States aboard ships. Science Applications International Corporation has developed a device that examines and photographs the contents of a container as it is passed through gamma ray. These units cost around $270,000, are very transportable, and are easily installed in one day's time.

(Courtesy Miami-Dade Police Department)

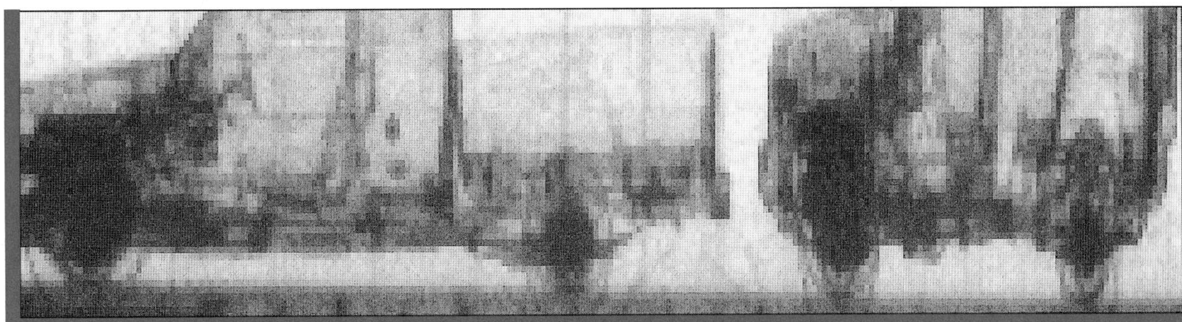

equipment and the return of such equipment to owners and insurers and promotes due diligence in the purchase of used equipment, thereby deterring the trade in stolen equipment. The NER organization is gearing up to provide training programs for law enforcement officers on equipment recovery and for owners on loss prevention.[24]

## LOCATING AND HANDLING VEHICLES

In recent years investigators have gotten seriously ill performing their jobs. Locating and handling the recovery of vehicles and parts can be very dangerous. Often, an investigator will climb or crawl around, through and over wrecks, in a remote area of a salvage yard in order to locate or identify a vehicle part. Not only is the physical work dangerous, but, unknowingly, the investigator may be exposed to toxic hazardous waste, which can cause permanent physical damage. Gloves should be worn at all times, along with protective clothing and a mask or breathing device, when encountering the unknown. Similarly, when investigating a vehicle fire, investigators must take precautions as toxic chemicals may be around that can cause serious long-term illness due to exposure.

## VEHICLE IDENTIFICATION

Often the most difficult and time-consuming task facing an investigator is the identification of a recovered vehicle. Although there are a number of ways by which motor vehicles can be identified, including a description by year, make and model, or license number, these items are easily generalized or alterable. For the investigator, identification is made by numbers affixed to or inscribed on the vehicle.

Since 1954 American automobile manufacturers have used a **vehicle identification number (VIN)** instead of an engine number as the primary means of identification. However, before 1968, VINs, although usually inscribed on metal plates, were not uniformly located on vehicles, nor was there any standard method for attaching a **VIN plate** to a vehicle. On varying makes and models, VIN plates were affixed with screws or rivets or were spot-welded on doors, doorposts, or dashes. Since 1968 VIN plates on almost all domestic and foreign cars have been attached to the left side of the dash on the instrument panel in such a fashion as to be visible through the windshield. Corvettes, prior to 1984, had the VIN plate attached to the left-side windshield post. Tractor and semitrailer manufacturers still lack consistency in the placement of VIN plates, as do construction and farm equipment manufacturers in the placement of product identification numbers (PINs).

VIN plates still are attached by a variety of methods. Several foreign manufacturers use a round-head "pop" rivet made of aluminum, stainless steel, or some plastic material. A six-petal "rosette" rivet made of aluminum or stainless steel has been used on General Motors products since 1966, on Chrysler-manufactured vehicles since 1968, and on Ford units since 1970. Sheet-metal screws are still occasionally used on some imports (see Figure 15–2).

**Figure 15-2** Attaching VIN Plates

(**Source:** National Insurance Crime Bureau, *2001 Passenger Vehicle Identification Manual* (Palos Hills, IL: NICB, 2001), p. 46. Used with permission of NICB.)

**ROUND-HEAD "POP" RIVET**
**ALUMINUM, STAINLESS STEEL, OR PLASTIC**

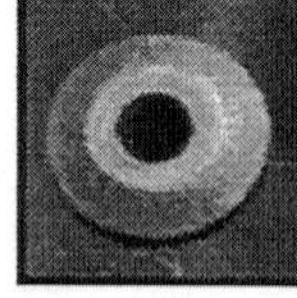

Used on early General Motors vehicles prior to 1965 after departure from "spot weld" method of attaching VIN plates. Still used by most foreign manufacturers.

**"ROSETTE"-TYPE RIVET**
**6 PETALS, ALUMINUM, OR STAINLESS STEEL**

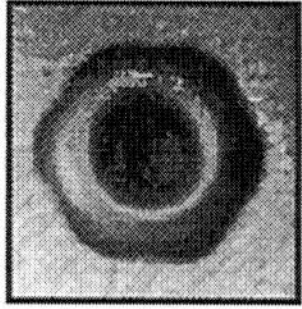

Used by General Motors Corp. since 1965, Chrysler Corp. since 1966, and Ford Motor Co. since 1970. There have been instances when round-head rivets were used at some assembly plants but only on very rare occasions.

**"ROSETTE"-TYPE RIVET**
**5 PETALS, ALUMINUM**

Used by Toyota since 1985, except for the 1985 Corolla front-wheel drive, diesel, and 1989 and 1990 Cressida models, which have round aluminum rivets.

**SHEET-METAL SCREWS**

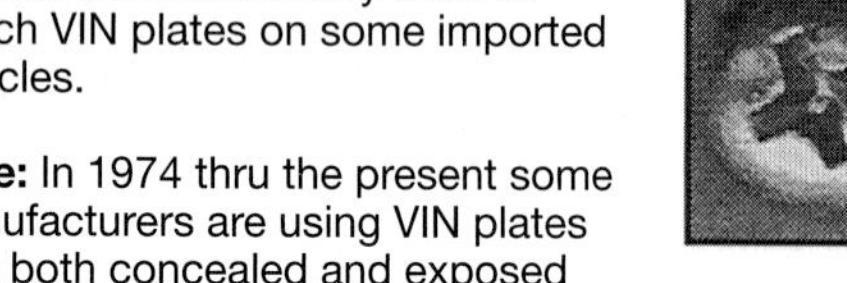

Screws are occasionally used to attach VIN plates on some imported vehicles.

**Note:** In 1974 thru the present some manufacturers are using VIN plates with both concealed and exposed rivets.

The use of a public VIN is designed to provide a positive, individualized means of identifying a motor vehicle. The 1981 adoption of a standardized 17-character VIN for all cars manufactured in or sold in the United States was certainly a forceful step in that direction. Previously, General Motors used a 13-digit VIN, Ford and Chrysler each used 11 characters, and imports used a host of other lengths. The standardized 17-character configuration is required of all imports manufactured for sale in the United States. The first 11 characters of the standardized VIN identify the country of origin, manufacturer, make, restraint system, model, body style, engine type, year, assembly plant, and a mathematically computed check digit that is used to verify all the other characters in the VIN. The last six characters are the sequential production number of the vehicle (see Figures 15–3 and 15–4). The letters "I," "O," "Q," "U," and "Z" are not used so as to avoid confusion with similar-looking numbers.

Under the standardized 17-character system, the check digit is always the ninth character in the VIN and is calculated using the formula process illustrated on the worksheet depicted in Figure 15–5. By assigning specified numerical values to each letter and number, then multiplying and dividing, the appropriate check digit can be determined and matched with the check digit on the VIN in question to ascertain whether there are any flaws in the construction of the VIN such as altered or transposed characters.

The tenth character of the VIN represents the year of manufacture or vehicle model year. The letter A was used to designate 1980, B for 1981, and so on. Without the letters "I," "O," "Q," "U," and "Z," the remaining 20 letters, followed by the use of numbers 1 to 9, establish a 30-year cycle before the possibility of an exactly duplicated VIN could result from the normal manufacturing process (see Figure 15–6).

On some newer vehicles, VIN plates also have a bar code that contains all the information represented by the alphanumeric characters of the VIN (see Figure 15–7). This makes attempted alteration of the VIN plate less effective because a reader can detect the true information in a second. Other manufacturers put a separate sticker on the door or doorpost that bears the VIN and bar code (see Figure 15–8).

## Gray-Market Vehicles

When the U.S. dollar is strong overseas, it becomes economically feasible for individuals to purchase motor vehicles in other countries and have them shipped to the United States for sale, resale, or personal use. This effort can be profitable even though it may cost up to several thousand dollars apiece to

Figure 15-3

Example of 17-Digit VIN System

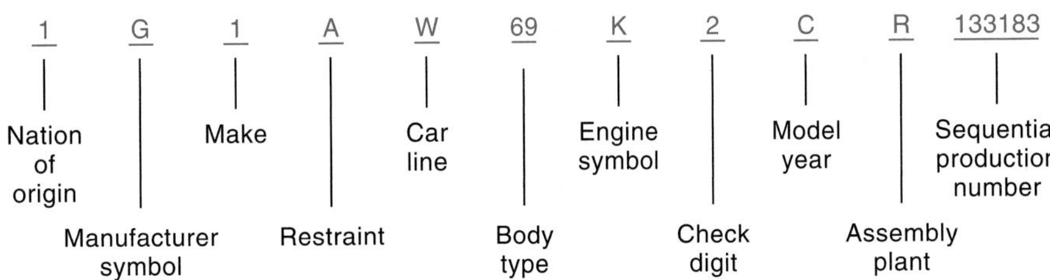


"legalize" the vehicles for use in the United States. Since such vehicles are not manufactured for sale in this country, they are not constructed to meet U.S. emission control or safety standards, nor do they have a 17-character standardized VIN. If **gray-market vehicles** are brought into this country legally, a bond for each must be posted with U.S. Customs until such time as the appropriate modifications have been made to bring the vehicle into compliance with the U.S. Environmental Protection Agency (EPA) emission control requirements and the safety standards promulgated by the U.S. Department of Transportation (DOT). When these steps have been accomplished and the modifications approved, the federal government will issue a replacement VIN plate that conforms with the 17-character standard.

Many vehicles are found operating on the streets and highways of this nation prior to or without conforming to the legal conversion requirements for gray-market vehicles. The operation of these vehicles is unlawful, and they are subject to seizure by U.S. Customs. The frequency of such seizures and the ability to ensure compliance with the EPA and DOT regulations are, of course, a direct function of the resources devoted to the programs and the priorities established. Not unlike state and local agencies, federal law enforcement programs also suffer from limited resources. In some years, gray-market imports have approached 100,000 vehicles.

The nonconforming VIN on a gray-market vehicle is sometimes nothing more than a Dymotape label stuck on the left-side dash and visible through the windshield. Often such a VIN is on a plate riveted in the appropriate place, but its construction does not satisfy the accepted format requirements. Learning the proper appearance and configuration of the accepted VIN format will aid investigators not only in identifying gray-market vehicles but also in detecting altered VINs.

## Attempts to Conceal the Identity of Vehicles

The methods used to change the identity of a motor vehicle, as discussed earlier in this chapter, include doing a salvage switch and altering genuine or counterfeiting ownership documents. Numbers can be intentionally transposed on documents, VIN plates can be counterfeited or removed, and other identifying numbers can be completely obliterated, altered, or defaced in an attempt to thwart any effort to accurately identify a vehicle.

Why is concealing a vehicle's identity so important? Simply, if a vehicle cannot be positively identified, it cannot be proved that the vehicle was stolen, when it was stolen, or from whom it was stolen. Thus, one who is in possession of such a vehicle cannot be prosecuted as a thief.

Even the most careful thief has extreme difficulty totally concealing the identity of a stolen vehicle. Although it does happen, total inability to identify a vehicle is rare if the investigator doesn't hesitate to call on his or her own or others' knowledge, training, and experience. Knowing how and when to call on outside resources is important to the successful investigation. NICB special agents and other highly qualified law enforcement officers know how and where to look for clues to a vehicle's identity.

The public VIN on the dash is not the only number that identifies a specific vehicle. The VIN may be stamped in several different places on the vehicle's body, frame, or component parts. The location of some of these secondary numbers is not a big secret, but others, referred to as **confidential VINs,** are stamped into frames or bodies in places supposedly known only to the manufacturer and to law enforcement agencies and officers who are specialists in vehicle identification and auto theft investigation, such as NICB special agents. Various other

Figure 15-4

World Manufacturer Identification Codes

(**Source:** Courtesy NICB, Palos Hills, Illinois)

| Code | Manufacturer | Code | Manufacturer |
|---|---|---|---|
| JH4 | ACURA | 1LN | LINCOLN |
| ZAR | ALFA ROMEO | SCC | LOTUS |
| 1AM | AMERICAN MOTORS | ZAM | MASERATI |
| SCF | ASTON MARTIN | JM1 | MAZDA |
| WAU | AUDI | WDB | MERCEDES BENZ |
| 12A | AVANTI | 1ME | MERCURY |
| ZBB | BERTONE | WF1 | MERKUR |
| WBA | BMW | JA3 | MITSUBISHI |
| 1G4 | BUICK | JN1 | NISSAN |
| 1G6 | CADILLAC | 1G3 | OLDSMOBILE |
| 1G1 | CHEVROLET | VF3 | PEUGEOT |
| 1C3 | CHRYSLER | ZFR | PININFARINA |
| 2E3 | EAGLE PREMIER | 1P3 | PLYMOUTH |
| JE3 | EAGLE SUMMIT | 1G2 | PONTIAC |
| VF1 | EAGLE MEDALLION | WPO | PORSCHE |
| SCE | DELOREAN | VF1 | RENAULT |
| 1B3 | DODGE | SCA | ROLLS ROYCE |
| ZFF | FERRARI | YS3 | SAAB |
| ZFA | FIAT | SAX | STERLING |
| 1FA | FORD | JF1 | SUBARU |
| KMH | HYUNDAI | JS3 | SUZUKI |
| JHM | HONDA | JT2 | TOYOTA |
| JAB | ISUZU | WVW | VOLKSWAGEN |
| SAJ | JAGUAR | YV1 | VOLVO |
| 1JC | JEEP | | |

parts such as engines and transmissions will be given an identification number when manufactured, but, because they are distinct component parts, often manufactured in different locales from the final assembly plant, the numbers may be totally different from the VIN. However, documents created and maintained by the manufacturer, and perhaps already in the databanks of the NICB computer system, can be checked to determine the VIN of the vehicle in which the part was installed.

Other parts or components of a vehicle manufactured or subassembled elsewhere may be designed to fit a specific vehicle. In such cases, the part may have a serial number that is related to but not identical to the VIN. It may have a number that is a derivative of the VIN or formed from parts of the VIN, as where a T-top may need to be matched to a vehicle of a specific body type denoted by the sixth and seventh characters of the VIN and the six-digit sequential number. Numerous combinations are possible and plausible; again, this is where the manufacturer's records become indispensable.

The numbers often used to match parts so as to foster accurate assembly of a vehicle may be written on components with pen, pencil, chalk, marking pen, or crayon. It does not matter what they are written with, as long as there are numbers that can lead an investigator to the end result of positively identifying a vehicle. Frequently, the various components subassembled elsewhere in the same plant or shipped from other plants will be accompanied by production order forms or written orders containing the VIN or a derivative number, which matches the parts for assembly. After the parts are matched and assembled, the production form has no use and may be left in some nook, cranny, or crevice of the assembly. If the investigator knows where to look, such a document may often be found and thus lead to vehicle identification.

## Federal Safety Certification Label

All cars distributed in the United States since 1970 must have a **federal safety certification label.** This sticker, in addition to the required

**Figure 15-5** Check-Digit Calculation Formula

(**Source:** Courtesy National Automobile Theft Bureau)

| | 1 | 2 | 3 | 4 | 5 | 6 | 7 | 8 | 9 | 10 | 11 | 12 | 13 | 14 | 15 | 16 | 17 | |
|---|---|---|---|---|---|---|---|---|---|---|---|---|---|---|---|---|---|---|
| A | | | | | | | | | | | | | | | | | | |
| B | | | | | | | | | | | | | | | | | | |
| C | 8 | 7 | 6 | 5 | 4 | 3 | 2 | 10 | 0 | 9 | 8 | 7 | 6 | 5 | 4 | 3 | 2 | |
| D | | | | | | | | | | | | | | | | | | = ____ Final sum |

On line A, enter the 17-digit VIN.

On line B, enter the assigned value of each character of the VIN, utilizing table B, shown below.

11 |

*Multiply the numbers in line B with the numbers in line C, for each of the 17 digits in the VIN. Record the product of each of these separate computations in the appropriate box in line D.

*Divide together all of the numbers recorded in line D and enter the final sum in the place provided.

*Divide the final sum by the number 11. The remainder of this division is the "check digit" (the ninth character of the 17-digit VIN). If the remainder of this division is a single-digit number, then it should match the check digit in the VIN exactly; if the remainder is the number 10, then the check digit is the letter X.

Table B

| | | | | |
|---|---|---|---|---|
| A-1 | J-1 | T-3 | 1-1 | 6-6 |
| B-2 | K-2 | U-4 | 2-2 | 7-7 |
| C-3 | L-3 | V-5 | 3-3 | 8-8 |
| D-4 | M-4 | W-6 | 4-4 | 9-9 |
| E-5 | N-5 | X-7 | 5-5 | 0-0 |
| F-6 | P-7 | Y-8 | | |
| G-7 | R-9 | Z-9 | | |
| H-8 | S-2 | | | |

Assign to each number in the VIN its actual value and record that value in the appropriate box in line B.

The letters I, O and Q are never used in the new 17-digit VIN's.

To determine the year of manufacture from the 17-digit VIN (character 10 of the VIN) use the listed table.

1980-A 1981-B 1982-C 1983-D 1984-E 1985-F 1986-G 1987-H

---

The decoding chart, shown above, may be photocopied to provide multiple blank work sheets for computing the check digits of the new 17-digit VIN's.

Example: 1981 Ford Mustang 1FABP12A4BR101093, final sum = 246

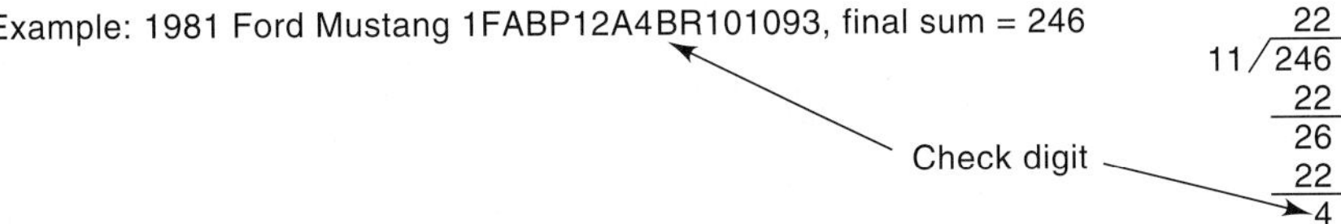


22
11/246
22
26
22
4

**Figure 15-6** Vehicle Model Year

| | | | | | |
|---|---|---|---|---|---|
| 1980 | A | 1995 | S | 2010 | A |
| 1981 | B | 1996 | T | 2011 | B |
| 1982 | C | 1997 | V | 2012 | C |
| 1983 | D | 1998 | W | | |
| 1984 | E | 1999 | X | | |
| 1985 | F | 2000 | Y | | |
| 1986 | G | 2001 | 1 | | |
| 1987 | H | 2002 | 2 | | |
| 1988 | J | 2003 | 3 | | |
| 1989 | K | 2004 | 4 | | |
| 1990 | L | 2005 | 5 | | |
| 1991 | M | 2006 | 6 | | |
| 1992 | N | 2007 | 7 | | |
| 1993 | P | 2008 | 8 | | |
| 1994 | R | 2009 | 9 | | |

certification statements, also contains the vehicle's VIN. If the sticker is removed, it leaves behind a "footprint" that often shows the word "void." Obviously, if the correct sticker is in place and the correct public VIN shows through the windshield, the VINs should match.

Shape and size of the labels, as well as the materials from which they are constructed, vary among manufacturers. More common among domestic manufacturers is a paper label covered with a clear Mylar-type plastic. The label is bonded to the vehicle with a mastic compound. Construction is such that the label should destruct if removal is attempted. Some foreign manufacturers construct the certifying label out of thin metal and attach it with rivets. In either case, security against removal and replacement is not absolute. However, investigators are encouraged not to use the VIN on the safety certification label as absolute proof of vehicle identification. The federal safety sticker will be located on the driver's door or on the doorpost.

## Federal Legislation

In an effort to reduce auto theft by easing the process of vehicle identification, Congress enacted the **Motor Vehicle Theft Law Enforcement Act** of 1984. Title I of the law requires that manufacturers place additional permanent identification numbers on up to 14 major parts of certain car lines. The car lines are selected each year for each manufacturer by the National Highway Traffic Safety Administration (NHTSA), the federal agency charged with setting the standards for the administration of the law. The car lines chosen each year for **parts marking** are those designated as high-theft lines. The parts requiring the additional identification are the major parts that are normally most sought in a chop-shop operation and include the following (see Figure 15–9):

- Engine
- Transmission
- Both front fenders
- Hood
- Both front doors
- Front and rear bumpers
- Both rear quarter panels
- Decklid, tailgate, or hatchback (whichever is applicable)
- Both rear doors (if present)

The numbers must either be inscribed on the designated parts or printed on labels attached to the parts. Labels must tear into pieces if removed; if completely removed, they must leave a "footprint," which becomes visible through certain investigative techniques such as using an ultraviolet light. The standards apply to the major parts of the designated new car lines and to replacement parts for the same car lines. The new-part labels must have the manufacturer's logo or other identifier printed on them and must use the full 17-character VIN for identification (see Figure 15–10); if, however, a VIN derivative of at least eight characters was being used to identify the engine and transmission on a particular covered line on the effective date of the law, that practice may continue. The identifier on covered replacement parts must carry the manufacturer's trademark, logo, or other distinguishing symbol, the letter "R" to reflect replacement, and the letters "DOT" (see Figure 15–10). The labels are to be affixed to the part on a surface that is not normally exposed to damage when the

**Figure 15-7** General Motors VIN Plate with Bar Code

(**Source:** IAATI-SE newsletter, 1997.)

**Figure 15-8** Federal Safety Certification Label with Bar Code

(**Source:** IAATI-SE newsletter, 1997.)

MFD.BY HONDA OF AMERICA MFG.,INC. 2/92
GVWR 3945LBS GAWR F 2140LBS R 1885LBS
THIS VEHICLE CONFORMS TO ALL APPLICABLE
FEDERAL MOTOR VEHICLE SAFETY,BUMPER,
AND THEFT PREVENTION STANDARDS IN EFFECT
ON THE DATE OF MANUFACTURE SHOWN ABOVE:

PASSENGER CAR MADE IN U.S.A.

part is installed, adjusted, or removed or damaged in an accident. When the part is removed from the vehicle, the label or inscription must be visible without the disassembling of the part.

The law limits the application of the requirements to no more than 14 production car lines for any one manufacturer, and the costs to the manufacturer for compliance cannot exceed $15 per vehicle, excluding the costs of marking the engine and transmission.

There is an exemption in the law, called a "black-box" exemption, which allows NHTSA to exempt from compliance with the standards up to two car lines per year for any single manufacturer if the vehicle line is equipped by the manufacturer with a standard equipment antitheft device determined by NHTSA to be as effective in deterring and reducing vehicle theft as would be compliance with the parts-marking requirements of the theft prevention standard.

The intent underlying the passage of the law, the promulgation of standards, and the marking of original and replacement parts was to reduce auto theft by ostensibly making it more difficult for the thief to conceal the identity of major parts, by providing fewer significant parts that would be untraceable, and by making it easier for law enforcement investigators to identify stolen parts.

Having determined that the parts-marking program initiated in 1984 was effective, Congress passed the Anti-Car Theft Act of 1992, which continued and extended the program. The 1992 legislation also called for the U.S. attorney general to conduct an initial evaluation, in 1997, of the effectiveness of the program in inhibiting chop-shop operations and deterring motor vehicle theft, with the objective of extending the parts-marking program to all lines (makes and models) by the end of 1997. The study recommended continuance of the program. The act required a long-range review of the program in 1999. In addition to evaluating whether chop-shop operations were impacted and theft had been deterred, the study was to determine whether the black-box exemptions were an effective substitute for parts marking in substantially reducing motor vehicle theft.

The act also required repair shops to check the VIN on all parts against a national file. Previously, this was the NCIC stolen-vehicle file, but the FBI, by direction of the act, established the National Stolen Parts Motor Vehicle Information System (NSPMVIS). Other provisions of the law made armed carjacking a federal crime; doubled the maximum penalty for importing, exporting, transporting, selling, or receiving a stolen vehicle; and directed U.S. Customs to spot-check vehicles and containers leaving the country.

To carry out the study mandate of the 1992 legislation, the attorney general directed the National

**Figure 15-9** Components Requiring Marking

(**Source:** Courtesy 3M Corporation)

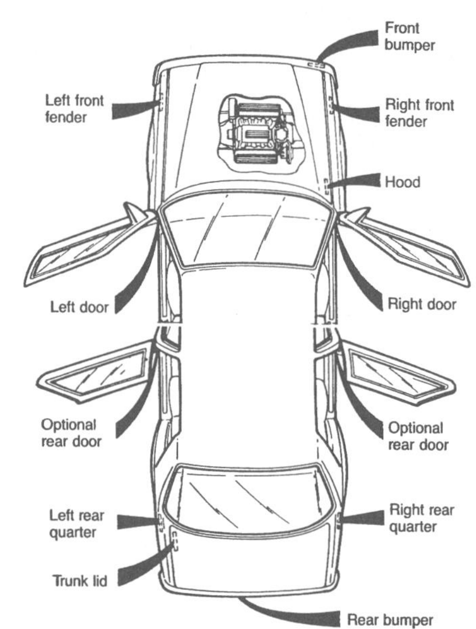

**Figure 15-10** Original- and Replacement-Part Labels for Selected Manufacturers

(**Source:** Courtesy 3M Corporation)

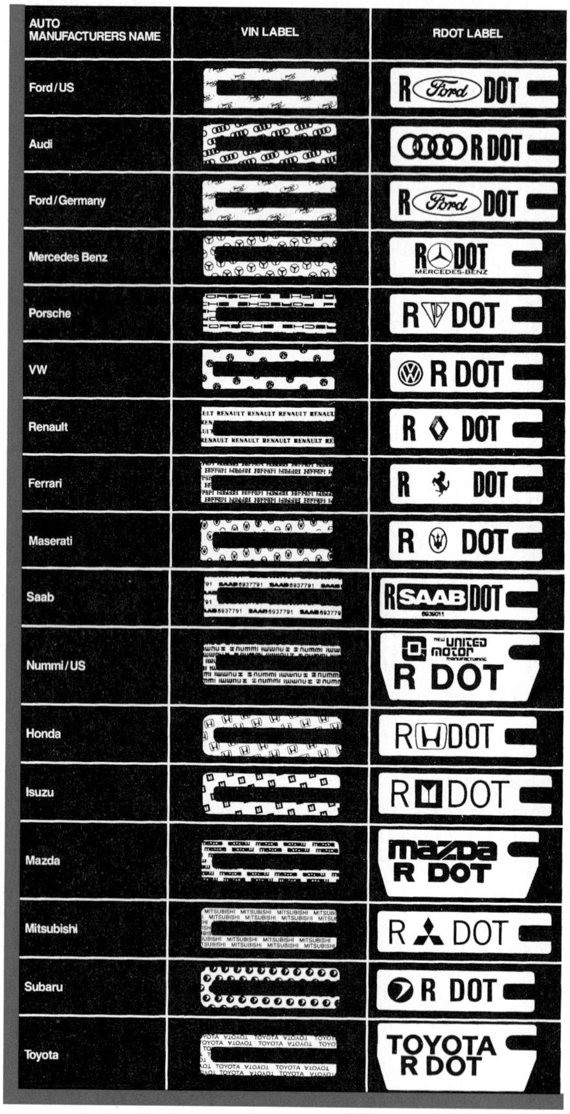

| AUTO MANUFACTURERS NAME | VIN LABEL | RDOT LABEL |
|---|---|---|
| Ford/US | | R Ford DOT |
| Audi | | R DOT |
| Ford/Germany | | R Ford DOT |
| Mercedes Benz | | R DOT MERCEDES-BENZ |
| Porsche | | R DOT |
| VW | | R DOT |
| Renault | | R DOT |
| Ferrari | | R DOT |
| Maserati | | R DOT |
| Saab | | R SAAB DOT |
| Nummi/US | | NEW UNITED MOTOR MANUFACTURING R DOT |
| Honda | | R DOT |
| Isuzu | | R DOT |
| Mazda | | mazda R DOT |
| Mitsubishi | | R DOT |
| Subaru | | R DOT |
| Toyota | | TOYOTA R DOT |

Institute of Justice to commission a study on the effectiveness of the parts-marking program. Attorney Janet Reno issued her report in the summer of 2000. The report concluded that the available evidence warrants application of the parts-marking standard to all motor vehicle lines. The decision was, in large measure, based on estimates and the absence of negative information. The study estimated that parts marking costs manufacturers about $5 per vehicle.[25] The study also concluded that between 33 and 158 fewer cars are stolen per 100,000 marked cars because of parts marking.[26] The research was unable to establish whether antitheft devices installed in vehicles were an effective alternative to parts marking.[27]

Manufacturers urged the attorney general not to expand the program, but the attorney general listened to law enforcement investigators who identified four ways that parts marking provides assistance. First, thieves often remove, alter, or obliterate the VIN plate and other numbers, but as long as one part number remains intact, the vehicle can be identified; this enables the owner to be identified and facilitates proving that the vehicle was stolen and securing an arrest. Second, auto theft investigators in many jurisdictions have been given authority to seize parts or vehicles when markings have been removed or destroyed. Third, the absence of markings causes investigators to inquire further and such investigations often lead to larger stolen-vehicle cases. Fourth, in jurisdictions requiring inspections of rebuilt vehicles prior to issuing a new certificate of title, a determination can be made as to whether stolen parts are being used in the rebuilding process.[28]

## VIN Editing and Reconstruction

In any investigation, even when it appears that the VIN has not been altered or defaced, it is incumbent on the investigator to check the validity of the identifying numbers. Using the worksheet in Figure 15–5 will only verify the correctness of the check digit as compared with and calculated from the other 16 characters. A VIN edit computer program available at many law enforcement agencies and state motor vehicle regulatory offices can readily determine if the entered VIN is "good." If the VIN is invalid, computer programs can analyze the available information and at least narrow the valid possibilities of a correct VIN. Such programs replace what formerly was a long drawn-out manual process accomplished by checking manufacturers' records. VINASSIST, available from NICB, is one such program and is currently being used by 7,000 insurers and law enforcement agencies. As noted earlier, the program edits, evaluates, and corrects vehicle identification numbers.

## VIN Restoration

The restoration of manufacturers' serial numbers altered or obliterated from metal is a process that can be performed by an investigator with the proper material at hand. There is no mystery involved in number restoration as long as the investigator is willing to do the necessary preparation and has the patience to await results that are often slow in developing.

When a die is struck on metal, the molecules beneath the die are compressed and it is on these compressed molecules that the restoration mediums are applied. The type of metal surface will dictate which of the three primary methods of restoration—heat, acid, or acid and electricity—should be used. In the heat process an oxygen-acetylene torch is used on cast iron only. An electrolytic process in which 5 to 6 volts of electricity at 2 to 3 amps are used in conjunction with a solution of hydrochloric acid is generally used on steel. For the etching of aluminum, one solution of potassium hydroxide and a second solution of hydrochloric acid and mercuric chloride are applied using a cotton or fiberglass swab.

Regardless of which type of surface is involved and which restoration process is used, the surface must be painstakingly prepared. All paint, oil, grease, or other foreign matter must first be removed by using any solution that will work, including paint remover or acetone. The surface is not to be scraped with a wire brush, knife, or any other tool, since one major purpose of preparation is to eliminate scratches and grind marks. Depending on how badly the surface is defaced, it may need to be polished with emery paper, a mill file, or a high-speed sanding or polishing disk to remove scratches or gouges. Polishing the surface to a mirrorlike finish is desirable. Sometimes careful preparation of the surface will make all or some of the numbers visible.

Documenting the surface before beginning the restoration process is advisable. This can be done by photographing the area to be restored, dulling the shine with the use of fingerprint powder or carbon paper, and then taking a tape lift of the area (similar to lifting a fingerprint from a metal surface) and/or making a large-scale drawing of the area. It is always advisable to check with the manufacturer to ascertain the structure of the numbers used on a factory identification number if it is not already known. For example, the investigator should ask whether O's are rounded or squared and if 3's have rounded or flat tops. Such information can assist the investigator in determining whether visible numbers are valid.

If the heat process is to be used on cast iron, the ignited torch should be slowly moved back and forth over the area to be processed and gradually brought closer to the surface in a manner that will not crack the block. When the top of the blue cone of the flame is being moved back and forth about half an inch above the surface, the surface will soon reach a cherry-red color. When that happens, the torch should gradually be drawn away from the surface until it is about 6 inches away, all the while being slowly moved back and forth. After the surface has cooled, it should be very lightly polished with emery paper to remove the carbon deposits. The restored numbers should show up as a lighter color than the surrounding metal. If no numbers appear, either too much of the metal was removed and restoration will not produce results or the surface was not heated to a high-enough temperature, in which case the process should be repeated.

In the electrolytic process of restoring numbers on steel, two pieces of number 12 or 14 braided wire, 18 to 24 inches in length with alligator clips attached to the ends, along with a 6- or 12-volt battery, are needed. Direct current may be used if a battery is not convenient. One wire should be connected to the positive pole, with the other end grounded somewhere near the area to be restored. The other wire, connected to the negative pole, should have a swab dipped in acid solution attached to the other end; the swab should be moved one way only over the surface until any numbers are restored. The acid, speeded by the electricity, eats the surrounding metal surface until the numbers (if not totally destroyed) are revealed. In this and all acid processing techniques, drawings or sketches should be made as individual numbers or letters are revealed because they may fade before more heavily ground characters are restored. Once the process is completed, the surface should be neutralized with water, dried, and coated with oil to prevent rust. In using any acid, good ventilation is imperative.

Good ventilation is also necessary in the acid process of restoring numbers on aluminum. Using potassium hydroxide solution and a swab, the surface area should be brushed in one direction for about 1 minute. The surface should be dried and brushed with a solution of hydrochloric acid and mercuric chloride in the same direction for 2 minutes. The surface should be dried again. This process constitutes one application. Often results will appear after two to four applications, but repeated applications may be made as often as necessary.[29]

## STOLEN-VEHICLE INDICATORS

The thorough investigator will become suspicious enough from the presence of the indicators listed below to pursue an investigation to determine if auto theft has occurred.

### Condition of Vehicle

Conditions such as the following may indicate that a vehicle is stolen:

- Missing or damaged ignition locks.
- Damaged doors, glove compartments, and trunks.
- Broken or missing door glass, particularly vent glass.
- Vehicle operated without lights at night.
- Vehicle being pushed or towed at night.
- Pry marks around windows, doors, glove compartment, or trunk.
- Vehicle parked or hidden in remote area.
- Missing parts, such as wheels, engine, or transmission.
- Missing accessories, such as radio, spare tire, or airbag.
- Vehicle illegally parked or abandoned long enough to accumulate dirt or debris under the wheels.
- Vehicle contains bullet holes.
- Vehicle used in other crimes.
- Windows open in inclement weather.
- Components such as four-speed transmission, bucket seats, or high-performance engine from a late-model vehicle on an older model.
- Vehicle showing evidence of having been lived in.
- Vehicle abandoned at the scene of an accident.
- Vehicle parked with engine running and no one around it.
- Vehicle with a new- or used-car lot identification number or sticker on it.
- Vehicle with license plates bent down, covered, or fastened with wire or vehicle with new bolts on old plates, or vice versa.
- Vehicle with nonmatching front and rear plates.
- Impacted insects on rear license plates.
- Out-of-state plates attached with a local dealer's license plate holder.
- Loose VIN plate or one showing evidence of tampering, such as scratches or different-style letters or numbers.
- VIN plate held by rivets that are loose or of the wrong type.
- Repainted VIN plate.
- Loose dashboard or loose ignition switch.
- Keys not original factory issue.
- Chisel or pull marks on ignition switch.
- Federal certification label tampered with or missing, or the VIN on the label does not match the plate on the dash.

### Suspicious Driver Behavior

Any of the following suspicious acts by a driver may be indications that a vehicle is stolen:

- The driver seems extremely nervous or attempts to avoid police vehicles.
- The driver appears unfamiliar with the operation of the vehicle.
- The driver is wearing gloves in warm weather.
- The driver leaves a service station without paying for gasoline.
- The driver has little or no regard for the property of others or for the vehicle.
- The driver does not fit the vehicle. Usually a vehicle reflects its owner's economic status and his or her personal characteristics.
- The driver attempts to escape from minor traffic violations.

## INVESTIGATION OF FRAUD CASES

The investigation of fraud cases is not unlike the investigation of other types of offenses. In the fraud case, the investigator should consider working very closely with any special investigative unit personnel available through an insurance company that may be involved in the case. Generally, the investigation of a motor vehicle fraudulent insurance claim case will center around questions involving the insured, the insurance policy, identification information on the vehicle, the police report, the status of the certificate of title, the condition of the vehicle, and any unusual conditions surrounding the claim.

The investigator should obtain all information and supporting documents regarding the purchase and possession of the vehicle and all the circumstances surrounding the alleged loss. It is important to determine whether the VIN on the stolen vehicle is consistent with the make and model and whether the VIN is, in fact, one that has been assigned to a manufactured vehicle. To determine the existence of and the condition of vehicles reported stolen, it is important that the investigator contact prior owners, lienholders, and insurers to verify information received on the reported loss. When information on a reported loss is supplied to a law enforcement agency, is any of the information inconsistent with the facts determined in the investigation? If the investigation centers on a possibly inflated theft loss, questions asked of people potentially having information should be directed to the condition of the vehicle immediately before the reported loss.

With only slight modification or expansion, the list of vehicle theft fraud indicators below can apply equally to accident and damage fraud cases, commercial vehicle theft fraud, false-vehicle claims, inflated-theft-loss frauds, and even some vehicle arson cases. At the very least, the profile indicators can serve as an excellent foundation for beginning an investigation.

## Indicators of Fraud Concerning the Insured

- Insured has lived at current address less than six months.
- Insured has been with current employer less than six months.
- Insured's address is a post office box or mail drop.
- Insured does not have a telephone.
- Insured's listed number is a mobile or cellular phone.
- Insured is difficult to contact.
- Insured frequently changes his or her address and/or phone number.
- Insured's place of contact is a hotel, tavern, or other place that is neither his or her place of employment nor his or her place of residence.
- Insured conducts all business in person, does not use mails.
- Insured is unemployed.
- Insured claims to be self-employed but is vague about the business and actual responsibilities.
- Insured has recent or current marital and/or financial problems.
- Insured has a temporary, recently issued, or out-of-state driver's license.
- Insured's driver's license has recently been suspended.
- Insured recently called to confirm and/or increase coverage.
- Insured has an accumulation of parking tickets on vehicle.
- Insured is unusually aggressive and pressures for quick settlement.
- Insured is very knowledgeable about claims process and insurance terminology.
- Insured's income is not compatible with value of insured vehicle.
- Insured is behind in loan payments on vehicle and/or other financial obligations.
- Insured avoids meetings with investigators.
- Insured cancels scheduled appointments for statements and/or examination under oath.
- Insured has a previous history of vehicle theft claims.

## Indicators of Fraud Related to the Vehicle

- Vehicle was purchased for cash with no bill of sale or proof of ownership.
- Vehicle is a new or late model with no lienholder.
- Vehicle was very recently purchased.
- Vehicle was not seen for an extended period of time prior to the reported theft.
- Vehicle was purchased out of state.
- Vehicle has a history of mechanical problems.
- Vehicle is a "gas guzzler."
- Vehicle is customized, classic, and/or antique.
- Vehicle displayed "for sale" signs prior to theft.
- Vehicle was recovered clinically or carefully stripped.

- Vehicle is parked on street although garage is available.
- Vehicle was recovered stripped, but insured wants to retain salvage and repair appears to be impractical.
- Vehicle is recovered by the insured or a friend.
- Vehicle purchase price was exceptionally high or low.
- Vehicle was recovered with old or recent damage, and coverage was high-deductible or no-collision coverage.
- Vehicle has an incorrect VIN (e.g., not originally manufactured, inconsistent with model).
- Vehicle VIN is different from VIN appearing on the title.
- Vehicle VIN provided to police is incorrect.
- Federal vehicle safety certification label is altered or missing.
- Federal vehicle safety certification label displays different VIN than that displayed on vehicle.
- Vehicle has theft and/or salvage history.
- Vehicle is recovered with no ignition or steering lock damage.
- Vehicle was previously involved in a major collision.
- Vehicle is late model with extremely high mileage (exceptions: taxi, police, utility vehicles).
- Vehicle is older model with exceptionally low mileage (i.e., odometer rollover or rollback).
- Vehicle is older or inexpensive model and insured indicates it was equipped with expensive accessories that cannot be substantiated with receipts.
- Vehicle is recovered stripped or burned or sustained severe collision damage within a short time after loss allegedly occurred.
- Vehicle is a leased vehicle with excessive mileage for which the insured would have been liable under the mileage limitation agreement.

## Indicators of Fraud Related to Coverage

- Loss occurs within one month of issue or expiration of the policy.
- Loss occurs after cancellation notice was sent to insured.
- Insurance premium was paid in cash.
- Coverage is for minimum liability with full comprehensive coverage on late model and/or expensive vehicle.
- Coverage was recently increased.

## Indicators of Fraud Related to Reporting

- Police report has not been made by insured or has been delayed.
- No report or claim is made to insurance carrier within one week after theft.
- Neighbors, friends, and family are not aware of loss.
- Title is junk, salvage, out-of-state, photocopied, or duplicated.
- Title history shows nonexistent addresses.
- Repair bills are consecutively numbered, or dates show work accomplished on weekends or holidays.
- An individual, rather than a bank or financial institution, is named as the lienholder.

## Other General Indicators of Vehicle Theft Fraud

- Vehicle is towed to isolated yard at owner's request.
- Salvage yard or repair garage takes unusual interest in claim.
- Information concerning prior owner is unavailable.
- Prior owner cannot be located.
- Vehicle is recovered totally burned after theft.
- Fire damage is inconsistent with loss description.
- VINs were removed prior to fire.
- Vehicle is alleged to have been stolen before titling and registration, and insured presents an assigned title that is still in the name of the previous owner as his or her proof of ownership.
- Appraiser had difficulty getting into body shop to view and estimate damage.
- Insurance agent did not view the vehicle before or at the time of issuing the policy.

- The last-known driver of a commercial vehicle is no longer employed by the owner, and the owner is unable to provide the driver's job application or any other identification.
- The history of a commercial vehicle shows many sale-ownership transactions that reflect low purchase prices compared to the stated value of the vehicle.
- Loss (theft) of a commercial vehicle occurred in an area not frequently traveled by the owner or driver or outside the scheduled route.
- The odometer on a recovered vehicle has been smashed to conceal high mileage.
- The insured or claimant is reluctant to provide the name of a previous insurance carrier.
- The insured or claimant does not call the police to the scene of a major accident but, rather, goes to the police station and makes an over-the-counter report.
- The insured is overly enthusiastic or candid about taking the blame for an accident.
- A phantom (not identified) vehicle caused the accident.
- The insured's or claimant's vehicle is not repaired locally but is driven or shipped out of state for repair.
- The reported accident occurred on private property near the residence(s) of those involved.[30]

## INVESTIGATION OF VEHICLE FIRES

Along with the general increase in crimes in the United States has come an increase in automobile fires. Many of the criminal fires occur when stolen vehicles have been stripped of valuable parts and the rest burnt to destroy the evidence. However, as in other fire investigations, the investigator first must eliminate natural and accidental causes of fire. Investigators who make unsubstantiated remarks about the origin of fires can damage their own and possible suspects' reputations.

### Inspection of Salvage

Before beginning the physical investigation of a vehicle fire scene, the investigator must understand that the crime scene examination includes both the vehicle and the area in which it was burned. Hence, the investigation must follow established principles by first recording the scene. Photographs should be taken immediately, before there is any disturbance of the crime scene. Measurements must be taken to establish the exact location of the vehicle in relationship to fixed objects, crossroads, houses, and so on. A description should be recorded of the terrain, nearby roadways, and weather conditions, including prevailing wind directions.

The successful investigation of automobile fire losses originates with basic lines of inquiry. First an inspection of the salvage must be completed for information on the origin and possible motive for the fire; second, an investigation must be made of the car owner for evidence of intent, motive, and opportunity; third, witnesses who might have information must be questioned; and last, the owner must be questioned to establish his or her knowledge of the fire and to verify information.

***External Inspection*** A thorough search should be made of the area for tire-tread marks, footprints, cans, bottles, other containers, unusual residue or materials, old tires, matches, or any other item that may be related to the case. Samples should be taken of soil, which may contain evidence of flammable liquids. When found, each item should be photographed before being moved, and then it should be properly packaged and marked as evidence.

***Internal Inspection*** Generally investigators inspect the burnt automobile before contacting the owner, and the inspection is made as soon after the fire as possible. The inspection starts where the fire apparently originated. In accidental fires, this will normally be the part of the vehicle that is the most badly damaged from the intensity of the heat. Accidental fires usually spread in diminishing degree from the point of origin according to prevailing conditions. Conditions include direction and velocity of wind and/or materials on which flames feed, such as gasoline in the tank, woodwork, or other similarly flammable parts of the vehicle. When there are significant variations in these patterns, arson emerges as a possibility. Arson fires started with flammable materials usually show intense heat in more than one place. The investigator should carefully note the extent of the fire and its path. This information may prove valuable in the later questioning of the owner or witnesses.

The car also should be inspected for the removal of equipment such as stereo, heater, air horns, fog lights, and so forth. Notice should also be made of other irregularities such as old tires on new cars or missing spare tires.

## Inspection of the Fuel System

***The Gas Tank*** The investigator should determine whether the cap to the gas tank was in place at the time of the fire. Sometimes gasoline to start the fire is siphoned from the tank and the cap is carelessly left off. If the cap is blown off, it will show effects of an explosion. The drain plug in the bottom of the tank should be checked. In addition, if it was removed or loosened before the fire, there might be evidence of fresh tool marks, especially pliers marks, on it.

***The Gas Lines*** The gas lines should be examined for breaks between the tank and the fuel pump. Breaks should be examined for tool marks. Some arsonists disconnect the line below the tank to obtain gasoline to start the fire and fail to replace the line.

***The Fuel Pump*** Gasoline to start the fire is sometimes obtained by disconnecting the line from the fuel pump and running the starter. If the fuel pump is melted, there should be evidence of fire on the sidepans. If the fuel pump was disconnected to allow the gasoline to run out and then be set on fire, there may be carbon deposits inside the gas line at the fuel pump.

The investigator should establish whether parts of the fuel pump are missing. If key parts of the fuel system are missing and the owner says that the vehicle was running at the time of the fire, then there is strong reason to suspect arson. This is true regardless of whether the vehicle is equipped with a mechanical pump in a low-pressure carbureted system or an electric pump in a high-pressure fuel-injected system.

## Inspection of the Electrical System

A short circuit in the electric wiring is the most common excuse offered for automobile fires. The chances of a modern automobile's burning up from a short in the wiring are negligible. Engineers have virtually eliminated this hazard. If a fire in fact did start from malfunctions in the electrical system, there generally is enough evidence to substantiate it.

The wires near where the fire started should be inspected. If the wires are not melted completely, a short can be located. A short melts the strands of wire apart and causes small beads of melted wire to form on the ends. Wires that are burnt in two have sharp points. If the fire started in an electrical system, the system must be close to a flammable substance for the fire to spread. If a fire started from a short while the motor was running, the distributor points will be stuck or fused.

## Inspection of the Motor, Radiator, and Parts under and near the Hood

The only possible place for an accidental fire to start at this location is around the fuel pump or carburetor and at the wiring. Any evidence of a fire on the front lower part of the motor not attributable to these parts indicates the use of flammables. If lead is melted from any lower or outside seams of the radiator, this is strong evidence of flammables. The fan belt does not usually burn in an accidental fire.

Gasoline on the motor sometimes causes the rubber cushions for the front of the motor to show evidence of fire. This evidence does not occur in accidental fires.

The radiator should also be checked. A badly burnt lower right corner indicates that the gas line from the fuel pump to the carburetor was disconnected, the starter was run to pump out gasoline through the fuel pump, and then the gasoline was set on fire.

## Inspection of the Body

The body of the car is usually so badly burnt as to afford little evidence. However, signs of the intensity of heat sometimes point to the use of an inflammable. An excessive amount of flammable material may run through the floor of the car and burn underneath, causing oil or gasoline soot to form on the underside of the car. An examination should be made for this soot. If the hood was raised during the fire, the paint on the top panels may be blistered but not be burnt off where the two panels touched. If the wind was blowing from the rear of the car to the front, the paint should be burnt for almost the length of the hood; the radiator core will be burnt; but there will not have been enough fire at the rear of the car to do much damage to the gasoline tank. If the paint on the hood is burnt only an inch or so from the rear toward the front, this would indicate that the wind was blowing from the front of the car toward the rear, in which case the gasoline tank may be badly damaged but the radiator will be intact.

### CONTACT WITH OWNERS

Before interviewing the owner of the car, the investigator should determine as completely as possible the character of the owner. This information may prove quite useful during the interview. The importance of preplanning the interview cannot be overemphasized. The more facts the investigator has available, the greater the probability of a successful clearance or later conviction.

Information should be obtained from the owner about the details of the purchase, such as date, cost, trade-in, down payment, amount of mortgage due, payments past due, name of salesperson, and so forth. The investigator should also inquire about the general condition of the car at the time of the fire and ask about defects, mileage, presence or absence of unusual equipment, and recent repairs.[31]

## PREVENTION PROGRAMS

Each year new and innovative approaches to the prevention and detection of crime and the apprehension of offenders are developed. Some of these are related to investigative techniques, whereas others are high-tech equipment developments that are designed to reduce the vehicle theft problem or assist law enforcement officers in their efforts. Other strategies are available to reduce the incidence of fraud.

### AUTO THEFT

Law enforcement officers and agencies in a number of jurisdictions now rely on integrated communications and computer networks of the FBI, state, and local police to identify and locate stolen vehicles. One unique system uses a small device called a micromaster, which is installed at random in a vehicle's electrical system. The micromaster is a microprocessor-controlled transceiver with its own unique code.

If a vehicle is stolen, the owner reports the theft to the local police in the usual way. The owner also tells the police that the vehicle is equipped with a micromaster. The police then announce through normal channels and the National Crime Information Center that a micromaster-equipped vehicle has been stolen. A computer then activates a transmitter that sends a signal with the stolen vehicle's own code. (The present system can manage up to 8 billion discrete micromaster codes.) The signal activates the micromaster's transceiver; it starts sending a signal identifying it as a stolen vehicle. The activation and tracking of the micromaster signal is under the control of law enforcement authorities. They have a homing device that gives them information about the location of the car. The system also allows police officers to identify micromaster signals and determine whether the stolen car has been involved in a crime.[32] Some of these tracking systems rely on signal relay towers, while others use a satellite-enhanced global positioning system (GPS) method of tracking. The law enforcement vehicles are equipped with tracking computers that bring up street maps that pinpoint location and direction of travel within very close proximity.

Many vehicles are now being manufactured with antitheft locks, starter disengagement systems (called ignition kill switches), and various other devices in an attempt to reduce the attractiveness of a particular model to the thief. Some of these are models that qualify for the black-box exemption to the labeling standards established under the guidelines of the Motor Vehicle Theft Law Enforcement Act of 1984.

In recent years, a number of private concerns have begun marketing antitheft devices that can be used effectively on older vehicles. It should be noted at the outset that no device can absolutely prevent motor vehicle theft, and one should look askance at any product or brand of product that is represented to be an absolute theft preventive.

Theft deterrent devices are of two types—passive or active. With a **passive system,** the driver does not need to do anything to activate the system, though he/she may be required to do something to deactivate the system. An **active system** requires that the operator do something every time the vehicle is driven or parked.

Audible alarm systems may be either passive or active and may be effective if anyone pays attention when an alarm is activated. Because some systems activate easily when someone passes the vehicle, a strong wind blows, or lightning strikes half a mile

**A Collar Affixed to a Steering Column**

Many innovative approaches to the prevention of vehicle theft are developed each year. Some involve high-tech equipment, while others are built to "harden the target" or make the particular vehicle less desirable to a thief. One such example is a collar constructed of steel or alloy, used to deter penetration of the steering column bowl.

(Courtesy Citizens for Auto-Theft Responsibility—C.A.R., Inc.)

away, many people pay little attention, beyond a passing glance, to a vehicle with an alarm blaring. Escape from the vicinity of the noise is more important than determining if a theft is occurring. The alarms are treated more as an annoyance than as a theft deterrent.

A boot is an active device installed under a front tire that prevents the vehicle from being moved until the boot is removed. Other active devices can key lock the transmission or the brakes.

"Collars," which are usually constructed of steel or an alloy, deter penetration of the steering column bowl associated with the General Motors and Chrysler "Saginaw steering column" (see photo). Passive collars are generally recommended over those that require driver interaction.

Many communities have instituted decal "alert" programs that provide decals for vehicles registered with the local law enforcement agency and authorize any law enforcement officer to stop the vehicle and question the driver if the vehicle is observed on the streets during certain hours (such as 2 A.M. to 6 A.M.).

A fuel shut-off device, which blocks the fuel line, may be activated by removal of the ignition key or by the throwing of a switch.

A case-hardened steering-column ignition lock that cannot be removed using a conventional slide hammer or lock puller can be effective, as can a case-hardened steel protective cap that fits over the ignition lock to prevent extraction of the ignition lock cylinder. The cap fastens to a steel collar that fits around the steering post and over the ignition lock. The ignition key fits through a slot in the cap.

Several manufacturers install a microchip or transponder in the ignition key that must be electronically read when inserted into the ignition in order for the vehicle to start. Early versions of some of these systems had only a few combinations, which could easily be defeated if a thief could procure a set of masters with all the combinations. However, General Motors' PASS-KEY III and Ford's Passive Anti-Theft System (PATS), as well as the newer systems on many other domestic and foreign-made brands, use much more advanced and sophisticated electronic systems that are deterring theft.

A steel or alloy post, rod, or collar may attach to the steering wheel, which can be extended and locked in place. The device prevents the steering wheel from making full rotations. This type of active device can be an effective deterrent to theft if used properly, but it is ineffective if the operator of the vehicle forgets or considers it an inconvenience to install it each time the vehicle is left unattended.

VIN etching is a process that helps identify vehicles recovered by the police after a theft has occurred. As noted earlier, thieves often attempt to conceal the identity of stolen vehicles by grinding numbers. When the VIN is permanently etched, using acid, on all the vehicle's windows, the identifying numbers are often overlooked by the thief or

**Figure 15-11**

The Layered Approach

(**Source:** Courtesy National Insurance Crime Bureau)

**1 LOCATION**

| City population | Points |
|---|---|
| Over 250,000 | 8 |
| 250,000 to 100,001 | 6 |
| 100,000 to 50,001 | 4 |
| 50,000 to 10,000 | 2 |
| Under 10,000 | 0 |

**2 VEHICLE STYLE**

| Vehicle owned | Points |
|---|---|
| Sports car | 5 |
| Luxury car | 4 |
| Sport-utility | 4 |
| Sedan | 3 |
| Passenger van | 1 |
| Station wagon | 0 |

**3 VEHICLE AGE**

| Age of vehicle | Points |
|---|---|
| 0 to five years | 1 |
| Six to eight years | 2 |
| Nine-plus years | 0 |

**4 BONUS POINT**

Add 1 point to your score if you live near an international port or border.

Your score tells how many layers of protection your vehicle needs. For example, if your vehicle scored a 4, the chance of theft is considered low and it should have a first layer of protection. If your vehicle scored a 12, it should have first, second and third layers. The scores:

**Layer 1 (0 to 4 points)**

**Common sense**—Remove keys from the ignition, lock the doors, close all windows, park in lighted areas.

**Layer 2 (5 to 10 points)**

**Visible or audible deterrent**—Steering wheel locks, steering column collars, theft-deterrent decals, tire locks, window etching.

**Layer 3 (11 to 14 points)**

**Visible immobilizer**— Smart keys, fuse cutoffs, kill switches, and starter, ignition or fuel disablers.

**Layer 4 (15 to 16 points)**

**Tracking systems**

require that the thief remove all the window glass to prevent identification, a major task a thief may not be willing to undertake.

Some programs focus on the responsibilities of vehicle owners to do their part in preventing vehicle theft. The Michigan affiliate of the American Automobile Association implements a law providing that if a car is stolen and the keys are anywhere in the passenger compartment, the owner, in addition to absorbing his or her insurance deductible, also absorbs an extra $500 plus 10 percent of the value of the vehicle. The total amount is deducted from the amount of the insurance payment made on the theft loss claim. The responsibilities of owners are also reflected in a survey initiated by the NICB that consists of scoring answers to some questions and taking necessary preventive actions on the basis of the total score. This is called a layered approach to theft deterrence (see Figure 15–11).

Some other prevention techniques include the following:

- If a lighter receptacle is used for a radio, telephone, or radar detector, remove the item when leaving the vehicle and reinsert the lighter. Thieves look for empty receptacles.
- Always lock the vehicle and remove the keys.
- Lock valuables in the trunk. Do not leave personal identification or credit cards in the vehicle.
- Do not leave a vehicle running while unattended.
- Photocopy registration and insurance papers and carry them on your person, not in the glove compartment.
- Park in a garage or in a well-lighted, heavily traveled area.
- When parking at a curb, turn the wheels toward the curb and use the emergency brake. This makes the vehicle harder to steal.
- Do not hide spare keys in or on the vehicle.
- Write the name of the owner and the VIN in crayon under the hood and in the trunk.
- Drop business cards down window channels into door interiors. This will make later identification easier.

Theft of vehicles from new- and used-car dealers is not a new phenomenon. Sometimes the dealership knows a vehicle is missing, such as when a vehicle taken on a test drive is not returned. Other times, if an inventory is large, a vehicle may be stolen overnight and not missed for several days. Key control is an essential crime prevention practice for a dealership. Keys should be kept in a locked cabinet with only a few people having access. Keys that are out for demonstration or sales purposes must be monitored. Customers should never be allowed to test-drive a vehicle without a salesperson going along. Display lots should be well lighted, and barriers should be erected that permit access and good observation from outside but are sufficient to deter theft at night and when the dealership is closed. Officers who are familiar with the concepts of crime prevention through environmental design should be consulted.

## CAR RENTALS

Car rental companies are generally knowledgeable about motor vehicle theft and techniques of prevention, but an investigator would be wise to understand some basics. In daily rental, the company is handing over the keys of a car to a person no one in the company has seen before or knows anything about. The rental agreement should be completely filled out, and the picture and information on the renter's driver's license should be carefully checked to make sure it matches the description of the person to whom the vehicle is being rented.

Rental companies generally require a credit card even for a cash rental. This not only serves as a good indication that the customer is a responsible person but also helps ensure that the contract will be paid. The employee of the rental company should make sure the credit card is current and check it against the driver's license to make sure the same name is on both documents.

Theft of rental vehicles generally occurs when a vehicle is not returned after it has been rented. At least one national rental company is in the process of installing tracking systems, as described earlier, which are traceable using radio-wave or GPS systems.

## HEAVY EQUIPMENT AND FARM EQUIPMENT

Tiny transponders that act as identification devices are now available. The device can be glued anywhere on the vehicle. Some agencies are experimenting with injecting the transponder into tires of construction or farm equipment. If attempts are made to completely conceal or alter a stolen vehicle's identity, a receiver can accurately distinguish the vehicle from all others.

Owners of construction and farm equipment are also encouraged to take the following actions:

- Use security devices such as ignition locks, stabilizer arm locks, and fuel shut-off valves.
- Record all product identification numbers, and participate in equipment identification programs.
- Photograph all equipment, paying particular attention to unique features such as dents, decals, and scratches, to aid in later identification.
- Leave equipment in well-lighted and fenced areas at job sites and equipment yards. Lock farm equipment in a secure building or an enclosed area that is kept locked.
- Know the location of all construction and farm equipment at all times.
- Keep law enforcement informed about where equipment is located and how long it will be maintained in a particular location.
- Take extra precaution on weekends. Most equipment thefts occur between 6 P.M. on Friday and 6 A.M. on Monday.
- Do not leave keys in any equipment that uses keys, and lock all machines that can be locked when not in use.
- Immediately report suspicious activity, such as a stranger taking photographs of equipment, to law enforcement officials.

Other methods of reducing or preventing theft of off-road equipment are available. Programs are available through private enterprise whereby heavy equipment can be registered, with each piece being assigned its own identification number. The equipment is "decaled" with its own number welded on at several locations. Should a law enforcement officer become suspicious, the dispatcher can call a toll-free number and remain on the line as the company calls the owner to verify the location of the equipment.

## FRAUD

The prevention of fraud can best be accomplished by knowing some things about the insured and about the vehicle. "Know your insured" is always sound advice for an insurance agent. Getting good identification on the person, learning why the person selected a particular agent or agency, and finding out how the insured learned of the agent or agency can all be useful in helping to determine whether the act of insuring is legitimate. Knowing about the insured vehicle is equally important in the fight against fraud.

Perhaps the most profound fraud prevention effort ever initiated is the preinsurance inspection program, particularly when photographs are required. Deceptively simple in concept and application, it is amazing that fewer than half a dozen states have even considered, much less adopted, mandatory legislation. The concept requires that before a vehicle can be insured, it must be physically inspected by a representative or an agent acting on behalf of the insurer.

A simple inspection requirement can immediately eliminate or substantially reduce two of the most prolific tactics in committing insurance fraud. First, it virtually eliminates the false-vehicle theft, which is normally based on insuring a "paper," or "phantom," car—in other words, a vehicle that does not exist—and subsequently reporting it stolen in order to file against and recover on an insurance policy. Second, a well-written preinsurance report can substantially reduce fraudulent claims about theft of expensive equipment on a vehicle or claims that damage actually present before issuance of the policy occurred when the substandard vehicle either was involved in a reported accident or was stolen.

Photographs supporting an inspection report make the program particularly effective, and color photographs are even more revealing. Photographs can show the exact condition of a vehicle at the time a policy was issued so as to dispel fraudulent damage claims filed later. It is recommended that at least two photographs be taken from diagonal corners so that one picture shows the front and one side of the vehicle and the other photo shows the rear and other side. These two photos will eliminate false damage claims, but there remains the question of proving that the photos are of the insured vehicle and not simply one of the same year, make, and model. To resolve this concern, a few of the jurisdictions having inspection programs require that a third photograph be taken of the federal motor vehicle safety certification label (often called the EPA label), which is usually found on the left door. This label contains, among other information, the vehicle identification number, which, as noted earlier, is the specific identifier for that vehicle as distinguished from all other vehicles; this reverifies the number contained in the written report, thus avoiding or explaining inadvertent omissions or accidental transposition of numbers.

An inexpensive instant-developing camera and film can be used for the program. In 1977, New York became the first state to enact legislation mandating photographic inspection prior to the issuance of insurance policies. The program initially required that two photographs be taken from a 180-degree angle, but the law was amended in 1986 to require the third photo of the federal motor vehicle safety certification label. Massachusetts was the next state to adopt a preinsurance inspection program. Legislation followed thereafter in New Jersey and Florida, although not all of these states have equally effective legislatively mandated programs. In addition to these states, two insurance companies have their own photographic inspection programs. Neither GEICO nor State Farm will insure a noninspected vehicle.

Is the program effective? Although it is difficult to measure how much crime (insurance fraud) is deterred by a photo inspection program, it has been estimated that in the state of New York, reduction in costs and in insurance fraud claims has saved well over $100 million, and these savings have been passed on to insurance buyers through premium reductions. Although insurance premiums have not actually been reduced in New York, the overall increase in premiums in that state has amounted to less than half of the national average.[33]

## ODOMETER FRAUD

One of the most costly consumer frauds of modern times is **odometer fraud,** also known by various other names including odometer tampering, rollbacks, and clocking. The National Highway Traffic Safety Administration estimates that over 3 million cars are clocked each year and that the cost of this fraud to American consumers surpasses $3 billion annually.

The most susceptible vehicles to odometer tampering are those that are relatively new with exceptionally high mileage. Of the total number of passenger cars sold in the United States each year, approximately half are sold to car rental or leasing companies or to others for business use. Each year, at least 4 million of these late-model high-mileage cars are replaced. Those that are taken off lease or are no longer used for business purposes find their way into the used-car market.

The reason for odometer rollbacks is to increase the value of used vehicles on the market. Obviously, a car with fewer miles should bring a higher price than one with high mileage. It has been conservatively estimated that on a small or intermediate-size car, the sales value increases $50 for each 1,000 miles that the odometer is set back; in larger vehicles, the value increases to around $65 per 1,000 miles the odometer reading is reduced. Thus, a late-model car that is clocked from 70,000 miles to 30,000 miles can increase its value to the seller by $2,000 to $2,600. This amounts to a nice additional profit for persons inclined to indulge in such deceitful conduct.

Besides the obvious profits to the seller of clocked vehicles, the costs to the purchaser can be even greater in the form of potential unanticipated safety problems and increased repair costs. Since cars are generally the largest purchase made by people after the cost of a home, the condition of a car and the anticipated costs for repair and maintenance figure prominently in the decision of whether to buy a particular car. But when the odometer has been clipped, mileage is not a dependable guide for estimating potential maintenance costs, since such a vehicle will be more costly to maintain and more likely to need expensive repairs. If the purchaser-owner is unable to afford the higher costs, the quality of maintenance and repairs may suffer, along with the safety and roadworthiness of the vehicle.

Because of the proliferation of this fraud, most states have created some type of investigative unit to deal with odometer tampering by accepting complaints from citizens and determining if there is any basis for enforcement action. When examining a late-model low-mileage vehicle that is suspected of being clocked, the investigator should check for extensive wear on the brake pedal, the driver's seat, and the seals around the trunk. Does the extent of wear conform with the claimed mileage? A check should be made for service stickers on the door, on the doorpost, and under the hood. If present, a date and odometer reading may be present; missing stickers may suggest tampering. The odometer wheels should be in alignment, should not rotate freely, and should not be scratched or nicked. Any of these conditions may be indicative of a rollback and warrant further inquiry. The investigator should order a vehicle history file through the state's motor vehicle titling agency and then check with each successive owner (including individuals, dealers, and auctioneers), obtain all odometer disclosure statements, piece together an odometer history, and attempt to determine if there has been a rollback. If a rollback seems likely, the investigator should determine the possessor of the vehicle when it was clocked. Standard investigative techniques should then be applied.

**Title fraud** is as big a part of the odometer rollback problem as is the act of clocking. Title alteration, discarding of title reassignment forms to complicate the tracing of ownership, manufacturing of false reassignments, and title laundering are criminal acts that violators often engage in to support and cover up odometer rollbacks.

To mandate better record keeping, reduce the opportunity for odometer tampering, and assist law enforcement in the investigation of cases, Congress enacted the **Truth in Mileage Act** in 1986. This act, along with amendments made in several subsequent years, attempts to improve the paper trail of odometer readings by requiring more tightly controlled documentation and recording of odometer readings each time ownership of a vehicle changes. The law attempts to close loopholes that permit the inception of fraudulent title schemes and to reduce the incidence of title washing between jurisdictions by requiring all states to adhere to strict record-keeping criteria, thus avoiding schemes to create confusing paper trails that intentionally avoid jurisdictional boundaries of courts and law enforcement agencies.

## MARINE THEFT

### SCOPE OF THE PROBLEM

**Marine theft** is a serious problem to the boating community. It includes the theft of boats, boat trailers, outboard motors, jet skis, and all equipment associated with boating or water activities. Marine theft is a "shadow crime." It is real but difficult to define because of the lack of accurate statistical information. The main reporting mechanism, the Uniform Crime Report (UCR), compiled and reported annually by the Federal Bureau of Investigation, enters the theft of an outboard motor in the burglary index, the theft of a boat trailer in the vehicle file, and other related thefts in different categories. As a result, the magnitude of the marine theft problem is hidden in other crime indexes. Marine insurance theft data are similarly disjointed because there are many types of policies—home owners', business, inland marine, yacht—that provide coverage for marine equipment. Nevertheless, it is estimated that nationwide losses resulting from marine theft exceed $250 million annually.

The majority of thefts occur from homes, businesses, or dry storage facilities. A boat and outboard motor on a boat trailer can be stolen in a matter of seconds by a thief who simply backs up to the trailer, hooks up, and drives away. Although locking mechanisms are available for boat trailers and may deter the amateur thief, such devices are easily overcome by the professional.

Theft by water is accomplished simply by towing the boat away with another boat or by starting the motor and driving away. Boats powered by outboard motors, under 25 horsepower, usually do not have keyed ignition switches. However, even on larger boats, a dozen master keys will start virtually any marine motor, whether outboard or inboard.

Approximately 87 percent of all boats stolen are under 20 feet in length. Of these, boats of 16 feet and less constitute 65 percent of the thefts. The National Crime Information Center reports over 27,000 boat thefts entered into the computer system. Law enforcement experts agree that most thefts are not investigated thoroughly (if at all) because of the difficulty investigators experience understanding marine equipment identification numbers and the lack of available ownership information.

Because of the absence of accurate statistical data, law enforcement is somewhat hampered in its efforts to address the problem. Consequently, there is a general lack of knowledge about marine theft and a resulting lack of commitment of resources to address the problems. In many agencies, marine theft reports are assigned to the auto theft or burglary unit and are treated as low-priority items.

Why are boats stolen? The number-one reason is profit. Marine theft is a high-profit, low-risk crime. Most often a boat, motor, and trailer are stolen and sold as a package at a fair market value. To reduce the possibility of identification, some organized theft rings operate a chop shop, switching stolen motors, trailers, and boats or selling them separately.

There is also a lucrative market for the exportation of stolen outboard motors. In Central and South America, a used outboard motor will sell for more than a new motor in the United States. In addition, as in auto theft, insurance fraud may be involved in 25 percent or more of the reported marine thefts.

The increase in marine theft has often been linked by the media to drug trafficking. Experts tend to disagree. If, in fact, 87 percent of the boats stolen are under 20 feet in length, it is unlikely that these are being used for drug trafficking. Boats 30 feet and longer could very well be involved in drug trafficking, but such thefts constitute only 3 percent of the problem. Of course, larger boats are also targets for professional thieves because of their high value. On the other hand, there may be some legitimate linkage between the theft of outboard motors and the drug problem. A 300-horsepower outboard motor, which retails for over $15,000, can be sold without any ownership documents.

Most small boats are stolen not by professionals but for the personal use of the thief or, occasionally, for joyrides. This is particularly true in the theft of personal watercraft. Approximately 20 percent of all boat thefts involve personal watercraft stolen by juveniles for their own use. Only occasionally are boats stolen to be used as transportation in other crimes, such as burglary of a waterfront home or business.

## HULL IDENTIFICATION

Effective November 1, 1972, the Federal Boating Safety Act of 1971 required boats to have a 12-character **hull identification number (HIN).** Prior to this, boat manufacturers assigned whatever numbers were needed for their own production records. The HIN was subsequently codified by federal regulation. The promotion of boating safety was the original purpose for the HIN. It enabled the U.S. Coast Guard to identify "batches" of boats produced by a manufacturer that failed to meet certain production standards. This consumer protection function soon became secondary after titling and registering authorities began using the HIN assigned to a boat to identify ownership in

**Marine Police on Lookout**
Marine theft, which includes theft of boats, trailers, and all associated equipment, is a serious problem in the boating community. In communities that have extensive waterways, local police often have a marine patrol unit that provides routine patrol and investigates theft of marine equipment.
(© Bonnie Kamin)

much the same manner as the VIN is used for a motor vehicle.

Although manufacturers are required to affix each HIN to the outside of the boat's transom in a "permanent manner" so that any alteration or removal will be evident, in reality this is rarely enforced. Many manufacturers attach the HIN using a plastic plate pop-riveted to the transom. This can be easily removed and replaced with a false HIN. Some manufacturers of fiberglass boats place the HIN on the outer layer of the gelcoat using a "Dymo label"-type device during the molding process. However, this can easily be scraped or gouged out by a thief with a screwdriver or knife. A professional thief will replace the removed HIN with automotive body filler that often matches the color of the gelcoat. Then, by stamping a false HIN into the body filler, it appears that the HIN was affixed by the manufacturer and the alteration often goes undetected. An additional problem occurs when the Coast Guard allows a manufacturer to alter a HIN on any boat that remains in inventory by changing the production dates or model year to reflect a newer model year. Even for an experienced marine investigator, it is difficult to recognize whether a HIN was altered to cover a theft or modified by a manufacturer to reflect a newer model year.

Figure 15–12 shows the three different HIN formats approved by the Coast Guard. The straight-year and model-year formats were used from November 1, 1972, until August 1, 1984, when a new format replaced them. The only differences between the three formats are the last four characters. In the straight-year format, the last four characters reflect the calendar month and year of production. In the model-year format, the ninth character is always the letter "M" followed by the model year and a letter indicating the month of production. The new format, optional on January 1, 1984, and mandatory as of August 1, 1984, uses the ninth and tenth characters to reflect the calendar month and year of production and the eleventh and twelfth characters to represent the model year.

The first three characters of the HIN are the manufacturer's identification code (MIC), assigned to each manufacturer by the Coast Guard. Since 1972, over 13,000 MICs have been assigned. Many codes have been reassigned after the original company went out of business. Because of this, it is very difficult even for the most experienced marine investigator to remain familiar with all the manufacturer's codes. In addition, large conglomerates such as Mercury Marine and Outboard Motor Corporation have purchased many boat manufac-

**Figure 15-12** Hull Identification Number Formats

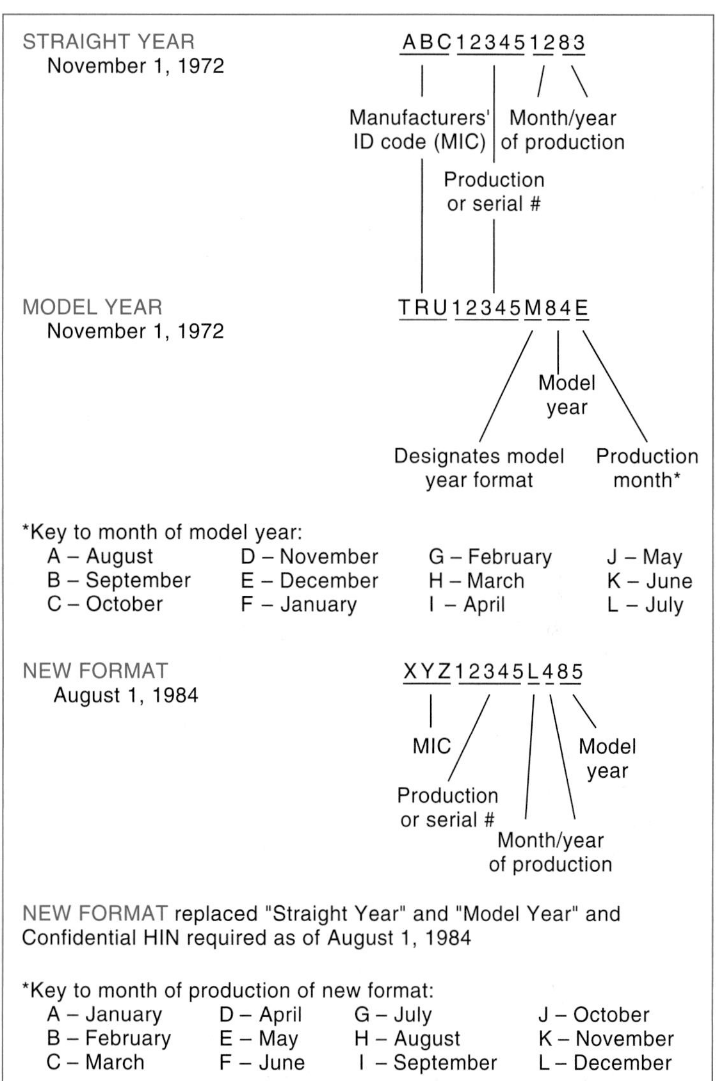


turers and used manufacturer's identification codes assigned to the parent corporation for multiple boat lines.

The middle five characters of the HIN are used as production numbers or serial numbers assigned by the manufacturer. Although the letters "I," "O," and "Q" cannot be used, any other letter can be used in combination with numbers. These "production" numbers can and often are repeated on a monthly basis for an entire year. Whereas the automobile VIN has a 30-year uniqueness and a check digit to avoid unintentional or deliberate omission of numbers and intentional or unintentional transposition of numbers, the HIN does not yet have these features.

## TITLE AND REGISTRATION ISSUES

There are approximately 12 million pleasure boats in the United States. Roughly 160,000 of these are federally registered by the Coast Guard and are referred to as "documented." Ownership and financial disputes over **documented vessels** can be resolved in the federal courts. The remainder of the pleasure boats are registered and/or titled by each state, except Alaska, in which registration issues are regulated by the Coast Guard.

Over 30 states require that boats be titled, but only a few states require the titling of outboard motors. Even in titling states, many boats are exempted by being less than a specified length or powered by less than a specified horsepower of motor. More than half the titling programs are administered by wildlife or natural resource agencies. The remainder are operated by motor vehicle agencies.

Many jurisdictions that title boats do not have computerized ownership records or do not retain the information for more than one year. The boat registration or title files in only a few states can be accessed using the National Law Enforcement Telecommunications System (NLETS). The inability of an investigator to obtain ownership information in a timely and efficient manner makes boat theft investigation very difficult.

## NCIC BOAT FILE

As noted earlier, over 27,000 stolen boats are included in the NCIC system, under the title "Boat File." The Boat File, one of the 17 NCIC 2000 files, records information on stolen boats, boat trailers, and boat parts. Information in the file is retrievable on an online basis by entering the registration or document number, the hull identification number, or the assigned NCIC number. Unless otherwise removed or located, information in the Boat File is maintained for the balance of the year of entry, plus four years. The exception to this is records that have no boat hull identification number or other number assigned by the owner that can be used for identification purposes. These remain in the file for only 90 days after entry.

The boat theft problem may be much greater than what the NCIC statistics display. There is no mandate requiring that boat thefts be entered into NCIC and, because of the difficulty of reporting, many thefts are not entered. According to marine theft experts, new edits installed in the NCIC Boat File in late 1993 contained errors, causing valid entries to be rejected and further discouraging the entry of stolen boat information by law enforcement agencies. Another major flaw in the system is that NCIC does not enter all the Coast Guard–assigned manufacturer's identification codes and, in some cases, has assigned codes that are not those recognized by the Coast Guard.

## INVESTIGATIVE RESOURCES

Marine theft investigations are often complex and time consuming. With the difficulty in obtaining ownership information, the tens of thousands of boat manufacturers, and the lack of computerized theft information, the success of an investigation is often predicated not on what the investigator knows but on whom he or she knows to contact for assistance. A major resource is the International Association of Marine Investigators. This organization has over 900 members who network with other law enforcement officers and agencies and insurance investigators throughout the United States, Canada, Europe, the Caribbean, and Central and South America. The organization holds an annual training seminar on marine theft issues.

## PREVENTIVE METHODS

There are several ways a boat owner can lessen the possibility of marine theft. For example, one individual who used to make his living by stealing boats and reselling them recommended that any boat with an electric starter should have a toggle switch that shuts off the electrical system when in the off position. The switch can be located under the dash or behind a panel. Typically, when a thief attempts to start the boat and cannot, the thief assumes that it is malfunctioning and gives up the effort to steal it.

To discourage theft, a boat owner may want to remove a vital engine part when the boat is left unattended. Trailered boats are more easily stolen than boats in the water. The best way to protect boats on trailers is to keep them out of the sight of thieves. They should be parked behind a house or behind a garage or inside a garage where they cannot be seen from the street.

Owners should never leave boats where they will tempt a potential thief. If a boat appears difficult to steal, the thief will seek an easier victim. The owner should never leave the keys or the registration on board when the vessel is not attended. Outboard motors should be bolted through the hull and secured with clamping locks. If the owner is to be away from the place where the boat is stored for an extended period of time, the engine should be disabled or one or more wheels should be removed from the trailer.

# AIRCRAFT AND AVIONICS THEFT

## SCOPE OF THE PROBLEM

With approximately 225,000 general-aviation aircraft in the United States, the theft of aircraft and burglary leading to the theft of avionics are certainly

### Stolen Aircraft Crashes into Bank Building

The theft of aircraft in the United States is a relatively rare event. However, breaking into an aircraft to steal electronic parts is relatively simple, since both door locks and ignition locks on many private planes can easily be picked. Thefts of aircraft are most likely to occur at airports that are poorly lit and unattended at night. The aircraft in the picture was stolen by a juvenile from a small airfield and ultimately crashed into a downtown bank building.
(© AFP/Corbis)

not as prevalent as motor vehicle theft. Nonetheless, they are significant criminal problems that law enforcement investigators may encounter.[34] In 2000, 11 aircraft were stolen in the United States. Although the number rose to 14 in 2001, these figures are the lowest since the pre-1990s.

The theft of aircraft electronic equipment, or **avionics,** can be a highly lucrative enterprise for thieves. Avionics include all the electronic radio and navigation equipment on board an aircraft—easily valued at over $10,000 in even the smallest aircraft. Many pieces of avionics look similar and can be accurately identified only by referring to the model number and/or name. Part of the difficulty encountered by many law enforcement officers is their unfamiliarity with such pieces of equipment. There were 76 burglaries in 2001, with 191 pieces of avionics stolen, valued at just over $477,500, a substantial reduction from the high of over $12.5 million worth of avionics stolen in 1994.

There are many reasons for equipment burglaries. One of the prime reasons is the lack of security at airports and the indifference on the part of many sales outlets regarding the identification and sources of used equipment. In addition, although most avionics contain stickers and plates identifying the manufacturer, model number, part number, and even the serial number, these are often easily removed and in some cases are just stick-on labels.

Most modern avionics are designed to be easily removed from the aircraft panel to facilitate frequent repair and maintenance of the equipment.

Stolen avionics are often resold through the used-parts market or to persons who need the items and are willing to overlook the source of such reasonably priced equipment.

Much of the stolen avionics equipment is exported to other countries. Some is resold using counterfeited VIN labels and VIN plates. Other equipment is switched so that the stolen equipment is never discovered, as illustrated by the following example: A thief will identify the type of equipment desired in a specific aircraft at a specific airport. The thief or thieves will then locate the same type of equipment in another aircraft at another airport. At the time of theft, the electronic equipment will be removed from the first aircraft and placed in the second aircraft after the second aircraft's equipment has been removed. The equipment from the second aircraft is then sold on the market; normally, the owner of the second aircraft doesn't even know the equipment is missing because the same material, stolen from the first aircraft, has been installed in his or her craft. The theft of equipment from the first aircraft is reported, but it is never recovered because it is already comfortably installed in aircraft number two.

## RESOURCES

An investigator who is unfamiliar with aircraft and aircraft thefts should not hesitate to obtain assistance from those who have the necessary expertise. It is advised that before undertaking a significant investigation, an investigator should visit a local airport, contact airport management, aircraft companies, flight schools, and so forth, to learn basic information about aircraft, avionics, and the theft of both. The Aviation and Crime Prevention Institute located in Hagerstown, Maryland, is an excellent source of assistance and support for law enforcement officers involved in the investigation of aviation theft.[35] The mission of the institute is to reduce aviation-related crime through information gathering, communication with law enforcement and the public, and education programs in theft prevention and security awareness.

## THEFT TECHNIQUES

The techniques thieves use to steal aircraft and burglarize aircraft for the avionics equipment are not that much different from, and most frequently parallel to, those used for stealing automobiles. Of course, if theft of the aircraft is the objective, it is unlikely that the thief will gain access by smashing a window. Indeed, smashing a window is generally not necessary. Perhaps the weakest security point of any aircraft is its locks. Most aircraft manufacturers use a limited number of key combinations, and a single key may open many aircraft of the same make. Occasionally, one manufacturer's key will open an aircraft of a different manufacturer.

Both door locks and ignition locks can easily be picked, and generally there are no antitheft devices on aircraft. Many of the more expensive aircraft don't even use ignition keys, so the only requirement for the thief is to enter the cabin.

Many of the techniques used to cover the theft of aircraft are similar to the processes used to conceal the theft of motor vehicles. The following illustrates a salvage switch involving aircraft: A thief decides on the type of aircraft desired and then purchases a total wreck of a similar aircraft from a junkyard. Rather than the certificate of title and VIN plate that come with a motor vehicle, the wrecked aircraft comes with its VIN plate and log book (a document required by the Federal Aviation Administration [FAA] that records the aircraft's history and repair record). The thief then steals (or has stolen) an aircraft of the same year, make, and model; switches the VIN plate; and installs the log book. After the thief adapts the registration markings and ensures that colors match the wrecked aircraft, the salvage switch is complete.

Thefts of aircraft are most likely to occur at airports that have poor lighting and are unattended at night, especially if they have little or no security, have no control tower, and perhaps are not even fenced.

## AIRCRAFT IDENTIFICATION

Aircraft have the same basic identification information as do motor vehicles. The major difference is that aircraft are regulated under a federal licensing system, whereas motor vehicles are regulated under state licensing systems. All aircraft are identified by a registration number, which is similar to a license plate number; a VIN; and make and model. The U.S. registration numbering system is part of a worldwide system under which each country has a letter and/or number code. In the United States, the code begins with the letter "N." Consequently, all U.S.-registered aircraft display an N number.

Most registered aircraft receive their N numbers when they are manufactured. It is possible for the purchaser of a used aircraft or of an aircraft currently being built to request a special N number. Such requests are processed by the FAA.

The N number is found on each side of the aircraft or on the vertical tail in large or small letter and numeral combinations. In some cases, such as on older aircraft, the N number may be displayed on the underside of one wing and the topside of the opposite wing. Helicopters have the N number displayed under the nose or undercarriage.

Most aircraft have a small plate on the instrument panel with the plane's N number on it. An investigator can look at the plate and determine whether the plate number matches the N number displayed on the exterior of the aircraft. If the plate is missing, further investigation is warranted.

Although each aircraft has a VIN, manufacturers design their own numbering systems, and the location of a VIN plate varies depending on the make. For example, on Cessna aircraft the VIN plate is found on the doorjamb; the door must be open to see the plate. The VIN plate on most single-engine and small twin-engine Beechcraft planes can be found on the right side above the wing flap; large Beechcraft planes have the VIN plate inside the main-cabin entry door frame. On Piper aircraft the VIN plate is usually found on the lower side of the tail on the aircraft's body.

As in any attempt to identify a vehicle, vessel, or aircraft, the investigator should understand the construction process well enough to know whether and where to look for identifiers. When aircraft are built, many of the parts are subassembled elsewhere in the plant, and such subassemblies are marked with the VIN number in Magic Marker or pencil so that the aircraft can later come together at the main assembly point. If the plate is missing, the investigator should look under seats, under carpeted areas, in inspection panels, and elsewhere for ID numbers relating to the VIN.

When trying to locate a VIN plate in aircraft other than those previously mentioned, the investigator should look in some of the most common locations, such as on the doorjamb on either side of the plane, on the lower tail section on either side of the plane, on the body where the main wing is attached, near the nose wheel, or on the lower body. In other words, when in doubt, the dedicated investigator will look over the entire aircraft in an attempt to find the attached plate, which will provide make, model, and VIN information.

## THEFT PREVENTION TECHNIQUES

Following are a few examples of the theft deterrent devices available and the actions an aircraft owner can take, some without cost, to reduce the chance of theft of the aircraft or the avionics:

- There are a number of alarm systems on the market, and some even have a pain generator, a second piercing alarm inside the cockpit that is most aggravating to the human ear.
- Ignition kills, which require entry of a security code into the control panel in the cockpit, are available. If the pilot fails to get the code right after a specific number of tries, the engine-starting circuits are disabled and, in some cases, a siren will sound.
- There should be a prearranged password known only to crew members and the airport operator. Thus a person who calls and directs that the plane be prepared for flight must know the password in order to get the plane. This technique has prevented the theft of many aircraft.
- A wheel-locking device, or "boot," prevents the plane from being towed or from moving under its own power.
- More secure locks can be installed.
- Airplanes should be parked at night at airports that are well lighted, fenced, and otherwise provided with security. Window covers should be used to conceal avionics.
- Avionics equipment should be checked to ensure that it is the manufacturer-installed equipment. Each piece should then be marked with a dot, paint, engraving, or scratch, and a detailed inventory should be made and recorded.
- Propeller chains and locks are available.
- Instrument panels can be equipped with a locking bar or locking cover.
- Flight operations personnel at airports should be given a list that identifies each crew

member and other persons permitted to be around the plane or to authorize service over the phone.

- Airport authorities should have a central point of contact available 24 hours a day.
- Vital aircraft records should not be kept in the aircraft.

## Key Terms

**AAMVANET**
**active system (theft deterrent)**
**avionics**
**cargo theft**
**chop shop**
**commercial-vehicle theft**
**confidential VIN**
**documented vessel**
**false-theft scheme**
**false-vehicle scheme**
**farm equipment**
**federal safety certification label**
**gray-market vehicles**
**heavy equipment**
**hull identification number (HIN)**
**inflated-theft-loss scheme**
**joyriding**
**marine theft**
**Motor Vehicle Theft Law Enforcement Act (1984)**
**National Motor Vehicle Title Information System (NMVTIS)**
**odometer fraud**
**off-road equipment**
**"paper vehicle"**
**parts marking**
**passive system (theft deterrent)**
**product information number (PIN)**
**professional theft (of vehicle)**
**quick strip (of vehicle)**
**salvage switch**
**salvage title**
**salvage vehicle**
**Stolen Auto Recovery (STAR) System**
**temporary theft (of vehicle)**
**title fraud**
**Truth in Mileage Act (1986)**
**vehicle fraud**
**vehicle identification number (VIN)**
**VIN plate**
**washing (of title)**

## Review Questions

1. Describe a chop-shop operation.
2. How does a salvage switch work?
3. Distinguish false-vehicle schemes, false-theft schemes, and inflated-theft-loss schemes.
4. What is a "paper" vehicle?
5. How is a certificate of title "washed"?
6. What are some of the factors contributing to the theft of off-road equipment?
7. What are the two major types of off-road equipment?
8. What is the National Insurance Crime Bureau, and what functions does it perform for law enforcement?
9. Why is vehicle identification the most difficult and time-consuming task faced by an investigator in an auto theft case?
10. Why do vehicles have a standardized identification numbering system?
11. What was the purpose behind passage of the Motor Vehicle Theft Law Enforcement Act of 1984?
12. Describe the three basic methods for restoring vehicle identification numbers.
13. What are some observable indicators that should lead to further investigation of a possible stolen car?
14. Describe some of the principal investigative steps in determining whether a vehicle fire is an accident or arson.
15. Describe the workings and benefits of a photographic preinsurance inspection program.
16. What is odometer fraud, and why is it a significant offense?
17. Discuss the nature and seriousness of marine theft.
18. What are avionics, and why is avionics theft prevalent?

## Internet Activities

1. Check on the Web to see if your state has law enforcement and/or insurance organizations that specialize in the investigation of motor vehicle and other related thefts. What types of investigative services do they provide? Are auto theft statistics available for your state? Does the site have auto theft prevention information? If you were a criminal investigator, what other information do you think should be available on the site?
2. Learn more about the export of stolen motor vehicles and other items by logging on to the U.S. Customs site at www.customs.ustreas.gov and the North American Export Committee site at www.naexportcommittee.org. The latter website also has several related links to insurance fraud and vehicle theft prevention.

## Notes


1. Federal Bureau of Investigation, *Crime in the United States, Uniform Crime Reports, 2000* (Washington, DC: Government Printing Office, 2001), pp. 52–55.
2. Citizens for Auto-Theft Responsibility, *CAR Newsletter*, Autumn 1992 (a quarterly publication of the not-for-profit public awareness and victim support organization, P.O. Box 3131, Palm Beach, FL 33480).
3. FBI, *Crime in the United States*, p. 55.
4. "NICB Goes Globe Trotting to Bring Back Stolen Cars," *APB* (official publication of the International Association of Auto Theft Investigators), November 1996, p. 63.
5. Jacques DeRemer, Conference Report, "United Nations Addresses International Auto Theft in Warsaw, Poland," *APB* (official publication of the International Association of Auto Theft Investigators), July 1997, p. 9.
6. National Automobile Theft Bureau, 1990 Annual Report, p. 15.
7. National Insurance Crime Bureau, *Fire Investigation Handbook* (Palos Hills, IL: NICB, 1995), p. 31.
8. Compiled by Sergeant Henry H. Brune, Motor Vehicle Theft Services, San Antonio, Texas, Police Department, December 2001.
9. Ibid.
10. Ibid.
11. John Green, "Gone in Four Minutes," *Implement and Tractor*, June 21, 1977, Vol. 92, No. 14, p. 48.
12. Gene Rutledge, "7 Character PIN for Off-Road Equipment Is Here," *APB* (journal of the International Association of Auto Theft Investigators), July 1999, pp. 17–19.
13. "There's More than One Way to Stop a Thief," *APB*, March 2001, pp. 52, 58–59.
14. FIA International Research, "Contraband, Organized Crime and the Threat to the Transportation and Supply Chain Function," study conducted on behalf of the National Cargo Security Council, a coalition of public and private transportation organizations, September 2001, Executive Summary, p. 1.
15. Ibid.
16. Ibid.
17. National Insurance Crime Bureau, *2001 Passenger Vehicle Identification Manual* (Palos Hills, IL: NICB, 2001).
18. National Automobile Theft Bureau, *Commercial Vehicle and Off-Road Equipment Identification Manual*, 7th ed. (Palos Hills, IL: NATB, 2000).
19. Ibid., p. 6.
20. Federal Bureau of Investigation, "The New Generation of NCIC," *CJIS: A Newsletter for the Criminal Justice Community*, Vol. 3, No. 2, 1999, pp. 5–6.
21. Ibid.
22. Ibid.
23. Glenn Wheeler, "North American Export Committee Update," *APB*, March 2001, p. 11.
24. David Shillingford, "National Equipment Register Update," *APB*, July 2000, p. 9.
25. "Attorney General Issues Report on Component Part Markings," IAATI Legal News column, *APB*, Nov. 2000, pp. 59, 61.
26. Ibid.
27. Ibid.
28. Ibid.

29. "Restoration of Altered or Obliterated Numbers," training bulletin, Alabama Department of Public Safety.
30. Most of the material in these lists is taken from handout materials produced by the National Insurance Crime Bureau.
31. National Insurance Crime Bureau, *Fire Investigation Handbook* (Palos Hills, IL: NICB, 1995), pp. 31–67; National Fire Protection Association International, *NFPA 921 Guide for Fire and Explosion Investigations, 2001 Edition* (Quincy, MA: NFPA International, 2001), pp. 921-171 to 921-182.
32. This information has been provided by the LoJack Corporation of Boston, Massachusetts.
33. Much of the material on this topic is drawn from Phillip J. Crapeau, "Photo Inspection Helps Deter Auto Theft," *National Underwriter,* Sept. 18, 1990.
34. Most of the material in this section is drawn from Aviation Crime Prevention Institute, *Aviation Identification and Information Manual for Police Officers* (Frederick, MD: ACPI and the Aviation Insurance Industry, 1987), and from information supplied by Robert Collins, Aviation Crime Prevention Institute, December 2001.
35. The address of the Aviation Crime Prevention Institute, Inc., is Post Office Box 30, Hagerstown, MD 21741-0030. Robert J. Collins, president of the institute, invites and welcomes inquiries and requests for assistance from law enforcement agencies and officers. Telephone numbers for the institute are 800-969-5473 and 301-791-9791. The website is www.acpi.org.

# SIXTEEN

# Computer Crime

**Robert W. Taylor and D. Kall Loper**
*University of North Texas*

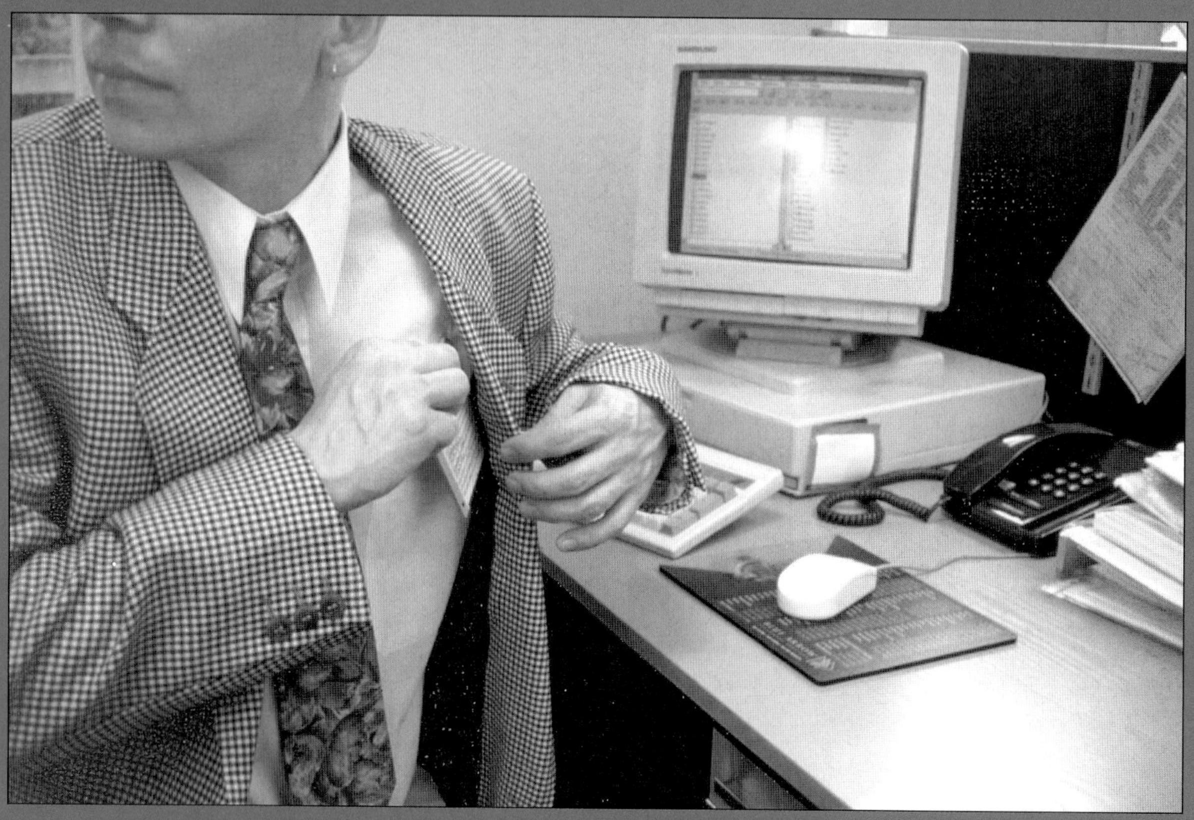

*Given the major advances in computer technology, it is not surprising that there are so many different types of computer crimes today. These range from network intrusion and data altering to the use of computers as facilitators for committing crimes. (© Hannah Gal/Corbis)*

## CHAPTER OUTLINE



## CHAPTER OBJECTIVES

1. Outline the types of crimes in which the computer is the target.
2. Discuss computers as an instrumentality of the crime.
3. Describe computers as incidental to the crime.
4. Explain crimes associated with the prevalence of computers.
5. Understand the tools that computer criminals use to commit crime.
6. Discuss debates regarding privacy issues concerning the regulation of the Internet.
7. Outline profiles of computer crime suspects.
8. Explain techniques for investigating computer crime.
9. Assess methods of preventing computer crime.

# INTRODUCTION

The first electronic computer was completed in 1945. The first long-distance electronic communication on the Internet was sent in 1969.[1] For a few years after this monumental communication event, computers and networks were safely enclosed in major university campuses and corporate research parks. Today, however, we have restructured our "information society" to depend on computers and networks in ways that no one could have predicted at the birth of computing or even the much later birth of large networks. In just a few short years, computers have become common fixtures of daily life. Students can register for or drop classes in real time from their homes by using a computer. People can withdraw money from their bank accounts at any time by using an automatic teller machine (ATM). They can get stock quotes, make flight reservations, browse reference libraries, shop at online stores, read the latest news, and make use of uncounted other resources almost instantaneously by clicking the mouse.

Being "connected" is now less about politics and more about online access to the World Wide Web, a global network of computers, through service providers such as America On-Line (AOL) and Prodigy or through a number of local, national, and international Internet service providers (ISPs) that offer access to the amazing arrays of information and databases.

The advance in computer and Internet technology, however, has provided new opportunities for criminal enterprise. Discoveries of computer crime committed both inside businesses, corporations, and network systems and through various means across the global network become more prevalent each day. The purpose of this chapter is to inform the reader about many issues concerning and related to computer crime. The first section of the chapter presents information on various types of computer crime, ranging from network intrusion and data altering to the use of the computer as a facilitator for committing crimes. Next, the chapter addresses discovery tools and delivery vehicles for viruses and worms used to commit computer crime. Profiles of the hacker and the computer criminal are also discussed. The next section highlights the investigation of computer crime, including crime scene techniques and the application of digital forensic analysis. The chapter concludes with a discussion on methods of preventing computer crime.

## TYPOLOGIES OF COMPUTER CRIME

The virtual explosion of the World Wide Web has dramatically increased communication between people, and the web has become a viable new conduit for business transactions. Stock quotes, flight schedules, reference libraries, online stores, the latest news, and uncounted other resources are available with a few clicks of the mouse. As is the case of many exciting developments, there is a dark side to this new information frontier—computer abuse and computer crime.

**Computer abuse** includes a range of intentional acts that may not be covered by criminal laws. Any intentional act involving knowledge of computer use or technology is computer abuse if the perpetrator could have made some gain and the victim could have experienced loss.[2] By contrast, **computer crime** is any illegal act in which knowledge of computer technology is used to commit the offense.[3]

Due to the rapid increase in and increasingly serious nature of these crimes, several federal agencies have formed units that deal exclusively with computer crimes. These units include the FBI's National Computer Crime Squad and the U.S. Department of Justice's Computer Crime Unit. The U.S. Secret Service and the Department of Defense (as well as special units with the Army, Air Force, and Navy) also have experts responsible for computer crime investigations, as do many other federal, state, and local agencies. The first computer crime unit at the local level was developed in the early 1980s at the Maricopa County Sheriff's Office in Phoenix, Arizona. Since that time, most large police departments have special units that focus on computer-related crimes. A number of nongovernment organizations have also been developed that perform varied tasks, including investigating computer crimes, providing computer security training and alerts, and acting as clearinghouses for both general and specific information regarding the technicalities of computer crime. These organizations are often called on as sources of experts who may be needed to assist law enforcement personnel conducting computer crime investigations. Two of the most prominent nongovernment organizations are the Computer Emergency Response Team (CERT) at Carnegie Mellon University and the Computer Security Institute (CSI), based in San Francisco, California.[4]

Today the opportunities for computer crime are greater than ever due to two basic facts: There are more computers, and they are increasingly connected to the Internet. To illustrate, Jay Nelson has scammed online auction users out of hundreds of thousands of dollars in the last two years. Using various identities, he has illegally influenced auction prices, sold merchandise he never delivered, and earned his way onto the Postal Inspector's

### Intellectual Property Theft Case

Theft of intellectual property—everything from stealing trade secrets to illegally reproducing copyrighted consumer goods such as music and movies—has incalculable costs. The Recording Industry Association of America (RIAA) has estimated its losses from the Napster music-swapping network to be in the billions. The *Metallica vs. Napster* suit was one of the first to challenge this concept of free music swapping.

(© Graham Douglas/Corbis Sygma)

Office's most-wanted list. By manipulating buyer's confidence through feedback on low-dollar purchases, he was able to defraud buyers on larger purchases. Buyers saw excellent service ratings for Nelson, but did not know they had been carefully manipulated. After making fraudulent sales, he collected the purchasers' money and then moved on to his next identity.[5] Ironically, the web alerted a vigilant coin shop owner that a regular customer was really the fugitive: Nelson.[6]

As Chapter 11, "Crimes against Children," explains, even our children are not safe from exploitation and victimization on the web. A young teenage girl began visiting online with someone she believed to be a young teenage boy. She gave him her telephone number. However, the person turned out to be a 51-year-old man who made a series of obscene calls to her before he was stopped.[7] In another case, a 27-year-old man enticed a 14-year-old boy into meeting him. The boy was blindfolded, handcuffed, shackled, and sexually abused by the man.

Other examples of online crimes include the interception of privileged information such as credit card numbers or passwords. Abuse of credit has reached epidemic proportions. In 1997, fraudulent Visa transactions were reported at $828 million. Theft of intellectual property, ranging from stealing trade secrets to illegally reproducing copyrighted consumer materials such as music and movies, has an incalculable cost. The Recording Industry Association of America (RIAA) has estimated its losses due to music swapping on the Napster network as being in the billions. Trading illicit information on the Internet has become a recurring theme in online crime. For example, a computer newsgroup, an archive of email messages, dealt specifically with ways to defeat security placed on digital satellite television.[8] Other forms of illicit information include child pornography, proprietary or privileged information leaked to websites, and illegal recordings of cellular phone calls.

Unfortunately, not all computer crimes are as restricted in their effects. "Hacktivists," politically motivated hackers, have attacked government websites, forcing sites to be shut down for days until the damage could be repaired. Other online vandals have launched denial-of-service attacks on corporations or ISPs, shutting them down for hours or days at a time. Government studies have shown that many corporations, government agencies, and utility companies are highly vulnerable to attacks from outsiders, who in some cases may be able to seriously affect large segments of the population through a single organization's computer system. According to the National Infrastructure Protection Center (NIPC), an interagency initiate led by the FBI, tampering with the vital-information infrastructure could result in serious harm. On the basis of the effects of recent power failures caused by bad weather and the California power crisis during the summer of 2001, the NIPC predicts serious national consequences from a failure in the power grid or communication infrastructure. One of the potential sources of such tampering is network intrusion conducted by terrorist organizations.

Not all computer crimes take place on the information superhighway. As shown in Figure 16–1, the National Institute of Justice recognizes six major categories of computer crime, many of which do not involve networked computers.[9] There are many other ways of categorizing computer abuse and crime. One way is in terms of vulnerabilities: hardware, software, networks, physical structures and buildings, information or data, and computer-controlled devices (such as phone switches, electric power, and airplanes being directed by air traffic controllers and their computers or automated equipment) are all vulnerable to electronic and physical attacks.

Another way to categorize computer crimes is in terms of the source of the threat: insiders or outsiders. Insider computer crimes are committed by persons who are employed by the targeted organization or have permission to be accessing its computer system. Outsider computer crimes are committed by persons from outside the organization. While these individuals may sometimes have legitimate access to part of the system for specific tasks (such as surfing an organization's website), often they do not. Many of the same types of crimes, such as hardware theft and destruction of data, can be done by both insiders and outsiders.

In 1976, Donn Parker made one of the first attempts to systematically define computer crimes by the activity involved. He developed the first typology[10] of computer crime based on accounts of the crimes.[11] Parker's typology remained the state of the art until Robert Taylor's "juvenile hacker profile" emerged in 1990.[12] David Carter modified both typologies to better suit the needs of criminologists and investigators.[13] Parker also created a new, more security focused, typology in 1998.[14] For our purposes, Carter's typology provides an excellent

**Figure 16-1** Categories of Computer Crime

(**Source:** Modified from C. H. Conely and J. T. McEwen. "Computer Crime," *NIJ Report*, January-February 1990, p. 3.)

**Internal Computer Crimes**
- Trojan horses
- Packet sniffers
- Salami techniques
- Back doors
- Logic bombs
- Viruses

**Telecommunication Crimes**
- Hacking
- Illegal bulletin boards
- Misuse of telephone systems

**Computer Manipulation Crimes**
- Embezzlement and fraud

**Support of Criminal Enterprises**
- Databases to support drug distributions
- Databases to keep records of client transactions
- Gambling and prostitution
- Money laundering

**Hardware and Software Thefts**
- Software piracy
- Thefts of computers
- Thefts of microprocessor chips
- Thefts of trade secrets

**Invasion of Privacy and Related Issues**
- Sexually explicit material
- Cookies

manner in which to categorize computer crimes. It is versatile enough to organize an increasing array of illegal, possibly illegal, and simply questionable actions called "computer crime."

## THE COMPUTER AS THE TARGET

Crimes in which the computer is the target include the denial of expected service and the alteration of data. The computer is defined as the target when an act effectively prevents the legitimate user or owner from receiving the service or data that he or she expects. Even without malicious intent, network intruders target the computer and may cause harm to the network owner. Crimes that target the computer are the most easily understandable examples of computer crime.

### Computer Manipulation Crimes

**Computer manipulation crimes** involve changing data or creating electronic records in a system for the specific purpose of advancing another crime, typically fraud or embezzlement. The simplest, safest, and most common form of computer crime—data diddling—falls within this category. In its most basic form, payroll records are changed so that a person is paid for more hours than he or she worked or paid at a higher rate. However, there is a great deal of variety in computer manipulation crimes.

For example, the price of a stock can be manipulated on the information superhighway. Stock shares in one little-known Canadian company, Wye Resources, Inc., were traded outside an established exchange. The value of the stock more than tripled after the company was hyped on messages posted on commercial bulletin board services and on the Internet.[15] The company reportedly owned a Zaire diamond mine where a major strike had been made. After the favorable online publicity had "pumped" up the stock's price, it was then "dumped," or sold for profit, by those in the know, and the stock collapsed.

According to the National Consumers League, the number of reported Internet frauds tripled, from an average of 32 per month in 1996 to nearly 100 per month in 1997.[16] The scams threaten the development of commerce on the Internet, as consumers need to feel confident that purchases are safe and secure. While many state and federal laws governing deceptive sales practices apply to online promotions, the Federal Trade Commission's Telemarketing Sales Rule does not. Efforts are under way to expand the rule to the Internet, thereby allowing regulators to crack down on promoters who offer phony services.[17] Frauds on the Internet are usually based on a traditional methodology of offering goods and services that are never provided or are of very poor quality for the price paid. Figure 16–2 outlines a number of common Internet scams.

**Computer Manipulation Crimes**
Computer manipulation crimes involve changing data or creating electronic records in a system for the purpose of advancing another crime, typically fraud or embezzlement. For example, electronic payroll records may be altered so that an employee is paid for more hours than he or she actually worked. Internet scams, such as the sale of merchandise that is never delivered, are another common type of fraud.
(© Corbis)

**Figure 16-2**

**Common Internet Scams**

(**Source:** *Dallas Morning News*, Feb. 16, 1998, p. 2D.)

According to the Internet Fraud Watch, these were the top 10 rip-offs on the Internet in 1997:

- *Web auctions:* Items bid for but never delivered by the sellers, value of items inflated, shills suspected of driving up bids, prices increased after highest bids accepted
- *Internet services:* Charges for services that were supposedly free, payment for online and Internet services that were never provided or falsely represented
- *General merchandise:* From toys to clothes, goods never delivered or not as advertised
- *Computer equipment and software:* Sales of computer products that were never delivered or were misrepresented
- *Pyramids and multilevel marketing:* Schemes in which profits were made only from recruiting others, not from sales of goods or services to the end users
- *Business opportunities and franchises:* empty promises of big profits with little or no work by investing in prepackaged businesses or franchise operations
- *Work-at-home plans:* Materials and equipment sold with false promises of payment for piecework performed at home
- *Easy credit cards:* False promises of credit cards to people with bad credit histories upon payment of up-front fees
- *Prizes and sweepstakes:* Requests for up-front fees to claim winnings that were never awarded
- *Book sales:* Genealogies, self-help improvement books, and other publications that were never delivered or were misrepresented

The advance of computerization has also opened new mechanisms for fraud. For instance, the Secret Service and FBI warned Congress in 1997 that a thriving new "point and click" counterfeiting scheme had been discovered that uses high-quality scanners to capture an original check, a personal computer to alter the data, and a quality laser printer to develop the counterfeit instrument.[18] Total cost for equipment used in such cases has averaged less than $5,000, providing criminals with the ability to pass phony checks that look "exactly like the originals." The Federal Reserve placed the cost of this type of check fraud to banks at $615 million in 1995, more than 10 times the $59 million attributed to bank robbery.[19] More alarming than the total amount of loss is the rapid growth and expansion of this type of crime. According to the FBI, counterfeit check schemes are the acts not just of lone, white-collar criminals but also of well-organized gangs and groups. A significant number of the cases discovered in 1997 were committed by organized ethnic enterprises, including Nigerians, Vietnamese, Russians, Armenians, and Mexicans. Some of these gangs were also heavily involved in the trafficking of guns and narcotics, extortion, and large-scale fencing of stolen property.[20]

Even the federal government is not exempt from computer manipulation crimes. Fraudulent Internal Revenue Service tax filings cost the federal government $5 billion a year. A multimillion-dollar portion of this was due to bogus electronic tax filings. Thieves would obtain or prepare false supporting documentation to justify a refund, such as W-2s. Then they would go to a tax preparer who completed a return based on this information and filed it electronically. Within 48 hours, the IRS would confirm that the return had been accepted and that the person was eligible for a refund anticipation loan (RAL). This confirmation came in the form of a direct-deposit indicator (DDI). In effect, the IRS served as credit reference, guaranteeing that the money would actually be forthcoming. With this information, the "filer" would obtain a loan from a bank, finance company, or the tax preparer and vanish. In 1994, the IRS announced new procedures for handling electronic filings to reduce such fraud.[21]

## Data Alteration or Denial

Data alteration or denial directly targets the computer by attacking the useful information stored or processed by the computer. Altered data may affect business decisions made by a company or may directly affect individuals by altering their records. In citing worst-case scenarios for data alteration, the changing of medical records often appears as an example. In a review of "shockers," author Jonathan Littman reported that a Berkeley researcher discovered a medical facility in the San Francisco Bay Area with open telephone lines to medical records.[22] An examination of medical records uncovers a great amount of personal information, but beyond the threat to privacy, alteration of those records by a single character can be fatal (in the case of blood type or a prescription). It is easy to understand why the alteration of medical data has received such attention.

Although malicious network intruders may alter critical data, the most common source of such damage is a disgruntled employee of the company affected. As an example, in 1999, the *Chicago Tribune* reported the theft of the only copy of air-traffic control software under development. Although no lives were placed in jeopardy, the theft of the software garnered national attention because it related to a public safety function. One of the few horror stories that rivals altering of medical records is tampering with air-traffic control data or software. Thomas Varlotta, the engineer who led a team that created vital air-traffic control software, destroyed the only copy of the source code when he left the employment of the Federal Aviation Administration (FAA) in June 1998.[23] The FAA launched an internal investigation and then enlisted the help of federal authorities, who obtained court authorization to search Varlotta's home. Luckily, authorities found a copy of the source code in the search. However, since the program had been encrypted by Varlotta, it took well over a year to gain access to the source code and retest the code. The FAA estimates that it may have taken years to reconstruct the program. The denial of access to this data may have severely hampered the nation's air-traffic control system and eventually placed lives in danger.

## Hacking, Cracking and Other Forms of Network Intrusion

**Hacking** or **cracking** is the process of gaining unauthorized entry into a computer system. For perhaps 99 percent of the people who do it, the hacking, or getting in, is the thrill. The remaining 1 percent hack for purposes ranging from pulling mild pranks to destroying or stealing data. To be able to hack, a person must get a password. People are often careless with their passwords, writing them down and leaving them in obvious places in their offices and homes, where hackers may discover them. Passwords can also be generated by using a special software program called a **hacker's dictionary.** A common hacker's tool, the dictionary generates millions of combinations of letters and numbers until it finds a combination that matches a password—and the hacker is in. The prime targets for hackers are secure sites found on the Internet.

**Packet sniffers** are also used in the hacking or cracking methodology. These unique programs are designed to monitor network communications and selectively keep records of sensitive information such as passwords and credit card numbers. In most computer networks, as information passes from its origin to its destination, it must pass through many computers along the way. Normally, these computers simply pass along the information, sometimes logging that it went through the system. By using a packet sniffer, it is possible to not only allow the information to pass but also to make a copy of it, undetected. While passwords and credit card numbers are often the information of choice, other sensitive information has been gathered this way by sniffers located on government and corporate networks, online networks, and Internet service provider networks and then used in blackmail schemes.

Interestingly, proactive law enforcement programs designed to catch criminals using the Internet are, essentially, highly advanced packet sniffers. Developed as a specialized network analyzer or "sniffer" program designed to work on a personal computer via Microsoft Windows, the FBI's monitoring program, DCS 1000 (formerly Carnivore) raises the ire of many civil libertarians.[24] Essentially, DCS 1000 "sniffs" or analyzes portions of selected network packets, and copies them to a separate file for further analysis by the FBI. These packets are defined by specific filters set within the program, which conform to a court order. The filter set can be extremely fine and can comply with applications developed from Title III interception orders, pen register court orders, and trap and trace court orders. The problem, of course, is discriminating between user messages that are legal and those that are not on the Internet. This is a complex issue. DCS 1000 does not search through the contents of every message and collect those that contain certain key words like "bomb" or "drugs." It selects messages on the basis of criteria expressly set out in a court order, for example, messages transmitted to or from a particular account or to or from a particular user.[25] If the device is placed at some point on a network where it cannot discriminate messages as set out in the court order, it simply lets all such messages pass by unrecorded. It is precisely the issue of discriminating among all messages that provokes such strong reaction from civil libertarians. For DCS 1000 to work, it must first "read" all messages passing over the network, those from suspect accounts named in the court order *and* those from others. Never before has the FBI had the authority or the capability to capture *all* the communications passing through a given network.

The primary difference between data alteration and network intrusion is the intent of the intruder. By reading or "browsing" through confidential files, the intruder actually creates a copy of the file. Thus, mere browsing may be theft, but it does not deprive the owner of the data or the use of the data. This makes the distinction between data alteration and intrusion more meaningful. It may be impossible for an investigator to determine whether data have been altered. While altered data may be used for committing fraud or for denying the expression of the owner's idea, the simple intruder might not cause actual harm. The story of Kevin Mitnick perfectly exemplifies this distinction. The prosecution of Mitnick relied on estimates of the value of software that he had downloaded but had not altered. Several major corporations placed a total value of hundreds of millions of dollars on the software Mitnick obtained. This amount was determined by using a method suggested by the FBI: the companies estimated the total development costs of the software. The amount was questioned at various stages in Mitnick's trial. Since Mitnick did not deprive the companies of the products of their research and development, it seems that the actual economic harm caused would be less than the total cost. This contention was supported by the failure of a single corporation on the list of Mitnick's victims to report the loss to the Securities and Exchange Commission (such reporting is required for losses suffered by a company that sells stocks).

On the other hand, the corporations had no way of knowing whether the data had been altered. They may have devoted significant effort to reestablishing their confidence in the data. It is also possible that Mitnick could have sold the information to rival companies. There is no evidence or even suggestion that he did so, but the initial estimate of value may have reflected this fear. Delays caused by the intrusion may have reduced the market advantage of some of the corporations affected. Thus, the calculation of actual damages is very difficult. In the three years Mitnick spent awaiting trial, the value of the Sun Microsystems operating system (Solaris) dropped from an estimated prerelease value of several million dollars to essentially zero. The delay may have had a direct financial impact, but attributing this loss to Mitnick for prosecution was virtually impossible.

When intrusion is discovered, it often leaves the owner or administrator of the affected system questioning the integrity, accuracy, and authenticity of data on the network. Although the legitimate user of the system and data is not denied access to either, there is no reasonable certainty of data's security in the system. Security measures often require the removal of web-based resources and restoration of data from, hopefully, unaffected backup copies. This is often a very timely and costly venture, as it appears that hackers are becoming much more destructive in their work. (See Figure 16–3.)

## Denial of Service

More direct than the subtleties of network intrusion, the denial of service leaves little room for argument about a negative effect. Although any resource may be denied to the rightful user, the most prominent example of this computer-targeting is the network denial-of-service attack. On February 7, 2000, the website of Yahoo was subjected to an unprecedented attack that effectively removed the site from the Internet for three hours, Other prominent Internet sites (e.g., Barnes and Noble, CNN, ABC) were also attacked. The initial reaction of law enforcement, security, and even hackers was shock that a site as large as Yahoo could be overwhelmed.[26] Subsequent investigation showed that the attacks had been aimed at choke points that funneled the majority of the site's traffic through a few routers. While not as bad as first suspected, the attack showed that even the largest sites on the Internet were not safe.

## Computer Vandalism

When an intruder removes valuable information from a computer system, the intruder prevents the legitimate user or owner from having access to that information. Such **computer vandalism** can result in a direct loss or represent a substantial loss of expected revenue. If the data were for direct sale, such as a computer program or music, it may be possible to estimate the value of the lost data. However, it is more likely that the disrupted data were provided to the public to generate goodwill or advertising income or for no commercial purpose. Even though a dollar value cannot be attached to the data, the owner still has a right to present the intended message and be free from disruption. Many educational organizations, like the University of Cambridge, maintain a web presence for no apparent commercial purpose other than recruitment and advertising. On May 13, 2001, the web camera at the University of Cambridge was replaced with the calling card of a computer vandal. The vandal wanted to express nothing more important than "Ne0tz owned u!"[27] In another example of data alteration, a group named "Hacking for Girlies" defaced the *New York Times* website. The defacement caused the *Times* embarrassment and the loss of advertising revenue for its free web-based service. Although an actual dollar value of loss was not disclosed by the *Times*, the incident drew national attention and affected interstate commerce.[28] Thus, the vandalism came under the jurisdiction of the FBI. To date, no arrests have been made for either of these incidents.

The web camera had to be moved on June 1, 2001; however, it may never be operational. Similarly, the *Times* web page had to be removed several times, once for an entire day, to clear the affected portions and add or repair security. In both cases, the legitimate owner was criminally deprived of the ability to express an idea through equipment and data legitimately owned for that purpose. The consequences of computer vandalism are similar to those of data alteration or denial of service; many instances of computer vandalism also include network intrusion. These offenses target the computer, and thus leave direct evidence of the crime for investigators to detect.

# THE COMPUTER AS AN INSTRUMENTALITY OF THE CRIME

An instrumentality of crime is a device used to commit a crime. Unlike the case with crimes targeting the computer, in computer-as-instrumentality crimes the perpetrator only *uses* the computer to further a criminal end; the computer and data contained therein are not the object of the crime.

## Theft

Under the common law definition of theft, a criminal actor deprives a legitimate owner of a good by taking that good. As in auto theft, simply borrowing the good or item is still a criminal deprivation of the owner. In an electronic environment, where data are more easily copied than deleted, depriving the owner of the property is relatively rare. Donn Parker, creator of the first computer crime typology, notes that market-sensitive proprietary information, financial information, trade secrets, process technology information, human resource information,

**Figure 16-3** Hacker Havoc

(**Source:** John Yaukey, Dallas Morning News, Oct. 15, 2001, Section D, pp. 1-2.)

When Maurice Paynter installed his new Internet security software, he got a sobering look at modern life online.

"I realized I'm being attacked constantly," he said. "It's like I'm in a war zone."

The software, which records attempts by hackers to infiltrate the host computer, showed Paynter was being scanned for vulnerable openings 30 to 40 times a day. Scarcely a day passes now that his software doesn't detect a virus.

"It's hard to believe how bad it's gotten," he said.

According to watchers of malicious codes, hacking is becoming pandemic, a national pastime for computer enthusiasts tempted to test their skills against the establishment.

Since 1998, the number of hacking attacks and virus releases has increased sevenfold. Viruses are being produced at a rate of a dozen or more per day, with some causing tens of millions of dollars in damages and lost productivity.

To make matters worse, many hackers are employing more intentionally destructive tools and tactics, some so callous that even their fellow code crackers have denounced them as a different breed.

Shortly after Sept. 11's terrorist attacks, some hackers exploited the catastrophe to spread a virus using what appeared to be an e-mail pleading for peace. When the message was opened, the virus loaded onto the recipient's computer and damaged files.

In what is perhaps the most disturbing new trend, hackers are infiltrating well-known news sites, including Yahoo! and the Orange County Register, and rewriting stories. These "subversion of information" attacks raise a host of concerns in the wake of the Sept. 11 events when news sites were a major source of information.

"There used to be a strong ethic among hackers—get in and look around, but do no harm," said William Knowles, a 32-year-old Chicago-based computer security analyst and a former "benign" hacker. "That's been lost on the younger masses."

Experts say it's changing the Internet the way crime changes a neighborhood.

People are now constantly on alert for suspicious e-mail and other applications that could potentially harbor malicious code. It's gotten so bad that several Internet service providers have been threatening to disconnect customers who don't use protective antivirus software.

**Meaner Viruses**

The modern hacker has a selection of tools and strategies to choose from, including viruses and worms that typically spread over networks and clog computers, and attacks, which they can launch against Web sites to disable them or change their contents.

Viruses and worms have typically been considered dangerous because once downloaded, say unwittingly from an e-mail attachment, they often destroy valuable files—and many still do that.

But new strains are being designed to add extra sting.

Consider the recent SirCam virus. It arrives in the form of a seemingly harmless e-mail attachment. If opened by the recipient, it sends itself to every name in the victim's address book. There's nothing special about that. But SirCam doesn't stop there. Before forwarding itself on, it raids your "My Documents" folder—where people often store their most sensitive material—and randomly selects a file that it sends out with the infected e-mail. Maybe it's a boring, meaningless file; maybe it's a file that gets you fired or divorced.

"With SirCam and some of these other recent releases you see a blending of standard basic virus making with some new, more sophisticated hacking tools," said Tom Powerledge, with security software maker Symantec.

But before a virus can do damage it has to enter a computer or network, and hackers have taken infiltration methods to new levels as well.

Most garden-variety viruses and worms enter computers when infected e-mail is downloaded.

This usually requires some sort of a trick euphemistically known as "social engineering." The Anna Kournikova virus released earlier this year as an e-mail attachment promised those who would download it a picture of the heartthrob tennis star.

But the recent Nimda virus was a different animal altogether, infecting e-mail, network servers, which regulate digital traffic, Web sites, and shared disk drives where it automatically copied itself without the need for anyone to download it.

Nimda was so persistent, it took several major efforts on the part of network managers around the world to finally suppress it.

"Nimda was certainly alarming but not unexpected," said Chad Dougherty, an Internet security analyst at Carnegie Mellon's federally funded Software Engineering Institute. "Hackers are now using best-of-breed methods for propagating malicious code, and viruses like Nimda are the result."

**Culture of Hacking**

Hacking wasn't always this destructive. In fact, it started at MIT in the 1960s as a perfectly innocent pastime, aimed at tweaking higher performance out of some of the first mainframe computers to appear on college campuses. The term hacker was taken from a model train club at the university that amused itself by "hacking" better performance out of electronic toys.

In the 1970s, college students known as "phone phreaks" turned their fascination with technology to hacking long distance telephone networks for free calls. Apple computer founders Steve Jobs and Steve Wozniak were among hacking's early gurus.

By the 1980s, as academic and defense research computer networks began rapidly expanding into what would become

**Figure 16-3** Hacker Havoc, *continued*

the Internet, the hobby had started turning dark. Phone phreaks turned to hacking these networks, exchanging passwords and techniques on some of the first electronic message boards.

Later, the first hacking groups formed while the movie "War Games" introduced the public to hacking with a story about a teenager who nearly sparks nuclear war by meddling with defense computers.

It wasn't until 1988 that hacking publicly shook the establishment with the Morris worm.

Created by Cornell graduate student Robert Morris Jr., the worm program spread through some 6,000 academic and defense computers, paralyzing many.

The spindly, bespectacled Morris typified the new computer nerd and showed the world what a few lines of renegade code could do. At his federal trial, covered on the front page of the *New York Times,* Morris told prosecutors that he never intended to crash computers, but rather only wanted to expose security flaws.

Until recently, this has been the credo of the hacker: Expose weaknesses so software venders will fix them. It took exceptional skill to do this, and indeed, Morris was the son of a federal computer security expert.

But as the Internet exploded and a new generation raised on computers has taken to hacking, the hobby has degenerated into what old school hackers call "crass vandalism" perpetrated by "script kiddies."

These are typically young, suburban males, in their late teens and 20s who create often highly destructive viruses using prewritten code such as the VBS Worm Generator downloaded from the Internet. The 20-year-old hacker who released the Kournikova virus was found by police to be in possession of hundreds of viruses he had collected off the Internet.

"This is point-and-click hacking," said a San Francisco–area "white hat" hacker who calls himself Pauly Morf. "It requires no skill or understanding of network vulnerabilities. I have no respect for it or this generation."

That said, the recent spike in hacking that the script kiddies are largely responsible for has helped send a wake-up call across the Internet that should eventually make it more secure.

Despite the occasional warning of a looming digital apocalypse, many hackers and security experts alike predict more awareness, especially among home computer users, and more secure software will help keep hackers in check, at least those attracted by the cheap thrill of hurling monkey wrenches.

"Hackers have had it pretty easy lately," said Pauly Morf. "But the bar will be raised."

## Viral Epidemic

Hackers have been churning out viruses and attacking networks and websites at an unprecedented rate. That's in part because creating a virus is considerably easier than it used to be.

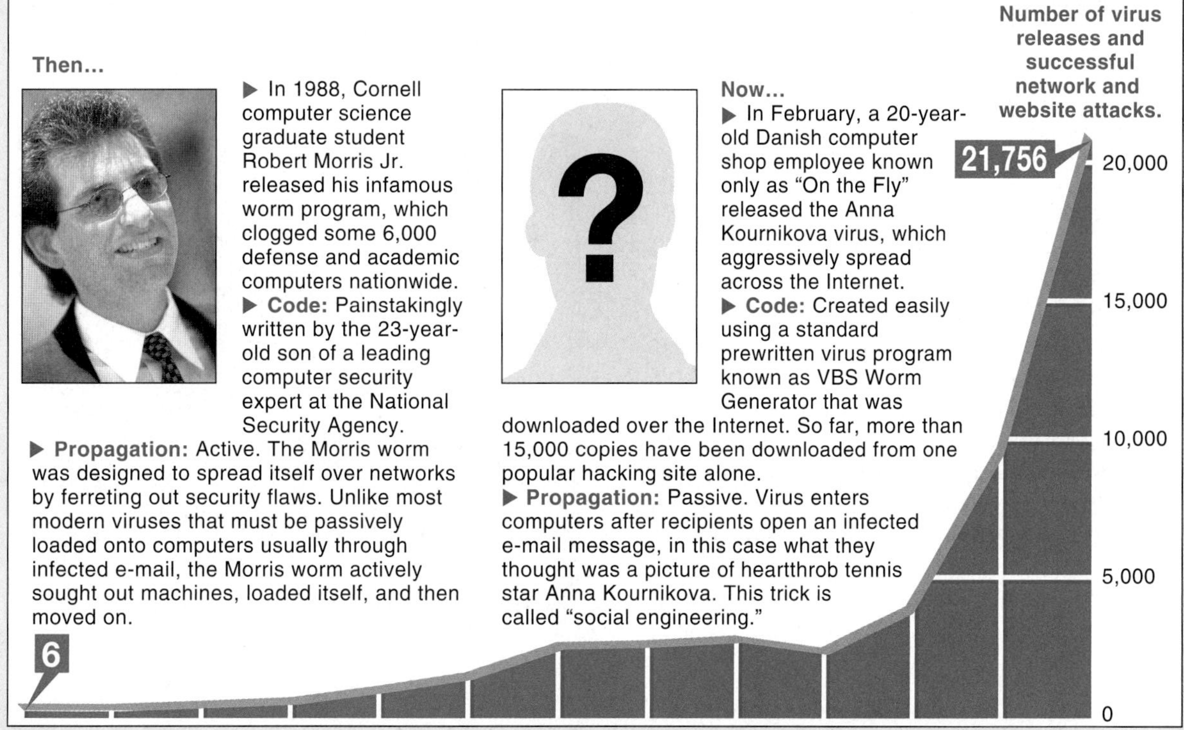

**Figure 16-3** Protecting Against Hackers

**TOOLS TO PROTECT YOURSELF**

Code and caution.

That double-pronged defense should keep malicious code out of your home computer.

On the code side, anyone on the Internet should be using an antivirus program at minimum. If you have an "always on" broadband connection, you should also have a firewall to prevent hackers from snooping around your computer.

Some of the leading security software includes:

- Symantec's Norton AntiVirus 2002 (www.symantec.com, $49.95).
- Norton Personal Firewall 2002 ($49.95).
- Norton Internet Security 2002 ($69.95), includes Norton AntiVirus 2002, Norton Personal Firewall 2002, Norton Privacy Control, Norton Parental Control, and ad blocking.
- McAfee's VirusScan (www.mcafee.com, $24.95 for one year, $39.95 for two years).

On the cautious side:

- Don't open suspicious e-mail attachments, especially any that end with the coding "VBS." VBS stands for Visual Basic Script, the favorite programming language of many hackers.
- Exercise caution when downloading files from the Internet. Ensure that the source is legitimate. Scan the file with antivirus software on the download site.
- Update antivirus software regularly. As a matter of habit you should keep tabs on virus activity by checking your security software provider's website at least once a week and downloading the updated antivirus software as needed. Most security software makers provide free updates to their customers via the web.

customer information, information products, transitory information, and security information can all have value to the owner.[29] To some degree, maintaining the value of such information requires that the owner either maintain confidence in the integrity of the information or control the distribution of the information. As in the Mitnick case, depriving the owner of sole possession or depriving the owner of the right to control distribution amounts to theft by reducing the value of the information.

Other, more blatant, examples of computerized theft actually deprive the legitimate owner of a tangible asset. The **salami-slice** technique is a money crime; it is an automated means of stealing assets from a large number of transactions. In the round-down salami technique, the computer is used to round calculated dollar amounts down to the nearest cent. Normally, gains and losses from rounding even out, so neither the merchant nor the customer loses on average. By always rounding down and diverting the rounded amount to a special account, the criminal deprives both merchant and consumer of assets; however, the amount is often trivial, like a slice from a salami, too thin to produce a noticeable effect. After a number of such slices are removed, the amount of missing salami becomes noticeable.

## Theft of Service

Although many services available on the Internet are free, some data and services are considered proprietary. This means the users must pay to use the data or service. Using proprietary services without paying is theft. Unlike the common law definition of theft, theft in this case does not necessarily include denial of the data or service to legitimate users. Many

### Computers as the Instrumentality of Crime

In some cases, the computer is used to actually commit the crime. For example, a computer may be used to steal assets from a large number of transactions. In the round-down salami technique, the computer is used to round calculated dollar amounts down to the nearest cent and then divert the rounded amounts to a special account operated by the thief.

(© Corbis)

providers invest in the ability to meet the demand for their services. In the mid-1990s, the Internet service provider America Online (AOL) failed to anticipate the demand for Internet access. As a result, many customers were not able to connect to AOL servers. To remedy this situation, AOL invested significant amounts of money on increasing its capacity. The amount of the increase was carefully planned to avoid spending too much. Although users had been temporarily deprived of service, this AOL incident was not theft of service. The damage from theft of service occurs when the criminal use of service forces the owner to invest in more capacity to meet the projected needs of legitimate users.

## Fraud

As in the common definition of fraud, fraud using a computer exploits the trust, guaranteed by law, in a business transaction. Fraud can be perpetrated by the buyer, seller, or peer in a transaction. **Shopping cart fraud** is an example of consumer fraud against a business. After purchases are selected, the computer criminal saves a copy of the purchase page and alters the prices. Once the altered prices are in place, the criminal submits the page as normal. Some merchants do not discover the fraud until they match inventory to purchases—possibly a month or more after the merchandise is shipped. Although basic security procedures or well-designed shopping cart programs can prevent this, many online merchants do not use either.

Other varieties of online fraud are simply high-tech variants of the methods described in Chapter 14, "Larceny and Fraud." Old scams have found a new source of victims on the Internet. Pyramid schemes feign legitimacy with professional-appearing websites and official-sounding web addresses.[30] For example, a basic pyramid scheme can claim association with a major retailer by using a trick URL, or web address.

The following URL will take a browser to Wal-Mart, the leading retailer in the United States:

www.walmart.com/index.gsp?cat=0&dept=0&path=0

The URL below will take a browser to the website of whoever had the $50 fee required to register this web address:

www.walmart.com@homeshoppingforyou.com

Without even registering a web domain name, a criminal can have URLs that provide access to his or her page from anywhere on the web. By using these URLs from a "front," the criminal can claim ignorance of where the links go. The links below can easily be altered to lead to anywhere on the Internet without changing anything in front of the "@" sign:

www.walmart.com@192.168.23.56

www.walmart.com@%C0%A8%17%38

### Computers Used in Shopping Fraud

Computer criminals can use the Internet to commit fraud against unsuspecting buyers. For example, professional-appearing websites and official-sounding web addresses can be established to resemble those of large retailers such as Wal-Mart. Customers and Wal-Mart both lose as the customers are lured to the fraudulent sites.

(© Sergio Dorantes/Corbis)

Both of these URLs go to the same place. Another way to perpetrate fraud by misusing a company's name is to register a URL similar to that of the company, such as the one below:

:www.wa1mart.com

Although it is difficult to distinguish, the "l" in Wal-Mart is actually the numeral one, "1." Most people would not make this mistake when typing but would fail to notice the difference on a link from a "front" page. Depending on which type font the browser uses, this phony URL may appear exactly like the authentic URL. The loss to Wal-Mart is obvious as potential customers are lured to fraudulent sites.

## Threat and Harassment

The U.S. Department of Justice (DOJ) maintains a website that details a range of threatening behaviors conducted on the Internet. In an early case of **cyberstalking,** a Maryland man, Warren Gray, pled guilty to sending five email messages that graphically threatened the lives of his victim and the victim's family. Gray had also slashed the victim's car tires and left a hatchet in the victim's office. In this case, cyberstalking coincided with real-world stalking, but the conviction under federal law stemmed from the use of "interstate wires" to transmit the threat.[31] While cyberstalking and real-world stalking have some similarities, there are a number of differences between the two.

### Major Similarities

- The majority of cases involve stalking by former intimates, although stranger stalking also occurs.
- Most victims are women; most stalkers are men.
- Stalkers are generally motivated by the desire to control their victims.

### Major Differences

- In offline stalking the perpetrator and the victim must generally be located in the same geographic area; in cyberstalking the perpetrator may be located across the street or across the country from the victim.
- It is much easier for a cyberstalker to encourage third parties to harass and/or threaten a victim (e.g., by posting inflammatory messages in the victim's name to bulletin boards and in chat rooms, causing readers of the messages to send threatening notes to the victim "author.")
- Cyberstalking has lower barriers to harassment and threats; with technology cyberstalkers can threaten victims more immediately and more easily than is typically possible with physical stalking.[31]

In another cyberstalking case, Carl Edward Johnson of Bienfait, Saskatchewan, Canada, was convicted of posting death threats against U.S. federal judges involved in the conviction of James Dalton Bell, an advocate of assassination politics. Johnson had sent the messages through "anonymous" remailers, but he was identified as the sender through technical testimony from a special agent of the U.S. Treasury's Inspector General for Tax Administration office. Convictions like this demonstrate that the myth of the "anonymous Internet" is overly optimistic about the Internet's ability to protect a criminal from investigation.[32]

Though falling short of cyberstalking, the case of Trung Ngo of Falls Church, Virginia, illustrates the use of the Internet to criminally harass a victim. Ngo pled guilty to sending anonymous harassing email to a former employer at the Department of Defense through his work account. The harassment began in 1995, shortly after Ngo left the Defense Information Systems Agency, where he had been a telecommunication specialist. At first, the harassment involved purchases and magazine subscriptions made by Ngo in the name of his former employer and delivered to the employer's home. In 1998, between April and July, Ngo sent as many as 50 unwanted email messages per day to his former employer.

The use of the computer as an instrumentality of crime introduces a new realm of investigative complications, but investigators trained in the collection and use of digital evidence also have a new realm of opportunities to pursue criminals. While the unprecedented ability of networked computers to reach individuals produces vast opportunities for criminals, it also produces huge amounts of evidence of criminal actions.

## THE COMPUTER AS INCIDENTAL TO THE CRIME

The computer is incidental to crime when "a pattern or incident of criminality uses a computer simply for ease in maintaining the efficacy of criminal transactions."[33] In this category the computer does not conduct the illegal transaction; it simply facilitates it.

## Money Laundering

As noted in Chapter 14, "Larceny and Fraud," money laundering provides criminals with the ability to spend illegally acquired money. The movement of money can be greatly facilitated and, to some degree, be done anonymously by using computer systems. Funds can be divided into groups that are too small to be noticed and that can be wired out of the country and merged together later in an offshore bank. Banks and casinos are closely regulated and heavily penalized for money laundering; however, the enormous volume of financial transactions in the United States makes it difficult for regulators to identify even relatively large questionable transactions. The number of such transactions is likely to increase as more businesses and consumers begin to use electronic funds transfer services.[34]

## Criminal Enterprise

Computers appeal to criminal enterprises or businesses for many of the same reasons they appeal to others: they are quick, reliable, and very accurate, and they perform many business-related tasks far faster than would be the case if the tasks were done manually. Thus, computers are used to support many different types of criminal enterprises, including loan-sharking and drug rings. A number of prostitution rings have used computers to keep track of customers and payroll. The richness of computers as sources of evidence has not been lost on investigators. The study of digital evidence has expanded beyond network intrusion. Detailed procedures and legal requirements of electronic evidence are available from a number of sources.[35]

## Child Pornography

Chapter 11, "Crimes against Children," details the use of the Internet for luring unsuspecting children to pedophiles and for distributing child pornography. The Internet has been the key communication medium for the sale and exchange of child pornography on both an international and a domestic basis. In September 1998, the largest child pornography sting operation in history occurred, resulting in the arrest of over 200 people in 21 countries.[36] Code named "Operation Cathedral," British police coordinated raids in Europe, Australia, and the United States, confiscating more than 100,000 indecent images of children. Most of the images were being traded among child pornographers over the Internet. While most of the people arrested were men, some were women who belonged to exclusive child pornography clubs throughout the world. One U.S.-based club, called "Wonderland," had images for sale depicting children as young as 2 years of age. The sheer size of the pornography network shocked the police as well as the general public. The United Nations called for a worldwide offensive to curb the exchange of pedophilia on the Internet, a very difficult task considering the vast number of jurisdictions and judicial systems present in the international community.[37]

## Pedophilia and Sexual Assault

Some crimes of violence are facilitated by the use of a computer. These crimes can be described in the familiar legal terms of "motive" and "opportunity." Motive reflects the encouragement violent or deviant persons find in the support they receive from their fellows online. Detective Toby Tyler of the San Bernardino County, California, Sheriff's Department described the child pornography problem before the Internet explosion: "Child pornography basically disappeared. . . . We thought this problem was behind us."[38] The problem is clearly back, with tens of thousands of known images available and new ones appearing daily.

If child pornographers use computer networks to exchange indecent images of children, those images must have been created with children. In 1996, a 10-year-old girl was molested at a slumber party by her host's father. Ronald Riva was sentenced in October 1997 for that act. Riva described his actions to a pedophile club via the Internet as he abused the girl. He also responded to requests from club members. The growing demand for fresh images has compelled pedophiles to new depths, including an act depicted in a series called "baby-rape." In regard to the Wonderland investigation, New York Attorney General Dennis C. Vacco stated, "These aren't nudie pictures. . . . These are graphic images of children being raped and sodomized. These are records of crimes."[39] Here we see the traffic of child pornography not only stimulating both the desire to consume more such images, showing greater levels of depravity and child victimization, but also stimulating the actual victimization of the children depicted.

In other instances, the Internet has been used to lure victims to pedophiles, thus providing opportunity. Adult users of chat rooms may use the supposed anonymity of the Internet to pose as teenagers in order to establish a rapport with their intended victims. Numerous sting operations have placed law enforcement officers in the same chat rooms, posing as children. As computer crime goes, investigations of solicitation of minors and of child pornography have been relatively productive for law enforcement. The *Organized Crime Digest* reports that a local and federal partnership in Maine has steadily increased the number of charges against distributors of child pornography over the last two and one-half years.[40]

Few would argue that children need to be protected from predators. It is fairly simple to set up stings for pedophiles using the Internet, and in some cases digital evidence can be linked to both motive and opportunity. Several criminal cases have introduced email as evidence of the state of mind of the accused. Hate speech online has been used to establish a racial or sexual bias for motive. Similarly, email has been used to actually trace the interaction of assailant and victim. Meetings discussed or demanded in email can be used to place the assailant at the crime scene. Unlike the trafficking of disturbing images, the desire to create those images directly stimulates an act. Where the act is assaulting, luring, or molesting children, the computer serves as the connection that provides motive or opportunity.

## CRIMES ASSOCIATED WITH THE PREVALENCE OF COMPUTERS

Computer crime investigators should be aware of new targets of crime. Crimes associated with the prevalence of computers make up a subset of computer crime that relies on the relatively new computer and information industry. Targets of these crimes are mainly the industry itself but also include its customers and even people who have avoided information technology.

### Intellectual-Property Violations

Intellectual-property violations are often described as **piracy.** The music trading service, Napster, has recently caused music piracy to replace software piracy in the public mind as the leading example of this crime.

The Business Software Alliance (BSA) is the principal software industry antipiracy resource. The BSA estimated that losses due to piracy were over $2.5 million in the United States alone during 2000. The worldwide estimate was over $11.7 million during 2000.[41] Figure 16–4 compares software-piracy losses by region. Another, often-quoted estimate places the total damage to the U.S. economy

**Figure 16-4** Costs of Software Piracy

(**Source:** International Planning and Research Corporation, *Sixth Annual BSA Global Software Piracy Study* (Washington, DC: Business Software Alliance, May 2001); retrieved from www.bsa.org/resources/2001-05-21.55.pdf, Aug. 30, 2001.)

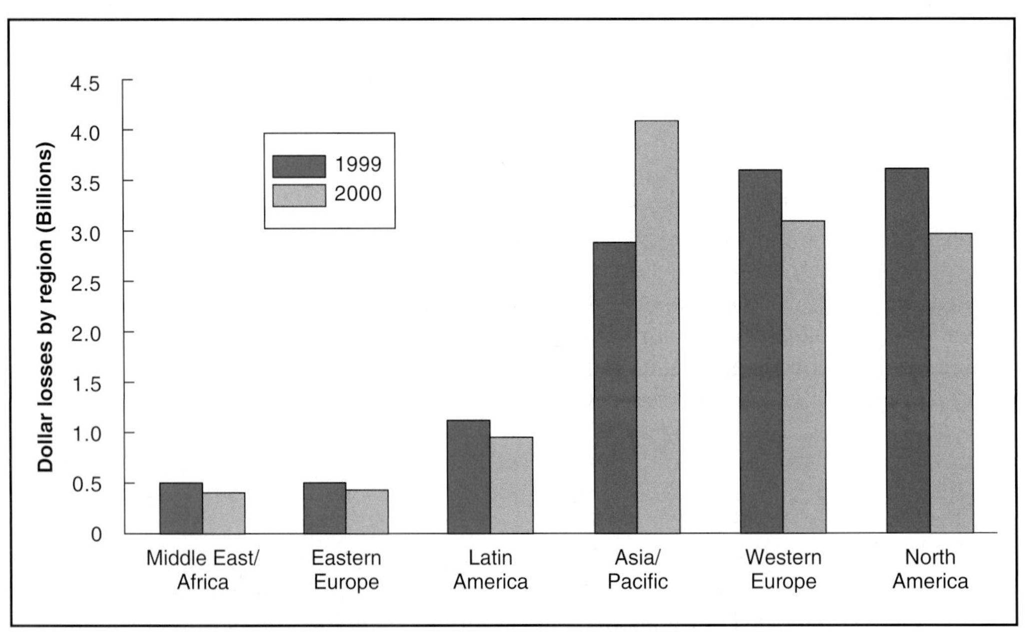

at over $10 billion.[42] Even if the BSA "tweaked" the figures somewhat to further heighten the attention drawn to the problem, this loss of revenue hurts not just the software industry but the national economy as well.

Large-scale software piracy began in Asia. The BSA reports that one person selling unauthorized copies of some 40 different popular programs in Singapore may have made several million dollars even though he charged as little as $15 for copies of programs that retailed for as much as $600.[43] Violation of U.S. copyright laws in China—particularly piracy of software, videotaped entertainment, and music—led the United States, in early 1995, to announce that it would place a 100 percent tariff on all products entering this country from China unless the Chinese government took action to eliminate such violations. This is one of the few incidents in history in which criminal activity actually influenced U.S. foreign policy.

Extensive software piracy now exists worldwide and is facilitated by the Internet. Dutch bulletin boards provided the nexus of "cracked" games and software during the 1980s.[44] Today, "WaRez Doods"[45] continue the tradition by racing to provide the first cracked edition of new software, often before it is released officially.[45] Microsoft operating systems are the favorite target of the Warez Doods. Another group of software pirates, from the Pacific Northwest, electronically raided the Lucas Arts Entertainment Company of San Rafael, California.[46] The prize was TIE Fighter, based on the three *Star Wars* movies. Intended for sale at about $60, the software had not yet been released. For about $300, a Lucas Arts employee attached a cellular modem to the back of his computer—so that there would be no company record of the call—and sent TIE Fighter to the waiting pirates. The copy protection was cracked, and the game was placed on an Internet "warez" site for distribution.

## Misuse of Telephone Systems

Telephone **phreakers** are people who trick telephone systems into believing that long-distance service and airtime are being legitimately purchased. In 1994, 1,000 hackers and phreakers gathered in the Hackers on Planet Earth Conference in New York City to attend seminars and exchange tips on their "hobby."[47] The interest of phreakers also extends to collateral areas, such as trying to break the code on magnetic subway cards for free rides and to decode the magnetic strips that are found on the back of some states' driver's licenses.[48]

In one phreaker case, a company employee figured out how to avoid the internal tracking system for long-distance charges and then sold time cheaply to friends to make telephone calls, which resulted in a $108,000 loss.[49] Cellular telephones are also subject to attack by phreakers. This is done by using one of two common fraud methods: cloning and tumbling.[50] Cellular telephones have two numbers: a mobile identification number (MIN) and an electronic serial number (ESN). Every time a call is made, the microchip in a cellular phone transmits both numbers to the local switching office for verification and billing. **Cloning** involves using a personal computer to change the microchip in one cellular phone so that it matches a legitimate MIN and ESN from numbers "hacked" from a phone company, bought from a telephone company insider, acquired from a cellular phone whose theft will not be quickly discovered, or "plucked" from the airways by a portable device—about the size of a notebook—that can be plugged into a car's lighter receptacle. The user with the cloned numbers can simply use them until service is cut off and then change the MIN and ESN and start

### Cloned Cellular Phone

Cloning involves the use of a personal computer to change the microchips in one cellular phone so that it matches legitimate mobile identification and electronic serial numbers "hacked" from a phone company. The use of cellular phones with cloned numbers is popular with criminals, particularly those dealing in drugs.

(© Thomas Brummett/PhotoDisc)

all over again. The use of cellular phones with cloned numbers is popular with criminals, particularly those dealing in drugs, who may lease them for up to $750 per day. In a related scam, a person leases a cloned cellular phone for a day and then sells international call time cheaply to immigrants or illegal aliens. **Tumbling** requires the use of a personal computer to alter a cellular phone's microchip so that its MIN and ESN numbers change after each call, making detection more difficult. One of the newest trends in cellular-phone fraud is to use a combination tumbler-clone, which affords the fraudulent user the untraceability of a tumbled phone with the free service of a cloned phone. There are two other types of cellular-telephone fraud: subscription fraud, in which free service is obtained through theft or forgery of subscriber information or through employee collusion; and network fraud, in which weaknesses in the cellular network's technology are exploited to defraud the cellular service provider.

## Component Theft

The theft of desktop and laptop computers, monitors, printers, scanners, modems, and other equipment has been decreasing. In 1999, laptop theft accounted for 10 percent of the total computer crime reported in the Computer Security Institute (CSI)/Federal Bureau of Investigation (FBI) annual survey. The figure dropped in 2000 to 3.9 percent and again in 2001 to 2.3 percent of the total. The actual dollar value has also been decreasing since the CSI/FBI survey began. The rapid growth of other types of computer crime and the rapidly dropping prices of computer systems are the most likely causes for this decline. While the value of laptops being stolen has dropped, there is significant evidence that laptop computers are now being stolen for the information contained on their hard drives, such as documents and passwords, rather than for the hardware itself. The largest category in the CSI/FBI survey is theft of proprietary information, which accounts for approximately 40 percent of total losses.[51] However, the full extent of computer theft is unknown because many thefts go unreported and because many police departments consider theft of computer hardware as just another stolen-property crime. Some computer owners do not even know what they own and therefore cannot provide the police with an accurate description, let alone the serial numbers. This problem is compounded by the inability of some police officers to accurately differentiate among computer equipment and peripherals.[52] The following story details such a case: A major telecommunication company had two server memory chips stolen from a card-access-only storage room, each worth about $1,200. When local police detectives searched the home of one of the suspects, they had to ask the suspect what the chips looked like, how big they

**Personal Computers and Components: Targets of Theft**

While recent data suggest the theft of desktop computers, printers, scanners, and modems are on the decline, they are still the favorite targets of some thieves. Today, personal computers are often stolen for their component parts, as well as for the proprietary information that may be stored within.

(© Jay Bryant/Getty Images/Stone)

were, and what type of machine they would fit. Fortunately, the suspect was very cooperative and pointed out the stolen chips, which were being used in a personal system.

## Corporate Crime

The rapid growth of the computer industry has caused many questionable business practices to develop and eventually be accepted as a part of doing business. Examples of such practices include rebate fraud, grossly one-sided end-user license agreements (EULAs), misleading advertising, component swapping, the resale of refurbished components in "new" systems, simple fraud, and many others. Rebates are a common practice in the computer industry. The Federal Trade Commission (FTC) has become involved in actions against several companies that promised mail-in rebates, but did not deliver. The first case to draw widespread attention involved the Iomega Zip Drive. With the unprecedented demand for the zip drive, the rebate fulfillment center contracted to handle the processing of rebates was overwhelmed. A large number of rebates were simply lost, and delays of a year or more were common. EULAs are contracts that specify the rights of the consumer when purchasing a license to use software.[53] Originally intended to prevent people from reselling copies of their software, EULAs have become so one-sided that they violate common tenets of contract law and consumer protection legislation. Common elements of EULAs include a stipulation that the software licensed need not function for any particular purpose, even if that function is advertised! Although it is legal to require a EULA, the contract's terms do not automatically supercede false-advertising legislation. There is also the assumption that an item sold is fit for use.

Component swapping and refurbishment fraud are practices that were fairly common among computer manufacturers. The Intel Inside campaign was a response by Intel, a computer processor manufacturer, to the use of chips by secondary suppliers. The Intel Inside logo assured consumers that they had a name-brand chip. In general, in the practice of **component swapping** manufacturers use parts from the lowest-cost supplier but do not inform the customer of the change. Other than processor chips, the most infamous example of this practice was the use of computer memory from a supplier in Taiwan. The memory used tin connectors instead of the industry standard, gold. The tin quickly corroded and the memory failed. **Refurbishment fraud** is a related practice in which working components from damaged or returned computers are used in the construction of new systems or simply resold as new systems. For several years, demand for computers rose as fast as or faster than manufacturing capability; a devastating earthquake and fire at one of the two memory fabrication facilities in the world added pressure to manufacturers. In response, manufacturers began to reuse components. These components were sometimes defective, but, more importantly, they were not the new systems advertised.

Simple fraud and misleading advertising are frequent facts in the computer industry. Simple fraud occurs when a company overextends its ability to supply products but continues to take orders. A frequent result of this situation is the bankruptcy or reorganization of the company. Even during the process of bankruptcy, it is fairly common for the company to continue to take new orders. While not rising to the level of fraud, several practices of the computer industry are considered misleading advertising by the FTC. Class-action lawsuits brought against monitor manufacturers claim that the actual dimensions of cathode ray tube (CRT) monitors are not the same as those advertised. For example, a 15-inch monitor actually measures only about 14.1 inches diagonally. While such dimensions are standardized across the industry, their use is misleading as to the actual size. Similarly, the page-per-minute (PPM) rating for printers is often based on questionable tests or simply on the theorized speed of the paper-feed mechanism.

# MALICIOUS CODE AND COMPUTER CRIME

Investigators should be aware of the tools that are unique to computer criminals. This section provides descriptions of the more common tools. In most cases, mere possession of these tools is not a crime; however, evidence of their use may be present on a suspect's system. Careful forensic analysis of such systems may produce useful leads or connect the suspect to the crime scene. Gene Spafford of Purdue University has made remarkable strides in linking compiled computer programs to an original source by, among other techniques, matching text-based commands and comments.[54] Analysis of malicious code may become an important tool for prosecution of computer criminals. At the very least, familiarity with such tools can help an investigator recognize their effects.

## DISCOVERY TOOLS

The first step in intruding into a system is finding the system. Most network intrusions attack targets of opportunity; this means that rather than select a target system, most intruders find a vulnerable system. A software tool called a port scanner can be used to probe for all computers on a given segment of the Internet. Once a target computer is discovered, the port scanner can be set to detect services available from that computer that have known vulnerabilities. When a computer is known to have a vulnerability, exploiting that vulnerability is as simple as entering the Internet address in another program called an exploit (see below).

The favorite port scanner of many intruders and network administrators alike is the NMAP program. NMAP uses several techniques to discover even hidden computers. It has a number of settings that allow a user to balance the speed, stealth, and thoroughness of the search.[55]

Another tool uses a similar technique to discover computers with modems. Modems are often not protected as well as Internet access points. A war dialer dials a sequence of numbers, for example 555-0000 through 555-9999, to discover computers.[56] When a person answers the phone, he or she hears silence or the squeaks of what sounds like a fax machine. The war dialer does not call back, so the incident is often dismissed. When a computer answers the phone, the war dialer notes the number and continues calling new numbers until the sequence is done. The would-be intruder is left with a list of phone numbers connecting to computers.

Although war dialing is being replaced with port scanning as the method of choice for intruders, it is still used. The most popular war dialer is ToneLoc, written by Christopher Lamprecht, a.k.a. "Minor Threat."[57] Lamprecht was convicted of charges unrelated to hacking in 1995. The age of this program indicates the waning interest in war dialing.

Not surprising, packet sniffers are another type of tool that gathers information. As mentioned earlier, sniffers are typically placed on a local area network (LAN) to discover traffic being sent across the network. Any computer capable of network communication can become a sniffer. There is no specific sniffing tool that stands above others, because sniffing is a basic technique for diagnosing and repairing LANs. However, sensitive information such as user names and passwords is often transferred unencrypted, making it a target for malicious sniffers. Even when passwords are encrypted, they can still be broken with cryptanalysis software.

## CRYPTANALYSIS SOFTWARE

Cryptanalysis software is not always malicious, but it is frequently used as an intrusion aid. One writer defines **cryptanalysis** as the art and science of accessing secured information without conventional means.[58] Functionally, cryptanalysis is about breaking encryption. L0pht Heavy Industries, now merged with a security company called @Stake, created a cryptanalysis tool called L0phtcrack to break Windows NT password security. Although there is no way to decrypt Windows NT passwords, this tool uses weaknesses in the NT password scheme to efficiently reproduce every possible password and find matches. When a match is found, the L0phtcrack user has the password and eventually every other password in the system. On a fairly common system running L0phtcrack, every possible password can be discovered in 480 hours, with 80 percent or more discovered in the first 5.5 hours.[59]

## EXPLOITS

**Exploits** are a generic class of programs that are written to take advantage of a security hole or **back door** program designed to evade normal security procedures. Programmers often use debugging aids that provide code breaks called back doors. Most of the time these breaks are removed before the software is released for general use, but sometimes their removal is overlooked or they are deliberately left in to provide easy maintenance of the program in the future. Back doors are often the victim of a specific exploit to gain access and privileges not normally available to the intruder. A common goal of intruders is to gain the privileges of the highest-level account: root or superuser in the Unix world and administrator in Windows environments.

Once the intruder "gets root," he or she enjoys unlimited access to virtually all areas of the computer's function. This allows the intruder to delete or alter privileged files called logs that may be useful in tracing the intruder. It also allows the intruder to install new software for his or her attack on the next target.

**Root kits** are specially designed exploit packages with tools that enable the intruder to maintain the level of access by installing back doors and secret accounts, as well as altering logs and basic system services. Different root kits are available for different operating systems. There are also exploits for obtaining and maintaining administrator privileges in Windows.

## ATTACK CODES

Unlike simple intrusion aids, which may cause damage incidental to the intrusion, an **attack code** is malicious software intended to impair or destroy the function of another computer or network resource. Attack codes are often designed simply to harass system users or administrators.

### Denial-of-Service Attacks

AOL punters, WinNuke, Bonk, Teardrop, mail bombs, and many other software tools have been developed with the sole function of annoying users. AOL punters can be used to force an AOL subscriber off of the network. Teardrop crashes the target's computer, also removing the user from the

#### Attack Codes Deny Service to Computer Users

An attack code is malicious software intended to impair or destroy the function of another computer or network source. Attack codes are often designed to harass system users or administrators. For example, AOL punters is a software tool that can be used to force subscribers off the network for the sole purpose of annoying users and administrators.

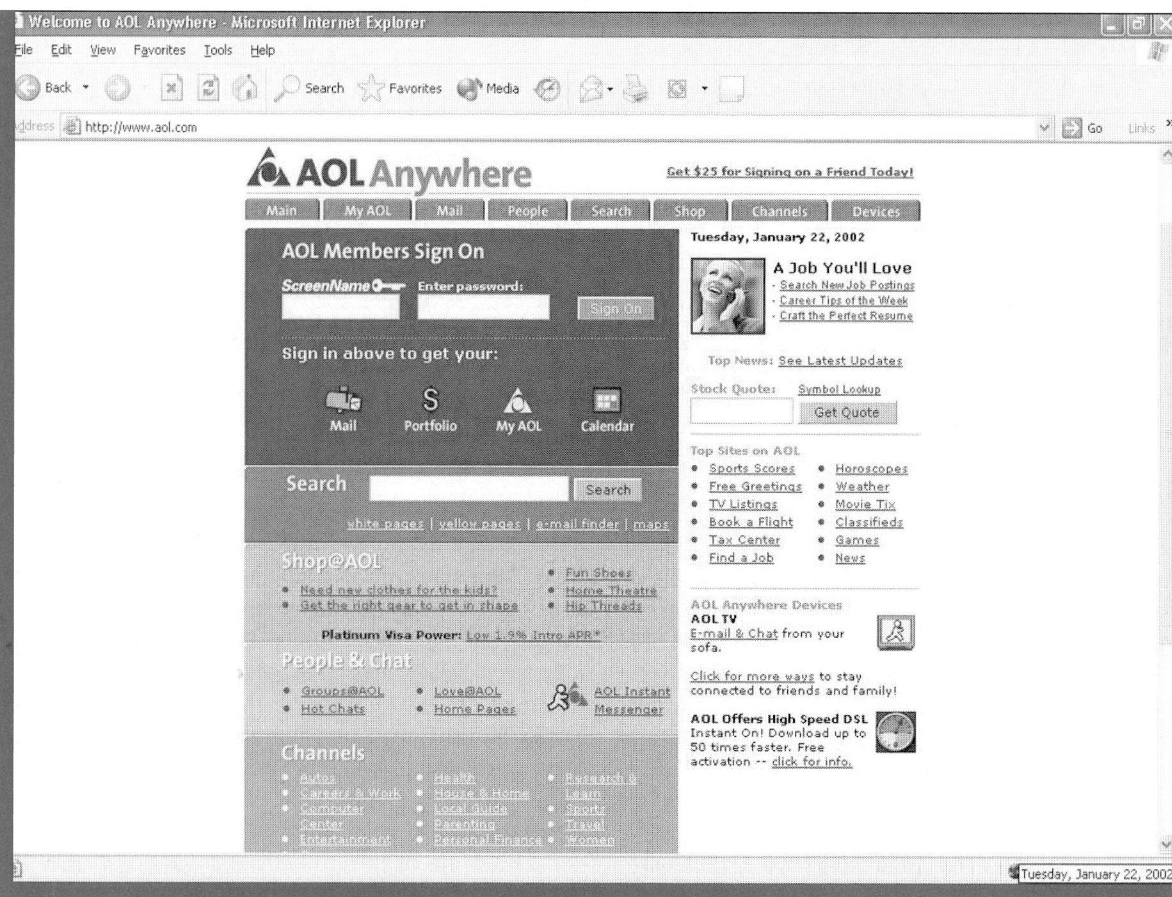

**Denial-of-Service Attack Software Creates Problems**

Recently, a particular subclass of denial-of-service attacks, known as the *distributed denial-of-service attack,* has drawn attention. Normally immune to simple denial-of-service attacks by virtue of their size and capacity, the largest Internet sites such as Yahoo and CMN have suffered from recent distributed attacks.

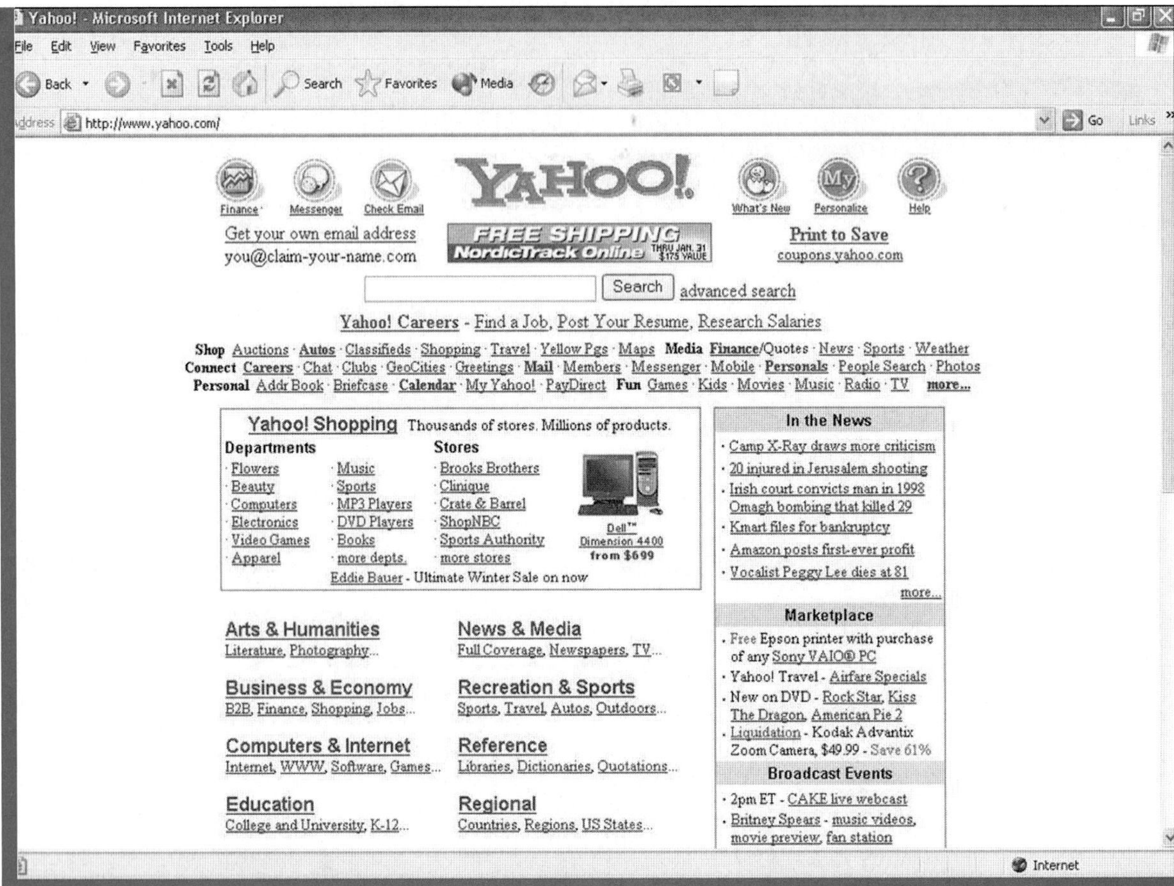


network. Mail bombs fill a user's email-box space quota and thereby deny the victim mail service. The use of any of these tools constitutes a denial-of-service attack.

Recently, a particular subclass of denial-of-service attacks has drawn attention: the distributed denial-of-service attack. Tools such as Trino and the Tribal Flood Network (TFN) have been used to deny service on a massive scale. Normally immune to simple denial-of-service attacks by virtue of their size and capacity, the largest Internet sites (e.g., Yahoo, Barnes & Noble, and CNN) have each suffered from distributed attacks.[60] Network-based denial-of-service attacks like the Yahoo attack are explained in Figure 16–5.

## Logic Bombs

The software tools mentioned above provide active attacks against a network target. Another means of attacking computers and the data structures they support is a **logic bomb.** Logic bombs use illegal program instructions and misuse legitimate instructions to damage data structures. "Data structure" is a broad term comprising the data, programmed uses of the data, instructions, and patterns that computers manipulate to provide requested results. Aside from damaging data structures, the primary distinction of logic bombs is that they operate at a specific time or periodically. A logic bomb may be executed on the basis of a specific date or time

**Figure 16-5** Denial-of-Service Attacks

The Internet was designed with several features that help network designers and administrators find problems. When misused, these features can provide an avenue for attackers to disable a single computer or even a whole portion of the network. One such feature is *Internet control message protocol (ICMP)*. The most common function of ICMP is the "ping." Like a submarine's sonar, a ping packet will be reflected from an active computer. This lets the sender know that the other computer is on the network and that it is possible to establish a connection.

**ICMP Flood Attack—Smurfing:** With this method, the attacker sends multiple pings to the broadcast address of an intermediate network: a staging network. The broadcast address passes the ping to every computer on the staging network. The ping tells the staging network to reply to the target computer instead of the sending computer. The target is overwhelmed by responses from every computer on the staging network. (See Figure A.)

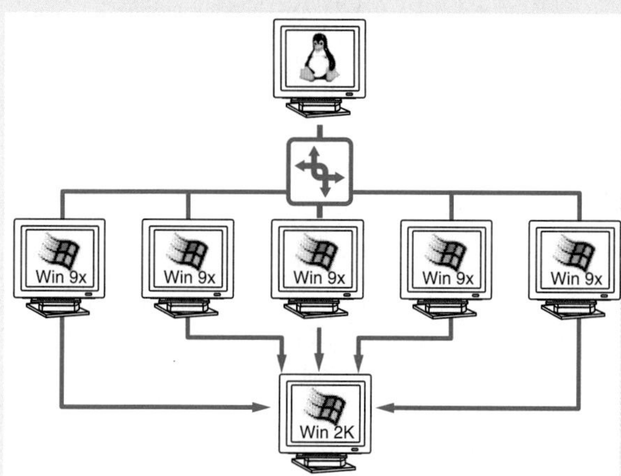


Figure A

**Malformed-Packet Attack—Ping of Death or Teardrop:** The Ping of Death uses a packet that exceeds the maximum size allowed by Internet protocol (IP); this is a supposedly impossible situation. (To transfer information, the Internet breaks large transmissions into packets and reassembles them upon arrival.) Vulnerable systems receiving this large packet may freeze, crash, or reboot. Teardrop exploits the way packets are reassembled upon arrival. By forging packets that overlap, when they are reassembled, Teardrop causes another impossible situation. An analogy is cutting a pie into 8 slices, having each person carry his or her own slice to the table, and then trying to place 11 slices back on the pie plate. Upon receiving this impossible packet, systems vulnerable to the Teardrop attack may freeze, crash, or reboot. (See Figure B.)

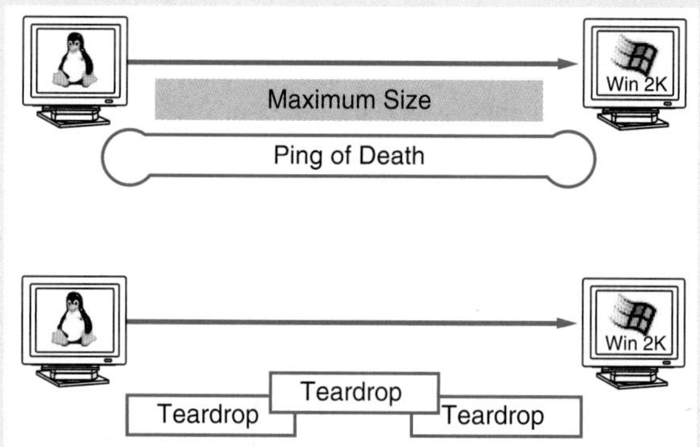


Figure B

**Half-Formed Connection Attack—SYN Flood:** When two computers on the Internet need to connect, the computer initiating the connection sends a SYN packet to synchronize a connection. The other computer replies with a SYN-ACK, or synchronization acknowledgment, packet. The first computer then acknowledges the connection with an ACK packet. This process is called a "three-part handshake." SYN flood attacks exploit this process by failing to send the final ACK. Most computers have a very limited capacity to hold such partial connections. If a SYN flood uses all the space, no new connections can be made. The target computer will hold each partial connection for a set time. As the time limit expires and the connection is dropped, the vast number of flooding SYN requests fills the space. (See Figure C.)

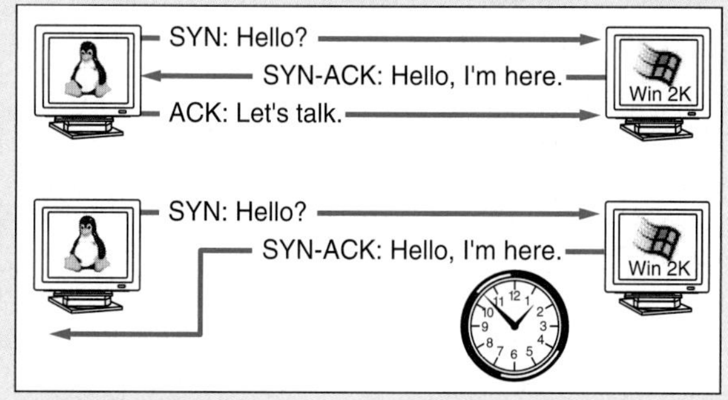


Figure C

or other instructions. For example, if a specific Social Security number is deleted from the salary database (meaning the employee has been fired), a logic bomb planted by that person might delete critical files.

## DELIVERY VEHICLES

**Delivery vehicles** provide computer criminals with a means of delivering their attack software. The most common varieties of delivery vehicles are

Trojan horses, viruses, and worms. Whether the vehicle delivers an intrusion code or attack code, it is distinguished by the method of delivery, not its effect. There is a history of legitimate research concerning the use of the delivery vehicles discussed below. Computer criminals often cite their contribution to this body of research as justification for their actions, but few, if any, have bothered to publish their discoveries.

## Trojan Horse Programs

The delivery vehicle of choice for exploit software, **Trojan horse** programs masquerade as legitimate programs. Technically, any program that is altered or designed to provide an unwanted or malicious function while appearing to provide a routine or benign function is a Trojan horse. This leaves a number of interpretations open for most commercial software with unadvertised functions or functions that may harm the user—such as copyright verification mechanisms. The most common Trojan horse involves replacing the normal password-verifying software with a "Trojaned" version that will capture user names and passwords to make them available to the intruder placing the Trojan. Login.c is a popular Trojan horse. Typical of Trojan horse programs, Login.c returns an error message to the user attempting to log on to the system and then activates the normal password verifier. Thus, the error may appear to be due to a typing mistake. When the user attempts to log on again, the system appears to function normally.

## Viruses and Worms

A computer **virus** is a malicious program that is secretly inserted into normal software or into the computer's active memory. The impact of such programs, which are relatively small, runs from annoying messages to more serious problems such as interference with the computer's normal operating procedures, extended run times, or deletion of data. The 2001 Annual CSI/FBI Computer Crime and Security Survey has estimated the damage due to viruses at 12 percent of the total damage caused by computer crime. From 1997 to 1999, the actual damage and the percentage of total damage from viruses declined steadily. However, the new generation of viruses, such as Love Letter and Melissa, brought the virus damage from a low of 4 percent of the total computer crime damage in 1999 to 12 percent in 2001.[61]

A virus is not a complete program; like its namesake, the computer virus is not active without a host. A computer virus attaches to a host by inserting instructions within the other program (i.e., infecting it). Thus, whenever the host program runs, the virus runs. A virus has two distinct components: propagation and payload. The propagation component allows the virus to spread. Common mechanisms include attaching to an executable program (e.g., MS Word), a system file (e.g., run32.dll), or a document with macros or scripts activated (e.g., My Document.doc). New variants can embed themselves in the scripts commonly found in web pages and html-based email. The virus payload can carry an attack code or intrusion code. It can issue commands to download Trojan horse programs from the web and install them in place of existing software. Fortunately, in many cases the payload is a trivial message: a symbolic "Gotcha!"

In the past, the most common methods of spreading viruses were by sharing infected floppy disks and by opening an infected file from the Internet (see Figure 16–6). Today, antivirus software has become extremely adept at catching known viruses. Modem viruses rely on stealth and speed. Stealth viruses hide themselves by intercepting requests to view the area where the virus is hiding. Early stealth viruses on floppy disks reported the virus area as unusable. Polymorphic viruses attempt to change their own codes too fast for antivirus vendors to provide updates. Some polymorphic viruses actually encrypt or compress themselves to hide telltale signs of viruslike code. Another variation on speed is rapid deployment. This strategy is most commonly used by worms.

The primary distinction between viruses and worms is that a **worm** does not rely on infecting a host program. This allows worms to be programmed to act faster. Worms such as Melissa attempt to spread rapidly, before antivirus software can be updated. The rapid-deployment variation has produced aggressive new strains that can spread through large portions of the Internet in a matter of hours. For example, the Melissa worm achieved most of its fame and destruction by spreading rapidly through email. The worm had run its course before the antivirus industry was able to respond. New heuristic virus detection technology no longer attempts to match viruses or worms to known samples; rather, it attempts to detect viruslike actions.

Figure 16-6

How Viruses Are Spread

(**Source:** *Houston Chronicle,* Aug. 8, 1988, p. 88; modified, 1998.)

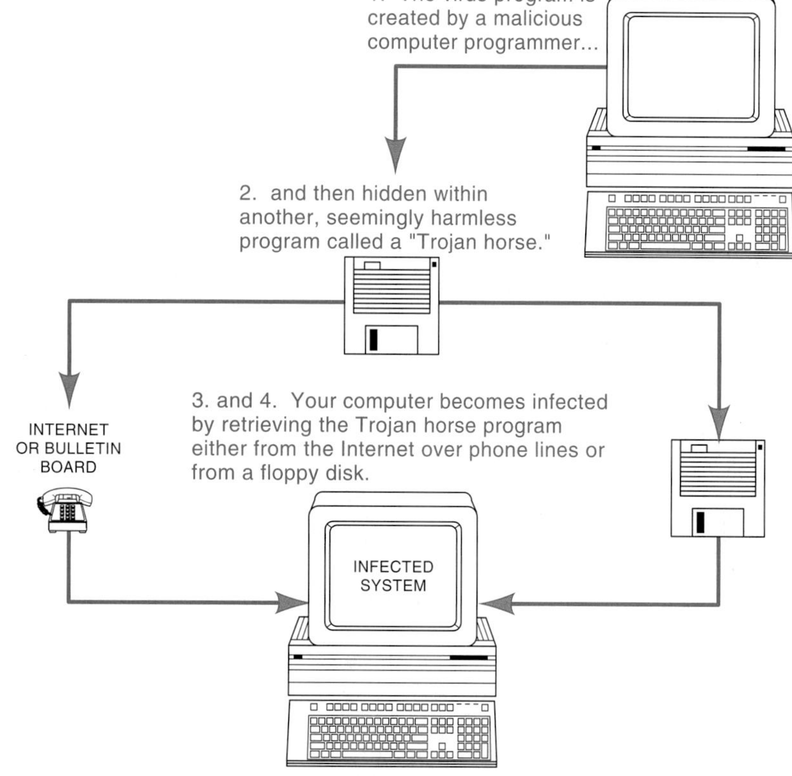


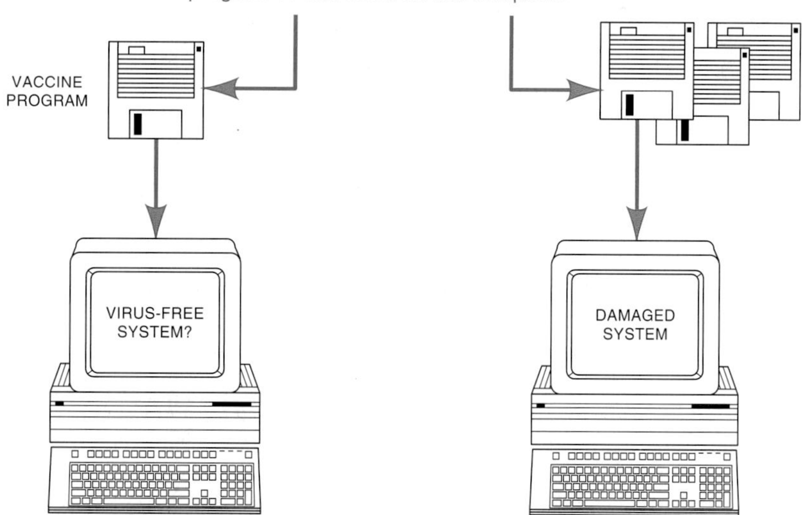

The next-generation viruses may find a way to adapt to this promising but imperfect technology.

# INVASION OF PRIVACY AND RELATED ISSUES

## SEXUALLY EXPLICIT MATERIAL

Nothing seems to spur more controversy than debate concerning regulation of the Internet. While several attempts have been made to limit access to unwanted material available on the web, no set standards have yet been approved as law.

One side of the debate typically focuses on the vast amount of pornographic and obscene material easily accessible via the Internet. This includes sites that not only depict partially clothed and nude individuals but also venture into the world of sexual perversion, including sadomasochism, bestiality, and online voyeurism. Proponents for regulation contend that the web should be treated like any other medium (i.e., radio, television, print material) and thus be required, through Internet service providers, to technically "ban" access to such material. This is a particularly strong argument when placed in the context of guarding minors from obtaining, receiving, and/or sending such material. Nowhere was this debate more intense than in the 1997 Supreme Court case involving the proposed Communications Decency Act of 1996.[62] The Court ruled that the act was much too broad and nonspecific. Further, the Court found that the requirement to limit such access was too burdensome and would essentially limit the free-speech clause of the First Amendment of the Constitution.[63] The Court added that parents and schools could use commercially available software that blocks sexually oriented sites to safeguard children from such material. Finally, it argued that significant federal statutes already existed that allowed authorities to act against obscenity—that is, hard-core pornography. Transmission of such material, especially that involving the depiction of children in a sexual venue, is *not* constitutionally protected and is a felony in the United States.[64]

The decision has had far-reaching effects. Adult sites continue to proliferate on the web. In fact, an adult website (amateurs.com) is the second-most-visited site on the entire Internet, just behind microsoft.com. And adult sites continue to be top money-making ventures on the web. There appears to be no end to the pornographic explosion as technology now allows interactive, live sex shows via the Internet. While the Communications Decency Act had a short, but eventful, life, its impact may well limit the government's ability to impose other controls on Internet content, such as restrictions on commodity trading, stock advice sites, and electronic junk mail.

## COOKIES

Debate over the Communications Decency Act sparked interest in maintaining personal privacy while on the web. New discussions concerning the potential for clandestine "spying" and invasion of personal privacy have reached national agendas. Much of the debate centers on **cookies,** which are small files planted by web pages on a visiting computer.[65] These files are stored within the user's browser (Netscape Navigator) or a separate file (Microsoft Explorer). They are used by a web server to identify past users. They can pass short bits of information, such as user name, from the web server back to itself the next time a visit occurs. Popular rumors about cookies describe them as evil programs that can scan a user's hard drive and gather information about the user, including passwords, credit card numbers, and lists of software on his or her computer. This is simply not true. Cookies cannot gather and transmit information from a hard drive and cannot plant viruses.[66] Figure 16–7 provides more detailed information on cookies and tips for Internet privacy. However, computer and security experts agree on one simple guideline for governing all Internet activity: Assume that nothing is absolutely private or safe!

# THE HACKER PROFILE

The computers that hackers use are typically far less sophisticated than those used by the systems they attack. Their weapon of choice is a fast computer with a large hard disk, a modem, and a telephone line through which they can access the information superhighway.

**Figure 16-7**

**Tips on Internet Privacy**

(**Source:** Cookie information prepared by Matt Taylor, CTC Communications, Waltham, Massachusetts, May 2002)

**Cookies:** A cookie is a small piece of information that is sent to a user's web browser by a particular website's server. The information is saved on the user's hard drive in a file and has a set expiration date, which may be so far into the future that the cookie will effectively never expire. Each subsequent time that the user visits the site, the server requests the information that it put in the cookie file. These transactions are usually conducted transparently and without the user's knowledge. The vast majority of net users are unaware of cookie files.

A cookie keeps track of what sites a computer has visited by providing users with unique identifiers. Cookies can be helpful, as they allow a web server to "remember" specific information about a user. Cookies can allow website personalization, quicker access to user-ID and password-protected websites, and the ability to return to the last actions at a specific site. Cookies can also be used by law enforcement during a computer crime investigation to view a history of potentially illicit activity while the suspect was on the Internet. They have been important tools in linking suspects to child molesting, pornography, terrorist organizations, and fraud crimes.

For more information on cookies, visit the following websites:

www.cookiecentral.com

www.luckman.com/products/anoncookie/index.html

www8.zdnet.com/pcmag/features/cookies/_open.htm

www.webattack.com/shareware/security/swcookie.html

ww.anu.edu.au/people/Roger.Clarke/II/Cookies.html#Appl

www.gc.maricopa.edu/2dts000/cis133/modules/m20a.htm

www.pcug.org.au/~amikkels/cookies.html

**Usenet news groups:** Remember the "Mom rule": Don't include anything you wouldn't want your mother to read.

**Chat rooms:** Even if you chat under an anonymous name, anyone can capture and rebroadcast the dialogue. With the "WHOIS" command, your real email address and those of others who conversed with you can be revealed.

**Email:** Messages are routed through possibly dozens of computers across the Internet. Any truly private information should be encrypted.

**Anonymous remailers:** They let whistleblowers send untraceable messages. Unfortunately, they are also available to junk mailers and harassers.

**Credit cards:** Credit card transactions on the Internet are as safe as phone and fax transactions as long as they occur on web pages with secure, encrypted connections.

Hackers can spring from any group, as illustrated by cases involving an airline pilot and a homemaker. However, such instances are somewhat unusual and do not meet the more typical hacker profile. On the basis of interviews with approximately 100 convicted hackers, most of them are relatively young, white males from middle-class environments.[67] Generally, they range from 14 to 25 years of age.

They are not socially integrated and tend to be loners, except when communicating by computer. They tend not to associate with their peer group or become actively involved in peer group behavior such as dating or participating in school activities. They take on the air of self-assurance only when they are with fellow phreakers, talking about their computers. One convicted teenager reported that "hacking is like cocaine . . . it's a rush you can't forget."[68] Most hackers are thrill seekers; the challenge of entering a secure data bank is exciting, just as mountain climbing is for people who climb mountains. Penetrating multiple levels of a computer system's security to get at the programs and files has been described as "orgasmic." One young man stated that "hacking is the next best thing to sex."[69] Often, the attacks cause little if any physical damage as the hacker "browses" through files looking for innocuous games to play.

Hackers' parents rarely suspect problems because hackers appear to be "model" young adults. As one investigator pointed out, "They [hackers] don't race cars, chase girls, drink beer, or get into trouble." Although hackers are smart, they tend to be underachievers in school. They stay in their rooms, working on their computers.

## THE COMPUTER CRIMINAL PROFILE

The most likely suspects in insider computer crime are programmers and system operators. Any other personnel who have inordinate amounts of autonomy, overlapping areas of responsibility, and freedom of movement within the electronic data processing (EDP) function of a business are also prime suspects. No one person should ever be allowed to control all—or overlapping—aspects of EDP operations. Within the government, computer criminals generally were found to be:

> young, good employees of a federal agency or a state, local, or private agency administering federal programs . . . their median age was thirty. Three-quarters had spent at least some time in college. They had been with their respective agencies for an average of five years before they committed their crimes. . . . Nearly three-quarters had been promoted and two-thirds reported receiving at least an above average performance rating. In fact, a quarter of the perpetrators told us they had received performance awards.[70]

When investigating what appears to be an insider computer crime, the investigator should consider the factors listed below.[71]

### Opportunities

- Familiarity with operations (including cover-up capabilities).
- Position of trust.
- Close associations with suppliers and other key people.

### Situational Pressures—Financial

- High personal debts.
- Severe illness in family.
- Inadequate income and/or living beyond means.
- Extensive stock market speculation.
- Loan-shark involvement.
- Excessive gambling.
- Heavy expenses incurred from extramarital involvement.
- Undue family, peer, company, or community expectations.
- Excessive use of alcohol or drugs.

### Situational Pressures—Revenge

- Perceived inequities (e.g., low pay or poor job assignment).
- Resentment of superiors.
- Frustration, usually with job.

### Personality Traits

- Lacks personal moral honesty.
- No well-defined code of personal ethics.
- A wheeler-dealer, that is, someone who enjoys feelings of power, influence, social status, and excitement associated with rapid financial transactions involving large sums of money.
- Neurotic, manic depressive, or emotionally unstable.
- Arrogant or egocentric.

- Psychopathic.
- Low self-esteem.
- Personally challenged to subvert a system of controls.

Investigators should also construct a "personal demography" on suspects. This consists of three factors: (1) criminal history, (2) list of associates, and (3) references.[72]

Among the persons who should raise suspicion are employees who work late (after hours) and refuse promotions and/or transfers. Any scams they may be working will be more lucrative than the promotions. Other suspects might be persons who show remarkable curiosity toward aspects of EDP outside their job requirements.

**Computer Criminal Studies Latest Prey**

Insider computer crimes are most often committed by programmers and systems operators. Other potential suspects would include anyone having significant autonomy, overlapping areas of responsibility, and freedom of movement within the electronic data processing function of a business. Within government agencies, many computer criminals have been otherwise good employees.

(© Michael Prince/Corbis)

## INVESTIGATING COMPUTER CRIME

Among the many problems confronting investigators is that some victims—such as financial institutions, consulting firms, and corporations—may not report the fraud or prosecute the offender because of the adverse publicity involved. They simply do not want depositors, potential clients, and shareholders to think them incapable of managing their affairs. Although no one wants bad publicity, this practice allows known violators to go free. Additionally, because many crimes go unreported, the police, prosecutors, and legislative bodies have only a partial understanding of the true scope of the problem.

Because computer crime is difficult to detect, the trail is often cold, records may be at a minimum, key people to interview may have gone on to other jobs, and investigators may not recognize key evidence or know what to ask for due to a lack of training and experience.[73]

The hacker(s) who attacked the Yahoo and CNN websites during the summer of 2001 used methods that were virtually antique yet was able to wreck havoc on the system. If that hacker was difficult for a computer expert to catch, consider how much harder it would be to investigate a crime committed by any of the 200 or so superelite hackers who use cutting-edge methods. However, investigators have a number of sources to which they can turn for information, training, and assistance when investigating computer crime.

The FBI (through the FBI Academy in Quantico, Virginia) has a growing role in computer crime investigation and training. It certainly is not the only federal agency heavily involved in this new area of criminal investigation. Federal Law Enforcement Training Centers in Georgia and Arizona offer excellent courses on computer crime investigation that state and local police officers can attend. In addition, the Secret Service, U.S. Postal Inspection Service, and the Department of Defense provide direct support to local and state agencies. There are also a number of private and public organizations that provide training and assistance in the investigation of computer crime. The following are three important groups:

- The National White Collar Crime Center (NW3C), Computer Crime Section, in Richmond, Virginia, has established the National Cybercrime Training Partnership linking numerous private corporations to the training and development of police agencies on a regional basis. Several important national conferences and summits have been sponsored by the NW3C group.[74]
- The International Association of Computer Investigative Specialists (IACIS) is a volunteer nonprofit corporation composed of law enforcement professionals throughout the world who are dedicated to training police personnel in the investigation of computer crime. IACIS is the only body to "certify," through advanced training, digital forensic examiners in the recovery of evidence from computer systems.[75]
- The High Technology Crime Investigation Association (HTCIA) is a law enforcement–based, nonprofit organization that has chapters across the United States and in several other countries. The chapters allow local investigators to collaborate, network, and assist each other on various computer crime cases. Many chapters also provide excellent training, and the parent organization sponsors an annual national conference for a similar purpose.[76]

## CRIME SCENE TECHNIQUES

Frequently, computer crime evidence will be seized by the execution of a search warrant.[77] This warrant should include information about the computer, data storage devices (including internal and external hard drives), floppy disks, tape backups, modems, programs, software manuals, user notes, hard-copy output, and any peripherals that may be of concern to investigators, such as scanners. Removing noninvestigative personnel from computers and terminals is a high priority. This prevents tampering or destruction of electronic evidence—intentional or unintentional. While a local network administrator may assist the efforts, only investigators should execute commands. In some cases, under the Electronic Communications Privacy Act (ECPA), the owner of a multiuser computer may not consent to a search of a user's files. Consult legal counsel if a multiuser system is to be searched. Another consideration is the potential use of the information to be seized. If there is a reasonable expectation that the owner will distribute such information to the public, special First Amendment protections reserved for publishers might apply, including protection of web pages.[78]

A computer expert—either an investigator specializing in this field or a civilian with the necessary expertise—should be consulted for assistance in specifying what is to be searched for by the warrant and also in seizing it. The computer and related equipment and material should not be touched or moved until thoroughly documented by photography or videotaping. In particular, the screen needs to be photographed immediately in order to secure the information on it. More than one criminal case has been won because an investigating officer noticed incriminating evidence on the screen and photographed it before the screen changed. It is also important that all connections and wires be photographed and portrayed. The keyboard should not be used in a premature attempt to locate evidence. After the system has been photographed, the first step is to unplug the computer; do not use the on/off switch. All wiring connections should be tagged with notes indicating where they were connected. If there is a modem, disconnect it by unplugging the connecting cable from the wall jack. The serial numbers for all equipment should be recorded. The hard disk should be secured for transportation to prevent damage. Before actually moving the computer, check the outer perimeter of the room in which the computer is located to make sure that there is no magnetic force that would erase evidence of the crime on storage devices. All computer evidence should be stored in an area free from dust, heat, dampness, and magnetic fields.

## DIGITAL FORENSIC ANALYSIS

**Digital forensic analysis** is the science of acquiring, preserving, retrieving, and presenting data that have been processed electronically and stored on computer media.[79] As a forensic discipline, nothing since DNA technology has had such a large potential effect on specific types of investigations and prosecution as has digital forensic analysis. It is important to note that the examination of computer media for evidence is not limited to computer crimes but is relevant to the investigation of almost any traditional fraud as well as a variety of common crimes. Thus, special care must be given to the recovery of electronic data to ensure the accuracy and integrity of this metaphysical evidence.[80]

Seized computers should be examined only by trained technicians who either are law enforcement officers or have appropriate training in search-and-seizure laws and procedures. The U.S. Department of Justice has published extensive documentation on federal guidelines for searching and seizing computers.[81] These should be consulted before computer equipment is likely to be seized or searched. There should never be just one investigator examining a seized computer, as additional observers may be able to provide the only supporting testimony regarding evidence seen on the computer screen. Seized computers should never initially be rebooted using their own disks. Seized hard disks should be write-protected with a jumper, and the system should then be booted with a clean boot disk. Unused floppy boot disks or a write-closed CD-R should be used for rebooting. The next step is to create a bit-stream copy—also called an image. A bit-stream copy exactly reproduces all the data on the hard drive, even if the data are invisible to the operating system or have apparently been deleted. All analyses should be performed on a copy while maintaining a clean copy to verify that evidence has not been altered. Figure 16–8 lists the types of evidence that are sought during the investigation of various crimes.

Not following these safeguards can have devastating consequences for a criminal investigation, either before or after law enforcement officers are involved in the case. In 1997, an employee of the information system department of a large telecommunication company was fired due to negligence of duty. The individual was escorted out of the company and not given access to his company computer. He had powered down his computer the night before, as he normally did before leaving for the evening. A few days later, a supervisor discovered e-mail that suggested that the employee possessed child pornography on the company computer. A cursory search of the employee's computer found several files of pornographic pictures of children. Within a couple of minutes of the files' being discovered, a coincidental power failure caused the computer to reboot. Once the computer had rebooted, the supervisor looked for the incriminating files in order to record their location for investigative purposes. The files and email were missing. The supervisor then started to determine what had happened to the files. It quickly became apparent that the employee had installed a trap on the machine. The trap was a custom-written software

### Investigator Examines Seized Computer

Digital forensic analysis is the science of acquiring, retrieving, and presenting data that had been processed electronically and stored on computer media. Special care must be given to the recovery of electronic data to ensure the accuracy and integrity of this metaphysical evidence in the investigation of crime.

(© Origlia Franco/Corbis Sygma)

## Figure 16-8 Forensic Examination by Crime Category or Type

The matrix lists the types of files (evidence) that are commonly found during forensic analyses of computers associated with specific crimes.

(**Source:** U.S. Department of Justice, Office of Justice Programs, *Electronic Crime Scene Investigation: A Guide for First Responders* [Washington, DC: NCRJS, July 2001].)

| | Sex Crimes | | Crimes against Persons | | | Fraud and Other Financial Crimes | | | | | | | | |
|---|---|---|---|---|---|---|---|---|---|---|---|---|---|---|
| | Child Exploitation/Abuse | Prostitution | Death investigation | Domestic Violence | E-mail Threats/ Harassment/Staffing | Auction Fraud | Computer Intrusion | Economic Fraud | Extortion | Gambling | Identity Theft | Narcotics | Software Piracy | Telecommunication Fraud |
| **General Information** | | | | | | | | | | | | | | |
| Databases | | ✔ | | | | ✔ | | ✔ | | ✔ | | ✔ | | |
| E-mail/notes/letters | ✔ | ✔ | ✔ | ✔ | ✔ | ✔ | ✔ | ✔ | ✔ | ✔ | ✔ | ✔ | ✔ | ✔ |
| Financial/asset records | | ✔ | ✔ | ✔ | ✔ | ✔ | | ✔ | | ✔ | | ✔ | | ✔ |
| Medical records | | ✔ | ✔ | ✔ | | | | | | | | | | |
| Telephone records | | | ✔ | ✔ | ✔ | ✔ | | | | | | | | ✔ |
| **Specific Information** | | | | | | | | | | | | | | |
| Account data | | | | | | ✔ | | | | | | | | |
| Accounting/bookkeeping software | | | | | | ✔ | | | | | | | | |
| Address books | | ✔ | ✔ | ✔ | ✔ | ✔ | ✔ | ✔ | | ✔ | | ✔ | | |
| Backdrops | | | | | | | | | | | ✔ | | | |
| Biographies | | | ✔ | | | | | | | | | | | |
| Birth certificates | | | | | | | | | | | ✔ | | | |
| Calendar | | ✔ | | | | ✔ | | ✔ | | ✔ | | ✔ | | |
| Chat logs | ✔ | | | | | ✔ | | | | | | | ✔ | |
| Check, currency. and money order images | | | | | | | | ✔ | | | ✔ | | | |
| Check cashing cards | | | | | | | | | | | ✔ | | | |
| Cloning software | | | | | | | | | | | | | | ✔ |
| Configuration files | | | | | | | ✔ | | | | | | | |
| Counterfeit money | | | | | | | | | | | ✔ | | | |
| Credit card generators | | | | | | | | | | | ✔ | | | |
| Credit card numbers | | | | | | | | | | | ✔ | | | |
| Credit card reader/writer | | | | | | | | | | | ✔ | | | |
| Credit card skimmers | | | | | | | | ✔ | | | | | | |
| Customer database/ records | | ✔ | | | | | | | | ✔ | | | | ✔ |
| Customer information/ credit card data | | | | | | ✔ | | ✔ | | ✔ | | | | |
| Date and time stamps | ✔ | | | | | | | | ✔ | | | | | |
| Diaries | | | ✔ | ✔ | ✔ | | | | | | | | | |
| Digital cameras/software/ images | ✔ | | | | | ✔ | | | | | ✔ | | | |
| Driver's license | | | | | | | | | | | ✔ | | | |
| Drug recipes | | | | | | | | | | | | ✔ | | |
| Electronic money | | | | | | | | | | ✔ | | | | |
| Electronic signatures | | | | | | | | | | | ✔ | | | |

**Figure 16-8** Forensic Examination by Crime Category or Type, *continued*

| | Sex Crimes | | Crimes against Persons | | | Fraud and Other Financial Crimes | | | | | | | | |
|---|---|---|---|---|---|---|---|---|---|---|---|---|---|---|
| | Child Exploitation/Abuse | Prostitution | Death investigation | Domestic Violence | E-mail Threats/Harassment/Stalking | Auction Fraud | Computer Intrusion | Economic Fraud | Extortion | Gambling | Identity Theft | Narcotics | Software Piracy | Telecommunication Fraud |
| **Specific Information (cont.)** | | | | | | | | | | | | | | |
| Erased Internet documents | | | | | | | | | | | ✔ | | | |
| ESN/MIN pair records | | | | | | | | | | | | | | ✔ |
| Executable programs | | | | | | | ✔ | | | | | | | ✔ |
| False financial transaction forms | | | | | | | | ✔ | | | | | | |
| False identification | | ✔ | | | | | | ✔ | | | | ✔ | | |
| Fictitious court documents | | | | | | | | | | | ✔ | | | |
| Fictitious gift certificates | | | | | | | | | | | ✔ | | | |
| Fictitious loan documents | | | | | | | | | | | ✔ | | | |
| Fictitious sales receipts | | | | | | | | | | | ✔ | | | |
| Fictitious vehicle registrations | | | | | | | | | | | ✔ | | | |
| Games | ✔ | ✔ | | | | | | | | | | | | |
| Graphic editing and viewing software | ✔ | | | | | | | | | | | | | |
| History log | | | | | | | | | | ✔ | | | | |
| "How to phreak" manuals | | | | | | | | | | | | | | ✔ |
| Images | ✔ | | ✔ | | ✔ | ✔ | | | | | | | | |
| Images of signatures | | | | | | | | ✔ | | | | | | |
| Image files of software certificates | | | | | | | | | | | | | ✔ | |
| Image players | | | | | | | | | | ✔ | | | | |
| Internet activity logs | ✔ | ✔ | ✔ | | ✔ | ✔ | ✔ | ✔ | ✔ | ✔ | | ✔ | ✔ | ✔ |
| Internet browser history/cache files | | | | | | ✔ | | | | | | | | |
| IP address and user name | | | | | | | ✔ | | | | | | | |
| IRC chat logs | | | | | | | ✔ | | | | | | | |
| Legal documents and wills | | | ✔ | | ✔ | | | | | | | | | |
| Movie files | ✔ | | | | | | | | | | | | | |
| Online financial institution access software | | | | | | ✔ | | ✔ | | ✔ | | | | |
| Online orders and trading information | | | | | | | | | | | ✔ | | | |
| Prescription form images | | | | | | | | | | | | ✔ | | |
| Records/documents of "testimonials" | | | | | | ✔ | | | | | | | | |

*(continued)*

**Figure 16-8** Forensic Examination by Crime Category or Type, *concluded*

| | Sex Crimes | | Crimes against Persons | | | Fraud and Other Financial Crimes | | | | | | | | |
|---|---|---|---|---|---|---|---|---|---|---|---|---|---|---|
| | Child Exploitation/Abuse | Prostitution | Death investigation | Domestic Violence | E-mail Threats/ Harassment/Staffing | Auction Fraud | Computer Intrusion | Economic Fraud | Extortion | Gambling | Identity Theft | Narcotics | Software Piracy | Telecommunication Fraud |
| **Specific Information (cont.)** | | | | | | | | | | | | | | |
| Scanners/scanned signatures | ✔ | ✔ | ✔ | ✔ | ✔ | ✔ | ✔ | ✔ | ✔ | ✔ | ✔ | ✔ | ✔ | ✔ |
| Serial numbers | | | | | | | | | | | | | ✔ | |
| Social Security cards | | | | | | | | | | | ✔ | | | |
| Software cracking information and utilities | | | | | | | | | | | | | ✔ | |
| Source code | | | | | | | ✔ | | | | | | | |
| Sports betting statistics | | | | | | | | | | ✔ | | | | |
| Stock transfer documents | | | | | | | | | | | ✔ | | | |
| System files and file slack | | | | | | | | | | | ✔ | | | |
| Temporary Internet files | | | | | | | | | ✔ | | | | | |
| User names | | | | | | | ✔ | | ✔ | | | | | |
| User-created directory and file names that classify copyrighted software | | | | | | | | | | | | | ✔ | |
| User-created directory and file names that classify images | ✔ | | | | | | | | | | | | | |
| Vehicle insurance and transfer documentation | | | | | | | | | | | ✔ | | | |
| Victim background research | | | | | ✔ | | | | | | | | | |
| Web activity at forgery sites | | | | | | | | | | | ✔ | | | |
| Web page advertising | | ✔ | | | | | | | | | | | | |

program that was automatically run whenever the machine was booted. The trap program looked for specific trap files, and if those files were not present, the program would delete the pornography files, email, and other incriminating data. Before shutting down his computer, the employee would manually run a program that he had written that would create several specifically titled trap files. When the computer was then rebooted, the trap program would look for those files, and if they were present, it would delete them but do nothing else. If the computer was later powered down without the manual file-creation program being run, as occurred when the power failed, the needed trap files would not be created and therefore would not be found when the trap program automatically ran on reboot. The incriminating files would then be deleted by the trap program, as they were when the computer rebooted after the power failure. Since the supervisor was the only witness to the event, and because the files were no longer present on the system, criminal charges were not filed against the ex-employee. While this case occurred before police investigators were involved, similar losses of evidence have occurred from seized computers when insufficiently trained law enforcement officials tried to access data stored on computers. When examining a seized computer, do not save anything to the hard disk or floppies seized, as this alters it and is likely to make it inadmissible in court. Investigators should remember that all equipment and software seized are the property of someone else. Damage done by an investigator to equipment, programs, or data (including the erasure of data) can open police agencies to legal action.

Finally, it is important to note that what may initially look like a computer crime may not actually prove to be an intentional or malicious act. Software bugs, hardware failures, and other noncriminal events can appear to be evidence that a crime has taken place. A failing modem may repeatedly try to dial a number, making it appear that someone is trying to break into a computer system. A software bug may inadvertently alter or delete data records. Poor communication within an organization may lead to the conclusion that hardware has been stolen when it was merely relocated. The complexity of computer crimes dictates that properly trained and technically competent individuals conduct the investigation or be consulted.

## PREVENTING COMPUTER CRIME

Historically, the focus of computer crime prevention has been on protecting software, hardware, and connected devices. Today, because of the rapid growth of the information economy, computer crime prevention is increasingly focusing on the protection of information. While a hard drive can be replaced, the information contained on the hard drive may be irreplaceable, and its loss may be catastrophic to a corporation. The increase in laptop computer thefts may stem not from the potential resale value of the machines but from the invaluable information contained on their hard drives. Imagine the value, to a competitor, of a major corporation's marketing plans for the next five years, contained on a senior executive's laptop that was stolen as he went through airport security. Protecting information, largely by making it inaccessible to unauthorized users, is a key element of preventing computer crimes.

### BACKUPS AND REDUNDANT FILE STORAGE

Creating backups is the most important security measure a company or individual can take. As noted in Carter's typology, most computer-as-target crimes involve data loss or alteration. The best protection against these attacks, and most natural disasters, is to back up the data. A backup is a copy of data. If data are lost, destroyed, or altered, the backup may be the only means of recovering the data. Although there is no rule on how often backups should be created, a good rule of thumb is to determine how much of the data you can afford to re-create. When you reach that amount, create a backup. Suppose a company pays 120 employees \$10 each per hour to enter data. A backup system capable of handling the firm's demands costs \$12,000. If the company creates a backup every 10 hours ($120 \times \$10 \times 10 = \$12{,}000$), the benefit is that it pays for the backup system only once (and thereafter incurs just small recurring costs, for tape and a portion of an administrator's time). Thus, if the company recovers data from a 10-hour shift once, the system has paid for itself. If the firm suspects that an intruder has tampered with the data, the company can simply compare it to a backup and restore the good data if necessary.

Mission-critical data (data that cannot be lost) are often protected with an instantaneous backup as the data are stored. A device called a redundant array of inexpensive disks (RAID) saves the data to two hard drives at once, making failure of a single drive less damaging.[82] Since RAID really makes only two copies of the hard drive, regular backups are also necessary to protect against alteration.

### FIREWALLS

Another way individuals and organizations protect their computer networks is by using firewalls. A **firewall** is a device or software that acts as a checkpoint between a network or stand-alone computer and the Internet. A firewall checks all data coming in and going out. If the data do not fit strict criteria, they do not go through. In the past, firewalls were not widely used because they could significantly reduce access from the protected network to the outside world. Firewalls have since been greatly improved and are now relatively fast and easily configured by the user. Software development, combined with rapidly increasing computer-based crime occurring through interconnected networks, has led to the widespread use of firewalls.

## ENCRYPTION

Cryptography is "the art and science of securing messages." Messages can be any data. **Encryption** is a technique of securing data by scrambling it into nonsense. The encrypted message (i.e., the scrambled message) can be stored or transmitted to another point with a reasonable expectation of security. A similar technique called hashing produces a unique signature of the original data. At the other end of the transmission, a new hash is calculated on the data and compared to the old hash. If they match, the data have not been altered. Using these two techniques together provides a reasonable expectation that the message is private and unaltered. A "reasonable expectation of security" does not mean absolute security. Any encryption can be broken. "If the cost required to break an [encryption technique] is greater than the value of the encrypted data, it is probably safe."[83] The most essential feature of encryption is that scrambled data can be returned to a useful form by the intended user and cannot be returned to a useful form by others.

Encryption is used to store passwords on home computer systems, store credit card numbers in "online wallets," and secure e-commerce transactions. Even though modern encryption can be broken, except for cases involving the most basic forms of encryption, such as that protecting Windows passwords, most criminals find it easier to look for other ways to get the data. For instance, e-commerce may be protected as it crosses the Internet, but credit information is often stored on unsecured computers at the merchant's site. It is important to remember that encrypted e-commerce data are decrypted at the other end. While e-commerce transactions are generally safe, few merchants have devoted the resources required to secure their whole computer systems.

## PASSWORD DISCIPLINE

The greatest problem in computer security is password protection. In addition to the basic dos and don'ts (see Figure 16–9), there are sophisticated software programs that address the issue. Several approaches have been taken in an attempt to solve the problem, including password-creation software, one-time password generators, and user authentication systems such as biometric devices. There are a variety of software programs that system administrators can use to improve password security. Some programs force users to change their passwords on a regular basis, perhaps every month or few months, or even every week. Other programs automatically create random pronounceable passwords for users, such as "jrk^wud," which is pronounced "jerk wood." The user remembers that the ^ character is between two words. Such pronounceable passwords are rarely compromised by dictionary attacks, are easily remembered by users, and do not relate to user information (such as a child's first name or a user's Social Security number) that might be easily determined by an intruder.

SecurID, from Security Dynamics Technologies, Inc. (see photo on page 622), is perhaps the most popular one-time password generator, with over 3 million users in 5,000 organizations worldwide. SecurID identifies and authenticates each individual user on the basis of two factors: (1) something secret that the user knows—a memorized personal identification number (PIN)—and (2) something unique that the user has—the SecurID card. Under this system, a computer user logging on first types in his or her PIN. Then the user types in the number currently displayed on his or her SecurID card, which changes every 60 seconds. Each individual SecurID card is synchronized with either hardware or software on the computer system that the user is attempting to access. The result is a unique access code that is valid only for a particular user during a 60-second period.

Kerberos is a program developed at MIT by the Athena Project. It is a leading network and data encryption system. Cygnus Support, a Mountain View, California, company, has developed Kerberos-based user-authentication software—Cygnus Network Security (CNS)—that eliminates the need to use clear, unencrypted text passwords on a network. In this system, an individual user is given an encryption key to encrypt and decrypt Kerberos passwords, log ins, and other computer system transactions. When this individual wants to access the network, he or she sends a message to the Kerberos server. This computer sends back an encrypted package that can be

**Figure 16-9**

**Guidelines for Password Protection**

(**Source:** Peter H. Lewis, "Some Password Do's and Don'ts," *New York Times*, Feb. 13, 1994, p. 9, with modification and additions.)

1. Don't use words found in an English or other dictionary because hackers' programs test different words very quickly.
2. The longer a password is, the more difficult it is to guess it.
3. Use a mixture of numbers, letters, and special characters if possible. Also, some passwords are case-sensitive—they can distinguish between lowercase and uppercase letters. This feature should be used if available. To illustrate, "K2jwE" is harder to guess than "Super Ace."
4. Don't use obvious or guessable passwords; don't use your child's name, birth date, car license number, Social Security number, or favorite sports team.
5. Don't write your password down where people can find it. Don't write it on the underside of your desk blotter or leave it in your wallet.
6. Change passwords as frequently as possible.
7. Don't disclose or lend your password to other people.
8. Don't allow people to watch what you type when you log on. Relatedly, when using your telephone calling-card number in public places, be aware of people watching you. Credit card and other numbers have been stolen by people using video cameras and telescopes.
9. Don't tell your password to anyone over the telephone.
10. Promptly report any unusual log-on experiences to your network administrator, as well as any suspicion that your password has been compromised.

read only with that user's secret key. The package also includes a temporary encryption key good for only that session on the computer. To prove his or her identity, the user then sends a message coded in the temporary encryption key back to the computer. The Kerberos computer then acknowledges the user's identity by sending a second encrypted message to the user, which can be decoded only by using the temporary encryption key previously sent to the user. In 1994, CNS was posted on the Internet, available without charge to any American or Canadian network that wants it. Cygnus Support does, however, charge for support services it provides for CNS adopters.

Kerberos is just one program that uses encryption. Many other programs, such as SecureShell (SSH), also create encrypted sessions between the user's computer and the destination computer, thus protecting passwords and other sensitive information from hackers using tools like packet sniffers. All that the hackers are able to retrieve are indecipherable streams of encrypted data. Other programs use encryption to safeguard email or files. Some can even encrypt the entire contents of a hard drive or floppy disk. The advent of widely available strong encryption products such as Pretty Good Privacy (PGP) has led the government and some law enforcement officials to become concerned about the possible misuse of encryption by criminals. Terrorists, for example, could use encrypted email to develop plans for a bombing in secrecy.[84] While some officials have proposed that software developers build trap doors for the government into their encryption programs, civil liberty advocates have strongly opposed such measures, noting that such trap doors could be abused by the government. Strict export regulations on strong encryption products restrict the legal export of such software from the United States. However, these regulations have not stopped the illegal smuggling of such software.

New technologies are altering the face of user identification. The use of tools such as digital fingerprint identification, retinal identification, and voice recognition greatly increases the accuracy of

**SecurID Card**

SecurID, from Security Dynamics Technologies Inc., is perhaps the most popular one-time password generator. It identifies and authenticates each individual user on the basis of two factors: one, something unique that the user knows—a memorized personal identification number—and two, something unique the user has—the SecurID card.

(Courtesy Security Dynamics Technologies, Inc., Bedford, Massachusetts)

user identification, sometimes replacing passwords. The future of computer security will continue to link user's unique physical attributes (those that do not change or cannot be easily altered) to known passwords or stored encryption keys. Biometrics do not provide absolute security, but by adding another level of complexity to passwords, they make it increasingly difficult for intruders to guess passwords but do not make it harder for users to remember them. A retinal scan and a short password are, effectively, a 10,000- to 20,000-digit password. The longer the password is, the harder it is to guess.

## Key Terms

**attack code**
**back doors**
**cloning**
**component swapping**
**computer abuse**
**computer crime**
**computer manipulation crime**
**computer vandalism**
**cookie**
**cryptanalysis**
**cyberstalking**
**delivery vehicles**
**digital forensic analysis**
**encryption**
**exploits**
**firewall**
**hacker's dictionary**
**hacking or cracking**
**logic bomb**
**packet sniffers**
**phreakers**
**piracy**
**refurbishment fraud**
**root kits**
**salami slice**
**shopping cart fraud**
**Trojan horse**
**tumbling**
**virus**
**worm**

## Review Questions

1. What are computer abuse and computer crime?
2. What is a computer manipulation crime? Describe some common Internet scams.
3. Define the activity of hacking or cracking.
4. What are the differences between real-world stalking and cyberstalking?
5. How do cloning and tumbling work?
6. Identify and describe the three tools that can help investigators recognize malicious code.
7. Identify and describe the three major types of delivery vehicles for malicious code.
8. Can you describe the "typical" hacker on the basis of seven different factors?

9. What is digital forensic analysis, and why is it so important in the investigation of computer-related crime?

10. Identify and describe the four major methodologies for protecting information and preventing computer crime.

## Internet Activities

1. Check out the U.S. Department of Justice's website on cyber crime at www.cybercrime.gov. This website provides policies, cases, press releases, and articles about intellectual-property, computer, and Internet crimes.
2. Search several Internet media sites for information on computer crime in your area. What types of computer crimes have been reported on within the last few years? Have arrests and/or convictions been made in these crimes? What estimates have been given on the cost of these crimes? Who investigated the crimes? What were the outcomes of the investigations?

## Notes

1. B. M. Leiner, V. G. Cerf, D. D. Clark, R. E. Kahn, L. Kleinrock, D. C. Lynch, J. Postel, L. G. Roberts, and S. Wolff, www.isoc.org/internet-history/brief.html, "A Brief History of the Internet. Version 3.31," retrieved Feb. 1, 2001.
2. Donn Parker, *Computer Crime: Criminal Justice Resource Manual* (Washington, DC: National Institute of Justice, 1989).
3. Catherine H. Conley and J. Thomas McEwen, "Computer Crime," *NIJ Reports,* January–February 1990, No. 218, p. 3.
4. CERT and CSI have extensive online services that provide detailed information on most computer crime units within federal, state, and local agencies. For more information, see www.cert.org and www.gocsi.org.
5. B. Sullivan, "Have You Seen This Geek?" zdnet.com/zdnn/stories/news/0,4586,2771692,00.html, June 8, 2001; retrieved Aug. 31, 2001.
6. U.S. Postal Inspection Service, "Net Fraudster Caught by Web," www.usps.gov/postalinspectors/NRNElson.htm, July 18, 2001; retrieved July 18, 2001.
7. Sandy Rovner, "Molesting Our Children by Computer," *Washington Post,* Aug. 2, 1994, p. 15.
8. David Mann and Michael Sutton, "Netcrime: More Changes in the Organization of Thieving," *British Journal of Criminology* 1998, Vol. 38, pp. 201–229.
9. Five of the six categories are identified in Catherine H. Conly and J. Thomas McEwen, "Computer Crime," pp. 2–7. The material in this chapter retains these basic categories and extends them considerably with current research.
10. A criminal typology is a tool for categorizing crime by type; similar crimes are grouped together. See Julian B. Roebuck, *Criminal Typology* (Springfield, IL: Charles C. Thomas, 1967).
11. Donn Parker, *Crime by Computer* (New York: Scribner, 1976).
12. See Robert W. Taylor, "Hackers, Phone Phreakers, and Virus Makers," paper presented at the Second Annual Conference on Computer Viruses, London, England, June 1990. This paper was developed into the chapter entitled "Computer Crime" in earlier editions of this book. See Charles R. Swanson, Neil C. Chamelin, and Leonard Territo, *Criminal Investigation,* 5th, 6th, and 7th ed. (New York: McGraw-Hill, 1992, 1996, and 2000).
13. David Carter, "Computer Crime Categories," *FBI Law Enforcement Bulletin,* 1995, Vol. 64, No. 21.
14. Donn Parker, *Fighting Computer Crime: A New Framework for Protecting Information* (New York: Wiley, 1998).
15. Robert W. Taylor and Deanne Carp, "Policing the Internet: Legal Issues on the Information Super-Highway," in J. Walker, ed., *Legal Issues in Policing* (Upper Saddle River, NJ: Prentice-Hall, 2002).
16. "Consumers' Group Wants Telemarketing Rules Expanded to Net," *Dallas Morning News,* Feb. 16, 1998, p. 2D.
17. Ibid.
18. "Congress Warned of New Fraud: Computers Simplify, Reduce Cost of Check Counterfeiting," *Dallas Morning News,* May 2, 1997, p. 5A.
19. Ibid.
20. Ibid.
21. Aaron Nathans, "IRS Moves to Block 'Rapid Refund' Scam Artists," *Los Angeles Times,* Oct. 27, 1994, p. A24.

22. J. Littman, "Hacker Shocker: Project Reveals Breaches Galore," www5.zdnet.com/zdnet.com/zdnn/content/zdnn/0918/zdn0010.html, retrieved Sept. 18, 1997.
23. The *Source code* is the version of a computer program that can be read and altered by humans.
24. See B. Steinhardt, "The Fourth Amendment and Carnivore," Statement for the Record before the U.S. House of Representatives, Committee on the Judiciary, Washington, DC, July 24, 2000; D. M. Kerr, "Internet and Data Interception Capabilities Developed by the FBI," Statement for the Record before the U.S. House of Representatives, Committee on the Judiciary, Washington, DC, July 24, 2000; and P. K. Craine, "Search Warrants in Cyberspace: The Fourth Amendment Meets the Twenty-First Century" www.smu.edu/~csr/sum96a2.htm, 1996.
25. Ibid.
26. A. Eunjung Cha and J. Schwartz, "Hackers Disrupt Yahoo Web Site," www.washingtonpost.comwp-dyn/business/A23174-2000Feb7.html, retrieved Feb. 14, 2000.
27. Attrition.org, "Video Cam: University of Cambridge" (defaced web page), www.attrition.org/mirror/attrition/2001/05/13/video.cbcu.cam.ac.uk/, retrieved Aug. 30, 2001.
28. Reuters, "Hacking Closes N.Y. Times Site," www.news.com/News/Item/0,4,26301.00.html, retrieved Sept. 13, 1998.
29. Parker, *Fighting Computer Crime.*
30. *Pyramid schemes* multilevel marketing arrangements in which higher-level members make money by finding new distributors and charging for initial stock rather than taking a portion of actual sales.
31. Janet Reno, *1999 Report on CyberStalking: A New Challenge for Law Enforcement and Industry.* www.cybercrime.gov/cyberstalking.htm, retrieved Aug. 30, 2001.
32. D. Kall Loper, "A Case Study in the Forensics of Computer Crime: E-Mail Spoofing," *Journal of Security Administration* 2001, Vol. 24.
33. David L. Carter and Andrea J. Bannister, "Computer Crime: A Forecast of Emerging Trends," paper presented at the Academy of Criminal Justice Sciences Annual Meeting, New Orleans, Louisiana, March 2000.
34. See B. Zagaris and S. D. McDonald, "Money Laundering, Financial Fraud and Technology: The Perils of an Instant Economy," *George Washington Journal of International Law and Economics,* Vol. 26, No. 1, pp. 61–90, and S. Walther, "Forfeiture and Money Laundering Laws in the United States: Basic Features and Some Critical Comments from the European Perspective," *Crime, Law, and Social Change,* Vol. 21, No. 1, pp. 1–13.
35. See Eoghan Casey, *Digital Evidence and Computer Crime: Forensic Science, Computers and the Internet* (San Francisco, CA: Academic Press, 2000).
36. Jill Sergeant, "Police Raid Global Internet Child Porn Club," *Reuters,* Sept. 2, 1998.
37. Ibid.
38. D. L. Vial, M. J. Fine, and R. Gebeloff, "Molesters Forming Network of Abuse," *Bergen Record,* Dec. 3, 1997; retrieved from www.bergen.com/news/childporn199712030.htm, Aug. 30, 2001.
39. Ibid.
40. "Web Stings Hit Child Porn Distributors," *Organized Crime Digest,* Vol. 22, No. 12, p. 3.
41. International Planning and Research Corporation, *Sixth Annual BSA Global Software Piracy Study* (Washington, DC: Business Software Alliance, May 2001).
42. Ibid.
43. "Stalking Asian Software Pirates," *Technology Review,* Vol. 95, No. 2, p. 15.
44. The telephone-based electronic bulletin board system (BBS) was the primary method by which most computer users communicated and exchanged software before Internet access became so widely available.
45. Warez Doods (pronounced "wheres [as in 'softWARE'] dudes") are software pirates.
46. A. Bauman, "The Pirates of the Internet," *Los Angeles Times,* Nov. 3, 1994, p. A1.
47. Jennifer Steinhauer, "Phreakers Take a Swipe at Turnstiles and Nynex," *New York Times,* Aug. 15, 1994, p. B3.
48. Ibid.
49. Conly and McEwen, "Computer Crime."
50. The information on cellular phones is taken from William G. Flanagan and Brigid McMenamin, "Why Cybercrooks Love Cellular," *Forbes,* Dec. 21, 1992, Vol. 150, No. 14, p. 189.
51. R. Powers, ed., "CSI/FBI Computer Crime and Security Survey," *Computer Security Issues and Trends* (San Francisco, CA: CSI, Spring 2001).
52. Social Security Administration, Office of the Inspector General, "Annual Audit Plan Fiscal Year 2001,"

www.ssa.gov/oig/adopbepdf/audit%20work%20plan.pdf, retrieved Aug. 30, 2001.

53. Software licenses grant the purchaser limited rights to use the compiled version, but not to reverse-engineer or sell copies. Thus, the purchaser does not buy the software; he or she buys only the right to *use* the software.

54. Most programs are written in a computer language such as C or C++. The original program or source code is readable by human beings. A special program called a compiler reduces the human-readable program to a set of computer instructions called the *compiled code.* Very few people can comprehend compiled code.

55. Fyodor, "Nmap Network Security Scanner Man Page," www.insecure.org/nmap/nmap_manpage.html, retrieved Aug. 30, 2001.

56. War dialers take their name from the 1983 movie *War Games.* The lead character, played by Matthew Broderick, used a program to dial numbers until he found a computer to "play" or intrude to alter or delete data.

57. D. Thomas, "Minor Threats, Major Sentence: Banning Hackers from the Net," *Online Journalism Review,* olj.usc.edu/indexf.htm?/sections/department/hackers.htm, retrieved June 7, 1998.

58. Bruce Schneier, *Applied Cryptography: Protocols, Algorithms, and Source Code in C* (New York: Wiley, 1996).

59. L0pht Heavy Industries, "L0phtcrack: NT Password Cracker," www.l0pht.com/l0phtcrack/, retrieved Oct. 17, 2000.

60. Cha and Schwartz, "Hacker Disrupt Yahoo Web Site."

61. Powers, "CSI/FBI Computer Crime and Security Survey."

62. David A. Price, "1st Amendment and the Internet," *Investor's Business Daily,* June 27, 1997, pp. A1, A24.

63. Ibid.

64. Ibid.

65. Peter Slover, "Cyber Eyes," *Dallas Morning News,* June 20, 1998, pp. 1F, 6F.

66. Ibid.

67. See Taylor, "Hackers, Phone Phreakers, and Virus Makers."

68. Ibid.

69. Ibid.

70. R. P. Kusserow, "An Inside Look at Federal Computer Crime," *Security Management,* May 1986, p. 75.

71. R. K. Elliot and J. J. Willingham, *Management Fraud: Detection and Deterrence* (New York: Petrocelli Books, 1980), pp. 223–226.

72. Ibid.

73. Richard C. Hollinger and Lonn Lanza-Kaduce, "The Process of Criminalization: The Case of Computer Crime Laws." *Criminology,* 1988, Vol. 26, pp. 101–126.

74. For more information on this organization, visit www.nw3c.org.

75. For more information on this organization, visit www.cops.org.

76. For more information on this organization, visit www.htcia.org.

77. This information on the search and seizure of computer crime evidence is drawn from "Crime Scene Computer Factsheet" (Washington, DC: National Institute of Justice), p. 1. For additional information on this subject, see U.S. Department of Justice, Office of Justice Programs, *Electronic Crime Scene Investigation: A Guide for First Responders* (Washington, DC: NCRJS, July 2001).

78. See U.S. Department of Justice, *Electronic Crime Scene Investigation.*

79. Michael G. Noblett, Mark M. Pollitt, and Lawrence A. Presley, "Recovering and Examining Computer Forensic Evidence," *Forensic Science Communications* (Washington, DC: FBI, October 2000).

80. Ibid.

81. See U.S. Department of Justice, *Electronic Crime Scene Investigation.*

82. RAID comes in a variety of schemes and options. For a more thorough discussion of RAID configurations, see www.whatis.com.

83. Schneier, *Applied Cryptography,* p. 18.

84. Several sources indicate that terrorists in the Al-Qaeda network used computers to communicate in secrecy and plot their attacks on the World Trade Center and Pentagon Building on Sept. 11, 2001. For further information on terrorist threats using computer and information system networks, see Dorothy E. Denning, *Information Warfare and Security* (Reading, MA: Addison-Wesley, 1999), and Winn Schwartau, *CyberShock: Surviving Hackers, Phreakers, Identity Thieves, Internet Terrorists and Weapons of Mass Disruption* (New York: Thunder's Mouth Press, 2000).

# SEVENTEEN

# Agricultural, Wildlife, and Environmental Crimes

*While it is difficult to accurately estimate the costs associated with environmental crimes, it is reasonable to conclude there are substantial losses associated with these crimes each year. Some states have established police agencies with the specific responsibility of investigating agricultural, wildlife, and/or environmental crimes. (Photo provided by William Sullivan, Massachusetts Environmental Police)*

## CHAPTER OUTLINE



## CHAPTER OBJECTIVES

1. Discuss the prevalence of timber theft.
2. Explain agrichemical theft.
3. Discuss cattle and horse rustling.
4. Outline several methods of horse and cattle identification.
5. Summarize measures to prevent rural and agricultural crimes.
6. Distinguish between situational and professional poachers.
7. Understand investigative techniques used in wildlife crimes.
8. List and describe the characteristics of hazardous waste.
9. Discuss methods of investigating environmental crimes.

## INTRODUCTION

Conventional wisdom says that crime is fundamentally, if not almost exclusively, an urban phenomenon. Yet, as with most matters, some aspects of crime do not immediately meet the eye. In the United States, 17 percent of the farms—or roughly one in every five—are located within Metropolitan Statistical Areas (MSAs), and thus crime on and against them contributes to the magnitude of reported crime in urban areas.[1] In addition, some crimes committed against wildlife, for example, have significant economic value. Poaching grizzly bears, polar bears, and elk, for skin, meat, and other parts of the animals, can yield thousands of dollars on several markets. A single instance of crime against wildlife, therefore, may produce more profit to the offender than does a single episode of a conventional crime such as burglary, robbery, or larceny. Similar to crimes against wildlife, agricultural crimes such as theft of agrichemicals, cattle and horse rustling, and tack theft can be equally profitable for criminals.

Investigations of wildlife and livestock crimes may be particularly challenging to criminal investigators. While investigative and surveillance techniques such as uniformed patrol, intensive hunting patrols, and covert investigations may help deter and effectively reduce wildlife crimes, wildlife officers generally spend only about 20 percent of their time in law enforcement activities. Further, in livestock crimes it is not uncommon for livestock to be stolen, transported, and disposed of before the theft is discovered. While the theft of horses may be discovered in a day to two weeks, the theft of range cattle may go undetected for months. Livestock investigation may also be unfamiliar territory to the uniformed officer, who may not recognize various aspects of livestock identification, breeds, scars, marks, tattoos, and brands.

The third section of this chapter is devoted to environmental crimes, such as those involving the illegal treatment, storage, transportation, and disposal of hazardous waste. Not only are these crimes a significant threat to public health, they also affect outdoor recreation and wildlife. The purpose of this chapter is to call attention to the nature and extent of crimes against agriculture, wildlife, and the environment and to provide information regarding their investigation.

## AGRICULTURAL CRIME AND ITS CITY CONNECTION

There is a natural but mistaken view that crimes against agriculture are of little overall economic consequence and are not within the sphere of interest for urban police officers. Although these themes are examined in detail from various perspectives in subsequent portions of this chapter, a few observations are warranted here. Estimates of the economic impact of rural and agricultural crime are as high as $5 billion annually.[2] This figure may be low when the size of the agricultural enterprise is considered. National membership in the American Farm Bureau Federation exceeds 4 million people.[3] By almost every estimate, farm products nationally are worth more than $1,000 billion annually. Just in San Diego County, California, agriculture ranks as the fourth-largest industry, with an economic impact of $3.9 billion annually.[4]

There is also evidence that urban-based criminals and criminal groups are involved as both planners and perpetrators of crimes in rural areas and on farms. In some instances these crimes are raid-like actions in which city-dwelling street gang members enter the rural setting, commit their crimes, and return to their familiar urban habitat swiftly on the interstate highways that are so conveniently positioned. In California and surrounding states, thieves are stealing cattle to support their drug addictions. Currently, it is estimated that drug-related incidents account for about 30 to 40 percent of all cattle stolen in California. One reason for this development is that rustlers can get full market value for their "stolen goods." A weaned calf, depending on its size and market conditions, will bring at least $375; quality steers and heifers can command prices of $700 to $900. Urban centers are also conduits for the disposal of some property stolen in rural areas; a portion of the extensive amount of farm machinery and equipment that is stolen is rapidly passed through big-city ports and shipped for sale in foreign countries, particularly those located in South America. Illegal "killer plants" or slaughterhouses have also been located in some cities and are used as part of a distribution system for stolen animals that are processed and sold as meat.

Another direct connection between rural crime and city dwellers results from the changing composition of labor used by farmers. There was a time when the principal source of farm labor was provided by the immediate family of the farm owner, neighbors, or laborers who lived in the vicinity of the farms. With the growth of large conglomerate farms and huge citrus orchards, the reliance on labor has by necessity shifted more and more to both migrants and city-based labor. When workers from the cities are employed, they typically travel to the farms or orchards on a daily basis and return to their homes in the cities at night. In some cases, these workers have returned to the farming areas for the purpose of committing crimes and have also, for a fee, tipped active criminals as to specific opportunities there.

Altogether, such illustrations provide substantial evidence that rural and agricultural crimes are economically significant and are of concern to both rural and urban police agencies.

## DIMENSIONS OF AGRICULTURAL, WILDLIFE, AND ENVIRONMENTAL CRIMES

We really don't know what agricultural, wildlife, and environmental crimes cost us. The information that is available is fragmented and often based on estimates or extrapolations from small data sets. However, from that information, it is reasonable to conclude that these problems are widespread and costly.

Ranchers, farmers, and others living in rural places are often the victims of thefts, including thefts of livestock, tack, pesticides, tractors, dirt bikes, all-terrain vehicles, drip lines, stock trailers, plants and timber, tools, hay, grains and citrus, irrigation pipes, and sprinkler heads. Often when the prices of crops and cattle increase, thefts of them may increase 20 percent or more. For example, when freezes kill oranges or droughts kill avocados—90 percent of which are grown in California[5]—prices rise on the remaining crops because there are less of them. The result is that thieves looking for an easy buck steal them. In the case of California avocados, thieves steal some $10 million worth annually, or about 5 percent of the total value of avocados statewide. A lone "night picker" can invade a grove and easily pick $300 to $500 worth of avocados and disappear. Or a worker commuting to a job beyond a grove might stop and tell a legal picker to "leave two burlap bags filled with avocados over there and I'll leave you $40 when I pick them up." The worker can get $200 for the two bags, pocketing a quick $160 in profit.[6]

Nationally, rustlers steal about 20,000 cattle worth $12.1 million.[7] Moreover, pigs, sheep, emu, and goats are also stolen. In a three-county area of North Carolina, hog rustlers made off with 300 pigs valued at $50,000 in less than 90 days.[8] Because livestock theft is at least 50 percent underreported, the total national loss due to rustling of all types of animals is at least double the known figure.

Private and public lands are being invaded by stealthy fossil hunters, who are also described as **bone rustlers.** They loot the land of fossils; a complete dinosaur skeleton may command as much as a $500,000 price. In South Dakota, thieves dug up the graveyard of rhinoceros-like mammals called titanotheres and made off with 18 skulls, each worth $5,000.[9] At Petrified National Forest, Arizona, U.S. park rangers marked fossils at several different sites with chemicals invisible to the unassisted eye. By inventorying these areas over a six-week period, they learned that 32,000 pounds of fossils had been stolen. One of the most successful fossil-poaching investigations was a joint local, state, and federal effort dubbed "Operation Rockfish," named after a fossil common in southwest Wyoming. There, Lincoln County Sheriff's Department Sergeant/Pilot Steve Rogers began noticing new holes in the ground in and around Fossil Butte National Monument. First suspecting that toxic chemicals were being dumped, he invited several federal agents to fly with him. On-the-ground investigation revealed that fossils were being stolen and sold both in the open and on black markets, some for prices in excess of $10,000. Nationally, Operation Rockfish resulted in the recovery of $7 million worth of stolen fossils. (See photo below.) The theft of bull semen

### Stolen Fossils Recovered as Evidence

Fossil thefts are more prevalent than was previously recognized. Today, private and public lands are being invaded by stealthy fossil hunters known as "bone-rustlers." These thieves dig up grave sites of dinosaurs or other highly sought fossils and sell them to collectors for a high price.

(Courtesy Steve Rogers, Sheriff's Office, Lincoln County, WY)

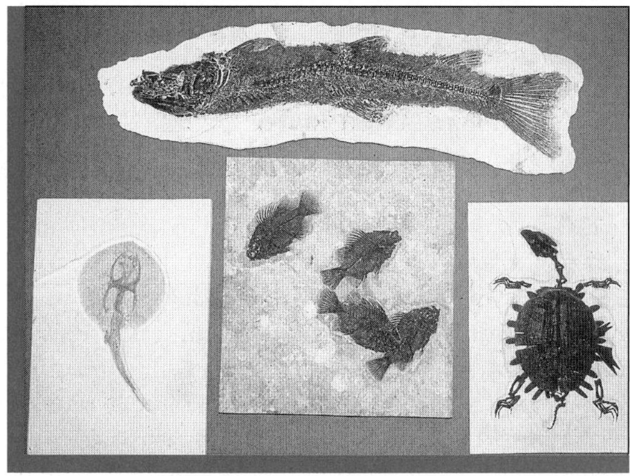

**Saguaro Cacti**
The theft of saguaro cacti from national lands in the West is a continuing problem. Saguaros grow very slowly; a 10-year one may only be 4 to 6 inches tall. They reach maturity in about 150 years and may live another 50 years beyond that, reaching a height of about 45 feet. Consequently, saguaro thefts amount to stealing part of our national heritage.
(©Jo MacDonald/Corbis)

from dairy farms has become a criminal enterprise.[10] The bull semen is essential to the operation of dairies because cows must be either pregnant or nursing to produce milk. A full tank of bull semen can be worth $10,000 and is easy to dispose of. In a number of places throughout the country, individuals and rings have been convicted of killing horses in order to collect the insurance money on them. Often the horses have been overinsured. Upon learning of convictions for these killings, groups such as the American Horse Shows Association have banned any members who were involved in the killings from attending their functions for periods up to life. Where there is lesser culpability, people have been banned for a period of years with the right to subsequently reapply for membership.[11] Radical environmentalists in Washington have used guerrilla tactics to halt the cutting of trees.[12] For example, spikes are driven into trees still in the forest, causing chain saws to shatter when an attempt is made to cut the tree down. Although when such tactics are used notices are often posted to warn loggers of the danger, serious injuries have resulted. Our national parklands are also victimized by plant poachers. Ginseng roots are prized by Asians as an aphrodisiac and as a treatment for infection, lack of vigor, and inflammation.[13] A dried pound of ginseng root can bring its harvester as much as $300. In the Great Smokies National Park, rangers seized two separate loads of illegally picked ginseng roots, each of which weighed 1,600 pounds. In the Northwest each fall, hundreds of people sweep through places like Crater Lake National Park in Oregon picking mushrooms. The prize is the matsutake, which is sold in Japan for up to $200 per pound. Local harvesters—who may pick as much as 50 pounds per day—sell their finds to roadside buyers, who give them a few hundred dollars and then sell them to Japanese outlets for considerably more. Although both ginseng and matsutake may be legally gathered, people often do so at illegal times or go onto lands where their permits are not valid. Saguaro cacti are being stolen from ranches and public lands in New Mexico, Arizona, and Nevada. Thieves place the stolen saguaros on their own land or sell the cacti through unscrupulous landscaping companies. The saguaros can be sold for about $50 for each foot of height, plus $100 for each arm on the cactus. The saguaro cactus can be dug up, loaded onto a truck, and removed from the scene in 15 to 25 minutes.[14] (See photo above.)

It must be observed that persons who live in rural areas and on farms, groves, vineyards, and ranches not only are crime victims but are themselves occasional offenders. For example, false reports of livestock or equipment theft are made to obtain insurance money, and the nature of crops may be misrepresented. In California when demand for wine outstrips the supply of grapes, prices increase dramatically. French colombard grapes, which usually sell for $150 per ton, have been sold as chardonnay grapes—at $1,500 per ton.[15]

## TIMBER THEFT

The U.S. Forest Service concedes that it doesn't know how much timber is stolen from national forests but says that the value may be as much as $100 million worth annually and amount to about 1 in every 10 trees cut down.[16] In East Texas, timber is the number-one ranking agricultural commodity, with 500,000 acres a year being harvested, producing a revenue of $900 million; at least another $20 million is lost annually to "tree rustlers."[17] Winter is the prime season for hunting burls, the huge gnarly root at the base of walnut trees. Burls, used to make fine clocks, wood trim in expensive sports cars, and fancy rifle stocks, can command up to $20,000 on the black market.[18] Burl thieves sneak into a walnut grove at night looking for a prime specimen. They dig a large hole to expose the burl, which may weigh up to 2,000 pounds. Then they place the soil loosely back into the hole and return the next night. They can easily shovel away the soil, cut the burl loose quickly with a chain saw, and leave as soon as they get it into a truck.[19]

"Tippers" or "brushers" are people who harvest the ends of branches on Christmas-type trees. These branches are ultimately made into Christmas wreaths. Many tippers operate legitimately on their own land or purchase the right to work someone else's under a permit. However, there are also tippers who operate illegally and are referred to as "branch rustlers."[20] This type of rustler goes onto land illegally and may steal the choice tips that someone else has a permit to harvest, causing economic loss to legitimate tippers and an occasional violent confrontation. Other tippers purchase a permit to harvest on a particular section of land but then gather their branches from a more desirable tract of land. In a single day or night a tipper or branch rustler may earn $250, but the rustlers' profit is generally higher because they operate without the expense of the permit from the landowner.

Investigations into the illegal cutting of timber involve a full range of investigative techniques. Examination of crime scenes continues to result in the discovery of evidence of paint transfers and tool marks on wood debris left behind by suspects. These marks and paint transfers result from the use of axes, wedges, and splitting mauls and serve to tie a suspect to a crime. Examination of tool marks on wood is based on established principles that it is possible to identify a suspect tool with the mark it leaves on a surface. In several cases, containers left at the scene of a timber theft have been processed and fingerprints developed. These fingerprints have been useful in identifying and placing suspects at the scene. In addition, casts of both shoe and tire impressions that were later identified as belonging to particular suspects and vehicles have been found at some crime scenes.[21] Increasingly, DNA is proving important as key evidence in many of the types of crimes discussed in this chapter, including plant and tree thefts, livestock rustling, and fish and wildlife poaching.

Although the crime scene examinations at the site of timber thefts are important, they are supplemented by the long process of interviewing potential witnesses to the crime, conducting investigations to develop witnesses in resort-type areas where thefts have occurred, and checking possible outlets where forest products might be sold. In order to conduct investigations concerning timber sales, law enforcement officers must become familiar with the variety of terms and techniques pertaining to a timber sale, from its inception to the eventual purchase.

In some urban areas, particularly along parkways and expressways in the month leading up to the Christmas holiday, Christmas-type trees "disappear" as motorists cut them down and cart the trees home to decorate. To combat such thefts, some cities chemical-coat trees that are likely targets, causing them to smell "awful." Another coating has an unnoticeable odor until it starts to heat up, and then it "smells worse than cat urine."

## THEFT OF AGRICHEMICALS

**Agrichemical** is a broad term whose meaning encompasses a variety of products used on farms, including pesticides, fertilizers, and herbicides. As a rule of thumb, fertilizers are not a target of theft because of their bulk and relatively low cost. In contrast, pesticides and herbicides can be costly; even a small pickup truck's load can be worth thousands of dollars. Although the theft of agrichemicals is a multimillion-dollar-per-year problem nationally, the exact type of agrichemical taken varies by geographic region, depending on what the predominant crop is.

In general, manufacturers do not have a theft problem because they can maintain tight security. As the product moves from the manufacturer to the distributor to the dealer to the ultimate consumer, the farmer, the problem increases. Distributors in particular have been vulnerable to the hijacking of trucks carrying agrichemicals, with resulting losses of $200,000 or more per incident. Dealers typically have been victimized by burglaries. One crime prevention tactic that is recommended to farmers is buying agrichemicals only in quantities that can be immediately used. While some farmers have adopted this practice, many have found it to be impractical given the time, inconvenience, and cost of repeat trips to make purchases.

Because the theft of agrichemicals may take the form of any of several different criminally chargeable acts, it would be possible for investigators in different parts of the same agency to be working on various activities by the same ring without knowing it. For example, the hijacking of a truck might be worked on by robbery investigators, the burglary of a dealership by the property section or burglary investigators, while personnel assigned to the ranch and grove unit might be working on the theft of pesticides from a local farmer. Although one ring might not exhibit a wide range of criminally chargeable behaviors, they may be sufficiently different to cause the fragmentation of investigative information.

To be effective in the investigation of agrichemical thefts, the investigator must become familiar with the legal supply channels and the principal agrichemicals that are used in his or her region. In particular it is important to know that the same basic chemical or formulation may be sold by several different manufacturers under different product names. For example, atrazine is manufactured and sold by Ciba-Geigy as AAtrex; it is used as a corn herbicide. Imagine the difficulty created for an investigation if a victim reports the theft of "50 gallons of atrazine" and it is entered into police records that way, when the victim was using "atrazine" as a synonym for "AAtrex." Another aspect of agrichemicals that requires a specialized knowledge is awareness of various security measures that have been taken by manufacturers, such as coded lot numbers and ultraviolet and chemical coding.

Finally, because of their precarious economic situation, some farmers will engage in the theft of agrichemicals or will readily purchase such commodities at "bargain prices." Because farmers are the end users of many agrichemicals, they know that a multigallon plastic jug of agrichemicals can be emptied in less than a minute, the jug readily and totally burned due to its high density, and the product immediately applied, making detection difficult. One method of identifying farmers who are possible illegal receivers of agrichemicals is to determine those whose purchasing patterns through legal supply channels are inconsistent with their crop needs.

## LIVESTOCK AND TACK THEFT

It is sometimes difficult to comprehend that a society that can land people on the moon and safely return them still has a serious rustling problem (see photo on page 633). Yet rustling did not disappear with the closing of the American frontier in 1890. While new and often sophisticated methods of theft are now used, the object of attack—livestock—remains the same, as do the motivations: profit or food.

**Livestock** refers to cattle, horses, sheep, goats, hogs, mules, jackasses, and other such species. **Tack** refers to saddles, bridles, harnesses, and related equipment. Certain generalizations can be made with respect to livestock and tack thefts:

1. Most livestock thefts are committed by persons who have been or are currently employed in some aspect of a livestock business. One significant exception to this broad observation is that in economically hard times rural areas adjacent to urban centers experience more thefts in which the physical evidence suggests that the motivation was food rather than profit. Such so-called **freezer crimes** typically involve only one or a few head of cattle, and when they are butchered at the scene, it is often in a manner that reflects only a crude understanding of the process.[22]
2. It is common for livestock to be stolen, transported, and disposed of before the theft is discovered. While the theft of horses may

be discovered in a day to two weeks, theft of range cattle may go undetected for months.

3. Except for small roadside slaughters committed as freezer crimes, livestock is stolen to be sold for economic gain. The excellent interstate systems that cross the country lend themselves—like the famous trails of frontier days—to transporting the stolen livestock rapidly for sale in states other than the one in which the crime took place.
4. Because horse owners are typically very attached to their animals, such thefts are often very emotional situations.
5. Horse thieves also tend to be tack thieves; statistically, for every stolen horse there are approximately 20 cases of tack theft.

As awareness of the livestock theft problem develops, law enforcement agencies have created specialized investigative units or designated a particular individual as the agency's specialist in such matters.[23] Regardless of whether the investigator works as part of a specialized unit or as the sole specialist, he or she must have or develop an expertise in the various aspects of livestock identification, including breeds, markings, blemishes, scars, marks, tattoos, and brands. In short, the investigator must be able to speak "livestock" in order to be effective.

The heaviest burden in livestock investigation often falls on the uniformed officer who takes the original offense report; this is true because such officers may have no knowledge, or only a rudimentary knowledge, of livestock and the applicable special laws.[24] Police agencies can help compensate for this by adopting forms similar to those depicted in Figures 17–1 and 17–2 and by providing training in their use. When such forms are not used, a good guide to follow is that an animal is property and can be described like any other type of property, although the language may be unfamiliar to the investigator. In such situations, the frank acknowledgment of a lack of familiarity or expertise will elicit a more systematic and detailed description from the owner than would otherwise be obtained. Subsequent to the taking of the original offense report, the progress of an investigation often hinges on the mutual assistance, cooperation, and free exchange of information that is given by ranchers, feedlot operators, stock auctions, farmers, sale yards, slaughterhouses, livestock associations, and other public agencies.

## CATTLE RUSTLING

The majority of cattle-rustling thefts are committed by one or two people who take the animal for their own use.[25] The usual method of operation is to drive to an isolated area, locate an animal, shoot it, and either butcher it there or load the carcass into a vehicle and butcher it at home. Butchering the animal at the scene means the thieves must spend more time there, but it avoids the problem of having to

**Stolen Horses**
Acting on a tip that rustlers in remote Nevada were driving horses from land belonging to the Pyramid Lake Paiute tribe, investigators located a hidden corral in which five wild horses were being kept. If sold to a rodeo or slaughterhouse, the five horses together would have brought a price of roughly $1,000. The horses were released back into the wild.
(©Marilyn Newton/Reno Gazette-Journal)

**Figure 17-1**

## Cattle Identification Form

(**Source:** Courtesy Los Angeles County, California, Sheriff's Department)

LOS ANGELES COUNTY SHERIFF'S DEPARTMENT

CATTLE IDENTIFICATION FORM

Classification Lost ( ) Found ( ) Theft ( ) Other ( )
File No.____________

Date & Time____________ Location____________

Victim ( )
Informant ( )

Address City Phone

Suspect____________

Name Address City Phone

DBO______Sex______Race______Age______Hair______Eyes______Ht.______Wt.______

Vehicle Year______Make______Body______Color______Lic.______

Trailer Horse Stock Rig Make Color # Axles Gooseneck

ON THE DRAWING INDICATE EAR MARKS, BLEMISHES, ODDITIES, DEFORMITIES, OR ANY INJURY THAT MAY BE USED TO IDENTIFY THIS ANIMAL. IF THE ANIMAL HAS DEWLAP OR WATTLE MARKINGS, SHOW TYPE AND LOCATION. ALSO HORNS CAN BE INDICATED.

Right Left

Brand

| Sex Bull ( ) Cow ( ) Steer ( ) Calf ( ) Heifer ( ) Breed | Also indicate Location on Animal & any other Brands. Type of Brand. | Method of Operation Check all that apply |
|---|---|---|
| Age____Wt______Color______ | Hot Iron______ ( ) | Trailered ( ) Driven ( ) |
| Polled______Horned______ | Chemical______ ( ) | Pasture ( ) Range ( ) |
| Ear Tag ( ) No. Color | Freeze______ ( ) | Barn ( ) Dairy ( ) Corral ( ) |
| | Hair Brand______ ( ) | Feed, Auction or Sale Yard ( ) |
| | Horn Brand______ ( ) | Residential ( ) Other ( ) |

Field Slaughter
Items used Gun ( ) Knife ( ) Axe ( ) Rope ( ) Hoist ( ) Chainsaw ( ) Other ( )

Carcass
Removed entire Carcass ( ) Hind Quarters ( ) Other ( )

Left at Scene Feet ( ) Head ( ) Hide ( ) Waste ( ) Other ( )

To move Animal Used Horses ( ) On Foot ( ) Dogs ( ) Motorcycle ( ) Lead ( ) Other ( )

Remarks____________

| Officer Reporting | Agency | Date |
|---|---|---|

dispose of unused remains later. At times the thieves will shoot the animal and then drive to a place where they can watch to see if anyone comes to investigate. If no one comes, they then butcher the animal. As these incidents often occur at night, they can see the headlights of approaching vehicles for some distance, giving them ample time to depart from the area. Freezer-crime rustlers are difficult to apprehend because they must be caught when they are committing the act or while they are transporting the carcass or meat. Surveillances that work well in urban areas are usually difficult to execute in rural areas. Their success depends on:

- The topography of the area.
- The availability of cover for concealment.
- The number and position of access roads.
- The size of the area containing the cattle.

One proven method for successful surveillances is for investigators to choose the area of the theft

**Figure 17-2** Horse Identification Form

(**Source:** Courtesy Kern County, California, Sheriff's Department)

KERN COUNTY SHERIFF'S DEPARTMENT

**HORSE IDENTIFICATION FORM**



Breed______ Sex______

Color______ Ht.____ Wt.____ Age____

Brands______ Tattoo______

Scars & Marks______

Other I.D. Info______

(USE REVERSE FOR SADDLES)

Owner______ (name) (address)

______ (city) (phone)

Date & Time Stolen______ Reported To______ (agency)

Date Reported______ File No.______

Method: Lead Away ( ) Trailer ( ) Ride Away ( )
Corral ( ) Barn ( ) Stall ( ) Pasture ( )
Other ( )

ATTACH PHOTOGRAPH OF HORSE

KC Sheriff #44 (12-73)

themselves.[26] This is accomplished by picking an area that maximizes the considerations important to investigators and then having the rancher move the cattle into this area. The rancher must not allow employees or other persons to learn that an operation is being set up. If others are involved in moving the cattle to the area selected, they should be given some reason for the change of pasture, such as a tally, brand check, or veterinary inspection.

Vehicles coming out of isolated areas should routinely be visually inspected for signs of blood on the rear bumper or trunk areas.[27] Because rustlers are invariably armed with some type of firearm, extreme caution must be used when approaching suspicious vehicles. Panicky suspects, who might not otherwise think of assaulting a peace officer, may do so impulsively. In addition to having firearms, this type of rustler will also often be carrying butcher knives and ropes.

In contrast to the modest equipment usually employed by the freezer thief, professional rustlers use more sophisticated means to commit their crimes, such as light planes or helicopters to spot vulnerable herds and watch for patrolling officers. The thieves coordinate their movements with walkie-talkies, and "dirt-bike cowboys" herd the cattle to where they will be killed and butchered, often by the use of chain saws. Refrigerated trucks with meat-processing equipment inside quickly transform the rough-butchered cattle into salable products.[28] Professionals may also have a full array of forged documents, such as a forged bill of sale and counterfeit U.S. Department of Agriculture inspection stamps. The professional rustling operation can be very profitable. Thirty head of cattle can be taken from the range, loaded onto a truck, and butchered in the truck; the waste is dumped off the road, and the 60 sides of beef are illegally stamped and delivered to the city at approximately $325 per side—a profit of $20,100 for a night's work.[29]

As a general matter, peace officers have a right to stop any conveyance transporting livestock on any public thoroughfare and the right to impound any animal, carcass, hide, or portion of a carcass in the possession of any person who they have reasonable cause to believe is not the legal owner or is not entitled to possession.[30] To transport cattle legally, certain written documents may be required, such as:

- Bill of sale.
- Certificate of consignment.
- Brand inspector's certificate.
- Shipping or transportation permit.[31]

Because these provisions vary by state, it is essential that every investigator know:

- What documentation is required for lawful transportation (e.g., a "horse-hauling permit").
- What the investigator's precise authority is in such matters.
- How to handle violations of law.[32]

Equipped with such knowledge, the investigator is better prepared to deal with issues related to transportation violation or a possible theft. Although the applicable state law may permit the officer to impound livestock or meat, there are several less drastic alternatives. Under unusual conditions or where only slight suspicion exists, investigators may elect to get a full description and identifying information of the driver and the rig and its contents. Other information essential for a useful follow-up inquiry is the origin and destination of the trip. If suspicion is more pronounced, specialists may be requested to come to the scene of the stop. Such specialists may come from the investigator's own agency, another local department, the state police or state investigative agency, or the Marks and Brands Unit of the state's department of agriculture. If the investigator is sufficiently confident that a shipping violation or theft exists, the arrest can be made and the load impounded. Live animals can be delivered to the nearest feedlot or sales yard, and meat can be placed in refrigeration storage. Such situations require that officers in the field have a basic working knowledge of the applicable laws and exercise sound judgment. They are not required to be experts in such matters, and their general investigative experience is a substantial asset in making an evaluation of the situation.

## HORSE RUSTLING

More than 50,000 horses are stolen each year,[33] as compared to about 20,000 cattle.[34] About 60 percent of the stolen horses end up in slaughter plants, where they are processed and sold as meat for human consumption in Europe and Japan.[35] The United States is the world's leading exporter of horse meat—which abroad commands a greater price than filet mignon.[36] Many of the slaughtered horses are bought at auction and are lame, unwanted, or just worn out. "Killer buyers" get them for a few hundred dollars a head and take them to the plants. Because some horse rustlers are not knowledgeable judges of livestock, a few very expensive horses end up being slaughtered too. In a Texas case, two unemployed men and a woman decided to "go into the rustling business." They loaded three horses worth $100,000 in a trailer and sold them to a buyer who promptly had them slaughtered.

There is not a great deal of variation in the way in which horse rustlers operate. If the horse is in a corral, the thief will park a vehicle and trailer nearby, walk up and take the horse, load it in the trailer, and drive off.[37] As such thefts usually occur during the hours of darkness, the rustler can be several hundred miles away before the theft is discovered. When horses are in pasture, the task of stealing them is only slightly more difficult. The thief walks into the pasture with a bucket of grain. One or more of the horses will usually approach him, and because they are herd animals, if one approaches, the others are also likely to follow along. The theft then proceeds in the same fashion as a corral theft. One tactic commonly used by horse rustlers is to knock down the corral or pasture fence after loading up the trailer with horses and chase any remaining horses down the road. The owner will think that the horses have gotten out on their own, and it may be several days before he or she realizes that some horses have been stolen. Thus, even if there is no clear evidence of a theft, the investigator should not assume that the horse has strayed off. As a minimum action, a lost report should be initiated. If the horse is later discovered to have been stolen, the incident can be reclassified.

## TACK THEFT

Simply stated, tack is equipment that is used with horses; the most common items are saddles, bridles, and horse blankets.[38] Of all stolen tack, approximately 80 percent is saddles—which often have base prices in excess of $2,000—and it is generally believed that 85 to 90 percent of all tack is unmarked for identification, making tracing a very difficult proposition. In order to help reduce tack thefts, particularly saddles, and to improve the low recovery rate, property-marking programs have been undertaken and specialized reporting forms, as depicted in Figure 17–3, adopted. These have been favorable developments, but tack theft remains a serious problem for several reasons: many owners prefer not to mark their equipment, feeling that even if the numbers are hidden, the tack, particularly saddles, is disfigured; owners think that the numbers can be altered or removed entirely from the tack with ease; and there is a ready market for the sale of tack, which is sufficiently diffuse to make detection a limited possibility in many situations. Some owners are now having microchips embedded in saddles to facilitate their recovery if stolen.[39]

# LIVESTOCK IDENTIFICATION

In any livestock theft case one key to a successful prosecution is the positive identification of a specific animal as belonging to a particular owner. It is therefore essential that investigators have a basic knowledge of the methods used to identify livestock.

This section addresses the identification of horses and cattle. In general, people are more willing to

**Figure 17-3** Saddle Identification Form

(**Source:** Courtesy Los Angeles County, California, Sheriff's Department)

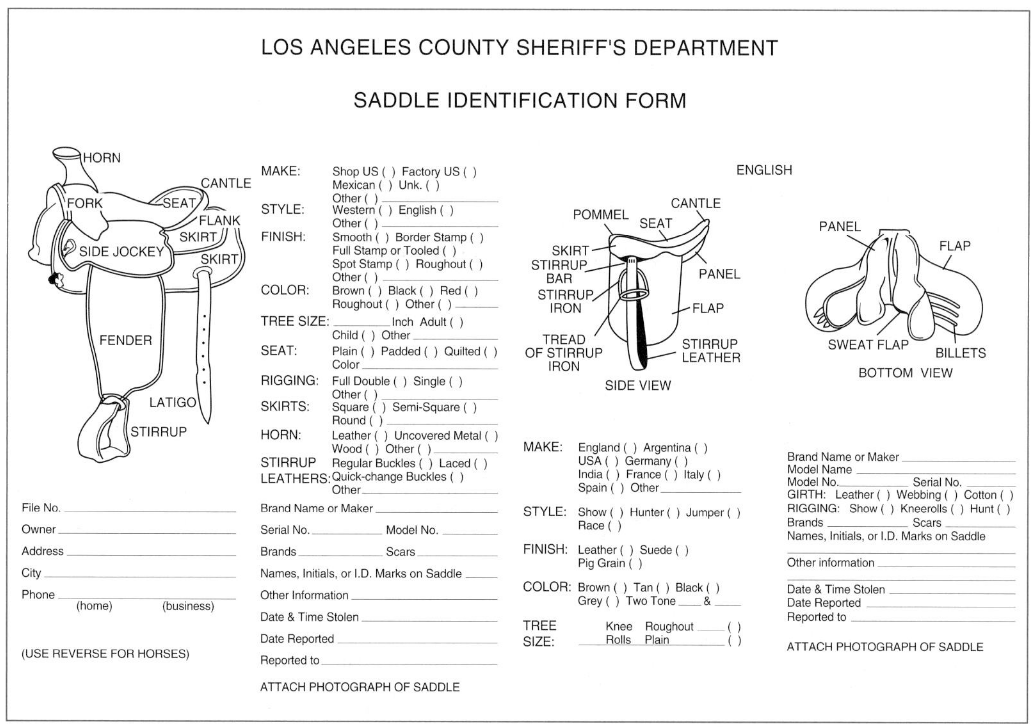

LOS ANGELES COUNTY SHERIFF'S DEPARTMENT

SADDLE IDENTIFICATION FORM



MAKE: Shop US ( ) Factory US ( ) Mexican ( ) Unk. ( ) Other ( ) ______
STYLE: Western ( ) English ( ) Other ( ) ______
FINISH: Smooth ( ) Border Stamp ( ) Full Stamp or Tooled ( ) Spot Stamp ( ) Roughout ( ) Other ( ) ______
COLOR: Brown ( ) Black ( ) Red ( ) Roughout ( ) Other ( ) ______
TREE SIZE: ______ Inch Adult ( ) Child ( ) Other ______
SEAT: Plain ( ) Padded ( ) Quilted ( ) Color ______
RIGGING: Full Double ( ) Single ( ) Other ( ) ______
SKIRTS: Square ( ) Semi-Square ( ) Round ( ) ______
HORN: Leather ( ) Uncovered Metal ( ) Wood ( ) Other ( ) ______
STIRRUP LEATHERS: Regular Buckles ( ) Laced ( ) Quick-change Buckles ( ) Other ______

File No. ______
Owner ______
Address ______
City ______
Phone ______ (home) (business)

(USE REVERSE FOR HORSES)

Brand Name or Maker ______
Serial No. ______ Model No. ______
Brands ______ Scars ______
Names, Initials, or I.D. Marks on Saddle ______
Other Information ______
Date & Time Stolen ______
Date Reported ______
Reported to ______

ATTACH PHOTOGRAPH OF SADDLE

ENGLISH



MAKE: England ( ) Argentina ( ) USA ( ) Germany ( ) India ( ) France ( ) Italy ( ) Spain ( ) Other ______
STYLE: Show ( ) Hunter ( ) Jumper ( ) Race ( )
FINISH: Leather ( ) Suede ( ) Pig Grain ( )
COLOR: Brown ( ) Tan ( ) Black ( ) Grey ( ) Two Tone ____ & ____
TREE SIZE: ______ Knee Rolls ( ) Roughout Plain ( )

Brand Name or Maker ______
Model Name ______
Model No. ______ Serial No. ______
GIRTH: Leather ( ) Webbing ( ) Cotton ( )
RIGGING: Show ( ) Kneerolls ( ) Hunt ( )
Brands ______ Scars ______
Names, Initials, or I.D. Marks on Saddle ______
Other information ______
Date & Time Stolen ______
Date Reported ______
Reported to ______

ATTACH PHOTOGRAPH OF SADDLE

**Figure 17-4**

Methods of Reading Brands

| Top to Bottom | | Left to Right | | Outside to Inside | |
|---|---|---|---|---|---|
| H̄ | Bar H | A+ | A cross | (K) | Circle K |
| 2/X | 2 bar X | /X | Slash X | ◊P | Diamond P |
| | D hanging C | ++ | Double cross | [M] | Box M |
| | Y lazy P | ◊/K | Diamond slash K | △S | Triangle S |
| | Rafter diamond | (E | Lazy E, quarter circle E | | Double circle, lazy K |

use a wider range of identification methods on cattle than they are on their horses, who are somewhat akin to being family members. For example, earmarking horses is unimaginable to most owners. Horses and cattle are commonly branded, and there are a lot of brands to read: over 26,000 different ones in Utah alone, some of which date back to 1847.[40] **Brands** are combinations of numbers, letters, marks, and shapes that establish a unique identification. Brands are registered with different agencies in various states; in some states registry is accomplished at the local county courthouse. By legislation some states require that brands be placed on the hide at predetermined locations, while in others the location is a choice made by the owner. As depicted in Figure 17–4, there are three ways to read brands. Treated as a separate category are picture brands, which simply mean what they represent (see Figure 17–5). Common methods of livestock identification are discussed below.

## HOT-IRON BRANDING

Hot-iron branding is a method of identification that has been used in this country for nearly 400 years. After a brand application has been approved by a state agency, it can be manufactured and used. The agencies often are located within a department of agriculture and may operate under a name similar to "Brands and Inspections" or "Animal Husbandry." In this method, an "iron" is heated in a fire and then the end bearing the brand is impressed on the hide of the animal, creating a permanent mark. Unless the hair grows over the mark, which is roughly 5 inches across, the brand can be easily read. Horse branding continues to lose favor as other methods of identification have become available.

In recording brands and their location (see Figure 17–6), the protocol is to record the brand first and then the location. Thus, "Circle A, RH" means that the brand is located on the right hip.

**Figure 17-5** Picture Brands

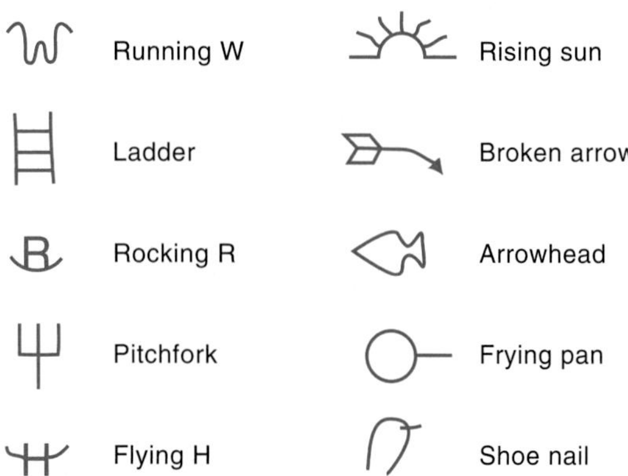

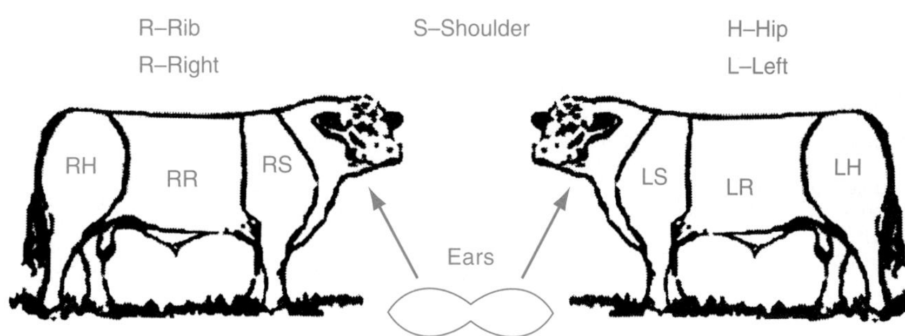


**Figure 17-6**

**Brand-Location Designations**

(**Source:** Courtesy California Bureau of Livestock Identification)

## TATTOOS

When used on horses, the tattoo is applied to the inside of the lip; on cattle, the inside of the ear is tattooed. In both cases, a permanent record of identity is made, which can be registered with law enforcement agencies or livestock associations. Tattoos are a combination of letters and numbers or symbols. In some systems the tattoo numbers are partially sequenced to help with herd management by establishing, for example, when the animal was born.

## EAR TAGS AND INJECTABLE IDENTIFICATION

In early applications, ear tags were metal or plastic, but in a number of cases they were simply lost while in use. Bar-code ear tags for cattle were an advancement for herd management because of the additional data that could be recorded. More recently, the National Farm Animal Identification and Records (FAIR) Program developed electronic ear tags, which provide even greater information about each animal and better animal tracking. These tags are finding favor among those in animal industries and became mandatory in Canada in 2002. Because they can be quickly read with PDA-type equipment, herd management information can be more quickly collected and acted on, which is especially important in disease control. Horses can be injected with a passive electronic transponder to establish their identities. When a handheld reader is passed over the site of an injected transponder, the transponder is activated and the implanted information is readable.

## FREEZE BRANDING

Special freeze-branding irons are chilled using dry ice or liquid nitrogen and then applied to the hide. Although the brand can immediately be seen, over the next three weeks to several months white hair fills the branded area, which is very effective with animals that have darker-colored hides. For lighter-colored animals, the chilled branding iron is left on longer and creates a permanent bald spot. Freeze branding is permanent and appears to be painless to horses and cattle.

## EARMARKS

Earmarks are often used in conjunction with branding because in some states earmarks alone are not legally sufficient to establish identification. Commonly used earmarks are shown in Figure 17–7. In reading them, the correct method is to use the animal's perspective, as indicated in Figure 17–7. Referring to the third column of the figure and the second illustration down, an investigator recording earmarks would make the notation "R—under half crop, L—under half crop." Earmarkings may use any of the combinations shown in Figure 17–7.

## DNA PROFILES

DNA profiles of expensive horses and bulls are common as a theft deterrent, required by some breed associations, and mandated by some insurance companies to prevent insurance scams (e.g., a less-expensive horse is killed and a claim is made for an expensive horse, which is sold, creating an additional source of "profit"). DNA can easily be obtained from animals by means of nasal swabs or mane or tail hair with the root attached.

# PHYSICAL EVIDENCE

The processing of a crime scene where an agriculture-related theft has occurred is in many respects no different from the processing of any other crime

Figure 17-7

Common Earmark Combinations

(Source: Courtesy California Bureau of Livestock Identification)

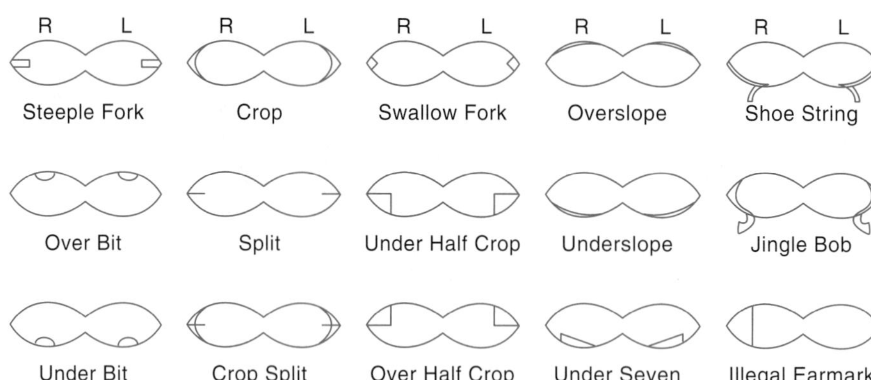


scene. For example, when cattle rustling occurs, the perpetrators frequently cut the barbed wire or locks securing a grazing area. The cut wire and lock will have tool marks left on them from the cutting tool. In addition, if the suspect's clothing came into contact with any of the barbed wire at the scene, pieces of fiber may be found adhering to the barbs. Shoe or tire impressions found at the crime scene may later be linked to a specific suspect and vehicle. Soil samples collected at the crime scene may also prove to be valuable, linking evidence to a suspect with similar soil on his or her shoes or clothes or on the vehicle used to transport the cattle. There is increasing movement toward the use of DNA evidence in livestock theft cases. The types of evidence discussed in Chapter 3, "Physical Evidence," can often be readily found and will be of great value to law enforcement officers in the investigation of agricultural crimes.

When their livestock has been stolen, farmers and ranchers often move equipment into the area of a theft and make immediate repairs to corrals, fences, and outbuildings or as otherwise needed. The predictable and unfortunate result is that physical evidence is either hopelessly contaminated or lost altogether. This contributes to a recovery rate for stolen livestock of only 20 percent.

## CRIME PREVENTION MEASURES

Information about how to prevent rural and agricultural crimes can be obtained from a variety of sources, including sheriff's departments, county police, state investigative agencies, state departments of agriculture, county extension agents, and various associations. Although some techniques developed in urban areas can be readily applied to the farm, others would create costs disproportionate to the benefits that could reasonably be expected to accrue to the rancher or farmer. Consequently, the technology in this area is sometimes familiar, sometimes takes advantage of unique aspects of the rural environment, and is continuously in the process of changing and developing. The suggestions that follow are organized around the object of attack; in general they are specialized and can be supplemented as may be appropriate by more conventional strategies, such as the use of case-hardened padlocks.

### Farm Equipment Theft

- Participate in equipment identification programs.
- Do not leave unattended equipment in remote fields for hours at a time or overnight. If it is necessary to do so for some reason, disable the engine by taking a vital part and use logging chains to secure other equipment. Even if such precautions are taken, equipment in remote areas should be hidden from view from roadways.
- Equipment is best protected, in reducing order of preference, by positioning it as follows: secured in a locked building near the main house or an inhabited house; secured in a gated area that is kept locked and is close to the main or an inhabited house; secured in one or more ways and not visible from commonly traveled roads.

- Immediately report all suspicious activity, such as strangers taking photographs of equipment, to local enforcement officials.

## Timber Theft

- Post the property.
- Check periodically to determine if any timber has been cut.
- Promptly report all losses.
- Take aerial photos of land.

## Agrichemical Theft

- End users, whenever feasible, should buy only in quantities that they can readily use.
- If quantity purchases cannot be avoided, they should be stored in a locked, lighted building very close to the main house or an inhabited house. If available, place a few geese or guinea hens inside as watch animals.
- Rural dealers should employ security personnel during the months when they have large inventories.
- Be suspicious of people offering unusually good buys on agrichemicals; the absence of a market helps deter thefts.

## Livestock and Tack Theft

- All livestock should be marked for identification; maximum deterrence is obtained when marks are readily visible.[41]
- A daily tally or count should be taken.
- Do not follow a set routine, such as going to the movies every Friday night, which would give a thief an advantage.
- Enter into cooperative arrangements with trusted neighbors to help watch one another's places.
- Avoid leaving animals in remote pastures or on faraway ranges whenever practical.
- Mark tack and keep it in a room that lends itself to security measures.
- Do not use "set guns" or "booby traps." They are often illegal and frequently injure innocent people or animals; surviving thieves have won damage suits because of the injuries that resulted.
- Keep photographic records of livestock and tack.

Investigators interested in obtaining more detailed information can contact any of the sources mentioned earlier if their departments do not have active prevention programs. These sources are typically generous with the materials they send and often will give permission for them to be reproduced for use with the public.

# WILDLIFE CRIMES

The transition from the topic of agricultural crimes to wildlife crimes is a natural one because of some overlaps. For example, in many states wildlife officers may be called on to assist local police officers in cases of livestock theft or slaughter because the basic physical evidence closely resembles the types of evidence that wildlife officers process in poaching cases. Within the respective states, the responsibility for enforcing game and fish laws is primarily that of a state-level agency.

Wildlife officers require many of the same types of knowledge and skills as do other peace officers, including knowledge of the laws of arrest, search, and seizure and skills such as interviewing people and interrogating suspects. They are also required to recognize, collect, mark, and identify physical evidence. In addition, wildlife investigators need to know specialized laws pertaining to their field and to be able to recognize the species and gender of wildlife. They also must be able to master unique skills, such as interpreting tracks and being able to follow a trail (see photo on page 642).

The U.S. Fish and Wildlife National Forensics Laboratory in Ashland, Oregon, is a premier source of assistance for wildlife investigators, as is the Wildlife Forensic DNA Laboratory at Trent University in Canada. In the United States, wildlife DNA programs have evolved at several state universities. These developments are of vital importance because conventional crime laboratories are awash in dealing with traditional offenses and often lack not only the time but also the expertise to handle physical evidence from wildlife investigations. In cases of poaching, DNA profiles can tie together the remains of a deer found at the location where it was field-dressed and dried bloodstains in the back of a pickup and then meat packages in the poacher's freezer. This creates scientific evidence that is very strong to overcome in court.

**Evidence of Poaching**

In the course of a major poaching investigation, wildlife investigators seized these boots, whose soles had been carved to resemble cattle hooves. By using them, the poacher tried to conceal his actual boot prints and thus mislead investigators.

(Photo courtesy Texas Parks & Wildlife ©2002, Earl Nottingham)

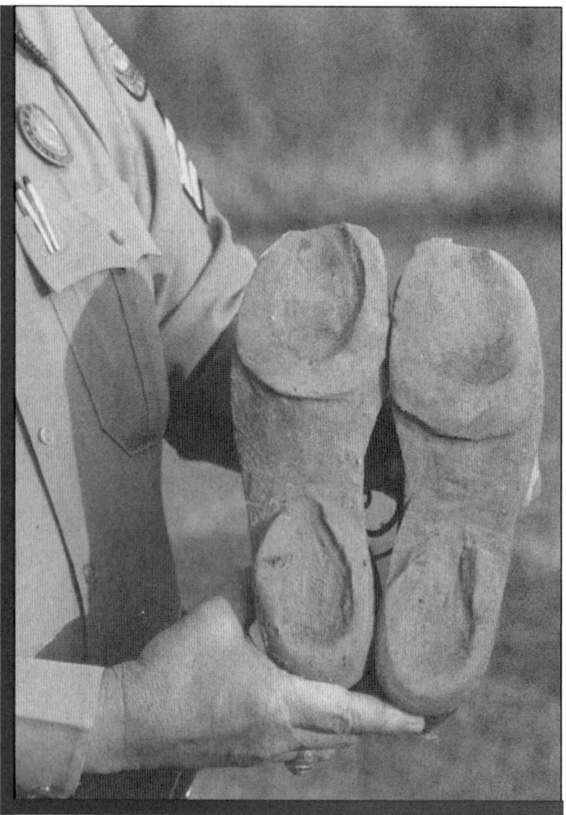

Because wildlife investigators often patrol alone in the wild, they encounter individuals and small groups of people who may be difficult or even deadly to deal with, including survivalists, fugitives, radical environmentalists, paramilitary units, drug smugglers, and persons engaged in illegal activities on public lands such as growing marijuana and operating clandestine drug labs.

A few urban restaurants occasionally knowingly buy poached game, telling their customers they have a legal source for it "in another state." The availability of such illegal markets helps sustain poaching. Conversely, restaurants are sometimes the victims of scams in which they are told they are getting one kind of meat when they are actually getting another. In one case, the restaurant was paying a premium price for wild alligator turtle or alligator "snapper" meat, when in fact it was simply getting less-expensive alligator meat, most of which is commercially farmed in the United States. There are also snapper turtle farms, where turtles are killed and butchered when they are 10 to 12 pounds in weight. In contrast, in the wild, alligator snapping turtles commonly reach 175 pounds.

## MAJOR THREATS TO WILDLIFE

There are a number of major threats to our wildlife. As urban areas continue their sprawl outward from the core city, more construction occurs, destroying habitats. The accidental release of chemicals, illegal dumping, land erosion, and oil spills produce the same effect. The illegal taking or possession of game, fish, and other wildlife—**poaching**—is the major threat that the next portion of this chapter addresses.

Poaching reduces the amount of wildlife that would otherwise be available. It makes "camera safaris" less meaningful, has the potential to reduce tourism, hampers the reestablishment of game species, and constitutes a significant threat to endangered species. Although the actual cost of poaching is not known, it is very substantial. Worldwide, there may be as much as a $10 billion market for trafficking in animal parts,[42] with as much as 40 percent of it based on poaching.[43]

## POACHERS AND POACHING

Poachers can be categorized into two types: situational poachers and professional poachers.

The largest number of poachers are situational, some being motivated by opportunity and others by circumstances. A normally law-abiding man or woman is driving home at night and suddenly sees an elk on the road frozen by the car's headlights. Impulsively, or after a quick deliberation, the person shoots the elk out of season, becoming a situational poacher. Others become situational poachers to feed their families because of economic circumstances. A few opportunistic poachers kill simply for the thrill of it (see photo on page 643).

Although fewer in numbers, professional poachers take much more game than do situational poachers because the more they take, the more they profit. Thus, while a situational poacher may take an elk or deer now and then, the professional will kill a half dozen or more in a single evening. It is estimated that for every incident in which a poacher is caught, there are another 30 to 50 incidents that go undetected or for which there will be no arrest made.[44]

Some trophy hunters pay to be taken into areas closed to hunters, to hunt out of season, or to have their guides use illegal hunting methods to ensure their success. One Alaskan admitted that every one of the 37 grizzlies that he had helped hunters bag—each of which was placed in the Boone and Crockett Club's record book—was illegally herded toward the hunters by use of an airplane.[45] Other "hunters" do not inconvenience themselves with actually going into the field; they just want the trophy to hang on the wall. They buy ready-to-mount bighorn sheep for \$20,000[46] and grizzlies for \$25,000.[47]

Poachers also shoot polar bears for the \$4,000[48] they can get for the skin and the additional \$2,000 or more for the gall bladder, valued by Asians for medical and aphrodisiac uses. About 65 days after they begin growing new antlers, elk and similar animals have the maximum amount of velvet on them; this velvet is a covering of blood vessels that nourish the antlers. Also believed to have medical and aphrodisiac qualities, this velvet sells for \$85 to \$135 per pound. A mature elk may have produced as much as 35 pounds of velvet, and even the velvet from small deer can bring \$1,000. The market for velvet has resulted in legal elk farms that supply it, but it has also increased the incentive to illegally trap elk for breeding purposes in order to avoid paying the much more substantial cost of legally raising elk.

### Elk Killed for Thrills

A thrill killer shot this elk in a clear-cut area off a logging road. No attempt was made by the poacher to retrieve the antlers or any meat from the carcass. Thrill killers are part of the category of poachers described as situational poachers. Situational poachers are generally motivated by opportunity or circumstance.

(Courtesy Wyoming Game and Fish Department)

## INVESTIGATIONS

Wildlife officers generally spend only about 20 percent of their time in law enforcement activities. The balance is spent in such activities as teaching hunting, boating, and snowmobile safety courses for the public, staffing exhibits at state and local fairs or other functions, participating in multiagency mock-disaster drills as part of emergency preparedness training, conducting various surveys for state and federal government, including counts of raccoon, deer, and midwinter waterfowl, as well as other censuses conducted on a one-time-only basis. When conducting law enforcement activities, wildlife officers use many of the same investigative techniques used by other types of peace officers.

### Information

Information is an essential commodity in combating poachers. With it, more investigative successes are experienced. In some states, 80 percent of all poacher arrests come from leads from citizens. To assist wildlife officers in getting information, a number of states have established special programs. In some states, these efforts are referred to as Citizens Against Poachers (CAP) programs and in other states as Turn in a Poacher (TIP) programs.

### Uniformed Patrol

Uniformed wildlife officers patrol in boats and cars to see if game is being taken out of season or by illegal means. They visit various sites to observe, to check licenses, and to examine each sportsperson's daily take. As a supplement to patrolling by car, airplanes can be used during the day to locate hunters, trappers, and camps in remote areas. At night, aircraft can also be useful in pinpointing places where it appears that artificial light is being used by poachers to take game, a tactic known as jacklighting. In both day and night uses of aircraft, the pilot or spotter will relay information to ground units so that they can take appropriate action. In some instances aircraft keep poachers leaving an area under surveillance and direct wildlife officers in cars on a course to intercept the poachers.

### Intensive Hunting Patrols

Wildlife officers also employ intensive hunting patrols, especially during the opening weekends for various types of game such as pheasant, wild turkey, waterfowl, grouse, and deer. Intensive patrols tend to be concentrated in areas of high public use, especially those with a history of excessive violations.

### Vehicle Check Stops

Vehicle check stops are strategically set up on carefully selected roads to check vehicles for bag limits, unplugged shotguns, and licenses and to determine whether necessary special stamps (e.g., duck hunting) have been acquired.

### Fishing Patrols

Fishing patrols check to see that no protected or endangered fish, eels (see photo on page 645), crabs, lobsters, or other aquatic life forms are being taken, that takable aquatic species are taken only by legal means during the proper seasons and times of day, that legal limits are being respected, and that the proper licenses have been obtained. Wildlife investigators are also vigilant in ferreting out the taking of sport and game fish by commercial fishing methods, such as the use of seines and trotlines.

### Resident License Verifications

In a common wildlife violation, nonresidents of a state claim residency so that they can be issued less-expensive hunting or fishing licenses. Periodically, wildlife officers go through copies of licenses to determine whether a purchaser may in fact have been a nonresident. The wildlife officer has many avenues to pursue in determining the actual legal residence of the license purchaser. Local utility companies are contacted for information concerning service by the individual, telephone books are checked, and driver's license records are examined, as are voter registration files. If the information indicates that the purchase is not by a resident of a state, the wildlife officer contacts the individual to attempt a personal interview. Once confronted, suspects will often make an admission.

### Covert Investigations

Covert investigations vary in their complexity. At the simplest, a wildlife officer who could not approach an area without being plainly visible for some distance may dress as a trout fisher and work his way along a stream watching for violations. Wildlife investigators also employ sophisticated sting operations. In Texas, some ranchers learned that their well-managed trophy deer herds were targets for poachers. The ranchers normally charge from $2,500 to more than $10,000 for the right to

**Elver Poaching**
Along the East Coast, American eels living in streams and marshes swim several thousand miles in the sea to spawn. When their juvenile offspring, called elvers, arrive back in the coastal waters, they are transparent in color and are therefore often called "glass eels." At this stage of development, they are considered a delicacy in Asia, bringing $300 per pound in good years. New Jersey is one of the states where elver poaching occurs.
(©Lynda Richardson/Corbis)

hunt their property legally. Undercover investigators agreed to take poachers out at night or to hunt from roads on the ranches. They received as little as $125 and a bag of marijuana from one "client." The sting operation netted dozens of arrests and broke the back of poaching for a number of ranchers.

## ENVIRONMENTAL CRIME

This planet—which we will pass on to our children—suffers from what the inhabitants do to it. Rain forests are being chopped down for their timber. The entry of raw (untreated) sewage into water systems threatens fish populations. Worldwide, smokestack industries pour carbon dioxide into the air, polluting it and further exacerbating our efforts to combat the greenhouse effect and its rising temperatures. Nuclear accidents render portions of countries uninhabitable. Swamps and marshes are disappearing at an alarming rate, along with their rich ecosystems. While not all of these events constitute environmental crimes, they do suggest that our planet is in some distress. Therefore, it is incumbent on us to enforce environmental laws.

### THE LEGAL AND ENFORCEMENT FRAMEWORK

There are roughly 18 major federal environmental laws that form the basis for Environmental Protection Agency (EPA) programs. These laws deal with a number of issues, including chemical safety and site security, clean air and water, oil pollution, toxic-substance control, emergency planning, and environmental cleanup. Many states have substantially similar laws on some of these issues, and a number of local jurisdictions have enacted their own laws to combat environmental crimes. From this maze of laws three patterns of enforcement emerge:

1. Acts over which only the federal government has jurisdiction.
2. Acts for which there is concurrent federal and state jurisdiction.
3. Acts for which there is unique state and/or local jurisdiction.

Individuals and businesses may be subject to criminal and civil fines for violating laws and consent decrees. Other sanctions that can be applied include the revocation of licenses and permits and the imposition of freezes on eligibility to receive federal grants.

The federal Resource Conservation and Recovery Act (RCRA) of 1976 and its subsequent amendments give the Environmental Protection Agency authority over hazardous waste from "its cradle to its grave." **Hazardous wastes** may be solids, liquids, sledges, or by-products of manufacturing processes. They may also be commercial products such as battery acid and household cleaning supplies. A waste is hazardous if it has one or more of the following characteristics (see Figure 17–8):

- *Ignitability:* Wastes that can create fires, those that can readily catch fire, and friction-sensitive substances (e.g., paints, degreasers, linseed oil, and gasoline).
- *Corrosivity:* Wastes that are acidic and those capable of corroding metal objects such as drums and tanks (e.g., cleaning fluids, battery acids, and rust removers).
- *Reactivity:* Substances that are unstable under normal conditions and that can create explosions and/or toxic fumes, gases, and vapors when mixed with water (e.g., sulphur-bearing wastes and cyanides).
- *Toxicity:* Substances that are harmful or fatal when ingested or absorbed and that, when improperly disposed of on land, may eventually pollute groundwater (e.g., mercury, certain pesticides, and lead).

## PROVISIONS OF STATE RCRA LAWS

Many states have enacted laws that are very similar to the federal RCRA. Among the common provisions of these laws are:

1. Identification and listing of hazardous wastes.
2. Establishment of permit and license systems regarding various types of hazardous waste, including their treatment, storage, and disposal (T/S/D).
3. A manifest or shipping-paper system that tracks hazardous waste from its cradle to its grave.
4. Identification of the responsibilities of the generators and transporters of hazardous waste.
5. Requirements for hazardous-waste management facilities, such as proof of financial reliability.
6. Designation of enforcement authority and criminal penalties.

**Figure 17-8** Characteristics of Hazardous Waste

(**Source:** Courtesy Environmental Protection Agency)

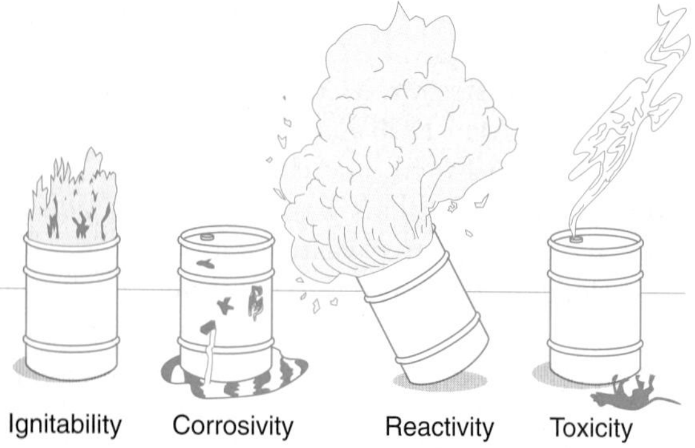


In a typical case, hazardous-waste crime charges are brought against one or more individuals and/or corporations involved in any combination of the three major components of the waste cycle:

- *Generating:* Among the companies engaging in activities that involve hazardous waste are chemical companies, which produce it as a by-product of their legal activity; furniture and wood manufacturing companies working with various solvents and ignitable wastes, which must periodically be disposed of; and vehicle maintenance operations, which involve lead-acid batteries, solvents, and heavy metal and inorganic wastes.
- *Transportation:* This component involves the hauling away of hazardous waste from industrial sites. False manifests may be prepared to make the loads look less harmful, thereby allowing for inexpensive disposal of the waste. Tankers in poor condition may leak hazardous waste as they are driven along highways, and illegal disposal of hazardous waste also occurs when tankers deliberately discharge the waste in small amounts onto the road.
- *Treatment, storage, and disposal:* **T/S/D crimes** are committed by companies that treat hazardous waste without a permit or treat it inadequately, store it without a permit to do so, improperly identify the nature of the waste or store it under inadequate conditions (see photo on page 647), discharge it into sewers, simply abandon it, mix it with regular waste for cheaper disposal, or store incompatible chemicals or amounts of chemicals beyond their permitted level.

Hazardous-waste generators vary in the level of regulatory requirements that they are required to meet (see Table 17–1). Regardless of generator

**Table 17-1** EPA Hazardous-Waste Generator Status

| Generator Category | Monthly Generation Rate | Maximum Quantity Accumulation Limit | Maximum Time Accumulation Limit |
|---|---|---|---|
| Conditionally exempt small-quantity generator (CESQG) | Less than 100 kg | 1,000 kg | None |
| Small-quantity generator (SQG) | 100 to 1,000 kg | 6,000 kg | 180 days |
| Large-quantity generator (LQG) | More than 1,000 kg | No storage limit | 90 days |

**Source:** Environmental Protection Agency.

status, all generators must comply with basic RCRA requirements, including the use of manifests to track waste shipments. Conditionally exempt small-quantity generators must obtain an EPA permit once they generate more than 100 kilograms of hazardous waste per month. In all cases, waste must be properly stored and labeled. The EPA's *universal waste* list identifies items thrown out in large numbers, including batteries, some lamps, obsolete pesticides, and thermostats. The T/S/D requirements for universal waste are less stringent and do not count against a generator's status.

The most frequent violators of hazardous-waste regulations and laws are the small to midsize generating firms. Companies in this group violate hazardous-waste laws to maintain their profitability by avoiding the cost of legal disposal. However, large companies (or their employees) that have violated state RCRAs or various federal environmental laws include such well-known businesses as Texaco, Ocean Spray Cranberries, Fleischmann's, Ashland Oil, B.F. Goodrich, and Kaiser Steel.

Investigators must be alert to the fact that traditional crimes are also involved in acts that constitute environmental crimes. Examples of these include falsification of records and forgery—typically involving manifests and T/S/D records—and bribery of public officials, such as regulation inspectors and landfill operators, who accept money to certify that the hazardous waste was properly disposed of when it actually ends up being illegally dumped or abandoned.

**Storage of Hazardous Waste under Inadequate Conditions**

Properly identified hazardous waste stored in a deteriorated drum. The federal government and many states have enacted laws to protect against hazardous waste violations that threaten both people and the environment. Treatment, storage, and disposal (T/S/D) violations are committed by companies that fail to follow specific guidlines, including those that identify proper conditions for storage of hazardous materials.

(Courtesy Environmental Protection Agency)

## INVESTIGATIVE METHODS

Patrolling officers should be alert for signs that indicate the possibility or presence of illegal dumping of hazardous waste. Some of these signs are similar to the signs of a mass chemical attack (see Chapter 2), but in illegal-dumping cases the scale is smaller. Among the signs to watch for are:

1. Suspicious discharges into waterways.
2. Discolored and dying vegetation that is unusual for the season.
3. An unusual number of dead animals, fish, and/or birds.
4. Unusual and persistent odors.
5. Odors that are accompanied by uncomfortable sensations (e.g., burning) affecting skin, eyes, and respiratory system.
6. New activity by trucks at closed businesses or abandoned buildings (see photo) or on secondary roads.
7. Tankers visiting waterways in which they might illegal dump their cargoes.

### Aerial Photograph

Aerial photograph of a New Hampshire business that cleaned out used toxic-waste barrels and recycled them, and crushed and disposed of drums that were unsalvageable. In the cleaning process, chemicals were washed into local groundwater and recreational lakes nearby, creating serious pollution problems. This photograph was important in refuting the defendant's claim in a sworn deposition that, as of a certain date, there were only 300 to 400 barrels on site. Analysts counted more than 3,000 barrels.

(Courtesy Environmental Protection Agency)

Officers should approach suspected hazardous-waste spills and toxic-waste sites with the wind at their backs and from the highest ground reasonably available. They should use binoculars to assess the scene in a standoff mode and notify their communications center as quickly as possible.

Leads on illegal hazardous-waste sites may be offered by disgruntled or former employees, occasionally by a current employee (who may have reservations about doing so because of the possibility of losing his/her job should the employer shut down, by home owners in the area of such sites, and by local pilots, boaters and fishers, competitors, building inspectors, and others. As in the case with other types of investigation, the most immediate concerns are determining the reliability and motive of the person bringing the information forward and assessing the public safety and health risks.

Surveillance is an excellent tool for gathering information, as it can establish illegal practices and the persons involved with them. Night photography equipment is essential and thermal imaging and nightscopes are very useful in investigating "midnight dumping." Aerial photographs of known hazardous-waste dumping areas can assist in locating the sites of additional illegal dumps and are useful in determining whether generators and disposal facilities are exceeding their legal or permit capacities (see photo on page 648).

For most environmental crimes, it is necessary to form a team to conduct the investigation. Access to an attorney or inclusion of one on the team is a must because of multiple, complex laws, consent decrees, and regulatory guidance. An attorney can be helpful in drafting or reviewing requests for search warrants, arrest warrants, and other legal documents. The team should also include people whose skills match the needs of the investigation, such as backhoe operators or hydrologists. Because of the dangers associated with hazardous-waste sites, investigators must wear PPE to protect themselves (see photo). Specialized investigators from federal and state agencies are often available to assist with complex investigations. The EPA's National Enforcement Investigations Center (NEIC) has multidisciplinary teams for conducting investigations, has one of the leading forensic environmental chemistry laboratories, and has an extensive library, all of which are available to federal, state, and local agencies.

## Trench Excavation

Excavation of a trench to locate hazardous-waste tanks that were illegally buried. Because of the danger associated with hazardous waste sites, investigators must wear specilized suits to protect themselves at such locations. In some cases it is necessary to use other specialists such as backhoe operators or hydrologists to assist in the investigation at these crime scenes.

(Courtesy Environmental Protection Agency)

## Key Terms

**agrichemical**
**bone rustlers**
**brands**
**freezer crimes**
**hazardous wastes**
**livestock**
**poaching**
**tack**
**T/S/D crimes**

## Review Questions

1. In what ways are the cities and agricultural crime linked?
2. What specialized knowledge is required by the investigator with respect to the theft of agri-chemicals?
3. What generalizations can be made about livestock and tack theft?
4. What are four concerns with respect to conducting stakeouts in rural areas?
5. The legal provisions for transporting cattle vary by state; at a general level what three things must investigators know regarding such matters?
6. What does "M RH R-crop L-split" mean?
7. State and briefly describe different methods of marking livestock for identification.
8. What are the two major categories of poachers, and how do they differ?
9. Identify and briefly discuss different investigative programs or techniques used by wildlife officers.
10. Identify and describe the three major components of the waste cycle.
11. Identify the common provisions of RCRA state laws.
12. Identify and briefly discuss the characteristics of hazardous waste.
13. Explain T/S/D.
14. List five of the seven signs of illegal dumping.

## Internet Activities

1. Check out the Environmental Protection Agency's website at www.epa.gov and find some recent EPA investigations on topics such as waste, pollution, and toxins. Also check out the EPA's National Enforcement Investigations Center at es.epa.gov/oeca/oceft/neic/index.html. What services does the NEIC laboratory perform? What information and resources does the site provide that would be helpful to criminal investigators?
2. What are the most frequent and most serious types of wildlife crimes in your area and/or state? To get started on your answer, check out the websites of your state's department of natural resources, of local, state, and/or national parks, and of local newspapers. If your state has a forensic laboratory that specializes in crimes against wildlife, this agency may also provide additional information.

## Notes

1. For an extension of this and related propositions, see Charles Swanson, "Rural and Agricultural Crime," *Journal of Criminal Justice*, 1981, Vol. 9, No. 1, pp. 19–27.
2. Charles Swanson and Leonard Territo, "Agricultural Crime: Its Extent, Prevention and Control," *FBI Law Enforcement Bulletin*, 1980, Vol. 49, No. 5, p. 10. We originally estimated $3 billion annually. The figure in the text is based on the assumption of an annual 3 percent increase in losses over the past 20 years.
3. San Diego County Farm Bureau, www.sdfarmbureau.org/index.html, Nov. 11, 1998.
4. Ibid.
5. Jerome Weeks, "California Story: Avocado vs. 'Nighttime Pickers'; One Year Theft Losses Amounted to 10 Million Dollars," *St. Louis Post-Dispatch*, Sept. 21, 1997.
6. Ibid.
7. E. N. Smith, "Modern Rustlers Steal Livestock Via the Highway," *Seattle Times*, June 7, 1998.
8. Craig Whitlock, "Police Strive to Lasso Hog Rustlers," *News and Observer* (Raleigh, NC), May 22, 1997.
9. Mike Toner, "Brazen Fossil Hunters Are Cleaning Out U.S. Dinosaur Heritage," *Atlanta Journal Constitution*, Aug. 23, 2001.

10. Mark Arax, "Rural Cops Battle Rising Crime in the Cropland," *Los Angeles Times*, Mar. 2, 1998, p. 1.
11. For example, see *American Horse Shows Assn.* v. *Ward*, New York Supreme Court, 186 Misc. 2d 571, 718 N.Y.S. 2d 593, Dec. 28, 2000.
12. Patricia A. Michaels, "Tree Spiking: Nailing the Trees to Save the Forest," *Environmental Issues*, Aug. 1, 2001, environment.about.com/library/aa080101a.htm.
13. Yvette La Pierre, "Poached Parklands," *American Horticulturist*, October 1994, Vol. 73, No. 10, p. 22. Our discussion of poached parklands is drawn from this source.
14. See Jerry Kammer, "Year in Prison for Cactus Thief," *Arizona Republic*, Oct. 31, 1998, and Frank J. Prial, "Feds Getting Tough on Outlaws Rustling Cactus," *Houston Post*, Mar. 4, 1990.
15. Frank J. Prial, "California Brings Grape-Fraud Suits," *New York Times*, June 28, 1990, p. C1.
16. Brad Knickerbocker, "U.S. Fight against Timber Thieves," *Christian Science Monitor*, Mar. 23, 1998, Internet edition.
17. Kate Thomas, "Illegal Logging Cases Sprout Up over U.S.: Increase in Rustling Due to Rise in Prices," *Journal of Commerce*, Mar. 10, 1997, Internet edition.
18. Arax, "Rural Cops Battle Rising Crime in Cropland," p. 2.
19. Ibid.
20. Jane Chavey, "Public's Help Needed to Fight Christmas Bough Thefts," Washington State Department of Natural Resources, News Release, www.wa.gov/dnr/htdocs/adm/comm/nr00091.htm, Dec. 8, 2000.
21. David Windsor, "Timber Theft: A Solvable Crime," *Indiana Woodland Steward*, Spring 2001, vol. 10, no. 1, pp. 1–3, www.fnr.purdue.edu/inwood/past%20issues/timberth.htm.
22. These points are drawn from Sgt. William Bacon, *Livestock Theft Investigation*, Los Angeles County Sheriff's Department, undated, p. 2, with modifications made by the authors.
23. Ibid., which is the source for the information in this paragraph.
24. Ibid.
25. Some of the information in this paragraph is drawn from ibid., pp. 5–6.
26. Ibid., p. 5.
27. Ibid.
28. E. N. Smith, "Modern Rustlers Steal Livestock via the Highway," *Seattle Times Com*, June 7, 1998, p. 1.
29. Ibid., p. 6, but recomputed in current dollars.
30. Ibid.
31. Ibid., p. 12.
32. Ibid.
33. Alex Kershaw, "Return of the Rustler," *Guardian* (London, England), Sept. 12, 1998.
34. Staff and Wire Reports, "Cattle Rustling Nowadays Uses Pickups, Not Ponies," *Columbus* (Ohio) *Dispatch*, July 14, 1998.
35. Kershaw, "Return of the Rustler."
36. Ibid.
37. Bacon, *Livestock Theft Investigation*, p. 16, from which this paragraph was obtained with restatement.
38. Ibid., p. 24.
39. St. Tammany Bureau, "Saddle Microchips Offered," *Times-Picayune*, Oct. 25, 1997.
40. See *Utah Livestock Brand Book*, Utah Department of Agriculture, 1996.
41. Several of these points were taken from Bacon, *Livestock Theft Investigation*, p. 17.
42. National Fish and Wildlife Service Forensics Laboratory, toltecs.lab.rl.fws.gov/lab/hpstory/cag/feature/9-97/index.html, September 1997.
43. Jeff Bernard, "Beauty Threatens Survival of Many Species," *Los Angeles Times*, Jan. 1, 1995.
44. David Van Biema, "The Killing Fields," *Time*, Aug. 22, 1994, Vol. 144, No. 8, p. 37.
45. "Poachers Enlisted to Save Big Game," *New York Times*, Dec. 26, 1990, p. A28.
46. Telephone interview, Fran Marcoux, Colorado Division of Wildlife, Mar. 3, 1995.
47. Van Biema, "The Killing Fields," p. 37.
48. Constance J. Poten, "A Shameful Harvest," *National Geographic*, September 1991, Vol. 180, No. 3, pp. 110, 131.

# EIGHTEEN

# Arson and Explosives Investigations

*Police use dog to check suspicious vehicle for explosives. Many federal and local law enforcement agencies now use dogs specifically trained to assist in locating illegal explosive materials.* (©Reuters NewMedia Inc./Corbis)

## CHAPTER OUTLINE



## OBJECTIVES

1. Discuss the steps in the preliminary investigation of arson.
2. Be familiar with various types of burn indicators.
3. Describe ignition devices that may be used in arson.
4. Assess several common motivations of arsonists for setting fires.
5. Explain the scientific methods used in arson investigation.
6. List several groups of people whom an arson investigator should interview.
7. List questions that investigators should ask in interviews and interrogations.
8. Explain the two types of explosions.
9. Outline the procedures for handling and investigating bomb threats.

# INTRODUCTION

The crime of arson has increased dramatically in recent years. It is estimated that more than 1,000 lives are lost each year due to arson fires. Another 10,000 injuries are sustained each year as a result of arson fires. Conservative estimates show that approximately $2 billion in property damage is caused each year by arsonists. This $2 billion is the tip of the iceberg when it comes to the total amount of money lost annually as a result of arson. The cost of fire services increases that figure by at least an additional $10 billion. Law enforcement spends additional time and money trying to bring arsonists to trial. The judicial system then must spend its time and many personnel hours on trying the cases. In the event of conviction, the penal system must house and feed the convicted arsonists. Even greater than the costs to government bodies are the costs to the person in the street. Untold thousands of jobs are lost when factories are burned for profit. Thousands of homes are lost each year, forcing home owners and tenants to relocate and, generally, incur higher house and rent payments.[1]

Arson is an inherently difficult crime to detect and prosecute, in part because the motivations for and methods of committing arson vary widely. While some arsonist may be troubled juveniles who start fires with matches or cigarettes, professional arsonists frequently use timing devices and accelerants. Arson investigation also falls between police responsibility and fire department responsibility, an area that is too often not effectively covered. Both the police and the fire services can legitimately claim authority in arson cases, but each also may rationalize that the responsibility belongs to the other. Unfortunately, in most jurisdictions neither is prepared to devote the resources needed to achieve identification, arrest, and conviction rates commensurate with other crimes. Arson investigators need cooperation and better training. Administrative officials need to help, but in order to help they need to give the problem a greater share of their attention. Probably the most urgent step in controlling arson rates is for top fire and police officials and local, state, and national governments to recognize the magnitude of the problem and then provide the necessary resources to combat it.[2]

## PRELIMINARY INVESTIGATION

Arson investigations entail several exceptions to fire service training. For example, the fire service has taught firefighters that fire loss is less and public relations are better if they clean premises of debris, water, and so forth. However, if arson is suspected, firefighters should not disarrange the premises, especially at the point of origin. Moving debris, even window glass, may destroy valuable physical evidence.[3]

In nearly all cases, there is little additional loss if the area encompassing the point of origin is not cleaned out, because this area is usually the most heavily damaged by the fire, with little salvage possible. Often it is necessary during overhauling to move large quantities of acoustical tile, plasterboard, canned goods, cartons, and other items. If this material is beyond salvage, it is natural to throw it into the worst-burned area of the building. But this is probably the area the investigator will want to examine carefully, and such discards will have to be moved again. In the confusion, the fire cause is likely to remain in doubt.

One effective way to determine fire causes is to determine the point of origin. Neighbors', onlookers', or others' ideas about the cause sometimes lead investigators astray. When the exact point of origin is established, the cause usually becomes obvious. For instance, a point of origin in the middle of a bare concrete basement floor probably eliminates defective heating appliances or wiring.

Points of origin sometimes are established by reconstructing furniture and walls, replacing loose boards and doors. Neighbors and occupants can help describe how things were before the fire. The direction of heat flow then can be followed by checks for deepest charring, indications of highest temperature, and duration of heat. Temperatures are indicated by the condition of metal, glass, wood, plastics, and other materials. Because heat rises, a general rule is to look for the lowest point of deep char as the point of origin. This rule, however, has many exceptions.

After the area of origin has been established, the investigator should check for the level of origin by examining the bottoms of shelves, ledges, moldings, and furniture and all sides of the legs, arms, and framework of reconstructed furniture. The investigator also should clean the floor carefully at the point of origin, examining and moving all objects to one side. After this is done, the floor or rugs should be swept as clean as possible for examination of burn patterns.

The floor and lower areas of the room produce the most clues to the cause of the fire, because they are the living area. Most equipment and contents are near floor level, actions of occupants are conducted near floor level, and most materials drop there during a fire.

## WHERE AND HOW DID THE FIRE START?

Once the fire is out, the primary task is to begin examining what is left of the building for physical evidence that may indicate how the fire began (see photo on page 655).

The point of origin can be a clue to possible arson. For example, if two or more distinct points of origin are found, two or more separate fires probably were deliberately set. Also, if the fires started in the middle of a large room or in a closet, then the index of suspicion should go up sharply.[4]

## TWO FACTORS NEEDED TO CAUSE FIRE

During the investigation, it should be borne in mind that a fire always has two causes: a source of heat and material ignited.

In checking for the fire cause at the point of origin, it is usually an advantage to use the **layer-checking technique.** Before any material is moved or shoveled out, the investigator should make notes and carefully examine the strata while working through to the floor. These layers often contain wood ash, plaster, melted aluminum, window glass, charred drapery fabric, and charred newspapers. They may give a picture of the sequence of burning. If, for example, charred newspapers were found beneath charred drapery fabric, this could indicate a set fire, particularly if papers would not usually be in the area or if they were of different types of dates. Aluminum and similar alloys melt fairly early in a fire (at about 1,150°F), often splash or run over other material near floor level, solidify, and protect the material from further

### Arson Investigators at Work

A team of arson investigators searching the scene of a suspected arson. Arson investigators have received numerous hours of specialized training in order to effectively conduct this type of investigation. In searching a scene of a suspected arson, investigators must be careful not to destroy potential evidence while sifting through soot and debris.

(Courtesy Thomas Evans, Pinellas County, Florida, Sheriff's Office)

damage. Draperies and heavy curtains may burn free and drop on flammable liquid, preventing it from being completely consumed, especially if the liquid is heavy or less volatile.[5]

## ACCIDENTAL FIRES

Once the point of origin has been discovered, the next step is to determine how the fire started. Even though arson may be suspected, the investigator must first investigate and rule out all possible accidental or natural causes. Many courts have held that this elimination of accidental causes is a firm basis for an arson charge. Also, if the investigator is put on the witness stand, it is likely that a question will be raised about the possibility of accidental causes. A failure to eliminate accidental causes could substantially weaken the prosecution's case.

Some of the more common accidental or natural causes of fire fall into the following categories:

- *The electric system:* Fuses in which pennies have been inserted; broken or rotted insulation; overloaded circuits; defective switches; and improperly installed wiring.
- *Electrical appliances and equipment:* Defective electrical units with short circuits; overheated irons; and light bulbs covered by paper shades.
- *Gas:* Leaks in gas pipes; defective stoves and heating units.
- *Heating units:* Overheated stoves or steam pipes; clothing being dried too close to fireplaces or open flames; faulty chimneys; explosions from kerosene stoves; and overturned space heaters.
- *Sunlight:* The concentration of sun rays on bubbles in glasses, windowpanes, or convex shaving mirrors placed near combustible materials such as paper or rags.
- *Matches:* Children playing with matches, especially in enclosed areas such as closets or utility rooms.
- *Smoking:* The careless disposal of cigars, cigarettes, pipe ashes, and other lighted devices into trash cans in the home; individuals who fall asleep while smoking in bed or in a chair.

Indications of cigarettes in furniture or mattresses are heavy charring of the unit and the floor; a char pattern on furniture frames, heaviest on the inside; heavy staining and blackening of mirrors and window glass in the area, indicating a long, slow fire; a burning time of from 1½ to 3 or 4 hours; collapsing of part or all of the core springs. Lying flat on a padded surface, cigarettes usually char a small hole and burn out. If the cigarette is partially covered at the sides or bottom, a fire usually results in an hour or so. Cigarettes ignite foam rubber padding to about the same degree as other padding. With foam rubber padding, fire occurs a little faster because smoldering rubber reaches an ignition temperature faster and burns with greater intensity.[6]

## SPONTANEOUS HEATING AND IGNITION

There are a few fundamental causes of spontaneous heating, but the conditions under which these factors may operate are numerous. Nearly all organic materials and many metals are subject to oxidation, fermentation, or both and, therefore, have some potential for spontaneous heating.

**Spontaneous heating** is produced in three major ways: chemical action, fermentation, and oxidation (the most common way). For example, chemical-action heating occurs when unslaked lime and water or sodium and water are combined. Fermentation heating is caused by bacterial action. Here, moisture is a prime factor. The most dangerous materials are those subject to combinations, such as fermentation and oxidation with drying. Fresh sawdust over 10 feet deep is subject to fermentation heating but rarely reaches ignition temperature. In oxidation heating, rapid oxidation must take place in the presence of a good insulating factor and an oxygen supply. Oxidation takes place in oils containing carbon, hydrogen, and oxygen. This combination is mostly found in vegetable and fish oils and, to some extent, in animal oils.

The susceptibility to spontaneous heating is usually determined by drying time. Unadulterated hydrocarbons, such as mineral and petroleum oils, are not considered subject to spontaneous ignition.

**Spontaneous ignition** is rare in residences and small businesses. It is considerably accelerated by external heat such as sunshine, steampipes, hot air ducts, or friction from wind or vibration. Spontaneous ignition is rather mysterious because of many unknowns. Therefore, it is often used as a catch-all explanation.

The usual time required to produce spontaneous ignition by oxidation or fermentation runs from several hours to several days or months. This form of ignition is characterized by internal charring of a mass of combustibles, and some of the remains of this material usually are found at the point of origin (if the firefighters have been careful and especially if fog was used), because it normally takes a considerable mass—several inches of fairly dense material—to create the factors necessary for spontaneous heating. Sometimes when material of the appropriate type is suspected and found to be deeply charred all the way through, investigators must satisfy themselves that external heat was not responsible. When not heated internally, sacks of meals, flour, and the like usually survive fire with only an inch or two of charring on the exposed surface.

Dust and polishing mops have often been accused of causing spontaneous ignition and probably have in some rare cases. Most fires originating near a mop in a closet or on a back porch are caused by a child playing with matches.[7] It is debatable whether the average mop would have enough bulk to provide the necessary insulation to raise the temperature to the ignition point, although with favorable conditions—such as a large mop, saturated with fast-drying oils, pressed in a corner with other brooms, and receiving outside heat from a steampipe or the sun's rays through a window—ignition could occur. During the several hours required for the material to ignite, it gives off very acrid odors. Linseed and similar oils are especially odorous. People in the area during that time usually would be aware of these odors.

## BURN INDICATORS

**Burn indicators** are the effects of heat or partial burning that indicate a fire's rate of development, points of origin, temperature, duration, and time of occurrence, and the presence of flammable liquids. Interpretation of burn indicators is a principal means for determining the causes of fires, especially arson. Some of the burn indicators used are the following:[8]

### Alligatoring

**Alligatoring** is the checking of charred wood, which gives the wood the appearance of alligator skin. Large, rolling blisters indicate rapid, intense heat; small, flat alligatoring indicates low heat. (See photo below.)

### Depth of Char

Analysis of the depth of char is most reliable for evaluating fire spread, rather than for establishing specific burn times or intensity of heat from adjacent burning materials. By measuring the relative depth and extent of charring, the investigator may be able to determine which portions of a material or construction were exposed the longest to a heat source. The relative depth of char from point to point is the key to appropriate use of **charring**—locating the places where the damage was most severe due to exposure, ventilation, or fuel placement. The investigator may then deduce the direction of fire spread, with decreasing char depths being farther away from the heat source. (See Figure 18–1.)

**Alligatoring**
Note the checked pattern on the burnt wood. Investigators carefully examine burned wood in order to determine the heat intensity of the fire. Large, rolling blisters indicate rapid, intense heat, whereas flat alligatoring indicates low-intensity heat.
(Courtesy Ron French, Ecorse, Michigan, Fire Department)

Depth of char is often used to estimate the duration of a fire. The rate of charring of wood varies widely depending on such variables as:

- Rate and duration of heating.
- Ventilation effects.
- Surface area-to-mass ratio.
- Direction, orientation, and size of wood grain.
- Species of wood (pine, oak, fir, etc.).
- Moisture content.
- Nature of surface coating.[9]

## Breaking of glass

If a pane of glass is mounted in a frame that protects the edges of the glass from the radiated heat of fire, a temperature difference occurs between the unprotected portion of the glass and the protected edge. Researchers estimate that a temperature difference of about 158° F (70°C) between the center of the pane of glass and the protected edge can cause cracks that start at the edge of the glass. The cracks appear as smooth, undulating lines that can spread and join together. Depending on the degree of cracking, the glass may or may not collapse from its frame. If a pane of glass has no edge protection from the radiated heat or fire, the glass breaks at a higher temperature difference. Research findings suggest that fewer cracks are formed and the pane is more likely to stay whole.

Glass that has received an impact will have a characteristic "cobweb" pattern: numerous cracks in straight lines. The glass may have been broken before, after, or during the fire.

If flame suddenly contacts one side of a glass pane while the unexposed side is relatively cool, a stress can develop between the two faces and the glass can fracture between the faces. Crazing is a term used in the fire investigation community to describe a complicated pattern of short cracks in glass. These cracks may be straight or crescent-shaped and may or may not extend through the thickness of the glass. Crazing has been theorized as resulting from the very rapid heating of one side of the glass while the other side remains cool. While this theory has not yet been confirmed, research has established that crazing can be created by the rapid cooling of glass brought on by the application of water spray in a hot environment. Occasionally with small-size panes, differential expansion between the exposed and unexposed faces may result in the pane's popping out of its frame.[10]

**Figure 18-1** Line of Demarcation in a Wood Section

(**Source:** Factory Mutual Engineering Corporation, Norwood, Massachusetts. Reprinted with permission.)

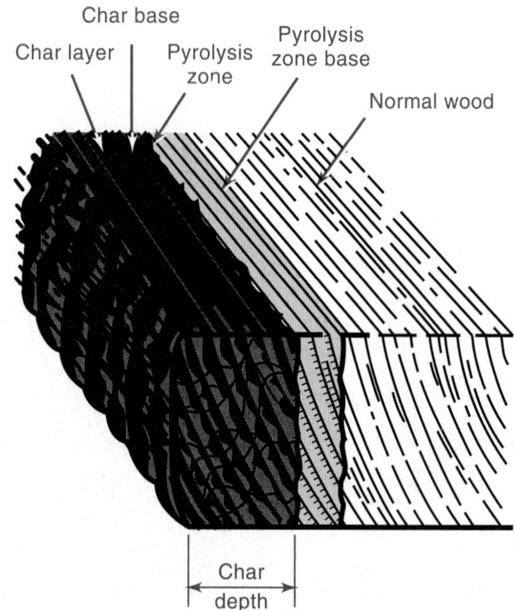


## Collapsed Furniture Springs

The collapse of furniture springs may provide the investigator with various clues concerning the direction, duration, or intensity of the fire. However, the collapse of the springs cannot be used to indicate exposure to a specific type of heat source or ignition, such as smoldering ignition or the presence of an ignitable liquid. The results of laboratory testing indicate that the annealed springs, and the associated loss of tension (tensile strength), are a function of the application of heat. The tests revealed that short-term heating at high temperatures and long-term heating at moderate temperatures over 750° F (400°C) can result in the loss of tensile strength and in the collapse of the springs. The tests also revealed that the presence of a load or weight on the springs while they are being heated increases the loss of tension.

By analyzing furniture springs, the investigator can compare the differences between the springs and other areas of the mattress, cushion, frame, and so forth. Comparative analysis of the springs can assist the investigator in developing hypotheses concerning the relative exposure of various items or areas to a particular heat source. For example, if the springs at one end of a cushion or mattress have lost their tension and those at the other end have not, then hypotheses may be developed. The hypotheses should take into consideration other circumstances, effects (such as ventilation), and evidence at the scene concerning duration or intensity of the fire, area of origin, direction of heat travel, and relative proximity of the heat. Areas characterized by the loss of tensile strength may indicate greater relative exposure to heat than do areas without the loss of strength.

Other circumstances and effects that may be considered are the loss of mass and material; the depth of char in a wood frame; and color changes, possibly indicating intensity, in metal frames. Comparative analysis should also include consideration of the covering material of the springs. The absence of material may indicate a portion closer to the source of heat, while the presence of material may indicate an area more remote from the heat source. The investigator should also consider the condition of the springs before the fire.[11]

## Spalling

**Spalling** is the breakdown in the surface tensile strength of concrete, masonry, or brick that occurs when exposure to high temperatures and rates of heating produces mechanical forces within the material. These forces are believed to result from one or more of the following:

- Moisture present in uncured or "green" concrete.
- Differential expansion between reinforcing rods or steel mesh and the surrounding concrete.
- Differential expansion between the concrete mix and the aggregate. (This is most common with silicon aggregates.)
- Differential expansion between the fine-grained surface or finished layers and the coarser-grained interior layers.
- Differential expansion between the fire-exposed surface and the interior of the slab.

Spalling of concrete or masonry surfaces may be caused by heat, freezing chemicals, or abrasion. It may be induced more readily in poorly formulated or finished surfaces. Spalling is characterized by distinct lines of striation and the loss of surface material, resulting in cracking, breaking, and chipping or in the formation of craters on the surface. Spalled areas may appear lighter in color that adjacent areas. This lightening can be caused by the exposure of clean subsurface material. Also, adjacent areas may tend to be sooted.

Spalling of concrete, masonry, brick, or painted surfaces such as plaster has often been linked to unusually high temperatures caused by burning accelerants (see photo below).

While spalling can result from high rates of heat release or a rapid change in temperature, an accelerant need not be involved. The primary mechanism of spalling is the expansion or contraction of the

### Spalling on Painted Plaster Surface

Arson investigators carefully examine their crime scenes to determine every fire's cause. They are aware that the spalling of painted plaster surfaces pictured here is often related to unusually high temperatures caused by burning accelerants.

(Courtesy NFPA International)

**Pulled Light Bulb**

As the side of the bulb facing the heat's source is heated and softens, the internal gases expand and bubble out. This "pulled" portion of the bulb will be in the direction of the heat's source.

surface while the rest of the mass expands or contracts at a different rate. Another factor in the spalling of concrete is the loading and stress in the material at the time of the fire. Since high-stress or high-load areas may not be related to the fire, spalling of concrete on the underside of ceilings or beams may not be directly over the origin of the fire.[12]

## Distorted Light Bulbs

Incandescent light bulbs can sometimes show the direction of heat impingement. As the side of the bulb facing the source of heat is heated and softens, the gases inside a bulb greater than 25 watts can begin to expand and bubble out of the softened glass. This has traditionally been called a "pulled" light bulb, although the action is really a response to internal pressure rather than pulling. The bulge, or pulled portion of the bulb, will be in the direction of the heat source.[13]

## Temperature Determination

If the investigator knows the approximate melting temperature of a material, an estimate can be made of the temperature to which the melted material was subjected. This knowledge may be of help in evaluating the intensity and duration of the heating, the extent of heat movement, or the relative rates of heat release from fuels.

When using such generic materials as glass, plastics, and white pot metals for making temperature determinations, the investigator must be aware of the wide variety of melting temperatures for these materials (see Table 18–1).

The best approach is to take a sample of the material and have its melting temperature ascertained by a competent laboratory, materials scientists, or metallurgist. Wood and gasoline burn at essentially the same flame temperature. The turbulent diffusion flame temperatures of all hydrocarbon fuels (plastics and ignitable liquids) and cellulosic fuels are approximately the same, although the fuels release heat at different rates.

The temperature achieved by an item at a given location within a structure or fire area depends on how much the item is heated. The amount of heating depends on the temperature and velocity of the airflow, the geometry and physical properties of the heated item, its proximity to the source of heat, and the amount of heat energy present. Burning metals and highly exothermic chemical reactions can produce temperatures significantly higher than those created by hydrocarbon- or cellulosic-fueled fires.

Identifiable temperatures achieved in structural fires rarely remain above 1,900°F (1,040°C) for long periods of time. These temperatures are sometimes called **effective fire temperatures,** for they reflect physical effects that can be defined by specific temperature ranges. The investigator can use the analysis of the melting and fusion of materials to assist in establishing whether higher-than-expected heat energy was present.[14]

**Table 18-1** Approximate Melting Temperatures of Common Materials

| Material | °F | °C |
|---|---|---|
| Aluminum (alloys) | 1,050–1,200 | 566–650 |
| Aluminum | 1,220 | 660 |
| Brass (yellow) | 1,710 | 932 |
| Brass (red) | 1,825 | 996 |
| Bronze (aluminum) | 1,800 | 982 |
| Cast iron (gray) | 2,460–2,550 | 1,350–1,400 |
| Cast iron (white) | 1,920–2,010 | 1,050–1,100 |
| Chromium | 3,350 | 1,845 |
| Copper | 1,981 | 1,082 |
| Fire brick (insulating) | 2,980–3,000 | 1,638–1,650 |
| Glass | 1,100–2,600 | 593–1,427 |
| Gold | 1,945 | 1,063 |
| Iron | 2,802 | 1,540 |
| Lead | 621 | 327 |
| Magnesium (AZ31B alloy) | 1,160 | 627 |
| Nickel | 2,651 | 1,455 |
| Paraffin | 129 | 54 |
| Plastics (thermo): | | |
| ABS | 190–257 | 88–125 |
| Acrylic | 194–221 | 90–105 |
| Nylon | 349–509 | 176–265 |
| Polyethylene | 251–275 | 122–135 |
| Polystyrene | 248–320 | 120–160 |
| Polyvinylchloride | 167–221 | 75–105 |
| Platinum | 3,224 | 1,773 |
| Porcelain | 2,820 | 1,550 |
| Pot metal | 562–752 | 300–400 |
| Quartz ($SiO_2$) | 3,060–3,090 | 1,682–1,700 |
| Silver | 1,760 | 960 |
| Solder (tin) | 275–350 | 135–177 |
| Steel (stainless) | 2,600 | 1427 |
| Steel (carbon) | 2,760 | 1,516 |
| Tin | 449 | 232 |
| Wax (paraffin) | 120–167 | 49–75 |
| White pot metal | 562–752 | 300–400 |
| Zinc | 707 | 375 |

**Source**: National Fire Protection Association, NFPA 921 Guide for Fire and Explosion Investigations (Quincy, MA: NFPA, 2001), pp. 921-30.

# FIRE SETTING AND RELATED MECHANISMS

It is the duty of an arson investigator to search the debris of a suspicious fire, particularly around the point of origin, to gather evidence pointing to the mechanism used by the fire setter in the arson effort.[15]

An arsonist may use the simplest of methods, a match and some paper, or elaborate mechanical or chemical methods. An **incendiary mechanism** may be mechanical or chemical. It consists of an ignition device, possibly a timing device, one or more "plants" to feed or accelerate the initial flame, and, frequently, "trailers" to spread the fire about the building or from plant to plant.

**Pipe Bomb and Gasoline**
A pipe bomb intended to be used in conjunction with a can of gasoline. A hole was cut out of the top of the gasoline can between the handle and the lid to allow the bomb to be inserted into the can. The pipe bomb was immersed into the can. It was at this point that the gasoline saturated the inner workings and got the gunpowder wet, therefore making it impossible to ignite.
(Courtesy Michael M. Gonzalez, Chief of Fire Investigations, Tampa Fire Department, Florida)

## IGNITION DEVICES

### Matches

Only juvenile arsonists and pyromaniacs seem to favor striking matches. Other fire setters want some delay, so they adapt the ordinary match to some timing mechanism.

Several matches may be affixed to a lighted cigarette with a rubber band or tape, the heads of the matches set about halfway down the cigarette from its glowing end. In some cases, matches are laid alongside a cigarette. Books of paper matches are also popular. Because cigarettes will continue to burn when laid on their sides, they are effective ignition devices; the slow-burning cigarette allows the fire setter a few minutes to get away from the scene before the fire makes any headway.

### Gasoline

Gasoline and other accelerants are very popular with many different types of arsonists. The investigator should remember that gasoline and many types of liquid accelerants burn at about 3,000°F as opposed to ordinary combustibles, which burn at 1,600°F. If, for example, the investigator observes a metal door melted in a pile, gasoline was probably used as an accelerant because steel generally reaches its melting at 3,000°F.

### Chemicals

Various chemical combustions have been used to set fires. Saboteurs have used such means for years. Units that provide for an acid to be released on some combination of chemicals are favorite devices, with the acid releasing itself by eating its way through the cork or even the metal of its container. The time lag from setting to ignition can be estimated with some certainty by an arsonist with a little knowledge of chemistry.

Various rubber receptacles, such as hot water and ice bags or contraceptives, have been used for a phosphorus and water ignition device. A pinhole is made in the rubber container, allowing the water to seep out. Once it drains below the level of the phosphorus, ignition takes place. As this chemical ignites upon contact with air, a time lag is secured by controlling the amount of water and the size of the hole in the container.

Even the ordinary fire setter sometimes uses a chemical that ignites upon contact with water. The device is activated by rain. Holes in a roof or a connection to the building's gutter system have been used to trigger such devices. Another device is used to divert the sewage line in a building. It is set up at night to trigger the next morning when the toilet is flushed for the first time.

Most chemical ignition units leave some residue, have a distinctive odor, or both. Debris must be analyzed at a laboratory if it is suspected that chemicals have been used as ignition devices. Fortunately, most arsonists do not know enough to use chemical ignition or timing devices, and the machinery and tools necessary for the construction of some of these devices are not always readily available. The devices usually are fairly simple. Most complex devices are used only in time of war by enemy agents.

## Gas

Although not commonly encountered, the combination of gas and the pilot light on the kitchen stoves of many residences is always a possibility. Illuminating gas rises to the ceiling, being lighter than air, and then slowly moves to floor level as it continues to escape. When it reaches a combustion buildup, it is close to the pilot-light level. An explosion, usually followed by fire, takes place. A candle placed in a room adjoining the kitchen has also been used as a means of ignition. Therefore, arson investigators must remember that although such explosions usually follow suicide attempts or accidents, arsonists may use an ordinary gas range as a tool.

In such cases, investigators should get help from an engineer at the local public utility. The time lag between the initial release of the gas and the explosion can be estimated from the size of the room involved, the number of openings, the type of gas, and related data. For example, a kitchen 10 by 15 feet with a ceiling 9 feet high equals a total volume of 1,350 cubic feet. When 71 cubic feet of gas are introduced into the room, the lowest limit of explosive range will have been reached. In a well-ventilated room, it is almost impossible to build up to this limit, but an arsonist seals off the room so that the gas builds up. In a fairly well sealed room, a single burner left open on a kitchen gas stove will deliver enough gas to explode in about 5 hours. The oven jets will build up the same volume in 2 hours; an oven plus four burners, 30 minutes to 1 hour.

The widespread use of gas as an arson tool has been thwarted because of its smell. Neighbors usually detect the smell, call the police or the fire department, or break in themselves, ruining a carefully planned arson attempt.

## Electrical Systems

Any wiring system, including doorbell and telephone circuits, can be used as a fire-setting tool. Ignition devices hooked to the wiring systems of buildings have been used throughout the country by arsonists. The time can be established by a study of the habits of those using the premises. Possibly a security guard switches on the light every hour while inspecting the various portions of the building, or employees turn on the lights at opening time, and so on.

Although a doorbell system can be used to trigger an ignition device, the bell may be rung by some chance visitor and the plans of the fire setter thwarted. Telephone timing devices have the same fault. A wrong number or an unexpected call can start the fire, possibly days ahead of schedule.

The photo below depicts an electrical timer, appliance cord, matches, and shredded paper used as an ignition device. Once the paper catches on fire, it would ignite the clothing in the closet.

**Arson Device**

An electrical timer used in conjunction with an appliance cord, matches, and shredded paper. Some arsonists have attached matches to the hammer of the clock, where they were pressed against an abrasive surface to ignite flammable material. In many cases, the mechanical devices such as the timer in this photo do not burn and can eventually be used as evidence in the prosecution of suspects.

(Courtesy Property Claim Services, American Insurance Association)

Electrical appliances have also been used to set off fires. An open heater is placed close to a flimsy set of curtains, and an apparently accidental fire results. An electrical circuit is deliberately overloaded with several appliances until it heats up. Sometimes an accelerant such as kerosene is dropped into a switch box. In a few cases, a length of normal wiring is removed and lighter wire substituted so that it will overheat and, without blowing the fuses, serve as an ignition device.

Investigators generally discover physical traces of electrical ignition devices after a fire.

### Mechanical Devices

Alarm clocks were once a favored weapon of arsonists. With a simple alarm clock, some wire, and a small battery, a fire setter was "in business." But a search of the fire debris usually sent the arsonist to prison. Some arsonists used the lead hammer in the clock to break a glass tube that fed flammable matter to a fixed flame. This action pushed one container of chemicals into another, closing an electrical circuit. Some arsonists attached matches to the hammer, where they were pressed against an abrasive surface to ignite flammable material. The clock was activated by setting the alarm for a certain time. The weights in a grandfather's clock have been used in a similar manner.

Some mechanical devices are childish, some are worthy of master craftsperson, and others are truly fiendish. Unfortunately for many of these ingenious incendiaries, their machines do not burn and can later be used in their prosecution.

## PLANTS

A **plant** is the material placed around the ignition device to feed the flame. Newspapers, wood shavings, rags, clothing, curtains, blankets, and cotton waste are some plants. Newspapers are the most frequently used; cotton waste is used extensively in factory or industrial fires.

**Accelerants,** or "boosters," to speed the progress of the fire are also part of the plant. Kerosene and gasoline are favored boosters; alcohol, lighter fluid, paint thinners, and other solvents are also popular. However, any flammable fluid or compound may be used to accelerate the blaze.

## TRAILERS

**Trailers** are used to spread the fire. A trailer is ignited by the blaze from the plant. It carries the fire to other parts of a room or building. Usually a trailer ends in a second plant, another pile of papers, or excelsior sprinkled with gasoline, kerosene, or some other booster. From the primary plant, the fire setter may lay four trailers to four secondary plants. Four separate fires thus result from one ignition device.

Rope or toilet paper soaked in alcohol or similar fluid, motion picture film, dynamite fuses, gunpowder, and other such substances have been used as trailers. Sometimes rags or newspapers are soaked in a fire accelerant and twisted into rope. Some arsonists use a fluid fire accelerant such as kerosene as a trailer by pouring a liberal quantity on the floor in a desired path.

## MISSING ITEMS

Sometimes items that are missing from the fire scene can prove valuable. For example, does it appear that many of the building's contents, especially furniture, clothing, or valuable items, were removed prior to the fire? Were house pets removed? Moving a pet to a kennel or the home of friends just before a fire should raise the suspicions of the investigator.

# ARSON FOR PROFIT

Understanding the motive of the arsonist is extremely important if the investigation is to be successful. There are several common motivations among arsonists for setting fires.

The motive behind committing arson for profit is economic gain, whether it be the enormous gain derived from inflating insurance coverage beyond the building's value or the limited economic gain derived from cutting one's losses before oncoming financial disaster.[16]

To decide where and how to begin the investigation, the investigator needs to determine whether the arson in question was due primarily to financial stress, to a fraud scheme (without much stress), or to a combination of some stress and the profitability of fraud.

## FINANCIAL STRESS AS THE PRIMARY CAUSE

The home owner or business owner who decides to arrange an arson fraud may do so out of submission

**Internal View of Pipe Bomb**
A pipe bomb with the cap removed. Pipe bombs have been a favorite device of arsonists for years, due to the inexpensive costs of the materials used to construct them. International and domestic terrorists have also used pipe bombs in their efforts to inflict pain and cause panic.

(Courtesy Michael M. Gonzalez, Chief of Fire Investigations, Tampa Fire Department, Florida)

to financial stress. In general, two primary factors influence the insured person's decision to commit arson fraud: (1) the desire for financial relief, and (2) greed—the desire for easily obtained financial assistance. One way to conceive of an arson-fraud scheme is to view it as the result of the interplay between these two factors. Experience in cases where owners have been caught in arson-fraud schemes indicates that the more extreme and immediately pressing the financial stress, the more desperate the insured becomes. Certainly, the number of insureds who are not persuaded to commit arson—no matter how severe their financial stress—is great, and the swelling bankruptcy court dockets reflect the prevailing honesty of most citizens. However, a rapidly developing situation of financial stress can place the insured in a position where he or she desperately examines all kinds of options both legal and illegal.

Perhaps we can understand the arson-fraud motive of a home owner who has just been fired or who faces mortgage foreclosure and burns a home or business. It is important to conduct a search for evidence for those forms of stress. The investigator is likely to find a great deal about such matters in court papers associated with divorces, foreclosures, bankruptcies, and liens. Although it is not fully accepted as a rule of thumb, the more severe the financial stress of an insured, the more likely the person is to either personally set the fire or involve a minimum number of people—usually a professional arsonist—in the crime.

Investigators often view real estate arson schemes as purely the result of the fraudulent motives of the owners. Actually, the motives for committing real estate arson split between those that are pure scams (discussed later) and those that result from the owner's or landlord's deteriorating financial position. Financial stress in the latter instance can result from any number of factors: strong net migration out of the neighborhood, a long and expensive backlog of code violation citations and fines, or steady deterioration in the quality of the housing—sometimes by design of the landlords. Whatever the specific reasons, housing that no longer produces net income for the owner or landlord can help place the person (and perhaps the coinvestors) in a financially precarious position. The clues to determining whether the financial condition of a building or real estate corporation would make arson-fraud attractive lie in the financial records of investment, income, and tax depreciation.

## Short-Term Business Problem

The businessperson on the brink of insolvency faces financial stress that is more severe than the one who faces a short-term problem, such as a slack period in a seasonal business or an unforeseen problem of cash flow. Because of the regularity with which insurance settlements occur (when claims are not denied), the businessperson who selects arson can be fairly sure of having much of the money or all of it in hand within a short period of time. One reason to suspect that a short-term business problem, rather than a more serious one, led to the arson is the absence of creditors threatening to force the owner into bankruptcy, and thus the absence of a bankruptcy filing. An examination of the business's books will enable the investigator (or accountant) to infer better whether the cash-flow problem was the likely motive for arson.

***Desire to Relocate or Remodel*** Arsons do occur in businesses that are subject to quickly shifting consumer tastes, and this type of arson-fraud scheme may be motivated by the desire of the owner to secure enough money to remodel or move. In this way, the insured feels able to keep up with changing tastes or to move to a more fashionable location with better market potential. Examples of businesses vulnerable to these trends are beauty salons, "theme" restaurants, and furniture stores. Frequently, such owners arrange for the arson because they realize that shifting tastes have caught them unprepared. However, an owner may also sense the onset of a new trend in its early stages and try to avoid financial distress and arrange for the arson to occur early enough to remodel or move by using the insurance proceeds. In cases where an inventory no longer sells because of shifting tastes, a variety of internal business and supplier records can help establish whether this was the motive. In this type of arson for profit, as in many other types, the actual discomfort of financial distress may not be the motive as much as the perception that the insured will soon be in such distress—unless he or she acts immediately.

***Buildup of Slow-Moving Inventory*** A short-term cash-flow problem can be caused by an unusually large buildup of slow-moving inventory. While the inventory problem may not appear to the investigator to be a logical motive for the arson, this issue may be easier to understand if the investigator becomes familiar with what are normal or abnormal levels of inventory for a particular type of business, for certain periods of the year. If an inventory problem led to the arson, it is likely that the insured has filed a full and possibly even inflated claim to recoup the value of the allegedly destroyed inventory. For this reason, such documentation may point toward the motive but in itself be insufficient to establish the motive. The investigator should look also for multiple points of fire origin and the attempt to destroy all inventory.

***Outmoded Technology*** Several years ago, two of the largest arson-for-profit cases prosecuted in this country involved companies that failed to keep pace with the technological progress of their competitors. The arson frauds involving the Sponge Rubber Products Company and the Artistic Wire Products Company originated partly because the technologies for making the respective products had changed to more efficient, profitable forms. For whatever reasons, the owners had not kept pace. Where an industrial concern may be destroyed because of these technological problems, telltale signs of arson for profit are usually present. First, professional arsonists, even good ones, can rarely destroy a large industrial facility simply by burning it. Incendiary devices, sometimes involving explosives, may be required. Remnants and residues of these can often point to a "professional" arson job. Second, books and business records of the companies will often reveal financial stress in ways such as corporate debt reorganizations as well as documented searches for new capital or drastic changes in marketing strategies prior to the arson. Third, since an owner involved in an industrial arson may claim that a labor-management grievance led to it, investigators should search for documentation on formally filed labor grievances, both with the local union and with state and federal regulatory bodies, in order to confirm or deny the validity of such a claim.

## Satisfaction of a Legal or Illegal Debt

The businessperson or home owner whose property is destroyed by fire does not always broadcast clear signals of financial stress. One reason for this is that the source of the stress may not be apparent. It may not show up in the books of a business or in other indicators such as divorce or bankruptcy records. For example, if the owner incurred an illegal loan-sharking debt that the lender has called in, the tremendous pressure and threats of violence can make an incendiary fire an acceptable risk to the business owner. On many occasions, the owner either sets the fire or arranges for it to be set. In others, however, the loan shark sets it or has it set, knowing that the businessperson has fire and perhaps other (e.g., business interruption) insurance in force.

Evidence of an illegal debt will be difficult to locate if the investigator follows only the "paper trail" from the insured to his or her business and personal records of transactions. If arson to satisfy an illegal debt is suspected, it is important for the investigator to seek out information on the owner's actions that led to the indebtedness, for example, a recent gambling junket, heavy betting during the sports season, or borrowing from a loan shark for a highly speculative venture that initially appeared to have enormous profit potential but later went sour. When the trail leads to an illegal debt involving the insured but his or her denial of any involvement is convincing, the investigator should examine the possibility that the loan shark arranged the fire without the insured's knowledge or consent.

## PURELY FRAUD SCHEMES AS THE PRIMARY MOTIVE

Many types of arson occur because of the actual or anticipated problem of financial stress; others result from schemes where there was not and probably would not be any financial problem. These types of arson-fraud schemes result from the planning and plotting of professional fraud schemers and their associates. Their objective is to defraud insurance companies, as well as banks and even creditors, of as much money as possible. Some of the common types of frauds encountered by investigators follow.

### Redevelopment

In cases where a defined tract has been designated for receipt of federal redevelopment funds, owners and investors may stand to make more money if existing buildings on the tract are razed at no cost to themselves. Arson is a convenient vehicle, for although it may not destroy the building, the city or redevelopment authority will usually raze the remains at no cost to the owner, especially if the building is a safety hazard. Investigators who study tracts designated for redevelopment can often plot which blocks and even which buildings may burn as a result of redevelopment fraud schemes. Owners who decide to arrange this type of arson realize that if the building is only partly damaged, the adjusted insurance settlement may pay for repairs (which they do not want) but not for rebuilding. Therefore, in the interest of ensuring maximum destruction, professional arsonists are likely to be called on for their expertise.

### Building Rehabilitation

In order to improve the condition of old or rundown dwellings, a variety of federal and state loan and loan insurance programs are available for housing rehabilitation. Certain unscrupulous owners, contractors, and others who know the "rehab" business realize that they stand to reap huge profits by obtaining funds to make repairs and then claiming that fire destroyed the rehabilitated unit. In most cases, the claimed repairs were not made, or they were only partially completed, or they were done with inferior (cheaper) materials. Therefore, in addition to reaping a profit from that portion of the loan that was not used to buy materials and pay laborers, this type of arsonist often files insurance claims for the full amount of the allegedly completed work. In addition to arson and insurance fraud, such persons commit a variety of frauds against the federal or state government that provides the rehabilitation program assistance. Financial records should indicate the cost of the work actually done.

### Real Estate Schemes

In many core urban areas, the most common form of arson for profit involves the destruction of dilapidated multifamily housing. While such housing is usually in an advanced state of disrepair, there may be little if any financial stress facing the owners. This is so because either the owner recouped the investment through depreciation of the building and through rent gouging or the owner recently purchased the building for a small fraction of the amount for which it was insured. The typical MO involves an owner purchasing the housing for a small cash down payment, often accompanied by a large, unconventional mortgage. The owner then sells the building to another speculator (usually an associate) for an inflated amount, again with little money down and a large mortgage. Often the building is insured not only for the inflated, artificial value of the second sale but for the replacement value of the building, which is even greater. Then the building burns, the policyholder is almost routinely paid, and the speculating schemers split the proceeds according to a preset formula.

To reap the maximum profit from this type of scheme, the speculators often involve one or more kinds of specialists:

- Several arsonists, so that one arsonist will not know all the plans or be easily recognized because of repeated trips to the neighborhood.
- A public insurance adjuster to help inflate the claim on the building.
- A realtor who scouts around for "bargain" properties to buy.
- An insurance agent who may be corrupted and who is helpful in insuring buildings far beyond what normal, reasonable underwriting standards would permit.

This type of real estate–arson scheme is very lucrative, and its perpetrators realize that the greater the number of buildings burned, the greater the profits. Soon another speculator, perhaps in league with a contractor or realtor, sees how "well" the first speculator is doing, and out of greed the latter begins the same type of arson scheme, creating a chain reaction. The idea spreads to still other speculators, and shortly an entire city can find itself in the midst of a real estate arson-for-profit epidemic.

### Planned Bankruptcy

Although this variation of arson for profit is not encountered often, its incidence does seem to be growing. In a typical bankruptcy fraud, the owner establishes a business and buys quantities of goods on credit. The owner pays the first few creditors quickly and in cash in order to increase the volume of merchandise he or she can then buy on credit. The inventory is then sold, often surreptitiously through another company or to a fence, and then the business declares bankruptcy. Often the creditors are left with large numbers of unpaid bills. One way to satisfy them is by paying them off with insurance proceeds obtained after a "mysterious" fire in the business. Additional money is generated from such a fraud scheme because the owner represents in the fire insurance claim that substantial amounts of inventory were destroyed, when in fact merchandise was purposely moved out before the fire. Occasionally, a cheaper grade of merchandise is substituted in its place. Because the creditors are paid, their incentive to complain or report the probable fraud is reduced. Because the destroyed records of such inventory are hard to reconstruct, it is difficult to determine exactly what was destroyed in the fire, and hence its value. Also, since bankruptcy-fraud fires always seem to destroy the office and files where the books are kept, it is difficult for the investigator to reconstruct the flow of money into and out of the business, as well as the flow of merchandise.

## ARSON GENERATED BY THIRD PARTIES

This is another broad category of arson for profit, where the beneficiary of the fire is not the owner-insured but a third party who arranges for the fire out of some economic motive. Because the insured is really the major victim here, rather than the culprit, it is important for the investigator to determine whether a third-party arson for profit did occur in order to avoid targeting the wrong individual. The following are some examples of major forms of third-party arson.

### Elimination of Business Competition

This type of scheme is motivated by someone who seeks to create a business monopoly or at least to maintain a competitive edge. Businesses most prone to this type of arson are those that stand to suffer from too great a concentration of similar businesses in a limited geographic area. Examples include restaurants, taverns, and sex-oriented establishments (e.g., topless bars, adult bookstores, and massage parlors), which need to generate a large volume of business in order to make a profit. Increased competition can pose an economic problem to similar businesses in a limited area, which can cause some or all of them a degree of financial distress. Consequently, the financial records of a burned business may indicate the existence of financial problems that could lead the investigator to the mistaken assumption that the owner arranged the fire in order to obtain relief from that condition. Actually, in this example, a competitor is more likely to set the arson in order to improve his or her business situation.

The following case illustrates the type of arson in this category:

A brand-new nightclub had recently been opened in fairly close proximity to an older nightclub. The new nightclub was highly successful and started to draw business away from the old nightclub. Two employees of the old nightclub thought they would take matters into their own hands and "torch" the new nightclub one night after it closed, in hopes that this would help get back some of the old club's customers. Sometime during the early morning hours these two individuals broke into the new nightclub and set out eight 2½-gallon cans of gasoline at strategic locations throughout the business. Three 12-inch pipe bombs were then inserted into three of the cans of gasoline. The fuses were lit and the individuals quickly fled the business and drove away. Unbeknownst to the would-be arsonists was the fact that the gasoline-soaked black powder could not be ignited. Thus, when the fuse finally made contact with the black powder, nothing happened. The following morning, when the business was reopened, the unexploded devices and cans of gasoline were found.

During the initial investigation, it was suspected that at least one of the possible motives for this attempted arson was to eliminate competition with the older nightclub. Thus, the investigators focused their efforts on the owners and employees associated with the older nightclub. Several days after the attempted arson, an investigative inquiry was made at the nightclub and it was determined that two employees had recently left town and were working in a companion business of the old club 260 miles away. Not surprisingly, the sudden departure of these individuals caused them to emerge as major suspects. Their fingerprints, which were on file, were compared with fingerprints found on the gasoline cans and a positive fingerprint identification was made of both suspects. The suspects has assumed that any fingerprints they left on the cans would be destroyed once the cans were ignited, so they failed to take any precautions to ensure that their fingerprints were not left on the cans. They were subsequently arrested and convicted of attempted arson. An interesting sidelight to this was the presence of a handwritten number on one of the pipes. After checking with several local hardware stores in the general area of both businesses, the investigators determined that the number was actually the price of the pipe and had been handwritten on the pipe by one of the hardware store employees. The employee who had written the number on the pipe was not able to make an identification of the individuals who had purchased it, but the possibility of an identification had to be considered by the investigators in their investigative process.

Although this was not considered to be an organized-crime-related attempted arson, the same category of arson is fairly common when an organized-crime figure maintains a financial interest in this type of business and either seeks a monopoly or offers to hire out his or her services to create the monopoly for a client or associates in that business. In either case it is important to involve investigators who are familiar with organized-crime intelligence gathering and investigation when elimination of business competition is suspected as a motive pattern behind arson.

## Extraction of Extortion Payments

The identity of the criminal who drives out competitors by burning them out may not be known to the victim. On the other hand, offenders who demand extortion payments to let someone remain in business will necessarily identify themselves (if only through their collectors) in order to effect timely payment. In this motive pattern, the arson may be a warning signal to a businessperson to "pay up or else," or it may be a signal to other businesspersons in that type of business to pay or wind up like the "example" of the burned-out victim. This pattern is similar to that found in the elimination of business competition, in that an organized-crime figure or someone who wants to appear to victims as such a figure (e.g., a juvenile gang leader) is often behind this type of scheme. Investigators who suspect this motive should examine the possibility of extortion payments being demanded of similar businesses in the locality.

## Labor-Management Grievances

Arsons in business establishments may be the result of an unresolved labor-management grievance for which the perpetrator felt there was insufficient redress or resolution. Investigators should be careful to distinguish whether this type of arson is part of a more regularized pattern of violent activity in the industry or whether it could have resulted from a lone disgruntled employee. It is important to approach the possibility of this motive pattern carefully, for it can occur in an industry that is feeling the effects of

**Figure 18-2** Establishing Arson-for-Profit Motive

The roles of people and paper in arson-for-profit enforcement.

(**Source:** C. L. Karchmer, M. E. Walsh, and J. Greenfield, *Enforcement Manual: Approaches for Combating Arson-for-Profit Schemes* [Washington, DC: U.S. Department of Justice, 1979], p. 31.)

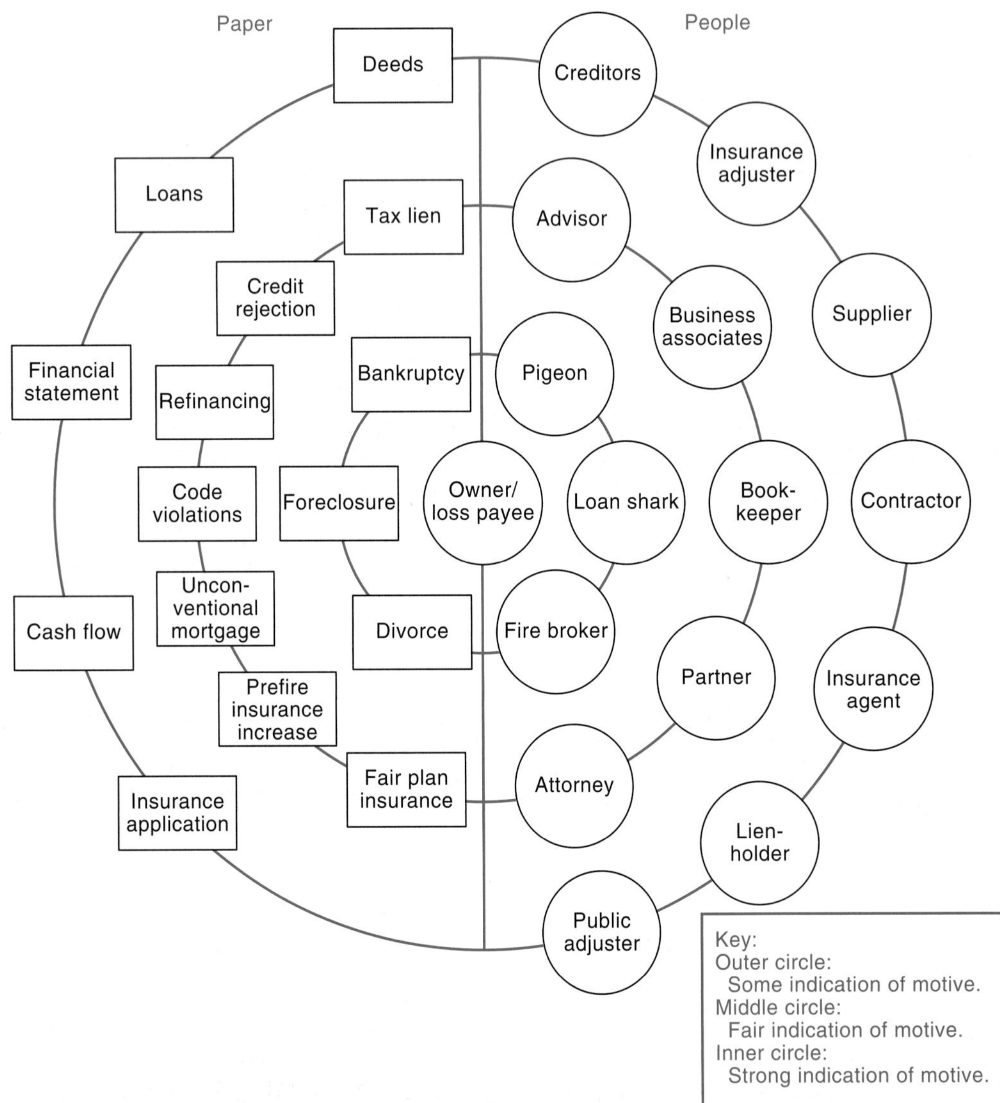


an economic downturn and thus the management may logically be reluctant to accede to labor demands because of their cost. Therefore, the financial records of the business, as well as of the entire industry, may signal financial stress. In reality the arson may have been caused by an employee unsympathetic to that economic condition. Investigators who suspect this motive pattern should examine the history of labor-management grievances in the business by reviewing records of complaints filed with state and federal labor regulatory agencies.

## PEOPLE AND PAPER EVIDENCE IN ARSON-FOR-PROFIT INVESTIGATIONS

Figure 18–2 briefly summarizes the people and documents that are most likely to provide information on motive. The presence of certain documents is a good, direct indicator of fraud, economic stress, or a combined fraud-stress motive. Other people and documents are more remote indicators and provide only a glimpse of a possible motive. The chart is intended merely as a guide to assist the investigator in determining motive.

## OTHER MOTIVES FOR ARSON

### REVENGE, SPITE, JEALOUSY

This category includes jilted lovers, feuding neighbors, disgruntled employees, quarreling spouses, people getting even after being cheated or abused, and people motivated by racial or religious hostility. Lovers' disputes and domestic squabbles are the greatest contributors to this category (see photo below). In some parts of the country, particularly in rural areas, disagreements result in the burning of homes or barns. Many arsonists drink alcohol before this kind of fire.[17]

### VANDALISM, MALICIOUS MISCHIEF

Vandals set fires for excitement and have no other motive. Many fires in vacant buildings, so common in recent years, are set by vandals. Vandals also set fires in abandoned cars, garbage cans, and so on; junk fires are also started as a protest to local conditions and for "instant urban renewal." Vagrants and drug users sometimes set fires. Vandalism fires seem to be increasing at a fairly rapid rate.[18]

### CRIME CONCEALMENT, DIVERSIONARY TACTICS

Criminals sometimes set fires to obliterate the evidence of burglaries, larcenies, and murders. The fire may destroy evidence that a crime was committed, may obscure evidence connecting the perpetrator to the crime, or may make visual identification of a murder victim impossible or difficult. (For a further discussion of fire deaths, see Chapter 9, "Injury and Death Investigations.")

People set fires to destroy records that contain evidence of embezzlement, forgery, or fraud. Arson has also been used to divert attention while the perpetrator burglarizes another building and to cover attempted escapes from jails, prisons, and state hospitals. The following case falls into this category:

AN individual went to a local U-Haul sales office and set fire to one of the trucks on the property in order to draw employees outside the business so that the individual could remove money from the cash register. The tactic worked and all the employees left, but one employee returned sooner than expected and observed the individual removing the contents from the cash register. Other employees were summoned, and

**Revenge Arson**

A female victim's car was set on fire by her boyfriend after she jilted him for another man. When the target of a suspected arson is personal property, such as a vehicle, investigators carefully review any recent occurrences in the victim's life that might reveal a potential motive for the crime.

(Courtesy Michael M. Gonzalez, Chief of Fire Investigations, Tampa Fire Department, Florida)

**Arson Fire Set as a Diversion**
A truck set on fire at a U-Haul sales office in an effort to draw employees outside of the business so that the fire setter could remove money from the cash register. Diversionary fires are also set by criminals who are trying to hinder the efforts of police investigators. For example, it is not uncommon for a person to be murdered and the scene made to appear as if he or she had been killed by fire.

(Courtesy Michael M. Gonzalez, Chief of Fire Investigations, Tampa Fire Department, Florida)

the individual was held by the employees and turned over to the police. (See photo above).

## PSYCHIATRIC AFFLICTIONS—THE PYROMANIAC AND SCHIZOPHRENIC FIRE SETTER

**Pyromaniacs** differ characteristically from other arsonists in that they lack conscious motivation for their fire setting. In fact, they are considered by many to be motiveless. They may derive sensual satisfaction from setting fires. Pyromaniacs have been described as setting their fires for no particular reason and no material profit. In one study, the pyromaniac represented 60 percent of the sample population. Of this number, 241 expressed receiving some sort of satisfaction from the fire. The remaining 447 offenders offered no special reason or persistent interest beyond the fact that something within them forced them to set fires.[19]

The urge to set fires has been referred to as an irresistible impulse. However, authorities should be cautioned against accepting this explanation. Some researchers have postulated that pyromania releases sexual tension; others reject that as a major motive. In another study of pyromania, only a small percentage of subjects claimed to receive sexual gratification from fire setting.[20]

Psychosis is generally defined as a severe form of personality disorganization characterized by marked impairment of contact with reality and personal and social functioning. Delusions, hallucinations, emotional blunting, and bizarre behavior may also be present in varying degrees. The most serious of all psychotic disorders is *schizophrenia,* which has been defined as "a group of psychotic disorders characterized by gross distortions of reality, withdrawal from social interaction, and disorganization and fragmentation of perception, thought, and emotion."[21]

In one study of 1,145 male fire setters, 13.4 percent could be classified as psychotic. These fire setters seemed distinct from others in that their fires were set for suicidal purposes, or their motives were delusional in character, or they manifested bizarre behavior during or immediately after the fire setting. Nonetheless, psychotic fire setters also fell into other categories, such as those of revenge fire setter and pyromaniac.[22]

## VANITY, HERO FIRES

On occasion the person who "discovers" a fire turns out to be the one who started it and did so to be a hero:

IN a recent case, a private guard company hired extra personnel and soon promoted one employee to sergeant. After a while, the company decided that the extra guards were not needed and discussed reducing the force. This reduction would have resulted in a demotion for the sergeant. Shortly thereafter, a fire was "discovered" by the sergeant. His quick action meant that the fire was confined, although it did cause thousands of dollars' worth of damage. A polygraph examination showed reactions indicative of deception, and the sergeant confessed to a police lieutenant that he had in fact set the fire. His criminal record revealed that he had recently been released from a mental institution in another state and that he had been sent there in lieu of being sent to state prison.

The fire investigator must look for any overlap among types of fires, such as pathological, profit for employment, and vanity.

The setting of fires by police officers and firefighters, although relatively rare, does occur. Although sometimes volunteer firefighters might set a fire with a profit motive, those who are paid on an hourly or individual basis most often do so because they like to fight fires and there is no activity in the neighborhood. They might also like to save people and property and be called heroes. Babysitters sometimes find a need to be "recognized"; they may start fires where they are working, discover the fire, and "save the child."[23]

## THE FEMALE FIRE SETTER

The female arsonist usually burns her own property, rarely that of an employer or neighbor. Her motives may be similar to those of male fire setters, but she seems to have more self-destructive tendencies. In one study of 201 female fire setters, most were found mentally defective. One-third were psychotic, primarily schizophrenic. They were described generally as older women who were lonely, unhappy, and in despair.[24]

## THE CHILD FIRE SETTER

Authorities on fire-setting behavior believe that repetitive or chronic fire setting by children represents a severe behavioral symptom or psychological disturbance. For the disturbed child, fire setting becomes an outlet for vengeful, hostile reactions, resentment, and defiance of authority.

In one study of 60 child fire setters, 60 percent were between 6 and 8 years of age and had the following characteristics:

- They set fires with fantasies of burning a member of the family who had withheld love or was a serious rival for parental attention.
- Most fires were started in or near their homes.
- The fires usually were symbolic, caused little damage, and were extinguished by the child.
- Prior to the fire settings, the children often had anxious dreams and fantasies of devils and ghosts.
- They suffered acute anxiety over their dreams, fantasies, and sexual preoccupations. All experienced sexual conflicts. Most actively masturbated; some participated in mutual masturbation, sodomy, and fellatio.
- Many were bed-wetters and also passive.
- Many had learning disabilities.
- Some had physical handicaps.
- They also demonstrated other forms of asocial behavior, including truancy, stealing, running away, and aggressive behavior.
- Some were orphans and institutionalized.
- Their home environments were pathological or broken. Many had absent or ineffective fathers.
- They lacked a sense of security, love, and attention.

## THE ADOLESCENT FIRE SETTER

There have been extensive studies on adolescent fire setting. One study of adolescent male fire setters showed that home-centered fire setting diminished as the age of the fire setter increased. Scenes of fires shifted to schools, churches, factories, and homes of strangers. These targets were preferred by adolescents age 12 to 16. The highest incidence of fire setting at schools involved 12- to 14-year-olds. Fires directed at schools were generally associated with adolescents who had school problems and were motivated by revenge. These fires often were preceded by theft, vandalism, and harassment of teachers. Defective intelligence was not found to be a factor in adolescent fire setting until perpetrators reached the age of 16.[25]

Common characteristics of adolescent fire setters include a history of delinquency, disruptive home environment, pathological personality development, sexual immaturity, aggressive or destructive behavior, poor social adjustment, emotional disturbance, and poor academic achievement. Some researchers have suggested that adolescents set fires for excitement.

Whatever the motive, vandalism fires appear to represent 80 percent of adolescent fire setting. Adolescent fire setters generally work in pairs or groups, in which one boy assumes a dominant role and the others assume a submissive role.

### Unusual Burn Patterns

Unusual burn patterns on wood floors should be closely examined. Flooring that was saturated with flammable liquid, like this, has deeply pronounced char. Burning between floorboards indicates that flammable liquid seeped down into the cracks. The area beneath the floor should also be examined for evidence of burning, and a sample of the burned floor should be sent to a laboratory for analysis.

(Courtesy Fire and Fraud Section, Aetna Casualty Surety Company)

## DETECTION AND RECOVERY OF FIRE-ACCELERANT RESIDUES

Because flammable liquids flow to the lowest level, heat travels from this level up, and the charring on the bottom of the furniture, ledges, and shelves will be as deep as, or deeper than, the charring on the top.[26]

After a fire has been extinguished, the floor should be carefully cleaned. Many signs may be found there, such as charred, inkblotlike outlines of flammable liquids. A rug that appears charred all over may, when dried out and swept with a stiff broom, show a distinct pattern of the flammable liquid. This pattern occurs because the liquid is absorbed into the nap of the rug and burns more heavily. Flammable liquid usually soaks into the joints of wooden flooring, and as a result the joints will be heavily burned (see photo above).

The baseboards and sills should be checked, because flammable liquid often runs under and chars them on the bottom. Corners of the rooms should also be checked, because few floors are perfectly level, and flammable liquid often runs into and burns out the corners. In most common household fires, the corners at floor level are least damaged. The depth of charring in the floor and ceiling should be compared. If the floor is charred as much as or more than the ceiling, this indicates a flammable material directly at floor level. In the average fire, the floor temperature is only about one-third that of the ceiling.

When gasoline or similar material is suspected to have been thrown on porches or buildings without basements, especially those with single constructed flooring, the soil beneath the burned area should be checked. The investigator should dig 1 or 2 inches into the earth and smell for the odor of flammable liquids. A vapor tester is better for this purpose, because flammables like alcohol have little or no odor in cold, wet earth.

If recovered material is suspected of containing flammable liquids, it should be sealed in an uncoated metal paint can, not in plastic bags or plastic containers. Uncoated metal paint cans can be purchased at auto supply houses. Plastic can give off hydrocarbons that contaminate the material. The container should be tightly sealed to minimize evaporation or contamination. Evidence tape should be used to ensure integrity of the chain of evidence. The container may also be marked for identification purposes with permanent ink.

Before they can be analyzed, accelerant residues must first be separated from the ashes, wood, carpeting, or other material in which they are found. This extraction is usually accomplished by simple, steam, or vacuum distillation. These are listed in increasing order of efficiency, particularly for petroleum products, and increasing complexity of apparatus. Steam distillation and vacuum distillation are capable of extracting 65 percent of any gasoline from debris; for fuel oil the efficiencies are 30 percent and 90 percent, respectively.[27]

## SCIENTIFIC METHODS IN ARSON INVESTIGATION

The presence of flammable liquids may establish arson and sometimes link a suspect to the fire.[28] The objection is sometimes raised that identifiable amounts of liquid fire accelerants rarely survive a fire and efforts to detect them would be largely wasted. But arson investigators often find accelerant residues, and accelerants can survive fires. One expert, for example, performed the following experiment: He poured 2½ gallons of kerosene over furniture and rugs in one room of a wooden building, and 1 gallon of gasoline over straw in another room, and then he left a trail of gasoline as a fuse. The building was allowed to burn freely and completely. He was able to extract identifiable amounts (more than 1 milliliter*) of both kerosene and gasoline from the debris.[29]

The areas most likely to contain residues of liquid fire accelerants—floors, carpets, and soil—are likely to have the lowest temperatures during the fire and may have insufficient oxygen to support the complete combustion of accelerant. Porous or cracked floors may allow accelerants to seep through to underlying earth. Numerous instances have been recounted of the excellent retention properties of soil for flammable liquid.[30] Another place where accelerants may be discovered is on the clothes and shoes of a suspect.

Because each method of accelerant detection (including the human nose) has a threshold of sensitivity, another question that arises is the vapor concentration that is produced by accelerant residues. Some idea of the order of magnitude can be obtained from the experiment of two experts. They burned small (2-milliliter) samples of various accelerants for 30 seconds and then measured vapor concentrations ranging upward from 60 parts vapor per million of air—within the range of detection of currently available portable detectors and generally, but not always, well above readings produced by hydrocarbons from such things as burnt wood and burnt mattresses.[31]

Another way of looking at the potential vapor concentration is to consider the following hypothetical case: Suppose that a gallon of gasoline is used to accelerate a fire in a 15- by 15- by 8-foot room and that 1 percent (39 milliliters) survives the fire in cracks in the floor. (The residue would consist of higher boiling-point components, such as naphthalene.) The subsequent evaporation of 1 milliliter (3 percent) of the residue would produce an average vapor concentration of 2.7 parts per million throughout the entire room. Such a concentration can be detected with available equipment. Ventilation of the room, of course, dissipates the vapor and generally causes the vapor concentration to be highest at the points where the residues are located, a situation that can be used to advantage in locating evidence samples to be preserved for laboratory analysis.

### DETECTION OF FIRE ACCELERANTS

Several types of portable equipment are available to the arson investigator for detecting residues of flammable liquids at fire scenes. Some of these use chemical color tests, catalytic combustion, flame ionization, gas liquid chromatographs, and infrared spectrophotometers and ultraviolet fluorescence. The sensitivities, limitations, advantages, and disadvantages of each of these are discussed next.

#### Olfactory Detection

The sensitivity of the human nose to gasoline vapor is about 1 part per 10 million. Gasoline is a complex mixture of chemical compounds, the proportions of which vary with the source of the crude oil and the type of process used in its manufacture. Benzene and other aromatic hydrocarbons, for example, may constitute from 0.1 to 40 percent of the mixture. Although no conclusive data on the sensitivity of the nose to gasoline are available, the sensitivity of the nose to benzene vapor is 0.015 part per million. Assuming that 15 percent (or more) of gasoline vapor consists of aromatic hydrocarbons to which the nose is as sensitive as it is to benzene, then the sensitivity to gasoline is 1 part in 10 million (or greater). Thus, the nose is as sensitive as any of the currently available detecting equipment. But there are flammable liquids to which the nose is not sensitive. Another problem is the tendency of the nose to lose its

*There are approximately 30 milliliters in 1 fluid ounce.

sensitivity to an odor after prolonged or intense exposure to it. Further, the odor of fire accelerants may be masked by another strong odor such as that of burnt debris. In fact, in one case an arsonist attempted to camouflage gasoline by mixing it with vanilla.[32] Finally, it may be impractical or impossible to search with the nose for accelerant odors along floors or in recessed areas.[33]

Increasingly, agencies are using specially trained canines for the detection of accelerants. They have proved to be quite effective. On occasion such dogs are even brought to the scene of the arson while the fire is occurring in the hopes that the dogs will be able to detect accelerants on individuals who may have set the fire and are in the crowd watching the fire. (See photo below).

## Chemical Color Test Detectors

Chemical color tests may be used to detect both liquid accelerant residues and their vapors. Certain dyes indicate the presence of hydrocarbons by turning red. Dyes are less sensitive and less specific to flammable liquids than other available methods. Dyes also may interfere with laboratory identification of the accelerant. Hydrocarbon vapors can be detected by pumping a suspected sample through a glass container of reagent that changes color in the presence of hydrocarbons. The reported sensitivity of this method is on the order of 1 part per 1,000. Again, the method is less sensitive and less specific (reacting to hydrocarbons that are not fire accelerants) than others available. Its main advantages are low cost (approximately $100 for the vapor detector) and simplicity.[34]

## Catalytic Combustion Detector

The most common flammable vapor detector operates on the catalytic combustion principle and is popularly known as a sniffer, combustible-gas indicator, explosimeter, or vapor detector. A **catalytic combustion detector** is portable, moderate in cost, and fairly simple to operate. Vapor samples are pumped over a heated, platinum-plated coil of wire that causes any combustible gas present to oxidize. The heat from the oxidation raises the electrical resistance of the coil, and this change in resistance is measured electronically. A sensitivity (to hexane vapor) on the order of a few parts per million can be achieved with this method. Because oxygen is required for the operation of the detector, its sensitivity is reduced in oxygen-deficient areas, but these are unlikely to occur in arson investigations. (An internal source of oxygen could be fitted to a detector if required.) Another problem is the gradual loss of sensitivity when this type of detector is exposed to gasoline containing lead. Lead deposits form on the platinum catalyst and interfere with its operation.[35]

## Flame Ionization Detector

In the **flame ionization detector,** the sample gas is mixed with hydrogen and the mixture is burned. Ionized molecules are produced in the flame in proportion to the amount of combustible organic gases in the sample. (Pure hydrogen, air, and water

**Accelerant Detecting Canine**
An ATF-certified accelerant-detecting canine from the Salt Lake City Sheriff's Office, working the scene of a warehouse arson in Utah. Investigators know many arsonists will stay close to the scene after they have set the fire. On occasion, dogs such as the one in the photo, are brought to the scene of the arson while the fire is burning—the goal being for the dog to detect accelerants on a person in a crowd of onlookers.

(Courtesy U.S. Department of the Treasury Bureau of Alcohol, Tobacco and Firearms)

vapor produce little ionization.) The degree of ionization is then measured by electrometer. The sensitivity of this method (to methane) is on the order of 1 part in 10 million. It is thus more sensitive but more complex and expensive than the catalytic combustion method.

### Gas Liquid Chromatograph

The portable **gas liquid chromatograph (GLC)** adapted for field use, sometimes called the arson chromatograph, is one of the most common detectors in arson investigations. The sample gas is first separated into components on the basis of the speed with which they travel through a tube filled with packing material. The amounts of each component are then measured by either a catalytic combustion or flame ionization detector. The sensitivity ranges from a few hundredths of a part per million to a few parts per million, depending on the type of detector used. The main advantage is specificity because of the preliminary separation process. The main disadvantages are its size, weight, and cost. Also, the time required for the analysis of each sample is about ½ hour, a disadvantage in some situations. In addition, there is a setup time of about 1 hour. The operation of the gas chromatograph requires a certain amount of technical training.

### Infrared Spectrophotometer

**Infrared spectrophotometers** can achieve high specificity to flammable liquids and high sensitivity (on the order of hundredths of a part per million). Infrared light of varying wavelengths is directed through the sample, and the amount of light passing through is plotted on a pen recorder. The recording is compared with those of known compounds to determine the identity of the sample. Because the chemical bonds in a compound determine how it absorbs infrared radiation, these recordings (called spectrograms) are unique for different compounds. However, evidence mixed with impurities must be purified before it can be successfully identified. In particular, since water vapor absorbs infrared light, it interferes with the identification of flammable vapors. This is a disadvantage in arson investigation, where water is commonly present. A final disadvantage is the high cost of this type of detector.

### Ultraviolet Fluorescence

**Ultraviolet fluorescence** consists of illuminating the darkened fire scene with an ultraviolet lamp. Certain substances, including constituents of gasoline and its residue, absorb the ultraviolet light and release it as visible light. They appear to glow against the darkened background. The color of the glow is affected by exposure to heat, and so the method also can be used to locate the point of origin of a fire. The only equipment required is an ultraviolet lamp and a portable power supply. The sensitivity of the method appears comparable to that of other methods of detection. The main disadvantage of the method is that it requires extensive testing, particularly to identify fire accelerants to which it does not respond.[36]

# INTERVIEWS

To establish possible motives and develop suspects, the arson investigator must interview people who might know about the fire and how it started. The following kinds of people may provide information.[37]

## POSSIBLE WITNESSES

Prospective witnesses include tenants, businesspeople, and customers from the burnt building and in surrounding buildings, as well as passersby, including bus drivers, taxi drivers, delivery people, garbage collectors, police patrols, and people waiting for buses and taxis.

### Questions to Ask

Did you observe the fire? At what time did you first observe the fire? In what part of the building did you observe the fire? What called your attention to the building? Did you see any people entering or leaving the building before the fire? Did you recognize them? Can you describe them? Did you observe any vehicles in the area of the fire? Can you describe them? Can you describe the smoke and the color of the flame? How quickly did the fire spread? Was the building burning in more than one place? Did you detect any unusual odors? Did you observe anything else?

## FIREFIGHTERS AT THE SCENE

Firefighters can be an invaluable source of information to arson investigators because of their technical knowledge and because of what they observe at a fire.

### Questions to Ask

What time was the alarm received? What time did you arrive at the scene of the fire? Was your route to the scene blocked? What was the extent of burning when you arrived? Were doors and windows locked? Were the entrances or passageways blocked? What kind of fire was it? What was the spread speed of the fire? In what area(s) did the fire start? How near was the fire to the roof? Was there evidence of the use of an accelerant? Was any evidence of arson recovered? Did the building have a fire alarm system? Was it operating? Was there any evidence of tampering with the alarm system? Did the building have a sprinkler system? Did it operate? Was there any evidence of tampering with the sprinkler system? Was there anyone present in the building when you arrived? Who was the person in the building? Did that person say anything to you? Were there any people present at the scene when you arrived? Who were they? Did you observe any vehicles at or leaving the scene when you arrived? Can you describe them? Were there contents in the building? Was there evidence that contents had been removed? Was the owner present? Did the owner make a statement? What did the owner say? What is the fire history of the building? What is the fire history of the area?

## INSURANCE PERSONNEL

The profit in many arson-for-profit cases is an insurance payment. Three people may be interviewed to determine if the profit centers around an insurance claim: the insurance agent or broker, the insurance adjuster, and the insurance investigator.

There may be restrictions on the amount of information insurance personnel can turn over without a subpoena, but the investigator should be able to determine enough to indicate whether a subpoena or search warrant would prove fruitful.

### Questions to Ask the Agent or Broker

Who is the insured? Is there more than one person insured? Is the insured the beneficiary? What type of policy was issued? What is the amount of the policy? When was it issued? When does it expire? What is the premium? Are payments up-to-date? Have there been any increases in the amount of coverage? What amount? When did the increase take effect? What was the reason for the increase? Are there any special provisions in the policy (e.g., interruption of business or rental income)? What are they, and when did they take effect? Does the insured have any other policies? Were there previous losses at the location of the fire? Were there losses at other locations owned by the insured?

### Questions to Ask the Insurance Claims Adjuster

Did you take a sworn statement from the insured? Did the insured submit documents regarding proof of loss, value of contents, bills of lading, value of building, and the like? Did you inspect the fire scene? Did you inspect the fire scene with a public insurance adjuster? Did you and the public adjuster agree on the cost of the loss? Have you dealt with this public adjuster before? Has he or she represented this owner before? Has the insured had any other losses with this company? (If so, get details.)

### Questions to Ask the Insurance Investigator

Were you able to determine the cause of the fire? Did you collect any evidence? Who analyzed the evidence? What were the results of the analysis? Was the cause of the fire inconsistent with the state of the building as known through an underwriting examination? Have you investigated past fires at the location? Have you investigated past fires involving the insured? What were the results of the investigations? Have you had prior investigations involving the public adjuster? Have you had prior investigations involving buildings handled by the same insurance agent or broker? What were the results of these investigations? Does this fire fit into a pattern of fires of recent origin in this area? What are the similarities? What are the differences? Have you taken any statements in connection with this burning? Whose statements did you take? What do they reveal?

### Property Insurance Loss Register

The insurance industry maintains a modern computerized data bank, the **Property Insurance Loss Register (PILR),** to keep track of fire, burglary, and theft claims. PILR is a listing of everyone who has an insurable interest in fire claims and a listing of *only* the insureds in burglary and theft claims. Thus, PILR is one of the most effective routes for determining a repeated pattern of claim activity on the part of individuals and organized rings. Most insurance companies are members of PILR and routinely submit data, listing insureds and claim details, to the registry after fire and burglary losses. The information is immediately entered into the PILR data bank; should the name of an insured (or of a person with an insurable interest, in the case of fire losses) have been entered before, a "hit" will be reported to the insurance company that submitted the entry. Hits can vary widely in significance, as shown by the following examples:

- *Probably insignificant:* A major landlord or mortgagee experienced a minor fire at another location 12 months prior to the immediate loss.
- *Inconclusive:* A home owner experienced a $4,000 burglary loss 18 months prior to the immediate fire loss.
- *Suspicious:* A business owner made two expensive burglary loss claims against two other insurers during the 12 months preceding the immediate, very suspicious fire loss under investigation. (Why is the owner having such bad luck, and why is he or she changing insurance companies so frequently?)
- *Highly suspicious:* A home owner or tenant experienced two expensive and suspicious fire losses at previous addresses during the 24 months prior to the immediate loss.
- *Probably incriminating:* An insured has made claims against two different insurers for the same immediate loss under investigation. There can be legitimate circumstances in which double claims are made; for example, the building and some of its contents may be insured by one carrier, while special inventory or equipment is insured by another.[38]

The insurance company that has made an entry is notified only when a hit occurs. Thus, the lack of a PILR response in the claim file may indicate either that there was no hit or that no entry was made. When obtaining the claim file, the investigator should ask the claims adjuster whether PILR entries were submitted and, if so, which individuals were listed on the entries. If no PILR entries were made or if the names of some of the possible suspects with an insurable interest were not included, the National Insurance Crime Bureau (NICB) can request PILR data if it is a party to the investigation.[39] If previous fire, burglary, or theft losses are reported by PILR, it then becomes possible to compare the claimed losses to see whether the same furnishings, inventory, or equipment were already reported lost, stolen, or destroyed. Likewise, PILR's records can be a means of constructing the "big picture" for an arson-for-profit conspiracy. By running the names of every possible suspect in one suspicious fire through PILR and/or the NICB's database, a dozen or more interrelated claims may be uncovered and used to develop evidence against the entire ring. In some states, model arson laws may allow the investigator to easily obtain the claim files for the previous losses from the insurance companies involved. In instances where such laws do not apply or where suspicious prior burglary claims are not covered by the laws, the NICB may be able to secure copies of the previous claims when it is a party to the investigation.[40]

## OTHER WITNESSES CONCERNING FINANCES OF THE INSURED

A number of other people may have information on the finances of the owner, including business associates, creditors, and competitors. This information may indicate how the owner stood to profit from the burning.

### Questions to Ask

How long have you known the owner/insured? What is the nature of your relationship with the owner/insured? Do you have any information on the financial position of the business? Is the owner/insured competitive with similar businesses? Have there been recent technological advances that would threaten the owner/insured's competitive position? Has there been a recent increase in competition that would affect the owner/insured's position? Have changes in the economy affected the owner/insured's position? Has the owner/insured had recent difficulty in paying creditors? Has the owner/insured's amount of debt increased recently? Has the owner/insured lost key employees lately? Has the location where the owner/insured does business changed for the worse recently? Has the owner/insured increased the mortgage or taken out a second or third mortgage? Has the owner/insured had difficulty making mortgage payments? Do you have any other information about the owner's/insured's financial position?

## NEWS MEDIA PERSONNEL

This category includes both the print and electronic media. Individuals affiliated with these groups may have noticed something of value to the investigator or perhaps have films of the fire and fire scene. For example, if the arsonist remained in the area after the fire and mingled with spectators, his or her presence may be captured on film and prove quite valuable in an investigation.

## THE MEDICAL EXAMINER

The autopsy should reveal whether any victim found dead in the fire was dead or alive before the fire started and what the cause of death was. It is not uncommon for a person to be murdered and the scene made to appear as if the person had been killed by fire. See Chapter 9, "Injury and Death Investigations," for a detailed discussion of fire deaths.

## INTERVIEWING A SUSPECT

The questions below are based on the assumption that the person to be interviewed is involved in arson for profit, that the investigator has enough evidence to make an arrest or to convince the subject that he or she is liable to arrest, and that the subject is more valuable to the investigation in a cooperative role than as a defendant.

### Questions to Ask the Suspect

Are you willing to cooperate in this investigation? How many other people are involved in the arson-for-profit scheme? How are they involved? What role does each person play in the scheme? Explain (in detail) how the scheme works. How did you first become involved in the scheme? How did you meet the other participants? Where did you meet the other participants? Are you still in contact with the other participants? How often do you see them? Where do you see them? What do you talk about when you meet with them? Would you be able to record your conversations with them? Are you willing to record your conversations with them? Would you be willing to introduce an undercover investigator into the group? Could you introduce an undercover investigator into the group without the other participants' becoming suspicious? How far in advance of an arson are you told about it? What role do you play in connection with the arson (torch, driver, pigeon, fence, and so forth)? Are you willing to swear to an affidavit for a search warrant? Are you willing to testify before a grand jury? Are you willing to testify at trial? Do you have information on other arson-for-profit schemes?

### Questions to Ask the Torch, Specifically

What method was used to accomplish the arson? Specify whether what was used was an incendiary

**Convicted Arsonist Julio Gonzalez**

While prosecutors were effective in convicting Julio Gonzalez, obtaining enough evidence to lead to the successful prosecution and subsequent conviction of an arsonist is no easy task. If physical evidence is not available, investigators must often rely on gathering circumstantial evidence and some provable facts from which valid conclusions regarding potential suspects can be drawn.

device, gasoline or another inflammable fluid, or some other means. If an incendiary device was used, be specific as to the type of device. Where did you obtain the incendiary device? If it was improvised, who made it? How much did it cost? Who paid for the incendiary device? Was it paid for by cash or check? If gasoline or another flammable fluid was used, where was it obtained? How much was obtained and used? Were any special techniques used in setting the fire (or causing an explosion) to avoid detection?

## INTERVIEWING THE TARGET AND THE OWNER

The target of the investigation may be an owner, landlord, fire broker, or the like. The interview should take place after obtaining the background information on the fire and after interviewing the individuals previously listed.

### Questions to Ask the Target

Tell me in your own words what you know about this fire. When did you first hear of the arson? Who told you? Where were you, and what were you doing before, during, and after the arson? Who was with you? Do you know who committed the arson? Do you have any knowledge of any previous fire at the building? Do you have any knowledge of any previous incidents of any kind and at any location owned or rented by the owner/occupant of the building? Do you know of any recent changes in insurance coverage? Do you know the owner of the arson property? Describe your relationship to the owner. Do you have any financial interest in the burned property?

### Questions to Ask the Owner

Tell me in your own words what you know about this fire. How long have you owned the burned property? What was the purchase price? What was the total amount of the mortgage? Who is your insurance company? Agent? Broker? Public adjuster? How much insurance do you carry? Is there more than one policy on this property? On its contents? On rental or business interruption? Have you increased your insurance coverage on the property in the past year? If so, why and at whose suggestion? Have you ever received an insurance cancellation notice on this property? Where were you at the time of the fire? When did you first hear of the arson? Who told you? When were you last in the building? Was the building secured? If so, in what manner? Who else has access to or keys to the building? Who was the last person to leave the building? Do you have any knowledge that the sprinkler system or burglar alarm system was on and working? Indicate the name and address of all lienholders. What is the amount of each lien? What was the value of the inventory on hand immediately before the fire? Can you provide documentation for this value? Was any inventory removed from the premises before the fire? If yes, by whom and for what purposes? Where did it go, and why was it removed? Was any inventory removed from the premises after the fire? If yes, by whom and for what purpose? List the inventory removed and its value. Did you set the fire or cause it to be set? Do you know who set it?

## INTERVIEWING A POTENTIAL INFORMANT WHO IS NOT A SUSPECT

Before interviewing a potential informant who is not a suspect, investigative efforts should be made to determine if the informant has any police record and, if so, if it could have any bearing on the reliability of the information provided. For example, if a potential informant was previously convicted of arson and perjury, then the investigator should be cautious about acting on that person's information.

### Questions to Ask a Potential Informant

How are you currently supporting yourself? Do you have any pending prosecutions against you? Where? What are you charged with? Do you have any information about arson for profit in this city, county, state? How did you acquire this information? Do you know anyone engaged in arson for profit? What roles does that person play in the scheme? How do you know this? What is your relationship with this person or persons—loan shark, bookmaker, fence, or the like? Where does this person live, frequent? Who are his or her associates? Do you know them? Are they part of the scheme? Have you been asked to involve yourself in the scheme? In what way? Have any of these people talked freely to you about their activities? Have they talked in your presence? What was said? Can you engage them in conversation about past arsons? Future arsons? Would they be suspicious of you? Could you wear a concealed recorder during conversation? Could you introduce an undercover officer into the group? Would you be willing to testify before a grand jury? Would you be willing to testify at trial? Would you be willing to swear to an affidavit for a search warrant? Would you be willing to swear to an eavesdropping warrant? What do you expect in return for your help?

# THE ARSON SUSPECT

In some arson investigations, a single prime suspect may emerge and investigative efforts will be focused accordingly. However, in most cases, a number of suspects emerge, and merely establishing that one or more of them had a motive to set the fire is not proof enough for an arrest and conviction. The investigator must also determine which of the suspects had the opportunity and the means to commit the crime. This determination must be related to the background, personal characteristics, past activities, and financial status of each of the suspects. For example, 10 people may have had a chance to set the fire, but only 4 or 5 may have had a motive, and of this number, perhaps only 1 or 2 would risk an arson conviction for the expected profit or satisfaction.

In probing an arson fire, seldom does direct evidence link a suspect with a fire. Because arsonists tend to take elaborate precautions not to be seen near the fire, they are seldom caught in the act. It may be best for the investigator to concentrate on gathering circumstantial evidence and some provable facts from which valid conclusions can be drawn. For example, let us assume that a warehouse fire was ignited by a timing device—a slow-burning candle attached to some flammable material triggered 2 hours before the fire actually started. The owner, who is also a prime suspect, is identified but can prove his whereabouts at the time of the fire. However, he cannot prove where he was 2 hours before the fire. In addition, the structure was locked when the fire department arrived to fight the fire, and the owner is the only one with a set of keys. The owner also took a large insurance policy out on the warehouse a short time ago.

Although far more evidence would likely be needed to arrest and convict the owner, there is sufficient justification for focusing a considerable amount of the investigation in his direction. If some other evidence is found to link him more directly to the fire (say, candles and flammable material found in the trunk of his car), then the circumstantial evidence becomes significant.

# PHOTOGRAPHING THE ARSON SCENE

## STILL PHOTOGRAPHY

Photographing a fire scene can be a challenge. Adverse conditions—poor lighting, time constraints, inconvenient angles, and so forth—necessitate the use of camera equipment that is reliable and quick because there rarely is time to adjust the focus on every shot or arrange perfect lighting. Therefore, the ideal still camera is one that is fully automatic, such as a 35-millimeter camera with a good-grade film. This type of camera is more than adequate for taking interior as well as exterior photos. The adjustable setting on a 35-millimeter camera allows close-up photos at approximately 3 feet. In cases where the crime scene photographer wants more detail, photos can be enlarged.

The photo session should take at least as long as the physical examination; however, it is not necessary to photograph every step. The investigator should follow the same path in photographing the structure as is followed in the physical examination—the path of the burn trail from the least to the greatest amount of damage. The photos are as important as the written report because they show what happened rather than merely telling what happened.

Ideally the investigator should be concerned with photographing things and areas that show, in detail, what happened. For example, if there are severely darkened ventilation patterns out of a window or a door, the investigator should photograph them. He or she should also photograph burn patterns at lower levels and those that show distinct lines of demarcation, melted or stained glass, areas where explosions occurred, broken locks, and areas where the electric service enters the building. If the investigator does not know what happened, detailed photos will help in assessing what took place.

In some cases it is necessary to compile a panoramic view. This can be accomplished with a composite of several photos that are taped together to create a much larger overview. The area of the fire's origin should be photographed twice, first before the rubble is disturbed and then after the debris has been removed. Severe burn patterns should be documented, especially patterns that show how the fire burned. Burn patterns at the base of doors and underneath door moldings are a strong indication that flammable liquids were used. This is because a fire spreading of its own accord burns upward, not downward.

If clocks are present, the investigator should always photograph the faces of the clocks showing the times they stopped. Fires often cause interruptions in electricity, which means electrical clocks will usually stop within 10 minutes to ½ hour after the time the fire started. Knowing when the fire started is crucial to the case.

### VIDEOTAPE

Another form of visual documentation is videotaping, discussed in Chapter 2, "Investigators, the Investigative Process, and the Crime Scene." While the average fire investigation does not require videotaping, it should be done if the investigator reasonably believes that the case will involve litigation.[41]

## EXPLOSIVES INVESTIGATION

Under the fire and explosion investigation definition, an **explosion** is a physical reaction characterized by the presence of four major elements: high-pressure gas, confinement or restriction of the pressure, rapid production or release of that pressure, and change or damage to the confining (restricting) structure, container, or vessel that is caused by the pressure release. Although an explosion is almost always accompanied by the production of a loud noise, the noise itself is not an essential element of an explosion.[42] The generation and violent escape of gases are the primary criteria of an explosion.

### TYPES OF EXPLOSIONS

There are two major types of explosions: mechanical and chemical. These types are differentiated by the source or mechanism by which the explosive pressures are produced.

#### Mechanical Explosions

In **mechanical explosions,** the high-pressure gas is produced by purely physical reactions. None of the reactions involves changes in the basic chemical nature of the substances. The most commonly used example of a mechanical explosion is the bursting of a steam boiler. The source of overpressure is the steam created by heating and vaporizing water. When the pressure of the steam can no longer be confined by the boiler, the vessel fails and an explosion results.

#### Chemical Explosions

In **chemical explosions,** the generation of high-pressure gas is the result of reactions in which the fundamental chemical nature of the fuel is changed. The most common chemical explosions are those caused by the burning of combustible hydrocarbon fuels such as natural gas, liquified petroleum gas, gasoline, kerosene, and lubricating oils.

An example of a chemical explosion is the one that destroyed the Alfred P. Murah Federal Building in Oklahoma City several years ago. In this case the convicted bomber, Timothy McVeigh, loaded a van with 4,000 pounds of ammonium nitrate (commonly used as a fertilizer) that had been soaked in fuel oil and detonated with high explosives. The explosion killed 167 people.[43] As the photo on page 684 shows, the destructive force of such a device is enormous.

### INVESTIGATING THE EXPLOSION SCENE

The objectives of the explosion scene investigation are no different from those for a regular fire investigation: to determine the origin, identify the fuel and ignition sources, determine the cause, and establish the responsibility for the incident. A systematic approach to the scene examination is just as important in an explosion investigation as in a fire

**Damage Resulting from a Chemical Explosion**

The effects of a chemical explosion that destroyed the Alfred P. Murah Federal Building in Oklahoma City. The destructive force of this chemical explosion killed 167 innocent people. Timothy McVeigh was eventually convicted and executed for committing this terrible crime.
(Courtesy UPI/Corbis-Bettman)

investigation—or even more so—because explosion scenes are often larger and more disturbed than fire scenes. Without a preplanned, systematic approach, explosion investigations become more difficult or even impossible to conduct effectively.[44]

The first duty of the investigator is to secure the scene of the explosion. First responders to the explosion should establish and maintain physical control of the structure and surrounding areas. Unauthorized persons should be prevented from entering the scene or touching blast debris remote from the scene itself because the critical evidence from an explosion (whether accidental or criminal) may be very small and may be easily disturbed or moved by people passing through. Evidence is also easily picked up on shoes and tracked out. Properly securing the scene also tends to prevent additional injuries to unauthorized and/or curious persons who may attempt to enter an unsafe area. As a general rule the outer perimeter of the incident scene should be established at one and a half times the distance of the farthest piece of debris found. Significant pieces of blast debris can be propelled great distances or into nearby buildings or vehicles, and these areas should be included in the scene perimeter (see photo on page 685). If additional pieces of debris are found, the scene perimeter should be widened.

The investigator should establish a scene pattern. Investigation team members should search the scene from the outer perimeter inward toward the area of greatest damage. The final determination of the location of the explosion's epicenter should be made only after all the scene has been examined. The search pattern itself may be grid, zone, or spiral shaped. (See Chapter 2 for a detailed description of these patterns.) Often the particular circumstances of the scene will dictate the nature of the pattern. In any case, the assigned areas of the search pattern should overlap so that no evidence will be lost at the edge of any search area.

It is often useful to search areas more than once. When this is done, a different searcher should be used on each search to help ensure that evidence is not overlooked. The number of actual searchers will depend on the physical size and complexity of the scene. The investigator in charge should keep in mind, however, that too many searchers can often be as counterproductive as too few. Searchers should be briefed as to the proper procedures for identifying, logging, photographing, marking, and mapping the location of evidence. The location of evidence may be marked with chalk marks, spray paint, flags, stakes, or other marking means. After being photographed, the evidence may be tagged, moved, and secured.

Structures that have suffered explosions are often more structurally damaged than those burned in a fire. The possibility that a floor, wall, ceiling, roof, or entire building will collapse is much greater and should always be considered. Explosion scenes that involve bombings or explosives have added dangers. Investigators should be on the lookout for additional devices and undetonated explosives. The modus operandi (MO) of some bomber-arsonists includes using secondary explosive devices specifically targeted for the law enforcement or fire service personnel who will be responding to the bombing incident.

## Proper Tools and Equipment

Having the proper tools and equipment is essential in emergency situations such as explosion or bombing scenes. Because responders and investigators may not know the details of the situation until arriving at the scene, prior preparation is vital. Although equipment and tool needs are, for the most part, determined by the actual scene, the items listed in Figure 18–3 are frequently used by investigative teams at explosion and bombing scenes. Not every item mentioned will be applicable at every scene, but the list can serve as a planning guide for equipment and tool needs.

## LOCATING AND IDENTIFYING ARTICLES OF EVIDENCE

Investigators should locate, identify, note, log, photograph, and map any of the many and varied articles of physical evidence. Because of the propelling nature of explosions, the investigator should keep in mind that significant pieces of evidence may be found in a wide variety of locations, including outside the exploded structure, embedded in the walls or other structural members of the exploded

**Damage from a Metal Pipe Bomb**

Clearly shown is the devastation that occurs when a metal pipe bomb is placed in the front seat of a vehicle and detonated. Explosive filler in the pipe bomb was 1.5 pounds of smokeless powder. When establishing the outer perimeter of crime scenes such as the one in this photo, investigators usually set it at 1½ times the distance of the furthest piece of debris. The search of the crime scene starts at this outer perimeter and moves toward the area of greatest damage.

(Courtesy Jack H. Adkins, Bomb Squad Commander, Big Bend Bomb Disposal Team, Tallahassee, Florida)

**Figure 18-3** Equipment and Tools for Explosion Scene Investigations

(**Source:** Office of Justice Programs, *Guide for Explosion and Bombing Scene Investigation*, Research Report, National Institute of Justice [Washington, DC: U.S. Department of Justice, June 2000], pp. 11-14.)

### *Safety*

- Biohazard materials (i.e., bags, tags, labels)
- First-aid kit
- Footwear, safety (i.e., protective shoes or boots)
- Glasses, safety
- Gloves, heavy and disposable (e.g., surgical, latex)
- Helmets, safety or hard hats
- Kneepads
- Outerwear, protective (e.g., disposable suits, weather gear)
- Personnel support items (e.g., food, water, hygiene items, shelter)
- Reflective tape
- Respiratory equipment (e.g., particle masks, breathing equipment)

### *General Crime Scene Equipment*

- Barrier tape and/or perimeter rope
- Batteries
- Binoculars
- Communication equipment (e.g., telephone, two-way radio)
- Evidence collection kits (e.g., latent print, bodily fluid, impression, tool mark, trace evidence)
- Flares
- Flashlights
- Generators
- Handtools (e.g., screwdrivers, crowbars, hammers)
- Knives, utility
- Lighting, auxiliary
- Tarps or tents
- Thermometer
- Trashcans, large
- Tweezers or forceps

### *Scene Documentation*

- Compass
- Computer and computer-aided design (CAD) program
- Consent-to-search forms
- Drawing equipment (e.g., sketchbooks, pencils)
- Logs (e.g., evidence recovery, photo)
- Measuring equipment (e.g., forensic mapping station, tape measure, tape wheel)
- Photographic equipment (e.g., 35-mm camera, Polaroid camera, video camera, digital camera, film, lenses, tripods)
- Tape recorder and cassettes
- Writing equipment (e.g., notebooks, pens, permanent markers)

### *Evidence Collection*

- Bags, new (e.g., sealable, nylon)
- Boxes, corrugated or fiberboard
- Brushes and brooms
- Cans, new (e.g. unlined)
- Evidence flags or cones
- Evidence placards
- Evidence tags
- Evidence sealing tape
- Gloves (i.e., disposable cotton, disposable latex)
- Grid markers
- Heat sealer
- Magnets
- Outerwear, protective (e.g., disposable suits, shoe covers)
- Rakes, spades, and shovels
- Sifters and/or screens
- Swabbing kits
- Trowels
- Vacuum

### *Specialized Equipment*

- Aerial survey and photography equipment (e.g., helicopter)
- Chemical test kits and vapor detectors
- Construction equipment, heavy
- GPS (global positioning system) equipment
- Ladders
- Trace-explosives detectors (e.g., sniffers) and/or detection canines

structure, in nearby vegetation, inside adjacent structures or vehicles, or embedded in adjacent structures. In the case of bombing incidents or incidents involving the explosion of tanks, appliances, or equipment, significant pieces of evidence debris may have pierced the bodies of victims or be contained in their clothing.

The clothing of anyone injured in an explosion should be obtained for examination and possible analysis. The investigator should ensure that photographs are taken of the injuries and that any material removed from a victim during medical treatment or surgery is preserved. This is true whether the person survives or not. Investigators should note the condition and position of any damaged and displaced structural components, such as walls, ceilings, floors, roofs, foundations, support columns, doors, windows, sidewalks, driveways, and patios. Investigators should also note the condition and position of any damaged and displaced building contents, such as furnishings, appliances, heating or cooking equipment, manufacturing equipment, victim's clothing, and personal effects. Investigators should note the condition and position of any damaged and displaced utility equipment, such as fuel gas meters and regulators, fuel gas piping and tanks, electrical boxes and meters, electrical conduits and conductors, heating-oil tanks, parts of explosive devices, or fuel vessels.

Investigators should identify, diagram, photograph, and note pieces of debris that indicate the direction and relative force of the explosion. They should keep in mind that the force necessary to shatter a wall is more than that necessary to merely dislodge or displace it and that the force necessary to shatter a window is less than that necessary to displace a wall but more than that necessary to blow out a window intact. The greater the force, the farther pieces of debris will be thrown from the epicenter.

Investigators should log, diagram, and photograph varying missile distances and directions of travel for similar debris, such as window glass. Larger, more massive missiles should be measured and weighed for comparison of the forces necessary to propel them. The distance as well as the direction of significant pieces of evidence from the apparent epicenter of the explosion may be critical. The location of all significant pieces should be completely documented on the explosion scene diagram, along with notes as to both distance and direction. This enables investigators to reconstruct the trajectories of various components.

## ANALYZING THE FUEL SOURCE

Once the origin, or epicenter, of the explosion has been identified, the investigator should determine what type of fuel was employed. This is done by comparing the nature and type of damage to the known available fuels at the scene.

The available fuel sources must be considered and eliminated until one fuel is identified as meeting all the physical damage criteria. For example, if the epicenter of the explosion is identified as a 6-foot crater of pulverized concrete in the center of the floor, escaping natural gas can be eliminated as the fuel. Chemical analysis of debris, soot, soil, or air samples can be helpful in identifying the fuel. For explosives or liquid fuels, gas chromatography, mass spectrography, or other chemical tests of properly collected samples may be able to identify their presence. (See Chapter 7, "The Crime Laboratory," for a detailed discussion of instrumental analysis).

Air samples taken in the vicinity of the area of origin can be used in identifying gases or the vapors of liquid fuels. For example, commercial "natural gas" is a mixture of methane, ethane, propane, nitrogen, and butane. The presence of ethane in an air sample may show that commercial natural gas was there rather than naturally occurring "swamp," "marsh," or "sewer" gas, which are all-methane.

Once a fuel is identified, the investigator should determine its source. For example, if the fuel is identified as a lighter-than-air gas and the structure is serviced by natural gas, the investigator should locate the source of gas that will most likely be at or below the epicenter, possibly a leaking service line or malfunctioning gas appliance. All gas piping—including that from the street mains or LP-gas storage tanks, up to and through the service regulator and meter, to and including all appliances—should be examined and leak-tested if possible.

Odorant verification should be part of any explosion investigation involving, or potentially involving, flammable gas, especially if there are indicators that no signs of leaking gas were detected by people present. Its presence should be verified.

# BOMB THREATS

Bomb threats are numerous and occur for a number of reasons. Since relatively few reported threats actually result in the finding of a bomb or explosive device, law enforcement officers may consider following the procedures discussed below.

## RESPONDING TO THREATS

### Telephone Call

There are generally several explanations for why someone would telephone to report that a bomb is about to go off in a particular location. First, the person may have definite knowledge or may believe that an explosive device has been or will be placed and may want to minimize the potential personal injury or property damage. Second, the caller may want to create an atmosphere of fear and/or panic, which will, in turn, possibly result in the disruption of normal activities.[45]

When a telephone bomb threat is made, the caller should be kept on the line as long as possible. The call should be taped or monitored on an extension telephone whenever possible. The person answering the call should determine the following:

- The time the call was received.
- The sex and age of the caller (on the basis of the caller's voice).
- Voice characteristics of the caller (such as accent, calm, stutter, giggling, stressed, disguised, slow, deep, nasal, sincere, crying, loud, angry, lisp, squeaky, slurred, broken, rapid, excited, normal).
- Background noises.

In addition, the person answering the call should ask questions designed to elicit:

- The location of the bomb.
- The caller's reason for placing the bomb.
- When the bomb is going to explode.
- What the bomb looks like.
- What kind of bomb it is.
- What will cause it to explode.
- Whether the caller placed the bomb.

### Evacuation

The decision to evacuate the premises should be made by the responsible party at the scene. If the responsible party decides to evacuate, law enforcement officers will generally recommend that the evacuation be completed, including all searchers, at least 15 minutes prior to the time designated by the suspect as the blast time and remain in effect for at least 15 minutes after the designated time. The officers should assist with the evacuation and crowd control if requested. If officers have reason to believe that an extreme emergency exists, they should take whatever action is necessary to save lives, including an order to evacuate the building.

### Industrial Plants, Shopping Centers, and the Like

When a bomb threat is reported at an industrial plant, office building, shopping center, or apartment complex, the assigned officer should contact the owner or manager of the scene and advise the responsible party that search procedures, evacuations, and so forth, are the responsibility of the building owner or person in charge. The law enforcement officer responding should request any specific equipment necessary (fire, utility, etc.). Employees of the business should be briefed on what to look for (e.g., unusual or out-of-place items) and cautioned that suspicious items should not be touched if located.

### Private Homes and Small Businesses

If it is necessary to search a private home or small business and there are no responsible persons present to do a search, officers should conduct the search themselves. Canine teams and/or bomb detail personnel may be contacted for assistance.

### Police and Public Safety Buildings

If a bomb threat is received against a police or public safety building by a civilian employee, the employee should refer the threats to a sworn officer and the chief of police should be notified. Usually, the chief will make arrangements to have a systematic search done of the facility. If a possible explosive device is located, the bomb detail should be notified and will then take charge.[46]

## SEARCHING FOR CONCEALED EXPLOSIVES

Search procedures should always stress measures for protecting life and property. To help detect anything suspicious or out of the ordinary, search procedures should include interviews with persons familiar with the buildings or structures to be searched. Such people include maintenance or security personnel, janitorial staff, and personnel in charge of specific areas. It is important to eliminate some areas in order to focus attention on others that are potentially more dangerous.[47] Search personnel must be cautioned not to move, jar, or touch any suspicious object.

In general, the following search techniques should be employed to ensure an orderly and systematic search: The suspected area should be cordoned off on all sides (by at least 300 feet, if possible). In multistory buildings, at least the floors directly above and below the suspected area should be evacuated. The doors and windows should be left open. All electrical equipment should be disconnected. However, the building's main power source should not be shut down. Entry and exit to the building should be controlled by management with police assistance. Traffic should be directed away from the scene. Radio and cellular-phone transmissions are prohibited in the area of a possible explosive device, that is, within 1,000 feet of a suspected area. Search team members should be selected from volunteer personnel who are most familiar with the building or area to be searched. Areas accessible to the general public should be searched first, unless there is reason to suspect some other location. Searchers should look for items that are foreign or out of place. The search area should be divided equally among search team personnel. A recommended technique is to stand still with eyes closed and listen for the sound of a mechanical timer. An attempt should be made to locate and determine the source of all noise. The search sweep should be systematic, left to right, ground to waist level, waist to eye level, and eye level to the highest level that can be searched. Each area should be marked and controlled upon completion of the search to avoid duplication and later contamination. Whenever a suspicious object is located, all search operations should be suspended within a radius of 300 feet. The object should be left untouched until the bomb technician determines that it is safe. (See photo below.)

## WHAT NOT TO DO

- Do not ignore bomb threats.
- Do not touch suspected explosives.
- Do not touch suspected bombs.
- Do not move suspected bombs.
- Do not move things if you do not know what they are.
- Do not open things if you do not know what they are.
- Do not place in water.
- Do not shake.
- Do not turn any suspicious objects.
- Do not cut wires.
- Do not pull wires.
- Do not cut any strings.
- Do not pull any fuses.
- Do not stamp out fuses.
- Do not undo glued packages.
- Do not pass metallic tools near suspected bomb.

### Bomb Squad Officers

Officer in a bomb suit preparing to respond to a bomb threat call. In searching a bomb threat site, searchers look for items that are foreign or out of place. If a suspicious object is located, all search operations should be suspended within a radius of 300 feet. The suspicious object should be observed but not touched until a trained bomb technician arrives and takes charge.

(Courtesy of Jack H. Adkins, Bomb Squad Commander, Big Bend Bomb Disposal Team, Tallahassee, Florida)

- Do not move switches.
- Do not release hooks.
- Do not smoke near suspected bombs.
- Do not carry the bomb outside.
- Do not carry the bomb, period.
- Do not place near heat.
- Do not place near vital equipment.
- Do not use insulating materials (bomb blankets or sandbags) unless you know how the bomb works.
- Do not move the bomb away from people—move the people away from the bomb.
- Do not get near bombs.
- Do not transmit on radios. Turn beepers and all other transmitters off.[48]

## POTENTIAL CONCEALMENT AREAS FOR BOMBS

### Buildings and Structures

- Elevator wells and shafts, including nooks, closets, false panels, walk areas, motors, cables, and so on.
- All ceiling areas.
- Rest rooms.
- Access doors.
- Crawl space in rest rooms and areas used as access to plumbing fixtures.
- Electrical fixtures.
- Utility and other closet areas.
- Space under stairwells.
- Boiler (furnace) rooms.
- Flammable storage areas.
- Main switches and valves.
- Indoor trash receptacles and covered ashtrays.
- Storage areas, including record-storage areas.
- Mailrooms.
- Ceiling lights with easily removable panels.
- Firehose racks and fire extinguishers.
- Basements.
- Around windows hidden by drapes or shades.
- Inside desks.
- Inside storage cabinets and containers.
- Under tables and chairs.

### Auditoriums and Theaters

- Under each seat and into cut seat cushions.
- Stage area.
- Microphones, cameras, and radios.
- Speaker platform.
- Crawlways.
- Tunnels.
- Trapdoors.
- Dressing rooms.
- Rest rooms.
- Storage areas.
- Ceilings.
- Props.
- Hanging decorations.
- Lighting fixtures.
- Sound system.
- Air-conditioning system.
- Roof.
- Heating system.
- Projection booths.
- Offices and personal articles.

### Outside Areas

- Street drainage systems.
- Manholes in street and sidewalk.
- Trash receptacles.
- Garbage cans.
- Dumpsters.
- Incinerators.
- Mailboxes.
- Parked cars, trucks, and carts and outside storage areas.[49]

## SUSPICIOUS PACKAGES AND LETTERS

It must be remembered that items do not have to be delivered by a carrier. Most bombers set and deliver the bombs themselves. The following are

Figure 18-4 Warning! Suspect Letter and Package Indicators

(**Source:** Courtesy U.S. Department of the Treasury, Bureau of Alcohol, Tobacco and Firearms)

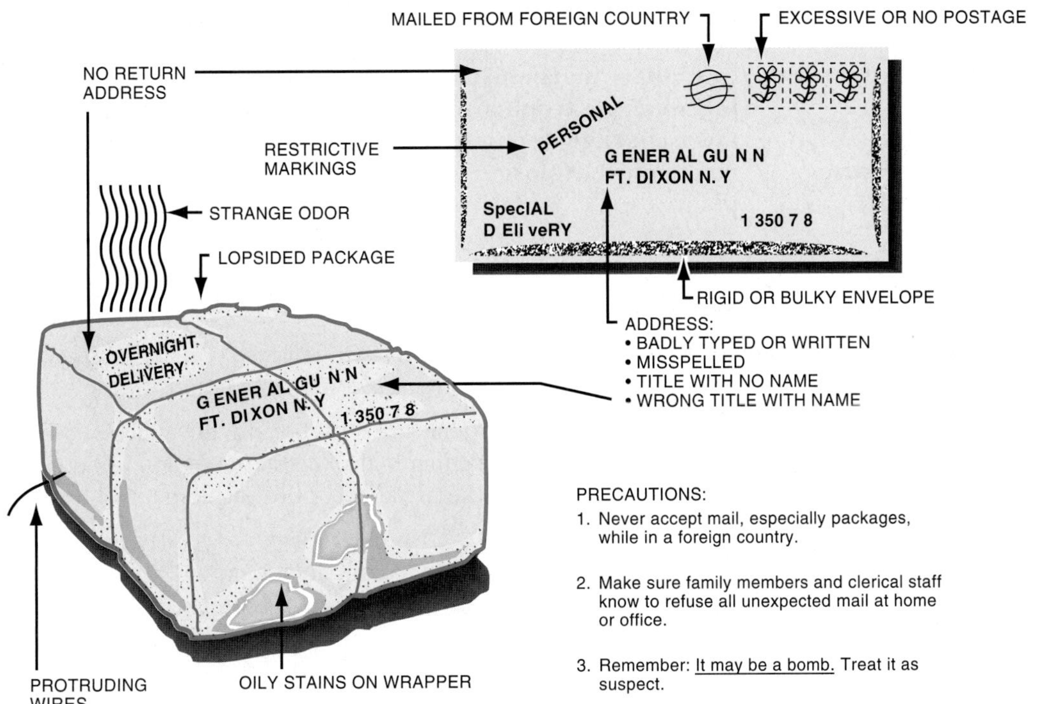


precautions that should be followed when encountering a suspicious package or letter:

- If delivered by carrier, inspect for lumps, bulges, or protrusions, without applying pressure.
- If delivered by carrier, balance-check to determine if it is lopsided or heavy-sided.
- If there is a handwritten address or label from a company, check to see if the company exists and if it sent the package or letter.[50]

Any of the following characteristics could denote a suspicious package or letter (see Figure 18–4):

- Packages wrapped in string, as modern packaging materials have eliminated the need for twine or string.
- Excess postage on small packages or letters, which indicates that the object was not weighed at a post office.
- Any foreign writing, address, or postage.
- Handwritten notes, such as "To Be Opened in the Privacy of . . .", "Confidential," "Your Lucky Day Is Here," and "Prize Enclosed."
- Improper spelling of common names, places, or titles.
- Generic or incorrect titles.
- Leaks, stains, or protuding wires, string, tape, and so on.
- Hand delivery or a "drop-off for a friend."
- No return address or a nonsensical return address.
- Delivery before or after a phone call from an unknown person asking if the item was received.[51]

## Key Terms

**accelerant**
**alligatoring**
**burn indicators**
**catalytic combustion detector**
**charring**
**chemical explosions**
**effective fire temperatures**
**explosion**
**flame ionization detector**
**gas liquid chromatograph (GLC)**
**incendiary mechanism**
**infrared spectrophotometer**
**layer-checking technique**
**mechanical explosions**
**plant**
**Property Insurance Loss Register (PILR)**
**pyromaniacs**
**spalling**
**spontaneous heating**
**spontaneous ignition**
**trailer**
**ultraviolet fluorescence**

## Review Questions

1. If arson is suspected, why should firefighters not disarrange the premises, such as by mopping up or overhauling the scene of the fire, especially at the point of origin?
2. What two factors are needed to cause a fire?
3. What is the layer-checking technique, and how can it assist in determining the cause and origin of a fire?
4. What are some of the more common causes of accidental or natural fires?
5. What types of burn indication can be examined by the arson investigator to assist in determining whether a fire is accidental or incendiary in nature?
6. What are some of the most commonly used ignition and timing devices in the commission of arsons?
7. Why can items missing from the fire scene be as valuable as things remaining at the scene?
8. What are some of the most common motives for arson?
9. What are the major characteristics of the child fire setter?
10. Why should uncoated metal paint cans (or similar containers), not plastic bags or containers, be used for the storage of material suspected of containing flammable liquids?
11. What are some of the advantages and disadvantages of olfactory detection in determining the presence of fire accelerants at the scene of a fire?
12. What types of individuals might be able to provide information relevant to the fire?
13. What is the purpose of the National Insurance Crime Bureau?
14. There are basically two types of explosions. What are they? Briefly describe each type.
15. What are the principal objectives of an explosion scene investigation?
16. What is the first duty of the investigator at the scene of an explosion?
17. Once the origin, or epicenter, of the explosion has been identified, the investigator should determine what type of fuel has been employed. How is this typically done?
18. In general, certain techniques should be employed to ensure an orderly and systematic search for explosive devices. What are they?

## Internet Activities

1. The Bureau of Alcohol, Tobacco and Firearms provides updates and statistics concerning arson and explosion incidents. Go the bureau's website at www.atf.treas.gov. Search the site for information on fire and explosion incidents for your state. The website also has information about arson and explosion training for police officers. What topics are covered in the training curriculum?
2. Many large police agencies and/or states have investigative units specializing in arson and bomb detection. Check several municipal and

state police agencies in your region by using websites such as www.officer.com and www.le-olinks.com. What are the functions and responsibilities of these units? Under what conditions do they respond (arson investigation, bomb threats, etc.)? Are any statistics provided concerning the number of cases they have responded to and/or investigated?

## Notes


1. This information was obtained from "Stop Arson Now," a brochure published by the Florida Advisory Committee on Arson Prevention.
2. K. D. Moll, *Arson, Vandalism, and Violence: Law Enforcement Problems Affecting Fire Departments* (Washington, DC: Government Printing Office, 1977), pp. 20–21.
3. C. W. Stickney, "Recognizing Where Arson Exists," *Fireman Magazine,* September–December 1960, p. 3.
4. *Touched Off by Human Hands,* 1979. This booklet was originally published by the Illinois Advisory Committee on Arson Prevention in cooperation with the Illinois Chapter of the International Association of Arson Investigation and was reprinted for distribution by the State Farm Fire and Casualty Company, Bloomington, Illinois. Much of the information in this section was taken from this source, pp. 7–11.
5. Stickney, "Recognizing Where Arson Exists," p. 4.
6. Ibid., p. 8.
7. Ibid.
8. C. W. Stickney, "Recognizing Where Arson Exists," *Fire and Arson Investigator,* October–December 1970; W. A. Derr, "Wildland Fire Investigation: Information from Objects," paper presented at the 18th Annual Fire and Arson Investigators Seminar, Palm Springs, California, June 14–18, 1971.
9. National Fire Protection Association *921 Guide for Fire and Explosion Investigations* (Quincy, MA: NFPA, 2001), pp. 921–27, 921-28.
10. Ibid., p. 921-33
11. Ibid., p. 921-33
12. Ibid., p. 921-29
13. National Fire Protection Association, *921 Guide for Fire and Explosion Investigations* (Quincy, MA: NFPA, 1992), pp. 921–942.
14. Ibid., pp. 921-30.
15. B. P. Battle and P. B. Weston, *Arson: A Handbook of Detection and Investigation* (New York: Arco, 1972), pp. 19–28. Much of the information in this section was taken with permission from this source.
16. C. L. Karchmer, M. E. Walsh, and J. Greenfield, *Enforcement Manual: Approaches for Combating Arson for Profit Schemes* (Washington, DC: U.S. Department of Justice, 1981), pp. 15–31. This discussion was adapted from this source.
17. B. S. Huron, *Elements of Arson Investigation* (New York: Reuben Donnelley, 1972), Chap. 1; Battle and Weston, *Arson: A Handbook of Detection and Investigation*, pp. 34–39.
18. J. A. Inciardi, "The Adult Firesetter, A Typology," *Criminology*, August 1970, pp. 145–155.
19. Anthony O. Rider, "The Firesetter—A Psychological Profile (Part 2)," *FBI Law Enforcement Bulletin*, July 1980, p. 12 (much of this discussion and accompanying references have been adapted with permission from this source, pp. 7–17); Nolan D. C. Lewis and Helen Yarnell, "Pathological Firesetting (Pyromania)," *Nervous and Mental Disease Monographs,* No. 82 (New York: Coolidge Foundation, 1951), pp. 228–242.
20. Louis H. Gold, "Psychiatric Profile of the Firesetter," *Journal of Forensic Science,* October 1962, p. 407; Lewis and Yarnell, "Pathological Firesetting," p. 118.
21. James C. Coleman et al., *Abnormal Psychology and Modern Life,* 6th ed. (Glenview, Ill.: Scott, Foresman & Co., 1980), p. 395.
22. Lewis and Yarnell, "Pathological Firesetting," pp. 376–377, 428.
23. E. B. Bates, *Elements of Fire and Arson Investigation* (Santa Cruz, CA: Davis, 1975), pp. 43–44.
24. Rider, "The Firesetter—A Psychological Profile," pp. 12–13.
25. Lewis and Yarnell, "Pathological Firesetting," pp. 286–287, 311–345.
26. Stickney, "Recognizing Where Arson Exists," 1960, pp. 11–12.
27. B. B. Caldwell, "The Examination of Exhibits in Suspected Arson Cases," *Royal Canadian Mounted Police Quarterly,* 1957, Vol. 22, pp. 103–108.
28. J. F. Bordeau, Q. Y. Kwan, W. E. Faragker, and G. C. Senault, *Arson and Arson Investigation*

(Washington, DC: Government Printing Office, 1974), pp. 77–83. Much of the information in this section was taken from this source.

29. J. D. Nicol, "Recovery of Flammable Liquids from a Burned Structure," *Fire Engineering*, 1961, Vol. 114, p. 550.
30. D. Q. Burd, "Detection of Traces of Combustible Fluids in Arson Cases," *Journal of Criminal Law, Criminology, and Police Science*, 1960, Vol. 51, pp. 263–264; P. Rajeswaran and P. L. Dirk, "Identification of Gasoline, Waves, Greases, and Asphalts by Evaporation Chromatography," *Microchemical Journal*, 1962, Vol. 6, pp. 21–29.
31. R. Milliard and C. Thomas, "The Combustible Gas Detector (Souffer), an Evaluation," *Fire and Arson Investigator*, January–March 1976, pp. 48–50.
32. D. M. Lucas, "The Identification of Petroleum Products in Forensic Science by Gas Chromatography," *Journal of Forensic Sciences*, 1960, Vol. 5, No. 2, pp. 236–243.
33. P. L. Kirk, *Fire Investigation* (New York: Wiley, 1969), pp. 43–44; E. C. Crocker and L. B. Sjostrom, "Odor Detection and Thresholds," *Chemical Engineering News*, 1949, Vol. 27, pp. 1922–1931; and H. Zwaardemaber, "Camera Inoorata," *Perfumery and Essential Oil Record*, 1921, Vol. 12, pp. 243–244.
34. P. L. Kirk, *Crime Investigation, Physical Evidence, and the Police Laboratory* (New York: Interscience, 1966), p. 717; H. P. Wonderling, "Arsonists—Their Methods and the Evidence," *International Association of Arson Investigators Newsletter*, October–December 1953, reprinted in *Selected Articles for Fire and Arson Investigators*, International Association of Arson Investigators, 1975; K. Ol'Khosvsbaya, "Colormetric Determination of Hydrocarbons, Gasoline, Kerosene and White Spent in the Air of Industrial Installations," *Gigiena Truda i Professional'nye Zabolevaniza*, 1971, Vol. 15, No. 11, pp. 57–58.
35. J. W. Girth, A. Jones, and T. A. Jones, "The Principle of Detection of Flammable Atmospheres by Catalytic Devices," *Combustion and Flame*, 1973, Vol. 21, pp. 303–312.
36. C. M. Lane, "Ultra-Violet Light . . . Gem or Junk," *Fire and Arson Investigator*, December 1975, Vol. 26, No. 2, pp. 40–42.
37. C. L. Karchmer, M. E. Walsh, and J. Greenfield, *Enforcement Manual: Approaches for Combating Arson for Profit Schemes* (Washington, DC: U.S. Department of Justice, 1981), pp. 249–252.
38. National Insurance Crime Bureau, *Fire Investigation Handbook* (Palos Hills, IL: NICB, 1995), pp. 24, 25.
39. The purpose of the National Insurance Crime Bureau is to investigate questionable insurance claims and cooperate with public law enforcement agencies in securing the prosecution of insurance criminals.
40. National Insurance Crime Bureau, *Fire Investigation Handbook*, p. 26.
41. John Barracato, *Burning: A Guide to Fire Investigation* (Stamford, CT: Aetna Casualty and Surety, 1986), pp. 14–16.
42. National Fire Protection Association, *Guide for Fire and Explosion Investigations*, pp. 921-94–921-100.
43. George Buck, *Preparing for Terrorism* (Albany, NY: Delmar, 1998), pp. xi–xii.
44. National Fire Protection Association, *Guide for Fire and Explosion Investigations*, 1992, pp. 921-103–921-107.
45. *Public Safety News*, December 1996, No. 34.
46. City of Phoenix Police Department, "Operations Order D-5, Explosives and Bomb Threat 495," p. 3.
47. Honolulu Police Department, "Procedure: Bomb Threat," Nov. 18, 1996.
48. Lesson plan prepared by the New Orleans Police Department, "Bombs and Hazardous Devices," Oct. 21, 1996, p. 8.
49. Ibid., p. 11. *Note:* Law enforcement and fire personnel should use the information in this chapter only within the framework of their training and departmental guidelines and policies. The departments having guidelines and police will always take precedence over the information discussed herein.
50. This checklist was provided by the U.S. Department of the Treasury, Bureau of Alcohol, Tobacco and Firearms, 1999.
51. Ibid.

# NINETEEN

# Recognition, Control, and Investigation of Drug Abuse

*Colombian drug kingpin Ochoa. The illegal drug industry is truly international in nature. The United States must often rely on foreign governments to assist in locating and apprehending drug fugitives. (© Reuters NewMedia Inc./Corbis)*

## CHAPTER OUTLINE



## CHAPTER OBJECTIVES

1. Identify and describe several opium-derived drugs.
2. List and describe synthetic narcotics.
3. Identify and distinguish among stimulants, depressants, and hallucinogens.
4. Outline techniques used in investigating dangerous drugs and narcotics.
5. Assess the motives, methods, and management of drug informants.
6. Describe the process of identifying and conducting raids on clandestine labs.
7. Explain the type of information necessary to establish probable cause and obtain search warrants.
8. Be familiar with drug evidence handling and potential security problems.

## INTRODUCTION

Currently, every major police department in the United States has assigned—with ample justification—a top priority to the control of drug abuse and related offenses. Most of the departments have narcotics or drug units that specialize in the identification, arrest, and prosecution of drug traffickers, ranging from low-level street dealers to leaders of organized-crime syndicates. As a result, many police agencies have allocated many resources for narcotics officers, undercover agents, drug surveillance and recovery equipment, and agreements with drug informants. The illegal importation, manufacture, sale, and use of drugs, however, have increased more rapidly than the resources for combating them.

Explanations for the phenomenal growth of drug abuse abound in the literature on this subject. Many cite variables associated with socioeconomic and political conditions. Others suggest that the inability of some individuals to deal with personal stress and emotional problems has led to the increase in drug abuse. Regardless of the contributing factors, police must deal with the violation itself, not the motivations and human conditions that produce it.

This chapter focuses on the categories of drugs that are most commonly encountered by law enforcement officers in their enforcement activities: opium-derived drugs, synthetic narcotics, stimulants, depressants, and hallucinogens. The procedures involved in narcotics investigations are also addressed. Most of the techniques used in investigating dangerous-drug and narcotics cases are the same as those used in investigating other cases. The identification of the source of the drug and the risk factors in apprehending a drug suspect, however, make investigations of these cases unique.

Another aspect of drug and narcotics cases that makes the investigation process atypical is the use of drug informants. Drug informants can provide valuable information on various types of drug activity, but compared with informants used in other investigations, they are perhaps the most difficult to manage. Drug informants have different motivations for helping the police, such as fear of punishment for criminal acts, revenge against their enemies, money, repentance, or altruism. Regardless of the motivation, informants who have entered into agreements with police agencies should initially be screened carefully and then, subsequently, be monitored. The chapter concludes with discussions on clandestine laboratories, search warrants, and evidence handling.

## THE OPIUM POPPY

Several drugs are derived from the opium poppy (Papaver somniferum). Known as **opiates,** they include opium, morphine, heroin, codeine, and other drugs less well known.

### OPIUM

One of the first drugs of abuse was **opium.** Its pleasurable effects were known to many ancient civilizations, including the Egyptians, as early as 1500 B.C. During the Renaissance in Europe, opium was employed in the treatment of hysteria, making it one of the early therapeutic agents in treating mental disorders.

In the seventeenth century, opium smoking spread throughout China, and opium dependence was recognized as a problem. Opium eating was known in the United States and England during the Revolutionary War. Opium was used by eighteenth-century doctors to treat venereal disease, cancer, gallstones, and diarrhea and to relieve pain at childbirth.

Opium comes from the poppy plant. Its pod is carefully cut to allow a milky white fluid to ooze onto the surface of the pod. There, after it air-dries into tan beads, it is carefully scraped by hand (see above photo) and allowed to further air-dry, after which it turns a blackish brown color. Raw opium has a pungent odor and may be smoked. The user appears sleepy and relaxed. Prolonged use creates both physical and psychological dependence. Raw opium is the source of morphine, heroin, and codeine.

**Traditional Method of Gathering Opium**
Historically, one of the first drugs to be abused was opium. Opium comes from the poppy plant. The poppy pod is cut to allow the milky, white fluid to come to the surface of the pod. After it is dried, it is hand scraped and allowed to be further air dried.
(Courtesy Drug Enforcement Administration)

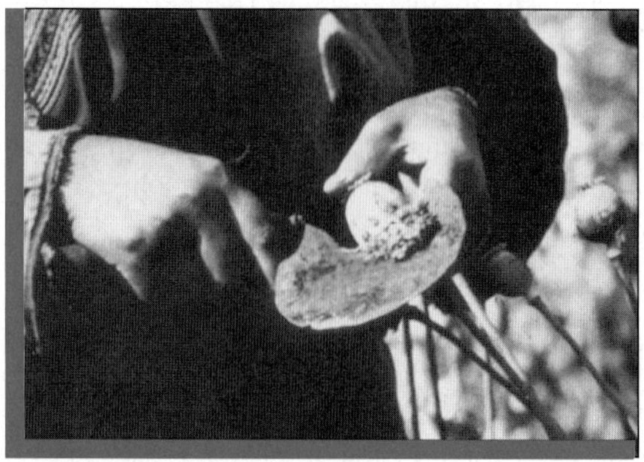

## MORPHINE

**Morphine** is obtained from raw opium; 10 pounds of raw opium yield 1 pound of morphine. A German named Sertürner first isolated the substance in 1804 and a few years later named it "morphine" after the Greek god of sleep, Morpheus. The drug was first used in medicine in 1825 as a painkiller and is still used as such today.

The use of morphine increased considerably with the invention of the hypodermic syringe by an Englishman around 1843. The hypodermic syringe was introduced into this country about 1853 and was used extensively for wounded Union troops during the American Civil War. Some developed physical and psychological dependence, for doctors did not clearly understand the addictive nature of opiates until around 1870.

Morphine appears in tablet, capsule, and liquid forms. It has no distinguishing color and provides the medical standards by which other narcotics are evaluated. Morphine is usually administered by injection. The drug creates both physical and psychological dependence in the user, who feels euphoric and seems sleepy or relaxed. The pupils of the eyes may constrict.[1]

## HEROIN (DIACETYLMORPHINE)

**Heroin** was developed in England in 1874, but it evoked little interest until about 1890, when it was found to be considerably stronger than morphine. Commercial production of heroin began in 1898 in Germany by the Bayer Company. Heroin was advertised as a cure for morphine dependence, but it was soon learned that heroin dependence was even more difficult to cure.

Heroin is an odorless, crystalline, white powder. It is usually sold in glassine paper packets, aluminum foil, or capsules. The darker the color, the more impurities it contains. Being about four to five times stronger than morphine, heroin is the principal drug of addiction among the opium derivatives. It is generally injected.

By the time the heroin reaches the addict, it often has been diluted considerably. Heroin reaching this country is perhaps 20 to 80 percent pure. (See Figure 19–1 and photo at right.) Deaths from overdoses are not uncommon and ordinarily occur because a dose was more pure than that to which the addict's body was accustomed. Addicts may also have a fatal allergic reaction to the drug or some substance used to "cut," or reduce, the purity level of the drug, such as powdered milk, sugar, or quinine. The fatal overdose is not always accidental. On occasion, addicts suspected of being police informers have been given "hot shots"—pure heroin—to eliminate them.

In addition to facing the perils of the law, withdrawal, and other aspects of addiction, the drug addict also faces the serious health problems associated with dirty needles. Many suffer venereal disease and serum hepatitis. Because both are transmitted diseases, those sharing needles with other drug abusers run the risk of injecting themselves with traces of blood from a disease carrier.[2] Drug users who administer their drugs through intravenous injections and share their needles with others face the additional danger of contracting the acquired immune deficiency syndrome (AIDS).

It should be noted that Colombia has become a major source of heroin production; the Drug Enforcement Administration (DEA) estimates that as much as 5 percent of the heroin in the United States comes from Colombia. Although this percentage may not seem to be high in comparison to the amount of heroin imported from other countries, it

### Heroin-filled Latex Balloons

In another method of smuggling heroin, couriers swallow heroin-filled latex balloons before boarding commercial airlines. Most heroin reaching the United States is 20 to 80 percent pure. It is smuggled into the United States in a variety of ways. The Drug Enforcement Administration (DEA) knows that much of the heroin entering the United States is produced in Colombia. Seizures of Colombian heroin by DEA have been 80 to 90 percent pure.
(Courtesy Drug Enforcement Administration)

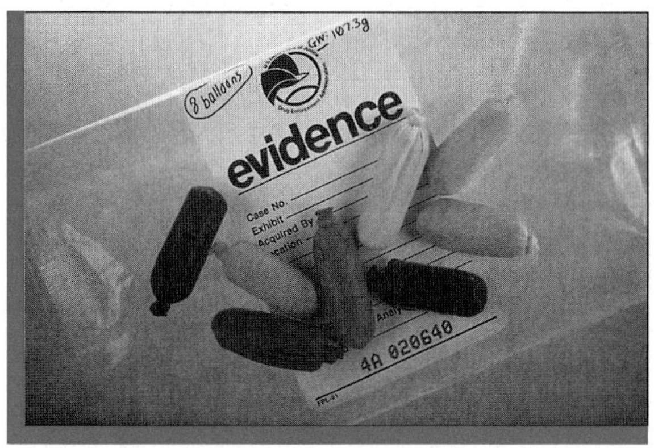

**Figure 19-1** Heroin-Trafficking Patterns

(**Source:** Bureau of Justice Statistics, U.S. Department of Justice.)

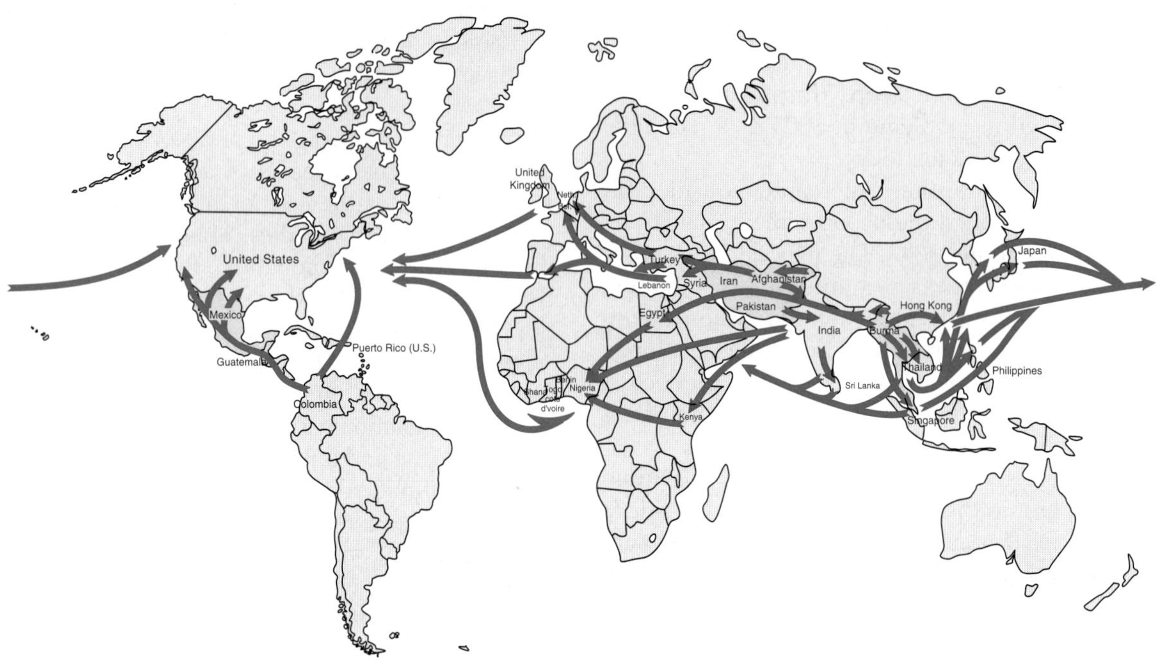


should be noted that the rate of importation has grown enormously since the early 1990s. Seizures of Colombian heroin by the DEA indicate that it is 80 to 99 percent pure. It is usually a light brown or tan powder. The poppies are being grown in the mountains of the Cauca Province around Popayan. It is anticipated that within the next several years Colombia will be the major source of heroin in the United States because the existing cocaine cartels have well-established routes from Colombia.

### CODEINE

The alkaloid **codeine** is found in raw opium in concentrations from 0.7 to 2.5 percent. It was first isolated in 1832 as an impurity in a batch of morphine. Compared to morphine, codeine produces less analgesia, sedation, and respiratory depression. It is widely distributed in products of two general types. Codeine to relieve moderate pain may consist of tablets or be combined with other products such as aspirin. Liquid codeine preparations for the relief of coughs (antitussives) include Robitussin AC, Cheracol, and terpin hydrate with codeine. Codeine is also manufactured in injectable form for pain relief.

### OTHER OPIUM DERIVATIVES

Other opium derivatives abused and stolen from pharmacies, hospitals, and physicians are Dilaudid, Papaverine, and Pantopon.

## SYNTHETIC NARCOTICS

**Synthetic narcotics,** though chemically related to the opium alkaloids, are produced entirely within the laboratory. A continuing search for a drug that kills pain but does not create tolerance and dependence has yet to yield a drug that is not susceptible to abuse. Two synthetic opiates are meperidine and methadone.

### MEPERIDINE (PETHIDINE)

The commercial name for **meperidine** is Demerol, and it was the first synthetic narcotic. Next to morphine, it is probably the most widely used drug for the relief of intense pain. It is available in pure form and in combination products. The drug is administered by mouth or by injection; the latter is the more common method of abuse.[3]

### METHADONE

**Methadone** is known by the commercial names Dolophine Hydrochloride and Methadone HCl Diskets. A heroin-dependent person can be treated with doses of methadone as a replacement for heroin. Methadone is manufactured in a solid form and administered orally. Methadone is a "maintenance drug." The drug is used to maintain a heroin addict at a stable level of opiate use and to remove the addict from the incidental dangers of heroin use.

The beneficial properties of methadone are that it is longer acting than most opiates and addicts do not build up tolerance. Also, oral administration is less potentially hazardous than injection, since it significantly reduces the addict's risk for diseases such as hepatitis and AIDS. As a rule of thumb, it takes about three weeks on methadone before a heroin addict completes the withdrawal stage and moves to the maintenance stage. However, it must be noted that the simultaneous use of methadone and heroin will not totally negate the physiological effect of the heroin on the user.

There is considerable controversy over the adoption of methadone maintenance programs. Critics argue that drug dependence is not cured. Proponents argue that it presents a cheaper way of supporting drug dependence and gets abusers out of crime and back to a conventional life. Proponents recognize that the programs need to include appropriate psychiatric help for overcoming the psychological dependence.[4]

## RECOGNIZING AN ADDICT

Drug abuse often falls into one of four categories: experimental, recreational, circumstantial, and compulsive or addictive.[5] The following list may be useful in identifying an individual who is addicted to natural or synthetic opiates:[6]

- The possession of addicting drugs without adequate medical explanation.
- A tendency on the part of the suspect to hide or conceal these drugs.
- The presence of needle marks in the form of black or blue spots resembling tattooing.
- The presence of elongated scars over the veins, especially those of the forearms and lower legs.
- The presence of boil-like abscesses over the veins or near where veins approach the surface.
- An appearance of drowsiness, sleepiness, or lethargy, especially if accompanied by a tendency to scratch the body, which sometimes indicates a slight overdose.
- Wide fluctuations in the size of the pupils of the eyes, with maximum constriction immediately after the suspect takes an injection.
- Possession of equipment for smoking opium.
- A tendency to wear long sleeves or other concealing clothing, even in hot weather, to cover needle marks.
- A tendency for the suspect to isolate himself or herself at regular intervals in order to take hypodermic injections.
- An obvious discrepancy between the amount of money the suspect earns and the amount he or she spends.
- The tendency of a person who has previously been reliable to resort to thievery, embezzlement, forgery, prostitution, and so forth.
- The tendency to develop withdrawal symptoms. The withdrawal symptoms from the denial of opium-derived drugs and synthetic opiates are quite similar: nervousness, anxiety, and sleeplessness; yawning, running eyes and nose, hoarseness, and perspiring; enlargement of the pupils of the eyes, goose flesh, muscle twitching; severe aches of the back and legs; hot and cold flashes; vomiting, diarrhea, and stomach cramps; increase in breathing rate, blood pressure, and body temperature; a feeling of desperation and an obsessive desire to secure more of the drug.
- Typically, the onset of symptoms occurs about 8 to 12 hours after the last dose. Symptoms increase for 72 hours, gradually diminish over

the next 5 to 10 days, and usually disappear entirely within 10 to 14 days; weakness, insomnia, nervousness, and muscle aches may persist for weeks.

## STIMULANTS

Drugs falling into the **stimulants** group directly stimulate the central nervous system, producing excitation, alertness, wakefulness, and, in some cases, a temporary rise in blood pressure and respiration rate. The major stimulants abused are cocaine, amphetamines, phenmetrazine, and methylphenidate. The effects of an overdose are agitation, increase in body temperature, hallucinations, convulsions, and possibly death. The withdrawal symptoms are apathy, long periods of sleep, irritability, depression, and disorientation.[7]

### COCAINE

**Cocaine** is a naturally occurring stimulant that is extracted from the leaves of the coca plant (Erythroxylon coca). The leaves of this western South American shrub have been chewed by Colombian, Bolivian, and Peruvian Indians since antiquity for religious, medicinal, and other reasons. Allegedly, the chewing of coca leaves has enabled the Indians to work in high altitudes and on inadequate diets. The chewing of the coca leaf, which continues to the present day, should not be confused with the use of the extracted drug, cocaine (see Figure 19–2). Coca leaves contain only about ½ to 1 percent cocaine; the cocaine contained within them is released more slowly, and the route of administration (oral) is different from that in most cocaine use.[8]

Because reports of native coca use generated considerable interest in Europe, efforts were made in the nineteenth century to isolate the purified psychoactive ingredient in coca leaves. When success was achieved in the 1880s, cocaine's potential value as a tonic, its general stimulant properties, its possible value for specific ailments, and its local anesthetic properties were explored. Its use as an anesthetic was particularly important because it could be used in eye surgery, for which no previous drug had been suitable. Cocaine also constricted blood vessels and limited bleeding in an anesthetized area. This property made it valuable for surgery of the nose and throat, areas that are richly supplied with blood. Although many of cocaine's uses as a therapeutic drug have been abandoned, it continues to be used as a local anesthetic.

Illicit cocaine is sold as a white, translucent, crystalline powder, frequently adulterated to about half its volume. The most common adulterants are sugars (especially lactose and glucose) and local anesthetics (Lidocaine, Procaine, and Tetracaine) similar in appearance and taste to cocaine. Amphetamines, other drugs with stimulant properties, are also used. Given the high cost of the drug, the temptation to adulterate at each level of sale is great (see photo below). The combination of high price and the exotic properties attributed to it have contributed to cocaine's street reputation as the status drug.

#### How Is It Used?

Cocaine is most commonly inhaled, or snorted, through the nose. It is deposited on the mucous linings of the nose, from which it is readily absorbed into the bloodstream. Repeated use often results in irritation to the nostrils and nasal mucous membranes. Symptoms may resemble those of a

**Powdered Cocaine**

Cocaine is a naturally occurring stimulant that is extracted from the leaves of coca plants. Illicit cocaine is sold as a white, translucent, crystalline powder. This powder is often adultered to about half its volume with sugars such as lactose or glucose. Given the high cost of the drug, it is often adultered at each level of sale by the drug dealers.

(Courtesy Drug Enforcement Administration)

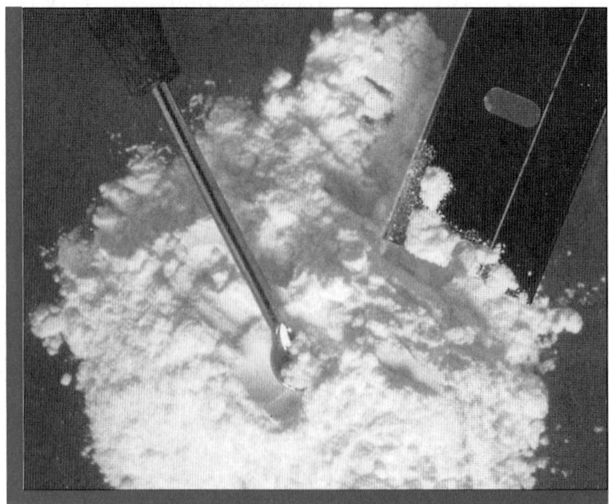

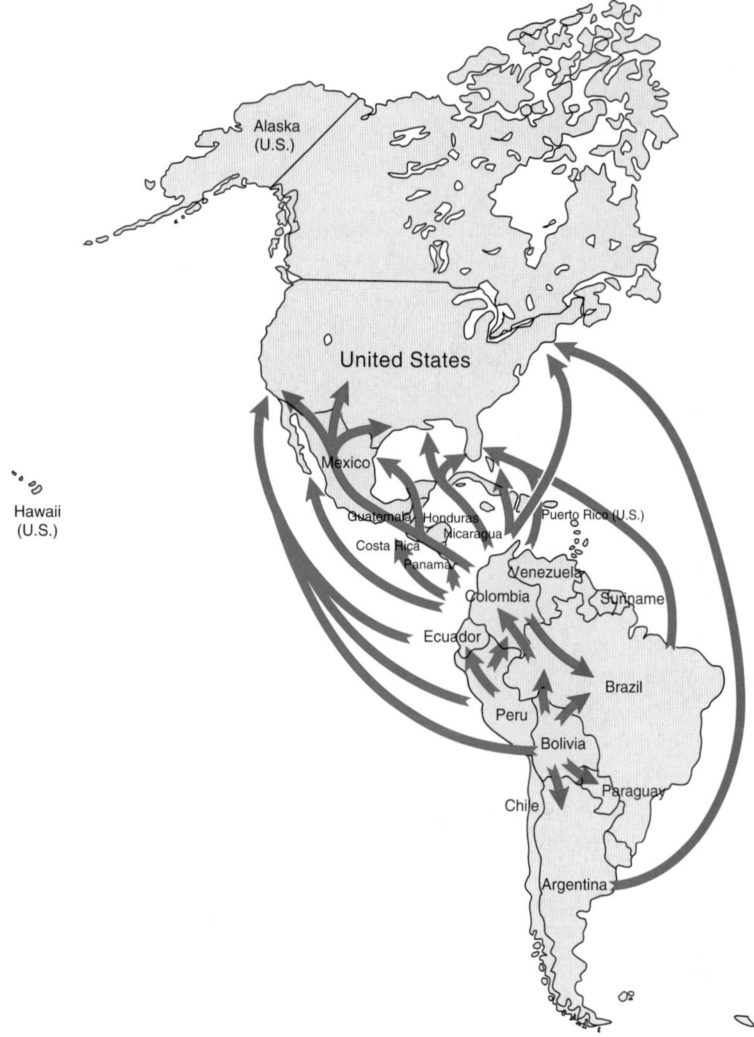


**Figure 19-2**

**Cocaine-Trafficking Patterns**

(**Source:** Bureau of Justice Statistics, U.S. Department of Justice.)

common cold, that is, congestion or a runny nose. Users therefore often resort to cold remedies, such as nasal sprays, to relieve their chronic nasal congestion. They may be unable to breathe comfortably without habitually using a spray.

A less common route of administration for cocaine is intravenous injection. The solution injected may be cocaine or a combination of heroin and cocaine. This route of administration carries the dangers of any intravenous use. Furthermore, intravenous injection introduces unknown quantities of cocaine or cocaine and heroin directly and suddenly into the bloodstream, leaving body organs wholly unprotected from the toxic effects of the drug. Cocaine deaths from intravenous injection are more numerous than from snorting, despite the greater prevalence of the latter method.

## Acute and Chronic Effects

Cocaine, like other drugs of abuse, has both fascinated and repelled people throughout history. It is little wonder, then, that a bewildering array of "effects," which may have little to do with the pharmacological action of the drug itself, have been attributed to it. Reassertion of often-repeated fictions does not, however, make them well-verified facts. Our need for certainty is not necessarily matched by equally adequate evidence to allay our doubts. Unfortunately, a lack of adequate information is sometimes interpreted as indicating that a drug is "safe" when it would be more accurate to admit that our knowledge is simply inadequate to specify the parameters of risk. Moreover, a substance that poses few hazards when used under conditions of relatively infrequent, low dosage may present quite a different picture when widely available and regularly used in larger amounts.

An important verified effect, when used medically, is cocaine's local anesthetic action as well as its ability to constrict blood vessels in the area to which it is applied. One consequence of this property when cocaine is used illicitly and snorted repeatedly is a tendency to cause a chronic inflammation of the nasal membranes, ulceration, and local tissue death. While perforation of the nasal septum (the wall dividing the two halves of the nose) is often mentioned, it is noteworthy that in the United States, at least, this consequence appears to be rare.

There is good evidence that cocaine in moderate doses (10 to 25 milligrams intravenously and 100 milligrams intranasally) significantly increases both heart rate and blood pressure. Increases following lower doses occur more rapidly when the drug is administered directly into the vein rather than when snorted. Heart rate increases from about 30 to 50 percent above normal nondrug levels. Increases in blood pressure when the heart is in its contracting phase (systolic pressure) are on the order of 10 to 15 percent.

In addition to the street reputation of the drug and historical accounts, even under conditions of carefully controlled laboratory administration, a sense of well-being—euphoria— subjectively characterizes cocaine use. Interestingly enough, however, when the drug is administered intravenously under laboratory conditions, the subjective effects are not easily distinguished from those of amphetamines (synthetic stimulants having more prolonged activity). A feeling of calmness and relaxation is described by most of the subjects who have participated in controlled laboratory studies; they also report diminished appetite. The observed and reported effects of several laboratory studies are generally consistent with accounts based on street use. However, there is much street lore and some clinical evidence emphasizing other effects that have not been systematically verified by controlled experimentation.

Clinical reports dating back to the 1800s have described a range of responses to heavier, more prolonged use of cocaine. Early reports by Freud and others also emphasized that there was wide individual variation in physiological and psychological responses to cocaine. Von Fleischl, who was encouraged to use cocaine by Freud to alleviate symptoms of nerve pain, rapidly progressed to heavy intravenous use (up to a gram per day). With heavier use, Fleischl's condition deteriorated into chronic intoxication, characterized by hallucinations of white snakes and insects creeping over and under his skin. A cocaine psychosis similar to paranoid schizophrenia has been described in the scientific literature. Tactile hallucinations similar to those experienced by Fleischl are a common aspect of this disorder. The hallucinations have been described as so real to the victims that they injure their skin in an attempt to remove the imagined parasites. Other paranoid delusions include fear of imaginary police and the belief that one is being watched.

## Cocaine Fatality

There is little question that cocaine can kill. By 1891 some 13 deaths had been attributed to the drug, and in 1924 a report was published of 26 cocaine deaths. These deaths were results of medical errors. They were virtually always rapid in onset and characterized by respiratory depression and cardiovascular collapse. In recent years, an increasing number of cocaine-related deaths among individuals who had snorted the substance have been reported. These deaths would seem to dispel the street wisdom and myth that snorting is completely safe.

## Freebasing

The practice of freebasing cocaine involves the dissolving of cocaine in a base solution, usually distilled water and calcium carbonate or lactose. The mixture is then shaken so that cocaine is dissolved completely. Several drops of ether are then added, and the mixture is shaken again. The cocaine is attracted to the ether, while the other additives are attracted to the base solution.

The ether-cocaine solution separates from the base (like oil and water), with the ether rising to the surface. An eyedropper is commonly used to suction off the ether-cocaine solution, which is then placed on an evaporating dish or crucible and allowed to evaporate naturally. This process can be accelerated by the use of a flame; however, this practice is extremely dangerous since the ether is highly flammable.

The cocaine crystals are then scraped off the dish with a metal spatula, placed in a glass pipe or bong (water pipe), and smoked.

The resultant high is alleged to be greater than that from simple snorting, although users remark that injection of the drug provides a more intense high than does freebasing.

The pleasant effects of freebasing begin to decrease in duration as usage increases, and users display changes in moods and irritability if a high cannot be maintained. As freebasing usage becomes chronic, a person can experience the same symptoms as a chronic nonfreebasing abuser of cocaine.

## Rock Cocaine (Crack)

A relatively inexpensive form of cocaine called **rock cocaine** or **crack** has grown tremendously in popularity among cocaine users (see photo at right). The drug is made by mixing ordinary cocaine with baking soda and water and heating the solution in a pot. The material, which is somewhat purer and more concentrated than regular cocaine, is dried and broken into tiny chunks that dealers sell as crack rocks. These little pellets are usually smoked in glass pipes and are frequently sold in tiny plastic vials. Rock cocaine is 5 to 10 times more potent than powdered cocaine; the high lasts about 5 minutes and leaves the user wanting more. According to mental health specialists, crack users are more likely to show serious psychiatric consequences, including intense paranoia, extreme depression, and often suicidal and even violent behavior. Part of the attraction to the dealer is the enormous profit that can be made by the sale of crack. For example, in Los Angeles an ounce of cocaine can sell for $1,000 to $1,500. Since each ounce contains 28 grams and each gram can produce up to six rocks selling for $25 each, the dealer can realize a profit of around $2,700.

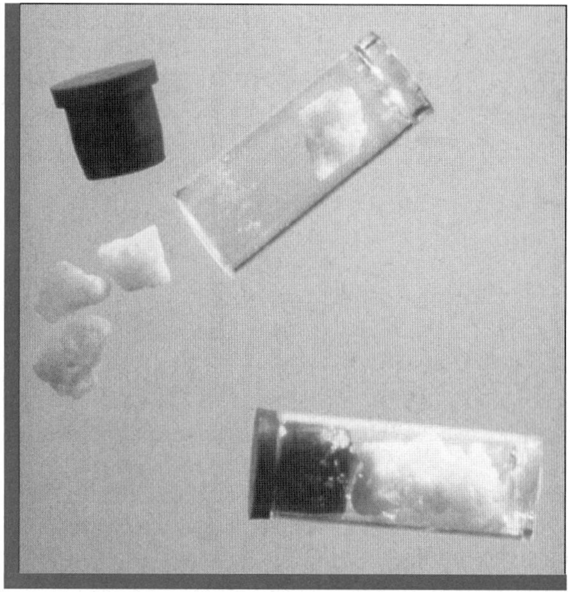

**Rock Cocaine/Crack**

Crack, the smokable form of cocaine, provides an immediate "rush." This form of cocaine is relatively inexpensive and very popular among cocaine users. The drug is made primarily by mixing ordinary baking powder and water and heating the solution in a pot. The resulting crack rocks are purer and more concentrated than regular cocaine.

(Courtesy Drug Enforcement Administration)

## Profiling and Tracing Cocaine

The prosecution of cocaine conspiracy cases—usually among the most difficult criminal cases to prove—can be made much easier if samples from several street-level dealers can be traced back to a single source. This task, no small feat in itself, is now more readily achieved, thanks to a sophisticated technique known as chromatographic impurity signature profile analysis (CISPA), developed by the North Carolina State Bureau of Investigation (SBI).[9]

Suspects in cocaine conspiracy cases are usually linked through telephone toll-call records, hotel receipts, surveillance of suspects, and coconspirator testimony. One of the nagging problems in drug enforcement has been the lack of a technique to match cocaine samples believed to have originated from the same source. Quite often, those at the top levels of a cocaine distribution ring are insulated from street-level dealing by several layers of intermediate buyers and sellers. Without proof that cocaine samples found in several different places all came from the same original source, it was very difficult to prosecute the heads of these rings.

The problem of cocaine analysis was made exasperatingly complex by the nature of cocaine distribution. Although large amounts of the drug may be imported in single batches, the lower-level dealers almost invariably adulterate, or "cut," the cocaine before resale (see photo on page 706). This is accomplished manually, by adding materials ranging from vitamin $B_{12}$ to Italian baby laxative. Because lower-level dealers do this on their own, the resulting street cocaine is composed of the original source cocaine plus whatever "cut" is added. Thus,

### Kilo Packages of Cocaine

Kilo packages of cocaine confiscated by the Drug Enforcement Administration from a warehouse in Guatemala. While cocaine may be smuggled into the United States in single batches, lower-level drug dealers usually adulterate or "cut" the cocaine before resale. This cutting of the drug means that enormous profits can be gained at each level of the sale.

(Courtesy Drug Enforcement Administration)

although the cocaine from several street-level dealers may have originated in the same source batch, the composition of each dealer's supply is different due to each dealer's manual dilution of his or her personal stock.

The processing of certain types of forensic evidence, such as drugs, is typically accomplished by visually comparing chromatographic signature patterns of the trace evidence with the signature pattern of a known reference. Because of the widely varying quantities and types of cut used with cocaine, this was both time consuming and inaccurate.

The challenge of CISPA, therefore, was to develop a system that could "see through" the adulterants and still distinguish between source groups of cocaine with a high degree of accuracy. The key to doing this is identifying impurities created during the original cocaine manufacturing process, as opposed to impurities added later as adulterants.

Because of the imprecise nature of the clandestine labs producing cocaine, the impurities created during manufacture vary too much between samples to provide for accurate identification even between samples manufactured using the same technique. The addition of other substances as cuts later on does not change the impurity signature of the underlying cocaine, which can still be identified as belonging to the same source batch.

Even knowing this, however, the job was far from done. Before impurity analysis could begin, the North Carolina SBI's forensic laboratory had to develop a reference signature of cocaine against which impurities could be measured. To learn more about the nature of cocaine, an SBI forensic chemist synthesized pure cocaine in the laboratory and developed a reference signature for it.

The chemist then spent several months synthesizing pure forms of 16 different impurities created by the various processes for cocaine manufacture and refinement. Once the impurities were identified, analyzed, and cataloged, it was possible to distinguish between source groups of cocaine by identifying both the type and quantity of individual impurities in each sample.

However, the visual comparison of samples remained very time consuming. The volume of cocaine imported into the country meant that the system needed to be able to pick out an original source from hundreds or even thousands of possible batches—and do so with almost no chance of error.

Cutting-edge computer technology and the Automated Fingerprint Identification System (AFIS) provided the answer. SBI chemists now had a good profile of pure cocaine and the impurities that could differentiate between batches, but they needed a means of rapidly identifying the batch.

Since a cocaine signature is in many ways analogous to a fingerprint, in that it is a unique pattern that can be digitized and stored in a computer, the AFIS system provided a good model. However, AFIS requires a large mainframe computer and many support systems, and the funds were simply not available for a similar system for CISPA. Working with the Research Triangle Institute, the SBI developed a lower-cost system using one of the newest techniques in artificial intelligence: neural networks.

Neural nets are interlocked computing nodes that have the capability of "learning" to recognize patterns. Once the network learns a pattern, it has no problem identifying other patterns as being either similar or dissimilar to the known pattern. It can also identify a pattern as being similar to a certain degree, represented as a percent figure. This allows a human operator to analyze only those patterns most similar to the sample in question, vastly cutting down on search time and costs.

CISPA, which was developed with the help of a $127,000 Federal Drug Control and System Improvement grant, has been used by local law enforcement agencies and prosecutors hundreds of times since it was developed. The speed and accuracy of CISPA allows it to be used on cases ranging from major distribution rings to the street-level dealer who denies that the 1-gram vial in his pocket came from the same source as the 1-ounce bag found in the street next to him.

Using the combination of "wet chemistry" in the lab and the world's newest computer techniques, the North Carolina SBI and the Research Institute have provided a significant and promising breakthrough in linking—and successfully prosecuting—cocaine distribution rings.

## AMPHETAMINES

Amphetamine, dextroamphetamine, and methamphetamine are so closely related chemically that they can be differentiated from one another only in the laboratory.[10] These compounds resemble the natural body hormones of epinephrine and norepinephrine. As a result of this similarity, they can act directly, by mimicking the natural hormones in their effects on nerve endings, and/or indirectly, by causing increased release of the natural hormones. In either case, the **amphetamines** stimulate certain areas of the nervous system that control blood pressure, heart rate, and respiratory and metabolic rates, all of which are increased. Appetite is markedly decreased, and the senses are hyperalert. The body is in a general state of stress, as if it were extremely threatened or expecting a violent fight. This group of drugs artificially intensifies and prolongs such stimulation, keeping the body in a state of tension for prolonged periods of time.[11] Many different classes of people employ amphetamines in abusive quantities, including middle-aged businesspeople, housewives, students, athletes, and truck drivers. Government studies indicate that young people are the greatest abusers. Drivers take them to stay awake on long trips; students take them while cramming for exams; and athletes take them for extra energy and stamina.[12] When the drug is prescribed, the dose frequently ranges between 2.5 and 15 milligrams per day. Abusers have been known to inject as much as 1,000 milligrams every 2 or 3 hours. Medical use of amphetamines is now limited to control of narcolepsy, appetite control, and control of hyperactivity in children.

## PHENMETRAZINE (PRELUDIN), METHYLPHENIDATE (RITALIN), AND PEMOLINE (CYLERT)

**Phenmetrazine** is related chemically to the amphetamines, and its abuse produces similar effects. Like phenmetrazine, methylphenidate is related chemically to amphetamines. It is prescribed for treatment of mild depression in adults and attention deficit disorder in children. Pemoline, like amphetamines, is a stimulant. It was developed early in 1975 and was approved for marketing as a drug to be used in the treatment of hyperactive children.

**Amphetamines**

Amphetamines stimulate areas of the central nervous system that control blood pressure, heart rate, and respiratory and metabolic rates, all of which are increased with the use of amphetamines. Many different classes of people take amphetamines in abusive quantities. Some studies indicate that young people are the greatest abusers of this drug.
(© Bonnie Kamin)

## CRYSTALLIZED METHAMPHETAMINE

"**Crystallized" methamphetamine,** better known as "crystal meth" and "speed" during the 1960s and 1970s, was originally taken as pills or injected. A new, smokable version, known as "ice," has now appeared on the drug market (see photo at right). In Hawaii, where ice first appeared in 1989, it was sold in $50 cellophane packets that contained about ⅒ gram, good for one or two smokes. Ice owes its special appeal to several factors:

- A puff of crack cocaine buoys its user for approximately 20 minutes, but the high from smoking ice endures for 12 to 24 hours. It does, however, share crack's addictive properties, and it produces similar bouts of severe depression and paranoia as well as convulsions.
- Ice can be manufactured in clandestine speed labs, whereas cocaine must be extracted from the leaf of the coca plant, refined, and imported by smugglers at considerable risk.
- Because it is odorless, ice can be smoked in public virtually without detection.

In its solid form the drug resembles rock candy or a chip of ice. When lighted in a glass pipe, the crystals turn to liquid and produce a potent vapor that enters the bloodstream directly through the lungs. Ice reverts to its solid state when it cools, thus becoming reusable and highly transportable.[13]

Ice has already become the number-one drug problem in Hawaii, where it is smuggled in from illegal labs in South Korea and the Philippines. Methamphetamine produced in California, Oregon, and Texas is making serious inroads across the United States. Drug enforcement officers have concluded that if an effort to stop the cocaine flow from Latin America makes crack hard to get, users will simply shift to easily available speed.[14]

**Drug "Ice"**

Crystallized methamphetamine, better known as "speed," was originally taken as a pill or injected. A newer, smokable version known as "ice" has arrived on today's drug market. In its solid form, ice resembles rock candy. Because it is odorless, ice can be smoked in public virtually without detection.

(© Bonnie Kamin)

## METHCATHINONE

**Methcathinone,** called "cat" or "goob," is a psychomotor stimulant with a chemical structure similar to methamphetamine.[15] Originally patented in Germany in 1928 and later used in the Soviet Union in the late 1930s and 1940s for the treatment of depression, methcathinone was all but unknown in the United States until 1957, when an American pharmaceutical firm received a patent for it and began animal studies to determine its potential as an appetite suppressant.

Because initial testing revealed that methcathinone was approximately one and a half times as potent as methamphetamine, clinical trials were never initiated and testing was discontinued. The formula for methcathinone languished in the archives of the pharmaceutical firm until 1989, when it was rediscovered and "liberated" by a college intern working for the firm. He shared the formula, and in 1990 a close friend set up a clandestine laboratory on the campus of Northern Michigan University (NMU) and attempted to develop a market for cat.

Although cat use did not take hold among the students at NMU, it rapidly found acceptance among the local population of Michigan's upper peninsula (UP). The relative ease with which cat is manufactured made it readily available, and its use and abuse rapidly spread throughout the UP and northern Wisconsin.

Methcathinone first came to the attention of law enforcement in the winter of 1990, when the Michigan State Police in the UP purchased a sample of what was purported to be a "new" drug more powerful than crack. The substance was analyzed to be methcathinone, closely related to but more powerful than methamphetamine. In January 1991, the Michigan State Police seized the first clandestine methcathinone lab ever discovered in the United States in a college dormitory room in Marquette, Michigan. Six months later, the DEA seized a methcathinone lab in Ann Arbor, Michigan. However, much to the surprise of law enforcement authorities, methcathinone was not a controlled substance under either Michigan state law or federal statute.

Since that time, 33 cat laboratories have been seized in Michigan, Wisconsin, Indiana, Illinois, and Colorado. Cat samples have been purchased or seized in several other states, including Illinois, Missouri, and Washington.

On May 1, 1992, under the DEA's emergency scheduling authority, methcathinone was placed in Schedule 1 of the Controlled Substances Act. After a scientific and medical evaluation, this classification was made permanent on October 7, 1993.

The effects of methcathinone on the human body are very similar to those of methamphetamine. Cat is reported by users to induce feelings of omnipotence and euphoria, marked by increased energy. Other reported effects include relief from fatigue, increased self-assurance, acute alertness, hyperactivity, talkativeness, a sense of invincibility, confidence, and increased sexual stimulation.

Cat is usually a white or off-white powdered substance, very similar in appearance to methamphetamine. It is usually sold in gram quantities for $75 to $100 and snorted in lines ranging from 1/10 to 1/4 of a gram. Because cat is usually sold in pure form, it reportedly can produce an immediate "rush," with a high that lasts 4 to 6 hours or more. There is typically a delay of 1 to 2 hours between dosages.

Users rapidly develop a tolerance for cat, requiring them to use larger amounts more frequently. Because cat destroys the sinus membranes, causing chronic nosebleeds and sinusitis, users may eventually resort to intravenous injection or oral ingestion.

Chronic cat use is characterized by binging. Addicts often go for up to eight days without sleep—eating very little, if at all—until they finally collapse. The onset of the "crash" occurs 4 to 6 hours after the last instance of use. Users often sleep for several days before beginning the cycle again.

Undesirable side effects reported by users include loss of appetite, weight loss, dehydration, stomachaches, profuse sweating, temporary blindness, deterioration of the nasal membranes, dry mouth, and an increased heart rate. Other side effects include anxiety, nervousness, depression, and hallucinations. The most consistently reported side effect—one with a serious implication for law enforcement officers—is extreme paranoia. In one case a cat abuser killed himself when he thought he was about to be arrested.

Symptoms of methcathinone intoxication can include profuse sweating, sweaty palms, increased heart rate, restlessness, increased body temperature, and uncontrollable shaking. Officers encountering suspected cat users should be particularly aware of withdrawal symptoms, which include irritability and argumentativeness. Other withdrawal symptoms include convulsions, hallucinations, and severe depression.

## DEPRESSANTS (SEDATIVES)

**Depressants** or **sedatives** depress the central nervous system and are prescribed in small doses to reduce restlessness and emotional tension and to induce sleep. The drugs most frequently abused are **barbiturates,** glutethimide, methaqualone, and meprobamate. Chronic use produces slurring of speech, staggering, loss of balance and falling, faulty judgment, quick temper, and quarrelsomeness. Overdoses, particularly in conjunction with alcohol, result in unconsciousness and death unless proper medical treatment is administered. Therapeutic doses cause minimal amounts of psychological dependence; chronic excessive doses result in both physical and psychological dependence. Abrupt withdrawal, particularly from barbiturates, can produce convulsions and death. Barbiturates are frequently nicknamed after the color of the capsule or tablet or the name of the manufacturer. The barbiturates most frequently abused are secobarbital and amobarbital.[16] These are among the short- and intermediate-acting barbiturates. The onset time is from 15 to 40 minutes, and the effects last for up to 6 hours.

## GLUTETHIMIDE (DORIDEN)

When introduced in 1954, **glutethimide** was wrongly believed to be a nonaddictive barbiturate substitute. The sedative effects of glutethimide begin about 30 minutes after oral administration and last 4 to 8 hours. Because the effects of this drug last for a long time, it is exceptionally difficult to reverse overdoses, and many result in death.

Glutethimide used with 16-milligram codeine tablets is one of the most popular pill combinations on the black market today. This combination gives a heroinlike effect and is known as "dors and 4's" or "D's and C's." It is commonly taken by oral ingestion.

## METHAQUALONE

**Methaqualone** was at one time very popular in the United States but has since been removed from the market. The drug was widely abused because it was mistakenly thought to be safe and nonaddictive and to have aphrodisiac qualities. Methaqualone caused many cases of serious poisoning. When administered orally, large doses produce a coma that may be accompanied by thrashing or convulsions. It was marketed in the United States under various names, including Quaalude, Parest, Optimil, Somnafac, and Soper. Most methaqualones found on the street today are counterfeit and usually test as diazepam (Valium).

## MEPROBAMATE

First synthesized in 1960 as a mild tranquilizer, **meprobamate** is distributed in the United States under the generic name as well as under brand names such as Miltown, Equanil, and Deprol. This drug is prescribed primarily for relief of anxiety, tension, and associated muscle spasms. The onset and duration of action are like those of intermediate-acting barbiturates, but this drug differs in that it is a muscle relaxant, does not produce sleep at therapeutic doses, and is less toxic. Excessive use, however, can result in psychological and physical dependence.[17]

## OXYCONTIN

Another powerful narcotic that is presently sold legally is **OxyContin** (see photo below). This drug, which is usually prescribed for cancer patients, has pushed aside marijuana, cocaine, and other narcotics as the drug of choice for addicts and teenage

### OxyContin

OxyContin is a powerful narcotic that is sold legally. This drug is usually prescribed for cancer patients. There is some evidence that it is more popular among addicts and teenagers than is marijuana and cocaine. Addicts can achieve an intensely pure high by crushing the pills and snorting or injecting them. OxyContin is often the target sought in pharmacy burglaries.

(©AP/Wide World Photos)

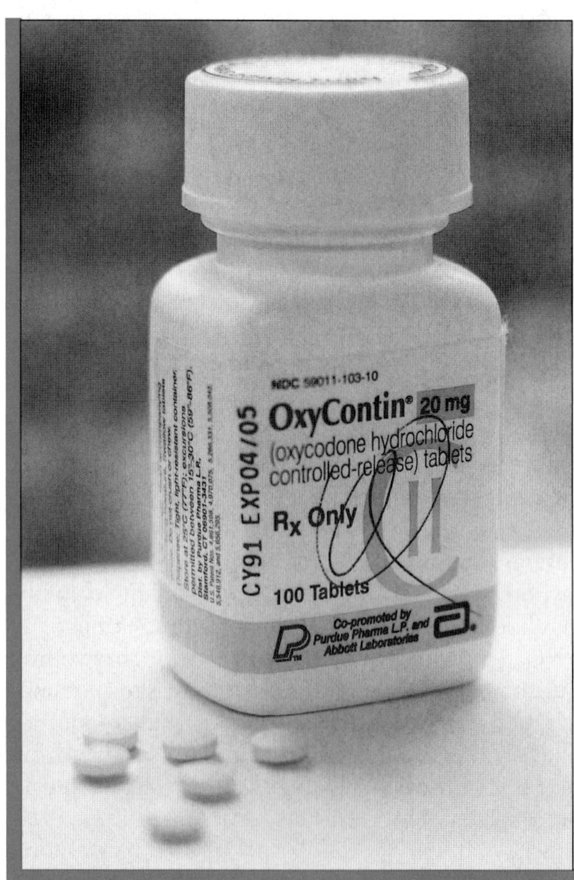

abusers. The active ingredient in OxyContin is a morphinelike substance called Oxycodone, which is also found in the prescription drugs Percodan and Tylox. But unlike those drugs, which need to be taken in repeated dosages, OxyContin is a time-released formulation that is effective for up to 12 hours. Experts say, however, that addicts can achieve an intensely pure high by crushing the pills and snorting or injecting them. A telltale piece of paraphernalia among adolescent users is a pill crusher, sold by drugstores to help elderly people swallow their medication.[18]

With the abuse of OxyContin on the rise, police in a least three states are reporting a record number of pharmacies being broken into. The homes of people with legitimate OxyContin prescriptions are being robbed, and home invasions are targeting the pills. These patients are often tracked down by relatives who know what is inside their medicine cabinets or by neighbors who hear talk about their prescriptions. Illegal users are even accosting drugstore customers in parking lots on the hunch that they might be carrying this sought-after drug.[19]

In an effort to deal with this growing problem, drug manufacturers have come up with blueprints for a "smart pill" that would make it more difficult to abuse the drug. The new painkiller is designed to destroy its own narcotic ingredients if crushed into powder for snorting or injecting—the typical manner in which OxyContin is abused to achieve a quick heroinlike high.

## SPEEDBALLING

**Speedballing** is a slang term that refers to the simultaneous ingestion, usually through injection, of heroin (a depressant) and cocaine (a stimulant). The cocaine provides the user with a tremendous euphoric "rush"; after the initial euphoria, the heroin provides a drowsy or depressing effect. An overdose of either drug can cause convulsions and death. Combined use greatly increases this risk.

## HALLUCINOGENS

The **hallucinogenic drugs,** natural or synthetic, distort perception of objective reality. In large doses, they cause hallucinations. Most of these drugs are processed in clandestine laboratories and have yet to be proved medically valuable. The effects experienced after taking hallucinogens are not solely related to the drug. They are modified by the mood, mental attitude, and environment of the user. The unpredictability of their effects is the greatest danger to the user. Users may develop psychological dependence but not physical dependence, so far as is known. The most commonly abused hallucinogens are PCP (phencyclidine), LSD 25 (lysergic acid diethylamide), mescaline (peyote), psilocybin, and psilocyn.

### PHENCYCLIDINE (PCP)

**Phencyclidine,** commonly called **PCP,** in pharmaceutically pure form is a solid white powder. Because the hydrochloride salt readily dissolves in water and as a street drug is often adulterated or misrepresented as other drugs, its appearance is highly variable. It is sold in powder form and in tablets, both in many colors. Often it is placed on parsley or on other leaf mixtures to be smoked as cigarettes (joints).[20]

When misrepresented, PCP is commonly sold as THC (the main psychoactive ingredient in marijuana, which in reality is rarely available on the street). But phencyclidine has also been sold as cannabinol (another marijuana constituent), mescaline, psilocybin, LSD, and even amphetamine or cocaine. Because of the variability in street names and appearance, and because PCP is sometimes found in combination with barbiturates, heroin, cocaine, amphetamine, methaqualone, LSD, and mescaline, users may be mistaken about its true identity. The mixture of marijuana and PCP has been thought to be common, but it has rarely been reported by street-drug analysis laboratories. At least one major laboratory on the West Coast that does such drug analysis has never encountered the combination.

Significantly adding to the risk of using PCP, especially when it is taken orally, is the wide variability in purity of the street drug. Even when PCP is not misrepresented, the percentage of PCP has been found to be quite variable. Depending on how carefully PCP is synthesized, it may contain impurities, including potassium cyanide. Generally, samples represented as "crystal" or "angel dust" tend to be purer than those sold under other names or misrepresented as other drugs.

In addition to phencyclidine, over 30 chemical analogues, some of which are capable of producing similar psychic effects, can also be synthesized and may appear on the street. Thus the problems of identifying and tracking the use of PCP and related drugs is unusually difficult.

THC is sometimes misrepresented as PCP. Unlike THC, PCP can be synthesized rather easily. The starting chemicals are widely available. Media accounts have sometimes exaggerated the ease with which phencyclidine can be made, but it is not particularly difficult for individuals with only modest technical training or elaborate equipment to make it.

Phencyclidine is used legally in veterinary medicine to immobilize primates. Although it was originally developed as an anesthetic for humans, it was later abandoned because it produced psychological disturbances and agitation in some patients. PCP made its first illicit appearance in the United States in 1965 on the West Coast. At that time it rapidly developed a bad street reputation and had only limited popularity. But in recent years use has markedly increased.

Because of its great variation in appearance, PCP is difficult to identify by sight. It is found in powder and tablet forms; on parsley, mint, oregano, or other leafy material; as a liquid; and in 1-gram "rock" crystals. When PCP is sold as a granular powder ("angel dust"), it may consist of 50 to 100 percent phencyclidine. Sold under other names and in other guises, the purity varies from 10 to 30 percent; leafy mixtures contain still smaller amounts of the drug.

## How Is It Used?

PCP is most commonly smoked or snorted. By smoking a leafy mixture on which the drug has been sprinkled, users can better regulate the dose. Because of the longer period before the drug takes effect and the greater purity, overdoses are probably worse when the drug has been taken orally.

## Clinical Aspects

The best-known effects of PCP would seem so unpleasant that many have wondered how it could possibly prove popular. For example, medical students volunteering for an experiment involving several hallucinogens and PCP were uniformly unwilling to return after having smoked moderate amounts of PCP. The drug made them feel weightless, smaller, out of touch with the immediate environment, and dying or dead. Common signs of PCP use include flushing, profuse sweating, involuntary eye movements, muscular incoordination, double vision, dizziness, nausea, and vomiting. Police officers have reported that individuals under the influence of PCP can be extremely violent and almost superhumanly strong.

Many PCP users do not knowingly take it again. Yet others use it chronically.

## Clinical Test for PCP

A 1-minute test to identify PCP was introduced by the Syva Company. The Emit PCP semiquantitative urine assay is similar to Emit drug-abuse assays and can be performed with existing laboratory equipment. It can be used in hospital emergency rooms and in parole, probation, and work-release programs.[21]

# METHYLENEDIOXY METHAMPHETAMINE (MDMA)

**Methylenedioxy methamphetamine,** commonly known as **MDMA** or **"ecstasy,"** is a bitter white powder. It enjoyed a brief period of popularity in the early 1970s as a substitute for methylenedioxy amphetamine (MDA), which was outlawed in the late 1960s, but it was not until the early to mid-1980s that ecstasy gained a regular following, in both Europe and the United States, in the nightclub and party scene. In recent years the drug's popularity has grown at an alarming rate. Although it is difficult to say exactly how many people are experimenting with the drug, law enforcement officials consider ecstasy to be one of the most troubling illicit drugs because of its widespread use.

Many ecstasy users are drawn to the drug by its ability to reduce inhibitions, promote euphoria, produce light hallucinations, and suppress the need to eat or sleep. One pill's effects can last as long as 6 hours, but users build up a tolerance. An overdose can cause accelerated heart beat, high blood pressure, aching muscle cramps, or panic attacks. According to many experts, ecstasy is psychologically addictive and can result in paranoia and psychosis.

The drug is manufactured, to a large extent, in laboratories in Belgium and the Netherlands. It can be manufactured for as little as $0.50, sold in the country of origin, and then smuggled into the United States, where it is sold for as much as $40 a pill. For the most part, Israeli organized-crime syndicates have been implicated as the main source of the drug's distribution in the United States. This so-called club drug has become increasingly popular

### Ecstasy Pills

These pills are street named "pirates" because of the skull and crossbones that are sometimes imprinted on them. The pills are manufactured in Belgium and the Netherlands for the most part. The use of ecstasy has gained a regular following in both Europe and in the United States on the nightclub and party scene. This drug has become increasingly popular among juveniles and is commonly used as a recreational drug at "raves." According to many experts, ecstasy is psychologically addictive and can result in paranoia and psychosis.

(Courtesy Sergeant Christopher McKissick and Detective Tyler Parks, Port Orange, Florida, Police Department)

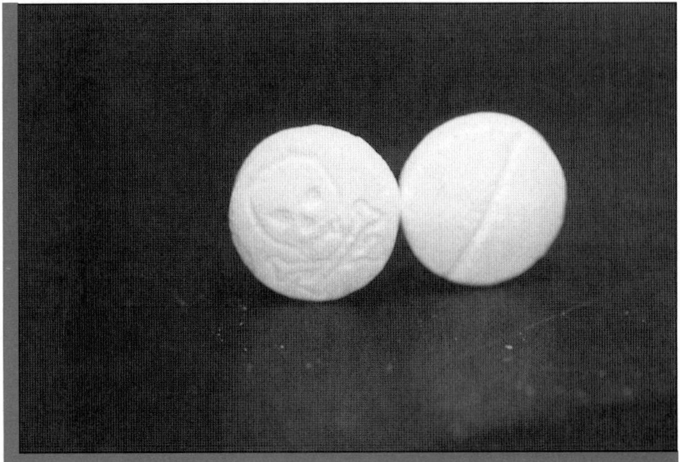

among juveniles and is commonly used as a recreational drug at large parties called "raves."[22]

## LYSERGIC ACID DIETHYLAMIDE (LSD 25)

**Lysergic acid diethylamide,** or **LSD** is a semisynthetic compound produced from lysergic acid, a natural substance found in ergot fungus, a disease that affects rye and wheat. An average dose of 30 to 50 micrograms—about the size of a pinpoint—will take the user on a "trip" lasting 10 to 12 hours. Drops of the solution are taken on a lump of sugar or on blotted paper. Along with experiencing mental changes, the user may have dilated pupils, lowered temperature, nausea, goose bumps, profuse perspiration, increased blood sugar, and rapid heart rate. Flashbacks are not uncommon.

Before 1972 there was no way to detect LSD in the body chemically. However, scientists of Collaborative Research, Inc., in Waltham, Massachusetts, developed a means for detecting it in small amounts in human blood and urine and for measuring the amount present. This discovery made it possible to study the distribution of LSD in the bodies of animals to determine the residual effect of the drug.[23] The DEA reports that LSD is making a comeback with juvenile circles and is also used frequently at raves.

## MESCALINE (PEYOTE)

The primary active ingredient of the peyote cactus is the hallucinogen **mescaline,** which is derived from the buttons of the plant. (See photo at right.) Mescaline has been used by the Indians of Central America and the southwestern United States for centuries in religious rites. Generally ground into a powder, it is taken orally. A dose of 350 to 500 milligrams of mescaline produces illusions and hallucinations for 5 to 12 hours. Like LSD, mescaline is not likely to produce physical dependence but may produce psychological dependence.

## PSILOCYBIN AND PSILOCYN

**Psilocybin** and **psilocyn** are obtained from mushrooms generally grown in Mexico. Like mescaline,

### Peyote

This photo is of a peyote cactus, from which the hallucinogen mescaline is derived. Mescaline is usually ground into powder and then taken orally. While mescaline does not produce physical dependence, it may cause psychological dependence.

(Courtesy Drug Enforcement Administration)

they have historically been used in Indian rites. They are taken orally, and their effect is similar to mescaline's, except that a smaller dose—4 to 8 milligrams—produces effects for about 6 hours.

## MARIJUANA

**Marijuana** (Cannabis sativa L.) is found in the sensimilla, the flowering tops and leaves of the unpollinated female Indian hemp plant. The leaves of the plant always grow in odd numbers. The plant grows in mild climates around the world, but the principal sources of import into the United States are Colombia, Mexico, and Jamaica (see Figure 19–3). Its most common nicknames are "pot," "reefer," "tea," "grass," "weed," "Maryjane," and "joint." Marijuana is made by crushing or chopping the dried leaves and flowers of the plant into small pieces. The cleaned or manicured leaves are then rolled into a cigarette and smoked, smoked in some other fashion, or mixed with food and eaten (see photo at right). The principal psychoactive substance is thought to be delta-9-tetrahydrocannabinol (THC), a chemical found nowhere else in nature. Low doses of the drug tend to produce initial restfulness and well-being, followed by a dreamy, carefree state of relaxation and an alteration of sensory perceptions, including an illusory expansion of time and space.

**Manicured Marijuana and Seeds**
Note smaller size of marijuana cigarette when compared to a regular cigarette on the left. The cleaned or manicured leaves of the marijuana plant are used to fill these "cigarettes." Low doses of the smoked drug tend to produce initial restfulness and a sense of well-being. Other effects include an alteration of sensory perceptions, including an illusory expansion of time and space.
(Courtesy Drug Enforcement Administration)

### Indoor Marijuana Operations

The move indoors has turned into a match of wits, pitting knowledgeable growers against seasoned narcotics agents.[24]

**Figure 19-3** Sources of Marijuana
(**Source:** U.S. General Accounting Office.)

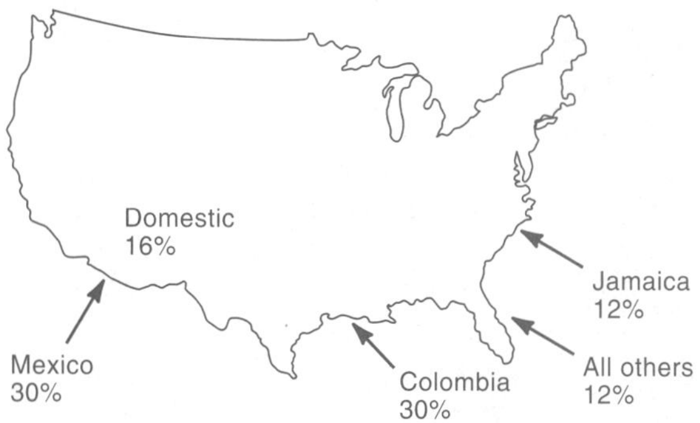


The outdoor marijuana growing season typically spans April to October. Not only do indoor growers hope to elude police by going inside; they are also able to control the climate, temperature, light, and soil conditions, thus being able to grow up to four crops a year. By controlling the crops, growers are also able to produce cannabis with a higher level of THC, the chemical found in the plant's flower tops that produces the mind-altering effects desired by marijuana smokers.[25]

The move to indoor growing operations, a trend seen on a nationwide scale, is a direct result of both police pressure and the ability to grow better marijuana. Growers are trying to hide their illicit crop more effectively from police because of the pressure from aerial surveillance.[26]

Another new trend is the growing of marijuana plants through hydroponics, which uses a growth medium other than soil. Unusually large purchases of hydroponic equipment are being more closely monitored these days.[27]

Domestic marijuana has come a long way in the United States. The DEA reports that the marijuana smoked in the 1960s had a THC level of about 2 percent. Today it is common to find marijuana in the United States with a THC level of 5 to 7 percent.[28]

**Customs Officer Looking at Fiber Found on Plant**
The marijuana plant grows in mild climates around the world, but the principal sources of import in the United States are Colombia, Mexico, and Jamaica. For years, the United States Border Patrol has expended considerable resources in attempting to reduce the flow of marijuana from neighboring Mexico.
(Photo by James R. Tourtellotte/U.S. Customs Service)

## HASHISH

A drug-rich resinous secretion from the flowers of the cannabis plant, **hashish** is processed by drying to produce a drug several times as potent as marijuana. The resin from the flowers is richer in cannabinols than the leaves and tops; the THC content ranges from 5 to 12 percent. (The leaves range from 0.27 to 4 percent in THC content.) Hashish is most commonly smoked in a small "hash pipe."

## HASHISH OIL

The Middle East is the main source of hashish entering the United States.[29] Liquid hashish, or **hashish oil,** is produced by concentrating THC. The liquid hashish so far discovered has varied between 20 and 65 percent THC. There is reason to suspect that methods are now being employed to make an even more powerful concentrate. The purity of the final product depends on the sophistication of the apparatus used.

Like other forms of the drug, liquid hashish can be used several ways. Because of its extraordinary potency, one drop of the material can produce a high. A drop may be placed on a regular cigarette, used in cooking, added to wine, and even smeared on bread. When smoked, a small drop of hashish oil is smeared inside the glass bowl of a special pipe with a flattened side. The user exhales deeply, tilts the bowl, and holds the flame from a match under the oil. In one inhalation, the smoker draws slowly on the pipe as the oil begins to bubble, continuing as it chars and burns.

There are many ways to produce hashish oil, but most clandestine operations use a basket filled with ground or chopped marijuana suspended inside a larger container, at the bottom of which is contained a solvent, such as alcohol, hexane, chloroform, or petroleum ether. Copper tubing or similar material is arranged at the top, and cold water circulates through it. The solvent is heated, the vapors rise to the top, they condense, and then they fall into the basket of marijuana. As the solvent seeps through the plant materials, the THC and other soluble chemicals are dissolved, and the solution drops back to the bottom of the container. Continued heating causes the process to recur. The solution becomes increasingly stronger until the plant material is exhausted of its THC.

## KETAMINE

**Ketamine** hydrochloride is a synthetic drug that was developed in the mid-1960s and is an anesthetic agent that has legitimate uses, mostly in veterinary medicine. Ketamine was used extensively in the Vietnam War because it is fast acting and has a relatively short duration, making it a drug of choice for "battlefield medicine." However, it soon became obvious that many humans who were anesthetized with ketamine often became agitated and suffered hallucinations when they awoke. It has since been replaced as an anesthetic for humans by other, more efficient agents with fewer side effects.

Ironically, the side effects that made ketamine unpopular and unsafe as a legitimate medical drug have spawned its use in the illegitimate market. On the street, ketamine is called "vitamin K," "kat," "kit," "special K," or "K." It has been closely associated with the all-night party phenomenons known as raves, where large crowds of young people listen to music and reportedly dance for 6 to 8 hours at a time. Ketamine causes hallucinations, excitement, and delirium similar to the drugs phencyclidine (PCP) and LSD; however, the effects are not as pronounced or as long in duration. Hallucinations caused by ketamine may last only an hour or two, but the intoxication-like effects of the drug may be noticeable for several hours. Because ketamine is an anesthetic, it may temporarily mask the feeling of pain. Users of ketamine can injure themselves and not know it.

Because ketamine is so difficult to produce, it is not manufactured in clandestine laboratories. Most of the ketamine abused today comes from stolen veterinary stock and is known by brand names such as Ketalar and Ketaset (see photo below). The legitimate drug is usually supplied in vials of liquid, although it can be in the form of white powder or pills.

In liquid form, ketamine may be injected into a large muscle. This route allows for a slower absorption and longer duration than the intravenous route. In powder form, ketamine is usually snorted in the same manner as cocaine. Both powder and liquid can be sprayed or sprinkled on vegetable matter and smoked or mixed with a drink. While it is not known if a person can become physically dependent on ketamine, tolerance and psychological dependence are distinct possibilities with frequent use.

The average street dose of ketamine ranges from 0.2 to 0.5 gram. The size and weight of the abuser, the desired effects, and the presence of other drugs in the abuser's system determine the ultimate effect. A vial of liquid ketamine is equivalent to approximately 1 gram of powder and sells for $100 to $200. A 0.2-gram dose of powder, or a "bump," commonly sells for $20. Ketamine may be packaged for sale in small plastic bags, aluminum foil, paper folds, or gelatin capsules. Obviously, an abuser must also possess hypodermic syringes and needles to abuse the drug by injection.

Ketamine is not a federally scheduled controlled dangerous substance. On the state level, it is controlled only in California, Connecticut, New Mexico, and Oklahoma. The DEA is presently collecting data on ketamine and may reevaluate the drug's nonscheduled status in the future.[30]

### Ketamine

Ketamine hydrochloride is a synthetic drug developed in the mid-1960s as an anesthetic agent. Two of the street names used for this drug are "vitamin K" and "special K." It has been closely associated with all-night parties called "raves." Ketamine causes hallucinations, excitement, and delirium similar to LSD or PCP. Because it is an anesthetic, it may temporarily mask pain—so much so that users can even injure themselves and not be aware of it.

(Courtesy Sergeant Christopher McKissick and Detective Tyler Parks, Port Orange, Florida, Police Department)

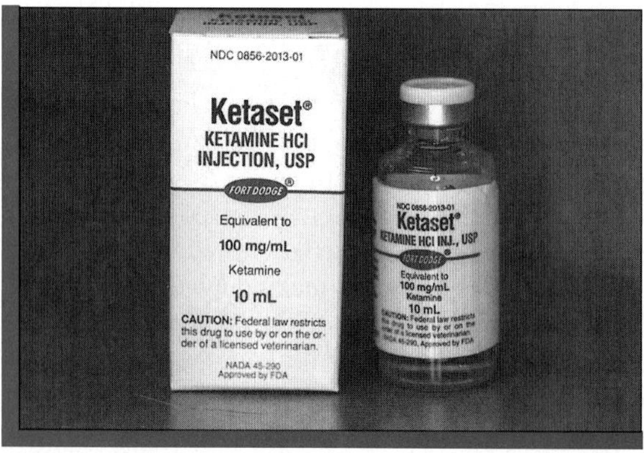


## FIELD TESTING FOR CONTROLLED SUBSTANCES

Chemical field tests, using reagents and test kits, give valuable clues about the identity of samples. Field tests are easy to perform. They are, however, only presumptive because they may produce false positives. Any drug that will be used as evidence must be positively identified by a qualified chemist. Additionally, a negative test does not preclude the possibility that another similar drug may be present.[31]

## INVESTIGATIVE PROCEDURES

Most of the techniques used in investigating dangerous-drugs and narcotics cases are the same as those used in investigating other cases; however, there are some unique procedures.[32]

Before undertaking any drug investigation, investigators should familiarize themselves with the street slang. Commonly used terms are defined in Figure 19–4.

### THE PURCHASE

One important aspect is identification of the source. This is accomplished through review of completed reports of investigation, through information received from an informant, or through surveillance and direct efforts to purchase drugs. It is desirable to make more than one direct purchase from a seller, if possible. This procedure gives investigators more opportunity to locate the peddler's cache of narcotics or source of supply. It also serves to identify other customers and to establish that the seller is not a one-time or opportunistic dealer. As a seller's sources of supply and customers are identified, the possibility of identifying key people in the network increases.

If an arrest is to be made immediately after a purchase, the currency used to make the buy should be dusted with fluorescent powder. The serial numbers of the currency should always be recorded for comparison with the numbers on currency recovered from other defendants, for a match may suggest an unsuspected link among traffickers and thus a conspiracy. Recovered currency should be treated as evidence.

If a peddler will sell only to an informant and not to an undercover investigator, the informant must be searched before the sale to make sure that he or she has no narcotics. Any money found on the informant should be removed. The informant should be searched immediately after the sale. At this time, money should be returned. Between the two searches, the informant must be kept under constant surveillance so that his or her testimony can be corroborated. Evidence obtained through "informant buys" is admissible in court, but the testimony of the informant may be required.

### THE APPREHENSION

All arrests should be as unobtrusive as possible to prevent them from becoming common knowledge on the street. This practice preserves the usefulness of the information the arrested party provides.

When approaching a drug suspect, the investigator must be particularly observant of the suspect's hands. The suspect may attempt to drop, throw, flush, eat, or otherwise dispose of drugs. If drugs are found on the ground or some distance away from the suspect, it may be extremely difficult, if not impossible, to connect the drug with the suspect. Because addicts can be dangerous, unpredictable, and uncooperative, investigators must exercise caution. Addicts may use a weapon or suddenly attack the unwary investigator. As soon as possible after apprehension, suspects should be required to place their hands directly in the air or behind their heads to preclude further disposal of evidence.

The investigator must ensure that drugs taken from the custody of persons suspected of a narcotics offense have not been prescribed. If certain seized drugs are necessary for a suspect's health, a physician's opinion should be sought on administering the drug.

Immediately after the apprehension or as soon as possible thereafter, a thorough search should be made of the suspect's person, clothing, and area of immediate control. The possession of even the minutest of drug particles may be sufficient to establish a connection.[33] Because the quantity of the drug may be small, hiding places are almost limitless. The law enforcement officer should use the full range of skills and imagination to search for them.

## DRUG INFORMANTS: MOTIVES, METHODS, AND MANAGEMENT

Informants in drug enforcement are unique among criminal informants and perhaps the most difficult to manage. However, investigators who know what motivates individuals to become informants can manage them more effectively.[34]

### INFORMANTS: MOTIVATIONS AND TYPES

Like most people, informants need motivation to produce. The more motivated they are, the more likely they are to apply themselves to the task at hand and remain committed to achieving success. Therefore, by identifying an informant's true motives, an investigator greatly enhances the potential success of

**Figure 19-4** Drug Terminology: Street Slang

**Acapulco gold:** High grade of marijuana.
**acid:** LSD, LSD 25 (lysergic acid diethylamide)
**acidhead:** Regular user of LSD.
**acid test:** Party at which LSD has been added to the punch, food, etc.
**agonies:** Withdrawal symptoms.
**all lit up:** Under the influence.
**angel dust:** Phencyclidine (PCP on parsley).
**artillery:** Equipment for injecting drugs; the works; the needle, eyedropper, spoon, bottle cap, cotton, and cloth, string, or belt for a tourniquet.
**baghead:** Someone involved in glue sniffing.
**bagman:** Supplier; person holding drugs for supplier.
**balloon:** A balloon containing approximately two doses of heroin.
**bang:** Injection of drugs.
**barbs:** Barbiturates.
**barrels:** LSD tablets.
**bathtub speed:** Methcathinone.
**bennies:** Benzedrine, an amphetamine.
**bindle:** Packet of narcotics.
**black beauties:** Amphetamines.
**blanks:** Extremely low-grade narcotics.
**blast:** Strong effect from a drug.
**blue acid:** LSD.
**blue angels:** Barbiturates (Amytal and amobarbital).
**blue birds:** Barbiturates (Amytal and amobarbital).
**blue devils:** Barbiturates (Amytal and amobarbital).
**blue heavens:** Barbiturates (Amytal and amobarbital).
**blue velvet:** Paregoric (camphorated tincture of opium) and pyribenzamine (an antihistamine) mixed and injected.
**bombed out:** High on marijuana.
**bombita:** Amphetamine injection, sometimes taken with heroin.
**brown:** Mexican heroin; usually of lower quality than white heroin.
**burn, burned:** To cheat; to be cheated out of money or drugs; to have identity disclosed.
**burned out:** Collapse of the veins from repeated injections.
**busted:** Arrested.
**buttons:** The sections of the peyote cactus.
**candy man:** Drug seller; one who deals in a variety of pills, tablets, and capsules of various shapes and colors.
**cannabinol:** Tetrahydrocannabinol (THC), active ingredient of cannabis.
**cartwheels:** Amphetamine powder (round, white, double-scored tablets).
**cat:** Methcathinone.
**china death:** Heroin containing strychnine or cyanide.
**china white:** An illicitly synthesized derivative of fentanyl (a designer drug); high-grade heroin from Southeast Asia.
**chipping:** Taking narcotics occasionally.
**clean:** Out of drugs; not using drugs.
**coke:** Cocaine.
**cold turkey:** Abrupt withdrawal from drugs, without medication; skin resembles the texture of a cold plucked turkey.
**come down:** End of a trip; drug effect wearing off.
**connection:** Source of supply.
**cooker:** Spoon or bottle cap for heating heroin and water.
**cop out:** Quit, take off, confess, inform, be defeated.
**cotton shot:** Drug-saturated cotton to which water is added to get whatever heroin is left.
**crack:** Rock cocaine; purer and more concentrated than regular cocaine.
**crack house:** Room, apartment building, or residence in which crack is sold and/or smoked.
**crank:** Methamphetamine or methcathinone.
**crash:** To collapse from exhaustion after continuous use of amphetamines; enjoyable sleep after smoking marijuana; to come down from an LSD trip.
**crash pad:** Place where the user withdraws from amphetamines.
**cut:** Dilute drugs by adding milk, sugar, or another inert substance.

Figure 19-4 Drug Terminology: Street Slang, *continued*

**dealer:** Drug supplier.
**deck:** Packet of narcotics.
**dexies:** Dexedrine, an amphetamine.
**dime bag:** $10 package of narcotics.
**dirty:** Possessing drugs; liable to be arrested if searched.
**doper:** Person who uses drugs regularly.
**downers:** Depressant drugs; barbiturates.
**dried out:** Cured of drug dependence (usually cold turkey).
**ecstasy:** MDMA.
**feed bag:** Container of narcotics or other drugs.
**feed store:** Place where drugs can be purchased.
**fifteen cents:** $15; a packet of drugs selling for $15.
**fire up:** Take a drug intravenously.
**fix:** Injection of narcotics.
**flash:** First euphoric sensation after taking a drug.
**flashback:** Unpredictable recurrence of an LSD trip long after the last drug trip was taken; may occur weeks or months after the last drug-induced trip.
**flip:** Become psychotic.
**floating:** Under the influence of drugs.
**freakout:** Bad experience with psychedelics; also, a chemical high.
**freebasing:** Chemical process used to increase the strength of cocaine.
**garbage:** Low-grade drug; no drug content.
**go:** Methcathinone.
**goob:** Methcathinone.
**good trip:** Happy experience with psychedelics.
**goofballs:** Barbiturates.
**grass:** Marijuana.
**H:** Heroin.
**H and C:** Mixture of heroin and cocaine (speedball).
**hard narcotics:** Opiates, such as heroin and morphine.
**hard stuff:** Heroin.
**hash:** Hashish, the resin of cannabis.
**hearts:** Dexedrine tablets (from the shape).
**heavenly blues:** Type of morning-glory seeds.
**high:** Euphoric; under the influence of a drug.
**hit:** Make a purchase; the effect of drugs; to steal drugs, money, or merchandise; to inject.
**holding:** Having drugs in one's possession.
**hooked:** Addicted.
**horse:** Heroin.
**hot load, hot shot:** Overdose; lethal drug dose; usually refers to drugs given deliberately to eliminate a troublesome customer, such as an informer; pure heroin or a heroin mixture containing a poison such as strychnine or cyanide.
**hustle:** Activities involved in obtaining money to buy heroin.
**hustler:** Prostitute.
**joint:** Marijuana cigarette.
**joy pop:** Occasional injection of narcotics (usually under the skin rather than in a vein).
**junkie:** Narcotics addict who injects drugs.
**K:** Ketamine hydrochloride.
**kat:** Ketamine hydrochloride.
**key:** One kilogram (2.2 pounds).
**kicking:** Withdrawal process.
**kicking cold:** Ceasing drug use without medical support.
**kicking the gong:** Usually refers to smoking marijuana or hashish.
**kilo:** Kilogram (2.2 pounds).
**kit:** (1) Equipment for injecting drugs; the works; (2) ketamine hydrochloride.
**loaded:** High on marijuana.
**loco weed:** Marijuana.
**ludes:** Quaaludes (methaqualone).
**M:** Morphine.
**mainline:** Inject drugs into a vein.
**maintaining:** Keeping at a certain level of drug effect.
**make:** To identify a police officer who is working undercover.
**make a reader:** Have a doctor write a prescription.
**(the) man:** Can be either the police or one's main supplier of drugs.

**Figure 19-4** Drug Terminology: Street Slang, *continued*

**manicure:** Remove the dirt, seeds, and stems from marijuana.
**Mary Jane:** Marijuana.
**mesc:** Mescaline, the alkaloid in peyote.
**meth:** Methamphetamine.
**methhead:** Habitual user of methamphetamine.
**monkey:** Drug habit; physical dependence.
**mule:** Transporter of drugs.
**nailed:** Arrested.
**narc:** Narcotics detective.
**nembies:** Nembutal (a barbiturate); pentobarbital.
**nickel bag:** $5 bag of drugs.
**nod:** The sleep and relaxation after a shot of heroin (on the nod).
**nose candy:** Cocaine.
**O.D.:** Overdose of narcotics.
**on a trip:** Under the influence of a hallucinogen.
**on the nod:** Sleepy from narcotics.
**oranges:** Amphetamines (orange colored, heart shaped); Dexedrine.
**paper:** Small quantity of drugs; prescription for drugs.
**peaches:** Amphetamines (Benzedrine).
**pep pills:** Amphetamines.
**persian white:** Fentanyls (designer drugs).
**peyote:** Hallucinogen from peyote cactus.
**pink hearts or pinks:** Dexedrine tablets.
**pirates:** Ecstasy pills.
**pop:** Inject beneath the skin.
**pot:** Marijuana.
**pothead:** Heavy user of marijuana.
**powder:** Heroin.
**pure:** Very good grade of heroin.
**purple hearts:** Dexamyl, a combination of Dexedrine and Amytal (from the shape and color).
**pusher:** Drug peddler.
**rainbows:** Tuinal (Amytal and Seconal), a barbiturate combination in a blue and red capsule.
**red birds, red bullets, red devils, reds:** A barbiturate (Seconal).
**reentry:** Return from a trip.
**roach:** Marijuana cigarette.
**rocks:** High-grade cocaine.
**satch cotton:** Cotton used to strain drugs before injection; may be used again if supplies are gone.
**score:** Make a purchase of drugs.
**scrip, script:** Prescription for drugs; money.
**script writer:** Sympathetic doctor; prescription forger.
**seccies, seccy:** Seconal.
**shit:** Drugs in general; heroin.
**shoot, shoot up:** Inject.
**shooting gallery:** Place where addicts inject drugs.
**shot down:** Under the influence of drugs.
**sick:** Going through drug withdrawal, usually from heroin.
**skin popping:** Injecting drugs under the skin.
**smack:** Heroin.
**snorting:** Inhaling drugs.
**snow:** Cocaine.
**special K:** Ketamine hydrochloride.
**speed:** Methamphetamine.
**speedball:** An injection of a stimulant and a depressant, originally heroin and cocaine.
**speedfreak:** Habitual user of speed.
**stash:** Supply of drugs in a secure place.
**step-on:** Dilution of a drug, typically heroin or cocaine, with some other substance.
**stomach addict:** An addict who eats heroin.
**stoned:** Under the influence of drugs.
**stoolie:** Informer.
**STP:** Hallucinogen (stands for "serenity, tranquility, and peace") related to mescaline and amphetamines.
**strung out:** Addicted.
**tea:** Marijuana.
**tea pad:** Place where marijuana is bought and smoked.
**tea party:** Get-together of marijuana smokers.
**THC:** Tetrahydrocannabinol; purified resin extract from the hemp plant, also synthetically produced; said to be the substance responsible for the mind-altering effects of cannabis.

**Figure 19-4** Drug Terminology: Street Slang, *concluded*

**tooies:** Tuinal.
**tools:** Equipment for injecting drugs.
**tracks:** Scars along veins after many injections.
**tripping out:** High on psychedelics.
**turkey trots:** Marks or scars from repeated injections.
**turned on:** Under the influence of drugs.
**turps:** Elixir of terpin hydrate and codeine, a cough syrup.
**25:** LSD (from its original designation, "LSD 25").
**uppers:** Stimulants, cocaine, and psychedelics.
**vtamin K:** Ketamine hydrochloride.
**weed:** Marijuana.
**whites:** Stimulants, generally amphetamines.
**works:** Equipment for injecting drugs.
**yellow jackets:** Nembutal, a barbiturate.
**yen shee:** Ashes of opium.
**yen shee suey:** Opium mixed with wine or other beverages.
**yen sleep:** A drowsy, restless state during the withdrawal period.
**zonked:** Heavily addicted; under the extreme influence of drugs.

an investigation. Initially, informants commonly voice a specific motive for providing assistance. However, as a case proceeds and a relationship with an investigator develops, other reasons may surface. Some of the more common motivational factors encountered by drug enforcement investigators are fear, revenge, money, repentance, and altruism.

The most frequently encountered motivational factor may be the confidential informant's (CI's) fear of punishment for criminal acts. Severe criminal penalties tend to increase the number of persons wanting to cooperate with drug enforcement authorities. Informants may also fear their criminal associates. Individuals wrongly accused by drug dealers of being informants may then become informants for self-preservation, money, or both.

Informants frequently cooperate with the government to seek revenge against their enemies. Jealousy may also prompt their acts of vengeance.

Some individuals provide information or services for money. These money-motivated informants, known as mercenaries, are usually the most willing to follow the directions of their handlers. Mercenaries frequently possess other motives as well.

Repentance can be a motivating factor. Informants often claim they cooperate in order to repent for past crimes. However, this is seldom their only motive for cooperating.

Some individuals are motivated by a sense of altruism. People with professional obligations or feelings of responsibility frequently provide information to the police. Examples of altruistic informants include airline ticket agents and private mail-service carriers.

## Problem Informants

Some informants have personalities that make them difficult, if not impossible, to manage. These individuals may also have questionable motives for offering their services to a law enforcement agency. Investigators who misjudge the true motives of informants experience tremendous control problems. This can create safety problems and place department resources and personnel in jeopardy. Therefore investigators should avoid recruiting certain types of individuals, if possible.

## Egotistical Informants

Egotistical informants, who are encountered frequently, may not have received positive reinforcement from their parents or schoolmates when growing up. Consequently, they seek positive feedback from their handlers as their primary reward. Investigators who provide this positive reinforcement motivate egotistical informants to continue supplying information. Unfortunately, these informants are often the hardest to handle because their egos prevent them from relinquishing control of the investigation entirely to their handlers.

## Informants with "James Bond Syndrome"

Some persons see their roles as informants as a way to have their lives imitate art. While working as informants, they imagine themselves in a police or spy drama. Sometimes they even attempt to orchestrate events to parallel a scene from a movie or novel. Frequently hard to handle, these informants often exaggerate their knowledge of criminal activity to enhance the likelihood of their becoming informants.

### Wannabe Informants

Wannabe informants are people who, for whatever reason, failed to qualify for a law enforcement position and now seek to become involved in law enforcement as informants. Because they lack criminal associates, these individuals usually cannot provide specific information about drug dealing. Therefore, they do not make good informants.

### Perversely Motivated Informants

The most dangerous and disruptive informants in drug law enforcement are perversely motivated CIs. They offer their services in order to identify undercover agents; learn the department's methods, targets, and intelligence; or eliminate their own competition in drug sales. Sometimes criminal organizations instruct these individuals to infiltrate departments and learn whatever they can to assist the traffickers. These individuals may even provide genuine information about specific events as a decoy to divert resources from more significant trafficking activity.

Therefore, investigators must question all walk-in and call-in informants (i.e., individuals who volunteer their services without prompting) because they may be, or have the potential to be, perversely motivated. After completing a thorough background investigation of CIs, investigators must constantly guard against providing more information than informants furnish in return. Furthermore, investigators should not discuss with informants specific details of methods and techniques used during drug investigations.

**Officer Talking to Drug Dealer Informant**
Informants in drug enforcement are unique and perhaps the most difficult to manage. This job can be made easier for investigators if they know what motivates the informants. Some of the more common motivational factors encountered by drug investigators are fear, revenge, money, repentance, and altruism.
(© Bonnie Kamin)

### Restricted-Use Informants

In addition to problem informants certain other informants, by virtue of their criminal background or other status, pose special management challenges to both investigators and supervisors.[35] Department managers should carefully scrutinize these individuals before using them as CIs. Examples include juveniles, individuals on probation or parole, individuals currently or formerly addicted to drugs, felons with multiple convictions, and individuals known to be unreliable.

Investigators should not use these individuals as informants until a supervisor approves them. In fact, because these informants require special scrutiny, only senior investigators should handle them. Furthermore, investigators must constantly reevaluate the motives of these individuals.

## DEPARTMENT POLICY

Agencies should not leave the management of drug informants exclusively to investigators. Formulating a written policy ensures consistency in the use and management of CIs and serves as a guide for inexperienced investigators.

The policy should indicate which investigators may maintain informants, as well as who will supervise these CIs. In addition, the policy should clearly establish that informants are assets of the department, not of individual investigators. In this regard, management should both authorize and encourage investigators to share informants. Also, checks and balances must be in place to ensure that the policy is followed.

Policy concerning the management of confidential informants should establish procedures in several areas. These include creating and documenting informant files, debriefing and interacting with informants, and determining methods and amounts of payments for services rendered.

## The Informant File

Investigators should formally establish files for CIs who regularly furnish information, as well as for those who expect compensation for information they supply. Informant files document investigators' interactions with CIs. In fact, investigators should not use any source that cannot be documented.

Although investigators should document their contacts with CIs, not everyone in the department needs to know an informant's identity or have access to informant files. Access should be on a need-to-know basis, including only the investigators and their supervisors who deal directly with the informant.

To further protect informants' identities, investigators should use code numbers in lieu of informants' names in investigative reports. Informants should keep the same number throughout their working relationships with the department.

The informant file should include information pertaining to the CI's vital statistics, such as physical description, work and home addresses, vehicles driven, contact telephone numbers, next of kin, and so forth. National Crime Information Center searches, performed before the informant is used and then systematically thereafter, ensure that the informant has no outstanding warrants. These records should be kept in the informant's file, along with the CI's photograph, fingerprints, and FBI and state "rap" sheets.

Establishing an informant file sends a not-so-subtle message to CIs that investigators document every encounter and verify all information that CIs supply. Such documentation may also deter a perversely motivated informant. In addition, informant files enhance the credibility of the department in the eyes of the court and the public, who view CIs as inherently unreliable and who may believe that the agency fabricated information. Therefore, every time an informant provides information concerning an actual or potential criminal matter, the agency should include a written report detailing this information in the CIs file. The original report should remain in that file, and a copy should be maintained in the case file.

The department must also document what steps it takes to corroborate information provided by a CI. This is especially important when informants act unilaterally. As a matter of policy, all CI information should be verified regardless of the CI's past reliability.

## Informant Debriefings

Each time investigators initiate investigations on the basis of information received from a CI, the designated handler should interview and debrief the CI in order to ascertain the informant's motive(s) and to advise the informant of the department's rules. For example, informants should know that they carry no official status with the department, that the department will not tolerate their breaking the law or entrapping suspects, and that the department cannot guarantee that they will not be called as witnesses in court.

At the end of the interview, the investigator should put this information in writing in an "informant agreement." This agreement should be signed by the informant, witnessed by the handler, and placed in the informant's file. Investigators should debrief their informants on a regular basis—for example, every 30, 60, or 90 days—to keep them active or, if necessary, to terminate their association with the department due to lack of productivity.

## Investigator-Informant Contact Procedures

The department must establish investigator-informant contact procedures and train employees in their use. For example, the handler should meet with the informant in private, if possible, but always in the presence of another investigator. In fact, the department should either strongly discourage or prohibit investigators from contacting informants alone, especially if the officer plans to pay the informant. Meeting with or paying a drug informant alone leaves the officer and the department vulnerable to allegations of wrongdoing.

Although informant handlers often develop special working relationships with their informants, department policies should preclude contact with informants outside the scope of official business. Investigators must keep their relationships with CIs strictly professional. This is particularly important when the informant and the investigator are not of the same sex. Policies should also expressly prohibit such contact as socializing with informants and/or their families, becoming romantically involved with informants, conducting nonpolice business with them, and accepting gifts or gratuities from them.[36]

To ensure adherence to department policy, supervisors should review informant files regularly. In addition, they need to attend debriefings periodically to oversee the entire informant management process.

Finally, department administrators must establish procedures for investigating alleged policy violations by investigators or informants. Thorough investigations of this type maintain the integrity of the department by dispelling any notion that the department does not enforce its own policies.

### Informant Payments

Payments to CIs can be divided into two distinct categories—awards and rewards. Awards take a monetary form. They are based on a percentage of the net value of assets seized during a drug investigation as a result of information provided by a CI. Advising the informant of the exact amount of the percentage at the beginning of the case provides incentive for the CI to seek out hidden assets that might otherwise go undetected. However, because payments based on seized assets are not universally accepted in the courts, the investigator should consult the case prosecutor before promising a specific amount to the informant.

Rewards, on the other hand, do not represent a percentage of the value of the seized assets. Amounts are usually determined by the type and quantity of drugs seized, the quality of the case produced, the number of defendants indicted, the amount of time and effort the CI exerted, and the danger faced by the CI during the course of the investigation. Unlike awards, rewards come directly from an agency's budget.

While an informant might receive money as a reward, many informants cooperate with law enforcement agencies to receive a reduced sentence for a pending criminal matter. Regardless of the form of compensation, the department's policy must address the circumstances under which an informant qualifies for an award and/or reward, who can authorize such payments, and the conditions under which payments will be granted.

Although many informants receive substantial awards when they locate the assets of drug dealers, agency budgets may limit the dollar amount of rewards paid to informants. For this reason, investigators should exercise caution when explaining the payment policy to informants. They should avoid mentioning a specific dollar amount that the informant will receive. Otherwise, the informant may try to hold the department to that amount, regardless of future budgetary constraints.

In addition to providing awards and rewards, departments can reimburse informants for expenses incurred during an investigation. In fact, the department may want to reimburse the CI with small amounts of money beyond actual expenses as added incentives to continue working.

It is highly recommended that informants be paid only in the presence of witnesses, with the final payment being made after all court proceedings have been completed to help ensure the informant's presence at the trial. Once a payment is made, a record documenting the date, exact amount, and payer must be included in the CI file in anticipation of future court inquiries.

## THE INVESTIGATOR'S PREVENTION RESPONSIBILITY

Investigators often can reduce the possibility that a physician or pharmacist will be victimized or can help reduce the magnitude of the loss. Ordinarily, investigators talk with such professionals during the investigation of an offense, while obtaining information not directly related to an offense or in the context of speaking before civic or professional groups. Physicians and pharmacists should be made aware of the precautions listed below.

### PRECAUTIONS FOR PHYSICIANS

Physicians should *not:*

- Leave unattended prescription pads in the open.
- Forget that prescriptions must be written in ink or indelible pencil or on a typewriter.
- Carry a large stock of narcotics in their medical bags.
- Store narcotics where patients can obtain easy access (near sinks or lavatories).
- Issue a narcotics prescription without seeing the patient.

- Write prescriptions for large quantities of narcotics unless absolutely necessary.
- Prescribe a narcotic because a patient says that another physician has been doing it.
- Leave signed blank prescriptions in the office for nurses to complete.
- Treat an ambulatory case of addiction.
- Dispense narcotics without making the necessary records.
- Purchase narcotics for office use with prescription blanks; the law requires an official order form.
- Act resentful if a pharmacist calls to confirm a prescription for narcotics (the pharmacist can be held responsible for filling forged prescriptions).
- Hesitate to call the local police department to obtain or give information.

### PRECAUTIONS FOR PHARMACISTS

Pharmacists should *not:*

- Leave or display narcotics near the cash register.
- Fail to scrutinize prescriptions written in a way that makes alterations possible, for example, "Morph. HT ½ #X" or "Morph. HT ¼ #10." In this illustration several "X" marks or zeros could be added to increase quantities. Physicians should be advised to spell out the prescription completely or to use brackets.
- Carry a large stock of narcotics; a three-month supply is advisable.
- Leave a key in the lock of the narcotics cabinet, which is locked at all times.
- Fail to keep all excess drugs in a safe, if possible.
- Place narcotics stock where it is accessible to others.
- Leave the prescription area unattended, if possible.
- Forget that a request for rapid filling of a prescription may be a ploy to distract them from checking a forged prescription.
- Fill telephone orders for narcotic drugs unless assured that a prescription will be available upon delivery.
- Be taken in by a person wearing a white uniform who presents a narcotics prescription.
- Refill narcotics prescriptions.
- Fill prescriptions for unusual quantities without checking with the physician.
- Hesitate to call a physician if the validity of a prescription is questioned.
- Supply a doctor's office needs from a prescription.
- Accept a narcotics prescription written in pencil.
- Leave prescription pads in accessible areas.

## DRUG ABUSE BY PRACTITIONERS

It has always been perplexing to investigators that a professional would become involved with drugs. But doctors do succumb to addiction. They have ready access to drugs and may turn to them out of fatigue, stress, or pain. Those who succumb may be only marginally adjusted to their environment.

They may function reasonably well at the onset of their addiction. An injection of Demerol, a tablet of codeine with aspirin, or a bottle of cough medicine may offer temporary euphoria and an escape from the pressure of living. Once the drug is used habitually, the doctor's ability to discern right from wrong falters. The doctor begins to rationalize, lie, connive, steal, and sometimes beg to perpetuate the habit. Physically, morally, and mentally, addiction becomes complete. The spouse may be initiated into the habit, whether for commiseration or to avoid censure.

Regardless of his or her previous social or professional position, the addicted doctor becomes unreliable. Each day is governed by the need to "get right," and maintenance of a routine is more and more difficult. Functioning by reflex works for a time, but discriminating judgments become increasingly less possible.

Well-meaning colleagues may become aware of the problem and try to assist. But the addict requires extensive assistance, usually beyond a colleague's "outpatient" approach. Discounting the criminal aspect, an adequate approach is hospitalization in a narcotics-free environment with extensive follow-up psychological treatment. The absence of responsible action may lead to tragedy.

Among the most common indications that a physician may be unlawfully diverting drugs are:

- A physician places excessively frequent orders for narcotics.
- A physician picks up and pays for filled narcotics prescriptions from a pharmacy.
- A physician places an emergency call for a narcotic medication to a pharmacy and requests delivery. The deliverer is met by the physician and given a prescription for the drugs. In some instances, no patient exists, or if one does exist the narcotics are retained by the physician and other medication is substituted.
- A narcotics prescription is issued to a patient by a physician with instructions to have it filled and to return with the drug for administration. Substitute medication is then given to the patient.
- In narcotics records, a physician uses fictitious or deceased people's names and addresses.
- The physician frequently requests that a prescription for an alleged patient be taken to the pharmacy by a nurse, a receptionist, or a member of the family and be returned to the doctor personally.
- While other physicians are in the operating room or making hospital rounds, the addict-physician searches their vehicles or medical bags for narcotics.
- A physician obtains a key to the narcotics locker in a hospital and has a duplicate made.
- A physician may place an order for a patient in a hospital; when the drug is prepared by a nurse, the doctor takes it over and either uses a substitute syringe containing a placebo or administers only a small portion of the drug.

If a case for prosecution is indicated against an addicted physician, an investigator must interview pharmacists, review prescriptions, and take statements from patients who allegedly received drugs prescribed by the doctor. The evidence thus obtained is used to secure an indictment.[37]

## CLANDESTINE DRUG LABORATORIES

**Clandestine drug laboratories** throughout the United States produce a variety of illegal drugs for sale and distribution. The processes used in production of these drugs range in their degree of sophistication from primitive to advanced. By the same token, those who operate such laboratories may range in expertise from the novice experimenter to the professional chemist. These factors alone can have a serious impact on the safety of the general public and on police and fire department personnel who may deal with these laboratories in enforcement and emergency situations.[38]

Raids conducted on clandestine drug laboratories are inherently dangerous, irrespective of the dangers associated with taking suspects into custody. The degree of danger is based largely on the types of chemicals that are typically used and the chemical processes employed. These dangers may be heightened by the operator's lack of expertise and experience and by the physical limitations and restrictions of the facility being used, as well as by weather conditions and other factors. Such dangers cannot be overemphasized. Major accidents resulting in loss of life have occurred during raids conducted on such facilities by those who are untrained, inexperienced, or careless in the dismantling, handling, transportation, storage, or disposal of the involved chemicals.

Normally, direct physical involvement with drug laboratories takes place during the execution of a search warrant on a suspect property. Under these circumstances, there is generally enough information to forewarn police officers about the nature of the operations and the types of chemicals that are most likely involved. Adequate safety precautions can thus be developed and employed. However, police officers may inadvertently encounter a laboratory operation while conducting other enforcement or investigatory operations. In such instances, unless there is imminent danger of loss of life, police officers and civilians alike should be restricted from entering laboratory premises. Clandestine laboratories typically employ processes using chemicals that are toxic, corrosive, caustic, and flammable. The laboratory environment may pose explosive toxic or carcinogenic risks that should be dealt with only by specially trained and equipped personnel.

## IDENTIFYING LABORATORY OPERATIONS

Clandestine laboratory operations are typically identified in one of four ways. In some instances, fire departments responding to the scene of a fire or explosion will find evidence of laboratory operations. Positive determinations, however, depend on the ability of emergency service personnel to recognize the type of substances and equipment typically used in such operations. It is important, therefore, that these personnel be trained in identification of clandestine lab operations. Since fire departments should be close at hand during police raids of drug laboratories, it is important that responsible personnel from both agencies develop a working relationship in dealing with problems that may arise from these types of operations.

Evidence of drug laboratory operations may also be generated through informants. Laboratory operators who are attempting to establish operations in a new community often need to determine sources for the purchase of specific chemicals. Plans for development of a lab and related involvement of suppliers or distributors frequently are revealed by confidential informants and intelligence gathered from arrestees.

The community at large may also provide valuable tips on laboratory operations on the basis of observations of unusual activities or circumstances. Many drug labs operate in urban or suburban residential communities where citizens who are alerted to the common signs of laboratory operations can provide valuable information to the police. These indicators include the following:

- A residence where one or more individuals visit but where no one lives. Laboratory operators are generally cautious about the risks of fire, explosion, or contamination and attempt to limit their exposure and risk.
- Residences or other buildings that have sealed doors and windows, although they are not abandoned facilities.
- The presence of ventilating fans that operate irrespective of weather conditions.
- Strong ammonia or related odor.
- An unfurnished "residence."
- A "resident" who frequently goes outside for a cigarette or to get some air.

Although these circumstances do not prove the existence of an illegal drug manufacturing operation, several of these factors together may be suggestive enough to warrant establishment of low-profile police surveillance.

## METH LABS

One of the fastest-growing types of clandestine laboratories is the methamphetamine lab. **"Meth labs"** have been around since the 1960s, when they were organized and operated by outlaw motorcycle gangs. To stop the spread of "clan labs," chemicals such as ether and ephedrine were restricted by the Chemical Diversion and Trafficking Act of 1988. Rogue chemical companies that sold to clan-lab precursors were prosecuted and put out of business by the DEA and other local, state, and federal law enforcement agencies.[39]

In the late 1980s and early 1990s, the biker manufacturers began to be edged out of the market by new and very violent methamphetamine manufacturers—the Mexican national methamphetamine organizations. Today, they dominate the meth manufacturing market. Their industrial-size labs are producing methamphetamine in mass quantities for distribution across the United States. This is evidenced by recent DEA operations that resulted in methamphetamine arrests in California, Texas, and North Carolina, as well as the seizure of three methamphetamine labs (see photo on page 728).

With the restriction of methamphetamine manufacturing chemicals, lab seizures started to decline in the late 1980s. Since then, however, the trend has been reversed with a vengeance, and lab seizures have started to skyrocket. One of the reasons for this increase is the Internet. Now all a methamphetamine manufacturer has to do is turn on his or her computer, point and click to find a recipe, and point and click again to find the chemicals. If the "meth cook" has any questions during the manufacturing process, he or she can simply visit one of the methamphetamine-manufacturing chat pages. These small "tweeker"-type labs are capable of making anywhere from ounce to pound quantities of methamphetamine. Size does not matter when it comes to clan labs; these small labs are just as dangerous for law enforcement officers as are the biker and Mexican national labs.

**Meth Lab**

Paraphernalia used in the production of methamphetamine discovered in a laboratory raided by special agents of the Drug Enforcement Administration. Today, the Mexican national methamphetamine organizations dominate the meth lab manufacturing. Their industrial-sized labs are producing methamphetamine in mass quantities for distribution across the United States. The Internet is also used by those interested in developing their own, smaller meth labs. The "meth cook" can visit a methamphetamine-manufacturing chat page to get questions answered. The smaller albs are capable of making anywhere from one-ounce to one-pound quantities, thus creating even more problems for law enforcement.

(Courtesy Drug Enforcement Administration)

Meth labs can be broken down into different styles:

- Biker or traditional
- Mexican national
- Cold-cook
- Pressure cooker
- Hydrogenation
- Tweeker

Chemicals used to manufacture methamphetamine are easily obtainable, even with chemical restrictions. Laboratory equipment used to manufacture methamphetamine runs the full spectrum from the scientific to the yard-sale purchase. Heating mantles, condensers, vacuum pumps, buchner funnels, and 22-liter reaction vessels are regularly seized at clandestine labs. Not wanting to attract attention of law enforcement, clandestine laboratory equipment manufacturers are turning to other types of clan-lab equipment. They now use pressure cookers, hot plates, mason jars, sun tea dispensers, nalgene containers, homemade compressed-gas cylinders, Pyrex bowls, sports bottles, microwave ovens, and other such material.[40]

## SEIZURE AND FORFEITURE

Laboratory operators may be arrested under a wide variety of circumstances, only the most typical of which are discussed here. Most laboratory operations are closed as the result of police raids following intensive investigative work.

On occasion, police officers will inadvertently discover a clandestine lab operation while responding to other public safety situations. It is essential that officers take only those steps necessary to protect their lives or the lives of bystanders and that they make arrests only if entry into the laboratory is not required. Normally, if the officer's presence has not been detected, this involves relaying information to supervisory personnel and/or other appropriate personnel in the department who have received specialized training in handling clandestine laboratories.

Once the scene is secure, it may be possible to interview neighbors in order to determine information on occupancy. Officers should make note of all vehicles parked in the immediate area of the laboratory.

Another means of interdiction involves the civil forfeiture of illicit chemicals and drug manufacturing paraphernalia. This procedure, which pertains to individual laboratory operators as well as chemical suppliers, allows federal agents to seize anything used or intended to be used to illegally manufacture, deliver, or import drugs. Most states have similar prohibitions, and officers should be familiar with the provisions and limitations of these laws. Use of the forfeiture statutes may be a reasonable alternative to attempts to establish a criminal case, particularly where staffing constraints limit surveillance and other operations, when suspects' discovery of surveillance may necessitate terminating the investigation, or when it is feared that the laboratory operation is preparing to relocate quickly. It should be noted that often the circumstances that justify a civil seizure will lead thereafter to successful prosecution under criminal statutes relating to conspiracy or the attempt to manufacture controlled substances.

When making a decision concerning civil seizure of illegal drugs and manufacturing materials, officers should contact their local prosecuting attorney for advice. Evidence not sufficient to support criminal prosecution may be adequate for a civil seizure. Normally, successful seizure requires that officers demonstrate the suspect's probable intent to manufacture a controlled substance. This can be accomplished by reference to the type and combination of chemicals and paraphernalia on hand, furtive activity, use of subterfuge, or other questionable practices.

Those who supply materials to clandestine laboratories with knowledge of their use are also subject to civil and criminal penalties under various federal and state laws. Chemical companies or supply houses may knowingly sell chemicals to laboratory operators without reporting the sales to the police, disguise sales records, assist buyers in using the chemicals, or otherwise assist in the preparation or merchandising process. It is normally possible to apply seizure and forfeiture actions to such merchants if investigation can establish any factor that shows the suppliers' "guilty knowledge" of the illegal uses of their merchandise.

An undercover purchase of chemicals from suspected suppliers is the most typical means of developing criminal cases against them. In addition, chemicals seized at drug laboratories may display manufacturers' labels, including lot numbers, and equipment may have manufacturers' plates and serial numbers that can be used to trace their sales or transfers.

Under proper circumstances, therefore, civil seizure may be an acceptable, if not preferred, approach to termination of illegal drug-manufacturing operations. Additionally, once such actions are taken, perpetrators will often cooperate with the police and provide intelligence that will assist in additional enforcement operations.

## CONDUCTING A LABORATORY RAID

Conducting a raid on an occupied laboratory requires careful planning. Normally, a planning meeting involves the police tactical unit, bomb squad, hazardous-material or chemical-waste disposal personnel, a chemist, and fire department representatives—all of whom are specially trained. The nature of the operation from initial entry to dismantling should be reviewed with particular attention to the types of chemicals most likely being used, the nature of the suspects involved, and contingency plans for emergency services should a fire, explosion, or toxic reaction take place.

The initial entry team should be outfitted with Nomex clothing, body armor, and goggles. Nomex will provide short-term protection from fire, and goggles will protect one's eyes from airborne fumes and thrown chemicals. The tactical unit is responsible only for securing the suspects and exiting the laboratory as quickly as possible and with the minimum amount of force.

It should be noted that to avoid unduly restricted movements, the tactical team should wear the minimum amount of protective clothing necessary. It is important, therefore, that the team's exposure to the laboratory environment be extremely limited. The team should make a mental note of the laboratory environment and report its findings to the assessment team members who will follow. Laboratory operators, in anticipation of possible raids, sometimes booby-trap the facility in order to destroy evidence. The ability to recognize traps and other potential hazards depends on the training and experience of team members, a factor that underscores the importance of special training for such operations. After leaving the facility, the tactical team should undergo decontamination.

After the site is secured, the assessment team is free to enter. Team members should wear Nomex clothing covered with disposable protective suits, as well as chemical-resistant gloves and boots covered with disposable gloves and boots. All seams of the suits should be taped with nonporous adhesive tape, and each team member should be equipped with a self-contained breathing apparatus. The team should be outfitted with two air-monitoring devices—a combustible-gas indicator and indicator tubes. (See photo on page 730.)

The combustible-gas indicator is an essential air-monitoring device that tests for oxygen levels, airborne gas particle levels, and the combustibility of the environment. The indicator tubes test for the presence and quantity of specific types of chemical

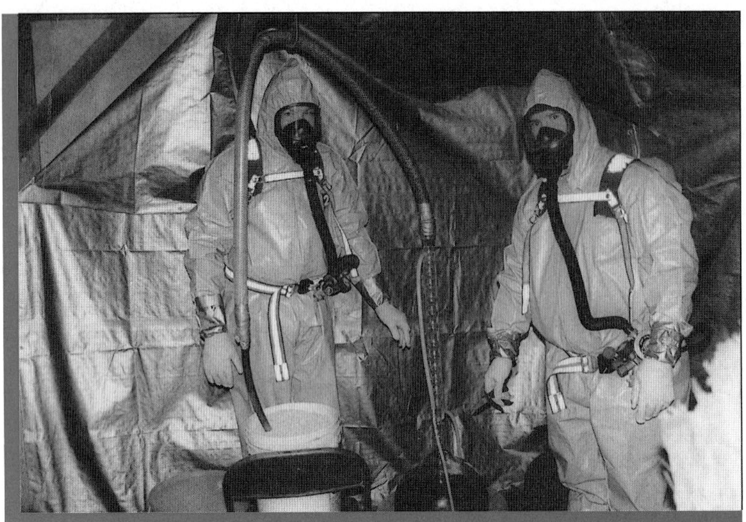

**Meth-Lab Raid**
The methamphetamine cooking process is extremely dangerous due to fumes and volatility of ingredients. After the site is secured, the assessment team (shown in the photo) enters the lab. Team members should wear Nomex clothing covered with disposable suits, as well as chemical resistant gloves and boots covered with disposable gloves and boots. Each team member should be equipped with a self-contained breathing apparatus. Finally, the team should have two air-monitoring devices.
(Courtesy Detective David Street, Riverside County, California, Sheriff's Deparment)

vapors. A pump is used to force air through the individual tubes.

Assessment team members test the lab environment at several locations and make notes of instrument readings. They should also make a diagram of the interior, noting any dangers or problems that may be encountered. When their work is completed, the assessment team should leave the facility, decontaminate, and give their report to the dismantling team.

The dismantling team should wear the same type of protective clothing as the assessment team. Even though dangerous substances may not have been found, there is always the possibility of spills and damage during dismantling, which could create a hazardous situation. A chemist trained in laboratory dismantling should be on hand to take samples of chemicals and of products being manufactured so that informed judgments can be made on safety in packaging, transportation, storage, disposal, and handling of evidence samples.

Crime scene personnel, under the close supervision of the dismantling team supervisor, should conduct standard crime scene processing procedures, including taking photographs and searching for latent fingerprints. Videotaping of laboratory operations is also helpful for evidentiary purposes and for court presentation.

The chemist can direct the proper packaging of chemical substances. Care must always be taken that only compatible chemicals are packaged together. Typically, chemicals are placed in drums filled with vermiculite or a similar absorbant, nonflammable substance. A waste disposal company approved by the Environmental Protection Agency (EPA) can be of great value in the packaging process.

Chemicals that are not being used in court because of potential hazards, together with contaminated clothing and equipment, must be packaged, transported, and stored or disposed of according to EPA guidelines.

## SEARCH WARRANTS AND PROBABLE CAUSE

Officers engaged in drug enforcement must understand the legal elements necessary to constitute probable cause for obtaining search warrants. The criteria for ascertaining probable cause vary somewhat even within judicial districts.

The vast majority of drug information provided to law enforcement officers comes from confidential informants. Therefore, it is particularly significant that certain guidelines be followed carefully by those responsible for drafting search warrants.

### LAW ENFORCEMENT BACKGROUND OF THE APPLICANT

Some factors to be considered in assessing the background of the law enforcement officer seeking the warrant are length of time employed by the agency, present position, familiarity with the offense in question, number of previous arrests made by the applicant for this type of offense, and, if applicable, familiarity with any paraphernalia used in connection with the offense.

### PAST RELIABILITY OF THE CONFIDENTIAL INFORMANT

The past reliability of the confidential informant is of considerable importance, especially when the effort to determine probable cause to obtain a search warrant is based exclusively on such information. One should consider the length of time the applicant has known the informant and the number of occasions on which reliable information was supplied. For example, how many times before did the confidential informant's information result in the seizure of contraband or paraphernalia on persons, on premises, or in vehicles, and how many of these offenses resulted in a conviction? To confirm that the confidential informant has been reliable, the officer should be prepared to cite specific instances of reliable information. Other considerations are the informant's familiarity with the type of offense involved in the affidavit and familiarity with paraphernalia used in connection with the offense.

### INFORMATION SUPPLIED BY THE INFORMANT

Information to be considered in this area includes the date, time, and place of the meeting between police and the informant; the substance and content of the information; and the date, time, and place that the information was obtained.

The law enforcement officer should try to elicit from the informant as many facts as possible that can be corroborated, for example, the telephone number and address of the suspect's residence, a physical description of the suspect, the occupation of the suspect, vehicles owned or operated by the suspect, a description of the vehicle and the tag number, and the time at which the suspect may be observed at the premises or within the described vehicle.

### CORROBORATION OF THE INFORMATION SUPPLIED

All efforts should be made to corroborate information supplied by a confidential informant. In some instances, corroboration is a simple check of the accuracy of portions of the information, such as the suspect's address, associates, vehicle, hangouts, patterns of behavior, and criminal record. When information is corroborated, careful records should be kept, including the date, time, and method of corroboration. Some jurisdictions have found it useful to attach a mug shot of the suspect and a photograph, diagram, or sketch of the property, vehicle, store, or other place to be searched.[41]

## EVIDENCE HANDLING AND SECURITY PROBLEMS

Aside from the burglaries, larcenies, and other crimes committed because of narcotics, there are additional related problems sprouting from the drug-culture vine. Some of these growths entwine the individual police officer and the overall police function. One offshoot, the handling and securing of narcotics and dangerous drugs after they are collected and seized, has emerged as an area of growing concern to police administrators for a number of reasons.

Once seized by the police, narcotic and dangerous-drug evidence requires protection so that it may be preserved in its original state until it is brought before a court or destroyed through legal process. It is during this period that the greatest demands are placed on personnel of the law enforcement agency concerned. Narcotic and dangerous-drug evidence must be protected not only against loss and outside threats of incursion, but, unfortunately, sometimes from internal intrusions as well.

Although relatively uncommon, there have been occasions when narcotic and dangerous-drug evidence has disappeared from a "secure" area under the control and within the confines of a police agency. The following methods for handling drug evidence will go far in addressing this concern and minimizing its occurrence.[42]

There are two recognized methods for introducing narcotic and dangerous-drug evidence into the processing sequence immediately after it is seized and marked. Neither method omits any of the processing steps; the difference is found in the manner in which the sequential steps are arranged.

The first method (the laboratory-first method) requires that all seized evidence (after it is field tested, marked, photographed, weighed, and initially inventoried) be transported immediately to the laboratory for analysis. Drop boxes are provided in the laboratory for the deposit of evidence during periods when the facility is not operational. All seized narcotic and dangerous-drug evidence is taken directly to a room in the vicinity of the laboratory. This room, known as an inventory or display room, is specially equipped for inventorying narcotic and dangerous-drug evidence and is not used for any other purpose. Weighing scales, camera, film holders, lighting equipment, evidence seals, evidence containers, appropriate forms, desk, typewriter, table or counter, and necessary administrative supplies are maintained in the room. When not in use, the room is locked and the keys (two) are retained in a secure location (normally, one key is kept in the laboratory and the other is controlled by the watch supervisor or desk officer). In order to achieve even greater control over inventory rooms, departments that have a high volume of narcotic evidence are employing more sophisticated entry-control systems, including "entry" or "swipe" cards on a system that records the cardholder's identity and time of entry and departure. Video cameras may also be used to record all behavior in the inventory room.

After seizure of the evidence and while en route to police headquarters, the seizing officer requests a witnessing officer of supervisory grade (at least one grade above that held by the seizing officer) and a member of the laboratory staff (technician on duty) or a technician from the mobile laboratory unit, if available, to meet with him or her at the narcotic and dangerous-drug inventory room. When the supervisory official arrives at the inventory room, the seizing officer displays the material seized (the witnessing officer does not handle any of the evidence). After the evidence package has been marked and displayed in the manner best suited for a photographic inventory, the laboratory technician photographs the evidence (the photographer does not handle any of the evidence). When photographs of the evidence have been taken, the evidence is weighed and inventoried under the direct supervision of the supervisory officer. Appropriate forms are then completed and witnessed, and the evidence is sealed in containers or envelopes provided for that purpose.

After these steps have been accomplished, in company with the witnessing officer and the laboratory technician, the seizing officer carries the evidence to the laboratory drop box and deposits it therein. If the drop box cannot accommodate the evidence package, the laboratory evidence-room custodian or an alternate is requested to come to the laboratory, assume custody of the evidence, and store it in the laboratory evidence room. If the evidence is taken to the laboratory during normal operational hours, the drop box is not used; the evidence is turned over directly to the laboratory evidence custodian or alternate.

On completion of the analytical process by the laboratory, the evidence is delivered to the narcotic and dangerous-drug evidence room in the property room. Here, the evidence custodian assumes control of the evidence and provides for its preservation and subsequent processing as required.

In the second method (the evidence-room-first method), seized narcotic and dangerous-drug evidence, after being field tested, marked, photographed, weighed, and inventoried, is sealed in an appropriate container and deposited in a drop box or delivered directly to the evidence room in the property room. There are variations to the procedure; in some cases certain intermediate steps (photographing the evidence, for example) are omitted or the initial processing (weighing, photographing, and inventorying) may be accomplished in the property room or evidence room. The single difference between the two methods is that in one the evidence is analyzed before it is stored whereas in the other the evidence is taken directly to the narcotic and dangerous-drug evidence room (or to an adjunct depository), receipted, and then removed to the laboratory for analysis.

Of the two methods used for introducing narcotic and dangerous-drug evidence into the processing sequence, the laboratory-first procedure is preferred and should be followed whenever possible. The main advantage of this method is that it reduces actual handling of the evidence and decreases the number of custody transfer points. By first delivering the evidence to the laboratory, the evidence must undergo only one journey to the narcotic and dangerous-drug evidence room, that is, after analysis, rather than before and after. Consequently, the exposure of the evidence to various loss hazards is reduced and its security is enhanced.

It must be recognized, however, that establishment of the laboratory-first method depends on the existence of certain features that are not available to many law enforcement agencies. The laboratory-first method requires that a mobile laboratory unit or laboratory technician be on call for around-the-clock operation. Second, this method requires an easily accessible laboratory—preferably located in the same building housing the headquarters of the police agency itself.

## Key Terms

**amphetamines**
**barbiturates**
**clandestine drug laboratories**
**cocaine**
**codeine**
**crystallized methamphetamine**
**depressants or sedatives**
**glutethimide (Doriden)**
**hallucinogenic drugs**
**hashish**
**hashish oil**
**heroin (diacetylmorphine)**
**ketamine**
**lysergic acid diethylamide (LSD)**
**marijuana**
**meperidine (Pethidine)**
**meprobamate**
**mescaline**
**meth labs**
**methadone**
**methaqualone**
**methcathinone**
**methylenedioxy methamphetamine (MDMA) or ecstasy**
**morphine**
**narcotics, synthetic**
**opiates**
**opium**
**OxyContin**
**phencyclidine (PCP)**
**phenmetrazine**
**psilocybin and psilocin**
**rock cocaine or crack**
**speedballing**
**stimulants**

## Review Questions

1. What major drugs of abuse are derived from opium?
2. What role does the drug methadone play in treating heroin addicts?
3. What factors may indicate that a person is addicted to opium-derived drugs or synthetic opiates?
4. What are the acute and chronic effects of cocaine use?
5. What is freebasing?
6. How is the chromatographic impurity signature profile analysis (CISPA) used in the investigation of drug distribution?
7. What is methcathinone?
8. Discuss OxyContin abuse.
9. What is speedballing?
10. What are some of the known side effects of PCP?
11. What are the positive and negative arguments for the use of MDMA?
12. Why has the indoor growing of marijuana become so popular in the past few years?
13. What types of drug-related confidential informants were discussed in the text?
14. What drug-theft preventive measures may physicians and pharmacists take to reduce the likelihood of being victimized?
15. What are the most common indications that a physician is unlawfully diverting drugs for his or her own use?
16. How are clandestine drug laboratory operations typically identified?
17. Which major factors should be considered when attempting to secure a search warrant solely on the basis of information supplied by a confidential informant?
18. What are the two recognized methods for introducing narcotics and dangerous drugs into the processing sequence immediately after they are seized and marked?

## Internet Activities

1. The U.S. Drug Enforcement Agency website, www.dea.gov, provides a variety of statistics and information on drug use in this country. For the most recent drug-use statistics, log on to the website and click on "Statistics." Find the report entitled "Collective Statistics Concerning Drug Use." This report summarizes statistics from many drug-use surveys including the National Household Survey on Drug Abuse, the Drug Abuse Warning Network, and the PRIDE Survey.
2. Find out about another frequently abused type of drug, inhalants, by logging on to the National Criminal Justice Reference Service website at www.ncjrs.org. Under the heading "Drugs and Crime," read the report entitled "Inhalants Fact Sheet."

## Notes

1. U.S. Department of the Army, *Field Manual—Military Police Criminal Investigation* (Washington, DC: U.S. Department of Defense, 1971), p. 28–5.
2. Ibid., pp. 28–5, 28–7.
3. John H. Langer et al., "Drugs of Abuse: Narcotics," in *Drugs of Abuse* (Washington, DC: Drug Enforcement Administration, 1975), pp. 10–13.
4. U.S. Department of the Army, *Field Manual*, p. 28–8.
5. Ian R. Tebbet, "A Pharmacist's Guide to Drugs of Abuse," *Drug Topics*, Sept. 3, 1990, Vol. 134, p. 58, with modification.
6. Malachi L. Harney and John C. Cross, *The Narcotics Officer's Notebook* (Springfield, IL: Charles C. Thomas, 1961), pp. 96–98.
7. Smith Kline and French Laboratories, *Drug Abuse* (Philadelphia, 1971), p. 10.
8. Robert C. Petersen, "Cocaine: An Overview," in *Drug Enforcement* (Washington, DC: Government Printing Office, 1977), pp. 9–12.
9. Keith Sarji and Jose Rosch, "Now Cocaine, Too, Can Be Profiled & Traced," *Law Enforcement News*, Apr. 30, 1993, Vol. 19, No. 379, p. 9. This discussion of profiling and tracing cocaine was obtained with permission from this source.
10. Langer et al., "Drugs of Abuse," p. 19.
11. John B. Williams, *Narcotics and Drug Dependence* (Encino, CA: Glencoe, 1974), p. 273.
12. U.S. Department of Health, Education, and Welfare, *Students and Drugs* (Washington, DC: Government Printing Office, 1969), pp. 8–9.
13. "Hawaii's Problems with 'Ice,'" *Police*, October 1989, p. 14.
14. Adapted from "The Menace of Ice," *Time*, Sept. 18, 1989, p. 28.
15. James McGiveny, "'Made in America': The New and Potent Methcathinone," *Police Chief*, April 1994, pp. 20–21 (this discussion was adapted with permission from this source). Methcathinone is also known as 2-methylamino-1-phenylpropan-1-one, n-methcathinone, monomethylproprion, and ephedrone; street names include "go," "goob," "sniff," "crank," "star," "wonder star," "bathtub speed," "gaggers," "wildcat," and "cat."
16. Drug Enforcement Administration, *Fact Sheets* (Washington, DC: Government Printing Office, 1973), p. 43.
17. Langer et al., "Drugs of Abuse," p. 16.
18. "Prescription Cancer Drug Is a Narcotic of Choice," *Law Enforcement News*, Feb. 14, 2001, p. 5.
19. Timothy Roche, "Potent Perils of a Miracle Drug," *Time*, Jan. 8, 2001.
20. Robert C. Petersen and Richard C. Stillman, "Phencyclidine Abuse," in *Drug Enforcement* (Washington, DC: Government Printing Office, 1978), pp. 19–20.
21. "Angel Dust—Abuse Diagnostic Test Introduced," *Police Chief*, November 1979, Vol. 46, No. 11, p. 12.
22. Raymond Hernandez, in "New Drug Battles, Use of Ecstasy among Young Soars," *New York Times* on the web, Aug. 2, 2000.
23. "Way Found to Detect LSD in Humans," *Tampa Tribune*, Sept. 8, 1972.
24. Loukia Louka, "Cropping Up Indoors," *Police*, November 1993, Vol. 17, No. 11, p. 38.
25. Ibid.
26. Ibid.
27. Ibid., p. 39.
28. Ibid., p. 90.

29. Drug Enforcement Administration, *Drugs of Abuse* (Washington, DC: Government Printing Office, 1988), p. 45.
30. John S. Farrell, "An Overview of Ketamine Abuse," *Police Chief*, February 1998, p. 47.
31. Drug Enforcement Administration, "Field Testing for Controlled Substances" (Washington, DC: National Training Institute, U.S. Department of Justice, 1973), pp. 1–6.
32. U.S. Department of the Army, *Field Manual*, pp. 28–16, 28–17.
33. Ibid., p. 28–18.
34. Gregory D. Lee, "Drug Informants, Motives, and Management," *FBI Law Enforcement Bulletin*, September 1993, pp. 10–15. This information was obtained with some modifications from this article.
35. Drug Enforcement Administration, *Agents Manual*, Appendix B, "Domestic Operations Guidelines," sec. B.
36. *DEA Integrity Assurances Notes*, August 1991, Vol. 1, No. 1.
37. Drug Enforcement Administration, "Addict Practitioners," handout material provided by the National Training Institute, Washington, DC.
38. Reprinted from Training Key 388, *Clandestine Laboratories* by L. Ray Brett. Copyright held by the International Association of Chiefs of Police, Inc., 1110 North Glebe Road, Suite 200, Arlington, VA 22201, U.S.A. Further reproduction without the express written permission from IACP is strictly prohibited.
39. Michael Cashman, "Meth Labs: Toxic Timebombs," *Police Chief*, February 1998, p. 44.
40. Ibid., pp. 44–45.
41. E. J. Salcines, "Checklist of Elements Constituting Probable Cause in Search Warrant Affidavits," prepared by the State Attorney's Office, Hillsborough County, Tampa, Florida, 1974.
42. Drug Enforcement Administration and International Association of Chiefs of Police. *Guidelines for Narcotic and Dangerous Drug Evidence Handling and Security Procedures* (Washington, DC: U.S. Department of Justice 1976). This discussion on the identification and recording of drug evidence was adapted from this source, pp. 42–54.

# TWENTY

# Terrorism

*Ground Zero, where the Twin Towers stood prior to the murderous Al-Qaeda attacks on September 11, 2001. This tragic act of terrorism brought about significant changes in the frequency and types of information shared between federal and local law enforcement regarding suspected terrorists and their organizations. (© AFP/Corbis)*

## CHAPTER OUTLINE



## CHAPTER OBJECTIVES

1. Explain mission-specific and sleeper cells.
2. Be familiar with different terrorist groups that threaten the United States and its allies.
3. Distinguish between right-wing and left-wing terrorists.
4. Describe four prominent national structures involved in terrorist intelligence, and outline their responsibilities.
5. Define joint terrorism task forces.
6. Identify the purpose of a suspicious-activity log.
7. Understand the process of critical thinking.
8. Describe the function of a reconnaissance operation.

# INTRODUCTION

The tragic events of September 11, 2001, were clearly the most horrendous and devastating terrorist acts ever to occur on U.S. soil. Few people would argue that 9/11 forever changed the lives of all Americans, not only in terms of coping with the loss experienced on that day but also in terms of living with the possibility of future terrorist threats.

This chapter discusses various aspects of terrorism and their relation to the work of a criminal investigator. The chapter opens with an overview of international terrorism and the international groups that have committed terrorist acts against and/or pose threats to the United States and its allies. Such acts of terrorism are not a recent phenomenon. While the significant terrorist events listed in this chapter occurred within the last few decades, they are only part of a long-standing pattern of worldwide violence. The chapter then turns to an examination of domestic terrorism and its perpetrators, including right-wing and left-wing terrorists and special-interest groups. The most publicized events of the past decade, such as the Branch Davidian incident in Waco, Texas, and the Oklahoma City bombing in 1995, are associated with right-wing terrorism. The next section addresses threat assessment, with a focus on the Al-Qaeda group and its potential for future terrorist acts against the United States. This is followed by a discussion of several U.S. national structures charged with the task of gathering information on terrorism, terrorism prevention and investigation, and counterterrorism.

While federal agencies are clearly important in assessing the threat of future terrorist acts, the role of criminal investigators at both the state and the local law enforcement levels should not be underestimated. The remainder of the chapter outlines the ways that criminal investigators can assist in the fight against terrorism. Confronting terrorism is not an occasional or seasonal venture; it is an ongoing responsibility. Now, more than ever, criminal investigators must be prepared to encounter and handle terrorist-incident crime scenes.

The world and the United States are not strangers to terrorism. The first U.S. plane hijacking occurred in 1961, when Puerto Rican Antuilo Ortiz, armed with a gun, diverted a National Airlines flight to Cuba, where he was given asylum.[1] A rebel faction in Guatemala assassinated the U.S. Ambassador John Mein by gunfire in 1968 after forcing his car from the road. Black September terrorists struck in Munich at the Olympics in 1972 and the following year killed U.S. Ambassador Cleo Noel in the Sudan. The Baader-Meinhof group and the Popular Front for the Liberation of Palestine (PFLP) seized a French airliner in 1976 and flew the 258 passengers to Uganda, precipitating the Entebbe hostage crisis. In 1979, the Italian Prime Minister was kidnapped and killed by Red Brigade members; the U.S. Embassy in Tehran was seized by Iranian radicals; and Mecca's Grand Mosque was taken over by 200 Islamic terrorists who took hundreds of pilgrims hostage, an incident that resulted in 250 people killed and 600 wounded.

Even a partial accounting of terrorist activities over the past two decades indicates a continuing pattern of such violence worldwide. Across the United States, people are wondering if the September 11, 2001, attacks were harbingers of the future or anomalies. They were not anomalies: the United States is opposed by international and domestic terrorist groups, and the likelihood of further incidents is quite real. Our nation's implacable enemies will have some successes because they are skilled and dedicated. However, Americans are not wanting for virtues, as was demonstrated by the courage of people in New York City and at the Pentagon in the wake of September 11 (see photo on page 740). Together, globally and locally, people have to work harder and smarter, with better tools, to eliminate, disrupt, minimize, and investigate terrorist attacks.

## INTERNATIONAL TERRORISM

"International terrorism involves violent acts or acts dangerous to human life that are the violation of the criminal laws of the United States or any state, or that would be a criminal act if committed within the jurisdiction of the United States or any state. Acts of international terrorism are intended to intimidate a civilian population, influence the policy of a government, or affect the conduct of a government. These acts transcend national boundaries in terms of the means by which they are accomplished, the persons they intend to intimidate, or the locale in which perpetrators operate."[2]

Although Osama bin Laden and Al-Qaeda ("the base") have dominated national attention recently, there are many other terrorist groups worldwide, including Al-Qaeda's allies, such as the Islamic Jihad (see Figure 20–1). Such groups include:

***Abu Nidal:*** Aliases include Fatwah Revolutionary Council, Arab Revolutionary Brigades, Revolutionary Organization of Socialist Muslims, and Black September. Split from the Palestine Liberation Organization in 1974, it since has launched terror attacks in more than 20 nations and killed or wounded more than 900 people. U.S. officials estimate membership at a few hundred. Abu Nidal is based in Iraq and sponsored by Iraq and Libya. Syria ended support in 1987.

***Abu Sayyaf:*** Affiliated with Al-Qaeda, it is the most radical Islamic separatist group in the southern Philippines. The group, led by Khadafi Janjalani, is under attack by the Philippine army and police. It engages in bombings, assassination, kidnapping, and extortion. U.S. officials believe it has about 200 hard-core fighters.

***Armed Islamic Group:*** Seeks to replace the secular Algerian government with an Islamic state.

**Figure 20-1** Partial Accounting of Global Terrorists

| Year | Group | Action |
|---|---|---|
| 1981 | Red Army | Bomb explosion on U.S. Airbase at Ramstein, then in West Germany |
| 1981 | Takflr Wal-Hajira sect | Assassination of Egyptian President Anwar Sadat during a troop review |
| 1983 | Islamic Jihad | U.S. Embassy bombing, Beruit |
| 1983 | Islamic Jihad | Suicide bomb truck, Marine Barracks, Beruit |
| 1984 | Hizballah | Bomb attack, Torrenjon, Spain, restaurant popular with U.S. service members |
| 1984 | Sikh terrorists | Seize the Golden Temple in India, 100 killed |
| 1985 | Narcotraffickers | In Mexico, kidnap, torture, interrogate a DEA agent and his pilot on orders from Rafael Cero |
| 1986 | North Korean agents | Detonate bomb at South Korea's Kimpo Airport in South Korea |
| 1987 | Libyan agents | Bomb attack in Berlin discoteque frequented by U.S. military members |
| 1988 | Organizafion of Jihad Brigades | Car bomb exploded outside of USI Club in Naples, Italy |
| 1988 | Libyan terrorists | Pan American flight 103 blown up over Lockerbie, Scotland |
| 1989 | New People's Army | Assassination of U.S. Army Colonel Rowe in Manila; he had survived long years of captivity during the war in South Vietnam |
| 1990 | New People's Army | Two U.S. airmen assassinated in the Phillipines |
| 1990 | Tupac Amaru Revolutionary Movement | Peru, U.S. Embassy bombed |
| 1993 | Followers of cleric Umar Abd al-Rahman | World Trade Center bombing, NYC |
| 1993 | Iraqi Intelligence Service | Attempted to assassinate President Bush during visit to Kuwait |
| 1994 | Baruch Goldstein | Jewish right-wing extremist, who was also an American citizen, uses machine gun at mosque, killing 29 and wounding an estimated 150 |
| 1995 | Unidentified gunmen | Karachi, Pakistan, assassination of two American diplomats |
| 1995 | Right-wing extremists | Bombing of U.S. Federal Building, Oklahoma City, killing 166 |
| 1995 | Unknown | A rocket propelled grenade (RPG) fired through the window of the U.S. Embassy in Moscow, perhaps as retaliation for U.S. air strikes against Serbian positions in Bosnia |
| 1996 | Irish Republican Army (IRA) | Bomb detonated in London, killing two and wounding more than 100 |
| 1996 | Tamil Tigers | Liberation Tigers of Tamil Eelam (LTTE) explode bomb in Colombo, Sri Lanka, 90 slain and over 1,400 injured |
| 1996 | Several groups claim responsibility | U.S. Military's housing facility in Dhahran, Khobar Towers, fuel truck carrying explosives kills 19 and wounds 515 |
| 1996 | Tupac Amaru | 23 members of the Tupac Amaru Revolution Movement (MRTA) take several hundred hostages at the Japanese Ambassador's residence in Lima, Peru |
| 1997 | Palestinian gunman | Observation Deck, Empire State Building, NYC, gunman opens fire on tourists from several countries, killing one and injuring others, kills himself. Note left by gunman states this was a punishment attack on "the enemies of Palestine" |
| 1998 | Al-Qaeda | Bombings of U.S. embassies in Nairobi, Kenya and Dar es Salaam, Tanzania, a total of 69 were killed in the attacks and some 5,077 wounded |
| 1999 | FARC | Three U.S. Citizens kidnapped by Revolutionary Armed Forces of Colombia and executed in Venezuela, one of numerous FARC attacks reported |
| 2000 | Al-Qaeda | U.S.S. destroyer Cole attacked by launch filled with explosives, causing major damage to the ship, killing 17, and injuring another 39 |
| 2001 | Al-Qaeda | Twin Towers and Pentagon attacks, producing horrific casualties |

**The Pentagon after Terrorist Attack**

This aerial photograph of the Pentagon shows some of the destruction caused when the hijacked American Airlines flight slammed into the building on September 11, 2001. The terrorist attack caused extensive damage to the west face of the building and followed similar attacks on the Twin Towers of the World Trade Center in New York City.

(© Reuters NewMedia Inc./Corbis)

Began violent activities in 1992 after the government voided the victory of the Islamic Salvation Front, Algeria's largest Islamic opposition party. The terror campaign has included wiping out villages and murdering more than 100 foreigners living in Algeria, mostly Europeans. The Salafi Group for Call and Combat is a splinter faction active since 1998. Group strengths are unknown. Sympathizers and members living abroad provide money and logistical support. Algeria alleges state sponsors include Iran and Sudan.

***Aum Supreme Truth:*** Also known as Aum Shinri-kyo, the group gained infamy for loosing sarin nerve agent in the Tokyo subway system, killing 12 people and injuring up to 6,000. Established in 1987, the Aum aimed to take over Japan, then the world. It adopted a view that the United States would initiate Armageddon by starting World War III with Japan. Control changed hands in 2000, and under Fumihiro Joyu, the Aum changed its name to Aleph and now claims to reject the teachings of its founder. Membership is 1,500 to 2,000.

***Basque Fatherland and Liberty:*** Known by its Basque initials, ETA, the group was founded in 1959 with the aim of establishing an independent, Marxist homeland in the border area between Spain and France. The group has killed more than 800 people and targets primarily Spanish officials. It finances activities through kidnapping, robbery, and extortion. Estimated membership is in the hundreds.

***Hamas:*** Also called the Islamic Resistance Movement, this group formed in late 1987 from the Palestinian branch of the Muslim Brotherhood. It has a political arm but includes terrorism in pursuit of an Islamic Palestinian state in place of Israel. Hamas works through mosques and social service institutions to recruit, raise money, organize activities, and distribute propaganda. Activists have attacked many Israeli civilians and soldiers. Officials estimate it has tens of thousands of supporters and sympathizers. It receives funds from Palestinian expatriates, Iran, and benefactors in moderate Arab states, Europe, and North America.

***Hezbollah:*** Its many aliases include Islamic Jihad, Revolutionary Justice Organization, Organization of the Oppressed on Earth, and Islamic Jihad for the Liberation of Palestine. This radical Shiite Muslim group is dedicated to increasing its political power in Lebanon and opposing Israel and the Middle East peace process. Hezbollah took part in the suicide truck bombing of the U.S. Embassy and U.S. Marine barracks in Beirut in October 1983. It has only a few hundred terrorist operatives but thousands of supporters. It is based in Lebanon but has cells worldwide. State sponsors include Iran and Syria.

***Al-Jihad:*** This Egyptian group seeks an Islamic state in Egypt and attacks U.S. and Israeli interests in Egypt and abroad. The original Al-Jihad was responsible for the 1981 assassination of Egyptian President Anwar Sadat. Several hundred hard-core members operate in Cairo, but the group's network outside Egypt includes Yemen, Afghanistan, Pakistan, Sudan, Lebanon, and the United Kingdom. Egypt claims Iran and Osama bin Laden support the Jihad.

***Kach and Kahane Chai:*** Israeli terrorists whose goal is to restore the biblical state of Israel. Radical Israeli American Rabbi Meir Kahane founded Kach. Kahane Chai, or "Kahane Lives," was founded by Binyamin Kahand following his father's assassination in New York in 1990. Both were declared terrorist groups by Israel in March 1994. The younger Kahane and his wife were murdered in a drive-by shooting in Israel on December 31, 2000. The Kahanes' groups protest against the Israeli government and harass and threaten Palestinians in Hebron and the West Bank. They receive support from sympathizers in the United States and Europe; their numbers are unknown.

***Kurdistan Workers' Party:*** Founded in 1974 as a Marxist-Leninist insurgent group, the party is primarily composed of Turkish Kurds bent on forming an independent Kurdish state in southeastern Turkey. Turkish authorities captured Chairman Abdullah Ocalan in 1999, tried him, and sentenced him to death. Ocalan announced a "peace initiative" in August 1999, ordering members to refrain from violence and to withdraw from Turkey and requesting dialogue with Ankara on Kurdish issues. Members supported the initiative and claim to use only political means to achieve a new goal of improving rights of Kurds. There are 4,000 to 5,000 supporters, most in northern Iraq, and thousands of sympathizers in Turkey and Europe. Syria, Iraq, and Iran have harbored party members and offered limited funds.

***Liberation Tigers of Tamil Eelam:*** Founded in 1976, it is the most powerful Tamil group in Sri Lanka. It uses overt and illegal methods to obtain funds and weapons and to publicize its cause of establishing an independent Tamil state. It began attacks on the Sri Lankan government in 1983 and relies on a guerrilla strategy that includes terrorism. One group, the Black Tigers, carries out suicide bombings and assassinations. Estimated to have 8,000 to 10,000 combatants in Sri Lanka, the Tigers control most of the northern and eastern coastal areas of Sri Lanka.

***Mujahedin-e-Khalq Organization:*** Known as MEK or MKO, this Iranian Marxist-Islamic group formed in the 1960s to counter "excessive Western influence" in the shah's regime. It is the largest, most active armed Iranian dissident group. While the West has been its historical bane, the group has shifted its aim to Iran's clerical regime. Based in Iraq, the group receives funds from Saddam Hussein.

***National Liberation Army:*** Based in Colombia, this Marxist insurgent group formed in 1965 and is currently in a dialogue with the Colombian government. The group's 3,000 to 6,000 armed combatants engage in kidnapping, hijackings, bombings, extortion, and guerrilla war. Its strength lies mostly in rural and mountainous areas of north, northeast, and southwest Colombia.

***Palestine Islamic Jihad:*** Originating among militant Palestinians in the Gaza Strip in the 1970s,

PIJ is one of many groups seeking the creation of an Islamic Palestinian state and the destruction of Israel. U.S. support of Israel makes America a target. The group also opposes moderate Arab governments "tainted by Western secularism." Its strength is unknown, but it has many sympathizers in Palestine and Israel. Based in Syria, it receives money from Iran and limited logistics aid from Syria.

***Palestine Liberation Front:*** Started as a breakaway from the Popular Front for the Liberation of Palestine—General Command in 1973 but later split into pro-PLO, pro-Syrian and pro-Libyan factions. The pro-PLO group, led by Muhammad Abbas, alias Abu Abbas, is known for air attacks against Israel and the 1985 attack on the cruise ship *Achille Lauro.* This faction is based in Iraq, which supports it.

***Popular Front for the Liberation of Palestine:*** A Marxist-Leninist group founded in 1967 by George Habash, it committed numerous international terrorist attacks during the 1970s. Since 1978, it has attacked Israeli and moderate Arab targets. With 800 hardliners, the group operates in Syria, Lebanon, Israel, and the occupied territories. Syria shelters the group and provides some money.

***Popular Front for the Liberation of Palestine–General Command:*** Violently opposes Yasser Arafat's PLO. Closely tied to Syria, its focus is on guerrilla operations in southern Lebanon and small-scale attacks in Israel, the West Bank, and Gaza Strip. Its several hundred members are based in Syria and receive funds from Iran.

***Revolutionary Armed Forces of Colombia:*** Established in 1964 by the Colombian Communist Party, FARC is Colombia's oldest, largest, most capable, and best-equipped Marxist insurgency. It operates with impunity in many areas of the country. It engages in bombings, murder, kidnapping, extortion, hijacking, and guerrilla and conventional war against Colombian political, military, and economic targets. There are 9,000 to 12,000 armed members and an unknown number of supporters, mostly in rural areas. Cuba provides some medical care and political consultation.

***Revolutionary Organization 17 November:*** A Greek radical leftist group established in 1975, it is named for the 1973 student uprising that protested Greece's military regime. It is against its government, the United States, Turkey, and the European Union. It wants Greece out of the EU and NATO and the Turkish military out of Cyprus. Responsible for killing U.S. officials and Greek public figures, its most recent victim was the British defense attachè in June 2000.

***Turkish Revolutionary People's Liberation Party/Front:*** Also called Dev Sol, this Marxist group formed in 1978 is virulently anti-American and anti-NATO. It finances activities through robbery and extortion. The Turks crippled Dev Sol in a series of attacks. Size is unknown.

***Sendero Luminoso:*** The "Shining Path" terror group of Peru is based on founder Abimael Guzman's belief in militant Maoist doctrine. Some 30,000 persons have died since Shining Path took up arms in 1980. Its stated goal is to replace Peruvian institutions with a communist peasant revolutionary regime. Peruvian counterterrorist operations, arrests, and desertions in recent years have reduced membership to an estimated 100 to 200 armed militants.

***Tupac Amaru Revolutionary Movement:*** A Peruvian group formed in 1983 that aims to establish a Marxist regime. The group's ability to operate has been sharply reduced by Peru's counterterrorism program, the imprisonment or deaths of senior leaders, infighting, and the loss of leftist support. In December 1996, the group seized the Japanese ambassador's residence in Lima and held 72 hostages for four months. Peruvian forces stormed the residence in April 1997, rescued all but one remaining hostage, and killed all 14 terrorists. The group now seems more interested in the release of jailed members than in terror operations. Officials estimate it has no more than 100 members.[3]

The above such groups have much closer ties than was thought previously, as revealed by international financial investigations that "follow the money trail" and by records originating in Afghanistan (see photo on page 743). They also have mission-specific cells and "sleeper" cells in dozens of countries.

## MISSION-SPECIFIC CELLS

**Mission-specific cells** are put together for the purpose of executing a specific mission. Information is often tightly compartmentalized to prevent the mission from being "blown" if one or more people are arrested. Individuals may know what skills they need to develop or keep sharp but not how their activities fit in the overall plan. That level of detail may be revealed only at the last moment.

The attacks on September 11, 2001, are a prime example of the operation of mission-specific cells. From the analysis of those attacks and the surrounding circumstances, a profile of the terrorists and their activities was developed.

## The Terrorists

The terrorists ranged in age from the early twenties to the mid-thirties and were from Middle Eastern countries. Their command of the English language was limited. They came in groups of three to four to open accounts at branch banks located in areas where there was a high Muslim population. Usually there was only one spokesman for the group, who wanted to deal with only one person and was somewhat reluctant to deal with a woman.[4] Sixteen of the 9/11 terrorists entered this country legally under business, tourist, or student visas; at least six of the hijackers attended flight schools abroad or attempted to get flight training in the United States.[5] For the most part, they lived quiet lives and at least one attacker used his family as a cover. The hijackers traveled across the country.

## Terrorists' Bank Accounts

With cash or its equivalent, attackers opened 24 domestic bank accounts in four different banks, averaging $3,000 to $5,000 per account. The identification used to open the accounts were visas issued through Saudi Arabia or the United Arab Emirates; none of the terrorists had a Social Security number. The addresses used for the accounts were often temporary (e.g., a mailbox) and changed frequently. Some of the terrorists used the same address and telephone number for their account records. No savings accounts were opened, nor were safety deposit boxes acquired. All accounts had debit cards.[6]

## Terrorists' Transactions

The accounts were funded primarily by cash and overseas wire transfers and were kept below $10,000 to avoid federal banking reporting requirements.[7] Account transactions did not reflect normal living expenses, such as rent, utilities, and insurance, nor was there any consistency with the timing of deposits and withdrawals. The terrorists made numerous balance inquiries, often exceeding their balances when making debit card withdrawals. The number of debit card transactions was much higher than the number of checks issued.

The profile of other terrorists operating in this country may or may not match this profile. Officers and investigators should look for anomalies in otherwise unremarkable data. Stated differently, they have to pick out the fish that really matters from the school in which it swims.

# SLEEPER CELLS

**Sleeper cells** are individuals or small groups who are in place in target or other countries. Potential terrorist or sympathizers who have been recruited

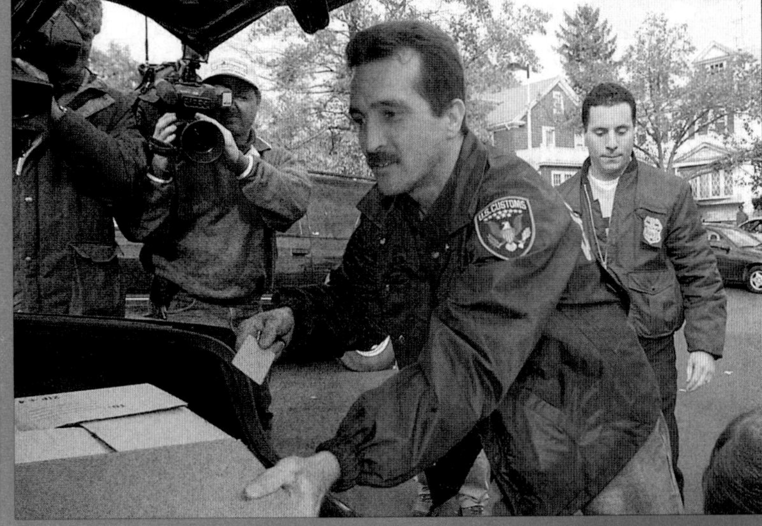

**Terrorist Records**
Information about Al-Qaeda and its allies being unloaded by FBI personnel. The boxes contain videotapes, maps, notebooks, and other documentary sources seized by military, intelligence, and law enforcement personnel in Afghanistan and brought to the United States for closer investigation.
(© AFP/Corbis)

are ordered to lead "everyday lives" and not bring attention to themselves. Classically, they may be in place for years before they are activated. Sleepers may also perform limited services for the group with which they are allied, including serving as couriers, providing financing, maintaining safe house, providing transportation, and engaging in reconnaissance tasks.

# DOMESTIC TERRORISM

"**Domestic terrorism** is the unlawful use, or threatened use, of violence by a group or individual based and operating entirely within the United States or its territories, without foreign direction, committed against persons or property to intimidate or coerce a government, the civilian population, or any segment thereof, in furtherance of political or social objectives."[8] It's perpetrators can be divided into three groups: right-wing terrorists, left-wing terrorists, and special-interest groups.

## RIGHT-WING TERRORISTS

"Domestic **right-wing terrorist** groups often adhere to the principles of racial supremacy and embrace antigovernment, antiregulatory beliefs."[9] They may also cling to antiabortion and survivalist views and the need for paramilitary training in "militias." In general, right-wing militias believe that inevitably there will be a "showdown" with the federal government, so they stockpile weapons and food. In contrast, patriot groups tend to be more focused on the overthrow and destruction of the federal government. There has been some movement toward "leaderless resistance," which is enacted by small groups autonomously. The Montana Freemen illustrate the antiregulatory attitude of some right-wing groups. They refused to register their cars or pay income taxes, filed liens on government property, established their own court system, announced rewards for the arrest of government officials, and forged financial documents such as money orders. A 960-acre farm was declared sovereign territory and named "Justus Township." The 21 armed freemen surrendered after being under siege from authorities for roughly 90 days in 1996. [10]

At the national level, examples of formal right-wing hate groups are the Aryan Nation, the World Church of the Creator (WCOTC), and the National Alliance.[11] They expressed their views via the Internet, through "white-power" music," and in publications. Some white-supremist groups have toned down the openness of their racial opinions in order to appeal to a broader audience.[12]

The incidents with the Weaver family at Ruby Ridge, Idaho, and the Branch Davidians in Waco, Texas, were catalysts for the militia and patriot groups.[13] There was subsequent upswing in right-wing terrorist incidents, the most destructive being the Oklahoma City bombing in 1995 (see photo on page 745), for which Tim McVeigh and Terry Nichols were later convicted; both men harbored antigovernment views and may have had some indirect ties to a militia.[14]

## LEFT-WING TERRORISTS

**Left-wing terrorists** generally profess a revolutionary socialist doctrine and view themselves as protectors of the people against the "dehumanizing effects" of capitalism and imperialism.[15] They advocate revolution as the means of transforming society; from the 1960s to the 1980s, leftists were the most serious domestic terrorist threat.[16] Their demise as a threat was brought about by law enforcement ef-

**Bombing in Centennial Park, Atlanta, During the 1996 Summer Olympics**

In early 2002, Eric Holder remained at large and on the FBI's 10 Most Wanted List for this fatal bombing, as well as one in Birmingham, Alabama, at a women's health clinic. Holder is also wanted for several other bombing attacks.

(© Wally McNamee/Corbis)

**The Oklahoma City Bombing**
The results of the blast at the Alfred P. Murrah Federal Building, where 168 people were murdered. This act of domestic right wing terrorism is considered the most destructive to date. Timothy McVeigh and Terry Nichols were later convicted for the crime.
(© AFP/Corbis)

forts and the fall of communism in Eastern Europe, which deprived them of ideological support.[17] The most significant of the existing left-wing terrorists are separatists in Puerto Rico, who want to establish an independent country. The Los Macheteros are suspected in several bombings in Puerto Rico in recent years.[18]

## SPECIAL-INTEREST GROUPS

Perhaps the most active special-interest groups in the United States are the Animal Liberation Front (ALF) and the Earth Liberation Front (ElF). Both are destructive of property but epouse a philosophy that discourages harm to "any animal, human or nonhuman." ELF has claimed responsibility for the arson fires set in Vail, Colorado, which caused $12 million in damages.[19]

# THREAT ASSESSMENT

Of necessity, threat assessments are ongoing and subject to change as usable intelligence about intentions and capabilities of existing and new groups is produced. The purpose of this section is to highlight patterns of terrorism in the Unites States and to assess known threats.

**Figure 20-2** Terrorism by Group Class, 1980–1999

(**Source:** Federal Bureau of Investigation, ***Terrorism in the United States*** [Washington, DC: FBI, 1999], p. 33.)

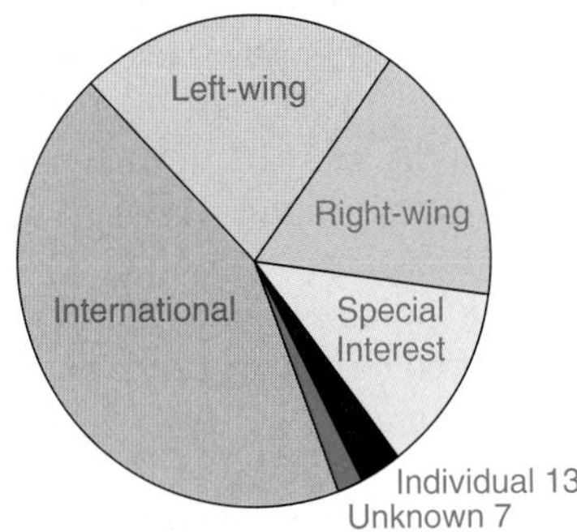


• Figures include terrorist incidents, suspected terrorist incidents, and preventions.

**Figure 20-3** Terrorism by Event, 1980-1999

(**Source:** Federal Bureau of Investigation, ***Terrorism in the United States*** [Washington, DC: FBI, 1999], p. 41.)

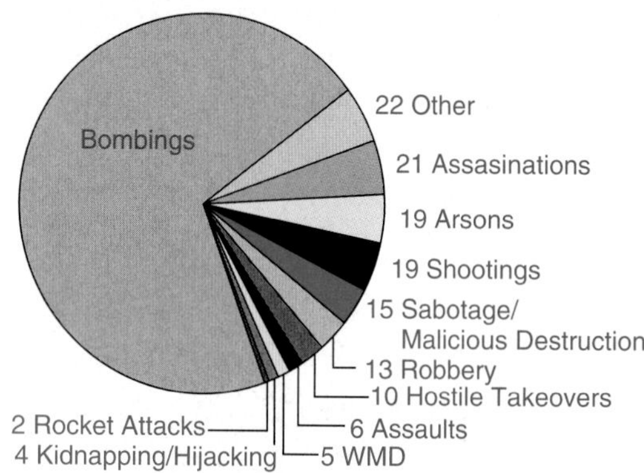


Since 1968, 14,000 international terrorist attacks have taken place throughout the world.[20] In the United States, between 1980 and 1999, there were 457 prevented, suspected, or actual terrorist acts, of which 163 involved international terrorists (see Figure 20–2). It is tempting to classify the Unabomber, Theodore Kaczynski, as a terrorist, although his mail bombings are actually classified as criminal acts because his intentions were unclear. Of the 457 terrorist acts, 321 were bombings (see Figure 20–3). As this data shows, the numbers of terrorist attacks is not high, and the terrorism is largely domestic in nature. Presently, the most serious internal threat comes from right-wing groups.

Externally, international terrorists are a formidable challenge because of the heretofore relaxed U.S. policies on obtaining visas and the presence of numerous lucrative and relatively "soft" American targets abroad, where access is less problematic for terrorists. The foreign threats are classified into three categories: (1) the radical international Jihad movement, largely consisting of Sunni Islamic extremists, such as those in Al-Qaeda, (2) formal terrorist groups, including Hamas and Hezbollah, and (3) state-sponsored terrorism, primarily by Iran, Iraq, Sudan, and Libya.[21]

The fatwahs, which are civil or religious rulings by Muslim clerics, encourage people to do or refrain from doing certain things. Bin Laden's policies against the United States are revealed in the following fatwahs, which he announced:

1. American forces stationed in the Horn of Africa, and particularly Somalia, should be attacked; subsequently, Al-Qaeda-trained Somalians killed 18 Americans in Mogadishu, in the "Blackhawk Down" incident.
2. "In compliance with God's order, we issue the following fatwah to all Muslims: the ruling to kill the Americans and their allies, including civilian and military, is an individual duty for every Muslim who can do it in any country in which it is possible to do it." This may have provided the religious justification for the

**Theodore Kaczynski**

While some consider the Unabomber a terrorist, his mail bombings are actually considered as criminal acts because his intentions were unclear. Determining the potential motivation of those who are willing to use explosive devices against innocent civilians can provide critical information for investigators. These cases are often complex and can take months or years to solve.

(© Reuters NewMedia Inc./Corbis)

bombings of two American Embassies in Africa, as well as other acts, such as Richard Reid's attempt to light explosives in his sneakers during an international flight to the United States.[22]

3. The acquiring of weapons of mass destruction (WMDs) is the religious duty of every Muslim.

Included in WMDs are chemical, biological, radiological, and nuclear (CBRN) weapons. A radiological weapon, also called a "dirty bomb," is a conventional weapon that has been filled with radiological materials. It kills people both by its initial explosion and through airborne radiation and contamination. Intelligence sources indicate that Al-Qaeda is close to acquiring nuclear capability and its operative have been trained in the use of biological and chemical agents. Other terrorist groups are also pursuing the acquisition of, and training in the use of, WMDs.

Radical Muslims regard the United States as an infidel because it is not governed according to their beliefs. In their view, the United States has provided support for other infidel regimes, particularly Saudi Arabia, Egypt, Israel, and the United Nations. Al-Qaeda opposed U.S. involvement in the Gulf War in 1991 and feels that Americans have violated its holy lands by their presence and are plundering the riches of Arabic countries. Moreover, Al-Qaeda is further aggrieved by the United States' arrest, conviction, and imprisonment of its members, and those of allied groups, for terrorist and criminal activities.[23]

Al-Qaeda and its allies are the greatest international terrorist threat to the United States because they have the money, equipment, training, and patience needed to carry out their murderous attacks.[24] Regardless of who is leading these terrorist groups, the United States can expect the following:

1. Future attacks on Americans at home and abroad are highly probable.
2. Everyone in the United States is considered a combatant; it is "open season" on American children, women, and men.
3. Targets will be selected on the basis of their economic and symbolic significance; there may be few attacks, but they will produce high casualties.
4. Softer, high-casualty-producing targets will be preferred.
5. The United States has preempted some terrorist strikes, but the opposing force continues to have the capability to launch sophisticated, multiple operations simultaneously with little or no warning.
6. To avoid detection and blame, the attackers will attempt to develop surrogates to conduct their operations.[25]

## NATIONAL STRUCTURES

A number of federal agencies are involved in intelligence gathering, foreign counterintelligence, terrorism prevention and investigation, and counterterrorism. This section describes four of the most prominent efforts.

The National Infrastructures Protection Center (NIPC) is responsible for protecting and investigating unlawful acts against U.S. computer and information technologies and unlawful acts, both physical and electronic, that threaten or target critical U.S. infrastructures.[26] NIPC manages computer intrusion technologies, coordinates specialized training related to its spheres of interest, and supports national security authorities when unlawful attacks go beyond crimes and become foreign-sponsored events. Founded in 1998, NIPC is housed by the FBI. In addition to protecting national security information, NIPC is engaged in preventing and investigating **cyberterrorism**, the use of electronic tools to disrupt or shut down critical components of our infrastructure, including energy, transportation, and government operations. For example, massive thefts of credit card numbers and other such acts could do serious harm to the public's confidence in using e-commerce transactions.[27]

As is the case with a number of investigative procedures, there is controversy regarding email intercepts conducted by law enforcement agencies. It usually focuses on the privacy expectations people have when using email versus the investigative need to read or view certain types of email transactions. Among these transaction are messages or images sent by terrorists, child molesters, and pornographers, as well as transactions involving people engaged in hacking crimes and espionage, people using the Internet to commit serious frauds and to launder money, and hostile groups or nations waging information warfare against the United States.[28]

Enacted in response to the September 11 attacks the U.S. Patriot Act of 2001 provides law enforcement with new, broadened electronic surveillance authority, DCS 1000 will continue to have a role in intercepting email. None of the new measures should be considered surprising in light of the prevalence of digital pagers, wireless telephones, fax machines, videoconferencing, encrypted emails, and other high-technology methods of communicating.

The Departments of Justice, Defense, Energy, and Health and Human Services, the Environmental Protection Agency, and the Federal Emergency Management Agency form the National Domestic Preparedness Office (NDPO). Established in 1998, it is responsible for assisting state and local authorities with the planning, equipment, and training, including health and medical support, needed to respond to a WMD attack.

The FBI Counterterrorism Center has steadily expanded since its creation in 1996. It operates on three fronts: international terrorism operations both within the United States and abroad, domestic terrorism operations, and counterterrorism measures at home and abroad.[29] The center is staffed by 18 participating agencies, including the Department of State, the Central Intelligence Agency, and the Secret Service.

Created in 2001 as an immediate response to the 9/11 attacks, the Office of Homeland Security was established by President Bush. Its mission is to develop and coordinate the implementation of a comprehensive national strategy of the federal executive branch to prevent, respond to, and recover from terrorist acts within the United States. Among its responsibilities are facilitating the exchange of information across agencies (such as immigration and visa matters), reviewing and assessing the adequacy of federal plans relating to terrorism, and increasing, as necessary, vaccine and other pharmaceutical stockpiles. The Office of Homeland Security has not yet proved its value, but it is a very new operation. Among the difficulties it faces is changing the thinking and behavior of well-established, entrenched bureaucracies, and the prospects for doing so are not bright unless the change is genuinely supported by agency personnel.

**Tom Ridge (Office of Homeland Security)**
In response to the attacks of 9/11, the Office of Homeland Security was established and Tom Ridge was selected to be its director. The office's mission is to develop and coordinate the implementation of a comprehensive national strategy of the Federal Executive Branch to prevent, respond to, and recover from terrorist acts within the United States.
(© Reuters NewMedia, Inc./Corbis)

## INVESTIGATION

Many officers will miss opportunities to investigate terrorism because they have not been provided with the resources needed to accurately determine whom they have stopped or what the persons' intentions are. In other instances, officers' information may be added as a piece to a puzzle being assembled by people with specialized training and experience. The role of state and local agencies in combating both domestic and, recently, international terrorism is rapidly evolving, but there are things that such agencies and/or their officers can do immediately:

***1. Participate in Joint Terrorism Task Forces*** Joint terrorism task forces (JTTFs) are responsible for gathering and acting on intelligence related to international and domestic terrorism, conducting investigations related to planned terrorist acts, preventing such acts, and investigating terrorist acts in their geographic areas of responsibility. Consisting of representatives of federal agencies and state and local enforcement officers, JTTFs are ultimately supervised by the FBI. Nationally, there are 27 JTTFs; the first one was established in 1980 in New York City.[30] That city's JTTF was instrumental in preventing two bombings by Shaykh Rahmain in 1993 and the attempted bombing of the New York City subway system in 1997.[31]

***2. Keep a Suspicious-Activity Log*** It is easy to forget details, especially if they seem only a little suspicious and probably inconsequential. To combat this possibility, keep a separate log of suspicious activities.[32] Using the disparate entries, it may be possible for you or others to "connect the dots" and foil an attack or some criminal activity. Do not just make records of events; apply critical thinking to them.

***3. Use Critical Thinking*** Critical thinking involves rigorously challenging your own views and those of others. "Challenging" does not mean being verbally confrontational at every encounter; rather, it means reasonably assessing the basis of assumptions and beliefs. Consider the following example:

WORKING the midnight shift in a newly assigned area, an officer would see a man in his seventies sitting on his home's porch from about 4:40 A.M. almost every day. People employed at a produce loading dock about half a mile away would often stop as they walked to work and talk briefly with the man. This observation was initially written off as someone with insomnia who had probably lived in the neighborhood for many years and knew everyone. What is more natural than an old man who can't sleep? Operating in his community-oriented mode, the officer periodically stopped and talked to the man, who was very pleasant. Over the next few mornings the officer waved at the older man as he drove past the man's home.

The officer mentally reviewed this situation and realized that nobody stopped to talk to the man when he was there, and this did not seem to fit the normal rhythm. The conclusion he came to, perhaps slowly, but correctly, was that the man was engaged in some illicit activity, which he was: selling drugs.

There are two generally recognized components of critical thinking: (1) possessing the knowledge and skills to be able to look at "data" and see it in a new light, and (2) having the personal and mental discipline to use the "new light" as a guide. In the case study just presented, the officer was able to see the data in a new light and verify his suspicion. Using critical thinking, he had begun his transformation from seeing to understanding. This is a skill that is useful in all phases of life.

***4. Be Alert for Reconnaissance Operations*** The execution of an attack is predated by reconnaissance, often involving multiple efforts, although not necessarily by the same person. While some of these efforts may be carried out in stealth at night, many of them will occur during normal business hours. Operatives may rent rooms that give them a view of the target and may recruit insiders who provide them with drawings or copies of plans. They may also take legitimate jobs that allow them to have access to sites (e.g., driving a delivery truck).

In a small town, alert police noticed an Arabic man, who was unknown to them, taking photographs of chemical tankers on a siding of a railroad track. He may have been an engineer or an employee of the railroad. He may also have been an operative or the dupe of an operative (e.g., a local photographer recruited by a legitimate-appearing businessman who said he had "insurance claims to be settled and needed some shots taken" of a specific siding). In Colorado in 2002, sensitive information about roads at Hoover dam was stolen, along with an engineer's identification badge. Is the dam being targeted? By whom? At the time of this writing these matters are under investigation.

***5. Apply and Update Your Knowledge Base*** Chapter 2 discusses procedures for approaching and handling potential and actual terrorist-incident crime scenes; Chapters 2 and 18 offer guidelines on recognizing suspicious packages and bombs. Review this information together with your own training and agency procedures because those sources will be the basis for your actions. Periodically, you must update your knowledge base by participating in appropriate training courses.

## TERRORIST CRIME SCENES

Terrorists have a wide range of tactics available to them, such as using various types of bombs or improvised explosive devices (IEDs), skyjacking planes, hijacking vehicles carrying hazardous materials, taking hostages, kidnapping, and engaging in assassination, ambushes, harassment raids, and sabotage, as well as launching biological, chemical, radiological, and nuclear attacks. It is beyond the scope of this section to cover the crime scene safety issues for every type of terrorist attack. Therefore, the section focuses on two areas of major concern: limited biological attacks and chemical attacks that produce mass casualties.

In the past, suspicious letters and packages might have contained explosives (see Chapter 18, "Arson and Explosive Investigations"). Today, they might also contain lethal biological agents. Fire departments have extensive training, appropriate equipment, and experience in handling hazardous-material (HAZMAT) situations. Because of this, they, along with public health officials and other specialists, play major roles in processing biological and chemical threat and attack sites.

## LIMITED BIOLOGICAL ATTACKS: ANTHRAX

**Biological agents** include both living microorganisms and the toxins produced by organisms. Their effect on humans ranges from various degrees of illness to death. Compared with chemical agents, biological agents are generally slower-acting. Among the biological agents that could be used in a terrorist attack are smallpox, anthrax, plague, botulism, tularemia, hemorrhagic fevers, and Q fever.

**Anthrax** is an acute infectious disease caused by a bacterium,[33] which has a one- to six-day incubation period, although in some unusual cases incubation may take as long as eight weeks. In nonwarfare situations, it most commonly occurs in hoofed animals, but it can also infect humans. There are three types of anthrax, each with its own means of transmission.

In cutaneous anthrax, a cut or abrasion in the skin allows the anthrax bacterium to enter the body. This type of anthrax develops fairly rapidly: the incubation period can be one to seven days but is usually two to five days. There is no latent period for its development. Starting as a raised itchy patch resembling the site of an insect bit, it progresses into a red-brown bump that becomes filled with fluid and may be accompanied by local swelling. This ruptures the skin, creating a painless ulcer 1 to 3 centimeters wide. At the center a black area emerges, which is caused by dying flesh (see photo). The disease may be accompanied by fever and sweating. The affected skin dries and falls off in one to two weeks, often leaving no scar.[34] Cutaneous anthrax can spread via the substantially clear fluid that oozes from the rupture site. Death is rare with appropriate antibiotic treatment, and even without it there is an 80 to 95 percent recovery rate.[35]

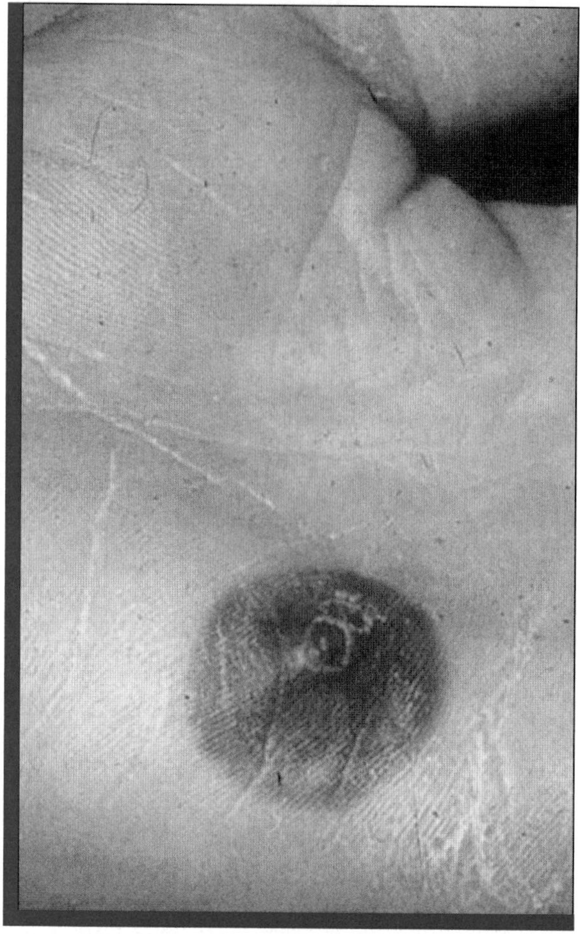

**Cutaneous Anthrax on Victim's Hand**
Note the darker spot, which is an area of dying flesh. Anthrax is an acute infectious disease caused by a bacterium. It is one of the biological agents that terrorists could use in an attack against the United States. In cutaneous anthrax, a cut or abrasion in the skin allows the anthrax bacterium to enter the body. Death is rare with appropriate antibiotic treatment.
(Courtesy U.S. Public Health Service)

Intestinal anthrax is contracted by eating anthrax-contaminated meat that has been insufficiently cooked; it produces an acute inflammation of the intestines. Initial symptoms are nausea, vomiting (including vomiting of blood), fever, abdominal pain, and severe, bloody diarrhea. The incubation period is one to seven days.[36] The mortality rate is estimated to be 25 to 75 percent;[37] the latter figure may indicate a lack of timely diagnosis and treatment.

Inhalation anthrax enters the body through the respiratory system; it has a usual incubation of one to six days, but there have been a few latent cases that did not reveal themselves until six weeks after exposure. During the first one to three days after exposure, the physical symptoms are similar to those of a cold or flu; thus they not very specific. They may include a sore throat, fever, fatigue, muscle aches, mild chest discomfort, and a dry, hacking cough. A period of brief improvement may follow, lasting from several hours to days. Then the symptoms return and quickly advance to severe respiratory distress, shock, and, typically, death. Death usually results within 24 to 36 hours of the onset of respiratory distress. Therefore, it is important to begin antibiotic treatment early. The effectiveness of treatment started after the onset of significant symptoms is limited,[38] and mortality rates at this stage are estimated to be 90 to 100 percent.

Inhalation anthrax is extremely unlikely to occur through person-to-person contact, so communicability is not a concern. The disease is spread by a deliberate act. Large amounts of high-quality, weapon-grade inhalation anthrax delivered in an aerosol form could produce horrific mass casualties. The Centers for Disease Control recommends getting annual flu shots to facilitate early differential diagnosis because flu presents many of the same symptoms as does inhalation anthrax. There is a vaccination for the anthrax virus, but it is not yet available to the general public.

## Biological Scene with No Overt Dissemination: Unopened Suspicious Letters and Packages

Workers have died from handling unopened mail containing inhalation anthrax. New precautions will reduce the potential for receiving anthrax-tainted mail through the U.S. Post Office and other major carriers. Guidelines have been issued to help spot suspicious mail (see Figure 20–4), postal workers are being trained to identify such mail, and many post offices are using electronic beams to kill biological bacteria such as anthrax. However, even at a **biological scene with no overt dissemination**—such as one in which suspicious mail is unopened, the situation is well controlled, and there is no known dissemination of a biological agent—precautions are warranted:

1. If individuals at the scene are not symptomatic—which is the most likely scenario—extensive PPE and respiratory protection may not be needed.[39] The Centers for Disease Control (CDC) recommends that the minimum level of respiratory protection for first responders at a biological-hazard site is the use of a half-mask or full-face-piece air-purifying respirator with particulate filters from N95 to P100.[40] Disposable hooded coveralls,

**Figure 20-4** Suspicious-Mail Indicators

*Inappropriate or Unusual Labeling*

- Excessive postage.
- Misspelled common words.
- Strange or no return address.
- Handwritten or poorly typed address.
- Incorrect title or a title with no name.
- No specific person as addressee.
- Restrictions (e.g., "personal," "confidential," or "Do not x-ray").
- Postmark from a city that does not match the return address.

*Appearance*

- Powdery substance, felt or seen, on the letter or package.
- Oily stains, discoloration, or odors.
- Lopsided or uneven.
- Excessive packaging material (e.g., masking tape or string).

*Other Suspicious Signs*

- Excessive weight.
- Ticking sound.
- Protruding wires or aluminum foil.

(**Source:** Centers for Disease Control, "Updated Information about How to Recognize and Handle a Suspicious Package or Envelope," www.bt.cdc/documents/app/anthrax/10312001/han50.asp, Oct. 31, 2001.)

shoe covers, and gloves are also warranted.[41] Currently, this equipment is not routinely carried in police cars. Therefore, wait for support specialists, such as a HAZMAT or public health team, if they are needed.

2. Control the scene and assess the threat (e.g., is it credible?). If the threat is credible, let other responding officers know what the situation is; the 911 dispatch center will notify the appropriate federal, state, and local agencies, which, in turn, will determine whether they accept the threat as credible. Direct people to leave the room, and close windows and doors. Have all people from the room in which the suspicious mail was discovered stay together in a room some distance away or, preferably, outside the building.
3. Allow only qualified emergency personnel to enter the scene.
4. You and other responders should not smell, shake, or handle the mail (except as necessary when seizing it as evidence).
5. The person handling the evidence should triple-bag the suspicious mail in heavy-plastic evidence pouches; limit handling of it to an absolute minimum, and do not drop the mail. When sealing the pouches, avoid creating a puff of air that could spread pathogens. This is most likely to happen if the pouches are sealed too vigorously or if they are noticeably larger than the size actually needed.[42]
6. Mark "Biohazard" on each evidence pouch. Place the evidence in a rigid, leakproof container, seal the container, and mark it "Biohazard." Repeat this process two more times. The evidence should then be taken by police courier to the appropriate public health laboratory.
7. Get the names of and locator information for everyone who was in the room, anyone who came into the room, and the primary handler of the mail. Determine how the mail traveled through the organization before it reached the point at which it was discovered. Consider the possibility of additional contaminated mail.
8. Do not conduct your preliminary investigation in or near the room where the suspicious mail was found.
9. Have the organization's health and safety officer advise persons who have been exposed to the biological threat about the precautions they should take and any follow-up health measures they should pursue.
10. Do not allow site decontamination to take place until the crime scene is released.
11. Inspect the ventilation system to see if it was tampered with, since other attack modes and agents could also be in operation.
12. Follow standard procedures for discarding disposable PPE items and for decontamination.

## Biological Scene with Limited Dissemination: Opened and Easily Bagged Letters and Packages

A somewhat higher level of PPE is required at a **biological scene with limited dissemination**—such as one in which dissemination occurs only through an opened letter or package (see photo on page 753)—even if the situation is still fairly contained:

1. A full-face-piece respirator, giving facial coverage roughly from the hairline to the chin, with a P100 filter or air-purifying respirator (PAPR) with a high-efficiency particulate air (HEPA) filter and appropriate PPE are needed for safety.[43] Disposable hooded coveralls, shoe covers, and gloves are sufficient for this situation.[44]
2. Control the scene and assess the threat; communicate the facts to other responders.
3. If the threat is credible, close windows and doors; direct people to leave the room immediately without taking anything with them or touching anything.
4. Ask the organization's health and safety officer to attend to the people who have been exposed and to consider turning off the ventilation system.
5. Proceed with your investigation along the lines outlined in the previous list.

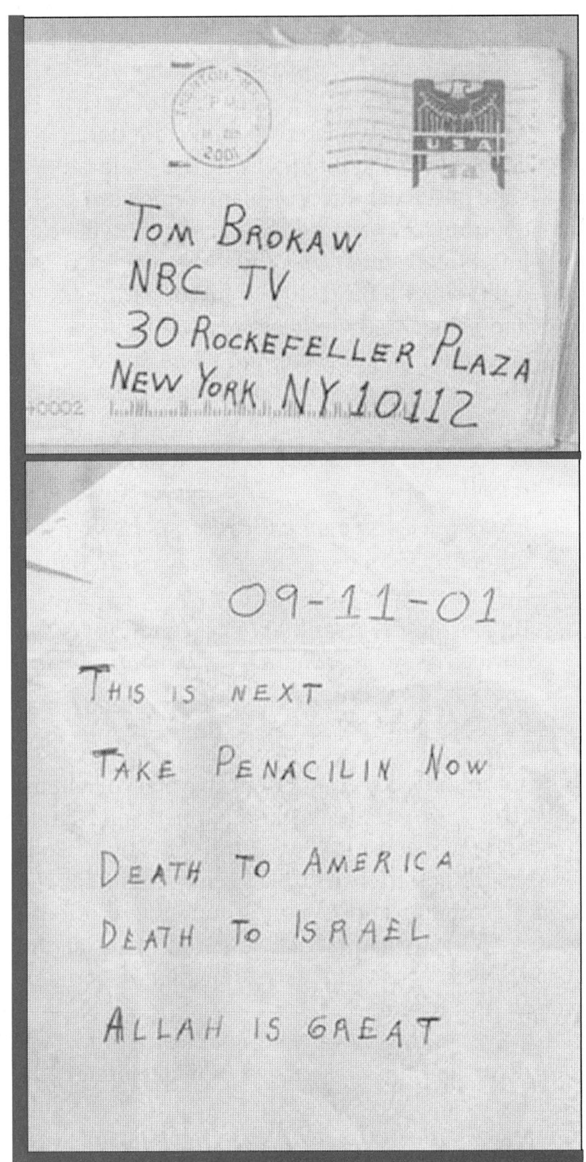
Tom Brokaw
NBC TV
30 Rockefeller Plaza
New York NY 10112

09-11-01

This is next
Take Penacilin Now

Death to America
Death to Israel

Allah is great

**An Opened Letter Containing Anthrax**
One of the ways terrorists or others can disseminate anthrax is through the use of the mail system. Following 9/11, numerous letters containing inhalation anthrax were discovered throughout the United States. One such letter was sent to NBC News Anchor Tom Brokaw. Following these discoveries, postal workers and others were given additional training on how to spot suspicious mail. Unfortunately, some individuals died as a result of their contact with mail containing inhalation anthrax.
(Courtesy Federal Bureau of Investigation)

## CHEMICAL ATTACKS: MASS CASUALTIES

Chemical attacks may be accomplished with V agents, mustard gas, sarin, soman, and tabun. With some **chemical agents,** incapacitation of victims occurs in only 1 to 10 minutes. We have no experience dealing with mass casualties from a chemical-agent attack. Depending on the size of the jurisdiction, the nature of the chemical agent, the method of dispersal, the timeliness of any warning that might be given, weather conditions, and other factors, casualties could number in the hundreds of thousands or even higher. Atropine autoinjectors are available to the military, emergency first responders, and civilians for use as an antidote for most nerve gases. They should not be used on children, who require a pediatric dose. Within the context of what we presently understand, the actions discussed below are appropriate if a chemical attack occurs and produces mass casualties.

### Initial Response to the Scenes

There may or may not be a warning before the attack; you must be on the alert for signs of danger when you patrol or are assigned to the scene of a possible chemical threat or to a **chemical attack scene.** If assigned to such a site, always approach with the wind at your back and from the high ground.[45] To achieve these favorable conditions, you may find it necessary to drive across open areas; remember, you are not restricted to driving on roads. Watch for the following signs of chemical attacks:

1. Lack of insects.
2. Birds falling from the sky, dying animals acting in an unusual manner, and dead animals.
3. Discoloration and withering of some types of grass, plants, shrubs, and trees. (These signs may become evident a few minutes to several days after the attack. The discoloration may be light or dark.)
4. Unexplained casualties, multiple victims, or victims with confused behavior, nausea, headaches, severe twitching, burning, or runny eyes, nose, or mouth, extremely small pupils, labored breathing, reddened or blistered skin, loss of bladder

or bowel control, convulsions, or cardiac arrest.

5. Unusual liquid droplets with an oily film. (Liquids may be any of several colors, e.g., clear, amber, or dark.)
6. Unexplained odors such as the smell from bitter almonds, freshly mown grass or hay, onions, sulfur, geraniums, garlic, mothballs, fruit, or fish. (Nerve gas has no odor.)
7. Vapor, mist, thin fog, or low clouds unrelated to the weather.
8. Unusual metal debris or unusual equipment such as abandoned sprayers and unexplained munitions.[46]

## Protection Measures

1. The most important thing you can do is resist the urge to rush in and help. First protect yourself; put on the highest level-PPE you have, including respiratory protection, immediately. Control the scene and assess the threat. The greatest contribution you can make is keeping others advised of conditions. You must be prepared to operate in somewhat of a standoff mode. Use binoculars, if you have them, to assess the scene.
2. In the absence of appropriate PPE, turn off your car's air conditioner and ventilation system, make sure windows are completely shut, and work from inside the car. It is crucial that you protect your respiratory system. Even placing a cloth or your sleeve over your mouth is beneficial.
3. Inform other responders about the dangerous conditions, as well as the direction in which suspicious plumes and clouds are moving the color and odor of such plumes and clouds, the scene condition, and the numbers, symptoms, and conditions of casualties.[47] Identifying the chemical agent or giving others sufficient information to do so is a high priority.
4. You will not be alone long; an integrated team will soon be there to help. Standing plans will immediately go into effect, and key federal agencies such as the Environmental Protection Agency (EPA), the Department of Defense (DOD), and the Federal Emergency Management Agency (FEMA), and the Centers for Disease Control (CDC) will handle tasks appropriate to their responsibilities regarding terrorist attacks. The FBI is designated as the lead federal agency for such incidents. At the same time, state and local terrorist plans, which are coordinated with the federal efforts, will go into effect. Fairly quickly, additional officers, public health officials, the fire department, and rescue and medical personnel will be arriving to help control the scene and to consider decontamination, triage, treatment, and transportation of living casualties.
5. Deny entry to the area to all but emergency responders.
6. Identify a staging area for responders.
7. Direct survivors to a single area; assure them that help is on its way.
8. Be alert to the possibility of secondary devices being present, e.g., command-detonated car bombs to kill rescuers. Watch for suspicious people.

After emergency responders arrive at the chemical attack scene, these better-equipped and trained specialists will enter and work the "hot zone." Your responsibilities then will be to help maintain the scene perimeter and to write the incident/offense report. When you are relieved from duty at the scene, follow your agency's postincident decontamination procedures.

Ideally, contingency planning, disaster preparedness drills, and the rapid arrival of an incident commander will relieve officers from the responsibility of making some of the decisions discussed above. If traffic or other conditions delay or prevent their arrival, officers must make the best decisions they can on the basis of their training and experience, the available resources, and the situation.

# LOOKING FORWARD

In addition to the dangers already discussed, other types of terrorist acts are possible, including agroterrorism, threats to water supplies, and the use of high-energy radio frequency (HERF) and electromagnetic pulse (EMP) weapons. **Agroterrorism** is the deliberate and malicious use of biological agents as weapons against the agricultural and food supply industries.[48] HERF weapons direct a high-energy radio signal at particular targets, such as computers and networks. They are essentially denial-of-service weapons. EMP bombs can destroy electromagnetic systems over a wide area when they are detonated.[49]

Confronting terrorism is not an occasional or seasonal venture; it is an ongoing responsibility. With the help of allies, the United States has the capacity to significantly disrupt terrorist groups and their finances and operations. Information systems must be improved and the products shared; genuine teamwork across numerous agencies will ensure progress. The United States must have the political will to be decisively and continuously engaged and the public must help sustain the effort and provide information. The greatest untapped resource in the fight against terrorism is local public safety officers: they are an army of eyes and ears on the nation's streets.

Domestic terrorists have murdered innocent people, and foreign ones have exhorted that Americans killed anywhere this can be done. The thousands of civilians killed on 9/11 is convincing proof of terrorists' willingness to do so, as are the international attacks. Ultimately, terrorists would like to destroy the United States and substitute another nation in its place.

## Key Terms

**agroterroism**
**anthrax**
**biological agents**
**biological scene with limited dissemination**
**biological scene with no overt dissemination**
**chemical agents**
**chemical attack scene**
**cyberterrorism**
**domestic terrorism**
**international terrorism**
**left-wing terrorists**
**mission-specific cells**
**right-wing terrorists**
**sleeper cells**

## Review Questions

1. What are mission-specific and sleeper cells?
2. Domestically, what are right- and left-wing terrorist groups?
3. Give an example of a domestic right-wing group, and discuss its activities.
4. What are special-interest terrorist groups?
5. In your view, was the Unabomber a terrorist?
6. What three categories can foreign terrorists be divided into?
7. What are fatwahs?
8. Assess the threats from domestic and foreign terrorists.
9. Discuss two of the four national structures that are engaged in antiterrorism efforts, and describe what they do.
10. Define JTTFs, and give two examples of their success.
11. What is critical thinking?
12. How do you use critical-thinking skills?
13. If you were concerned about a reconnaissance operation where you live, what would you look for?

## Internet Activities

1. Since September 11, 2001, several police departments and law enforcement institutes throughout the country have begun to offer training for police personnel on preparing for, investigating, and responding to terrorist crime incidents. Search the web for information on this training. What types of training are available? What topic areas do they cover? Do you

think the training would be helpful to a criminal investigator? Why or why not? Is there any specific type of training that you think should be provided but is not available?

2. Many large police agencies have posted information on their websites about homeland defense and preparation for terrorism incidents. Check out the websites of several large police agencies in your region. What type of information do they provide? Is any of the information useful to criminal investigators? (For an example, check out the Las Vegas municipal police department's site at www.lvmpd.com/home/homeland_safety.htm.)

## Notes

1. Office of the Historian, *Significant Terrorist Incidents*, 1961–2001 (Washington, DC: U.S. Department of State, 2002), 10 pp. The information in this paragraph was extracted, with restatement, from this source.
2. Phillip W. Thomas (Special Agent in Charge, Memphis Division, Federal Bureau of Investigation), "Statement for the Record before the House Committee on Government Reform, Subcommittee on Government Efficiency, Financial Management, and Intergovernmental Relations," Mar. 1, 2002, p. 1.
3. Jim Garamore, "Terrorism Inc.: Who's Who in the State Department List," Defend America, U.S. Department of Defense, Feb. 20, 2002, 3 pp.
4. Dennis M. Lormel, (Chief, Financial Crimes Investigations, Federal Bureau of Investigation), "Statement for the Record before the House Committee on Financial Services, Subcommittee on Oversight and Investigations," Feb. 12, 2002, p. 9.
5. Kellie Arena, *"Hijacking Suspects Quietly Entered the United States,"* www.cnn.com/2001/us/09/20/inv.howtheygother/, Sept. 20, 2001, pp. 1-2.
6. Lormel, "Statement for the Record," p. 5.
7. Ibid.
8. Dale L. Watson (Executive Assistant Director, Counterterrorism and Counter intelligence, Federal Bureau of Investigation), "Statement for the Record on the Terrorist Threat Confronting the United States, before the Senate Select Committee on Intelligence," Feb. 6, 2002, p. 3.
9. Ibid.
10. Federal Bureau of Investigation, *Terrorism in the United States* (Washington, DC: FBI, 1996), p. 7.
11. Watson, "Statement for the Record."
12. Ibid.
13. Federal Bureau of Investigation (FBI), *Terrorism in the United States* (Washington, DC: FBI, 1999), p. 30.
14. Ibid.
15. Watson, "Statement for the Record," p. 4.
16. Ibid.
17. Ibid.
18. Ibid.
19. FBI, *Terrorism in the United States,* 1999, p. 15.
20. Ibid.
21. J. T. Caruso (Deputy Executive Assistant Director, Federal Bureau of Investigation), "Statement for the Record on Combating Terrorism" before the House Subcommittee on National Security, Veteran's Affairs, and International Relations, pp. 1–10, March 21, 2002.
22. J. T. Caruso (Deputy Executive Assistant Director, Federal Bureau of Investigation), "Statement for the Record on Al-Qaeda" before the Senate Subcommittee on International Operations and Terrorism, pp. 2–3, December 18, 2001.
23. Ibid., pp. 1–2.
24. Ibid., p. 4.
25. George Tenet (Director of Central Intelligence), "World Wide Threat 2001, Statement before the Senate Select Committee on Intelligence," Feb. 7, 2001.
26. National Infrastructure Protection Center, www.nipc.gov, Mar. 12, 2001, p. 1.
27. Watson, "Statement for the Record," pp. 7–8.
28. Donald M. Kerr (Assistant Director, Laboratory Division, Federal Bureau of Investigation), "Statement for the Record on Carnivore Diagnostic Tool" before the Senate Committee on the Judiciary, pp. 1–12, September 6, 2000.
29. Ibid., p. 8.
30. Federal Bureau of Investigation, *Terrorism in the United States,* 1999, p. 44.
31. Watson, "Statement for the Record," p. 11.
32. International Association of Chiefs of Police, *Leading from the Front: Law Enforcement's Role in Combating Terrorism* (Alexandria, VA: IACP, 2001), p. 7.
33. The singular of "bacteria."

34. Thomas V. Inglesby et. al., "Anthrax as a Biological Weapon," *Journal of the American Medical Association,* Vol. 281, 1999, p. 7.

35. U.S. Department of Defense, "Information Paper: Anthrax as a Biological Warfare Agent," www.defenselink.mil/other_info/agent.html, June 1998, p. 2.

36. Centers for Disease Control, "Use of Anthrax Vaccine in the United States," *Morbidity and Mortality Report,* Dec. 15, 2000 (Vol. 49, No. RR-15), p. 3.

37. Centers for Disease Control, "Anthrax," www.cdc.gov/ncidod/dbmd/diseaseinfo/anthrax_t.htm, last reviewed Oct. 30, 2001, p. 1.

38. Ibid.

39. National Domestic Preparedness Office, "On-Scene Commanders Guide for Responding to Biological and Chemical Threats" (Washington, DC: Nov. 1, 1999), p. 19.

40. Centers for Disease Control, "Interim Guidelines for Firefighters and Other First Responders for the Selection and Use of Protective Clothing and Respirators," www.bt.cdc.gov/docuementsapp/anthrax/protective/10242001.asp, Oct. 14, 2001, p. 2.

41. Ibid.

42. Ibid., p. 3.

43. Ibid.

44. Ibid., p. 4.

45. National Domestic Preparedness Office, "On-Scene Commanders," p. 4, with minor additions by the authors.

46. Ibid., pp. 9–10.

47. Ibid., p. 10.

48. Steve Cain, Agroterrorism: A Purdue Extension Backgrounder (West Lafayette, IN: Purdue University 2001), p. 1.

49. Federal Bureau of Investigation, *Terrorism in the United States,* 1999, p. 240.

# TWENTY-ONE

# The Investigator and the Legal System

*The investigation, arrest, and subsequent prosecution of organized crime figures is quite interesting to many Americans. Local and federal investigators work closely with the prosecutors' office to ensure their cases will meet the highest standards of the legal system.*
*(© Stephen Frischling/AP/Wide World Photos)*

## CHAPTER OUTLINE



## CHAPTER OBJECTIVES

1. Distinguish among detention, arrest, and charging.
2. Explain the benefit of a police officer's making an arrest under the authority of a warrant.
3. Define and describe probable cause.
4. Discuss the risk factors involved in making a premature arrest.
5. Briefly outline the steps in a trial process.
6. Assess the importance of a criminal investigator's knowing the rules of evidence.
7. Describe the hearsay rule and the philosophy under which the exceptions to this rule have evolved.
8. Explain the reason for the existence of evidentiary privileges.
9. Discuss the role of an investigator as a witness in a criminal trial.
10. Explain the purpose of cross-examination.

# INTRODUCTION

At some point during the investigation of a crime, the investigator will decide to invoke the processes of the judicial system. If preparing for and taking a case to court were not the goal or, at least, one of the goals of a criminal investigation, there would be little point to investigating. That goal, however, may not always mesh with reality. Sometimes, despite the high level of investigative work done by the law enforcement agency, cases may not be prosecutable. First, even if a case is investigated as thoroughly as possible, many investigators at some time throughout their careers will be faced with the fact that the suspect simply cannot be identified. Second, if there is a suspect, investigators may not have enough evidence to arrest and later convict the perpetrator. Third, there may be situations in which legal requirements, such as probable cause, Miranda rights, and evidence-collection rules, are violated. Finally, because of certain rules of evidence or evidentiary privileges, some information garnered in an investigation may not be admissible. In short, investigators should always be aware of potential factors that may prevent or impede the prosecution of a criminal case.

The time at which the judicial system becomes involved during the course of an investigation is not uniform. The decision to begin involving the judicial system may come at the conclusion of the investigation, or it may occur at some earlier point. That decision will be based on a variety of factors, including identification of a suspect, collection of essential evidence and information for the case, and cooperation of witnesses and victims. Regardless of when the decision is made, the first step is bringing the accused before the court. How, when, where, and why this is done are the topics of the first part of this chapter. Next, the chapter discusses the trial process, including the order in which a trial is conducted and the elements of a criminal trial. This is followed by sections on the rules of evidence, evidentiary privileges, and the investigator as a witness.

## ARREST

There are a number of definitions of the term **arrest.** They range from "any interference with a person which, if not privileged, would constitute false imprisonment," to "interfering with the freedom of a person who is suspected of criminal conduct to the extent of taking him to the police station for some purpose," to "the taking of custody upon sufficient and proper evidence for the purpose of prosecution."[1] Each of these definitions is valid and depends on context. For example, what may appear to be a simple street stop or field interrogation may, in fact, constitute an arrest according to the first definition. Taking a person to the police station for interrogation may fit the second definition. When an investigator intends to incarcerate and charge a person with a crime, the third definition applies.

### Ingredients

There are three essential ingredients of an arrest:

1. Intention
2. Authority
3. Custody

The officer must have the intention of taking the suspect into custody. This factor distinguishes an arrest from a lesser form of detention, but actual or expressed intention is not always the controlling factor. The intention may be inferred by a court if its estimate of all the conduct and circumstances indicates that an arrest occurred, despite any contrary intent on the part of the police officer.

The officer must have real or assumed legal authority for taking the person into custody. The officer must have the actual authority to make a legal arrest or at least believe this to be the case. For example, an investigator may make an arrest under a defective warrant but not know about the defect. The third ingredient is that the person arrested must come within the custody and control of the law. This element can be satisfied either by physical restraint (see photo on page 762) or by the arrestee's voluntary submission to the custody and control of the arresting officer.

### Arrest Distinguished from Detention

**Detention** is a temporary and limited interference with the freedom of a person for investigative purposes. Sometimes called investigative detention, it is also commonly referred to by police as a "street stop" or "field interrogation." In this instance, police are justified in employing "stop and frisk" measures—patting down the outer clothing—if they suspect that the person being questioned may be armed and their safety is in jeopardy.[2]

There is a fine line between detention and arrest. Because an officer does interfere with the freedom of the individual stopped, even for only a few minutes, some theorists view any such action as constituting arrest. Most people and most courts recognize the validity of street stops and uphold them as not being arrests if conducted properly.

A valid detention must be brief and made for good reason. The officer must limit questioning and investigation and must then either release the subject or decide to arrest. Detention for an undue length of time could be construed as an arrest if later challenged in court.

## Arrest Distinguished from Charging

As noted earlier, one definition of arrest is to interfere with the freedom of a person suspected of involvement in a crime to the extent that the person is taken to the police station. But investigators do not always intend to prosecute or have the ability to prosecute at that time. Formally **charging** a suspect with a crime does not automatically flow from an arrest. Charging follows a decision to prosecute. This decision may be made by the police, by the prosecutor, or by both. But they may also decide not to bring charges. For example, the evidence that justified the arrest may not be sufficient to warrant charges, because the prosecutor believes he or she cannot prove the case beyond and to the exclusion of every reasonable doubt. Perhaps additional information may come to light after the arrest that points to the accused's innocence. Maybe an arrest was unlawful or evidence was obtained in violation of constitutional standards.

# ARREST PROCEDURES

The laws of most jurisdictions permit an arrest in at least three types of situations:

1. When a crime is committed in the presence of an arresting officer.
2. When a warrant has been issued.
3. When an officer has probable cause to believe that the suspect being arrested has committed a felony.

Any offense committed in the presence of an officer, whether felony or misdemeanor, can be the basis of arrest without a warrant. The in-presence requirement is usually thought of in the narrow context of sight. However, to satisfy the legal requirements, perception of some or all of the elements of an offense as they occur, through the use of any or all of the five senses—sight, hearing, taste, touch, or smell—can justify a warrantless arrest.

The most preferred method of effecting an arrest is under the authority of a warrant. In fact, if one were to read the constitutional requirements in their strictest sense, arrests can be justified only if made with a warrant. Of course, the courts have chosen to be more liberal in their interpretation so that warrantless arrests can be made in certain situations. But there are sound reasons for both the warrant requirements and the exceptions created by judicial case law. In the U.S. constitutional system, the functions of government—executive, legislative, and judicial—are each the responsibility of a separate branch. The police function is an executive one, while the judicial responsibility obviously belongs to the courts. Although the mechanism of arrest is an executive function, it is subject to judicial scrutiny and review. This position is supported by the very wording of the Fourth Amendment to the U.S. Constitution:

> and no warrant shall issue but upon probable cause, supported by oath or affirmation, particularly describing the . . . persons . . . to be seized.

The two major benefits derived from securing prior judicial approval for arrests through the warrant process are that the approval relieves the police of the burden of proving the legality of the arrest—so that officers need not fear charges of false arrest, malicious prosecution, or other civil suits—and it provides for an independent evaluation of the evidence.

Even the most objective, well-trained, and well-intentioned investigators sometimes become so involved in a case that their involvement may affect their ability to evaluate the case's merits objectively. Presenting the case before a qualified judge has the benefits of allowing an independent third party, with no emotional involvement in the investigation and with the knowledge of legal standards that must be met, to assist the investigator in determining whether those standards have been achieved. It is also logical to assume that the validity of an arrest made after this review and the issuance of a warrant is more likely to be upheld if later challenged in court than an arrest based solely on an officer's own determination of the sufficiency of the evidence. The wise police officer recognizes the value of obtaining a warrant whenever practical. The word "practical" has significance with regard to the propriety of securing an arrest warrant. The law recognizes that the innumerable situations encountered by police officers in daily activities and the

### An Arrest

A suspect restrained by handcuffs and under the close control of officers. In this case, the sheriff's deputies will transport the arrestee to a booking facility located at the sheriff's headquarters. At the booking facility, the arrestee will be formally identified if possible, will be fingerprinted, and will have his photograph taken.
(Courtesy Los Angeles County Sheriff's Department)

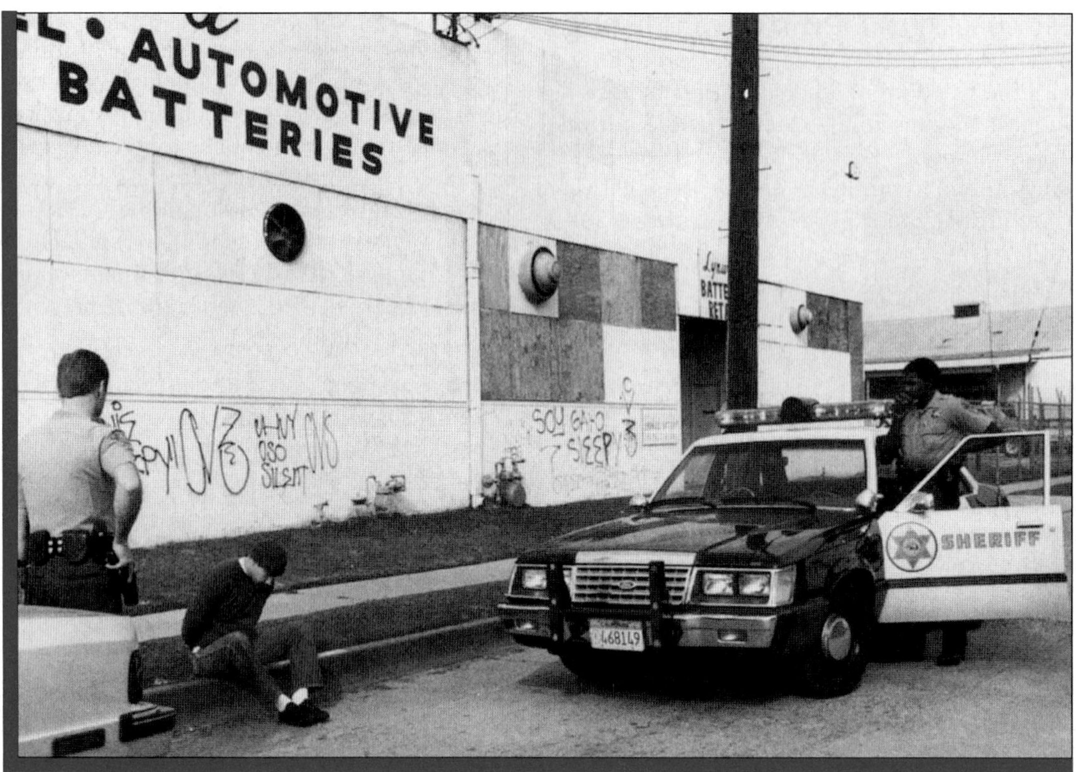


variety of conditions inherent in the nature of the police function make it impossible and unrealistic to expect an officer to obtain a warrant in every situation before effecting an arrest—hence, the exceptions to the warrant requirement. One of those exceptions, the in-presence condition, has already been discussed; another, probable cause, is discussed later in this chapter.

The procedure required for obtaining a warrant is often time consuming and inconvenient. Frequently, the process in major felony cases requires that the investigator seek out the prosecutor; present the facts, which will be reduced to paper in affidavit form; find a judge who is authorized to issue warrants; present the case again for a determination of the sufficiency of the grounds for arrest; and then wait for the warrant to be typed up and signed. In many cases the procedure can take many hours, even during the normal workday. On weekends and late at night it may take even longer, as the prosecutor, judge, or both are located or roused from bed. As a consequence, officers sometimes tend to take the easy way out by making a warrantless arrest, hoping they are right and believing they have sufficient grounds to act. By conducting themselves in this manner, they neglect the basic rule of thumb—get a warrant—and its underlying rationale. But the warrantless arrest is not always a shortcut. As clear as the law may appear to be on the need for warrants, each case must rest on its own facts. There are relatively few cases in which it is obvious that an arrest can be made without a warrant. Similarly, the clear-cut instances for which a warrant is absolutely needed are relatively few. The majority of cases fall within that vast plane requiring evaluation of the merits of each case. An arrest without a warrant, however, does not save time. In reality, the time an officer spends on justifying this decision in motion hearings demanded by the defense attorney will equal or exceed the time it would have taken to get a warrant in the first place. The potential consequence is that the case may be dismissed for want of a valid arrest, or that important evidence, seized as a result of the arrest, may be suppressed.

## THE ARREST WARRANT

The investigator is not relieved of all responsibility for the legality of the arrest simply because a warrant was obtained. The investigator must be aware of what constitutes a valid warrant to ensure that the one he or she possesses permits a legal arrest.

An **arrest warrant** is a judicial order commanding the person to whom it is issued or some other person to arrest a particular individual and to bring that person promptly before a court to answer a criminal charge. The arrest warrant generally must be written. By legislation, some jurisdictions allow for verbal authorization supported by written authorization in warrant form that is issued later.

In most cases, particularly major felonies, the warrant must be issued by a judge who personally reviews the facts to determine the existence of reasonable grounds as required by the Constitution. The warrant must be supported by an **affidavit**—a written statement of the information known to the officer that serves as the basis for the issuance of the warrant. In major cases, the requirements vary on whether the warrant must be issued in the county in which the offense occurred, but once issued, major case warrants can be served anywhere in the state.

The contents of a warrant are fairly standard and incorporate constitutional as well as statutory requirements. Most modern warrants, samples of which appear in Figures 21–1, 21–2, and 21–3, simply require that blanks be filled in. The form and contents usually include:

1. The authority under which the warrant is issued (the name of the state).
2. The person who is to execute the warrant (generally addressed to any peace officer of the state).
3. The identity of the person to be arrested.
4. The designation of the offense.
5. The date, time, and place of the occurrence.
6. The name of the victim.
7. A description of the offense and how it occurred.

Blank warrants are not constitutionally valid. Before a warrant can be issued, the identity of the perpetrator must be known. The mere fact that a crime has been committed by someone unknown will not support a warrant's issuance. The Constitution requires that the warrant contain a particular description of the suspect. This description must be specific enough to permit an officer not acquainted with the case to identify the person to be arrested with reasonable certainty. Aliases may be used. If the suspect's name is not known, "John Doe" may be used provided there are other methods of particularly describing the person to be arrested, such as place of residence, occupation, and a physical description.

## THE PROBABLE-CAUSE REQUIREMENT

The third and final major category in which a lawful arrest is generally permitted involves offenses not committed in the officer's presence and for which a warrant has not been issued. The law allows an officer to make warrantless arrests in felony cases provided reasonable grounds or probable cause exists to make the arrest. (As previously noted, probable cause also must be shown in an affidavit to support the issuance of a warrant.)

Probable cause is a difficult term to define because in no two instances are circumstances identical. One acceptable definition of **probable cause** is that it is more than suspicion but less than actual knowledge. It is suspicion plus facts and circumstances that would lead a reasonable person exercising ordinary caution to believe that a crime has been, is being, or is about to be committed. Probable cause may be based on a number of sources of information, not all of which have to be the kind of evidence admissible at trial. However, if prosecution is an aim of the arrest, there must also be sufficient evidence to take the case to court. In addition, the probable cause must exist at the time the arrest is made and may not be developed by subsequently acquired evidence.

**Figure 21-1**

Front of Arrest Warrant

(**Source:** Courtesy Geauga County, Ohio, Sheriff's Department)

National Graphics Corp., Cols., O.
Form No. M66-12

THE STATE OF OHIO

______________________ Municipal Court

______________________ County, Ohio
(City) (Name of County)

vs

No. ______________

Name

Address

**WARRANT ON COMPLAINT**
**(Rule 4)**

**************************************************

**FORM VII**

TO ______________________________
(officer authorized to execute a warrant)

A complaint, a copy of which is attached hereto, has been filed in this court charging

______________________________
(describe the offense and state the numerical designation of the applicable statute or ordinance)

______________________________

______________________________

You are ordered to arrest ______________ (defendant) and bring (him)(her) before this court without unnecessary delay.

You (may) (may not) issue summons in lieu of arrest under Rule 4(A)(2) or issue summons after arrest under Rule 4(F) because ______________________________
(state specific reasons if issuance of summons restricted)

______________________________

Special instructions to executing officer:

______________________________
Judge—Officer designated by Judge(s)
Clerk—Deputy Clerk—Municipal Court

**************************************************

**SUMMONS ENDORSEMENT**
**Use only in appropriate case**

This warrant was executed / by arrest and / by issuing the following summons:

TO ______________________________
(defendant)

You are hereby summoned and ordered to appear at ______________ o'clock ____ M.,

______________ (day), ______________ (month), 19____ (date), at the above captioned Court.

If you fail to appear at the time and place stated above you may be arrested.

______________________________
Issuing Officer, Title
**See Rule 4(A)(2) Rule 4(F) and Return Forms**

**NOTICE TO DEFENDANT: For information regarding your duty to appear call** ______________
(fill in telephone number(s))

**The address of the Court is:** ______________________________

Mere suspicion is not enough to justify an arrest; there must be supporting facts and circumstances. Certain factors may help to decide the existence of probable cause. The most common is the personal knowledge of the investigator. Information obtained from informants also may be of value, although that information may not be admissible at a subsequent hearing or trial. The investigator must be able to establish the reliability of the information and the informant by indicating the length of

**Figure 21-2**

Return of Executed Warrant

(**Source:** Courtesy Geauga County, Ohio, Sheriff's Department)

**RECEIPT OF WARRANT BY EXECUTING AUTHORITY**

| *First Receipt* | *Subsequent Receipt* |
|---|---|
| Received this warrant on ______________, 19___, | Received this (alias) (warrant) on ______________, |
| at______________o'clock___m. | 19___, at______________o'clock___m. |
| ______________________ Officer | ______________________ Officer |
| By______________________ Title | By______________________ Title |

****************************************************

**RETURN OF EXECUTED WARRANT**

**Fees** Mileage $__________ ; __________ ; __________ ; __________ ; __________ ; **Total $**__________

1. **Execution By Arrest**
I received this warrant on ________________________, 19____, at ____________o'clock ___m. On ________________________, 19____, I arrested______________________and gave / him/her / a copy of this warrant with complaint attached and brought / him/her / to____________________ (state the place)

______________________ Arresting Officer, Title

**Fees** Mileage $__________ ; __________ ; __________ ; __________ ; __________ ; **Total $**__________

2. **Execution By Issuance Of Summons Under Rule 4(A)(2) By Executing Officer**
I received this warrant on ________________________, 19____, at ____________o'clock ___m. On ________________________, 19____, I executed this warrant by issuing____________________a summons by / personal service / residence service / which ordered him/her to appear at______________ (time) ______________ (day) ______________ (date) ______________ (room) at the captioned Court. The summons was endorsed upon the warrant and accompanied by a copy of the complaint.

______________________ Issuing Officer, Title

**Fees** Mileage $__________ ; __________ ; __________ ; __________ ; __________ ; **Total $**__________

3. **Execution By Arrest And Issuance Of Summons Under Rule 4(F) By Arresting Officer**
I received this warrant on ________________________, 19____, at ____________o'clock ___m. On ________________________, 19____, I arrested______________________and after arrest I issued him/her a summons by personal service which ordered him/her to appear at captioned Court at__________ (time) ______________________ (day, date, room). The summons was endorsed upon the warrant and accompanied by a copy of the complaint.

______________________ Arresting-Issuing Officer, Title

4. **Execution By Arrest And Issuance Of Summons Under Rule 4(F) By Superior Of Arresting Officer**
On ____________________, 19____, ____________________was arrested by____________________ (name of arresting officer) and I issued____________________________a summons by personal service which ordered / him/her / to appear at ______________________ (time, day, date, room) at the captioned Court. The summons was endorsed upon the warrant and accompanied by a copy of the complaint.

______________________ Issuing Officer, Title

****************************************************

**RETURN OF UNEXECUTED WARRANT**

**Fees** Mileage $__________ ; __________ ; __________ ; __________ ; __________ ; **Total $**__________

I received this warrant on ________________________, 19____, at ____________o'clock ___m. On ________________________, 19____, I attempted to execute this warrant but was unable to do so because______________ ______________________ (state specific reason or reasons and) ______________________ (additional information regarding defendant's whereabouts)

______________________ Executing Officer, Title

****************************************************

**RETURN OF UNEXECUTED WARRANT**

**Fees** Mileage $__________ ; __________ ; __________ ; __________ ; __________ ; **Total $**__________

I received this warrant on ________________________, 19____, at ____________o'clock ___m. On ________________________, 19____, I attempted to execute this warrant but was unable to do so because______________ ______________________ (state specific reason or reasons and) ______________________ (additional information regarding defendant's whereabouts)

______________________ Executing Officer, Title

time the investigator has known or dealt with the informant, the general character and reputation of the informant, the number of tips received from the informant in the past, the accuracy of previous information, whether the informant is paid for the information, and the informant's motives for volunteering the information.

Other sources of probable cause include information from a police department or from other law enforcement agencies, such as notice of outstanding

**Figure 21-3**

Application for Complaint

(**Source:** Courtesy Boston Police Department)

**APPLICATION FOR COMPLAINT** NUMBER

**Trial Court of Massachusetts**
**Boston Municipal Court Department**

Boston Municipal Court
Criminal Division, Room 411 —
Fourth Floor, New Court House
Boston, MA 02108

☐ ARREST ☐ HEARING ☐ SUMMONS ☐ WARRANT

The within named complainant requests that a complaint issue against the within named defendant, charging said defendant with the offense(s) listed below.

| DATE OF APPLICATION | DATE OF OFFENSE | PLACE OF OFFENSE |
|---|---|---|
| | | |

NAME, ADDRESS AND ZIP CODE OF COMPLAINANT

NAME, ADDRESS AND ZIP CODE OF DEFENDANT

| NO. | OFFENSE | G.L. Ch. and Sec. |
|---|---|---|
| 1. | | |
| 2. | | |
| 3. | | |
| 4. | | |

IF ADDITIONAL OFFENSES CHECK HERE. ☐ AND ATTACH.

**DEFENDANT IDENTIFICATION INFORMATION** — Complete data below if known.

| C.C. # | DATE OF BIRTH | SEX | RACE | HEIGHT | WEIGHT | EYES | HAIR | SOCIAL SECURITY NUMBER |
|---|---|---|---|---|---|---|---|---|
| | | | | | | | | |

COURT USE ONLY ⟶ A hearing upon this complaint application will be held at the Boston Municipal Court, Rm. 411 on DATE OF HEARING AT TIME OF HEARING COURT USE ⟵ ONLY

**CASE PARTICULARS — BE SPECIFIC**

| NO. | NAME OF VICTIM Owner of property, person assaulted, etc. | DESCRIPTION OF PROPERTY Goods stolen, what destroyed, etc. | VALUE OF PROPERTY Over or under $100. | TYPE OF CONTROLLED SUBSTANCE OR WEAPON Marijuana, gun, etc. |
|---|---|---|---|---|
| 1 | | | | |
| 2 | | | | |
| 3 | | | | |
| 4 | | | | |

OTHER REMARKS:

X ____________________
SIGNATURE OF COMPLAINANT

IF PROCESS IS ORDERED, THIS APPLICATION MUST BE PRESENTED AT ONCE TO PLEADING CLERK AT ROOM 411

| NAMES OF WITNESSES | Recog. to S.C. | Give place of business or employment, if in Boston, otherwise, residence | ST. NO. |
|---|---|---|---|
| | | | |
| | | | |
| | | | |
| | | | |
| | | | |

State if defendant is arrested ____________ Date of Arrest ____________

COMPLAINANT'S COPY

BMC-CR-2 (5/85) **FOR ADDITIONAL REMARKS OR WITNESSES-USE REVERSE OF ORIGINAL AND CHECK HERE** ☐

warrants, the past criminal record of the suspect, physical evidence found at the scene of the crime, other evidence detected in the follow-up investigation, crime laboratory analyses, and reports of victims and eyewitnesses.

## EVALUATING THE CASE

The decisions investigators must make involve a great deal of discretion. Investigators must consider what may be termed risk factors. As suggested by Figure 21–4, the fact that probable cause exists does not require that the arrest be made at the moment, nor does it mean that the investigation is complete. Certain disadvantages may result from a premature arrest, even one that is valid. In Figure 21–4, B1 through B7 represent the alternative times when arrest may take place between the establishment of probable cause and the existence of certainty requiring arrest as a prerequisite to prosecution. (The spacing and numbering are arbitrary and are intended for graphic purposes only.)

One prime consideration is whether the suspect is likely to flee if allowed to remain free. If there is a high risk of this, the investigator should make an arrest as soon as probable cause can be established and complete the investigation while the suspect is in custody. In evaluating the likelihood of flight, the investigator will consider such factors as the nature and seriousness of the offense, whether the suspect is a transient or an established member of the community, the suspect's occupation and income, and whether the suspect has a family to support.

Another risk that must be considered by the investigator deals with the potential danger posed to others if the suspect is allowed to remain free. Again, the nature of the offense along with any past criminal record or history of the suspect must be carefully evaluated. If the case under investigation involves a violent crime or one that tends to reveal violent propensities on the part of the suspect, early arrest is most probably the wisest course of action.

The investigator should also consider the hardships imposed on the suspect by early incarceration. Although this is often overlooked, it is one additional portion of the investigator's responsibility in evaluating the case.

## THE TRIAL PROCESS

Some police officers and criminal investigators are not fully aware of the order in which a trial is conducted because time often prohibits them from attending a complete trial from beginning to end. Also, witnesses are often sequestered from the courtroom before and after giving testimony. This very common practice is used to minimize the possibility that a witness's testimony might be affected by other witnesses' testimony.

The courtroom process begins with the selection and swearing in of the jury. Then the trial starts with the prosecutor's and defense attorney's opening statements. These statements acquaint the jury with the allegations in the case. The prosecutor tells the jury how he or she will attempt to prove that a crime was committed and that it was committed by the defendant. The defense tells how it will attempt to convince the jury that either no crime was committed or the crime was not committed by this defendant.

Then the prosecution presents its case, calling witnesses and introducing evidence to establish that a crime was committed and that it was committed by the defendant. While the prosecution is presenting its case, the questioning of witnesses it calls to testify on behalf of the prosecution is called **direct examination.** When the same witness is questioned by the defense attorney, the process is called **cross-examination.** In most jurisdictions, the scope of cross-examination is limited to matters brought up during direct examination. If on cross-examination the defense attorney manages to confuse a point raised on direct examination the prosecutor has the opportunity to conduct a **redirect examination** after the defense attorney has completed cross-examination, and likewise the defense later has an opportunity to conduct a **re-cross-examination** of each witness.

When the prosecution finishes introducing all its evidence and presenting all its witnesses, the defense attorney usually moves to dismiss the charge on the grounds that the state failed to prove that a

Figure 21-4

Case Evaluations

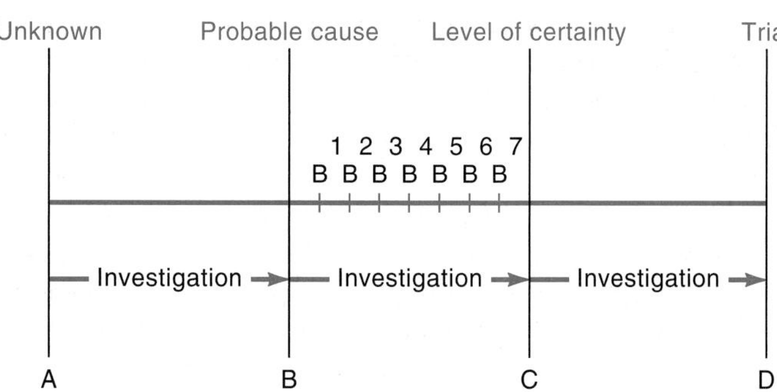

**Amy Fisher in Court**

It is not unusual for lovers' triangles to end in a tragic act; many such relationships are highly volatile in nature. In one such case, Amy Fisher, of Long Island, New York, shot her lover's wife in the face.

(© Michael Albans/AP/Wide World Photos)

crime was committed or that the defendant committed it. This is a normal procedural response to the state's case by the defense attorney. If, in fact, the judge is convinced that the prosecution did substantially fail to establish that a crime was committed or that the defendant is guilty, charges are dismissed and the trial ends. But if the judge feels that the jury could reasonably decide that the defendant is guilty after hearing the defense case, the motion is denied and the defense attorney is permitted to present the case for the defendant.

The presentation of the defense case follows the same pattern as that for the state. Evidence is introduced at the appropriate time and witnesses are called. Witnesses called by the defense are directly examined by the defense attorney and cross-examined by the prosecutor. The procedures for redirect and re-cross-examination are applicable.

After the defense rests its case the prosecution has an opportunity for **rebuttal**. New evidence may be presented, or witnesses may be reexamined to clarify earlier testimony. If the prosecutor uses the opportunity to present rebuttal evidence, then the defense is given equal opportunity to rebut this, through the process called **surrebuttal.** After the introduction of all evidence by both sides, each attorney may make a closing argument. They summarize for the jury the evidence they have presented. The prosecutor attempts to show the jury that sufficient evidence has been presented to indicate that the defendant is guilty of the particular crime charged, that it should find guilt, and that it should punish accordingly. The defense attorney attempts to persuade the jury that the prosecution has failed to prove its case against the defendant and that the jury should acquit.

Once closing statements are completed, the judge has the responsibility of instructing the jury on the law applicable to the case and of advising the jury of its responsibilities: to weigh the testimony of witnesses and the evidence presented. The judge also tells the jury the various decisions it may reach in terms of guilt or innocence and the elements of the crimes—including lesser offenses—of which they may find the defendant guilty. The judge advises the jurors of the degree to which they must be convinced of guilt or acquit the defendant.

## THE RULES OF EVIDENCE

Every police officer must have a working knowledge of the rules of evidence. This requirement is particularly true for the criminal investigator, on whose shoulders falls the responsibility of collecting and preserving evidence that will be useful to the prosecutor in presenting the state's case in court. Therefore, the investigator must be able to distinguish between factual material that is admissible in court and that which is worthless as evidence.

The language and terminology used in the field of law are quite different from those that most of us are accustomed to using. In the rules of evidence, many terms have specific meanings that investigators must know and understand. Many of these are set forth in this chapter.

## EVIDENCE

**Evidence** can be defined as anything that tends logically to prove or disprove a fact at issue in a judicial case or controversy. Simply put, anything that might have the slightest bearing on the outcome of a case can be broadly classified as evidence, provided it has a logical tendency to relate to the outcome of the case. In a criminal case, if the matter has a bearing on the guilt or innocence of the defendant, it is evidence. The word "anything" should be emphasized because, in its broadest sense, anything can be evidence.

## THE FIRST RULE OF EVIDENCE

The rules of evidence are designed primarily to keep a jury from hearing or seeing improper evidence, and the first rule of evidence is designed to set parameters on the above definition of evidence. Because evidence can be anything having a bearing on the outcome of the case, the first rule of evidence provides that anything is admissible as evidence unless there is some rule that prohibits its admissibility. Thus this first rule provides that all the other rules of evidence may limit the things that a jury is entitled to hear, see, and decide on. From this it can be surmised that most of the rules are stated in negative form.

## PROOF

Many people confuse proof with evidence. They are separate but related elements of the judicial process. As noted, evidence consists of individual facts submitted to the jury for its consideration. **Proof** may be defined as the combination of all those facts—of all the evidence—in determining the guilt or innocence of a person accused of a crime. Thus, in referring to Figure 21–5 one can see that the entire pie might constitute proof of guilt, while slices of the pie are matters of evidence.

## TESTIMONY

Although testimony and evidence often are considered to be interchangeable, they are distinct. **Testimony** is simply evidence given in oral form. It consists of spoken facts of which witnesses have knowledge. Although the gun found at the scene, fingerprints, and tire treads are evidence, they require testimony to explain their significance to the case. In Figure 21–5, it is apparent that all six segments of the pie constitute evidence. But only segments 2, 3, and 5 are testimonial evidence.

## ADMISSIBILITY

**Admissibility** is the essence of the rules of evidence. The rules of admissibility protect the trier of fact, generally a jury, from hearing improper evidence that may be unreliable or untrustworthy and that may prejudice the case unjustifiably against the defendant. The majority of the rules of evidence deal with what is admissible. Questions of admissibility are decided by the judge, and these decisions are made out of the hearing of the jury.

### Relevance

One of the rules governing the admissibility of evidence requires that the evidence be relevant. The evidence must have a bearing on the issues in the case being tried. The relevance of a particular piece of evidence can easily be determined by the answer to this question: "Does this piece of evidence have probative value?" Alternatively stated, "Will it aid in proving or disproving a particular point that the jury should consider in determining the guilt or innocence of the defendant?" If it cannot throw some light on the case, it is irrelevant.

### Materiality

Admissibility is also governed by the test of materiality. Even assuming that a particular piece of evidence is relevant, if it is such an insignificant and unimportant point that its admissibility will not affect the outcome of the case, it may be ruled inadmissible. Admissibility may be denied on the basis of immateriality. Thus, materiality deals with the importance of the item of evidence in question.

### Competence of Evidence

The test of competence of evidence relates to evidence's legal significance to the case. Because of certain statutory requirements or other rules of evidence, a particular item of evidence may not be admissible. For example, there is a rule of evidence to

Figure 21-5 The Relation of Evidence and Proof

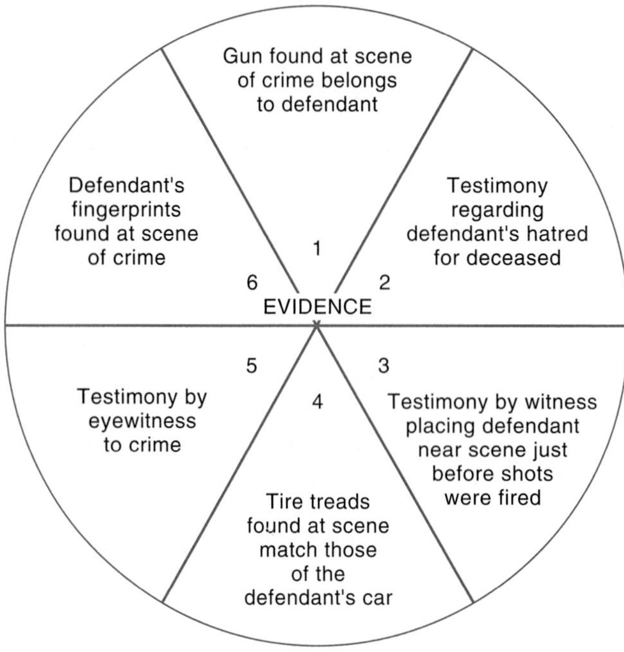


the effect that the defendant's character cannot be attacked by the prosecution unless and until the defendant tries to show that he or she is of good character. Hence, unless the defendant did proceed in this direction, any attempt by the prosecution to introduce evidence of the defendant's character would be inadmissible on the grounds of incompetence.

The competence of physical evidence must also be established as a condition of admissibility. This is done through a process known as laying a foundation. For instance, the admissibility of a tape-recorded conversation would have to be prefaced by testimony about the date, time, place, and circumstances under which the recording was made; the satisfaction of legal requirements in the making of the recording; proper identification of the voices on the tape; assertions about the functioning of the recorder and tape at the time of the recording; and assurances about the absence of editing or modification of the tape.

## COMPETENCE OF WITNESSES

Regardless of their knowledge of the facts of a case, certain individuals are not permitted by law to testify for or against a defendant in a criminal case. For example, the rules of evidence generally prohibit people who have been declared legally insane from testifying in a criminal case. A child "of tender years" may or may not be declared a competent witness. A person intoxicated by alcohol or drugs at the time of testifying will not be permitted to relate his or her knowledge in court. In some circumstances, a witness may be competent to testify regarding particular aspects but be held incompetent to testify regarding other matters. One spouse may be competent to testify for or against the other spouse on certain matters but not others. This aspect of competence of witness is discussed in greater detail later in the chapter.

## WEIGHT OF EVIDENCE

Once evidence has been admitted into the trial, it must be weighed by the jury. The object of the attorney for either side in a case is to persuade the jury to believe his or her side's view of the facts at issue and the responsibility of the defendant. The jury must then weigh all the evidence and determine which is the more believable. Guilt or innocence then is determined. **Weight** then deals with the elements of persuasion and believability.

Within certain guidelines, discussed below, the jury is free to give whatever weight it desires to the evidence presented to it. In essence, the entire judicial system in the United States is directed toward persuading the jury to weigh one side more favorably than the other.

### Presumptions

Among the guidelines that the jury is required to follow in weighing and applying evidence are those regarding presumptions. There are two types of presumptions: conclusive and rebuttable. A conclusive presumption is one that the jury must follow without alternatives. For example, when the prosecution creates a reasonable belief in guilt, and the defense does not contradict any of the prosecution's case, the jury must follow a conclusive presumption that guilt has been established and must find the defendant guilty. A rebuttable presumption requires that a specific conclusion be drawn unless that conclusion has been dispelled or rebutted by evidence presented to the jury for its consideration. The presumption that one is innocent until proven guilty is an example of a rebuttable presumption. Another presumption of this type is that all persons are presumed sane at the time they commit criminal acts. This presumption can be rebutted by the introduction of evidence to the contrary indicating insanity.

### Inferences

An inference is similar to a presumption but differs in that the jury has more latitude in accepting or rejecting an inference. Thus an inference is a permissible deduction that the jury may make. An inference is a natural conclusion arrived at by deduction, in logical sequence, from given facts. For example, if fact A—the gun found at the scene of the crime belongs to the defendant—and fact B— testimony by a witness placing the defendant near the scene just before the shots were fired—are both all known facts, this is not conclusive proof that the defendant committed the crime. However, on the basis of these known facts, the jury may logically infer that the defendant did in fact commit the crime. But it is equally free to reject that inference if it feels that the evidence is not sufficient for that conclusion.

## BURDEN OF PROOF

In each criminal case, the prosecution has the responsibility of affirmatively proving the allegations on which it has based its accusation. This is known as the **burden of proof.** The burden of proof is on the prosecution and never shifts to the defense. The defendant is never required to prove innocence. Innocence is presumed. The state must prove guilt. Assuming that both the prosecution and the defense present evidence in the trial in support of their theories of the case, the prosecution must establish proof beyond and to the exclusion of every reasonable doubt. The jurors must be convinced that the prosecution has proved the defendant guilty beyond any doubt to which they can attach a reason. Often only the defendant knows positively whether he or she is guilty or innocent. Because juries are composed of human beings, they are subject to some doubt in every case and must rely on testimony and physical evidence in reaching their decision. However, if the prosecution so thoroughly convinces the jurors of the defendant's guilt that they cannot give a reasonable explanation of why they doubt that guilt, then the burden of proof has been satisfied beyond and to the exclusion of every reasonable doubt. The word "reasonable" is included to separate human fallibility from the alleged infallibility of machines.

There is one exception to the requirement that the state prove its case beyond reasonable doubt. When the prosecution shows sufficient facts to indicate that the defendant more likely did commit the crime than did not, it has a prima facie case. The prosecution has satisfied its burden of proof if it presents a prima facie case, provided that there is no contradiction by the defense. Figure 21–6 illustrates these relationships.

## BURDEN OF GOING FORWARD

The requirements concerning burden of proof do not mean that a defendant has no responsibility for convincing the jury of his or her innocence. The defense carries a **burden of going forward** with evidence. That responsibility is a great deal less than the burden of proof carried by the prosecution. The burden of going forward with evidence is placed on the defense so that is will present evidence that creates a reasonable doubt of guilt. In other words, the defense need present only enough evidence to overcome the prosecution's contentions and create a reasonable doubt of guilt in the minds of the jurors. When a unanimous decision by the jury is necessary to find the defendant

**Figure 21-6**

Relations among Burden of Proof, Burden of Going Forward, and Preponderance of Evidence

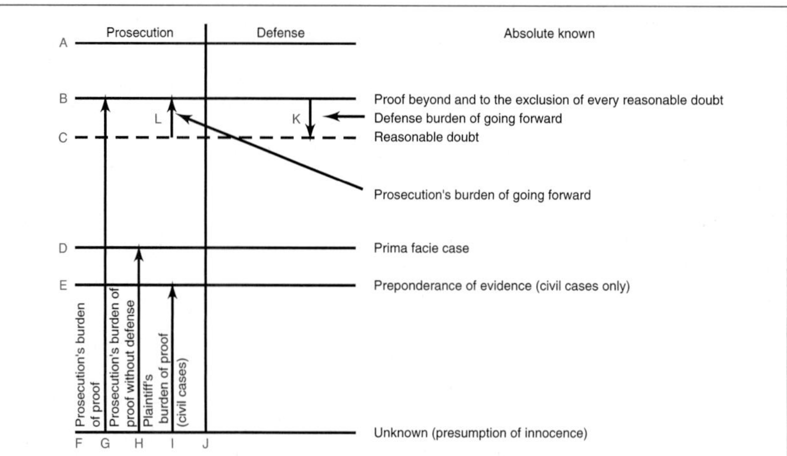


| | |
|---|---|
| Line A | Represents truth generally known only to the defendant. |
| Line B | Level of proof needed to convict. Area between lines A and B represents human doubt but not reasonable doubt. |
| Line C | Can be anywhere below line B and represents reasonable doubt. |
| Line D | Represents prima facie case (level of proof needed to convict if no defense is offered). |
| Line E | Level of proof needed for decision in civil case. |
| Line F | Starting point–presumption of innocence. |
| Arrow G | Represents prosecution's burden of proof. |
| Arrow H | Represents prosecution's burden of proof necessary to convict if no defense is offered. |
| Arrow I | Plaintiff's burden of proof in civil cases. |
| Line J | Represents the continuum between unknown and absolute known. |
| Arrow K | Defense burden of going forward with evidence to create a reasonable doubt (line C). |
| Arrow L | Prosecution's burden of going forward with evidence to overcome reasonable doubt created by defense, thereby elevating level of proof (pushing line C up to overlie line B). |

guilty, the burden is even lighter, for the defense need create that reasonable doubt in the mind of only one juror to avoid a verdict of guilty.

This explanation sounds as though every benefit is being given to the defendant, and it is. The very essence of our entire criminal justice system is to place the heaviest responsibility on the accuser—the prosecution.

The prosecution also has a burden of going forward with evidence. If the prosecution presents a prima facie case that is contradicted by evidence presented on behalf of the defendant, the state must then erase the reasonable doubt by presenting evidence that contradicts that offered by the defense.

## PREPONDERANCE OF EVIDENCE

In civil case, the party allegedly wronged is called the **plaintiff.** The plaintiff may be an individual, a group, a business, or a representative of some other private concern. The plaintiff in a civil action is not required to prove allegations beyond and to the exclusion of every reasonable doubt. All that is required is a **preponderance of evidence**—that is, that the evidence the plaintiff presents be considered weightier by the jury than the contrary evidence presented by the defendant. Thus if the civil jury believes that the plaintiff's story offers a higher probability of being true than does the defendant's contention, the plaintiff will win the case. But the defendant wins if the jury gives greater credibility to the defense. In nonlegal terms, if evidence had to be weighed on a 100-point scale of probability, 51 percent believability would win.

### ORDER OF PROOF

Court procedures generally require that the prosecuting attorney prove the existence of the corpus delicti at trial before attempting to show the guilt of the defendant. The **corpus delicti** is the combination of all the element of the crime. It is, of course, only logical that the prosecution be required to show that a crime has been committed before it can begin proving the defendant's guilt. Trial judges rarely exercise their discretionary power to allow evidence to be submitted to prove a point out of order. The judge has the prerogative of allowing the introduction of evidence to establish the guilt of the defendant prior to the prosecution's showing the existence of all the elements of the crime. However, this is done only on rare occasions, when to maintain the order of proof might be a major inconvenience to a particular witness. Permission is given only on the condition that the prosecution guarantee it will later establish the corpus delicti. If the guarantee is made and the prosecution later cannot show the corpus delicti, grounds exist for a mistrial or a directed verdict of innocence.

## JUDICIAL NOTICE

The doctrine of judicial notice is an evidentiary shortcut. Judicial notice is designed to speed up the trial and eliminate the necessity of formally proving the truth of a particular matter when that truth is not in dispute. **Judicial notice,** then, is proof without evidence and may be taken in three situations:

1. Judicial notice may be taken of matters of common knowledge that are uniformly settled and about which there is no dispute. If the fact is known to most reasonably informed people in the community where the trial is being held, judicial notice may be taken of that fact. For example, the fact that a particular intersection, located in a city where an accident occurred, is a business district might well be a matter of common knowledge of which judicial notice could be taken if the trial is held in that city. Since most reasonably informed people in a community would know that a particular intersection was a business area, the court would accept that as a given fact without requiring formal proof.
2. Judicial notice may be taken of laws. A state court, for example, is required to take judicial notice of the state statutes of the jurisdiction in which the court operates; a municipal court takes judicial notice of municipal ordinances.
3. Judicial notice may be taken of matters that may be ascertained as true by referring to common authoritative sources such as books or official agencies. Included in this category are scientific facts, medical facts, historical facts, and meanings of words, phrases, and abbreviations. Examples would include the official time of sunset on a particular date by reference to a weather bureau; the fact that the abbreviation "M.D." following a name stands for "medical doctor;" the fact that the hair and blood types of human beings differ from those of animals; and the fact that no two individuals have identical fingerprints.

Judicial notice must be distinguished from judicial knowledge. The latter refers to knowledge possessed by a judge. The fact that the judge may know a fact is not material in applying the doctrine of judicial notice. Personal knowledge may not be substituted for common knowledge in the community or for facts capable of being ascertained.

Judicial notice may be taken only on a collateral or minor point of fact in a case. Judicial notice may never be used to prove a fact that the jury is required to decide in determining the proper charge and verdict. For example, in the case of a defendant on trial for stealing a car, the court may not take judicial notice of the value of the car if that value will determine the seriousness of the charge against the defendant. Even if it is a matter of common knowledge that a brand new Cadillac El Dorado is worth more than $100, judicial notice may not be taken, because the value is an important element that the prosecution must prove to ensure the propriety of the charge placed against the defendant.

## TYPES OF EVIDENCE

There are many ways of classifying evidence. Not all authorities agree on the classifications, but the differences are immaterial as long as the principles are understood. Five types of evidence are defined below.

### DIRECT EVIDENCE

Direct evidence usually is the testimony of witnesses that ties the defendant directly to the commission of the crime, such as the testimony of an eyewitness who can positively state that the defendant committed the crime. It is based on the firsthand knowledge of the witness regarding the guilt of the defendant.

### REAL EVIDENCE

Sometimes referred to as "physical evidence," real evidence is connected with the commission of the crime and can be produced in court. Items of physical evidence found at a crime scene, such as a weapon used to commit a homicide, a crowbar used to pry open a window, and fingerprints, all constitute real evidence that can be observed by the jury.

### DEMONSTRATIVE EVIDENCE

Demonstrative, or illustrative, evidence is not identical to real evidence even though the items introduced are tangible. It consists of maps, diagrams, sketches, photographs, tape recordings, videotapes, X-rays, and visual tests and demonstrations produced to assist witnesses in explaining their testimony. When testimony alone would be inadequate to describe a victim or crime scene, photographs taken by police officers are used to help the jury understand the conditions that existed.

The use of demonstrative evidence is governed by complex and highly restrictive rules to ensure that the jury is not prejudiced against the defendant.

### CIRCUMSTANTIAL EVIDENCE

It is a myth that one cannot be convicted of a crime solely on circumstantial evidence. The broad definition of circumstantial evidence encompasses all evidence other than direct evidence, provided that it logically relates the defendant to the crime. Circumstantial evidence is sometimes referred to as "indirect evidence" for this reason. Circumstantial evidence is used in a criminal case by inferring from a series of known facts the existence of an unknown fact. In other words, by the process of deductive reasoning, inferences are logically drawn from a series of known facts, and a conclusion is

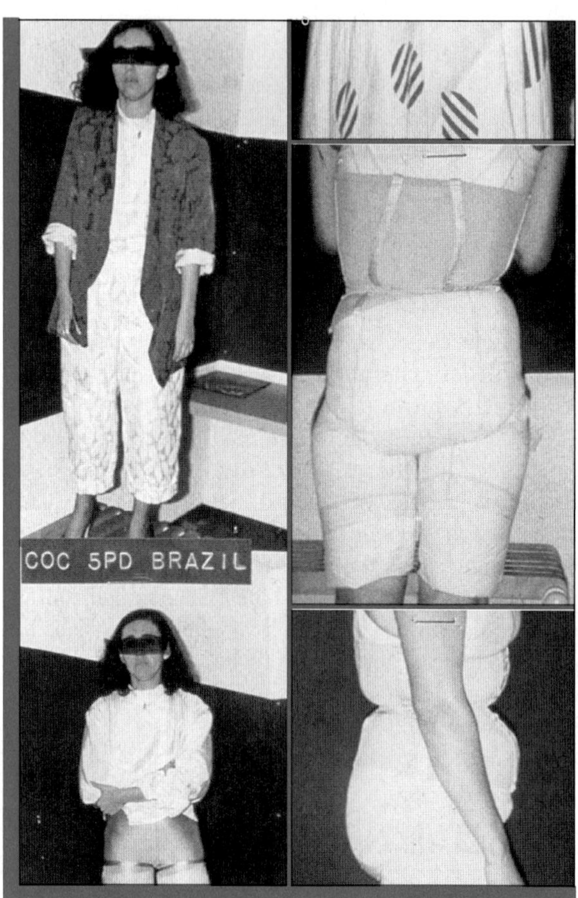


**Cocaine Smugglers**

These individuals, known in the investigative world as "mules," were arrested at an airport and were found to have bags of cocaine taped under their clothes. The key witness for the prosecution in this case will be an observant airport security officer who noted suspicious behavior on the part of the suspects. At the trial, the credibility of the security officer as a witness will be evaluated—which means that the security officer's presentation and demeanor will be evaluated by the jury, as will the substance of his testimony.

(Francis Apesteguy/Getty Images)

reached. For example, the fact that the defendant's fingerprints are detected on a weapon found at the scene of a homicide does not necessarily mean that the defendant committed the crime. The fingerprints tie the defendant to the gun, and finding the gun at the scene of the crime may be a circumstance relating the gun to the commission of the crime. Likewise, testimony that the defendant was seen near the scene of the crime shortly after its commission does not necessarily constitute guilt; but again, it may lead the jury to infer guilt.

It is possible that an accumulation of circumstantial evidence may be nothing more than a series of unfortunate coincidences for which the defendant may have a logical and truthful explanation. How much circumstantial evidence is required for a jury to convict someone of a crime varies form case to case and depends largely on the composition of the jury.

Circumstantial evidence can be considered analogous to links in a chain. Each link might be an unfortunate coincidence, but the greater the number of links, the more a jury is likely to infer guilt by joining the links into a chain of overwhelming circumstantial evidence.

## OPINION EVIDENCE

Witnesses ordinarily are not permitted to give their opinions or draw conclusions on matters about which they are testifying. Their function is to present the facts about which they have firsthand knowledge. It is within the province of the jury to determine the truthfulness of those facts and to draw whatever conclusions it believes are necessary. However, there are a few exceptions to that general rule. Everything a human being perceives through the senses is generally expressed in the form of a conclusion. It is difficult, if not impossible, to describe something perceived as an absolute fact without expressing it in the form of a conclusion. The only things on which a nonexpert may give opinion evidence are matters of description in which fact and opinion are so interwoven that they cannot be separated without losing most of their probative value. Matters of description in which a nonexpert may give an opinion include color, size, shape, speed, mental condition, identity, race, and language.

An expert is someone with special skills or knowledge not ordinarily possessed by others. The skills or knowledge may be acquired through experience, study, observation. or education. To be an **expert witness**, one need not necessarily have a formal education. The expert witness is permitted to interpret facts and give opinions about their significance; the lay witness may present only facts that are a matter of firsthand knowledge. The expert witness is called on to assist the jurors in understanding facts that they are ordinarily not sufficiently trained to understand, such as the results of medical examinations, chemical analyses, ballistics reports, and findings from questioned documents. Results of DNA analysis, for example, would certainly require the supporting testimony of an expert witness.

### The Introduction of Demonstrative Evidence at Trial

Demonstrative evidence is sometimes referred to as "illustrative evidence." Demonstrative evidence consists of visual tests and demonstrations such as pictures produced to assist the witness with the testimony.

(© Bob Daemmrich/The Image Works)

# THE HEARSAY RULE

## HEARSAY EVIDENCE

Most people have heard a story from several different sources and recognized how different the versions sound. Whether these alterations are caused by poor memory or deliberate attempts to spice up the truth is immaterial in a legal context. The fact that stories tend to be changed when they are repeated makes their reliability and truthfulness questionable. For this reason, the hearsay rule was created. **Hearsay** is derived from "heard say." Testimony in court that repeats what others were heard to say means testifying to a second version of what actually happened. The witness has no personal knowledge of the facts in question. Thus, the truth of the testimony depends on the truthfulness and the competence of the person from whom the information was heard rather than of the person testifying. For these reasons the hearsay rule is perhaps one of the most important yet most confusing rules of evidence.

Inaccuracy, unreliability, and untrustworthiness are only some of the reasons why hearsay evidence is excluded. The inability of the judge and jury to observe the demeanor or conduct of the person who actually has firsthand knowledge of the information is another.

Other reasons for generally excluding hearsay rely on protections guaranteed in the Constitution. The Sixth Amendment guarantees a defendant the right to be confronted by the witnesses against him or her and the right to cross-examine those witnesses. Because the person with firsthand knowledge is not present in court, that person cannot be confronted or cross-examined by the defendant.

Hearsay is a version of the truth repeated in court by one who does not know whether the assertion is true. People may assert things lightly and casually out of court without being overly concerned about the truth; but they would likely be more careful about speaking truthfully in court, when an individual's life or liberty may be at stake and when they are testifying under oath.

The hearsay rule also excludes written statements by people not in the courtroom to testify. Because the writer's personal knowledge is in his or her head, writing that knowledge makes it secondhand information.

If the out-of-court assertion is being offered as evidence not to prove the truth of a matter but only to show that it was said, it is not hearsay and thus may be admissible. This is one of the rare occasions in which the hearsay rule would not be applicable. For example, a homicide victim may have made threats against the defendant. These threats can be repeated in court to show the defendant's state of mind when he or she killed the victim and to support a claim of self-defense. The truth or falsity of the threats is not the issue.

A second exception deals with reputation. The reputation of a defendant or a witness in a trial may be questionable. A third party may testify about what he or she has heard concerning another's reputation. Because an individual's reputation is representative not of actual character but, rather, of what other people think of that person, the truth of the reputation is immaterial. But the fact that such a reputation exists is admissible. For example, if the defendant presents evidence in a trial for assault that he or she is a calm individual, a witness may testify to having heard that the defendant is extremely short-tempered.

In these situations, evidence is offered only to show that the statements were made, not that they are true. Because the witness has personal knowledge, it is not hearsay, and because the statements are not offered for the truth of their contents, they are admissible.

The hearsay rule is based on the recognition that human beings have human weaknesses and that the testimony of human witnesses provides the majority of evidence presented to juries in modern trials. Because we will continue to rely on the testimony of human beings as the principal source of information for trying cases, the law must continue to impose standards to ensure the most accurate and reliable testimony possible. Unequivocal application of the hearsay rule to all situations does, however, present certain injustices in our modern judicial system. For this reason, a number of specific exceptions to the hearsay rule have developed.

## EXCEPTIONS TO THE HEARSAY RULE

The sheer number of exceptions often creates doubt about whether the hearsay rule has any merit. Among the many reasons for the existence of the hearsay rule, two stand out as the most critical: the unreliability and the untrustworthiness of declarations repeated under oath in court. The exceptions to the rule can be justified only if these two major drawbacks can be overcome. If the circumstances surrounding the hearsay evidence can ensure a high degree of trustworthiness and reliability, that evidence is admissible as an exception to the rule in order to minimize any injustice. Thus, each exception must meet many tests to satisfy the criteria of reliability and trustworthiness before it is admissible. Several decisions by the courts have eliminated the concern over the constitutional issues involved. These decisions, in effect, have held that allowing the admissibility of the exceptions does not violate the Sixth Amendment guarantees of confrontation and cross-examination, nor does it violate the due process guarantees of the Fourteenth Amendment. Some exceptions apply in both civil and criminal cases; others apply only to civil or criminal cases. The following paragraphs discuss several exceptions applicable in criminal cases.

## Confessions

A **confession** is an acknowledgment by a person accused of a crime that he or she is guilty of that, crime. To constitute a confession, the admission of guilt must apply to all the elements of the crime and exclude any reasonable doubt about the possibility of innocence. Confessions are generally of two types. A judicial confession is an in-court confession made before a judge. A judicial confession can also take the form of a guilty plea. Judicial confessions do not fall within the hearsay rule, because they are in-court assertions of the truth of the matter asserted by the person directly involved.

Confessions made out of court fall within the hearsay rule. For such confessions to be admissible, they must meet the tests of admissibility and overcome the assumptions of unreliability and untrustworthiness.

The admissibility of a confession usually raises questions about constitutionality. First, it must be shown that the confession satisfies constitutional requirements of voluntariness. A confession that is obtained involuntarily certainly would not be admissible under modern law. Second, courts admit confessions as an exception to the hearsay rule on the theory that it is highly unlikely that a person will say something against his or her own interest unless it is true. Therefore, a confession tends to establish the reliability and trustworthiness of the truth of the matter asserted. People do not often deliberately make statements that jeopardize their own life or liberty unless those statements are true. Based on this assumption, the major objections to admitting confessions, as hearsay, are overcome.

## Admissions

One who makes an **admission** does not acknowledge all the facts surrounding the crime necessary to constitute guilt but does admit to certain facts or circumstances from which guilt may be inferred by the jury For example, without confessing to the crime, an accused may admit having been at or near the scene of the crime at the time it occurred, having a motive to commit the crime against the victim, possessing the gun used in the crime, having foot impressions that match those found outside the window of the victim's house, and leaving town the day after the crime was committed. These admissions may be introduced in the trial by a witness who overheard the accused make these statements or in the form of a written document repeating these statements. They may be introduced for basically the same reasons as confessions are admissible. The contents of the admissions are certainly against the interest and welfare of the defendant and, like confessions, must have been made voluntarily to be admissible. If these factors exist, it is unlikely that a defendant would make such admissions unless they were true. Therefore, the courts allow the admissions on the basis that the principal objections to the hearsay rule—unreliability and untrustworthiness—have been overcome.

## Spontaneous and Excited Utterances

Human nature is such that speaking the truth is an instinctive reaction. Therefore, if one makes a spontaneous or excited utterance after something startling or unusual has happened, the utterance may be admissible as an exception to the hearsay rule when testified to by one who heard it made. It may be offered to prove the truth of the matter asserted. The spontaneity of the utterance and its declaration under startling and unusual circumstances lend credence to its reliability and trustworthiness. To illustrate, a 5-year-old girl, observing a playmate struck at a railroad crossing, was heard by a passerby to scream, "The engine runned over Billy!" The passer-by was permitted to testify in court about what he had heard the girl say,

### Dying Declarations

A declaration concerning the facts and circumstances of the fatal injury made by the victim of a homicide who is about to die, expects to die, and does not hope to recover is admissible as an exception to the hearsay rule. The theory is that a person about to die has no reason to lie. Statements admissible under this exception must concern the injury inflicted to the declarant and are admissible only in the trial of the person charged with the declarant's death.

### Former Testimony

Written or oral testimony in a hearing or trial falls within the hearsay rule if that testimony is sought to be introduced in a later judicial proceeding. For example, if a witness testifies against the defendant in a preliminary hearing to determine probable cause to hold the defendant for trial, the court record is not admissible in the later trial unless it meets the tests of the former-testimony exception to the hearsay rule. Because the testimony was given in a court under oath, it is presumed reliable and trustworthy and is admissible provided the two judicial proceedings involve the same defendant, charged with committing the same act, under the same circumstances. In addition, the witness who originally testified at the former hearing must be unavailable for testimony before the transcript of the hearing is admissible, and, to show that constitutional requirements have been satisfied, it must be proved that the defendant had the right to cross-examine the witness in the former hearing or trial.

## EVIDENTIARY PRIVILEGES

Defendants and other witnesses have a right to have certain matters of communication barred from disclosure in court—for example, confidential communications between husband and wife, confidential communications between attorney and client, and grand jury proceedings that are confidential requirements of law are barred.

The **evidentiary privileges** may vary from state to state. Some are universally recognized as necessary and have existed since the early days of common law. Others exist only if the state legislature has created the privilege by statute. Some of the more common evidentiary privileges fall into four basic categories. The first might be called professional privileges and includes those that exist between attorney and client, physician and patient, priest and penitent, and journalist and informant. Government communications and information, state secrets, and matters of diplomacy are classified as political privileges. The third category is social privileges and includes confidential communications between husband and wife or between a guidance counselor and a child. Finally, judicial privileges include grand jury proceedings, communications among jurors deliberating a verdict, and the privilege against self-incrimination guaranteed by the Fifth Amendment.

All these privileges can be waived by the person against whom the evidence is to be used or who would suffer from its disclosure. Thus an attorney cannot disclose evidence of a confidential communication between attorney and client unless so directed by the client. Likewise, a spouse cannot testify against a mate without the latter's express permission, unless the spouse is the victim of the mate's crime.

Although only confidential communications are excluded by the privilege, it is the relationship, not the communication, that is privileged. The theory underlying evidentiary privileges creates a balance between the disclosure of truth and the welfare of society. The assumption is that the public benefits more by protecting these relationships than it does by requiring disclosure of the truth to seek to convict one defendant.

## WITNESSES

Until a few hundred years ago, witnesses appeared at a trial voluntarily. There were no legal means to compel attendance. With the advent of the rules of evidence, procedures had to be established for requiring the presence of people who possessed knowledge of the facts of the case. The **subpoena** is used for this purpose. It is a written order commanding the person named to appear in court at a specified date and time to testify, under oath, before a judicial tribunal, to facts within the witness's personal knowledge that are pertinent to the case. A subpoena duces tecum commands the individual to bring certain records or documents in his or her possession. Refusal to obey subjects the individual to punishment for contempt. Likewise, refusal to testify or answer specific questions may be grounds for contempt unless valid grounds exist, such as the self-incrimination protections guaranteed in the Constitution. People who possess firsthand knowledge have a duty, not a right, to appear in court.

In early common law, defendants had no right to call witnesses on their behalf. Therefore, the prosecution was required to call all witnesses having knowledge of facts, regardless of which side those facts favored. Today, the defense has an equal right to compel the attendance of witnesses. Hence, the state may use only those witnesses it chooses. Witnesses may also be called by the judge, but this power is rarely exercised.

Once in court, the witness's competence to testify must be ascertained. Competence of witnesses was discussed earlier in this chapter. If the witness is not insane, intoxicated, or excluded for other reasons, and if the testimony will not fall within any of the evidentiary privileges, he or she will be presumed competent to testify, though this must first be asserted by taking an oath or affirmation.

In common law, taking an **oath** was a process by which individuals swore to tell the truth on the basis of their sacred belief in a supreme being. Today, of course, the oath is still a recognized means of establishing a witness's competence, but it is no longer the only method. The affirmation is also used for people who refuse, for personal reasons, to take the oath. Because they are otherwise competent to testify, some guarantee that they will tell the truth is necessary. A witness may be declared competent if he or she understands and undertakes the obligation of an oath. This obligation is to tell the truth with a realization of the penalties for perjury. As long as the witness understands and undertakes the obligation, even without swearing to a supreme being, the witness is considered competent to testify. This process is called **affirmation.**

A declaration of a witness's competence in no way guarantees the credibility of the testimony. Credibility deals with believability, which, like the weight of any other evidence, is determined by the jury. Attitude, personality, appearance, hygiene, and general demeanor all affect a witness's credibility, along with the substance of the testimony.

## THE INVESTIGATOR AS WITNESS

The success or failure of a criminal investigation is often ultimately measured in terms of the quality and effectiveness of an officer's presentation of evidence to court and jury. Because one aim of the entire process of criminal investigation is to bring about the apprehension and prosecution of violators of the criminal laws, the presentation of the case in court must be of paramount concern to the investigator from the moment of arrival at the crime scene. Inability to understand and appreciate this crucial role in the judicial process not only adversely affects the investigator's performance as a witness but reflects on the investigator's overall professional effectiveness.

Every police witness, whether a uniformed officer or criminal investigator, must become skilled at testifying on the witness stand. Preparation should include a knowledge of the rules of evidence so that the officer not only can perform in the field more effectively but also can have a better understanding of courtroom procedures and the functions of the prosecution and the defense. To prepare a case adequately, the investigator must understand the rules of admissibility and the relevance of evidence collected. The best witnesses are those who have an understanding and appreciation of their role in the courtroom and their relationship to other participants in the judicial process.

### THE ROLE OF THE POLICE WITNESS

The function of any witness in the courtroom, including the investigator, is to present firsthand knowledge of facts to the jury for its consideration. The investigator must inform the jury of the matters investigated in the case and present this information so that the jury understands the sequence of events and their significance. But the investigator may not offer personal conclusions.

To understand his or her role in the courtroom completely, the witness must also understand the functions of the other participants in the criminal process. Specifically, the witness must understand the functions of the judge and the jury in relation to the role of a witness.

As mentioned earlier, the function of any witness is to present facts from firsthand knowledge. The jury's function is to weigh the facts presented by witnesses from both prosecution and defense and to interpret these facts, giving appropriate weight and credibility to the evidence and to the witnesses for the purpose of reaching a decision regarding the guilt or innocence of the defendant. The responsibility of the judge is twofold. The judge functions as a referee to ensure compliance with the rules of evidence and interprets the law as applicable to the facts of a case.

### Credibility

A police officer is not entitled to any more credibility in the courtroom than any other witness. The officer has an equal responsibility, through presentation, appearance, demeanor, and the substance of testimony, to persuade the jury to believe the facts being related.

The issue of credibility is of special concern to the police witness. Few people from the general population ever view a criminal offense or act as witnesses in court. It is likely that the trauma of such an event would be so vivid for them that remembering it would not be difficult. However, police officers regularly deal with criminal cases and investigate some with striking similarities. Thus, for officers, the frequency and similarities of, and the time lag between, investigations and court appearances may create difficulties in the presentation of testimony.

A related area that may affect the credibility of the police witness stems from public expectations and perceptions of the police role. Many citizens expect nothing less than perfection from police officers in both the performance of their duties and their presentation of testimony in court. They often lose sight of the fact that police officers are subject to human frailties. An officer's credibility may suffer if his or her recall is less than perfect.

Another issue in the investigator's credibility relates to the perceptions of the jurors. Some individuals regard as suspect any statements made by police officers. The predisposition of jurors with this attitude may be reinforced by defense attorneys who, on cross-examination, seek to discredit the testimony of the officer on the basis of his or her occupation.

The police witness can overcome all these barriers by preparing meticulously for testimony and by giving straightforward, unemotional responses.

## CHARACTERISTICS OF A GOOD WITNESS

The successful testimony of the investigator is based on adequate preparation of the case, familiarity with the rules of evidence and with how juries think and react, knowledge of trial processes, and maintenance of proper appearance and conduct at all times.

Preparation for testimony, as has already been indicated, is of extreme importance and cannot be overemphasized. For the police witness the first step in preparation is to ensure that a complete investigation was conducted, that all leads were followed and all avenues explored. It must be remembered that the prime responsibility of the investigator is not to convict but to ascertain the facts objectively. The investigator must also prepare complete and accurate notes on information obtained and evidence gathered. Before appearing in court, the investigator must review all notes; on the stand, he or she must recall events in as much detail as possible with minimal referral to notes. In addition to reviewing notes, it is critical that the investigator thoroughly review all written reports, all evidence, and any deposition that may have been given prior to trial to ensure that his or her memory is complete and accurate.

The investigator should review the case with prosecuting officials so that they will know the testimony the investigator can offer and the evidence available. This review also gives the investigator a chance to learn the nature of the questions that might be asked on direct examination. Admittedly investigators rarely can spend much time with the prosecutor before a trial. The demands on prosecutors' time and the caseloads that most prosecutors carry make in-depth preparation with each witness a virtual impossibility. But even a short time spent in preparation is valuable.

### Understanding the Jury

The jury's task is unique. In theory, it is constrained in what it may consider by rules of evidence and other procedural requirements. In practice, juries are composed of human beings who are subject to influences other than those that might appear in

**An Officer on the Witness Stand**
In the American criminal justice system, cases which ultimately result in trials are relatively few. However, for those that do go to trial, the courtroom testimony by investigators can be very important. The success or failure of a criminal investigation may ultimately be measured in terms of the quality and effectiveness of an officer's presentation of evidence to the court and jury. Every police witness, whether a uniformed officer or criminal investigator, must become skilled at testifying on the stand.
(Courtesy Los Angeles County Sheriff's Department)

written rules and regulations. The study of jury psychology is fascinating, for it points out the flexibility and fallibility of the human mind and, in turn, the absurdity of some of the procedural requirements imposed on the jury. The good police witness will, at the very least, understand and appreciate the fact that juries do not make their determination of guilt or innocence solely on the substance of testimony and evidence offered. The appearance and demeanor of the defendant, attorneys, and witnesses; the manner in which witnesses make their presentations and answer questions; the professionalism displayed by police officers while in the courtroom; and the way in which witnesses respond to cross-examination all bear on the reactions of individual jurors. A good witness is conscious of these factors at all times.

## Appearance and Demeanor

Law enforement authorities disagree as to whether police officers should wear uniforms or civilian clothes to court. Some believe that a police officer should always wear a uniform when testifying in court for immediate identification by the jurors. Others contend that civilian clothing is proper dress because the uniform presents an authoritarian appearance that may be offensive to the jury. A third group takes the view that the officer should wear the type of dress—that is, uniform or civilian clothes—worn at the time of the arrest. Often this decision is largely a matter of departmental policy.

In any event, dress should be clean and neat. If civilian clothes are worn, a degree of formality is appropriate. Conservative clothes are less likely to offend members of the jury than are wild, flashy outfits, even though neat. Identifying items such as jewelry representing a specific occupation or association membership should be avoided. Lapel pins from specific civic clubs or tie tacks with emblems of handcuffs or service revolvers should not be worn. Although these are extremely small points, one can never predict who might be offended. Additionally, all the fundamentals pertaining to personal hygiene should be scrupulously observed.

Police witnesses should be conscious of their demeanor from the time they arrive at the courthouse. Prior to trial or during recesses, jurors may be standing around the courthouse. If an officer makes a bad impression through his or her appearance or actions, this may be remembered by a juror when the officer takes the stand and may adversely affect the credibility of the officer in that juror's mind. Consequently, any actions that could be offensive to jurors are to be avoided. The police officer should avoid talking to the prosecutor, court clerks, or judges and should refrain from acting overly friendly to anyone involved in the trial. Although there is nothing inherently wrong with idle talk or friendliness, jurors may perceive it as collusion.

### TAKING THE WITNESS STAND

From the moment the police witness enters the courtroom, people are forming opinions. The officer should walk naturally when approaching the witness stand, not look at or speak to the prosecutor, and not frown at the defendant. If the jury sees these expressions, it interprets them as signs of partiality. The police witness should stand erect while being sworn in and, when permitted to be seated, should sit erect, facing the jury. The investigator should not continually cross his or her legs or fidget uncomfortably. Hands should be kept comfortably in the lap or on the arms of the chair.

Nervousness is natural for anyone who appears as a witness. Usually it disappears with experience. However, if the police witness is properly prepared and answers all questions accurately and truthfully to the best of his or her knowledge, nervousness is minimized.

Eye contact and speaking voice are extremely important. Many authorities contend that the witness should maintain eye contact with the jury while answering questions rather than watching the prosecutor or defense attorney. But this skill must be developed. It is difficult for most people to look at the jury when responding to a question from an attorney who may be standing on the opposite side of the courtroom. If the jury cannot hear or understand what the witness is saying, the testimony is worthless. Witnesses should speak loudly enough for people in the back of the courtroom to hear clearly and understand what they are saying. Then they can be sure that the jury, the attorneys, and the judge also can hear them.

## Answering Questions

The ability to answer questions under direct and cross-examination is usually developed through experience. The police witness must answer without emotion or partiality. Sarcasm, witty remarks, or an attitude of "I'm out to get the defendant" must be avoided at all times. The good police witness must be positive and firm in answering all questions and should readily admit not knowing an answer if this is the case. The witness who constructs an answer to avoid embarrassment jeopardizes the case for the prosecution. Even the slightest fabrication of testimony is perjury and is likely to be discovered on cross-examination. It should be remembered that to err is human. It is not impossible for police witnesses to make mistakes in their testimony. Although it is slightly embarrassing, the witness should not hesitate to admit having made a mistake. This acknowledgment should be accompanied by an explanation. Even if the mistake is not discovered until after testimony is complete, the witness should immediately advise the prosecutor of the mistake so that the prosecutor will have the opportunity to correct it before the conclusion of the trial.

The requirement of being positive and firm in responding to questions also means that the witness must avoid the use of such expressions as "I think," "I believe," or "as I recall." It is difficult to avoid using expressions such as these because they are part of everyday usage of the English language, but in court they can raise questions as to the definitiveness of the officer's testimony and can be a factor in the degree of credibility given to the testimony by the jury.

There are two basic methods by which witnesses are examined. The narrative technique allows the witness to tell the facts in his or her own words as they are known to be, in response to a question such as, "Now tell us what you found at 1234 Elm Street." This technique is used if the examiner knows the witness well and has confidence that the witness will relate only relevant, unobjectionable matters. The advantage of the narrative technique is that it permits the witness to relate details chronologically and make them clearer to the jury. The obvious disadvantage is that an inexperienced witness may ramble, give objectionable or irrelevant testimony, or expose the jury to tainted evidence, potentially causing a mistrial. Hence, prosecutors use this technique sparingly.

Usually attorneys use the question-and-answer technique for examining witnesses. They ask a single, pointed question and receive an answer to it. When the question-and-answer technique is used, the police witness should hesitate momentarily before answering. This allows time for the opposing attorney to raise any objections. It also gives the witness an opportunity to digest the question to make sure it has been clearly understood. If not, the witness should ask that the question be repeated as many times as necessary. If the question does not make any sense after several repetitions, the witness may ask that the question be phrased in different terms. The witness should not volunteer information.

Courtesy and respect are important qualities of an effective witness. The judge should always be addressed as "Your Honor." The witness's language should be intelligible and understandable to the jury. Police witnesses should deliberately avoid the use of slang and words unique to the police service, for these may not be understood by the jury. Profanity should not be used in the courtroom unless the witness is repeating a direct quote. If such is the case, the officer should have no hesitation in using the exact words that were used during the investigation.

Occasionally a yes or no answer may be demanded of a witness, particularly on cross-examination. Sometimes such an answer is not an appropriate response to the question. If this occasion arises, the witness should not be pressured into an inaccurate response for the sake of brevity. The witness is always permitted to qualify answers and should persist in this right, if necessary asking the judge for permission to qualify the answer. But if the question can be accurately answered with a simple yes or no, the witness should respond accordingly.

## Cross-Examination

The purpose of cross-examination is to ensure that testimony given under direct examination has been accurate and truthful. Through cross-examination the attorney attempts to impeach witnesses called by the opposing side. **Impeachment** is the process of discrediting or contradicting the testimony of the witness to show that the witness is unworthy of belief. It is designed to weaken or destroy the effect of the testimony presented under direct examination and thus to destroy the credibility of the witness in the eyes of the jury. Cross-examination tests the reliability of the witness by attempting to detect whether testimony was intentionally slanted or whether an error or misstatement was made.

The five basic methods for attacking the credibility of a witness are:

1. Showing that the witness's previous statements, personal conduct, or conduct of the investigation is inconsistent with the witness's testimony in court.
2. Showing that the witness is biased or prejudice for or against the state or the defendant because of a close relationship, personal interest in the outcome of the case, hostility toward the opposing party, or similar biases.
3. Attacking the character of the witness—revealing prior criminal convictions or other irrefutable characteristics that would render testimony unworthy of belief.
4. Showing the witness's incapacity to observe, recollect, or recount due to mental weakness, a physical defect, influence of drugs or alcohol, or the like.
5. Showing that the witness is in error, that the facts are otherwise than as testified.

Cross-examination tactics used by attorneys vary widely, but they fall into two basic categories. Browbeating or belligerent cross-examination is designed to put the witness under pressure to provoke an unprofessional reaction. The attorney may ask a series of questions rapidly in an attempt to confuse the witness and force inconsistent responses. The attorney may try to reverse the witness's words or may continually repeat the same questions in an attempt to elicit inconsistent or conflicting answers.

The cross-examiner who assumes a friendly, condescending role attempts to lull the witness into a false sense of security to bring about less caution in listening to and answering questions. Once the witness's guard is down, the cross-examiner often resorts to leading questions. Leading questions suggest the answer desired. Although leading questions are not permitted in direct examination, they are permitted in cross-examination.

Another danger that should be avoided in cross-examination involves questions regarding whether the officer has talked with anyone about the case. Police witnesses often have the impression that this kind of question is designed to attack their integrity by attempting to show that they discussed the details of the case with the press or others in an attempt to create prejudice toward the defendant. In fact, discussing the case with the prosecutor before the trial is perfectly permissible. If the officer answers no to the question and this later turns out to be false, his or her credibility suffers. Likewise, if the witness responds no to the question, "Did the prosecutor tell you how to testify?" the answer is only partly complete. Obviously, the prosecutor generally has instructed the witness to testify to firsthand knowledge of facts and to tell the truth. But the question is designed in such a manner as to imply that an affirmative response means the prosecutor told the witness exactly how to answer each question. The best way of handling this type of situation is to respond, "Yes, I talked with the prosecutor about the case. The prosecutor advised me to relate the facts about which I had firsthand knowledge."

### Use of Notes on the Stand

It is permissible for witnesses to use notes to help refresh their memory while testifying; the human mind can retain only so much information. The witness is not and cannot be expected to remember minute details such as dates and numbers that are of lesser importance than the major facts of the case. However, the witness should constantly be aware of the proper use of notes and the ramifications of their use.

There are two reasons why a witness may refer to notes. The first is a need to remember a particular fact in question. In this case, the officer does remember the case and is permitted to use the notes to help recall minor details. This use of notes is perfectly permissible. On the other hand, if the officer's references to the notes are necessitated by an inability to remember anything about the events preceding the trial, the consequences of referring to notes are entirely different.

In the rules of evidence, using notes simply to refresh the memory is referred to as past recollection refreshed. As indicated, this is permissible but should be used with restraint, for it may indicate a lack of pretrial preparation. When notes are used by a police officer in direct examination, the defense attorney has an absolute right to examine those notes and test the witness's memory before allowing the witness to continue testifying under direct examination. This is done to ensure that the witness is, in fact, testifying from memory.

In the event that the witness cannot remember the facts of the case but uses the notes as the sole basis of testimony without any independent recall, the term applied is past recollection recorded. In this instance the oral testimony of the police officer becomes worthless, as the knowledge is entirely based on the notes. Should this occur, the prosecutor most likely will, at the insistence of the defense attorney, dismiss the police officer as a witness and introduce the notes as evidence in the trial. If the notes are meaningless to everybody but the police officer who took them, the entire substance of the knowledge will be excluded from evidence.

For the various reasons described above, it is highly recommended that police officers use loose-leaf notebooks during their investigations. In this way, materials not relevant to the particular case at hand can be removed before the trial and only the notes that are pertinent will be brought into the courtroom. If this is not done, the defense attorney may question the officer on any irrelevant part of the contents of the notebook and perhaps, by embarrassment, decrease the officer's credibility with the jury.

## LEAVING THE WITNESS STAND

How witnesses leave the witness stand is just as important as how they enter, because the eyes of the jury follow them. It is improper for the witness to rise and leave the witness stand on completion of cross-examination. The prosecutor may conduct a redirect examination, or the defense attorney may think of a last-minute question. During this time, the witness should be careful not to be caught off guard. A common tactic in cross-examination is to ask a last-minute question while the witness is preparing to leave the stand, in hopes of catching the witness in an error after the pressure of testifying seems over. The witness should wait to be excused by the judge and should leave the courtroom without smiling, speaking, or glaring at anyone.

## Key Terms

**admissibility**
**admission**
**affidavit**
**affirmation**
**arrest**
**arrest warrant**
**burden of going forward**
**burden of proof**
**charging**
**confession**
**corpus delicti**
**cross-examination**

**detention**
**direct examination**
**evidence**
**evidentiary privileges**
**expert witness**
**hearsay**
**impeachment**
**judicial notice**
**oath**
**plaintiff**
**preponderance of evidence**
**probable cause**
**proof**
**rebuttal**
**re-cross-examination**
**redirect examination**
**subpoena**
**surrebuttal**
**testimony**
**weight (of evidence)**

## Review Questions

1. Define arrest.
2. Distinguish arrest from detention.
3. Distinguish arrest from charging.
4. What are the benefits to a police officer and the case if an arrest is made under the authority of a warrant?
5. Is a "John Doe" arrest warrant valid under any circumstances? Explain.
6. Define and describe probable cause.
7. During an ongoing criminal investigation, what factors must the criminal investigator consider in deciding whether to make an arrest and when to make it?
8. Why must a criminal investigator know the rules of evidence?
9. Define the following concepts:
   (a) Evidence
   (b) Proof
   (c) Testimony
   (d) Admissibility
   (e) Relevancy
   (f) Materiality
   (g) Competency of evidence
   (h) Competency of witnesses
   (i) Weight
10. Distinguish between burden of proof and burden of going forward with evidence.
11. What is the purpose of judicial notice?
12. Describe the manner in which circumstantial evidence is used in a criminal prosecution.
13. Why does the opinion rule of evidence exist?
14. What is the hearsay rule, and why does it exist?
15. What is the philosophy under which exceptions to the hearsay rule have evolved?
16. Describe the philosophy underlying the existence of evidentiary privileges.
17. What is the role of the investigator as a witness?
18. What factors affect the credibility of the investigator as a witness?
19. What are the characteristics of a good witness?
20. How important are a witness's appearance and demeanor to credibility?
21. What is the function of cross-examination?
22. When and how may a witness use notes on the witness stand?

## Internet Activities

1. Find out what investigative methods may or may not be protected from disclosure in court by going to the **FBI's Law Enforcement Bulletin** website, www.fbi.gov/publications/leb/leb.htm. Find the article entitled "The Qualified Privilege to Protect Sensitive Investigative Techniques from Disclosure" in the May 2000 issue. Under what conditions have courts recognized privilege for investigative techniques?
2. Search your state statutes for information on privileged communications. Legal research websites such as www.megalaw.com and www.Findlaw.com are good places to start. What types of communication are privileged in your state?

## Notes

1. Wayne R. LaFave, Arrest: The Decision to Take a Suspect into Custody (Boston: Little, Brown, 1965), pp. 3–4.
2. Terry v. Ohio, 392 U.S. 1 (1968).

# GLOSSARY

**AAMVANET** Maintained by the American Association of Motor Vehicle Administrators, a computerized network linking state and Canadian province agencies on driver's license and motor vehicle matters of highway usage and safety.

**accelerant** In fire starting, any flammable fluid or compound that speeds the progress of a fire. Also called *booster*.

**action stereotyping** Occurs when an officer expects an event will unfold in a particular way; it can result in the officer's failure to see the event the way it actually occurred.

**active system (theft deterrent)** A type of vehicle antitheft device which requires that the driver do something to activate and deactivate the system every time the vehicle is parked or driven.

**administrative log** A written record of the actions taken by the crime scene coordinator, including assignments and release of the scene.

**admissibility** A legal criterion used to determine whether an item of evidence can be presented in court; requires that the evidence have relevance, materiality, and competence.

**admission** A person's acknowledgment of certain facts or circumstances that tend to incriminate him or her with respect to a crime but are not complete enough to constitute a confession.

**affidavit** A sworn, written statement of the information known to an officer that serves as the basis for the issuance of an arrest warrant.

**affirmation** The process in which a witness acknowledges that he or she understands and undertakes the obligation of an oath (i.e., to tell the truth with a realization of the penalties for perjury); a means of establishing a witness's competence.

**AFIS** *see* **Automated Fingerprint Identification System.**

**agrichemical** Any of various chemical products used on farms; includes pesticides, fertilizers, and herbicides.

**agroterrorism** The use of biological agents as weapons against the agricultural and food supply industries.

**AIDS** *see* **human immunodeficiency virus**.

**algor mortis** The decrease in body temperature that occurs after death.

**alligatoring** The checking of charred wood, which gives it the appearance of alligator skin.

**ALS** *see* **alternative light systems.**

**alternative light systems (ALSs)** Portable lasers and handheld ultraviolet lighting used to locate physical evidence at the crime scene; particularly helpful in locating trace evidence.

**amateur burglars** Burglars who operate on the basis of impulse or opportunity, with no planning; often use sheer force to enter, ransack the premises for anything of value, and may become violent if detected and commit secondary crimes (e.g., murder, rape).

**ambush** A robbery that involves virtually no planning and depends on surprise and the use of force against victims; usually produces a small score.

**American Society of Crime Laboratory Directors (ASCLD)** An international society devoted to maintaining the highest standards of practice at crime laboratories; conducts an accreditation program for laboratories and education programs for lab personnel.

**amido black** A dye that is sensitive to blood and thus is used in developing fingerprints contaminated with blood.

**amphetamines** Stimulants that increase blood pressure and heart, respiratory, and metabolic rates; produce decreased appetite, hyperalert senses, and a general state of stress that last a prolonged period.

**anthrax** An acute infectious disease with three forms (cutaneous, intestinal, and inhalation), which differ in means of transmission, symptoms, and lethality; also, a biological agent.

**anthropometry** Developed by Alphonse Bertillon in the late 19th century, the study and comparison of body measurements as a means of criminal identification.

**archaeological looting** The illegal, unscientific removal of archaeological resources from public, tribal, or private land.

**arrest** The process of taking a person into legal custody to answer a criminal charge.

**arrest warrant** A judicial order commanding that a particular person be arrested and brought before a court to answer a criminal charge.

**assignment sheets** Written reports completed by persons assigned tasks at a crime scene that document what they have done and found.

**associative evidence** Bidirectional evidence that connects the perpetrator to the scene or victim or connects the scene or victim to the perpetrator.

**attack code** A malicious software program intended to impair or destroy the functioning of a computer or a network resource.

**autoerotic death** Death from accidental asphyxiation as a result of masochistic activities of the deceased. Also called *sexual asphyxia*.

**Automated Fingerprint Identification System (AFIS)** A computerized system, maintained by the FBI, that stores and compares millions of fingerprints and is used to find matches for identification purposes.

**autopsy** The medical examination of a body to determine the time of and cause of death; required in all cases of violent or suspicious death.

**avionics** The electronic equipment (e.g., radio, navigation) on an aircraft.

**back doors** Code breaks used in debugging a computer program that are designed to evade normal security procedures; targeted by exploit programs as a means of illegal access to files.

**barbiturates** Short-, intermediate-, and long-lasting depressants (e.g., secobarbital, amobarbital) strongly associated with the tendency for abrupt withdrawal to cause convulsions and death; nicknamed after the capsule or pill color or the manufacturer's name.

**basic yellow 40** Used after superglue fuming, a dye that causes latent prints to fluoresce under alternative lighting.

**battered-child syndrome** The clinical term for the injuries sustained by a physically abused child.

**be-on-the-lookout (BOLO)** Part of the preliminary investigation, a notification broadcast to officers that contains detailed information on suspects and their vehicles.

**behavioral evidence analysis (BEA)** A deductive and evidence-based method of criminal profiling.

**Biggers-Brathwaite Factors Test** A test that balances the reliability of eyewitness identification (as determined by five factors specified by the Supreme Court) with the corrupting effect of any suggestive procedures; enables a highly reliable identification to be used in court even if something jeopardized the fairness of the identification procedure.

**biological agents** Certain microorganisms and toxins produced by organisms (e.g., smallpox, anthrax, plague, botulism) that cause human illness or death and could be used as terrorist weapons; typically slower acting than chemical agents.

**bobbies** A colloquial term used in reference to British police constables; derived by the public from the first name of Sir Robert Peel, whose efforts led to the creation of the first metropolitan police force in London.

**body language** Gestures, demeanor, facial expressions, and other nonverbal signals that convey, usually involuntarily, a person's attitudes, impressions, truthfulness, and so on.

**BOLO** *see* **be-on-the-lookout**.

**bone rustlers** Unauthorized fossil hunters, who loot public and private lands.

**booster bag** Used by shoplifters, a large shopping bag lined with an inner bag of tin foil and duct tape; renders useless the electronic security tags on items placed within it.

**boosters** *see* **commercial shoplifters**.

**bore** The diameter of a gun barrel's interior between its opposing high sides (the lands).

**Bow Street Runners** Established by Henry Fielding in 1748, a group of volunteer, nonuniformed home owners who helped catch thieves in London by rushing to crime scenes and beginning investigations, thus acting as the first modern detective force. By 1785, some were paid government detectives.

**brands** On livestock, registered combinations of numbers, letters, marks, and shapes that establish unique identifications.

**burden of going forward** In a criminal trial, the responsibility of the defense to present enough evidence to create a reasonable doubt of guilt in the jurors' minds; an optional burden, as the defense is not required to present any evidence.

**burden of proof** In a criminal trial, the requirement that the prosecution establish the defendant's guilt beyond and to the exclusion of every reasonable doubt.

**burglary** The crime of breaking and entering a house or other building belonging to another with the intent to commit a crime therein.

**burglary tools** Tools used in the commission of burglary; often are ordinary household tools, but may be modified for increased effectiveness in breaking and entering.

**burn indicators** Any effects of heat or partial burning that indicate a fire's rate of development, points of origin, temperature, duration, and time of occurrence and the presence of flammable liquids.

**cadaver dogs** Trained dogs, sensitive to the odor of decomposing human remains, that assist in locating bodies buried in the ground or submerged in water.

**cadaveric spasm** The instantaneous tightening of an extremity or other part of the body at the time of death. Also called *death grip*.

**caliber** The diameter of a bullet; somewhat larger than the bore of the weapon from which the bullet is fired.

**cargo theft** The theft of items from or in commercial motor vehicles.

**carjacking** The crime of taking a motor vehicle from the motorist or passenger, or from his or her immediate presence, by use of force, fear, or threat of force, with the intent to temporarily or permanently deprive the owner of its use.

**catalytic combustion detector** A portable device that oxidizes any combustible gases in a sample; used to detect residues of flammable-liquid accelerants at fire scenes. Also called *sniffer, combustible-gas indicator, explosimeter,* and *vapor detector*.

**chain of custody** The witnessed, unbroken, written chronological record of everyone who had an item of evidence and when each person had it; also accounts for any changes in the evidence.

**charging** The act of formally asserting that a particular person is to be prosecuted for a crime.

**charring** The scorching of materials by fire; used to deduce the direction of fire spread by comparing relative depths of char throughout the scene.

**check fraud** Any activity involving the creation or use of phony or altered checks (e.g., counterfeiting, identity assumption, payroll-check schemes).

**check washing** The process of altering checks by using an acid-based chemical solution to erase amount and payee information.

**chemical agents** Rapidly acting substances (e.g., mustard gas, sarin, V agents) that produce a variety of incapacitating symptoms or death; as weapons, can cause mass casualties and devastation.

**chemical explosions** Explosions in which the high-pressure gas is produced by reactions that involve changes in the basic chemical nature of the fuel; commonly caused by the burning of hydrocarbon fuels (e.g., natural gas, gasoline, lubricating oils).

**child** An individual under the age of 18.

**child pornography** The sexually explicit visual depiction of a minor (as defined by statute); includes photographs, negatives, slides, magazines, movies, videotapes, and computerized images.

**chop shop** An illegal operation at which stolen cars are disassembled and their traceable parts are altered or disposed of so that untraceable parts can be sold to repair shops, salvage yards, and indiscriminate buyers.

**CID** *see* **Criminal Investigation Department.**

**clandestine drug laboratories** Illicit operations that produce a variety of illegal drugs for sale and distribution; due to the chemicals, processes used, and workers' inexperience, pose serious danger to police and firefighters, as well as the public.

**class characteristics** Characteristics of physical evidence that are common to a group of objects or persons.

**cleared by arrest** The classification assigned to an offense when the suspect has been arrested and there is sufficient evidence to file a formal charge.

**cloning** The illegal programming of cellular phones by overwriting their access codes with the codes of legitimate cellular customers; done through a personal computer or cloning "black box."

**cocaine** A natural stimulant extracted from the leaves of the coca plant; illegally sold as a white, translucent, crystalline powder, which is often adulterated.

**codeine** An opiate in tablet, liquid, and injectable forms that produces less analgesia, sedation, and respiratory depression than morphine.

**CODIS** *see* **Combined DNA Index System**.

**cognitive interview technique** An interviewing approach in which a witness is asked to recall events and details in different ways as a means of fostering the witness's recollections.

**Combined DNA Index System (CODIS)** Developed by the FBI, a database of convicted-offender and known- and unknown-subject DNA profiles that is used to find matches and to link unsolved crimes in multiple jurisdictions.

**commercial shoplifters** or **boosters** Persons who steal merchandise for the purpose of reselling it.

**commercial-vehicle theft** The theft of vehicle tractor units and trailers.

**competency (of a witness)** A witness's personal qualification for testifying in court, which depends on circumstances that affect the person's legal ability to function as a sworn witness (e.g., age, mental state).

**component swapping** A fraudulent practice in which manufacturers (e.g., of computers) use parts from the lowest-cost supplier but do not inform consumers that the parts are nonstandard.

**computer abuse** Any intentional act involving knowledge of computer use or technology in which the perpetrator could have made a gain and the victim could have experienced a loss; includes acts that may not be covered by criminal laws.

**computer crime** Any illegal act in which knowledge of computer technology is used to commit the offense.

**computer manipulation crime** Any act that involves changing data or creating records in an electronic system for the purpose of facilitating another crime, typically fraud or embezzlement.

**computer vandalism** The unauthorized removal of valuable information from a computer system, thereby preventing the legitimate user or owner from having access to that information.

**concentric fractures** Lines that roughly circle the point of impact in a glass window.

**confabulation** In hypnosis, the subject's fabrication of recollections to fill in gaps in his or her actual memory.

**confession** The acknowledgment by a person accused of a crime that he or she is guilty of that crime and committed every element of the offense; must exclude any reasonable doubt about the possibility of innocence.

**confidence artists** Individuals who use guile in a person-to-person relationship to swindle the other person by gaining his or her confidence.

**confidential VIN** A duplicate vehicle identification number stamped into a vehicle's frame or body in a place known only to the manufacturer and law enforcement specialists in vehicle identification and auto theft investigation.

**contact burns** Burns on the skin caused by contact with flames or hot solid objects (e.g., irons, cigarettes).

**contaminated/visible prints** Prints created when fingers contaminated with blood, face powder, or a similar material touch a clean surface.

**cookie** A small file that some web pages plant within the browser of a visiting computer; can pass its limited data (e.g., user name) back to the web server on subsequent visits but cannot gather additional information.

**corpus delicti** Literally, "body of the crime"; consists of all the elements of the crime.

**corpus delicti evidence** Evidence that substantiates elements whose commission or omission must be demonstrated to have occurred in order to prove a case.

**crack** *see* **rock cocaine.**

**cracking** *see* **hacking**.

**credibility (of a witness)** That quality of a witness that renders his or her testimony worthy of belief; established in terms of presence, consciousness, and attentiveness during interviews.

**credit card fraud** Any activity involving the creation or use of phony, altered, stolen, or fraudulently acquired credit cards.

**crime** The commission of any act that is prohibited or the omission of any act that is required by the penal code of an organized political state.

**crime analysis** The use of systematic analytical methods to acquire timely and pertinent information on crime patterns and trend correlations; subdivided into administrative, strategic, and tactical analysis.

**crime bulletins** Prepared by crime analysts, publications used to disseminate information on specific topics (e.g., most active criminals, crime series and trends); may be in printed or electronic form.

**crime laboratory** A scientific organization that analyzes material collected from crime scenes and suspects to help determine whether a crime was committed and, if so, how, when, and by whom it was committed.

**crime scene** The location at which a crime was committed.

**crime scene entry log** A written chronological record of all persons who enter and leave the crime scene and the times they do so, along with their reason for entering.

**crime scene release** The end of crime scene processing and the return of the premises or area to the owner or another responsible person; determined by the scene coordinator.

**Criminal Identification Bureau (Chicago)** Established in 1884, the first municipal organization in the United States devoted specifically to assisting detectives with identifying criminals.

**Criminal Investigation Department (CID)** Established in London in 1878, a centralized organization of detectives responsible for investigating crimes; located at Scotland Yard but, to correct internal abuses, kept separate from the Metropolitan Police.

**criminal investigative analysis** The process of analyzing crime scene patterns to determine the personality and behavioral characteristics of offenders who commit serial murders or rape and homicide; formerly called *psychological profiling*.

**criminal profiling** The process of inferring distinctive personality characteristics of individuals who commit crimes.

**criminalistics** The application of scientific disciplines, such as geology, physics, chemistry, biology, and mathematics, to criminal investigation and the study of physical evidence.

**crimogen** (1) An individually known offender who is responsible for a large number of crimes; (2) one victim who reports a large number of crimes.

**cross-contamination** The unwanted transfer of material between two or more sources of physical evidence.

**cross-examination** In a trial, the questioning of a witness who was initially called by the opposing party.

**cryptanalysis** The process of accessing secured information by breaking encryption; in computers, often done intrusively with cryptanalysis software.

**crystal violet** A dye used to develop latent prints on the adhesive side of almost any kind of tape.

**crystallized methamphetamine** A long-acting stimulant originally in pill or injectable form *(crystal meth, speed)* but now in a smokable, odorless version *(ice)*; in solid form, resembles an ice chip but liquefies when lighted.

**CUPPI** Acronym for "circumstances undetermined pending police investigation"; refers to a case on which the medical examiner, after autopsy, wants clarification before signing the death certificate.

**cyberstalking** The crime of harassing or threatening victims by means of electronic technologies (e.g., through email and Internet chat rooms or news groups).

**cyberterrorism** The use of electronic tools to disrupt or shut down critical infrastructure components, such as energy, transportation, and government operations.

**dactylography** The study and comparison of fingerprints as a means of criminal identification; first used systematically for that purpose in England in 1900, but a means of identification since the first century.

**date-rape drugs** Drugs that facilitate rape by debilitating the victim; include Rohypnol, GHB, and many depressants and benzodiazapines.

***Daubert* v. *Merrell Dow Pharmaceuticals, Inc.*** A 1993 case in which the Supreme Court held that the admissibility of an expert's testimony or a scientific technique's results depends on a preliminary assessment, made by the trial judge, of the principles and methodology involved.

**DEA** *see* **Drug Enforcement Administration.**

**deductive reasoning** The thought process that moves from general premises to specific details; e.g., a hypothesis about the crime is developed and then tested against the factual situation to arrive at a conclusion.

**defense wounds** Wounds suffered by victims while attempting to protect themselves from an assault; often inflicted by a knife or club.

**delay-in-arraignment rule** Based on a 1943 Supreme Court decision, the principle that the failure to take a prisoner before a committing magistrate without unnecessary delay will render his or her confession inadmissible even if it was freely obtained.

**delivery vehicles** Software programs used by criminals to implant intrusion codes or attack codes in computer systems.

**dental identification** The identification of an individual on the basis of dental records (or, sometimes, "smiling" photographs); performed by a forensic dentist, who compares before-death records with after-death findings to see if there is a match.

**dental stone** The preferred material for casting tire, footwear, and foot impressions; stronger and faster setting than plaster of paris and provides more detailed impressions.

**deoxyribonucleic acid (DNA)** A nucleic acid consisting of the molecules that carry the body's genetic material and establish each person as separate and distinct.

**depressants** or **sedatives** Drugs that depress the central nervous system, reducing tension and inducing sleep; can cause, in chronic use, loss of balance, faulty judgment, and quick temper and, in overdose, unconsciousness and death.

**detention** A temporary and limited interference with a person's freedom for investigative purposes. Also called *investigative detention, street stop,* and *field interrogation.*

**DFO (diazafluren-9-one)** A very effective chemical for developing latent prints on paper; produces red prints that may be visible to the naked eye and that fluoresce under most laser and alternative lighting.

**digital forensic analysis** The process of acquiring, preserving, analyzing, and presenting evidentiary electronic data relevant to an investigation or prosecution.

**direct examination** In a trial, the questioning of a witness by the party that calls the witness to testify.

**disposition (of incident report)** After approval of an incident report, the determination of how the case will be handled (i.e., unfounded, inactivated, retained for investigation by officers, referred to plainclothes investigators); usually made by the supervisor of the officer who wrote the report.

**DNA** *see* **deoxyribonucleic acid.**

**DNA typing** The process of isolating and reading deoxyribonucleic acid—a genetic blueprint unique to every human (except for identical twins), which can be used as a means of criminal identification. Also called *DNA fingerprinting*.

**document** Anything on which a mark is made for the purpose of transmitting a message.

**documented vessel** A boat that is registered by the U.S. Coast Guard.

**domestic terrorism** The use or threatened use of violence against persons or property by a group (or an individual) whose operations are entirely within the victims' nation, without foreign direction, and are done to further political or social objectives.

**Drug Enforcement Administration (DEA)** Created in 1973, the federal agency responsible for enforcing laws on illicit drugs and fighting international drug traffic; also trains state and local police in investigative work regarding illegal drugs, surveillance, and use of informants.

**due process revolution** An appellation applied to the period from 1961 to 1966, during which a series of Supreme Court decisions established important rights for suspects and defendants regarding search and seizure and legal representation.

**ecstasy** *see* **methylenedioxy methamphetamine.**

**effective fire temperatures** In structural fires, identifiable temperatures which reflect physical effects that can be defined by specific temperature ranges.

**email intercept** An intelligence technique in which email is intercepted and analyzed to obtain information about terrorists, pornographers, hackers, and other criminals and their crimes; requires a showing of reasonable cause.

**emotional approach** An interrogation technique in which the interrogator appeals to the suspect's sense of honor, morals, family pride, religion, etc.; works better with women and first-time offenders.

**encryption** A means of data security in which the data are scrambled into nonsense for storage or transmission and then unscrambled, as needed, by legitimate users.

**Enderby cases** Two rape-murder cases in England that involved the first use of DNA typing, in 1987, in a criminal case. DNA samples recovered from both victims led to the release of an innocent man and the subsequent arrest and conviction of the killer.

**evidence** Anything that tends logically to prove or disprove a fact at issue in a judicial case or controversy.

**evidence recovery log** A chronological record of each item of evidence, listing who collected it, where and when it was collected, who witnessed the collection, and whether it was documented by photos or diagrams.

**evidential intelligence** Factual, precise information that can be presented in court.

**evidentiary privileges** Certain matters of communication that defendants and other witnesses have a right to have barred from disclosure in court; classified as professional, political, social, and judicial.

**exceptionally cleared** The classification assigned to an offense when a factor external to the investigation results in no charge being filed against a known suspect (e.g., the death of the suspect).

**exchangeable traces** Particulates, lubricants, and spermicide added to condoms by manufacturers; can help identify particular brands and indicate condom use.

**excusable homicide** The killing of a person in which the slayer is to some degree at fault but the degree of fault is not enough to constitute a criminal homicide.

**expert witness** A person who is called to testify in court because of his or her special skills or knowledge; permitted to interpret facts and give opinions about their significance to facilitate jurors' understanding of complex or technical matters.

**exploits** Software programs written to take advantage of security holes or "back doors" and thereby provide the user with illegal access to computer files.

**explosion** A physical reaction characterized by the presence of high-pressure gas, confinement of the pressure, rapid release of the pressure, and change or damage to the confining structure, container, or vessel as a result of the pressure release.

**eyewitness identification** The identification of someone or something involved in a crime by a witness who perceives the person or thing through one or more senses.

**facial identification systems** Manual kits or computer programs for preparing a likeness of a suspect; creates a composite from individual facial features.

**facial recognition software** Any of various computer programs that compare video images of persons' faces (taken by cameras at arenas, airports, hotels, etc.) with mug shots of known offenders for the purpose of identifying and apprehending wanted persons.

**false-theft scheme** An insurance fraud in which the owner of a vehicle reports the vehicle stolen but has actually hidden or disposed of it.

**false-vehicle scheme** An insurance fraud in which a person insures a vehicle that does not exist, has already been salvaged, or belongs to someone else and later reports the vehicle stolen.

**farm equipment** Motorized equipment used on farms and on lawns; usually does not require a title or registration. Also called *off-road equipment*.

**FBI** *see* **Federal Bureau of Investigation.**

**FBI Crime Laboratory** A comprehensive forensic laboratory that conducts a broad range of scientific analyses of evidence and provides experts to testify in relation to analysis results; provides its services without charge to state and local law enforcement agencies.

**Federal Bureau of Investigation (FBI)** Created in 1908 as the Bureau of Investigation and given its current name by Congress in 1935, the primary agency responsible for investigating crimes within the federal jurisdiction; influences law enforcement countrywide through its crime laboratory, training courses, and databanks, all available to state and local police.

**federal safety certification label** The sticker certifying a vehicle's safety and including its VIN; usually on the driver's door or doorpost.

**felonious assault** An assault committed for the purpose of inflicting severe bodily harm or death; usually involves use of a deadly weapon.

**felonious homicides** Killings that are treated and punished as crimes; include murder and manslaughter.

**felony** A serious violation of the criminal code; punishable by imprisonment for one or more years or by death.

**fences** or **receivers** Persons who knowingly purchase stolen property at a fraction of its cost and then resell it at a considerable profit, but still at a good price, to a consumer.

**field interview/information report** A form on which a patrolling officer notes details about a person or vehicle that seems suspicious but is not connected with any particular offense.

**field notes** The shorthand written record made by a police officer from the time he or she arrives at a crime scene until the assignment is completed.

**Financial Crimes Enforcement Network (FinCen)** Part of the Department of the Treasury, an agency responsible for investigating major financial crimes (e.g., money laundering); provides assistance to law enforcement agencies.

**FinCen** *see* **Financial Crimes Enforcement Network.**

**fingerprint classification** A system used to categorize fingerprints on the basis of their ridge characteristics.

**fingerprint patterns** Patterns formed by the ridge detail of fingerprints; primarily loops, whorls, and arches.

**fingerprints** Replicas of the friction ridges (on palms, fingers, toes, and soles of the feet) that touched the surfaces on which the prints are found.

**firearm identification** This extends well beyond comparing two fired bullets; it encompasses slide, ejector, firing-pin impressions, and other markings caused by the action of the firearm, restoration of obliterated serial numbers, estimation of the distance between a fired gun's muzzle and the victim, as well as knowledge of design and functioning of firearms.

**firewall** A device or software program that acts as a checkpoint between a network or stand-alone computer and the Internet; blocks any incoming or outgoing data that do not fit specified criteria.

**flame ionization detector** A device that produces ionized molecules in proportion to the amount of combustible organic gases in a sample; used to detect residues of accelerants at fire scenes.

**fluorescent powders** Powders, dusted on areas being examined, that chemically enhance latent prints viewed under UV, laser, or alternative light illumination.

**follow-up investigation** The process of gathering information after the generation of the incident report and until the case is ready for prosecution; undertaken for cases receiving a supervisory disposition for further investigation.

**footwear impressions** Impressions that result when footwear, feet, or tires tread on a moldable surface such as earth, clay, or snow.

**footwear prints** Prints that result when footwear, feet, or tires contaminated with foreign matter such as mud, grease, or blood are placed on a smooth, firm surface (e.g., a floor, a chair, paper). Also called *residue prints.*

**forensic accountants** Accountants who specialize in analyzing financial evidence and testifying as expert witnesses in cases of white-collar crime.

**forensic dentistry** A medical specialty that relates dental evidence to investigation.

**forensic pathology** The study, by physicians, of how and why people die; can also include examination of the living to determine physical or sexual abuse.

**forensic photograph analysis** The comparison of photos from a security surveillance camera with file pictures of suspects to identify a perpetrator or acquire information about him or her.

**forensic science** The examination, evaluation, and explanation of physical evidence in terms of law.

**forgery** Any falsification or alteration of a document; can be traced, simulated, or freehand.

**fracture match** The alignment of the edges of two items of evidence, thereby showing that both items were previously joined together.

**free-and-voluntary rule** Based on a number of Supreme Court decisions since 1936, the principle that the exertion of any kind of coercion, physical or psychological, on a suspect to obtain a confession will render the confession inadmissible.

**freezer crimes** Thefts of livestock (usually only one or a few animals) in which the motivation is food rather than profit.

***Frye* v. *United States*** A 1923 federal case which established that the results of a scientific technique would be admissible only if the technique had gained general acceptance in its field. (Per *Daubert,* this was superceded by the federal rules of evidence.)

**gamma hydroxybutyrate (GHB)** A central nervous system depressant used to perpetrate sexual attacks; mixed into a victim's food or drink, can induce relaxation or unconsciousness, leaving the victim unaware of the attack; can also cause seizures or death.

**gas liquid chromatograph** A portable device that separates a sample gas into measurable components; used to detect residues of accelerants at fire scenes.

**geographic profiling** or **geoprofiling (GP)** An investigative strategy in which the locations of a series of crimes (or, sometimes, the scenes of a single crime) are used to determine the most probable area of the offender's residence.

**GHB** *see* **gamma hydroxybutyrate**.

**glutethimide (Doriden)** A depressant with long-lasting effects that make it very difficult to reverse overdoses, many of which result in death.

**GP** *see* **geographic profiling.**

**gray-market vehicles** Vehicles purchased abroad and shipped to the United States; may require modifications to meet U.S. emission control and safety standards.

**grooves** In a firearm's rifled bore, the low cuts that separate the higher lands.

**hacker's dictionary** A software program that provides unauthorized access to computer systems by generating millions of alphanumeric combinations until it finds one that matches a password.

**hacking** or **cracking** The process of gaining unauthorized entry into a computer system.

**hallucinogenic drugs** Natural or synthetic drugs that distort perception of objective reality and, in large doses, cause hallucinations; lead to unpredictable effects based on user and environment.

**hashish** A natural hallucinogen, derived from resinous secretions of the cannabis plant, that is more potent than marijuana; sold in soft lumps and usually smoked in a small hash pipe.

**hashish oil** An extremely potent hallucinogen, derived by distilling THC from marijuana, that produces a high from a single drop; smoked in a cigarette or glass-bowled pipe or ingested in food or wine.

**hazardous wastes** Solid, liquid, sludge, and manufacturing by-product wastes that are ignitable, corrosive, reactive, and/or toxic; may pose serious threat to human health and the environment if improperly managed.

**hearsay** Testimony by a witness that repeats something which he or she heard someone say out of court and which the witness has no personal factual knowledge of; inadmissible in court.

**heavy equipment** Heavy construction equipment; usually does not require a title or registration. Also called *off-road equipment*.

**Hemident** A reagent used in preliminary or presumptive field tests for the presence of blood.

**Henry system** Devised by Edward Henry, the fingerprint classification system that facilitated the use of fingerprints in criminal identification; adopted in England in 1900 and today used in almost every country

**hepatitis B (HBV)** and **hepatitis C (HCV)** Viruses present in blood (and, for HBV, other bodily fluids) that attack the liver and can lead to death; a health hazard at scenes where bodily fluids are exposed.

**heroin (diacetylmorphine)** An opiate that is much stronger than morphine and often causes death due to its purity or diluents; an odorless, crystalline white powder, which is usually sold diluted and is injected.

**HIN** *see* **hull identification number**.

**HIR** *see* **home-invasion robbery.**

**home-invasion robbery (HIR)** A crime in which one or more offenders deliberately enter a home to commit robbery; characterized by gangs who target individuals rather than residences and use violence to terrify and control their victims.

**homicide** The killing of a human being by another human being; can be felonious or nonfelonious.

**hot spot** A location where various crimes are committed on a regular basis, usually by different offenders. Also called *hot dot*.

**hull identification number (HIN)** Identification number assigned to boats.

**human immunodeficiency virus (HIV)** The blood-borne pathogen, also present in other bodily fluids, that can progress into AIDS, which reduces the body's defenses against diseases and leaves victims vulnerable to infections from which they die; a health hazard at scenes where bodily fluids are exposed.

**hypercompliance** In hypnosis, the situation in which the desire to please the hypnotist or others leads the subject to provide information that does not reflect his or her actual memories.

**hypersuggestibility** In hypnosis, the subject's heightened degree of suggestibility, which creates the possibility of the hypnotist's influencing the subject, intentionally or inadvertently, to give false information.

**hypnosis** A state of heightened awareness in which subconscious memories may surface that can be of help to an investigation.

**IAFIS** *see* **Integrated Automated Fingerprint Identification System.**

**identity theft** The assumption of another person's identity for use in fraudulent transactions that result in a loss to the victim; accomplished by acquiring personal information about the victim (e.g., date of birth, address, credit card numbers).

**immersion burns** Burns on the skin that occur when part or all of the body falls into or is placed into a tub or other container of hot liquid.

**impeachment** In a trial, the process of discrediting or contradicting the testimony of a witness to show that he or she is unworthy of belief.

**in-custody interrogation** The legal condition under which the *Miranda* warnings are required, although case decisions vary on the definitions of "custody" and "interrogation."

**incendiary mechanism** A fire-starting mechanism that consists of an ignition device, possibly a timing device, one or more plants to accelerate the flame, and, often, trailers to spread the fire; can be mechanical or chemical.

**incest** Broadly, any sexual abuse of a minor by an adult who is perceived by the minor to be a family member; also, under some statutes, sexual activity between closely related adults.

**incident report** The first written investigative record of a crime, usually compiled by the uniformed officer assigned to the call, who conducts the preliminary investigation.

**incised wounds** Wounds inflicted with a sharp-edged instrument such as a knife or razor; typically narrow at the ends and gaping at the center, with considerable bleeding. Also called *cutting wounds*.

**indicative intelligence** Information pertaining to emerging and new criminal developments; may include fragmentary or unsubstantiated information, as well as hard facts.

**individual characteristics** Characteristics of physical evidence that can be identified as coming from a particular person or source.

**inductive reasoning** The thought process that moves from specific details to a general view; e.g., the facts of a case are used to arrive at a logical explanation of the crime.

**infant abduction** The taking of a child less than 1 year old by a nonfamily member; classified by the FBI as kidnapping, although the motive is usually to possess the child rather than to use the child as a means to something else (e.g., money, sex, revenge).

**inflated-theft-loss scheme** An insurance fraud in which the owner of a stolen vehicle reports a greater financial loss, based on alleged current value, damage, or stolen parts, than is the case.

**informant** A person who regularly provides information to a particular investigator in return for money, a reduced charge or lenient sentence, or some personal motive such as rivalry or self-aggrandizement.

**infrared spectrophotometer** A device that identifies samples by recording the amount of infrared light that passes through them; used to detect residues of flammable-liquid accelerants at fire scenes.

**Integrated Automated Fingerprint Identification System (IAFIS)** Maintained by the FBI, a national online fingerprint and criminal-history database with identification and response capabilities; may be accessed by local law enforcement agencies.

**intelligence/analytical cycle** A five-part process designed to produce usable information for the client.

**international terrorism** The use or threatened use of violence against persons or property by a group (or an individual) whose operations transcend national boundaries and are done to further political or social objectives.

**interrogation** A conversation between an investigator and a suspect that is designed to match acquired information to the suspect and secure a confession.

**interviewing** The process of obtaining information from people who have knowledge that might be helpful in a criminal investigation.

**investigation** The process of establishing that a crime was committed, identifying and apprehending the suspect, recovering stolen property if any, and assisting in the prosecution of the person charged with the crime.

**investigative psychology** A criminal-profiling approach based on interpersonal coherence, significance of time and place, criminal characteristics, and the offender's criminal career and forensic awareness.

**investigator** An official who gathers, documents, and evaluates evidence and information in the investigation of a crime.

**iodine** A dye used in developing latent prints on porous (particularly paper) and nonporous surfaces; one of the oldest and most proven means of locating prints.

**Jacob Wetterling Crimes against Children and Sexually Violent Offender Registration Act** A 1994 federal act requiring that states create and maintain registries of sex offenders. See also **Megan's law**.

**jail booking report** A document containing complete personal information about a suspect, including a photograph, fingerprints, and a list of the suspect's personal property at the time of booking.

**joyriding** The theft and use of a motor vehicle solely to drive it, after which it is abandoned; usually committed by teenagers.

**judicial notice** An evidentiary shortcut whereby the necessity of formally proving the truth of a particular matter is eliminated when that truth is not in dispute.

**justifiable homicide** The necessary killing of a person in the performance of a legal duty or the exercise of a legal right when the slayer is not at fault.

**ketamine** A synthetic hallucinogen that produces hallucinations, excitement, and delirium of less intensity and shorter duration than the effects of PCP and LSD; sold as liquids, tablets, or white powder and injected, smoked, or ingested in a drink.

**kinesics** The relationship between body language (limb movements, facial expressions, etc.) and the communication of feelings and attitudes.

**known samples** (1) Standard or reference samples from known or verifiable sources; (2) control or blank samples from known sources believed to be uncontaminated by the crime; (3) elimination samples from sources who had lawful access to the crime scene.

**lacerations** Wounds inflicted by blunt objects such as clubs, pipes, and pistols; typically open and irregularly shaped, bruised around the edges, and bleeding freely.

**lands** The high sides in a firearm's rifled bore.

**larceny** The crime of taking and carrying away personal property of another, with the intent to permanently deprive the owner of its use.

**laser illumination** A method of developing latent prints in which lasers are used to illuminate a crime scene, causing otherwise-undetectable fingerprints to fluoresce when viewed through a special lens.

**latent fingerprints** Any prints (plastic, contaminated/visible, and latent/invisible) found at the scene of the crime or on items of investigative interest.

**latent/invisible prints** Fingerprints created when friction ridges deposit body perspiration and oil on surfaces they touch; typically invisible to the naked eye.

**Law Enforcement Online (LEO)** Maintained by the FBI, an intranet system through which enforcement officers can communicate, obtain critical information, and participate in educational programs and focused dialogs.

**layer-checking technique** In arson investigation, the process of examining the strata of debris, working through to the floor; may indicate the sequence of burning.

**left-wing terrorists** Terrorists who, usually, profess a revolutionary socialist doctrine and view themselves as protecting the people against capitalism and imperialism.

**LEO** *see* **Law Enforcement Online**.

**lifted-prints log** A written record of lifted-prints evidence that contains the same type of information as that listed in the evidence recovery log.

**lifters** Various materials and devices used to "lift" evidence, especially fingerprints and footwear prints, from a surface and preserve it; include flap, electrostatic, rubber-gelatin, and clear-tape lifters.

**ligature strangulation** Pressure on the neck applied by a constricting band that is tightened by a force other than body weight; causes death by occluding the blood vessels that supply oxygen to the brain.

**lineup** A procedure in which a number of similar-looking persons, including the suspect, are shown simultaneously or sequentially to a witness who may be able to identify one of them as the perpetrator; can also be conducted with photos.

**livestock** Farm and ranch animals raised for profit.

**livor mortis** Soon after death, a purplish color that appears under the skin on the portions of the body that are closest to the ground; caused by settling of the blood.

**logic bomb** A computer program that uses illegitimate instructions or misuses legitimate instructions to damage data structures; operates at a specific time, periodically, or according to other instructions.

**logical approach** An interrogation technique in which the interrogator bases his or her appeals to the suspect on common sense and sound reasoning; works better on men with criminal records, educated persons, and mature adults.

**loiding (of a lock)** The act of slipping or shimming, by means of a celluloid strip or credit card, a spring-bolt lock that does not have an antishim device.

**lookouts** Accomplices of a robber who watch for police and may provide armed backup for the offender.

**LSD** see **lysergic acid diethylamide.**

**lysergic acid diethylamide (LSD)** A semisynthetic hallucinogen that produces mental changes lasting up to 12 hours; taken as drops on a sugar lump or blotted paper, was popular in the 1960s and now making a comeback among juveniles.

**macroscopic scene** The "large view" of a crime scene, including things such as locations, the victim's body, cars, and buildings.

**mail fraud** Any scheme that involves the use of mail to defraud individuals (e.g., chain letters, foreign-lottery scams).

**manslaughter** A criminal homicide that is committed under circumstances not severe enough to constitute murder but that cannot be classified as justifiable or excusable.

**manual strangulation** Pressure on the neck applied by a hand, forearm, or other limb that compresses the neck's internal structures; causes death by occluding the blood vessels that supply oxygen to the brain.

**marijuana** A natural hallucinogen, derived from certain hemp plants, that produces a dreamy, carefree state and an alteration of sensory perceptions; in the form of crushed dried leaves and flowers, is smoked or eaten in food.

**marine theft** The theft of boats, boat trailers, outboard motors, jet skis, and all equipment associated with boating or water activities.

**MDMA** *see* **methylenedioxy methamphetamine**.

**MDT** *see* **mobile data terminal**.

**mechanical explosions** Explosions in which the high-pressure gas is produced by purely physical reactions; commonly caused by steam (e.g., the bursting of a steam boiler).

**media statement** Information released to the news media; must not prejudice the suspect's right to a fair and impartial trial.

**Megan's law** An amendment to the Jacob Wetterling act, legislation requiring that states disclose information about registered sex offenders to the public.

**meperidine (pethidine)** A synthetic narcotic that in illicit use is usually injected but can be taken orally; the first synthetic opiate.

**meprobamate** A mild tranquilizer and muscle relaxant that is less toxic than barbiturates.

**mescaline** A natural hallucinogen, derived from the peyote cactus, that produces hallucinations for up to 12 hours; ground into a powder and taken orally.

**meth labs** Illegal laboratories that manufacture methamphetamine; range from industrial-size organizations to one-person tweeker labs, with prevalence skyrocketing due to availability of "recipes" and chemicals via the Internet.

**methadone** A synthetic narcotic used to maintain a heroin addict at a stable level of opiate use during and after withdrawal from heroin; administered orally, thus reducing dangers from injection.

**methaqualone** A strong depressant that can cause poisoning and convulsive comas; removed from the legal U.S. market and usually counterfeit on the street.

**methcathinone** A psychomotor stimulant chemically similar to methamphetamine but more potent, often producing extreme paranoia; usually a white or off-white powder that is sold pure and snorted. Also called *cat* and *goob*.

**methylenedioxy methamphetamine (MDMA)** or **ecstasy** A hallucinogen that produces reduced inhibitions, euphoria, light hallucinations and can result in paranoia and psychosis; sold as a white powder, with usage increasing alarmingly.

**Metropolitan Police Act (1829)** An act of Parliament that created the London Metropolitan Police, the first centralized, professional police force in Britain, which soon became the international model of professional policing.

**microscopic scene** A crime scene viewed in terms of specific objects and pieces of evidence associated with the crime, such as knives, guns, hairs, fibers, and biological fluids.

**minutiae** The characteristics of friction ridges on palms, fingers, toes, and soles of the feet.

***Miranda* v. *Arizona*** The 1966 case in which the Supreme Court established that law enforcement officers must advise a person of his or her constitutional rights before beginning an in-custody interrogation.

**mirror** To match a person's words, actions, and mannerisms in order to eliminate communication barriers, foster trust, and create the flow of desired information.

**misadventure** A death that occurs during the commission of a lawful or unlawful act when the slayer has no intent to hurt and there is no criminal negligence.

**misdemeanor** A violation of the criminal code that is less serious than a felony; often punishable by imprisonment for no more than one year and/or a fine of no more than $500.

**mission-specific cells** In terrorist organizations, small units put together for the purpose of executing a specific assignment.

**mitochondrial DNA (mtDNA)** DNA found in the mitochondria of a cell; inherited only from the mother and thus serves as an identity marker for maternal relatives.

**mobile data terminal (MDT)** An electronic system in a police car that provides features such as secure communication with 911 and among police units, direct access to national and local databases, and computer functions (e.g., email, Internet access, computing, word-processing).

**money laundering** The process of making illegally obtained money seem legitimate by filtering it through a business and falsifying the business's accounts and invoices.

**morgue** A crime lab that determines cause of death; when the cause is questionable or is other than a known disease, conducts analyses that produce investigative information.

**morphine** An opiate in tablet, capsule, and liquid form (but usually injected) that produces euphoria, drowsiness, and relaxation; provides the medical standards by which other narcotics are evaluated.

**Motor Vehicle Theft Law Enforcement Act (1984)** Federal legislation requiring that manufacturers place permanent identification numbers on major parts of certain car lines.

**MSBP** *see* **Munchausen syndrome by proxy.**

**mugging** *see* **strong-armed robbery.**

**Mulberry Street Morning Parade** Instituted by Chief Detective Thomas Byrnes in New York City in the late 1800s, an innovative approach to criminal identification in which all new arrestees were marched each morning before detectives so that the detectives could make notes and later recognize the criminals.

**Munchausen syndrome by proxy (MSBP)** A psychological disorder in which a parent or caretaker attempts to elicit medical attention for himself or herself by injuring or inducing illness in a child.

**murder** The killing of any human being by another with malice aforethought.

**narcotics, synthetic** Narcotics that are chemically related to the opiates but are produced entirely within laboratories; primarily used as painkillers.

**narrative style** In incident reports, the officer's written chronological account of events at the crime scene from the time he or she arrived until the assignment is completed.

**National Center for the Analysis of Violent Crime (NCAVC)** Operated by the FBI, an organization that provides investigative and operational assistance to agencies dealing with violent crimes; consists of the BEA, CASMIRC, and VICAP.

**National Crime Information Center (NCIC)** The FBI's online system of extensive databases on criminals and crime; available to federal, state, and local agencies.

**National Incident-Based Reporting System (NIBRS)** An FBI program for crime reporting that features a detailed report format documenting far more data than does a basic incident report; involves voluntary participation, but made mandatory by some states.

**National Integrated Ballistic Information Network (NIBIN)** A joint program of the

ATF and the FBI, a computerized database of crime gun information that stores images of ballistic evidence (projectiles and casings), against which new images are compared for identification.

**National Motor Vehicle Title Information System (NMVTIS)** Under development, a computerized database that will include complete histories of vehicles in all states and will prevent title laundering between states.

**NCAVC** *see* **National Center for the Analysis of Violent Crime**.

**NCIC** *see* **National Crime Information Center**.

**negative match** In DNA analysis, a lack of a match between a suspect's DNA and that found on evidence at the crime scene.

**neighborhood canvass** A systematic approach to interviewing residents, merchants, and others who are in the immediate vicinity of a crime and may have useful information.

**neuro-linguistic programming (NLP)** An approach used in interviewing and interrogating that emphasizes establishing rapport, through mirroring, as a means of improving communication and thus obtaining useful information.

**NIBRS** *see* **National Incident-Based Reporting System.**

**ninhydrin** A chemical used in developing latent prints on paper and cardboard; produces purplish prints, making it unsuitable for use with money.

**NLP** *see* **neuro-linguistic programming**.

**NMVTIS** *see* **National Motor Vehicle Title Information System.**

**nonfelonious homicides** Killings that are not treated as crimes; include justifiable and excusable homicides.

**nuclear DNA** DNA found in the nucleus of a cell; inherited from both the mother and the father.

**oath** A formal attestation in which a witness swears to tell the truth on the basis of his or her belief in a supreme being and acknowledges a realization of the penalties for perjury; a means of establishing a witness's competence.

**odometer fraud** The crime of rolling back a vehicle's odometer so that it shows a lower mileage than is the case and obtaining or altering paperwork to support the fraud. Also called *odometer tampering*, *rollback*, and *clocking*.

**off-road equipment** Heavy construction equipment and farm equipment.

**opiates** Drugs derived from the opium poppy (e.g., opium, morphine, heroin, codeine).

**opium** An opiate in the form of blackish brown, pungent-smelling beads of dried fluid, which are smoked; produces drowsiness and relaxation and is the source of morphine, heroin, and codeine.

**organized/disorganized-offender model** A criminal-profiling approach in which offenders are categorized as organized or disorganized on the basis of personal and crime scene characteristics. Mixed organized-disorganized crimes reflect aspects of both patterns.

**OxyContin** A powerful narcotic consisting of oxycodone, a morphinelike drug, in a time-release formulation that, when crushed and snorted or injected, produces an intense heroinlike high; the latest drug of choice among addicts and teenage abusers.

**packet sniffers** Computer programs designed to monitor network communications and selectively record sensitive information (e.g., passwords, credit card numbers); used by hackers and, with court order, by the FBI.

**palo verde seedpod case** A 1992 murder case in Phoenix, Arizona, in which DNA analysis of plant evidence was used, for the first time in criminal proceedings, to help secure a conviction.

**"paper vehicle"** A vehicle that does not exist but is insured on the basis of a counterfeit title or manufacturer's certificate of origin so that it can later be reported stolen.

**paralanguage** Characteristics of speech, such as volume, pitch, tone, and tempo, that communicate, often unconsciously, meanings and attitudes of the speaker that may not be evident in the words themselves.

**parts marking** The process, mandated by law, of attaching VIN labels to the major parts of vehicles in high-theft lines.

**passive system (theft deterrent)** A type of vehicle antitheft device which activates automatically but may require that the driver do something to deactivate the system.

**pattern (crime)** A crime characteristic in which the same crime is committed repeatedly over a short period of time, sometimes by the same offender.

**pawnshop databases** Computer databases maintained by state and individual agencies to monitor secondhand-merchandise transactions; include data on the items and the persons pawning (or selling) and buying them.

**PCP** *see* **phencyclidine.**

**PDA** *see* **personal digital assistant.**

**Pennsylvania State Police** Created in 1905, the prototype for modern state police organizations in the United States.

**personal digital assistant (PDA)** A handheld device that prints out traffic citations, sends digital copies to the station, and provides communication and other capabilities.

**personal protection equipment (PPE)** Equipment and clothing designed to protect individuals at high-risk crime scenes from injury and infection.

**phencyclidine (PCP)** A hallucinogen in powder *(angel dust)*, tablet, liquid, leafy mixture, and rock-crystal forms that produces unpleasant effects and can cause extreme violence and strength; as a street drug, often adulterated and misrepresented, yet usage increasing notably.

**phenmetrazine** A stimulant chemically related to the amphetamines; when abused, produces amphetamine-like effects.

**photographic log** A written record listing the photographs taken at a crime scene and detailing who took them, where and when they were taken, and under what conditions.

**phreakers** People who misuse telephone systems through a variety of fraudulent methods that make it seem as if long-distance service and airtime are being legitimately purchased.

**physical stereotyping** Occurs when an officer expects that the robber will fit a preconceived description; can result in the escape of a suspect or harm to the officer.

**picking (of a lock)** The process of manipulating a lock into an unlocked position by using picks.

**pilferers** Persons who steal merchandise for the purpose of their own private use.

**PILR** *see* **Property Insurance Loss Register.**

**PIN** *see* **product information number**.

**Pinkertons** Private detectives in the National Detective Agency, formed in 1850 by Allan Pinkerton and Edward Rucker; the only consistently competent detectives in the United States for over 50 years.

**piracy** A term used in reference to intellectual-property violations; in electronic media, the act of stealing or copying data or software and then selling or distributing unauthorized copies.

**plaintiff** In a civil case, the party that was allegedly wronged and that files the lawsuit.

**planned operation** A robbery that involves careful planning and no planned use of force; has less likelihood of apprehension and generates a large score.

**plant** In arson, the material placed around the ignition device to feed the flame.

**plastic prints** Prints created when fingers touch moldable material, such as newly painted surfaces, the gum on stamps, putty, and the sticky side of adhesive tape.

**poaching** The illegal taking or possessing of game, fish, and other wildlife.

**police spies** In early-19th-century England, a derogatory term used in reference to plainclothes detectives; coined by persons who feared that the use of such officers would reduce civil liberties.

**polygraph** A mechanical device that records physiological changes that occur in a person while he or she is being questioned, with deviations from normal readings indicating deception; can be used only with subject's voluntary consent. Also called *lie detector*.

**Ponzi sales schemes** *see* **pyramind sales schemes**.

**positive match** In DNA analysis, an identical match of a suspect's DNA with that found on evidence at the crime scene.

**postmortem interval** The period between the time of death and the time that the body is found.

**PPE** *see* **personal protection equipment.**

**preferential child molester** A person who molests children because he or she has a definite sexual preference for children.

**preliminary investigation** The process undertaken by the first officer (usually a patrol officer) to arrive at the scene of a crime; includes assessment, emergency care, scene control, BOLO, scene determination, incident report, and, sometimes, evidence procedures.

**preponderance of evidence** The burden of proof in civil cases; requires only that the evidence presented by one side be seen by the jury as more believable than the evidence presented by the opposing side.

**primary scene** The location at which the initial offense was committed.

**probable cause** A condition in which an officer has suspicion about an individual and knowledge of facts and circumstances that would lead a reasonable person to believe that a crime has been, is being, or is about to be committed.

**product information number (PIN)** The 17-character identification number assigned to every new-model heavy-equipment vehicle manufactured worldwide since 2000.

**professional burglars** Burglars who thoroughly plan their crimes; go for big scores, know in advance what they intend to steal, and usually use a ruse if detected to get away without violence.

**professional theft (of vehicle)** The theft of a vehicle to fill a specific order or to resell the parts.

**proof** The combination of all the evidence in determining the guilt or innocence of a person accused of a crime.

**Property Insurance Loss Register (PILR)** An insurance industry database that lists the insureds in burglary and theft claims and everyone with an insurable interest in fire claims; detects repeated patterns of claim activity.

**protective order** A court order prohibiting the defendant from communicating with the victim and from entering the victim's residence, workplace, school, or property and any place the victim frequents.

**proximity** The amount of space between the participants in a conversation—neither too close, which causes discomfort, nor too far apart, which causes a loss of connectivity.

**psilocybin** and **psilocyn** Natural hallucinogens, derived from certain mushrooms, that produce hallucinations for about 6 hours; taken orally.

**psilocyn** *see* **psilocybin.**

**psychological autopsy** An analysis of a decedent's thoughts, feelings, and behavior, conducted through interviews with persons who knew him or her, to determine whether a death was an accident or suicide.

**puncture wounds** Wounds inflicted with piercing instruments such as leather punches, screwdrivers, and ice picks; typically small, with little or no bleeding.

**pyramid**, or **Ponzi, sales schemes** Fraudulent marketing programs in which people buy the right to sell others the right to sell a specified product; based on misrepresentation of investors' ability to recoup their initial investments. Also called *chain-referral schemes*.

**pyromaniacs** Arsonists who lack conscious motivation for their fire setting.

**QUAD** *see* **rapid response deployment.**

**quick action deployment** *see* **rapid response deployment.**

**quick strip (of vehicle)** The process of removing from a stolen vehicle valuable parts (e.g., seats, stereos, tires) that have no identifying numbers and thus can be easily sold.

**Racketeering Records Analysis Unit (RRAU)** Part of the FBI laboratory, the unit that examines documents from suspected money-laundering businesses to establish a link between illegal funds and their original source.

**radial fractures** Lines that move away from the point of impact in a glass window.

**rape** or **sexual battery** The crime of having sexual relations with a person against her or his will; with a person who is unconscious or under the influence of alcohol; or with someone who is insane, feeble-minded, or under the age of consent.

**rape-murder** Murder that results from or is an integral part of the rape of the victim; either unplanned response (of increasing aggression or panic over sense of failure) or planned act (of revenge or sadism).

**rapid response deployment** or **quick action deployment (QUAD)** An intervention approach in which patrol officers are trained in the principles and tactics of rapid deployment for critical incidents so that responding officers can take action immediately rather than wait for a SWAT team.

**rapport** In interviews and interrogations, the harmonious relationship with the witness or suspect that must be established by the investigator to foster trust and meaningful communication.

**rebuttal** In a trial, the optional process in which the prosecution, after the defense has closed its case, presents new evidence or calls or recalls a witness; occurs at the discretion of the prosecution.

**receivers** *see* **fences**.

**reconstruction (of crime)** May be part of the incident report, a narration of the probable manner in which the crime was committed, based on interviews, evidence, and examination of the scene.

**re-cross-examination** In a trial, the requestioning of a witness initially called by the opposing party.

**redirect examination** In a trial, the requestioning of a witness by the party that called the witness.

**reflected ultraviolet imaging system (RUVIS)** Lighting and imaging system in which ultraviolet light applied to undetected fingerprints is "bounced" back, highly intensifying the prints.

**refurbishment fraud** A practice in which working components from damaged or returned items (e.g., a computer) are used in the construction of new items or are resold as new items.

**rhodamine 6G** An excellent fluorescing chemical for enhancing developed latent prints and revealing others; used on metal, glass, plastic, wood, and other nonabsorbent surfaces.

**rifling** The lands and grooves in the rifled bore of a firearm.

**right-wing terrorists** Terrorists who, usually, espouse racial supremacy and antigovernment, antiregulatory beliefs; often hold antiabortion and survivalist views and call for paramilitary training in "militias."

**rigor mortis** The increasing rigidity of the body's muscles and joints that begins soon after death; reaches completion in 10 to 15 hours and starts to subside 24 to 36 hours later. Also called *postmortem rigidity* or *rigor*.

**robbery** The crime of taking and carrying away personal property of another, with the intent to permanently deprive the owner of its use, by means of force, fear, or threat of force.

**rock cocaine** or **crack** The pellet form of cocaine; more concentrated, somewhat purer, and much more potent (though shorter acting) than the powdered form and relatively inexpensive.

**rogues gallery** Instituted by the New York City Police Department in 1857, a display in which photographs of known offenders were arranged by criminal specialty and height for detectives to study so that they might recognize criminals on the street.

**Rohypnol** A benzodiazapine used to perpetrate sexual attacks; mixed into a victim's food or drink, can induce sedation, memory impairment, or unconsciousness, leaving the victim unaware of the attack. Also called *flunitrazepam*.

**root kits** Exploit packages that enable computer-system intruders to maintain the highest level of access by installing back doors and secret accounts and altering logs and basic system services.

**rough sketch** A drawing made at the crime scene; not drawn to scale, but indicates accurate dimensions and distances.

**rules of evidence** Federal evidentiary rules which state that scientific, technical, or other specialized knowledge is admissible if it will help the trier of fact understand the evidence or determine a fact at issue.

**RUVIS** *see* **reflected ultraviolet imaging system.**

**safes** Locked receptacles for protecting valuables; classified as fire-resistant safes (protection from fire but minimum security) or money chests (security and reasonably good protection from fire).

**salami slice** A computerized-theft technique in which dollar amounts are automatically rounded down and the difference is diverted to the perpetrator's special account.

**salvage switch** A method of disguising a stolen vehicle whereby the title and VIN plate of a salvage vehicle are transferred to an identical stolen vehicle, which can then be sold in the legitimate market.

**salvage title** The title issued to an insurance company after it has paid a total-loss claim; remains with the vehicle until it is destroyed.

**salvage vehicle** A vehicle that has been damaged to such an extent that the cost of repairing it is more than its fair market value.

**SBS** *see* **shaken-baby syndrome**.

**scald burns** Burns on the skin caused by contact with hot liquids, either through spills/splashes or immersion; most common type of burn injury to children.

**Scotland Yard** The original headquarters of the London Metropolitan Police, so-called because the building formerly housed Scottish royalty. Since 1890, the headquarters have been located elsewhere, but known as New Scotland Yard.

**search patterns, crime scene** Specific approaches for searching an entire crime scene for evidence; include the spiral, strip/line, grid, zone/quadrant, and pie/wheel patterns.

**secondary scenes** The locations of all events subsequent to and connected with the event at the primary scene.

**Secret Service, U.S.** The federal agency created by Congress in 1865 to combat counterfeiting; since 1903, responsible for guarding the president.

**selective raid** A robbery that involves a minimal amount of casual planning and may be repeated several times in rapid succession; generates a low to moderate score.

**semen** A grayish-white fluid produced in the male reproductive organs and ejaculated during orgasm; has a chlorinelike odor and dries to a starchlike consistency.

**serial murder** Usually, a series of sexual attacks and resulting deaths of at least three or four persons committed by a killer who tends to follow a distinct physical or psychological pattern.

**series (crime)** A crime characteristic in which crimes of the same type are committed over a short period of time, usually by the same offender.

**sex offenses** Crimes related to sexual activity; classified as serious (e.g., rape), nuisance (e.g., voyeurism, exhibitionism), and mutual consent (e.g., adultery, prostitution).

**sexual battery** *see* **rape**.

**shaken-baby syndrome (SBS)** Severe intracranial trauma caused by the deliberate application of violent force (shaking) to a child.

**Shoeprint Image Capture and Retrieval (SICAR) System** Computer software that classifies, archives, and identifies shoe prints.

**shopping cart fraud** A computer crime in which the offender selects purchases at an online store, saves a copy of the purchase page and lowers the prices, and then submits the altered page and continues the checkout process.

**SICAR** *see* **Shoeprint Image Capture and Retrieval System.**

**SIDS** *see* **sudden infant death syndrome**.

**situational child molester** A person who molests children because the opportunity exists to do so or because of his or her inadequacy, regressed personality, or desire for experimentation; does not have a sexual preference for children.

**situational stereotyping** Occurs when an officer's knowledge and experience with a location creates the expectation that the present situation will be the same as past situations; increases the officer's vulnerability.

**sleeper cells** In terrorist organizations, small groups of recruits who are in place in target and other countries, living ordinary lives until activated for the cause; may also perform services for their immediate group (e.g., courier and reconnaissance tasks).

**small particle reagent (SPR)** A chemical used in developing latent prints on objects that have been immersed in water, dew- or rain-soaked cars, surfaces covered with a residue such as ocean salt, and waxed materials, plastics, tile, and glass.

**smooth bore** A bore without rifling; characteristic of most shotguns.

**smooth sketch** A finished sketch of the crime scene, often drawn to scale using information contained in the rough sketch.

**Snow Print Wax** An aerosol wax sprayed on footwear impressions in snow to tint the highlights so that the impressions can be photographed before being cast.

**spalling** The breakdown in the surface tensile strength of concrete, masonry, or brick that occurs when exposure to high temperatures and rates of heating produces mechanical forces within the material.

**speedballing** The simultaneous ingestion of heroin (a depressant) and cocaine (a stimulant); produces a euphoric rush followed by a drowsy or depressing effect and can cause convulsions and death.

**sperm** Tadpolelike organisms that are contained in and travel through semen to fertilize the female egg.

**spill/splash injuries** Burns on the skin that occur when a hot liquid falls from a height and splashes onto the body.

**spontaneous heating** An increase in temperature that results from a natural process; caused by chemical action, fermentation, or oxidation.

**spontaneous ignition** The catching afire of materials subjected to spontaneous heating; usually requires several hours to several months of oxidation or fermentation.

**SPR** *see* **small particle reagent**.

**spree (crime)** A crime characteristic in which crimes of the same type are committed at almost the same time by the same offender.

**staged crime** A crime that the offender has contrived or altered to mislead investigative efforts.

**stalking** Harassing or threatening behavior toward a specific victim that the perpetrator engages in repeatedly (e.g., following a person, making harassing phone calls).

**STAR** *see* **Stolen Auto Recovery System.**

**statement analysis** An examination of a suspect's statement that focuses on how the person expressed things (the words and tenses used, e.g.); aids in understanding the suspect and detecting deception.

**stimulants** Drugs that directly stimulate the central nervous system, producing excitation, alertness, wakefulness, and, sometimes, a temporary increase in blood pressure and respiration rate; in overdose, can cause hallucinations, convulsions, and death.

**sting operation** In combating fences, a tactic in which undercover officers pose as fences in a "front" business to gain information; effective means of identifying criminals, penetrating criminal organizations, and recovering property.

**Stolen Auto Recovery (STAR) System** A method of examining and photographing the contents of shipping containers, by means of gamma rays, while they are entering a port or being loaded onto a vessel; used to identify stolen vehicles being shipped abroad.

**strategic intelligence** Information that is gathered and analyzed over time and usually confirms new or recently discovered patterns of criminal activity.

**striae** Tiny furrows made by the action of a tool on an object's surface (e.g., marks left on a door's hinge from an attempt to force the door open with a pry bar).

**strong-armed robbery** A robbery in which the perpetrator attacks and beats the victim but no weapons are involved.

**subpoena** A written order commanding a particular person to appear in court at a specified date and time to testify as a witness.

**sudden infant death syndrome (SIDS)** The sudden and unexpected death of an apparently healthy infant, usually during sleep, the cause of which has yet to be determined.

**superglue fuming** The process of heating cyanoacrylate in a high-humidity chamber so that the condensing of the resultant fumes develops any latent prints.

**surrebuttal** In a trial, the process in which the defense, after a rebuttal by the prosecution, presents new evidence or calls or recalls a witness; permitted only if the prosecution conducts a rebuttal.

**surreptitious entries** Burglaries in which no apparent force is used and thus a point of entry or exit cannot be established; may indicate loiding, picking, an unlocked door, a perpetrator with authorized access, or an occupant-staged crime.

**surveillance** The secretive and continuous observation of persons, places, and things to obtain information concerning the activities and identity of individuals.

**suspect** A person who is seen as possibly being guilty of the crime under investigation.

**suspect description form** An information-gathering aid for recording details of a suspect's physical description; may include description of any vehicle used in the crime.

**T-men** Agents of the Bureau of Internal Revenue (which enforced Prohibition), so-called because the bureau was part of the Department of the Treasury.

**tack** The equipment used with horses (e.g., saddles, bridles, horse blankets).

**tactical intelligence** Information that implies immediate action and can lead to arrests or the collection of additional information; may be derived from surveillance, informants, and intelligence analysis.

**telephone record analysis** An intelligence technique in which telephone records are compiled and analyzed to obtain information on the relationships between the subscriber and the numbers called.

**temporary theft (of vehicle)** The theft of a motor vehicle for use in the commission of another crime, after which it is abandoned.

**testimony** A witness's oral presentation of facts about which he or she has knowledge.

**threat** An expression of the intent to do harm or act out violently against someone or something; can be spoken, written, or symbolic.

**threat assessment** The process of determining the risk level posed by a threat and whether law enforcement should be called in and a criminal prosecution pursued; includes evaluation of the threatener.

**three-strikes laws** State laws mandating that persons convicted repeatedly of serious crimes be sentenced to lengthy imprisonment or to imprisonment without parole.

**time-event chart (TEC)** A crime analysis tool that displays the major events relating to a crime or an offender in chronological order.

**title fraud** For motor vehicles, any act that involves altering, laundering, or counterfeiting a title or title reassignment form; often engaged in to support and cover up odometer rollbacks.

**tool mark** Any impression, cut, gouge, or abrasion made when a tool comes into contact with another object.

**totality of the circumstances** In determining the applicability of the *Miranda* warnings, an approach that takes all the circumstances into consideration, rather than imposing a strict interpretation based on formal procedures.

**toxicologist** A scientist who specializes in poisons, their effects, and their antidotes.

**trace evidence** Evidence that is extremely small or microscopic in size or is present only in limited amounts.

**tracing evidence** Evidence that helps identify and locate the suspect.

**traditional powders** The basic powders, available in a number of colors, that have been used for decades for developing latent fingerprints.

**trailer** In arson, any substance used to spread the fire from the plant to other parts of a room or building.

**trend (crime)** A general tendency in the occurrence of crime across a large geographic area over an extended period of time.

**trespassory** Illegal taking.

**Trojan horse** Any computer program that is altered or designed to perform an unwanted or malicious function while appearing to perform a routine or benign function.

**Truth in Mileage Act (1986)** Federal legislation that requires more tightly controlled documentation and recording of odometer readings each time ownership of a vehicle changes.

**T/S/D crimes** Any illegal acts involving the treatment, storage, and disposal of hazardous wastes.

**tuberculosis (TB)** A chronic bacterial infection, spread by air, that usually infects the lungs and can lead to death if untreated; a health hazard for anyone in contact with high-risk individuals such as drug addicts and homeless persons.

**tumbling** The illegal altering of a cellular phone's microchip so that its access codes change after each call, making it difficult to trace the fraudulent user; done through a personal computer.

**ultraviolet fluorescence** A technique in which a darkened fire scene is illuminated with an ultraviolet lamp so that certain substances glow; used to detect residues of accelerants and to locate the point of a fire's origin.

**Uniform Crime Reports** Statistics on crime, including numbers of offenses, published annually by the FBI.

**unknown** or **questioned samples** (1) Recovered crime scene samples whose sources are in question; (2) questioned evidence that may have been transferred to an offender during the commission of a crime and may have been taken away by him or her; (3) questioned evidence recovered at multiple crime scenes that associates a particular tool, weapon, or person with each scene.

**vehicle canvass** A systematic approach to documenting every vehicle in the immediate vicinity of a crime as a means of locating the suspect's vehicle.

**vehicle fraud** Any fraudulent activity involving motor vehicles; includes theft of vehicles, fraud perpetrated on purchasers of vehicles, and fraud committed by owners (or persons acting on their behalf) against insurance companies.

**vehicle identification number (VIN)** The 17-character identification number assigned to every car manufactured or sold in the United States.

**victim** A person or an organization that has suffered injury or loss as the result of a crime.

**VIN** *see* **vehicle identification number**.

**VIN plate** The plate that contains the VIN of a vehicle; usually attached to the upper left side of the dashboard so that it is visible through the window.

**violation** In some states, a minor transgression of the law; often punishable by a fine of no more than $250; e.g., littering.

**virus** A malicious program that is secretly inserted into normal software or a computer's active memory and runs when the host runs; causes effects ranging from annoying messages and deletion of data to interference with the computer's operation.

**walk-through (of crime scene)** The investigator's initial overview of the crime scene, performed by walking through the area, to locate and view the body, identify evidence, and determine procedures for examination and documentation of the scene and body.

**washing (of title)** The process a fabricating a vehicle's sale to a purchaser in a jurisdiction that does not issue salvage titles or carry title brands forward and thereby obtaining a clean title on the vehicle.

**weight (of evidence)** The amount of believability a jury gives to the testimony of a witness or the presentation of an item of evidence.

**West case** A 1903 incident in which two criminals with the same name, identical appearances, and nearly identical measurements were distinguished only by fingerprints, thus significantly advancing the use of fingerprints for identification in the United States.

**white-collar crime** Any illegal act committed by concealment or guile, rather than physical means, to obtain money or property, avoid payment or loss of money or property, or obtain business or personal advantage.

**witness** A person who has firsthand knowledge regarding a crime or who has expert information regarding some aspect of the crime.

**worm** A malicious program that attacks a computer system directly, rather than infecting a host program; spreads rapidly through the Internet or email.

# INDEX